ARCHITECTURAL DRAFTING
RESIDENTIAL AND COMMERCIAL

THOMAS OBERMEYER

REGISTERED ARCHITECT

ARCHITECTURAL TECHNOLOGY PROFESSOR
MINNEAPOLIS TECHNICAL COLLEGE
MINNEAPOLIS, MINNESOTA

GLENCOE
Macmillan/McGraw-Hill

New York, New York   Columbus, Ohio   Mission Hills, California   Peoria, Illinois

LIBRARY OF CONGRESS CATALOGING-IN-PUBLICATION DATA

OBERMEYER, THOMAS L.
 ARCHITECTURAL DRAFTING : RESIDENTIAL AND COMMERCIAL / THOMAS OBERMEYER.
 P.   CM.
 ISBN 0-02-800415-9
 1. ARCHITECTURAL DRAWING--TECHNIQUE. I. TITLE
NA2708.024   1992
720'.28'4--DC20   92-38564
                                                                  CIP

COPYRIGHT © 1993 BY THE GLENCOE DIVISION OF MACMILLAN/McGRAW-HILL
SCHOOL PUBLISHING COMPANY. PRINTED IN THE UNITED STATES OF AMERICA.
ALL RIGHTS RESERVED. EXCEPT AS PERMITTED UNDER THE UNITED STATES
COPYRIGHT ACT, NO PART OF THIS PUBLICATION MAY BE REPRODUCED OR
DISTRIBUTED IN ANY FORM OR BY ANY MEANS, WITHOUT THE PRIOR WRITTEN
PERMISSION OF THE PUBLISHER.

SEND ALL INQUIRIES TO:

GLENCOE DIVISION
MACMILLAN/McGRAW-HILL
936 EASTWIND DRIVE
WESTERVILLE, OHIO 43081

PRINTED IN THE UNITED STATES OF AMERICA

    2 3 4 5 6 7 8 9 0 MAZ 99 98 97 96 95 94 93

CONTENTS

P	PREFACE
UNIT 1	INTRODUCTION
UNIT 2	DRAFTING TOOLS
UNIT 3	ARCHITECTURAL DRAFTING
UNIT 4	ARCHITECTURAL PRINTING
UNIT 5	DRAFTING SYMBOLS
UNIT 6	DIMENSIONS
UNIT 7	PROJECT ASSEMBLY TECHNIQUES
UNIT 8	COMPUTER AIDED DRAFTING
UNIT 9	DETAILS
UNIT 10	REFERENCE SOURCES
UNIT 11	PROBLEM SOLVING
UNIT 12	BUILDING MATERIALS
UNIT 13	SITE PLANS AND DETAILS
UNIT 14	FLOOR PLANS
UNIT 15	EXTERIOR ELEVATIONS

UNIT 16	BUILDING SECTIONS
UNIT 17	WALL SECTIONS
UNIT 18	STAIRS AND ELEVATORS
UNIT 19	SCHEDULES
UNIT 20	DETAIL ASSEMBLY
UNIT 21	BIRCH LAKE CABIN
UNIT 22	12/12 PITCH ROOF HOUSE
UNIT 23	SKYWAY HOUSE
UNIT 24	PROJECT DESIGN
UNIT 25	FIRE STATION
UNIT 26	MOTEL AND RESTAURANT
UNIT 27	STUDENT LIBRARY
UNIT 28	PRESENTATION DRAWINGS
UNIT 29	STUDY MODELS
A	APPENDIX
G	GLOSSARY

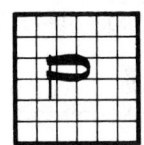

PREFACE

THE PRACTICE OF ARCHITECTURE BLENDS DESIGN AND TECHNOLOGY INTO A UNIQUE PROFESSION. A BUILDING PROJECT IS BEGUN BY DEFINING ELEMENTS THAT WILL AFFECT THE DESIGN, SUCH AS WHERE TO LOCATE A BUILDING ON A SITE, WHO WILL USE THE BUILDING, WHAT KIND OF SPACES ARE DESIRED, AND HOW MUCH MONEY CAN BE SPENT. ONCE A DESIGN IS DEVELOPED, AN EQUALLY IMPORTANT TASK MUST BE COMPLETED: THE ASSEMBLY OF A TECHNICAL SET OF DRAWINGS THAT WILL DEFINE EVERY PHASE OF THE CONSTRUCTION PROCESS. THE TECHNOLOGY OF CONSTRUCTION IS SO CLOSELY LINKED TO ARCHITECTURAL PRACTICE THAT YOU CAN'T SUCCESSFULLY DESIGN A BUILDING THAT FAILS TECHNICALLY.

A BRIEF GLANCE AT THIS BOOK WILL TELL YOU THAT THIS ISN'T AN ORDINARY TEXT ON ARCHITECTURAL DRAFTING. THE FIRST THING YOU'LL NOTICE IS THE ARCHITECTURAL PRINTING FONT USED THROUGHOUT THE BOOK; THIS PRESENTS THE MATERIAL IN A STYLE THAT REMINDS YOU, ON EVERY PAGE, THAT THIS IS A BOOK ABOUT ARCHITECTURE. A FURTHER REVIEW WILL SHOW YOU THAT THE TEXT USES THREE RESIDENTIAL AND THREE COMMERCIAL PROJECTS AS EXAMPLES IN MOST UNITS. THE RESIDENTIAL PROJECTS INCLUDE A SMALL LAKE CABIN, A POST-MODERN HOUSE WITH HALF-ROUND WINDOWS, AND A FLAT-ROOF HOME WITH A SKYWAY CONNECTING THE HOUSE AND TWO BEDROOMS OVER THE GARAGE. THE COMMERCIAL PROJECTS INCLUDE A FIRE STATION, A UNIQUE MOTEL AND RESTAURANT BUILT OVER A LAKE, AND A COLLEGE LIBRARY. PAGE TO THE BACK OF THE BOOK TO SEE THAT CUT-OUT MODELS OF THE SIX PROJECTS ARE PRESENTED ON LIGHT CARDBOARD. IN ADDITION, EACH PROJECT IS "UNFOLDED" IN A WAY THAT EXPLAINS THE TECHNOLOGY OF EACH SPECIAL CONSTRUCTION SYSTEM. THE

BOOK CONTAINS OVER 1,500 ARCHITECTURAL ILLUSTRATIONS THAT ARE INTENDED TO PROVIDE YOU WITH A FUNDAMENTAL UNDERSTANDING OF BUILDING.

THERE ARE A NUMBER OF ADDITIONAL FEATURES THAT MAKE THIS BOOK UNIQUE. THERE IS A UNIT ON PROBLEM-SOLVING CONSTRUCTION CONDITIONS THAT PRESENTS STEP-BY-STEP PROCEDURES IN DETERMINING BUILDING ASSEMBLY. ONE UNIT DISCUSSES THE PROCESS OF BUDGETING YOUR TIME IN ORDER TO COMPLETE A PROJECT ON SCHEDULE, AND ANOTHER PRESENTS INFORMATION ON HOW TO USE REFERENCE SOURCES TO DETERMINE CONSTRUCTION SYSTEMS. INFORMATION REGARDING THE USES OF BUILDING PRODUCTS AND HOW THEY ARE INCORPORATED IN CONSTRUCTION IS ALSO PRESENTED. IN ADDITION THE BOOK PROVIDES HUNDREDS OF TIPS ON CONVENTIONAL "HAND" DRAFTING AND PRINTING PLUS A PRESENTATION ON COMPUTER AIDED DRAFTING (CAD). IN THE TEXT YOU WILL FIND HUNDREDS OF ARCHITECTURAL CONSTRUCTION DETAILS THAT DEFINE THE TECHNOLOGY OF BUILDING; ONE UNIT PRESENTS OVER SIXTY LARGE-SCALE DETAILS THAT SHOW RESIDENTIAL AND COMMERCIAL ASSEMBLY TECHNIQUES.

THE INTENT OF THE TEXT IS TO INTRODUCE YOU TO THE TECHNOLOGY OF ARCHITECTURAL DRAFTING BY PRODUCING WORKING DRAWING PACKAGES FOR SIX PROJECTS. ASSIGNMENTS RANGE FROM STUDYING THE FUNDAMENTALS OF CONCRETE TO THE ASSEMBLY OF A "STUDY MODEL" FOR EACH PROJECT. EVERY ARCHITECTURAL PROJECT PRESENTS A SET OF UNIQUE PROBLEMS; THIS TEXT WILL PROVIDE YOU WITH THE TOOLS NEEDED TO SOLVE A WIDE RANGE OF BEGINNING CONSTRUCTION CONDITIONS.

I WOULD LIKE TO THANK MR. THOMAS NATHAN OF NATHAN EVANS POUNDERS & TAYLOR, ARCHITECTS, FOR HIS PERMISSION TO USE THE REELFOOT LAKE STATE PARK PROJECT IN TIPTONVILLE, TENNESSEE. I WOULD ALSO LIKE TO THANK MR. ARTHUR MILLIKEN, ACORN STRUCTURES, INC., FOR HIS PERMISSION TO USE THE ARCHITECTURAL PRESENTATION DRAWINGS FOUND IN UNIT 28.

TO MY WIFE BETH, WITHOUT HER UNDERSTANDING AND SPIRIT, THIS BOOK WOULDN'T HAVE BEEN WRITTEN.

PREFACE   P-2

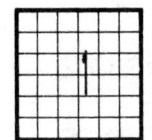

INTRODUCTION

The practice of architecture requires a blend of art and technology. A building could be described as a piece of sculpture that has to "work"; by that we mean that it must meet structural requirements, it shouldn't leak, building codes must be adhered to, and construction materials must be properly used.

An architect's job involves dealing with two completely different groups of people: clients and contractors. In the first phase of a project, an architect must deal with the needs of the client. This phase involves the development of a design concept and its presentation to the building owner; a document called a <u>program</u> is prepared to define the requirements of every room in the project. The second stage of an architectural project involves taking the design concept and organizing it into a drawing package that can be given to a contractor for construction. In this phase, the architect is preparing drawings that will act as a legal contract between the owner and contractor.

The development of an architectural contract is commonly divided into five phases, beginning with the design process

SCHEMATICS ⇒ DESIGN DEVELOPMENT ⇒ WORKING DRAWINGS ⇒ BIDDING ⇒ CONSTRUCTION

and ending with the building phase. We will use the assembly of a small cabin to explain the steps from schematics through construction.

INTRODUCTION 1-1

SCHEMATICS

THE SCHEMATIC PHASE STARTS WITH AN ANALYSIS OF A CLIENT'S REQUIREMENTS AND OF SITE CONDITIONS. BASED ON THESE CONSIDERATIONS, A ROUGH DESIGN IS FORMED. IN THE CASE OF THE CABIN PROJECT, THE ARCHITECT WOULD MEET WITH THE OWNER TO DETERMINE EXACTLY WHAT HE OR SHE NEEDED FOR A WEEKEND GET-AWAY. THE DISCUSSION WOULD INCLUDE SUCH POINTS AS THE FOLLOWING: HOW WOULD THE CABIN BE USED, HOW MANY PEOPLE WOULD BE STAYING OVER A WEEKEND, IF THE CABIN WOULD BE USED DURING COLD MONTHS, AND HOW MUCH THE PROJECT SHOULD COST. THE WRITTEN DOCUMENT (CALLED THE PROGRAM) AND ROUGH SKETCHES (CALLED THE SCHEMATIC DRAWINGS) WOULD BE USED TO PROVIDE THE CLIENT WITH A PRELIMINARY VIEW OF THE BUILDING DESIGN.

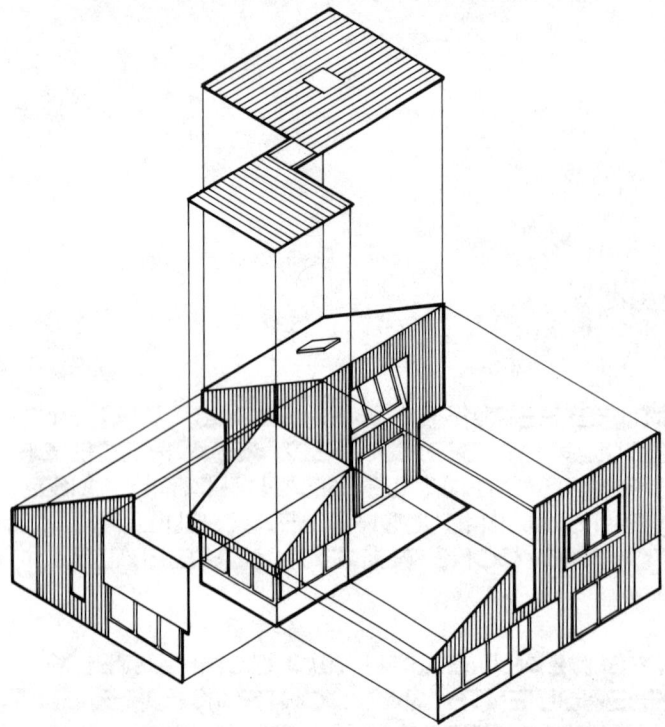

IN ADDITION TO CLIENT REQUIREMENTS, THE SITE OF A PROPOSED PROJECT IS ALSO A DETERMINING FACTOR IN THE SCHEMATIC DESIGN PHASE. A SITE ANALYSIS EVALUATES SUCH ITEMS AS VIEWS, ROADS, PRIVACY FACTORS, LAKE SETBACK REQUIREMENTS, SOLAR ANGLES, AND THE SLOPE OF THE SITE. A DESIGN STATEMENT WOULD BE FORMED THROUGH MEETINGS WITH THE OWNER TO MERGE THE REQUIREMENTS OF THE PROJECT WITH THE BUILDING FORM DEVELOPED BY THE ARCHITECT. THE FINAL SCHEMATICS TYPICALLY TAKE THE SHAPE OF "ROUGH" SKETCHES AND MODELS THAT DEMONSTRATE THE DESIGN SOLUTION. THE SCHEMATIC PHASE ENDS WHEN THE OWNER AGREES THAT THE DESIGN MEETS THE PROJECT CONDITIONS.

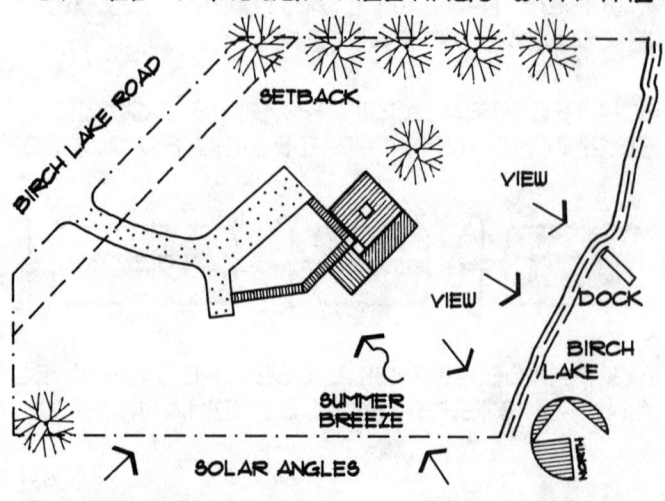

INTRODUCTION   1-2

DESIGN DEVELOPMENT

IN THE DESIGN DEVELOPMENT PHASE, THE COMPLETED SCHEMATIC PACKAGE IS USED AS A STARTING POINT FOR REFINING THE PROJECT INTO A MORE WORKABLE SYSTEM. IN OTHER WORDS, THIS PHASE STARTS WITH A SKETCH WHICH EVOLVES INTO A FUNCTIONAL DESIGN. THIS PROCESS INVOLVES SUCH TASKS AS LOCATING AND SIZING DOORS AND WINDOWS, LAYING OUT HEATING AND VENTILATING SYSTEMS, DESIGNING THE PRELIMINARY STRUCTURAL MEMBERS, AND MAKING DETAILED DRAWINGS OF THE SCHEMATIC PLANS. IN THE CABIN PROJECT, WE WOULD BEGIN WITH THE OWNER-APPROVED SET OF SKETCHES AND DEVELOP THEM INTO A TECHNICALLY CORRECT SET OF DRAWINGS. FOR EXAMPLE, THE DESIGNER WOULD LAY OUT THE STRUCTURAL FRAMING FOR BOTH FLOORS AND THE ROOF. THE LAYOUT WOULD TAKE INTO ACCOUNT THE STRENGTH OF ROOF RAFTERS, THE SIZE OF PLYWOOD SHEETS NEEDED, AND THE SPECIAL REQUIREMENTS OF THE PROPOSED SKYLIGHT FRAMING. THE FINAL DESIGN DEVELOPMENT PACKAGE WOULD CONSIST OF ACCURATELY DRAWN SCALE DRAWINGS SHOWING THE FLOOR PLANS, EXTERIOR ELEVATION VIEWS, AND DETAIL CUTS THROUGH THE CABIN (CALLED SECTIONS). KEEP IN MIND THAT IN THIS PHASE THE ARCHITECT IS STILL STUDYING THE BUILDING DESIGN.

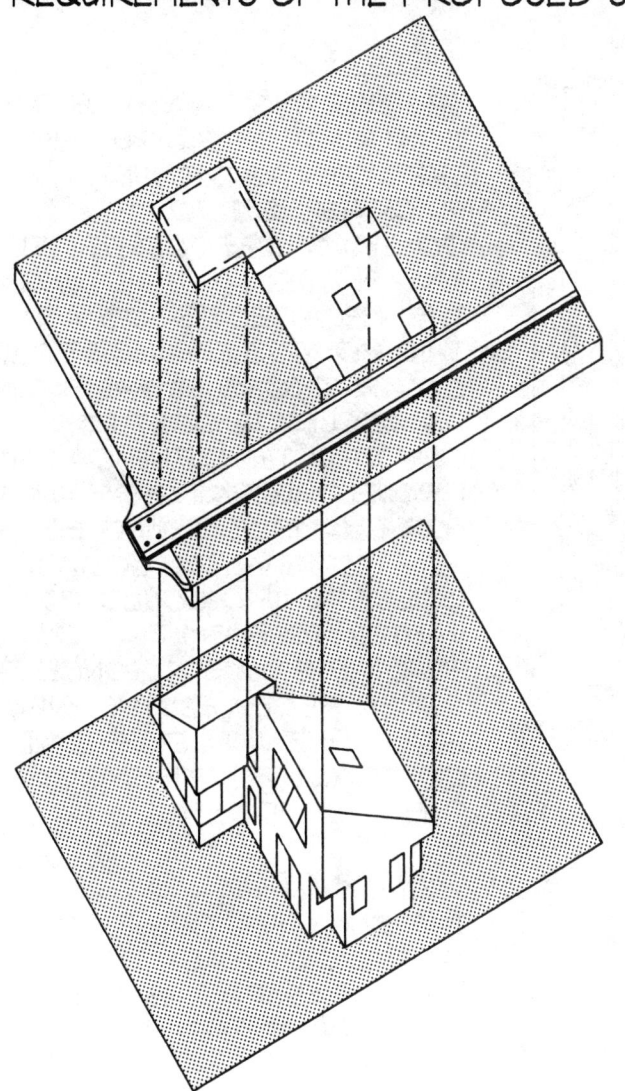

WORKING DRAWINGS

THE WORKING DRAWING PHASE FURTHER REFINES THE DESIGN INTO A PACKAGE OF DRAWINGS THAT CAN BE GIVEN TO A CONTRACTOR FOR CONSTRUCTION. IN THE DRAWINGS, ALL ELEMENTS ARE LOCATED BY DIMENSION AND ALL MATERIALS TO BE USED ARE DEFINED. AT THIS POINT, THE DRAWINGS BECOME THE BASIS FOR A CONTRACT BETWEEN THE OWNER AND THE BUILDER AND TECHNICAL ACCURACY IS OF THE UTMOST IMPORTANCE: WINDOWS

MUST BE SPECIFIED AND LOCATED BY DIMENSION, ROOF AND WALL INTERSECTIONS MUST BE DETAILED, AND THE BUILDING MUST BE DIMENSIONED FROM THE PROPERTY LINES. IN THE CABIN PROJECT, DRAWINGS WOULD BE DEVELOPED INTO A SET OF PLANS, ELEVATIONS, AND SECTION VIEWS THAT WOULD DIRECT ALL WORK THAT THE CONTRACTOR IS TO PERFORM. FOR EXAMPLE, THE DECK WOULD BE DRAWN AS SHOWN BELOW, INCLUDING NOTES SPECIFYING THE QUALITY OF WOOD TO BE USED AND THE SIZE AND SPACING OF THE PIECES. AS WE SAID BEFORE, THE DRAWING SET IS THE DOCUMENT THAT THE OWNER AND CONTRACTOR USE TO FORM A LEGAL CONTRACT TO BUILD THE CABIN: THE CONTRACTOR AGREES TO BUILD ALL ITEMS ON THE DRAWINGS TO THE QUALITY SPECIFIED, AND IN RETURN THE OWNER AGREES TO PAY THE CONTRACTOR FOR HIS OR HER WORK. JUST AS THE CONTRACTOR IS REQUIRED TO PERFORM ALL OF THE WORK SHOWN ON THE DRAWINGS, HE OR SHE IS NOT REQUIRED TO COMPLETE WORK THAT IS NOT INCLUDED.

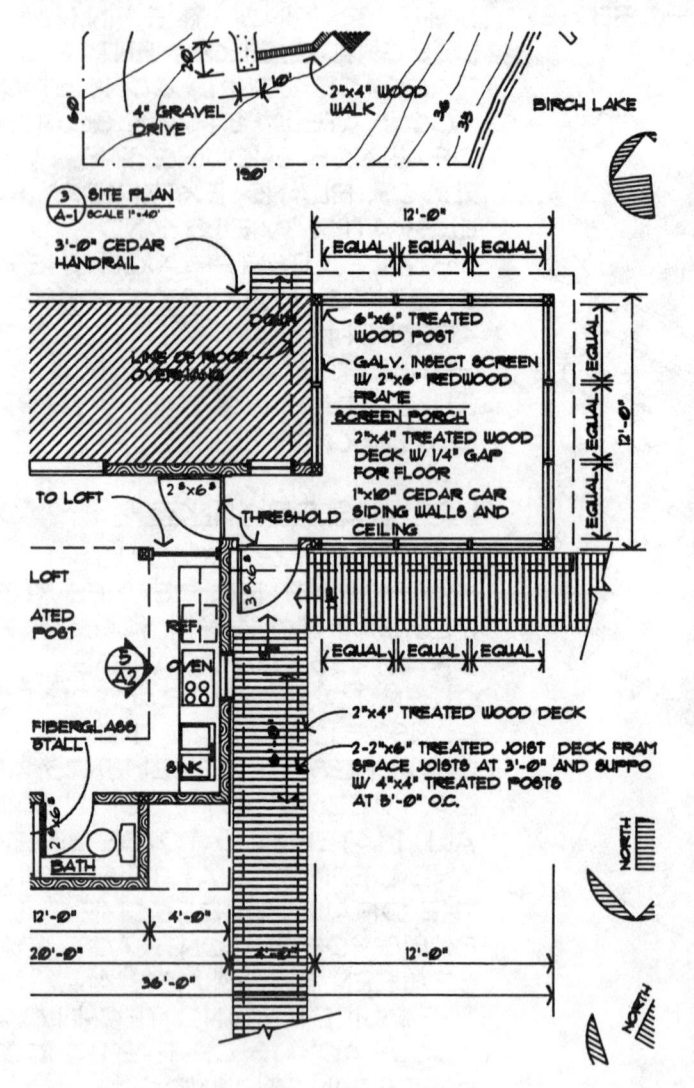

BIDDING

THE BIDDING PHASE OF THE CONTRACT INVOLVES SENDING THE WORKING DRAWING PACKAGE OUT TO CONTRACTORS FOR REVIEW AND SUBSEQUENT BIDDING. THE ARCHITECT'S JOB AT THIS POINT IS TO ASSIST THE CONTRACTORS IN PREPARING AN ACCURATE COST FOR CONSTRUCTION. THE CABIN PROJECT WORKING DRAWINGS, FOR EXAMPLE, WOULD BE SENT TO SEVERAL LOCAL BUILDERS WHO WOULD BE INVITED TO SUBMIT A COST FOR THE PROJECT. ONCE THE OWNER RECEIVED THE BIDS, HE OR SHE WOULD SELECT A CONTRACTOR, TYPICALLY THE LOW BIDDER.

CONSTRUCTION

THE CONSTRUCTION PHASE OF THE CONTRACT ENCOMPASSES THE ACTUAL BUILDING OF THE PROJECT.

INTRODUCTION 1-4

DURING THIS PHASE, THE ARCHITECT INTERPRETS THE WORKING DRAWINGS FOR THE CONTRACTOR AND MAKES PERIODIC VISITS TO THE BUILDING SITE TO ASSURE QUALITY CONTROL OVER MATERIALS AND CONSTRUCTION. IN THE CABIN PROJECT, THE CONTRACTOR AND ARCHITECT WOULD BE IN FREQUENT CONTACT WITH EACH OTHER TO DECIDE HOW DETAILS SHOULD BE BUILT. THE ARCHITECT WOULD ALSO APPROVE THE CONTRACTOR'S MONTHLY REQUEST FOR PAYMENT (THE AMOUNT OF PAYMENT WOULD BE DETERMINED BY THE AMOUNT OF WORK COMPLETED AND THE COST OF MATERIALS USED IN THE CABIN'S CONSTRUCTION).

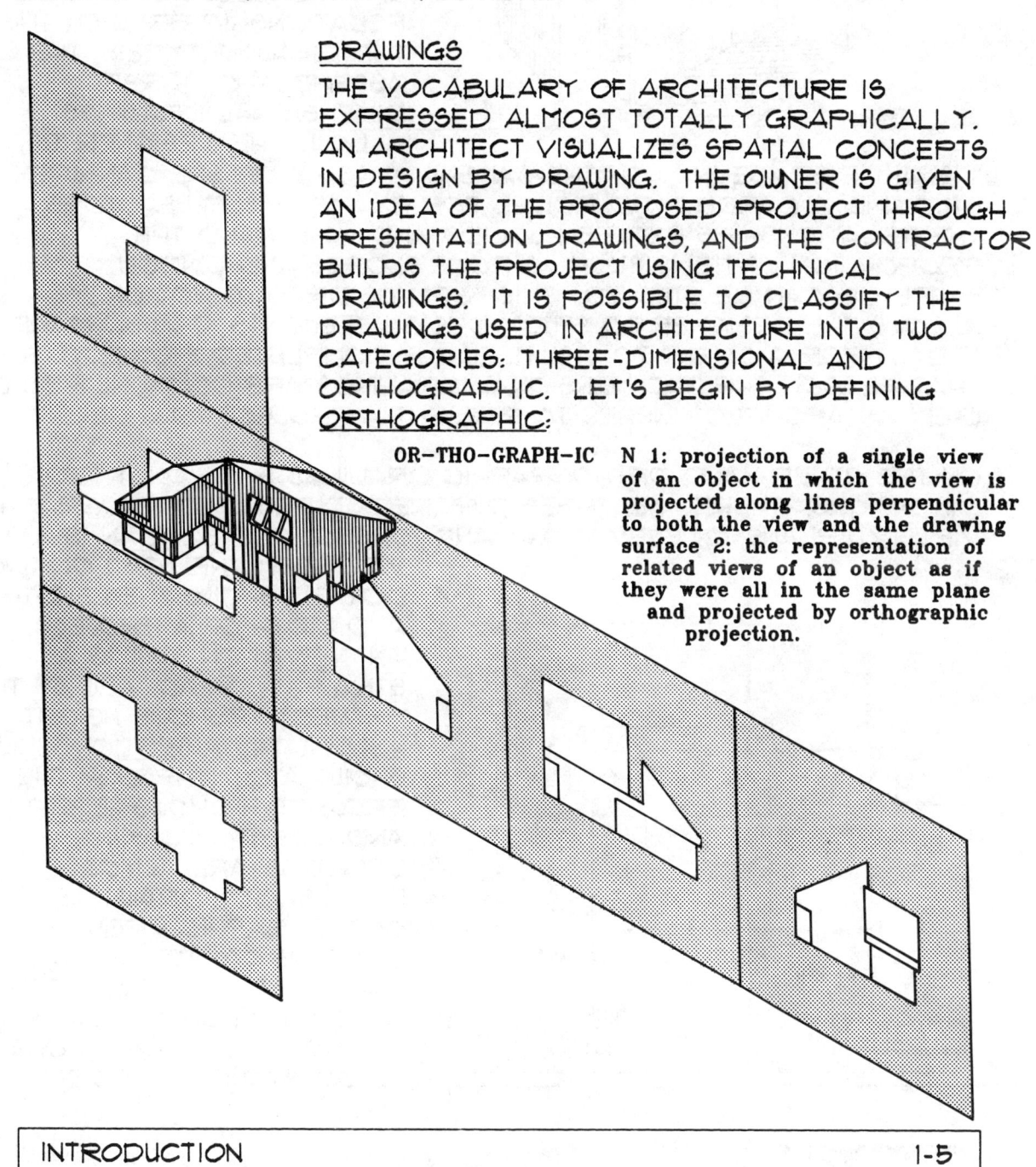

DRAWINGS

THE VOCABULARY OF ARCHITECTURE IS EXPRESSED ALMOST TOTALLY GRAPHICALLY. AN ARCHITECT VISUALIZES SPATIAL CONCEPTS IN DESIGN BY DRAWING. THE OWNER IS GIVEN AN IDEA OF THE PROPOSED PROJECT THROUGH PRESENTATION DRAWINGS, AND THE CONTRACTOR BUILDS THE PROJECT USING TECHNICAL DRAWINGS. IT IS POSSIBLE TO CLASSIFY THE DRAWINGS USED IN ARCHITECTURE INTO TWO CATEGORIES: THREE-DIMENSIONAL AND ORTHOGRAPHIC. LET'S BEGIN BY DEFINING ORTHOGRAPHIC:

OR-THO-GRAPH-IC N 1: projection of a single view of an object in which the view is projected along lines perpendicular to both the view and the drawing surface 2: the representation of related views of an object as if they were all in the same plane and projected by orthographic projection.

INTRODUCTION 1-5

THREE-DIMENSIONAL DRAWINGS, SUCH AS ISOMETRIC, AXNOMETRIC, AND PERSPECTIVE VIEWS, ARE GENERALLY USED TO PRESENT PROJECTS TO A CLIENT. TWO-DIMENSIONAL ORTHOGRAPHIC DRAWINGS ARE COMMONLY USED IN THE PRODUCTION OF CONSTRUCTION DRAWINGS.

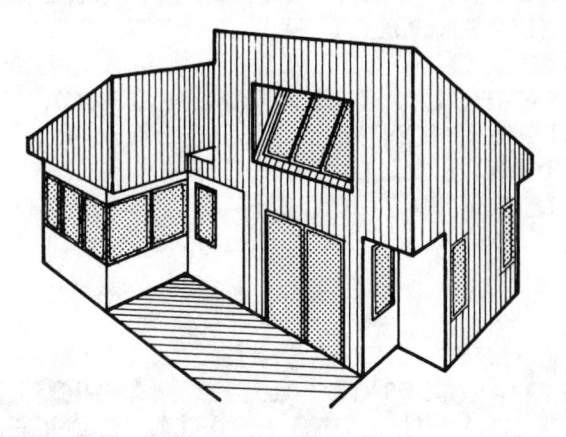

USING THE CABIN AS AN EXAMPLE, LET'S STUDY THE RELATIONSHIP BETWEEN THE TWO DRAWING TYPES. THE ASSEMBLY OF THREE-DIMENSIONAL DRAWINGS ALLOWS THE DESIGNER TO VISUALIZE SPACE IN MUCH THE SAME WAY AS HE OR SHE CAN WHEN STUDYING A CARDBOARD MODEL; FOR EXAMPLE, SUCH FACTORS AS THE RELATIONSHIPS BETWEEN SOLIDS AND VOIDS AND THE PROPORTION OF ITEMS SUCH AS ROOF SLOPES AND WINDOW PATTERNS CAN BE STUDIED. THIS FORM OF DRAWING NOT ONLY ALLOWS THE DESIGNER TO STUDY DESIGN ELEMENTS, IT ALSO MAKES IT EASY FOR A CLIENT TO VISUALIZE THE COMPLETED PROJECT. FOR THAT REASON, THREE-DIMENSIONAL DRAWINGS ARE COMMONLY USED WHEN AN ARCHITECT WISHES TO PRESENT A PROJECT TO A CLIENT.

ON THE OTHER HAND, ORTHOGRAPHIC DRAWINGS SHOW ONLY TWO DIMENSIONS. THERE ARE THREE DIFFERENT TYPES OF ORTHOGRAPHIC VIEWS: (1) PLANS, (2) ELEVATIONS, AND (3) SECTIONS. A PLAN IS A VIEW FROM THE TOP LOOKING DOWN; IT SHOWS THE LENGTH AND WIDTH OF A PROJECT. AN ELEVATION VIEW IS A STRAIGHT-AHEAD VIEW OF THE PROJECT; IT SHOWS HEIGHT AND WIDTH. A SECTION VIEW SHOWS A CUT THROUGH THE PROJECT; IT SHOWS HEIGHT AND LENGTH. WORKING DRAWINGS ARE ALMOST EXCLUSIVELY DRAWN AS ORTHOGRAPHIC VIEWS. A BUILDING CANNOT BE BUILT USING JUST ONE VIEW; IT TAKES A COMBINATION OF PLANS, ELEVATIONS, AND SECTIONS TO CONSTRUCT A PROJECT.

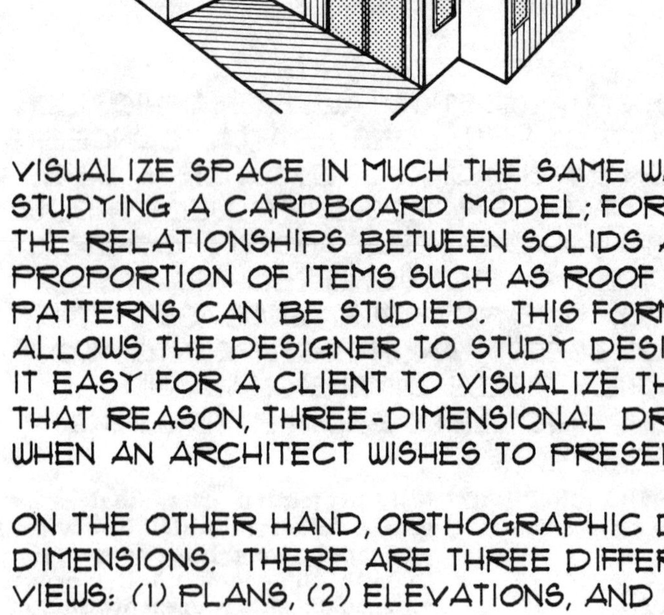

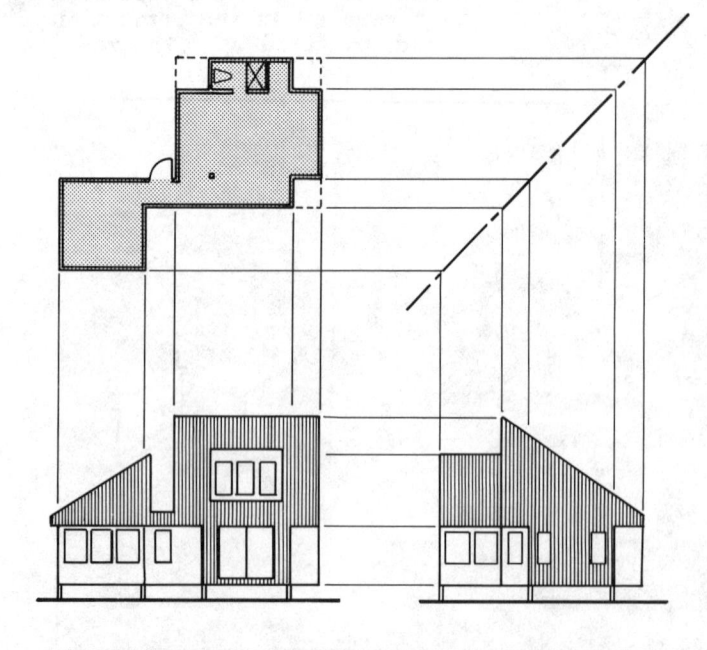

INTRODUCTION 1-6

WORKING DRAWINGS

THIS SECTION WILL INTRODUCE YOU TO THE PACKAGE OF DRAWINGS TYPICALLY FOUND IN A SET OF ARCHITECTURAL WORKING DRAWINGS AND WILL PROVIDE A BRIEF OVERVIEW OF THE 29 UNITS IN THIS TEXT. A SIMPLE DEFINITION OF <u>WORKING DRAWINGS</u> IS THAT THEY ARE THE GRAPHIC REPRESENTATION OF ALL THE INFORMATION A CONTRACTOR NEEDS TO KNOW IN ORDER TO BUILD A PROJECT. WORKING DRAWINGS MUST THEREFORE BE PRECISELY DRAWN TO SHOW DETAILED CONSTRUCTION CONDITIONS. THEY ARE PLACED IN THE SET OF DRAWINGS IN AN ORDER THAT BASICALLY CORRESPONDS TO THE PATTERN THAT THE CONTRACTOR FOLLOWS WHEN BUILDING A PROJECT. THE ORDER IS AS FOLLOWS:

1. SITE PLAN
2. FLOOR PLAN(S)
3. ELEVATIONS
4. SECTIONS

USING THE CABIN AS AN EXAMPLE, LET'S STUDY THE DRAWINGS THAT WOULD BE USED TO MAKE UP THE DRAWING PACKAGE.

SITE PLAN

THE SITE PLAN, OR "SITE," AS IT IS COMMONLY CALLED, IS AN ORTHOGRAPHIC PLAN SHOWING THE LENGTH AND WIDTH OF THE PROPERTY. THE SITE INDICATES (1) THE CONDITIONS THAT A CONTRACTOR CAN EXPECT TO FIND ON THE SITE BEFORE CONSTRUCTION, (2) THE ITEMS THAT THE CONTRACTOR MUST BUILD (OR CHANGE), AND (3) THE LOCATION OF THE BUILDING. A GOOD WAY TO VISUALIZE A SITE PLAN IS TO IMAGINE THE ORTHOGRAPHIC VIEW YOU WOULD SEE IF YOU WERE TO FLY OVER A PROJECT ONCE IT WAS COMPLETED. THE SITE DRAWING TO THE LEFT LOCATES THE CABIN BY DIMENSION FROM THE PROPERTY LINES. THE CURVED LINES (CALLED <u>TOPOGRAPHIC CONTOURS</u>) REPRESENT THE VERTICAL HEIGHTS ON THE SITE. THE SITE PLAN ALSO INDICATES THE SIZE AND LOCATION OF THE GRAVEL DRIVE THAT IS TO BE BUILT. IN OTHER WORDS, THE SITE DRAWING DIRECTS ALL CHANGES THAT ARE TO BE MADE BY THE CONTRACTOR.

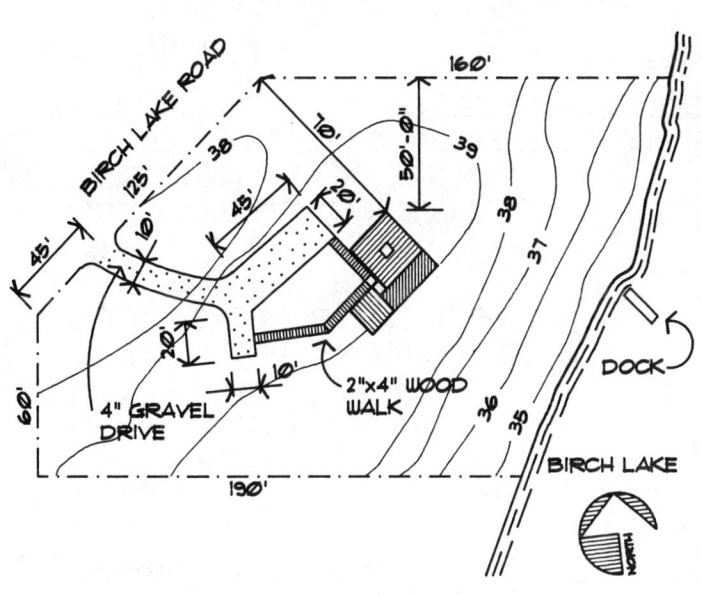

INTRODUCTION 1-7

FLOOR PLAN

THE FLOOR PLAN SHOWS AN ORTHOGRAPHIC VIEW OF THE WIDTH AND LENGTH OF THE BUILDING AND INCLUDES SUCH ITEMS AS WALLS, DOORS, WINDOWS, AND DECKS. ITEMS ON A FLOOR PLAN TYPICALLY ARE REPRESENTED IN THREE WAYS: (1) THEY ARE ACCURATELY DRAWN TO SCALE, (2) THEY ARE LOCATED BY DIMENSION, AND (3) THEY ARE GRAPHICALLY CODED (USING CROSSHATCHING) TO IDENTIFY THE CONSTRUCTION MATERIAL TO BE USED. A WAY TO VISUALIZE A FLOOR PLAN IS TO IMAGINE MAKING A HORIZONTAL CUT THROUGH THE BUILDING ABOUT 3' OFF THE FLOOR AND THEN LOOKING STRAIGHT DOWN TO THE FLOOR. THE CABIN ILLUSTRATED ABOVE SHOWS WHAT ITEMS ARE TYPICALLY INCLUDED ON THE PLAN VIEW.

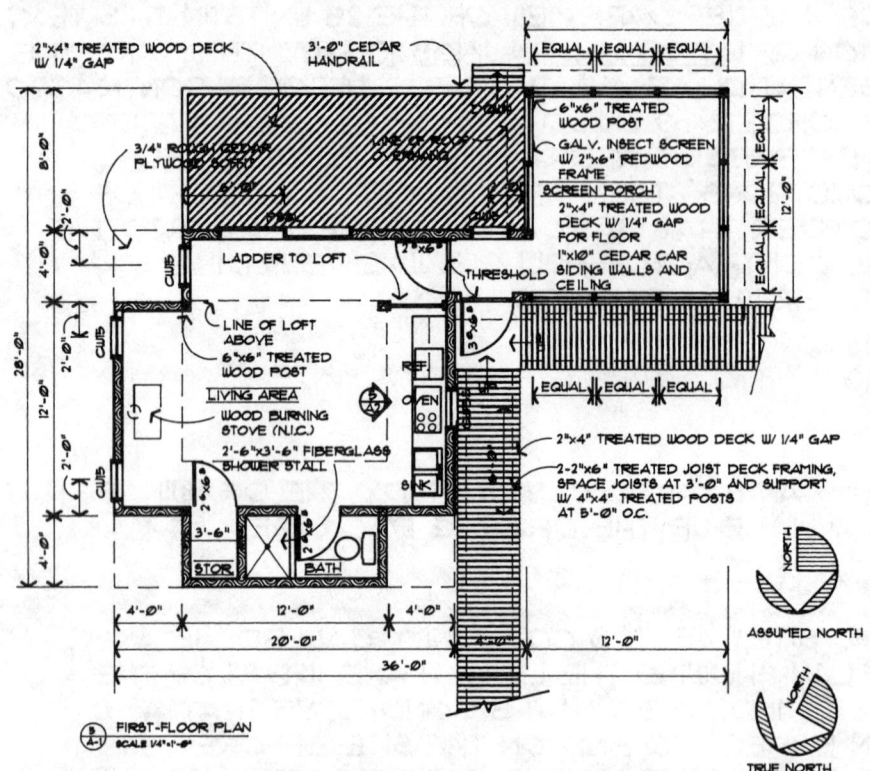

ELEVATIONS

ELEVATIONS SHOW AN ORTHOGRAPHIC VIEW OF THE HEIGHT AND WIDTH OF A BUILDING AND INCLUDE SUCH EXTERIOR ITEMS AS WINDOWS AND ROOF SLOPES. AN ELEVATION VIEW IS RATHER EASY TO VISUALIZE SINCE IT IS THE VIEW SEEN WHILE LOOKING AT THE PROJECT FROM THE OUTSIDE. ELEVATIONS ARE INTENDED TO REPRESENT ITEMS THE WAY THEY WOULD LOOK AFTER ASSEMBLY; FOR EXAMPLE, WINDOW FRAMES ARE DRAWN WITH DOUBLE LINES, AND SIDING IS DRAWN TO SHOW THE LAP SPACING.

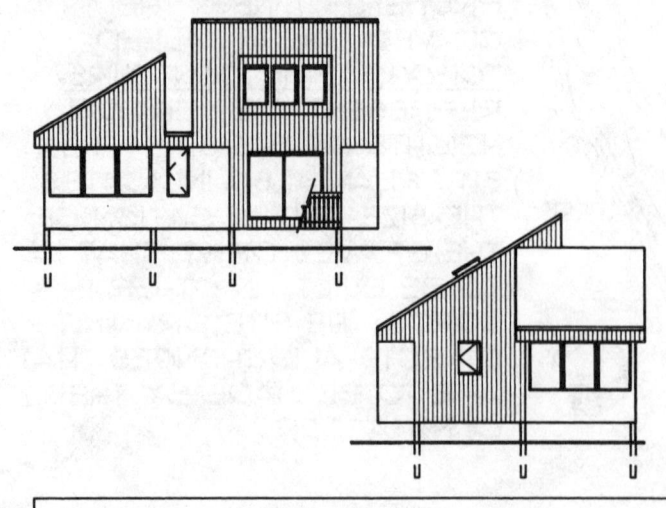

INTRODUCTION   1-8

SECTIONS

A SECTION VIEW SHOWS A VERTICAL CUT THROUGH A BUILDING. THE ORTHOGRAPHIC-VIEW DRAWING INDICATES CONSTRUCTION DETAILS THAT COULD ONLY BE SHOWN BY CUTTING APART THE FLOOR, WALLS, AND ROOF OF THE PROJECT. IT IS COMMON TO DRAW SECTIONS AT THREE DIFFERENT SCALES: (1) A BUILDING SECTION IS DRAWN AT A SMALL SCALE TO SHOW THE ENTIRE BUILDING; (2) A LARGER-SCALE WALL SECTION IS DRAWN IN ORDER TO ENLARGE INDIVIDUAL WALLS AND SHOW GREATER DETAIL; AND (3) BUILDING DETAILS ARE DRAWN AT A LARGE SCALE TO SHOW THE CONTRACTOR PRECISE CONSTRUCTION ASSEMBLY.

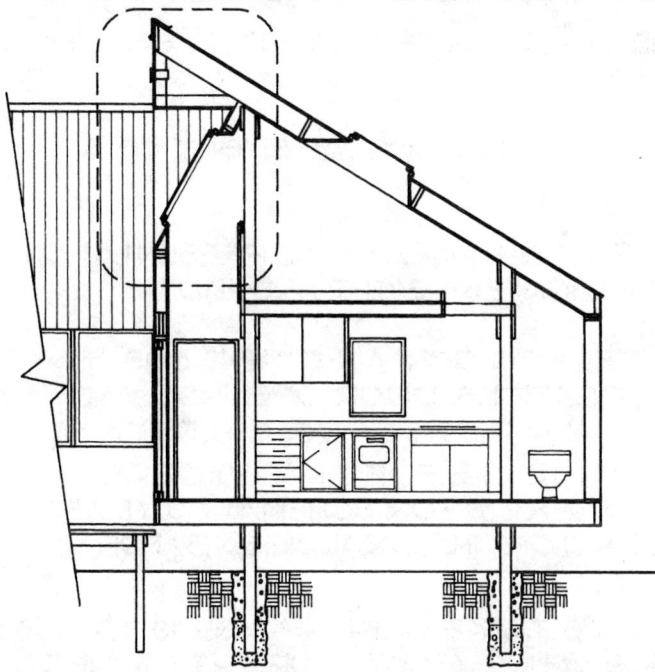

ABOVE IS A BUILDING SECTION CUT THROUGH THE CABIN. IT SHOWS THE SLOPED WINDOW AND SECOND-FLOOR LOFT, ITEMS THAT COULDN'T BE SHOWN ACCURATELY IN THE ORTHOGRAPHIC FLOOR PLANS AND ELEVATIONS. THE DRAWING TO THE LEFT IS A DETAIL DRAWING OF THE SLOPED WINDOW AND ROOF. SECTIONS DISPLAY INFORMATION REGARDING THE CONSTRUCTION TECHNIQUES USED TO ASSEMBLE THE BUILDING.

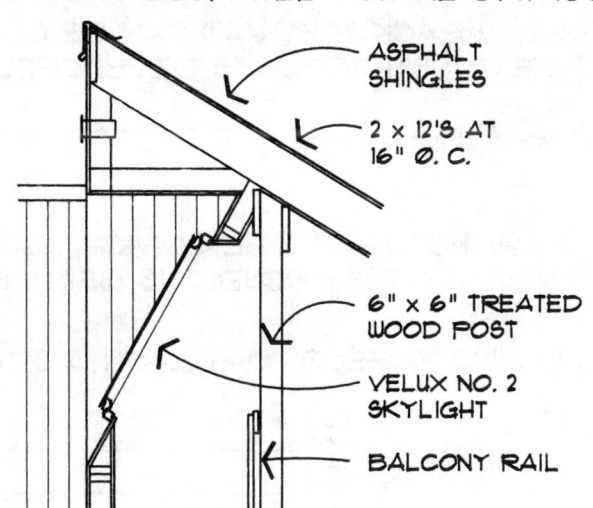

A WORKING DRAWING SET TRANSLATES A THREE-DIMENSIONAL DRAWING INTO TWO-DIMENSIONAL DRAWINGS IN ORDER TO GIVE THE BUILDER AN ACCURATE VIEW OF EVERY ASPECT OF A PROJECT. WORKING DRAWINGS SHOULD DIRECT THE CONTRACTOR IN MEETING QUALITY REQUIREMENTS AND COMPLETING THE TECHNICAL ASSEMBLY OF ALL PARTS OF THE BUILDING PROCESS. KEEP IN MIND THAT THESE DRAWINGS FORM PART OF THE LEGAL CONTRACT THAT THE OWNER HAS ENTERED INTO WITH THE CONTRACTOR.

INTRODUCTION

REPLAY

QUESTIONS 1 THROUGH 4 DEAL WITH ORTHOGRAPHIC VIEWS: ANSWER (P) FOR PLAN, (E) FOR ELEVATION, AND (S) FOR SECTION.

_____ 1. THIS VIEW SHOWS THE LOCATION OF A BUILDING ON THE SITE.

_____ 2. THIS VIEW SHOWS THE CONSTRUCTION ASSEMBLY OF A SKYLIGHT IN A ROOF.

_____ 3. THIS VIEW SHOWS A "STRAIGHT-AHEAD" REPRESENTATION OF A BUILDING AND INDICATES HEIGHT AND WIDTH.

_____ 4. THIS VIEW IS MOST LIKELY TO CONTAIN DIMENSIONS INDICATING WINDOW LOCATIONS, DOOR OPENINGS, AND THE OVERALL LENGTH AND WIDTH OF THE BUILDING.

QUESTIONS 5 THROUGH 8 PERTAIN TO THE FIVE PHASES OF AN ARCHITECTURAL CONTRACT: ANSWER (S) FOR SCHEMATICS, (D) FOR DESIGN DEVELOPMENT, (WD) FOR WORKING DRAWINGS, (B) FOR BIDDING, OR (C) FOR CONSTRUCTION.

_____ 5. ONE OF THE ARCHITECT'S TASKS IN THIS PHASE IS TO ASSIST CONTRACTORS IN PREPARING A COST FOR THE PROJECT.

_____ 6. IN THIS PHASE A ROUGH BUILDING DESIGN IS CREATED.

_____ 7. IN THIS PHASE A DRAWING PACKAGE THAT CAN BE GIVEN TO A CONTRACTOR FOR CONSTRUCTION IS DEVELOPED.

_____ 8. A MAIN GOAL IN THIS PHASE IS TO REFINE THE PRELIMINARY DESIGN CONCEPT.

_____ 9. IN THIS PHASE THE ARCHITECT MAKES PERIODIC VISITS TO THE SITE TO DETERMINE THAT THE PROJECT IS BEING BUILT ACCORDING TO THE PLANS.

10. LIST FOUR ITEMS THAT YOU WOULD EXPECT TO FIND ON A SITE PLAN.

(A) _____   (C) _____
(B) _____   (D) _____

11. LIST SIX ITEMS THAT YOU WOULD EXPECT TO FIND ON A FLOOR PLAN.

(A) _____   (D) _____
(B) _____   (E) _____
(C) _____   (F) _____

INTRODUCTION   1-10

2 DRAFTING TOOLS

THIS UNIT WILL REVIEW THE TOOLS THAT ARE NEEDED FOR DRAFTING. EACH TOOL ILLUSTRATION IS ACCOMPANIED BY A BRIEF NARRATIVE GIVING TIPS ON USE AND DESCRIBING POINTS TO LOOK FOR WHEN PURCHASING EQUIPMENT. THE LEAST EXPENSIVE TOOL ISN'T ALWAYS THE BEST BUY. A QUALITY TOOL CAN EASILY LAST SEVERAL TIMES LONGER THAN A CHEAPER ONE. IN ADDITION TO DETERMINING QUALITY, SELECT A TOOL THAT FEELS RIGHT IN YOUR HAND.

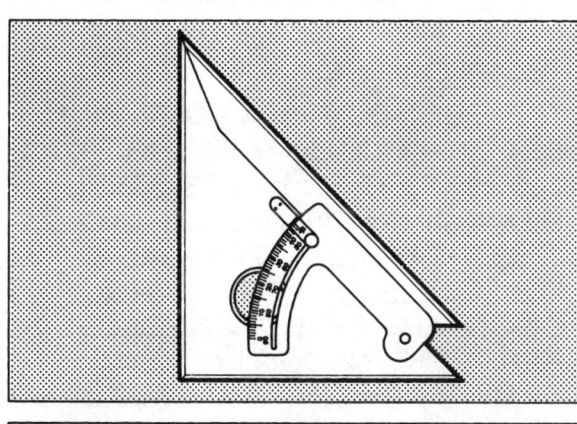

ADJUSTABLE TRIANGLE

SELECT A TRIANGLE MADE OF GOOD-QUALITY ACRYLIC. IT SHOULD FLEX SLIGHTLY WHEN BENT. A 10" SIZE IS THE BEST CHOICE. A BEVELED EDGE WILL PERMIT USING A TECH PEN. TAPE THREE DIMES UNDER THE TRIANGLE WHEN USING INK.

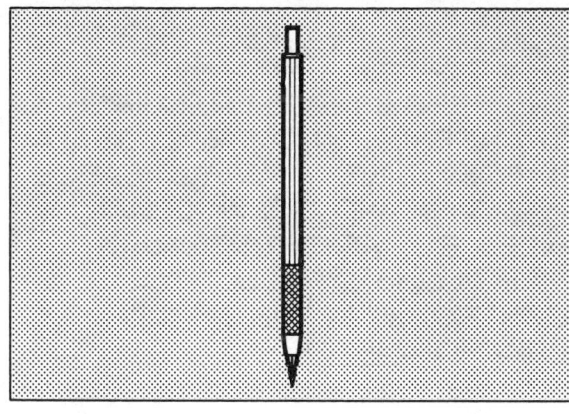

LEAD HOLDER (2 mm LEAD)

A LEAD HOLDER SHOULD HAVE PROPER BALANCE AND WEIGHT. CHECK THE KNURLING AT THE BASE OF THE HOLDER TO DETERMINE ITS FEEL. BUY HOLDERS WITH DIFFERENT COLORED ENDS TO IDENTIFY DIFFERENT LEAD WEIGHTS.

DRAFTING TOOLS

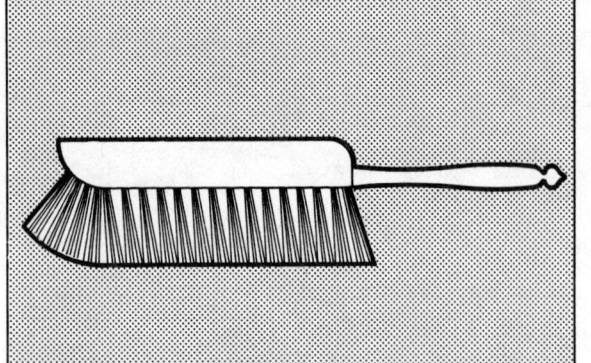

DRAFTING BRUSH

SELECT A COMPACT BRUSH WITH NATURAL BRISTLES.

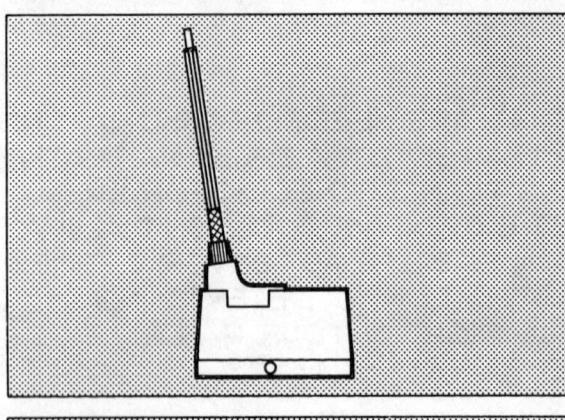

LEAD POINTER

SELECT A POINTER THAT WILL SIT ON A DRAFTING BOARD WITHOUT ROLLING OFF. THE POINTER SHOULD BE EASY TO EMPTY. LOOK FOR A UNIT WITH A VARIABLE LEAD-POINT LENGTH THAT WILL PRODUCE A SMOOTH TIP.

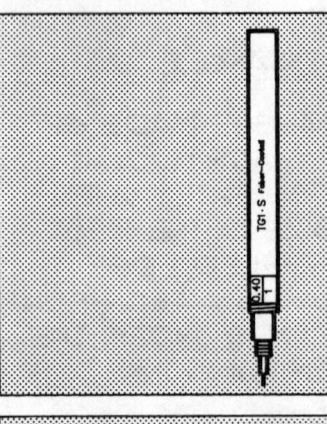

TECHNICAL PEN

THE BEST BUY IS A FOUR-PEN SET WITH POINTS RANGING FROM Ø.3 mm TO Ø.6 mm. USE STEEL PEN POINTS ON VELLUM AND JEWEL-TIP PENS ON PLASTIC FILM. SELECT A PEN WITH A GOOD AIR SEAL TO REDUCE PEN POINT CLOGGING.

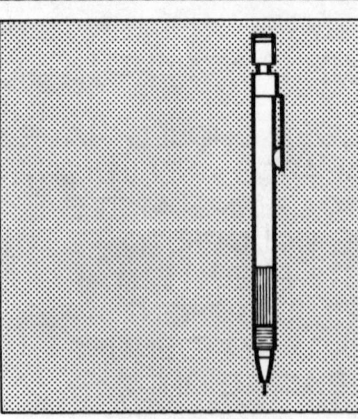

MECHANICAL PENCIL

THE PENCIL NEVER REQUIRES SHARPENING AND PRODUCES A UNIFORM LINE. IT IS AVAILABLE IN Ø.3 mm AND Ø.5 mm LEAD SIZES, BUT ARCHITECTURAL PRINTING IS DIFFICULT TO CONTROL WITH THE SMALL LEAD DIAMETER.

DRAFTING TOOLS

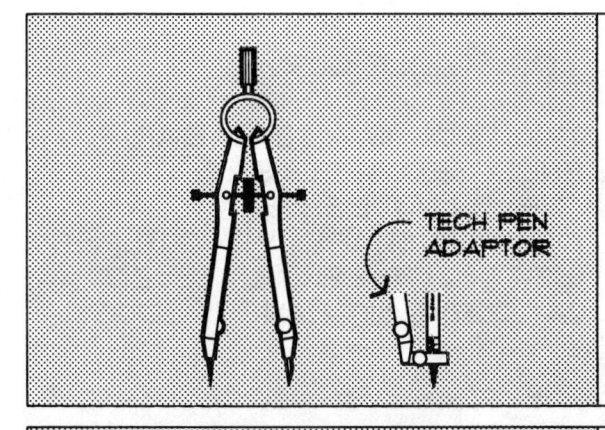

BOW COMPASS

A BOW COMPASS WORKS WELL IN MAKING CIRCLES REQUIRING FINE ADJUSTMENT. A SINGLE COMPASS IS A BETTER BUY THAN A DRAFTING SET. A TECH PEN ADAPTOR IS USEFUL FOR DRAWING INK-LINE CIRCLES.

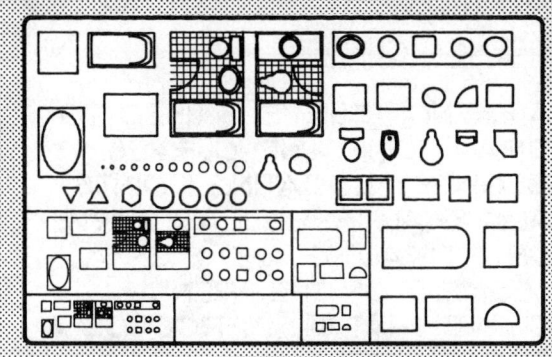

TECH PEN ADAPTOR

TOILET TEMPLATE

SELECT A TEMPLATE WITH A VARIETY OF FIXTURE TYPES. FIXTURES SHOULD BE SHOWN AT 1/4", 1/8", AND 1/16" SCALES. CHECK THE TEMPLATE TO DETERMINE THAT THE HOLES ARE CUT IN A SMOOTH MANNER.

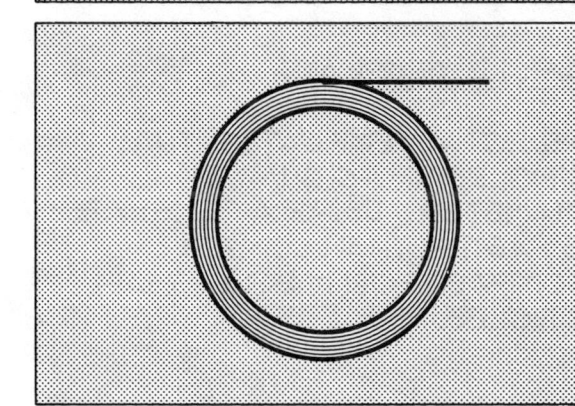

DRAFTING TAPE

SELECT A QUALITY-BRAND DRAFTING TAPE; DON'T USE MASKING TAPE (IT IS TOO STICKY). TAPE CIRCLES ARE ALSO AVAILABLE.

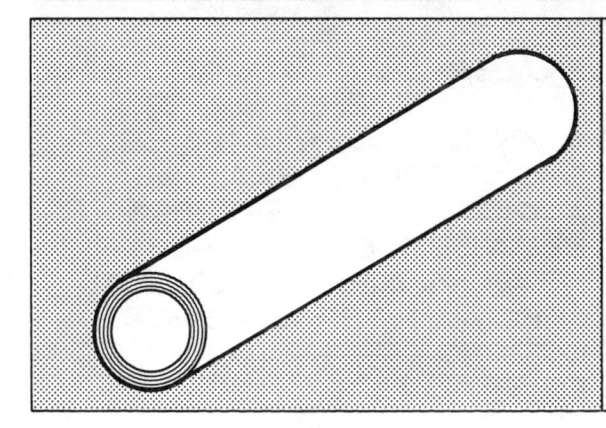

SKETCH PAPER

THIS IS THE PAPER THAT ARCHITECTS USE FOR SKETCHING DETAILS. THE PAPER (USUALLY LIGHT YELLOW IN COLOR) WILL ALLOW PENCIL, INK, OR FELT-TIP PEN DRAWING. SELECT A 12"- OR 18"-WIDE ROLL.

DRAFTING TOOLS

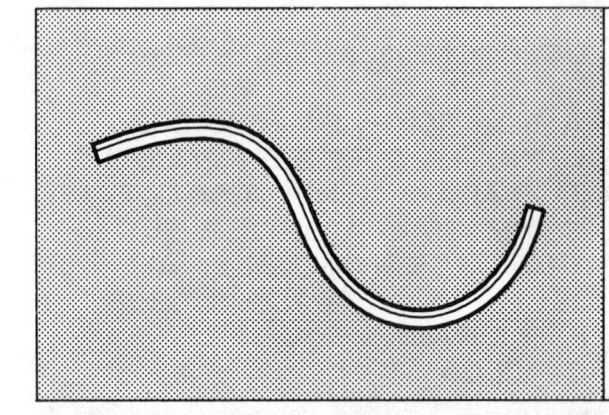

ADJUSTABLE CURVE

THIS TOOL IS A LEAD BAR ENCLOSED IN PLASTIC. THE CURVE MAY BE BENT TO A DESIRED SHAPE AND OUTLINED WITH INK OR PENCIL. SELECT A 24" CURVE WITH AN INK EDGE.

FRENCH CURVE

A FRENCH CURVE IS USED TO DRAW COMPOUND CURVES. BEGIN BY LOCATING POINTS ALONG AN IRREGULAR CURVE ON A DRAWING AND PICK A SEGMENT ON THE FRENCH CURVE THAT WILL PRODUCE A SMOOTH LINE.

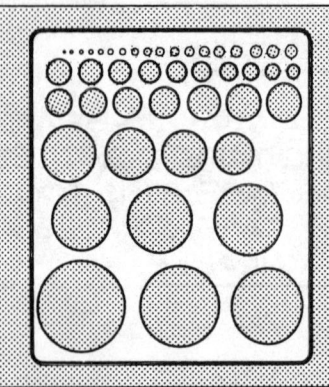

CIRCLE TEMPLATE

SELECT A TEMPLATE WITH CIRCLES UP TO 2 1/4" IN DIAMETER. USING A TEMPLATE IS FASTER THAN USING A COMPASS FOR MAKING SMALL CIRCLES.

ERASER

A VINYL ERASER IS THE BEST CHOICE FOR GENERAL USE. AVOID HARD INK ERASERS BECAUSE THEY MAR THE DRAFTING SURFACE. SELECT SPECIAL INK ERASERS FOR WORKING WITH INK ON PLASTIC DRAFTING FILM.

DRAFTING TOOLS 2-4

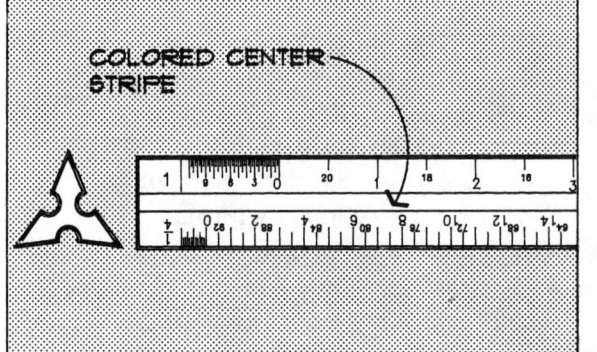

ARCHITECT'S SCALE

SELECT A GOOD-QUALITY 12" TRIANGULAR SCALE WITH ENGRAVED NUMBERS. A SCALE WITH A WOOD CORE IS MORE EXPENSIVE THAN SOLID PLASTIC. A SCALE WITH A COLORED CENTER STRIPE MAKES SCALE SELECTION EASY.

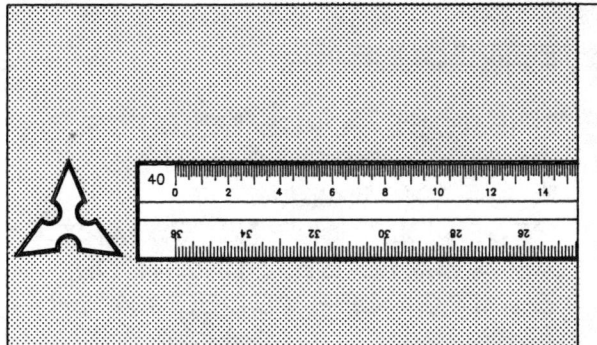

COLORED CENTER STRIPE

ENGINEER'S SCALE

FIND A SCALE SIMILAR IN QUALITY TO YOUR ARCHITECT'S SCALE. LESS EXPENSIVE TOOLS HAVE PAINTED NUMBERS RATHER THAN ENGRAVED; THESE RUB OFF WITH USE.

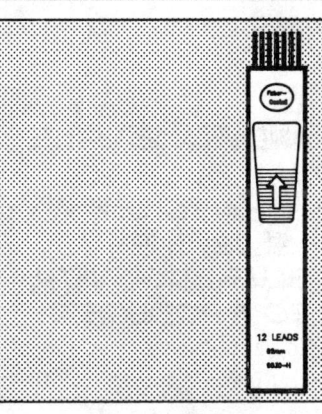

DRAFTING LEAD

SELECT A QUALITY BRAND-NAME LEAD (2H AND H WEIGHTS). POOR QUALITY LEAD CAN CAUSE A LOT OF PROBLEMS. USE PLASTIC LEAD WHEN DRAWING ON MYLAR DRAFTING FILM.

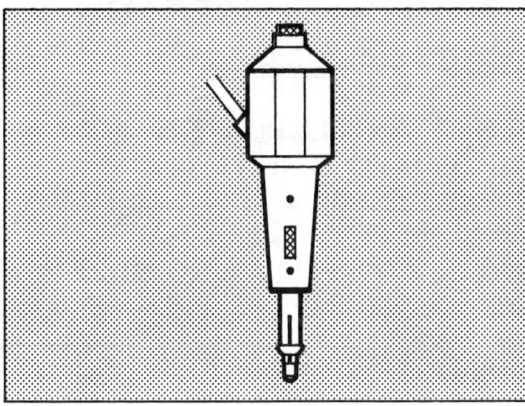

ELECTRIC ERASER

THIS TOOL IS EXPENSIVE AND CAN BE SKIPPED UNTIL YOU GET VERY INVOLVED WITH DRAFTING. IT DOES SAVE TIME ON LARGE PROJECTS, BUT, WHEN USING IT, YOU MUST BE CAREFUL NOT TO RUB A HOLE IN THE PAPER.

DRAFTING TOOLS

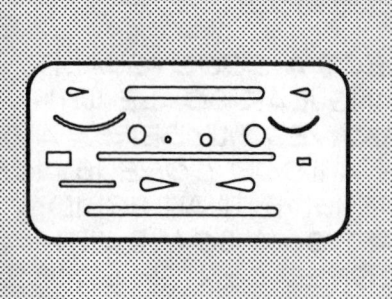

ERASING SHIELD

THIS IS A VERY USEFUL TOOL. USE IT WHENEVER YOU ARE ERASING IN TIGHT SPACES. SELECT A SHIELD WITH A VARIETY OF ROUND AND SQUARE HOLES. PICK A THIN SHIELD AND PUT A SLIGHT BEND IN IT TO ALLOW EASY PICKUP.

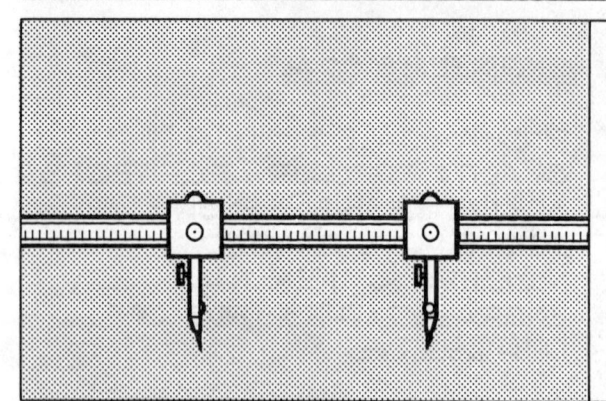

BEAM COMPASS

THIS TOOL WORKS WELL FOR DRAWING CIRCLES WITH MORE THAN A 4" RADIUS. IT PROBABLY ISN'T NECESSARY AS A BASIC DRAFTING TOOL, BUT IT CAN BE ADDED LATER.

GLUE

SELECT A BRAND-NAME WHITE GLUE FOR MODEL BUILDING. IT IS A GOOD IDEA TO USE A THIN COAT OF GLUE; THEN SPREAD THE GLUE EDGE WITH YOUR FINGER TO PRODUCE A UNIFORM BEAD.

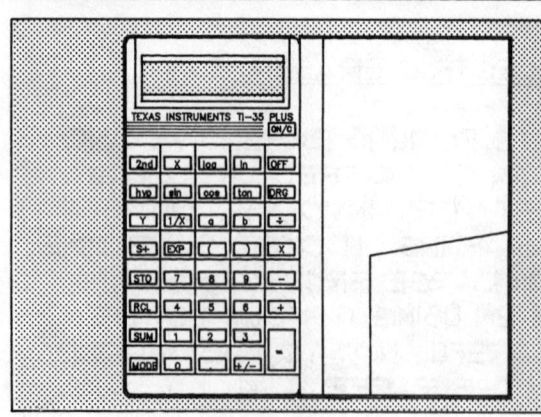

POCKET CALCULATOR

SELECT A CALCULATOR THAT HAS TRIG FUNCTIONS AND SCIENTIFIC NOTATION (NUMBERS UP TO 99 DECIMALS). A CALCULATOR WITH AN AUTO SHUT-OFF SAVES BATTERIES.

DRAFTING TOOLS

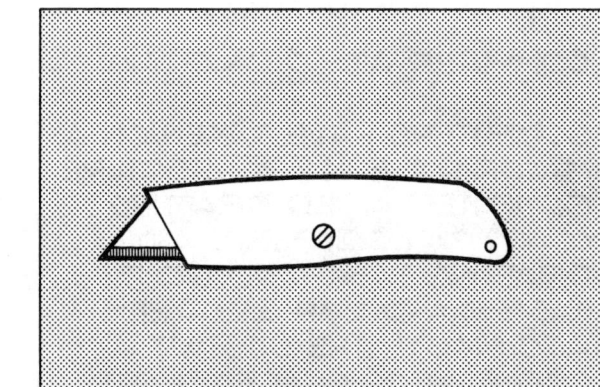

MAT KNIFE

THIS KNIFE IS A GOOD CHOICE FOR JOBS RANGING FROM CUTTING PAPER TO MAKING MODELS. THE SIZE OF THE TOOL ALLOWS YOU TO APPLY PRESSURE WHEN CUTTING CARDBOARD. ALWAYS USE A SHARP BLADE.

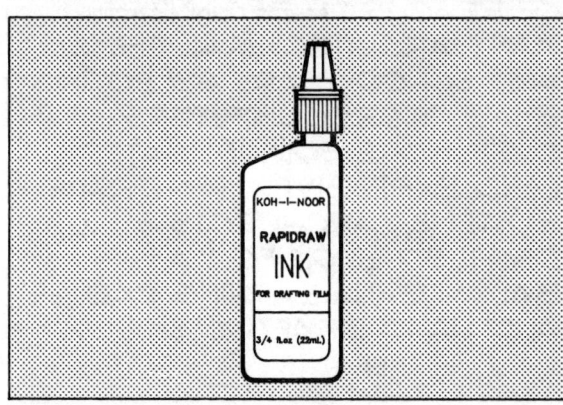

DRAFTING INK

THERE IS A VARIETY OF DRAFTING INKS AVAILABLE; MAKE SURE YOU SELECT THE PROPER INK FOR THE JOB. SOME INK DRIES VERY FAST FOR SUMMER USE BUT TENDS TO CLOG PENS IN LOW HUMIDITY.

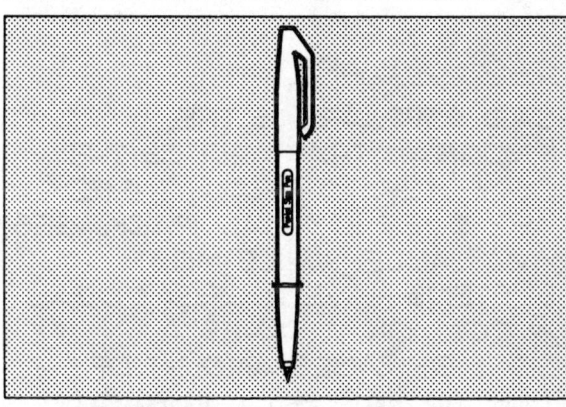

FELT-TIP PEN

SELECT A PEN WITH A GOOD TIP (ARCHITECTS TEND TO USE BROAD POINTS). THE PRIMARY USE OF THE PEN WILL BE TO DRAW DETAILS ON SKETCH PAPER. MAKE SURE THE PEN YOU SELECT DOESN'T SMEAR

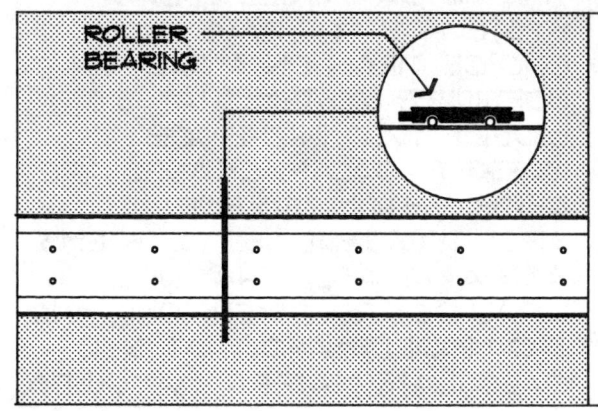

PARALLEL BAR

A PARALLEL BAR CAN COST NEARLY AS MUCH AS ALL OF THE OTHER TOOLS DISCUSSED IN THIS UNIT PUT TOGETHER. SELECT A QUALITY BAR WITH ROLLER BEARINGS ALONG THE UNDERSIDE. NEVER USE THE EDGE AS A CUTTING SURFACE.

DRAFTING TOOLS

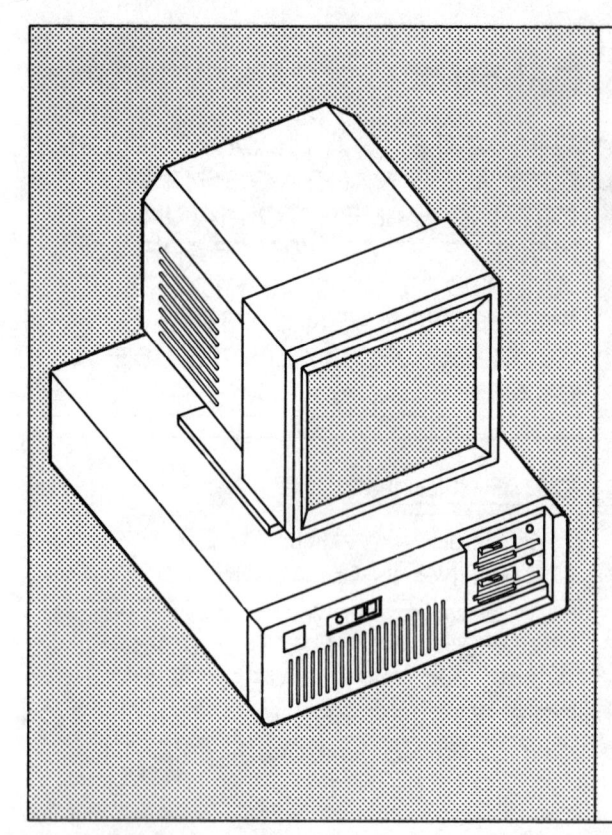

COMPUTER AIDED DRAFTING

COMPUTERS HAVE TAKEN ON A MAJOR ROLE IN ARCHITECTURE. COMPUTER AIDED DRAFTING (CAD) CAN COMPLETE ANY DRAFTING TASK—AND DO IT FASTER AND WITH GREATER ACCURACY. THE COST OF A CAD STATION PLACES IT OUT OF REACH FOR BEGINNERS. MANY ARCHITECTURAL FIRMS AND SCHOOLS ARE SELECTING SMALL MICROCOMPUTERS OVER MORE SOPHISTICATED (AND EXPENSIVE) MAIN-FRAME SYSTEMS. ARCHITECTS STILL DRAW, SO LOOK FOR A BALANCE IN LEARNING CAD AND HAND DRAFTING SKILLS.

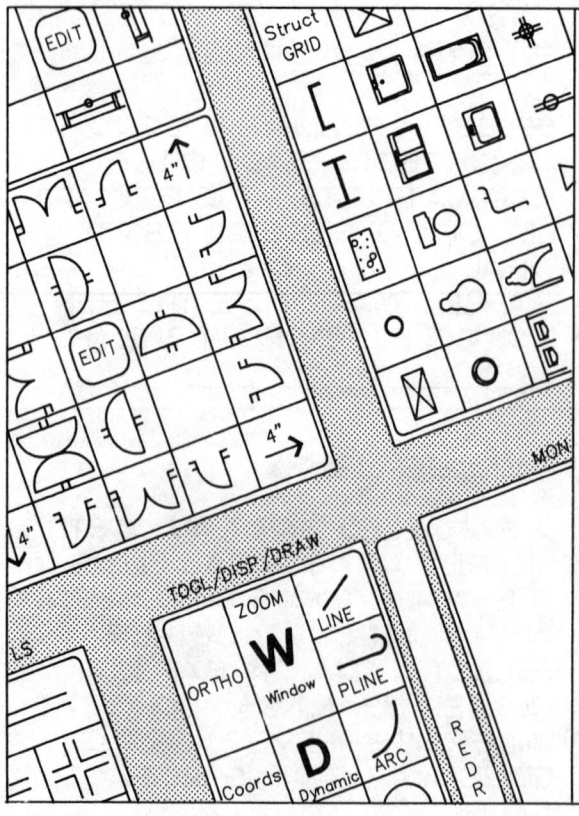

CAD SOFTWARE

CAD SOFTWARE IS THE PROGRAM THAT ALLOWS THE COMPUTER TO DRAW. THERE ARE OVER 100 CAD PACKAGES AVAILABLE. WHILE MOST SYSTEMS HAVE A GREAT DEAL IN COMMON, IT TAKES A CONSIDERABLE AMOUNT OF TIME TO GAIN SKILL IN EACH SYSTEM. IF YOU HAVE A CHOICE, TRAIN ON A CAD SOFTWARE SYSTEM THAT IS WIDELY USED IN THE JOB MARKET. CAD PACKAGES ARE QUITE CUSTOMIZED FOR ARCHITECTURAL USE. SYSTEMS ARE AVAILABLE THAT WILL DRAW DOORS, DIMENSIONS, AND 3-D MODELS, AND THAT WILL CALCULATE MATERIAL AMOUNTS.

DRAFTING TOOLS 2-8

TOOL USE TIPS
THIS PAGE OFFERS SEVERAL TIPS FOR USING DRAFTING TOOLS.

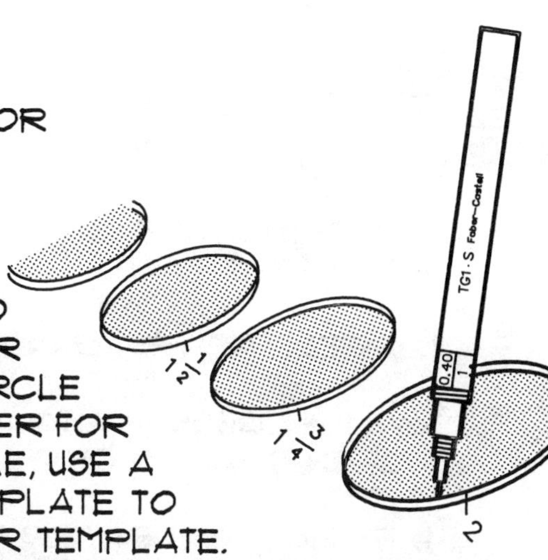

1. INK DRAFTING
WHEN DRAFTING WITH INK, PLACE ONE TEMPLATE OVER ANOTHER TO PREVENT INK FROM FLOWING UNDER THE EDGE. SELECT A LARGER CIRCLE ON THE BOTTOM TO ACT AS SPACER FOR THE TOP TEMPLATE. FOR EXAMPLE, USE A 2 1/2" CIRCLE ON THE BOTTOM TEMPLATE TO DRAW A 2" CIRCLE WITH THE UPPER TEMPLATE. THE SPACE BETWEEN THE UPPER TEMPLATE AND THE DRAWING WILL PREVENT INK FROM FLOWING UNDER THE TEMPLATE.

2. ERASING
AN ERASING SHIELD WILL ALLOW YOU TO PUT MORE PRESSURE ON YOUR ERASER. A SLIGHT AMOUNT OF EXTRA FORCE TENDS TO CAUSE LESS SMEARING AND MAKES THE TASK GO FASTER. THERE ARE A VARIETY OF ERASERS DESIGNED TO WORK WITH INK OR PENCIL ON PAPER OR PLASTIC FILM; BE SURE TO SELECT THE PRODUCT DESIGNED FOR THE JOB.

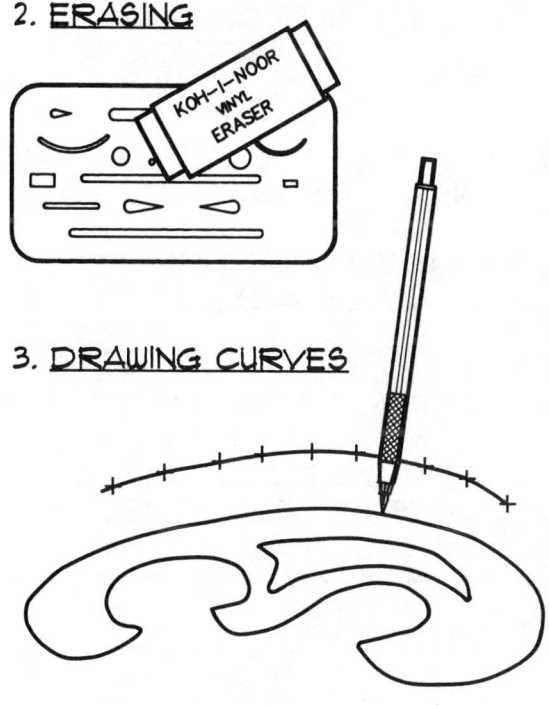

3. DRAWING CURVES
USE A FRENCH CURVE TO DRAW AN IRREGULAR CURVE. BEGIN THE DRAWING BY MARKING THE POINTS THAT ARE TO LIE ALONG THE LINE. THEN SELECT A SEGMENT OF THE FRENCH CURVE THAT MATCHES THE DRAWING AND USE IT AS A DRAWING EDGE.

4. MARKING SEGMENTS
MARK UNIFORM SEGMENTS ON A DRAWING BY MAKING A PHOTO-COPY OF YOUR ARCHITECT'S SCALE. PLACE THE PAPER COPY OF THE SCALE UNDER THE DRAWING SHEET TO ELIMINATE MARKING THE POINTS WITH A PENCIL.

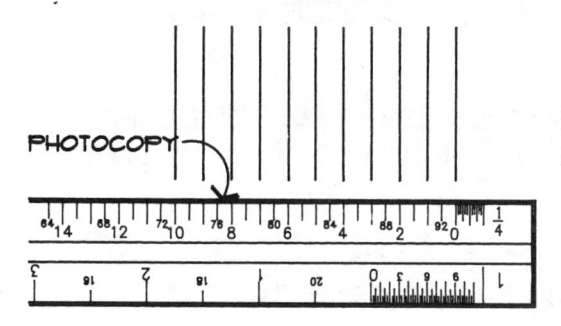

DRAFTING TOOLS 2-9

REPLAY
CIRCLE (T) IF THE STATEMENT IS TRUE AND (F) IF THE STATEMENT IS FALSE.

T F   1. MASKING TAPE IS AN ACCEPTABLE SUBSTITUTE FOR DRAFTING TAPE.

T F   2. A FELT-TIP PEN CAN BE USED ON SKETCH PAPER.

T F   3. IT IS NECESSARY TO USE A JEWEL-TIP TECHNICAL PEN WHEN DRAWING ON PLASTIC DRAFTING FILM.

T F   4. IT WOULD BE EASIER TO DRAW A SMALL CIRCLE (FOR EXAMPLE, 1/4" DIAMETER) BY USING A CIRCLE TEMPLATE THAN BY USING A BOW COMPASS.

T F   5. THE SMALL LEAD DIAMETER IN A ⌀.3 mm MECHANICAL PENCIL MAKES IT DIFFICULT TO CONTROL ARCHITECTURAL PRINTING.

T F   6. WHEN BUILDING A CARDBOARD MODEL, A WIDE BEAD OF WHITE GLUE WORKS BETTER THAN A THIN COAT.

T F   7. AN ERASING SHIELD SHOULD BE USED WHEN YOU ARE ERASING LARGE AREAS (FOR EXAMPLE, A 2" x 3" DRAWING).

T F   8. IF YOU WERE DRAWING 50 LINES SPACED 1/16" APART, IT WOULD BE FASTER TO MAKE A PHOTOCOPY OF YOUR ARCHITECT'S SCALE AND PLACE IT UNDER YOUR DRAFTING SHEET THAN TO PLACE TICK MARKS AT EACH POINT.

T F   9. WHILE MOST CAD PACKAGES HAVE A LOT IN COMMON, IT TAKES A GREAT AMOUNT PRACTICE TO GAIN SKILL IN EACH SYSTEM.

T F   10. IT WOULD BE BETTER TO SELECT A BEAM COMPASS THAN A BOW COMPASS TO DRAW A CIRCLE WITH A 1" RADIUS.

T F   11. PLASTIC DRAFTING LEAD SHOULD BE SUBSTITUTED FOR STANDARD DRAFTING LEAD WHEN DRAWING ON MYLAR DRAFTING FILM.

T F   12. AN IRREGULAR CURVE SHOULD BE CONSTRUCTED BY USING A BOW COMPASS WITH SHORT ARCS THAT CONNECT.

DRAFTING TOOLS

3 ARCHITECTURAL DRAFTING

THIS UNIT ON ARCHITECTURAL DRAFTING PRESENTS THE GRAPHICS USED TO ASSEMBLE TECHNICAL WORKING DRAWINGS. VIRTUALLY EVERYTHING ASSEMBLED IN AN ARCHITECTURAL FIRM INVOLVES DRAWING LINES. THE UNIT WILL DISCUSS THE TECHNIQUES THAT YOU MUST MASTER TO DEVELOP QUALITY DRAFTING. ARCHITECTURAL DRAFTING IS DEVELOPED WITH PRACTICE—USE THE TIPS TO IMPROVE YOUR STYLE.

GOOD DRAFTING IS ESSENTIAL TO THE ARCHITECT. IT IS THE VOCABULARY THAT HE OR SHE USES TO EXPRESS IDEAS TO AN OWNER OR CONTRACTOR. THE FIRST SKILL TO BE MASTERED IN ARCHITECTURAL DRAFTING IS PRECISION. LINES SHOULD BE LOCATED BY PLACING TICK MARKS AT EACH END. ALWAYS USE A SCALE TO PLACE OBJECTS AND TAKE TIME TO BE ACCURATE. WITH PRACTICE, IT IS POSSIBLE TO COME WITHIN 1" IN SCALE USING AN 1/8"=1'-0" ARCHITECT'S SCALE. THE SECOND SKILL TO MASTER IS THE STYLE OF ARCHITECTURAL DRAFTING. IT IS A BLEND OF THE RIGID TECHNICAL DRAFTING USED IN MECHANICAL DRAWING WITH AN ARTISTIC QUALITY. THIS UNIT WILL PRESENT TIPS AND EXAMPLES SHOWING GOOD ARCHITECTURAL DRAFTING. THE SKILL CAN BE MASTERED THROUGH PRACTICE AND CONSTANT EVALUATION OF YOUR WORK.

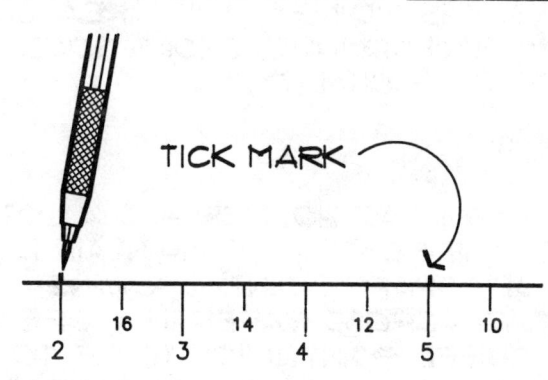

LINE QUALITY
LINE QUALITY DEALS WITH THE TECHNIQUE USED TO DRAW A LINE. THE OBJECT IS TO DRAW LINES THAT APPEAR CRISP RATHER THAN

FUZZY. THE QUALITY OF A LINE CAN BE CONTROLLED BY
1. THE PRESSURE YOU PLACE ON YOUR LEAD HOLDER
2. THE SHARPNESS OF THE DRAFTING TIP
3. THE LEAD WEIGHT

PRACTICE DRAFTING USING DIFFERENT AMOUNTS OF PRESSURE ON YOUR LEAD HOLDER. AN EVEN PRESSURE, FOR EXAMPLE, WILL PRODUCE UNIFORM LINES RANGING FROM LIGHT GUIDELINES TO HEAVY DETAIL OUTLINES. THE ILLUSTRATION BELOW SHOWS EXAMPLES OF BOTH GOOD AND POOR LINE QUALITY.

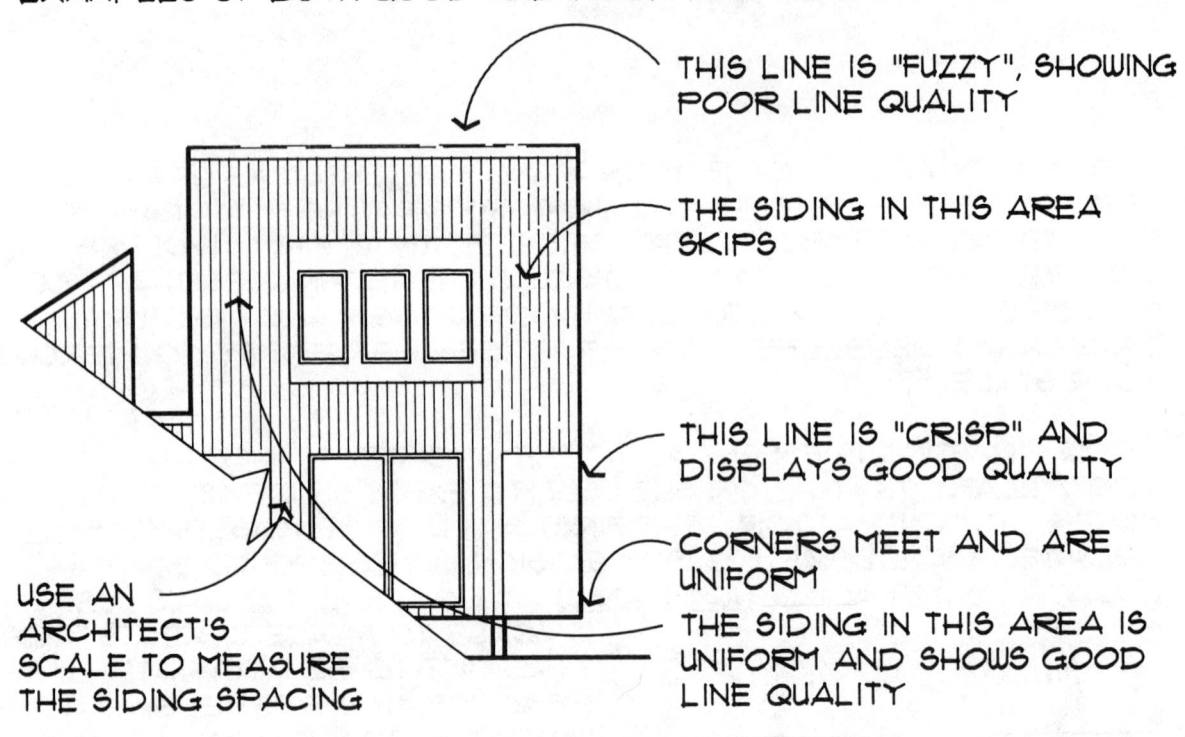

THIS LINE IS "FUZZY", SHOWING POOR LINE QUALITY

THE SIDING IN THIS AREA SKIPS

THIS LINE IS "CRISP" AND DISPLAYS GOOD QUALITY

CORNERS MEET AND ARE UNIFORM

THE SIDING IN THIS AREA IS UNIFORM AND SHOWS GOOD LINE QUALITY

USE AN ARCHITECT'S SCALE TO MEASURE THE SIDING SPACING

THE SHARPNESS OF THE POINT ON YOUR LEAD HOLDER HAS A LOT TO DO WITH THE QUALITY OF A LINE. THE BEST TIP TO MAINTAIN IS A SEMISHARP POINT. DRAWING LEAD ACROSS PAPER WILL CREATE A CHISEL POINT WHICH TENDS TO MAKE A FUZZY LINE. DEVELOP A TECHNIQUE OF SLOWLY ROTATING YOUR LEAD HOLDER BETWEEN YOUR THUMB AND INDEX FINGER WHEN YOU DRAW. PRACTICE MAKING ONE ROTATION IN ABOUT 24" OF LINE. THIS TECHNIQUE WILL MAINTAIN A UNIFORM POINT.

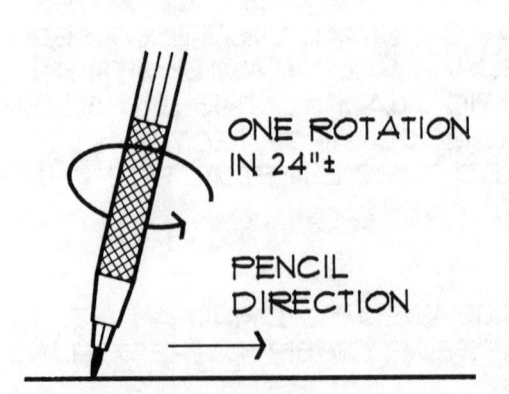

ONE ROTATION IN 24"±

PENCIL DIRECTION

ARCHITECTURAL DRAFTING   3-2

DRAFTING LEAD IS MADE BY MIXING CLAY AND GRAPHITE. THE PROPORTIONS OF THE TWO MATERIALS DETERMINE THE HARDNESS OR SOFTNESS OF THE LEAD. THE FOLLOWING ILLUSTRATION SHOWS THE RANGE OF DRAFTING LEADS.

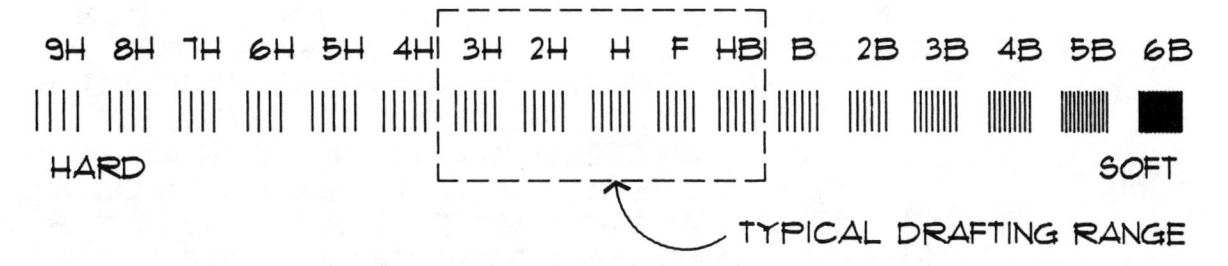

9H 8H 7H 6H 5H 4H 3H 2H H F HB B 2B 3B 4B 5B 6B

HARD   SOFT

TYPICAL DRAFTING RANGE

THE BEST LEAD WEIGHT TO START DRAFTING WITH IS 2H. A HARDER LEAD WEIGHT (3H AND UP) WILL PRODUCE A THIN, LIGHT LINE THAT DOESN'T PRINT WELL. A LEAD WEIGHT IN THE "B" RANGE IS TOO SOFT FOR WORKING DRAWINGS AND PRODUCES FUZZY LINES THAT SMEAR EASILY.

LINE WEIGHT
IN ARCHITECTURE, CHANGES IN LINE WEIGHT ARE USED TO STRESS IMPORTANT POINTS IN THE DETAIL. THE WEIGHT OF A LINE IS VARIED BY CHANGING THE AMOUNT OF PRESSURE ON THE LEAD HOLDER AND THE WIDTH OF THE LINE. THE ILLUSTRATION BELOW SHOWS AN <u>ELEVATION VIEW</u> OF THE CABIN AND THE VARIETY OF LINE WEIGHTS USED TO DRAW IT. (AN ELEVATION SHOWS THE HEIGHT AND WIDTH OF A BUILDING SIMILAR TO THE VIEW IN A PHOTOGRAPH.)

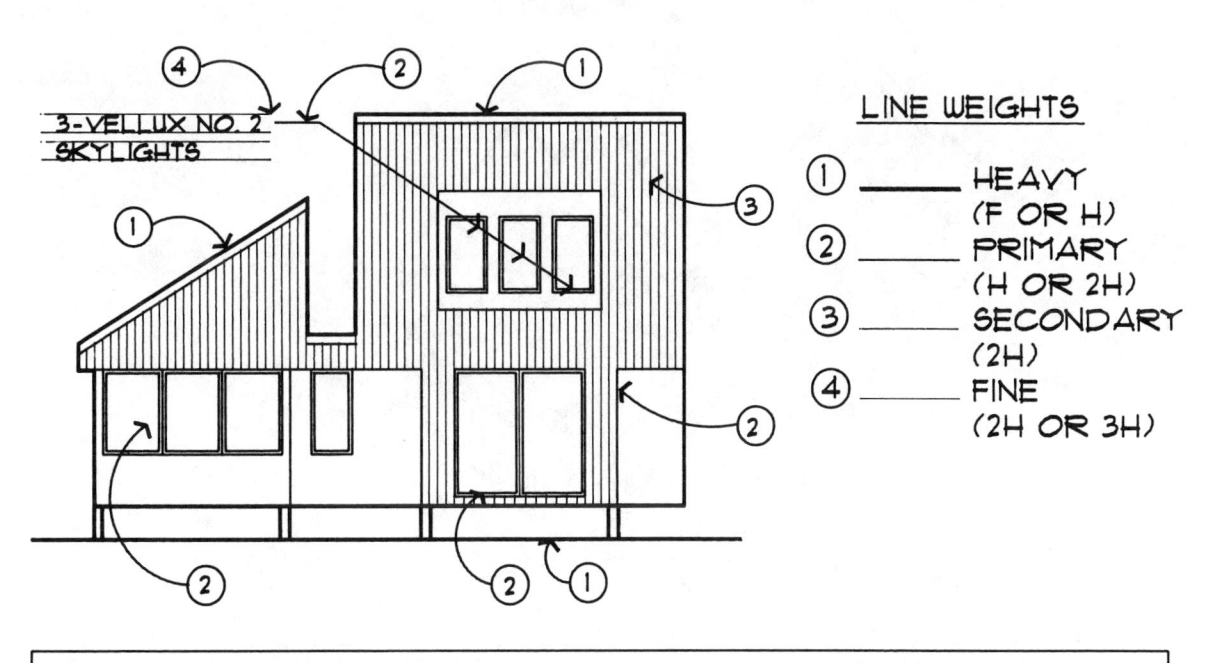

LINE WEIGHTS

① HEAVY (F OR H)
② PRIMARY (H OR 2H)
③ SECONDARY (2H)
④ FINE (2H OR 3H)

3-VELLUX NO. 2 SKYLIGHTS

ARCHITECTURAL DRAFTING   3-3

THE ELEVATION SHOWS FOUR DISTINCT LINE WEIGHTS. A HEAVY LINE IS DRAWN BY MAKING A PRIMARY LINE SLIGHTLY WIDER, WHILE SECONDARY AND FINE LINES ARE MADE BY VARYING THE PRESSURE ON THE LEAD HOLDER. A RULE OF THUMB FOR LINE WEIGHT IS BASED ON THE IMPORTANCE OF THE OBJECT BEING DRAWN: IMPORTANT ITEMS WOULD BE DRAWN WITH A HEAVIER LINE WEIGHT THAN LESS IMPORTANT ONES. AS AN EXAMPLE, A WINDOW IS MORE IMPORTANT THAN WOOD SIDING, SO IT WOULD BE DRAWN WITH A HEAVIER LINE WEIGHT. TYPICALLY, THE SILHOUETTE AROUND THE PERIMETER OF AN ELEVATION IS DRAWN WITH A HEAVY LINE TO ACCENT THE DRAWING'S DETAIL. AN EASY WAY TO DARKEN THE LINE IS TO USE A TECHNICAL PEN WITH INK. IT IS A GOOD IDEA TO WAIT UNTIL THE END OF THE PROJECT TO PUT INK ON VELLUM IN ORDER TO MINIMIZE CORRECTIONS. THE TREATMENT OF LINES THIS WAY IS BASED ON ARTISTIC CONSIDERATIONS RATHER THAN ON A TECHNICAL DRAFTING SET OF RULES. IT IS ONE OF THE POINTS THAT SETS ARCHITECTURAL DRAFTING APART FROM MECHANICAL DRAFTING.

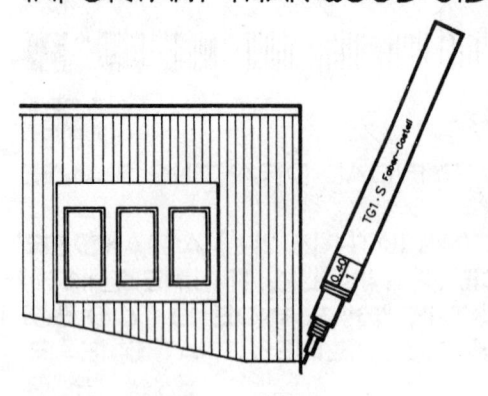

A PLAN VIEW IS GENERATED BY HORIZONTALLY CUTTING A PLANE THROUGH THE BUILDING (AS IF YOU WERE USING A KNIFE). THE TOP PORTION IS REMOVED AND THE REMAINING VIEW IS DRAWN. THE ILLUSTRATION BELOW GIVES YOU AN EXAMPLE.

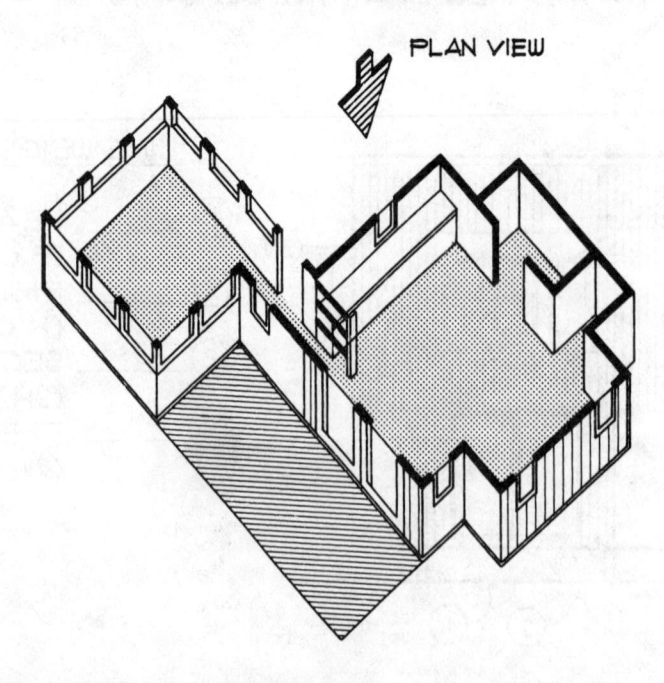

PLAN VIEW

ARCHITECTURAL DRAFTING 3-4

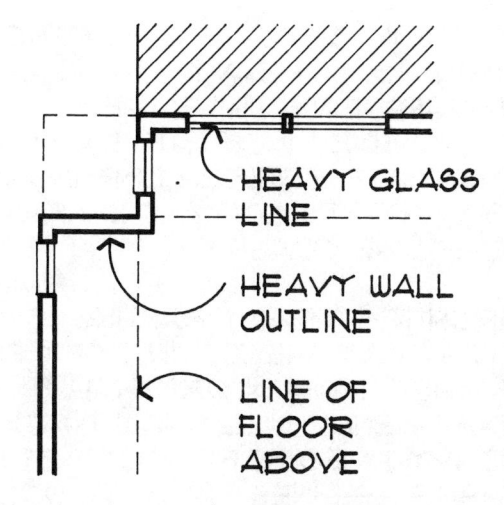

THE PLAN VIEW IS DRAWN WITH LINE WEIGHTS RANGING FROM 1 TO 4 SIMILAR TO THOSE USED IN THE ELEVATIONS. DETERMINE WEIGHT BY THE IMPORTANCE OF THE DETAIL. FOR EXAMPLE, THE INDIVIDUAL BOARDS ON THE DECK ARE NOT AS SIGNIFICANT AS THE DOOR AND WINDOW LOCATIONS SO THEY WOULD BE DRAWN WITH A SLIGHTLY LIGHTER LINE WEIGHT. THE HEAVIEST LINE WEIGHT WOULD BE USED WHERE THE SECTION IS CUT THROUGH THE BUILDING. USING THIS TECHNIQUE, THE OUTSIDE FACE OF THE WALLS WOULD APPEAR HEAVIER TO INDICATE THE SECTION CUT. NOTE THAT THE CUT THROUGH THE WINDOW WOULD ACCENT THE GLASS RATHER THAN THE OUTSIDE LINES OF THE SILL. FOR THAT REASON, THE TWO OUTSIDE LINES OF THE FRAME WOULD BE PRIMARY LINES, WHILE THE GLASS LINES WOULD BE HEAVY.

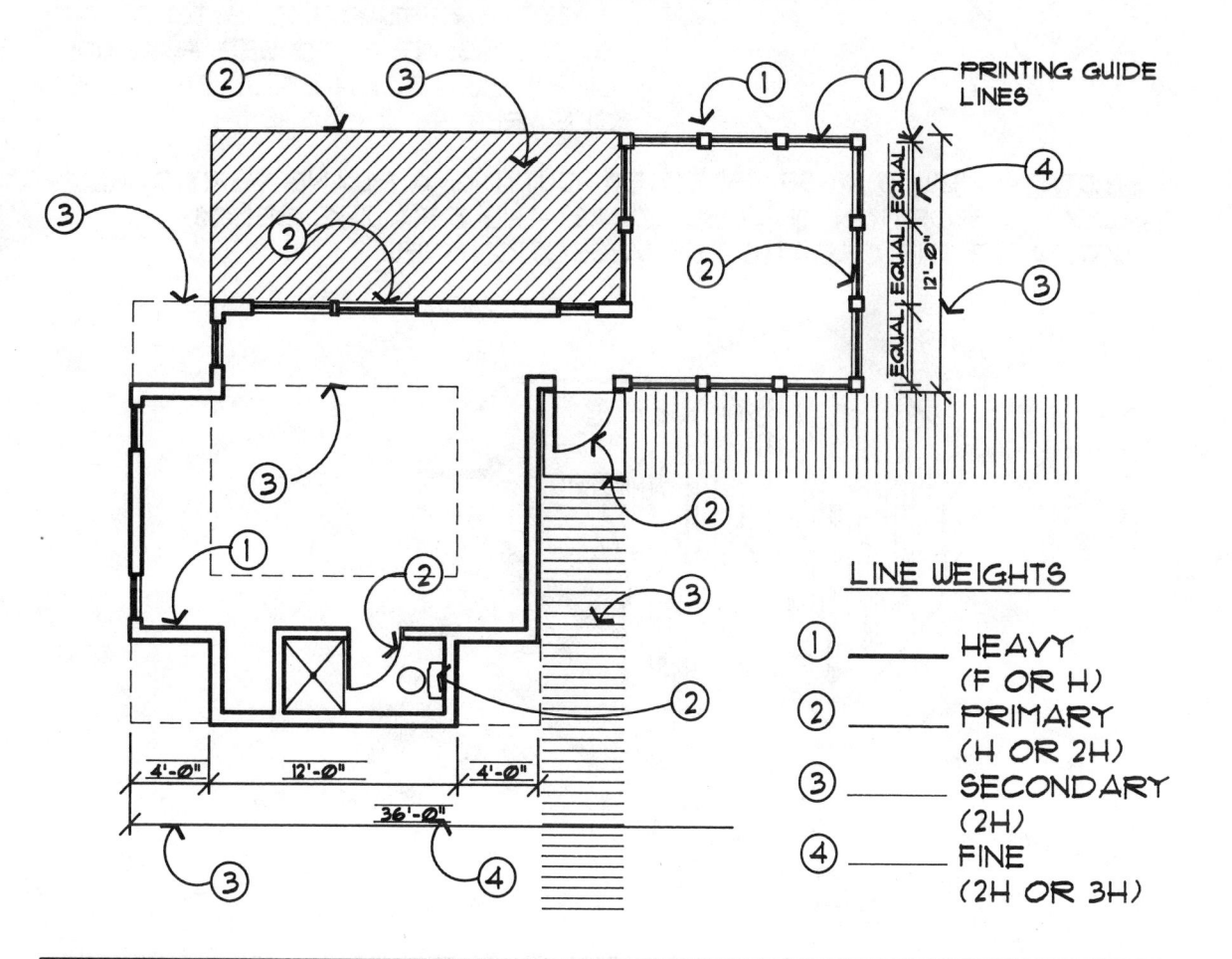

LINE WEIGHTS

1. HEAVY (F OR H)
2. PRIMARY (H OR 2H)
3. SECONDARY (2H)
4. FINE (2H OR 3H)

ARCHITECTURAL DRAFTING 3-5

KEEP IN MIND THAT THERE IS NOT A GREAT DEAL OF DIFFERENCE BETWEEN EACH OF THE FOUR LINE WEIGHTS. A HEAVY LINE IS ROUGHLY TWICE THE WIDTH OF A PRIMARY LINE, WHILE THE DIFFERENCE BETWEEN SECONDARY AND FINE LINES IS EVEN MORE SUBTLE. IT IS IMPORTANT TO DIFFERENTIATE BETWEEN LINE WEIGHT AND LINE QUALITY. THE FOUR LINES VARY IN WIDTH AND DARKNESS, BUT THEY ARE ALL DRAWN WITH CRISP LINE QUALITY.

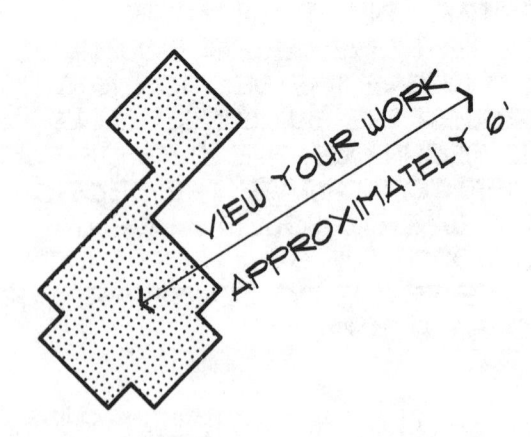

ARCHITECTURAL DRAFTING IS TYPICALLY VIEWED IN COPY FORM RATHER THAN IN ORIGINAL. EXPERIENCE WILL SHOW THAT HEAVY LINES REPRODUCE BETTER THAN FINE LINES. IT IS A GOOD PRACTICE TO EVALUATE YOUR LINE WEIGHT AS YOU DRAW. FOR EXAMPLE, MOST OF YOUR LINES WILL APPEAR TO HAVE GOOD LINE WEIGHT WHEN YOU VIEW THEM AT A DISTANCE OF 9" TO 1' AWAY. A BETTER PRACTICE IS TO STAND BACK ABOUT 6' TO SEE IF YOUR LINE WEIGHT CAN STILL BE VIEWED CLEARLY.

A <u>SECTION VIEW</u> IS ASSEMBLED BY CUTTING A PLANE VERTICALLY THROUGH A PORTION OF A BUILDING. THE DRAWING BELOW ILLUSTRATES THE CREATION OF A SECTION VIEW.

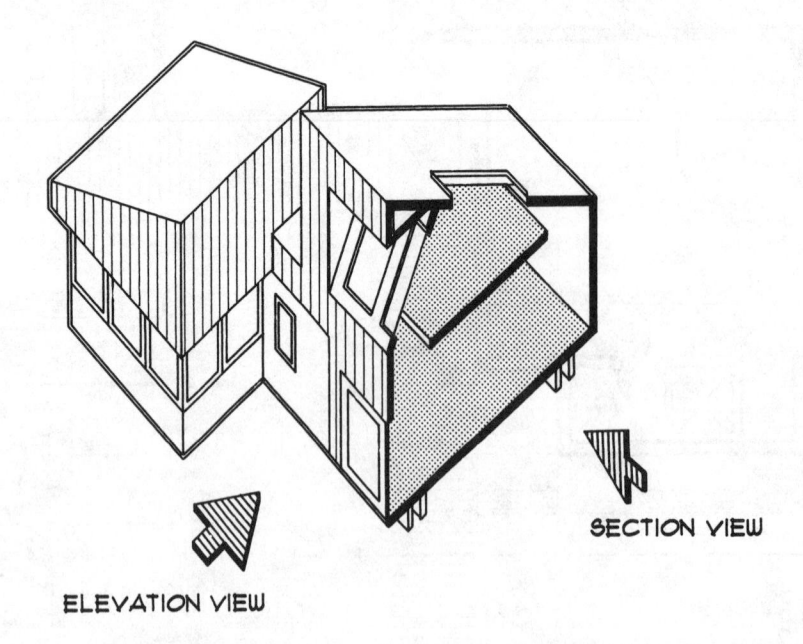

ELEVATION VIEW

SECTION VIEW

ARCHITECTURAL DRAFTING

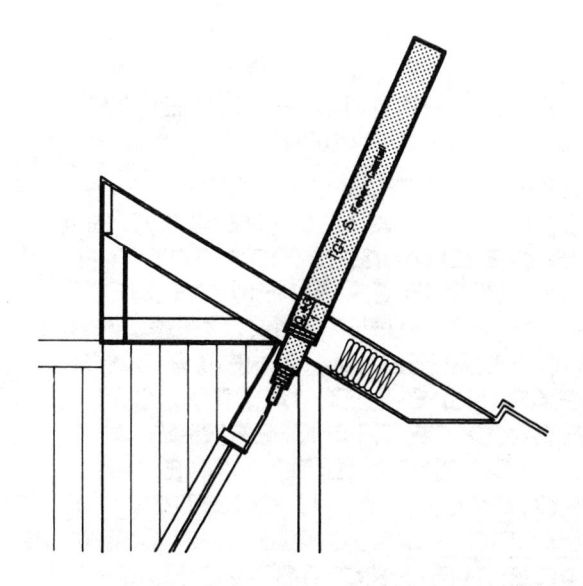

AS IN THE CASE OF PLAN AND ELEVATION VIEWS, THE LINE WEIGHTS USED TO DRAW A SECTION ACCENT THE IMPORTANCE OF MATERIALS. THE PREVIOUS ILLUSTRATION SHOWS THAT THE VERTICAL SIDING (SEEN IN ELEVATION) HAS A LESSER LINE WEIGHT THAN A DETAIL SUCH AS THE WINDOW FRAME. THE SECTION CUT LINE THROUGH THE BUILDING HAS THE HEAVIEST LINE WEIGHT TO CLEARLY SHOW THE CONTRACTOR WHERE THE CUT OCCURS. WAIT UNTIL THE SECTION CUT IS NEARLY COMPLETE BEFORE YOU ACCENT THE SECTION CUT LINE. ONE WAY TO DARKEN THIS LINE IS TO DRAW OVER THE DETAIL WITH A TECHNICAL PEN.

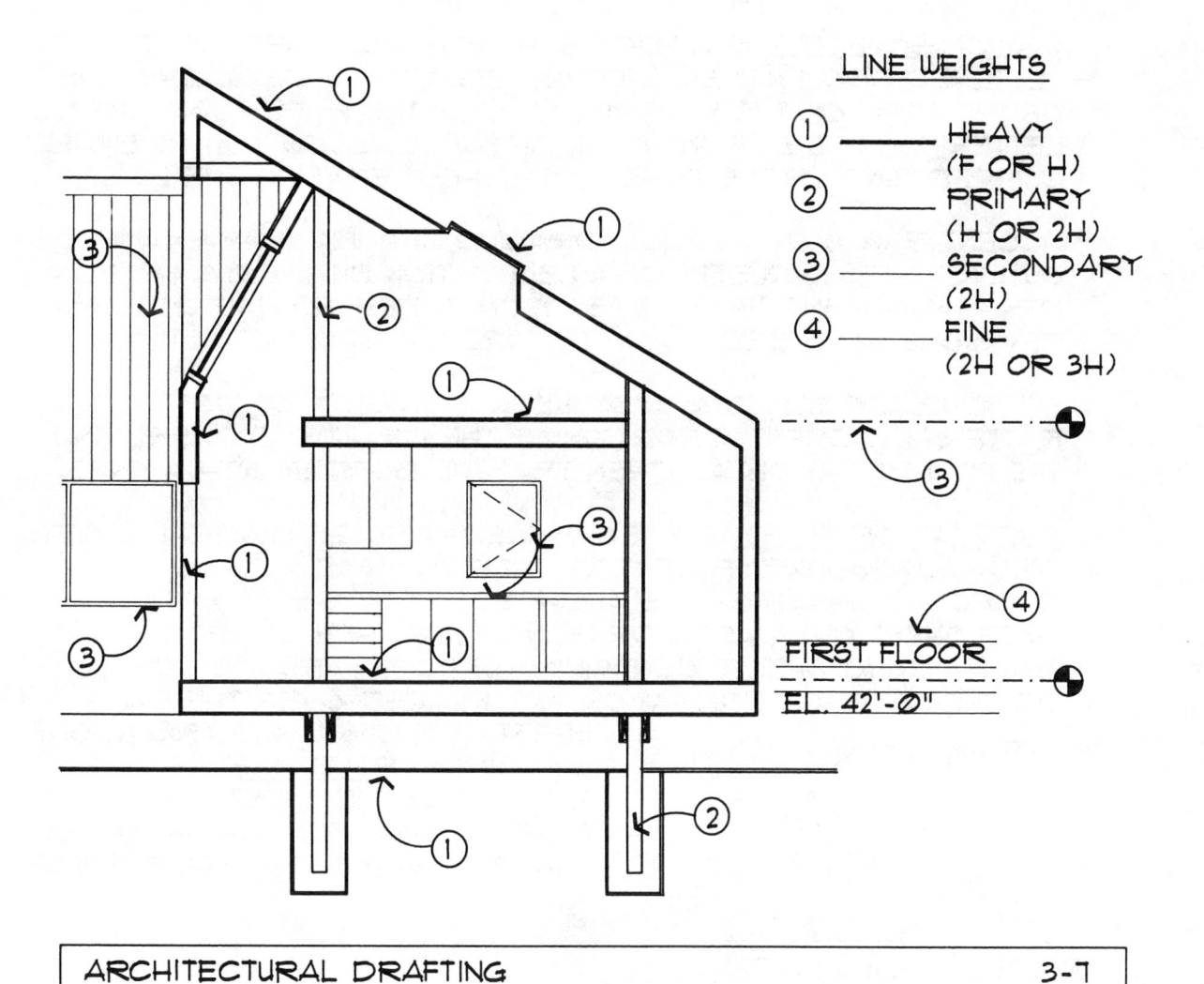

LINE WEIGHTS

① ———— HEAVY (F OR H)
② ———— PRIMARY (H OR 2H)
③ ———— SECONDARY (2H)
④ ———— FINE (2H OR 3H)

FIRST FLOOR
EL. 42'-0"

ARCHITECTURAL DRAFTING   3-7

DRAFTING SHORTCUTS

SEVERAL TECHNIQUES HAVE BEEN DEVELOPED TO REDUCE THE TIME THAT IT TAKES TO ASSEMBLE A SET OF DRAWINGS.

1. <u>PASTE-UP DRAFTING</u> IS A PROCESS FOR TRANSFERRING A PHOTOGRAPH OF AN EXISTING DETAIL TO A NEW DRAWING SHEET. (THE DETAIL CAN BE USED AS-IS OR CHANGED TO MEET THE CONDITIONS OF A NEW PROJECT.) THE PASTE-UP IS PHOTOGRAPHED AND PLACED ON A NEW PLASTIC DRAFTING SHEET. A LESS COSTLY METHOD OF TRANSFERRING A PHOTOGRAPH IS TO MAKE A PHOTOCOPY OF IT ON <u>STICKY-BACK PLASTIC FILM</u>. ONCE THE COPY IS MADE, THE PROTECTIVE BACK SHEET OF THE FILM CAN BE REMOVED AND THE COPY OF THE PHOTOGRAPH CAN BE APPLIED TO THE NEW DRAWING.

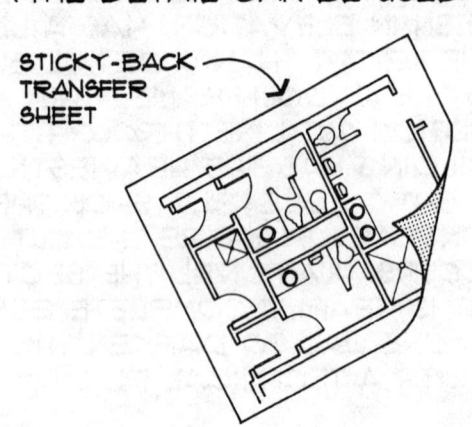

   STICKY-BACK TRANSFER SHEET

2. A <u>ROOM SCHEDULE</u> IS A FORM CONSISTING OF LINED BOXES WITH LETTERED ROOM NAMES AND FINISHES. TRY DRAWING THE LINES OF THE FORM ON THE REVERSE SIDE OF THE PAPER AND DO THE LETTERING ON THE FRONT SIDE. THIS WILL ALLOW YOU TO ERASE CORRECTIONS ON THE SCHEDULE WITHOUT ERASING THE LINES.

3. ACCENT PARTS OF A PENCIL DRAWING WITH INK. FOR EXAMPLE, OUTLINE THE SILHOUETTE OF AN ELEVATION WITH A Ø.6 mm TECH PEN. INK DOESN'T ERASE EASILY ON PAPER, SO WAIT UNTIL ALL REVISIONS HAVE BEEN MADE BEFORE DRAWING THE OUTLINE.

4. STICKY-BACK FILM IS AVAILABLE IN A VARIETY OF DOT PATTERNS. ACCENT A PORTION OF THE DRAWING BY APPLYING THE FILM TO THE DETAIL; THEN TRIM THE BORDER WITH A KNIFE.

5. <u>OVERLAY DRAFTING</u> IS A TECHNIQUE THAT USES SEVERAL SHEETS OF DRAWINGS ASSEMBLED TOGETHER TO MAKE A FINAL COMPOSITE DRAWING. THE ARCHITECT STARTS BY DRAWING A BASE SHEET ON PLASTIC DRAFTING FILM. THEN, OTHER TRANSPARENT SHEETS CONTAINING SPECIFIC ARCHITECTURAL OR ENGINEERING INFORMATION ARE PLACED OVER THE BASE SHEET. THE DRAWINGS ARE ALIGNED BY USING A <u>PIN BAR STRIP</u> ALONG THE TOP OF THE SHEET. EACH SHEET IS PUNCHED WITH 1/4" HOLES THAT FIT OVER THE METAL PIN BAR.

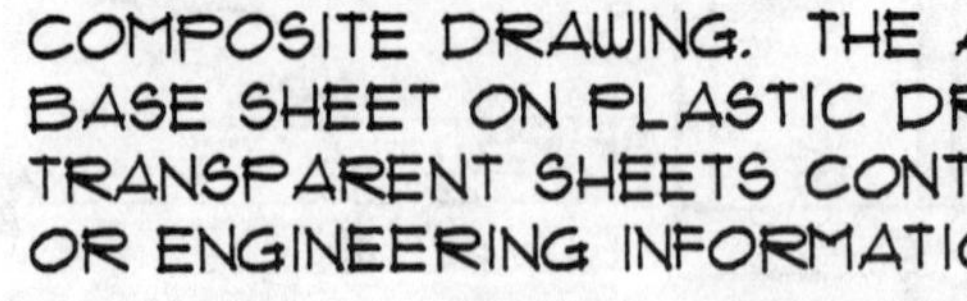

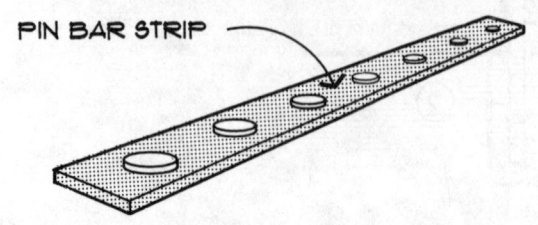

   PIN BAR STRIP

ARCHITECTURAL DRAFTING

THE OVERLAY DRAWING BELOW SHOWS AN EXAMPLE OF A FLOOR PLAN COMPOSED OF FOUR SHEETS. A STRUCTURAL ENGINEER WOULD USE THE BASE SHEET COMBINED WITH A SEPARATE TITLE SHEET AND A THIRD OVERLAY CONTAINING STRUCTURAL NOTES AND DETAILS. PRINTS OF OVERLAY DRAWINGS ARE MADE BY USING A SPECIAL VACUUM-FRAME PRINT MACHINE OR BY PHOTOGRAPHING THE SHEETS.

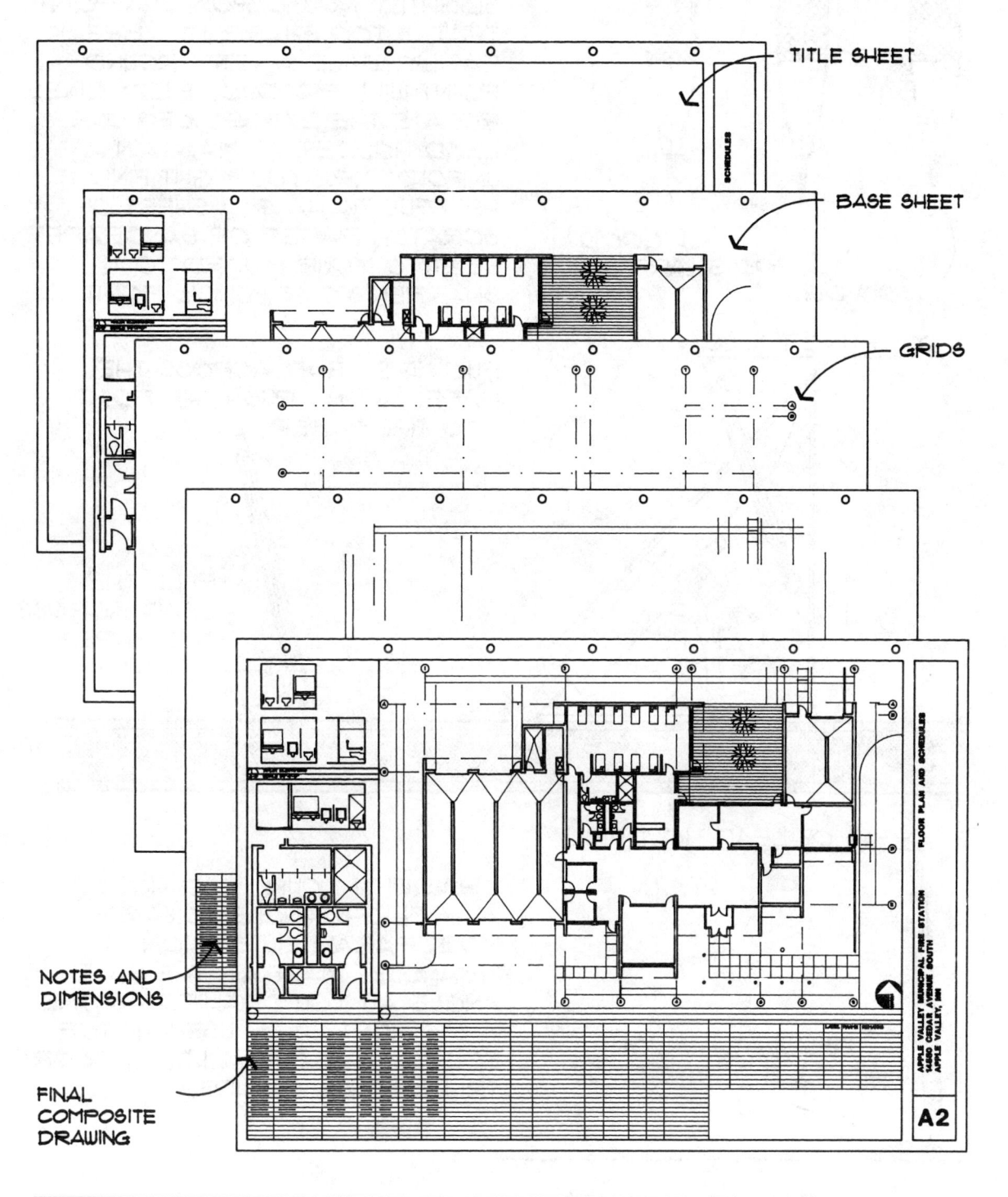

ARCHITECTURAL DRAFTING 3-9

DRAFTING TIPS
THE NEXT SEVERAL PAGES DISCUSS TIPS FOR IMPROVING YOUR DRAFTING TECHNIQUE.

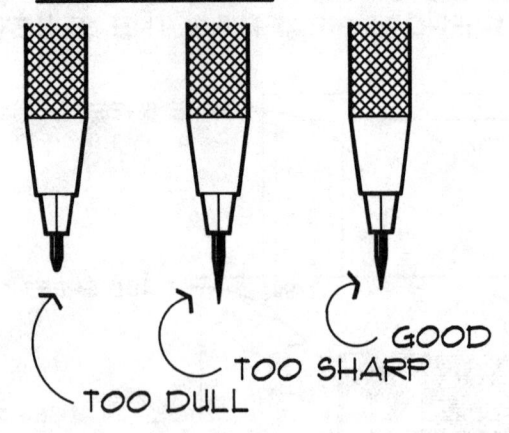

1. <u>PENCIL POINT</u>

YOUR LEAD TIP SHOULD HAVE A SLIGHTLY ROUND POINT. A POINT THAT IS TOO SHARP WILL BREAK EASILY, WHILE A VERY ROUND POINT WILL PRODUCE FUZZY LINES. ROTATE THE BARREL OF YOUR LEAD HOLDER TO MAINTAIN A UNIFORM TIP. YOU MIGHT FIND IT HELPFUL TO HAVE A SHEET OF SCRATCH PAPER OR SANDPAPER NEXT TO YOUR BOARD TO SHARPEN YOUR PENCIL POINT.

TOO DULL   TOO SHARP   GOOD

2. <u>DRAFTING TOOLS</u>

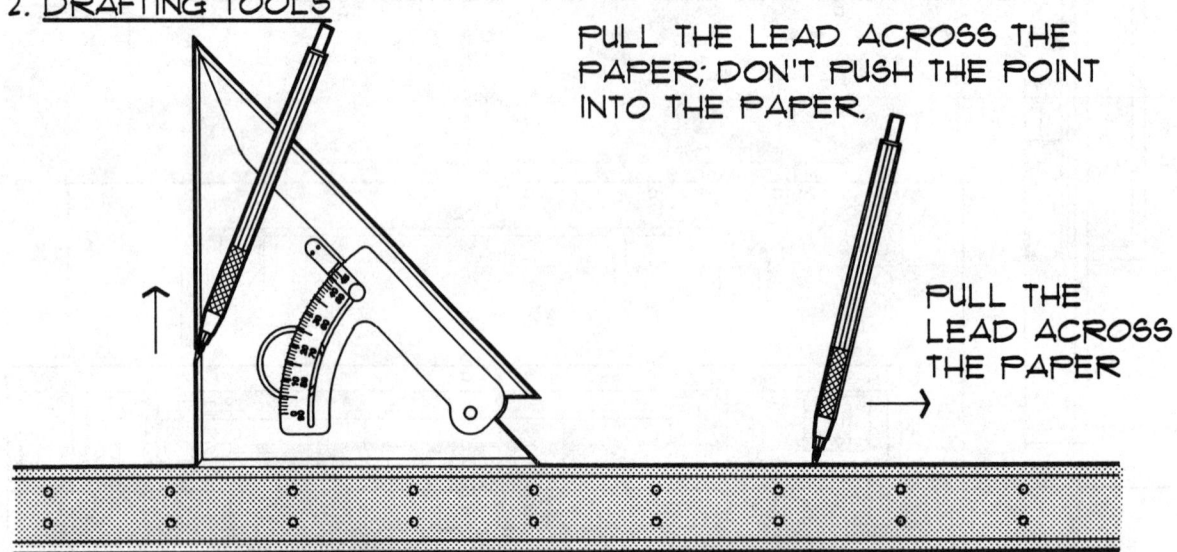

PULL THE LEAD ACROSS THE PAPER; DON'T PUSH THE POINT INTO THE PAPER.

PULL THE LEAD ACROSS THE PAPER →

3. <u>ANGLE OF LEAD HOLDER</u>

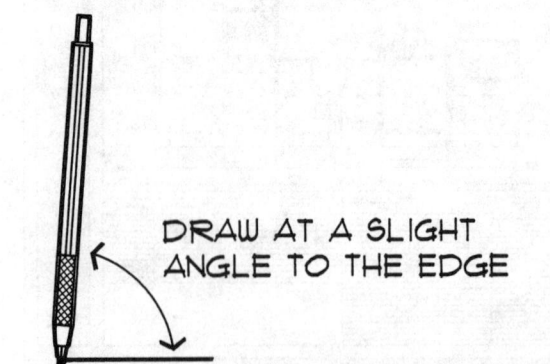

DRAW WITH YOUR LEAD HOLDER AT A SLIGHT ANGLE TOWARD YOUR PARALLEL BAR OR TRIANGLE. MAINTAIN THE SAME ANGLE AS YOU DRAW TO ASSURE A STRAIGHT LINE. USE THE TOP EDGE OF THE PARALLEL BAR OR TRIANGLE AS A GUIDE.

DRAW AT A SLIGHT ANGLE TO THE EDGE

ARCHITECTURAL DRAFTING

4. CORNERS

GOOD
CORNERS OVERLAP
CORNERS DON'T MEET

CORRECT CORNER INTERSECTION OF LINES IS VERY IMPORTANT. CORNERS SHOULD MEET AT A CRISP POINT. LINES THAT DON'T TOUCH OR LINES THAT OVERLAP DISTRACT FROM THE DETAIL. WHILE SOME FIRMS ALLOW OVERLAPPED LINES, THE STANDARD IS TO MAKE THEM TOUCH.

5. LINE TYPES

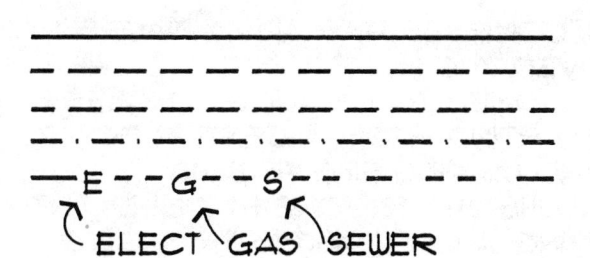

THE ILLUSTRATION SHOWS A VARIETY OF LINE TYPES USED ON ARCHITECTURAL DRAWINGS.

(SOLID) MATERIAL LOCATIONS
(DASHED) OBJECTS ABOVE PLANE
(DASHED) TOPOGRAPHY
(PHANTOM) PROPERTY LINES
(DASHED) UTILITY LINES

—E— —G— —S—
ELECT GAS SEWER

6. MECHANICAL PENCIL

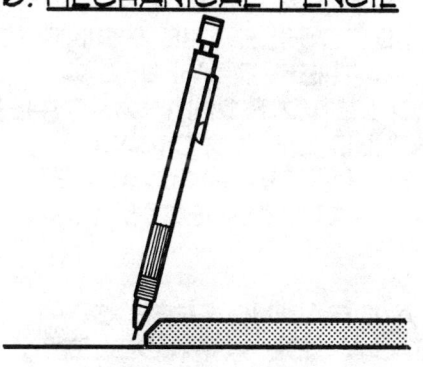

A Ø.5 mm MECHANICAL PENCIL PRODUCES A UNIFORM LINE AND DOESN'T REQUIRE SHARPENING. LEAD WEIGHTS ARE AVAILABLE IN THE SAME GRADE AS 2 mm LEAD. HEAVY LINE WEIGHTS CAN BE DRAWN BY DRAWING LINES TWICE.

7. TECHNICAL PEN

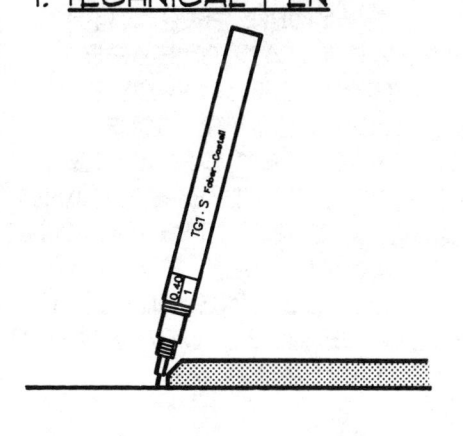

A TECHNICAL DRAFTING PEN PRODUCES A CRISP INK LINE THAT REPRODUCES MUCH BETTER THAN PENCIL LEAD. SOME FIRMS USE INK ON ALL WORKING DRAWINGS. WHILE YOU ARE LEARNING TO USE INK, TAPE THREE DIMES TO THE BOTTOM OF YOUR TRIANGLE TO PREVENT INK FROM FLOWING UNDER THE EDGE. REMEMBER TO CHECK THE LINE TO SEE IF IT IS DRY BEFORE MOVING TOOLS OVER IT.

ARCHITECTURAL DRAFTING

8. CIRCLES

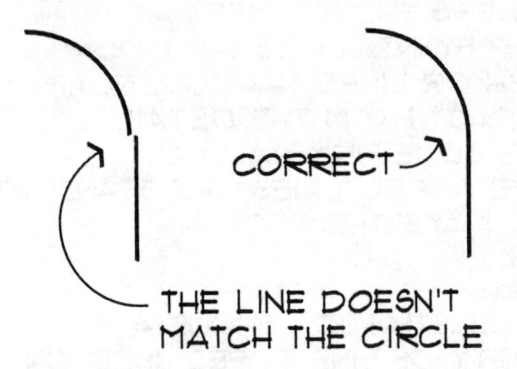

ONE DIFFICULTY IN DRAWING CIRCLES IS INTERSECTING THEM CORRECTLY WITH LINES. A SOLUTION IS TO DRAW THE CIRCLE FIRST, THEN DRAW THE LINE SEGMENT FROM THE CIRCLE.

CORRECT

THE LINE DOESN'T MATCH THE CIRCLE

9. COMPASS

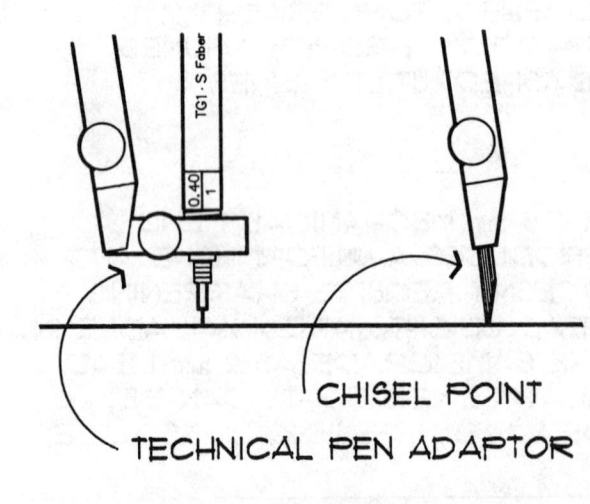

A COMPASS HAS ADVANTAGES OVER A CIRCLE TEMPLATE WHEN IT COMES TO DRAWING CIRCLES STARTING FROM A CENTER POINT AND MAKING FINE RADIUS ADJUSTMENTS. ONE PROBLEM WITH USING A COMPASS IS TRYING TO MAINTAIN A UNIFORM LEAD POINT WHILE DRAWING A CIRCLE. A SOLUTION IS TO FILE THE POINT TO A CHISEL RATHER THAN USE A STANDARD LEAD POINT. ANOTHER OPTION WOULD BE TO DRAW CIRCLES WITH A TECHNICAL PEN ADAPTOR THAT CONNECTS TO A COMPASS.

CHISEL POINT
TECHNICAL PEN ADAPTOR

10. CLEANING DRAWINGS

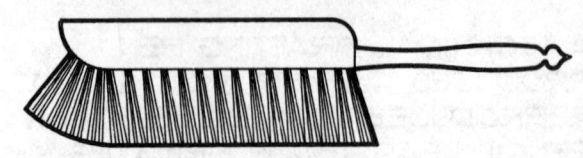

KEEPING A DRAWING FREE OF GRAPHITE CAN BE A PROBLEM. USE A DRAFTING BRUSH OR BLOW OFF LINES WITH YOUR BREATH. SOFTER WEIGHT LEAD SMEARS EASILY, SO TRY NOT TO MOVE DRAFTING TOOLS OVER YOUR WORK. INSTEAD, TRY DRAWING FROM THE TOP OF THE SHEET AND WORK DOWN. A DRAFTING ERASING POWDER IS AVAILABLE, BUT IT TENDS TO REDUCE LINE QUALITY AND SHOULD BE USED SPARINGLY. (DON'T USE IT WITH INK.)

ARCHITECTURAL DRAFTING

REPLAY

1. USE A PENCIL OR FELT-TIP PEN TO DARKEN THE <u>HEAVY</u> AND <u>PRIMARY LINES</u> THAT WOULD BE USED TO ACCENT THE ELEVATION SHOWN BELOW. (SEE PAGE 3-3 FOR THE DEFINITION OF THESE TWO LINE WEIGHTS.)

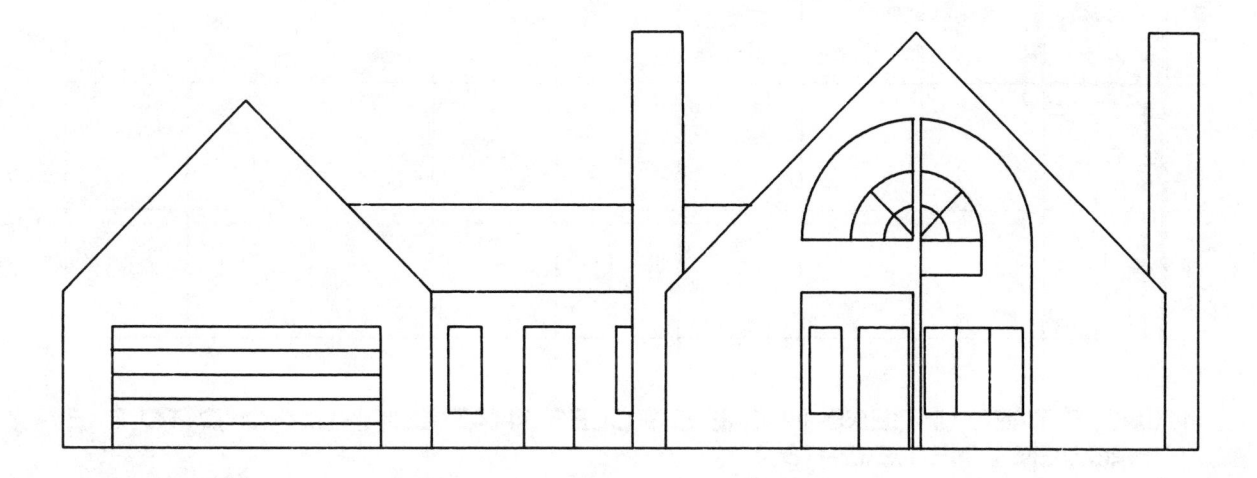

2. USE A PENCIL OR FELT-TIP PEN TO ACCENT THE SECTION CUT LINE ON THE PLAN BELOW. YOUR HEAVY LINE SHOULD ILLUSTRATE CUTS THROUGH WALLS, GLASS, AND DOORS.

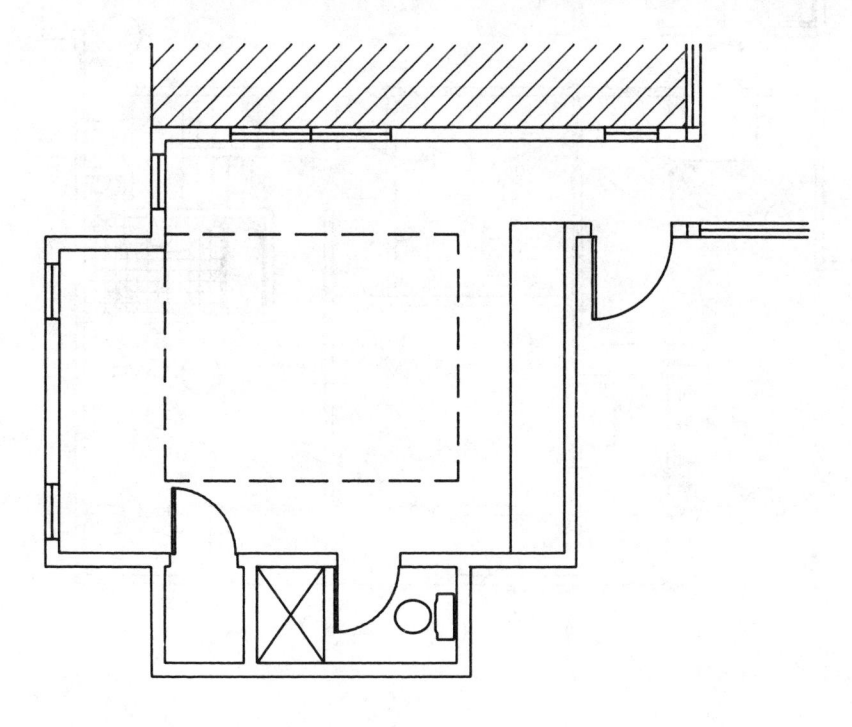

ARCHITECTURAL DRAFTING 3-13

3. USE A 2H LEAD HOLDER AND TRIANGLE TO DRAW THE DETAIL
   ON THE LEFT OF THE ILLUSTRATION BELOW. YOUR LINE WEIGHT AND
   QUALITY SHOULD MATCH THE DETAIL.

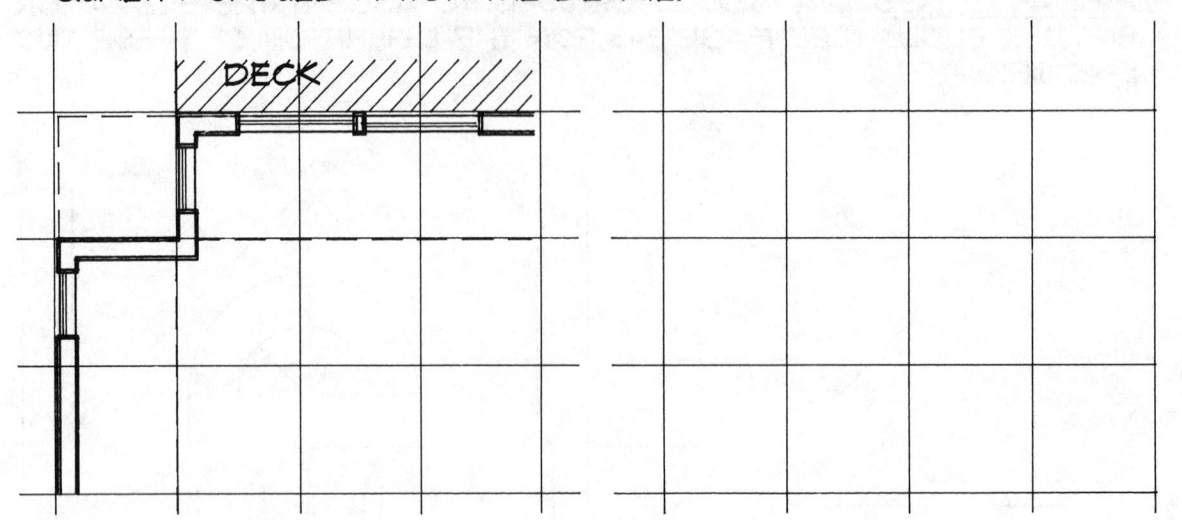

4. WRITE THE NUMBERS IN THE CIRCLES THAT CORRESPOND TO THE
   PROPER LINE WEIGHTS.

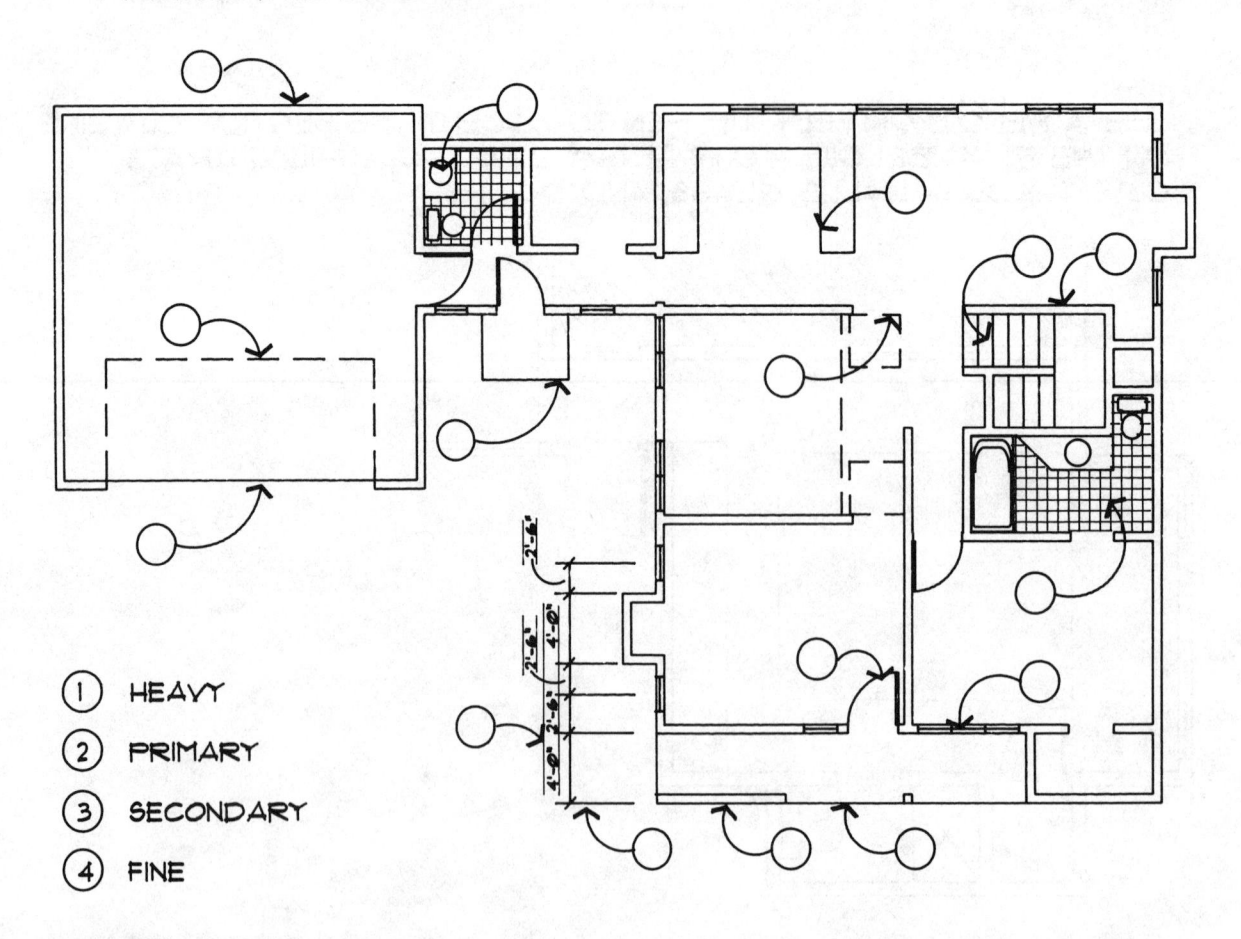

① HEAVY
② PRIMARY
③ SECONDARY
④ FINE

ARCHITECTURAL DRAFTING   3-14

ARCHITECTURAL PRINTING

ARCHITECTURAL PRINTING IS A FORM OF CALLIGRAPHY THAT IS UNIQUE TO THE PROFESSION. THIS STYLE OF LETTERING IS AN EXTREMELY IMPORTANT SKILL FOR THE ARCHITECT TO MASTER. IN FACT, MANY ARCHITECTS CONSIDER IT A "BADGE" THAT MUST BE EARNED IN ORDER TO FIND EMPLOYMENT. IN ADDITION TO BEING A SOURCE OF PROFESSIONAL PRIDE, UNIFORM PRINTING ALLOWS SEVERAL PEOPLE TO WORK ON THE SAME SHEET OF DRAWINGS WITHOUT SHOWING THEIR DIFFERENT STYLES. KEEP IN MIND THAT DEVELOPING GOOD PRINTING REQUIRES A LOT OF WORK— TAKE OUT A SHEET OF PAPER AND PRACTICE WHENEVER YOU CAN.

FIRST, LET'S LOOK AT THE ALPHABET TO DETERMINE A STYLE FOR EACH LETTER. YOU WILL FIND A VARIETY OF LETTER STYLES IN ARCHITECTURAL PRINTING; THE ONE THAT IS PRESENTED HERE WILL BE ACCEPTED BY MOST FIRMS.

A B C D E F G H I J K L M N O P Q R
S T U V W X Y Z   0 1 2 3 4 5 6 7 8 9

IT IS TYPICAL TO PRINT WITH AN ALL UPPER-CASE ALPHABET, BUT SOME FIRMS USE A STYLE THAT ALSO INCLUDES LOWER-CASE LETTERS LIKE THOSE SHOWN BELOW.

a b c d e f g h i j k l m n o p q r
s t u v w x y z

ARCHITECTURAL PRINTING   4-1

DON'T READ THE MATERIAL IN THIS UNIT ONCE AND EXPECT TO REMEMBER ALL OF THE GUIDELINES PRESENTED. QUALITY PRINTING WILL ONLY BE ACHIEVED WITH A LOT OF PRACTICE. OPEN YOUR BOOK TO THIS UNIT OFTEN AND FOLLOW THE GUIDELINES UNTIL YOU MASTER THE TECHNIQUE.

THE FOLLOWING TIPS WILL HELP YOU TO DEVELOP YOUR PRINTING STYLE:

1. MAKE YOUR LETTERS FIT INTO A SQUARE. FOR MOST BEGINNERS THAT MEANS MAKING LETTERS WIDER THAN YOU TYPICALLY WOULD. OBVIOUSLY, LETTERS LIKE I AND J WON'T FIT THIS RULE, BUT THE MAJORITY OF THE ALPHABET SHOULD BE AS BROAD AS THEY ARE HIGH. THIS TECHNIQUE IS IMPORTANT; CONCENTRATE ON THIS POINT WHEN YOU PRACTICE.

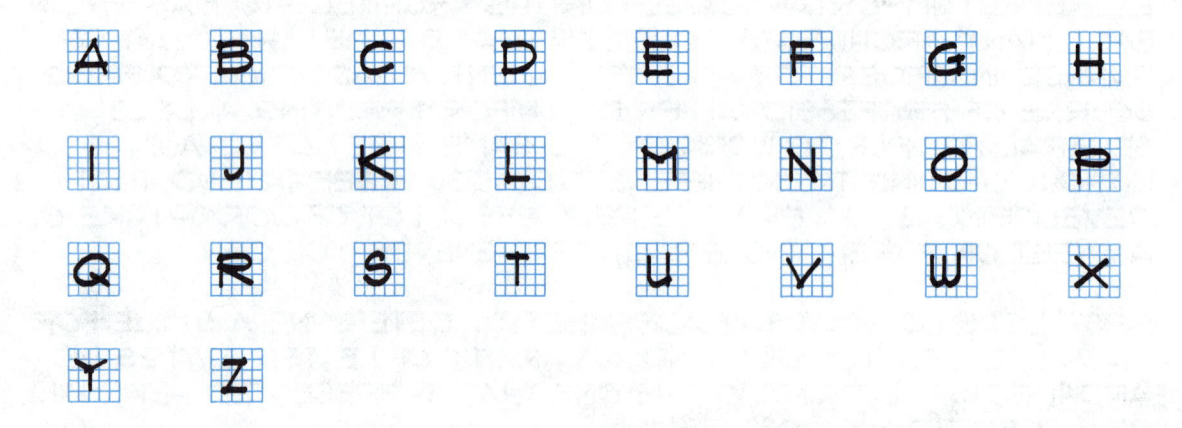

A B C D E F G H
I J K L M N O P
Q R S T U V W X
Y Z

NUMBERS SHOULD FIT INTO THE SAME SQUARE GRID.

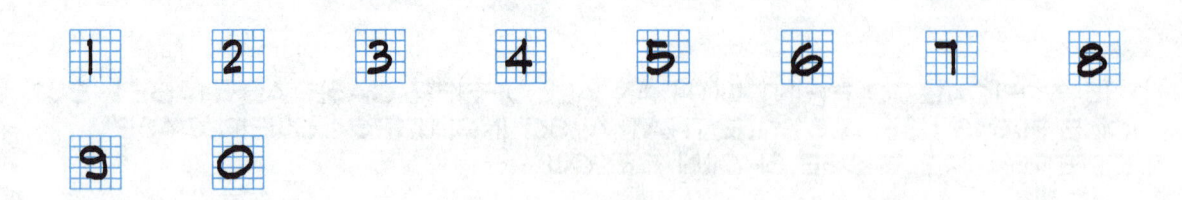

1 2 3 4 5 6 7 8
9 0

2. CONCENTRATE ON MAKING YOUR VERTICAL LETTER STROKES AS STRAIGHT UP AND DOWN AS POSSIBLE. LETTERS SUCH AS B, H, D, AND E SHOULD BE STARTED WITH THE VERTICAL STROKE FIRST. WORK ON THIS WHEN YOU PRACTICE; ONCE IT IS MASTERED,

ARCHITECTURAL PRINTING 4-2

YOUR PRINTING WILL START TAKING ON A MORE PROFESSIONAL LOOK.

LETTERS WITH VERTICAL STROKE LINES

| B | D | E | F | H | I | J | K | L | M | N | R | T | U | W |

3. ROUND LETTERS, SUCH AS B, C, D, AND G SHOULD BE CONSTRUCTED WITH QUICK, SMOOTH, EVEN STROKES. MAKE ROUND LETTERS IN ONE OR TWO MOTIONS AND CONCENTRATE ON THE CURVED LINE.

ROUND-STROKE LETTERS

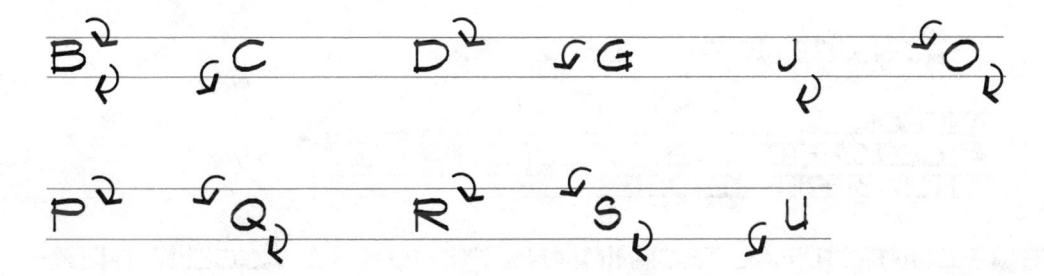

B C D G J O

P Q R S U

4. USE A SOFTER LEAD WEIGHT FOR PRINTING (ONE STEP BELOW THE LEAD YOU USE TO DRAW WITH). THE POINT ON THE LEAD SHOULD BE SLIGHTLY MORE DULL THAN THE TIP USED FOR DRAFTING. THE COMBINATION OF A SOFTER AND A ROUNDED POINT WILL ALLOW YOUR LETTERING TO TAKE ON MORE OF AN ARCHITECTURAL CHARACTER. EXPERIMENT WITH AN H OR F LEAD AND TWIST YOUR LEAD HOLDER OFTEN TO MAINTAIN AN EVEN POINT WHEN YOU PRINT.

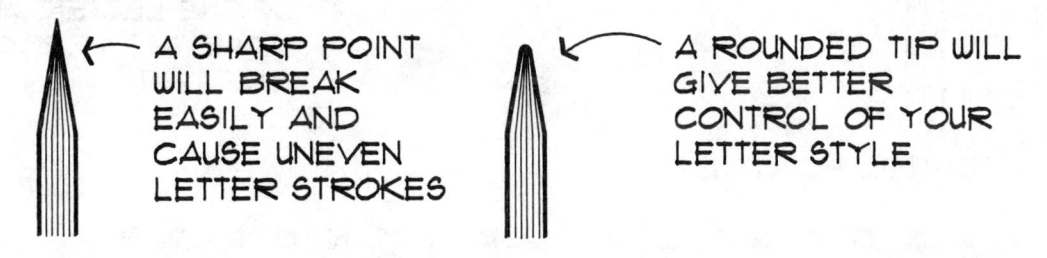

← A SHARP POINT WILL BREAK EASILY AND CAUSE UNEVEN LETTER STROKES

← A ROUNDED TIP WILL GIVE BETTER CONTROL OF YOUR LETTER STYLE

5. LETTER WITH A 2 mm LEAD HOLDER RATHER THAN A Ø.3 mm OR Ø.5 mm MECHANICAL PENCIL. THE LARGER DIAMETER LEAD WILL GIVE YOUR PRINTING A BROADER CHARACTER THAN WILL THE FINER LEAD OF A MECHANICAL PENCIL.

ARCHITECTURAL PRINTING   4-3

6. DRAW GUIDELINES FOR THE UPPER AND LOWER LIMITS OF YOUR PRINTING. GUIDELINES SHOULD BE LIGHTLY DRAWN SO THEY DON'T COMPETE WITH OTHER LINES ON YOUR DRAWING. NOTES AND DIMENSIONS SHOULD BE DRAWN 1/8" HIGH WITH A 1/16" GAP BETWEEN LINES OF TEXT. TITLES SHOULD BE DRAWN 3/16" HIGH. AVOID THE TENDENCY TO PRINT SMALLER IN TIGHT SPACES; IT REDUCES THE OVERALL QUALITY OF YOUR DETAIL.

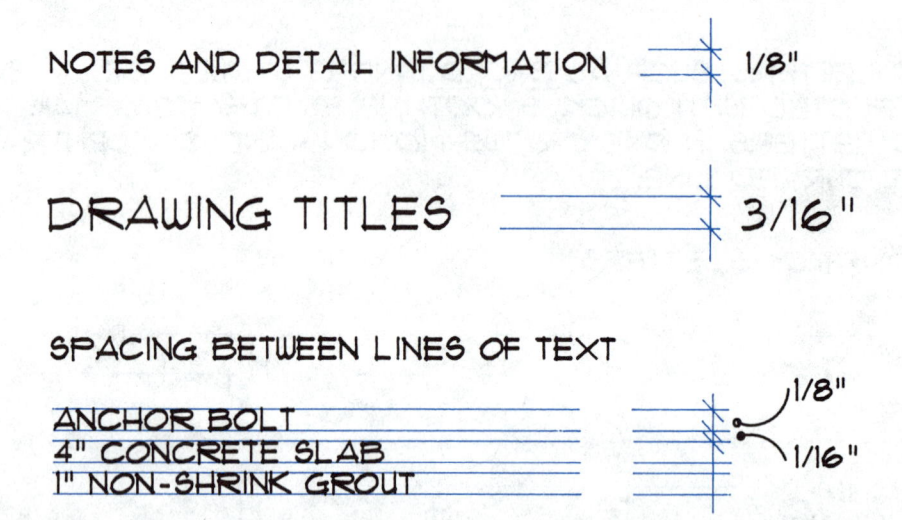

NOTES AND DETAIL INFORMATION — 1/8"

DRAWING TITLES — 3/16"

SPACING BETWEEN LINES OF TEXT

ANCHOR BOLT
4" CONCRETE SLAB
1" NON-SHRINK GROUT

1/8"
1/16"

7. SOME ARCHITECTURAL TECHNICIANS PREFER TO ACCENT THE HORIZONTAL STROKE OF A LETTER BY USING A CHISELED LEAD. CHISEL POINT LETTERING IS SLIGHTLY MORE DIFFICULT TO MASTER, BUT IT HAS A VERY DISTINCTIVE STYLE. THE SHARPER EDGE OF THE LEAD IS USED TO MAKE THE DOWNWARD VERTICAL STROKE, AND THE FLATTER FACE OF THE LEAD IS ROTATED TO DRAW HORIZONTAL AND ROUND PORTIONS OF THE LETTER.

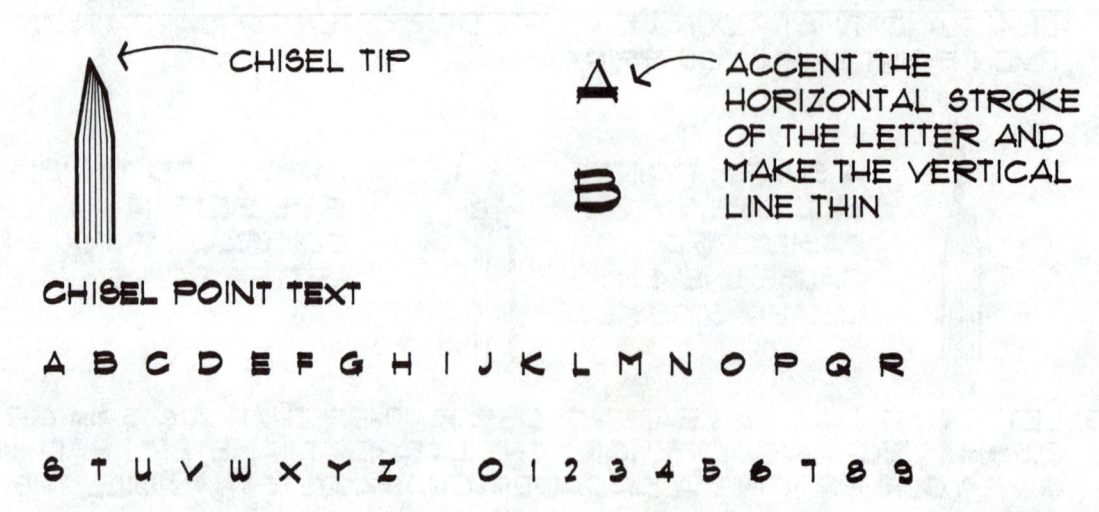

← CHISEL TIP

A ← ACCENT THE HORIZONTAL STROKE OF THE LETTER AND MAKE THE VERTICAL LINE THIN
B

CHISEL POINT TEXT

A B C D E F G H I J K L M N O P Q R

S T U V W X Y Z   0 1 2 3 4 5 6 7 8 9

ARCHITECTURAL PRINTING   4-4

8. THE DISTANCE BETWEEN LETTERS IS REFERRED TO AS <u>SPACING</u>. SOME LETTERS SHOULD BE SPACED MORE CLOSELY TOGETHER TO SET A PROPER PROPORTION. THIS IS DEFINITELY AN ARTISTIC DECISION RATHER THAN ONE BASED ON AN ACCEPTED TECHNICAL FORMULA. WHILE A TYPEWRITER SPACES THE LETTERS <u>I</u> AND <u>O</u> EVENLY, ARCHITECTURAL PRINTING USES UNEVEN SPACING TO PRODUCE A BETTER PROPORTION. VERTICAL LETTERS, SUCH AS <u>H</u>, <u>I</u>, <u>M</u>, AND <u>N</u>, SHOULD BE SPACED SLIGHTLY FURTHER APART TO GIVE THEM A PERCEIVED "BETTER" PROPORTION. ROUND LETTERS, SUCH AS <u>B</u>, <u>C</u>, <u>D</u>, AND <u>O</u>, SHOULD HAVE LESS SPACE AROUND THEM TO ACHIEVE GOOD BALANCE. THE SPACE PARTIALLY SURROUNDING EACH LETTER (EXCEPT THE LETTER <u>I</u>) IS CALLED THE <u>COUNTER SPACE</u>. YOUR PRINTING SHOULD REFLECT THE COUNTER SPACE PROPORTION BETWEEN LETTERS. FOR EXAMPLE, THE TWO LETTER <u>O</u>'S IN WOOD CREATE A "LIGHT" COUNTER SO THEY LOOK BETTER SLIGHTLY CLOSER TOGETHER.

LETTER SPACING ADDRESSES THE AREA BETWEEN LETTERS

MORTAR JOINT

THIS SPACING IS TOO WIDE

MORTAR JOINT

THIS SPACING IS BETTER

MORTAR JOINT

ROUND LETTERS NEED LESS AREA BETWEEN THEM

WOOD   WOOD

THIS SPACING IS TOO WIDE

AN ARCHITECTURAL DRAWING COULD BE VIEWED AS HAVING THREE SEPARATE LAYERS: (1) THE BASE LAYER WOULD DISPLAY THE DRAWING LINE WORK, (2) THE SECOND LAYER WOULD CONSIST OF GRIDS AND DIMENSIONS, AND (3) THE FINAL LAYER WOULD CONTAIN PRINTING. IT IS COMMON TO COMPLETE MOST OF THE DRAFTING BEFORE THE DIMENSIONS AND PRINTING ARE ADDED. IT IS IMPORTANT

TO KNOW WHERE PRINTING WILL FIT INTO THE ENTIRE "SCHEME" OF A
DRAWING BEFORE YOU BEGIN. KEEP IN MIND THAT PRINTING SHOULD

- LINE UP VERTICALLY
- HAVE PROPER SPACING
- BALANCE THE DRAWING

A GOOD WAY TO ORGANIZE YOUR DRAWING IS TO MAKE A
TRACING PAPER OVERLAY USING A FELT-TIP PEN. START BY
PLACING THE TRACING PAPER OVER YOUR ORIGINAL LINE DRAWING.
ORGANIZE THE PLACEMENT OF YOUR DIMENSIONS AND NOTES ON
THIS SKETCH BEFORE YOU LOCATE THEM ON THE FINAL DRAWING.
THIS STEP CAN BE ACCOMPLISHED IN UNDER A MINUTE, BUT IT COULD
SAVE YOU A GREAT DEAL OF ERASING.

THRU-WALL FLASHING

ROPE-WICK WEEPS AT
16" O. C.

W 18 x 45 WIDE FLANGE BEAM

WELD BLOCK TIES TO BEAM

FILL MASONRY CAVITY SOLID
W/ GROUT

PLACE A LIGHT
LINE TO ALIGN
TEXT VERTICALLY

USE LIGHT GUIDELINES TO SET
HORIZONTAL LETTERS

PRINTING IS OBVIOUSLY VERY IMPORTANT TO AN ARCHITECTURAL
DETAIL; WITH IT MATERIALS ARE "CALLED-OUT," DIMENSIONS ARE
SHOWN, AND SPECIFIC CONSTRUCTION TECHNIQUES ARE ORDERED.
IN THIS UNIT, WE ARE ADDRESSING THE ARTISTIC RATHER THAN THE
PRACTICAL ASPECTS OF PRINTING. AN ARCHITECTURAL DETAIL
APPEARS "NAKED" WITHOUT PRINTING. IT IS UP TO THE TECHNICIAN'S
SENSE OF PROPORTION TO POSITION NOTES ON THE DRAWING IN
ORDER TO FILL THE VOID AND BALANCE THE DRAWING.

THE NEXT PAGE SHOWS THE LOCATION OF ARCHITECTURAL NOTES
ON A DETAIL. STUDY THE DRAWING TO DETERMINE WHY NOTES
ARE PLACED WHERE THEY ARE ON A DRAWING.

ARCHITECTURAL PRINTING

THE DRAWINGS ON THIS PAGE ILLUSTRATE THE PLACEMENT OF
NOTES ON AN ARCHITECTURAL DETAIL. THE UPPER DRAWING
REPRESENTS THE BASE DRAWING BEFORE NOTES HAVE BEEN
ADDED.

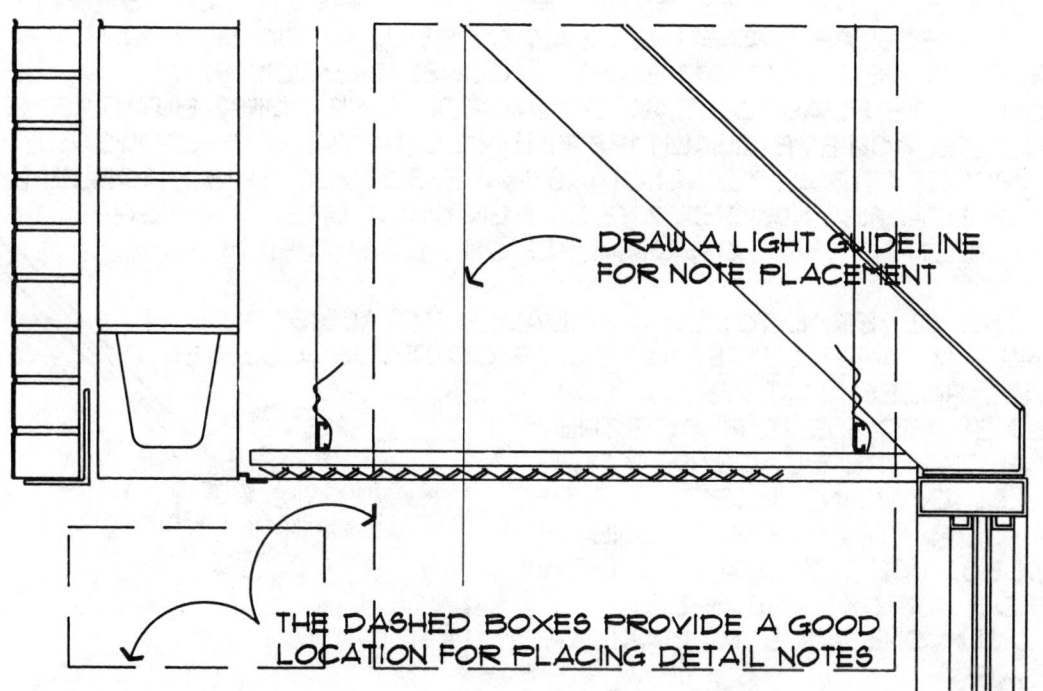

DRAW A LIGHT GUIDELINE
FOR NOTE PLACEMENT

THE DASHED BOXES PROVIDE A GOOD
LOCATION FOR PLACING DETAIL NOTES

THE DASHED BOXES ILLUSTRATE OPEN SPACES ON THE DETAIL
WHERE NOTES COULD BE CLUSTERED. NOTES SHOULD BE ALIGNED,
SPACED, AND ORGANIZED SO LEADER ARROWS DON'T CROSS.

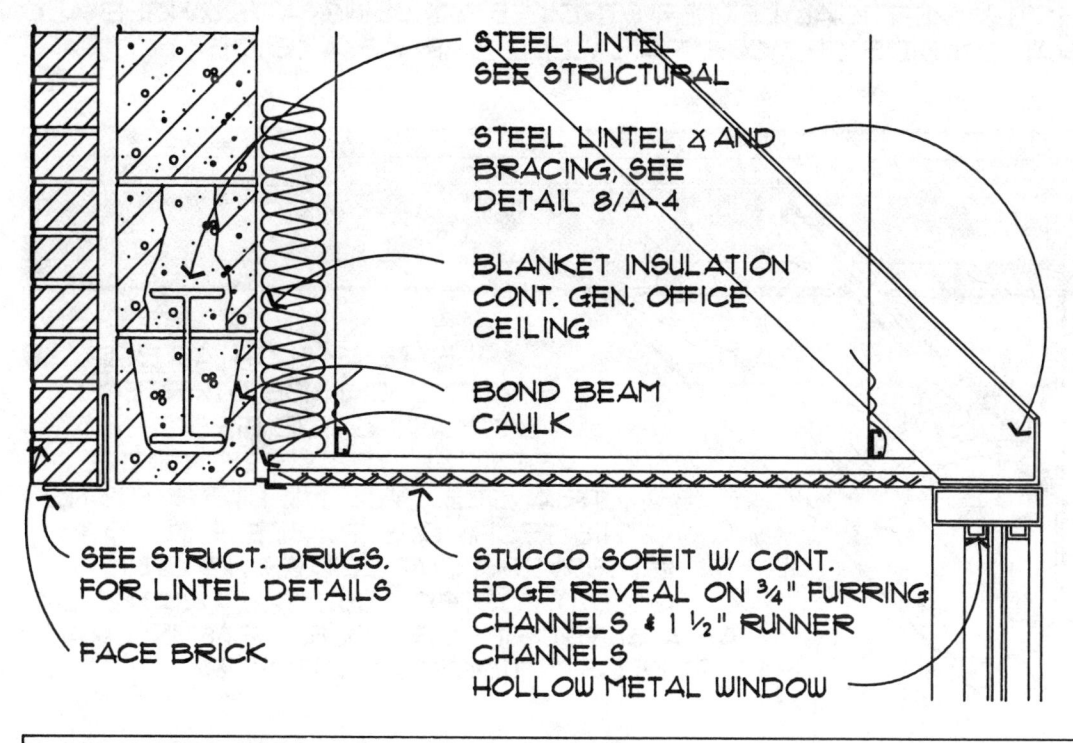

STEEL LINTEL
SEE STRUCTURAL

STEEL LINTEL & AND
BRACING, SEE
DETAIL 8/A-4

BLANKET INSULATION
CONT. GEN. OFFICE
CEILING

BOND BEAM
CAULK

SEE STRUCT. DRWGS.
FOR LINTEL DETAILS

STUCCO SOFFIT W/ CONT.
EDGE REVEAL ON ¾" FURRING
CHANNELS & 1 ½" RUNNER
CHANNELS

FACE BRICK

HOLLOW METAL WINDOW

ARCHITECTURAL PRINTING | 4-7

PLASTIC DRAFTING FILM (MYLAR) HAS BECOME VERY POPULAR AMONG ARCHITECTURAL FIRMS. PLASTIC FILM IS A MUCH MORE PERMANENT MEDIUM THAN 100% RAG BOND VELLUM. UNFORTUNATELY, THAT PRESENTS PROBLEMS WHEN IT COMES TO PRINTING. REGULAR DRAFTING LEAD DOESN'T WORK WELL ON MYLAR; IT TENDS TO SMEAR EASILY. CONSEQUENTLY, FIRMS COMMONLY USE PLASTIC LEAD OR INK FOR LINE WORK, BUT IT IS DIFFICULT TO ACHIEVE QUALITY PRINTING WITH THESE PRODUCTS. MOST ARCHITECTURAL TECHNICIANS HAVE SOLVED THIS PROBLEM BY USING EITHER A NUMBER 2 TECH PEN OR A SPECIAL HIGH-DENSITY FELT-TIP PEN FOR DRAWING ON PLASTIC FILM.

THERE ARE SEVERAL TOOLS AVAILABLE TO ASSIST YOU IN PRINTING. AN AMES LETTERING GUIDE CONTAINS A SERIES OF SMALL HOLES THAT ALLOW YOU TO DRAW GUIDELINES. TO USE IT, PLACE THE GUIDE ALONG THE BLADE OF YOUR PARALLEL BAR AND INSERT THE TIP OF YOUR DRAFTING LEAD IN ONE OF THE HOLES. USE THE LEAD TO DRAW THE GUIDE ACROSS THE SHEET. MOVE DOWN ONE HOLE TO MAKE THE NEXT LINE.

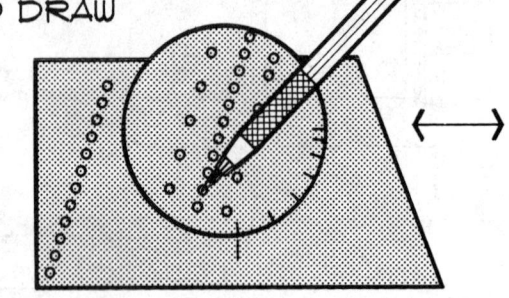

SOME ARCHITECTS CONSIDER THIS NEXT TIP TO BE A "CRUTCH" THAT SHOULDN'T BE USED. IT IS POSSIBLE, HOWEVER, TO ACHIEVE PERFECTLY VERTICAL LETTER STROKES BY USING A TRIANGLE ALONG THE BOTTOM SIDE OF YOUR PARALLEL BAR AS A GUIDE.

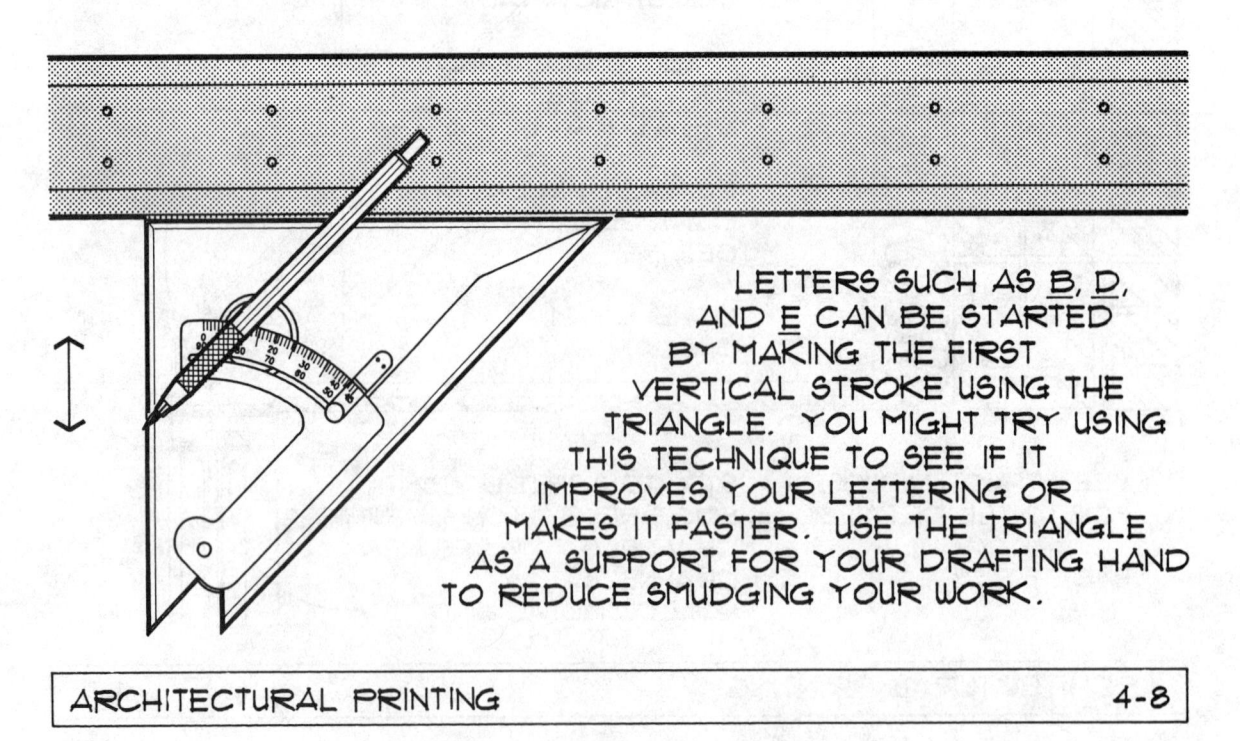

LETTERS SUCH AS B, D, AND E CAN BE STARTED BY MAKING THE FIRST VERTICAL STROKE USING THE TRIANGLE. YOU MIGHT TRY USING THIS TECHNIQUE TO SEE IF IT IMPROVES YOUR LETTERING OR MAKES IT FASTER. USE THE TRIANGLE AS A SUPPORT FOR YOUR DRAFTING HAND TO REDUCE SMUDGING YOUR WORK.

ARCHITECTURAL PRINTING

THESE TIPS WILL HELP TO IMPROVE YOUR PRINTING:

- USE GUIDELINES FOR ALL PRINTING.
- MAINTAIN A UNIFORM POINT ON YOUR LEAD HOLDER.
- MAKE VERTICAL LINE STROKES FIRST.
- PLACE A PIECE OF PAPER UNDER YOUR HAND TO PROTECT YOUR DRAWING.
- CLEAN THE GRAPHITE OFF YOUR DRAWING (EITHER WITH A BRUSH OR BY BLOWING IT OFF).
- BE CRITICAL ABOUT YOUR LETTERING.
- PRACTICE PRINTING BY LETTERING ONE OR TWO 8 1/2" x 11" SHEETS EACH WEEK. USE THE EXAMPLES IN THIS CHAPTER AS A GUIDE.

REPLAY

1. PRACTICE MAKING EACH LETTER STROKE FIVE TIMES.

A   B   C   D   E
F   G   H   I   J
K   L   M   N   O
P   Q   R   S   T
U   V   W   X   Y
Z   0   1   2   3
4   5   6   7   8
9

2. PRINT THE TIPS SECTION AT THE TOP OF THIS PAGE.

ARCHITECTURAL PRINTING   4-9

PLACE THE NOTES IN THE DASHED BOX ON THESE DETAILS.

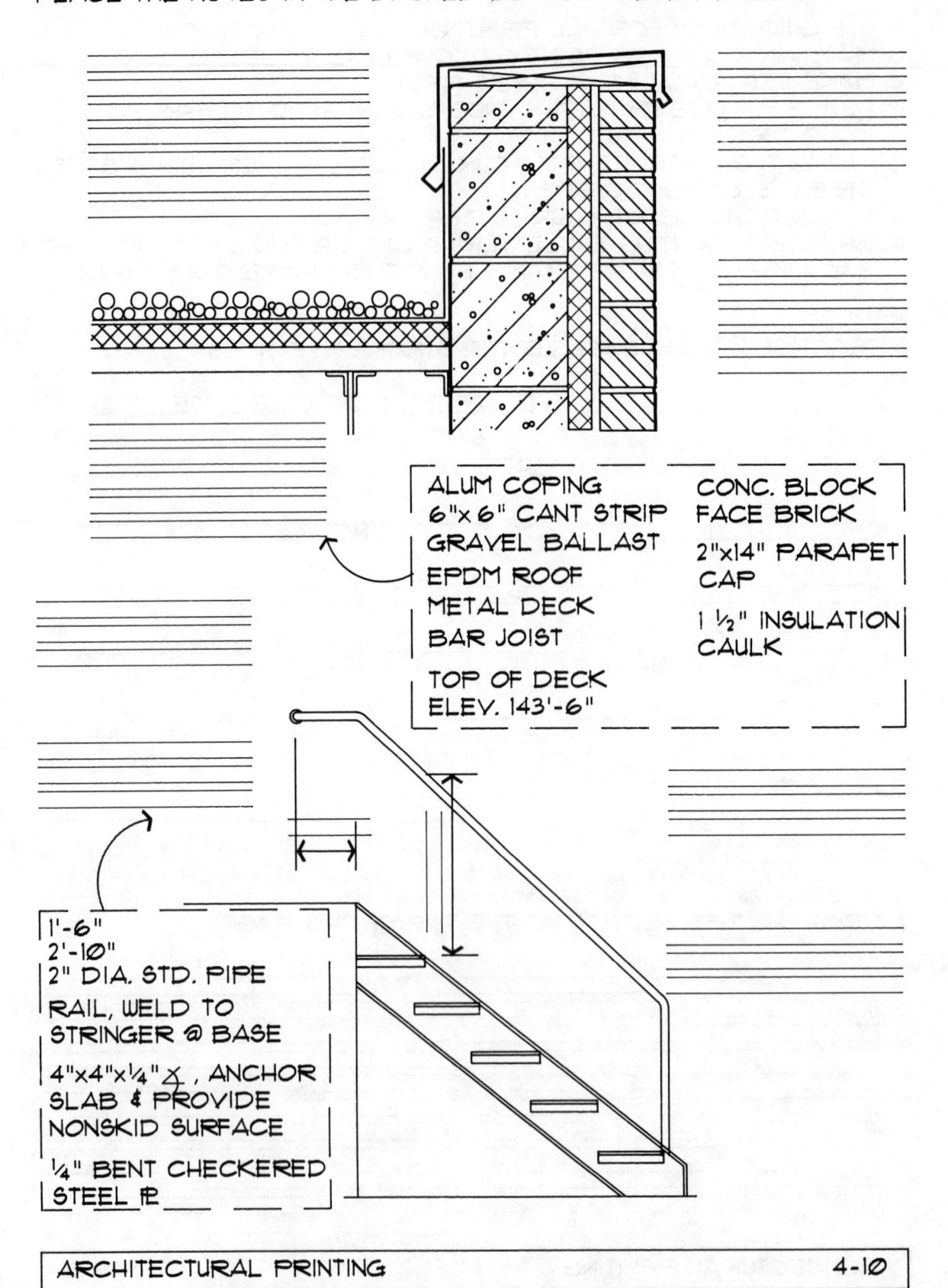

```
ALUM COPING            CONC. BLOCK
6"x 6" CANT STRIP      FACE BRICK
GRAVEL BALLAST         2"x14" PARAPET
EPDM ROOF              CAP
METAL DECK
BAR JOIST              1 ½" INSULATION
                       CAULK
TOP OF DECK
ELEV. 143'-6"
```

```
1'-6"
2'-10"
2" DIA. STD. PIPE
RAIL, WELD TO
STRINGER @ BASE

4"x4"x¼" ∠, ANCHOR
SLAB & PROVIDE
NONSKID SURFACE

¼" BENT CHECKERED
STEEL ℞
```

ARCHITECTURAL PRINTING   4-10

DRAFTING SYMBOLS

THIS UNIT PRESENTS THE SYMBOLS USED IN ARCHITECTURAL WORKING DRAWINGS. THE MATERIAL IS DIVIDED INTO THREE AREAS: (1) MATERIAL HATCHING, (2) ARCHITECTURAL SYMBOLS, AND (3) SIZES OF STANDARD ARCHITECTURAL ITEMS. THE MATERIAL IN EACH SECTION IS PRESENTED WITH EXAMPLES SHOWING HOW THEY ARE INCORPORATED INTO WORKING DRAWINGS.

MATERIAL HATCHING

A FLOOR PLAN OR SECTION IS GENERATED BY CUTTING A PLANE (A KNIFE BLADE) THROUGH A PORTION OF THE BUILDING. THE CONSTRUCTION MATERIALS THAT ARE EXPOSED IN THE SECTION CUT ARE CROSSHATCHED, OR MARKED WITH VARIOUS PATTERNS, TO IDENTIFY THE DIFFERENT MATERIALS. THIS APPLIES ONLY TO ITEMS THAT ARE CUT, NOT ITEMS THAT ARE SHOWN IN ELEVATION BEYOND THE CUT. THE DETAIL BELOW ILLUSTRATES THE HATCHING SYMBOLS USED FOR MATERIALS IN A FOUNDATION WALL CONDITION. (THE SYMBOLS SHOWN IN THIS UNIT ARE USED IN EXAMPLES THROUGHOUT THE TEXT; THEY MAY DIFFER SLIGHTLY AMONG ARCHITECTS.)

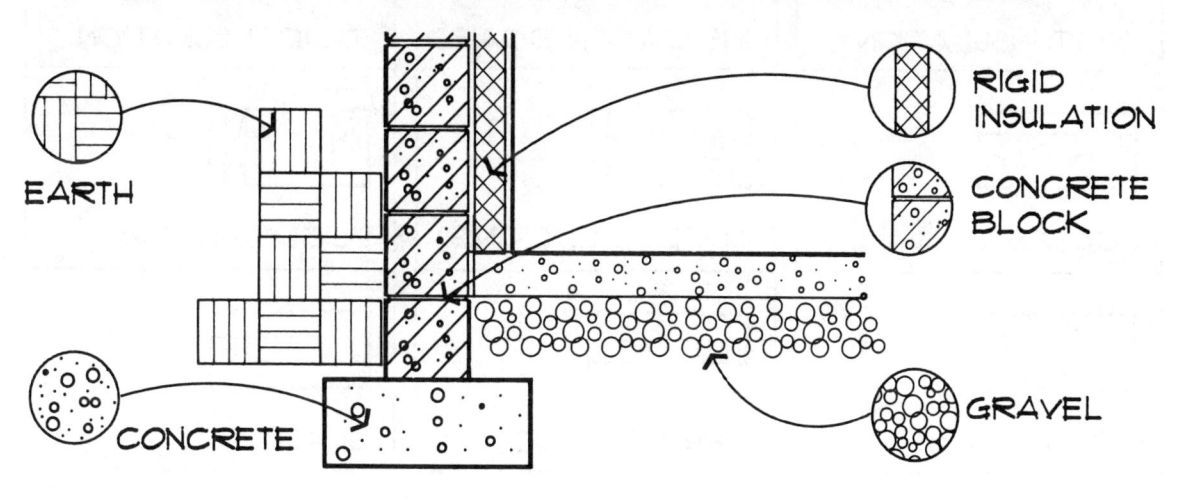

DRAFTING SYMBOLS 5-1

MATERIAL HATCHING	CARPET	METAL STUD WALL
EARTH	CLAY	STEEL
GRAVEL	SAND	PLASTER
BRICK	STONE	GASKET
CONCRETE BLOCK	CONCRETE	PLYWOOD
BATT INSULATION	INSULATION BOARD	RIGID INSULATION
WOOD STUD WALL	WOOD (BLOCKING)	WOOD (ROUGH)
WOOD (FINISHED)	CERAMIC TILE	GLASS

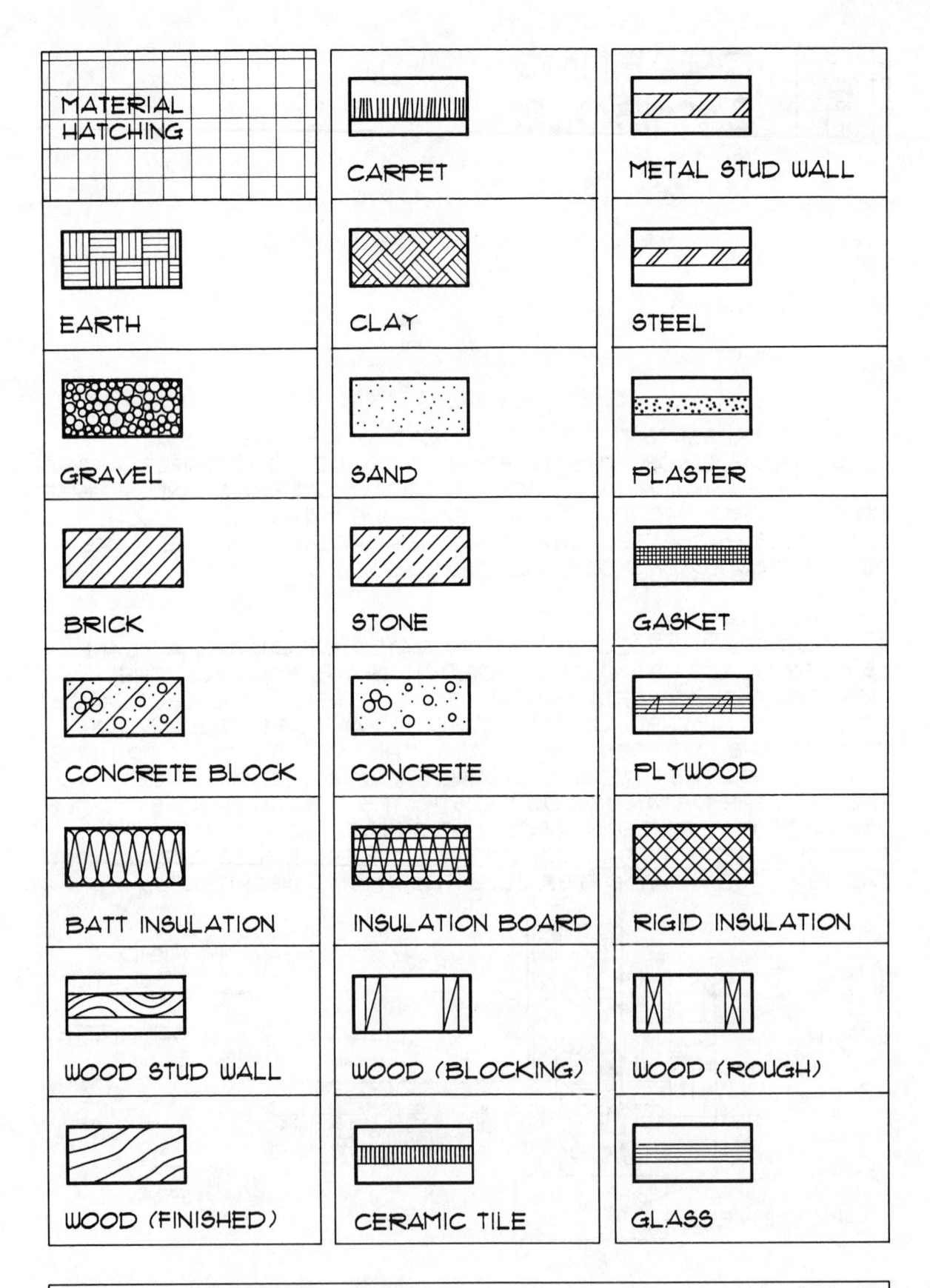

DRAFTING SYMBOLS 5-2

USE THE FOLLOWING TIPS WHEN DRAWING MATERIAL HATCHING:

1. DRAW HATCHING WITH A SLIGHTLY LIGHTER LINE QUALITY SO IT WON'T COMPETE WITH THE DETAIL.

DRAW THE CONTINUOUS WAVY LINE FOR A WOOD STUD WALL FIRST, THEN FILL IN THE SHORT ARCS

USE A 4H LEAD WEIGHT AND DRAW "CRISP" LINES

2. THE DOTS IN CONCRETE ARE DIFFICULT TO PLACE IN ORDER TO MAKE THEM DARK ENOUGH TO READ WHEN THEY ARE PRINTED. USE A Ø.35 mm OR Ø.50 mm TECHNICAL PEN TO MAKE THE DOTS. REMEMBER THAT INK DOESN'T ERASE EASILY, SO MAKE SURE THAT THE MATERIAL IS IN THE RIGHT LOCATION BEFORE YOU START DRAWING.

PLACE EACH DOT WITH A TECH PEN—ONE POINT AT A TIME WORKS BETTER THAN A SERIES OF FAST STIPPLE "PECKS."

3. ACCURATELY MEASURE THE SPACES USED FOR MATERIAL SUCH AS RIGID INSULATION.

A 1/16" DISTANCE IS GOOD SPACING BETWEEN DIAGONAL LINES. ONE TECHNIQUE FOR EASIER SPACING IS TO MAKE A PHOTOCOPY OF YOUR ARCHITECT'S SCALE AND PLACE IT UNDER THE DETAIL. THIS SAVES MAKING TICK MARKS.

4. THERE ARE SEVERAL DIFFERENT HATCHING PATTERNS FOR WOOD. THE PATTERN USED IS DETERMINED BY THE VIEW (PLAN OR SECTION).

THIS IS A WOOD STUD WALL IN PLAN

THE SAME WOOD STUD WALL IS HATCHED WITH INSULATION IN A SECTION VIEW

THIS IS A CONTINUOUS PIECE OF WOOD (SUCH AS A JOIST) IN SECTION

THIS IS A CUT PIECE

DRAFTING SYMBOLS   5-3

THIS EXAMPLE SHOWS THE HATCHING SYMBOLS USED FOR A PORTION OF A COMMERCIAL BUILDING.

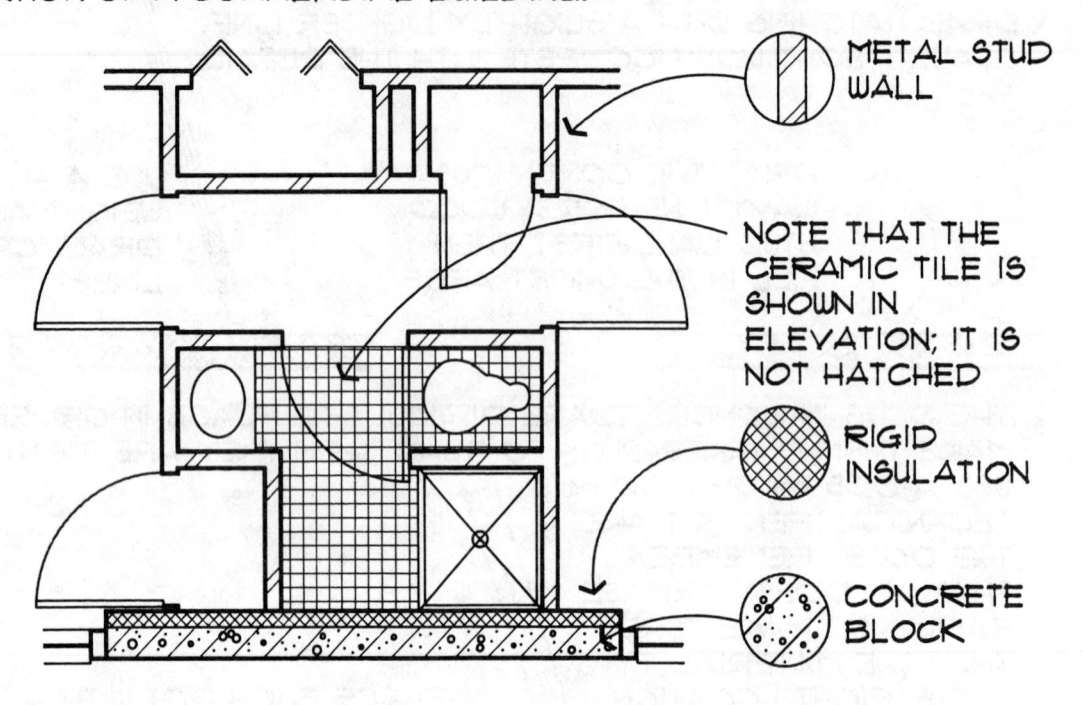

- METAL STUD WALL
- NOTE THAT THE CERAMIC TILE IS SHOWN IN ELEVATION; IT IS NOT HATCHED
- RIGID INSULATION
- CONCRETE BLOCK

THE ILLUSTRATION BELOW SHOWS HATCHING EXAMPLES FOR A SECTION THROUGH A PARAPET WALL AND GLUE-LAMINATED BEAM.

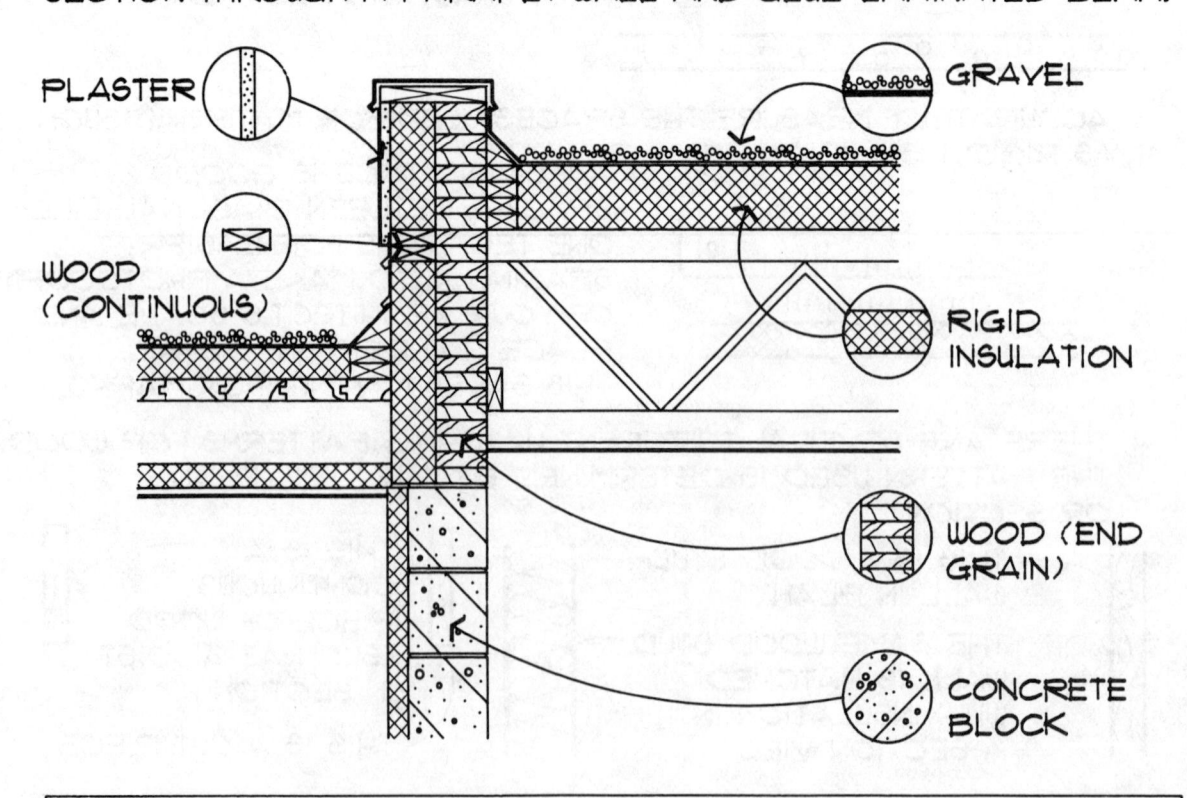

- PLASTER
- WOOD (CONTINUOUS)
- GRAVEL
- RIGID INSULATION
- WOOD (END GRAIN)
- CONCRETE BLOCK

DRAFTING SYMBOLS 5-4

ARCHITECTURAL SYMBOLS

THERE ARE A NUMBER OF SYMBOLS THAT ARE STANDARD IN ARCHITECTURAL DETAILS. THESE SYMBOLS ARE USED AS "SIGNS" TO INFORM THE CONTRACTOR READING A DETAIL ABOUT SPECIFIC CONDITIONS. A DASHED LINE, FOR EXAMPLE, INDICATES THE EXISTING TOPOGRAPHY OF A SITE, WHILE A SOLID LINE REPRESENTS A CHANGE. THE SYMBOLS USED ARE FREQUENTLY LISTED IN AN ARCHITECT'S SPECIFICATION SHEET TO MAKE SURE THAT ALL PARTIES USING IT CLEARLY UNDERSTAND THEIR MEANING. THE ILLUSTRATION AT THE LEFT SHOWS SEVERAL SYMBOLS THAT ARE COMMONLY FOUND ON ELEVATIONS. THE 2 SYMBOL INDICATES WHAT WINDOW TYPE SHOULD BE USED FOR THE UPPER WINDOWS. THE CONTRACTOR CAN USE THIS SYMBOL TO REFER TO ANOTHER PART OF THE DRAWING SET WHERE SPECIFIC INFORMATION ABOUT THE WINDOWS, INCLUDING CATALOG NUMBERS, IS LISTED. THE SYMBOL FIRST FL. 700'-0" SHOWS THAT THE ELEVATION OF THE FIRST FLOOR IS 700'-0" ABOVE SEA LEVEL. THE SYMBOL 7/A-6 REFERENCES THE CONTRACTOR TO DETAIL 7 ON SHEET A-6.

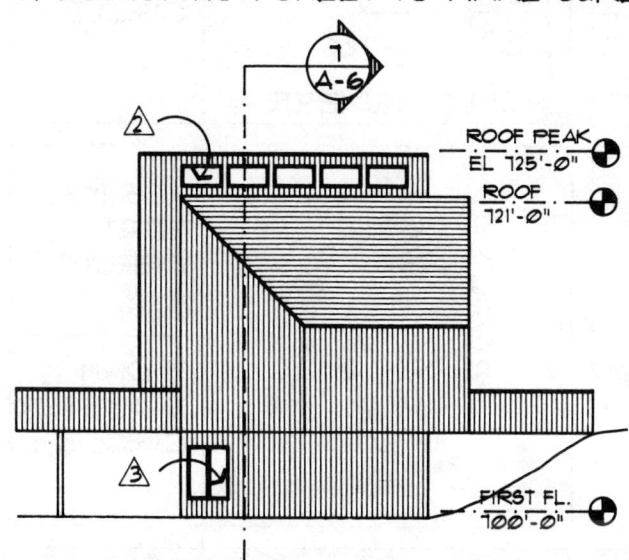

THE PARTIAL FLOOR PLAN BELOW ILLUSTRATES A NUMBER OF SYMBOLS COMMON TO ARCHITECTURE. THE NEXT SEVERAL PAGES WILL PROVIDE MORE EXAMPLES OF FREQUENTLY USED SYMBOLS.

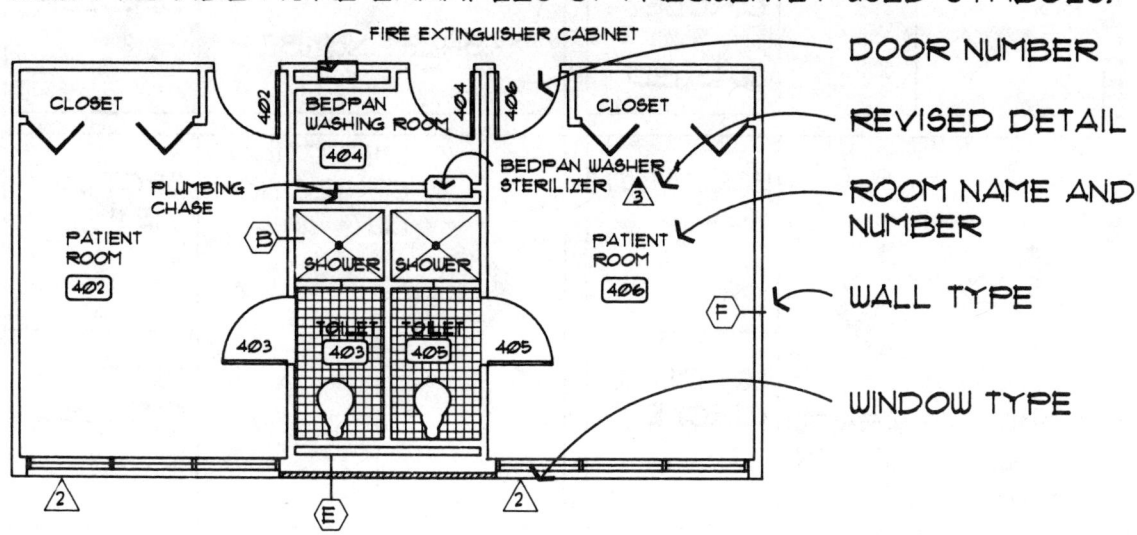

DRAFTING SYMBOLS   5-5

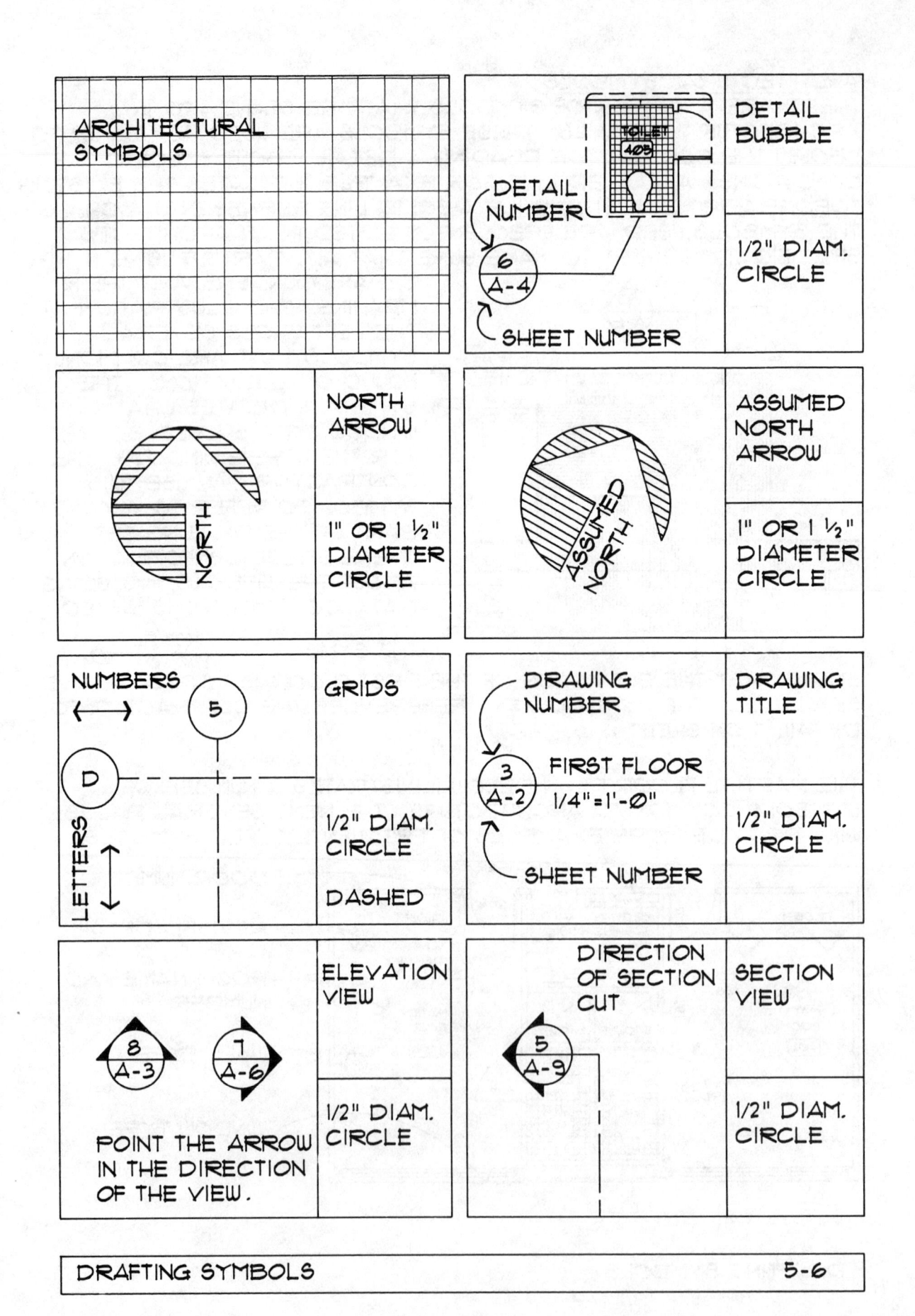

ARCHITECTURAL SYMBOLS

DETAIL BUBBLE — Detail Number / Sheet Number	1/2" DIAM. CIRCLE
NORTH ARROW	1" OR 1 1/2" DIAMETER CIRCLE
ASSUMED NORTH ARROW	1" OR 1 1/2" DIAMETER CIRCLE
GRIDS (Numbers / Letters)	1/2" DIAM. CIRCLE — DASHED
DRAWING NUMBER / SHEET NUMBER — 3/A-2 FIRST FLOOR 1/4"=1'-0"	**DRAWING TITLE** — 1/2" DIAM. CIRCLE
ELEVATION VIEW — 8/A-3, 7/A-6. Point the arrow in the direction of the view.	1/2" DIAM. CIRCLE
DIRECTION OF SECTION CUT — 5/A-9	**SECTION VIEW** — 1/2" DIAM. CIRCLE

DRAFTING SYMBOLS 5-6

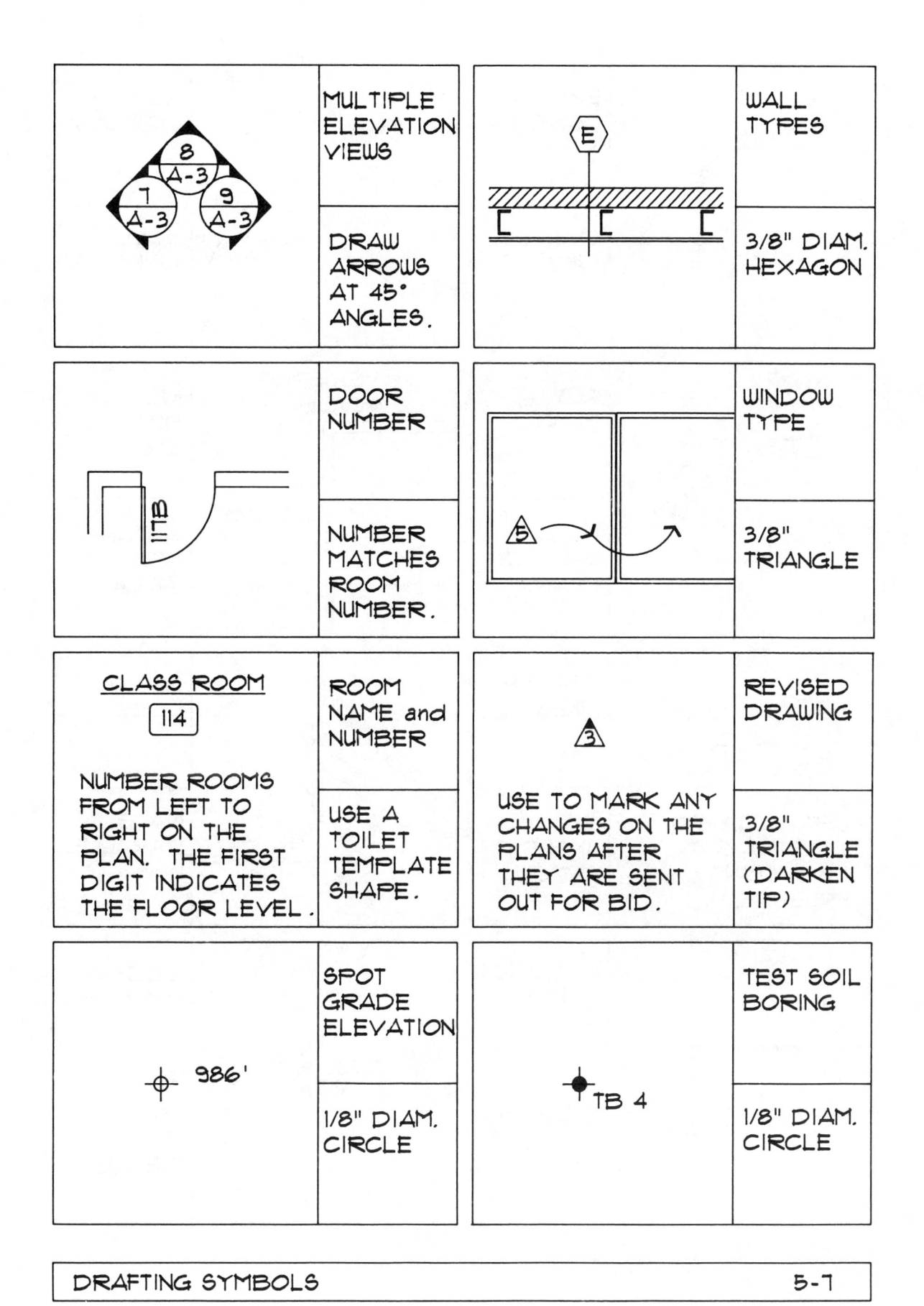

(diamond with circles 7/A-3, 8/A-3, 9/A-3)	MULTIPLE ELEVATION VIEWS	(hexagon with E over hatched wall section)	WALL TYPES
	DRAW ARROWS AT 45° ANGLES.		3/8" DIAM. HEXAGON
(door symbol with 117B)	DOOR NUMBER	(window with circled 5 arrow)	WINDOW TYPE
	NUMBER MATCHES ROOM NUMBER.		3/8" TRIANGLE
CLASS ROOM [114] NUMBER ROOMS FROM LEFT TO RIGHT ON THE PLAN. THE FIRST DIGIT INDICATES THE FLOOR LEVEL.	ROOM NAME and NUMBER	(triangle with 3)	REVISED DRAWING
	USE A TOILET TEMPLATE SHAPE.	USE TO MARK ANY CHANGES ON THE PLANS AFTER THEY ARE SENT OUT FOR BID.	3/8" TRIANGLE (DARKEN TIP)
⊕ 986'	SPOT GRADE ELEVATION	⦿ TB 4	TEST SOIL BORING
	1/8" DIAM. CIRCLE		1/8" DIAM. CIRCLE

DRAFTING SYMBOLS   5-7

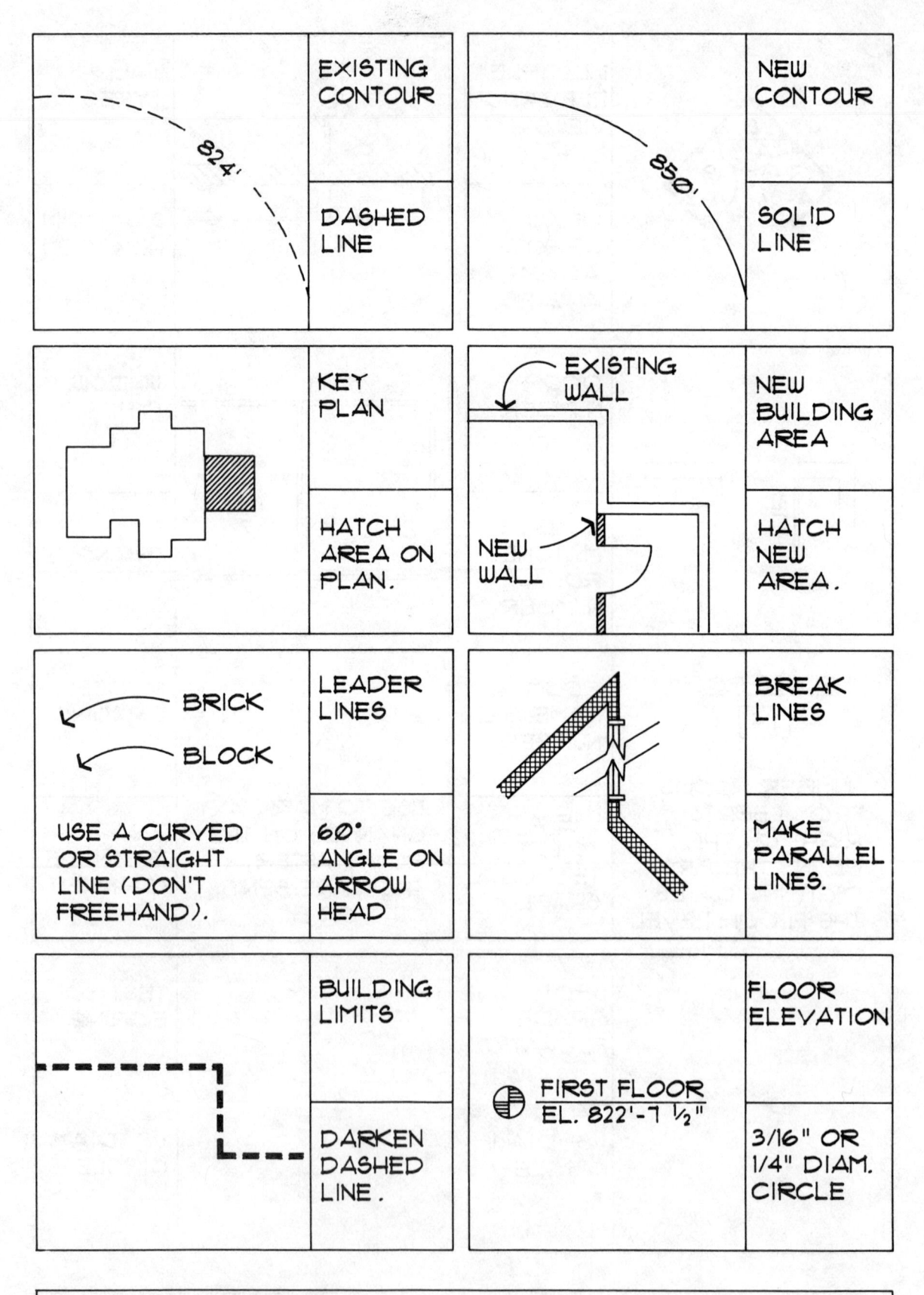

(dashed arc labeled 824')	EXISTING CONTOUR / DASHED LINE	(solid arc labeled 850')	NEW CONTOUR / SOLID LINE
(key plan shape with hatched area)	KEY PLAN / HATCH AREA ON PLAN.	(wall detail with EXISTING WALL and NEW WALL labels)	NEW BUILDING AREA / HATCH NEW AREA.
BRICK ↙ / BLOCK ↙ — USE A CURVED OR STRAIGHT LINE (DON'T FREEHAND).	LEADER LINES / 60° ANGLE ON ARROW HEAD	(break line symbol between hatched walls)	BREAK LINES / MAKE PARALLEL LINES.
(dashed rectangle outline)	BUILDING LIMITS / DARKEN DASHED LINE.	⌖ FIRST FLOOR / EL. 822'-7 ½"	FLOOR ELEVATION / 3/16" OR 1/4" DIAM. CIRCLE

DRAFTING SYMBOLS

THE PLAN BELOW ILLUSTRATES SEVERAL SYMBOLS ASSOCIATED WITH SITE DRAWINGS.

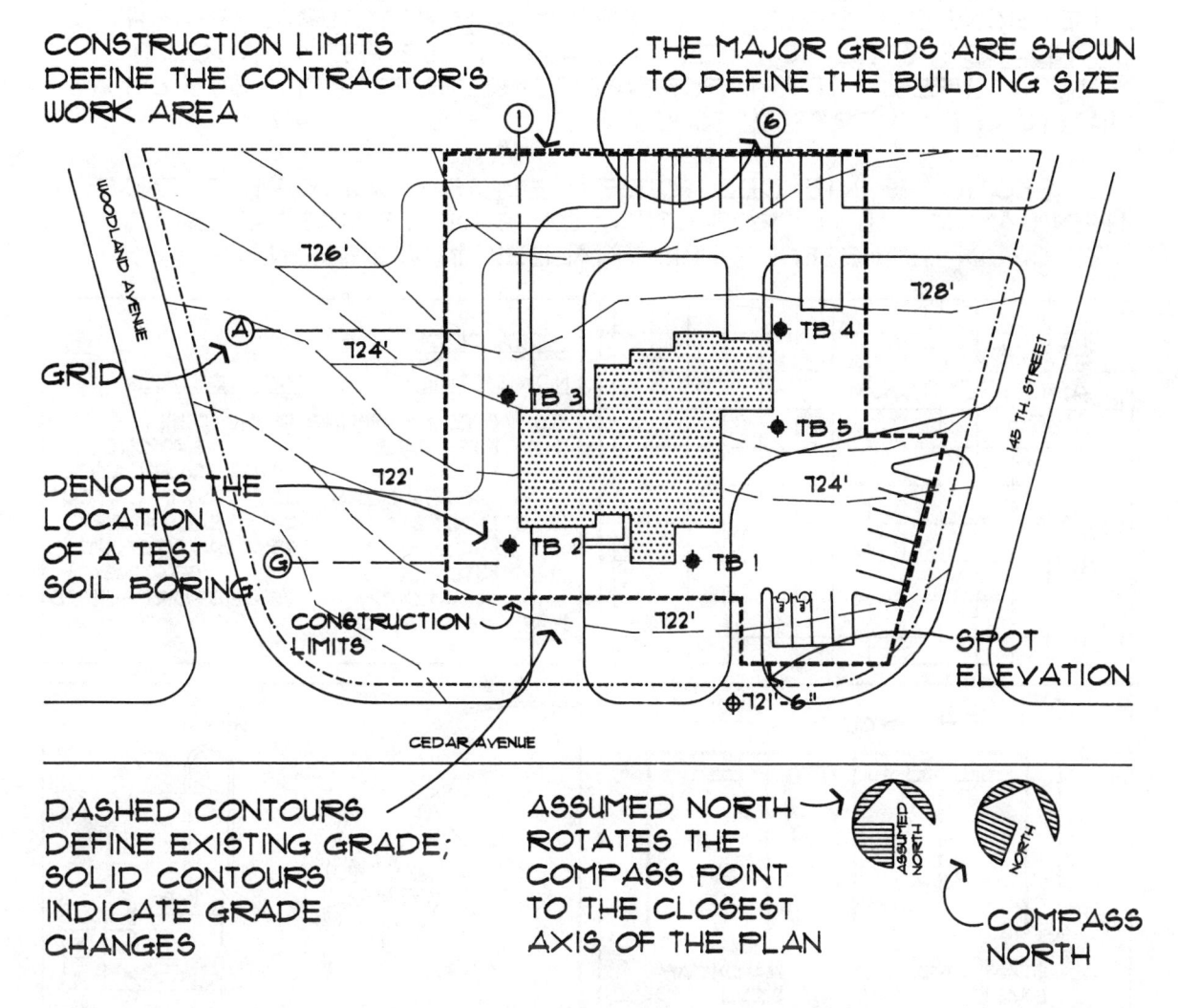

CONSTRUCTION LIMITS DEFINE THE CONTRACTOR'S WORK AREA

THE MAJOR GRIDS ARE SHOWN TO DEFINE THE BUILDING SIZE

GRID

DENOTES THE LOCATION OF A TEST SOIL BORING

CONSTRUCTION LIMITS

SPOT ELEVATION

DASHED CONTOURS DEFINE EXISTING GRADE; SOLID CONTOURS INDICATE GRADE CHANGES

ASSUMED NORTH ROTATES THE COMPASS POINT TO THE CLOSEST AXIS OF THE PLAN

COMPASS NORTH

USE THE FOLLOWING TIPS WHEN DRAWING ARCHITECTURAL SYMBOLS:

1. DRAW SYMBOLS WITH A LIGHT LINE QUALITY, USING A 2H OR 4H LEAD.

2. PLACE SYMBOLS AFTER THE MAJORITY OF THE DETAIL AND DIMENSIONS ARE DRAWN. MOST SYMBOL LOCATIONS ARE FLEXIBLE AND CAN BE FIT ON THE DRAWING.

3. MANY OF THE SHAPES USED FOR ARCHITECTURAL SYMBOLS CAN BE FOUND ON A TOILET TEMPLATE. FOR EXAMPLE, THE BOX WITH ROUNDED CORNERS USED FOR ROOM NUMBERS IS A 1/4" SCALE SINK ON THE TEMPLATE.

| DRAFTING SYMBOLS | 5-9 |

STANDARD SIZES

IT IS NECESSARY TO KNOW THE SIZE OF HUNDREDS OF ITEMS USED IN ARCHITECTURE TO BE ABLE TO DETAIL A PROJECT. GENERAL DIMENSIONS CAN BE OBTAINED FROM <u>ARCHITECTURAL GRAPHIC STANDARDS</u>; SPECIFIC SIZES ARE AVAILABLE FROM PRODUCT MANUFACTURERS. IT IS IMPORTANT TO RESEARCH THE SIZE OF A MATERIAL RATHER THAN TO GUESS.

THIS SECTION IS INTENDED TO BE USED AS A QUICK REFERENCE WHEN LAYING OUT A PROJECT. ALWAYS DETERMINE THE EXACT SIZE OF AN ITEM BEFORE IT IS FINALIZED IN A DESIGN.

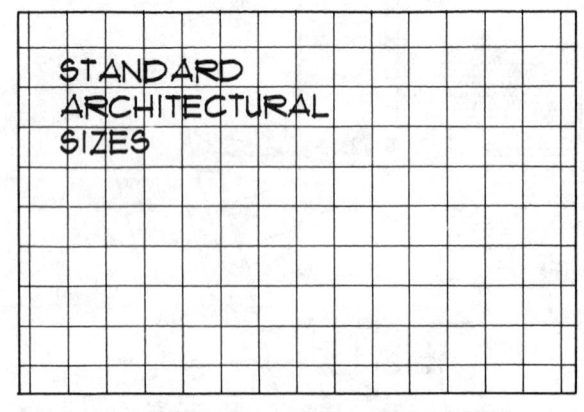

STANDARD ARCHITECTURAL SIZES

INDEX OF DETAILS

NO	DETAIL	NO.	DETAIL
1-6	SITE & PARKING	18-19	TOILET LAYOUT
7-8	FURNITURE	20-22	STAIR LAYOUT
9	KITCHEN & BATH SIZES	23	RAMP LAYOUT
10-12	DOORS & CLOSETS	24	ELEVATOR
13-14	KITCHEN LAYOUT	25	AUDITORIUM SEATING
15-17	BATH LAYOUT	26-28	SPORT FIELDS

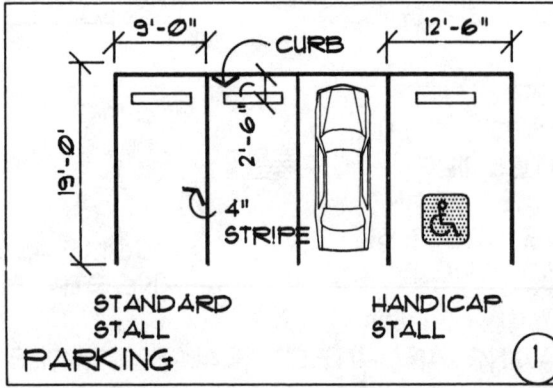

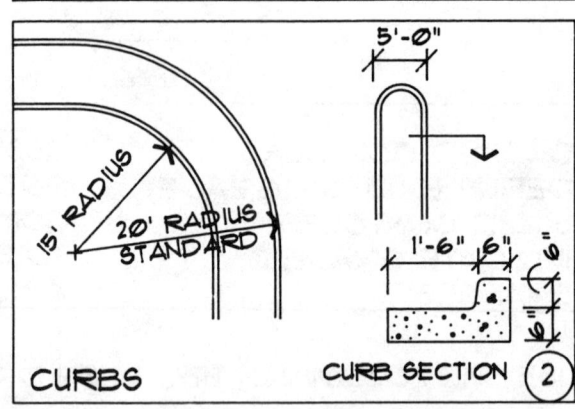

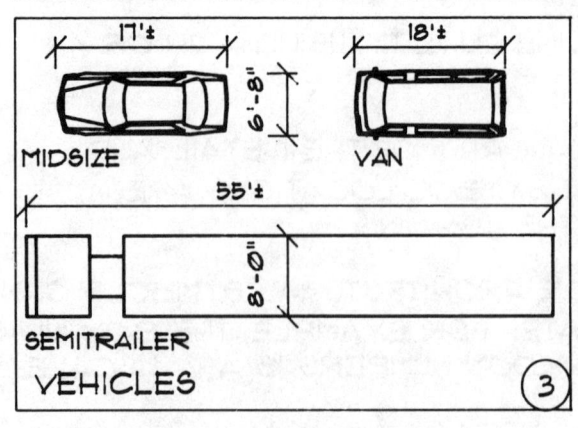

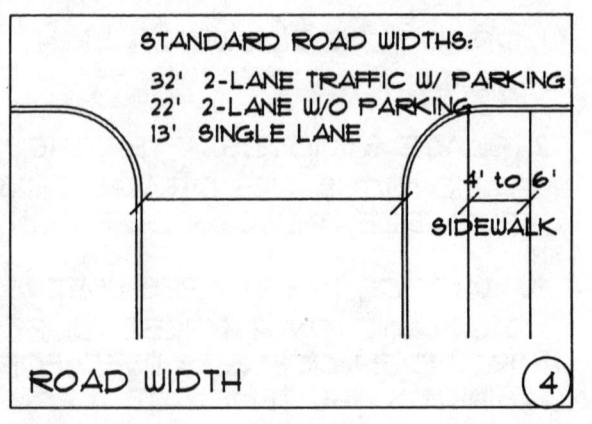

1. PARKING — STANDARD STALL 9'-0" × 19'-0", HANDICAP STALL 12'-6", CURB, 2'-6", 4" STRIPE

2. CURBS — 15' RADIUS, 20' RADIUS STANDARD, 5'-0". CURB SECTION: 1'-6", 6", 6", 6"

3. VEHICLES — MIDSIZE 17'± × 6'-8", VAN 18'±, SEMITRAILER 55'± × 8'-0"

4. ROAD WIDTH — STANDARD ROAD WIDTHS:
- 32' 2-LANE TRAFFIC W/ PARKING
- 22' 2-LANE W/O PARKING
- 13' SINGLE LANE

4' to 6' SIDEWALK

DRAFTING SYMBOLS — 5-10

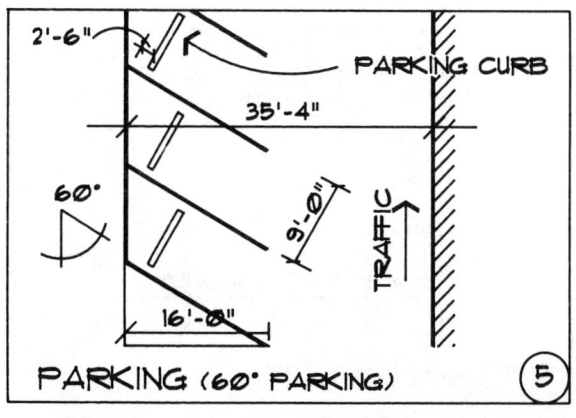

PARKING (60° PARKING) ⑤

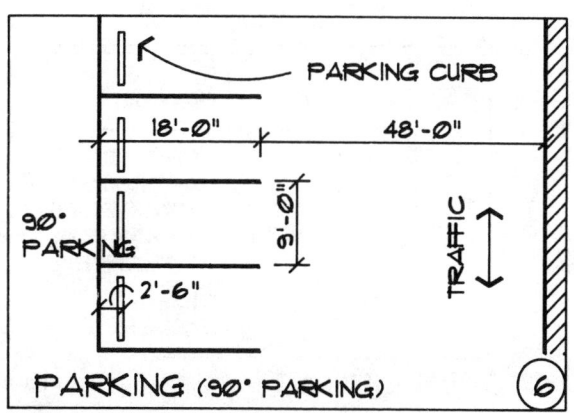

- 2'-6"
- 35'-4"
- 60°
- 9'-0"
- 16'-0"
- PARKING CURB
- TRAFFIC

PARKING (90° PARKING) ⑥

- 18'-0"
- 48'-0"
- 90° PARKING
- 9'-0"
- 2'-6"
- PARKING CURB
- TRAFFIC

FURNITURE ⑦

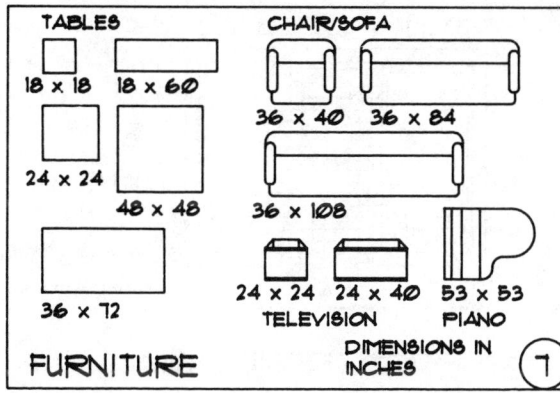

TABLES
- 18 x 18
- 18 x 60
- 24 x 24
- 48 x 48
- 36 x 72

CHAIR/SOFA
- 36 x 40
- 36 x 84
- 36 x 108

- 24 x 24 TELEVISION
- 24 x 40
- 53 x 53 PIANO

DIMENSIONS IN INCHES

BED SIZES ⑧

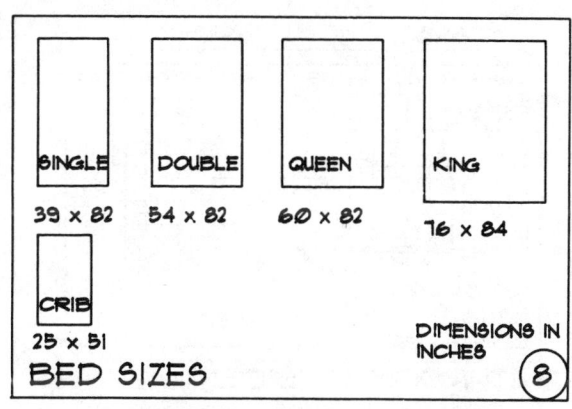

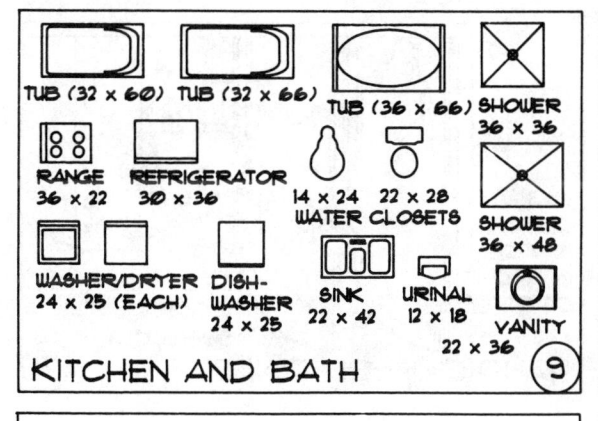

- SINGLE 39 x 82
- DOUBLE 54 x 82
- QUEEN 60 x 82
- KING 76 x 84
- CRIB 25 x 51

DIMENSIONS IN INCHES

KITCHEN AND BATH ⑨

- TUB (32 x 60)
- TUB (32 x 66)
- TUB (36 x 66)
- SHOWER 36 x 36
- RANGE 36 x 22
- REFRIGERATOR 30 x 36
- WATER CLOSETS 14 x 24, 22 x 28
- SHOWER 36 x 48
- WASHER/DRYER 24 x 25 (EACH)
- DISHWASHER 24 x 25
- SINK 22 x 42
- URINAL 12 x 18
- VANITY 22 x 36

⑩

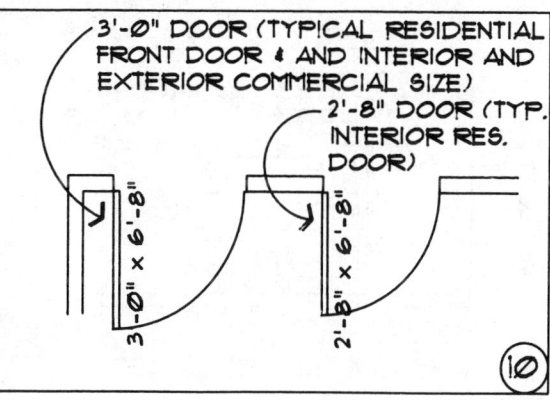

- 3'-0" DOOR (TYPICAL RESIDENTIAL FRONT DOOR & AND INTERIOR AND EXTERIOR COMMERCIAL SIZE)
- 2'-8" DOOR (TYP. INTERIOR RES. DOOR)
- 3'-0" x 6'-8"
- 2'-8" x 6'-8"

CLOSET ⑪

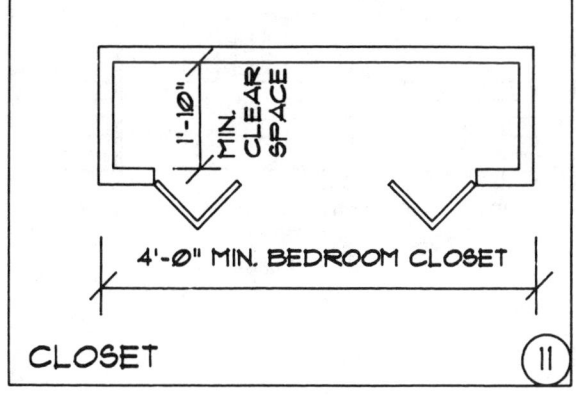

- 1'-10" MIN. CLEAR SPACE
- 4'-0" MIN. BEDROOM CLOSET

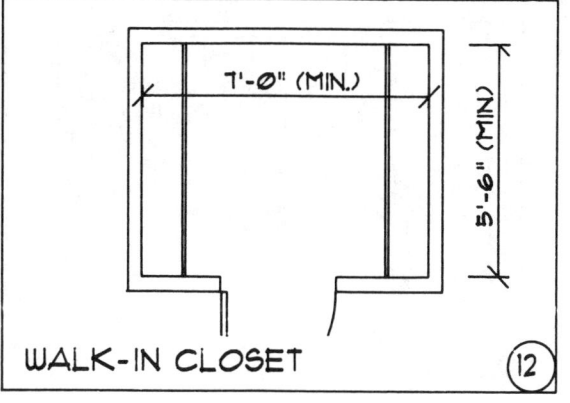

WALK-IN CLOSET ⑫

- 7'-0" (MIN.)
- 5'-6" (MIN)

DRAFTING SYMBOLS   5-11

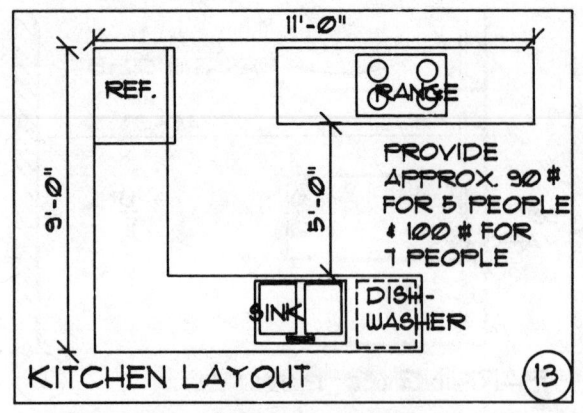

KITCHEN LAYOUT (13)

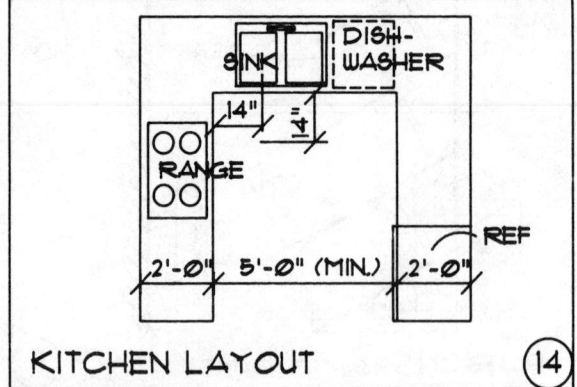

- 11'-0"
- 9'-0"
- 5'-0"
- REF.
- RANGE
- SINK
- DISH-WASHER
- PROVIDE APPROX. 90 # FOR 5 PEOPLE & 100 # FOR 7 PEOPLE

KITCHEN LAYOUT (14)

- SINK
- DISH-WASHER
- 14"
- 14"
- RANGE
- REF
- 2'-0"
- 5'-0" (MIN.)
- 2'-0"

BATHROOM (RESIDENTIAL) (15)

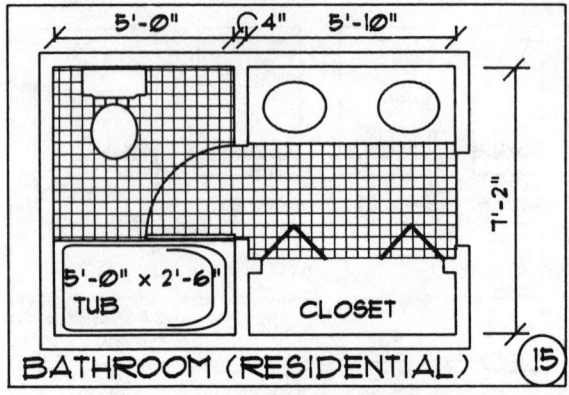

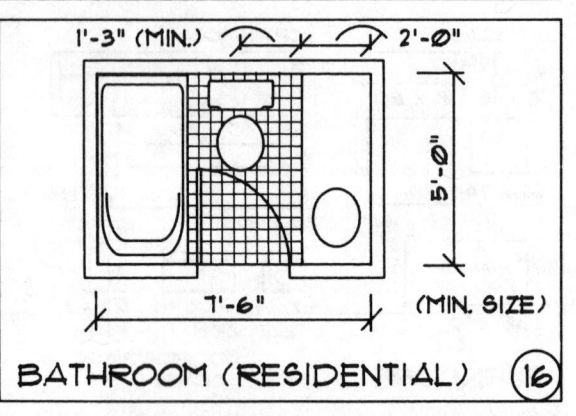

- 5'-0"
- 4"
- 5'-10"
- 7'-2"
- 5'-0" x 2'-6" TUB
- CLOSET

BATHROOM (RESIDENTIAL) (16)

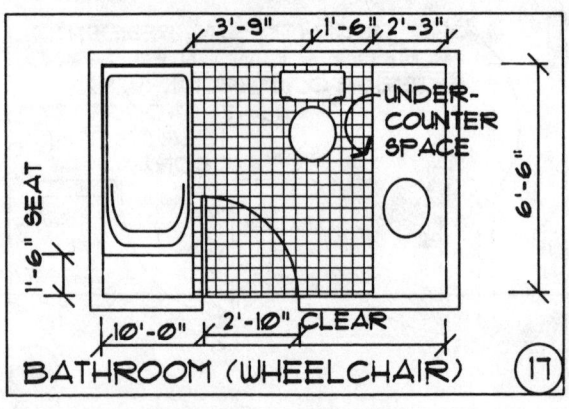

- 1'-3" (MIN.)
- 2'-0"
- 5'-0"
- 7'-6"
- (MIN. SIZE)

BATHROOM (WHEELCHAIR) (17)

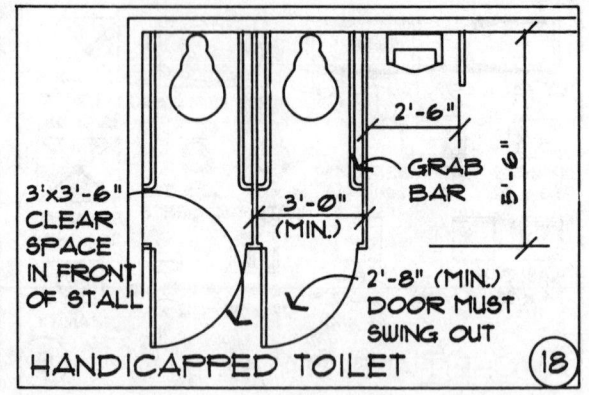

- 3'-9"
- 1'-6"
- 2'-3"
- UNDER-COUNTER SPACE
- 6'-6"
- 1'-6" SEAT
- 10'-0"
- 2'-10" CLEAR

HANDICAPPED TOILET (18)

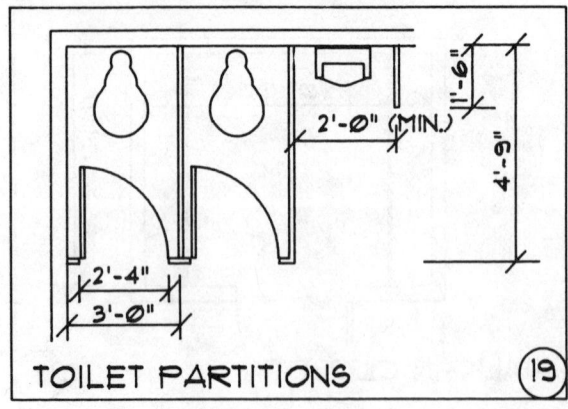

- 2'-6"
- GRAB BAR
- 3' x 3'-6" CLEAR SPACE IN FRONT OF STALL
- 3'-0" (MIN.)
- 5'-6"
- 2'-8" (MIN.) DOOR MUST SWING OUT

TOILET PARTITIONS (19)

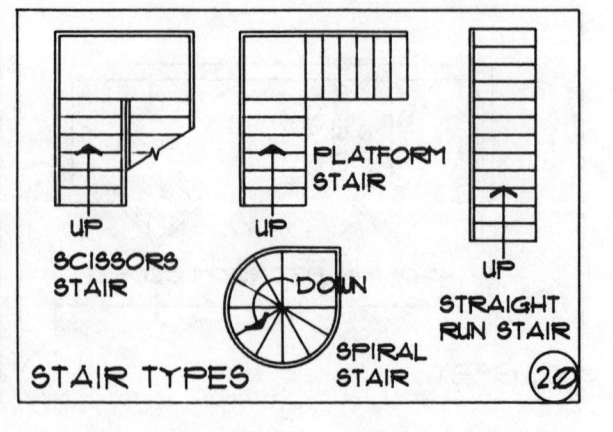

- 1'-6"
- 2'-0" (MIN.)
- 4'-9"
- 2'-4"
- 3'-0"

STAIR TYPES (20)

- UP — SCISSORS STAIR
- UP — PLATFORM STAIR
- UP — STRAIGHT RUN STAIR
- DOWN — SPIRAL STAIR

DRAFTING SYMBOLS 5-12

RESIDENTIAL STAIR (21)

A RULE OF THUMB IS: T + R = 17 ½"

10" T.
7 ¾" R
8" RISER IS MAX. FOR RESIDENTIAL
MEASURE HANDRAIL FROM EDGE OF TREAD TO TOP OF RAIL

6'-4"
3'-0" IS TYP FOR RES.
6 TREADS @ 10" = 5'-0"
7 TREADS @ 7 ¾" = 4'-6"
2'-8"
8'-0"
UP
CHECK LOCAL CODES

COMMERCIAL STAIR (22)

A 7" RISER IS MAXIMUM WITH SOME BUILDING CODES FOR COMMERCIAL

3'-6" IS TYPICAL FOR COMMERCIAL
2'-8" HANDRAIL
7" RISER
11" TREAD
5"
LANDING
UP
CHECK LOCAL CODES

HANDICAP RAMP (23)

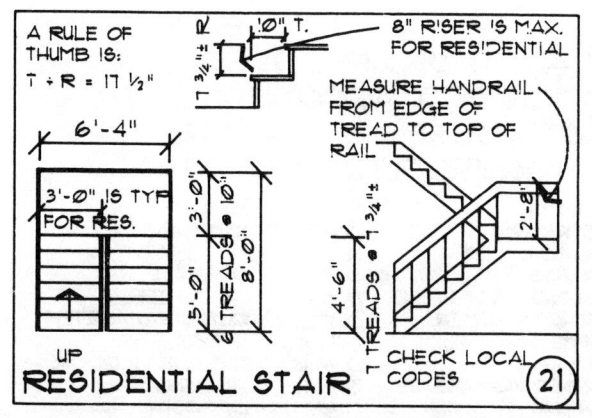

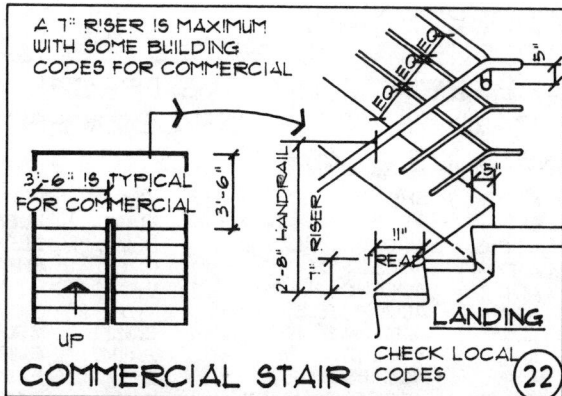

1:12 (4° 43" ANGLE) IS THE MAXIMUM SLOPE FOR A HANDICAP RAMP

RAMPS STEEPER THAN 1:15 MUST HAVE LANDINGS AT THE TOP AND BOTTOM PLUS AN INTERMEDIATE LANDING FOR EVERY 5' OF VERTICAL RISE

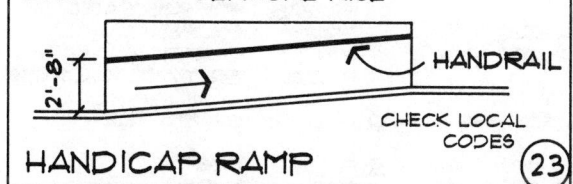

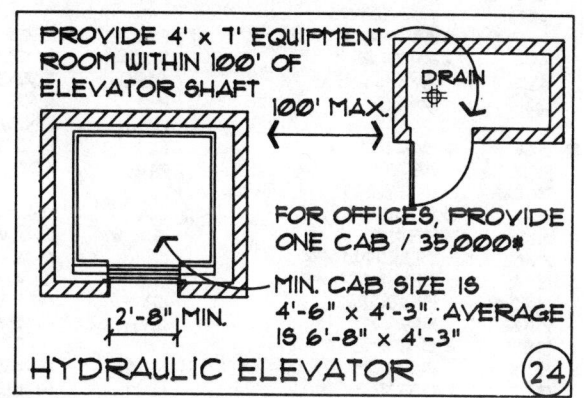

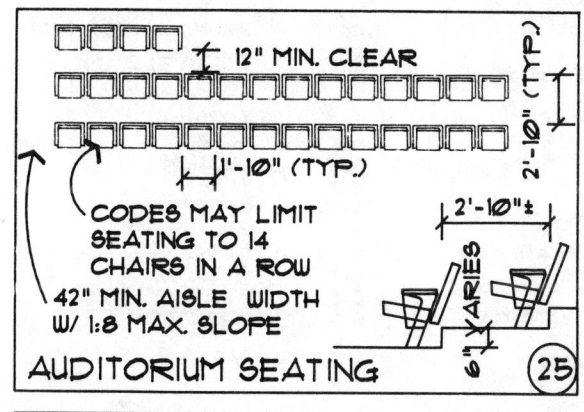

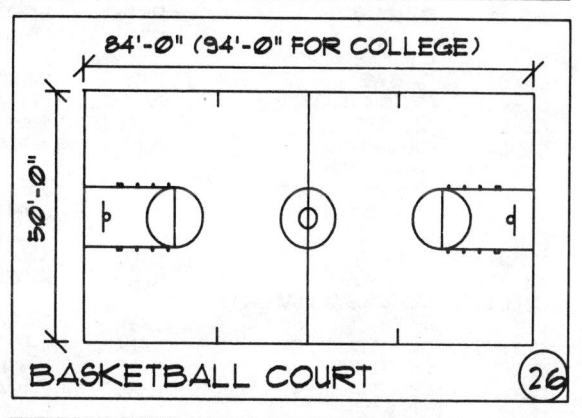

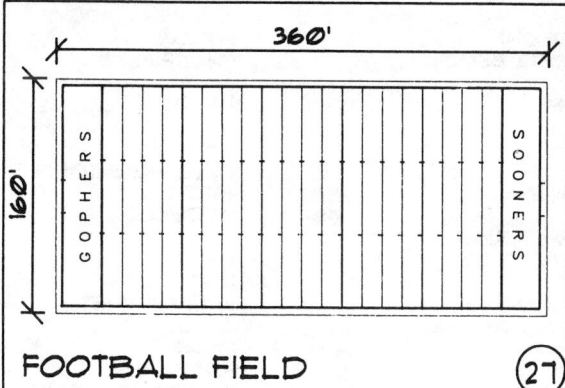

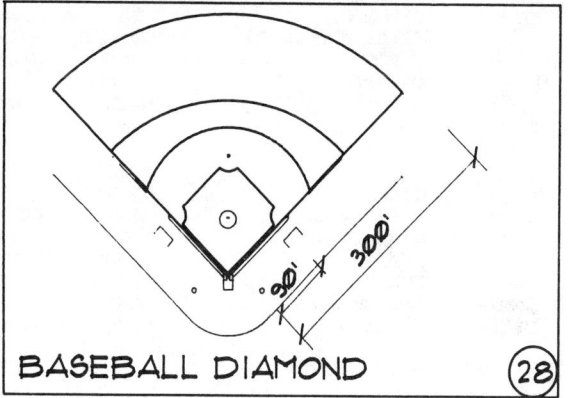

2'-8"
HANDRAIL
CHECK LOCAL CODES

HYDRAULIC ELEVATOR (24)

PROVIDE 4' x 7' EQUIPMENT ROOM WITHIN 100' OF ELEVATOR SHAFT
100' MAX.
DRAIN

FOR OFFICES, PROVIDE ONE CAB / 35,000#

MIN. CAB SIZE IS 4'-6" x 4'-3"; AVERAGE IS 6'-8" x 4'-3"

2'-8" MIN.

AUDITORIUM SEATING (25)

12" MIN. CLEAR
1'-10" (TYP.)
2'-10" (TYP.)
2'-10"±
6" VARIES

CODES MAY LIMIT SEATING TO 14 CHAIRS IN A ROW
42" MIN. AISLE WIDTH W/ 1:8 MAX. SLOPE

BASKETBALL COURT (26)

84'-0" (94'-0" FOR COLLEGE)
50'-0"

FOOTBALL FIELD (27)

360'
160'
GOPHERS
SOONERS

BASEBALL DIAMOND (28)

90'
300'

DRAFTING SYMBOLS   5-13

ABBREVIATIONS

ARCHITECTURAL OFFICES PUBLISH A LIST OF APPROVED ABBREVIATIONS IN THE SPECIFICATION THAT ACCOMPANIES THE DRAWINGS. IF THE OFFICE DOES NOT ABBREVIATE A WORD, FOR INSTANCE <u>GLASS</u> TO GL., YOU ARE REQUIRED TO SPELL IT OUT.

A &	AND	ELEV.	ELEVATION	#	NUMBER
@	AT	ELEC.	ELECTRICAL	NOM.	NOMINAL
ACOUS.	ACOUSTIC(AL)	ELEV.	ELEVATOR		
A.D.	ACCESS DOOR	ENT.	ENTRANCE	**O** O.A.	OVERALL
ADD'L	ADDITIONAL	EPDM	ETHYLENE PROPYLENE	O.C.	ON CENTER
ADJ.	ADJUSTABLE		DIENE MONOMER	O.D.	OUTSIDE DIAMETER
ALUM.	ALUMINUM	EQUIP.	EQUIPMENT	OFF.	OFFICE
AMT.	AMOUNT	EXIST.	EXISTING	O.H.D.	OVERHEAD DOOR
A.P.	ACCESS PANEL	EX. AGG.	EXPOSED AGGREGATE	OPNG.	OPENING
APPROX.	APPROXIMATE(LY)	E.W.	EACH WAY	OPP.	OPPOSITE
ASB.	ASBESTOS			ORN.	ORNAMENTAL
ASPH.	ASPHALT	**F** FT.	FEET (FOOT)		
AVE.	AVENUE	F.D.	FLOOR DRAIN	**P** PERP.	PERPENDICULAR
AVG.	AVERAGE	FDN.	FOUNDATION	P.I.	POINT OF INTERSECTION
∠	ANGLE	F.E.	FIRE EXTINGUISHER	PL.	PLATE
		FIN.	FINISH(ED)	PLAS.	PLASTER
B BD.	BOARD	FL.	FLOOR	PLYWD.	PLYWOOD
BET.	BETWEEN	FTG.	FOOTING	PR.	PAIR
BLDG.	BUILDING			PRCST.	PRECAST
BK.	BLOCK	**G** GA.	GAUGE	PREFAB.	PREFABRICATED
BM.	BEAM	GALV.	GALVANIZED	PROP.	PROPERTY
B.M.	BENCH MARK	G.I.	GALVANIZED IRON	PTN.	PARTITION
B.R.	BEDROOM	GL	GLASS	P.V.C.	POLYVINYL CHLORIDE
BRDG.	BRIDGING	GYP.	GYPSUM		
BRK	BREAK	GYP. BD.	GYPSUM BOARD	**Q** Q.T.	QUARRY TILE
BSMT.	BASEMENT				
BTM.	BOTTOM	**H** H.B.	HOSE BIB	**R** R	RISER
BTR.	BETTER	H.M.	HOLLOW METAL	RAD.	RADIUS
BITUM.	BITUMINOUS	HORIZ.	HORIZONTAL	R.D.	ROOF DRAIN
		HT.	HEIGHT	REINF.	REINFORC(ED)(ING)
C C.	COURSE(S)			REQD.	REQUIRED
CABT.	CABINET	**I** I.D.	INSIDE DIAMETER	R.O.	ROUGH OPENING
C.B.	CATCH BASIN	INSTALL.	INSTALLATION		
CEM.	CEMENT	INSUL.	INSULATION	**S** S.	SOUTH
CER.	CERAMIC	INT.	INTERIOR	SCHED.	SCHEDULE
C.I.	CAST IRON			SECT.	SECTION
C.J.	CONTROL JOINT	**J** JAN.	JANITOR	SHT.	SHEET
℄	CENTER LINE	JT.	JOINT	SPEC.	SPECIFICATION(S)
CLG.	CEILING			▫	SQUARE FEET
COL.	COLUMN	**K** K.P.	KICK PLATE	STD.	STANDARD
CONC.	CONCRETE	KIT.	KITCHEN	STL.	STEEL
C.M.U.	CONCRETE MASONRY			S.S.	STAINLESS STEEL
	UNIT	**L** LAB.	LABORATORY	STRUCT.	STRUCTURAL
CONST.	CONSTRUCTION	LAD.	LADDER		
CONT.	CONTINUOUS	LAM.	LAMINATED	**T** T.	TREAD
CONTR.	CONTRACTOR	LAV.	LAVATORY	T.F.E.	TOP OF FOOTING
CNTR.	COUNTER	LDG.	LANDING		ELEVATION
CTR.	CENTER	LT.	LIGHT	T&G	TONGUE & GROOVE
C. TO C.	CENTER TO CENTER	LW. C.B.	LIGHTWEIGHT	TYP.	TYPICAL
CU.	CUBIC		CONCRETE BLOCK	T.O.S.	TOP OF SLAB
⊏	CHANNEL				
		M MACH.	MACHINE	**U** U.	URINAL
D DET.	DETAIL	MAS.	MASONRY		
D.F.	DRINKING FOUNTAIN	MAT.	MATERIAL	**V** V.	VINYL
DIAG.	DIAGONAL	MAX.	MAXIMUM	V.A.T.	VINYL ASBESTOS TILE
⌀	DIAMETER	MECH.	MECHANICAL	VERT.	VERTICAL
DISHW.	DISHWASHER	MET.	METAL	VEST.	VESTIBULE
DIV.	DIVISION	MFG.	MANUFACTURING		
DN.	DOWN	MFGR.	MANUFACTURER	**W** W.	WEST
DR.	DOOR	MIN.	MINIMUM	W/	WITH
DRWG.	DRAWING	MISC.	MISCELLANEOUS	W.C.	WATER CLOSET
DWLS.	DOWELS	M.O.	MASONRY OPENING	WD.	WOOD
				WDW.	WINDOW
E E.	EAST	**N** N.	NORTH	WF.	WIDE FLANGE
EA.	EACH	N.I.C.	NOT IN CONTRACT	W.W.M.	WELDED WIRE MESH

DRAFTING SYMBOLS 5-14

REPLAY

1. CROSSHATCH THE MATERIALS IDENTIFIED IN THE DETAIL BELOW.

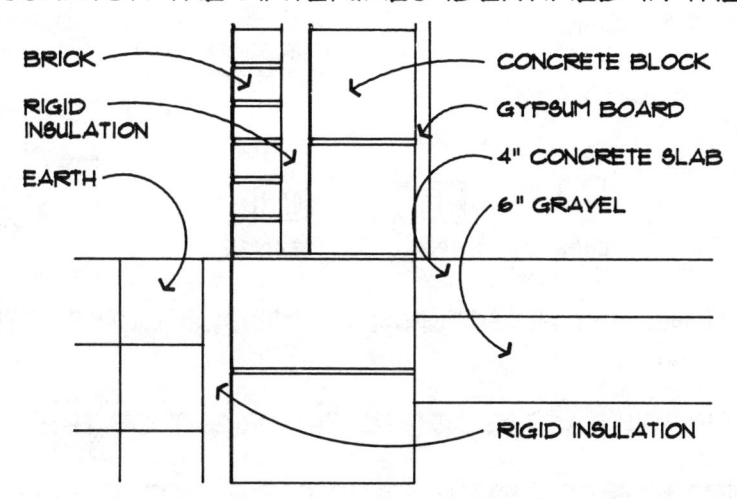

- BRICK
- RIGID INSULATION
- EARTH
- CONCRETE BLOCK
- GYPSUM BOARD
- 4" CONCRETE SLAB
- 6" GRAVEL
- RIGID INSULATION

2. PRODUCE A ROUGH SKETCH USING THE FEATURES LISTED NEXT TO THIS PLAN. THE FIXTURES AND FURNITURE SHOULD BE DRAWN AT THE SAME SCALE AS SHOWN ON PAGES 5-10 THROUGH 5-13.

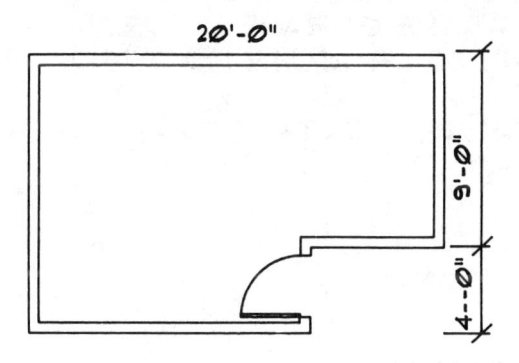

USING THE FIXTURES FROM DETAIL 9, SKETCH A MEN'S TOILET THAT CONTAINS
- 2 STANDARD TOILET PARTITIONS
- 1 HANDICAP TOILET PARTITION
- 2 URINALS
- 3 SINKS BUILT INTO A VANITY

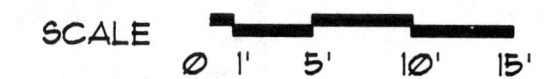

SCALE 0 1' 5' 10' 15'

THE PLAN TO THE RIGHT IS A ONE-BEDROOM APARTMENT. USE DETAILS 7 AND 9 TO DETERMINE SIZES. YOUR SKETCH SHOULD INCLUDE A KITCHEN WITH APPLIANCES, A BATH WITH A TUB, A BEDROOM WITH A QUEEN-SIZED BED AND CLOSET, AND A LIVING ROOM WITH A SOFA, TWO CHAIRS, AND A DINING ROOM TABLE.

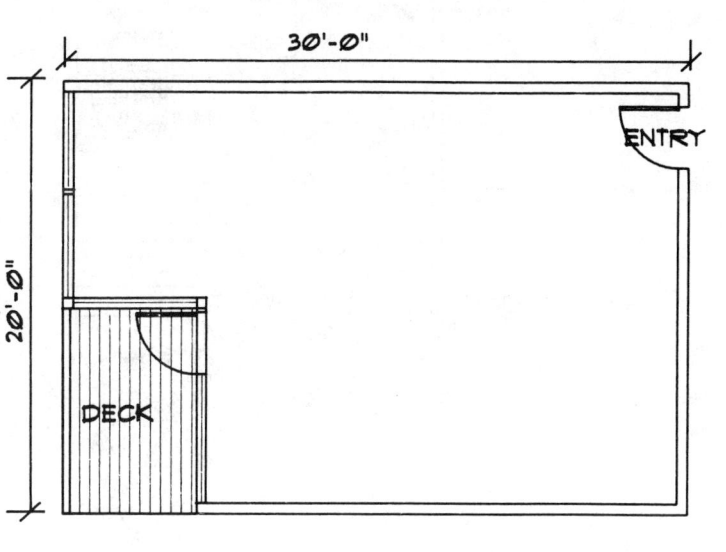

DRAFTING SYMBOLS 5-15

REPLAY QUESTION 2 (CONTINUED)
THE PARTIAL FLOOR PLAN TO
THE RIGHT SHOWS A KITCHEN
LAYOUT WITH A HALF BATH.
LOCATE THE APPLIANCES BELOW
ON THE PLAN.

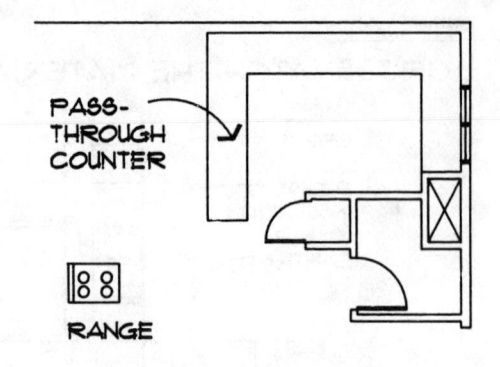

VANITY   W.C.   REF.   DISH-WASHER   SINK   RANGE

3. USING THE FOLLOWING ARCHITECTURAL SYMBOLS, COMPLETE THE
   FLOOR PLAN BELOW:

- DRAW A NORTH ARROW FACING 30° TO THE RIGHT OF THE TOP
  OF THE SHEET.
- DRAW AN ASSUMED NORTH ARROW FACING THE TOP OF THE SHEET.
- INDICATE A BLOW-UP DETAIL OF THE HALF BATH PLAN LOCATED
  ON SHEET A-4, DETAIL 2.
- INDICATE AN ELEVATION OF THE KITCHEN CABINET WHICH
  CONTAINS THE SINK LOCATED ON SHEET A-2, DETAIL 5.
- SHOW A SPOT ELEVATION OF 624'-5" AT THE GARAGE DOOR.
- INDICATE A SECTION CUT THROUGH THE STAIR TOWER LOCATED
  ON SHEET A-4, DETAIL 1.
- TITLE THE PLAN FIRST-FLOOR PLAN, DETAIL 1 ON SHEET A-2.
  THE SCALE OF THE DRAWING IS 1/4"=1'-0".
- NUMBER THE ROOMS AND DOORS.

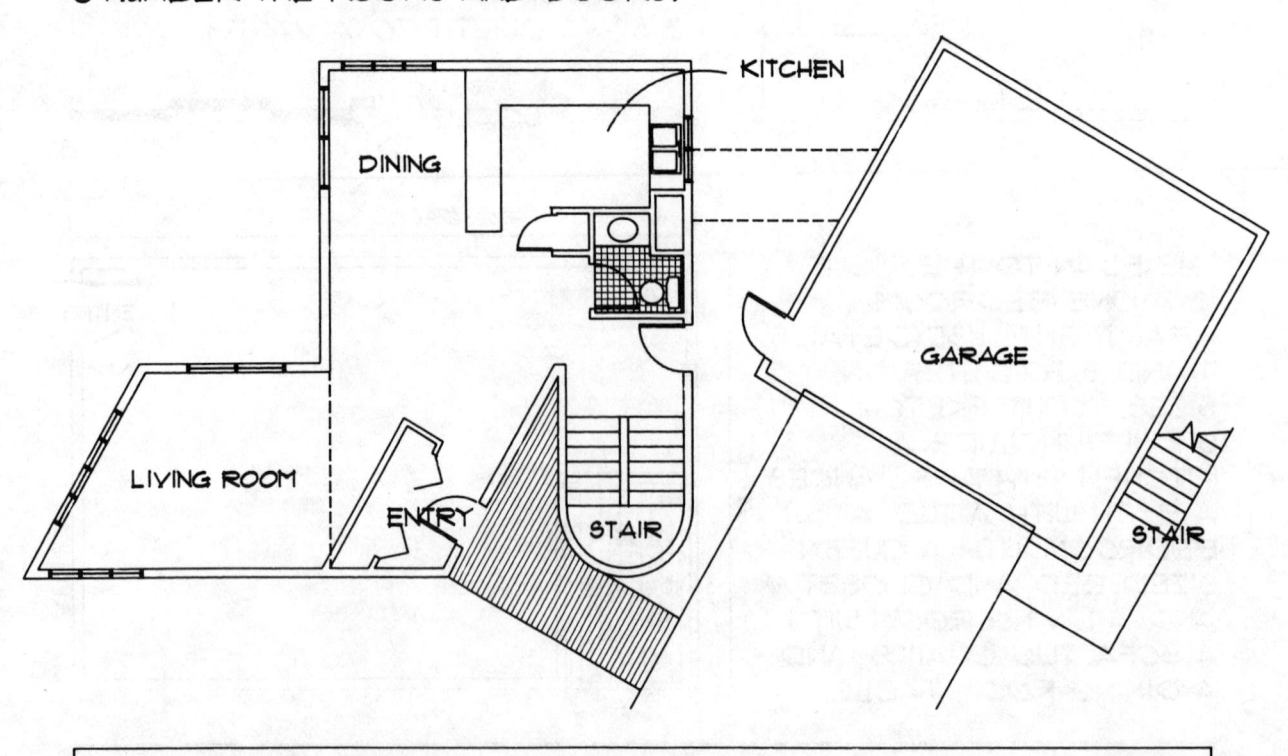

DRAFTING SYMBOLS   5-16

6 DIMENSIONS

A DISCUSSION OF DIMENSIONING SHOULD BEGIN WITH THE STATEMENT THAT IS FOUND IN MOST ARCHITECTURAL SPECIFICATIONS: "THE CONTRACTOR SHALL NOT SCALE THE DRAWINGS." THIS DOESN'T MEAN THAT DRAWINGS SHOULD BE ASSEMBLED OUT OF SCALE. INSTEAD THE STATEMENT MEANS THAT EVERYTHING ON A PLAN, INCLUDING WINDOW OPENINGS, WALL WIDTHS, BUILDING CORNERS, AND DOOR PLACEMENT, SHOULD BE LOCATED BY DIMENSION. THIS UNIT WILL DISCUSS THE RULES ESTABLISHED FOR DIMENSIONING A DRAWING, PLUS IT WILL PROVIDE TIPS FOR MAKING THE TASK EASIER.

SCALES

ARCHITECTURAL PLANS ARE DRAWN TO A SCALE TO ALLOW THEM TO FIT ON A SHEET OF DRAWINGS. THERE ARE 11 SCALES FOUND ON A TRIANGULAR ARCHITECT'S SCALE. THE CHART BELOW LISTS THE MOST TYPICAL SCALES USED ON PLANS AND DETAILS.

DRAWING	RESIDENTIAL	COMMERCIAL
SITE PLAN	1"=20' to 1"=40'	1"=20' to 1"=40'
FOUNDATION PLAN	1/4"=1'-0"	1/8"=1'-0"
FLOOR PLAN	1/4"=1'-0"	1/8"=1'-0" or 1/16"=1'-0"
FRAMING PLAN	1/8"=1'-0"	STRUCTURAL DRAWINGS
ELEVATIONS	1/8"=1'-0"	1/8"=1'-0"
BUILDING SECTIONS	3/8"=1'-0"	1/8"=1'-0" or 1/4"=1'-0"
WALL SECTIONS	1/2"=1'-0"	1/2"=1'-0" or 3/4"=1'-0"
DETAILS	1 1/2"=1'-0"	1 1/2"=1'-0" or 3"=1'-0"
INTERIOR ELEVATIONS	1/4"=1'-0"	1/4"=1'-0"

READING AN ARCHITECT'S SCALE (DON'T CALL IT A RULER) IS QUITE SIMPLE. EACH SCALE STARTS AT THE 0 POINT AND READS TO THE RIGHT OR LEFT. ONE FOOT IS BROKEN INTO SMALLER INCREMENTS

IN THE OPPOSITE DIRECTION ALONG THE SCALE. REVIEW THE EXAMPLES BELOW TO DETERMINE THE DISTANCES INDICATED.

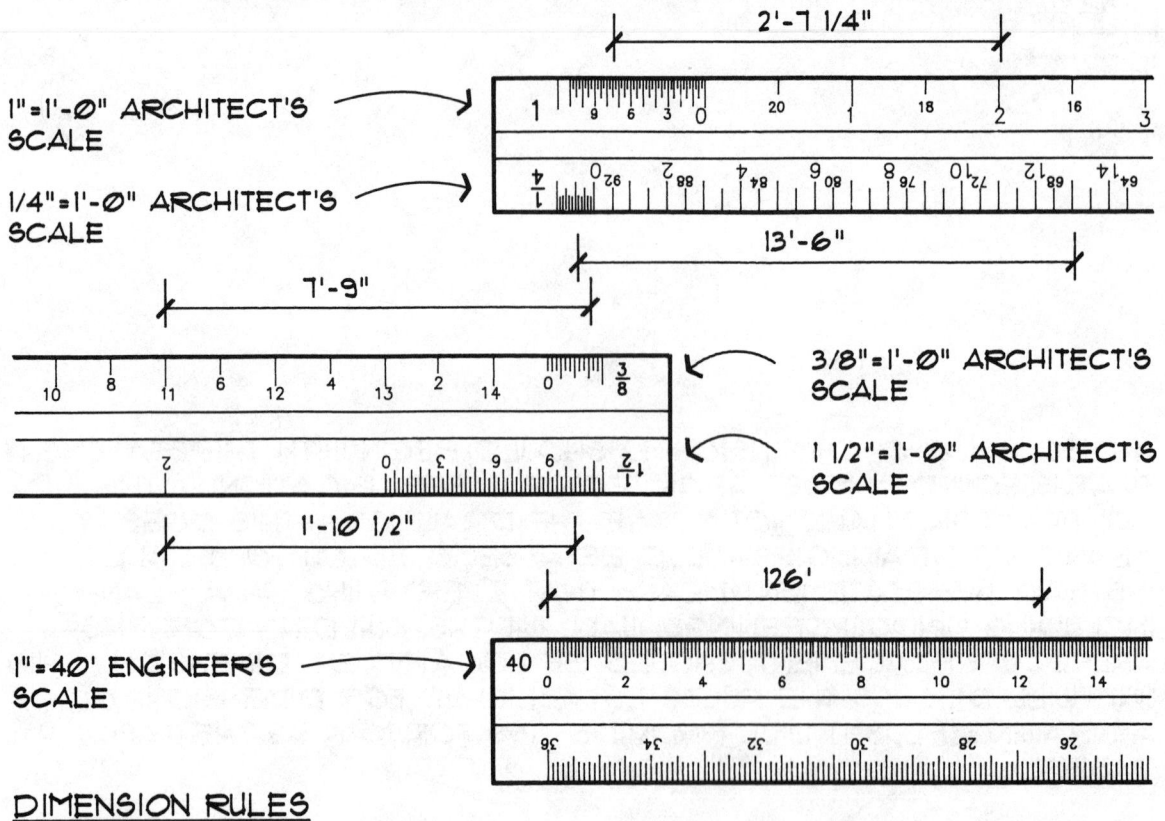

1"=1'-0" ARCHITECT'S SCALE → 2'-7 1/4"

1/4"=1'-0" ARCHITECT'S SCALE → 13'-6"

7'-9"

3/8"=1'-0" ARCHITECT'S SCALE

1 1/2"=1'-0" ARCHITECT'S SCALE

1'-10 1/2"

126'

1"=40' ENGINEER'S SCALE

DIMENSION RULES

LET'S ESTABLISH SEVERAL GROUND RULES CONCERNING DIMENSIONS.

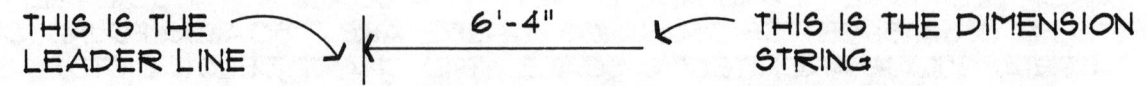

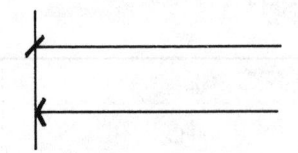

THIS IS THE LEADER LINE   6'-4"   THIS IS THE DIMENSION STRING

A 45° (HEAVY STROKE) SLASH LINE OR A 60° (HEAVY STROKE) ARROW HEAD ARE GENERALLY ACCEPTED AS SYMBOLS FOR TERMINATING DIMENSION STRINGS.

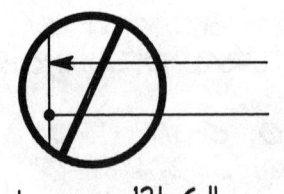

THE TWO SYMBOLS TO THE LEFT ARE TYPICALLY USED ON MECHANICAL DRAWINGS AND ARE NOT USED IN ARCHITECTURE.

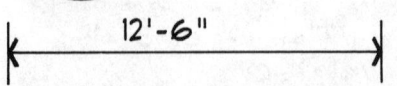

12'-6"

12'-6"

ARCHITECTURAL DIMENSIONS SHOULD BE LOCATED ABOVE THE STRING.

MECHANICAL DIMENSIONS ARE PLACED BETWEEN THE STRING. DON'T USE THIS TECHNIQUE ON ARCHITECTURAL DRAWINGS.

DIMENSIONS   6-2

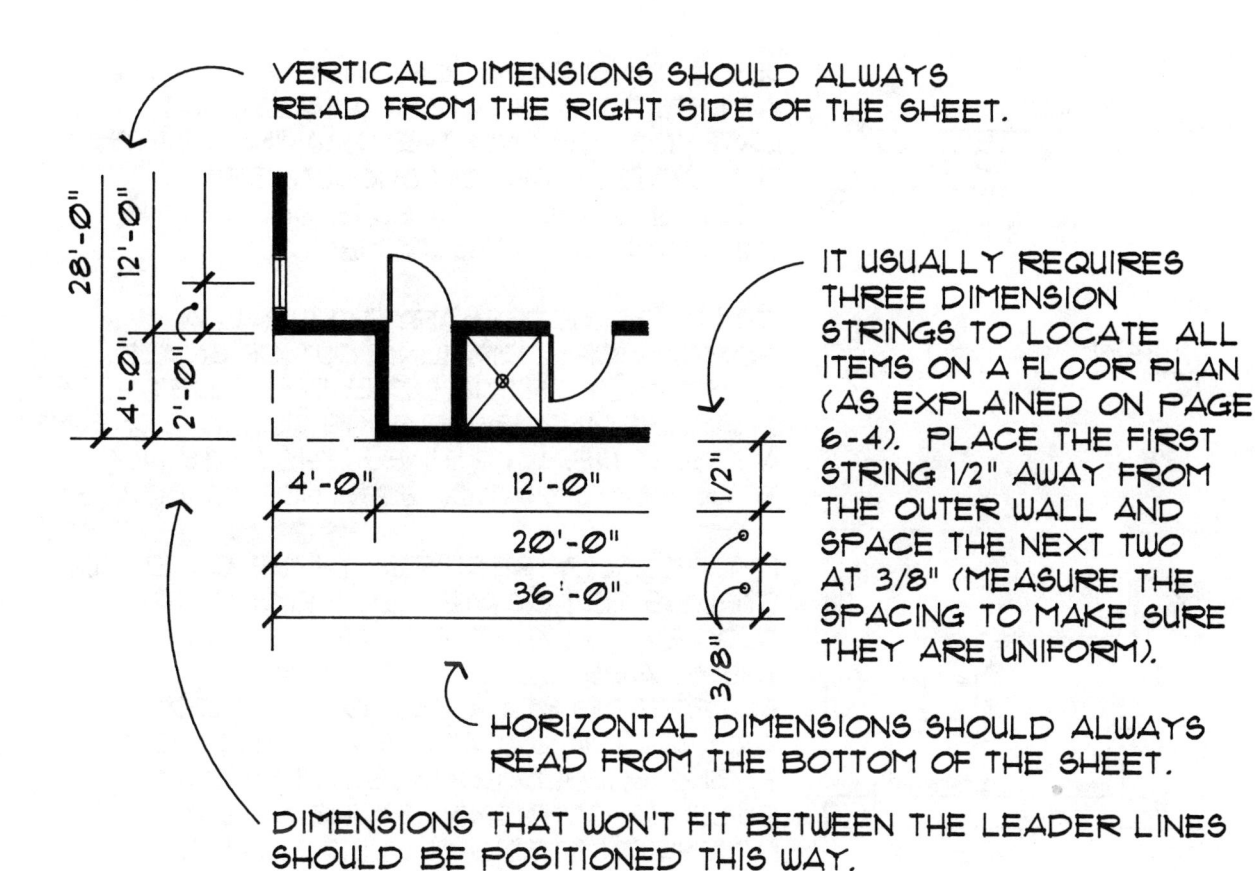

VERTICAL DIMENSIONS SHOULD ALWAYS READ FROM THE RIGHT SIDE OF THE SHEET.

IT USUALLY REQUIRES THREE DIMENSION STRINGS TO LOCATE ALL ITEMS ON A FLOOR PLAN (AS EXPLAINED ON PAGE 6-4). PLACE THE FIRST STRING 1/2" AWAY FROM THE OUTER WALL AND SPACE THE NEXT TWO AT 3/8" (MEASURE THE SPACING TO MAKE SURE THEY ARE UNIFORM).

HORIZONTAL DIMENSIONS SHOULD ALWAYS READ FROM THE BOTTOM OF THE SHEET.

DIMENSIONS THAT WON'T FIT BETWEEN THE LEADER LINES SHOULD BE POSITIONED THIS WAY.

DIMENSIONS SHOULD BE SHOWN IN FEET AND INCHES FOR ALL DISTANCES OVER ONE FOOT.

DIMENSIONS UNDER A FOOT ARE SHOWN IN INCHES (USE 1'-0" RATHER THAN 12").

THE ONE EXCEPTION TO THE RULE ABOUT FEET AND INCHES IS FOUND ON SITE DRAWINGS. CIVIL ENGINEERS TYPICALLY DIMENSION DISTANCES IN HUNDREDTHS OF A FOOT (ONE INCH = 0.0833 FEET).

DIMENSIONS SHOULD NOT BE LESS THAN 1/8" (1/4" IS COMMON) FOR MOST CONSTRUCTION CONDITIONS.

ALWAYS ADD DIMENSION STRINGS TO DETERMINE IF INTERIOR DISTANCES ADD UP TO THE EXTERIOR DIMENSION.

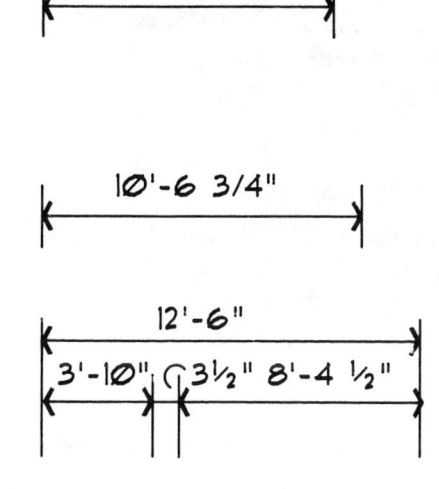

DIMENSIONS 6-3

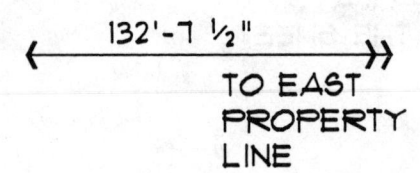

USE A DIMENSION CONDITION AS SHOWN AT LEFT TO INDICATE A STRING THAT EXTENDS BEYOND THE DRAWING LIMITS. THE DOUBLE ARROW SHOULD BE ACCOMPANIED BY A NOTE SPECIFYING THE POINT OF MEASUREMENT.

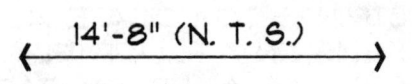

IT MAY BE NECESSARY TO DRAW A PORTION OF A DRAWING OUT OF SCALE. (TYPICALLY THIS IS DONE IF THE DETAIL IS CHANGED AND REDRAWING WOULD CONSUME A GREAT DEAL OF TIME.) THE NOTE N. T. S. IS AN ABBREVIATION FOR "NOT TO SCALE."

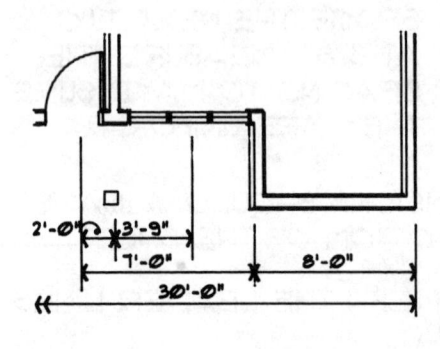

IT TYPICALLY REQUIRES THREE DIMENSION STRINGS TO LOCATE ALL ITEMS ON A FLOOR PLAN: (1) THE STRING CLOSEST TO THE PLAN SHOULD DIMENSION THE SHORTEST DISTANCES (USUALLY DOOR AND WINDOW LOCATIONS); (2) THE MIDDLE STRING SHOULD LOCATE INTERMEDIATE BUILDING CORNERS; (3) THE OUTER DIMENSION STRING SHOULD SHOW THE OVERALL LENGTH OF THE BUILDING FROM CORNER TO CORNER.

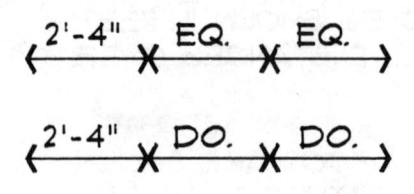

A REPETITIVE SET OF DIMENSIONS (SUCH AS WINDOW OPENINGS) CAN BE SHOWN WITH THE ABBREVIATIONS EQ. (FOR EQUAL) OR DO. (FOR DITTO) AFTER THE FIRST DIMENSION IS INDICATED.

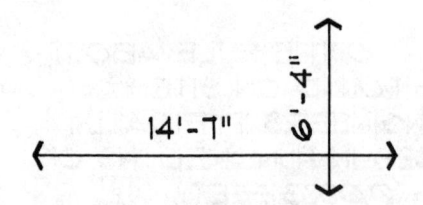

AVOID CROSSING DIMENSION STRINGS; THE TECHNIQUE COULD CAUSE A CONTRACTOR TO MISREAD THE MEASUREMENT. THE SOLUTION IS TO CAREFULLY PLAN THE LOCATION OF DIMENSIONS.

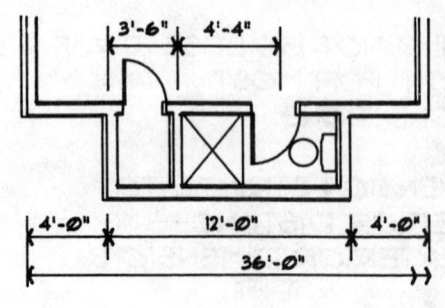

LOCATE INTERIOR DIMENSIONS ON THE INSIDE OF A PLAN AND EXTERIOR DIMENSIONS ON THE OUTSIDE. WHILE THIS ISN'T ALWAYS POSSIBLE, IT IS A GOOD PRACTICE TO FOLLOW WHEN YOU CAN.

DIMENSIONS 6-4

USE THE FOLLOWING TIPS WHEN LAYING OUT DIMENSIONS

1. THE KEY TO LAYING OUT DIMENSIONS IS TO ORGANIZE THE LOCATION OF ALL STRINGS ON TRACING PAPER BEFORE YOU BEGIN TO DRAW THEM ON YOUR FINAL DRAWING. USE A FELT-TIP PEN TO ORGANIZE THE LOCATION OF NOTES AND DIMENSION STRINGS.

2. THERE ARE THREE ELEMENTS (OR LAYERS) INVOLVED IN SHEET COMPOSITION: (1) THE DRAWING, (2) THE DIMENSIONS, AND (3) THE NOTES. IT IS A GOOD IDEA TO FINISH THE DRAWING BEFORE POSITIONING DIMENSIONS AND NOTES.

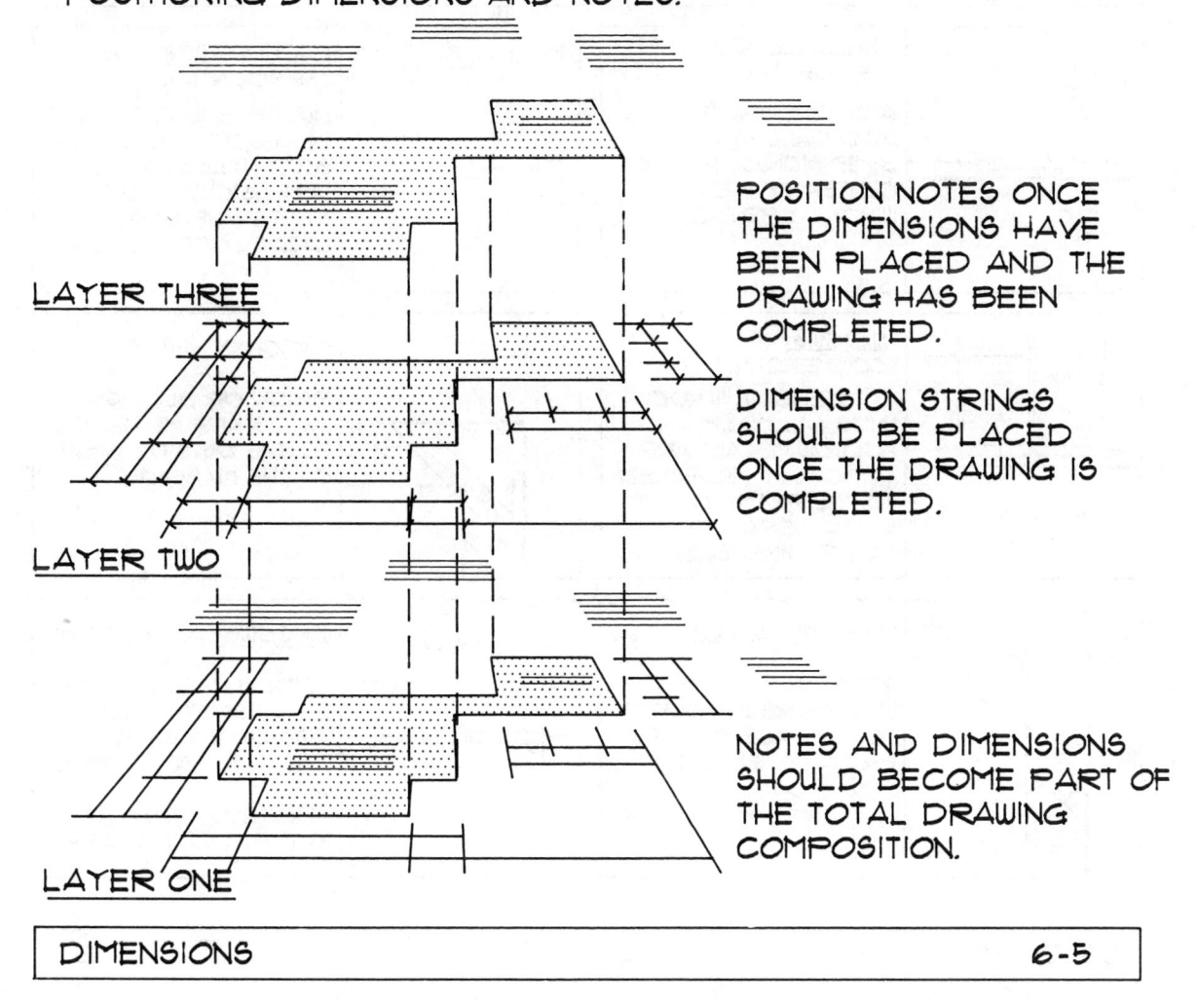

LAYER THREE

LAYER TWO

LAYER ONE

POSITION NOTES ONCE THE DIMENSIONS HAVE BEEN PLACED AND THE DRAWING HAS BEEN COMPLETED.

DIMENSION STRINGS SHOULD BE PLACED ONCE THE DRAWING IS COMPLETED.

NOTES AND DIMENSIONS SHOULD BECOME PART OF THE TOTAL DRAWING COMPOSITION.

| DIMENSIONS | 6-5 |

THE STANDARD DETAILS USED ON ARCHITECTURAL DRAWINGS ARE SHOWN BELOW. IT'S A GOOD IDEA TO REFER TO THIS MATERIAL BEFORE YOU BEGIN LOCATING DIMENSION STRINGS.

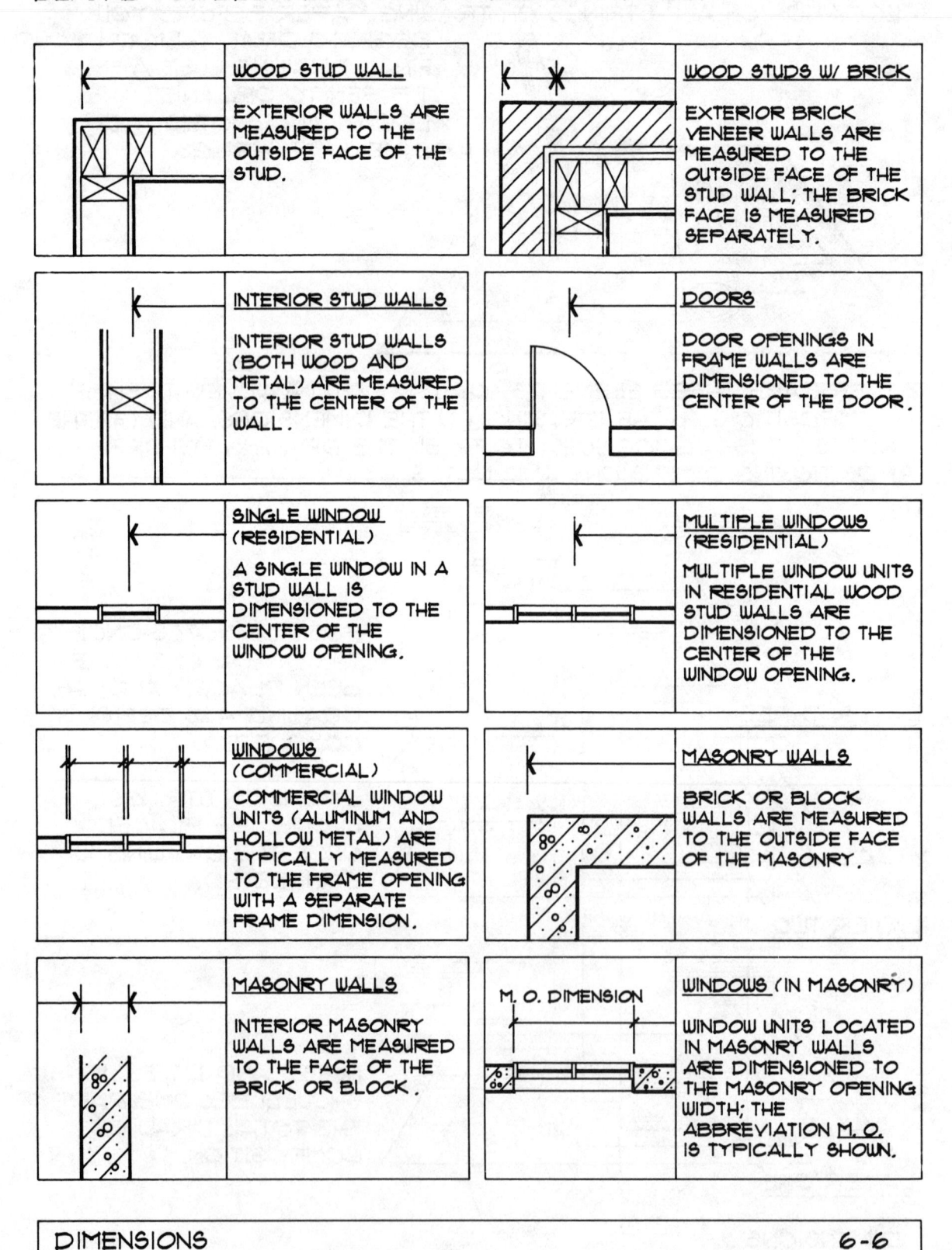

WOOD STUD WALL
EXTERIOR WALLS ARE MEASURED TO THE OUTSIDE FACE OF THE STUD.

WOOD STUDS W/ BRICK
EXTERIOR BRICK VENEER WALLS ARE MEASURED TO THE OUTSIDE FACE OF THE STUD WALL; THE BRICK FACE IS MEASURED SEPARATELY.

INTERIOR STUD WALLS
INTERIOR STUD WALLS (BOTH WOOD AND METAL) ARE MEASURED TO THE CENTER OF THE WALL.

DOORS
DOOR OPENINGS IN FRAME WALLS ARE DIMENSIONED TO THE CENTER OF THE DOOR.

SINGLE WINDOW (RESIDENTIAL)
A SINGLE WINDOW IN A STUD WALL IS DIMENSIONED TO THE CENTER OF THE WINDOW OPENING.

MULTIPLE WINDOWS (RESIDENTIAL)
MULTIPLE WINDOW UNITS IN RESIDENTIAL WOOD STUD WALLS ARE DIMENSIONED TO THE CENTER OF THE WINDOW OPENING.

WINDOWS (COMMERCIAL)
COMMERCIAL WINDOW UNITS (ALUMINUM AND HOLLOW METAL) ARE TYPICALLY MEASURED TO THE FRAME OPENING WITH A SEPARATE FRAME DIMENSION.

MASONRY WALLS
BRICK OR BLOCK WALLS ARE MEASURED TO THE OUTSIDE FACE OF THE MASONRY.

MASONRY WALLS
INTERIOR MASONRY WALLS ARE MEASURED TO THE FACE OF THE BRICK OR BLOCK.

WINDOWS (IN MASONRY)
WINDOW UNITS LOCATED IN MASONRY WALLS ARE DIMENSIONED TO THE MASONRY OPENING WIDTH; THE ABBREVIATION M.O. IS TYPICALLY SHOWN.

DIMENSIONS 6-6

BUILDING EXAMPLES

STUDY THE FOLLOWING RESIDENTIAL EXAMPLES TO DETERMINE THE PROCEDURE USED TO DIMENSION PLANS. THE CABIN FLOOR PLAN ON THIS PAGE PROVIDES A CONTRACTOR WITH DIMENSION STRINGS TO LOCATE ALL DOORS, WINDOWS, AND WALLS IN THE PROJECT.

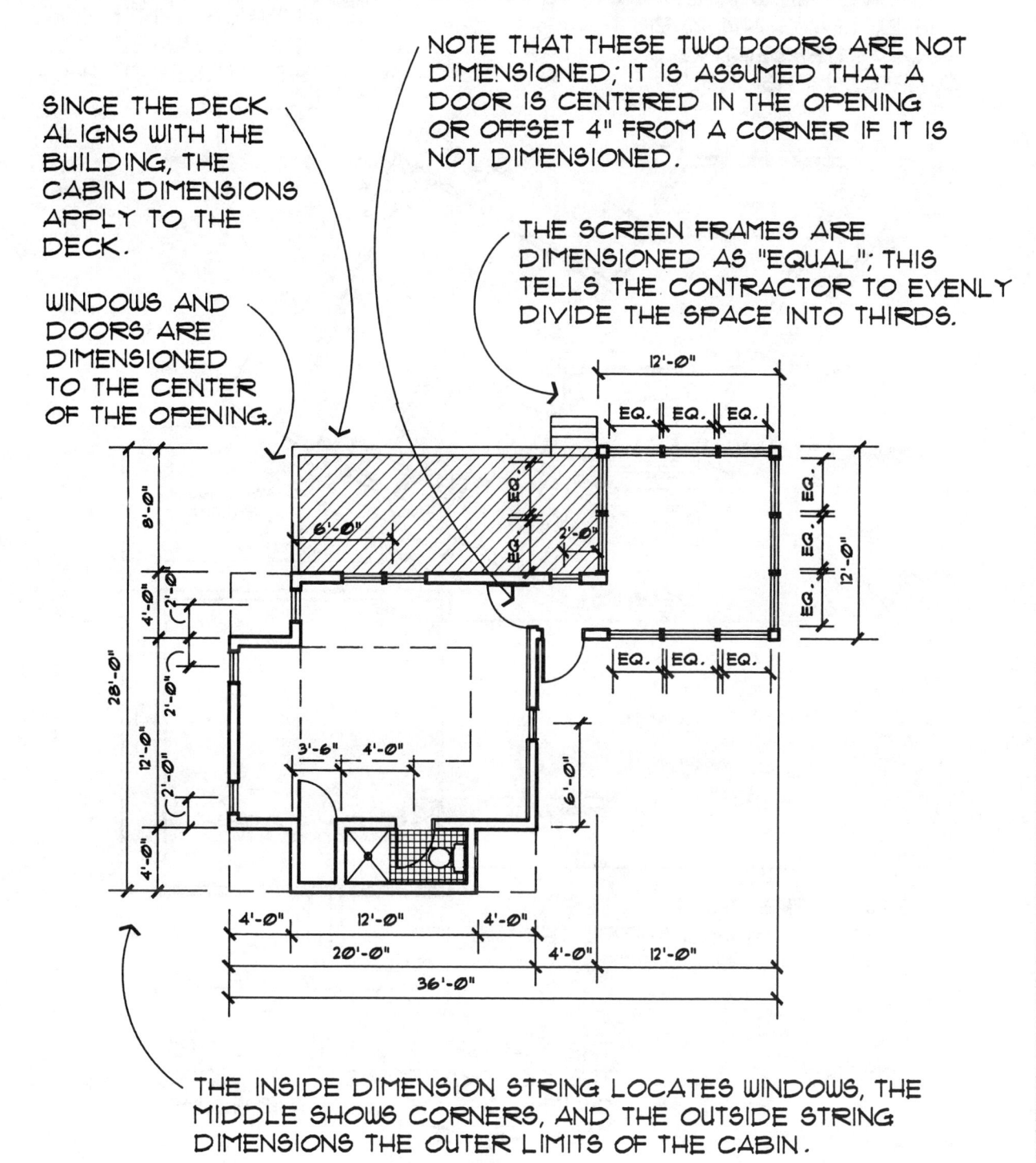

NOTE THAT THESE TWO DOORS ARE NOT DIMENSIONED; IT IS ASSUMED THAT A DOOR IS CENTERED IN THE OPENING OR OFFSET 4" FROM A CORNER IF IT IS NOT DIMENSIONED.

SINCE THE DECK ALIGNS WITH THE BUILDING, THE CABIN DIMENSIONS APPLY TO THE DECK.

THE SCREEN FRAMES ARE DIMENSIONED AS "EQUAL"; THIS TELLS THE CONTRACTOR TO EVENLY DIVIDE THE SPACE INTO THIRDS.

WINDOWS AND DOORS ARE DIMENSIONED TO THE CENTER OF THE OPENING.

THE INSIDE DIMENSION STRING LOCATES WINDOWS, THE MIDDLE SHOWS CORNERS, AND THE OUTSIDE STRING DIMENSIONS THE OUTER LIMITS OF THE CABIN.

| DIMENSIONS | 6-7 |

THE SECOND EXAMPLE SHOWS A HOUSE WITH A GARAGE AT AN ANGLE TO THE MAIN STRUCTURE.

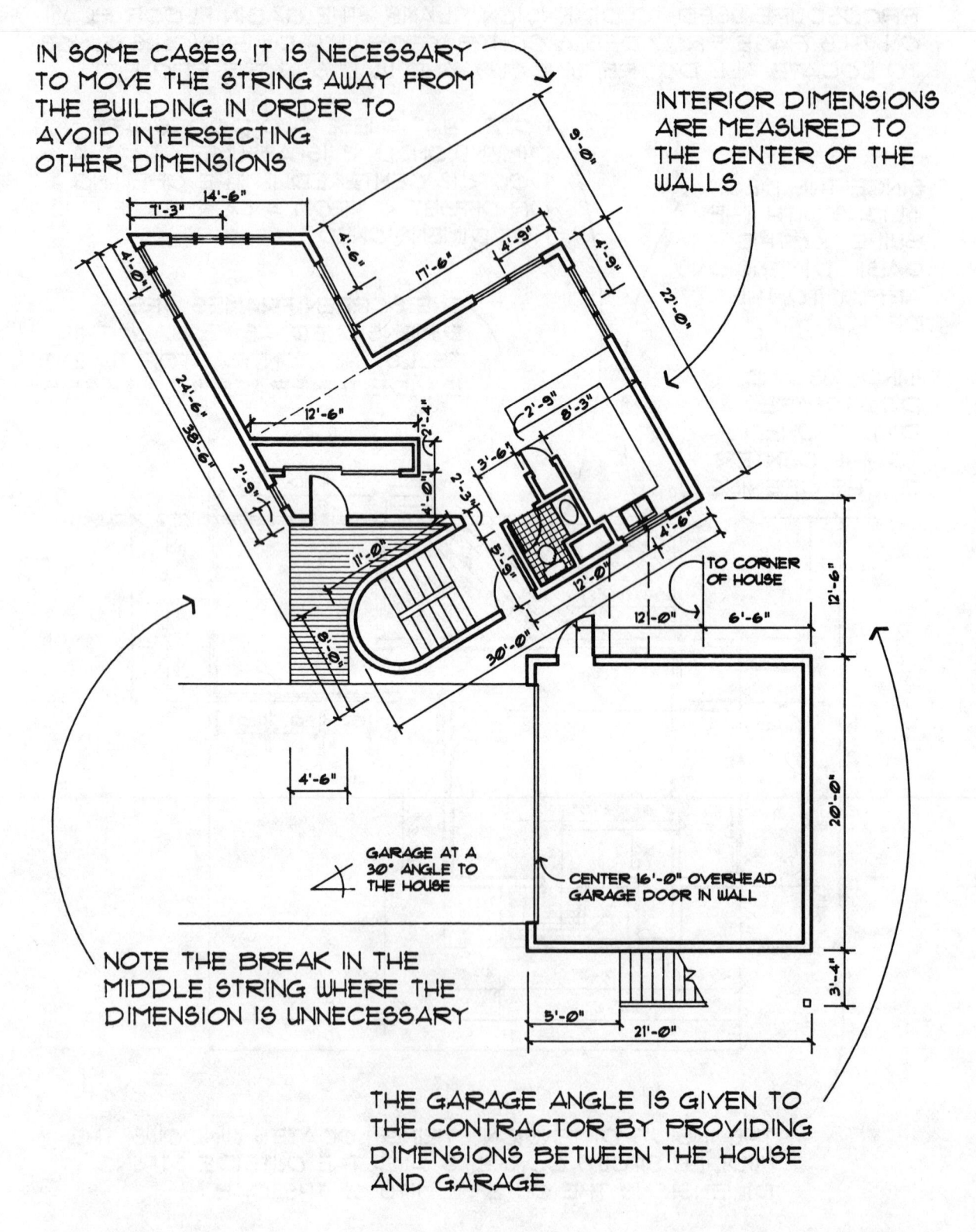

IN SOME CASES, IT IS NECESSARY TO MOVE THE STRING AWAY FROM THE BUILDING IN ORDER TO AVOID INTERSECTING OTHER DIMENSIONS

INTERIOR DIMENSIONS ARE MEASURED TO THE CENTER OF THE WALLS

TO CORNER OF HOUSE

GARAGE AT A 30° ANGLE TO THE HOUSE

CENTER 16'-0" OVERHEAD GARAGE DOOR IN WALL

NOTE THE BREAK IN THE MIDDLE STRING WHERE THE DIMENSION IS UNNECESSARY

THE GARAGE ANGLE IS GIVEN TO THE CONTRACTOR BY PROVIDING DIMENSIONS BETWEEN THE HOUSE AND GARAGE

| DIMENSIONS | 6-8 |

THIS EXAMPLE ILLUSTRATES THE DIMENSIONING OF A PORTION OF A COMMERCIAL MASONRY STRUCTURE.

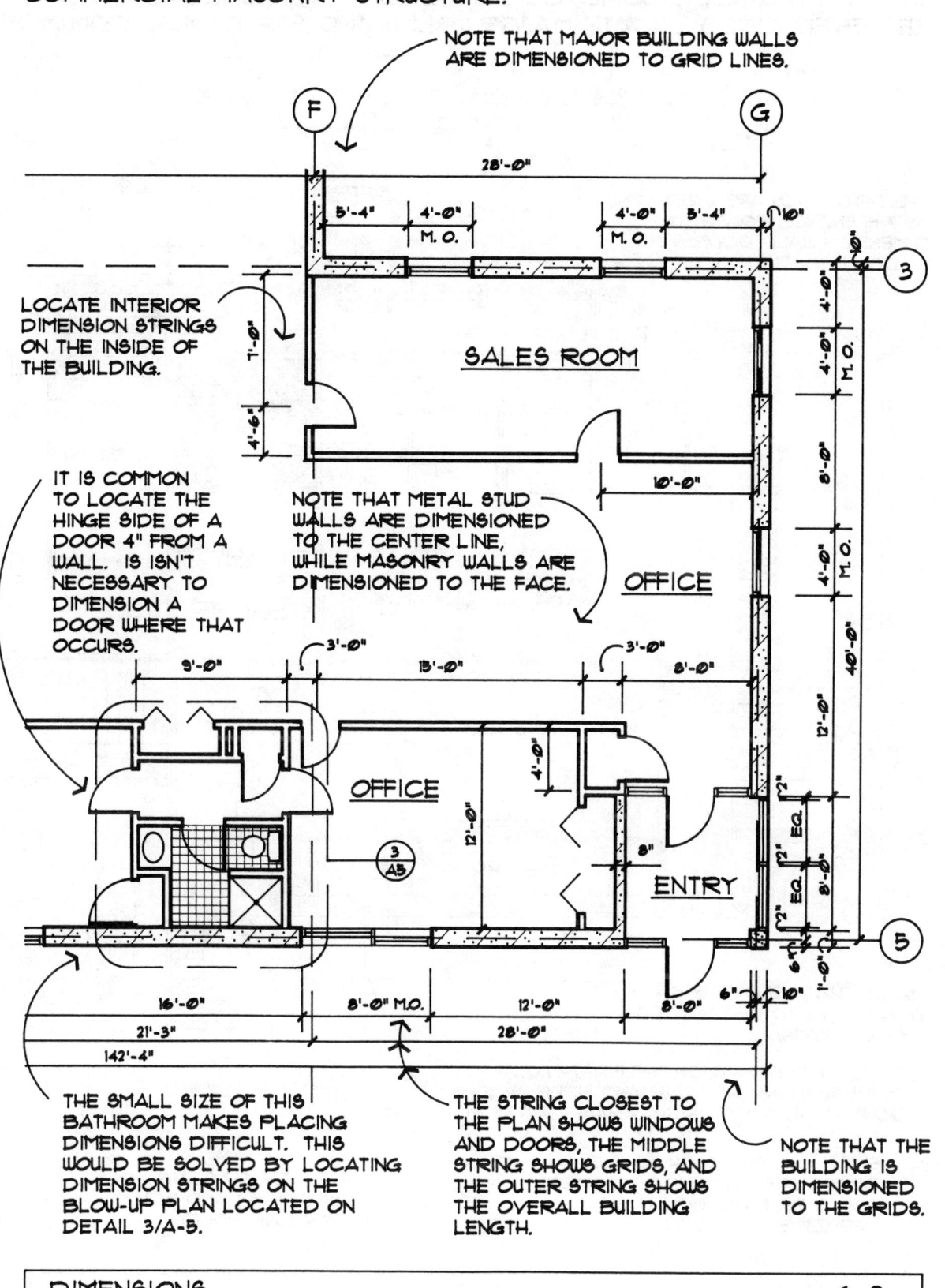

NOTE THAT MAJOR BUILDING WALLS ARE DIMENSIONED TO GRID LINES.

LOCATE INTERIOR DIMENSION STRINGS ON THE INSIDE OF THE BUILDING.

IT IS COMMON TO LOCATE THE HINGE SIDE OF A DOOR 4" FROM A WALL. IS ISN'T NECESSARY TO DIMENSION A DOOR WHERE THAT OCCURS.

NOTE THAT METAL STUD WALLS ARE DIMENSIONED TO THE CENTER LINE, WHILE MASONRY WALLS ARE DIMENSIONED TO THE FACE.

THE SMALL SIZE OF THIS BATHROOM MAKES PLACING DIMENSIONS DIFFICULT. THIS WOULD BE SOLVED BY LOCATING DIMENSION STRINGS ON THE BLOW-UP PLAN LOCATED ON DETAIL 3/A-5.

THE STRING CLOSEST TO THE PLAN SHOWS WINDOWS AND DOORS, THE MIDDLE STRING SHOWS GRIDS, AND THE OUTER STRING SHOWS THE OVERALL BUILDING LENGTH.

NOTE THAT THE BUILDING IS DIMENSIONED TO THE GRIDS.

DIMENSIONS

6-9

THE STUDENT LIBRARY PLAN BELOW ILLUSTRATES THE USE OF DIMENSION STRINGS COMBINED WITH GRIDS. THE NUMBERED AND LETTERED GRIDS LOCATE MAJOR WALLS AND STRUCTURAL COLUMNS.

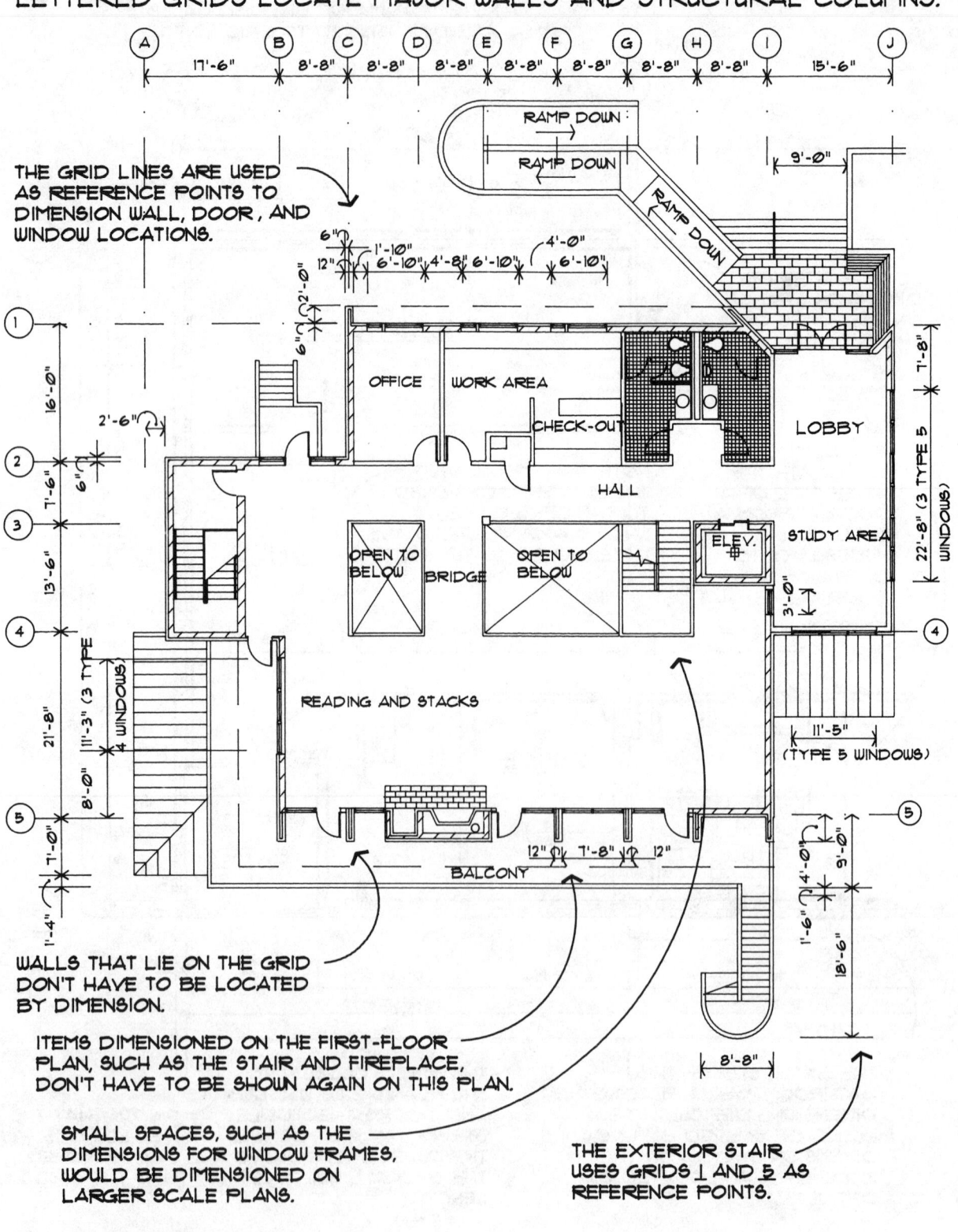

THE GRID LINES ARE USED AS REFERENCE POINTS TO DIMENSION WALL, DOOR, AND WINDOW LOCATIONS.

WALLS THAT LIE ON THE GRID DON'T HAVE TO BE LOCATED BY DIMENSION.

ITEMS DIMENSIONED ON THE FIRST-FLOOR PLAN, SUCH AS THE STAIR AND FIREPLACE, DON'T HAVE TO BE SHOWN AGAIN ON THIS PLAN.

SMALL SPACES, SUCH AS THE DIMENSIONS FOR WINDOW FRAMES, WOULD BE DIMENSIONED ON LARGER SCALE PLANS.

THE EXTERIOR STAIR USES GRIDS 1 AND 5 AS REFERENCE POINTS.

DIMENSIONS   6-10

THIS EXAMPLE ILLUSTRATES THE TYPICAL DIMENSIONS FOUND ON A BUILDING ELEVATION. NOTE THAT THE DIMENSION STRINGS ARE LIMITED TO SHOWING VERTICAL DISTANCES (HORIZONTAL DIMENSIONS ARE SHOWN ON PLANS).

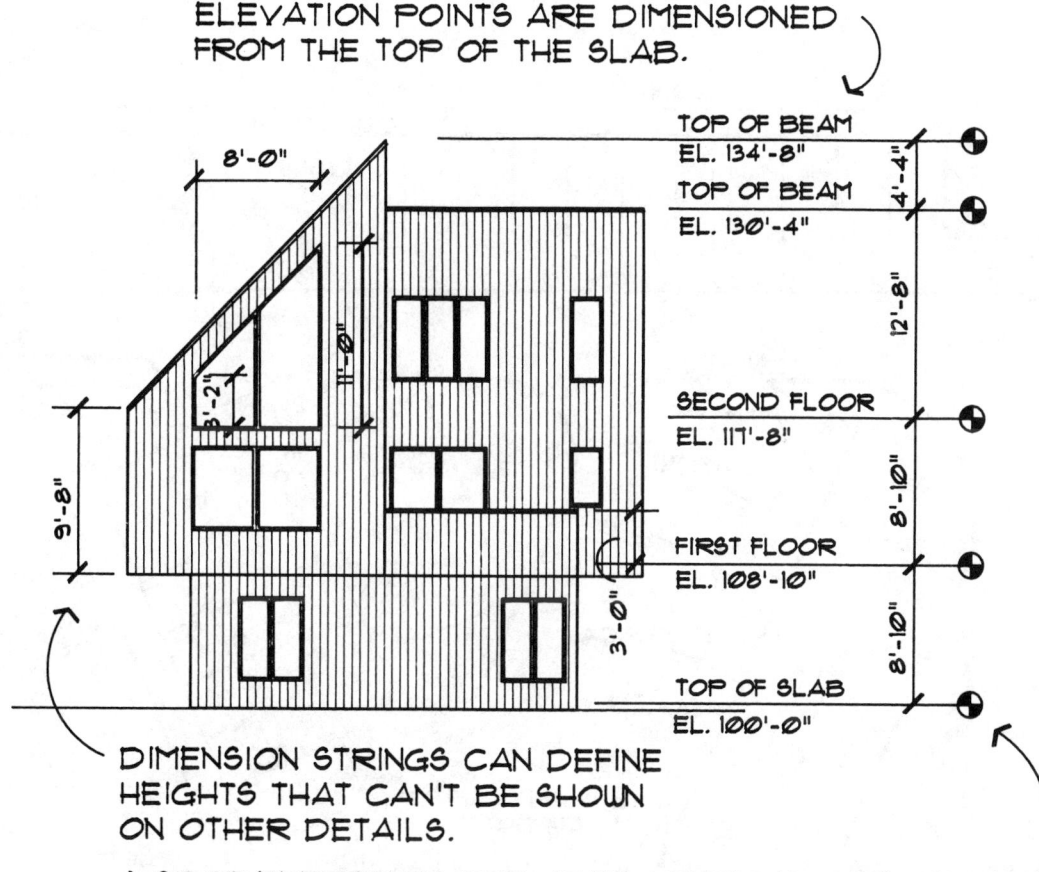

ELEVATION POINTS ARE DIMENSIONED FROM THE TOP OF THE SLAB.

DIMENSION STRINGS CAN DEFINE HEIGHTS THAT CAN'T BE SHOWN ON OTHER DETAILS.

A SPOT ELEVATION PROVIDES VERTICAL DIMENSIONS ABOVE A KNOWN HEIGHT ON THE SITE (CALLED A <u>BENCH MARK</u>). THE CIRCLE SYMBOL ⊕ IS USED TO INDICATE SPOT ELEVATIONS. KEEP THE CONSTRUCTION PROCESS IN MIND WHEN LOCATING THESE POINTS. IT IS BETTER TO LOCATE A STRUCTURAL POINT, SUCH AS A STRUCTURAL LINTEL, THAN A CONDITION THAT WOULD BE DIFFICULT TO LOCATE, SUCH AS THE TOP OF A METAL CANT STRIP.

AS IN THE CASE OF FLOOR PLAN DIMENSIONS, SPOT ELEVATIONS SHOULD BE ORGANIZED SO THEY WON'T CLUTTER THE DRAWING. TECHNIQUES SUCH AS ALIGNING NOTES AND DRAWING DIMENSION STRINGS WITH A LIGHTER LINE WEIGHT WILL ADD TO THE QUALITY OF THE DRAWING. DIMENSIONS, ALONG WITH NOTES, SHOULD BE PLACED ON DRAWINGS IN A METHODICAL WAY IN ORDER TO FULLY DEFINE THE EXACT LOCATION OF BUILDING COMPONENTS AND TO ADD TO THE OVERALL COMPOSITION OF THE DRAWING.

DIMENSIONS

THE FINAL EXAMPLE ILLUSTRATES THE DIMENSION STRINGS USED TO DETAIL A PORTION OF A COMMERCIAL OFFICE BUILDING SITE PLAN.

NOTE THAT PROPERTY DIMENSIONS ARE TYPICALLY SHOWN IN HUNDREDTHS OF A FOOT.

USE THE PROPERTY LINE AS THE BASE FOR DIMENSIONS.

MULTIPLE PARKING STALL DIMENSIONS ARE TYPICALLY SHOWN THIS WAY (RATHER THAN DIMENSIONING EACH STALL).

THE DOUBLE ARROW INDICATES A DIMENSION THAT EXTENDS BEYOND THE DRAWING.

NOTE THAT THE BUILDING WALL LINE IS USED TO DIMENSION SITE ITEMS SUCH AS CURBS AND PARKING STRIPES.

DIMENSIONS　　　　　　　　　　　　　　　　6-12

MASONRY DIMENSIONING

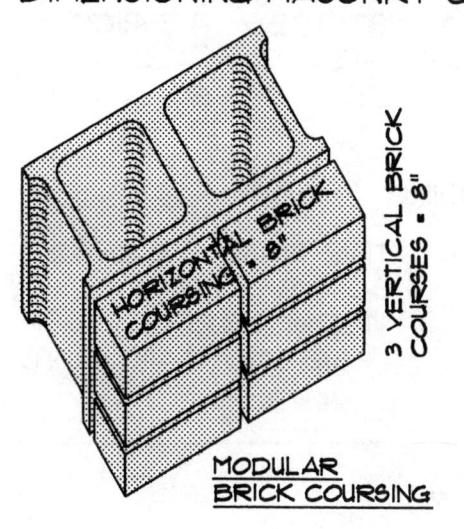

DIMENSIONING MASONRY CONDITIONS (BRICK OR BLOCK) REQUIRES MORE PREPLANNING THAN DIMENSIONING OTHER CONDITIONS. MASONRY OPENINGS AND CORNERS SHOULD BE LOCATED TO REDUCE CUTTING THE MATERIAL TO A MINIMUM. THE FACE OF A CONCRETE BLOCK (PLUS A MORTAR JOINT) IS 16" WIDE AND 8" HIGH. THIS IS CALLED A <u>BLOCK COURSE</u>. IT TAKES THREE VERTICAL MODULAR BRICK COURSES AND TWO HORIZONTAL COURSES (PLUS THEIR MORTAR JOINTS) TO MATCH THE 8" × 16" SIZE OF A BLOCK. MODULAR DIMENSIONING USES EQUAL BRICK AND BLOCK SIZES FOR WALL DIMENSIONS AND OPENINGS. THE TABLE BELOW SHOWS THE NOMINAL SIZES OF OTHER BRICK TYPES.

MODULAR BRICK COURSING
- HORIZONTAL BRICK COURSING = 8"
- 3 VERTICAL BRICK COURSES = 8"

BRICK TYPE	MODULAR COURSING	HEIGHT 2 2/3"	HEIGHT 3 1/5"	HEIGHT 4"	LENGTH 8"	LENGTH 12"	DEPTH 4"	DEPTH 6"
STANDARD MODULAR	3C = 8"	●			●		●	
NORMAN	3C = 8"	●				●	●	
SCR BRICK	3C = 8"	●				●		●
ENGINEER	5C = 16"		●		●		●	
ECONOMY	1C = 4"			●	●		●	
UTILITY	1C = 4"			●		●	●	

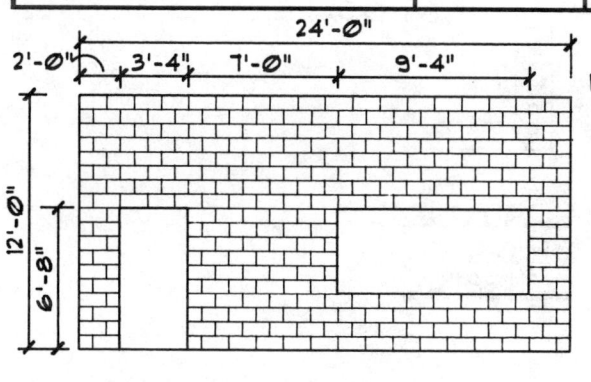

THIS BLOCK WALL ELEVATION SHOWS A WINDOW AND DOOR THAT IS DIMENSIONED USING 8" VERTICAL AND HORIZONTAL COURSING.

THIS WALL IS DIMENSIONED 4" DIFFERENT FROM THE FIRST EXAMPLE. THE DARK HATCHED BLOCKS INDICATE THE MORE THAN 80 UNITS THAT MUST BE CUT TO MEET THE DIMENSION CHANGES.

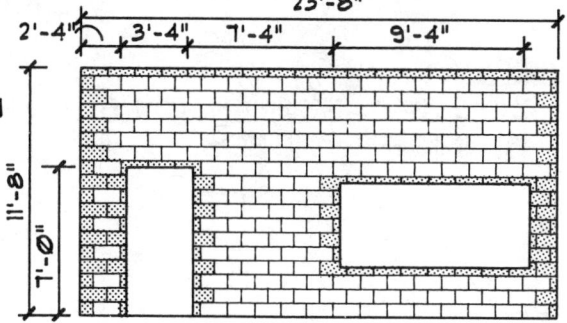

DIMENSIONS

6-13

THE ILLUSTRATION BELOW SHOWS A PORTION OF A BRICK SCALE. CARDBOARD OR PLASTIC SCALES ARE AVAILABLE FROM MANY MASONRY SUPPLIERS OR LOCAL MASONRY INSTITUTES. A BRICK SCALE IS USED IN THE SAME WAY AS AN ARCHITECT'S SCALE AND IS USUALLY AVAILABLE IN THE FOLLOWING SIZES: 1/4"=1'-0", 1/2"=1'-0", AND 3/4"=1'-0".

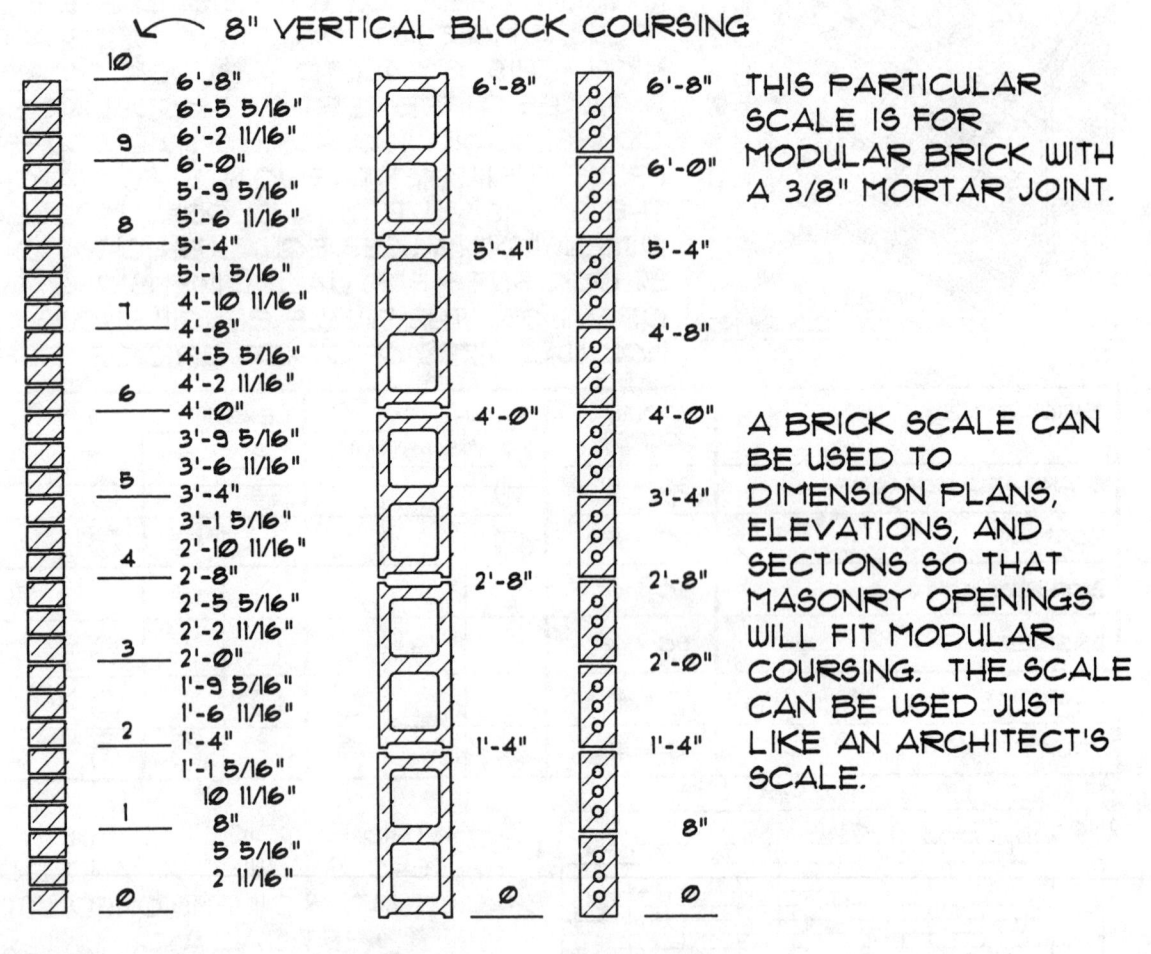

↙ 8" VERTICAL BLOCK COURSING

Vertical Brick Coursing	Horizontal Block Coursing	Horizontal Brick Coursing
10 — 6'-8" 6'-5 5/16" 6'-2 11/16" 9 — 6'-0" 5'-9 5/16" 8 — 5'-6 11/16" 5'-4" 5'-1 5/16" 7 — 4'-10 11/16" 4'-8" 4'-5 5/16" 6 — 4'-2 11/16" 4'-0" 3'-9 5/16" 5 — 3'-6 11/16" 3'-4" 3'-1 5/16" 4 — 2'-10 11/16" 2'-8" 2'-5 5/16" 3 — 2'-2 11/16" 2'-0" 1'-9 5/16" 2 — 1'-6 11/16" 1'-4" 1'-1 5/16" 1 — 10 11/16" 8" 5 5/16" 2 11/16" 0	6'-8" 5'-4" 4'-0" 2'-8" 1'-4" 0	6'-8" 6'-0" 5'-4" 4'-8" 4'-0" 3'-4" 2'-8" 2'-0" 1'-4" 8" 0

THIS PARTICULAR SCALE IS FOR MODULAR BRICK WITH A 3/8" MORTAR JOINT.

A BRICK SCALE CAN BE USED TO DIMENSION PLANS, ELEVATIONS, AND SECTIONS SO THAT MASONRY OPENINGS WILL FIT MODULAR COURSING. THE SCALE CAN BE USED JUST LIKE AN ARCHITECT'S SCALE.

REPLAY
1. ADD UP THE DIMENSION STRINGS AND WRITE THE TOTAL IN THE BLANK PROVIDED.

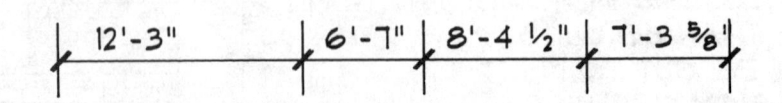

| 12'-3" | 6'-7" | 8'-4 1/2" | 7'-3 5/8" |

DIMENSIONS 6-14

|—— 9'- 3 ¾" ——|—— EQUAL ——|—— EQUAL ——|—— EQUAL ——|

|—6'-4"—|2"|—6'-4"—|2"|—6'-4"—|2"|—6'-4"—|2"|—6'-4"—|2"|—6'-4"—|

|— 8'-7 ⅞" —|— 6'-1 ⅜" —|— 9'-4 ¾" —|— 7'-4 ⅝" —|— 11'-9 ½" —|

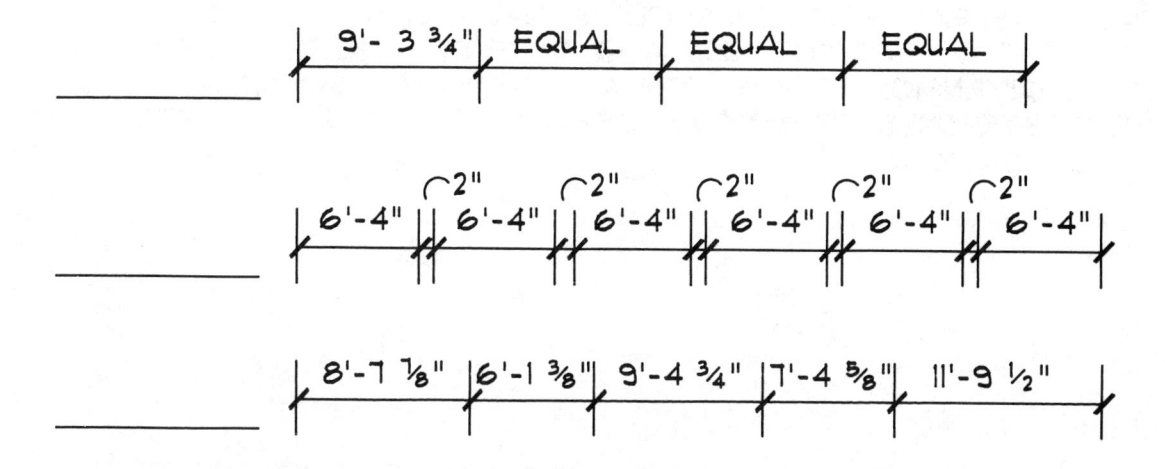

2. USE AN ARCHITECT'S SCALE TO MEASURE THE LENGTH OF THE LINES SHOWN BELOW.

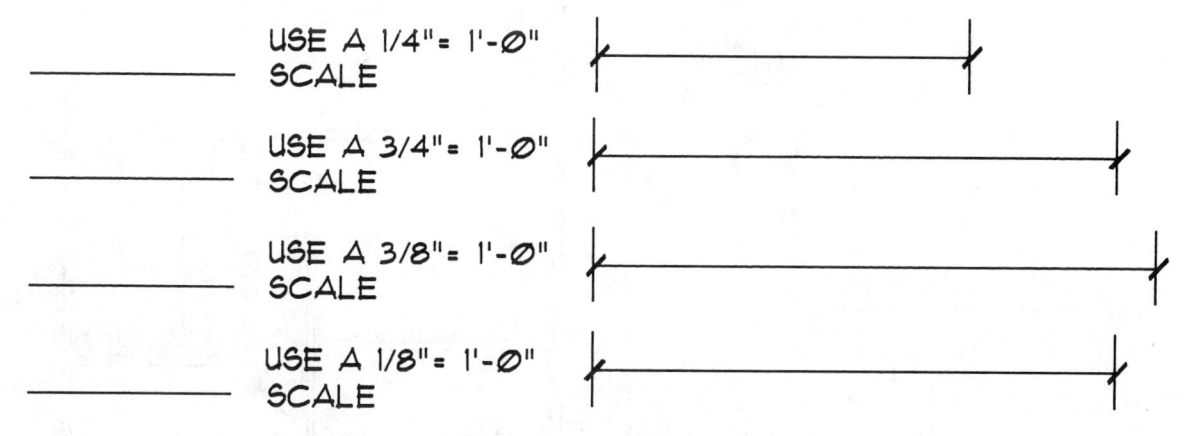

_____   USE A 1/4"= 1'-0" SCALE

_____   USE A 3/4"= 1'-0" SCALE

_____   USE A 3/8"= 1'-0" SCALE

_____   USE A 1/8"= 1'-0" SCALE

3. USE AN 1/8"= 1'-0" ARCHITECT'S SCALE TO MEASURE THE SECTION OF THE MASONRY BUILDING SHOWN BELOW. WRITE EACH DIMENSION IN ITS PROPER LOCATION ON THE STRING.

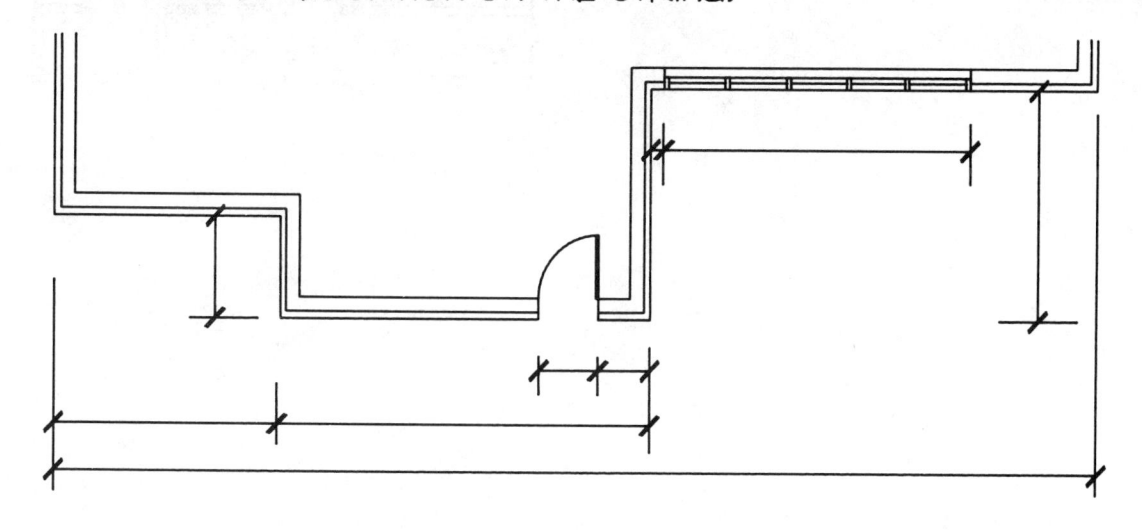

DIMENSIONS   6-15

4. THE ILLUSTRATION BELOW SHOWS A FIRST-FLOOR PLAN OF A RESIDENTIAL PROJECT. USE A FELT-TIP PEN OR PENCIL TO DRAW DIMENSION STRINGS FOR ALL ITEMS THAT WOULD HAVE TO BE DIMENSIONED (IT IS NOT NECESSARY TO ACTUALLY WRITE THE DIMENSION).

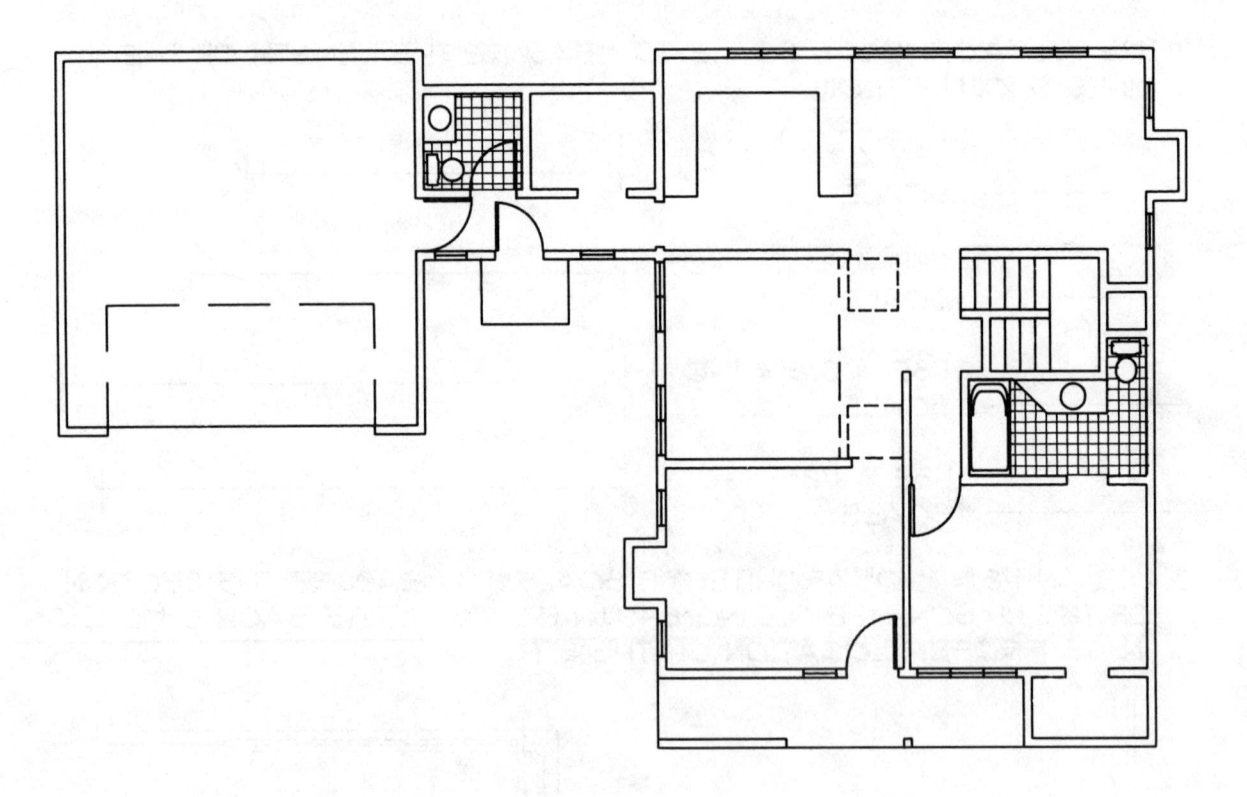

DIMENSIONS 6-16

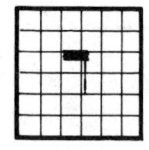

PROJECT ASSEMBLY TECHNIQUES

THIS UNIT WILL PRESENT SEVERAL TECHNIQUES THAT WILL MAKE THE ASSEMBLY OF A WORKING DRAWING PACKAGE EASIER. THE PREVIOUS UNITS HAVE DISCUSSED HOW TO DRAW; THIS UNIT WILL CONCENTRATE ON WHAT TO DRAW. THE MATERIAL WILL ADDRESS (1) SELECTION OF DRAWINGS TO BE INCLUDED IN A WORKING DRAWING PACKAGE, (2) STRUCTURAL FRAMING, AND (3) SHEET LAYOUT. THE LIST COULD BE MUCH LONGER, BUT THESE THREE ITEMS TEND TO CAUSE CONCERN WITH BEGINNING TECHNICIANS.

WHAT TO DRAW

EVERY WORKING DRAWING PACKAGE REQUIRES A DECISION ON WHAT SHOULD BE DRAWN. REMEMBER THAT THE DRAWINGS ARE A MAJOR PORTION OF THE LEGAL CONTRACT BETWEEN THE OWNER AND CONTRACTOR. THE CONTRACTOR IS OBLIGATED TO CONSTRUCT ALL ITEMS SHOWN ON THE PLANS AND SPECIFICATIONS. EQUALLY CRUCIAL, THE CONTRACTOR IS NOT OBLIGATED TO PROVIDE ITEMS THAT HAVE BEEN OMITTED.

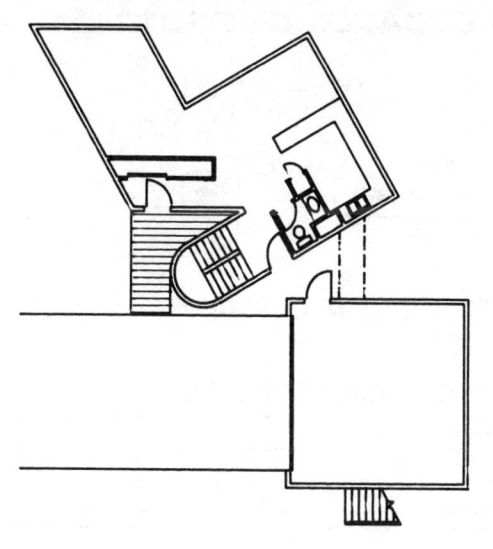

THIS UNIT WILL DISCUSS THE ASSEMBLY OF TWO PROJECTS, THE HOUSE SHOWN TO THE LEFT AND A FIRE STATION. (BOTH PROJECTS WILL BE COMPLETELY DETAILED IN UNITS 23 AND 26.) THE MATERIAL IN THIS UNIT WILL ADDRESS THE DECISION ON WHAT ITEMS SHOULD BE INCLUDED IN THE RESPECTIVE DRAWING SETS.

THERE IS A SIMILARITY IN THE ORGANIZATION OF MOST SETS OF

PROJECT ASSEMBLY TECHNIQUES 7-1

WORKING DRAWINGS. RESIDENTIAL PROJECTS TYPICALLY FOLLOW THIS PATTERN:

SITE PLAN
THE FIRST DRAWING SHOWS THE SITE WITH THE HOUSE DIMENSIONED FROM THE PROPERTY LINES. THE SITE PLAN INDICATES ALL CHANGES THAT ARE TO BE MADE TO THE EXTERIOR OF THE PROJECT.

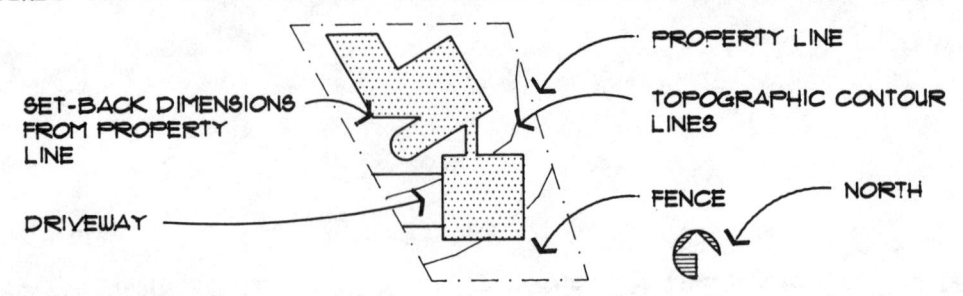

FLOOR PLAN(S)
THE NEXT SET OF DRAWINGS ARE THE FLOOR PLANS, STARTING WITH THE LOWEST LEVEL. THE PLANS MUST BE FULLY DETAILED TO SHOW THE CONTRACTOR ITEMS SUCH AS STAIRS, WINDOWS, DOORS, AND PLUMBING FIXTURES.

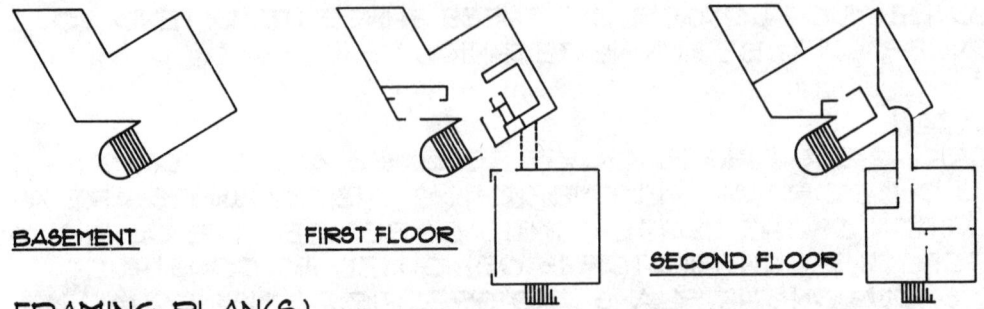

FRAMING PLAN(S)
IT IS TYPICAL TO PROVIDE THE CONTRACTOR WITH REDUCED SCALE FRAMING PLANS SHOWING THE SIZE AND LOCATION OF COLUMNS, BEAMS, AND JOISTS.

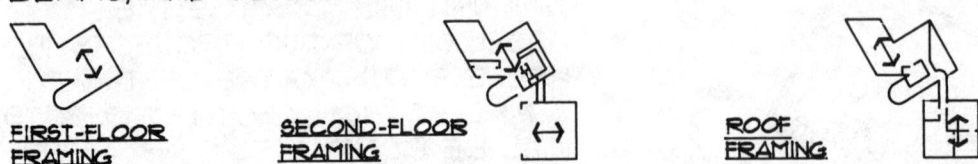

SCHEDULES
ROOM FINISH AND DOOR SCHEDULES PROVIDE A DETAILED ROOM-BY-ROOM SPECIFICATION FOR THE PROJECT.

PROJECT ASSEMBLY TECHNIQUES   7-2

INTERIOR ELEVATIONS
THE DRAWING PACKAGE INCLUDES ELEVATIONS OF ALL INTERIOR DETAILS THAT MUST BE DEFINED. THIS COVERS ITEMS SUCH AS KITCHEN AND BATHROOM CABINETS AND WALLS THAT HAVE SPECIAL CONDITIONS.

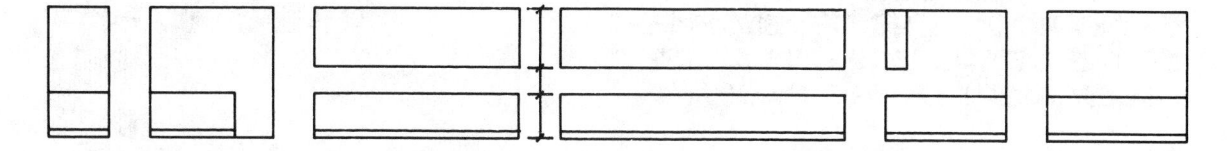

EXTERIOR ELEVATIONS
ALL EXTERIOR ELEVATIONS OF THE BUILDING MUST BE DRAWN. ELEVATIONS SHOW MATERIALS, ROOF HEIGHTS, AND WINDOW AND DOOR LOCATIONS.

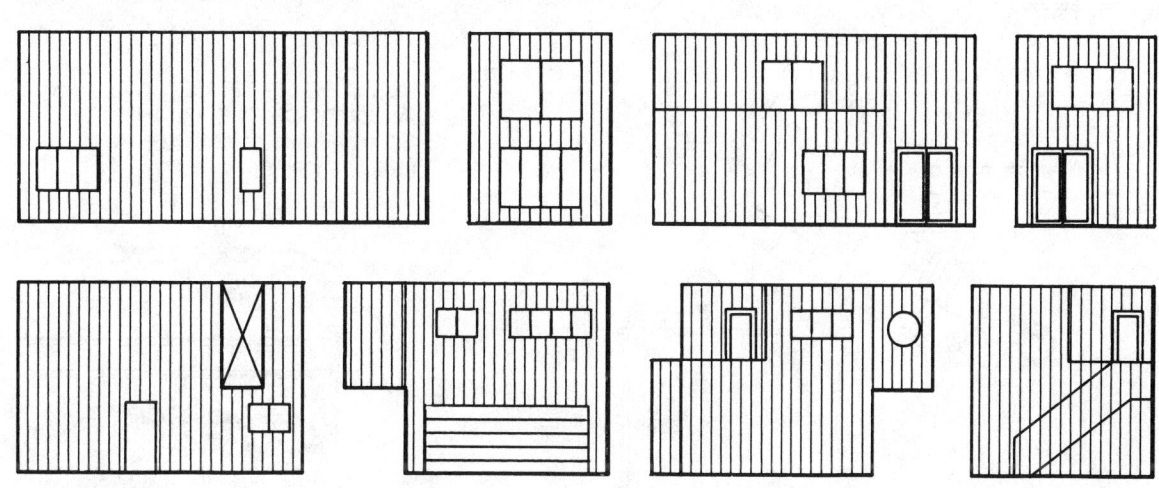

SECTIONS
THE FINAL SET OF DRAWINGS SHOWS SECTION CUTS THROUGH THE BUILDING. DETERMINING THE LOCATION OF THESE CUTS IS POSSIBLY THE MOST DIFFICULT TASK IN THE ASSEMBLY OF A WORKING DRAWING PACKAGE. THE FOLLOWING POINTS WILL HELP YOU TO DETERMINE THE PORTIONS THAT SHOULD BE DRAWN:

1. MAKE SURE YOU UNDERSTAND THE BUILDING DESIGN EXTREMELY WELL BEFORE YOU DETERMINE SECTION CUTS. PROBABLY THE BEST WAY TO DO THIS IS TO CONSTRUCT ONE OR MORE STUDY MODELS TO DETERMINE BUILDING CONDITIONS THAT MUST BE DEFINED.
2. EVERY UNUSUAL DETAIL IN THE BUILDING MUST BE DEFINED FOR THE CONTRACTOR. THESE COULD INCLUDE, FOR EXAMPLE, STAIRS, TWO-STORY SPACES, SKYLIGHTS, A BALCONY, OR WINDOWS.
3. WORK WITH THE FLOOR PLANS TO DETERMINE WHERE SECTION CUTS SHOULD BE MADE. USE A FELT-TIP PEN TO MARK UNUSUAL CONDITIONS ON A COPY OF THE PLAN.

PROJECT ASSEMBLY TECHNIQUES 7-3

THE FLOOR PLAN SHOWN BELOW ILLUSTRATES THE TECHNIQUE OF MARKING WALL CONDITIONS THAT SHOULD BE DETAILED. FOR EXAMPLE, THE SECTION MARKED ① IS CUT THROUGH THE TWO-STORY LIVING ROOM. THE DEVELOPMENT OF THE DETAIL IS SHOWN AT THE LOWER RIGHT OF THIS PAGE.

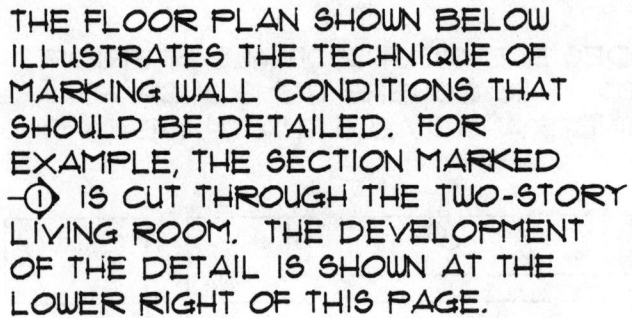

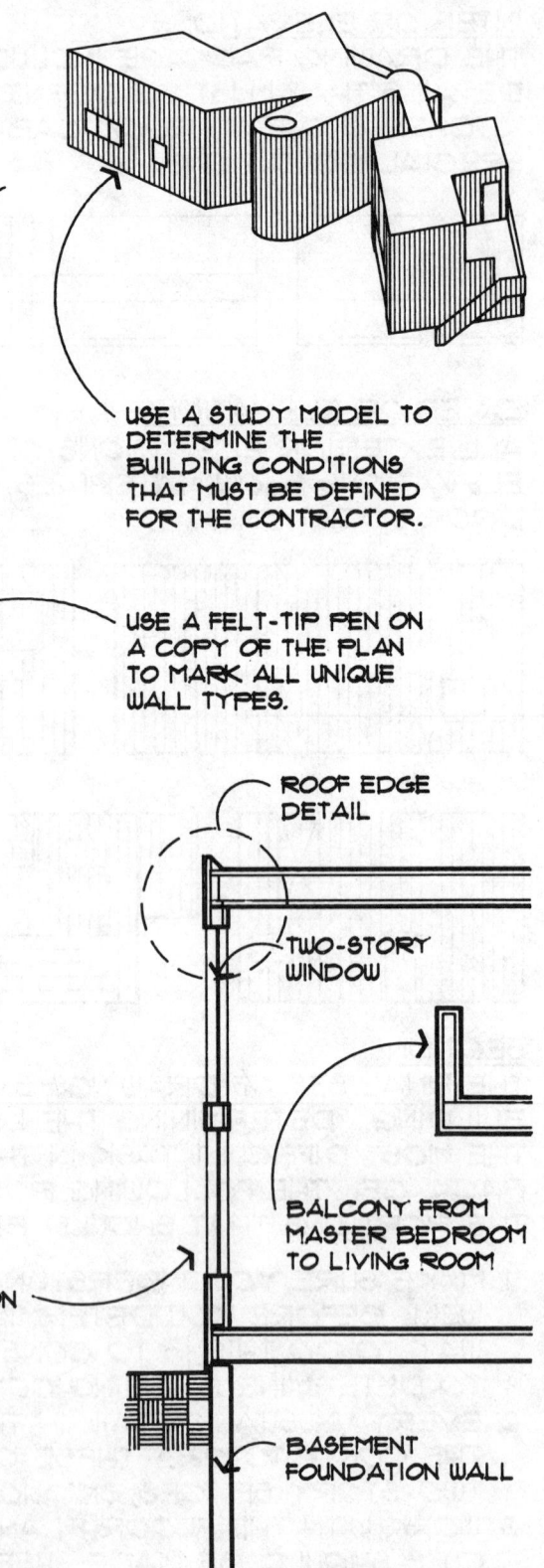

USE A STUDY MODEL TO DETERMINE THE BUILDING CONDITIONS THAT MUST BE DEFINED FOR THE CONTRACTOR.

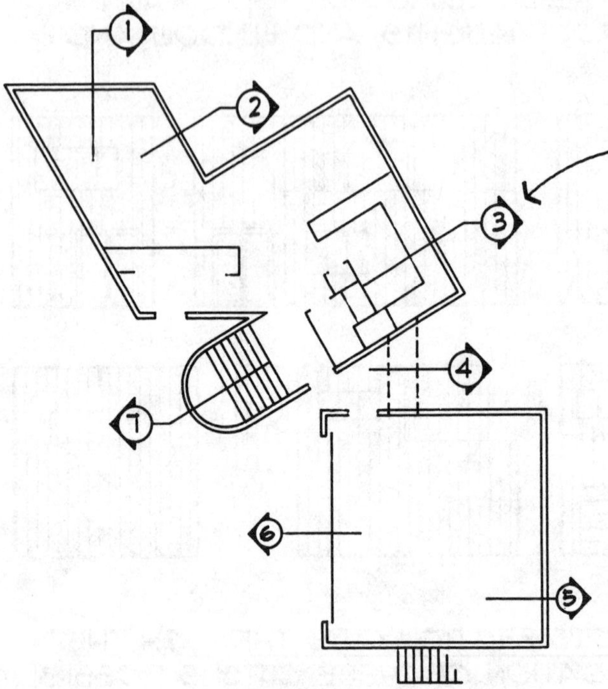

USE A FELT-TIP PEN ON A COPY OF THE PLAN TO MARK ALL UNIQUE WALL TYPES.

ROOF EDGE DETAIL

TWO-STORY WINDOW

BEGIN DRAWING A BUILDING SECTION BY LOCATING FLOORS AND WALLS; USE THE FLOOR PLAN AS A REFERENCE FOR THE DETAIL.

BALCONY FROM MASTER BEDROOM TO LIVING ROOM

BASEMENT FOUNDATION WALL

SECTION 1

PROJECT ASSEMBLY TECHNIQUES 7-4

GRAVEL STOP
BUILT-UP ROOF

FIBERGLASS INSULATION

3- 2" x 12" LINTEL

PELLA WINDOW UNIT

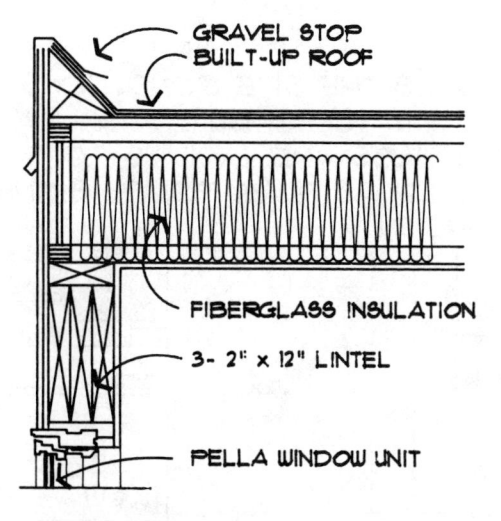

ROOF EDGE DETAIL

THE SCALE USED TO DRAW SECTION CUTS CAN RANGE FROM 1/8"=1'-0" UP TO 3"=1'-0". THE SECTION TO THE LEFT SHOWS A ROOF EDGE DETAIL FROM THE HOUSE. SECTION DETAILS ARE ILLUSTRATED TO SHOW THE CONTRACTOR SPECIFIC BUILDING CONDITIONS. FOR EXAMPLE, THE BUILDING SECTION SHOWN ON PAGE 7-4 IS USED TO INDEX THE LARGER SCALE ROOF EDGE DETAIL. THE ENLARGED DRAWING ALLOWS AN ARCHITECTURAL TECHNICIAN TO SOLVE WINDOW, LINTEL, AND ROOF CONDITIONS IN A WAY THAT WOULDN'T BE POSSIBLE USING A SMALLER SCALE.

OUR SECOND PROJECT INVOLVES THE FIRE STATION SHOWN BELOW. THE DECISIONS ON WHAT TO DRAW FOR THIS PROJECT ARE VERY SIMILAR TO THE ONES MADE FOR THE HOUSE PROJECT JUST DISCUSSED. IN ORGANIZING A DRAWING PACKAGE THESE TWO PRINCIPLES ARE TYPICALLY FOLLOWED: (1) THE DRAWINGS FIRST SHOW THE EXTERIOR OF THE BUILDING AND WORK THEIR WAY TO THE INTERIOR, AND (2) THE SCALE OF THE DRAWINGS STARTS WITH THE SMALLEST (THE SITE) AND WORKS UP TO THE LARGEST (THE DETAILS).

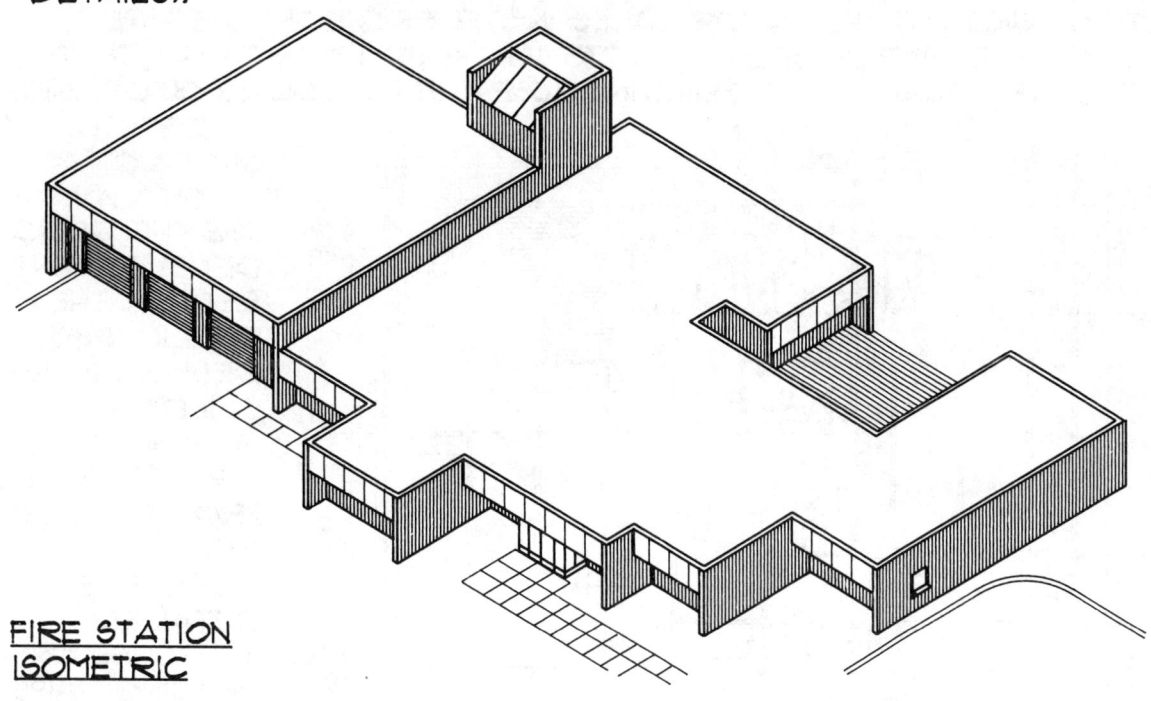

FIRE STATION
ISOMETRIC

PROJECT ASSEMBLY TECHNIQUES

SITE PLAN AND DETAILS
THE FIRST GROUP OF DRAWINGS ADDRESSES THE SITE CONDITIONS. THE SITE PLAN IS DRAWN SHOWING ALL ITEMS TO BE BUILT, TOPOGRAPHY CHANGES, LOCATIONS OF CURBS AND DRIVES, TO NAME SEVERAL. IN ADDITION, DETAILS SUCH AS FLAG POLES, SIGNS, HANDICAP CURBS, AND BENCHES ARE SHOWN.

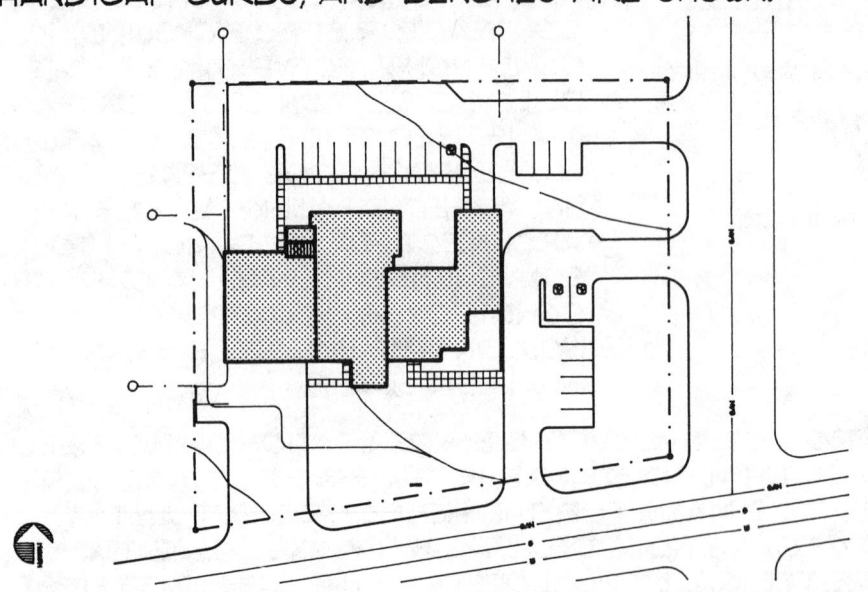

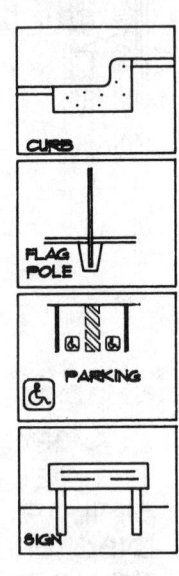

SITE DETAILS

FLOOR PLANS
COMMERCIAL FLOOR PLANS ARE ASSEMBLED SHOWING WALLS, DOORS, WINDOWS, AND DIMENSIONS. START A FLOOR PLAN BY BLOCKING OUT THE MAJOR WALLS IN THE PROJECT. THE FIRE STATION EXAMPLE BELOW STARTS WITH GRID LINES THAT DEFINE THE STRUCTURE OF THE BUILDING. USE THE FOLLOWING GUIDELINES TO BEGIN TO CONSTRUCT A FLOOR PLAN: 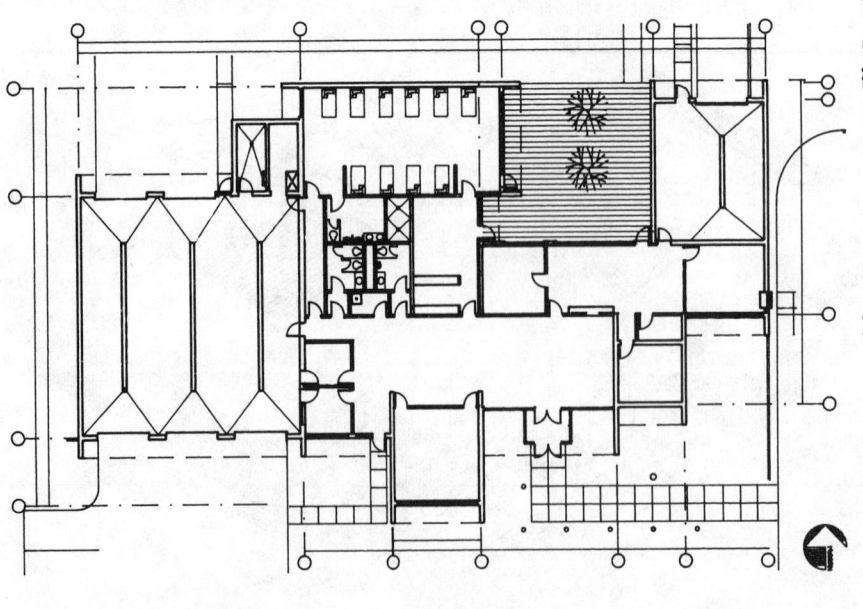
1. USE THE DESIGN DEVELOPMENT SET FOR THE PRELIMINARY DESIGN OF THE BUILDING.
2. REFER TO DRAWING SETS FROM SIMILAR PROJECTS.
3. ASSEMBLE DETAILED SKETCHES ON TRACING PAPER.

PROJECT ASSEMBLY TECHNIQUES   7-6

INTERIOR PLAN BLOW-UPS AND ELEVATIONS

MOST COMMERCIAL PLANS ARE DRAWN AT A 1/8"=1'-0" SCALE. THIS SMALL SCALE USUALLY REQUIRES THAT HIGH-DETAIL AREAS, SUCH AS TOILETS, BE ENLARGED TO ALLOW DIMENSIONS AND TIGHT CONDITIONS TO BE SHOWN. IT IS ALSO COMMON TO DRAW LARGER SCALE ELEVATIONS OF WALLS CONTAINING PLUMBING FIXTURES.

PLAN BLOW-UP   TOILET ELEVATIONS   DOOR PANELS

                                       DOOR FRAMES

SCHEDULES

ROOM FINISH SCHEDULES SHOULD BE DETAILED TO SHOW FLOOR, WALL, AND CEILING FINISHES. A DOOR SCHEDULE INDICATES THE SIZE AND FINISH OF ALL DOORS IN THE PROJECT. SCHEDULES RELATE TO THE FLOOR PLANS AND SHOULD BE LOCATED ON THE SAME SHEET OR ON A SHEET NEAR THE PLAN SHEET(S).

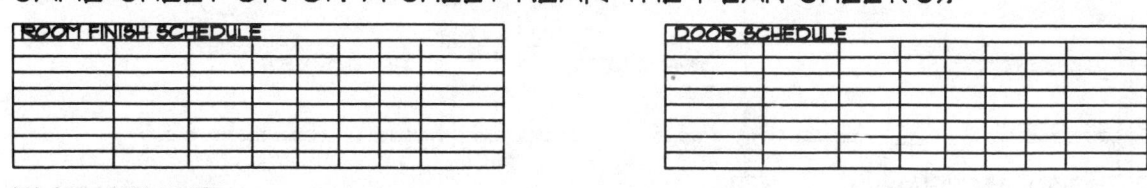

ROOM FINISH SCHEDULE   DOOR SCHEDULE

ELEVATIONS

EXTERIOR ELEVATIONS DETAIL ROOF AND WALL HEIGHTS, AND ALL CONSTRUCTION MATERIALS ARE CALLED OUT IN THEM. ELEVATIONS SHOULD ALSO ILLUSTRATE WINDOW AND DOOR LOCATIONS.

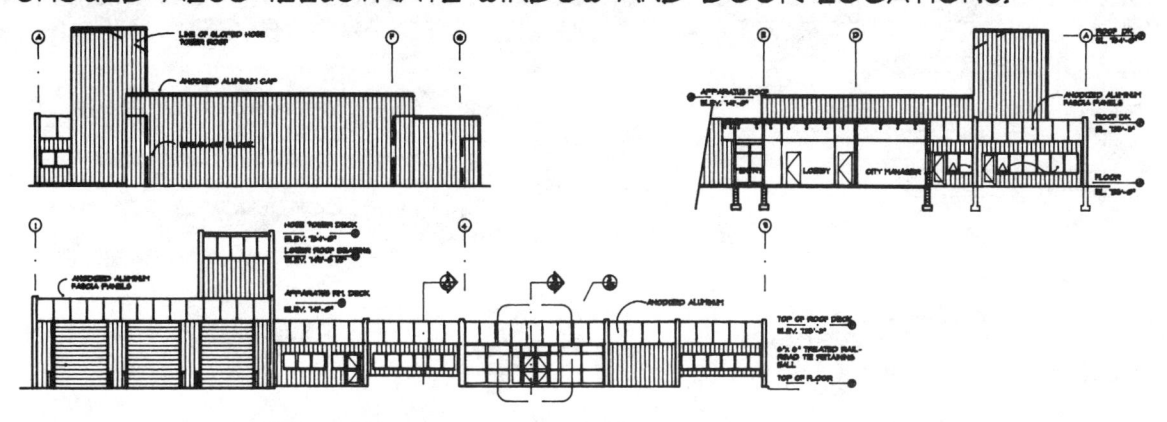

PROJECT ASSEMBLY TECHNIQUES   7-7

SECTIONS

THE FINAL SET OF DRAWINGS IN THE PACKAGE CONTAINS THE SECTION VIEWS. THE DETAILS BEGIN WITH CUTS THROUGH THE LONG AXIS OF THE BUILDING (LONGITUDINAL) AND THROUGH THE SHORT AXIS (TRANSVERSE).

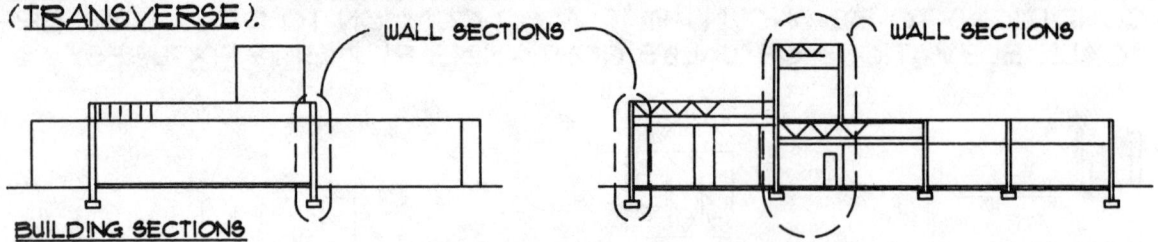

BUILDING SECTIONS

THE SMALL-SCALE BUILDING SECTIONS ARE USED AS AN INDEX TO DETERMINE WALL CONDITIONS THAT SHOULD BE ENLARGED. THE EXAMPLE ABOVE IDENTIFIES THREE WALLS THAT NEED TO BE FURTHER DEFINED BY DRAWING LARGER-SCALE WALL SECTIONS. THE THREE WALLS ENLARGED ARE ILLUSTRATED BELOW.

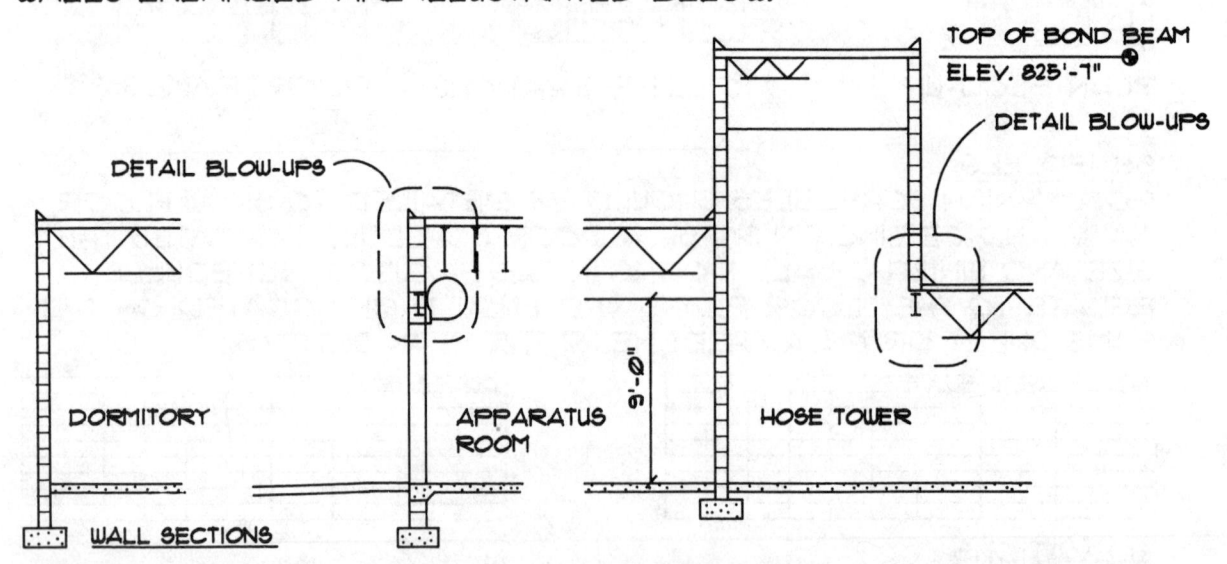

WALL SECTIONS

THE FINAL SET OF DRAWINGS IN THE SECTION PACKAGE IS MADE UP OF BLOW-UP DETAILS OF THE WALL SECTIONS. USE THE BUILDING SECTIONS AS AN INDEX TO HELP YOU DETERMINE WHAT DETAILS YOU WILL USE. DON'T FORGET THAT YOU NEED TO SHOW EVERY UNIQUE WALL CONDITION.

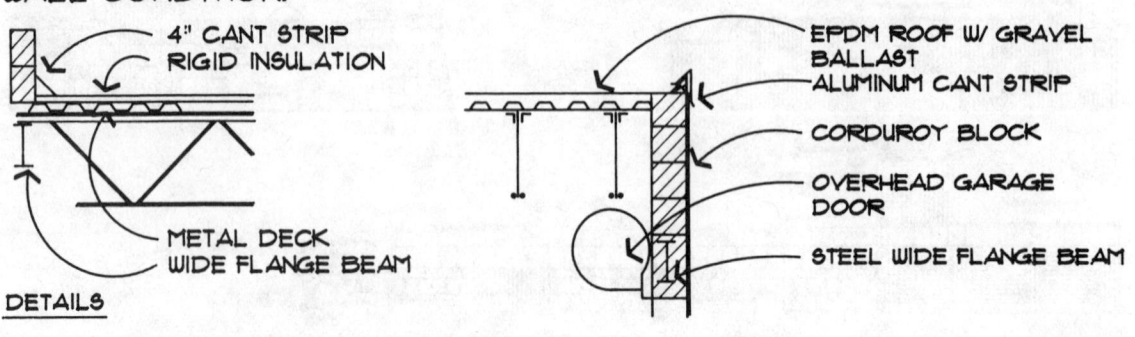

DETAILS

PROJECT ASSEMBLY TECHNIQUES 7-8

STRUCTURAL FRAMING

ONE OF THE FIRST STEPS IN THE ASSEMBLY OF A PROJECT IS TO DEVELOP A STRUCTURAL SKELETON FOR THE BUILDING. IT IS ESSENTIAL TO ANALYZE A BUILDING DESIGN TO DETERMINE A WORKABLE FRAMING SYSTEM BEFORE A FINAL DRAWING PACKAGE CAN BE STARTED. MOST BUILDING FRAMING FOLLOWS A PATTERN USING POST AND BEAM CONSTRUCTION WITH JOISTS OR LOAD-BEARING WALLS WITH JOISTS. THE FOLLOWING DETAILS ILLUSTRATE SEVERAL FRAMING TECHNIQUES FREQUENTLY USED IN RESIDENTIAL AND COMMERCIAL CONSTRUCTION.

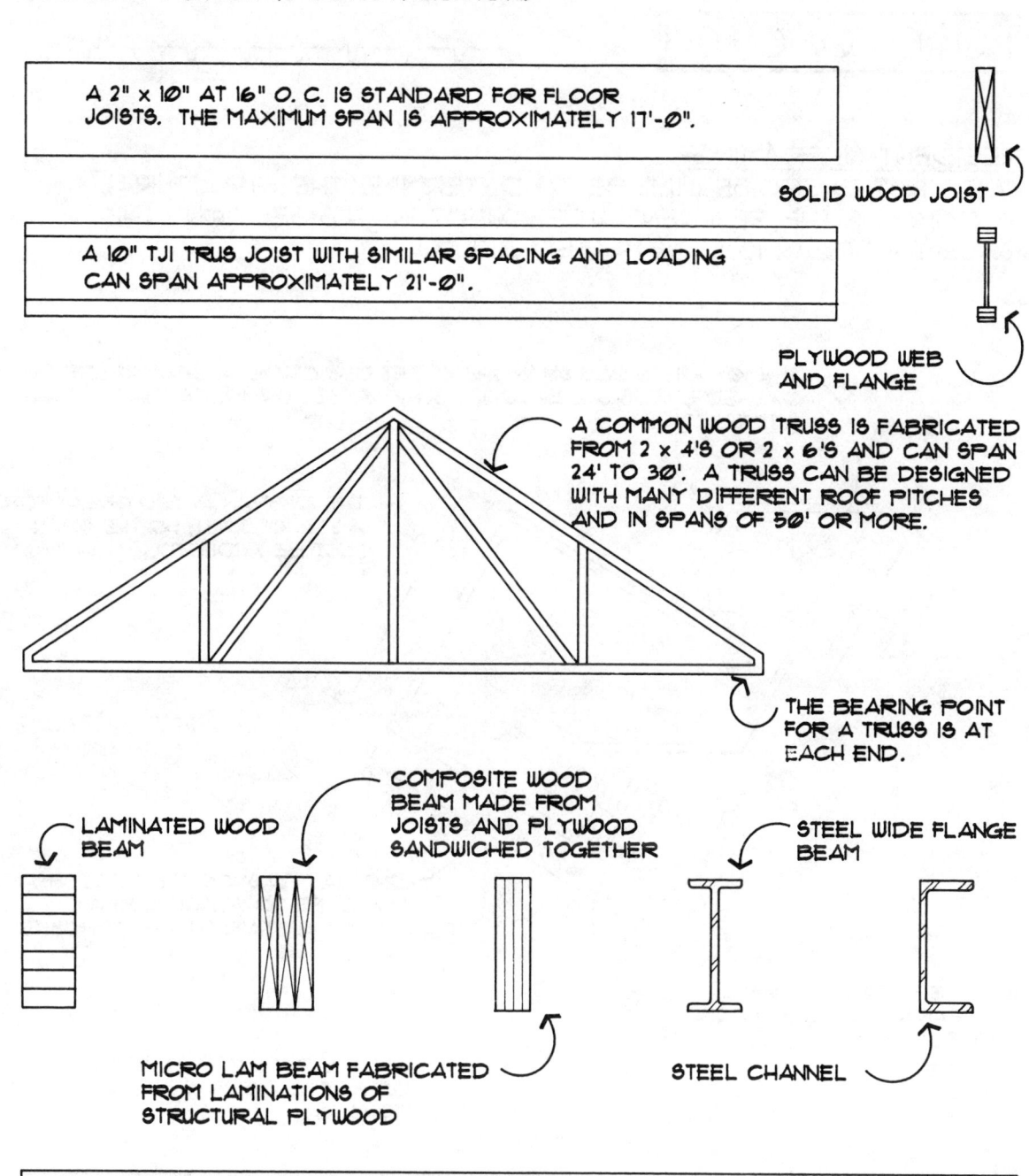

A 2" x 10" AT 16" O.C. IS STANDARD FOR FLOOR JOISTS. THE MAXIMUM SPAN IS APPROXIMATELY 17'-0".

SOLID WOOD JOIST

A 10" TJI TRUS JOIST WITH SIMILAR SPACING AND LOADING CAN SPAN APPROXIMATELY 21'-0".

PLYWOOD WEB AND FLANGE

A COMMON WOOD TRUSS IS FABRICATED FROM 2 x 4'S OR 2 x 6'S AND CAN SPAN 24' TO 30'. A TRUSS CAN BE DESIGNED WITH MANY DIFFERENT ROOF PITCHES AND IN SPANS OF 50' OR MORE.

THE BEARING POINT FOR A TRUSS IS AT EACH END.

LAMINATED WOOD BEAM

COMPOSITE WOOD BEAM MADE FROM JOISTS AND PLYWOOD SANDWICHED TOGETHER

STEEL WIDE FLANGE BEAM

MICRO LAM BEAM FABRICATED FROM LAMINATIONS OF STRUCTURAL PLYWOOD

STEEL CHANNEL

PROJECT ASSEMBLY TECHNIQUES   7-9

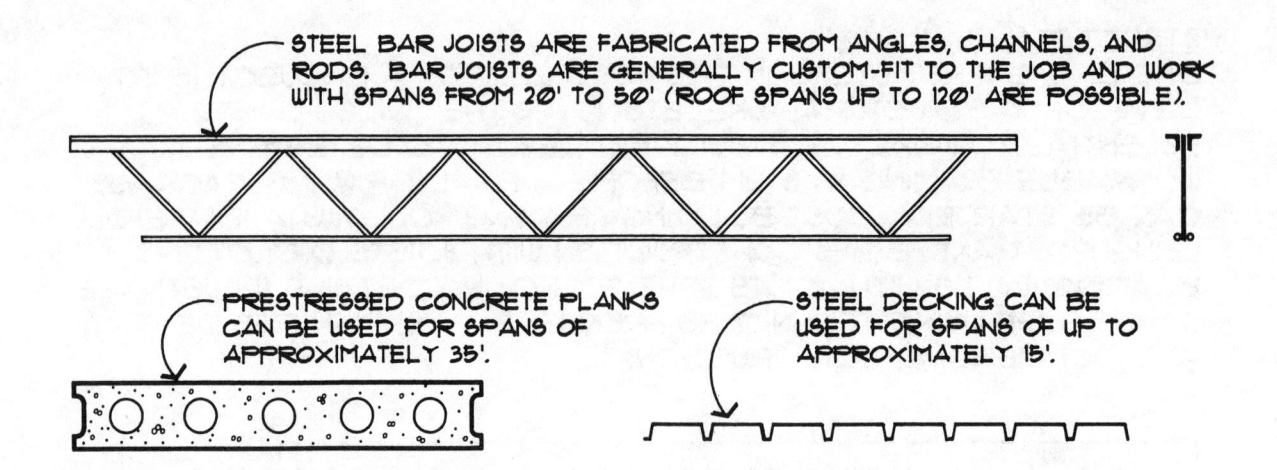

STEEL BAR JOISTS ARE FABRICATED FROM ANGLES, CHANNELS, AND RODS. BAR JOISTS ARE GENERALLY CUSTOM-FIT TO THE JOB AND WORK WITH SPANS FROM 20' TO 50' (ROOF SPANS UP TO 120' ARE POSSIBLE).

PRESTRESSED CONCRETE PLANKS CAN BE USED FOR SPANS OF APPROXIMATELY 35'.

STEEL DECKING CAN BE USED FOR SPANS OF UP TO APPROXIMATELY 15'.

RESIDENTIAL FRAMING

OUR FIRST EXERCISE WILL BE TO DETERMINE THE STRUCTURAL FRAMING OF THE RESIDENTIAL PROJECT IN THIS SECTION. THE BASEMENT PLAN IS ILLUSTRATED BELOW.

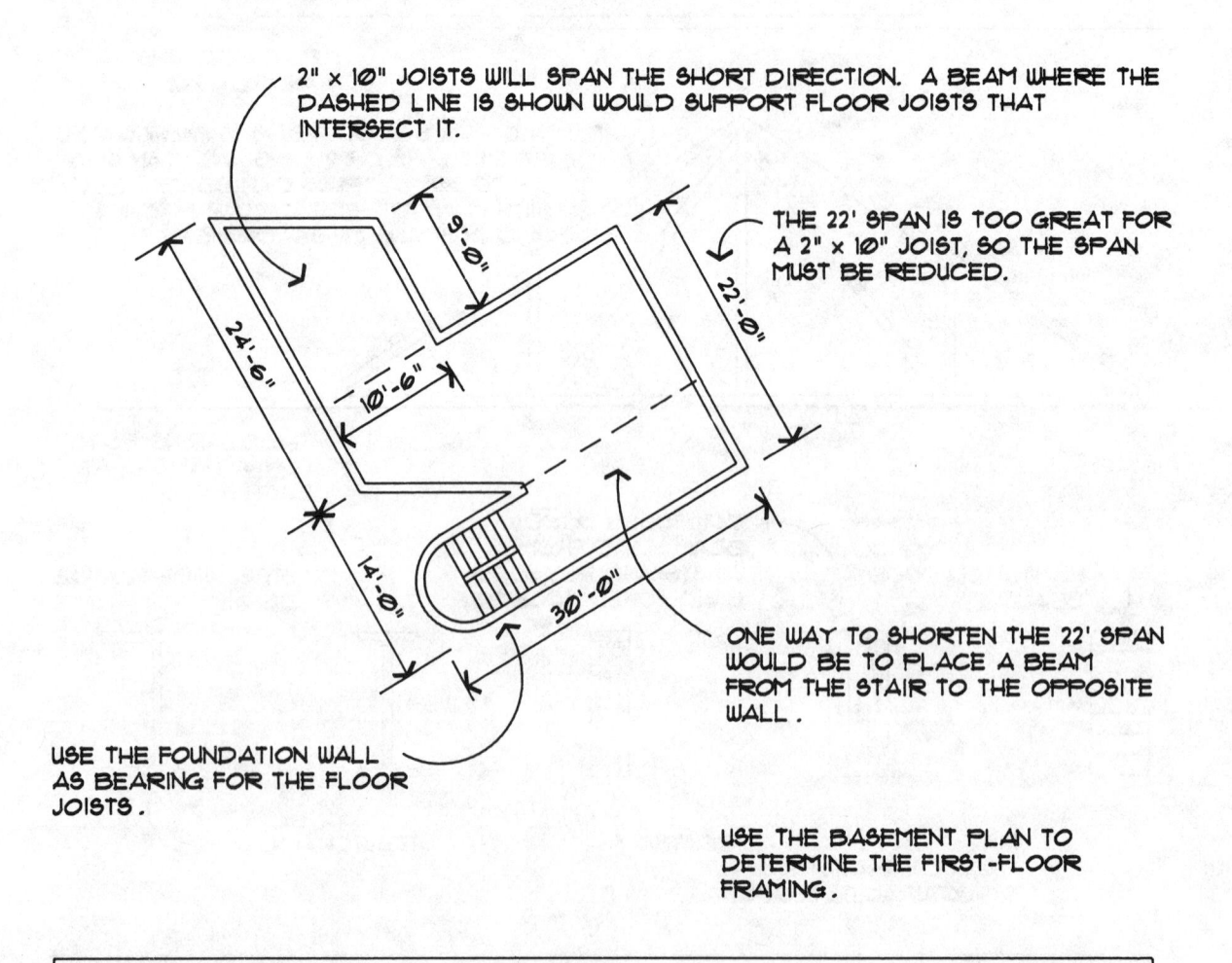

2" x 10" JOISTS WILL SPAN THE SHORT DIRECTION. A BEAM WHERE THE DASHED LINE IS SHOWN WOULD SUPPORT FLOOR JOISTS THAT INTERSECT IT.

THE 22' SPAN IS TOO GREAT FOR A 2" x 10" JOIST, SO THE SPAN MUST BE REDUCED.

ONE WAY TO SHORTEN THE 22' SPAN WOULD BE TO PLACE A BEAM FROM THE STAIR TO THE OPPOSITE WALL.

USE THE FOUNDATION WALL AS BEARING FOR THE FLOOR JOISTS.

USE THE BASEMENT PLAN TO DETERMINE THE FIRST-FLOOR FRAMING.

PROJECT ASSEMBLY TECHNIQUES 7-10

THE FIRST-FLOOR FRAMING PLAN SHOWN BELOW ILLUSTRATES ONE SOLUTION TO THE QUESTION OF THE PLACEMENT OF JOISTS AND BEAMS.

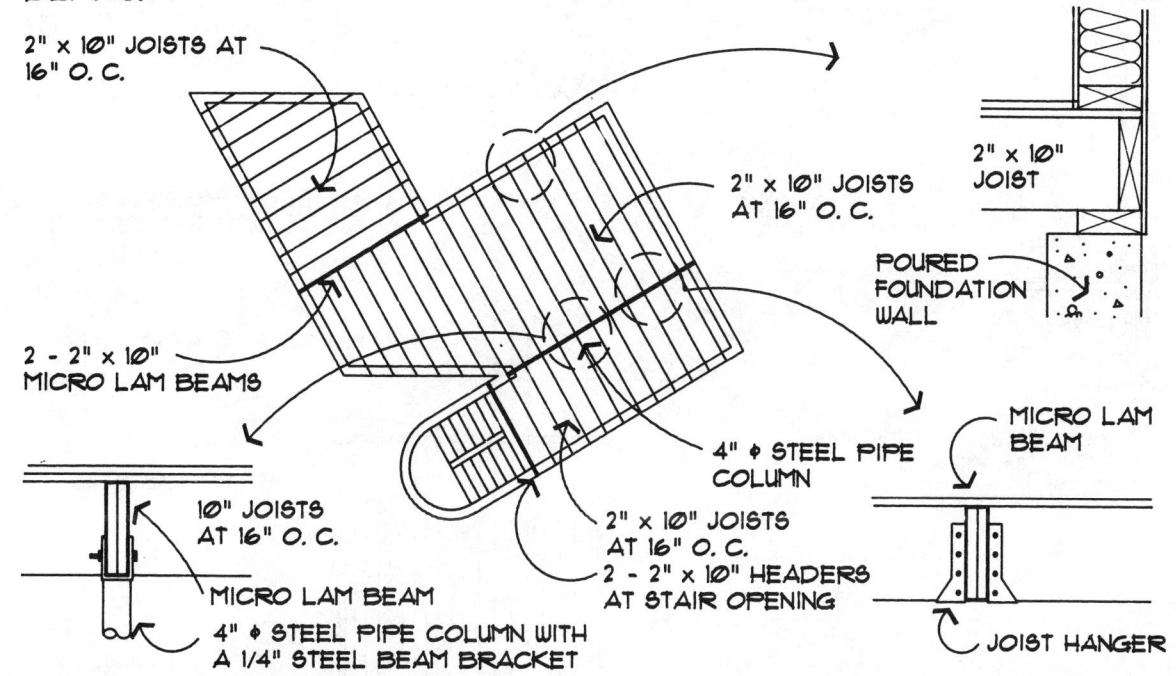

2" x 10" JOISTS AT 16" O.C.

2" x 10" JOISTS AT 16" O.C.

2" x 10" JOIST

POURED FOUNDATION WALL

2 - 2" x 10" MICRO LAM BEAMS

MICRO LAM BEAM

10" JOISTS AT 16" O.C.

MICRO LAM BEAM

4" ⌀ STEEL PIPE COLUMN WITH A 1/4" STEEL BEAM BRACKET

4" ⌀ STEEL PIPE COLUMN

2" x 10" JOISTS AT 16" O.C.

2 - 2" x 10" HEADERS AT STAIR OPENING

JOIST HANGER

SECOND-FLOOR FRAMING SHOULD ADDRESS THE CONDITIONS NOTED ON THE PLAN BELOW.

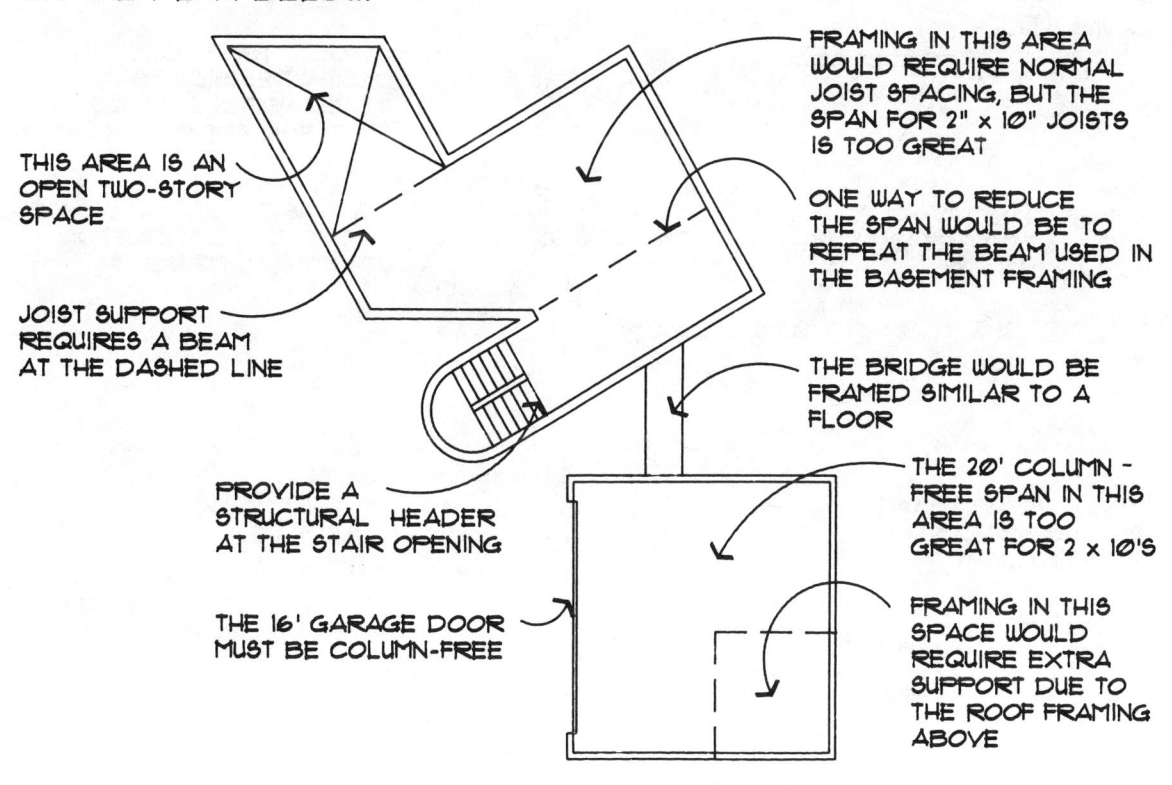

FRAMING IN THIS AREA WOULD REQUIRE NORMAL JOIST SPACING, BUT THE SPAN FOR 2" x 10" JOISTS IS TOO GREAT

ONE WAY TO REDUCE THE SPAN WOULD BE TO REPEAT THE BEAM USED IN THE BASEMENT FRAMING

THIS AREA IS AN OPEN TWO-STORY SPACE

JOIST SUPPORT REQUIRES A BEAM AT THE DASHED LINE

THE BRIDGE WOULD BE FRAMED SIMILAR TO A FLOOR

THE 20' COLUMN-FREE SPAN IN THIS AREA IS TOO GREAT FOR 2 x 10'S

PROVIDE A STRUCTURAL HEADER AT THE STAIR OPENING

THE 16' GARAGE DOOR MUST BE COLUMN-FREE

FRAMING IN THIS SPACE WOULD REQUIRE EXTRA SUPPORT DUE TO THE ROOF FRAMING ABOVE

PROJECT ASSEMBLY TECHNIQUES   7-11

THIS SECOND-FLOOR FRAMING PLAN SHOWS ONE METHOD OF INCLUDING THE NECESSARY DESIGN CONDITIONS (SEE PAGE 7-11).

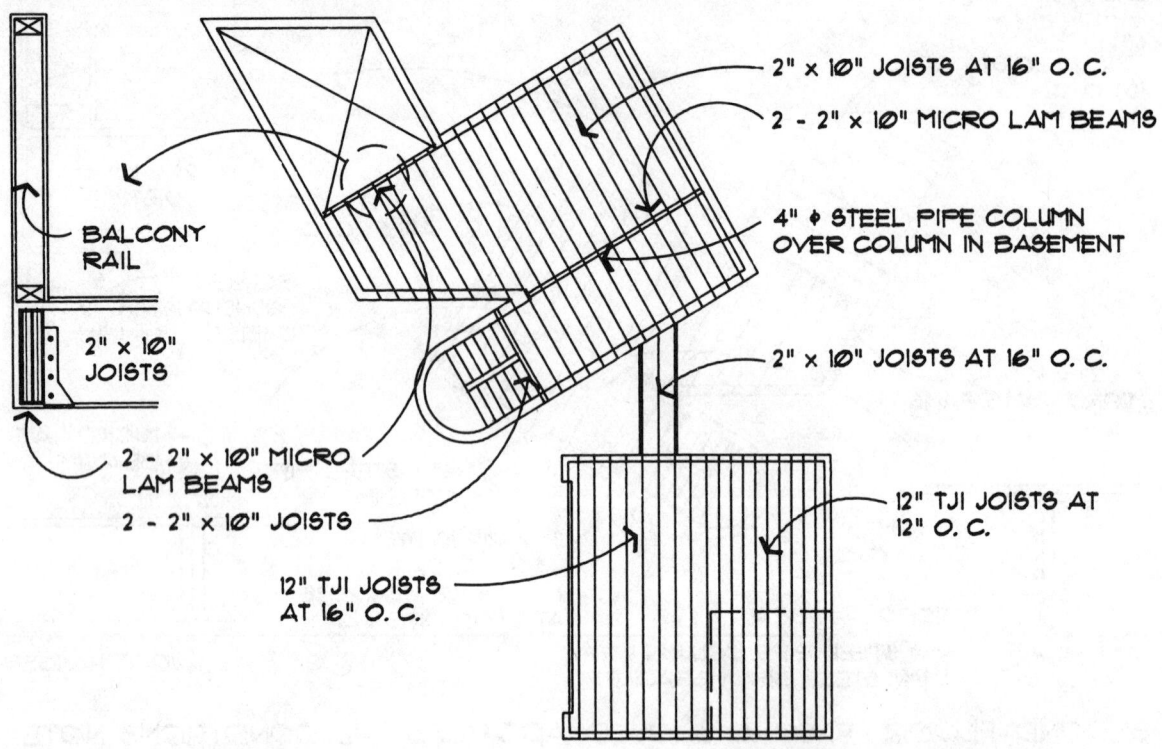

- 2" x 10" JOISTS AT 16" O.C.
- 2 - 2" x 10" MICRO LAM BEAMS
- 4" ⌀ STEEL PIPE COLUMN OVER COLUMN IN BASEMENT
- 2" x 10" JOISTS AT 16" O.C.
- 12" TJI JOISTS AT 12" O.C.
- 12" TJI JOISTS AT 16" O.C.
- 2 - 2" x 10" JOISTS
- 2 - 2" x 10" MICRO LAM BEAMS
- 2" x 10" JOISTS
- BALCONY RAIL

THE ROOF BELOW CONTAINS NOTES THAT PERTAIN TO FRAMING CONDITIONS.

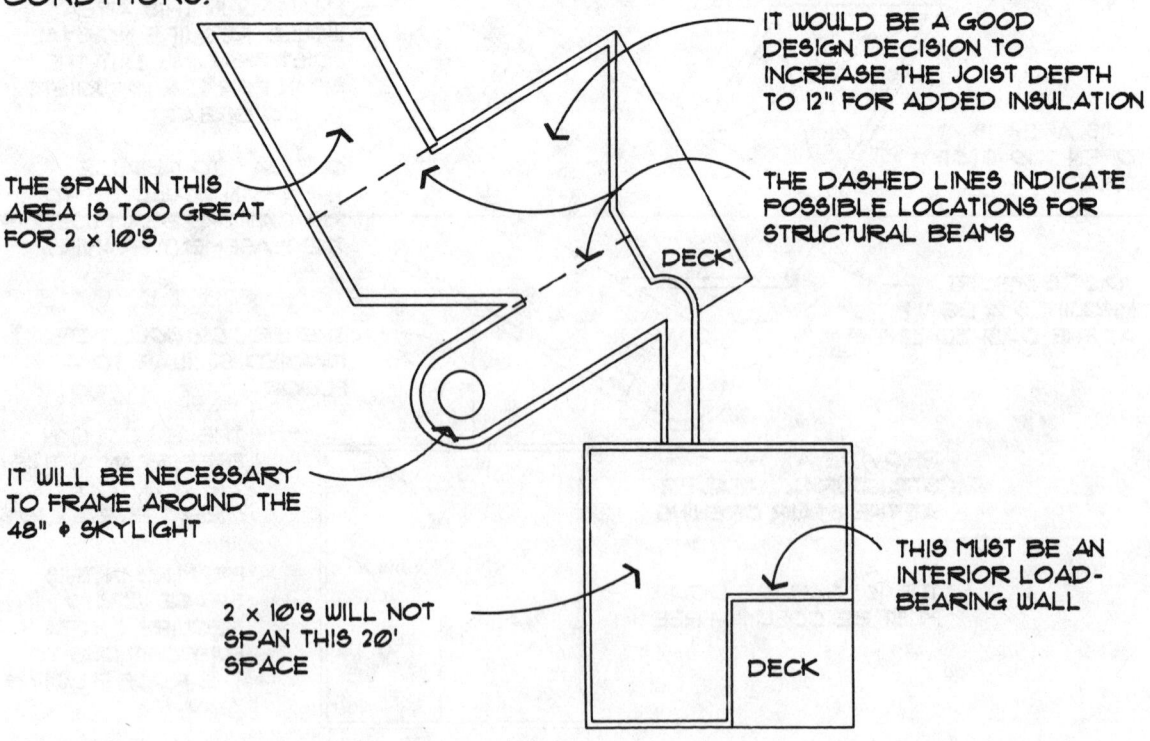

- IT WOULD BE A GOOD DESIGN DECISION TO INCREASE THE JOIST DEPTH TO 12" FOR ADDED INSULATION
- THE DASHED LINES INDICATE POSSIBLE LOCATIONS FOR STRUCTURAL BEAMS
- THE SPAN IN THIS AREA IS TOO GREAT FOR 2 x 10'S
- IT WILL BE NECESSARY TO FRAME AROUND THE 48" ⌀ SKYLIGHT
- 2 x 10'S WILL NOT SPAN THIS 20' SPACE
- THIS MUST BE AN INTERIOR LOAD-BEARING WALL
- DECK
- DECK

PROJECT ASSEMBLY TECHNIQUES 7-12

THIS ROOF FRAMING PLAN ILLUSTRATES ONE METHOD OF ADDRESSING THE CONDITIONS MENTIONED ON PAGE 7-12.

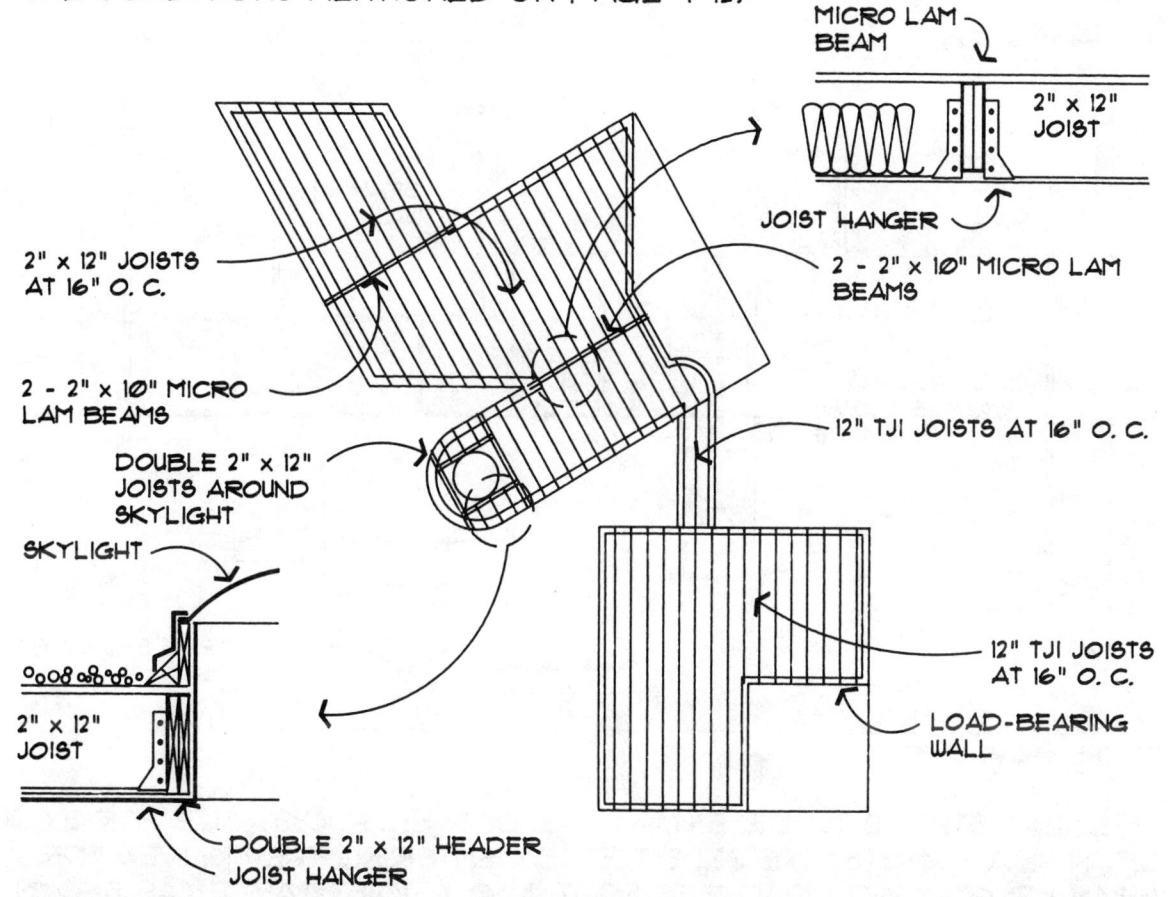

- MICRO LAM BEAM
- 2" x 12" JOIST
- JOIST HANGER
- 2" x 12" JOISTS AT 16" O.C.
- 2 - 2" x 10" MICRO LAM BEAMS
- 2 - 2" x 10" MICRO LAM BEAMS
- DOUBLE 2" x 12" JOISTS AROUND SKYLIGHT
- 12" TJI JOISTS AT 16" O.C.
- SKYLIGHT
- 2" x 12" JOIST
- 12" TJI JOISTS AT 16" O.C.
- LOAD-BEARING WALL
- DOUBLE 2" x 12" HEADER JOIST HANGER

CONSIDER THE FOLLOWING TIPS WHEN LAYING OUT THE STRUCTURAL FRAMING FOR A BUILDING:

- USE A ROLL OF TRACING PAPER FOR MARKING THE STRUCTURAL CONDITIONS ON EACH LEVEL OF THE FLOOR PLAN.
- START FROM THE LOWEST LEVEL OF THE BUILDING AND WORK UP TO THE TOP LEVEL.
- CONSIDER ONE "PIECE" OF THE FRAMING AT A TIME.
- MARK THE DIRECTION OF JOIST FRAMING ON TRACING PAPER TO SHOW EACH FLOOR CONDITION.
- REVIEW JOIST TABLES TO DETERMINE SIZES.

<u>FIRE STATION FRAMING</u>

NEXT WE WILL EXAMINE THE FRAMING REQUIREMENTS FOR THE FIRE STATION PROJECT. THE FIRST STEP IN FIGURING THE FRAMING IS TO MAKE A DECISION ABOUT THE MATERIALS TO BE USED. (IN THIS EXAMPLE, WE WILL USE STEEL BAR JOISTS WITH LOAD-BEARING WALLS.) BAR JOIST MANUFACTURERS PUBLISH CATALOGS CONTAINING JOIST TABLES THAT WILL PROVIDE A JOIST SIZE WHEN THE SPAN (IN FEET) AND LOAD (IN POUNDS) ARE ENTERED.

PROJECT ASSEMBLY TECHNIQUES

THE PLAN BELOW SHOWS THE CONDITIONS THAT WOULD APPLY TO THE ROOF FRAMING.

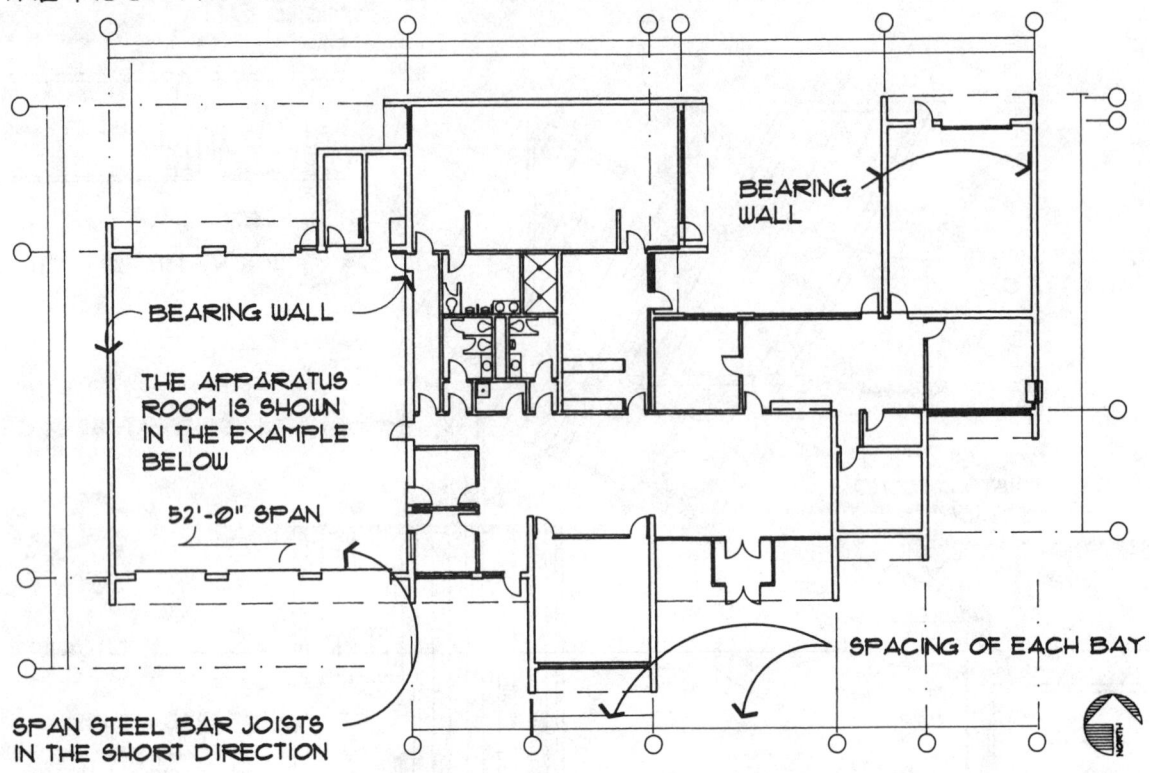

- BEARING WALL
- BEARING WALL
- THE APPARATUS ROOM IS SHOWN IN THE EXAMPLE BELOW
- 52'-0" SPAN
- SPAN STEEL BAR JOISTS IN THE SHORT DIRECTION
- SPACING OF EACH BAY

THE NEXT STEP IS TO DETERMINE THE CORRECT JOIST SIZE FOR EACH SPAN. BAR JOISTS ARE SELECTED BY ENTERING THE FIGURES FOR SPAN LENGTH AND LOAD PER FOOT INTO A JOIST TABLE (AS SHOWN ON PAGE 7-15). THE JOIST IS DETERMINED BY SETTING THE SPACING OF EACH JOIST AND USING A LOAD PER FOOT. A FAIRLY COMMON DESIGN FOR BAR JOISTS IS TO SPACE THEM 4'-0" ON CENTER WITH A ROOF LOAD OF 60 POUNDS FOR EVERY SQUARE FOOT OF ROOF SURFACE. THE ILLUSTRATION BELOW SHOWS THAT A 60-POUND-PER-SQUARE-FOOT ROOF LOAD WOULD TRANSFER 240 POUNDS PER FOOT TO THE JOIST.

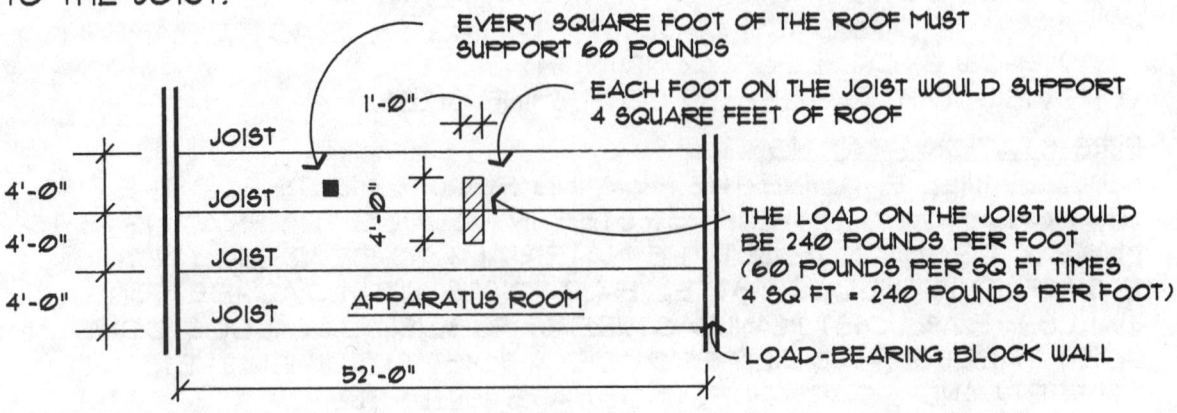

- EVERY SQUARE FOOT OF THE ROOF MUST SUPPORT 60 POUNDS
- EACH FOOT ON THE JOIST WOULD SUPPORT 4 SQUARE FEET OF ROOF
- THE LOAD ON THE JOIST WOULD BE 240 POUNDS PER FOOT (60 POUNDS PER SQ FT TIMES 4 SQ FT = 240 POUNDS PER FOOT)
- LOAD-BEARING BLOCK WALL
- APPARATUS ROOM
- 52'-0"

PROJECT ASSEMBLY TECHNIQUES — 7-14

DETERMINE THE STEEL JOIST SIZE FOR THE 52'-0" SPAN BY ENTERING THE TABLE BELOW.

③ READ UP TO SEE THAT A 30K10 BAR JOIST WILL SPAN THE DISTANCE

STANDARD LOAD TABLE / OPEN WEB STEEL JOISTS, K-SERIES

JOIST SPAN (MEASURED IN FEET)	JOIST DESIGNATION					
	30K7	30K8	30K9	30K10	30K11	30K12
46'	241	266	290	344	380	380
47'	230	255	277	329	372	372
48'	221	244	266	315	362	365
49'	212	234	255	303	347	357
50'	203	225	245	291	333	350
51'	195	216	235	279	320	343
52'	188	208	226	268	308	336
53'	181	200	218	258	296	330
54'	174	192	209	249	285	324

① ENTER THE 52'-0" SPAN HERE

② SELECT THE FIRST LOAD THAT EXCEEDS THE REQUIRED LOAD PER FOOT (IN THIS CASE IT IS 240#)

ONE WAY OF DRAWING THE FRAMING PLAN FOR THE ROOF STRUCTURE IS SHOWN BELOW.

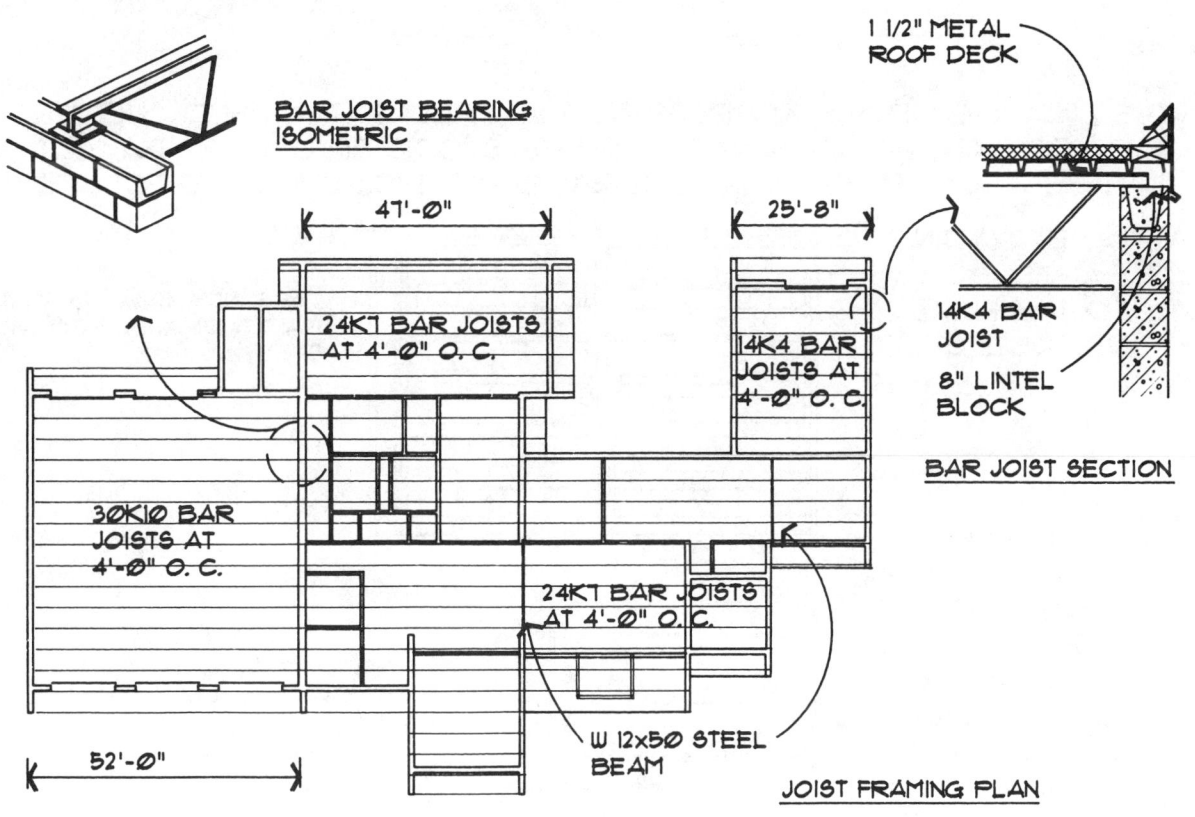

BAR JOIST BEARING ISOMETRIC

1 1/2" METAL ROOF DECK

47'-0"

24K7 BAR JOISTS AT 4'-0" O.C.

25'-8"

14K4 BAR JOISTS AT 4'-0" O.C.

14K4 BAR JOIST

8" LINTEL BLOCK

BAR JOIST SECTION

30K10 BAR JOISTS AT 4'-0" O.C.

24K7 BAR JOISTS AT 4'-0" O.C.

W 12x50 STEEL BEAM

52'-0"

JOIST FRAMING PLAN

PROJECT ASSEMBLY TECHNIQUES 7-15

SHEET LAYOUT

THE FINAL PORTION OF THIS UNIT DEALS WITH THE LOCATION OF DRAWINGS IN A PACKAGE. ORGANIZATION OF THE VARIOUS DRAWINGS IN THE SET IS CALLED <u>SHEET LAYOUT</u>. IT IS NECESSARY FOR YOU TO BE AWARE OF ALL OF THE DRAWINGS THAT WILL BE INCLUDED IN THE WORKING DRAWINGS BEFORE YOU BEGIN TO ORGANIZE YOUR LAYOUT. THIS SECTION WILL DEMONSTRATE THE DEVELOPMENT OF A SHEET LAYOUT FOR THE FIRE STATION.

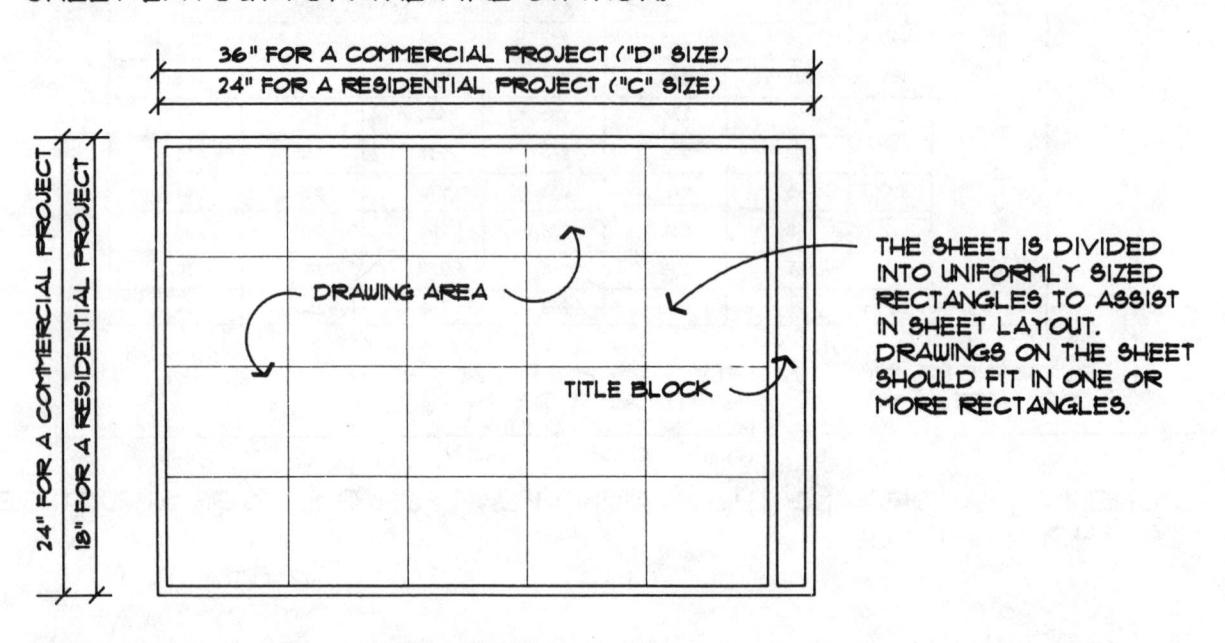

36" FOR A COMMERCIAL PROJECT ("D" SIZE)
24" FOR A RESIDENTIAL PROJECT ("C" SIZE)

24" FOR A COMMERCIAL PROJECT
18" FOR A RESIDENTIAL PROJECT

DRAWING AREA
TITLE BLOCK

THE SHEET IS DIVIDED INTO UNIFORMLY SIZED RECTANGLES TO ASSIST IN SHEET LAYOUT. DRAWINGS ON THE SHEET SHOULD FIT IN ONE OR MORE RECTANGLES.

THE DRAWING ABOVE REPRESENTS TWO FREQUENTLY USED SHEET SIZES FOR ARCHITECTURAL DRAWINGS. SUCCESSFUL SHEET LAYOUT CAN BE ACCOMPLISHED IN SEVERAL WAYS, INCLUDING THE FOLLOWING:

1. TAPE TRACING PAPER SKETCHES TO THE FINAL DRAWING SHEET.

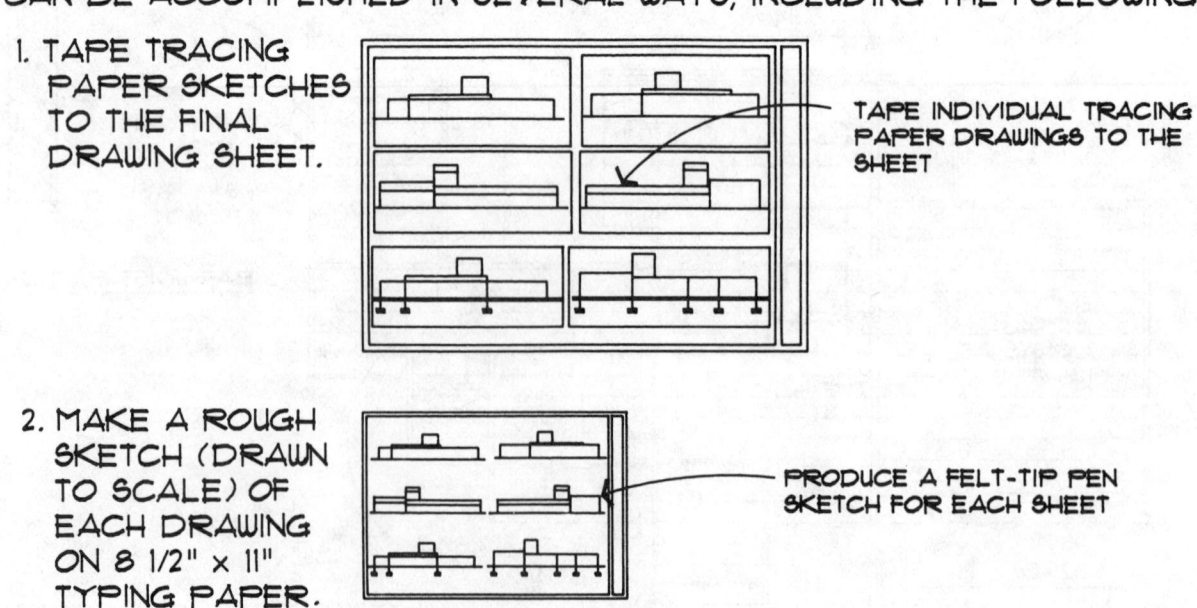

   TAPE INDIVIDUAL TRACING PAPER DRAWINGS TO THE SHEET

2. MAKE A ROUGH SKETCH (DRAWN TO SCALE) OF EACH DRAWING ON 8 1/2" x 11" TYPING PAPER.

   PRODUCE A FELT-TIP PEN SKETCH FOR EACH SHEET

PROJECT ASSEMBLY TECHNIQUES 7-16

THE FOLLOWING GUIDELINES SHOULD ASSIST YOU IN ORGANIZING A SHEET LAYOUT:

- DEVELOP SKETCHES OF ALL ITEMS THAT WILL BE INCLUDED IN THE DRAWING PACKAGE.
- ATTEMPT TO LINE UP DRAWINGS ON THE SHEET. FOR EXAMPLE, LINE UP FIRST- AND SECOND-FLOOR PLANS IN EITHER A VERTICAL OR HORIZONTAL PATTERN ON THE SHEET.

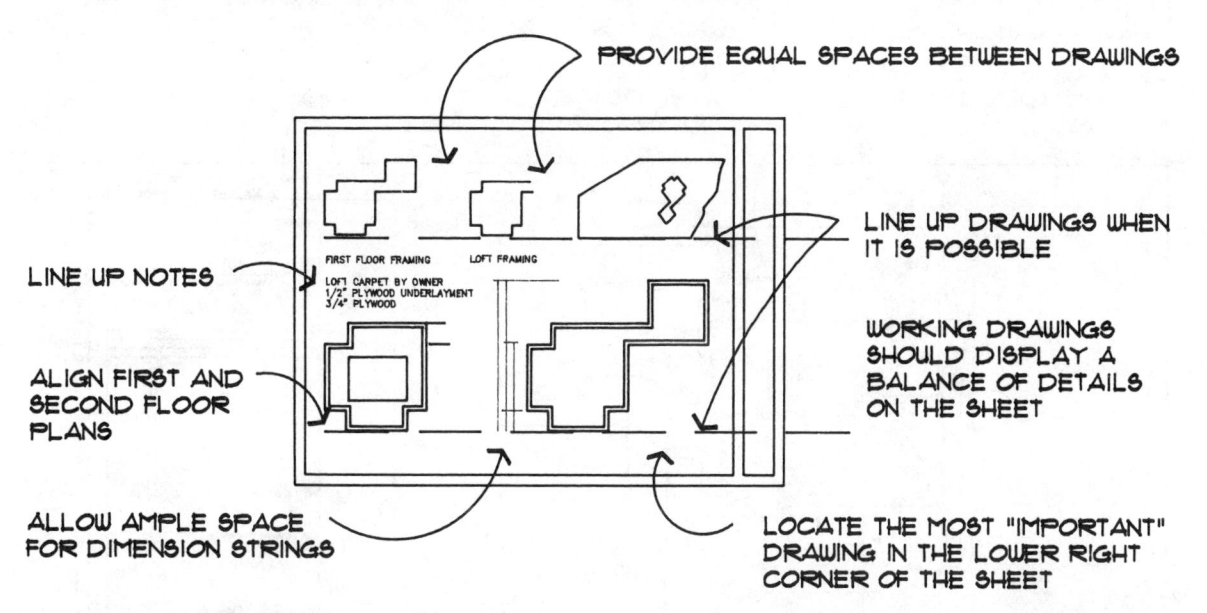

PROVIDE EQUAL SPACES BETWEEN DRAWINGS

LINE UP NOTES

FIRST FLOOR FRAMING   LOFT FRAMING
LOFT CARPET BY OWNER
1/2" PLYWOOD UNDERLAYMENT
3/4" PLYWOOD

LINE UP DRAWINGS WHEN IT IS POSSIBLE

ALIGN FIRST AND SECOND FLOOR PLANS

WORKING DRAWINGS SHOULD DISPLAY A BALANCE OF DETAILS ON THE SHEET

ALLOW AMPLE SPACE FOR DIMENSION STRINGS

LOCATE THE MOST "IMPORTANT" DRAWING IN THE LOWER RIGHT CORNER OF THE SHEET

- PLACE DRAWINGS THAT ARE SIMILAR AT THE SAME LOCATION ON EACH SHEET. FOR EXAMPLE, IF THREE FLOOR PLANS OF A BUILDING ARE TO BE PLACED ON SHEETS A-2, A-3, A-4, LOCATE THE PLAN IN THE SAME POSITION ON EACH SHEET.
- WORKING DRAWINGS READ LIKE A BOOK (WITH THE EDGE BINDING ALONG THE LEFT OF THE PAGE). IF POSSIBLE, LOCATE THE MORE "IMPORTANT" ITEMS ON THE RIGHT SIDE OF THE SHEET, MAKING THEM MORE ACCESSIBLE WHEN THE DRAWING SET IS OPENED.
- ONCE DRAWINGS HAVE BEEN LINED UP, DRAW LIGHT GUIDELINES TO ALIGN NOTES AND DIMENSIONS.
- VIEW SHEET LAYOUT AS SIMILAR TO A JIGSAW PUZZLE; MOVE DRAWINGS AROUND THE SHEET UNTIL THEY FIT AN ORGANIZED PATTERN.
- THE MAJOR DRAWINGS IN THE PACKAGE SHOULD FOLLOW THIS ORDER: (1) SITE PLAN, (2) FLOOR PLANS (LOWEST LEVEL FIRST), (3) ELEVATIONS, (4) BUILDING SECTIONS, (5) WALL SECTIONS, AND (6) DETAILS.
- THIS FINAL POINT DEALS WITH AN ARCHITECT'S VIEW OF A DRAWING PACKAGE—THE DRAWINGS SHOULD "LOOK GOOD." THIS INVOLVES BALANCE, GOOD ORGANIZATION, AND THE TRADE-OFF BETWEEN LIGHT AND DARK DETAIL MASSING.

PROJECT ASSEMBLY TECHNIQUES

THE NEXT FIVE PAGES SHOW ONE POSSIBLE LAYOUT FOR THE FIRE STATION. FACTORS CONSIDERED IN ORGANIZING THE MATERIAL ARE NOTED.

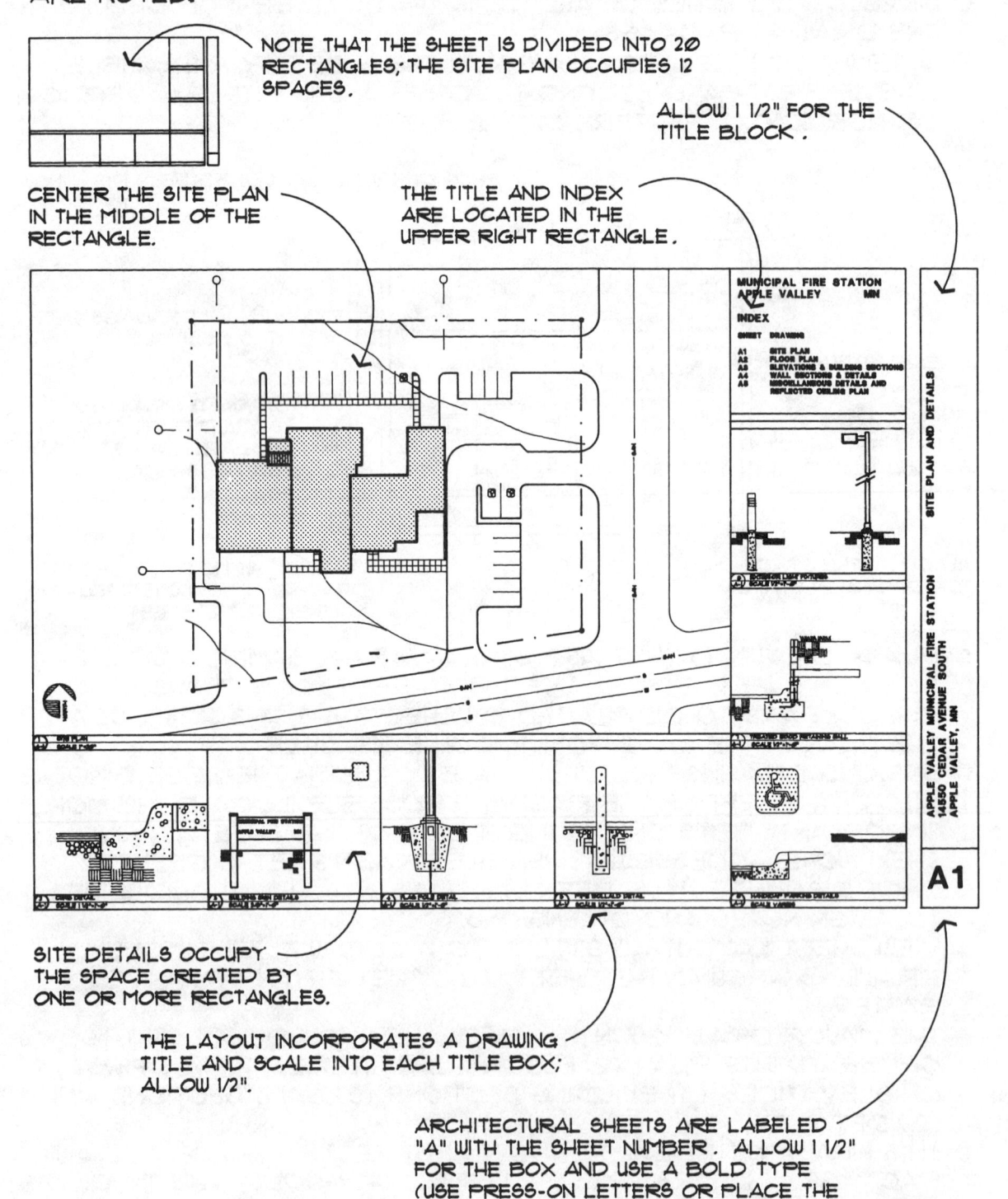

NOTE THAT THE SHEET IS DIVIDED INTO 20 RECTANGLES; THE SITE PLAN OCCUPIES 12 SPACES.

ALLOW 1 1/2" FOR THE TITLE BLOCK.

CENTER THE SITE PLAN IN THE MIDDLE OF THE RECTANGLE.

THE TITLE AND INDEX ARE LOCATED IN THE UPPER RIGHT RECTANGLE.

SITE DETAILS OCCUPY THE SPACE CREATED BY ONE OR MORE RECTANGLES.

THE LAYOUT INCORPORATES A DRAWING TITLE AND SCALE INTO EACH TITLE BOX; ALLOW 1/2".

ARCHITECTURAL SHEETS ARE LABELED "A" WITH THE SHEET NUMBER. ALLOW 1 1/2" FOR THE BOX AND USE A BOLD TYPE (USE PRESS-ON LETTERS OR PLACE THE PRESS-ON LETTERS UNDER THE SHEET AND TRACE).

PROJECT ASSEMBLY TECHNIQUES　　　7-18

THE ILLUSTRATION BELOW DEMONSTRATES HOW THE LAYOUT OF THE THE FLOOR PLAN SHEET IS ORGANIZED.

TOILET PLANS POSE A PARTICULAR PROBLEM WITH DIMENSIONS DUE TO THE SMALL SCALE. USE THE 1/4" SCALE BLOW-UP TO LOCATE MOST DIMENSION STRINGS.

START THE PROJECT BY LOCATING STRUCTURAL GRIDS.

DIMENSION STRINGS SHOULD SHOW GRID SPACING AS WELL AS OVERALL BUILDING LENGTHS.

PROVIDE AMPLE SPACE FOR NOTES AND DIMENSIONS AROUND THE FLOOR PLAN.

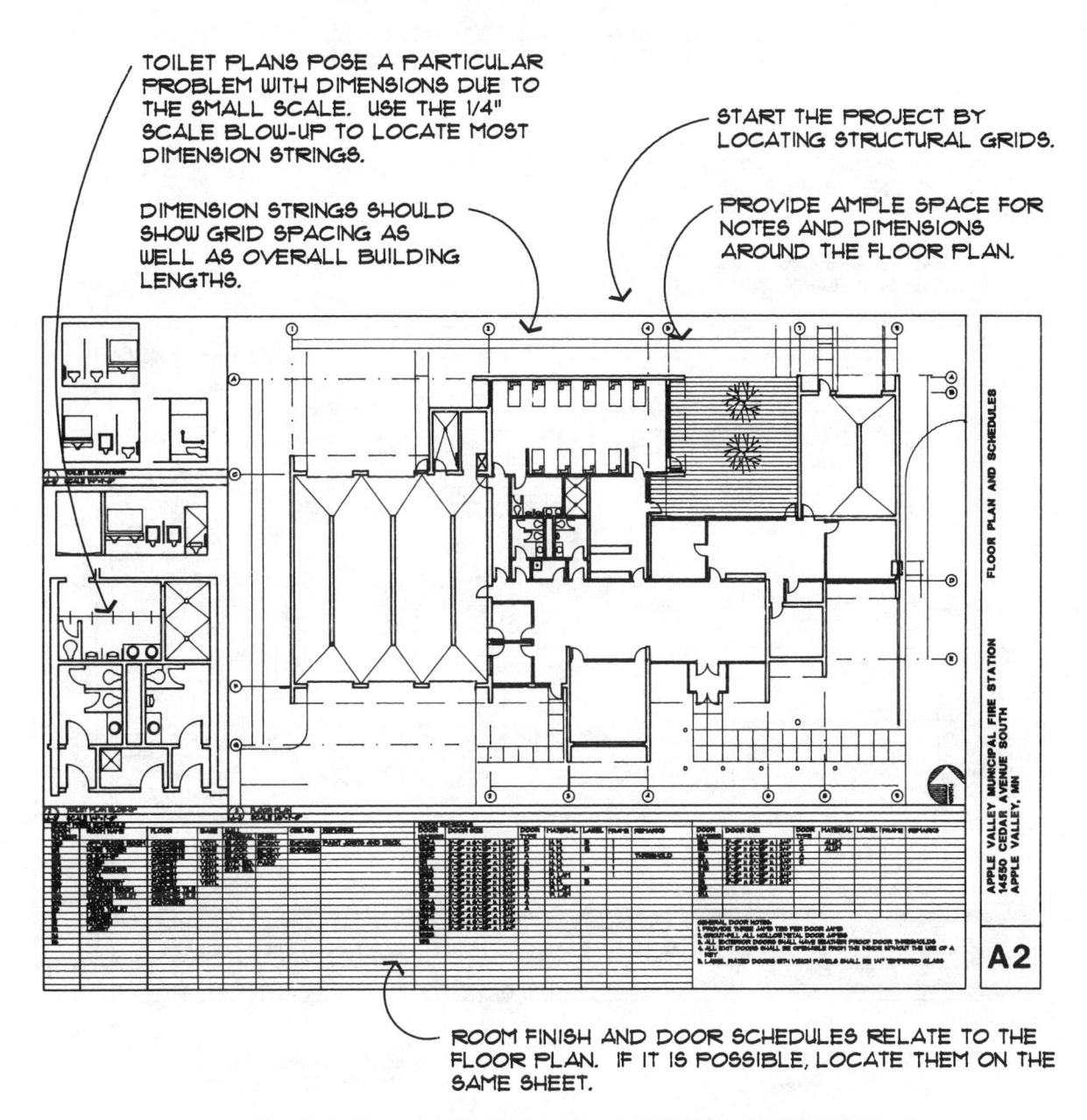

ROOM FINISH AND DOOR SCHEDULES RELATE TO THE FLOOR PLAN. IF IT IS POSSIBLE, LOCATE THEM ON THE SAME SHEET.

WITH THIS TECHNIQUE OF SHEET LAYOUT, USE AS MANY BOXES AS ARE NEEDED TO ACCOMMODATE THE DETAIL, BUT DON'T USE A PARTIAL BOX. THIS METHOD ASSURES GOOD ORGANIZATION.

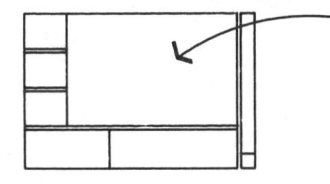

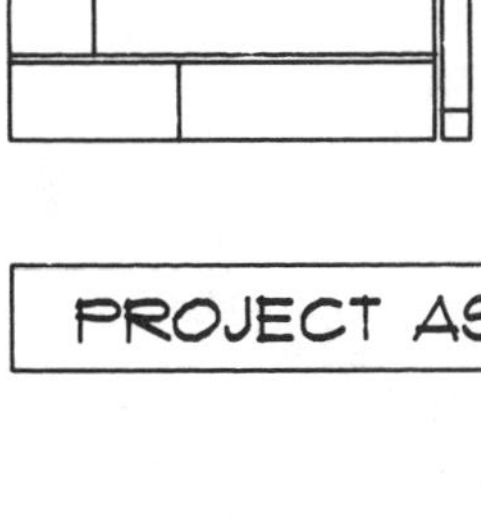

THE SHEET LAYOUT USES 12 RECTANGLES FOR THE FLOOR PLAN. THE THREE SPACES TO THE RIGHT ARE USED FOR TOILET PLAN AND ELEVATION BLOW-UPS. THE FIVE RECTANGLES ALONG THE BOTTOM OF THE SHEET ARE USED FOR ROOM FINISH AND DOOR SCHEDULES.

PROJECT ASSEMBLY TECHNIQUES   7-19

THE ILLUSTRATION BELOW SHOWS A PROPOSED LAYOUT FOR THE ELEVATIONS AND WALL SECTIONS ON SHEET A-3.

MISCELLANEOUS DETAILS (IN THIS CASE, WINDOW TYPES, WALL TYPES, AND CABINETS) CAN BE LOCATED IN AVAILABLE RECTANGLES.

SPACE THE ELEVATIONS WITHIN EACH RECTANGLE. ALLOW SPACE FOR NOTES AND ELEVATION SYMBOLS ALONG ONE SIDE OF THE DRAWING.

ALIGN THE THE DRAWINGS IN EACH RECTANGLE (WHEN POSSIBLE).

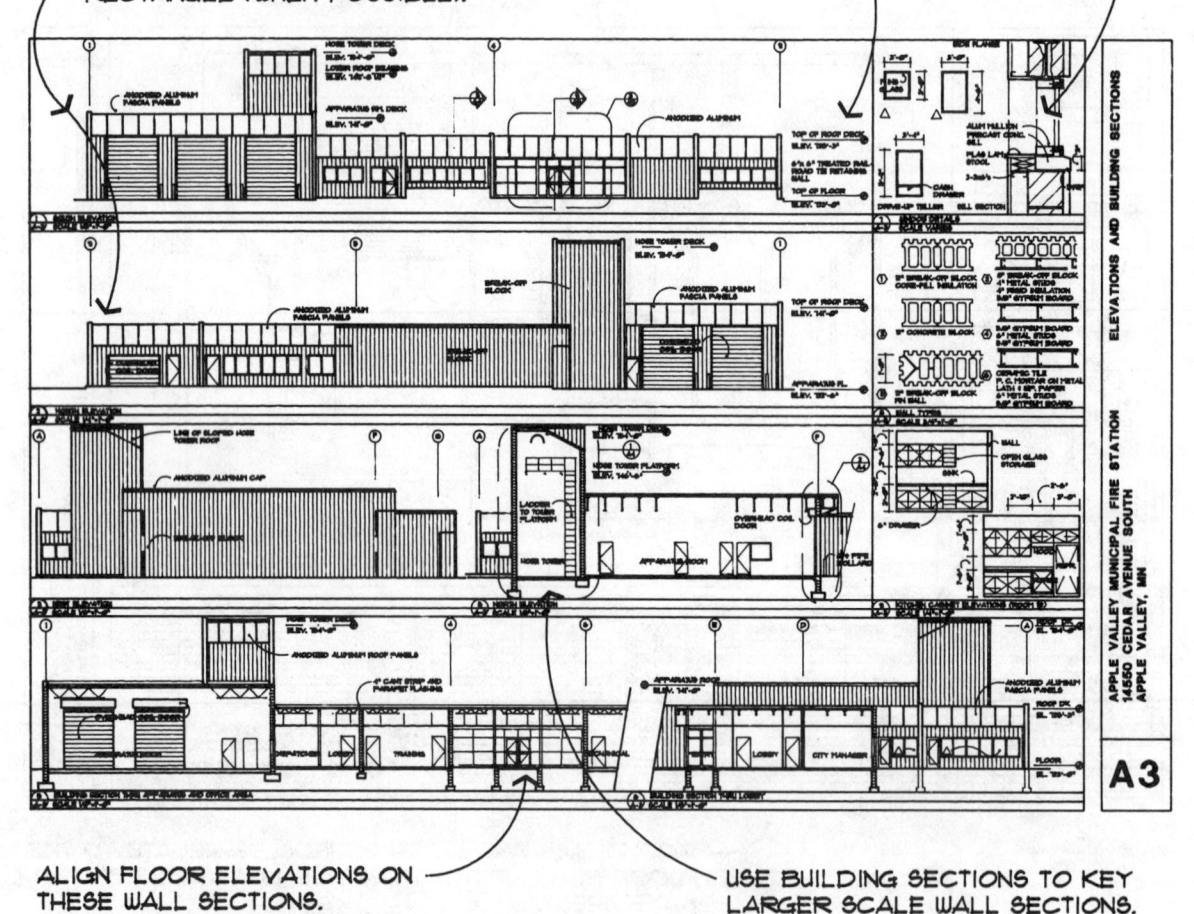

ALIGN FLOOR ELEVATIONS ON THESE WALL SECTIONS.

USE BUILDING SECTIONS TO KEY LARGER SCALE WALL SECTIONS.

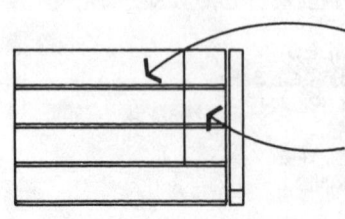

THIS SHEET LAYOUT CONSISTS OF FOUR MAIN HORIZONTAL RECTANGLES. THE ELEVATIONS WON'T FIT THE VERTICAL DIVISIONS, SO THE LINES WERE OMITTED.

MISCELLANEOUS DETAILS ARE LOCATED IN BOXES NOT USED; IT ISN'T WRONG TO LEAVE A BOX BLANK IF NOTHING FITS IN IT.

PROJECT ASSEMBLY TECHNIQUES   7-20

THE ILLUSTRATION BELOW SHOWS ONE POSSIBLE LAYOUT FOR THE FIRST OF TWO WALL-SECTION SHEETS.

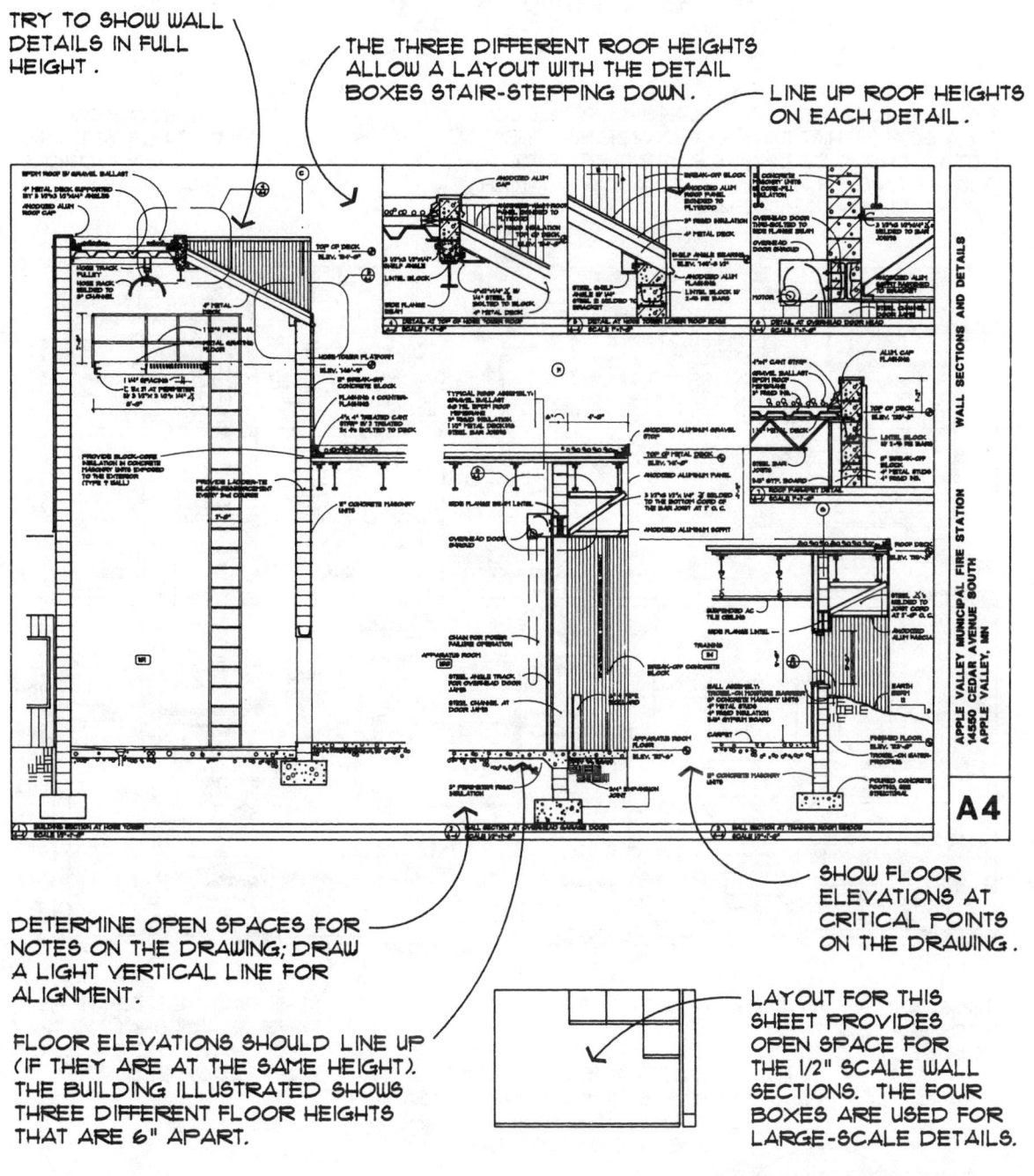

TRY TO SHOW WALL DETAILS IN FULL HEIGHT.

THE THREE DIFFERENT ROOF HEIGHTS ALLOW A LAYOUT WITH THE DETAIL BOXES STAIR-STEPPING DOWN.

LINE UP ROOF HEIGHTS ON EACH DETAIL.

SHOW FLOOR ELEVATIONS AT CRITICAL POINTS ON THE DRAWING.

DETERMINE OPEN SPACES FOR NOTES ON THE DRAWING; DRAW A LIGHT VERTICAL LINE FOR ALIGNMENT.

FLOOR ELEVATIONS SHOULD LINE UP (IF THEY ARE AT THE SAME HEIGHT). THE BUILDING ILLUSTRATED SHOWS THREE DIFFERENT FLOOR HEIGHTS THAT ARE 6" APART.

IT IS NOT NECESSARY TO REPEAT NOTES ON EVERY SIMILAR DETAIL. FOR EXAMPLE, A NOTE INDICATING ROOF CONSTRUCTION WILL BE ASSUMED TO BE THE STANDARD UNLESS IT IS NOTED OTHERWISE.

LAYOUT FOR THIS SHEET PROVIDES OPEN SPACE FOR THE 1/2" SCALE WALL SECTIONS. THE FOUR BOXES ARE USED FOR LARGE-SCALE DETAILS.

THIS DRAWING SHOWS A GOOD BALANCE BETWEEN (1) THE DRAWING, (2) NOTES, AND (3) DIMENSIONS. STAND BACK FROM THE SHEET TO REVIEW THE LAYOUT.

PROJECT ASSEMBLY TECHNIQUES   7-21

THE SHEET LAYOUT FOR THE FINAL DRAWING IN THE PACKAGE IS ILLUSTRATED BELOW. THIS SHEET CONTAINS WALL SECTIONS AND MISCELLANEOUS DETAILS.

DOOR JAMBS ARE SHOWN ON THIS SHEET AND KEYED TO THE FLOOR PLAN SHEET.

THE REFLECTED CEILING PLAN WAS REDUCED TO A SCALE THAT FIT SIX RECTANGLES. THE DETAIL SHOWS CEILING TILE, AIR DIFFUSERS, AND SPRINKLER HEADS, SO DRAWING IT AT AN 1/8" SCALE ISN'T NECESSARY.

THE TWO ROOF DETAILS ARE DRAWN WITH ROOF DECKS THAT ALIGN.

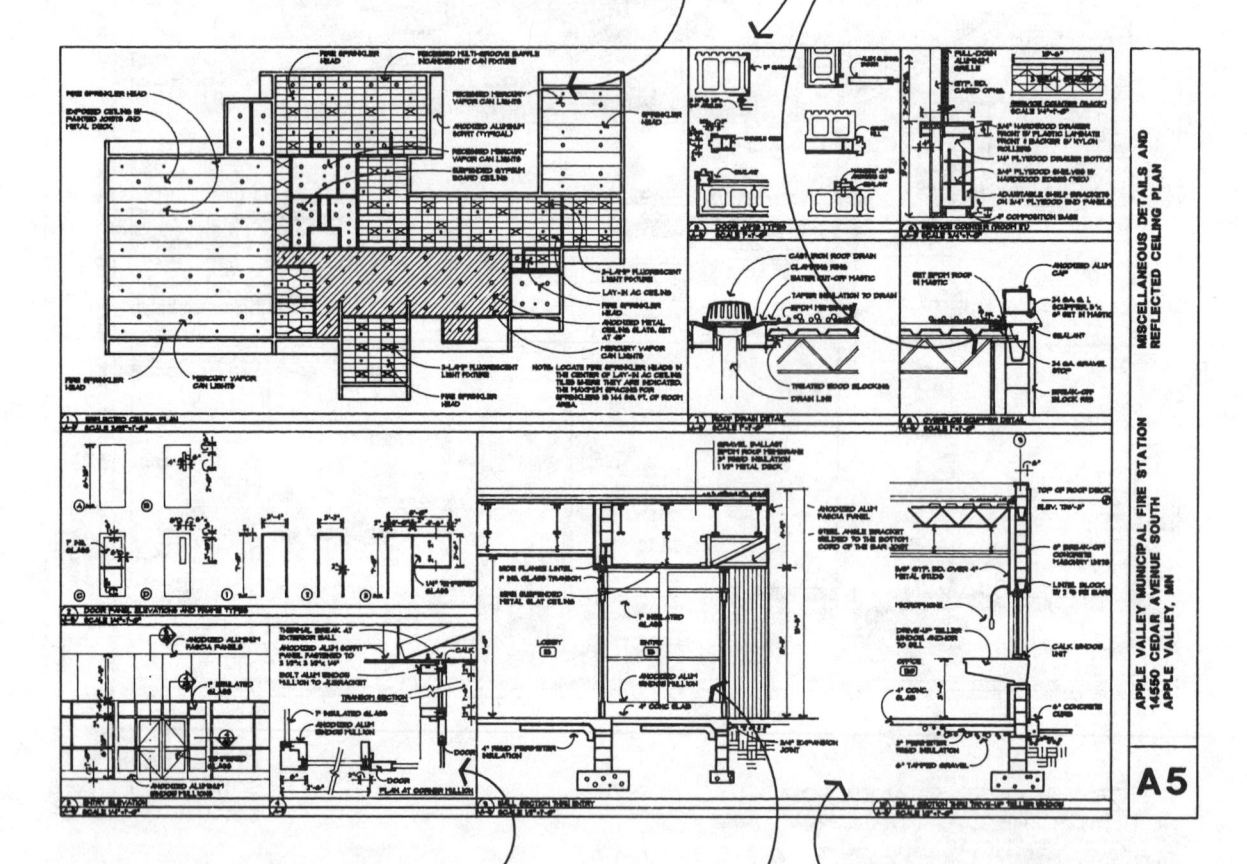

DOOR AND ENTRY DETAILS ARE GROUPED TOGETHER IN THE FOUR RECTANGLES.

THE TWO WALL SECTIONS ARE DRAWN SHOWING THAT THEY HAVE THE SAME ROOF AND FLOOR ELEVATIONS.

THIS DETAIL IS A GOOD EXAMPLE OF NOTE AND DIMENSION LOCATION. USE TRACING PAPER TO ASSIST IN THE LAYOUT.

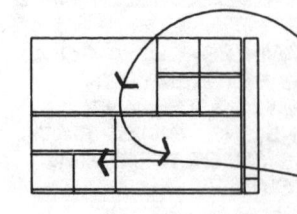

THIS SHEET LAYOUT USES SIX RECTANGLES EACH FOR THE REFLECTED CEILING AND WALL SECTIONS.

ENTRY DOOR DETAILS ARE LOCATED IN THIS AREA.

PROJECT ASSEMBLY TECHNIQUES

7-22

REPLAY

1. DEVELOP FRAMING FOR THE SECOND-FLOOR AND ROOF PLANS BELOW. USE 2 x 10'S FOR THE FLOOR JOISTS, TRUSSES FOR THE GARAGE ROOF AND LINK, AND TJI TRUS JOISTS FOR THE SLOPED ROOF ON THE HOUSE. DRAW A LINE ON THE PLAN FOR EACH JOIST OR TRUSS.

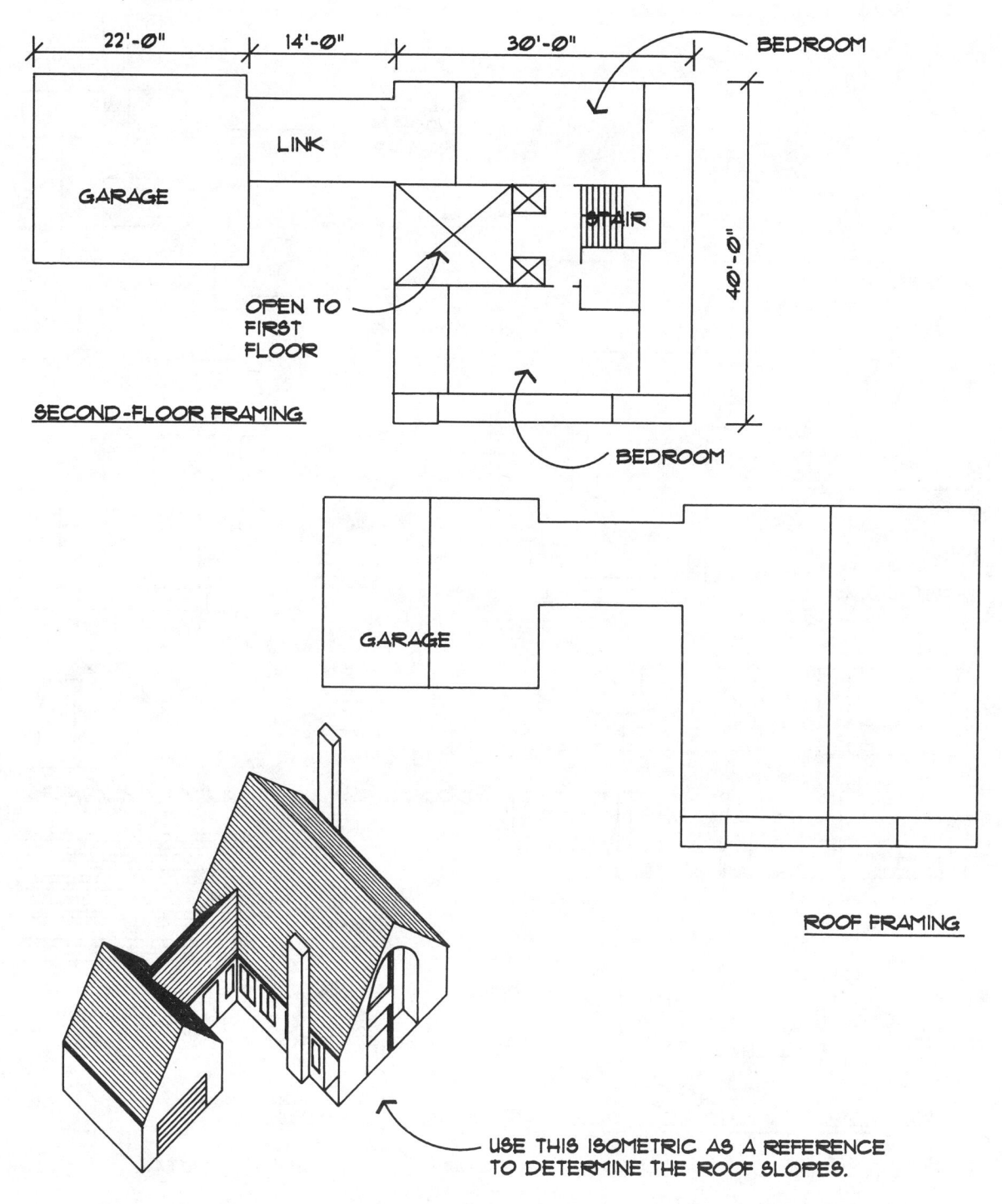

22'-0" | 14'-0" | 30'-0"

GARAGE | LINK | BEDROOM

40'-0"

STAIR

OPEN TO FIRST FLOOR

BEDROOM

SECOND-FLOOR FRAMING

GARAGE

ROOF FRAMING

USE THIS ISOMETRIC AS A REFERENCE TO DETERMINE THE ROOF SLOPES.

PROJECT ASSEMBLY TECHNIQUES   T-23

2. USE THE DRAWINGS ON THIS PAGE TO ASSEMBLE A SHEET LAYOUT FOR THE HOUSE PROJECT SHOWN ON PAGE 2-23. SKETCH YOUR SOLUTION FOR SHEETS A-1 THROUGH A-5 ON PAGES 7-24 AND 7-25 (USE THE SAME SCALE SHOWN ON THIS PAGE FOR YOUR SKETCH.)

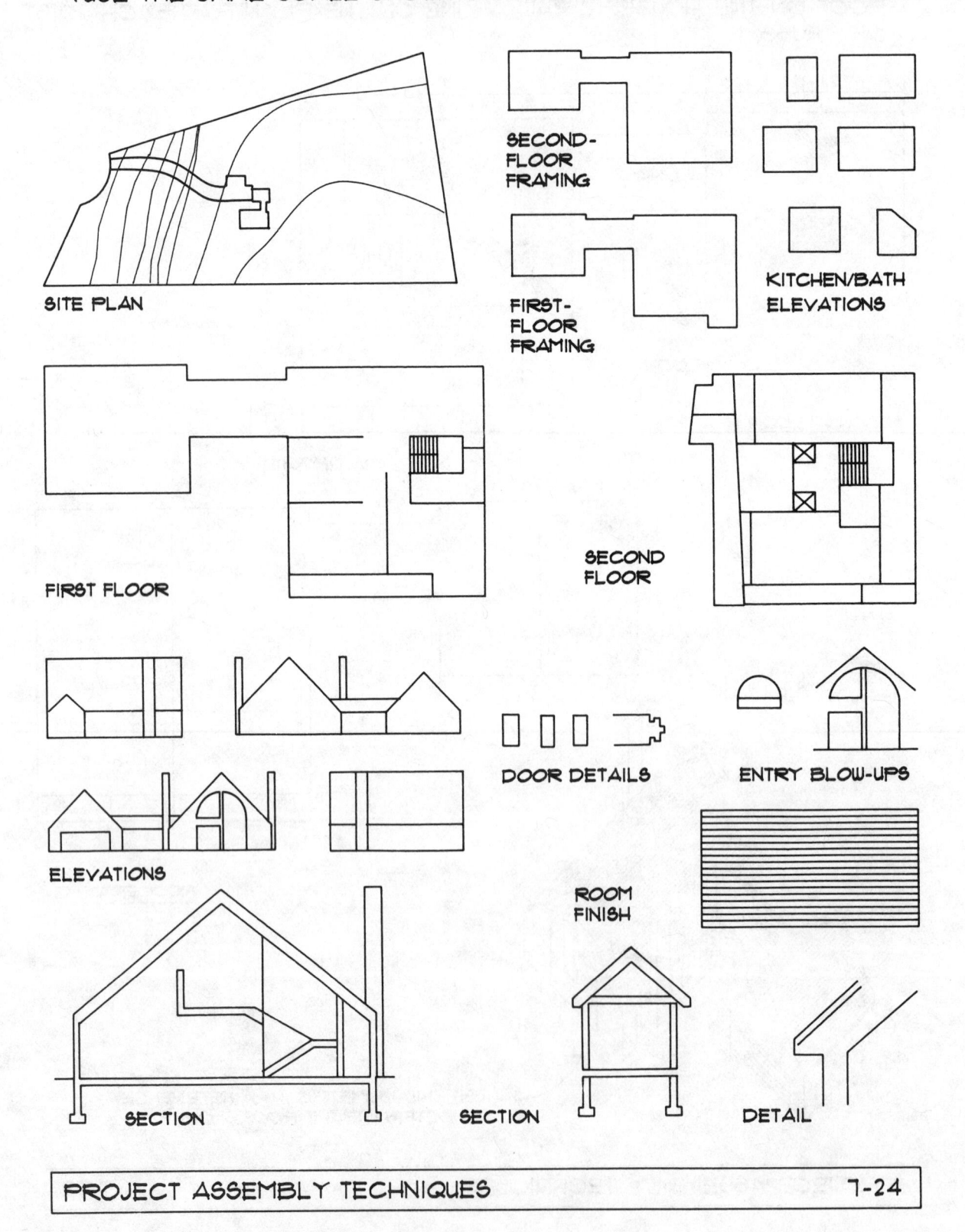

SITE PLAN

SECOND-FLOOR FRAMING

FIRST-FLOOR FRAMING

KITCHEN/BATH ELEVATIONS

FIRST FLOOR

SECOND FLOOR

DOOR DETAILS

ENTRY BLOW-UPS

ELEVATIONS

ROOM FINISH

SECTION

SECTION

DETAIL

PROJECT ASSEMBLY TECHNIQUES 7-24

USE THIS SPACE FOR
LAYOUT OF SHEET A-1

A-1

A-2

USE THIS SPACE FOR
LAYOUT OF SHEET A-2

USE THIS SPACE FOR
LAYOUT OF SHEET A-3

A-3

PROJECT ASSEMBLY TECHNIQUES 7-25

USE THIS SPACE FOR
LAYOUT OF SHEET A-4

A-4

USE THIS SPACE FOR
LAYOUT OF SHEET A-5

A-5

PROJECT ASSEMBLY TECHNIQUES 7-26

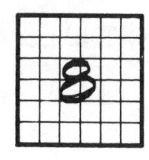

8 COMPUTER AIDED DRAFTING

COMPUTER AIDED DRAFTING (CAD) HAS HAD A DRAMATIC EFFECT ON THE ASSEMBLY OF ARCHITECTURAL WORKING DRAWINGS. CAD IS NOT SIMPLY A DIFFERENT WAY TO DRAW LINES; IT IS A SMARTER WAY TO DRAW. THIS UNIT WILL EXPLORE SEVERAL CHARACTERISTICS THAT MAKE CAD DRAFTING UNIQUE.

SINCE THERE ARE MORE THAN 100 CAD PACKAGES ON THE MARKET, THIS MATERIAL WILL NOT ATTEMPT TO ADDRESS SPECIFIC DRAFTING TASKS, BUT WE WILL REVIEW MANY EXAMPLES OF WHAT MAKES COMPUTER DRAFTING FASTER AND SMARTER. IF ONE WORD COULD BE USED TO SUM UP THE QUALITIES OF CAD, IT WOULD BE MANIPULATE. THIS MEANS THAT WITH CAD A DRAWING IS NO LONGER FIXED TO A PIECE OF PAPER; IT CAN BE MOVED, COPIED, ROTATED, CHANGED IN SCALE, OR PLACED ON A SEPARATE LAYER. THERE HAS TRADITIONALLY BEEN A GREAT DEAL OF REPETITION IN ARCHITECTURAL DRAWING; CAD, HOWEVER, ALLOWS DETAILS TO BE TRANSFERRED FROM SET TO SET WITHOUT REPEATED DRAWING. FIRST, LET'S REVIEW SOME CAD TASKS.

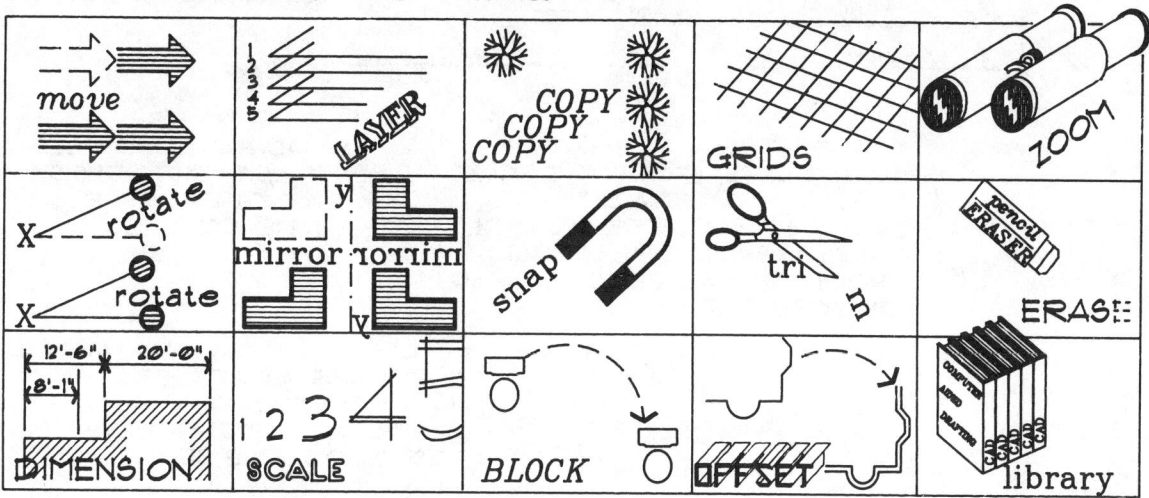

move	LAYER	COPY COPY COPY	GRIDS	ZOOM
rotate	mirror	snap	trim	ERASE
DIMENSION	SCALE	BLOCK	OFFSET	library

COMPUTER AIDED DRAFTING — 8-1

THE NEXT SEVERAL PAGES ILLUSTRATE CAD TECHNIQUES THAT WILL MAKE THE ASSEMBLY OF DRAWINGS FASTER.

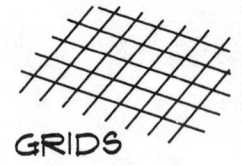

GRIDS — CAD SYSTEMS HAVE A GRID SETTING THAT WILL MAKE PLAN LAYOUT FASTER. THE PLAN BELOW WAS DRAWN USING A 12" GRID SETTING.

library — A CAD LIBRARY ALLOWS THE USE OF DRAWINGS FROM OTHER FILES. THIS PLAN SHOWS ITEMS SUCH AS DOORS AND WINDOWS THAT HAVE BEEN TRANSFERRED FROM ANOTHER DRAWING.

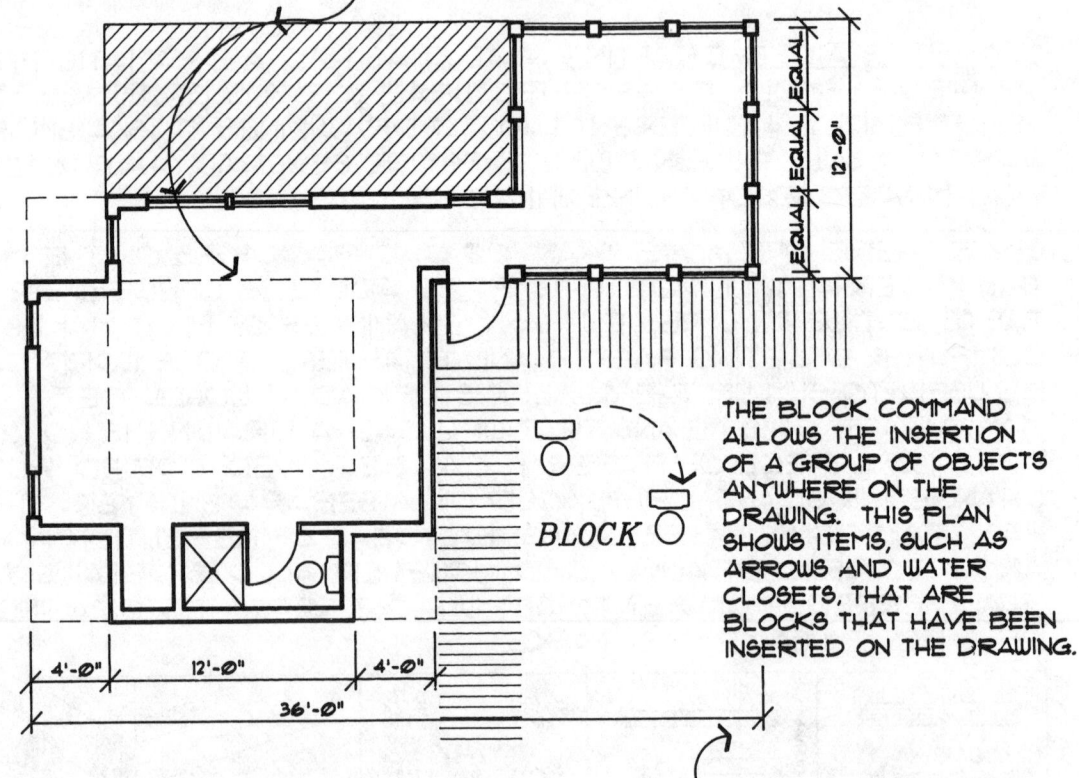

LINE TYPES (SUCH AS DASHED) AND HEAVIER LINES CAN BE EASILY SET WITH CAD.

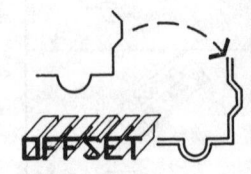

BLOCK — THE BLOCK COMMAND ALLOWS THE INSERTION OF A GROUP OF OBJECTS ANYWHERE ON THE DRAWING. THIS PLAN SHOWS ITEMS, SUCH AS ARROWS AND WATER CLOSETS, THAT ARE BLOCKS THAT HAVE BEEN INSERTED ON THE DRAWING.

OFFSET — THE OFFSET TASK ALLOWS ITEMS SUCH AS LINES, ARCS, AND CIRCLES TO BE DUPLICATED A SET DISTANCE FROM THE ORIGINAL. THIS PLAN SHOWS DOUBLE WALL LINES THAT HAVE BEEN GENERATED USING OFFSET.

CAD PACKAGES WILL ALLOW YOU TO DESIGN ARROWHEADS FOR DIMENSION LINES.

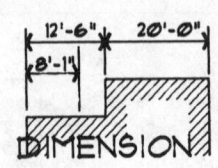

DIMENSION — THE DIMENSION TASK AUTOMATICALLY PLACES ARROWS, LEADER LINES, AND DIMENSION STRINGS ON A DRAWING. ALL DIMENSIONS ON THESE PLANS HAVE BEEN PLACED USING THE COMMAND.

COMPUTER AIDED DRAFTING 8-2

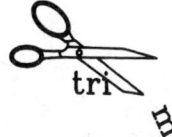

THE TRIM COMMAND ESTABLISHES AN OBJECT THAT ACTS AS A CUTTING-EDGE TO TRIM ALL OBJECTS. TRIM WAS USED ON THIS ELEVATION TO CUT THE SIDING OFF AT THE ROOF LINE.

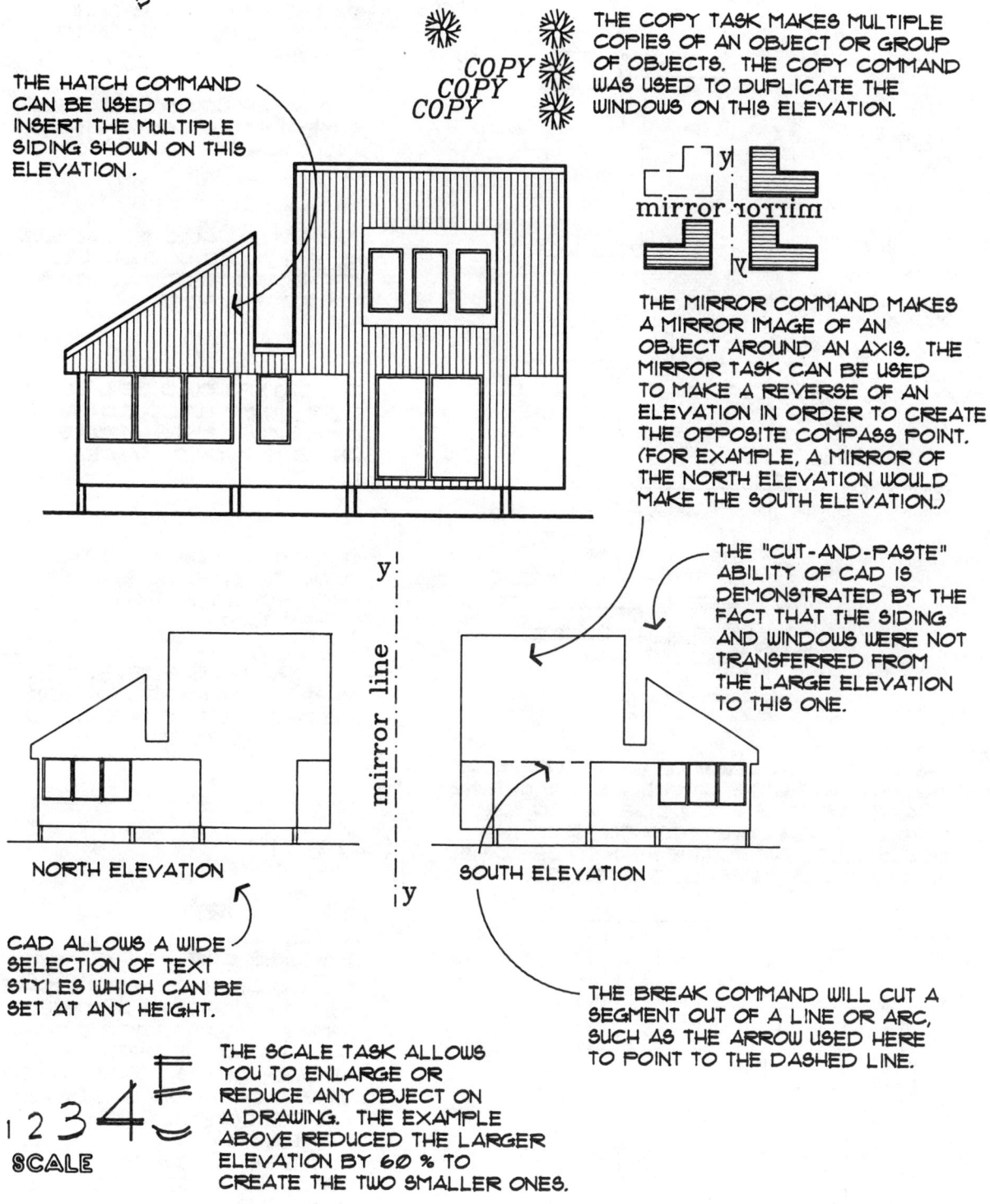

THE COPY TASK MAKES MULTIPLE COPIES OF AN OBJECT OR GROUP OF OBJECTS. THE COPY COMMAND WAS USED TO DUPLICATE THE WINDOWS ON THIS ELEVATION.

THE HATCH COMMAND CAN BE USED TO INSERT THE MULTIPLE SIDING SHOWN ON THIS ELEVATION.

THE MIRROR COMMAND MAKES A MIRROR IMAGE OF AN OBJECT AROUND AN AXIS. THE MIRROR TASK CAN BE USED TO MAKE A REVERSE OF AN ELEVATION IN ORDER TO CREATE THE OPPOSITE COMPASS POINT. (FOR EXAMPLE, A MIRROR OF THE NORTH ELEVATION WOULD MAKE THE SOUTH ELEVATION.)

THE "CUT-AND-PASTE" ABILITY OF CAD IS DEMONSTRATED BY THE FACT THAT THE SIDING AND WINDOWS WERE NOT TRANSFERRED FROM THE LARGE ELEVATION TO THIS ONE.

NORTH ELEVATION

SOUTH ELEVATION

CAD ALLOWS A WIDE SELECTION OF TEXT STYLES WHICH CAN BE SET AT ANY HEIGHT.

THE BREAK COMMAND WILL CUT A SEGMENT OUT OF A LINE OR ARC, SUCH AS THE ARROW USED HERE TO POINT TO THE DASHED LINE.

THE SCALE TASK ALLOWS YOU TO ENLARGE OR REDUCE ANY OBJECT ON A DRAWING. THE EXAMPLE ABOVE REDUCED THE LARGER ELEVATION BY 60 % TO CREATE THE TWO SMALLER ONES.

COMPUTER AIDED DRAFTING | 8-3

USING LAYERS IS SIMILAR TO PLACING PORTIONS OF A DRAWING ON SHEETS OF GLASS. IT IS POSSIBLE TO TURN LAYERS "ON" OR "OFF," WHICH ALLOWS PRINTING SELECTIVE PORTIONS OF THE DRAWING.

A CROSSHATCH PATTERN CALLED DOTS WAS USED TO DEFINE THE PLANS SHOWN TO THE LEFT.

BASE

THIS LAYER COULD BE LABELED BASE; IT WOULD CONTAIN THE WALLS FOR THE PLAN.

NOTE

THIS LAYER COULD BE LABELED NOTE; IT WOULD CONTAIN ALL OF THE ARCHITECTURAL NOTES FOR THE PROJECT.

DIMENSION

THIS LAYER COULD BE LABELED DIMENSION; IT WOULD CONTAIN DIMENSION STRINGS, ARROWS, AND DIMENSION DISTANCES.

THIS DRAWING DISPLAYS THE PLAN WITH BASE, NOTE, AND DIMENSION LAYERS ALL TURNED "ON."

THIS DRAWING WAS DEVELOPED USING A 3-D TASK THAT ALLOWS THE DRAWING TO CONVERGE TO A VANISHING POINT.

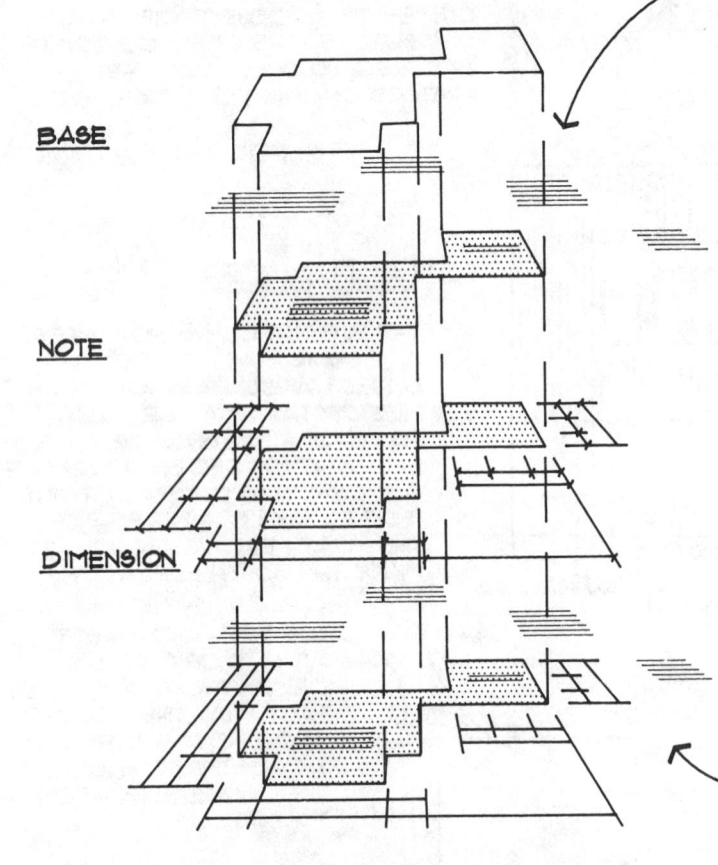

THE LAYER TASK COULD BE USED TO DEVELOP THE FRAMING PLAN SHOWN BELOW. THE OUTLINE PLAN (LAYER BASE) COULD BE TURNED "ON" WITH ALL OTHER LAYERS TURNED "OFF." THIS WOULD ALLOW THE OUTLINE PLAN TO BE COPIED WITHOUT TRANSFERRING OTHER OBJECTS.

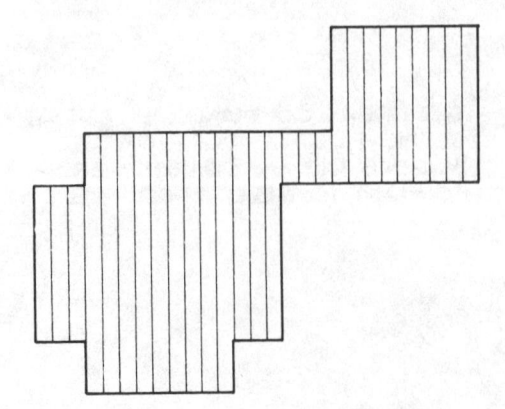

array

THE ARRAY COMMAND WILL MAKE MULTIPLE COPIES OF AN OBJECT. ARRAY DIFFERS FROM THE COPY TASK IN THAT THE DISTANCE BETWEEN COPIES, AS WELL AS THE NUMBER OF COPIES, CAN BE KEYED INTO THE COMPUTER WITH ARRAY. THE FRAMING PLAN ILLUSTRATED TO THE LEFT USED ARRAY TO DUPLICATE FLOOR JOISTS AT 16" ON CENTER.

COMPUTER AIDED DRAFTING 8-4

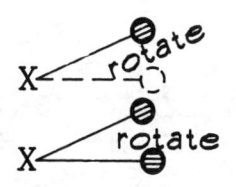

THE ROTATE COMMAND ALLOWS YOU TO TURN AN OBJECT AROUND A POINT. THE SECTION BELOW USED ROTATE TO CHANGE THE ANGLE OF THE SKYLIGHT FROM THE ROOF TO THE SLOPED WALL.

THE ERASE TASK WILL DELETE SELECTED OBJECTS ON A DRAWING. ERASE MAY BE USED TO ELIMINATE INDIVIDUAL ITEMS OR ENTIRE SPACES USING A WINDOW COMMAND.

THE ORIGINAL CAD SECTION HERE WAS DRAWN USING VARIOUS COLORS. THIS TRANSLATES TO CHANGES IN LINE WEIGHT WHEN THE DRAWING IS PLOTTED.

THE ZOOM TASK ALLOWS PORTIONS OF THE DRAWING TO BE MAGNIFIED. THIS COMMAND CAN BE USED TO ADD DETAIL TO VERY SMALL PORTIONS OF A DRAWING.

THIS DRAWING WAS DEVELOPED BY COPYING AND SCALING ONE OF THE ELEVATIONS.

A PRECISE ANGLE (IN THIS CASE A 7/12 ROOF PITCH) CAN BE EASILY DRAWN WITH CAD.

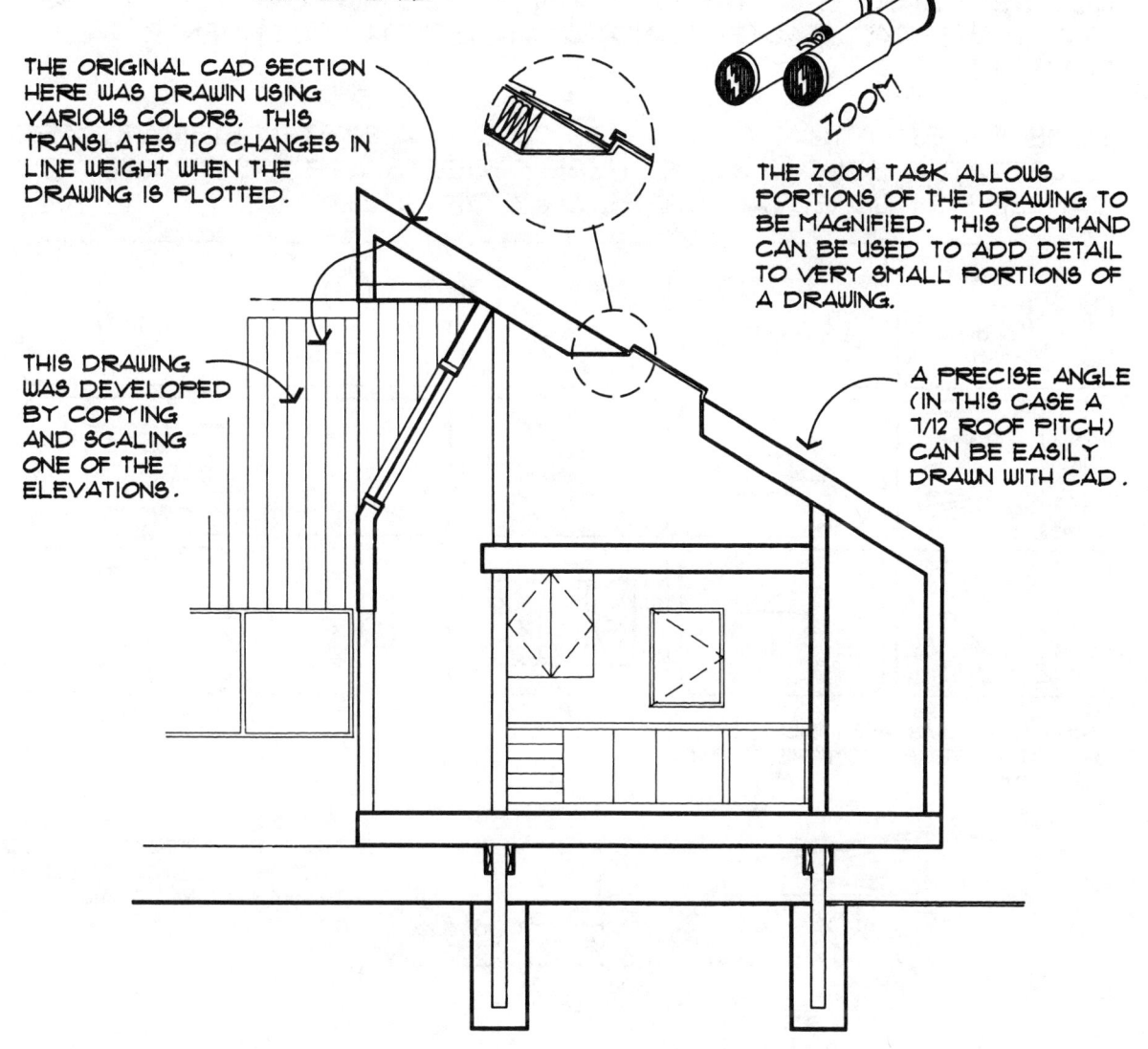

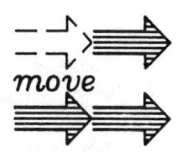

THE MOVE COMMAND WILL ALLOW OBJECTS TO BE RELOCATED ON THE DRAWING. THIS ENTIRE SECTION DRAWING WAS MOVED SLIGHTLY TO THE LEFT BY PLACING A WINDOW AROUND THE SPACE.

MOST CAD PACKAGES CONTAIN A VARIETY OF SNAP COMMANDS THAT ALLOW PRECISE LOCATION OF LINES. SOME OF THESE TASKS WILL LOCK ON TO THE FOLLOWING: THE END POINT OF A LINE, ITS MIDDLE, THE CENTER OF A CIRCLE, OR THE INTERSECTION OF TWO LINES.

COMPUTER AIDED DRAFTING — 8-5

THE FIRST PORTION OF THIS UNIT ILLUSTRATED SEVERAL CAD TASKS THAT ARE COMMON TO SYSTEMS SUCH AS AUTOCAD, CADVANCE, AND CADKEY. MOST CAD PACKAGES CAN BE CUSTOMIZED TO MEET THE SPECIFIC NEEDS OF THE USER. FOR EXAMPLE, AN ARCHITECTURAL FIRM WOULD REQUIRE A VERY DIFFERENT CUSTOMIZED SYSTEM FROM THE ONE NEEDED BY A CIVIL ENGINEERING OFFICE. THIS SECTION WILL REVIEW SOME OF THE COMMANDS SPECIFIC TO ARCHITECTURE THAT MAKE CAD "FASTER" AND "SMARTER" THAN CONVENTIONAL DRAFTING.

SOME SYMBOLS THAT COULD BE FOUND IN A SYSTEM LIBRARY ARE ILLUSTRATED BELOW. SINCE THESE OBJECTS ARE PREDRAWN, THEY CAN BE POSITIONED ANYWHERE ON A DRAWING.

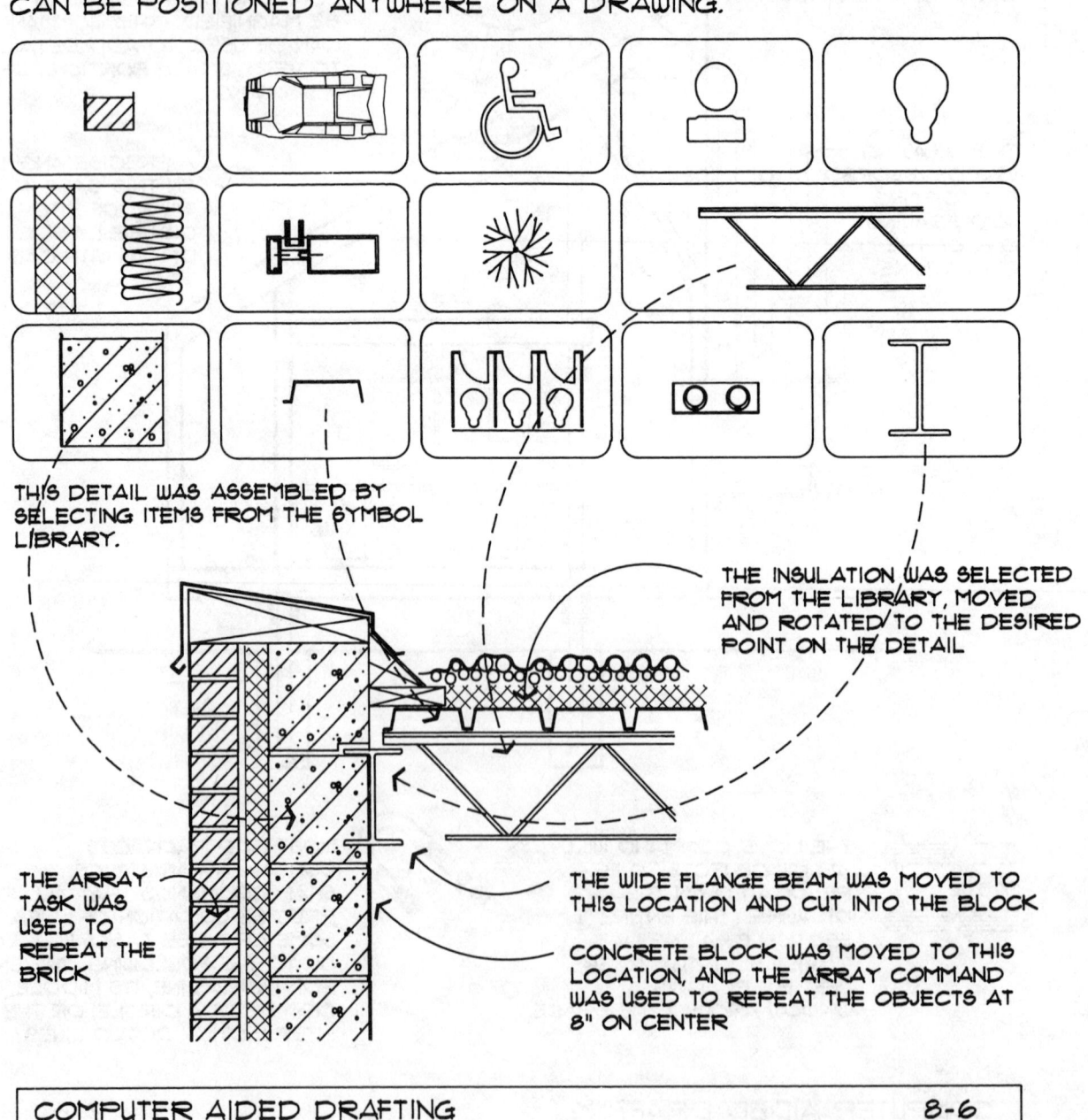

THIS DETAIL WAS ASSEMBLED BY SELECTING ITEMS FROM THE SYMBOL LIBRARY.

THE INSULATION WAS SELECTED FROM THE LIBRARY, MOVED AND ROTATED TO THE DESIRED POINT ON THE DETAIL

THE ARRAY TASK WAS USED TO REPEAT THE BRICK

THE WIDE FLANGE BEAM WAS MOVED TO THIS LOCATION AND CUT INTO THE BLOCK

CONCRETE BLOCK WAS MOVED TO THIS LOCATION, AND THE ARRAY COMMAND WAS USED TO REPEAT THE OBJECTS AT 8" ON CENTER

COMPUTER AIDED DRAFTING   8-6

THE SYMBOLS JUST ILLUSTRATED ARE SITUATED IN BLOCKS THAT CAN BE SELECTED FROM A MENU AND LOCATED ANYWHERE ON A DRAWING. THE FOLLOWING SECTION WILL ILLUSTRATE A NUMBER OF SPECIFIC COMPUTER TASKS THAT USE A BLOCK WITH A SET OF INSTRUCTIONS FOR ITS PLACEMENT (AUTOCAD CALLS THIS "AUTOLISP"). A GOOD WAY TO UNDERSTAND THIS PRINCIPLE IS TO STUDY THE DOOR PLACEMENT TASK SHOWN BELOW.

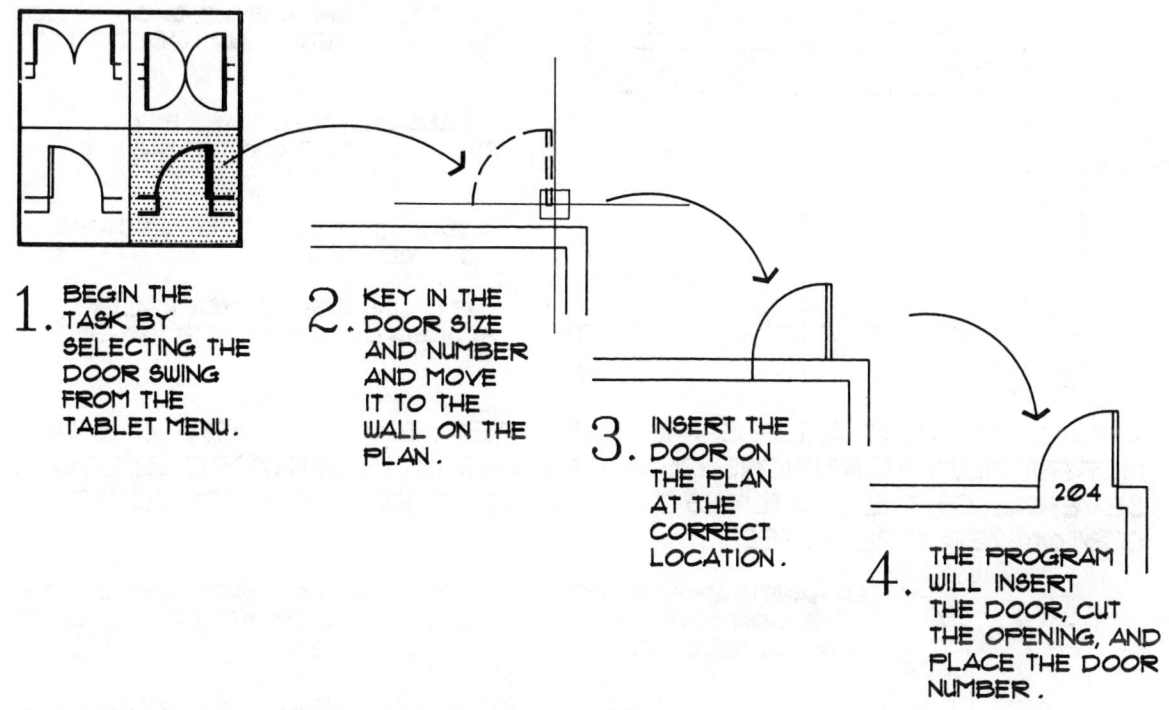

1. BEGIN THE TASK BY SELECTING THE DOOR SWING FROM THE TABLET MENU.

2. KEY IN THE DOOR SIZE AND NUMBER AND MOVE IT TO THE WALL ON THE PLAN.

3. INSERT THE DOOR ON THE PLAN AT THE CORRECT LOCATION.

4. THE PROGRAM WILL INSERT THE DOOR, CUT THE OPENING, AND PLACE THE DOOR NUMBER.

A TASK THAT SPEEDS DRAWING FLOOR PLANS WILL AUTOMATICALLY CLEAN UP WALL INTERSECTIONS. THE FOLLOWING STEPS SHOW THE PROCESS OF TRIMMING A TEE WALL.

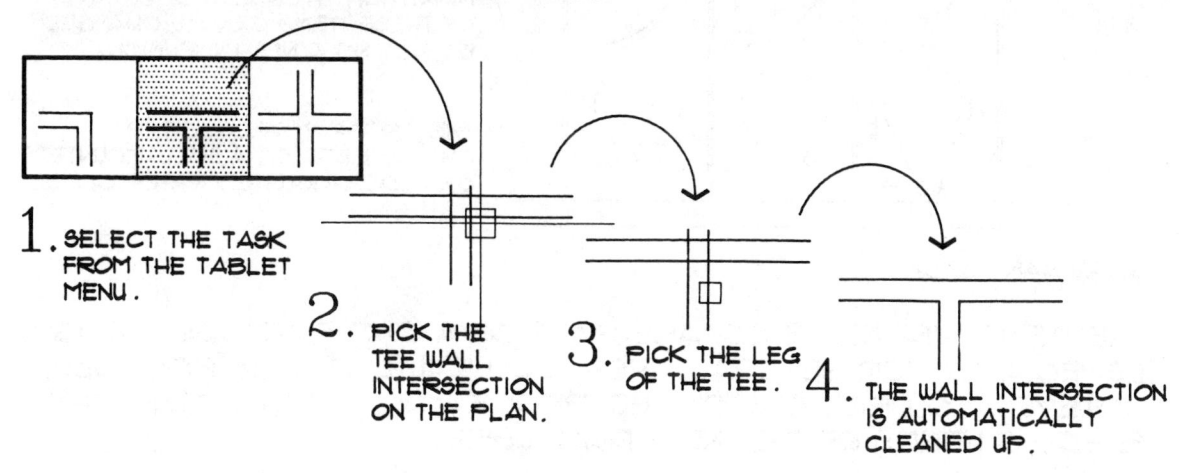

1. SELECT THE TASK FROM THE TABLET MENU.

2. PICK THE TEE WALL INTERSECTION ON THE PLAN.

3. PICK THE LEG OF THE TEE.

4. THE WALL INTERSECTION IS AUTOMATICALLY CLEANED UP.

COMPUTER AIDED DRAFTING 8-7

THE NEXT SEVERAL EXAMPLES ILLUSTRATE CAD PROGRAMMING FEATURES THAT ALLOW USER INPUT. THE FIRST COMMAND WE WILL LOOK AT PLACES STRUCTURAL GRID MARKERS ON A DRAWING. IN ADDITION TO SETTING THE GRID LINE, THIS FUNCTION AUTOMATICALLY NUMBERS (OR LETTERS) THE GRID AND POSITIONS THE NEXT LINE AT A DISTANCE THAT HAS BEEN KEYED.

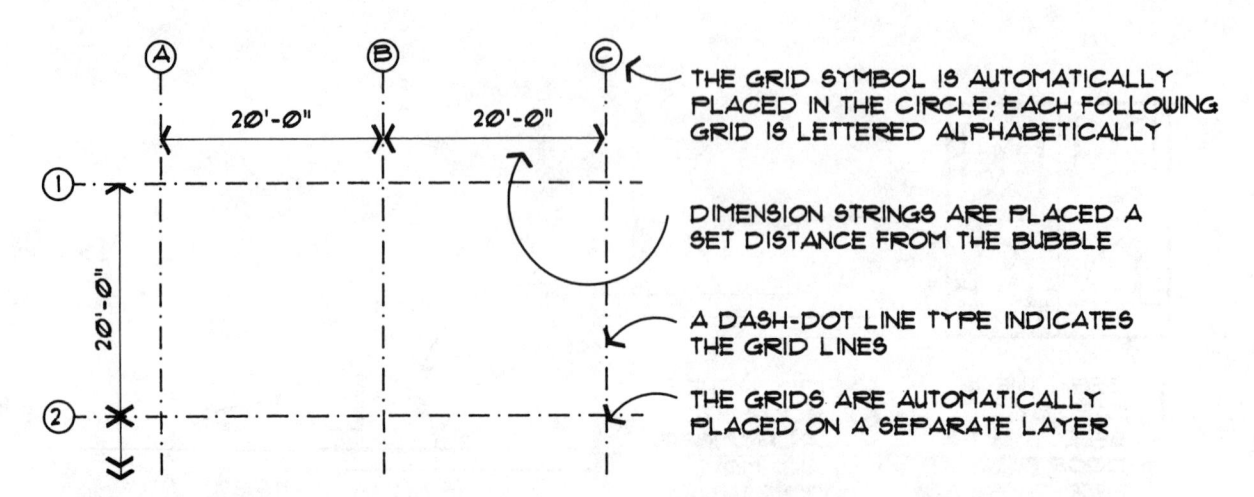

THE GRID SYMBOL IS AUTOMATICALLY PLACED IN THE CIRCLE; EACH FOLLOWING GRID IS LETTERED ALPHABETICALLY

DIMENSION STRINGS ARE PLACED A SET DISTANCE FROM THE BUBBLE

A DASH-DOT LINE TYPE INDICATES THE GRID LINES

THE GRIDS ARE AUTOMATICALLY PLACED ON A SEPARATE LAYER

A FUNCTION THAT ALLOWS THE CAD OPERATOR TO INSERT ONE OR MORE TOILET PARTITIONS ON A DRAWING IS ILLUSTRATED BELOW. SEVERAL OF THE FEATURES THAT ALLOW THESE OBJECTS TO BE CUSTOMIZED ARE NOTED.

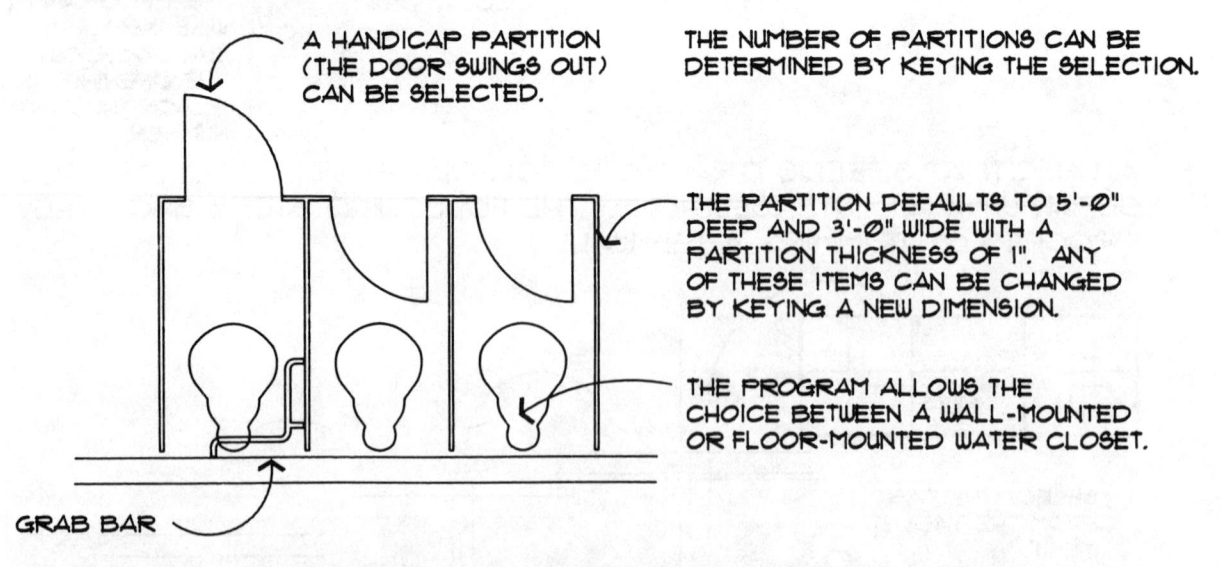

A HANDICAP PARTITION (THE DOOR SWINGS OUT) CAN BE SELECTED.

THE NUMBER OF PARTITIONS CAN BE DETERMINED BY KEYING THE SELECTION.

THE PARTITION DEFAULTS TO 5'-0" DEEP AND 3'-0" WIDE WITH A PARTITION THICKNESS OF 1". ANY OF THESE ITEMS CAN BE CHANGED BY KEYING A NEW DIMENSION.

THE PROGRAM ALLOWS THE CHOICE BETWEEN A WALL-MOUNTED OR FLOOR-MOUNTED WATER CLOSET.

GRAB BAR

THE ITEMS JUST REVIEWED ARE PART OF A CAD PACKAGE DESIGNED ESPECIALLY FOR GENERAL ARCHITECTURAL USE. IT IS POSSIBLE, HOWEVER, TO WRITE CUSTOMIZED PROGRAMS THAT WILL MEET THE SPECIFIC NEEDS OF THE INDIVIDUAL USER.

| COMPUTER AIDED DRAFTING | 8-8 |

SCALE

ALL DRAWINGS DONE IN CAD ARE DRAWN AT FULL SCALE. SCALE IS INTRODUCED ONLY WHEN THE DRAWING IS PLOTTED. THE DIMENSIONS OF A DRAWING MUST BE CONSIDERED WHEN THE FINAL COPY IS PRINTED. THIS IS ACCOMPLISHED BY USING THE SCALE FACTOR OF THE DRAWING. THE SCALE FACTOR IS THE RATIO BETWEEN THE ARCHITECTURAL SCALE AND THE FULL-SIZED DRAWING. FOR EXAMPLE, THE SCALE FACTOR OF A FLOOR PLAN PLOTTED TO 1/8"=1'-0" WOULD BE 96 (8 UNITS PER INCH TIMES 12 INCHES = 96). IN OTHER WORDS, AN 1/8"=1'-0" DRAWING WOULD BE ENLARGED 96 TIMES TO MAKE IT FULL SIZE. THE EXAMPLE BELOW SHOWS AN 18" x 24" SHEET THAT WILL BE DRAWN AT A 1/4"=1'-0" SCALE (THAT SCALE WOULD SET THE SCALE FACTOR AT 48). THE SHEET SIZE OF THE DRAWING WOULD USE THE INDICATED LIMITS TO PLOT AT THE PROPER SCALE.

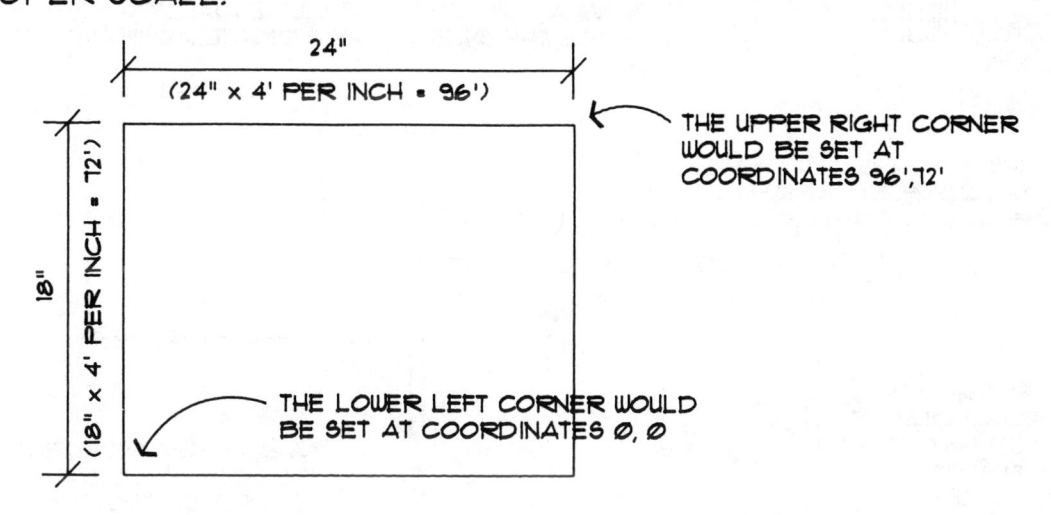

24"
(24" x 4' PER INCH = 96')
18"
(18" x 4' PER INCH = 72')

THE UPPER RIGHT CORNER WOULD BE SET AT COORDINATES 96',72'

THE LOWER LEFT CORNER WOULD BE SET AT COORDINATES 0, 0

CABIN CAD PROJECT

THE FINAL SECTION OF THIS UNIT WILL ILLUSTRATE A STEP-BY-STEP ASSEMBLY OF THE FIRST SHEET OF DRAWINGS FOR A CABIN PROJECT. THE NOTES WILL CONCENTRATE ON HOW USING CAD TASKS WOULD DIFFER FROM DRAWING A PROJECT MANUALLY.

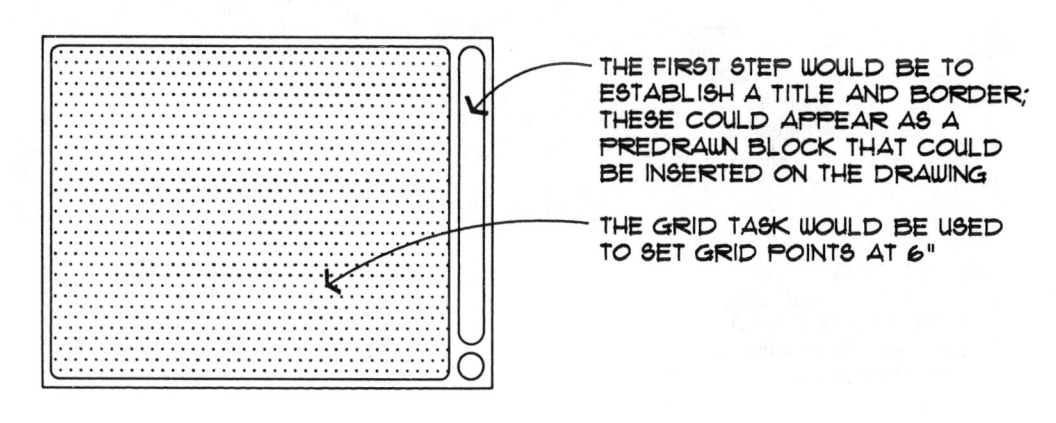

THE FIRST STEP WOULD BE TO ESTABLISH A TITLE AND BORDER; THESE COULD APPEAR AS A PREDRAWN BLOCK THAT COULD BE INSERTED ON THE DRAWING

THE GRID TASK WOULD BE USED TO SET GRID POINTS AT 6"

COMPUTER AIDED DRAFTING

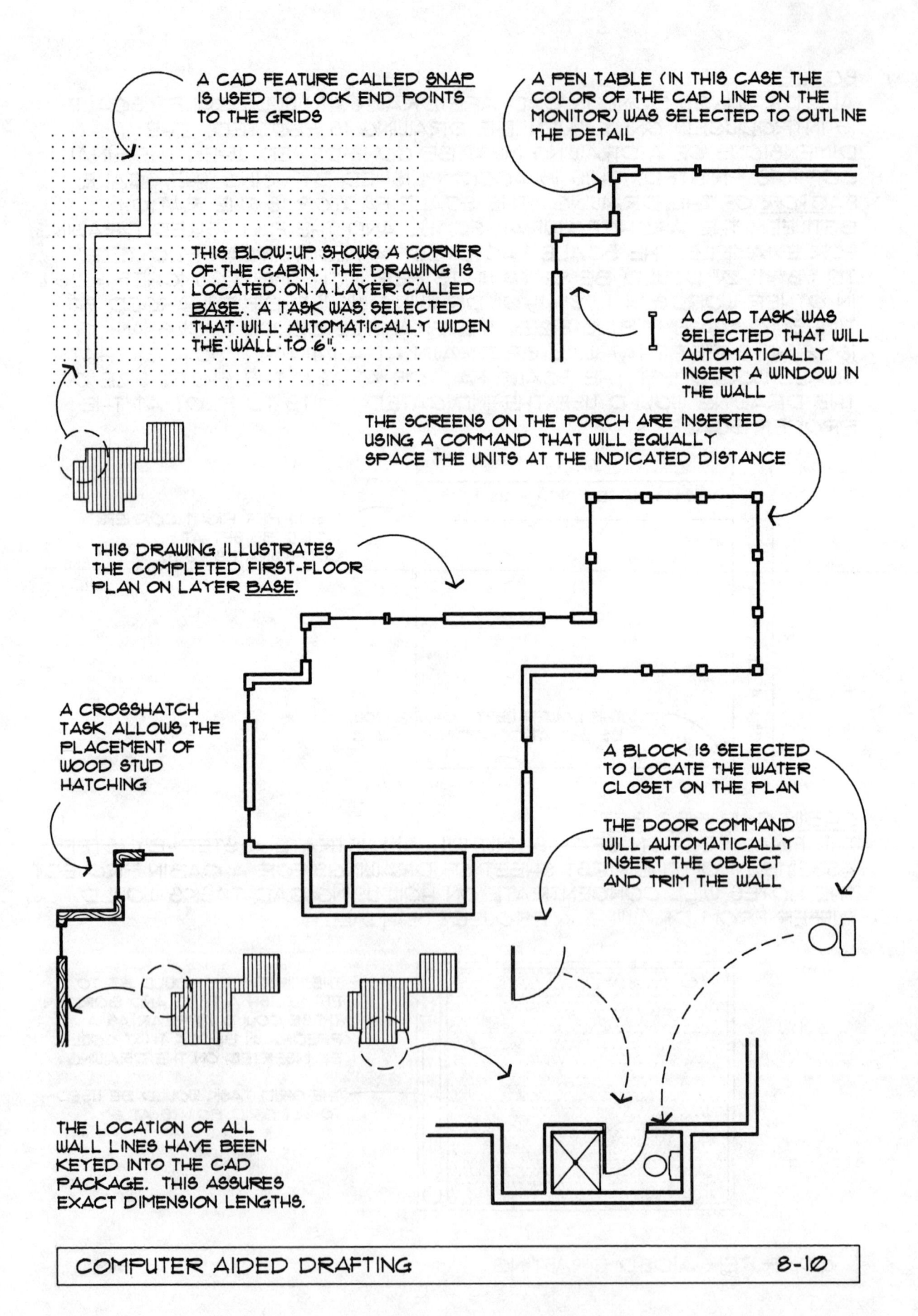

A CAD FEATURE CALLED SNAP IS USED TO LOCK END POINTS TO THE GRIDS

A PEN TABLE (IN THIS CASE THE COLOR OF THE CAD LINE ON THE MONITOR) WAS SELECTED TO OUTLINE THE DETAIL

THIS BLOW-UP SHOWS A CORNER OF THE CABIN. THE DRAWING IS LOCATED ON A LAYER CALLED BASE. A TASK WAS SELECTED THAT WILL AUTOMATICALLY WIDEN THE WALL TO 6".

A CAD TASK WAS SELECTED THAT WILL AUTOMATICALLY INSERT A WINDOW IN THE WALL

THE SCREENS ON THE PORCH ARE INSERTED USING A COMMAND THAT WILL EQUALLY SPACE THE UNITS AT THE INDICATED DISTANCE

THIS DRAWING ILLUSTRATES THE COMPLETED FIRST-FLOOR PLAN ON LAYER BASE.

A CROSSHATCH TASK ALLOWS THE PLACEMENT OF WOOD STUD HATCHING

A BLOCK IS SELECTED TO LOCATE THE WATER CLOSET ON THE PLAN

THE DOOR COMMAND WILL AUTOMATICALLY INSERT THE OBJECT AND TRIM THE WALL

THE LOCATION OF ALL WALL LINES HAVE BEEN KEYED INTO THE CAD PACKAGE. THIS ASSURES EXACT DIMENSION LENGTHS.

| COMPUTER AIDED DRAFTING | 8-10 |

THE DECK IS PLACED USING THE HATCH TASK. THE HATCHING IS SET AT 45° AND IS PLACED ON A LAYER CALLED DECK; A PEN TABLE WAS SELECTED FOR A LIGHTER LINE WEIGHT.

ALL NOTES ARE PLACED ON A LAYER LABELED NOTE. LAYERS NOTE, DIMENSION, AND DECK COULD BE TURNED "OFF." THE PLAN DRAWING WOULD THEN BE DISPLAYED SEPARATELY.

DIMENSION STRINGS ARE PLACED ON A LAYER LABELED DIMENSION. THIS TASK AUTOMATICALLY POSITIONS THE DIMENSION AND ARROWS WHEN THE END POINTS ARE SELECTED.

LINE OF ROOF OVERHANG

6" x 6" TREATED WOOD POST

SCREEN PORCH

ENTRY

LINE OF LOFT ABOVE

LIVING AREA

6" x 6" TREATED POST

TREATED 2 x 6'S FOR DECK FRAMING SPACED 3'-0" APART AND SUPPORTED BY 4" x 4" TREATED POSTS

FIRST-FLOOR PLAN

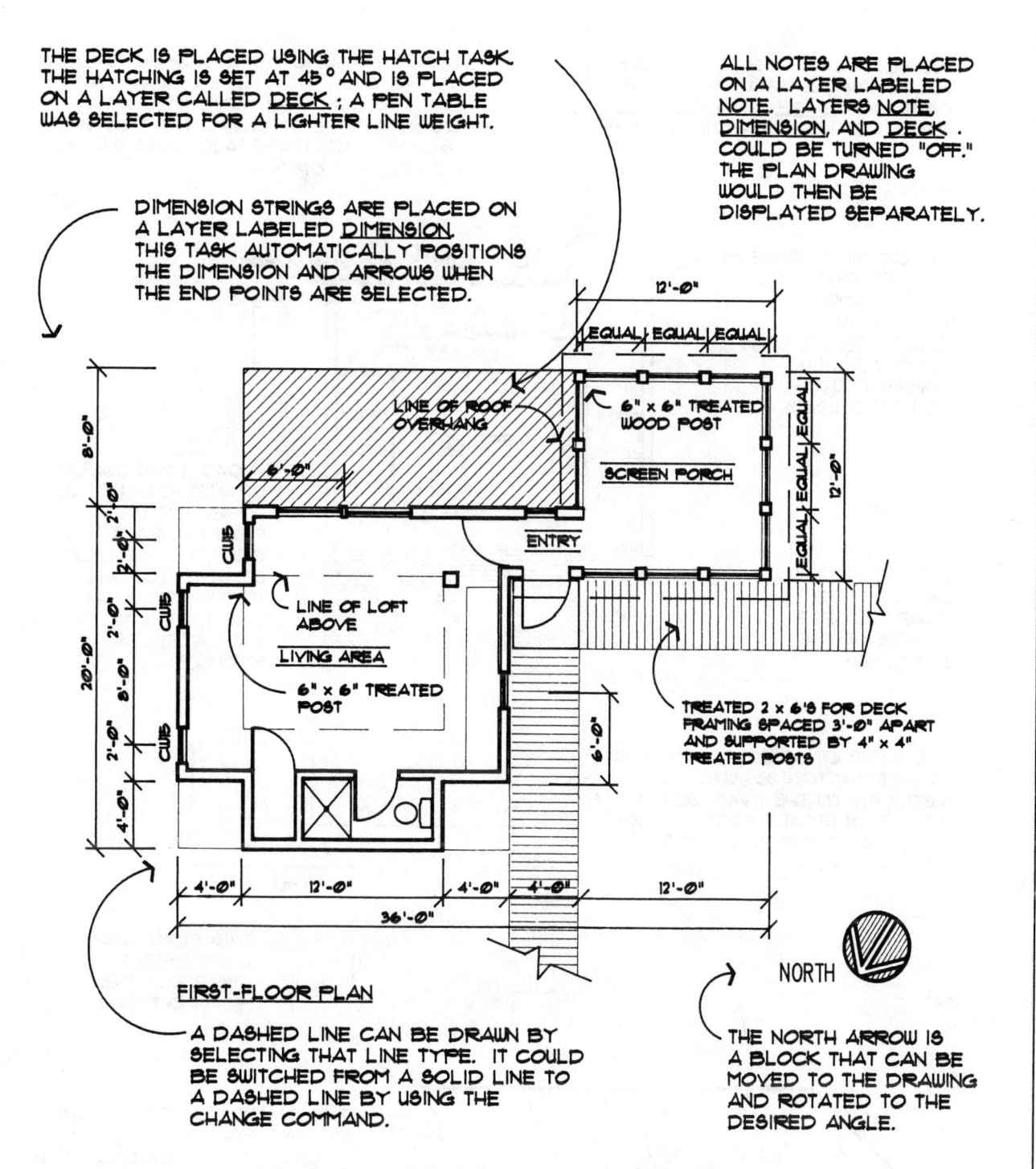

A DASHED LINE CAN BE DRAWN BY SELECTING THAT LINE TYPE. IT COULD BE SWITCHED FROM A SOLID LINE TO A DASHED LINE BY USING THE CHANGE COMMAND.

NORTH

THE NORTH ARROW IS A BLOCK THAT CAN BE MOVED TO THE DRAWING AND ROTATED TO THE DESIRED ANGLE.

THE DRAWING ABOVE ILLUSTRATES THE COMPLETED FIRST-FLOOR PLAN. RECALL THAT ANY OF THE TEN LAYERS USED TO ASSEMBLE THE DRAWING CAN BE TURNED OFF TO ASSIST IN CREATING ADDITIONAL PLANS. THIS WAS DONE IN THIS PROJECT TO PRODUCE COPIES OF THE THREE FRAMING PLANS, THE SECOND-FLOOR PLAN, AND THE SITE PLAN.

| COMPUTER AIDED DRAFTING | 8-11 |

THE SECOND-FLOOR PLAN SHOWN BELOW WAS GENERATED BY COPYING THE LAYER BASE. THIS REDUCED THE AMOUNT OF NEW DRAFTING BY 80%.

A CAD DRAWING BEING COPIED IS IDENTICAL TO THE ORIGINAL IN EVERY WAY. TASKS SUCH AS COPY OR MOVE WILL NOT DEGRADE THE ORIGINAL; THE TRANSFER IS DONE ELECTRONICALLY AND EACH NEW PLOT IS ORIGINAL.

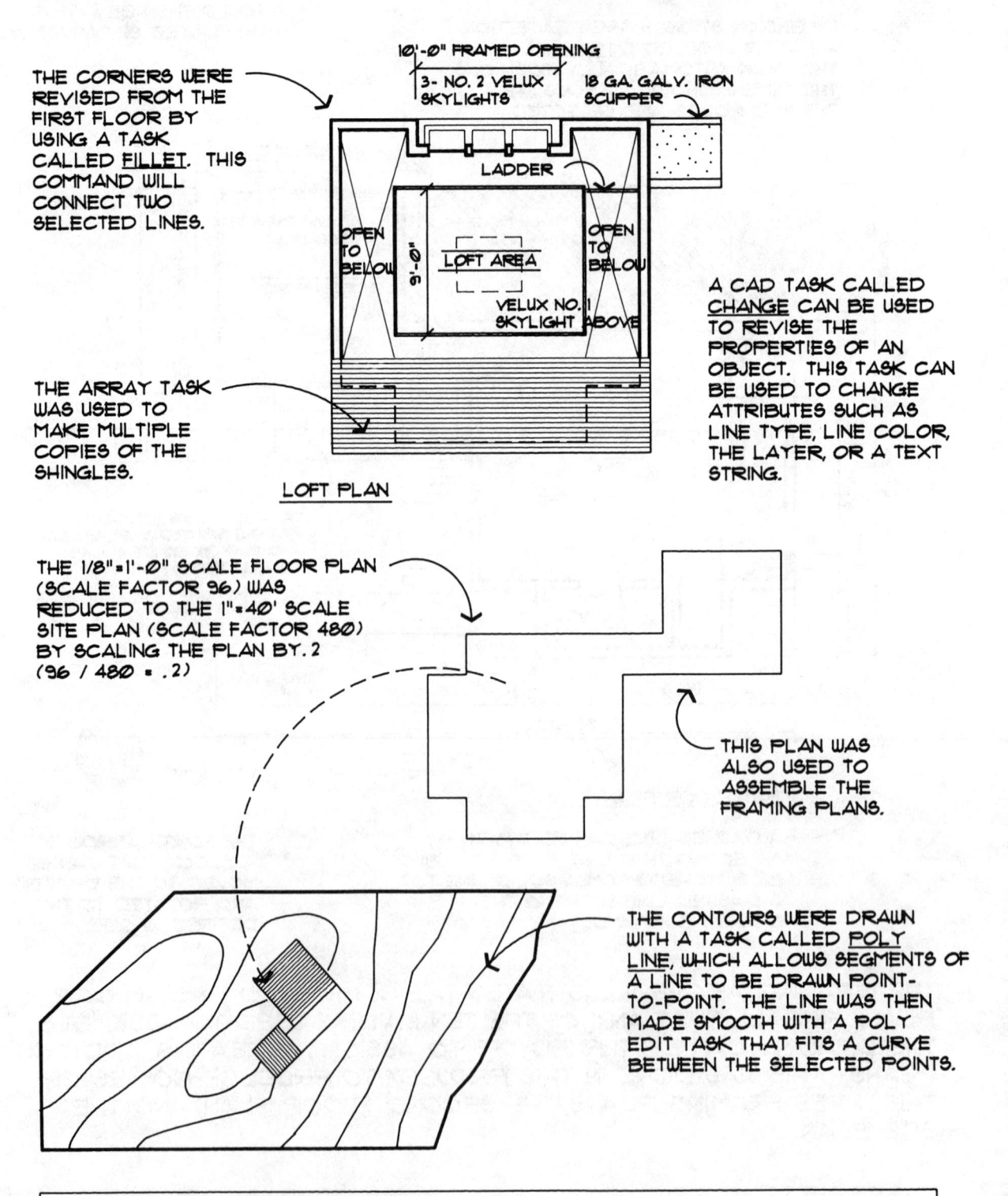

THE CORNERS WERE REVISED FROM THE FIRST FLOOR BY USING A TASK CALLED FILLET. THIS COMMAND WILL CONNECT TWO SELECTED LINES.

10'-0" FRAMED OPENING
3- NO. 2 VELUX SKYLIGHTS
18 GA. GALV. IRON SCUPPER
LADDER
OPEN TO BELOW
9'-0"
LOFT AREA
OPEN TO BELOW
VELUX NO. 11 SKYLIGHT ABOVE

A CAD TASK CALLED CHANGE CAN BE USED TO REVISE THE PROPERTIES OF AN OBJECT. THIS TASK CAN BE USED TO CHANGE ATTRIBUTES SUCH AS LINE TYPE, LINE COLOR, THE LAYER, OR A TEXT STRING.

THE ARRAY TASK WAS USED TO MAKE MULTIPLE COPIES OF THE SHINGLES.

LOFT PLAN

THE 1/8"=1'-0" SCALE FLOOR PLAN (SCALE FACTOR 96) WAS REDUCED TO THE 1"=40' SCALE SITE PLAN (SCALE FACTOR 480) BY SCALING THE PLAN BY .2 (96 / 480 = .2)

THIS PLAN WAS ALSO USED TO ASSEMBLE THE FRAMING PLANS.

THE CONTOURS WERE DRAWN WITH A TASK CALLED POLY LINE, WHICH ALLOWS SEGMENTS OF A LINE TO BE DRAWN POINT-TO-POINT. THE LINE WAS THEN MADE SMOOTH WITH A POLY EDIT TASK THAT FITS A CURVE BETWEEN THE SELECTED POINTS.

COMPUTER AIDED DRAFTING   8-12

A CARDBOARD STUDY MODEL WAS CREATED BY PRINTING THE 1/4" SCALE FLOOR PLAN AT HALF-SCALE (THIS WOULD MAKE IT AN 1/8" PLOT). THE PLAN, COUPLED WITH THE 1/8" SCALE ELEVATIONS, WOULD ALLOW THE ASSEMBLY OF A QUICK MODEL.

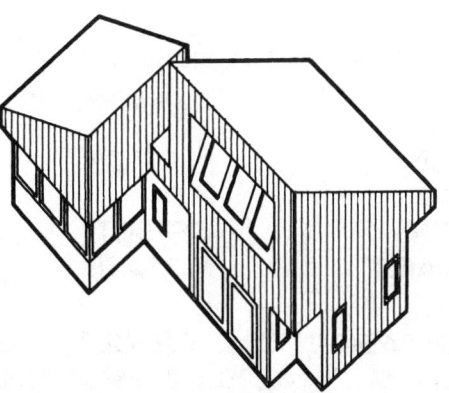

THE PROJECT WAS CREATED AS A THREE-DIMENSIONAL COMPUTER MODEL. THIS ALLOWED THE CREATION OF A WIRE-FRAME FORM THAT WAS USED TO ASSEMBLE ELEVATIONS AND SECTIONS FOR THE REMAINDER OF THE WORKING DRAWING PACKAGE.

THE DRAWING BELOW SHOWS THE COMPLETED SHEET LAYOUT. NOTES ON THE PAGE PERTAIN TO CAD TASKS THAT WILL MAKE THE DRAWING ASSEMBLY EASIER.

THE FRAMING PLANS WERE DEVELOPED BY COPYING THE SILHOUETTE OF THE FLOOR PLAN. ONCE THE PLAN IS MOVED, IT CAN BE SCALED TO HALF-SIZE.

THE MOVE TASK WAS USED TO ALIGN THE DRAWINGS ON THE SHEET.

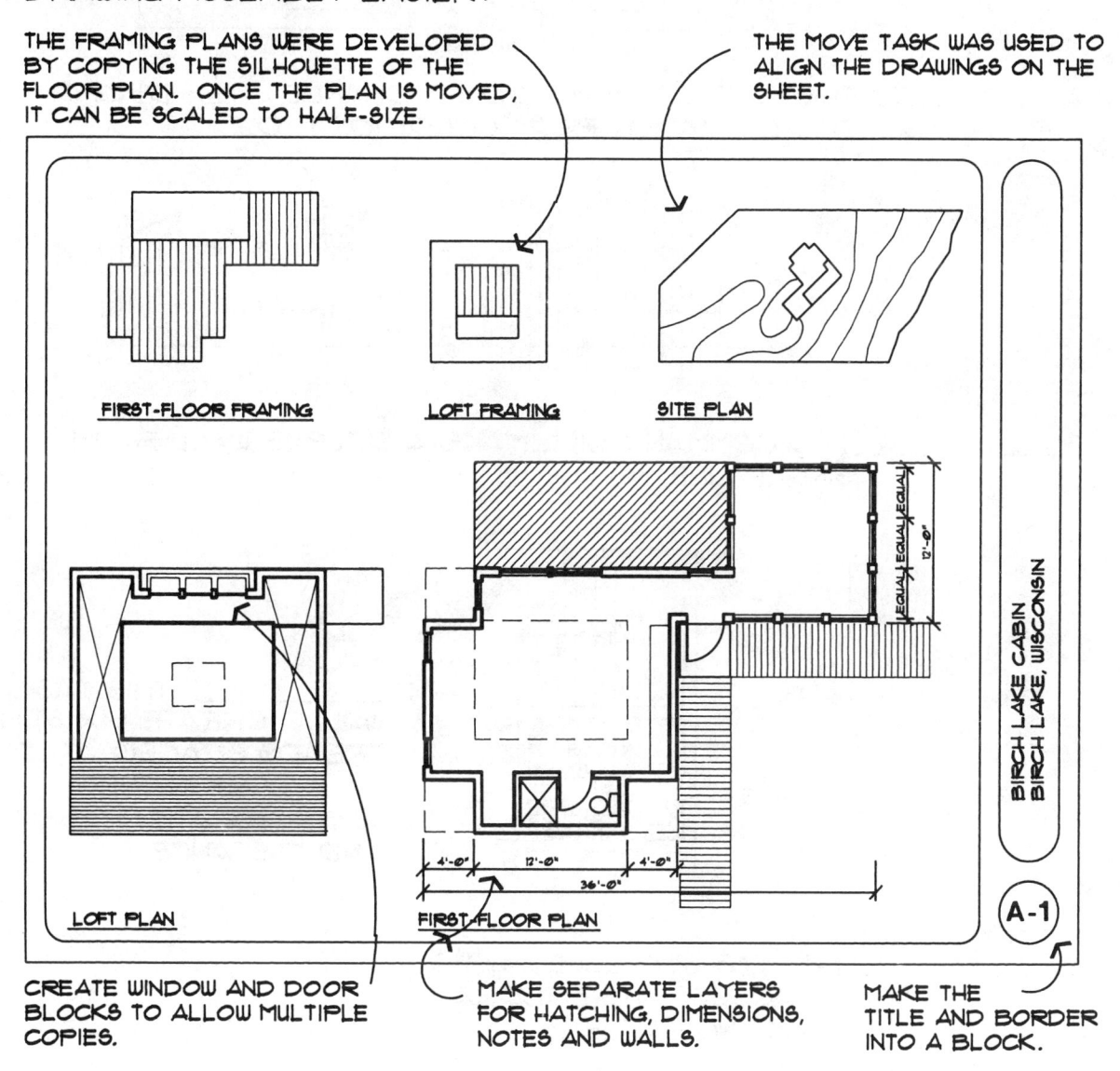

FIRST-FLOOR FRAMING   LOFT FRAMING   SITE PLAN

LOFT PLAN   FIRST-FLOOR PLAN

BIRCH LAKE CABIN
BIRCH LAKE, WISCONSIN

A-1

CREATE WINDOW AND DOOR BLOCKS TO ALLOW MULTIPLE COPIES.

MAKE SEPARATE LAYERS FOR HATCHING, DIMENSIONS, NOTES AND WALLS.

MAKE THE TITLE AND BORDER INTO A BLOCK.

COMPUTER AIDED DRAFTING   8-13

REPLAY
MATCH THE CAD TASKS LISTED BELOW WITH THE APPROPRIATE STATEMENT OR SKETCH.

ARRAY	ERASE	MIRROR	SCALE
BLOCK	GRIDS	MOVE	SNAP
COPY	LAYER	OFFSET	TRIM
DIMENSION	LIBRARY	ROTATE	ZOOM

1. _____ THIS CAD TASK WOULD RESULT IN CHANGING THE ELEVATION SHOWN BELOW FROM CONDITION 1 TO 2.

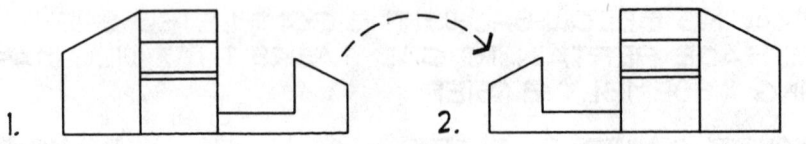

2. _____ THIS CAD COMMAND WOULD CHANGE THE SIDING ON THIS ELEVATION FROM CONDITION 1 TO 2.

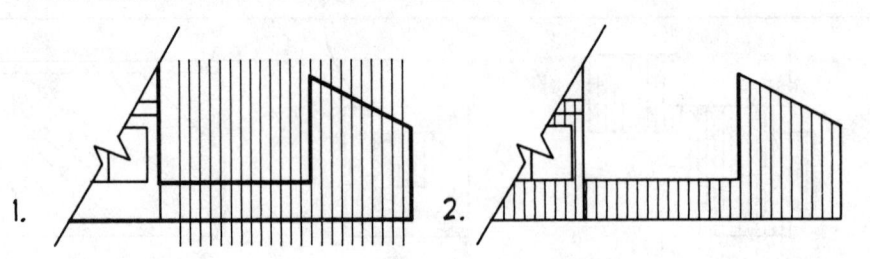

3. _____ THIS COMMAND WILL MAKE A DOUBLE WALL FROM A SINGLE LINE.

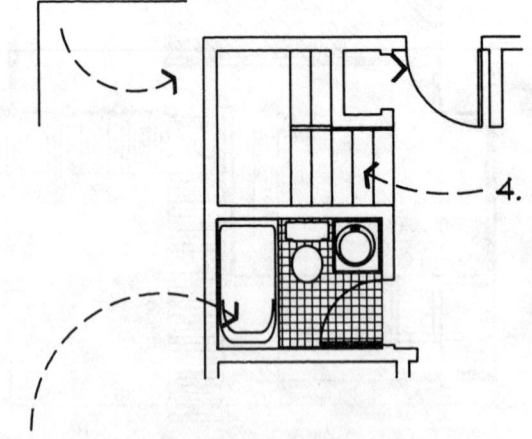

4. _____ THIS TASK WOULD CREATE SIX STAIR TREADS SPACED AT 10" BY KEYING IN THE APPROPRIATE NUMBER AND DISTANCE.

5. _____ THIS TASK WOULD BE USED TO ACCESS THE PREDRAWN PLUMBING FIXTURES.

COMPUTER AIDED DRAFTING   8-14

6. _____ THIS CAD TASK WOULD ALLOW THE WINDOW IN THE ELEVATION BELOW TO BE ENLARGED AS SHOWN.

7. _____ THIS CAD TASK WOULD ALLOW THE ASSEMBLY OF THE WINDOW INTO A SINGLE OBJECT THAT COULD BE USED ON OTHER DRAWINGS.

8. _____ THIS CAD COMMAND WOULD ALLOW TURNING ITEMS SUCH AS DOORS AND PLUMBING FIXTURES "ON" OR "OFF" SEPARATELY FROM THE REMAINING PLAN SHOWN BELOW.

9. _____ THIS CAD TASK WOULD CONNECT THE END POINTS OF A NEW LINE TO ONE THAT IS EXISTING.

10. _____ THIS CAD FUNCTION WOULD SET POINTS ON THE DRAWING AT 6" O. C. (ON CENTER) TO ALLOW THE EXACT LOCATION OF WALLS.

11. _____ THIS CAD COMMAND WOULD CHANGE THE ANGLE OF THE NORTH ARROW SHOWN IN THE ILLUSTRATION ABOVE.

12. _____ THIS COMMAND WOULD ALLOW RELOCATING THE ENTIRE FLOOR PLAN TO A DIFFERENT POINT ON THE DRAWING.

COMPUTER AIDED DRAFTING

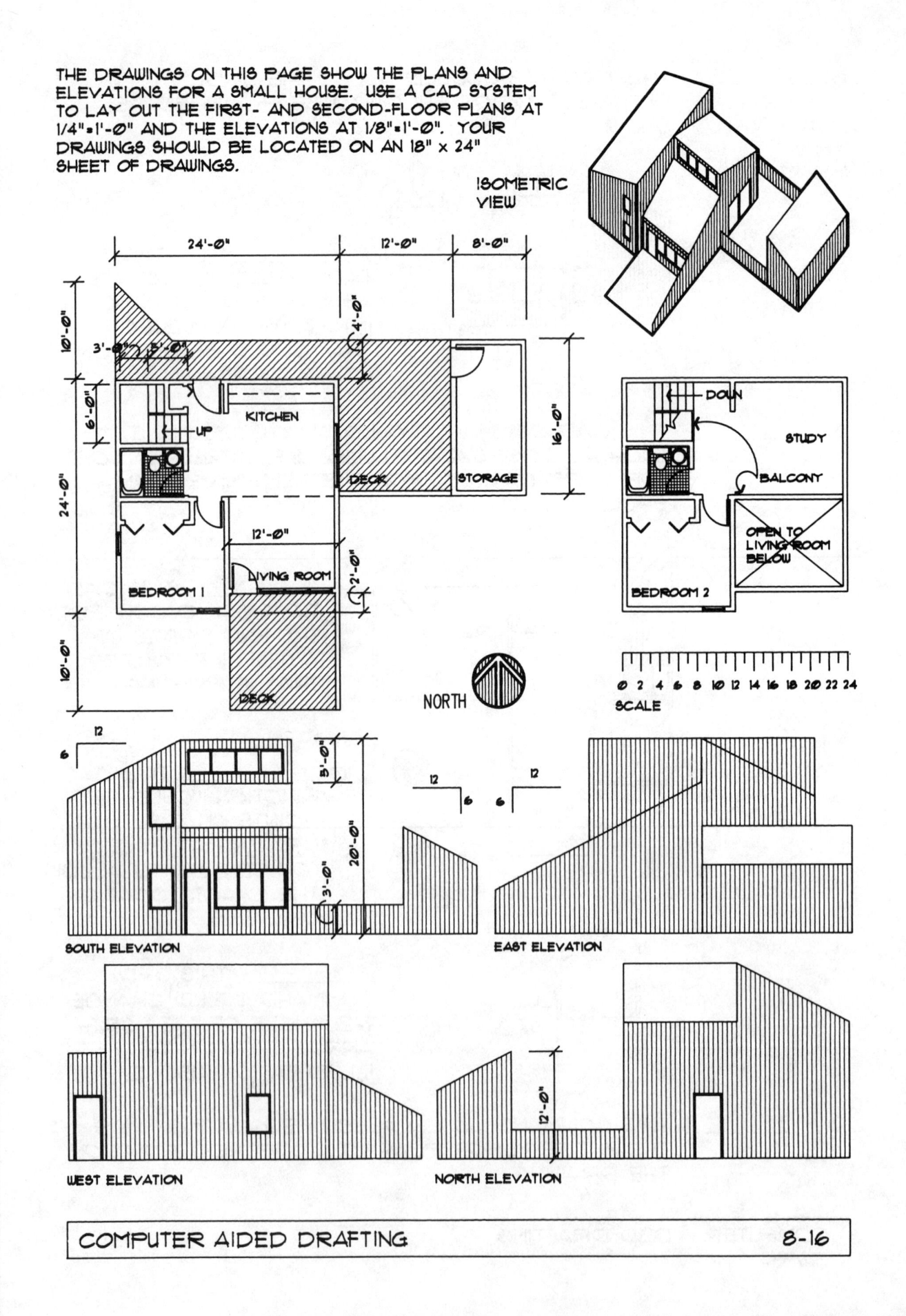

THE DRAWINGS ON THIS PAGE SHOW THE PLANS AND ELEVATIONS FOR A SMALL HOUSE. USE A CAD SYSTEM TO LAY OUT THE FIRST- AND SECOND-FLOOR PLANS AT 1/4"=1'-0" AND THE ELEVATIONS AT 1/8"=1'-0". YOUR DRAWINGS SHOULD BE LOCATED ON AN 18" x 24" SHEET OF DRAWINGS.

ISOMETRIC VIEW

SOUTH ELEVATION

EAST ELEVATION

WEST ELEVATION

NORTH ELEVATION

COMPUTER AIDED DRAFTING   8-16

9 DETAILS

THIS UNIT WILL PRESENT A SERIES OF ARCHITECTURAL DETAILS THAT YOU CAN USE AS A GUIDE WHEN ASSEMBLING A PACKAGE OF WORKING DRAWINGS. YOU SHOULD STUDY THE DETAILS IN ORDER TO UNDERSTAND A PRODUCT'S ASSEMBLY AND ITS ADAPTABILITY TO ANY PARTICULAR CONDITION YOU MIGHT FIND. EVERY BUILDING PRESENTS HUNDREDS OF PROBLEMS THAT MUST BE SOLVED. KEEP IN MIND THAT THE SOLUTION YOU CHOOSE MUST FIT YOUR BUILDING EXACTLY.

THE DRAWINGS BELOW ILLUSTRATE THE STAGES USED IN DETAIL DEVELOPMENT. BEGIN WITH THE MOST IMPORTANT FEATURE (USUALLY A STRUCTURAL MEMBER) AND BUILD THE DRAWING AROUND IT.

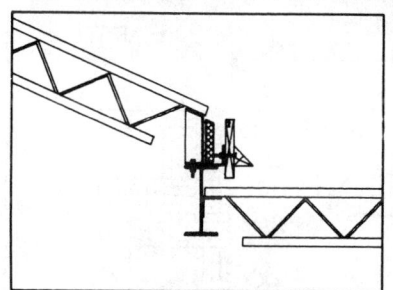

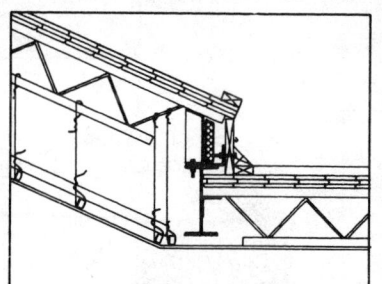

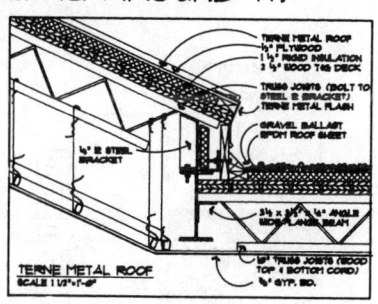

INDEX	
DETAIL	PAGE
SITE CONDITIONS	9-2 THROUGH 9-6
DOOR FRAMES	9-7
WALL TYPES	9-8
LINTEL AND DOOR CONDITIONS	9-9 THROUGH 9-11
STAIRS	9-12 THROUGH 9-13
RESIDENTIAL WALL CONDITIONS	9-14 THROUGH 9-16
COMMERCIAL WALL CONDITIONS	9-17 THROUGH 9-22
COMMERCIAL ROOF CONDITIONS	9-23 THROUGH 9-30

DETAILS

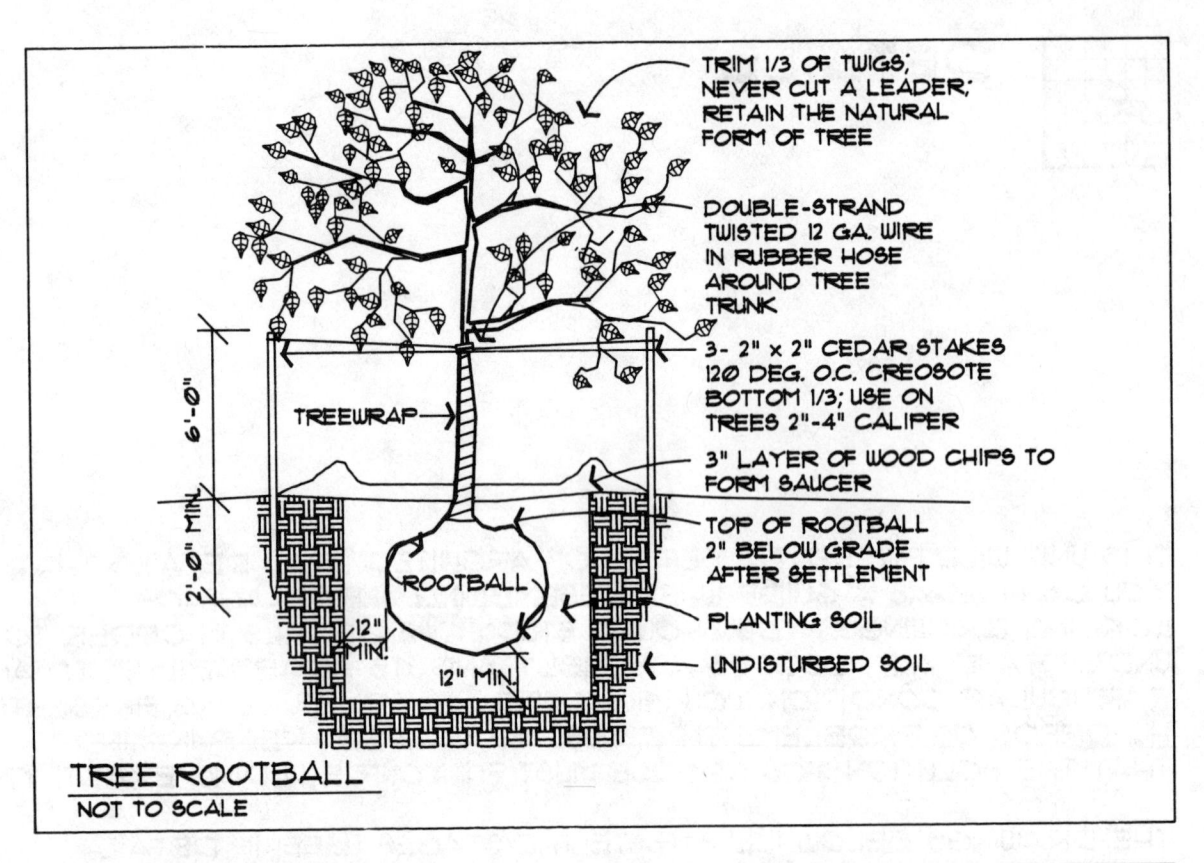

TREE ROOTBALL
NOT TO SCALE

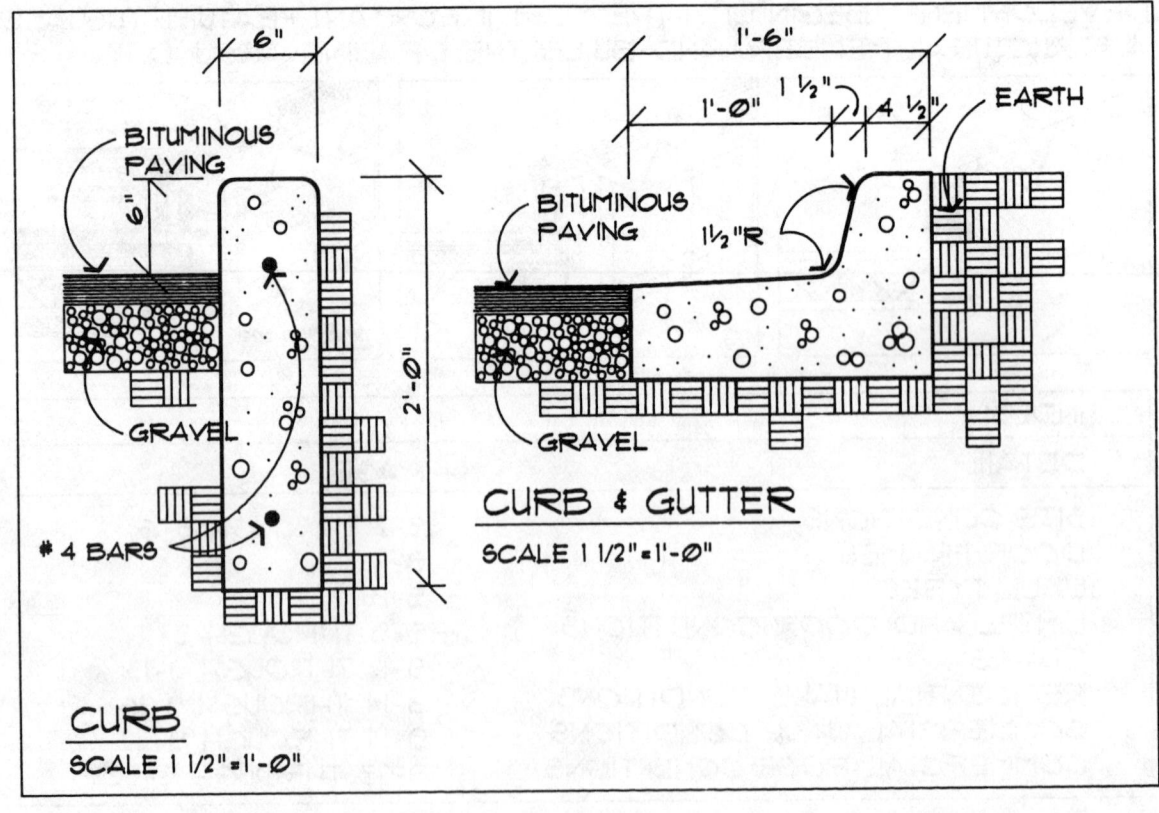

- TRIM 1/3 OF TWIGS; NEVER CUT A LEADER; RETAIN THE NATURAL FORM OF TREE
- DOUBLE-STRAND TWISTED 12 GA. WIRE IN RUBBER HOSE AROUND TREE TRUNK
- 3- 2" x 2" CEDAR STAKES 120 DEG. O.C. CREOSOTE BOTTOM 1/3; USE ON TREES 2"-4" CALIPER
- 3" LAYER OF WOOD CHIPS TO FORM SAUCER
- TOP OF ROOTBALL 2" BELOW GRADE AFTER SETTLEMENT
- PLANTING SOIL
- UNDISTURBED SOIL
- TREEWRAP
- ROOTBALL
- 6'-0"
- 2'-0" MIN.
- 12" MIN.
- 12" MIN

CURB
SCALE 1 1/2" = 1'-0"

- BITUMINOUS PAVING
- GRAVEL
- #4 BARS
- 6"
- 6"
- 2'-0"

CURB & GUTTER
SCALE 1 1/2" = 1'-0"

- BITUMINOUS PAVING
- GRAVEL
- EARTH
- 1 1/2" R
- 1'-6"
- 1'-0"
- 1 1/2"
- 4 1/2"

DETAILS

9-2

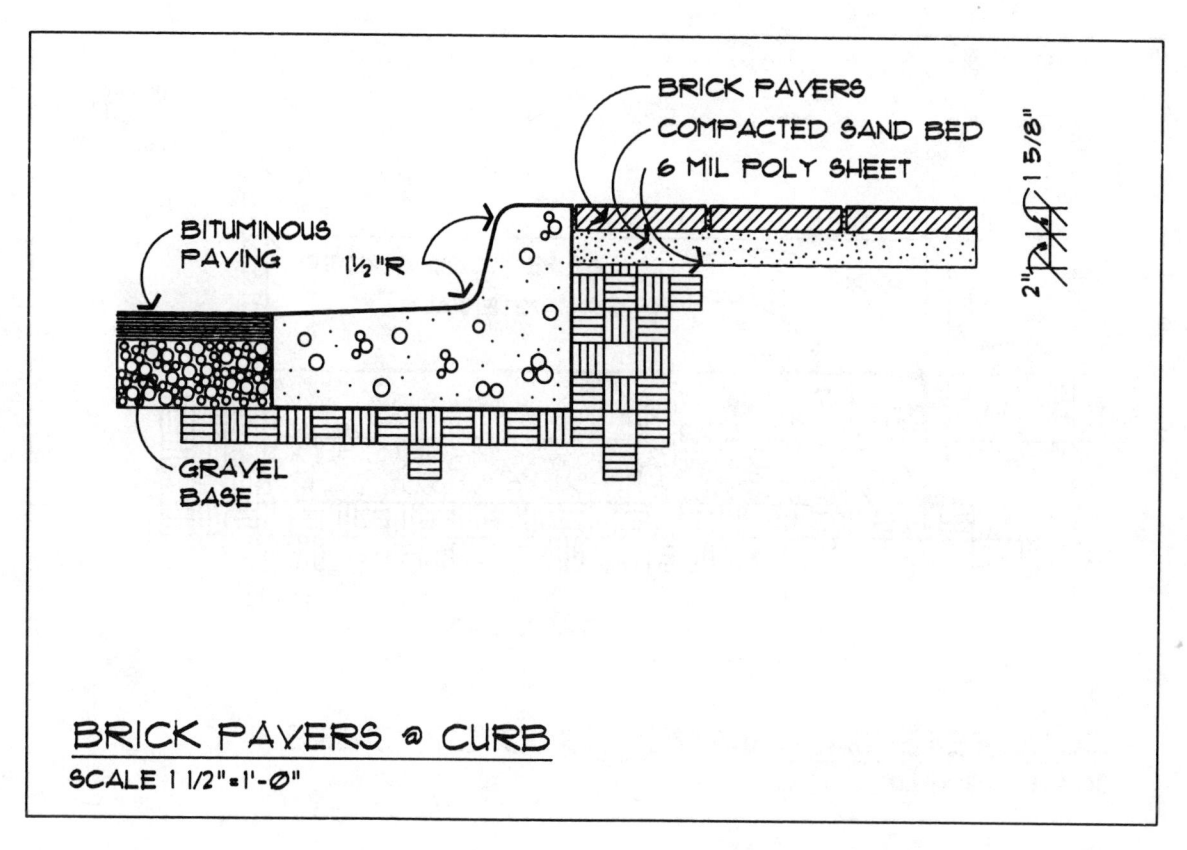

BRICK PAVERS @ CURB
SCALE 1 1/2"=1'-0"

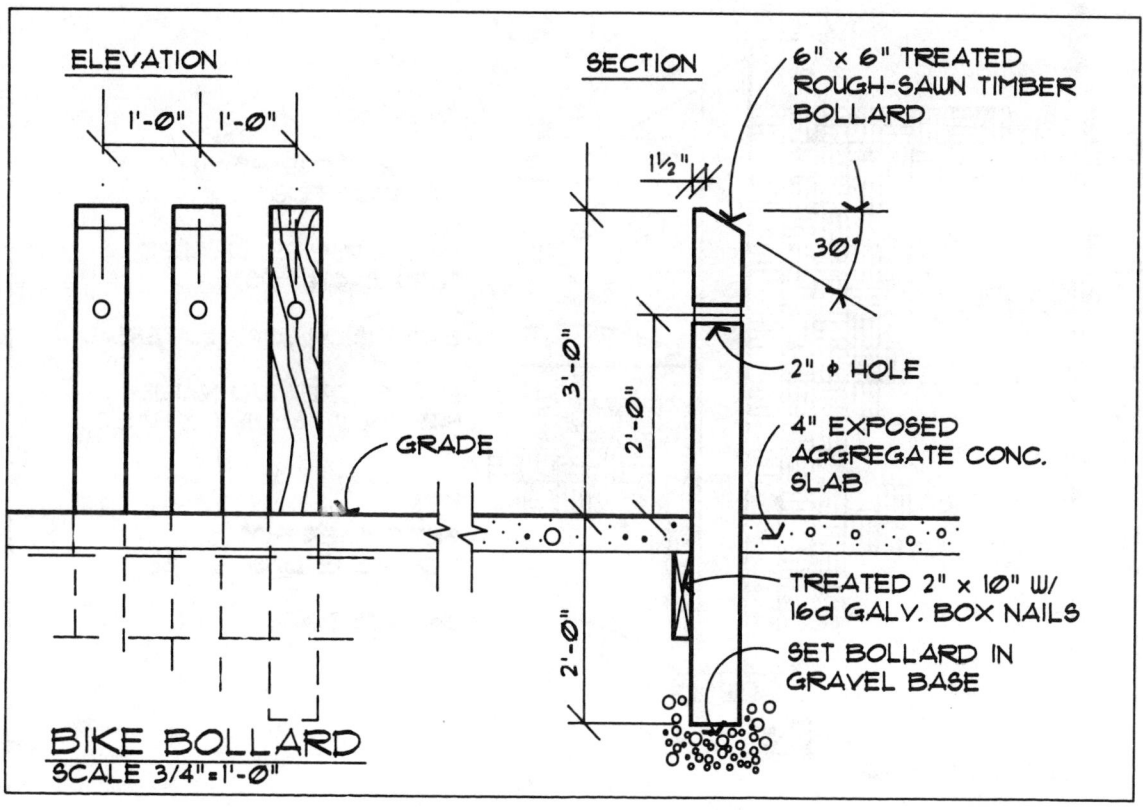

- BRICK PAVERS
- COMPACTED SAND BED
- 6 MIL POLY SHEET
- BITUMINOUS PAVING
- 1 1/2"R
- 2" / 1 5/8"
- GRAVEL BASE

BIKE BOLLARD
SCALE 3/4"=1'-0"

ELEVATION — 1'-0" / 1'-0"

SECTION

- 6" x 6" TREATED ROUGH-SAWN TIMBER BOLLARD
- 1 1/2"
- 30°
- 3'-0"
- 2'-0"
- 2" ⌀ HOLE
- 4" EXPOSED AGGREGATE CONC. SLAB
- GRADE
- TREATED 2" x 10" W/ 16d GALV. BOX NAILS
- 2'-0"
- SET BOLLARD IN GRAVEL BASE

DETAILS

9-3

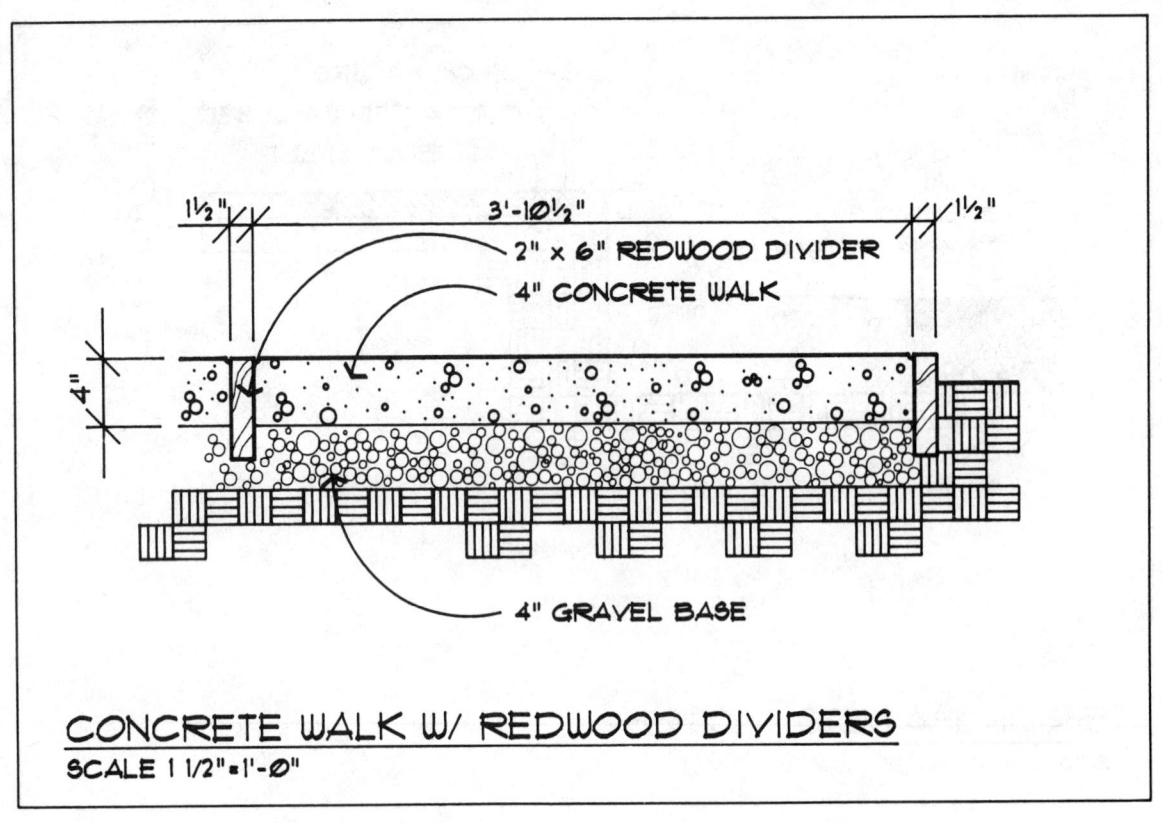

CONCRETE WALK W/ REDWOOD DIVIDERS
SCALE 1 1/2"=1'-0"

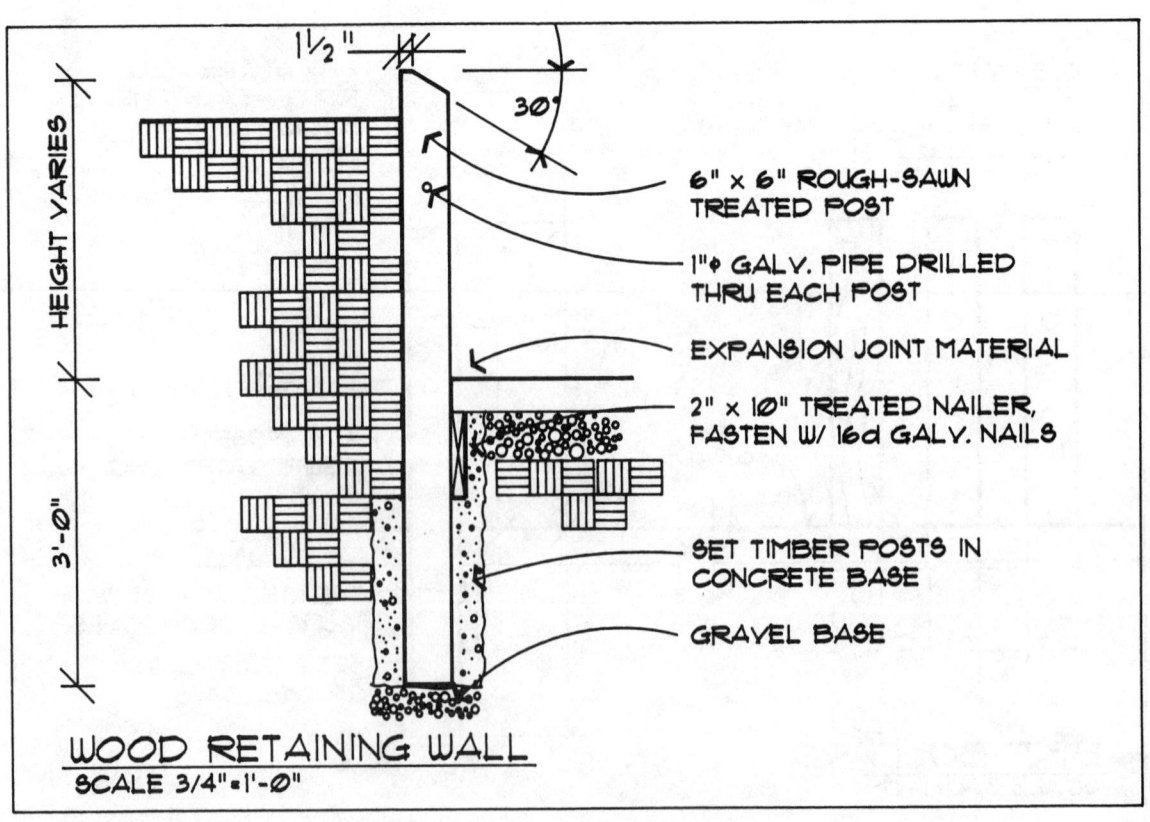

- 1½"
- 3'-10½"
- 1½"
- 2" x 6" REDWOOD DIVIDER
- 4" CONCRETE WALK
- 4"
- 4" GRAVEL BASE

WOOD RETAINING WALL
SCALE 3/4"=1'-0"

- 1½"
- 30°
- HEIGHT VARIES
- 3'-0"
- 6" x 6" ROUGH-SAWN TREATED POST
- 1"⌀ GALV. PIPE DRILLED THRU EACH POST
- EXPANSION JOINT MATERIAL
- 2" x 10" TREATED NAILER, FASTEN W/ 16d GALV. NAILS
- SET TIMBER POSTS IN CONCRETE BASE
- GRAVEL BASE

DETAILS

9-4

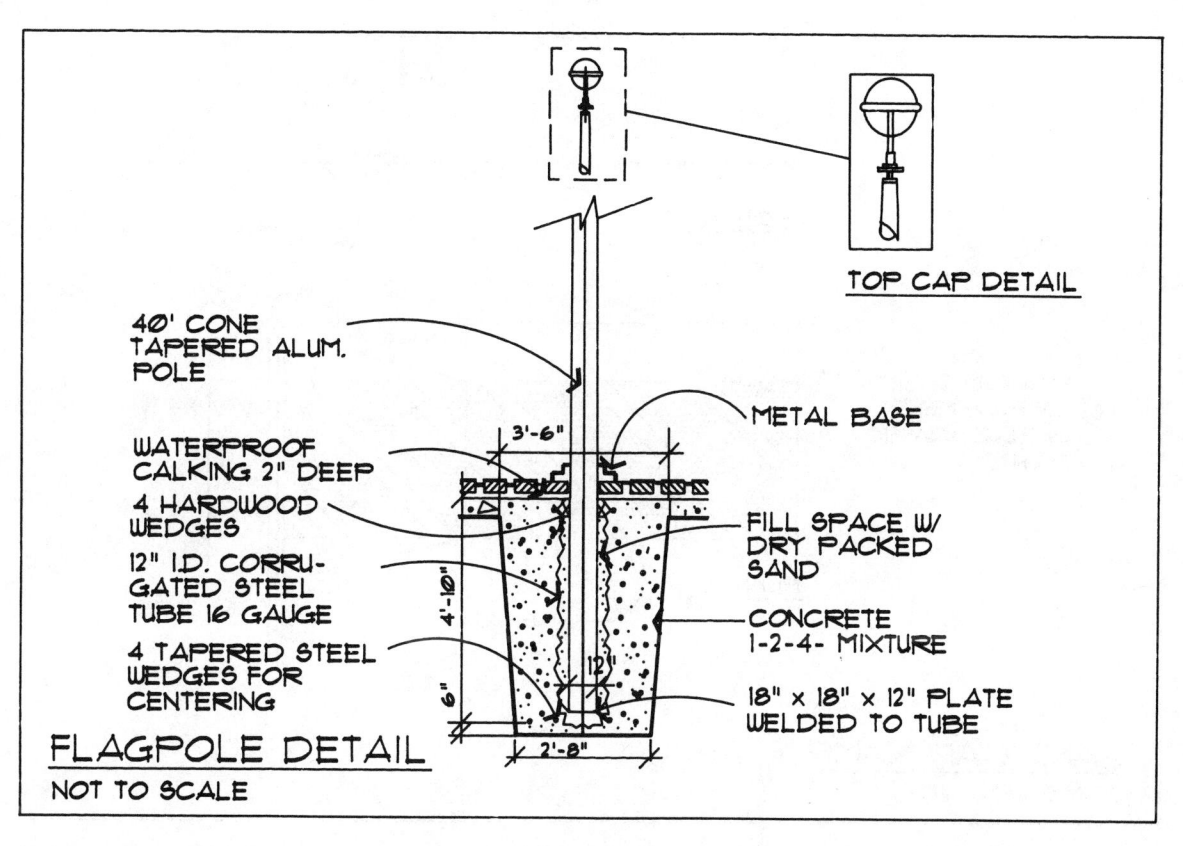

FLAGPOLE DETAIL
NOT TO SCALE

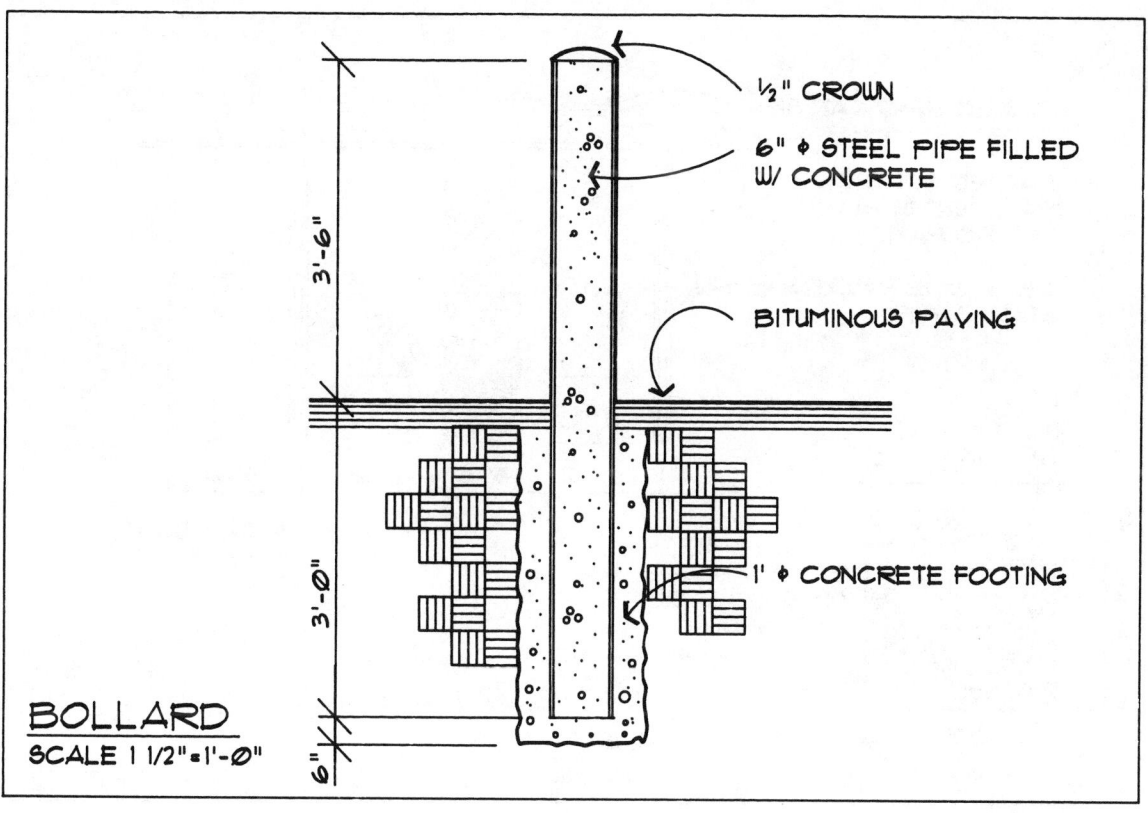

- 40' CONE TAPERED ALUM. POLE
- WATERPROOF CALKING 2" DEEP
- 4 HARDWOOD WEDGES
- 12" I.D. CORRUGATED STEEL TUBE 16 GAUGE
- 4 TAPERED STEEL WEDGES FOR CENTERING
- METAL BASE
- FILL SPACE W/ DRY PACKED SAND
- CONCRETE 1-2-4- MIXTURE
- 18" x 18" x 12" PLATE WELDED TO TUBE

Dimensions: 3'-6", 4'-0", 6", 2'-8", 12"

TOP CAP DETAIL

BOLLARD
SCALE 1 1/2" = 1'-0"

- 1/2" CROWN
- 6" ⌀ STEEL PIPE FILLED W/ CONCRETE
- BITUMINOUS PAVING
- 1' ⌀ CONCRETE FOOTING

Dimensions: 3'-6", 3'-0", 6"

DETAILS 9-5

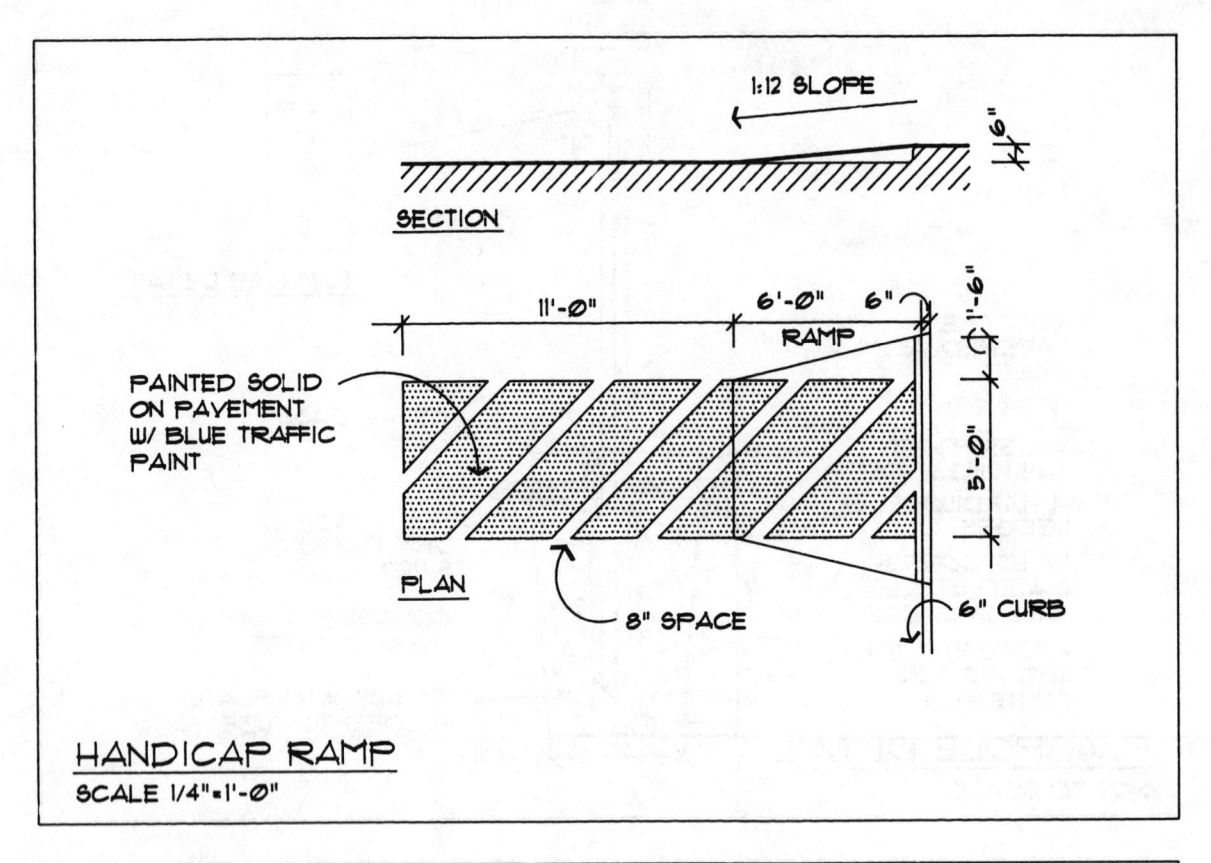

HANDICAP RAMP
SCALE 1/4"=1'-0"

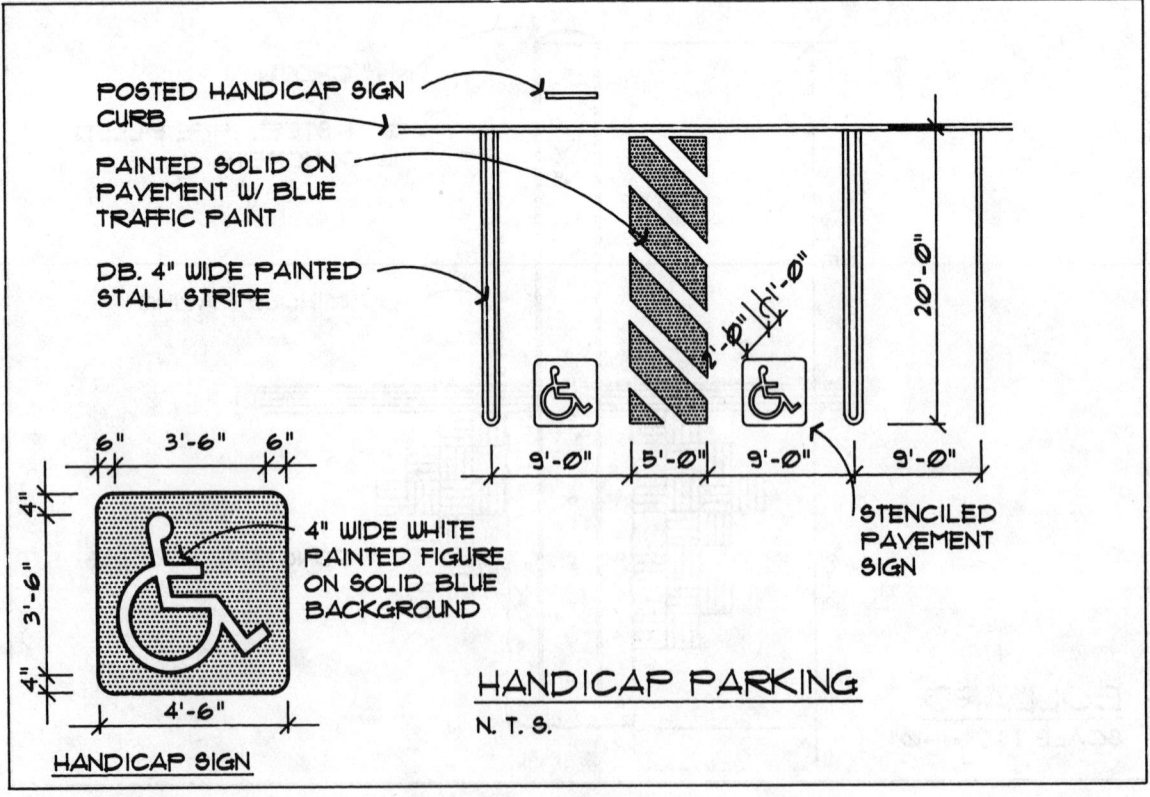

- 1:12 SLOPE
- 6"
- SECTION
- 11'-0"
- 6'-0"
- 6"
- RAMP
- 1'-6"
- 5'-0"
- PAINTED SOLID ON PAVEMENT W/ BLUE TRAFFIC PAINT
- PLAN
- 8" SPACE
- 6" CURB

HANDICAP PARKING
N.T.S.

- POSTED HANDICAP SIGN
- CURB
- PAINTED SOLID ON PAVEMENT W/ BLUE TRAFFIC PAINT
- DB. 4" WIDE PAINTED STALL STRIPE
- 20'-0"
- 2'-0" 1'-0"
- 9'-0" 5'-0" 9'-0" 9'-0"
- STENCILED PAVEMENT SIGN

HANDICAP SIGN
- 6" 3'-6" 6"
- 4"
- 3'-6"
- 4"
- 4'-6"
- 4" WIDE WHITE PAINTED FIGURE ON SOLID BLUE BACKGROUND

DETAILS 9-6

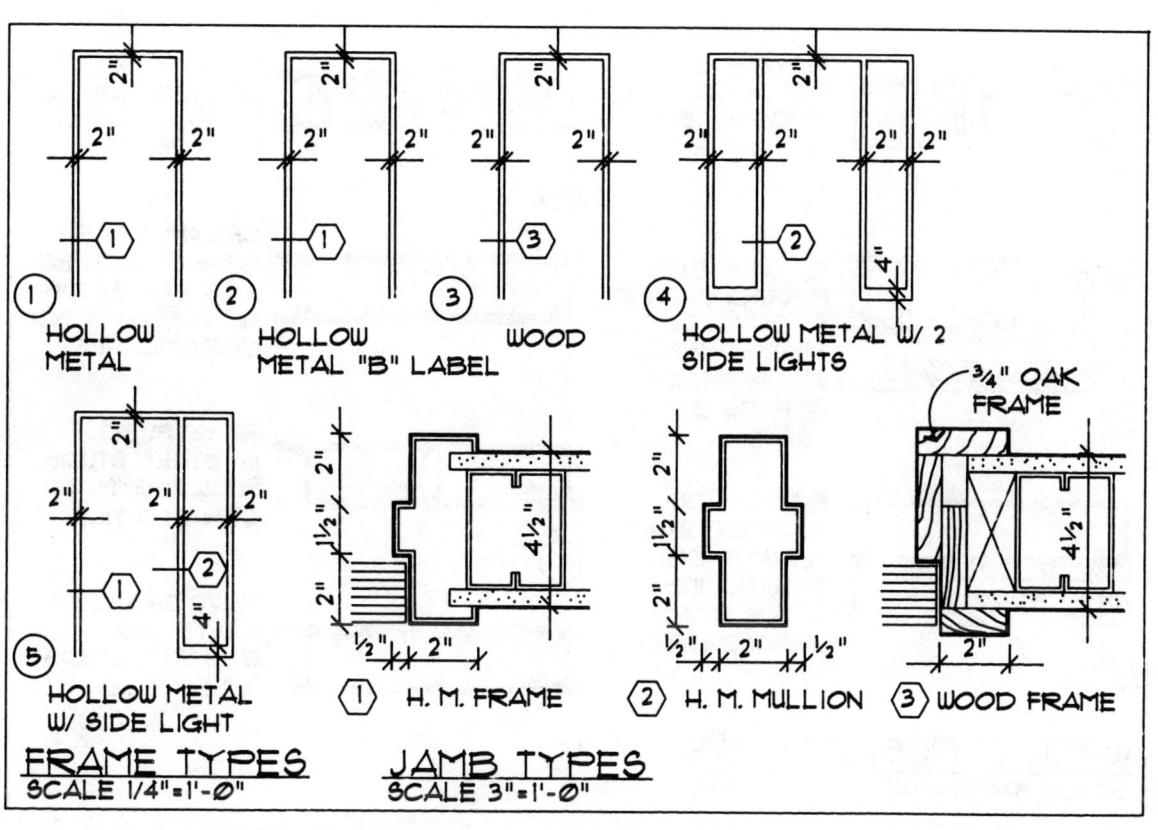

FRAME TYPES
SCALE 1/4"=1'-0"

① HOLLOW METAL
② HOLLOW METAL "B" LABEL
③ WOOD
④ HOLLOW METAL W/ 2 SIDE LIGHTS
⑤ HOLLOW METAL W/ SIDE LIGHT

JAMB TYPES
SCALE 3"=1'-0"

① H. M. FRAME
② H. M. MULLION
③ WOOD FRAME (3/4" OAK FRAME)

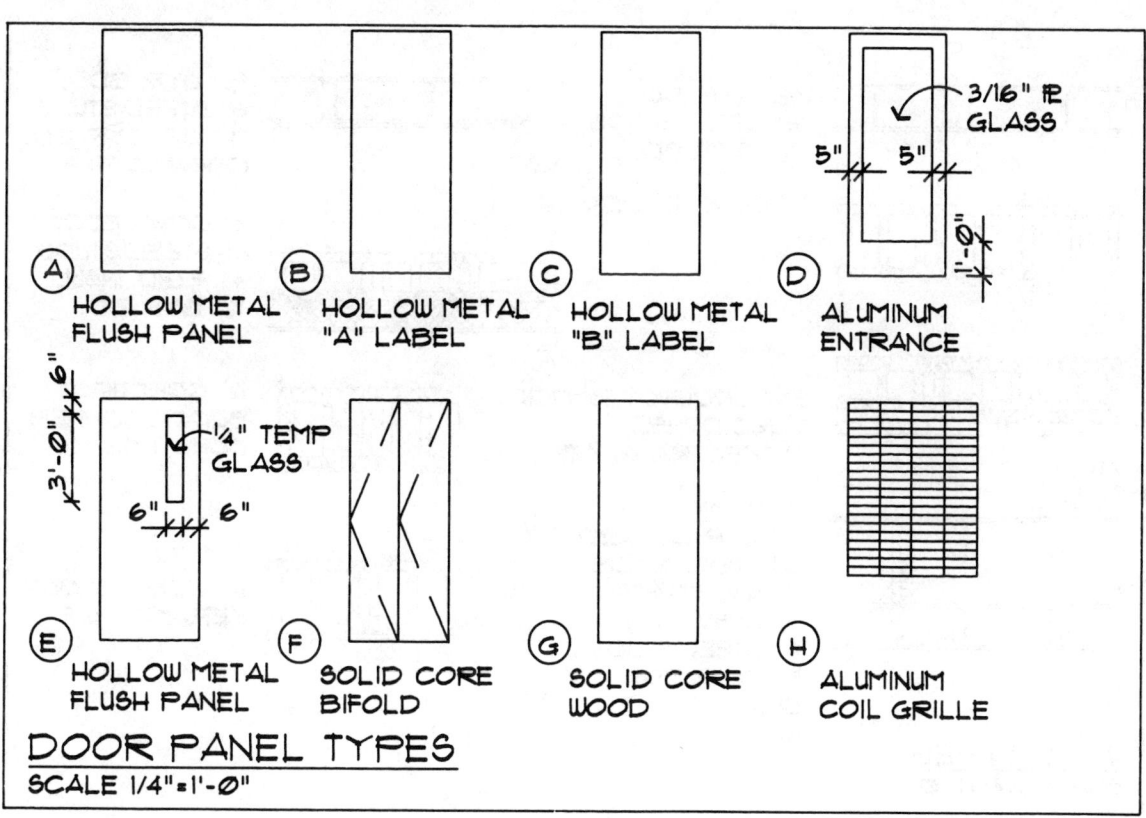

DOOR PANEL TYPES
SCALE 1/4"=1'-0"

Ⓐ HOLLOW METAL FLUSH PANEL
Ⓑ HOLLOW METAL "A" LABEL
Ⓒ HOLLOW METAL "B" LABEL
Ⓓ ALUMINUM ENTRANCE (3/16" φ GLASS)
Ⓔ HOLLOW METAL FLUSH PANEL (1/4" TEMP GLASS)
Ⓕ SOLID CORE BIFOLD
Ⓖ SOLID CORE WOOD
Ⓗ ALUMINUM COIL GRILLE

DETAILS   9-7

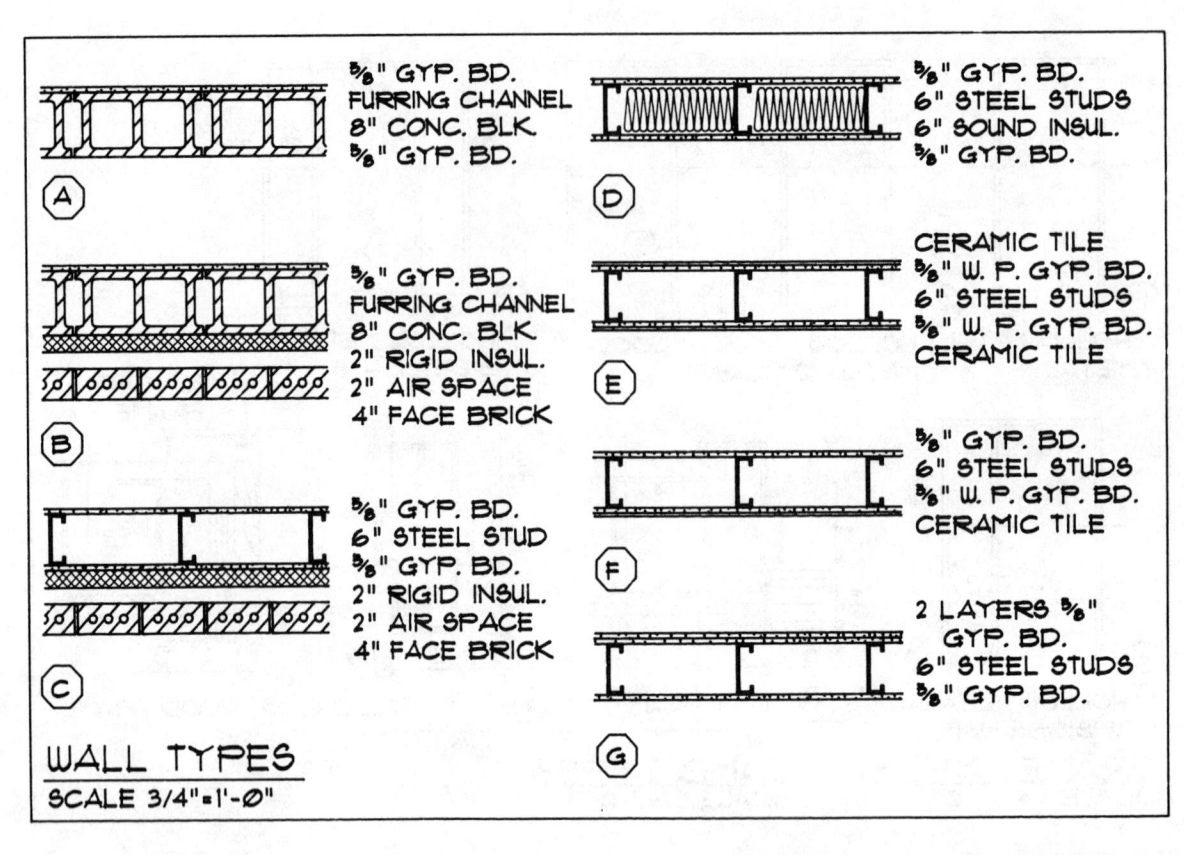

A
⅜" GYP. BD.
FURRING CHANNEL
8" CONC. BLK
⅜" GYP. BD.

B
⅜" GYP. BD.
FURRING CHANNEL
8" CONC. BLK
2" RIGID INSUL.
2" AIR SPACE
4" FACE BRICK

C
⅜" GYP. BD.
6" STEEL STUD
⅜" GYP. BD.
2" RIGID INSUL.
2" AIR SPACE
4" FACE BRICK

D
⅜" GYP. BD.
6" STEEL STUDS
6" SOUND INSUL.
⅜" GYP. BD.

E
CERAMIC TILE
⅜" W.P. GYP. BD.
6" STEEL STUDS
⅜" W.P. GYP. BD.
CERAMIC TILE

F
⅜" GYP. BD.
6" STEEL STUDS
⅜" W.P. GYP. BD.
CERAMIC TILE

G
2 LAYERS ⅜"
GYP. BD.
6" STEEL STUDS
⅜" GYP. BD.

WALL TYPES
SCALE 3/4"=1'-0"

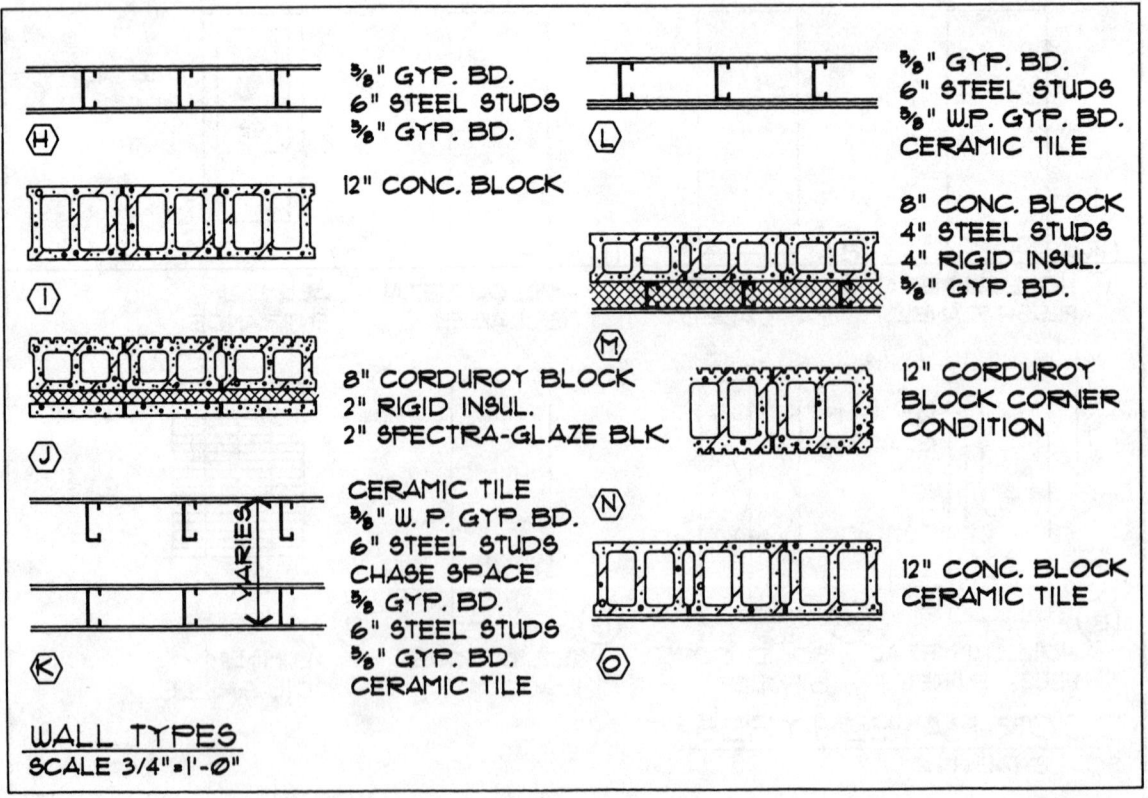

H
⅜" GYP. BD.
6" STEEL STUDS
⅜" GYP. BD.

I
12" CONC. BLOCK

J
8" CORDUROY BLOCK
2" RIGID INSUL.
2" SPECTRA-GLAZE BLK.

K
CERAMIC TILE
⅜" W.P. GYP. BD.
6" STEEL STUDS
CHASE SPACE
⅜" GYP. BD.
6" STEEL STUDS
⅜" GYP. BD.
CERAMIC TILE

L
⅜" GYP. BD.
6" STEEL STUDS
⅜" W.P. GYP. BD.
CERAMIC TILE

M
8" CONC. BLOCK
4" STEEL STUDS
4" RIGID INSUL.
⅜" GYP. BD.

N
12" CORDUROY
BLOCK CORNER
CONDITION

O
12" CONC. BLOCK
CERAMIC TILE

WALL TYPES
SCALE 3/4"=1'-0"

DETAILS

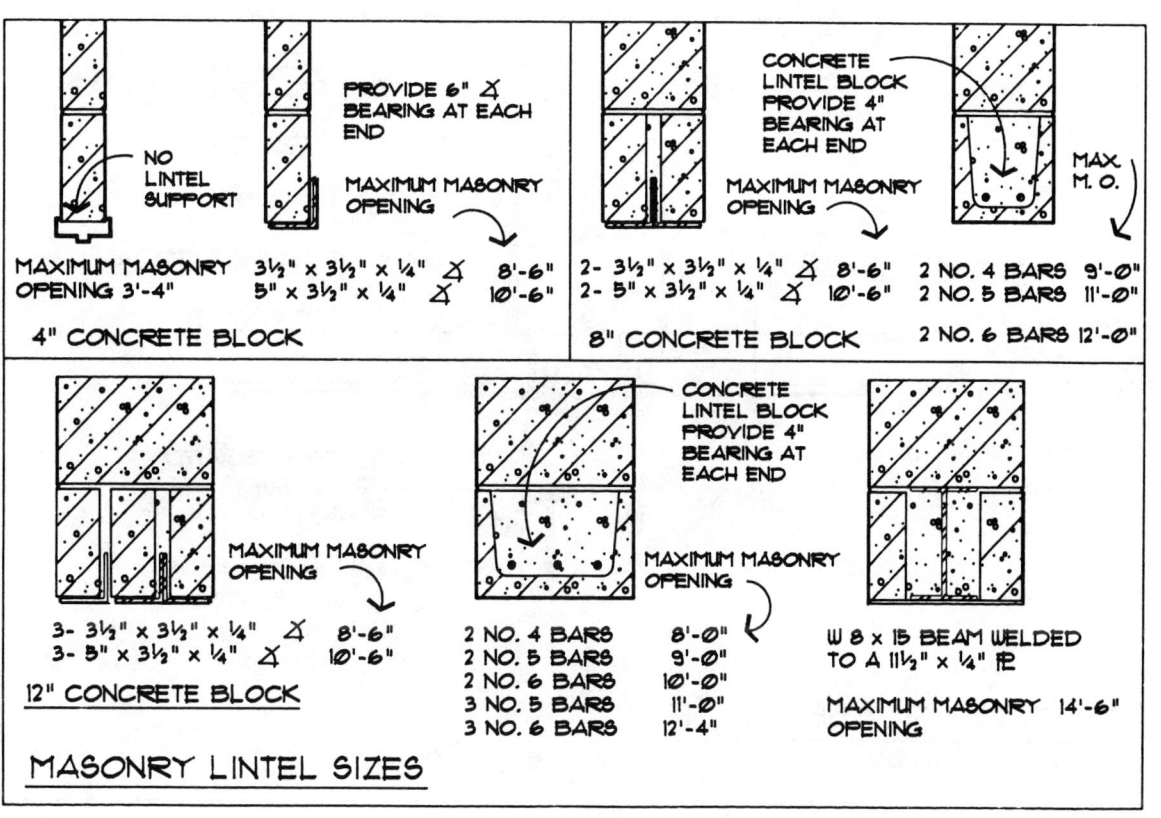

MASONRY LINTEL SIZES

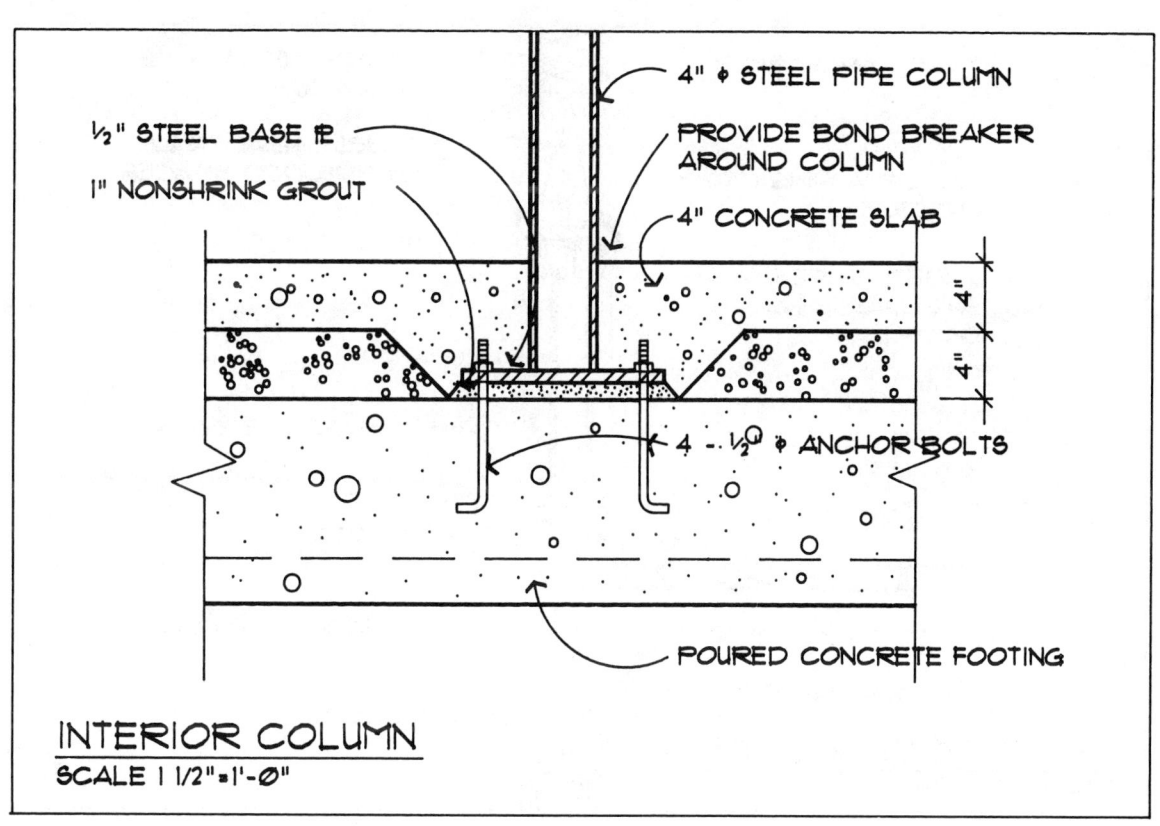

4" CONCRETE BLOCK

- NO LINTEL SUPPORT — MAXIMUM MASONRY OPENING 3'-4"
- PROVIDE 6" BEARING AT EACH END, MAXIMUM MASONRY OPENING:
  - 3½" x 3½" x ¼" ∠ — 8'-6"
  - 5" x 3½" x ¼" ∠ — 10'-6"

8" CONCRETE BLOCK

- CONCRETE LINTEL BLOCK, PROVIDE 4" BEARING AT EACH END, MAXIMUM MASONRY OPENING:
  - 2 - 3½" x 3½" x ¼" ∠ — 8'-6"
  - 2 - 5" x 3½" x ¼" ∠ — 10'-6"
- MAX. M.O.:
  - 2 NO. 4 BARS — 9'-0"
  - 2 NO. 5 BARS — 11'-0"
  - 2 NO. 6 BARS — 12'-0"

12" CONCRETE BLOCK

- MAXIMUM MASONRY OPENING:
  - 3 - 3½" x 3½" x ¼" ∠ — 8'-6"
  - 3 - 5" x 3½" x ¼" ∠ — 10'-6"
- CONCRETE LINTEL BLOCK, PROVIDE 4" BEARING AT EACH END, MAXIMUM MASONRY OPENING:
  - 2 NO. 4 BARS — 8'-0"
  - 2 NO. 5 BARS — 9'-0"
  - 2 NO. 6 BARS — 10'-0"
  - 3 NO. 5 BARS — 11'-0"
  - 3 NO. 6 BARS — 12'-4"
- W 8 x 15 BEAM WELDED TO A 11½" x ¼" ℞ — MAXIMUM MASONRY OPENING 14'-6"

INTERIOR COLUMN
SCALE 1 ½" = 1'-0"

- 4" ⌀ STEEL PIPE COLUMN
- ½" STEEL BASE ℞
- 1" NONSHRINK GROUT
- PROVIDE BOND BREAKER AROUND COLUMN
- 4" CONCRETE SLAB
- 4 - ½" ⌀ ANCHOR BOLTS
- POURED CONCRETE FOOTING

DETAILS

9-9

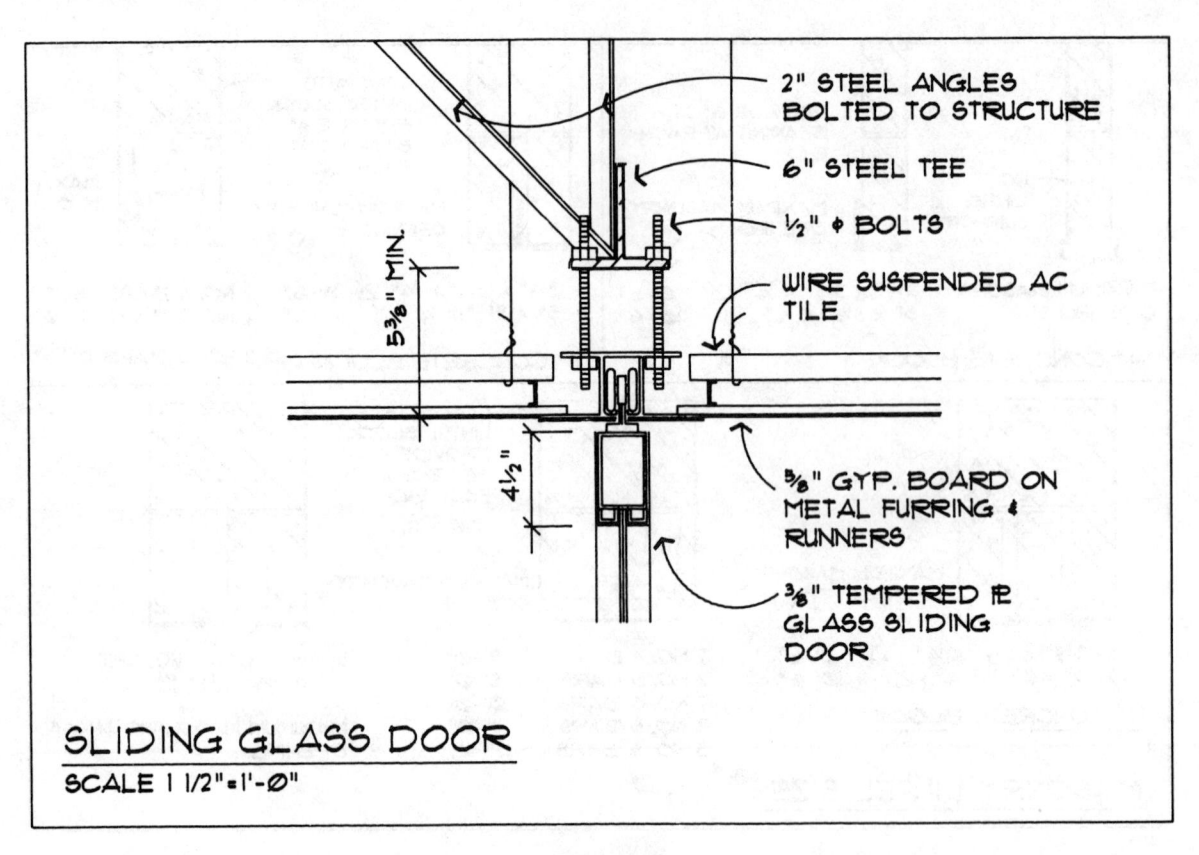

SLIDING GLASS DOOR
SCALE 1 1/2" = 1'-0"

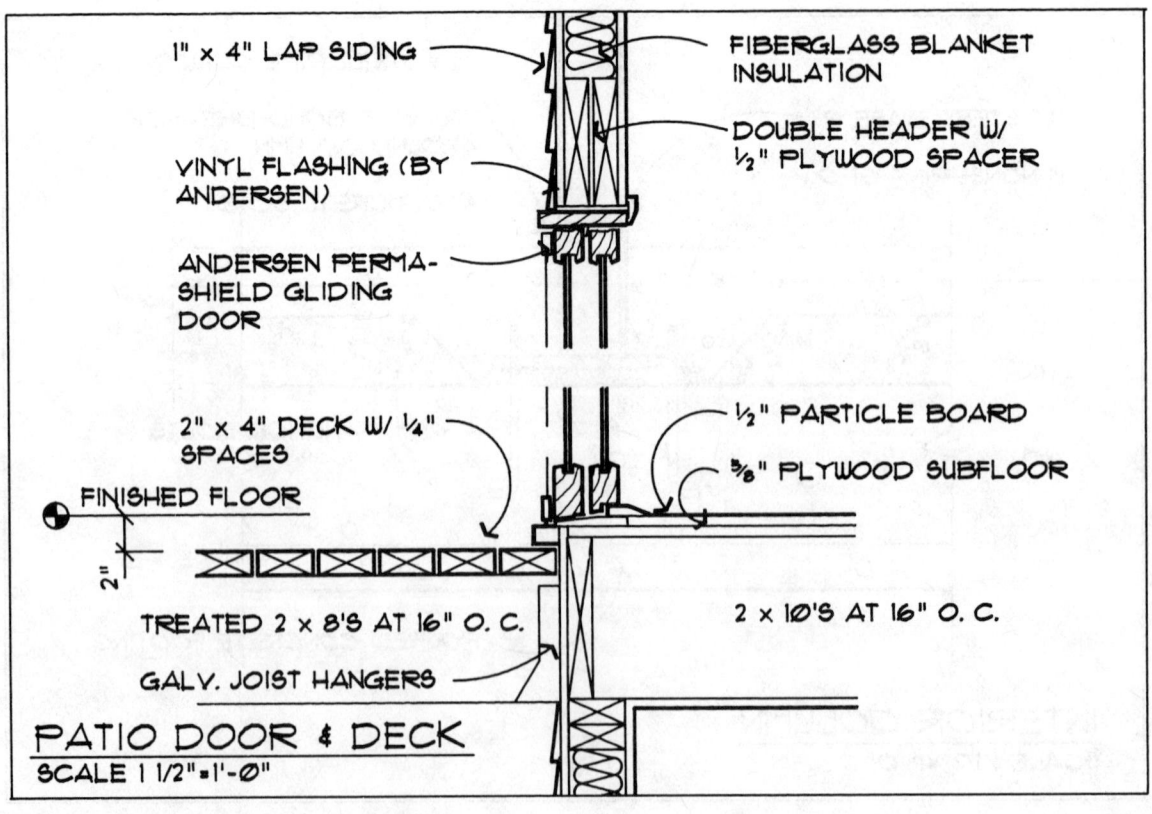

- 2" STEEL ANGLES BOLTED TO STRUCTURE
- 6" STEEL TEE
- 1/2" ⌀ BOLTS
- WIRE SUSPENDED AC TILE
- 5/8" GYP. BOARD ON METAL FURRING & RUNNERS
- 3/8" TEMPERED ℗ GLASS SLIDING DOOR

5 3/8" MIN.
4 1/2"

PATIO DOOR & DECK
SCALE 1 1/2" = 1'-0"

- 1" x 4" LAP SIDING
- VINYL FLASHING (BY ANDERSEN)
- ANDERSEN PERMA-SHIELD GLIDING DOOR
- 2" x 4" DECK W/ 1/4" SPACES
- FINISHED FLOOR
- TREATED 2 x 8'S AT 16" O.C.
- GALV. JOIST HANGERS
- FIBERGLASS BLANKET INSULATION
- DOUBLE HEADER W/ 1/2" PLYWOOD SPACER
- 1/2" PARTICLE BOARD
- 5/8" PLYWOOD SUBFLOOR
- 2 x 10'S AT 16" O.C.

2"

DETAILS 9-10

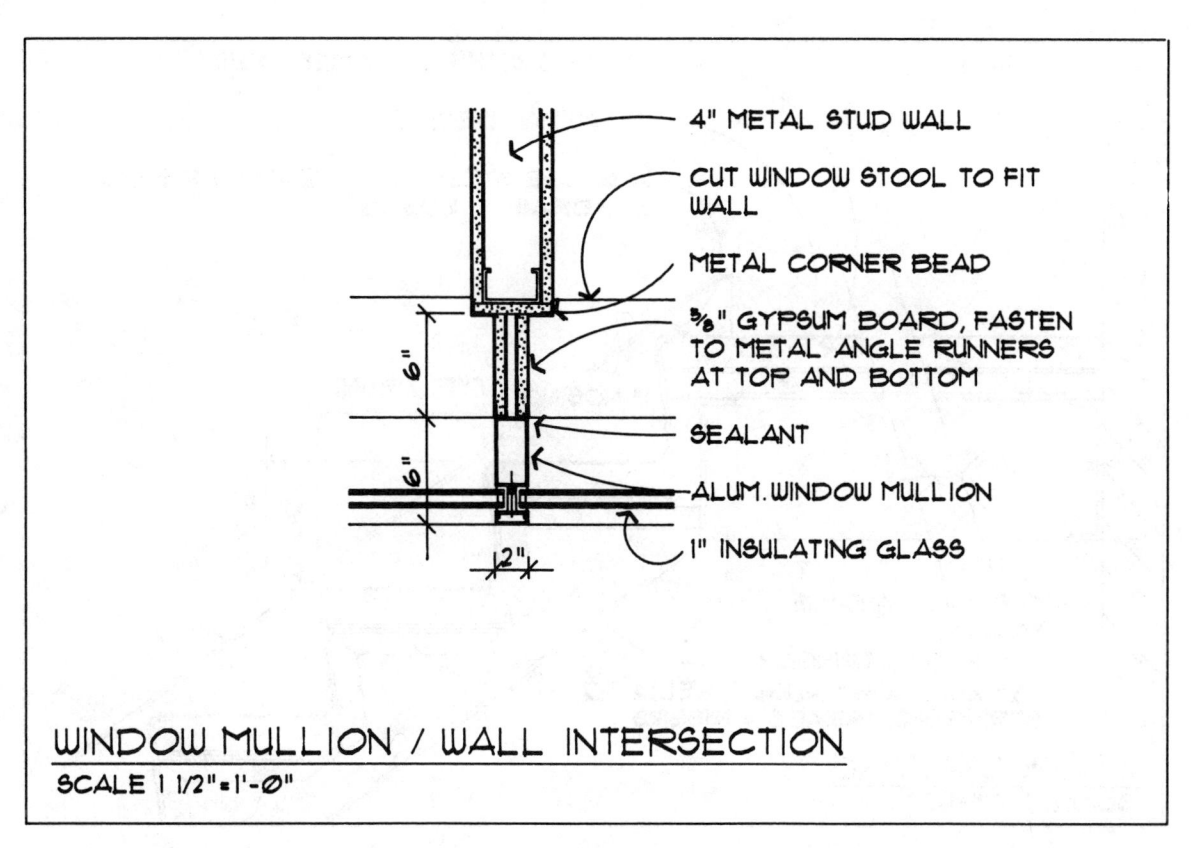

WINDOW MULLION / WALL INTERSECTION
SCALE 1 1/2"=1'-0"

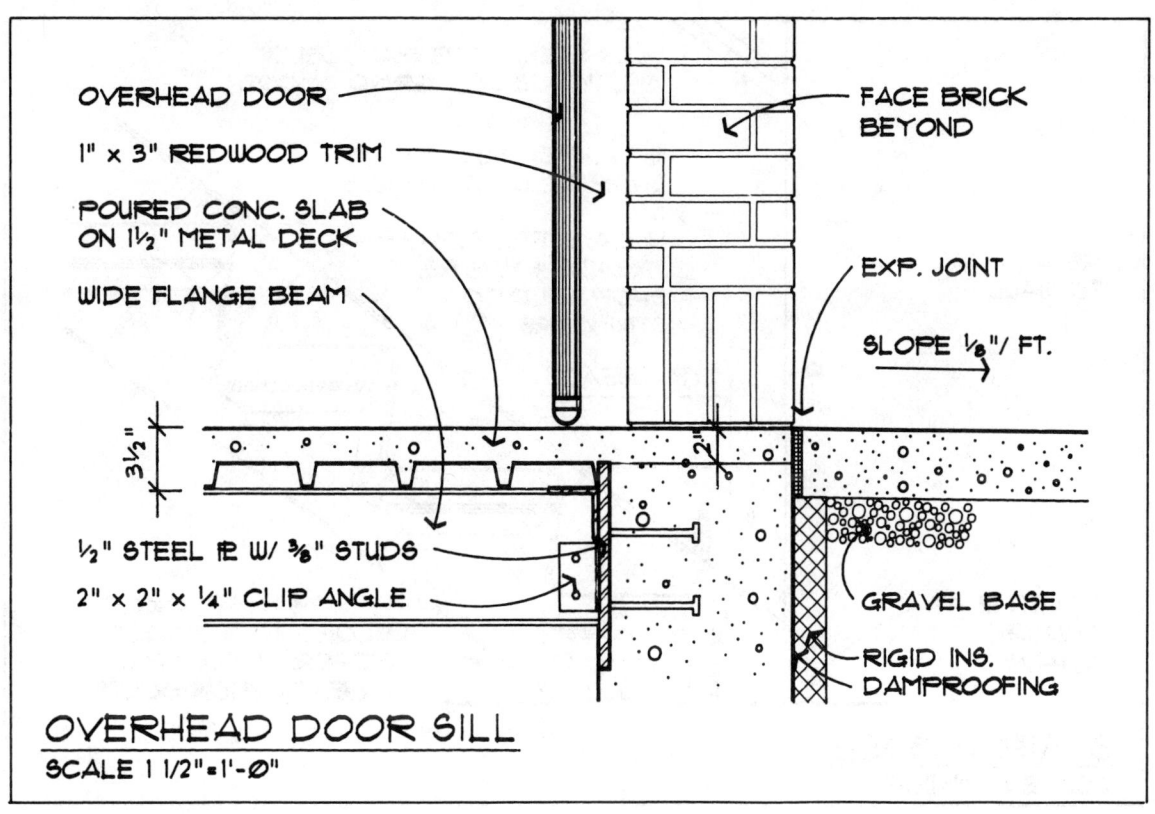

- 4" METAL STUD WALL
- CUT WINDOW STOOL TO FIT WALL
- METAL CORNER BEAD
- 3/8" GYPSUM BOARD, FASTEN TO METAL ANGLE RUNNERS AT TOP AND BOTTOM
- SEALANT
- ALUM. WINDOW MULLION
- 1" INSULATING GLASS

OVERHEAD DOOR SILL
SCALE 1 1/2"=1'-0"

- OVERHEAD DOOR
- 1" x 3" REDWOOD TRIM
- POURED CONC. SLAB ON 1 1/2" METAL DECK
- WIDE FLANGE BEAM
- 1/2" STEEL ℞ W/ 3/8" STUDS
- 2" x 2" x 1/4" CLIP ANGLE
- FACE BRICK BEYOND
- EXP. JOINT
- SLOPE 1/8"/ FT.
- GRAVEL BASE
- RIGID INS. DAMPROOFING

DETAILS 9-11

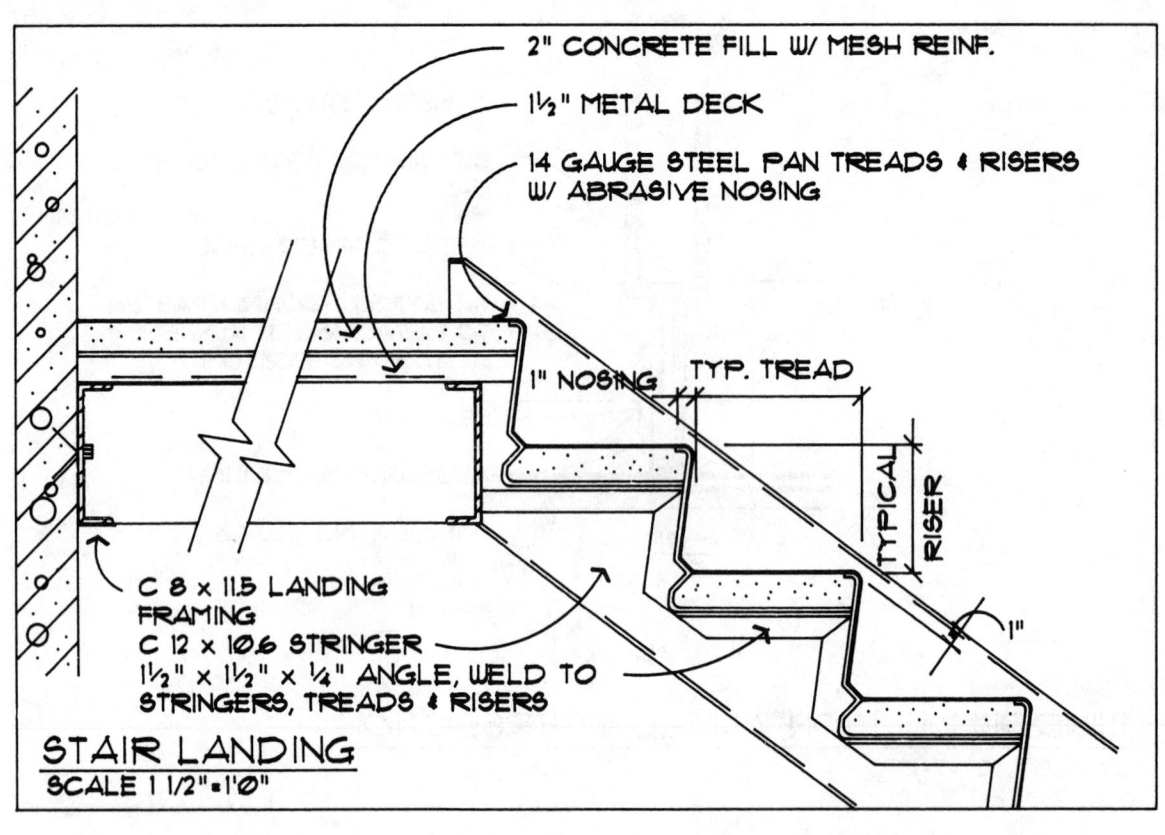

STAIR LANDING
SCALE 1 1/2" = 1'-0"

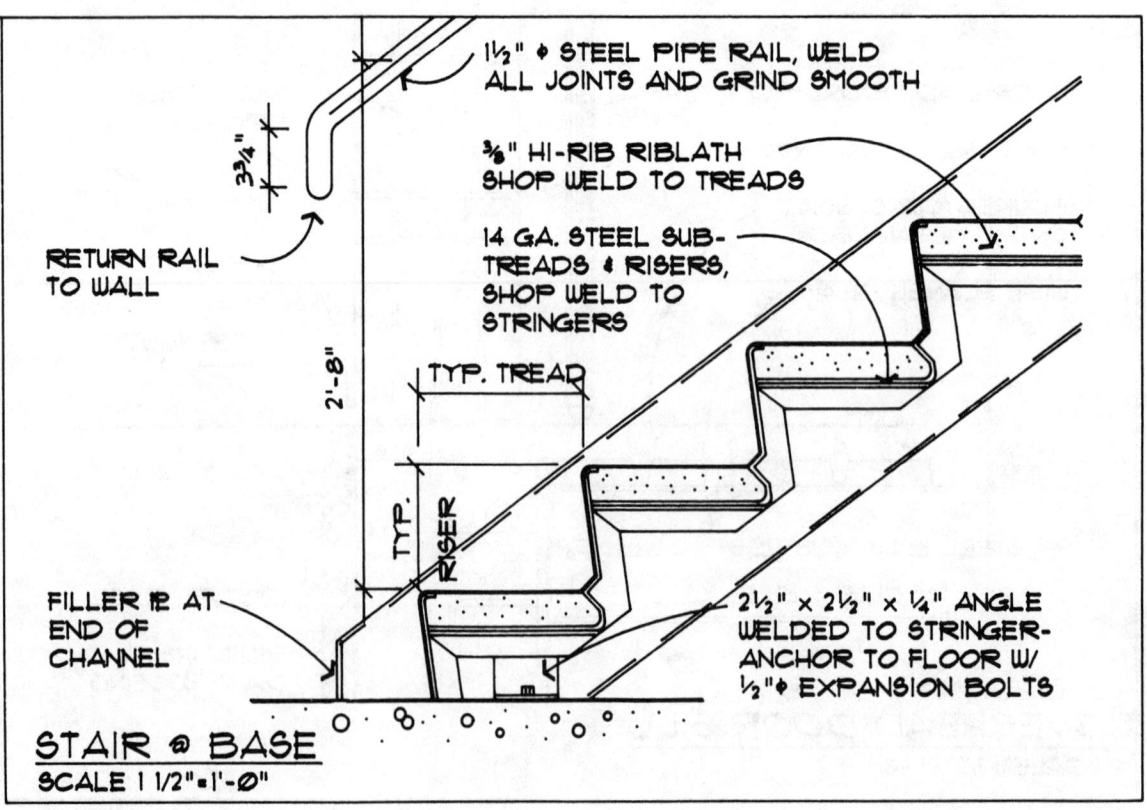

- 2" CONCRETE FILL W/ MESH REINF.
- 1½" METAL DECK
- 14 GAUGE STEEL PAN TREADS & RISERS W/ ABRASIVE NOSING
- 1" NOSING
- TYP. TREAD
- TYPICAL RISER
- 1"
- C 8 × 11.5 LANDING FRAMING
- C 12 × 10.6 STRINGER
- 1½" × 1½" × ¼" ANGLE, WELD TO STRINGERS, TREADS & RISERS

STAIR @ BASE
SCALE 1 1/2" = 1'-0"

- 1½" ⌀ STEEL PIPE RAIL, WELD ALL JOINTS AND GRIND SMOOTH
- ⅜" HI-RIB RIBLATH SHOP WELD TO TREADS
- 14 GA. STEEL SUB-TREADS & RISERS, SHOP WELD TO STRINGERS
- 3¾"
- RETURN RAIL TO WALL
- 2'-8"
- TYP. TREAD
- TYP. RISER
- FILLER ℔ AT END OF CHANNEL
- 2½" × 2½" × ¼" ANGLE WELDED TO STRINGER - ANCHOR TO FLOOR W/ ½" ⌀ EXPANSION BOLTS

DETAILS

9-12

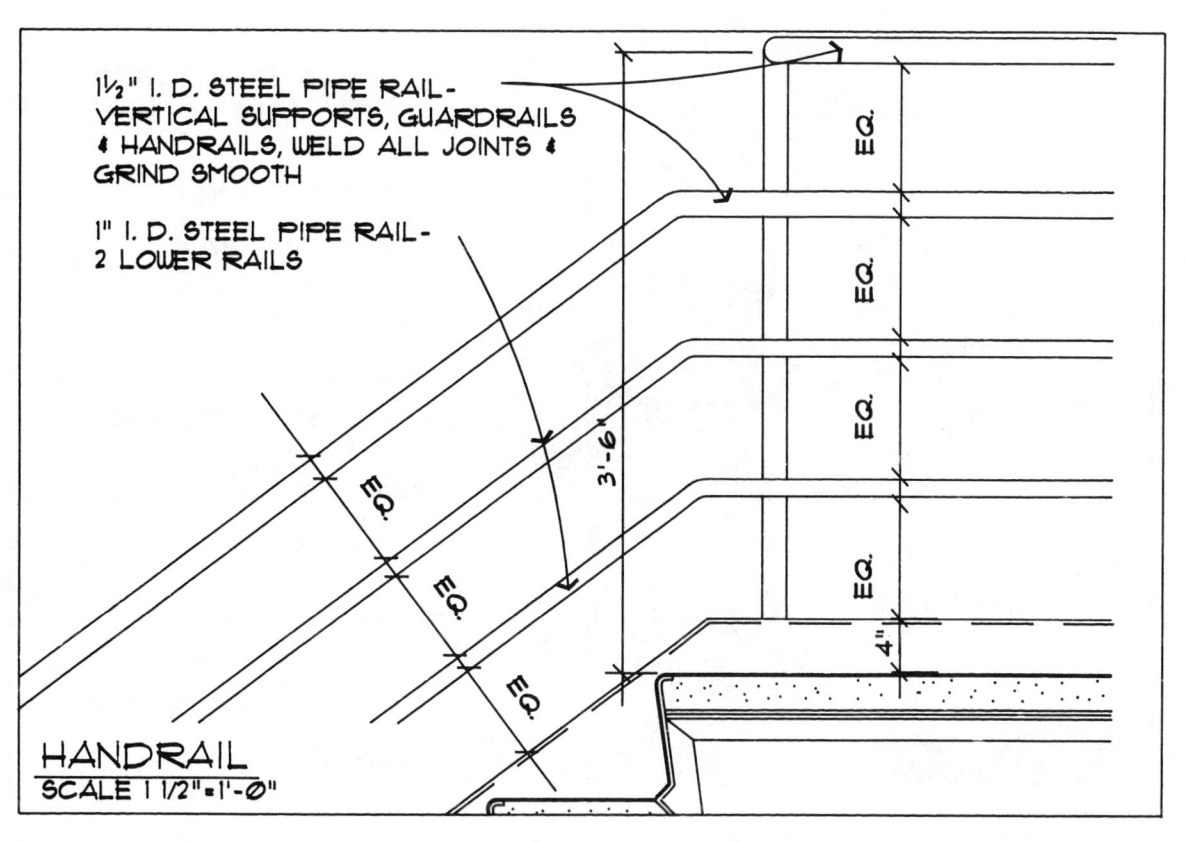

HANDRAIL
SCALE 1 1/2" = 1'-0"

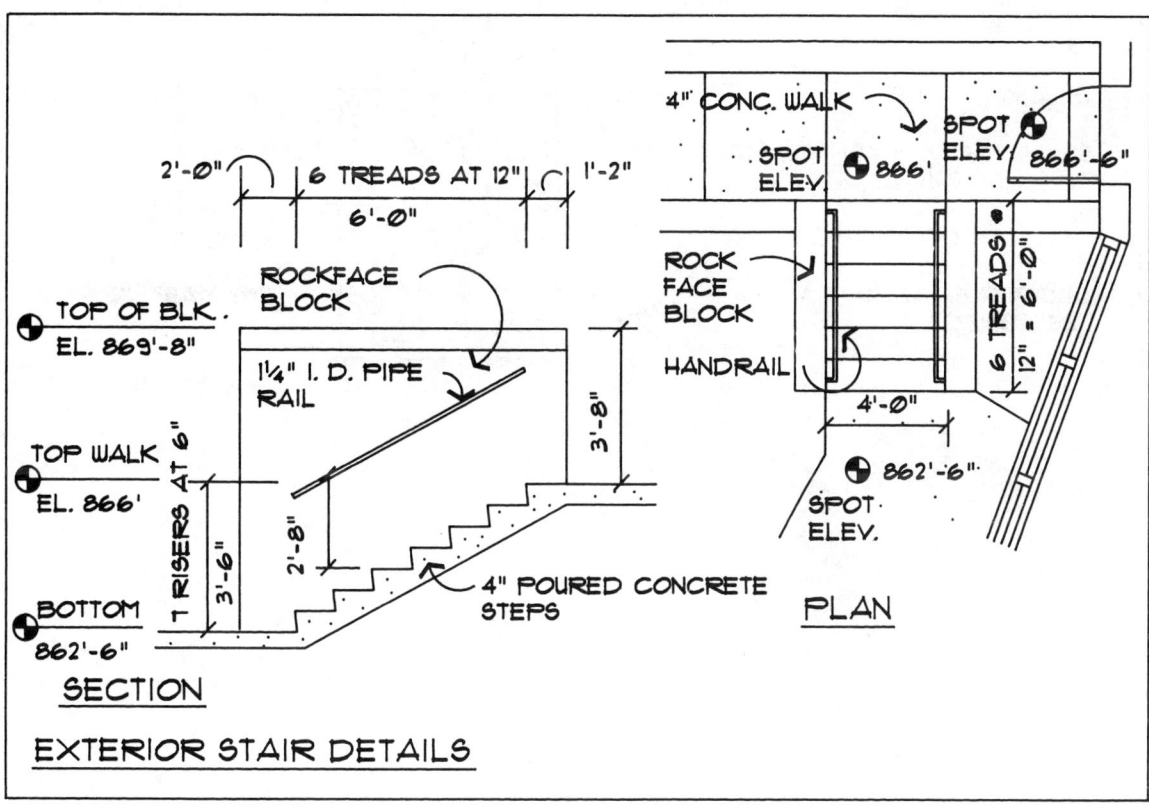

1 1/2" I.D. STEEL PIPE RAIL - VERTICAL SUPPORTS, GUARDRAILS & HANDRAILS, WELD ALL JOINTS & GRIND SMOOTH

1" I.D. STEEL PIPE RAIL - 2 LOWER RAILS

EQ. / 3'-6" / 4"

EXTERIOR STAIR DETAILS

SECTION

- 2'-0"
- 6 TREADS AT 12"
- 1'-2"
- 6'-0"
- ROCKFACE BLOCK
- 1 1/4" I.D. PIPE RAIL
- TOP OF BLK. EL. 869'-8"
- TOP WALK EL. 866'
- BOTTOM 862'-6"
- 7 RISERS AT 6"
- 3'-6"
- 2'-8"
- 3'-8"
- 4" POURED CONCRETE STEPS

PLAN

- 4" CONC. WALK
- SPOT ELEV. 866'
- SPOT ELEV. 866'-6"
- ROCK FACE BLOCK
- HANDRAIL
- 4'-0"
- SPOT ELEV. 862'-6"
- 6 TREADS 12" = 6'-0"

DETAILS

9-13

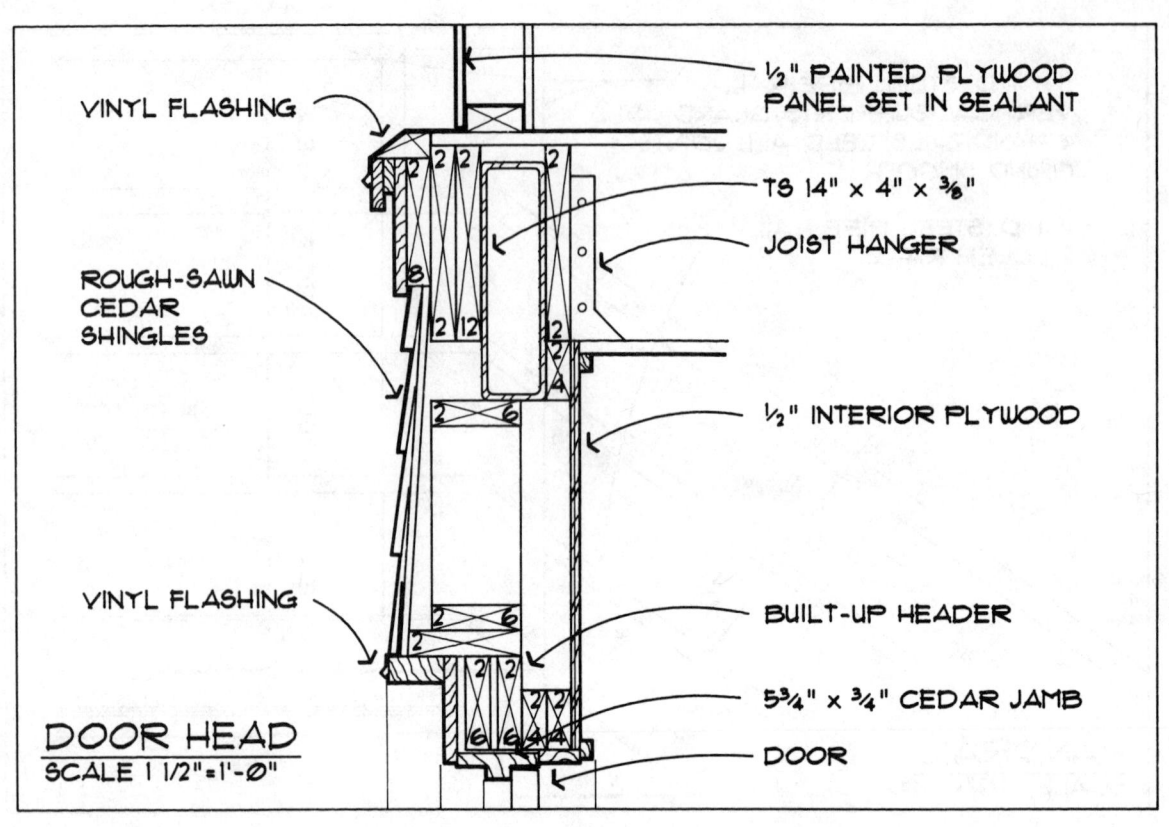

DOOR HEAD
SCALE 1 1/2"=1'-0"

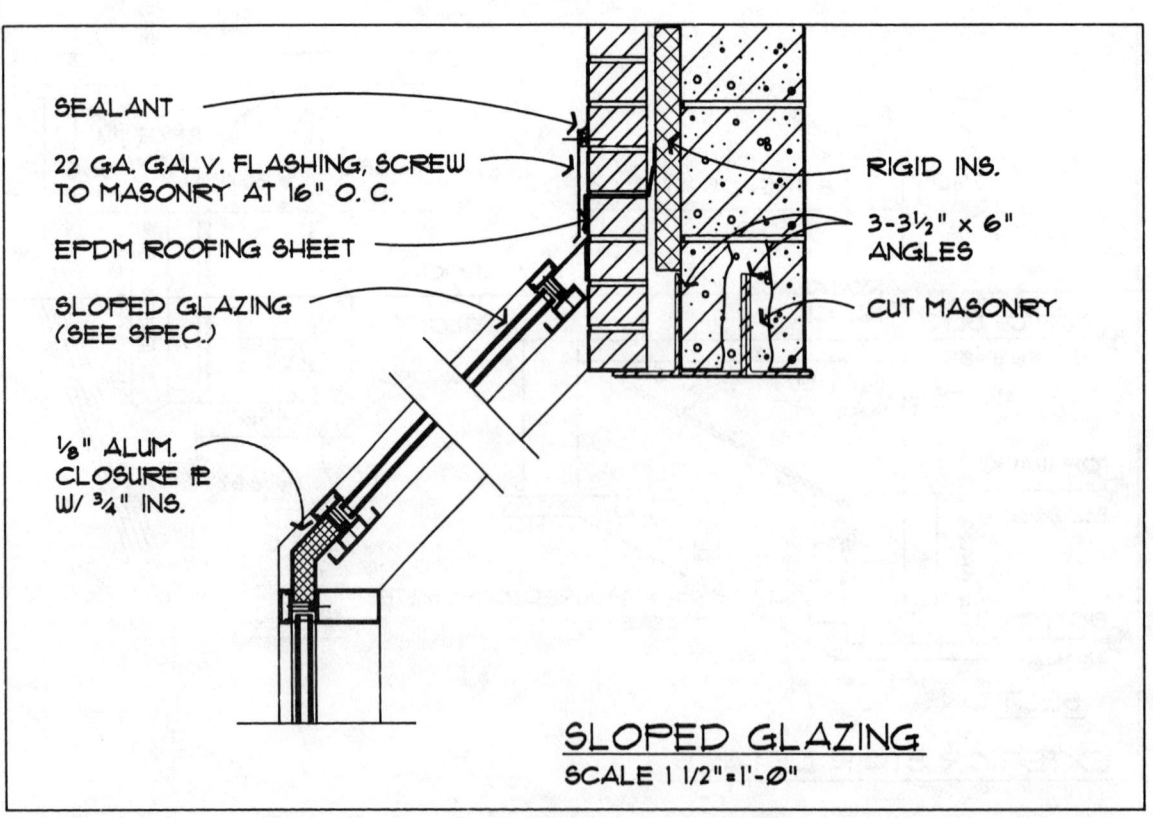

- VINYL FLASHING
- ROUGH-SAWN CEDAR SHINGLES
- VINYL FLASHING
- 1/2" PAINTED PLYWOOD PANEL SET IN SEALANT
- TS 14" x 4" x 3/8"
- JOIST HANGER
- 1/2" INTERIOR PLYWOOD
- BUILT-UP HEADER
- 5 3/4" x 3/4" CEDAR JAMB
- DOOR

SLOPED GLAZING
SCALE 1 1/2"=1'-0"

- SEALANT
- 22 GA. GALV. FLASHING, SCREW TO MASONRY AT 16" O.C.
- EPDM ROOFING SHEET
- SLOPED GLAZING (SEE SPEC.)
- 1/8" ALUM. CLOSURE PL W/ 3/4" INS.
- RIGID INS.
- 3-3 1/2" x 6" ANGLES
- CUT MASONRY

DETAILS 9-14

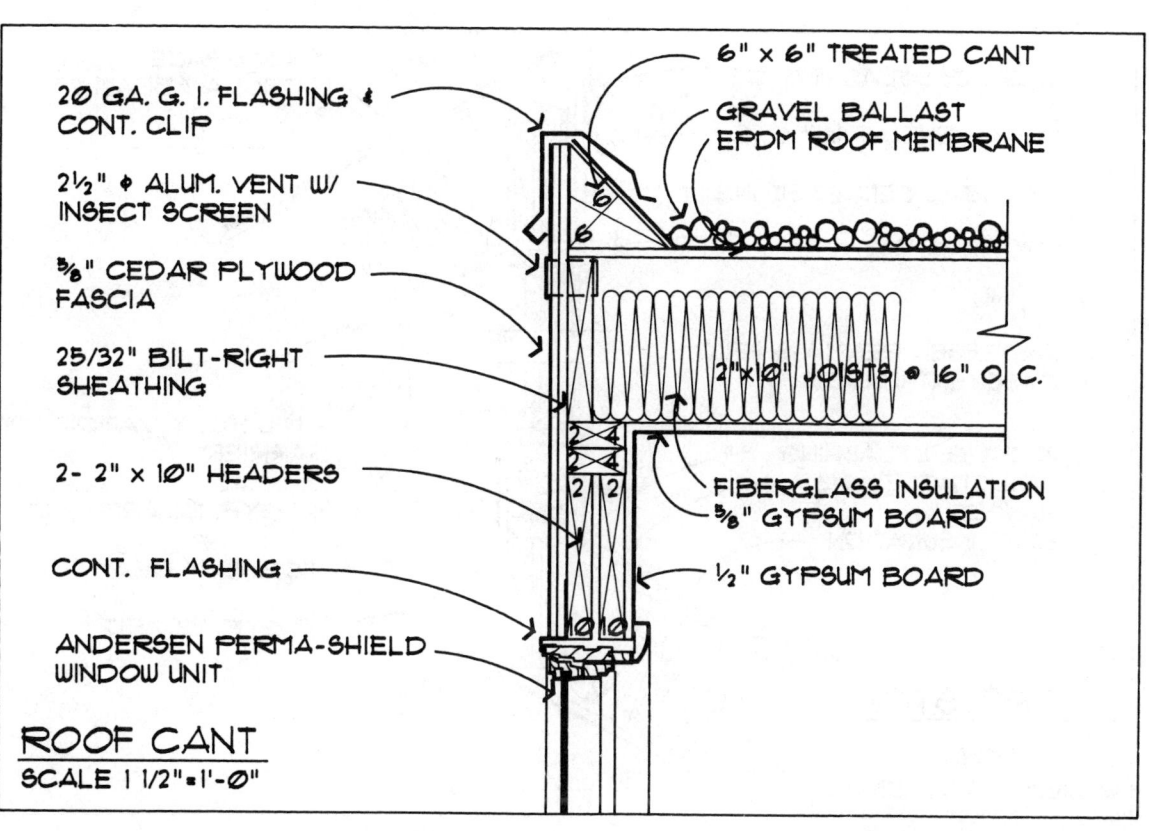

ROOF CANT
SCALE 1 1/2" = 1'-0"

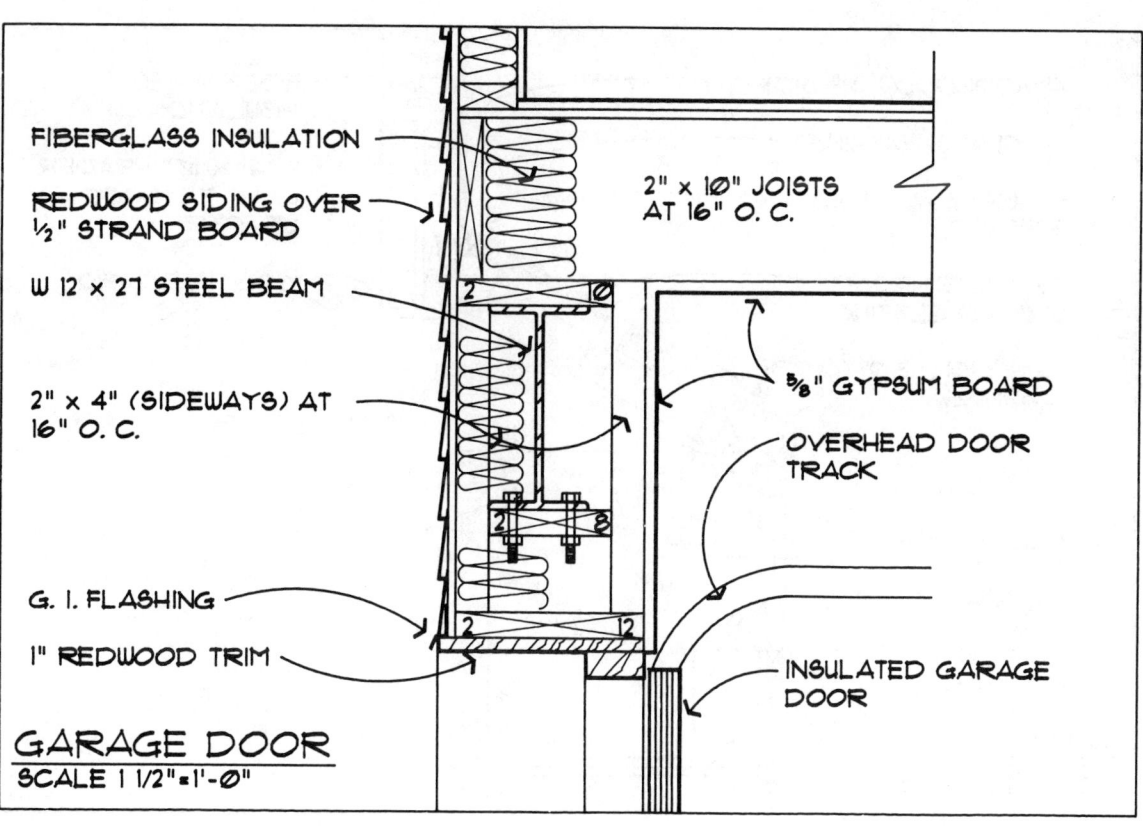

- 20 GA. G. I. FLASHING & CONT. CLIP
- 2 1/2" Ø ALUM. VENT W/ INSECT SCREEN
- 3/8" CEDAR PLYWOOD FASCIA
- 25/32" BILT-RIGHT SHEATHING
- 2- 2" x 10" HEADERS
- CONT. FLASHING
- ANDERSEN PERMA-SHIELD WINDOW UNIT
- 6" x 6" TREATED CANT
- GRAVEL BALLAST
- EPDM ROOF MEMBRANE
- 2" x 10" JOISTS @ 16" O.C.
- FIBERGLASS INSULATION
- 5/8" GYPSUM BOARD
- 1/2" GYPSUM BOARD

GARAGE DOOR
SCALE 1 1/2" = 1'-0"

- FIBERGLASS INSULATION
- REDWOOD SIDING OVER 1/2" STRAND BOARD
- W 12 x 27 STEEL BEAM
- 2" x 4" (SIDEWAYS) AT 16" O.C.
- G. I. FLASHING
- 1" REDWOOD TRIM
- 2" x 10" JOISTS AT 16" O.C.
- 5/8" GYPSUM BOARD
- OVERHEAD DOOR TRACK
- INSULATED GARAGE DOOR

DETAILS 9-15

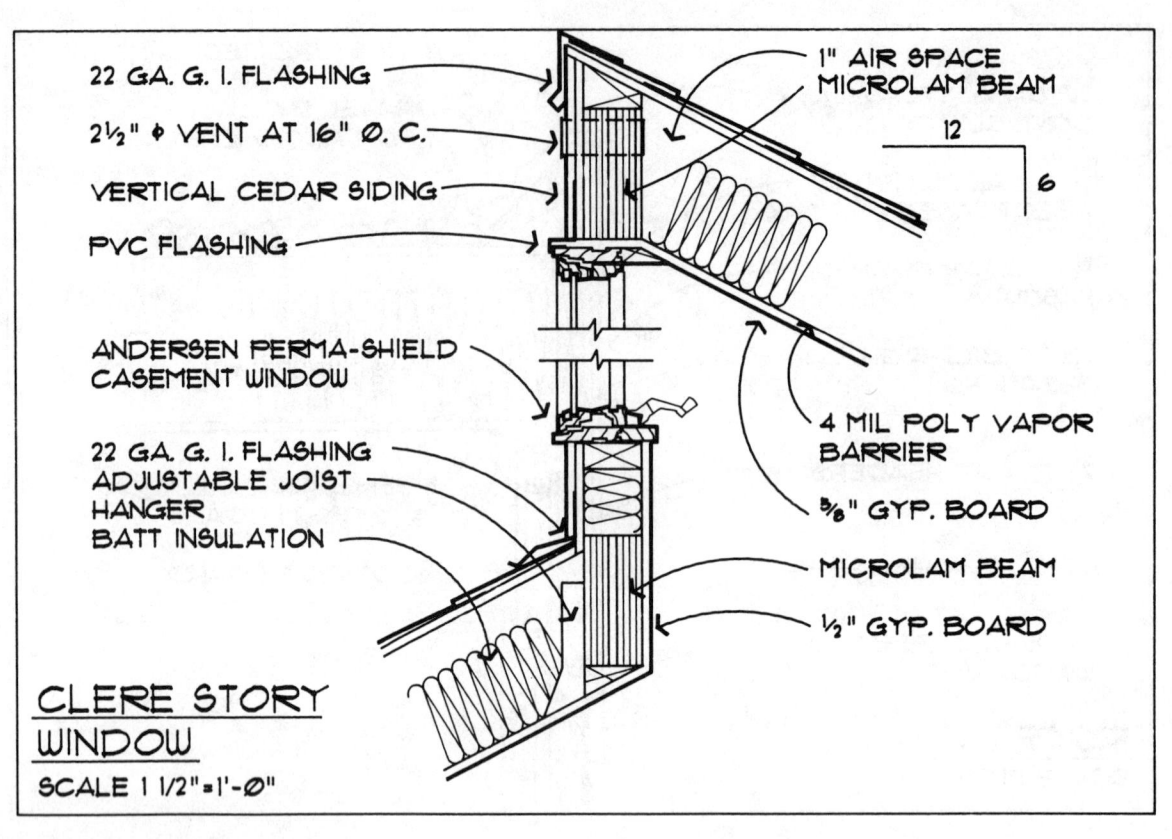

CLERE STORY WINDOW
SCALE 1 1/2"=1'-0"

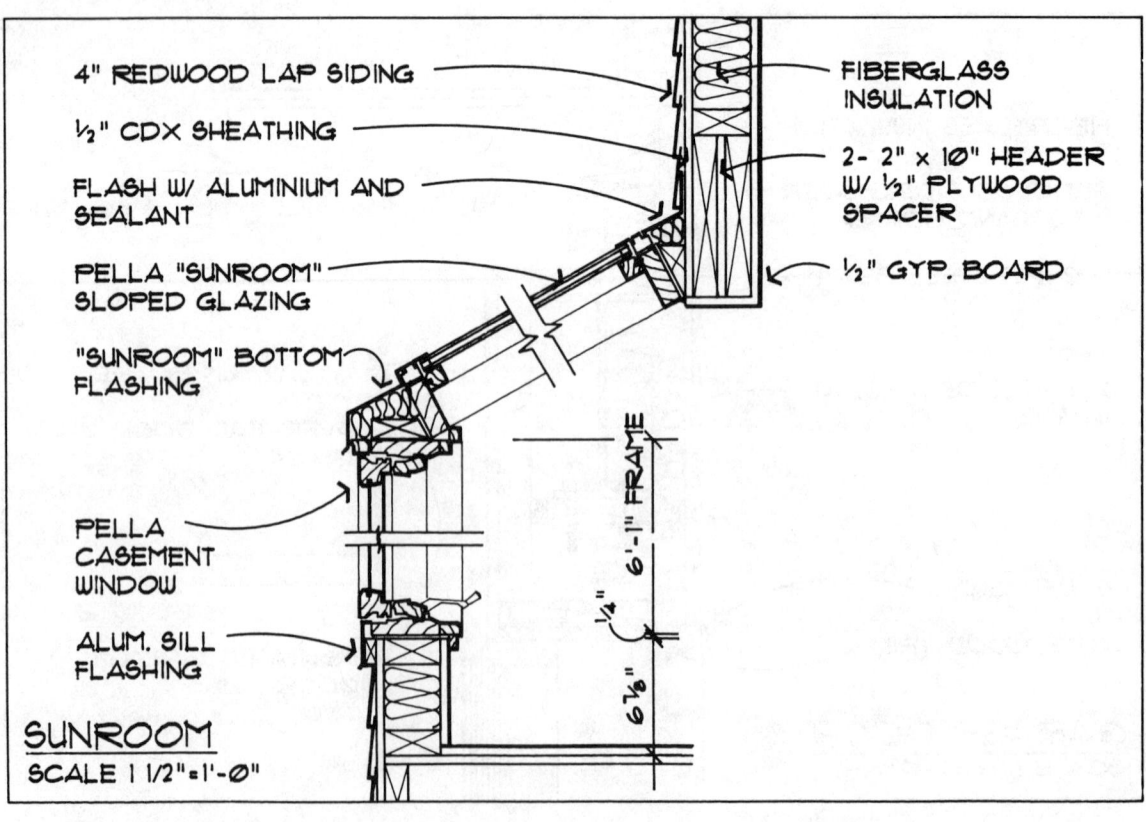

- 22 GA. G. I. FLASHING
- 2½" ⌀ VENT AT 16" O. C.
- VERTICAL CEDAR SIDING
- PVC FLASHING
- ANDERSEN PERMA-SHIELD CASEMENT WINDOW
- 22 GA. G. I. FLASHING
- ADJUSTABLE JOIST HANGER
- BATT INSULATION
- 1" AIR SPACE
- MICROLAM BEAM
- 12 / 6
- 4 MIL POLY VAPOR BARRIER
- 5/8" GYP. BOARD
- MICROLAM BEAM
- ½" GYP. BOARD

SUNROOM
SCALE 1 1/2"=1'-0"

- 4" REDWOOD LAP SIDING
- ½" CDX SHEATHING
- FLASH W/ ALUMINIUM AND SEALANT
- PELLA "SUNROOM" SLOPED GLAZING
- "SUNROOM" BOTTOM FLASHING
- PELLA CASEMENT WINDOW
- ALUM. SILL FLASHING
- FIBERGLASS INSULATION
- 2- 2" x 10" HEADER W/ ½" PLYWOOD SPACER
- ½" GYP. BOARD
- 6'-1" FRAME
- ¼"
- 6⅞"

DETAILS 9-16

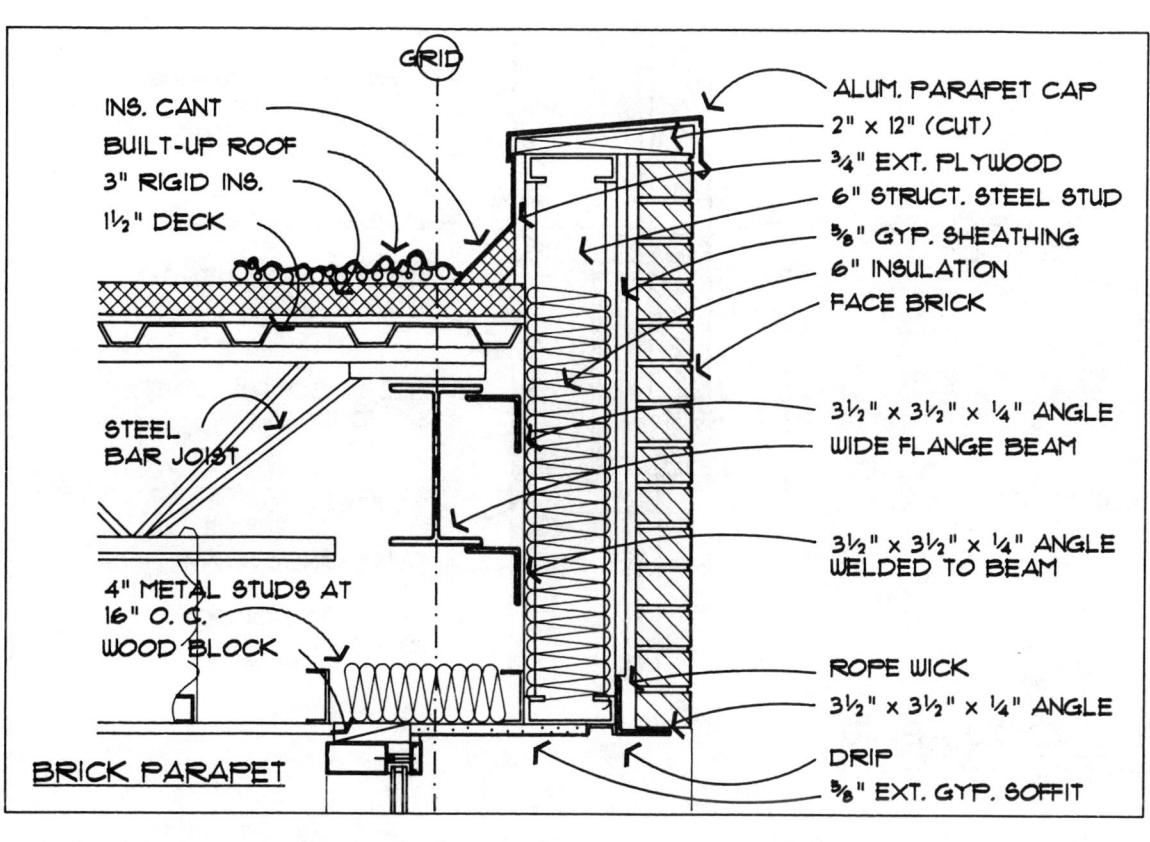

BRICK PARAPET

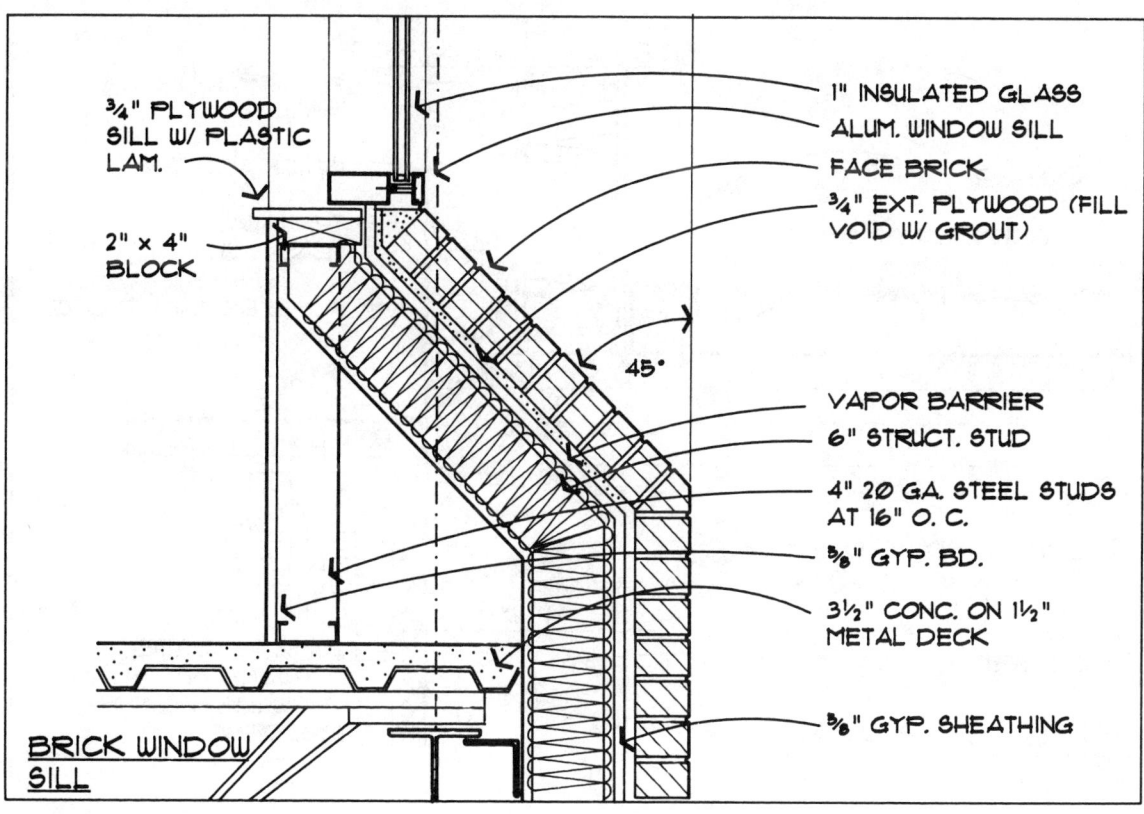

- INS. CANT
- BUILT-UP ROOF
- 3" RIGID INS.
- 1½" DECK
- STEEL BAR JOIST
- 4" METAL STUDS AT 16" O.C.
- WOOD BLOCK

- GRID
- ALUM. PARAPET CAP
- 2" × 12" (CUT)
- ¾" EXT. PLYWOOD
- 6" STRUCT. STEEL STUD
- ⅝" GYP. SHEATHING
- 6" INSULATION
- FACE BRICK
- 3½" × 3½" × ¼" ANGLE
- WIDE FLANGE BEAM
- 3½" × 3½" × ¼" ANGLE WELDED TO BEAM
- ROPE WICK
- 3½" × 3½" × ¼" ANGLE
- DRIP
- ⅝" EXT. GYP. SOFFIT

BRICK WINDOW SILL

- ¾" PLYWOOD SILL W/ PLASTIC LAM.
- 2" × 4" BLOCK

- 1" INSULATED GLASS
- ALUM. WINDOW SILL
- FACE BRICK
- ¾" EXT. PLYWOOD (FILL VOID W/ GROUT)
- 45°
- VAPOR BARRIER
- 6" STRUCT. STUD
- 4" 20 GA. STEEL STUDS AT 16" O.C.
- ⅝" GYP. BD.
- 3½" CONC. ON 1½" METAL DECK
- ⅝" GYP. SHEATHING

DETAILS

9-17

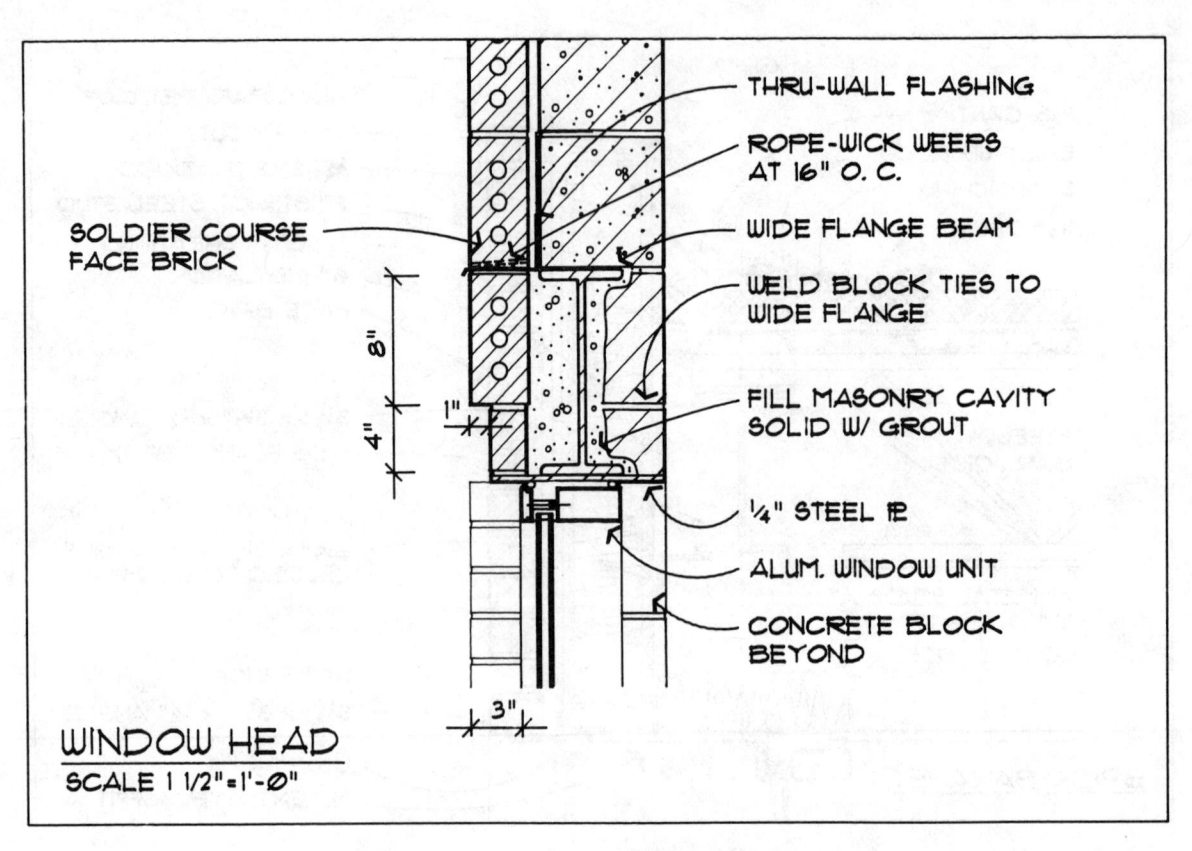

WINDOW HEAD
SCALE 1 1/2" = 1'-0"

- THRU-WALL FLASHING
- ROPE-WICK WEEPS AT 16" O.C.
- WIDE FLANGE BEAM
- WELD BLOCK TIES TO WIDE FLANGE
- FILL MASONRY CAVITY SOLID W/ GROUT
- 1/4" STEEL PL
- ALUM. WINDOW UNIT
- CONCRETE BLOCK BEYOND
- SOLDIER COURSE FACE BRICK

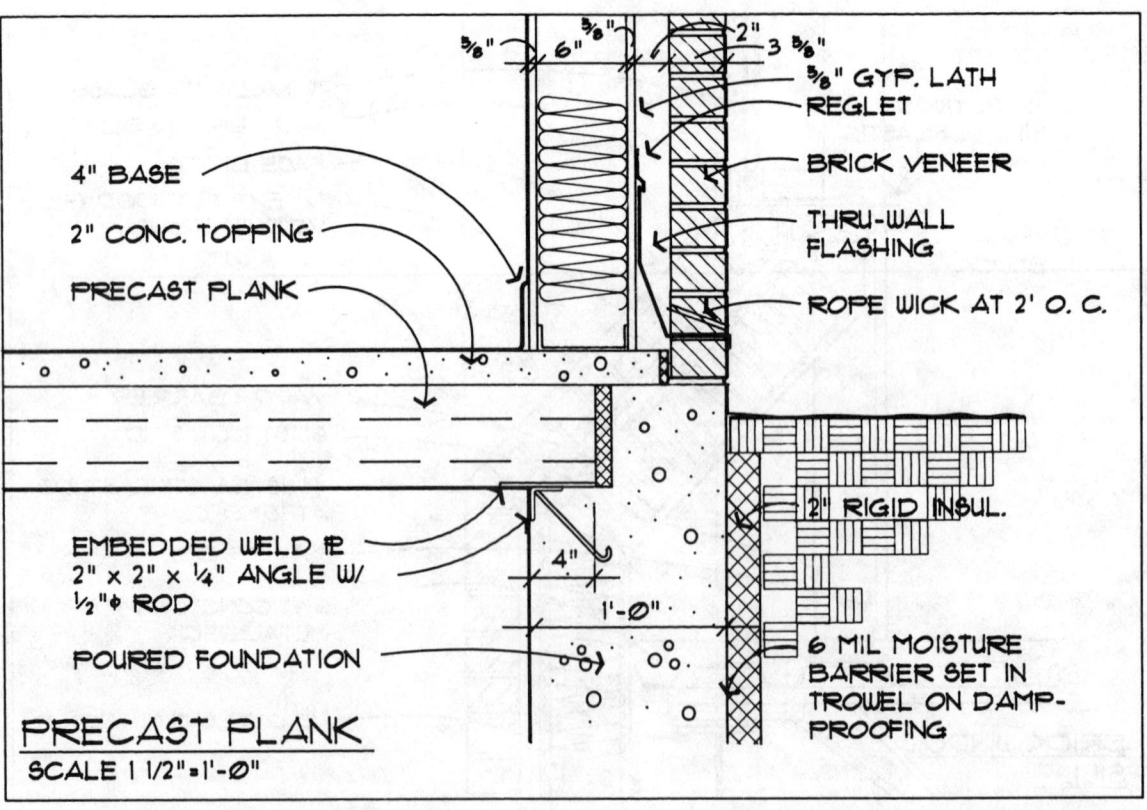

PRECAST PLANK
SCALE 1 1/2" = 1'-0"

- 3/8" GYP. LATH REGLET
- BRICK VENEER
- THRU-WALL FLASHING
- ROPE WICK AT 2' O.C.
- 4" BASE
- 2" CONC. TOPPING
- PRECAST PLANK
- EMBEDDED WELD PL 2" x 2" x 1/4" ANGLE W/ 1/2" ⌀ ROD
- POURED FOUNDATION
- 2" RIGID INSUL.
- 6 MIL MOISTURE BARRIER SET IN TROWEL ON DAMP-PROOFING

DETAILS 9-18

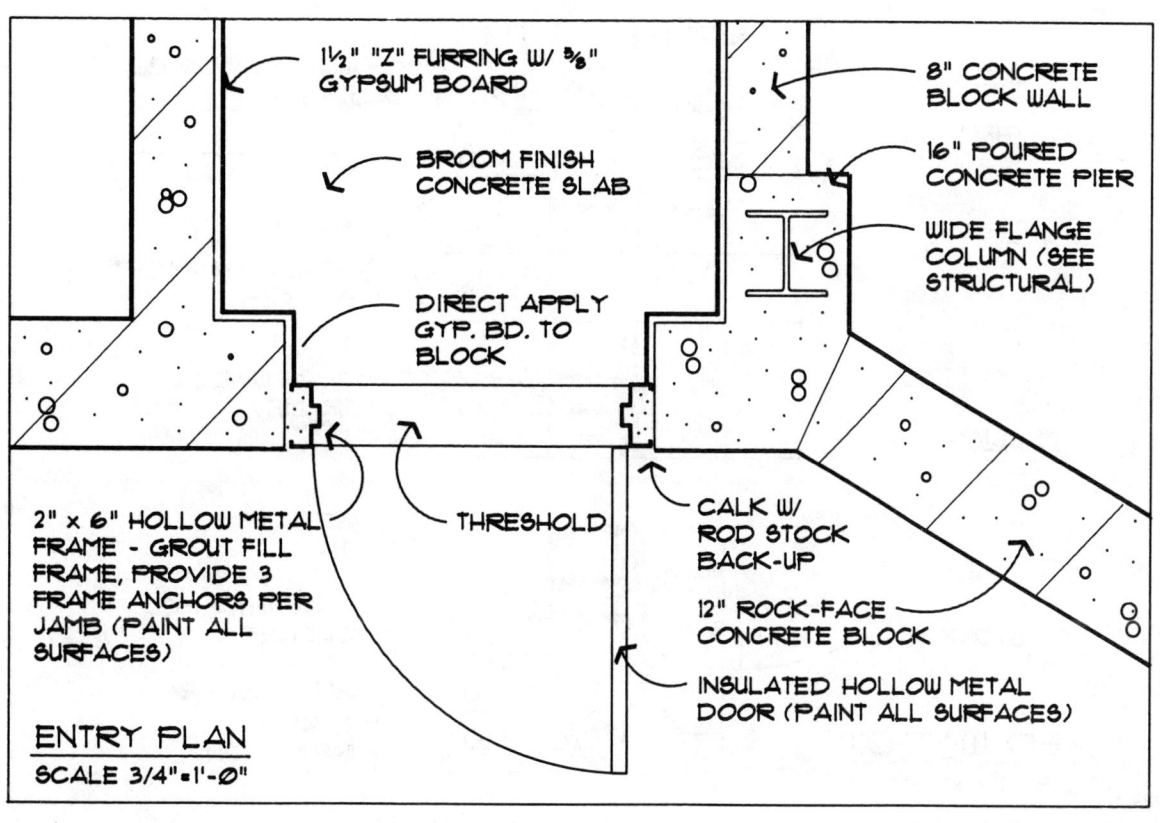

ENTRY PLAN
SCALE 3/4" = 1'-0"

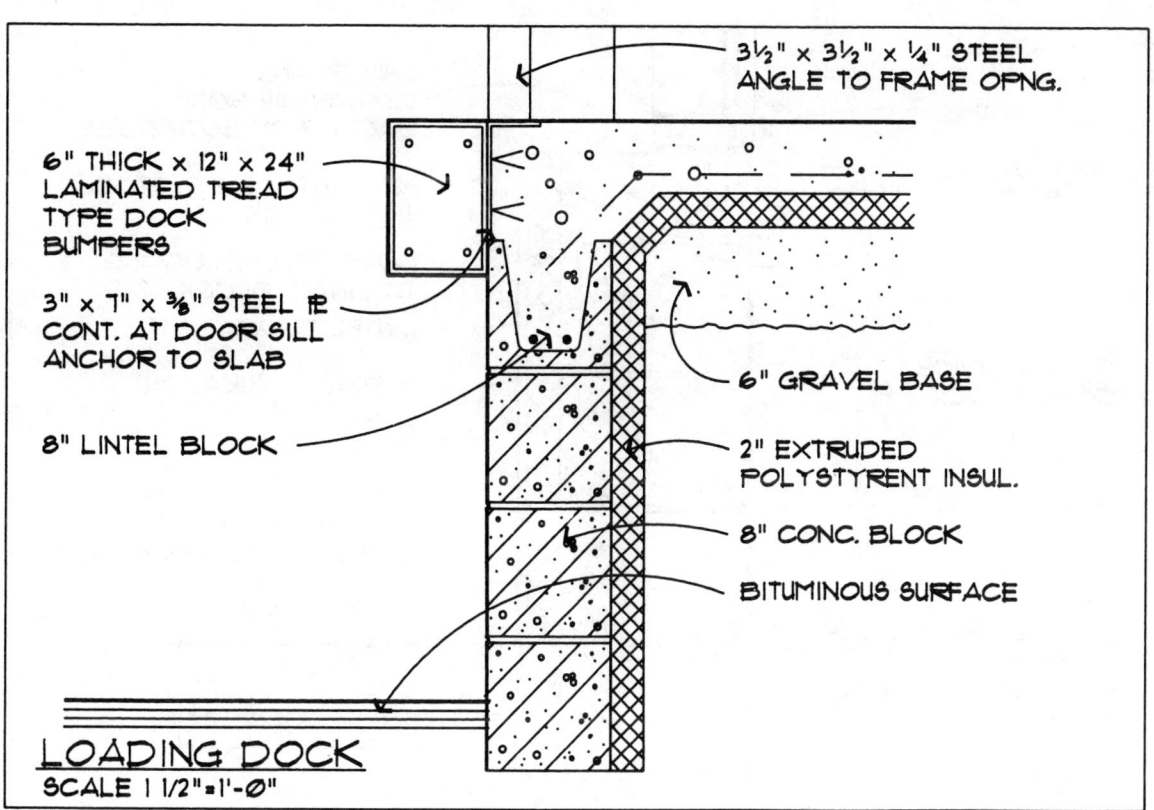

- 1½" "Z" FURRING W/ ⅝" GYPSUM BOARD
- BROOM FINISH CONCRETE SLAB
- 8" CONCRETE BLOCK WALL
- 16" POURED CONCRETE PIER
- WIDE FLANGE COLUMN (SEE STRUCTURAL)
- DIRECT APPLY GYP. BD. TO BLOCK
- 2" x 6" HOLLOW METAL FRAME - GROUT FILL FRAME, PROVIDE 3 FRAME ANCHORS PER JAMB (PAINT ALL SURFACES)
- THRESHOLD
- CALK W/ ROD STOCK BACK-UP
- 12" ROCK-FACE CONCRETE BLOCK
- INSULATED HOLLOW METAL DOOR (PAINT ALL SURFACES)

LOADING DOCK
SCALE 1 1/2" = 1'-0"

- 3½" x 3½" x ¼" STEEL ANGLE TO FRAME OPNG.
- 6" THICK x 12" x 24" LAMINATED TREAD TYPE DOCK BUMPERS
- 3" x 7" x ⅜" STEEL ₧ CONT. AT DOOR SILL ANCHOR TO SLAB
- 8" LINTEL BLOCK
- 6" GRAVEL BASE
- 2" EXTRUDED POLYSTYRENT INSUL.
- 8" CONC. BLOCK
- BITUMINOUS SURFACE

DETAILS

9-19

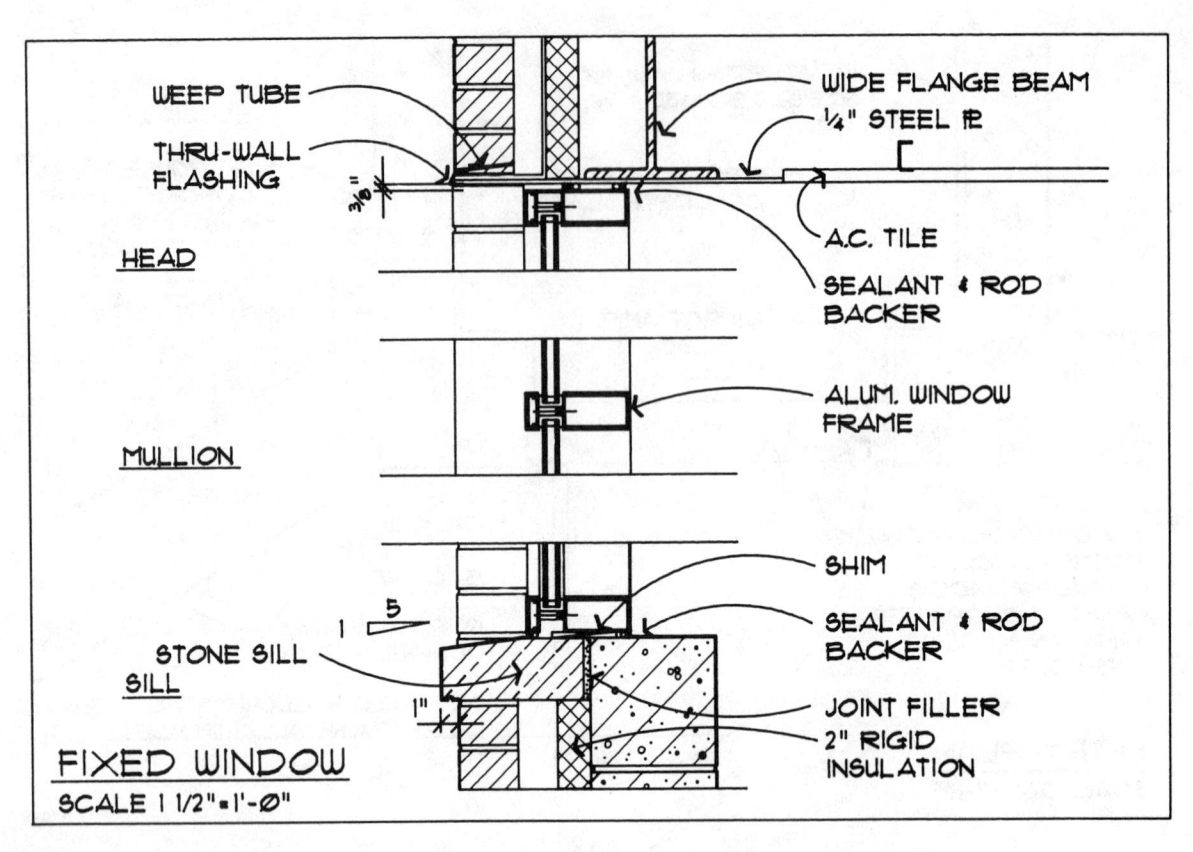

FIXED WINDOW
SCALE 1 1/2" = 1'-0"

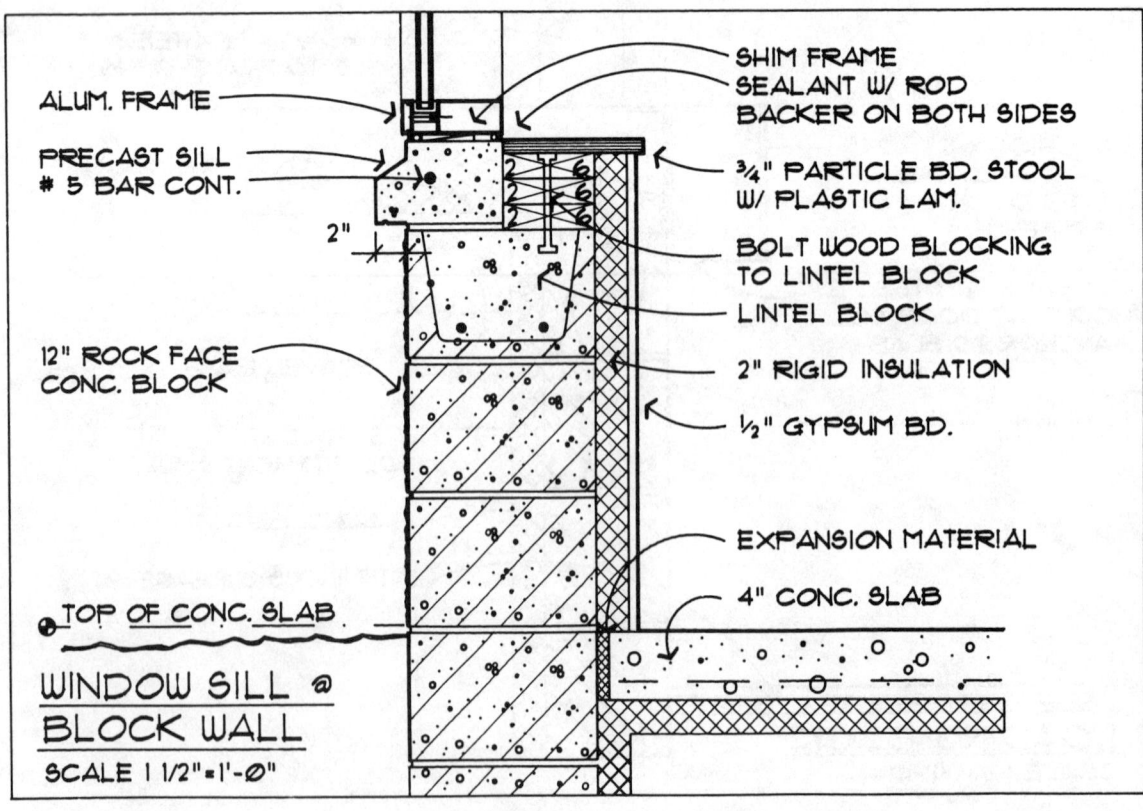

- WEEP TUBE
- THRU-WALL FLASHING
- 3/8"
- HEAD
- WIDE FLANGE BEAM
- 1/4" STEEL PL
- A.C. TILE
- SEALANT & ROD BACKER
- ALUM. WINDOW FRAME
- MULLION
- STONE SILL
- SILL
- 1"
- SHIM
- SEALANT & ROD BACKER
- JOINT FILLER
- 2" RIGID INSULATION

WINDOW SILL @ BLOCK WALL
SCALE 1 1/2" = 1'-0"

- ALUM. FRAME
- PRECAST SILL #5 BAR CONT.
- 2"
- 12" ROCK FACE CONC. BLOCK
- TOP OF CONC. SLAB
- SHIM FRAME
- SEALANT W/ ROD BACKER ON BOTH SIDES
- 3/4" PARTICLE BD. STOOL W/ PLASTIC LAM.
- BOLT WOOD BLOCKING TO LINTEL BLOCK
- LINTEL BLOCK
- 2" RIGID INSULATION
- 1/2" GYPSUM BD.
- EXPANSION MATERIAL
- 4" CONC. SLAB

DETAILS

9-20

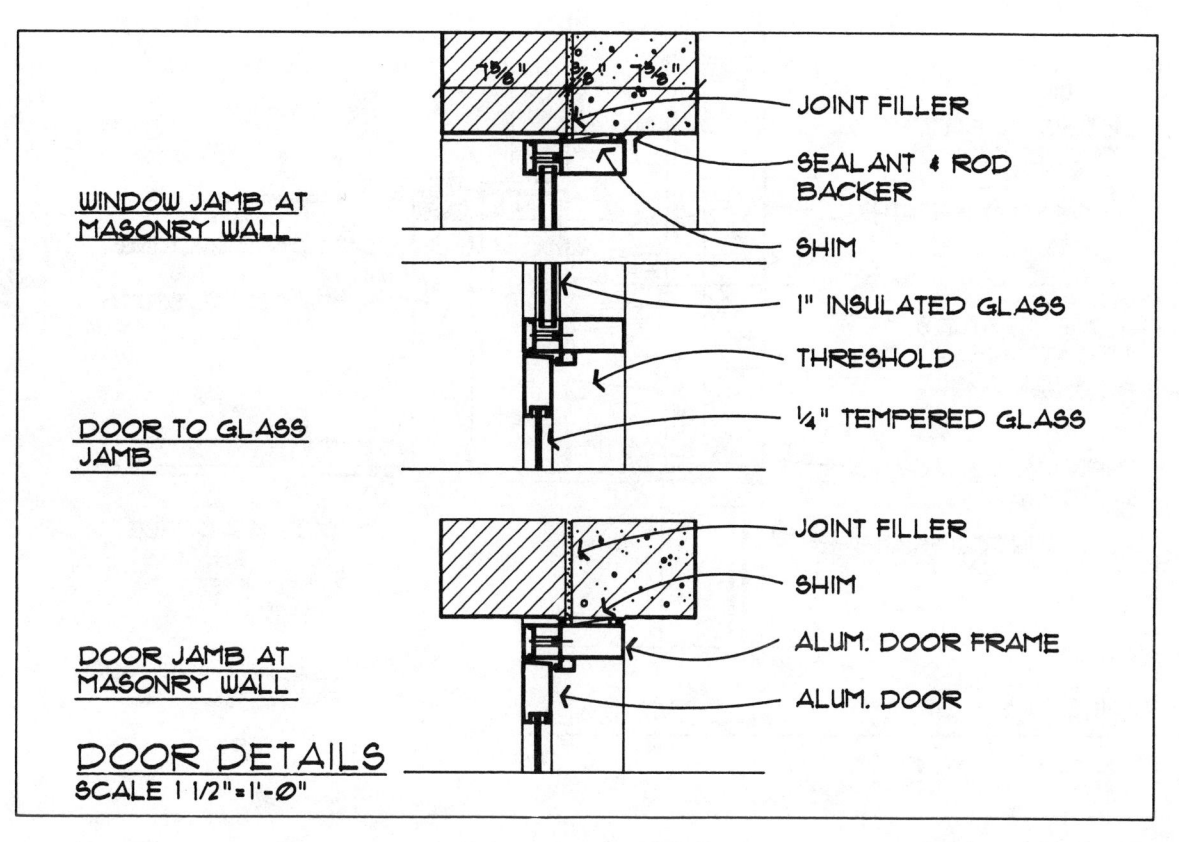

DOOR DETAILS
SCALE 1 1/2" = 1'-0"

- WINDOW JAMB AT MASONRY WALL
- DOOR TO GLASS JAMB
- DOOR JAMB AT MASONRY WALL

Labels:
- JOINT FILLER
- SEALANT & ROD BACKER
- SHIM
- 1" INSULATED GLASS
- THRESHOLD
- 1/4" TEMPERED GLASS
- JOINT FILLER
- SHIM
- ALUM. DOOR FRAME
- ALUM. DOOR

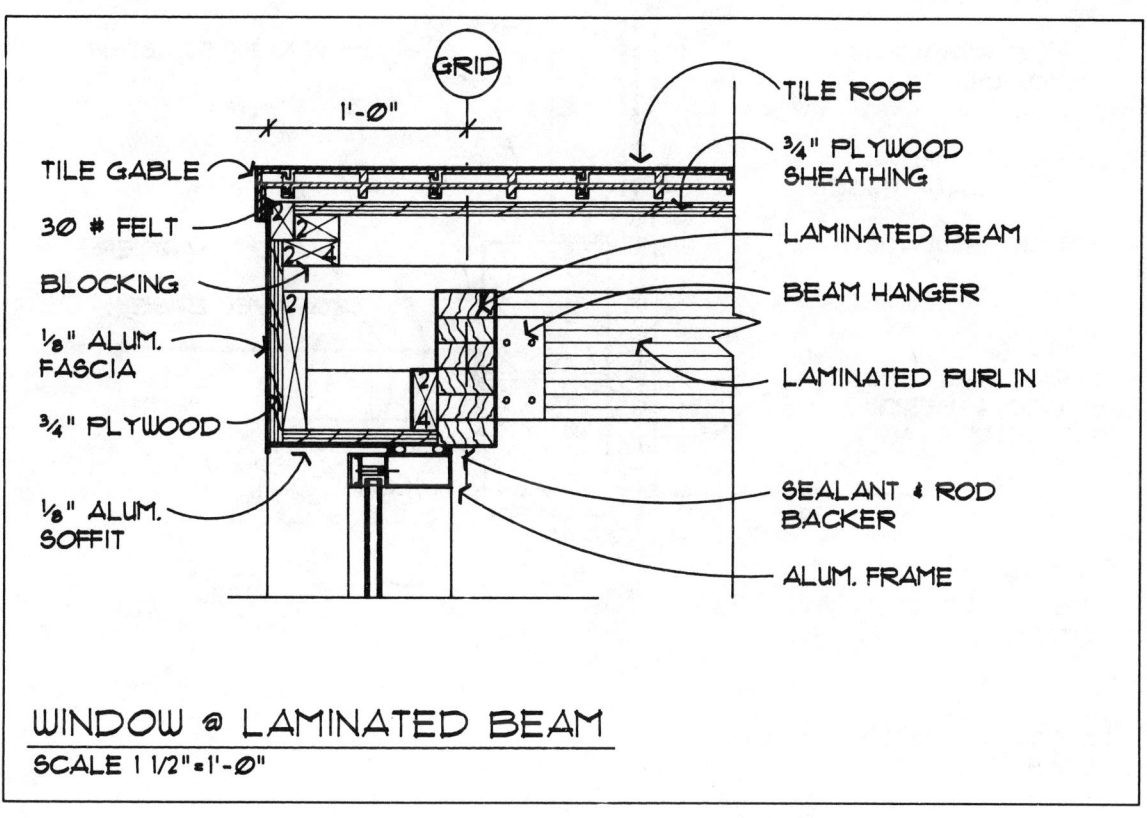

WINDOW @ LAMINATED BEAM
SCALE 1 1/2" = 1'-0"

Labels:
- TILE GABLE
- 30 # FELT
- BLOCKING
- 1/8" ALUM. FASCIA
- 3/4" PLYWOOD
- 1/8" ALUM. SOFFIT
- GRID
- TILE ROOF
- 3/4" PLYWOOD SHEATHING
- LAMINATED BEAM
- BEAM HANGER
- LAMINATED PURLIN
- SEALANT & ROD BACKER
- ALUM. FRAME

DETAILS

9-21

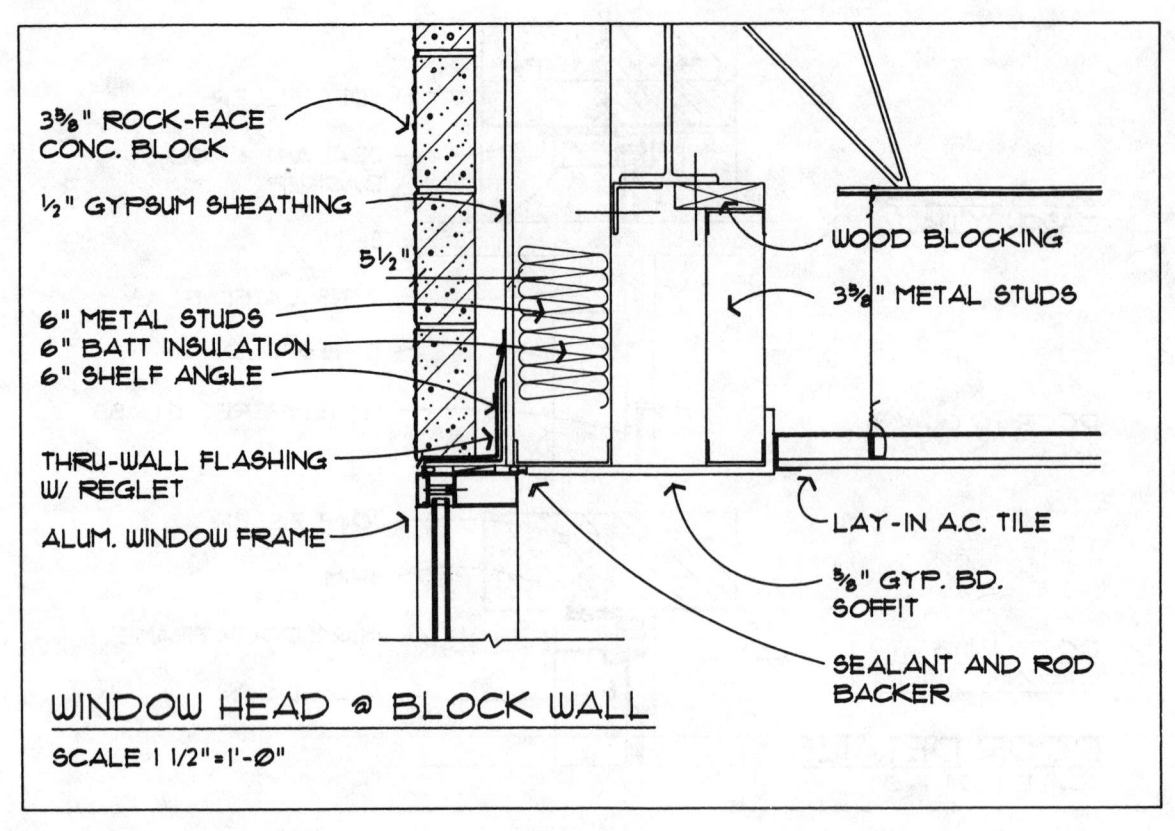

WINDOW HEAD @ BLOCK WALL
SCALE 1 1/2" = 1'-0"

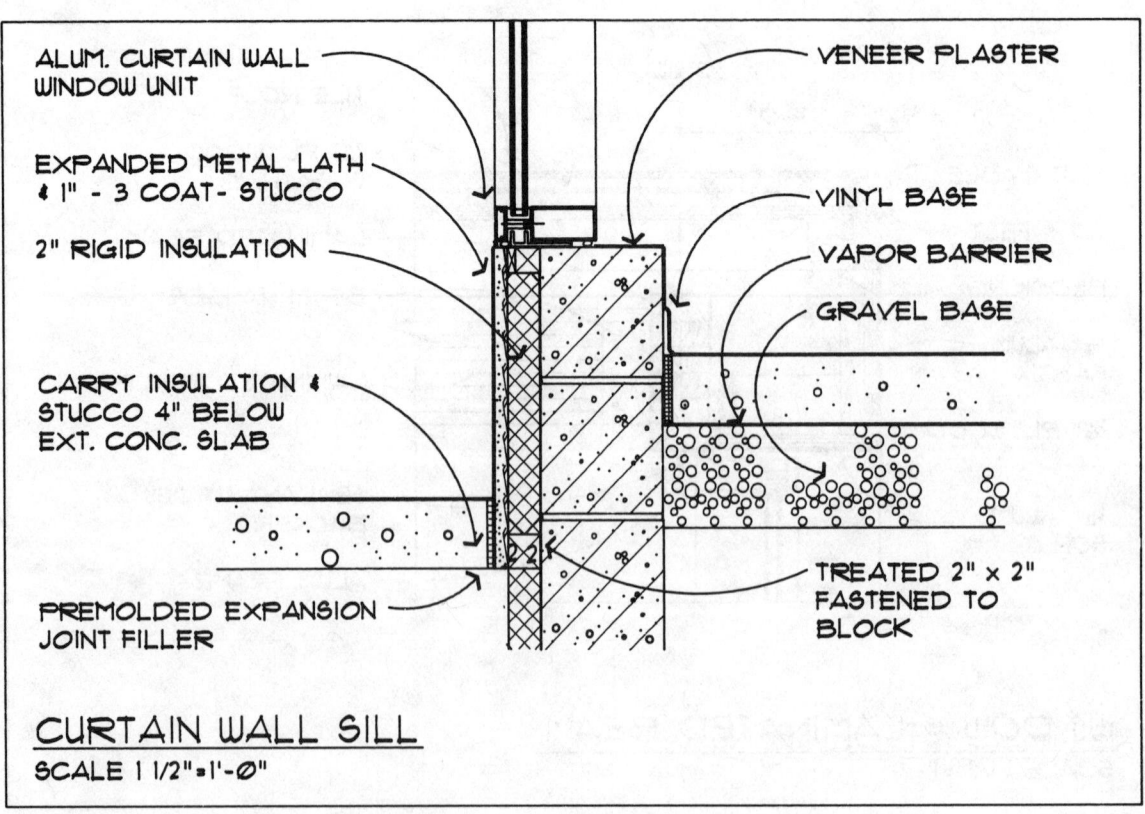

- 3 5/8" ROCK-FACE CONC. BLOCK
- 1/2" GYPSUM SHEATHING
- 5 1/2"
- 6" METAL STUDS
- 6" BATT INSULATION
- 6" SHELF ANGLE
- THRU-WALL FLASHING W/ REGLET
- ALUM. WINDOW FRAME
- WOOD BLOCKING
- 3 5/8" METAL STUDS
- LAY-IN A.C. TILE
- 5/8" GYP. BD. SOFFIT
- SEALANT AND ROD BACKER

CURTAIN WALL SILL
SCALE 1 1/2" = 1'-0"

- ALUM. CURTAIN WALL WINDOW UNIT
- EXPANDED METAL LATH & 1" - 3 COAT- STUCCO
- 2" RIGID INSULATION
- CARRY INSULATION & STUCCO 4" BELOW EXT. CONC. SLAB
- PREMOLDED EXPANSION JOINT FILLER
- VENEER PLASTER
- VINYL BASE
- VAPOR BARRIER
- GRAVEL BASE
- TREATED 2" x 2" FASTENED TO BLOCK

DETAILS

9-22

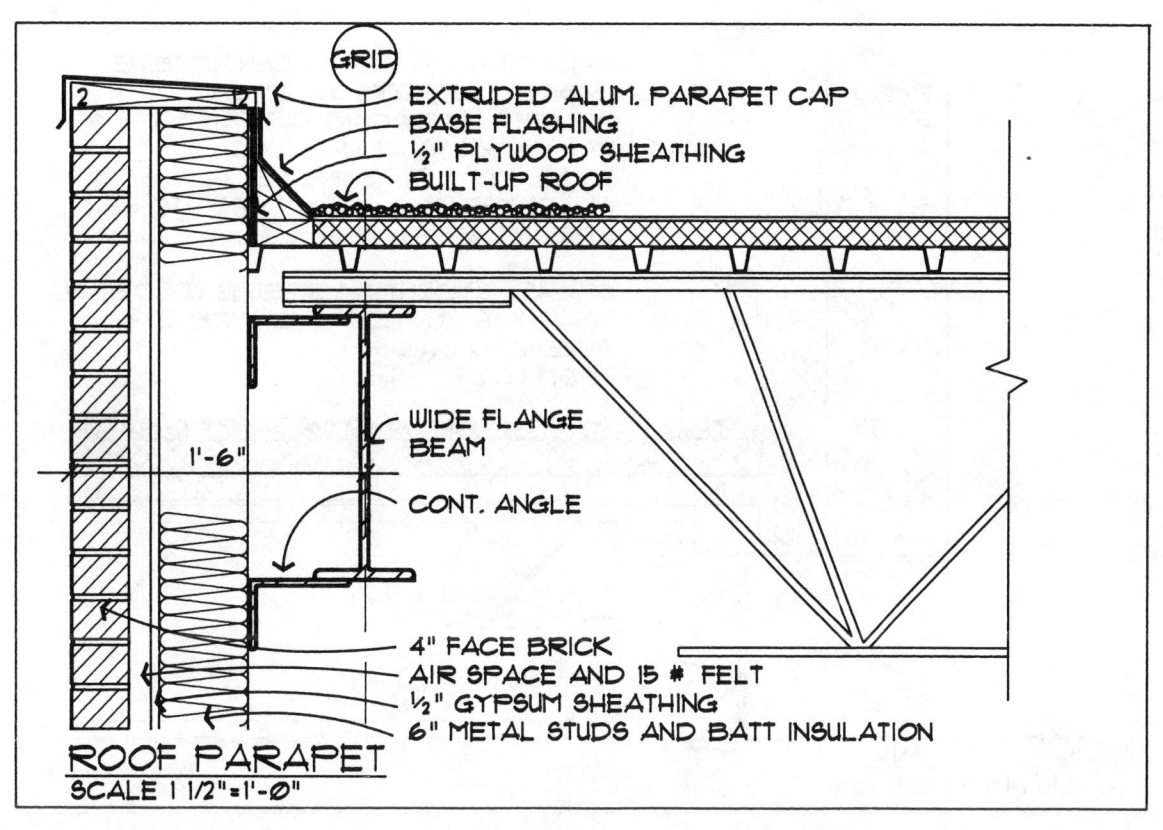

ROOF PARAPET
SCALE 1 1/2" = 1'-0"

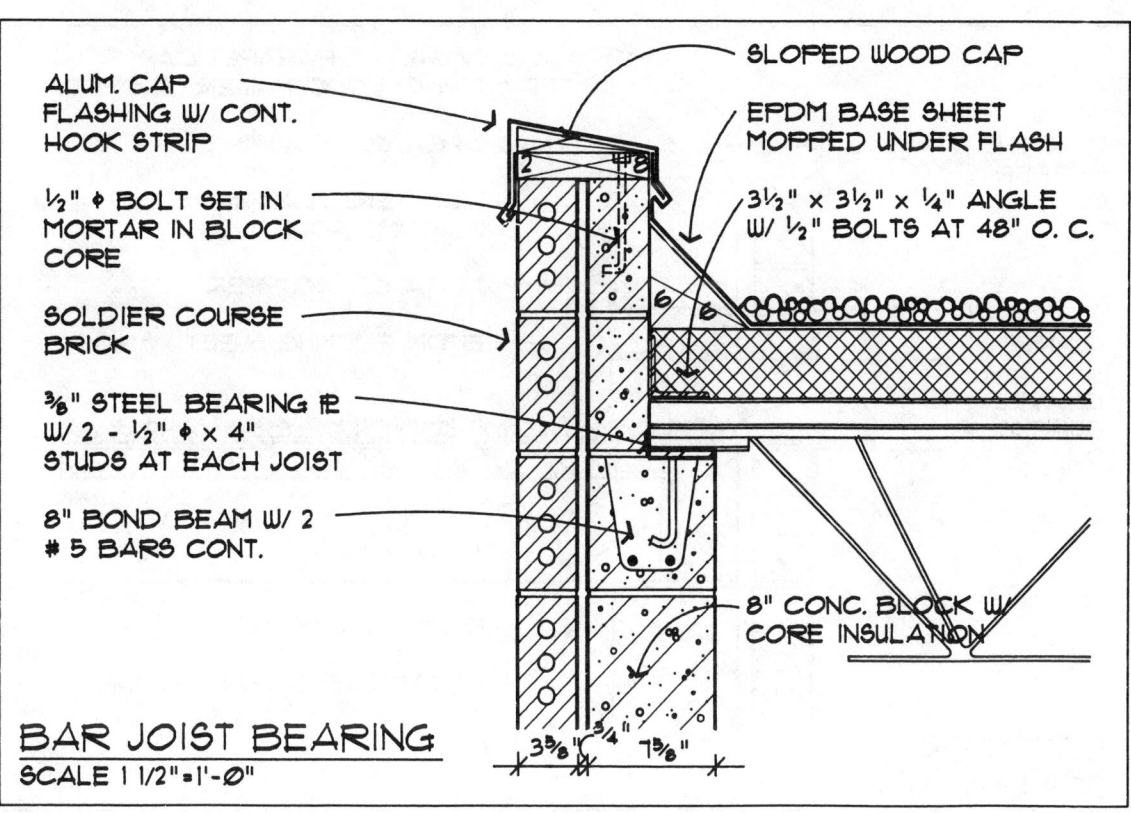

- GRID
- EXTRUDED ALUM. PARAPET CAP
- BASE FLASHING
- 1/2" PLYWOOD SHEATHING
- BUILT-UP ROOF
- WIDE FLANGE BEAM
- CONT. ANGLE
- 4" FACE BRICK
- AIR SPACE AND 15 # FELT
- 1/2" GYPSUM SHEATHING
- 6" METAL STUDS AND BATT INSULATION

1'-6"

BAR JOIST BEARING
SCALE 1 1/2" = 1'-0"

- ALUM. CAP FLASHING W/ CONT. HOOK STRIP
- 1/2" ⌀ BOLT SET IN MORTAR IN BLOCK CORE
- SOLDIER COURSE BRICK
- 3/8" STEEL BEARING ℔ W/ 2 - 1/2" ⌀ x 4" STUDS AT EACH JOIST
- 8" BOND BEAM W/ 2 # 5 BARS CONT.
- SLOPED WOOD CAP
- EPDM BASE SHEET MOPPED UNDER FLASH
- 3 1/2" x 3 1/2" x 1/4" ANGLE W/ 1/2" BOLTS AT 48" O.C.
- 8" CONC. BLOCK W/ CORE INSULATION

3 5/8" 7 5/8"

DETAILS 9-23

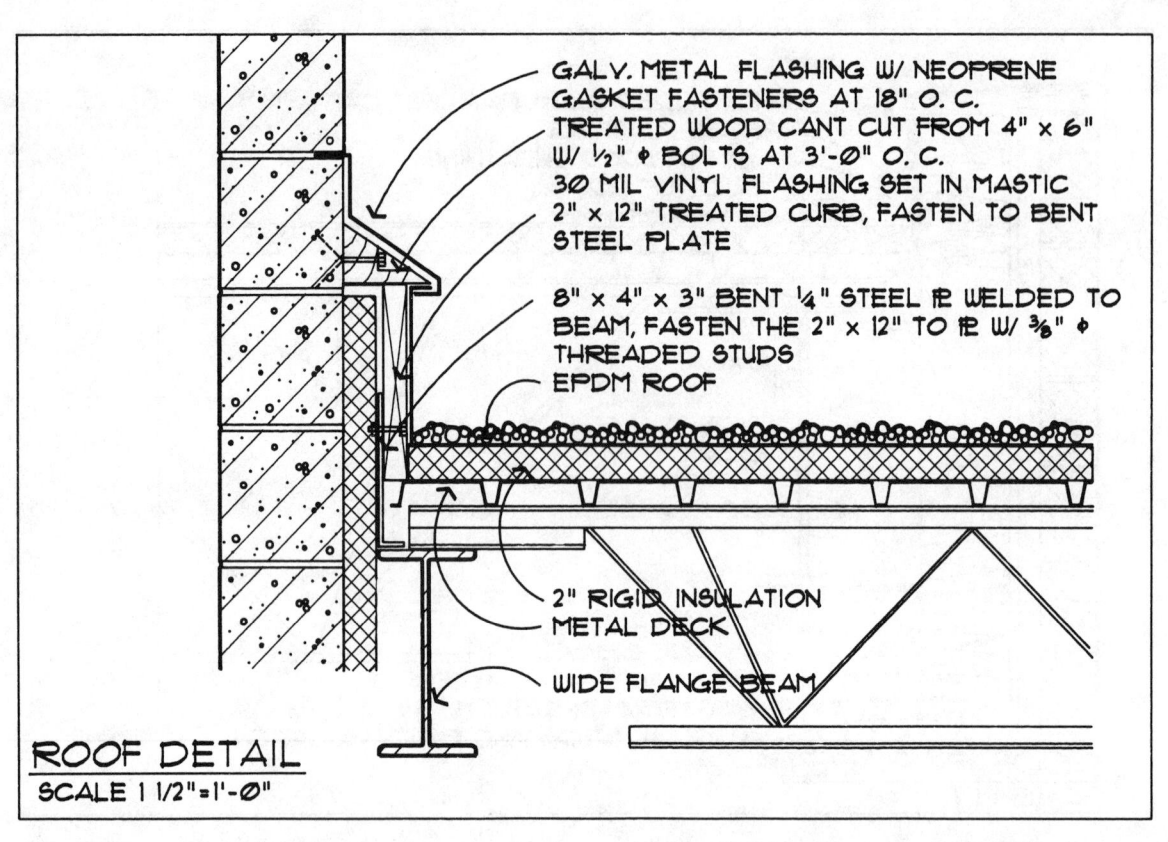

ROOF DETAIL
SCALE 1 1/2" = 1'-0"

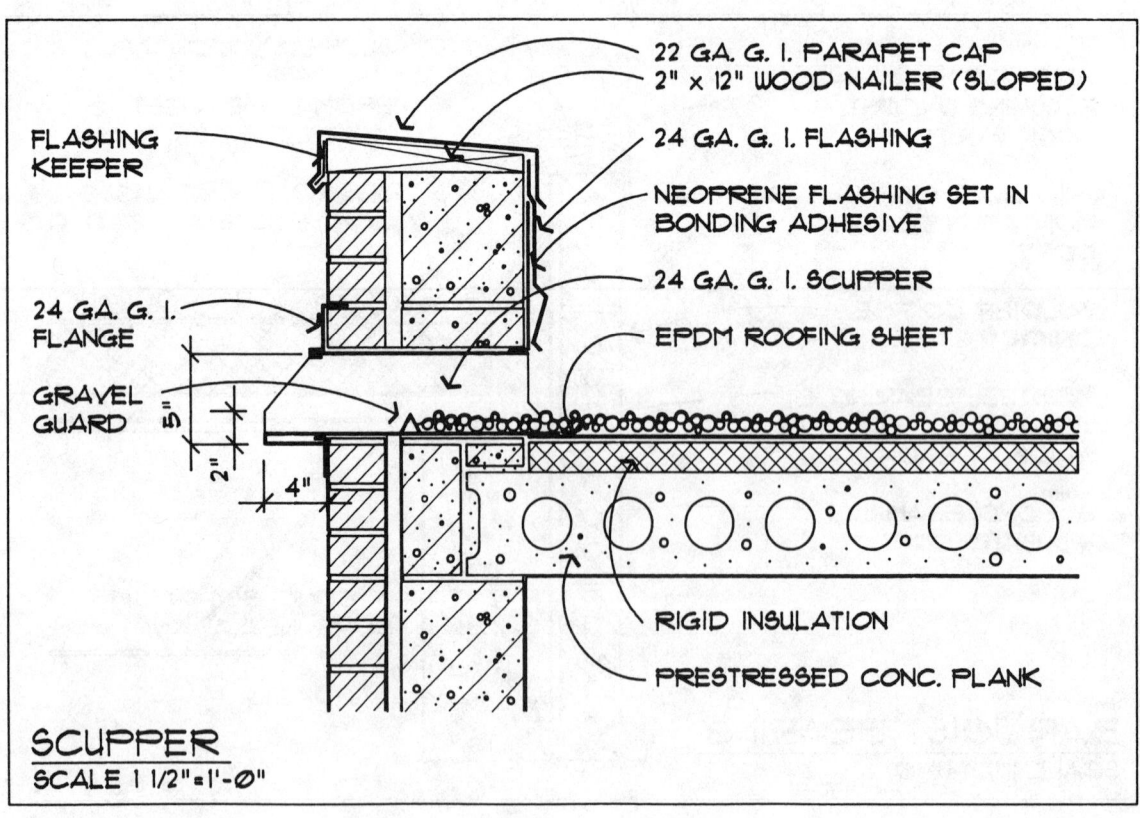

- GALV. METAL FLASHING W/ NEOPRENE GASKET FASTENERS AT 18" O.C.
- TREATED WOOD CANT CUT FROM 4" x 6" W/ 1/2" ⌀ BOLTS AT 3'-0" O.C.
- 30 MIL VINYL FLASHING SET IN MASTIC
- 2" x 12" TREATED CURB, FASTEN TO BENT STEEL PLATE
- 8" x 4" x 3" BENT 1/4" STEEL ℙ WELDED TO BEAM, FASTEN THE 2" x 12" TO ℙ W/ 3/8" ⌀ THREADED STUDS
- EPDM ROOF
- 2" RIGID INSULATION
- METAL DECK
- WIDE FLANGE BEAM

SCUPPER
SCALE 1 1/2" = 1'-0"

- 22 GA. G. I. PARAPET CAP
- 2" x 12" WOOD NAILER (SLOPED)
- 24 GA. G. I. FLASHING
- NEOPRENE FLASHING SET IN BONDING ADHESIVE
- 24 GA. G. I. SCUPPER
- EPDM ROOFING SHEET
- FLASHING KEEPER
- 24 GA. G. I. FLANGE
- GRAVEL GUARD
- RIGID INSULATION
- PRESTRESSED CONC. PLANK

DETAILS   9-24

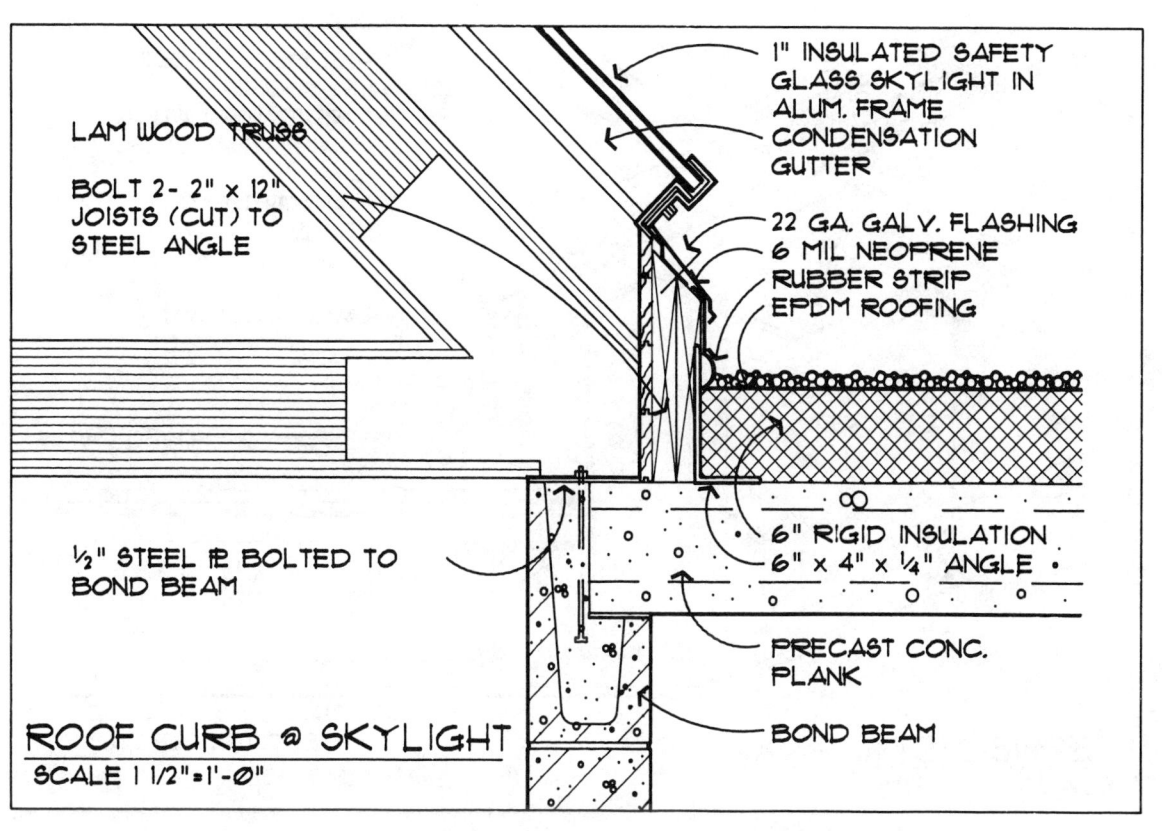

ROOF CURB @ SKYLIGHT
SCALE 1 1/2" = 1'-0"

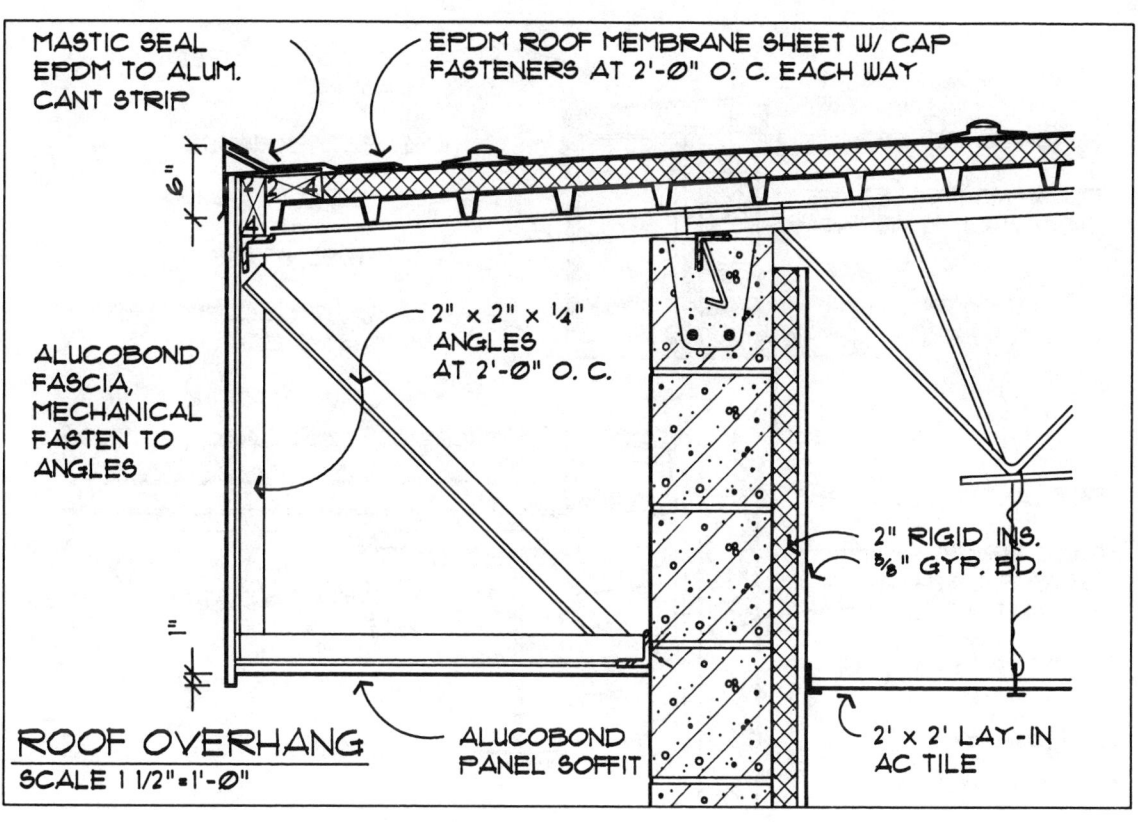

- LAM WOOD TRUSS
- BOLT 2- 2" x 12" JOISTS (CUT) TO STEEL ANGLE
- 1" INSULATED SAFETY GLASS SKYLIGHT IN ALUM. FRAME CONDENSATION GUTTER
- 22 GA. GALV. FLASHING
- 6 MIL NEOPRENE RUBBER STRIP
- EPDM ROOFING
- 1/2" STEEL PL BOLTED TO BOND BEAM
- 6" RIGID INSULATION
- 6" x 4" x 1/4" ANGLE
- PRECAST CONC. PLANK
- BOND BEAM

ROOF OVERHANG
SCALE 1 1/2" = 1'-0"

- MASTIC SEAL EPDM TO ALUM. CANT STRIP
- EPDM ROOF MEMBRANE SHEET W/ CAP FASTENERS AT 2'-0" O.C. EACH WAY
- 6"
- ALUCOBOND FASCIA, MECHANICAL FASTEN TO ANGLES
- 2" x 2" x 1/4" ANGLES AT 2'-0" O.C.
- 2" RIGID INS.
- 5/8" GYP. BD.
- 1"
- ALUCOBOND PANEL SOFFIT
- 2' x 2' LAY-IN AC TILE

DETAILS   9-25

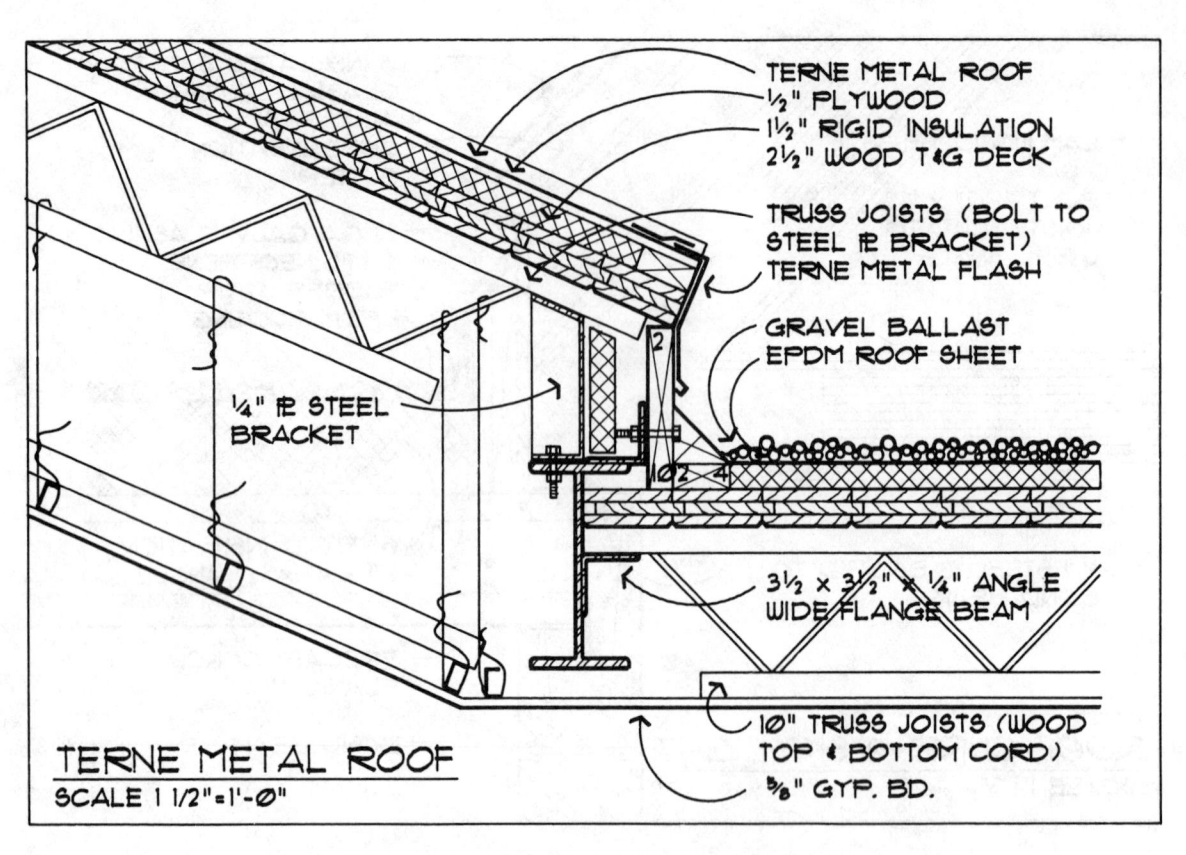

TERNE METAL ROOF
SCALE 1 1/2"=1'-0"

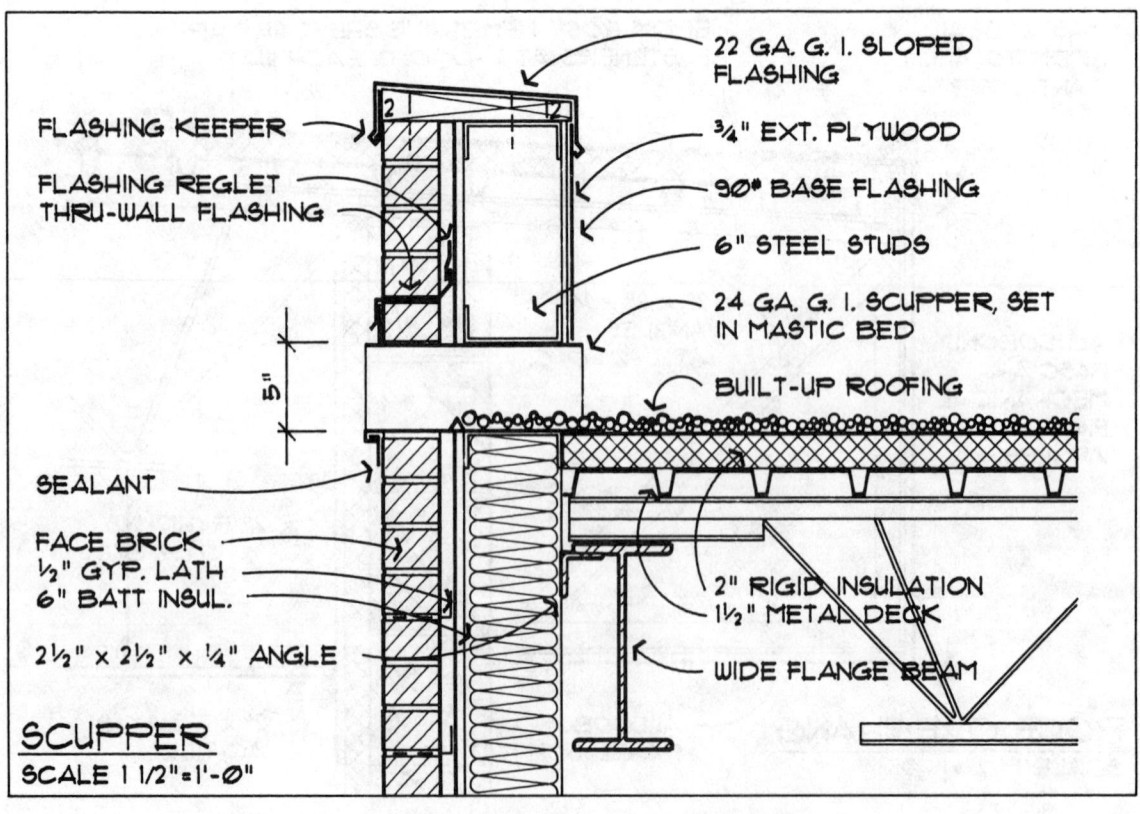

- TERNE METAL ROOF
- 1/2" PLYWOOD
- 1 1/2" RIGID INSULATION
- 2 1/2" WOOD T&G DECK
- TRUSS JOISTS (BOLT TO STEEL ℔ BRACKET)
- TERNE METAL FLASH
- GRAVEL BALLAST
- EPDM ROOF SHEET
- 1/4" ℔ STEEL BRACKET
- 3 1/2" x 3 1/2" x 1/4" ANGLE
- WIDE FLANGE BEAM
- 10" TRUSS JOISTS (WOOD TOP & BOTTOM CORD)
- 5/8" GYP. BD.

SCUPPER
SCALE 1 1/2"=1'-0"

- 22 GA. G. I. SLOPED FLASHING
- FLASHING KEEPER
- 3/4" EXT. PLYWOOD
- FLASHING REGLET
- THRU-WALL FLASHING
- 90# BASE FLASHING
- 6" STEEL STUDS
- 24 GA. G. I. SCUPPER, SET IN MASTIC BED
- BUILT-UP ROOFING
- 5"
- SEALANT
- FACE BRICK
- 1/2" GYP. LATH
- 6" BATT INSUL.
- 2 1/2" x 2 1/2" x 1/4" ANGLE
- 2" RIGID INSULATION
- 1 1/2" METAL DECK
- WIDE FLANGE BEAM

DETAILS 9-26

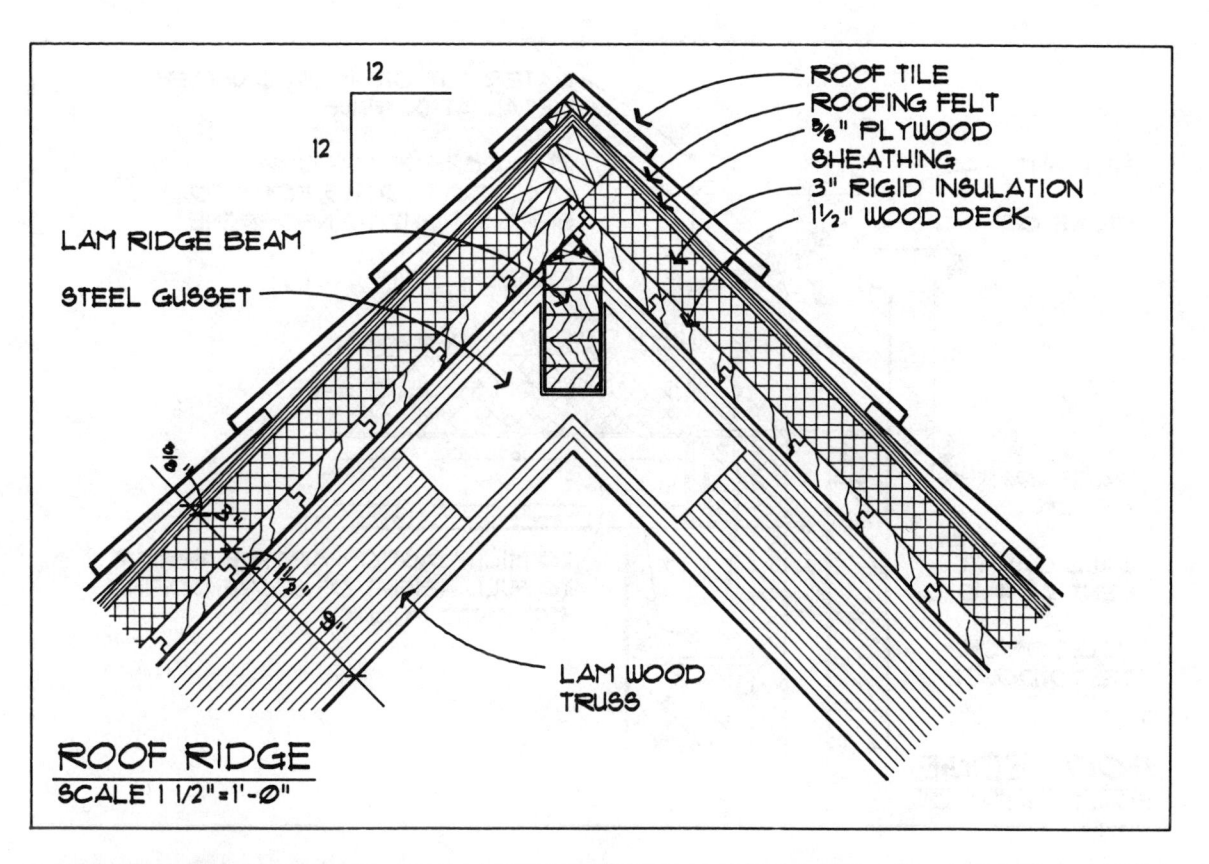

ROOF RIDGE
SCALE 1 1/2"=1'-0"

Labels:
- 12/12
- ROOF TILE
- ROOFING FELT
- 3/8" PLYWOOD SHEATHING
- 3" RIGID INSULATION
- 1 1/2" WOOD DECK
- LAM RIDGE BEAM
- STEEL GUSSET
- LAM WOOD TRUSS

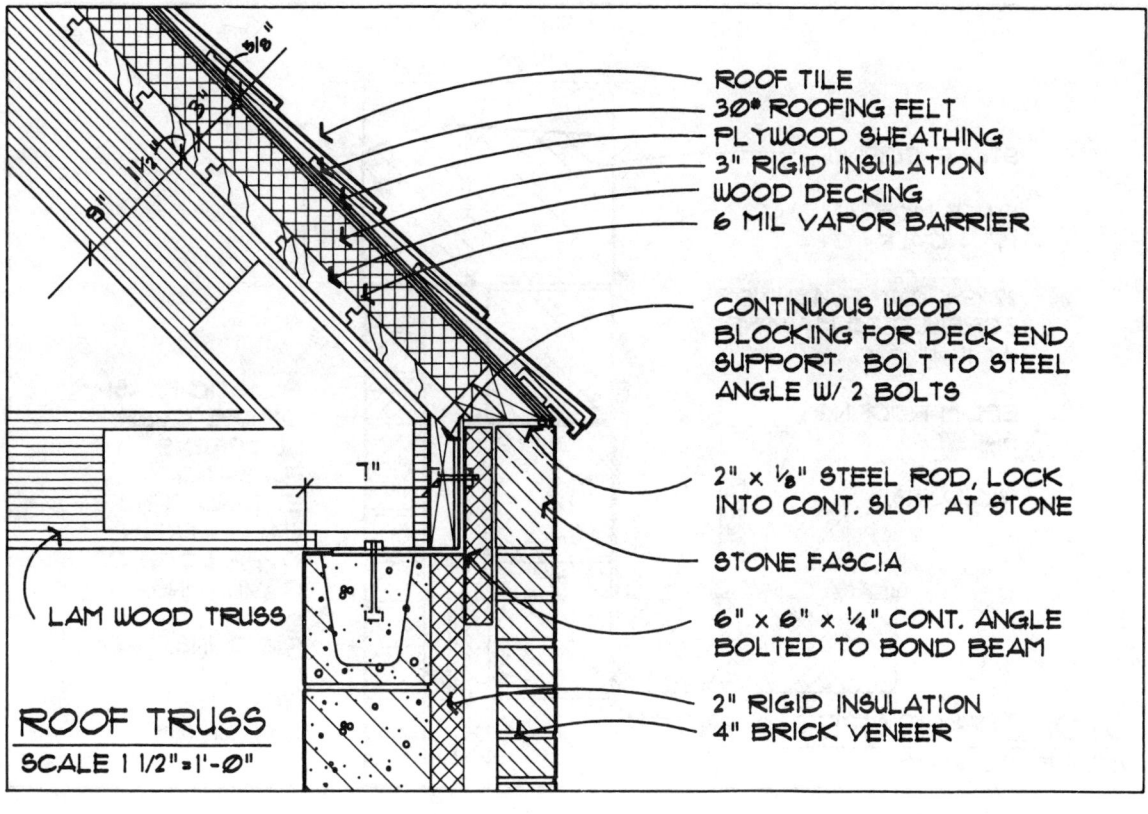

ROOF TRUSS
SCALE 1 1/2"=1'-0"

Labels:
- ROOF TILE
- 30# ROOFING FELT
- PLYWOOD SHEATHING
- 3" RIGID INSULATION
- WOOD DECKING
- 6 MIL VAPOR BARRIER
- CONTINUOUS WOOD BLOCKING FOR DECK END SUPPORT. BOLT TO STEEL ANGLE W/ 2 BOLTS
- 2" x 1/8" STEEL ROD, LOCK INTO CONT. SLOT AT STONE
- STONE FASCIA
- 6" x 6" x 1/4" CONT. ANGLE BOLTED TO BOND BEAM
- 2" RIGID INSULATION
- 4" BRICK VENEER
- LAM WOOD TRUSS
- 7"

DETAILS 9-27

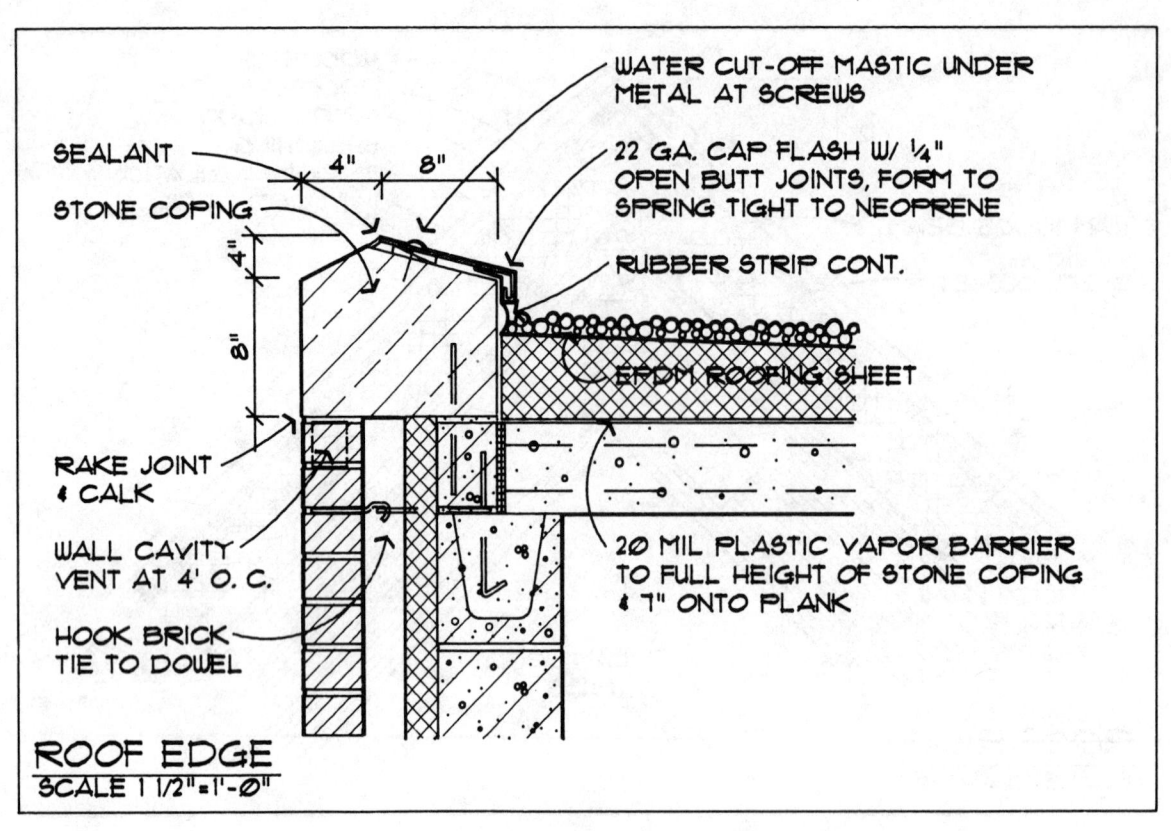

ROOF EDGE
SCALE 1 1/2" = 1'-0"

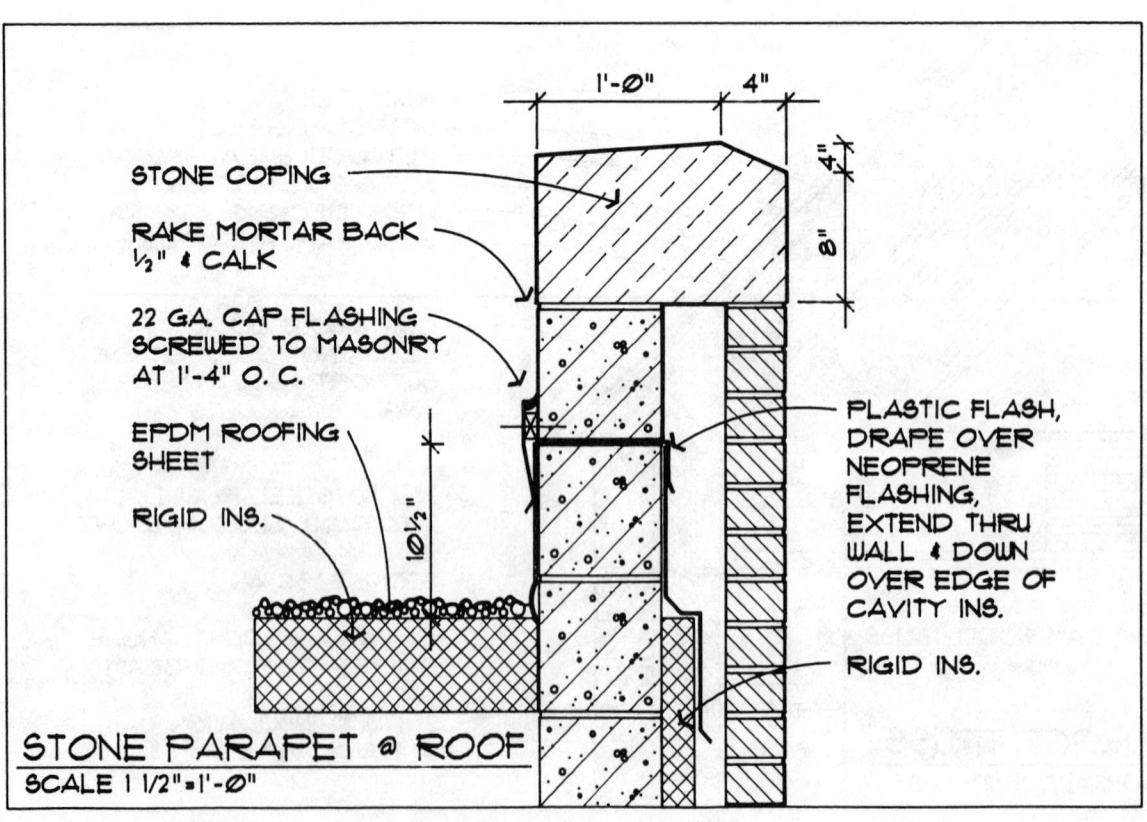

- SEALANT
- STONE COPING
- WATER CUT-OFF MASTIC UNDER METAL AT SCREWS
- 22 GA. CAP FLASH W/ 1/4" OPEN BUTT JOINTS, FORM TO SPRING TIGHT TO NEOPRENE
- RUBBER STRIP CONT.
- EPDM ROOFING SHEET
- RAKE JOINT & CALK
- WALL CAVITY VENT AT 4' O.C.
- HOOK BRICK TIE TO DOWEL
- 20 MIL PLASTIC VAPOR BARRIER TO FULL HEIGHT OF STONE COPING & 7" ONTO PLANK

Dimensions: 4", 8", 4", 8"

STONE PARAPET @ ROOF
SCALE 1 1/2" = 1'-0"

- STONE COPING
- RAKE MORTAR BACK 1/2" & CALK
- 22 GA. CAP FLASHING SCREWED TO MASONRY AT 1'-4" O.C.
- EPDM ROOFING SHEET
- RIGID INS.
- PLASTIC FLASH, DRAPE OVER NEOPRENE FLASHING, EXTEND THRU WALL & DOWN OVER EDGE OF CAVITY INS.
- RIGID INS.

Dimensions: 1'-0", 4", 4", 8", 10 1/2"

DETAILS

9-28

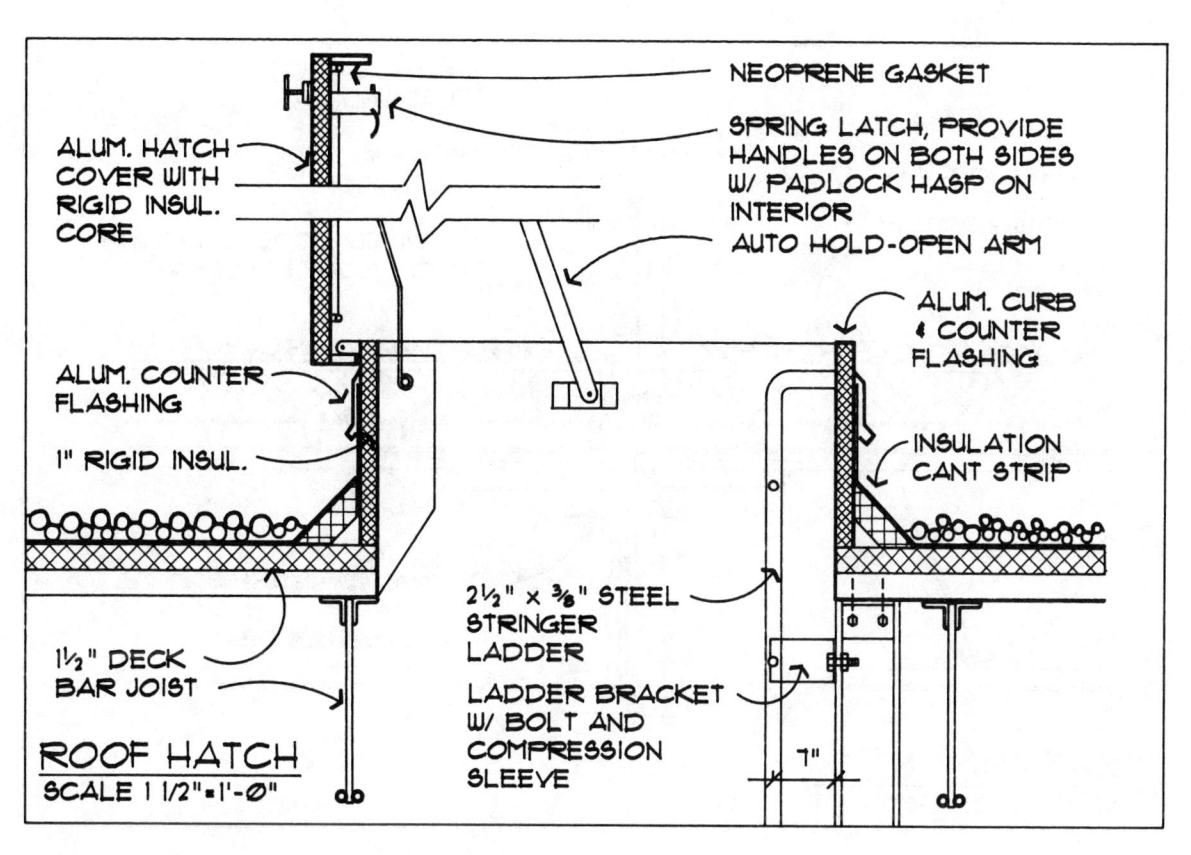

ROOF HATCH
SCALE 1 1/2" = 1'-0"

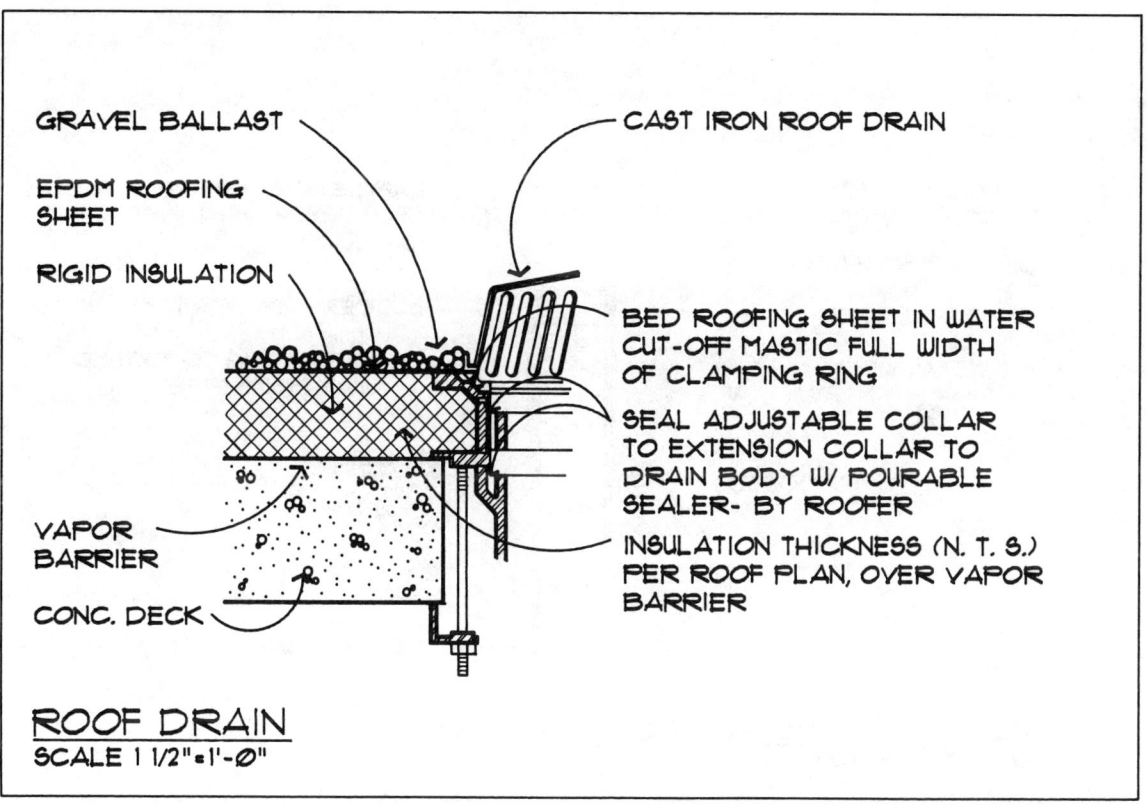

- NEOPRENE GASKET
- SPRING LATCH, PROVIDE HANDLES ON BOTH SIDES W/ PADLOCK HASP ON INTERIOR
- AUTO HOLD-OPEN ARM
- ALUM. HATCH COVER WITH RIGID INSUL. CORE
- ALUM. CURB & COUNTER FLASHING
- ALUM. COUNTER FLASHING
- 1" RIGID INSUL.
- INSULATION CANT STRIP
- 2 1/2" x 3/8" STEEL STRINGER LADDER
- 1 1/2" DECK BAR JOIST
- LADDER BRACKET W/ BOLT AND COMPRESSION SLEEVE
- 7"

ROOF DRAIN
SCALE 1 1/2" = 1'-0"

- GRAVEL BALLAST
- CAST IRON ROOF DRAIN
- EPDM ROOFING SHEET
- RIGID INSULATION
- BED ROOFING SHEET IN WATER CUT-OFF MASTIC FULL WIDTH OF CLAMPING RING
- SEAL ADJUSTABLE COLLAR TO EXTENSION COLLAR TO DRAIN BODY W/ POURABLE SEALER - BY ROOFER
- VAPOR BARRIER
- INSULATION THICKNESS (N.T.S.) PER ROOF PLAN, OVER VAPOR BARRIER
- CONC. DECK

DETAILS

9-29

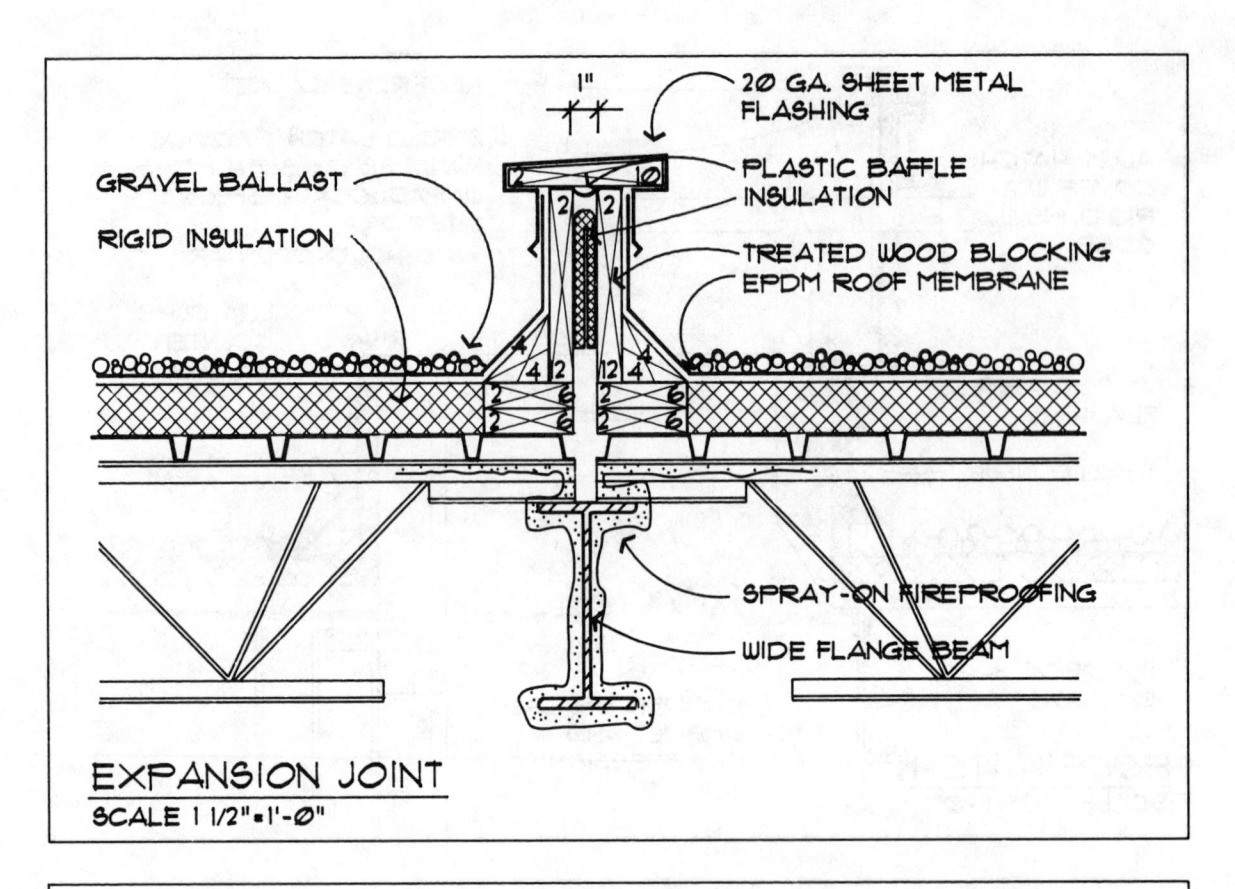

EXPANSION JOINT
SCALE 1 1/2"=1'-0"

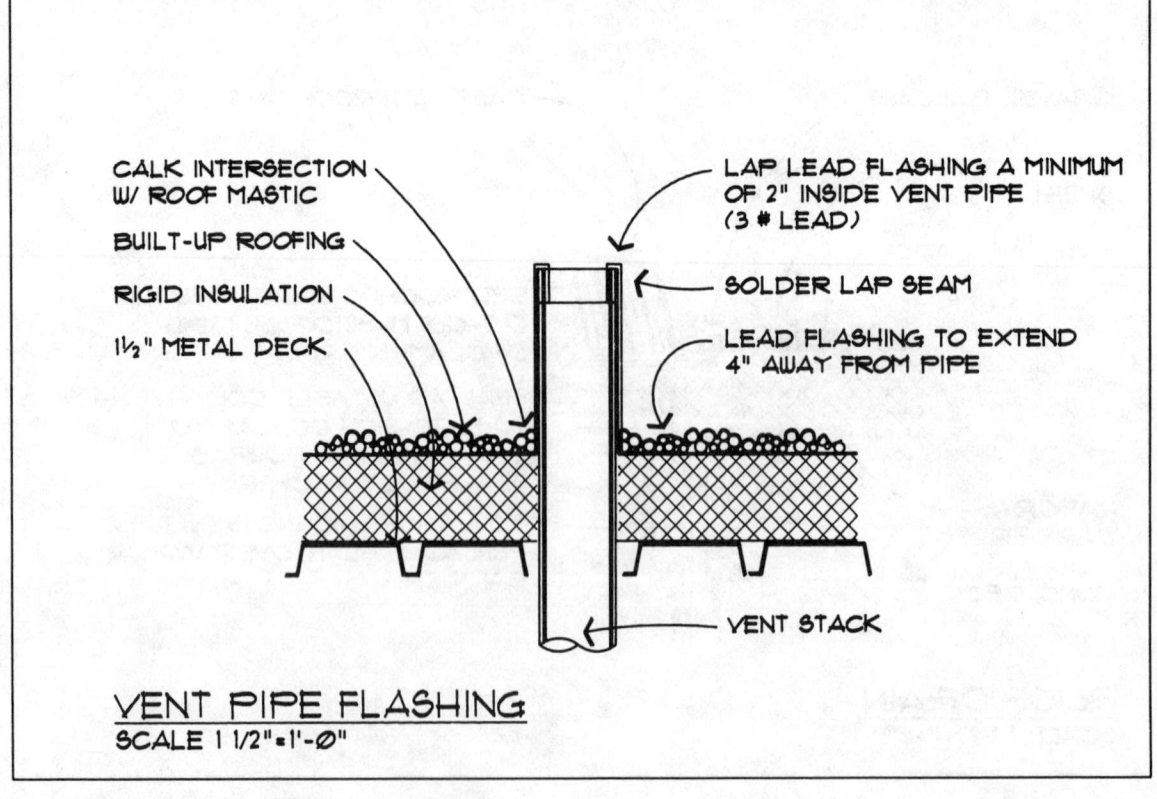

- 20 GA. SHEET METAL FLASHING
- PLASTIC BAFFLE INSULATION
- TREATED WOOD BLOCKING
- EPDM ROOF MEMBRANE
- GRAVEL BALLAST
- RIGID INSULATION
- SPRAY-ON FIREPROOFING
- WIDE FLANGE BEAM

VENT PIPE FLASHING
SCALE 1 1/2"=1'-0"

- CALK INTERSECTION W/ ROOF MASTIC
- BUILT-UP ROOFING
- RIGID INSULATION
- 1 1/2" METAL DECK
- LAP LEAD FLASHING A MINIMUM OF 2" INSIDE VENT PIPE (3 # LEAD)
- SOLDER LAP SEAM
- LEAD FLASHING TO EXTEND 4" AWAY FROM PIPE
- VENT STACK

DETAILS

9-30

REPLAY
1. USE THE 1/8" GRIDS TO SKETCH THE ROOF OVERHANG SHOWN ON PAGE 9-25.

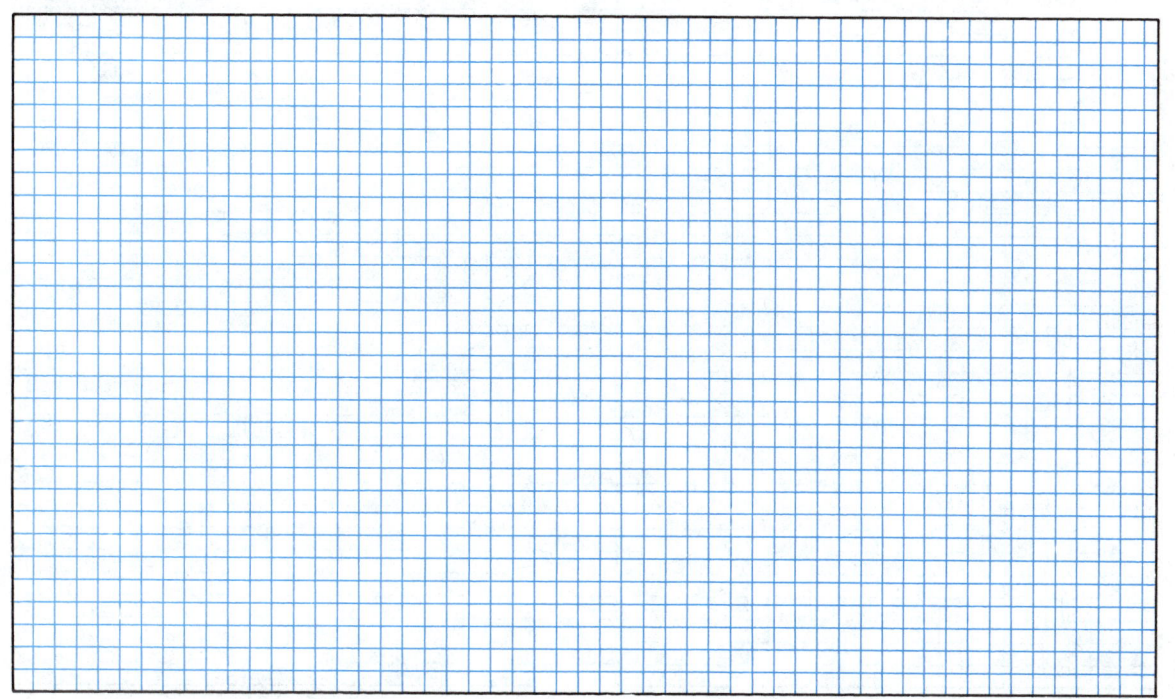

2. USE THE 1/8" GRIDS TO SKETCH THE SLOPED GLAZING SHOWN ON PAGE 9-14.

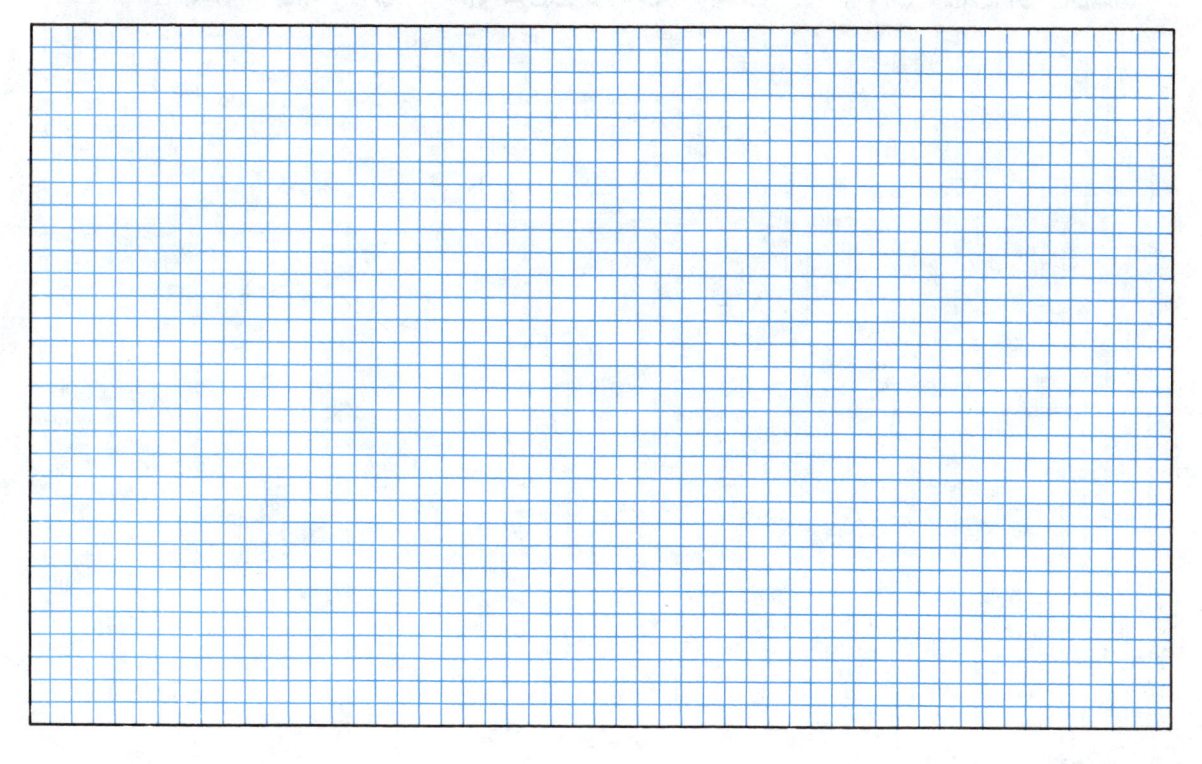

DETAILS 9-31

3. USE THE 1/8" GRIDS TO SKETCH THE CLERE STORY WINDOW SHOWN ON PAGE 9-16.

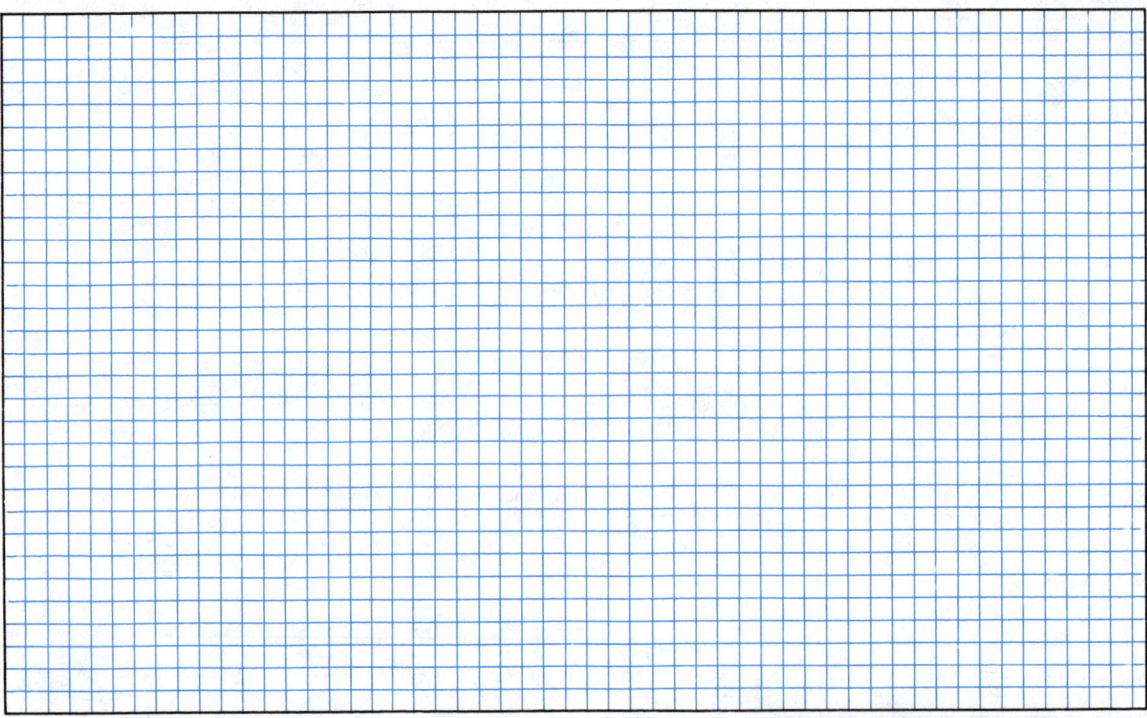

4. USE THE LINTEL DETAILS (PAGE 9-9) TO SKETCH A DOOR DETAIL THAT WILL SUPPORT A 10"-0" OPENING IN THE BRICK AND BLOCK WALL SHOWN ON THE "BAR JOIST BEARING" DETAIL (PAGE 9-23).

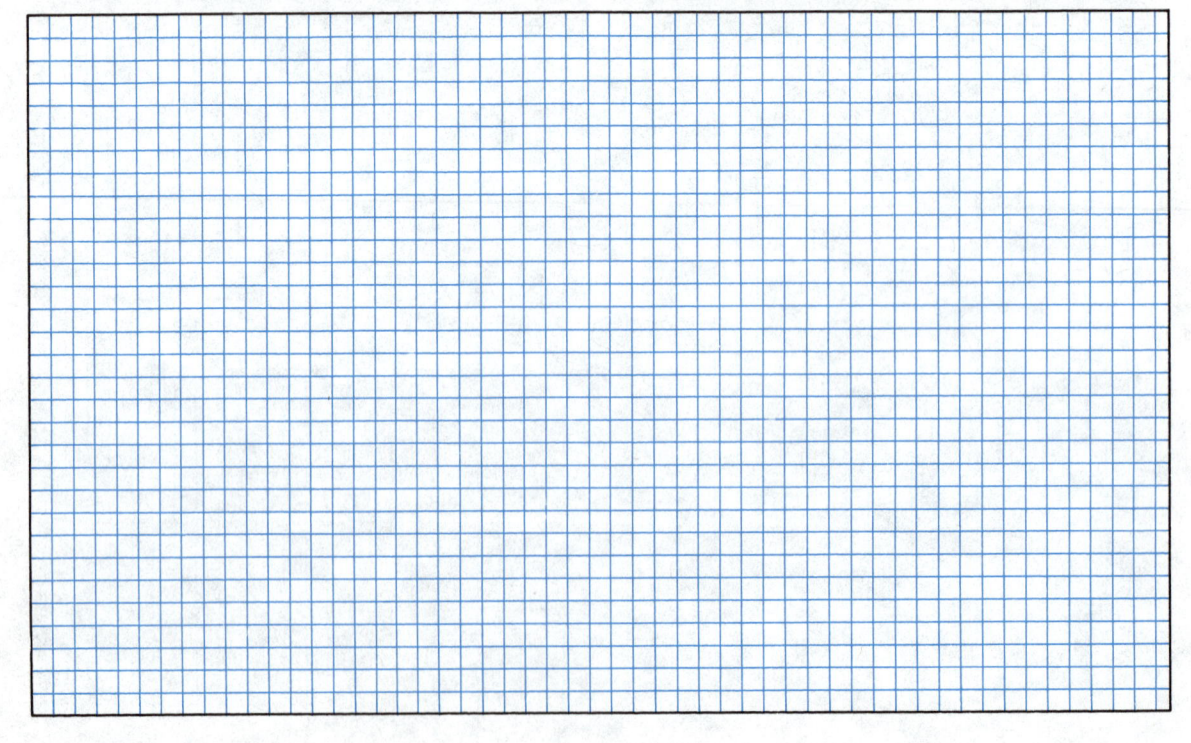

DETAILS

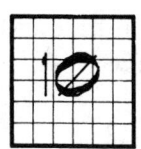

REFERENCE SOURCES

NEARLY EVERY ARCHITECTURAL PROJECT WILL INVOLVE UNIQUE CONDITIONS THAT MUST BE RESEARCHED - RESEARCH WILL BE NECESSARY FOR ACTIVITIES RANGING FROM SELECTING A SKYLIGHT FOR A HOUSE TO ASSEMBLING AN OVERHEAD DOOR FOR A FIRE STATION. THIS UNIT WILL REVIEW THE SOURCES OF CONSTRUCTION MATERIALS AND THE PROCEDURES THAT SHOULD BE FOLLOWED IN SELECTING THEM.

SPECIFICATION WRITERS BELONG TO AN ORGANIZATION CALLED THE CONSTRUCTION SPECIFICATION INSTITUTE (C.S.I.). THE C.S.I. HAS DEVELOPED A UNIFORM SYSTEM USED TO NUMBER VIRTUALLY EVERY PRODUCT USED IN CONSTRUCTION. THE C.S.I. FORMAT ORGANIZES BUILDING MATERIALS INTO THE 16 MAJOR GROUPS LISTED BELOW:

DIVISION	DESCRIPTION
1	GENERAL REQUIREMENTS
2	SITEWORK
3	CONCRETE
4	MASONRY
5	METALS
6	WOOD
7	THERMAL AND MOISTURE PROTECTION
8	DOORS AND WINDOWS
9	FINISHES
10	SPECIALTIES
11	EQUIPMENT
12	FURNISHINGS
13	SPECIAL CONSTRUCTION
14	CONVEYING SYSTEMS
15	MECHANICAL
16	ELECTRICAL

IF, FOR EXAMPLE, YOU NEEDED INFORMATION ON PELLA WINDOWS,

THE RELEVANT DATA WOULD BE INDEXED IN DIVISION 8 OF THE C.S.I. FORMAT. THERE ARE FOUR IMPORTANT REFERENCE SOURCES THAT USE THE C.S.I. NUMBERING SYSTEM TO CATALOG INFORMATION: (1) SWEET'S CATALOG FILE (COMMONLY CALLED SWEET'S FILE) (2) ARCHITECTURAL GRAPHIC STANDARDS, (3) MANUFACTURERS' PRODUCT INFORMATION, AND (4) ARCHITECT'S SPECIFICATIONS. THESE FOUR SOURCES ARE DESCRIBED BELOW.

SWEET'S CATALOG FILE

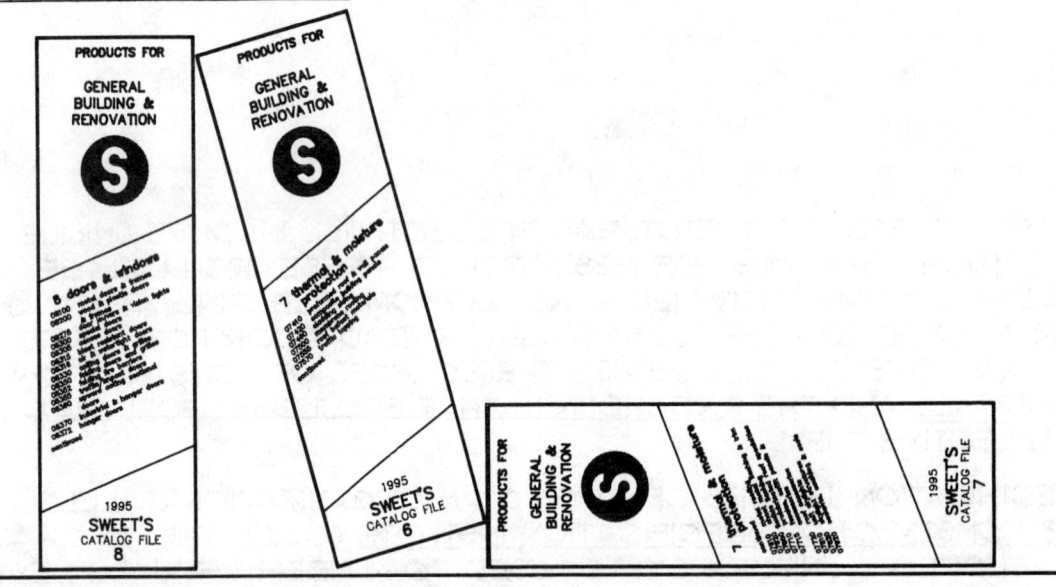

SWEET'S FILE IS ASSEMBLED BY BINDING PRODUCT CATALOGS FROM SEVERAL THOUSAND SUPPLIERS INTO A SERIES OF VOLUMES — COMPILING THIS INFORMATION WOULD BE COMPARABLE TO FILLING A SHOPPING CART WITH INFORMATION AT A BUILDING PRODUCT CONVENTION. SWEET'S FILE PROVIDES A COMPLETE INDEX TO ALL PRODUCTS AT THE BEGINNING OF EACH VOLUME. PRODUCTS ARE INDEXED BY (1) PRODUCT, (2) TRADE NAME, AND (3) FIRM NAME. FOR EXAMPLE, THE PRODUCT SHOWN BELOW WOULD BE INDEXED IN THREE WAYS.

FIRM NAME   TRADE NAME

ANDERSEN PERMA-SHIELD WINDOWS

PRODUCT NAME

IN EACH CASE, THE INDEX WOULD DIRECT YOU TO SECTION 08610. THE FIRST TWO DIGITS (08) INDICATE THE MAJOR C.S.I. HEADING, WHILE THE FINAL THREE DIGITS REFER TO THE SUBHEADING. SWEET'S FILE IS PUBLISHED EVERY YEAR TO INSURE THAT THE PRODUCT INFORMATION CONTAINED IN IT IS CURRENT. IF THERE IS A DOWNSIDE TO SWEET'S FILE, IT WOULD BE THAT ITS ADVERTISING COSTS TEND TO

REFERENCE SOURCES   10-2

LIMIT THE FIRMS INCLUDED IN IT TO MAJOR SUPPLIERS. FOR EXAMPLE, THERE IS VERY LITTLE INFORMATION ON CONCRETE MASONRY IN SWEET'S FILE BECAUSE BLOCK COMPANIES TEND TO BE LOCAL. ON THE OTHER HAND, SOME LARGE NATIONAL FIRMS INSERT OVER 100 PAGES OF PRODUCT INSTALLATION INSTRUCTION'S IN SWEET'S. THE LAST PAGE OF MOST CATALOGS CONTAIN THE ADDRESS AND TELEPHONE NUMBER OF PRODUCT REPRESENTATIVES.

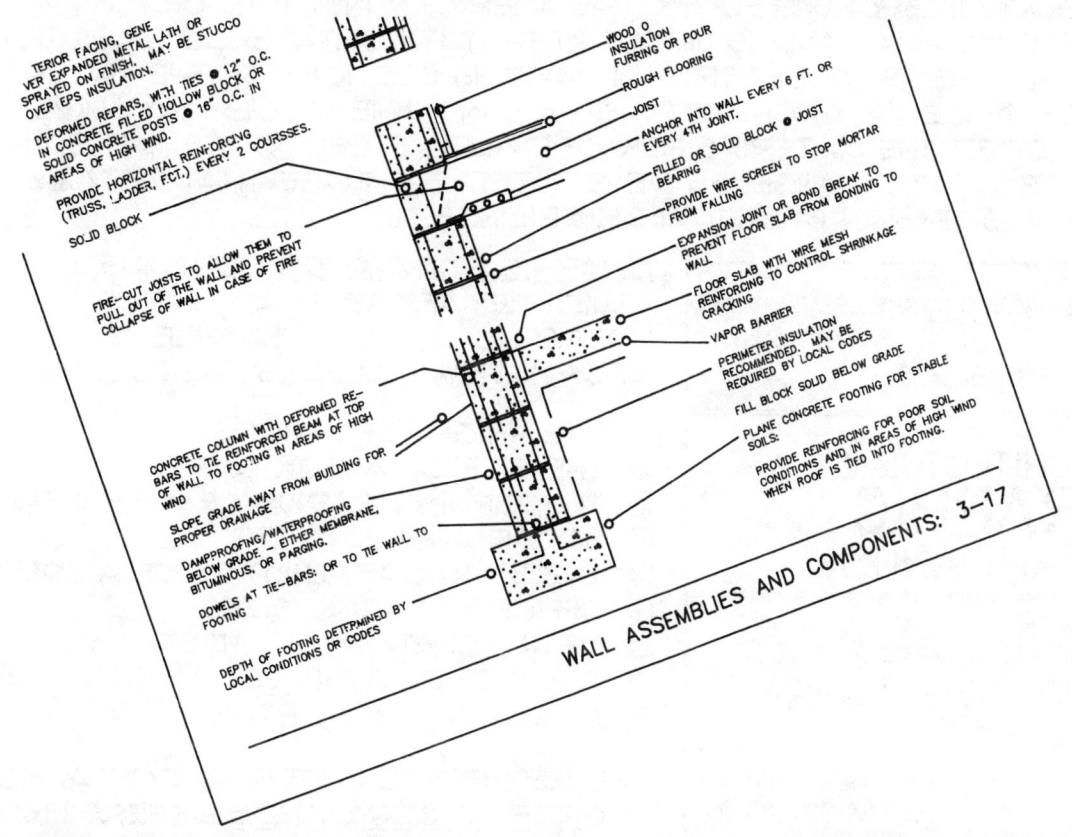

SWEET'S CATALOG FILE ALSO CONTAINS AN IMPRESSIVE REFERENCE SOURCE IN VOLUME ONE TITLED "SELECTION DATA." THE NEARLY 800 PAGES ARE SEPARATED INTO SIX BUILDING CATEGORIES:
1. ENCLOSURE
2. ROOF/FLOOR ASSEMBLIES AND COMPONENTS
3. WALL ASSEMBLIES AND COMPONENTS
4. MATERIALS- SPECIFIC USE
5. MATERIALS- MULTIUSE
6. SERVICES

THE SELECTION DATA UNIT BEGINS WITH GENERAL DESIGN MATERIAL ON VARIOUS BUILDING ENCLOSURES. CHAPTERS 2 AND 3 EXAMINE THE COMPONENTS THAT MAKE UP VARIOUS WALL AND ROOF SYSTEMS. THE PAGE SHOWN ABOVE ILLUSTRATES THE CONDITIONS THAT MAKE UP A MASONRY WALL. CHAPTERS 4 AND 5 REVIEW THE TECHNICAL

REFERENCE SOURCES | 10-3

SPECIFICATION ON HUNDREDS OF BUILDING PRODUCTS. CHAPTER 6 REVIEWS BUILDING SERVICES SUCH AS FIRE PROTECTION, HEATING, AND ELECTRICAL LIGHTING.

ARCHITECTURAL GRAPHIC STANDARDS
ARCHITECTURAL GRAPHIC STANDARDS IS PROBABLY THE MOST IMPORTANT REFERENCE SOURCE AVAILABLE TO THE PROFESSION. THIS BOOK IS SPONSORED BY THE AMERICAN INSTITUTE OF ARCHITECTS (AIA), AND IS UNIQUE IN THAT IT CONTAINS CONTRIBUTIONS FROM HUNDREDS OF EXPERTS IN VARIOUS SECTIONS OF THE MATERIAL. FOR EXAMPLE, AN ARCHITECT'S OFFICE IN MINNEAPOLIS MAY HAVE DEVELOPED THE MATERIAL FOR OPEN-WEB STEEL JOISTS, WHILE AN ARCHITECT IN LOS ANGELES DEVELOPED THE PAGE THAT DETAILS METAL SUSPENSION SYSTEMS FOR CEILINGS.

GRAPHIC STANDARDS CONTAINS A TRULY REMARKABLE AMOUNT OF MATERIAL. A SMALL SAMPLE OF THIS INFORMATION INCLUDES THE FOLLOWING:

- THE HEIGHT OF A HORSE
- THE SIZE OF A BOX CAR
- THE TURNING RADIUS OF A SEMI TRUCK
- SOLAR ANGLES IN THE U.S.
- THE SPAN CAPABILITIES OF A JOIST
- OFFICE FURNITURE SIZES
- METAL CURTAIN WALL DETAILS
- THE SIZE OF A 747 JET
- ROOF FLASHING DETAILS

THE REFERENCE MATERIAL CONTAINED IN GRAPHIC STANDARDS DIFFERS FROM THE MATERIAL IN SWEET'S FILE IN THAT IT IS INTENDED TO PROVIDE GENERIC DESIGN INFORMATION. FOR EXAMPLE, GRAPHIC STANDARDS CONTAINS SEVERAL PAGES ON RESIDENTIAL SKYLIGHTS, GIVING GENERAL DESIGN INFORMATION, SUCH AS HEAD AND SILL DETAILS AND FLASHING CONDITIONS. IT WOULD BE NECESSARY TO REFER TO A COMPANY CATALOG, SUCH AS THE VELLUX WINDOW CATALOG, TO DETERMINE THE EXACT SIZE AND FLASHING CONDITIONS FOR A SPECIFIC MANUFACTURED PRODUCT.

THE MATERIAL IN ARCHITECTURAL GRAPHIC STANDARDS IS ORGANIZED USING THE C.S.I. FORMAT. FOR EXAMPLE, WOOD FRAMING DETAILS ARE ILLUSTRATED IN CHAPTER SIX, WHILE MASONRY CONDITIONS ARE IN CHAPTER FOUR. THE FEATURES THAT MAKE THIS BOOK UNIQUE ARE THE QUALITY DETAILS AND BRIEF

EXPLANATIONS THAT ADDRESS THE TECHNICAL FABRICATION OF EACH PRODUCT. THE EXAMPLE BELOW ILLUSTRATES THE DESIGN CONSIDERATIONS FOR USING A SEALANT IN A JOINT.

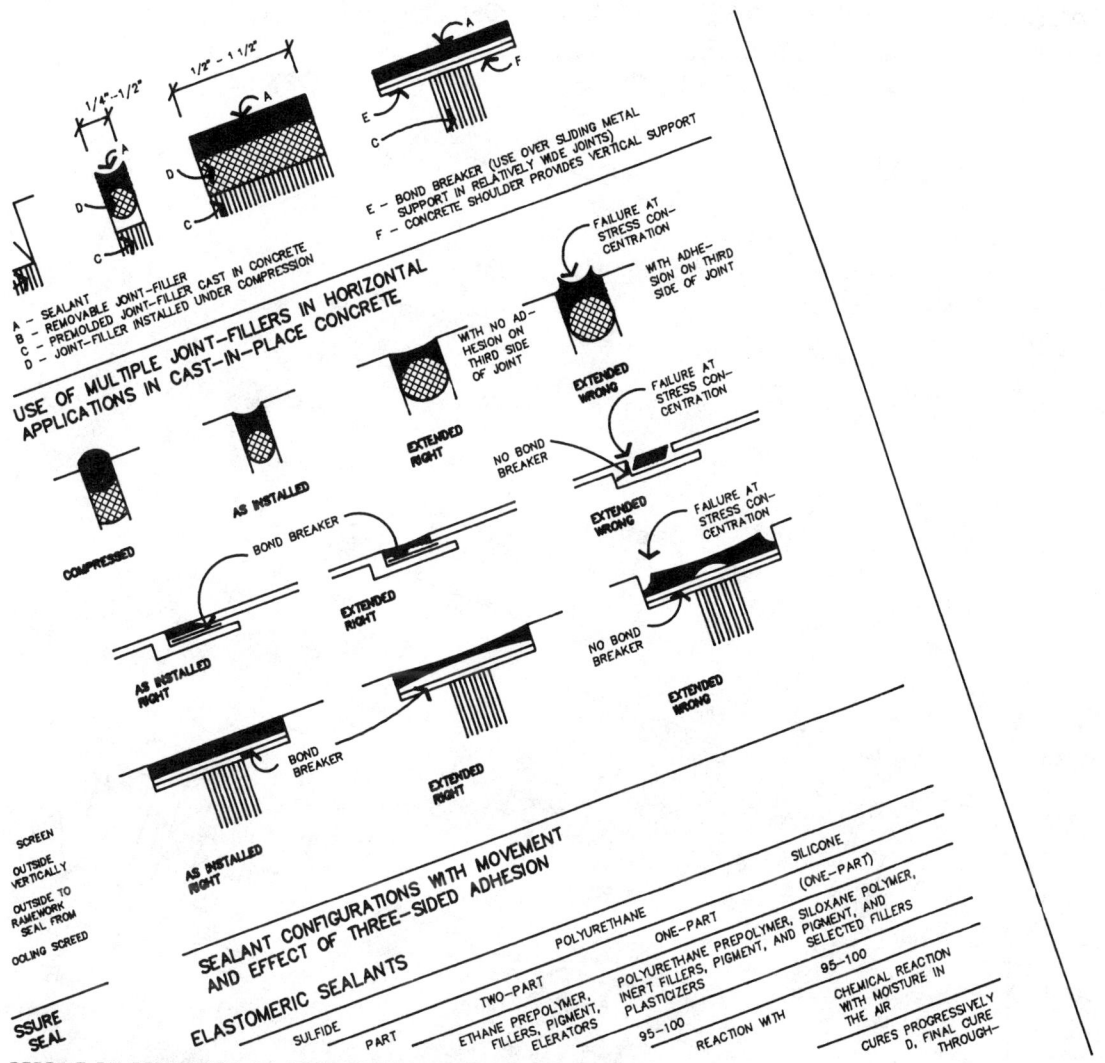

REPRINT BY PERMISSION OF JOHN WILEY & SONS, INC. © 1989

<u>GRAPHIC STANDARDS</u> SHOULD BE ONE OF THE FIRST REFERENCE SOURCES THAT YOU CONSULT WHEN RESEARCHING A CONDITION. MOST OF THE SECTIONS ARE ONLY TWO OR THREE PAGES LONG; BE SURE TO REVIEW ALL OF THE DATA BEFORE DEVELOPING A DETAIL.

IF GRAPHIC STANDARDS HAS A DOWNSIDE, IT WOULD BE THE COST (OVER $150). THE PUBLISHER HAS PRINTED A STUDENT EDITION FOR ABOUT ONE-THIRD OF THE TYPICAL PRICE. THIS SOFT COVER EDITION IS A REPRINT OF THE PREVIOUS ISSUE. ALTHOUGH SOME OF THE CHARTS HAVE BEEN DELETED IN THIS EDITION, THE ILLUSTRATIONS AND NOTES REMAIN THE SAME.

REFERENCE SOURCES | 10-5

MANUFACTURERS' DATA

THERE ARE SEVERAL THOUSAND MANUFACTURERS OF BUILDING PRODUCTS. MOST OF THESE COMPANIES PRINT TECHNICAL DATA CATALOGS WHICH PROVIDE INFORMATION ON PRODUCT SIZE, INSTALLATION, AND SPECIFICATIONS. CATALOGS ARE TYPICALLY 8 1/2" x 11" AND ARE ORGANIZED USING THE C.S.I. FORMAT.

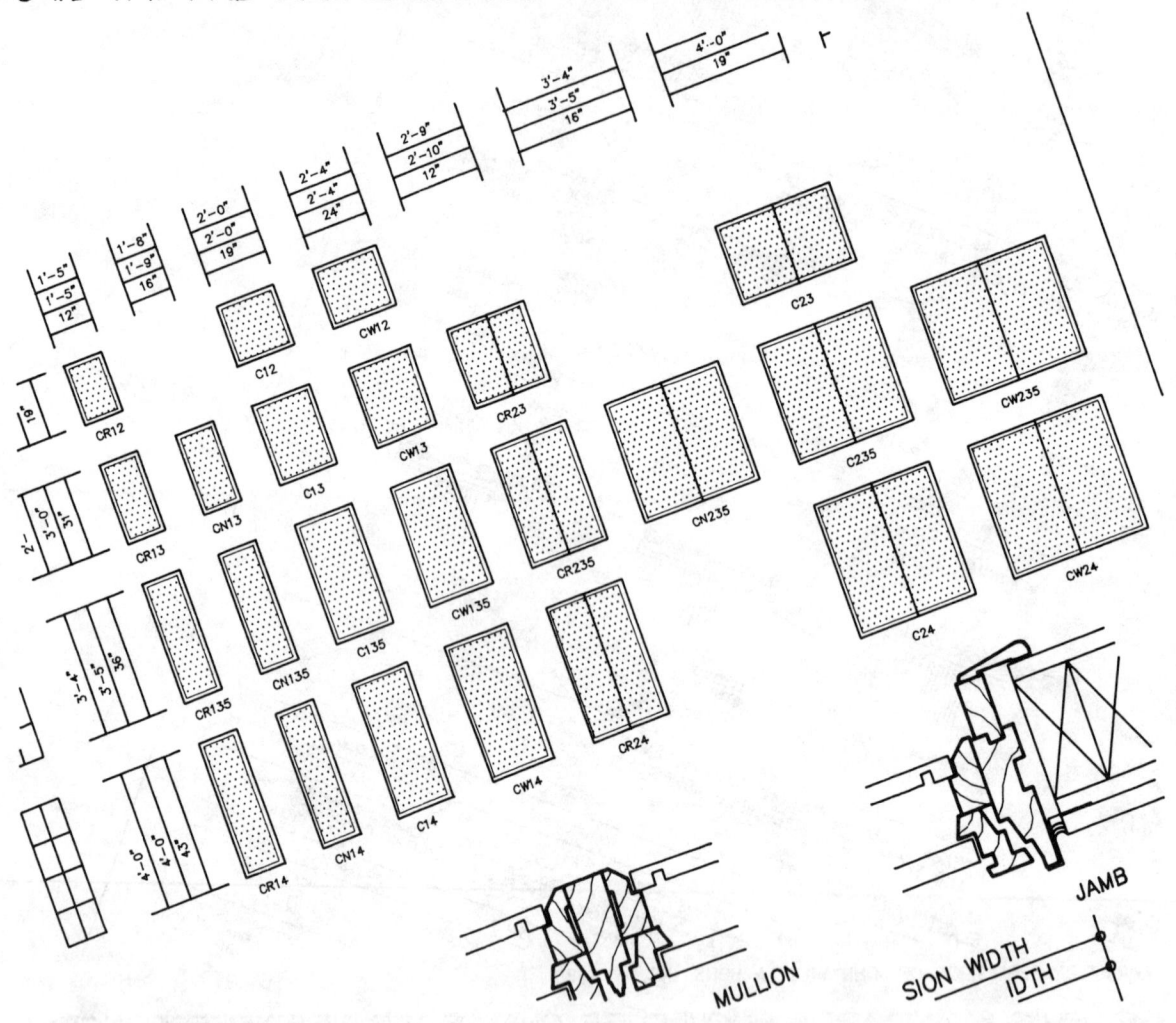

THE ILLUSTRATION ABOVE SHOWS A PAGE FROM A CATALOG ON WOOD CASEMENT WINDOWS. THIS MATERIAL PROVIDES EXACT SIZES OF EACH UNIT, THE ROUGH OPENING, AND THE GLASS DIMENSIONS. IN ADDITION, THE DETAILS INDICATE THE CONDITIONS USED TO INCORPORATE THE WINDOW INTO WOOD FRAME AND MASONRY WALLS.

SOME COMPANIES PROVIDE A GREAT DEAL MORE INFORMATION IN THEIR COMPANY CATALOG THAN IN THE ONE THEY SUPPLY TO SWEET'S FILE. COMPANY CATALOGS TYPICALLY PROVIDE INFORMATION IN

REFERENCE SOURCES   10-6

THE FOLLOWING WAYS:

- EXACT PRODUCT DIMENSIONS ARE GIVEN.
- SECTION CUTS THROUGH THE PRODUCT ARE SHOWN.
- DETAIL DRAWINGS SHOW THE PRODUCT INSTALLED IN THE BUILDING.
- TECHNICAL SPECIFICATIONS ARE WRITTEN FOR THE PRODUCT.
- THE LOCAL PRODUCT REPRESENTATIVE'S ADDRESS IS PROVIDED.

EXISTING DRAWINGS
AN EXCELLENT AID IN THE ASSEMBLY OF A DRAWING PACKAGE IS THE REVIEW OF EXISTING ARCHITECTURAL DRAWINGS. WHILE EVERY BUILDING IS UNIQUE, THERE ARE MANY DETAILS ON DIFFERENT BUILDINGS THAT ARE SIMILAR.

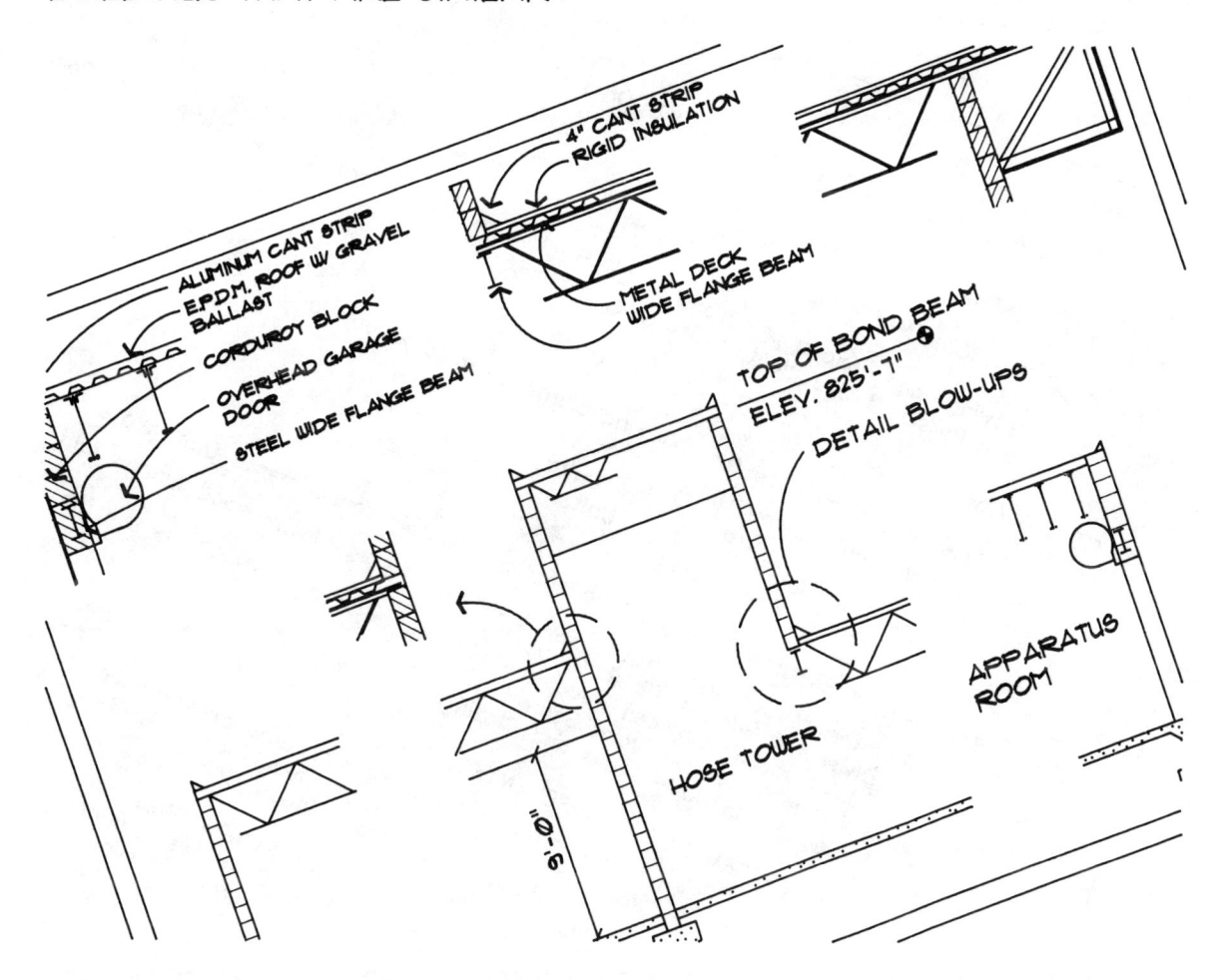

USE THE FOLLOWING TIPS WHEN SELECTING DRAWINGS:

- THE CONSTRUCTION TECHNIQUES SHOULD BE SIMILAR.
- STUDY (AND UNDERSTAND) THE DETAILS.
- USE PROFESSIONAL DRAWINGS (STUDENT WORK COULD CAUSE YOU TO DUPLICATE INCORRECT WORK).

REFERENCE SOURCES

ARCHITECT'S SPECIFICATIONS

THE CONSTRUCTION DRAWINGS BASICALLY INDICATE THE <u>QUANTITY</u> OF MATERIALS USED FOR A BUILDING - HOW MUCH BRICK, HOW MANY WINDOWS, ETC. SPECIFICATIONS INDICATE THE <u>QUALITY</u> OF MATERIALS USED FOR THE PROJECT - THE TYPE OF MORTAR TO USE, INSULATION STANDARDS FOR WINDOWS, ETC. SPECIFICATIONS CAN BE AN EXCELLENT REFERENCE SOURCE FOR TECHNICAL DATA ON A PRODUCT. SIMILAR TO THE OTHER REFERENCES IN THIS UNIT, MOST ARCHITECTURAL SPECIFICATIONS ARE ORGANIZED USING THE 16-SECTION C.S.I. FORMAT. IN THE FOLLOWING SECTION, WE WILL STUDY THE SPECIFICATION ON WOOD CLAD WINDOWS (SECTION 08610) FOR THE MOTEL AND RESTAURANT PROJECT SHOWN IN CHAPTER 26.

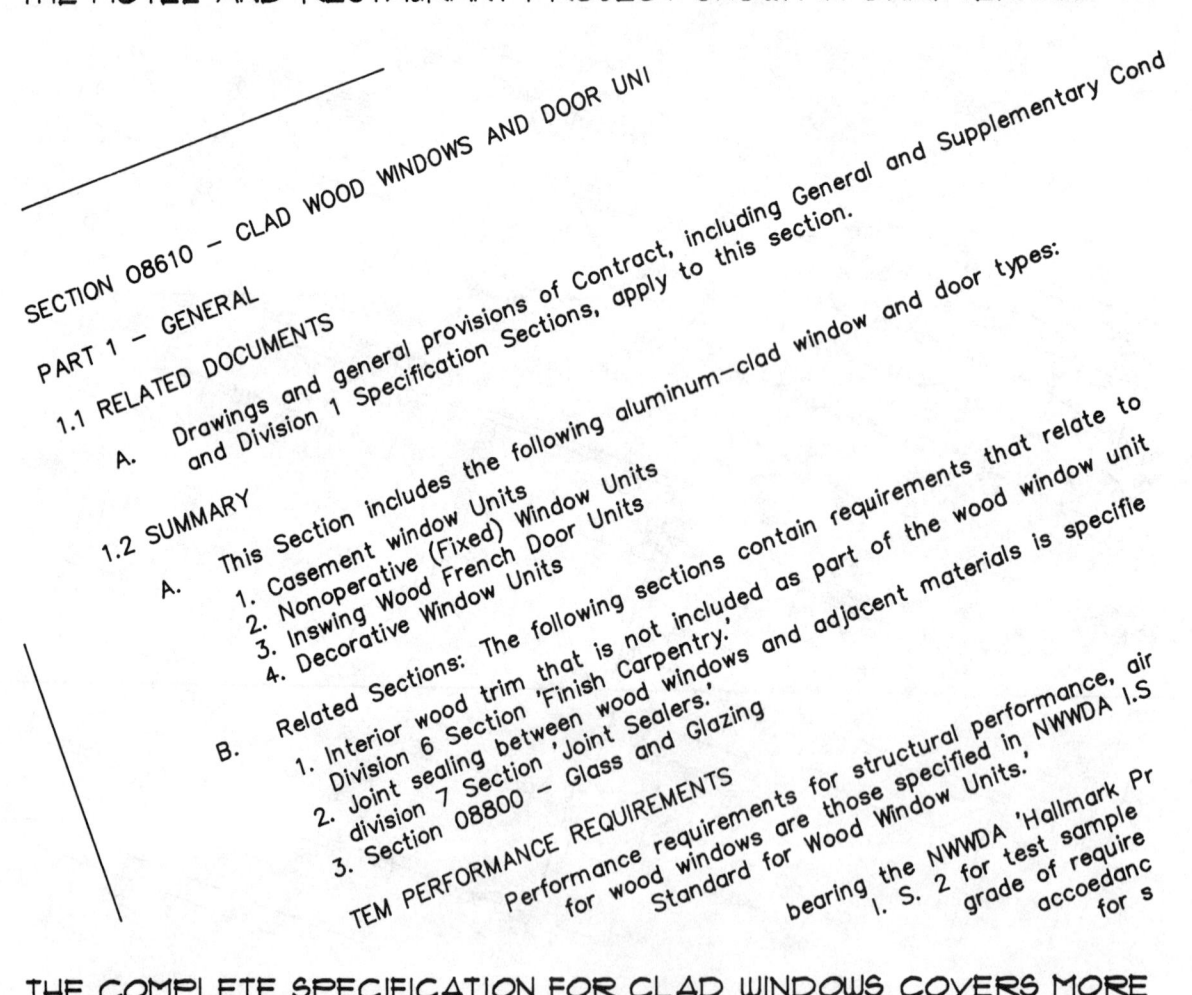

SECTION 08610 - CLAD WOOD WINDOWS AND DOOR UNI

PART 1 - GENERAL

1.1 RELATED DOCUMENTS

   A. Drawings and general provisions of Contract, including General and Supplementary Cond and Division 1 Specification Sections, apply to this section.

1.2 SUMMARY

   A. This Section includes the following aluminum-clad window and door types:
      1. Casement window Units
      2. Nonoperative (Fixed) Window Units
      3. Inswing Wood French Door Units
      4. Decorative Window Units

   B. Related Sections: The following sections contain requirements that relate to the wood window unit
      1. Interior wood trim that is not included as part of the wood window unit Division 6 Section 'Finish Carpentry.'
      2. Joint sealing between wood windows and adjacent materials is specifie division 7 Section 'Joint Sealers.'
      3. Section 08800 - Glass and Glazing

TEM PERFORMANCE REQUIREMENTS

Performance requirements for structural performance, air for wood windows are those specified in NWWDA I.S Standard for Wood Window Units.'

bearing the NWWDA 'Hallmark Pr I. S. 2 for test sample grade of require accoedanc for s

THE COMPLETE SPECIFICATION FOR CLAD WINDOWS COVERS MORE THAN TEN PAGES; THIS SECTION HIGHLIGHTS THE MAJOR POINTS. THE SECTIONS OF A SPECIFICATION ARE TYPICALLY WRITTEN TO "STAND ALONE." THIS MEANS THAT THE SECTION ON CLAD WOOD WINDOWS, FOR EXAMPLE, IS INDEPENDENT FROM OTHER ELEMENTS IN THE DOCUMENT.

REFERENCE SOURCES   10-8

A SUPPLIER IS THEREFORE ABLE TO OBTAIN ALL NECESSARY INFORMATION BY CONSULTING A SPECIFIC SECTION OF THE SPECIFICATION. A COMMON STRATEGY IN ORGANIZING A SPECIFICATION IS TO BREAK EACH DIVISION INTO THREE SECTIONS: (1) GENERAL INFORMATION, (2) PRODUCTS, AND (3) EXECUTION. THE WINDOW SPECIFICATION WILL BE USED TO EXPLAIN EACH OF THESE SECTIONS.

<u>GENERAL INFORMATION</u> IN THE SPECIFICATIONS COVERS ITEMS SUCH AS THE PERFORMANCE REQUIREMENTS FOR THE PRODUCT.

SYSTEM PERFORMANCE REQUIREMENTS

Performance Requirements (Grade 60 Windows): Each required window unit shall comply with the following performance requirements:
1. Air Infiltration: Not more than 0.10 cfm per sq. ft. of overall frame area at an inward test pressure of 1.57 lbs per sq. ft.
2. Water Penetration: No water penetration as defined in the test method at an inward test pressure of 6.24 lbs per sq. ft.
3. Structural performance: No glass breakage, damage to hardware, permanent deformation that would impair operation of the unit, or residual deflection greater than 0.4 percent of the span at a positive (inward) and negative (outward) test pressure of 60 lbs per sq. ft.
4. Forced Entry Resistance: Provide window units that comply with requirements for Performance Level 40 when tested in accordance with ASTM F 588.

SPECIFICATIONS FREQUENTLY REQUIRE THE CONTRACTOR TO PROVIDE INFORMATION TO THE ARCHITECT IN THE FORM OF SHOP DRAWINGS AND SAMPLES OF THE PRODUCT.

SUBMITTALS

A. General: Submit the following in accordance with the General Conditions of the Contract
   1. Product data for each type of wood window required, including:
      a. Standard construction details and fabrication methods
      b. Profiles and dimensions of individual components
      c. Data on hardware, accessories and finishes
      d. Recommendations for maintenance and cleaning exterior surfaces
   2. Shop drawings for each type of window specified
      a. Layout and installation details, including anchors
      b. Typical window unit elevations at 3/4 inch scale
      c. Full-size details of typical and composite members
      d. Hardware, including operators
      e. Glazing details

FINAL POINTS IN THE SECTION ON GENERAL INFORMATION ADDRESS QUALITY ASSURANCE, PROJECT CONDITIONS, AND WARRANTY.

WARRANTY

A. Wood Window Warranty: Submit written warranty, executed by the window manufacturer, agreeing to repair or replace units that fail in materials or workmanship within the specified warranty period. Failures include, but are not necessarily limited to:
   1. Structural failures, including excessive deflection, excessive leakage, or air infiltration
   2. Faulty operation of window sash or hardware
   3. Deterioration of metals, finishes, and other materials beyond normal weathering
B. Warranty Period: 3 years after the date of Substantial Completion
   1. The warranty shall not deprive the Owner of other rights or remedies that the Owner may have under other provisions of the Contract Cocuments.

THE NEXT SECTION OF A SPECIFICATION DEFINES THE PRODUCTS THAT THE CONTRACTOR MAY USE. IN THIS CASE, A SELECTION OF FOUR MANUFACTURERS IS GIVEN, AND PELLA WINDOW UNITS ARE NAMED AS THE STANDARD SHOWN ON THE CONSTRUCTION DRAWINGS.

MANUFACTURERS

A. Manufacturer: Subject to compliance with requirements, provide window units by one of the following:
   1. Hurd Millwork Co.
   2. Marvin Windows
   3. Rolscreen Co. (Pella)
   4. Weather Shield Mfg., Inc.
B. Pella Clad casement units, clad fixed frame units and clad traditional inswing french door units as manufactured by Rolscreen Company, Pella, Iowa are the standard of quality for this specification. Other manufacturers must submit for approval in accordance with section 01630.

THE PRODUCTS SECTION CONTINUES TO DEFINE THE MATERIALS THAT MAY BE USED IN THE BUILDING. THIS PORTION OF THE SPECIFICATION IS PRECISE (AND QUITE LONG). A PORTION OF THE WINDOW MATERIAL IS SHOWN BELOW.

MATERIALS

A. General: Comply with requirements of NWWDA I. S. 2.

   Wood: Clear Ponderosa Pine or other suitable fine-grain lumber that has been kiln dried to a moisture content of 6 to 12 percent at time of fabrication and is free of visible finger joints, blue stain, knots, pitch pockets and surface checks larger than 1/32 inch wide by 2 inches long.

   1. Lumber shall be water-repellent preservative treated after machining in accordance with NWWDA I. S. 4.
   2. Frame: Water repellent preservative treated in accordance with NWWDA I. S. 4: interior exposed surfaces clear Western Pine, exterior surfaces clad with aluminum, components assembled with screws and concealed corner locks. Overall frame depth: 5 inches.
   3. Sash: Western Pine, water repellent preservative treated in accordance with NWWDA I. S. 4, finished on edges; exterior surfaces clad with aluminum, lap-jointed and sealed. Corners mortised and tenoned, glued and secured with metal fasteners. Sash thickness: 1 3/4 inch.

THE EXECUTION SECTION OF A SPECIFICATION COVERS ITEMS SUCH AS INSPECTION, INSTALLATION, ADJUSTMENT, CLEANING, AND PROTECTION OF PRODUCTS. A REQUIREMENT FOR THE WINDOW INSPECTION IS SHOWN BELOW.

INSPECTION

A. Inspect openings before beginning installation. Verify that the opening is correct and the sill plate is level. Do not proceed with installation of window units until unsatisfactory conditions have been corrected.

   1. Masonry surfaces shall be visibly dry, and free of excess mortar, sand, and other debris.
   2. Metal frame walls shall be dry, clean, sound and well-screwed, free of voids, and without offsets at joints. Ensure that screw heads are flush with surfaces in the opening.
   3. Coordinate window installation with wall flashing and other built-in components.

REFERENCE SOURCES

MATERIAL RESEARCH

THE NEXT SEVERAL PAGES WILL EXAMINE THE STEPS USED TO RESEARCH BUILDING MATERIALS. IN OUR FIRST EXAMPLE, WE WILL SELECT WINDOWS FROM THE ANDERSEN WINDOW CATALOG. THE RELEVANT DATA ARE AVAILABLE (IN SECTION 08610/AND) FROM THE MANUFACTURER'S CATALOG.

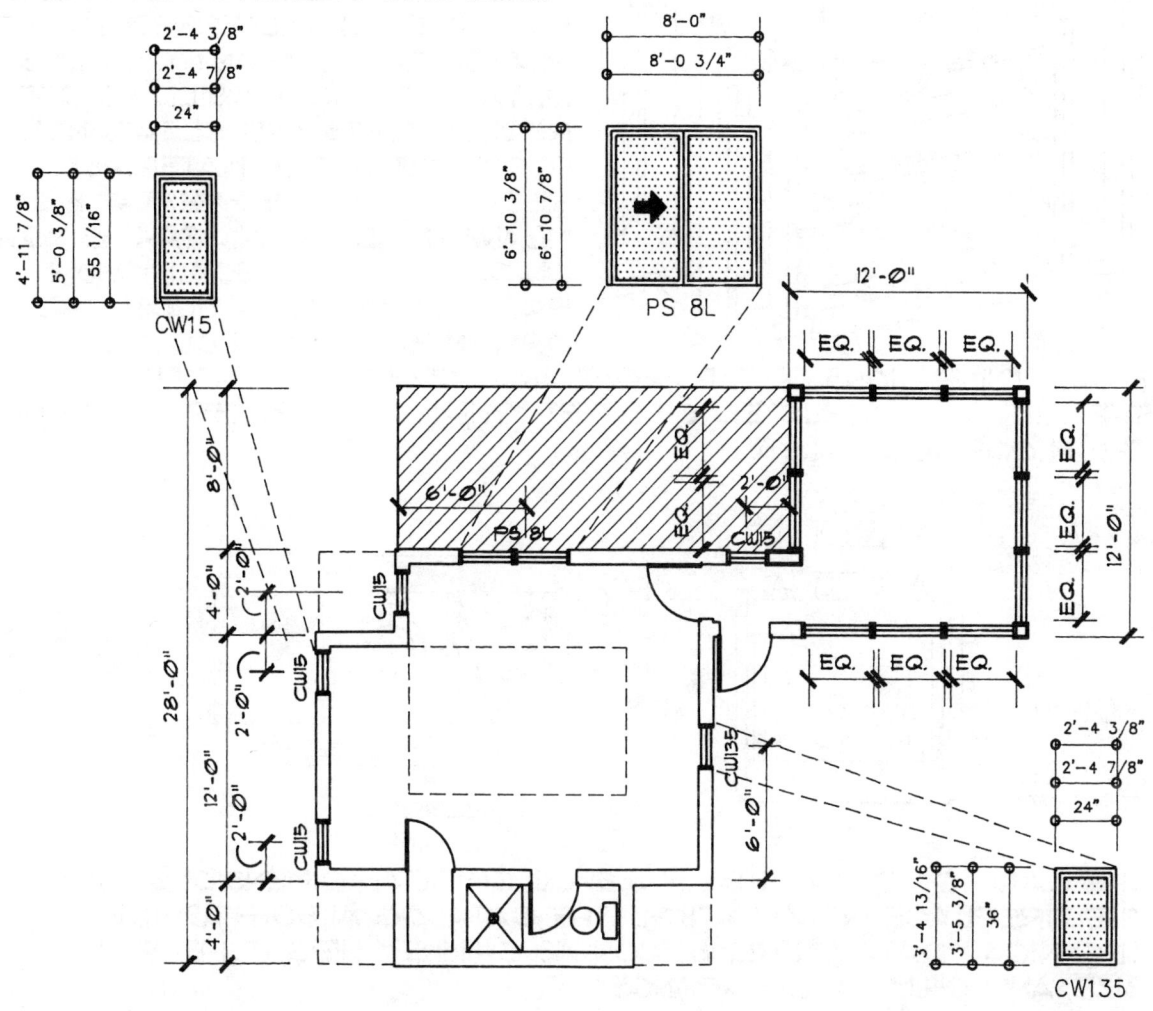

THE DRAWING ABOVE CONTAINS ELEVATIONS OF CASEMENT WINDOWS AND A GLIDING PATIO DOOR UNIT. NOTE THAT WINDOWS ARE GIVEN THREE DIMENSION STRINGS: THE INTERIOR DIMENSION IS THE GLASS SIZE; THE MIDDLE STRING IS THE ROUGH OPENING; AND THE OUTSIDE NUMBER IS THE UNIT DIMENSION. REFER TO THE JAMB SECTION AT THE LEFT TO DETERMINE THE DIFFERENCE BETWEEN THE UNIT DIMENSION AND ROUGH OPENING.

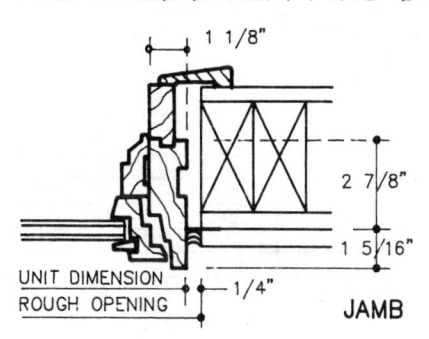

REFERENCE SOURCES   10-11

IN THE NEXT EXAMPLE, THE REQUIREMENTS FOR THE PREFABRICATED FIREPLACE IN THE 12/12 PITCH ROOF HOUSE IN CHAPTER 22 WILL BE DETERMINED. THE MATERIAL SHOWN BELOW IS FROM THE MANUFACTURER'S CATALOG. ONCE THE FIREPLACE IS SELECTED, THE RELEVANT DIMENSIONS AND NOTES SHOULD BE TRANSFERRED TO THE PLANS. THE COMPANY CATALOG DETAILS CRITICAL BUILDING CODE REQUIREMENTS AND CLEARANCES FOR COMBUSTIBLE MATERIALS. RESEARCHING THE FIREPLACE UNIT MEANS READING AND TAKING NOTES ON ALL OF THE PRECAUTIONS IN THE PRODUCT SPECIFICATIONS. THE DRAWINGS BELOW SHOW THE EXACT DIMENSIONS OF THE FRONT AND TOP VIEW OF THE FIREPLACE. THE UNIT IS CONSTRUCTED OF SHEET METAL WITH FIRE BRICK LINING THE FLOOR AND WALLS.

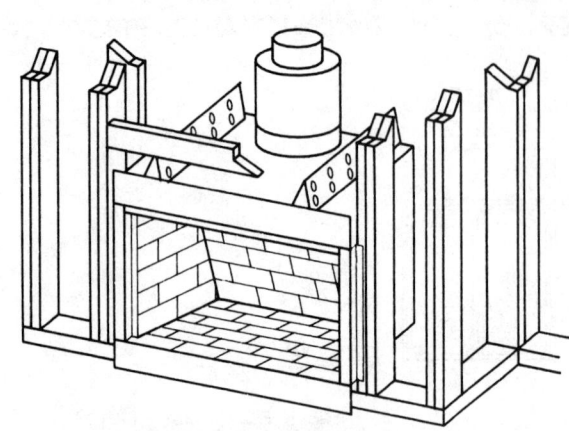

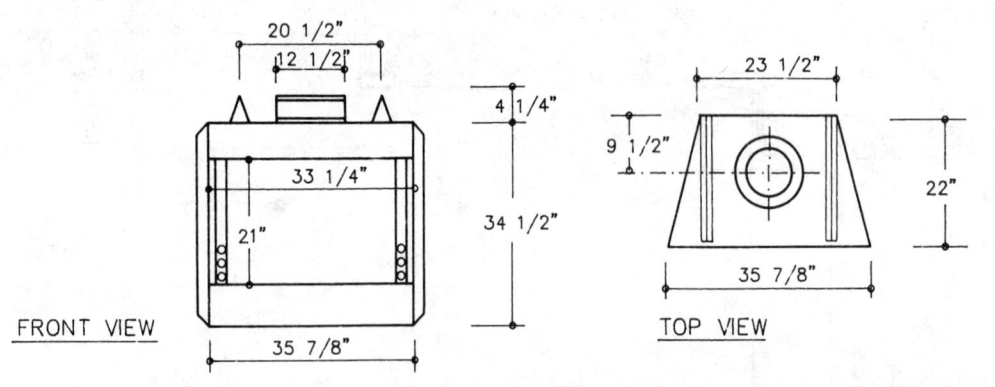

FRONT VIEW

TOP VIEW

THE CATALOG DETAILS BELOW SHOW CRITICAL DIMENSIONS FOR THE FIREPLACE INSTALLATION. THE CATALOG ALSO PROVIDES TECHNICAL DATA ON ITEMS SUCH AS CHIMNEY HEIGHT, HEARTH SIZE, AND CHIMNEY CLEARANCE.

FIREPLACE FRAMING FRONT ELEVATION

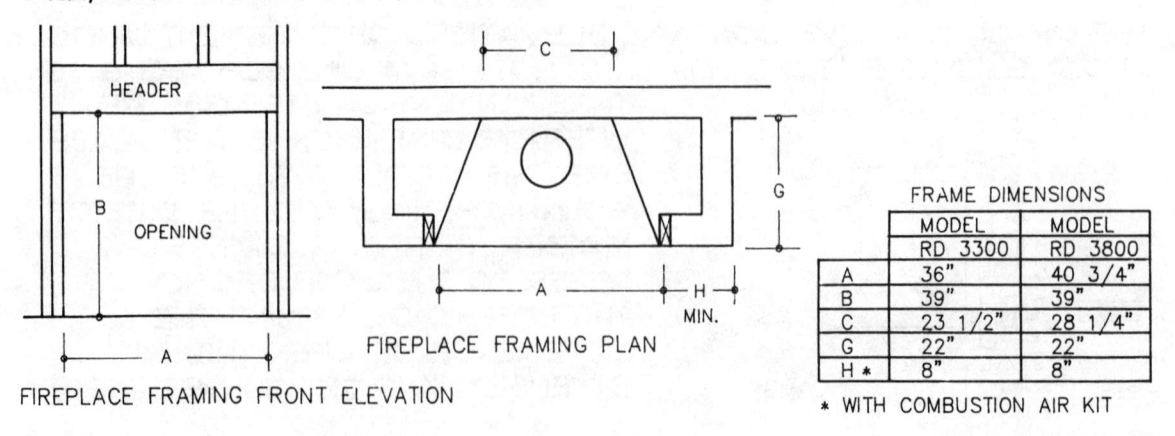

FIREPLACE FRAMING PLAN

FRAME DIMENSIONS

	MODEL RD 3300	MODEL RD 3800
A	36"	40 3/4"
B	39"	39"
C	23 1/2"	28 1/4"
G	22"	22"
H *	8"	8"

* WITH COMBUSTION AIR KIT

REFERENCE SOURCES

IN THIS EXAMPLE, WE WILL LOOK AT THE PLACEMENT OF A SKYLIGHT UNIT IN THE STUDENT LIBRARY PROJECT (CHAPTER 27). THE UNIT IS SET INTO AN EPDM (RUBBER SHEET) ROOF THAT MUST BE FLASHED PROPERLY TO PREVENT LEAKAGE. THE DEVELOPMENT OF THE SKYLIGHT BEGINS WITH A REVIEW OF TWO PRODUCT CATALOGS: ROOFING AND SKYLIGHTS. THE DETAIL SHOWN AT THE LEFT INDICATES CATALOG DESIGN CRITERIA FOR AN EPDM ROOF MEMBRANE. THIS DETAIL WAS SELECTED FROM THE 20-PAGE MANUFACTURER'S TECHNICAL BROCHURE BECAUSE IT CLOSELY RESEMBLED THE LIBRARY ROOF CONDITION. THE FINAL CONSTRUCTION DRAWING AND SPECIFICATIONS MUST REFLECT THE NOTES AND DETAILS FROM THE SUPPLIER. THE DETAIL SHOWS THE FLAT ROOF SHEET SECURED TO THE DECK WITH A FASTENER. A SECOND STRIP IS ATTACHED TO THE VERTICAL CURB (WITH ADHESIVE) AND LAPPED OVER THE FLAT ROOF SHEET. THE LAP JOINT IS SECURED WITH SPLICING CEMENT. THE SECOND AREA OF RESEARCH INVOLVES FINDING A SKYLIGHT MANUFACTURER. THE DRAWING AT THE RIGHT SHOWS A SECTION DETAIL FOR A UNIT THAT WILL FIT THE LIBRARY ROOF CONDITION. A NOTE ON THE DETAIL STATES: "ROOFING BY OTHERS." THIS MEANS THAT THE TWO CONDITIONS, SKYLIGHT AND ROOFING, MUST BE COMBINED TO DEVELOP A SKYLIGHT ON AN EPDM ROOF. THE FINAL WORKING DRAWINGS FOR THE SKYLIGHT SHOULD INCLUDE THE MINIMUM 9" CURB HEIGHT, SEALANT LOCATIONS, FASTENING REQUIREMENTS, AND A DETAILED PROFILE OF THE UNIT.

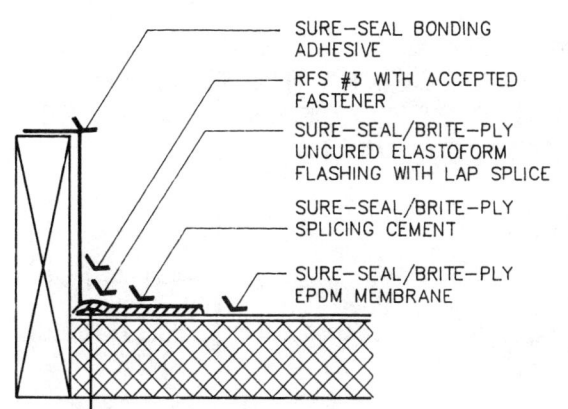

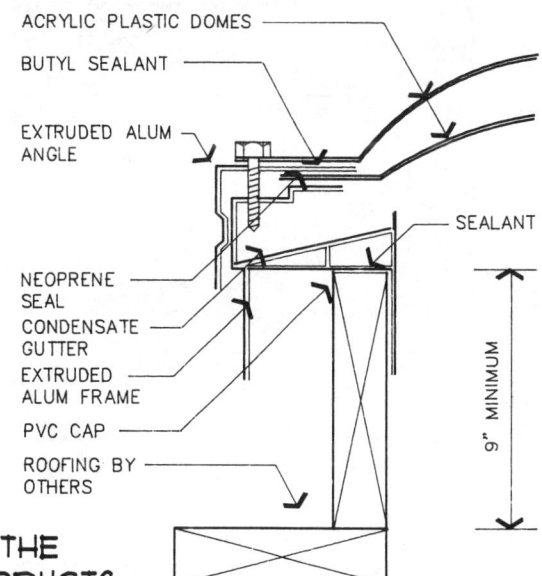

MOST SPECIFICATIONS WILL ALLOW THE CONTRACTOR A SELECTION OF PRODUCTS. FOR EXAMPLE, THERE ARE SEVERAL SKYLIGHT UNITS THAT WOULD FIT THE GENERAL REQUIREMENTS FOR THE LIBRARY UNIT. IF THE CONTRACTOR WERE TO SELECT A DIFFERENT PRODUCT FROM THOSE SPECIFIED, HOWEVER, HE OR SHE WOULD BE REQUIRED TO SUBMIT DETAILED SHOP DRAWINGS TO THE ARCHITECT FOR APPROVAL.

REFERENCE SOURCES   10-13

A PORTION OF THE LIBRARY WALL SECTION IS SHOWN BELOW. THE DETAIL RESEARCH INVOLVES DETERMINING HOW TO HANG A STONE BALCONY HANDRAIL FROM CANTILEVERED STEEL BEAMS. THE DESIGN MUST DEVELOP A STAINLESS STEEL STONE HANGER THAT IS FASTENED TO THE BEAM. WORK ON THE DETAIL WOULD BEGIN BY SKETCHING SECTION CUTS THROUGH THE BALCONY. THE NEXT STEP WOULD BE TO CONSULT A STONE TECHNICAL CATALOG.

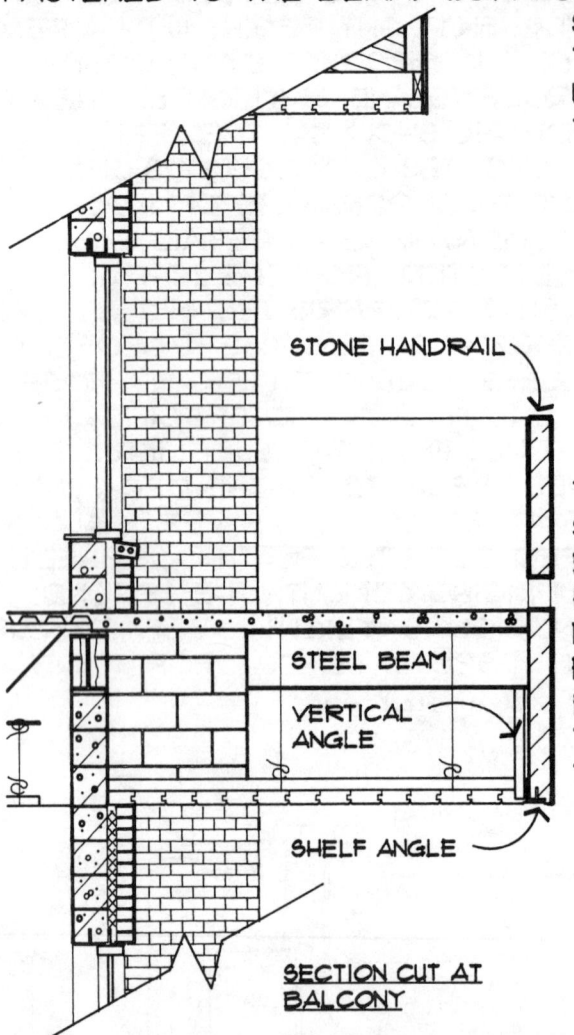

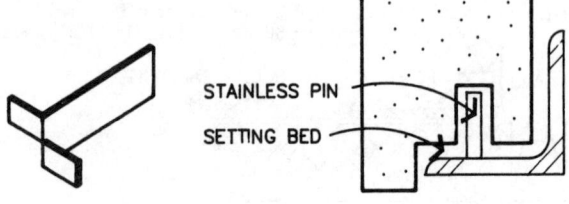

STAINLESS STEEL STONE ANCHOR

STAINLESS STEEL SHELF ANGLE

STONE HANDRAIL

THE TWO DETAILS ABOVE WERE SELECTED FROM THE STONE BROCHURE TO SUPPORT THE HANDRAIL. THE ANCHOR IS A NONLOAD-BEARING STRAP THAT FITS IN A SLOT CUT IN THE STONE PANEL. THE ANCHORS ARE USED TO TIE PANELS TOGETHER ALONG THE VERTICAL JOINT.

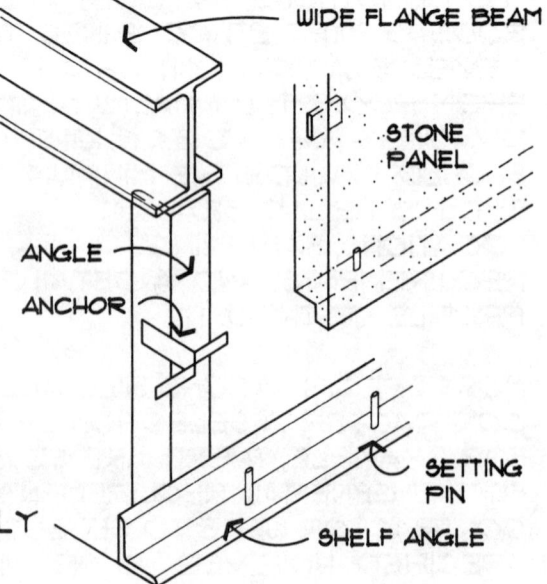

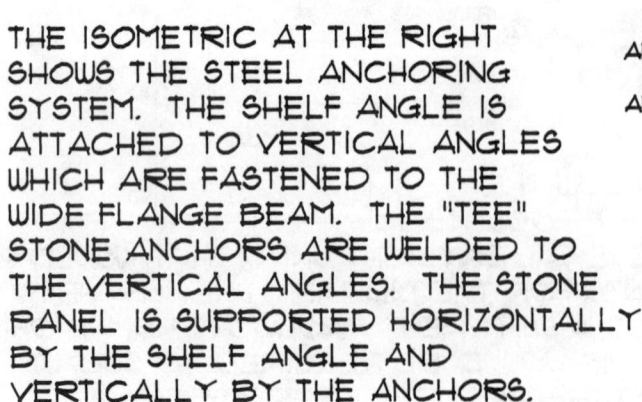

STEEL BEAM
VERTICAL ANGLE
SHELF ANGLE

SECTION CUT AT BALCONY

THE ISOMETRIC AT THE RIGHT SHOWS THE STEEL ANCHORING SYSTEM. THE SHELF ANGLE IS ATTACHED TO VERTICAL ANGLES WHICH ARE FASTENED TO THE WIDE FLANGE BEAM. THE "TEE" STONE ANCHORS ARE WELDED TO THE VERTICAL ANGLES. THE STONE PANEL IS SUPPORTED HORIZONTALLY BY THE SHELF ANGLE AND VERTICALLY BY THE ANCHORS.

WIDE FLANGE BEAM
STONE PANEL
ANGLE
ANCHOR
SETTING PIN
SHELF ANGLE

REFERENCE SOURCES | 10-14

REPLAY

GIVE THE C.S.I. DIVISION NUMBERS (1 THROUGH 16) THAT CORRESPOND TO THE CONSTRUCTION PRODUCTS LISTED BELOW.

1. _____ WOOD WINDOW
2. _____ ELEVATOR
3. _____ PAINT
4. _____ LIGHT FIXTURE
5. _____ SOD
6. _____ ALUMINUM WINDOW
7. _____ MORTAR FOR CONCRETE BLOCK
8. _____ ASPHALT SHINGLES
9. _____ STEEL BAR JOISTS
10. _____ FIBERGLASS INSULATION
11. _____ HOT-WATER FURNACE
12. _____ COPPER ROOF

THIS UNIT EXAMINED FOUR REFERENCE SOURCES. USING THE FOLLOWING ABBREVIATIONS, INDICATE WHICH OF THE FOUR IS REFERRED TO BY EACH STATEMENT BELOW: S—SWEET'S CATALOG FILE; A—ARCHITECTURAL GRAPHIC STANDARDS; M—MANUFACTURER'S DATA; AND E—EXISTING DRAWINGS.

13. _____ THIS SOURCE WOULD PROVIDE THE GREATEST AMOUNT OF TECHNICAL INFORMATION ON A PELLA WINDOW UNIT.

14. _____ THIS SOURCE PROVIDES GENERAL INFORMATION ON HOW TO PROVIDE LIGHTNING PROTECTION FOR A BUILDING.

15. _____ THIS REFERENCE CONTAINS INFORMATION ABOUT MOST MAJOR BRANDS OF WOOD WINDOWS ON THE MARKET.

16. _____ USE THIS SOURCE TO DETERMINE HOW AN ARCHITECT DETAILED A ROOF CONDITION ON A PROJECT SIMILAR TO THE BUILDING YOU ARE DRAWING.

17. _____ USE THIS REFERENCE SOURCE TO DETERMINE THE SIZE OF A SWIMMING POOL.

18. _____ THIS SOURCE WOULD SUPPLY THE GREATEST AMOUNT OF TECHNICAL DATA ON THE INSTALLATION OF A CARLISLE EPDM ROOF.

REFERENCE SOURCES

CIRCLE THE STATEMENT THAT CORRECTLY ANSWERS THE QUESTIONS ABOUT THE WINDOW SPECIFICATION FOUND ON PAGES 10-9 AND 10-10.

19. THIS STATEMENT CONCERNING THE WOOD THAT MUST BE USED TO CONSTRUCT THE WINDOWS IS CORRECT.
    A. THE WINDOW SASH MUST BE A MINIMUM OF 1 1/2" THICK.
    B. WOOD MUST BE DRIED TO A MINIMUM MOISTURE CONTENT OF 15%.
    C. THE WINDOW SASH SHALL BE MADE OF WESTERN PINE.
    D. WOOD CAN HAVE A CHECK (GRAIN SEPARATION) OF 1/4" BY 2".

20. WHICH OF THESE WINDOW MANUFACTURERS IS NOT ACCEPTABLE FOR USE ON THIS PROJECT?
    A. ANDERSEN
    B. PELLA
    C. MARVIN
    D. HURD

21. WHICH OF THESE WARRANTY ITEMS DOESN'T APPLY TO THE WOOD WINDOWS IN THE SPECIFICATION?
    A. THE MANUFACTURER MUST REPLACE A UNIT THAT ALLOWS EXCESSIVE AIR INFILTRATION.
    B. THE MANUFACTURER MUST WARRANT THE WINDOW FOR THREE YEARS.
    C. THE MANUFACTURER MUST REPLACE A UNIT WITH FAULTY HARDWARE.
    D. THE WARRANTY COVERS GLASS BREAKAGE FOR THREE YEARS.

22. BASED ON THE WINDOW MANUFACTURER'S CATALOG INFORMATION ON PAGE 10-6, WHAT IS THE SIZE OF A "C135" WINDOW?
    A. 4'-0" x 1'-8"
    B. 3'-4" x 1'-8"
    C. 3'-4" x 2'-0"
    D. 3'-4" x 2'-4"

23. BASED ON THE PREFABRICATED FIREPLACE CATALOG INFORMATION ON PAGE 10-12, WHAT IS THE FRAME OPENING WIDTH AND HEIGHT FOR A MODEL RD 3800 UNIT?
    A. 36" (WIDE) x 39" (HIGH)
    B. 40 3/4" (WIDE) x 39" (HIGH)
    C. 39" (WIDE) x 28 1/4" (HIGH)
    D. 36" (WIDE) x 22" (HIGH)

REFERENCE SOURCES

PROBLEM SOLVING

IT IS NECESSARY TO DEVELOP GOOD PROBLEM-SOLVING SKILLS IN ARCHITECTURE. EVERY ACTIVITY INVOLVED IN DESIGN OR WORKING DRAWINGS REVOLVES AROUND DECISIONS THAT COULD AFFECT OTHER PARTS OF THE PROJECT. THIS UNIT WILL CONCENTRATE ON TECHNIQUES USED TO SOLVE PROBLEMS IN DETAIL DRAFTING AND TIME MANAGEMENT.

WORKING DRAWINGS

THE FOLLOWING STATEMENT IS QUITE SIMPLE, BUT IT IS THE KEY TO DEVELOPING A STRATEGY IN SOLVING WORKING DRAWING PROBLEMS: "DRAW WHAT YOU KNOW — AND SOLVE WHAT YOU DON'T KNOW." IT'S A COMMON EXPERIENCE FOR AN ARCHITECTURAL STUDENT TO STARE AT A BLANK PIECE OF PAPER AND SIMPLY NOT KNOW WHERE TO START. THE SOLUTION LIES IN SKETCHING ALL OF THE KNOWN FACTS OF THE DETAIL AND FILLING IN THE BLANKS. THIS UNIT CAN'T GIVE YOU ALL THE ANSWERS; IN FACT, ARCHITECTS WITH MANY YEARS OF EXPERIENCE STILL GET STUMPED WITH DETAILS. STUDYING THE EXAMPLES PRESENTED, HOWEVER, WILL HELP YOU TO UNDERSTAND THE PROCESS OF SOLVING PROBLEMS.

1. FLOOR FRAMING

   THE ILLUSTRATION BELOW SHOWS A BASEMENT AND FIRST-FLOOR PLAN.

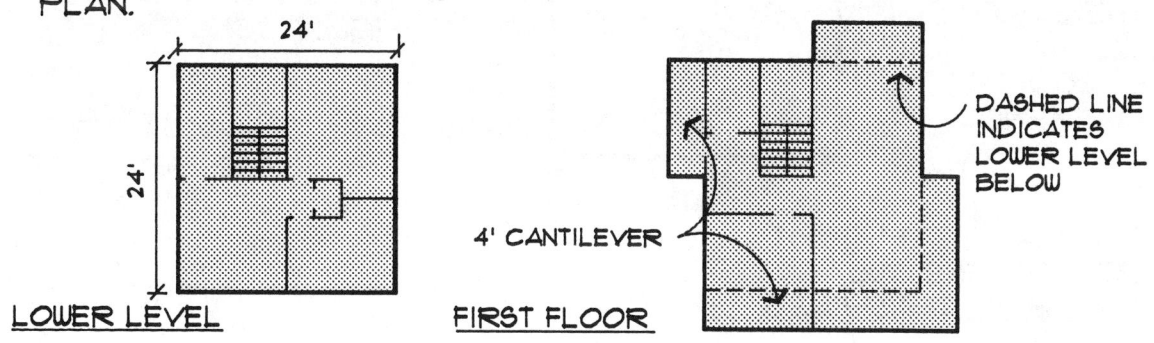

LOWER LEVEL (24' × 24')

FIRST FLOOR — 4' CANTILEVER — DASHED LINE INDICATES LOWER LEVEL BELOW

PROBLEM SOLVING 11-1

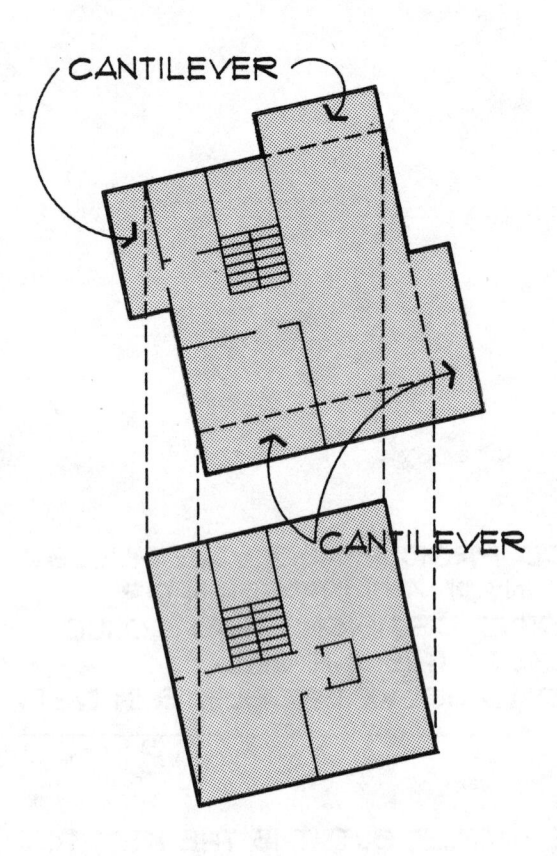

THE EXPLODED FLOOR PLAN VIEW TO THE LEFT INDICATES THAT THE SECOND FLOOR HAS SEVERAL CANTILEVER (OR OVERHANGING) CONDITIONS. A CANTILEVERED JOIST MUST BE PERPENDICULAR TO THE SUPPORT WALL WITH A USUAL ONE-THIRD MAXIMUM OVERHANG AND TWO-THIRDS JOIST SUPPORT BEHIND THE WALL.

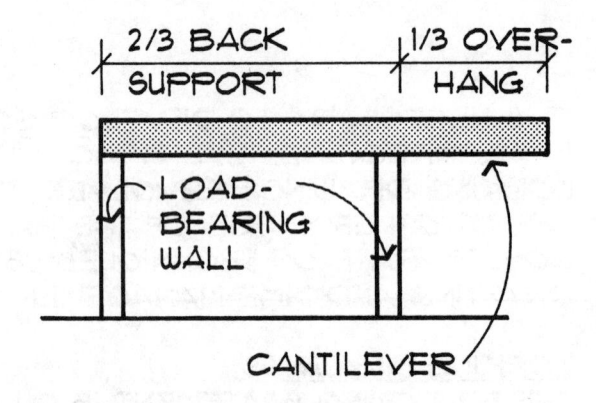

THE PROBLEM-SOLVING TASK IS TO DESIGN A JOIST FRAMING CONDITION THAT WILL SUPPORT THE FLOOR. LET'S START WITH A ROLL OF SKETCH PAPER AND DRAW THE FIRST-FLOOR PLAN. THE NOTES ON THE SKETCH INDICATE THE ASSUMPTIONS THAT ARE MADE IN THE DESIGN.

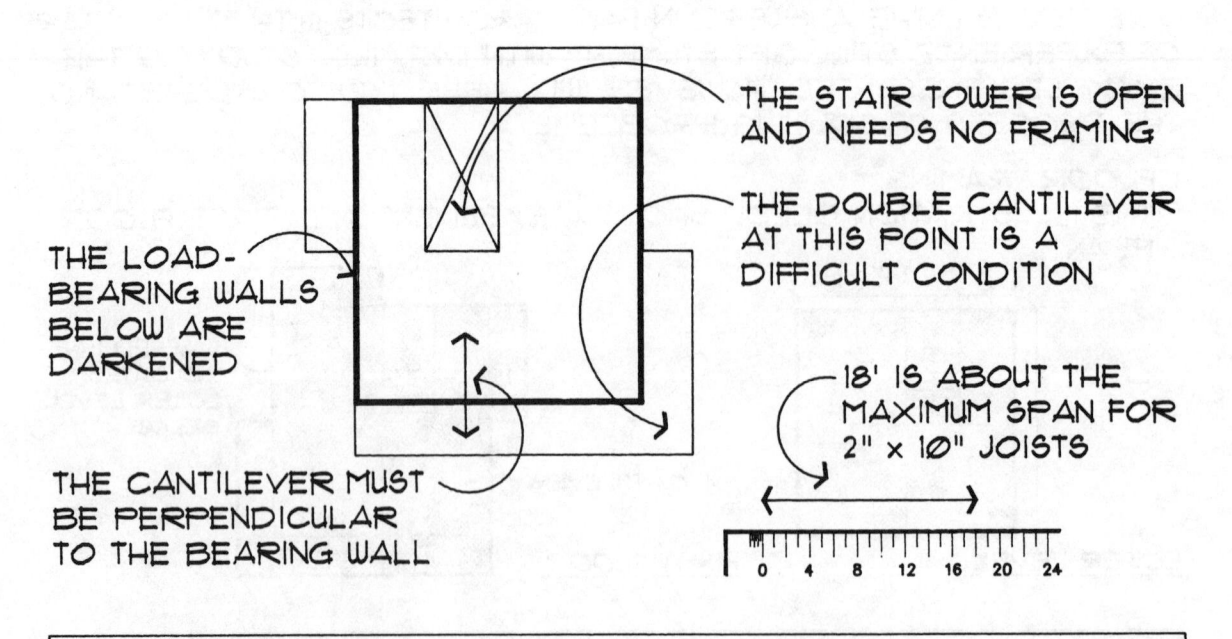

THE LOAD-BEARING WALLS BELOW ARE DARKENED

THE CANTILEVER MUST BE PERPENDICULAR TO THE BEARING WALL

THE STAIR TOWER IS OPEN AND NEEDS NO FRAMING

THE DOUBLE CANTILEVER AT THIS POINT IS A DIFFICULT CONDITION

18' IS ABOUT THE MAXIMUM SPAN FOR 2" x 10" JOISTS

PROBLEM SOLVING   11-2

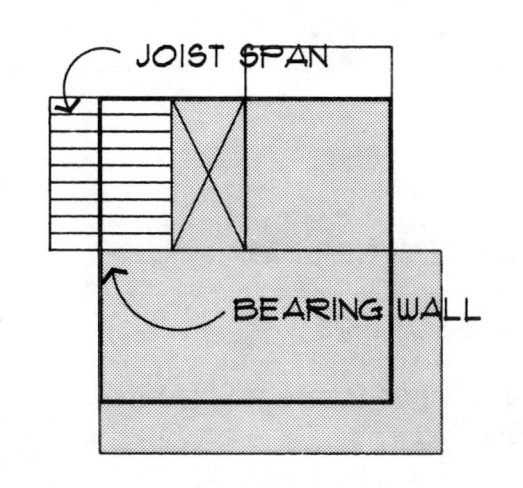

A KEY TO SOLVING FRAMING PROBLEMS IS TO BREAK THE PLAN INTO INDIVIDUAL SPAN OPENINGS (CALLED <u>BAYS</u>). THE JOIST SPAN TO THE LEFT IS SOLVED BY PLACING JOISTS AT 16" O.C. (ON CENTER) PERPENDICULAR TO THE BEARING WALL.

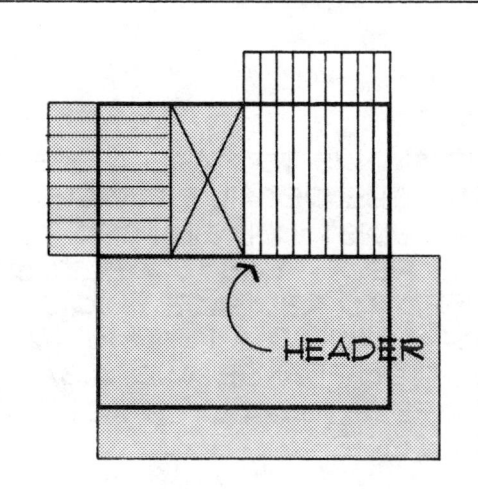

THE SECOND BAY IS SOLVED BY SPANNING THE JOISTS AT A RIGHT ANGLE TO THE BEARING WALL.

A BEAM (CALLED A <u>HEADER</u>) WOULD HAVE TO BE LOCATED IN THE CENTER OF THE HOUSE TO SUPPORT THE END OF THE JOISTS.

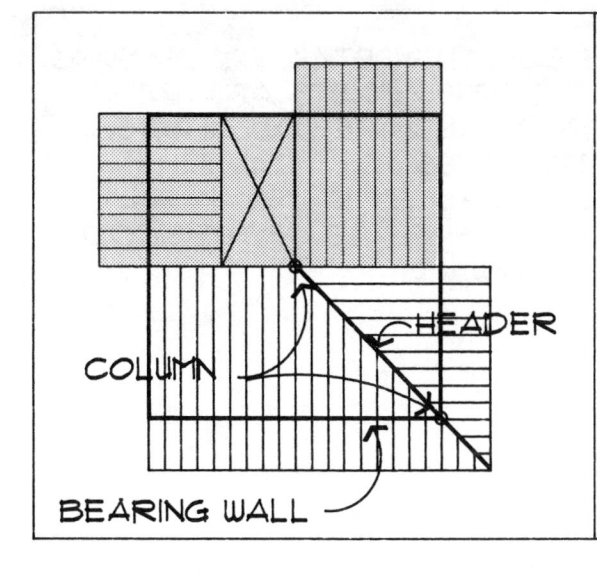

THE FINAL BAY FRAMING PROBLEM IS THE MOST DIFFICULT TO SOLVE. THE DOUBLE CANTILEVER CAN BE FRAMED BY USING A DIAGONAL HEADER. THE BEAM WOULD BE SUPPORTED BY COLUMNS LOCATED IN THE STAIR WALL AND THE LOWER RIGHT CORNER OF THE HOUSE.

PROBLEM SOLVING

2. ROOF OVERHANG

THIS PROBLEM CONCERNS A ROOF OVERHANG ON THE 12/12 PITCH ROOF SHOWN BELOW. THE NOTES ON THE DRAWING INDICATE THE LIMITING FACTORS ON THE DETAIL.

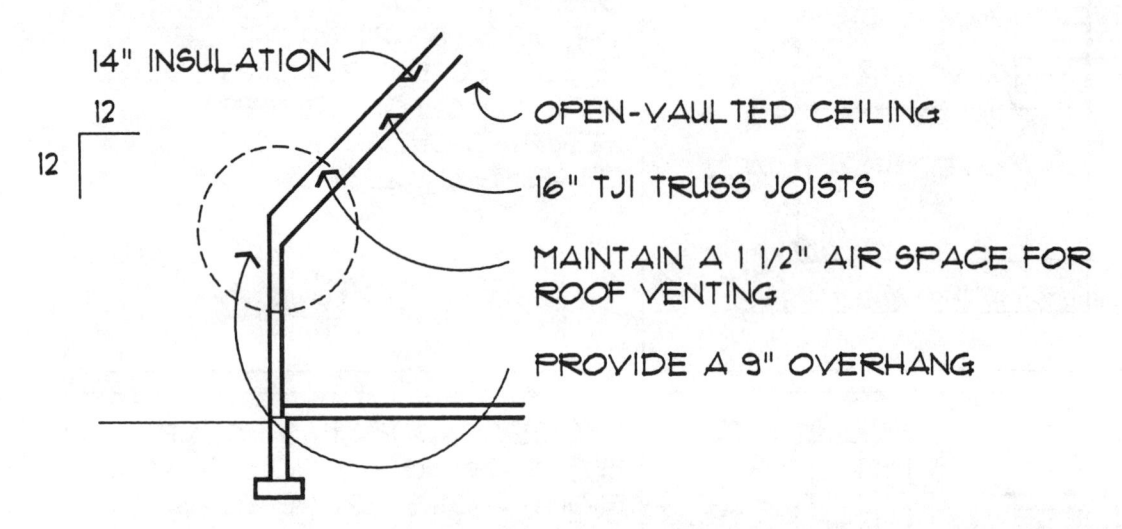

- 14" INSULATION
- OPEN-VAULTED CEILING
- 16" TJI TRUSS JOISTS
- MAINTAIN A 1 1/2" AIR SPACE FOR ROOF VENTING
- PROVIDE A 9" OVERHANG

THE FIRST STEP IN SOLVING THIS CONDITION IS TO MAKE A SKETCH SHOWING THE POINTS THAT ARE KNOWN. THE DETAIL INDICATES THAT A 16" TJI JOIST WILL BE USED TO SUPPORT THE ROOF. THIS IS A PLYWOOD PRODUCT USED TO REPLACE A JOIST OR RAFTER. A TJI HAS A 1 3/4" x 1 1/2" TOP AND BOTTOM FLANGE AND A 3/8" WEB. THEY ARE TYPICALLY SPACED AT 24" O.C. (ON CENTER).

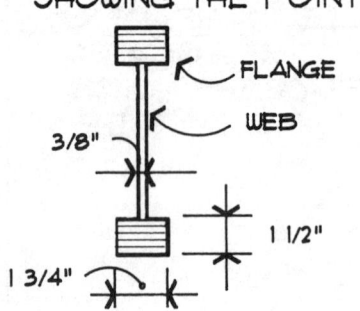

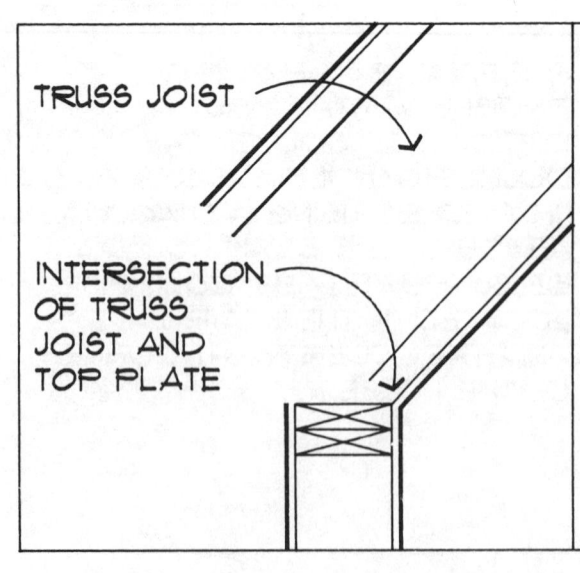

- FLANGE
- WEB
- 3/8"
- 1 1/2"
- 1 3/4"

TRUSS JOIST

INTERSECTION OF TRUSS JOIST AND TOP PLATE

BEGIN THE DETAIL BY DRAWING THE TRUSS JOISTS AT A 12/12 PITCH AND THE WALL STUDS. THE TRUSS JOIST CAN BE LOCATED BY LINING IT UP WITH THE TOP PLATE OF THE WOOD STUD WALL.

PROBLEM SOLVING   11-4

EXTEND TRUSS JOIST

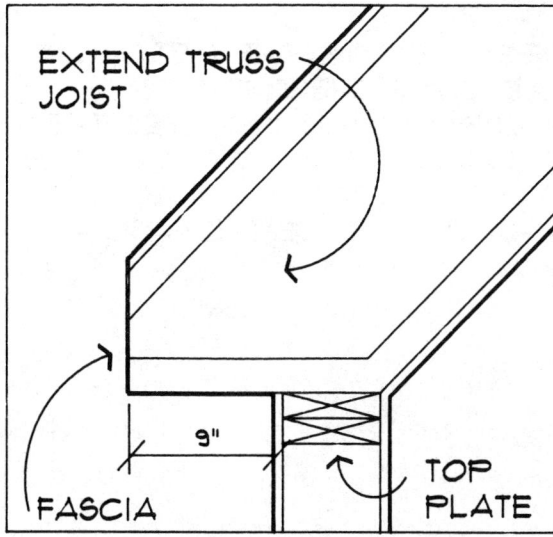

FASCIA — 9" — **TOP PLATE**

THE NEXT STEP IS TO EXTEND THE ROOF FASCIA OUT 9" AND ALLOW IT TO INTERSECT WITH THE ROOF SLOPE. THE BOTTOM OF THE TRUSS JOIST IS CUT SO THAT IT RESTS ON THE TOP PLATE OF THE STUD WALL.

THIS STEP OF THE DETAIL HAS BASICALLY SOLVED THE ROOF EXTENSION PROBLEM.

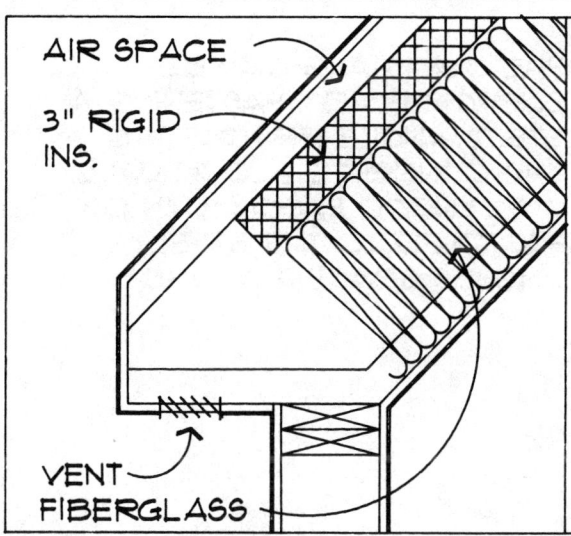

AIR SPACE

3" RIGID INS.

VENT

FIBERGLASS

THE FINAL STEP IN SOLVING THE DETAIL IS TO DETERMINE A WAY TO MAINTAIN AN AIR SPACE BETWEEN THE ROOF SHEATHING AND THE INSULATION. THE SOLUTION IS TO USE 3" OF RIGID INSULATION AT THE TOP EDGE OF THE ROOF DECK. THE FLANGE OF THE TRUSS JOIST WILL MAINTAIN THE AIR SPACE. THE REMAINING SPACE CAN BE FILLED WITH FIBERGLASS.

3. ROOF FASCIA

THIS PROBLEM INVOLVES PLACING A 4'-0" FASCIA ON THE CONCRETE BLOCK AND BAR JOIST WALL ILLUSTRATED BELOW. THE NOTES ON THE SECTION INDICATE THE LIMITING FACTORS.

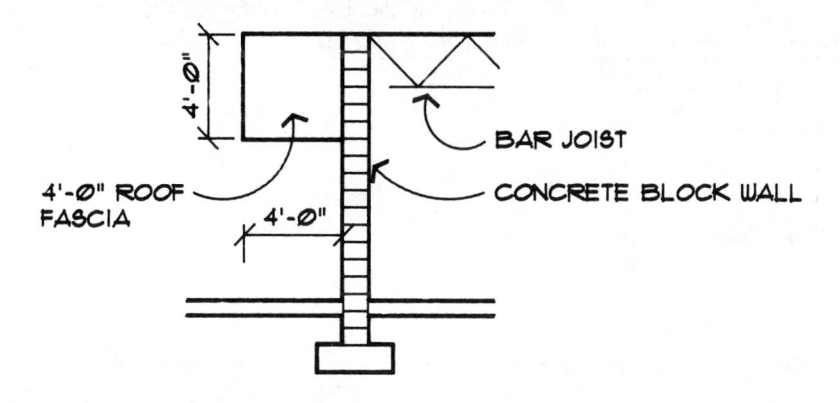

4'-0" ROOF FASCIA — 4'-0" — BAR JOIST — CONCRETE BLOCK WALL

PROBLEM SOLVING — 11-5

FASCIA
ROOF DECK
BLOCK
BAR JOIST
4'-0"

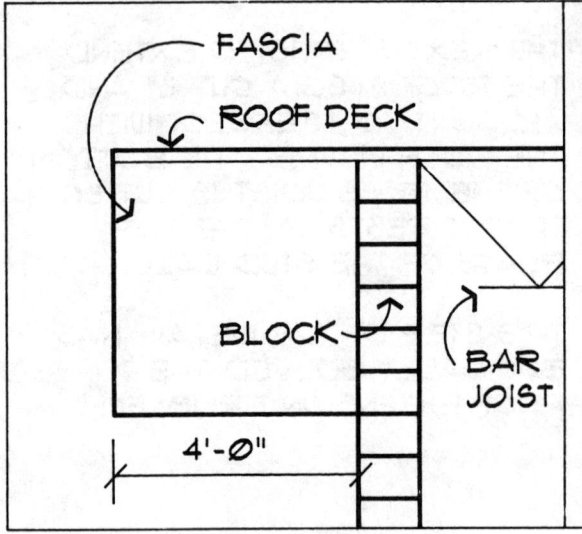

BEGIN SOLVING THE DETAIL BY SKETCHING THE KNOWN ELEMENTS. THIS INCLUDES THE 12" CONCRETE BLOCK WALL, THE BAR JOIST, AND THE 4'-0" x 4'-0" OUTLINE OF THE FASCIA.

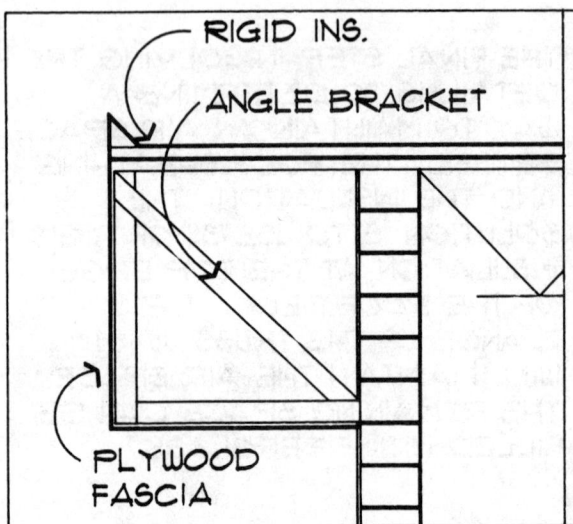

RIGID INS.
ANGLE BRACKET
PLYWOOD FASCIA

THE OVERHANG CAN BE SUPPORTED BY FASTENING A STEEL ANGLE BRACKET TO THE CONCRETE BLOCK WALL. A PLYWOOD FASCIA CAN BE FASTENED TO THE STEEL ANGLES SPACED AT 2'-0" O.C.

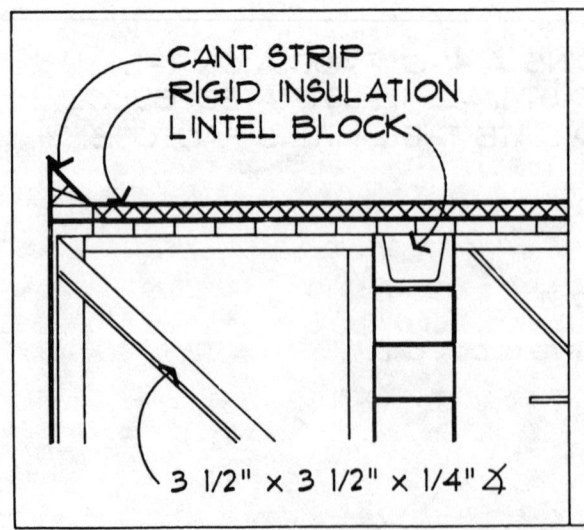

CANT STRIP
RIGID INSULATION
LINTEL BLOCK
3 1/2" x 3 1/2" x 1/4" ∠

A BLOW-UP OF THE DETAIL SHOWS THE ADDITIONAL CONSTRUCTION ITEMS ADDED TO THE FASCIA TO SOLVE THE CONDITION.

PROBLEM SOLVING   11-6

4. STAIR LAYOUT

THIS PROBLEM INVOLVES LAYING OUT A STAIR IN A RESIDENCE. THE DESIGN HAS EVOLVED TO PLACING A STAIR TOWER WITH A ROUND LANDING AT A 30° ANGLE TO THE MAIN AXIS OF THE HOUSE. A SECOND-FLOOR BATH IS QUITE TIGHT, AND IT IS DESIRABLE TO USE ANY AVAILABLE SPACE IN THE STAIR TOWER FOR PLUMBING FIXTURES.

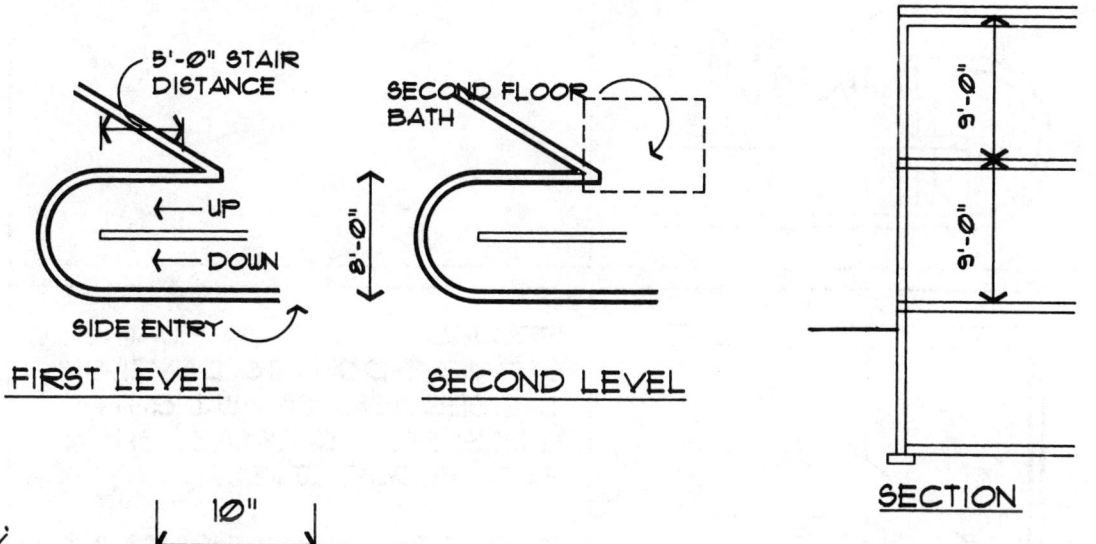

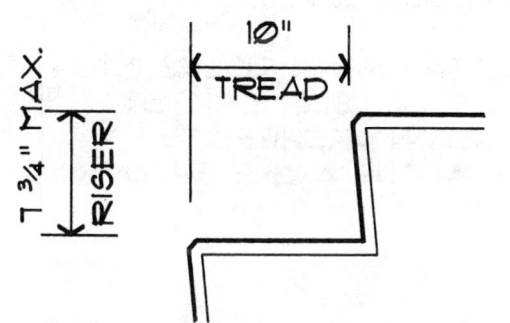

FIRST LEVEL

SECOND LEVEL

SECTION

THE SKETCH ABOVE SHOWS A STAIR LENGTH OF 5'-0" AND A FLOOR-TO-FLOOR HEIGHT OF 9'-0". ASSUME THE STAIR DESIGN IS A 10" TREAD WITH A MAXIMUM RISE OF 7 3/4".

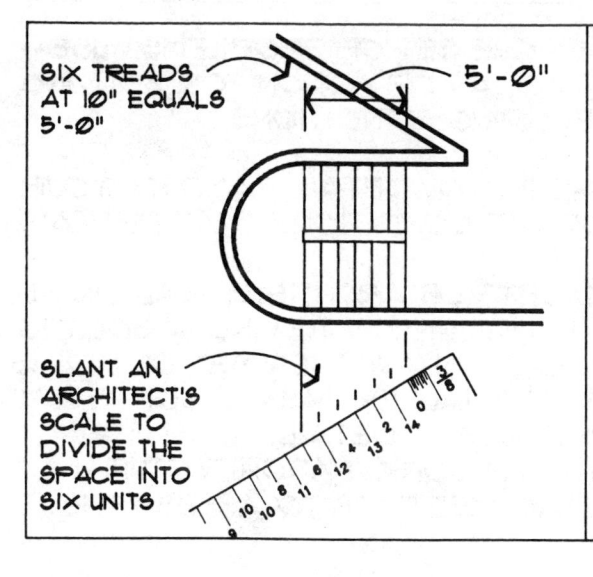

BEGIN THE STAIR LAYOUT BY SKETCHING THE FIRST-FLOOR PLAN. CALCULATE THE NUMBER OF STAIR RISERS BY DIVIDING THE FLOOR-TO-FLOOR HEIGHT (9'-0" OR 108") BY THE 7 3/4" STAIR-RISER HEIGHT. THE ANSWER IS ROUNDED UP TO 14 RISERS. THIS WOULD PROVIDE SEVEN RISERS AND SIX TREADS FROM THE FLOOR TO THE LANDING. SIX 10" TREADS WOULD EQUAL 5'-0" FOR THE STAIR LENGTH.

PROBLEM SOLVING 11-7

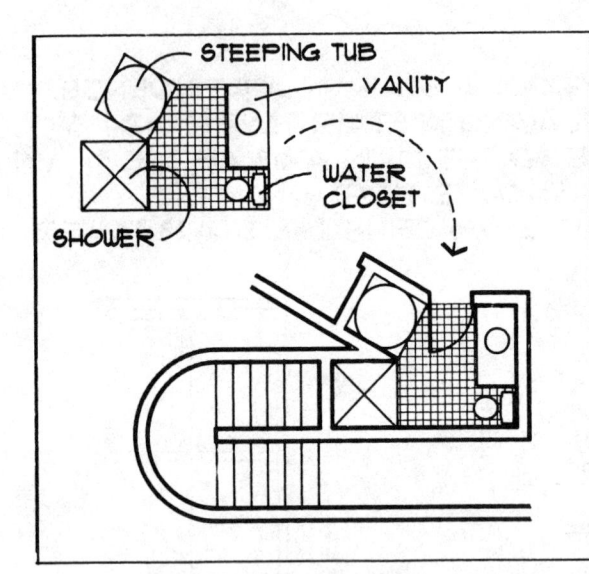

BEGIN THE SECOND-FLOOR STAIR AND BATH CONDITION BY LAYING OUT THE PLUMBING FIXTURES. USE THE FIRST-FLOOR STAIR PLAN AS AN OVERLAY.

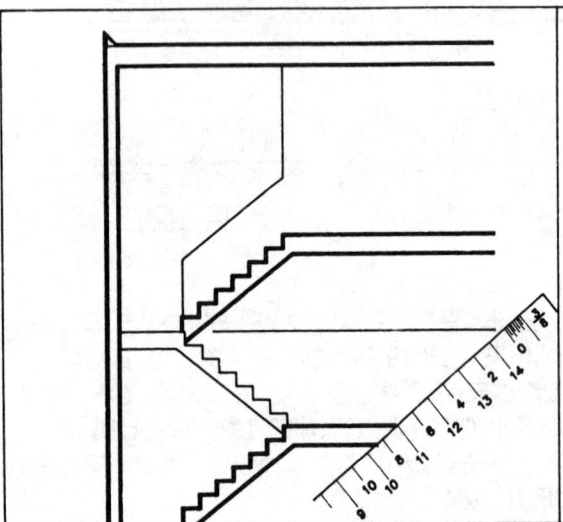

PROJECT THE STAIR-PLAN VIEW STRAIGHT DOWN TO DEVELOP THE SECTION. DRAW LIGHT GUIDELINES TO ESTABLISH EACH FLOOR LEVEL.

DIVIDE THE STAIR RISERS INTO SEVEN EQUAL SEGMENTS BY PLACING AN ARCHITECT'S SCALE AT THE ANGLE SHOWN.

EVERY PROJECT WILL PRESENT A UNIQUE SET OF PROBLEMS. USE THE FOLLOWING TIPS TO DEVELOP A PLAN OF ACTION FOR SOLVING THE PROBLEMS INVOLVED IN DEVELOPING CONDITIONS.

1. USE SKETCH PAPER TO DRAW THE INITIAL DETAIL LAYOUT. YOUR SKETCH SHOULD CONTAIN ALL OF THE CONDITIONS THAT PERTAIN TO THE DRAWING.
2. USE REFERENCE MATERIALS AND SETS OF ARCHITECTURAL DRAWINGS TO SOLVE DETAIL CONDITIONS. IT IS COMMON TO FIND A SOLUTION TO A PROBLEM YOU ARE WORKING ON IN ANOTHER SET OF PLANS.
3. BREAK A DETAIL INTO A SERIES OF SMALLER TASKS. SOLVE EACH PART AND COMBINE THEM TO PRODUCE A DETAIL.
4. SEEK ASSISTANCE IN REVIEWING YOUR WORK. ARCHITECTURAL OFFICES CONDUCT FREQUENT DETAIL MEETINGS TO ASSESS THE QUALITY OF A DETAIL SOLUTION.

PROBLEM SOLVING

SCHEDULING

SCHEDULING CAN BE DEFINED AS ORGANIZING A JOB INTO A TIME FRAME. ANOTHER TERM REFERRING TO THE SAME TASK IS TIME MANAGEMENT. JUST ABOUT EVERY PROJECT THAT YOU WILL WORK ON WILL REQUIRE A SCHEDULE. THE CREATION OF A WORKABLE TIME SCHEDULE IS A SKILL THAT MUST BE LEARNED. THE FOLLOWING TIPS SHOULD HELP:

1. YOU SHOULD KNOW THREE THINGS AT THE BEGINNING OF A PROJECT IN ORDER TO ORGANIZE A SCHEDULE: (1) THE BEGINNING DATE OF THE JOB, (2) THE DATE FOR FINAL COMPLETION, AND (3) THE SCOPE OF THE WORK. THE MOST DIFFICULT TASK IN BEGINNING THE SCHEDULING PROCESS IS DETERMINING THE AMOUNT OF WORK TO BE DONE.

LET'S USE THE 12/12 PITCH ROOF HOUSE (SHOWN IN CHAPTER 22) AS AN EXAMPLE. THE SHEET LAYOUT BELOW INDICATES THE FIVE DRAWINGS INCLUDED IN THE ARCHITECTURAL PACKAGE.

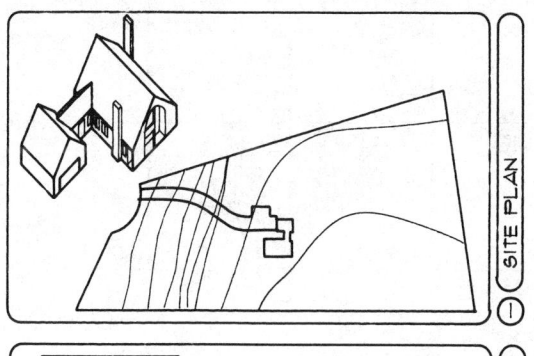

SHEET 1 — SITE PLAN
SHEET 2 — FIRST-FLOOR PLAN
SHEET 3 — SECOND-FLOOR PLAN
SHEET 4 — ELEVATIONS
SHEET 5 — BUILDING SECTIONS

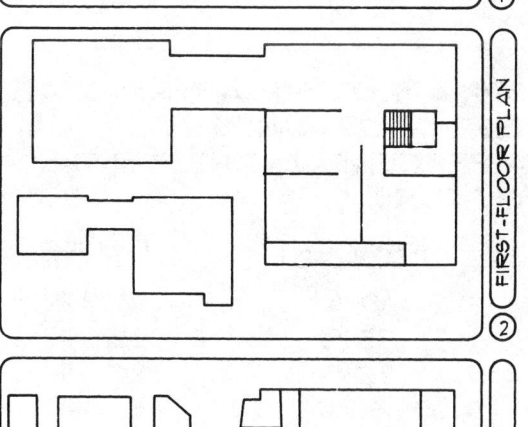

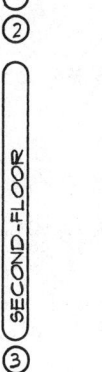

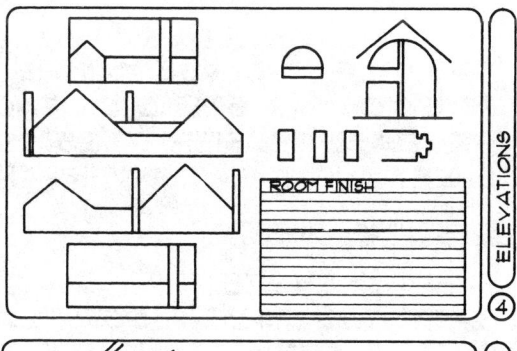

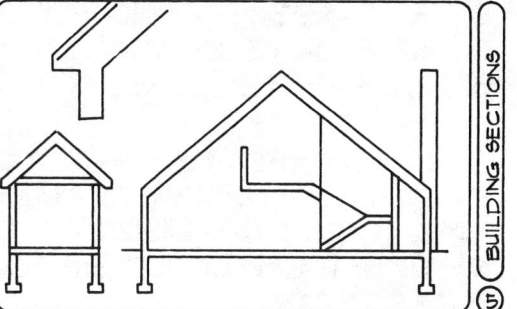

PROBLEM SOLVING

2. THE NEXT STEP IS TO DETERMINE THE AMOUNT OF TIME THAT YOU CAN SPEND ON THE ASSEMBLY OF THE PROJECT. WRITE DOWN CLASS TIME (MINUS LECTURES AND LUNCH) AND WORK TIME AT HOME ON EVENINGS AND WEEKENDS.

USING THE HOUSE AS AN EXAMPLE, ASSUME THAT YOU HAVE THREE WEEKS TO WORK ON THE PROJECT WITH A TOTAL TIME OF 100 HOURS. THE CALENDAR BELOW SHOWS A ROUGH SCHEDULE OF THE HOURS IN EACH DAY THAT CAN BE SPENT WORKING ON THE ASSIGNMENT.

	SUN	MON	TUE	WED	THU	FRI	SAT
OCTOBER	START PROJECT → 8	5 HR 9	6 HR 10	5.5 HR 11	6 HR 12	5 HR 13	4 HR 14
	3 HR 15	6 HR 16	5 HR 17	5 HR 18	5.5 HR 19	5 HR 20	5 HR 21
	5 HR 22	7 HR 23	6 HR 24	5 HR 25	6 HR 26	5 HR ← PROJECT DUE 27	28

3. THIS STEP INVOLVES MAKING AN ESTIMATE OF THE APPROXIMATE TIME YOU WILL SPEND ON EACH SHEET OF DRAWINGS. IT IS PROBABLY EASIER TO ESTIMATE A PERCENT AMOUNT FOR THE SHEET AND THEN CONVERT THAT TO HOURS.

DRAWING SHEET	PERCENT	HOURS
SHEET ONE (SITE)	10 %	10 HR
SHEET TWO (FIRST-FLOOR PLAN)	35 %	35 HR
SHEET THREE (SECOND-FLOOR PLAN)	20 %	20 HR
SHEET FOUR (ELEVATIONS)	15 %	15 HR
SHEET FIVE (SECTIONS)	20 %	20 HR

THIS STEP REQUIRES THAT YOU CAREFULLY ANALYZE THE DRAWING PACKAGE IN ORDER TO MAKE A REASONABLE ESTIMATE OF THE TIME. THE PLANS WILL TYPICALLY TAKE THE GREATEST AMOUNT OF TIME; THESE WOULD BE FOLLOWED BY SECTIONS, ELEVATIONS, AND SITE DRAWINGS.

PROBLEM SOLVING

4. THE FINAL STEP IN CREATING A SCHEDULE IS TO ASSIGN SPECIFIC TASKS TO EACH DAY ON THE CALENDAR. THE GOAL IS TO START EACH DAY OF THE PROJECT WITH A LIST OF WHAT NEEDS TO BE ACCOMPLISHED THAT DAY.

RATHER THAN TREAT A SHEET OF DRAWINGS AS A SINGLE JOB, BREAK IT INTO A SERIES OF SMALLER PROJECTS. FOR EXAMPLE, THE FLOOR-PLAN SHEET WOULD REQUIRE THE FOLLOWING TASKS:

- SHEET LAYOUT
- WINDOW AND DOOR SIZES
- STAIR ROUGH-IN
- BATH LAYOUT
- FIREPLACE LAYOUT
- KITCHEN LAYOUT
- MATERIAL HATCHING
- WALL ROUGH-IN
- WINDOW AND DOOR LAYOUT
- HARD-LINE WALLS
- DIMENSION LAYOUT
- DIMENSION STRINGS
- FRAMING PLAN ROUGH-IN
- HARD-LINE FRAMING PLAN

BASED ON THIS BREAKDOWN, SEVERAL DAYS OF THE CALENDAR ARE ILLUSTRATED BELOW, EACH CONTAINING A GUIDE FOR DETERMINING WHAT DAILY ACTIVITIES CAN BE COMPLETED ON THE PROJECT.

HOURS EACH DAY

SHEET LAYOUT (45 min) WALL ROUGH-IN (4 hr) WINDOW SIZES (1 hr 15 min)	DOOR ROUGH-IN (1 hr) STAIR ROUGH-IN (1 hr 30 min) BATH LAYOUT (1 hr) FIREPLACE/KITCHEN (2 hr)	HARD-LINE WALLS (4 hr) DIM STRING LAYOUT (1 hr) DIMENSION STRINGS (1 hr)
6	5.5	6
10 — (A2)	11 — (A2)	12 — (A2)

DATE *SHEET NUMBER*

THE ASSEMBLY OF A DAILY SCHEDULE ISN'T EASY, BUT IT IS IMPORTANT. YOU SHOULD CONSULT YOUR SCHEDULE EACH DAY TO DETERMINE YOUR PROGRESS ON A PROJECT. LOOK AT THE SCHEDULE AS A FLEXIBLE DOCUMENT THAT CAN BE CHANGED IF THE WORK ISN'T CORRESPONDING WITH THE HOURS YOU HAVE SCHEDULED. IT IS A GOOD POLICY TO SCHEDULE HIGH-PRIORITY TASKS NEAR THE END OF THE PROJECT. FOR EXAMPLE, THE TASK OF DIMENSIONING A FLOOR PLAN IS MORE CRITICAL THAN OUTLINING AN ELEVATION WITH INK, SO IT SHOULD BE GIVEN A HIGHER PRIORITY ON THE SCHEDULE. LOOK AT POSSIBLE WAYS OF EXPANDING THE TIME YOU CAN SPEND ON A PROJECT, SUCH AS TAKING FEWER BREAKS OR GETTING TO CLASS EARLIER.

PROBLEM SOLVING

REPLAY
1. THE DRAWING BELOW SHOWS THE INTERSECTION OF A SLOPED ROOF AND A FLAT ROOF. SKETCH YOUR SOLUTION TO THE DETAIL IN THE GRIDS AT THE BOTTOM OF THIS PAGE.

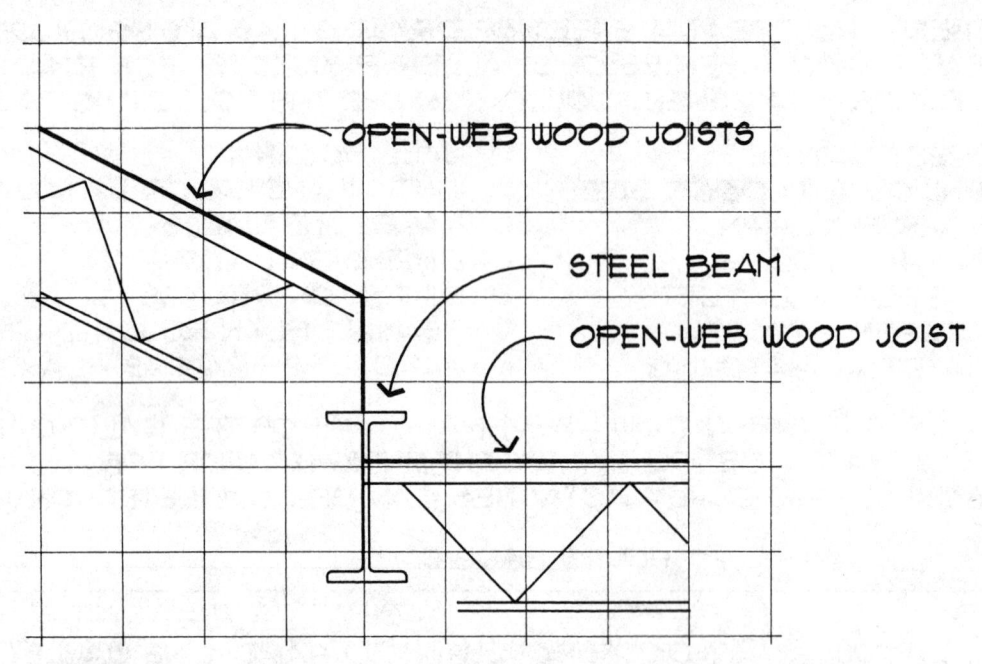

YOUR SKETCH SHOULD INCLUDE THE FOLLOWING CONDITIONS: PUT 2" WOOD DECKING ON THE FLAT AND SLOPED ROOF; DESIGN A SUPPORT DETAIL FOR BOTH SETS OF JOISTS; DESIGN ROOFING AND FLASHING FOR THE INTERSECTION.

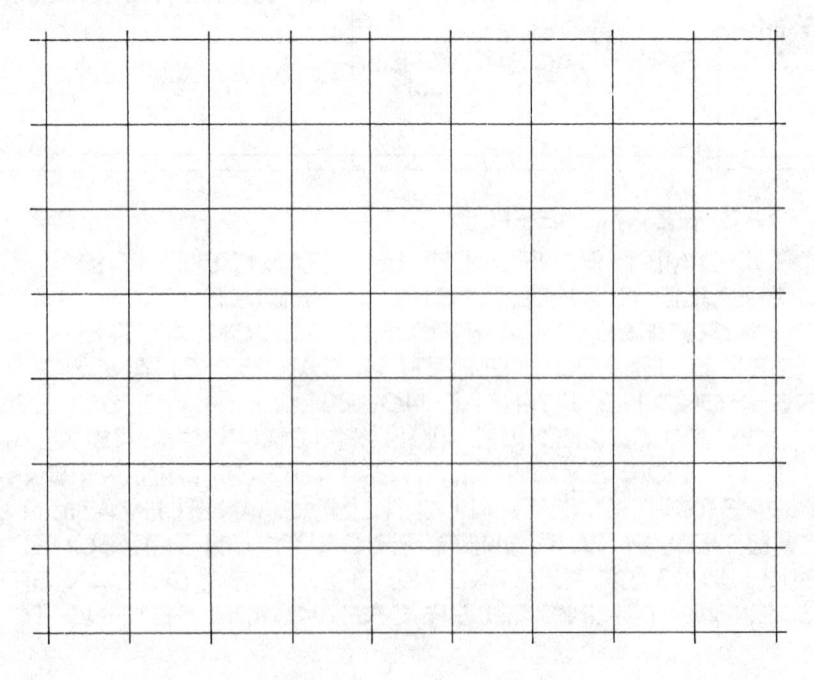

PROBLEM SOLVING   11-12

2. THE FLOOR PLAN BELOW SHOWS A PORTION OF A MASTER BEDROOM. SKETCH A PLAN FOR THE BATHROOM/SAUNA THAT INCLUDES THE ITEMS IN THE DASHED BOX BELOW (SKETCH THE ITEMS AT THE SAME SCALE).

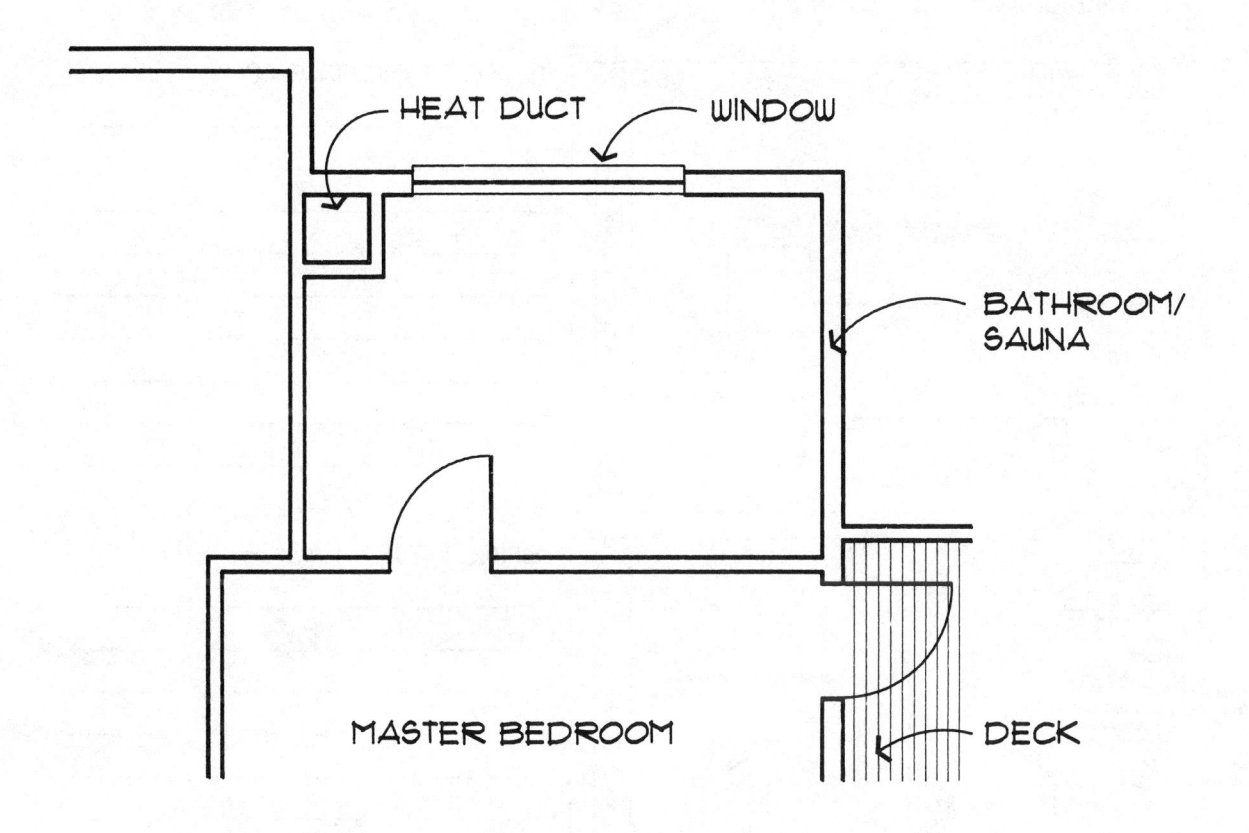

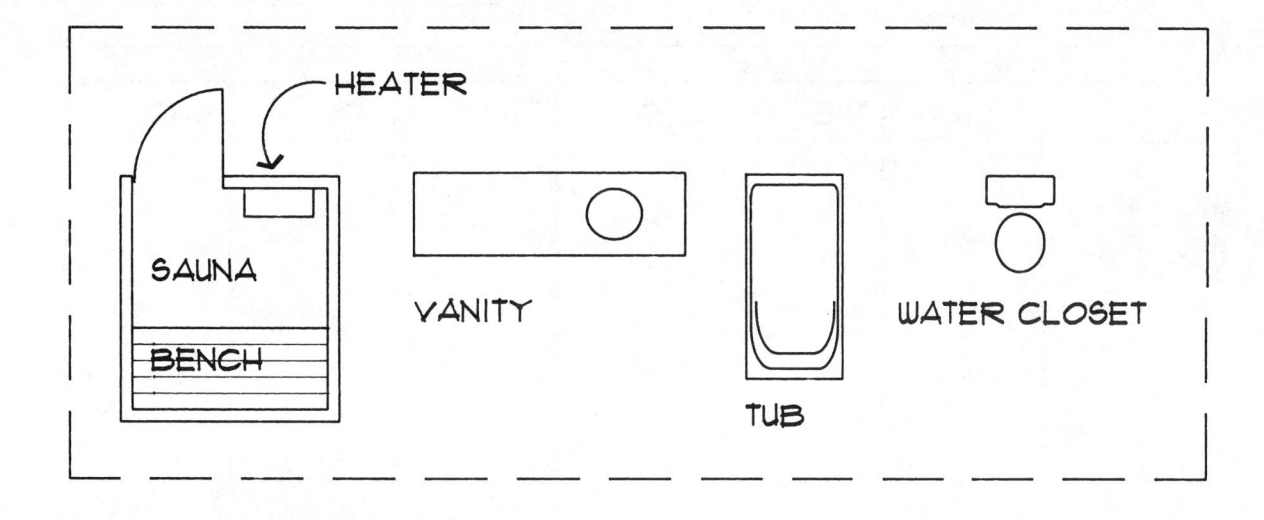

PROBLEM SOLVING

11-13

3. THIS PROJECT CONSISTS OF TWO SHEETS OF WORKING DRAWINGS FOR A TWO-STORY CABIN. PREPARE A TASK ANALYSIS OF THE STEPS NECESSARY TO DRAW THE PROJECT AND TO SCHEDULE THE TIME IT WILL TAKE TO ASSEMBLE THE PROJECT. THE PROJECT MUST BE FINISHED WITHIN TEN DAYS AND SHOULD TAKE A MAXIMUM OF 46 HOURS.

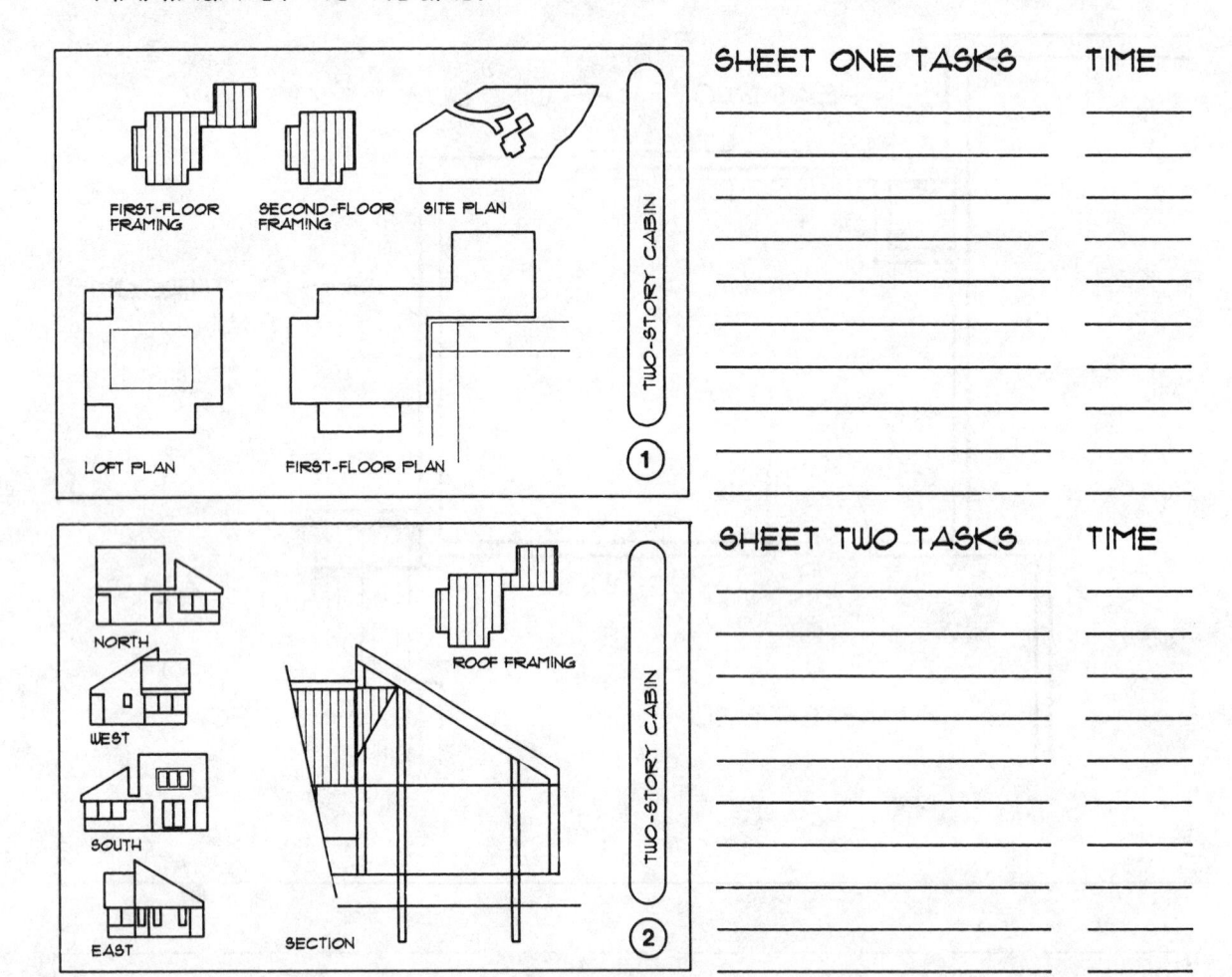

SHEET ONE TASKS	TIME

SHEET TWO TASKS	TIME

SUN	MON	TUE	WED	THU	FRI	SAT

PROBLEM SOLVING   11-14

12 BUILDING MATERIALS

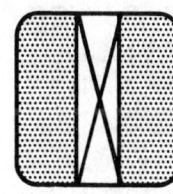

WOOD

WOOD IS THE MOST IMPORTANT MATERIAL USED IN RESIDENTIAL CONSTRUCTION. SOME REASONS ARE THE FOLLOWING:

1. THE MATERIAL IS REASONABLY PRICED AND IS FOUND IN MOST PARTS OF THE COUNTRY.
2. WOOD IS RELATIVELY STRONG.
3. WOOD IS EASILY FASTENED TOGETHER (WITH NAILS OR GLUE).
4. A LARGE SEGMENT OF THE CONSTRUCTION LABOR FORCE IS TRAINED TO BUILD WITH WOOD.

WOOD CAN BE SEPARATED INTO TWO CATEGORIES: SOFT WOOD AND HARD WOOD. SOFT WOOD, CALLED <u>CONIFEROUS</u>, IS FROM CONE AND NEEDLE-BEARING TREES. SOME OF THE MORE POPULAR SPECIES IN THIS GROUP ARE

SOUTHERN PINE	CEDAR	HEMLOCK
FIR	REDWOOD	LARCH
DOUGLAS FIR	WHITE PINE	SPRUCE

OVER 90% OF THE LUMBER USED IN CONSTRUCTION IS SOFT WOOD. WOODS SUCH AS PINE AND FIR ARE USED FOR STUDS AND JOISTS, WHILE CEDAR AND REDWOOD HAVE UNIQUE PRESERVATIVE PROPERTIES THAT ALLOW THEM TO BE USED OUTSIDE FOR DECKS AND SIDING. HARD WOOD TREES, CALLED <u>DECIDUOUS</u>, ARE BROAD LEAF SPECIES SUCH AS OAK, BIRCH, AND MAPLE. NEARLY ALL HARD WOOD IS USED FOR FINISH WORK THAT WILL BE EXPOSED (EXAMPLES WOULD BE OAK KITCHEN CABINETS AND MAPLE

FLOORING). REMEMBER THAT THE TERMS <u>HARD WOOD</u> AND <u>SOFT WOOD</u> REFER TO HAVING LEAVES OR HAVING CONES, RESPECTIVELY. SOME SOFT WOOD SPECIES ARE ACTUALLY STRONGER THAN SOME HARD WOODS.

<u>MILLING</u>
SEVERAL THINGS MUST BE DONE TO WOOD BEFORE IT APPEARS AS DIMENSION LUMBER. TREES ARE SELECTED BECAUSE OF THEIR SIZE, SPECIES, AND THE EFFECT THAT CUTTING WILL HAVE ON THE FOREST. A LARGE PORTION OF TREES USED FOR CONSTRUCTION ARE FROM REPLANTED FORESTS (MUCH LIKE FARMS). ONCE A LOG HAS BEEN CUT AND SENT TO A SAWMILL, THE FIRST STEP IN PROCESSING IS TO REMOVE THE BARK. THIS IS DONE WITH A ROTARY CUTTER SIMILAR TO A PENCIL SHARPENER, OR WITH HIGH-PRESSURE WATER. THE LOG IS THEN MOVED INTO A SERIES OF SAWS THAT CUT THE WOOD INTO ROUGH BOARD SIZES. THE ORIGINAL LOCATION OF THE CUT BOARD IN THE LOG HAS A GREAT DEAL TO DO WITH THE WAY THE BOARD WILL WARP OR TWIST. THE ILLUSTRATION ABOVE SHOWS SEVERAL EXAGGERATED EXAMPLES.

TANGENTIAL SHRINKAGE IS NEARLY TWICE AS GREAT AS RADIAL

<u>GRADING</u>
THE NEXT STEP IS TO GRADE THE WOOD BY ITS STRENGTH AND APPEARANCE. THIS IS DONE BY HUMAN INSPECTORS AND BY MACHINE. THE GRADING PROCESS WILL SEPARATE A SPECIES LIKE DOUGLAS FIR INTO MORE THAN 20 CATEGORIES. GRADES, SUCH AS <u>INDUSTRIAL</u>, <u>SELECT STRUCTURAL</u>, AND <u>CONSTRUCTION</u>, INDICATE THE STRENGTH AND GENERAL USE OF THE WOOD. THE STRONGEST GRADE OF DOUGLAS (<u>DENSE SELECT STRUCTURAL</u>) IS NEARLY TWICE AS STRONG AS THE LEAST STRONG (<u>CONSTRUCTION DECKING</u>). THE UNIT OF MEASURE FOR THE STRENGTH OF WOOD IS A <u>BENDING FIBER</u>. IT IS MEASURED IN POUNDS PER SQUARE INCH (PSI). THE BENDING FIBER FOR DENSE SELECT STRUCTURAL IS 2,300 PSI, WHILE CONSTRUCTION DECKING HAS A STRENGTH OF 1,200 PSI. A COMMON STRENGTH REQUIREMENT FOR JOISTS, STUDS, AND RAFTERS IS 1,500 PSI. LOCAL BUILDING CODES WILL SPECIFY A MINIMUM STRENGTH FOR WOOD USED IN FRAMING. A BETTER GRADE OF WOOD WILL COST MORE, SO IT WOULD BE A WASTE OF MONEY TO USE A HIGHER GRADE THAN NECESSARY.

BUILDING MATERIALS

SEASONING

THE NEXT STEP IN MILLING WOOD IS CALLED <u>SEASONING</u>. A MICROSCOPIC SECTION OF WOOD SHOWS HOLLOW CELLS MADE FROM VEGETABLE FIBERS (CALLED <u>CELLULOSE</u>) BONDED TOGETHER WITH A NATURAL GLUE (CALLED <u>LIGNIN</u>). THE HOLLOW CELLS CAN HOLD AS MUCH AS 200% MOISTURE COMPARED TO THE WEIGHT OF THE WOOD FIBER JUST AFTER CUTTING. A <u>MOISTURE CONTENT</u> (MC) ABOVE 30% FILLS THE HOLLOW TUBES AROUND THE CELLS, WHILE AN MC BELOW 30% IS ABSORBED IN THE CELL FIBER. IT IS THE CELL FIBER MOISTURE (30% MC TO 0% MC) THAT IS CRITICAL TO WOOD FRAMING. A 2" x 10" JOIST WILL SHRINK 3/4" IN THE 10" DIMENSION WHEN THE MC IS LOWERED FROM 30% TO 0%. WOOD WILL NATURALLY LOWER TO AN MC OF AROUND 15% TO 20% ONCE IT HAS BEEN INCORPORATED INTO A COVERED HOUSE. ALLOWING A CONTRACTOR TO USE "GREEN" WOOD WITH AN MC OF OVER 19% CAN CAUSE SERIOUS PROBLEMS WHEN THE FRAMING DRIES AND SHRINKS. SEASONING IS ACCOMPLISHED BY LOWERING THE MOISTURE CONTENT TO AN ACCEPTABLE LEVEL. WOOD WITH A GRADE STAMP OF "S-DRY" MUST HAVE AN MC BELOW 19%, WHILE WOOD MARKED "MC-15" MUST BE BELOW 15%. WOOD WITHOUT ONE OF THESE STAMPS COULD HAVE A MOISTURE CONTENT ABOVE 19%. IT IS COMMON FOR MILLS TO PAINT OR WAX COAT THE BUTT ENDS OF MOISTURE-DRIED WOOD TO PREVENT THE MATERIAL FROM ABSORBING WATER IN A LUMBER YARD OR ON THE JOB BEFORE THE PROJECT IS ENCLOSED. THE COMMON WAY TO CONTROL THE MOISTURE CONTENT IS TO PUT THE WOOD INTO A LOW-TEMPERATURE KILN (THIS WOULD BE STAMPED "KD" FOR KILN DRIED). A LESS SCIENTIFIC WAY IS TO LOOSELY STACK AND COVER THE CUT WOOD UNTIL IT DRIES SUFFICIENTLY. THIS IS CALLED <u>AIR</u> OR <u>RICK</u> <u>DRYING</u>. A SIMPLE BATTERY-OPERATED ELECTRIC PROBE CAN BE INSERTED IN THE WOOD TO PROVIDE AN INSTANT READING OF ITS MOISTURE CONTENT.

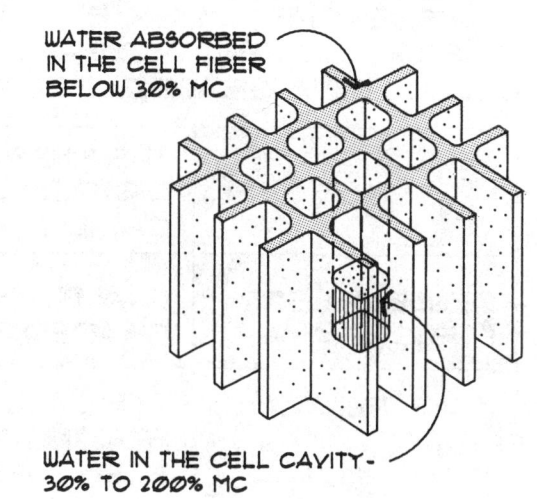

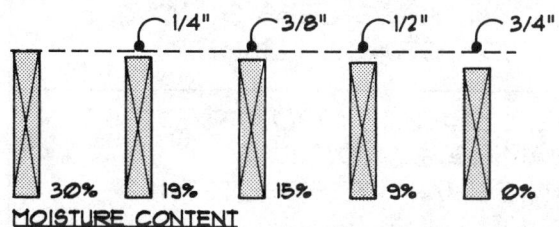

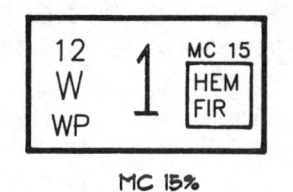

BUILDING MATERIALS 12-3

FINISHED LUMBER

THE FINAL STEP IN MILLING WOOD IS CALLED <u>PLANING</u>. THIS SHAPING PROCEDURE GIVES THE SEASONED MATERIAL A FINISHED SURFACE AND SIZE. THE LUMBER IS THEN STAMPED WITH A GRADE AND MOISTURE CONTENT AND SHIPPED TO LUMBER YARDS. THE CHART BELOW SHOWS GRADING USED FOR CONSTRUCTION LUMBER.

SELECT	THE FINEST APPEARANCE GRADE; A AND B GRADES CAN BE NATURALLY FINISHED WHILE C AND D GRADES ARE SUITABLE FOR PAINT
DENSE SELECT STRUCTURAL	QUALITY FRAMING LUMBER, TYPICALLY GRADED FROM 1 (THE BEST) TO 3
CONSTRUCTION	TYPICALLY USED FOR CONSTRUCTION FRAMING; THE WOOD CONTAINS MORE BLEMISHES THAN SELECT
STANDARD	A LESSER GRADE LUMBER USED IN FRAMING; IT TYPICALLLY CAN BE 1/3 LESS STRONG THAN CONSTRUCTION GRADE LUMBER
UTILITY	GENERALLY THE LOWEST WOOD GRADE, IT IS USED IN NONFRAMING CONDITIONS. IT TYPICALLY CAN BE 1/2 THE STRENGTH OF STANDARD GRADE LUMBER.

THE ACTUAL SIZE OF CONSTRUCTION LUMBER IS TYPICALLY 1/2" LESS THAN THE STATED SIZE. FOR EXAMPLE, A 2" x 6" IS ACTUALLY 1 1/2" x 5 1/2". LUMBER IS COMMONLY SOLD IN 2-FOOT LENGTHS FROM 6' TO 24'. THE ILLUSTRATION BELOW DEFINES THE PROPER TERMS THAT SHOULD BE USED WHEN REFERRING TO WOOD PRODUCTS. A 1" x 4" WOULD BE CALLED A <u>BOARD</u> AND A 6" x 10" WOULD BE CALLED <u>TIMBER</u>.

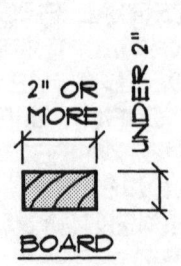

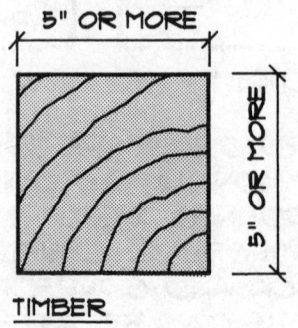

LUMBER TERMS

BOARD: 2" OR MORE, UNDER 2"
DIMENSION LUMBER: 2" OR MORE, 2" TO 5"
TIMBER: 5" OR MORE, 5" OR MORE

BUILDING MATERIALS

THE ILLUSTRATION BELOW SHOWS THE APPROXIMATE SPAN LIMITS FOR "CONSTRUCTION" GRADE LUMBER. IT IS COMMON FOR LOCAL BUILDING CODES TO LIMIT JOIST SPANS BY IMPOSING LOADS OF 40 POUNDS TO 60 POUNDS PER SQUARE FOOT. FOR EXAMPLE, THE ILLUSTRATION INDICATES THAT A 2" x 10" SPACED AT 16" O.C. WILL SPAN 16'-9" WITH A UNIFORM FLOOR LOAD OF 40 POUNDS PER SQUARE FOOT.

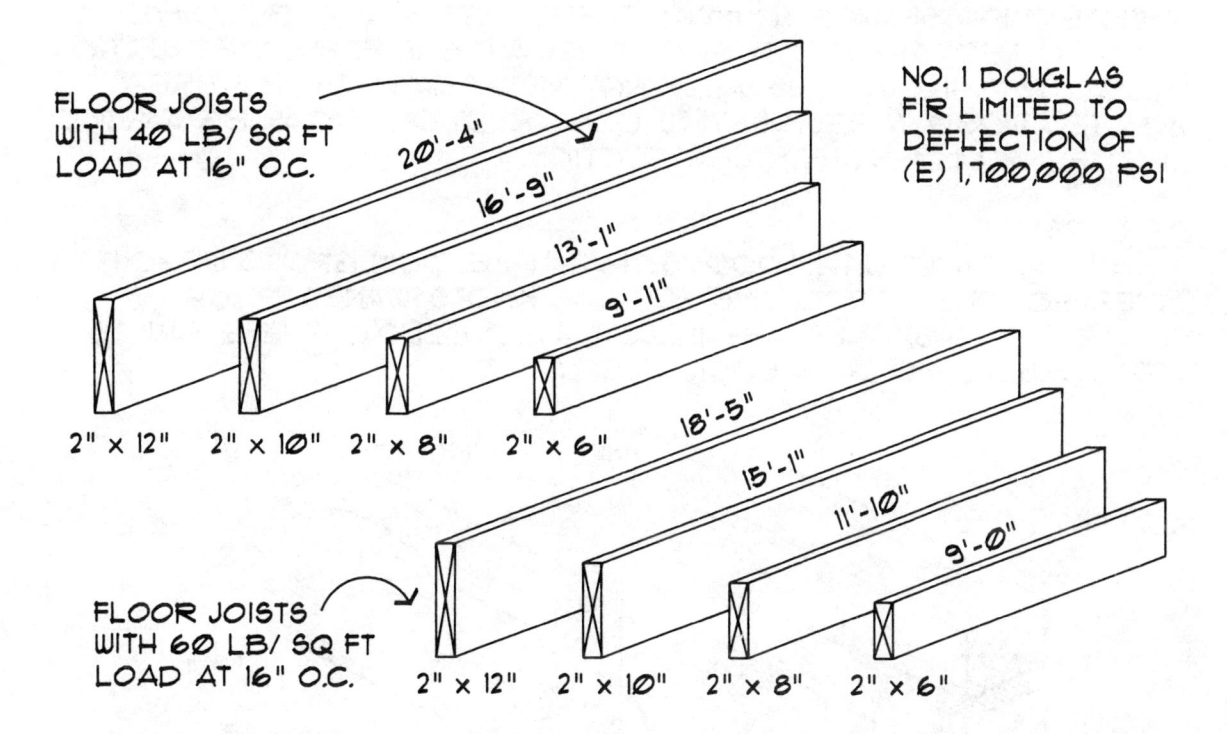

FLOOR JOISTS WITH 40 LB/ SQ FT LOAD AT 16" O.C.

NO. 1 DOUGLAS FIR LIMITED TO DEFLECTION OF (E) 1,700,000 PSI

20'-4"   2" x 12"
16'-9"   2" x 10"
13'-1"   2" x 8"
9'-11"   2" x 6"

FLOOR JOISTS WITH 60 LB/ SQ FT LOAD AT 16" O.C.

18'-5"   2" x 12"
15'-1"   2" x 10"
11'-10"   2" x 8"
9'-0"   2" x 6"

LIMITATIONS

WOOD IS NOT WITHOUT ITS FAULTS. ONE OF THE CHIEF CONCERNS IS DRY ROT. THIS IS A CONDITION IN WHICH THE LIGNIN BREAKS DOWN AND CAUSES THE FIBERS TO DISINTEGRATE. THREE THINGS MUST BE PRESENT FOR WOOD TO DRY ROT: (1) THE TEMPERATURE MUST BE ABOVE FREEZING; (2) THE WOOD MUST BE IN THE PRESENCE OF MOISTURE; AND (3) THE WOOD MUST BE IN THE PRESENCE OF AIR. IF ONE OF THESE CONDITIONS IS ALLEVIATED, WOOD WILL NOT ROT.

THERE ARE SEVERAL PRESERVATIVE METHODS THAT CAN BE USED TO PROTECT WOOD. THE MOST COMMON IS TO PAINT OR STAIN THE SURFACE. A SECOND COMMON TREATMENT IS TO PRESSURE-TREAT WOOD WITH A SALT-BASED PRESERVATIVE (SUCH AS CHROMATED ZINC CHLORIDE). WOOD IS PRESSURE-TREATED BY PLACING IT IN A VACUUM AND IMMERSING IT IN A VAT OF PRESERVATIVE. WOOD CAN ALSO BE PRESERVED BY PRESSURE-TREATING IT WITH A PETROLEUM-BASED PRODUCT (SUCH AS CREOSOTE).

BUILDING MATERIALS

PRESERVATIVES ACT AS A POISON TO ELIMINATE THE ORGANISMS THAT ATTACK THE CELLS OF WOOD. CEDAR AND REDWOOD CONTAIN A NATURAL PRODUCT THAT PROVIDES THE SAME PROTECTION. THIS IS THE REASON THESE TWO SPECIES CAN BE USED OUTDOORS WITHOUT SPECIAL TREATMENT.

WOOD CAN BE PRESSURE-TREATED WITH A CHEMICAL SUCH AS AMMONIUM PHOSPHATE TO MAKE IT FIRE-RESISTANT. BUILDING CODES DIRECT THE COMBUSTION PRECAUTIONS FOR CONSTRUCTION PRODUCTS; WHILE IT IS USUALLY NOT NECESSARY TO USE FIRE-TREATED WOOD IN RESIDENTIAL CONSTRUCTION, IT CAN BE A GOOD CHOICE IN COMMERCIAL CONSTRUCTION.

DEFECTS
A NATURAL FAULT WITH WOOD IS THAT IT SELDOM GROWS WITHOUT IMPERFECTIONS. PROBLEMS, SUCH AS KNOTS, WANES, PITCH POCKETS, AND SHAKES ARE ILLUSTRATED BELOW. THESE FAULTS ARE CONSIDERED WHEN WOOD IS GRADED.

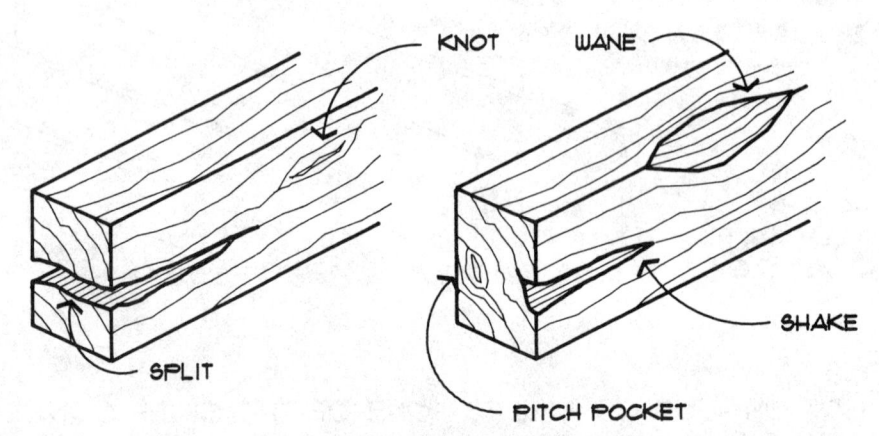

PRODUCTS
THE SELECTIVE PROCESS USED IN CUTTING WOOD IN A MILL MANAGES TO CUT AROUND MOST OF THE IMPERFECTIONS. THE WOOD INDUSTRY HAS DEVELOPED MANUFACTURING TECHNIQUES THAT MAKE A NUMBER OF IMPROVEMENTS OVER THE NATURAL MATERIAL. WOOD PRODUCTS ARE TYPICALLY REPROCESSED (1) TO MAKE A MATERIAL THAT IS STRONGER THAN FOUND IN NATURE, OR (2) TO MAKE A PRODUCT THAT IS OF GREATER SIZE THAN IS NATURALLY FOUND. PLYWOOD IS A GOOD EXAMPLE OF ENHANCED STRENGTH. WOOD IS CONSIDERABLY MORE RESISTANT TO BREAKING PERPENDICULAR TO ITS GRAIN. A KARATE EXPERT DEMONSTRATES THIS WHEN BREAKING BOARDS — A BOARD IS ALWAYS BROKEN PARALLEL TO ITS GRAIN (THE WEAKER DIRECTION). IN PLYWOOD THE GRAIN DIRECTION IS ALTERNATED BY 90° IN EACH LAYERING (CALLED A VENEER), PRODUCING A PRODUCT THAT HAS UNIFORM STRENGTH.

BUILDING MATERIALS　　　　　　　　　　12-6

PLYWOOD

PLYWOOD IS PRODUCED BY SLOWLY ROTATING A LOG INTO A LARGE KNIFE BLADE. A CONTINOUS THIN SHEET OF WOOD IS UNWRAPPED FROM THE LOG. THE SHEET IS CUT TO SIZE, DRIED, AND GLUE-LAMINATED INTO VENEER PLYWOOD. PLYWOOD IS FABRICATED INTO SHEETS RANGING IN THICKNESS FROM 1/4" TO 1 1/8". THE MOST COMMON THICKNESSES USED IN CONSTRUCTION ARE: 1/2", 5/8", AND 3/4". THE EXPOSED FACES OF PLYWOOD ARE GRADED A THROUGH D. AN A GRADE SURFACE MUST BE SMOOTH AND PAINT GRADE, WHILE D FACED SHEETS ALLOW UP TO 2 1/2" OPEN KNOTS. PLYWOOD IS ALSO MARKED INTERIOR OR EXTERIOR, INDICATING THE TYPE OF GLUE USED TO LAMINATE THE SHEETS TOGETHER. EXPOSED PLYWOOD, SUCH AS SHEATHING, SHOULD BE EXTERIOR GRADE TO PREVENT IT FROM DELAMINATING DURING CONSTRUCTION. THE GRADE STAMP ABOVE SHOWS THE QUALITY AND USE FOR A SHEET OF PLYWOOD. THE NUMBERS 32/16 INDICATE THAT THE SHEET WILL SPAN 32" IF IT IS USED FOR ROOF SHEATHING AND 16" IF IT IS USED FOR FLOOR UNDERLAYMENT. A COMMON GRADE OF PLYWOOD USED FOR WALL SHEATHING IS 1/2" CDX. THE MATERIAL IS 1/2" THICK, ONE FACE OF THE SHEET IS C GRADE AND THE OTHER IS D GRADE; THE X INDICATES EXTERIOR GRADE GLUE. THE MOST TYPICAL SHEET SIZES FOR PLYWOOD ARE 4' x 8' AND 4' x 12'. THE 4'-0" WIDTH ALLOWS THE MATERIAL TO SPAN THREE EQUAL 16" JOIST OR STUD SPACES. PLYWOOD HAS A VARIETY OF USES, RANGING FROM ROOF AND WALL SHEATHING, TO SIDING AND CABINETS. IT CAN ALSO BE USED TO CONSTRUCT FORMS FOR POURED CONCRETE.

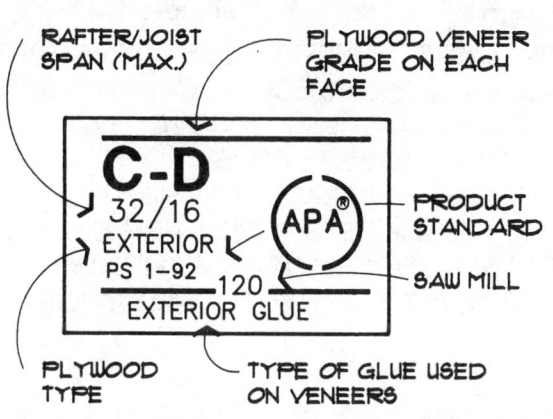

PARTICLE BOARD

PARTICLE BOARD IS AVAILABLE IN MANY OF THE SAME SHEET SIZES AND THICKNESSES AS PLYWOOD. THIS PRODUCT IS MADE BY MIXING SAWDUST WITH GLUE (RESIN) AND PRESSING IT INTO SHEET SIZES. PARTICLE BOARD SHOULD NOT BE SUBSTITUTED FOR PLYWOOD TO SPAN STRUCTURAL JOISTS, RAFTERS, AND STUDS. IT IS FREQUENTLY USED AS AN UNDERLAYMENT MATERIAL ON FLOORS (UNDER CARPET) AND AS A BASE MATERIAL FOR CABINETS. THE GLUE USED TO MAKE THIS PRODUCT CAN BREAK DOWN IF MATERIALS ARE GLUED TO ITS SURFACE. FOR THAT REASON, KITCHEN AND BATHROOM TILE AND VINYL FLOORS SHOULD HAVE PLYWOOD RATHER THAN PARTICLE BOARD AS AN UNDERLAYMENT. PARTICLE BOARD, HOWEVER, DOES MAKE AN EXCELLENT DENSE SUBFLOOR

BUILDING MATERIALS

MATERIAL IN OTHER ROOMS.

FLAKE BOARD

FLAKE BOARD (OR OSB FOR ORIENTED STRAND BOARD) IS A RELATIVELY NEW MATERIAL USED IN BUILDING. THIS PRODUCT RESEMBLES PARTICLE BOARD IN THAT IT IS PRODUCED BY GLUING CHIPS OF WOOD TOGETHER INTO A SHEET. IT IS DIFFERENT FROM PARTICLE BOARD, HOWEVER, BECAUSE IT IS PRODUCED FROM LARGE WOOD CHIPS (SOME ARE 1 1/2"). OSB HAS STRUCTURAL PROPERTIES SIMILAR TO THOSE OF PLYWOOD AND CAN BE USED AS A PLYWOOD SUBSTITUTE IN FLOOR, ROOF, AND WALL SHEATHING. IT IS TYPICALLY PRICED SLIGHTLY LOWER THAN PLYWOOD. OSB BOARD IS FABRICATED BY MAKING A VENEER SHEET OF WOOD CHIPS THAT ALIGN IN ONE DIRECTION. THREE OR FIVE SHEETS ARE THEN GLUED TOGETHER TO FORM THE PRODUCT. AS IN PLYWOOD, EACH LAYER IS PLACED AT A RIGHT ANGLE TO THE NEXT LAYER TO PRODUCE UNIFORM STRENGTH.

INSULATED SHEATHING

INSULATION BOARD IS MANUFACTURED BY PRESSING WOOD PULP INTO SHEETS. THIS MATERIAL IS USED ALMOST EXCLUSIVELY AS EXTERIOR WALL SHEATHING. WHILE THE MATERIAL HAS VERY LITTLE STRENGTH, IT IS LESS EXPENSIVE THAN PLYWOOD OR OSB. IT CAN BE IDENTIFIED BY ITS DARK BROWN OR BLACK COLOR AND CAN BE QUITE EASILY BROKEN IF BENT. THE LOW STRENGTH FOUND IN INSULATION BOARD REQUIRES THAT DIAGONAL TIES OR PLYWOOD CORNER BRACING MUST BE USED IN WALL SHEATHING.

LAMINATED BEAMS

A LARGE SOLID PIECE OF TIMBER CAN BE QUITE EXPENSIVE AND DIFFICULT TO OBTAIN. LAMINATED WOOD PROVIDES A VERY GOOD ALTERNATIVE. IN MANY CASES, THE WOOD LAMINATED BEAM (CALLED A GLUE LAM) IS OF BETTER QUALITY THAN A SOLID PIECE.

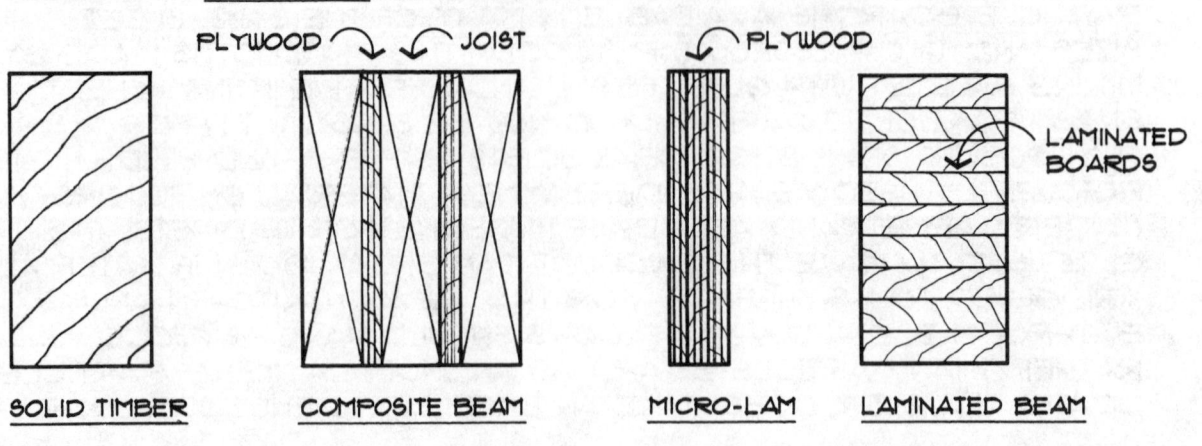

SOLID TIMBER | COMPOSITE BEAM (PLYWOOD, JOIST) | MICRO-LAM (PLYWOOD) | LAMINATED BEAM (LAMINATED BOARDS)

BUILDING MATERIALS 12-8

GLUE LAM BEAMS ARE FABRICATED BY GLUING SMALLER BOARDS (TYPICALLY 1 1/2" THICK) INTO A SINGLE PIECE. BEAMS ARE GRADED PREMIUM (BEST APPEARANCE), ARCHITECTURAL (SOME KNOTS), AND CONSTRUCTION (APPEARANCE IS NOT IMPORTANT). LAMINATED BEAMS ARE MADE FROM WOOD PIECES WITH IMPERFECTIONS CUT AWAY AND WITH A GLUE STRONGER THAN THE NATURAL LIGNIN. THE RESULT IS A PRODUCT THAT IS STRONGER AND MORE WARP-FREE THAN A SOLID TIMBER.

ENGINEERED JOISTS

SEVERAL ENGINEERED PRODUCTS ARE AVAILABLE FOR WOOD FRAMING. TWO OF THE MOST FREQUENTLY USED ARE KNOWN BY THEIR TRADE NAME, "TRUS JOIST." TRUS JOIST FABRICATES A "MICRO-LAM" BEAM THAT IS FREQUENTLY USED TO REPLACE STEEL IN JOIST BEARING CONDITIONS. A MICRO-LAM BEAM RESEMBLES A SOLID PIECE OF 1 3/4" PLYWOOD FOUND IN DEPTHS SIMILAR TO STANDARD WOOD JOISTS. A SECOND TRUS JOIST PRODUCT, CALLED A "TJI JOIST," IS SHOWN IN THE ILLUSTRATION. THE JOIST RESEMBLES A CROSS SECTION OF A STEEL BEAM AND IS MADE OF PLYWOOD. A TJI JOIST IS LIGHTER AND STRONGER THAN A SOLID WOOD JOIST (IT IS ALSO MORE COSTLY). TJI'S ARE AVAILABLE IN DEPTHS SIMILAR TO WOOD JOISTS.

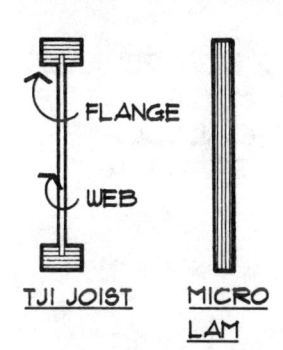

BOARD FEET

BOARDS, DIMENSION LUMBER, AND TIMBER ARE ALL MEASURED IN A UNIT CALLED A BOARD FOOT. ONE BOARD FOOT IS 1" DEEP, 12" WIDE, AND 12" LONG. A 1" x 12" BOARD 12" LONG WOULD BE 1 BOARD FOOT. AN EASY WAY TO CALCULATE BOARD FEET IS TO

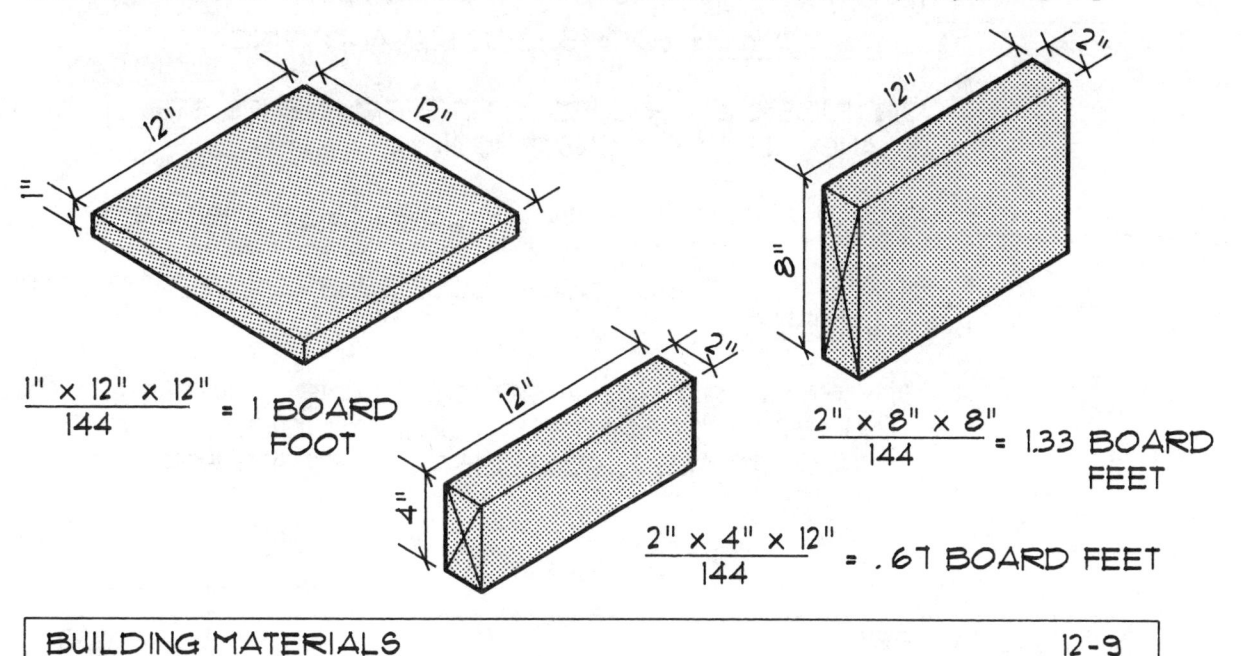

$$\frac{1" \times 12" \times 12"}{144} = 1 \text{ BOARD FOOT}$$

$$\frac{2" \times 4" \times 12"}{144} = .67 \text{ BOARD FEET}$$

$$\frac{2" \times 8" \times 8"}{144} = 1.33 \text{ BOARD FEET}$$

BUILDING MATERIALS　　　　12-9

REMEMBER THAT A BOARD FOOT EQUALS 144 CUBIC INCHES OF WOOD (12" x 12" x 1" = 144 CUBIC INCHES). CALCULATE BOARD FEET BY FIGURING THE VOLUME OF A 12" TRIAL SECTION OF A BOARD AND DIVIDE IT BY 144 CUBIC INCHES. ONCE A ONE-FOOT TRIAL SECTION IS FIGURED, MULTIPLY THE LENGTH OF THE BOARD BY THE BOARD FEET IN THE ONE-FOOT TRIAL SECTION. FOR EXAMPLE, CALCULATE THE NUMBER OF BOARD FEET IN A 2" x 10" PIECE OF DIMENSION LUMBER 12'-0" LONG.

$$\frac{2" \times 10" \times 12"}{144} = 1.6 \text{ BOARD FEET (B.F.)}$$ (12" TRIAL SECTION)

1.6 B.F. x 12' = 19.2 BOARD FEET (THE LENGTH OF THE LUMBER IS 12')

MOST LUMBER YARDS SELL WOOD BY THE THOUSAND BOARD FEET (ABBREVIATED BY THE ROMAN NUMERAL FOR 1,000 – M). IF THE PRICE FOR 12' LONG 2 x 10'S WAS MARKED "$460 M," CALCULATE THE NUMBER OF PIECES THAT COULD BE PURCHASED FOR $460.

$460 = 1,000 BOARD FEET OF LUMBER

$$\frac{1,000 \text{ B.F.}}{19.2 \text{ B.F.}} = 52 \text{ PIECES}$$

(THE BOARD FEET IN ONE 12' LONG 2" x 10")

REPLAY

MARK (T) IF THE STATEMENT IS TRUE. IF THE STATEMENT IS FALSE, MARK (F) AND CHANGE THE UNDERLINED WORD(S) TO A WORD THAT WOULD MAKE THE STATEMENT TRUE.

_____ ( )1. STUDS AND JOISTS ARE COMMONLY MADE FROM DECIDUOUS WOODS LIKE FIR AND PINE.

_____ ( )2. LUMBER IS GRADED TO DETERMINE ITS STRENGTH AND USE FOR CONSTRUCTION.

_____ ( )3. A 2" x 14" THAT IS 16'-0" LONG IS 32.3 BOARD FEET.

_____ ( )4. A 2" x 12" FLOOR JOIST WOULD BE CALLED FRAMING LUMBER.

_____ ( )5. IF PLYWOOD HAS A GRADE STAMP WITH THE NUMBERS "24/16," THE 24 WOULD INDICATE THE MAXIMUM ALLOWABLE SPAN IN INCHES FOR FLOOR JOISTS.

BUILDING MATERIALS

_____ ( )6. D GRADE PLYWOOD IS A SMOOTH, PAINT GRADE
MATERIAL.

7-10. MARK (T) IF THE MATERIAL NOTED IN THIS ILLUSTRATION WOULD
BE A GOOD CHOICE FOR THE CONDITION INDICATED. MARK (F)
AND CHANGE THE NOTE IF THE MATERIAL WOULDN'T BE A GOOD
CHOICE.

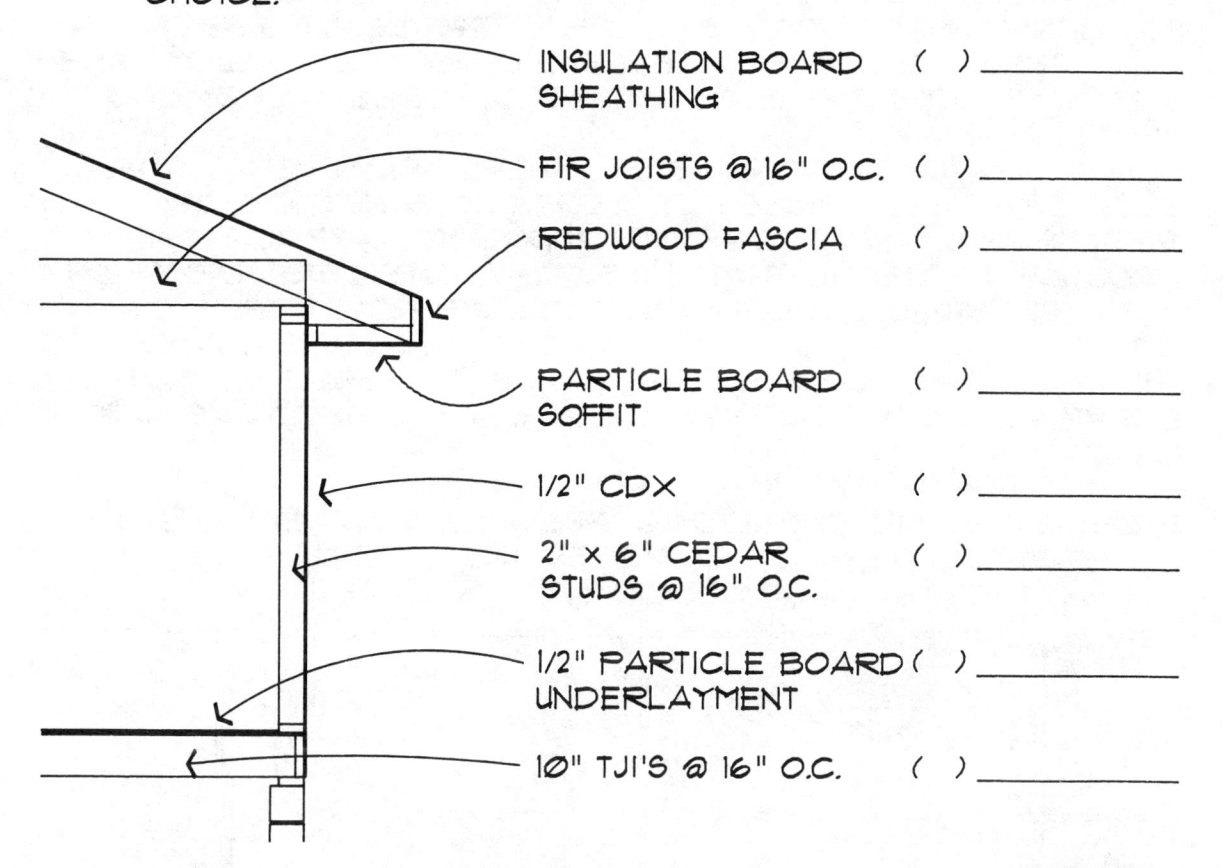

INSULATION BOARD ( ) _____
SHEATHING

FIR JOISTS @ 16" O.C. ( ) _____

REDWOOD FASCIA ( ) _____

PARTICLE BOARD ( ) _____
SOFFIT

1/2" CDX ( ) _____

2" x 6" CEDAR ( ) _____
STUDS @ 16" O.C.

1/2" PARTICLE BOARD ( ) _____
UNDERLAYMENT

10" TJI'S @ 16" O.C. ( ) _____

STEEL

STEEL IS NOT A NATURAL MATERIAL BUT IS MADE FROM IRON
THROUGH A PROCESS OF MELTING AND PURIFICATION. ARCHITECT'S
SPECIFICATIONS FREQUENTLY REFER TO STEEL PRODUCTS AS
"FERROUS METAL"; THIS SIMPLY MEANS THAT IT IS IRON-BASED.
ONCE IRON HAS BEEN MINED, IT IS MELTED ALONG WITH CARBON
(CALLED COKE) TO FREE IT FROM THE OXYGEN IT IS COMBINED WITH
IN NATURE. THE RESULTING PRODUCT, CALLED PIG IRON, IS QUITE
BRITTLE AND MUST BE FURTHER REFINED. STEEL IS MADE BY
INJECTING OXYGEN INTO MOLTEN PIG IRON. THIS CAUSES SOME OF

| BUILDING MATERIALS | 12-11 |

THE CARBON IN THE IRON TO BURN OFF. MOST STRUCTURAL STEEL CONTAINS AROUND 1% CARBON COMPARED TO THE 3% TO 5% FOUND IN IRON. THE RESULTING MATERIAL IS STRONGER AND MORE FLEXIBLE AND CAN BE ROLLED INTO STRUCTURAL SHAPES. THE MOST COMMON STEEL USED IN CONSTRUCTION IS CALLED A-36. THE SECTION ON WOOD INDICATED THAT THE MEASURE FOR STRENGTH OF A MATERIAL IS ITS BENDING FIBER. A COMMON BENDING FIBER FOR CONSTRUCTION WOOD IS 1,500 P.S.I.; THE BENDING FIBER FOR A-36 STEEL IS 36,000 P.S.I. SEVERAL OTHER STEEL ALLOYS ARE USED IN CONSTRUCTION, SOME WITH BENDING FIBERS OF 50,000 P.S.I.

IN ADDITION TO STRUCTURAL STEEL, THERE ARE SEVERAL OTHER BLENDS OF STEEL FREQUENTLY USED IN CONSTRUCTION. STAINLESS STEEL IS AN EXAMPLE: CHROMIUM AND NICKEL ARE ADDED TO PRODUCE A MATERIAL THAT IS STRONG AND RESISTS CORROSION. "COR-TEN" STEEL IS A BLEND THAT HAS APPROXIMATELY 1/2% COPPER ADDED TO MAKE IT "WEATHER." THIS STEEL CAN BE USED ON THE EXTERIOR OF A BUILDING WITHOUT ANY SPECIAL PROTECTION. COR-TEN WILL EVENTUALLY OXIDIZE (RUST) TO A BROWN-BLACK COLOR.

STEEL IS FASTENED BY WELDING OR DRILLING AND BOLTING THE MEMBERS TOGETHER. STEEL ANGLES ARE TYPICALLY USED TO

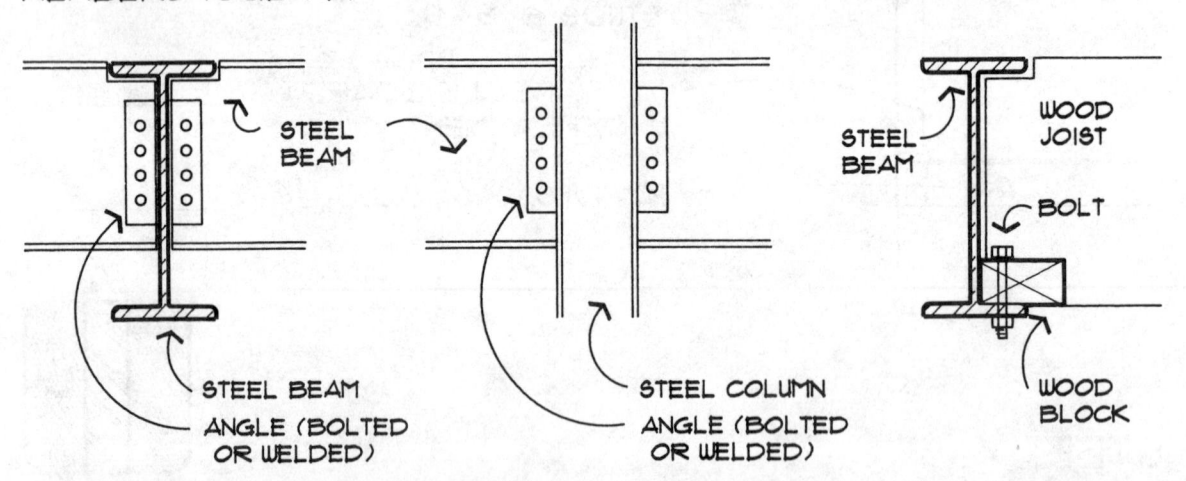

FASTEN BEAMS TO OTHER BEAMS OR COLUMNS. WOOD CAN BE FASTENED TO STEEL BY BOLTING A NAILING BLOCK TO THE FLANGE.

STEEL IS FINISHED BY ROLLING A RED-HOT PIECE (CALLED A BILLET) THROUGH A SERIES OF SHAPING ROLLERS. EACH PASS SLIGHTLY MODIFIES THE SHAPE OF THE PIECE AND GIVES IT ADDED STRENGTH. THE MOST COMMON SHAPES USED IN CONSTRUCTION ARE BEAMS AND COLUMNS. THE TOP AND BOTTOM PARTS OF A STEEL BEAM ARE CALLED THE FLANGE; THE VERTICAL PIECE IS THE WEB.

BUILDING MATERIALS

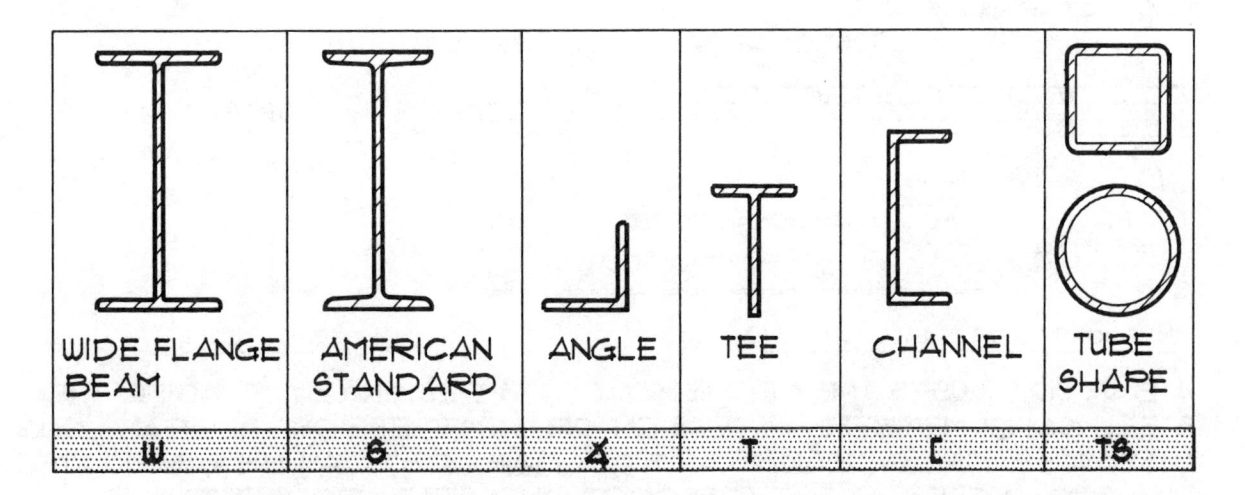

WIDE FLANGE BEAM	AMERICAN STANDARD	ANGLE	TEE	CHANNEL	TUBE SHAPE
W	S	A	T	C	TS

THE FIRST BEAM USED IN CONSTRUCTION WAS AN I BEAM (NOW CALLED AN AMERICAN STANDARD). A MORE EFFICIENT DESIGN IS A WIDE FLANGE SHAPE. A WIDE FLANGE IS TYPICALLY STRONGER THAN AN AMERICAN STANDARD BECAUSE A CROSS SECTION THROUGH THE BEAM CONTAINS MORE STEEL IN ITS FLANGE. STEEL BEAMS ARE CATEGORIZED USING THREE CRITERIA: (1) SHAPE, (2) HEIGHT (IN INCHES), AND (3) WEIGHT (IN POUNDS PER FOOT). FOR EXAMPLE, A W 12 × 45 BEAM WOULD BE A WIDE FLANGE SHAPE THAT IS 12" HIGH AND WEIGHS 45 POUNDS PER FOOT. A C 10 × 30 IS A CHANNEL SHAPE THAT IS 10" HIGH AND WEIGHS 30 POUNDS PER FOOT. STEEL IS PURCHASED BY THE POUND SO A LIGHTER BEAM WILL PRODUCE A MORE EFFICIENT DESIGN.

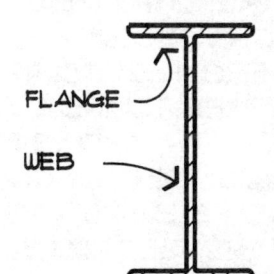

A MAJOR CONCERN WITH USING STEEL FRAMING IN COMMERCIAL CONSTRUCTION IS ITS POOR RESISTANCE TO FIRE. STEEL DOESN'T BURN, BUT IT LOSES ITS STRUCTURAL PROPERTIES WHEN SUBJECTED TO FIRE. STRUCTURAL STEEL FRAMES ARE REQUIRED (BY BUILDING CODES) TO BE PROTECTED WITH MASONRY, GYPSUM, OR SPRAY-ON FIREPROOFING.

SPRAY-ON STEEL BEAM

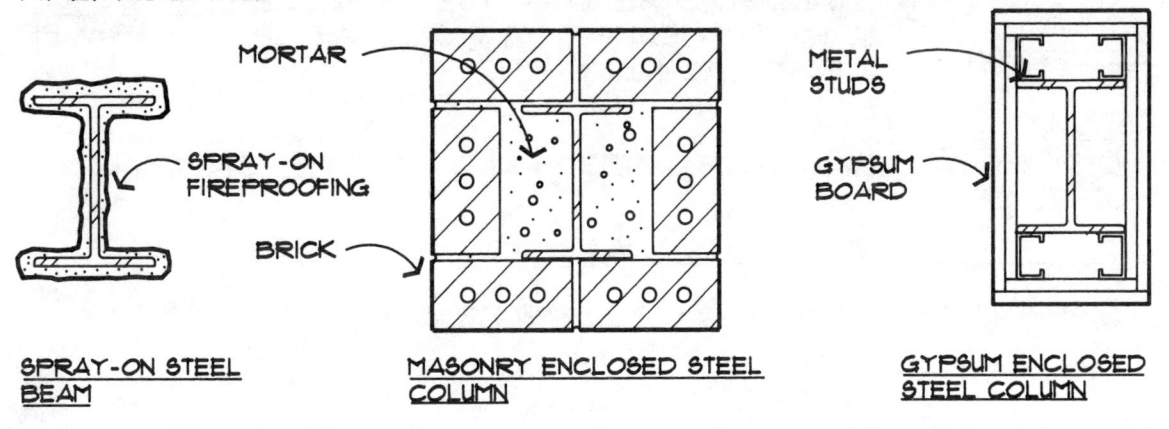

MASONRY ENCLOSED STEEL COLUMN

GYPSUM ENCLOSED STEEL COLUMN

BUILDING MATERIALS 12-13

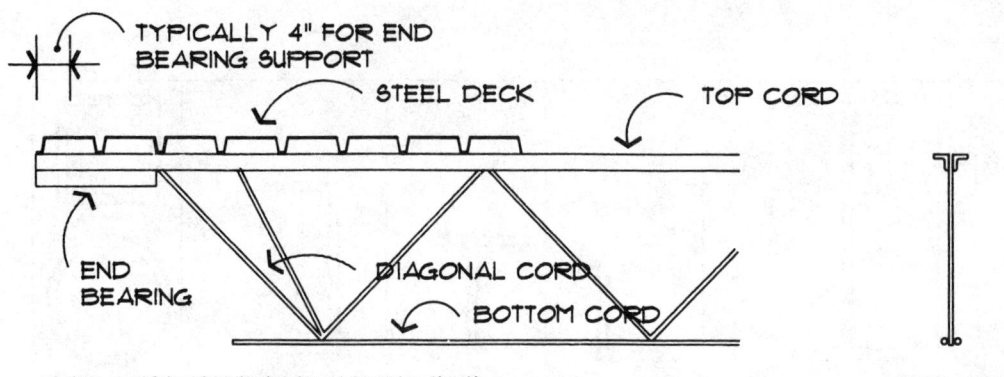

BAR JOIST (SIDE ELEVATION VIEW) — labels: TYPICALLY 4" FOR END BEARING SUPPORT, STEEL DECK, TOP CORD, END BEARING, DIAGONAL CORD, BOTTOM CORD

END VIEW

A BAR JOIST USES THE GEOMETRY OF ITS DESIGN (BY PLACING THE STEEL CORD MEMBERS IN TENSION OR COMPRESSION) TO SPAN LONG DISTANCES. WHILE DESIGNS VARY, A BAR JOIST CAN BE FABRICATED WITH TWO ANGLES AT THE TOP CORD AND STEEL RODS FOR THE DIAGONAL AND BOTTOM CORDS. BAR JOISTS ARE COMMONLY SPACED AT 2'-0" O.C. OR MORE. BAR JOISTS ARE LABELED H, J, AND K SERIES, WHICH SPECIFY THE STRENGTH OF THE STEEL USED IN THE JOIST (H IS LOW, J IS STRUCTURAL, AND K IS HIGH STRENGTH). BAR JOISTS ARE ALSO DESIGNATED L (LONG SPAN), WHICH ARE 18" TO 48" DEEP, AND DL (DEEP LONG SPAN), WHICH ARE FROM 52" TO 72" DEEP. A BAR JOIST IS IDENTIFIED USING THREE FIGURES TO INDICATE: (1) THE JOIST DEPTH (IN INCHES), (2) THE STEEL STRENGTH, AND (3) THE CORD. FOR EXAMPLE, A "28 LH 05" JOIST IS A 28" DEEP, LONG-SPAN JOIST FABRICATED FROM H SERIES STEEL, AND #5 BARS ARE USED FOR ITS DIAGONAL CORDS. BAR JOISTS CAN BE USED TO SPAN DISTANCES IN EXCESS OF 100 FEET.

STEEL RE BAR — labels: BAR SIZE (IN EIGHTHS OF AN INCH) 8; STEEL PSI (IN THOUSANDS) 75

STEEL REINFORCING BARS ARE USED TO ADD TENSION STRENGTH TO CONCRETE. "RE BARS" ARE IDENTIFIED BY A WHOLE NUMBER SIZE WHICH REFERS TO A BAR'S DIAMETER IN EIGHTHS OF AN INCH. FOR EXAMPLE, A NUMBER 7 BAR WOULD BE 7/8" IN DIAMETER. ANOTHER TYPE OF STEEL REINFORCING MATERIAL IS WELDED WIRE MESH. THE MESH IS SET INTO A CONCRETE SLAB TO GIVE IT ADDED STRENGTH. THE MESH LABEL 6" x 6" x 10/10 WWM MEANS THAT #10 GAUGE WIRE IS SPACED APART EACH WAY.

REPLAY

1. IDENTIFY THE MEANING OF NUMBERS AND LETTERS FOR A W 10 x 18 STEEL BEAM.

    W _____ 10 _____ 18 _____

2. GIVE THE DIAMETER OF A NUMBER 5 RE BAR.

    _____

BUILDING MATERIALS

3. IDENTIFY THE MEANING OF THESE LABEL COMPONENTS FOR A BAR JOIST THAT IS A 60 DLK 8.

    60 _____ DLK _____ 8 _____

4. WHAT IS THE USUAL CARBON CONTENT IN STRUCTURAL STEEL?

    _____ %

5. WHAT ARE THE TWO MOST COMMON METHODS USED TO FASTEN STEEL MEMBERS TOGETHER?

    1. _____ 2. _____

6. IF STEEL COST $ 0.30 PER POUND, WHAT WOULD BE THE PRICE OF A W 18 × 30 BEAM THAT IS 24'-0" LONG?

    $ _____

7. LIST THREE COMMON METHODS USED TO FIREPROOF A STEEL COLUMN.

    1. _____ 2. _____ 3. _____

8. IDENTIFY THESE SYMBOLS FOR STEEL SHAPES:

    W _____ S _____ TS _____

    [_____ ∠ _____

9. SKETCH AND LABEL A DETAIL THAT WILL FASTEN 2" × 10" WOOD JOISTS TO BOTH SIDES OF THE STEEL CHANNEL.

    [8 × 11.5

10. WHAT IS THE BENDING FIBER OF A-36 STEEL?

    _____ PSI

BUILDING MATERIALS 12-15

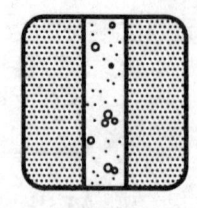

CONCRETE

CONCRETE IS A MANUFACTURED PRODUCT THAT HAS BEEN USED FOR SEVERAL THOUSAND YEARS. THIS MATERIAL IS ACTUALLY A COMBINATION OF FOUR MATERIALS: CEMENT, SAND, AGGREGATE (CRUSHED ROCK OR GRAVEL), AND WATER. CEMENT IS THE SINGLE INGREDIENT THAT IS NOT A NATURAL MATERIAL. IT IS PRODUCED BY BURNING LIMESTONE (AT 2,000° F) AND CRUSHING IT TO A FINE POWDER. CEMENT HAS THE ONE-TIME PROPERTY OF BECOMING ROCK HARD WHEN IT IS MIXED WITH WATER. THIS REACTION IS A CHEMICAL PROCESS (CALLED <u>CURING</u> OR <u>HYDRATION</u>) RATHER THAN SIMPLE DRYING. THE QUALITY OF MANUFACTURED CEMENT IS CERTIFIED BY AN ORGANIZATION CALLED THE PORTLAND CEMENT ASSOCIATION. THERE ARE MANY DIFFERENT COMPANIES THAT PRODUCE "PORTLAND CEMENT," BUT ALL OF THEM MAKE PRODUCTS THAT HAVE SIMILAR CURING AND STRUCTURAL PROPERTIES. REMEMBER TO CALL CONCRETE BY ITS CORRECT NAME; IT IS NO LONGER CEMENT ONCE SAND, AGGREGATE, AND WATER HAVE BEEN ADDED.

<u>DESIGN MIX</u>

WHILE CEMENT IS A KEY INGREDIENT IN CONCRETE, IT IS IMPORTANT TO ASSURE THE QUALITY OF WATER, SAND, AND AGGREGATE IN THE MIX. SPECIFICATIONS TYPICALLY REQUIRE THAT THE WATER USED TO MAKE CONCRETE BE DRINKABLE (<u>POTABLE</u>). THE SAND USED SHOULD BE CLEAN AND FREE OF CLAY AND ORGANIC MATERIALS SUCH AS DIRT. THE FINAL INGREDIENT, THE AGGREGATE, CONSISTS OF EITHER CRUSHED ROCK OR GRAVEL, SIZES OF WHICH MAY VARY FROM 1/4" IN DIAMETER TO 1 1/2".

THE PROPORTIONS USED IN MAKING CONCRETE ARE QUITE CRITICAL TO THE QUALITY OF THE FINISHED PRODUCT.

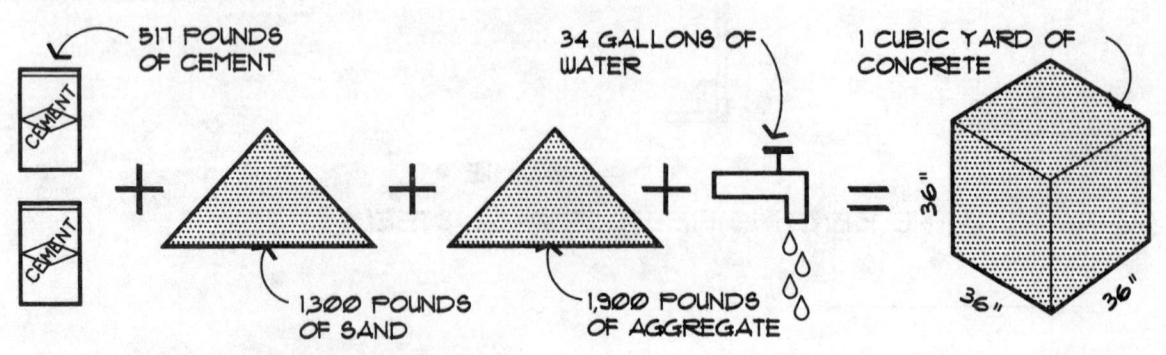

517 POUNDS OF CEMENT + 1,300 POUNDS OF SAND + 1,900 POUNDS OF AGGREGATE + 34 GALLONS OF WATER = 1 CUBIC YARD OF CONCRETE (36" × 36" × 36")

<u>DESIGN MIX FOR A CUBIC YARD OF CONCRETE</u>

| BUILDING MATERIALS | 12-16 |

CONCRETE IS MEASURED IN CUBIC YARDS (THINK OF A CUBIC YARD AS A BOX 36" ON EACH SIDE). A TYPICAL DESIGN MIX FOR A CUBIC YARD OF CONCRETE WOULD BE 5 1/2 BAGS OF CEMENT (A BAG WEIGHS 94 POUNDS), 1,300 POUNDS OF SAND, 1,900 POUNDS OF AGGREGATE, AND 34 GALLONS OF WATER. CONCRETE IS FREQUENTLY ORDERED BY ITS "DESIGN MIX." FOR EXAMPLE, A 1:2:4 MIX WOULD CONSIST OF ONE PART CEMENT, TWO PARTS SAND, AND FOUR PARTS AGGREGATE. A 1:2:4 MIX WOULD BE A GOOD CHOICE FOR A FOOTING, WHILE A 1:2:3 MIX WOULD BE A GOOD CHOICE FOR A SLAB IN WHICH A SMOOTHER FINISH IS DESIRED.

STRENGTH
THE STRENGTH OF CONCRETE IS MEASURED IN THE AMOUNT OF CRUSHING FORCE (OR COMPRESSION) THAT IT WOULD TAKE TO BREAK THE MATERIAL. COMPRESSIVE FORCES RANGE FROM A LOW OF ABOUT 2,500 PSI FOR A RESIDENTIAL SIDEWALK TO A HIGH OF 5,000 PSI TO 7,000 PSI FOR COLUMNS AND BEAMS. STRENGTHS UP TO 12,000 PSI ARE POSSIBLE TO OBTAIN BUT EXPENSIVE. TWO ITEMS GENERALLY DETERMINE THE COMPRESSIVE STRENGTH OF CONCRETE: (1) THE NUMBER OF BAGS OF CEMENT USED PER YARD ON CONCRETE, AND (2) THE WATER/CEMENT RATIO (MEASURED IN GALLONS OF WATER PER SACK OF CEMENT). MOST CONCRETE COMES PREMIXED TO THE SITE IN A READY MIX TRUCK. A READY MIX COMPANY WILL CUSTOM MIX THE MATERIAL TO MEET THE REQUIREMENTS OF THE JOB. IT IS COMMON TO OVERDESIGN THE MIX BY 20% TO COMPENSATE FOR ANY ERRORS. FOR EXAMPLE, 4,000 PSI CONCRETE WOULD BE MIXED TO TEST AT 4,800 PSI.

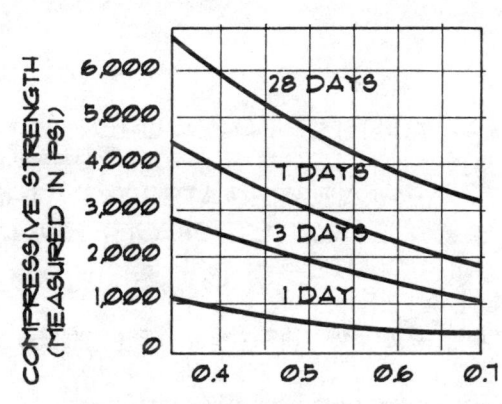

A VERY IMPORTANT FACTOR IN DETERMINING THE STRENGTH OF CONCRETE IS THE WATER/CEMENT RATIO. THE RATIO MEASURES THE GALLONS OF WATER USED DIVIDED BY THE SACKS OF CEMENT. THE CHART AT LEFT INDICATES THAT A SLIGHT INCREASE IN THE RATIO WILL RESULT IN A CONSIDERABLE REDUCTION IN THE FINAL STRENGTH OF CONCRETE. IN ORDER TO COUNTERACT THIS TENDENCY, A WATER-REDUCING AGENT IS ADDED TO READY MIX CONCRETE TO REDUCE THE AMOUNT OF WATER NEEDED TO COMPLETE HYDRATION. THE CHART SHOWS THE COMPRESSIVE STRENGTHS FROM 1 DAY TO 28 DAYS. A COMMON WATER/CEMENT RATIO IS AROUND 0.45 TO 0.5. CONCRETE STRENGTH IS INCREASED BY (1) REDUCING WATER, AND (2) INCREASING CEMENT.

BUILDING MATERIALS

THE OPTIMUM TEMPERATURE FOR CONCRETE PLACEMENT IS 73° F. IT IS GENERALLY NOT CRITICAL IF THE TEMPERATURE RANGES 25° ON EITHER SIDE OF THAT FIGURE. PRECAUTIONS MUST BE TAKEN, HOWEVER, IF THE TEMPERATURE IS ABOVE 100° F OR BELOW 40° F.

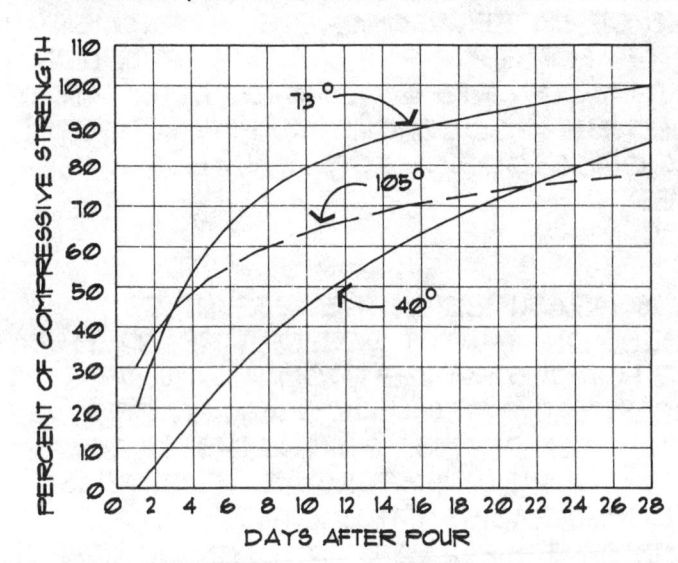

COLD WEATHER CONSTRUCTION GENERALLY REQUIRES THAT THE AREA AROUND THE CONRETE FORMS MUST BE HEATED BY ENCLOSING THE AREA WITH PLASTIC AND HEATING IT WITH A PORTABLE HEATER.

THERE ARE SEVERAL TYPES OF CEMENT WITH DIFFERENT CURING PROPERTIES. TYPE 1 PORTLAND CEMENT MUST REMAIN AT A TEMPERATURE ABOVE 50° FOR SEVEN DAYS AFTER IT HAS BEEN PLACED. TYPE III PORTLAND CEMENT (CALLED HIGH-EARLY STRENGTH) MUST BE HEATED TO 50° FOR THREE DAYS AFTER IT HAS BEEN PLACED. THE SELECTION OF TYPE III CEMENT, RATHER THAN TYPE I, WOULD REDUCE WINTER CONSTRUCTION HEATING COST. PLACING CONCRETE IN TEMPERATURES ABOVE 100° CAN BE ACCOMPLISHED BY USING CHILLED WATER IN THE MIX OR BY SPRAYING THE SLAB WITH WATER ONCE IT HAS CURED FOR SEVERAL HOURS.

PRECAUTIONS
THERE ARE SEVERAL PRECAUTIONS THAT MUST BE TAKEN WHEN PLACING CONCRETE:
- TO PREVENT SEPARATION OF THE HEAVIER AGGREGATE FROM THE SAND AND CEMENT, WET CONCRETE SHOULD NOT BE DROPPED MORE THAN 3'-0" FROM THE READY MIX CHUTE.
- DEPOSIT CONCRETE IN 12" (MAXIMUM) LAYERS.
- CONCRETE SHOULD BE PLACED IN THE FORMS WITHIN 1 1/2 HOURS OF WHEN IT WAS MIXED WITH WATER.
- CONCRETE SHOULD BE KEPT IN THE PRESENCE OF WATER FOR AS LONG A PERIOD OF TIME AS POSSIBLE. THIS COULD BE DONE BY FLOODING THE SLAB, BY PLACING A PLASTIC VAPOR BARRIER UNDER THE SLAB, OR BY KEEPING THE FORMS ON FOUNDATION WALLS FOR AN EXTENDED PERIOD.
- IT IS COMMON TO VIBRATE CONCRETE TO FILL VOIDS IN THE MIX. CARE SHOULD BE TAKEN NOT TO OVERVIBRATE THE MATERIAL, HOWEVER, BECAUSE IT COULD CAUSE THE MORE DENSE AGGREGATE TO SETTLE TO THE BOTTOM.

BUILDING MATERIALS

TESTING

THERE ARE SEVERAL TESTS THAT MAY BE USED TO DETERMINE THE QUALITY OF CONCRETE. IN A <u>COMPRESSION TEST</u>, A TEST CYLINDER IS USED TO DETERMINE THE COMPRESSIVE STRENGTH OF CONCRETE. THE TEST IS MADE BY FILLING A 6" DIAMETER BY 12" HIGH CARDBOARD CYLINDER WITH THREE LAYERS OF CONCRETE TAKEN FROM A READY MIX TRUCK. EACH LAYER IS THEN "RODDED" 25 TIMES WITH A STEEL DOWEL TO COMPACT THE MIX. ONCE THE MATERIAL BEING TESTED HAS CURED FOR 28 DAYS, THE CARDBOARD IS STRIPPED OFF AND THE REMAINING CONCRETE CYLINDER IS CRUSHED UNTIL IT BREAKS. A DIRECT READING SCALE ON THE PRESS DISPLAYS THE COMPRESSIVE STRENGTH (IN PSI). ONE PROBLEM WITH THIS TEST IS THAT THE RESULTS AREN'T AVAILABLE FOR 28 DAYS AFTER THE CONCRETE HAS BEEN PLACED.

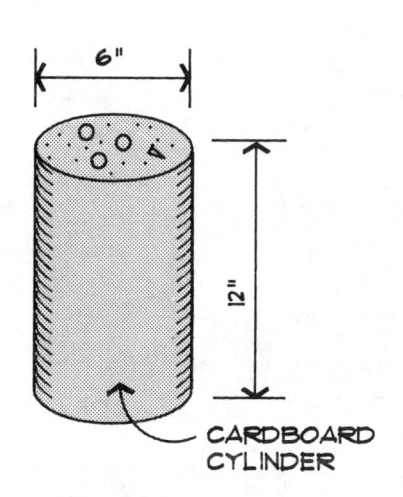

A <u>SLUMP TEST</u> PROVIDES A ROUGH INDICATOR ON THE WATER/CEMENT RATIO OF CONCRETE. THE TEST DEVICE IS A SHEET METAL CONE (WITH NO TOP OR BOTTOM) THAT IS 12" HIGH, 4" IN DIAMETER AT THE TOP, AND 8" IN DIAMETER AT THE BASE. THE CONE IS FILLED AND RODDED WITH THREE LAYERS OF CONCRETE AND STRUCK SMOOTH AT THE TOP. THE CONE IS THEN CAREFULLY LIFTED, CAUSING THE WET CONCRETE TO "SLUMP" DOWN. A CARPENTER'S LEVEL AND A RULER ARE USED TO MEASURE THE DIFFERENCE IN HEIGHT BETWEEN THE CONCRETE AND THE METAL TEST CONE. THE MEASUREMENT, IN INCHES, IS RECORDED AS THE <u>SLUMP</u> OF THE CONCRETE. A RECOMMENDED SLUMP FOR A FLOOR SLAB WOULD BE 1" TO 3", WHILE A BEAM OR REINFORCED WALL COULD HAVE A 1" TO 4" SLUMP.

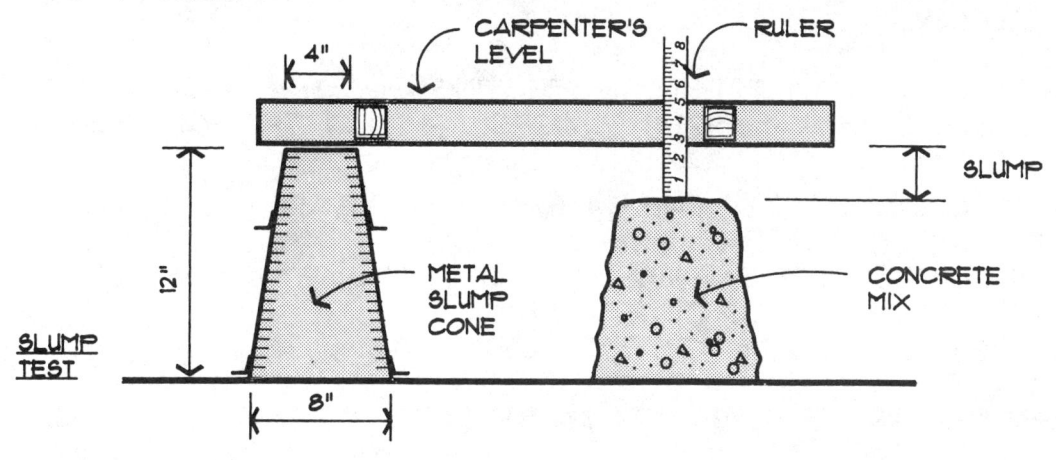

BUILDING MATERIALS   12-19

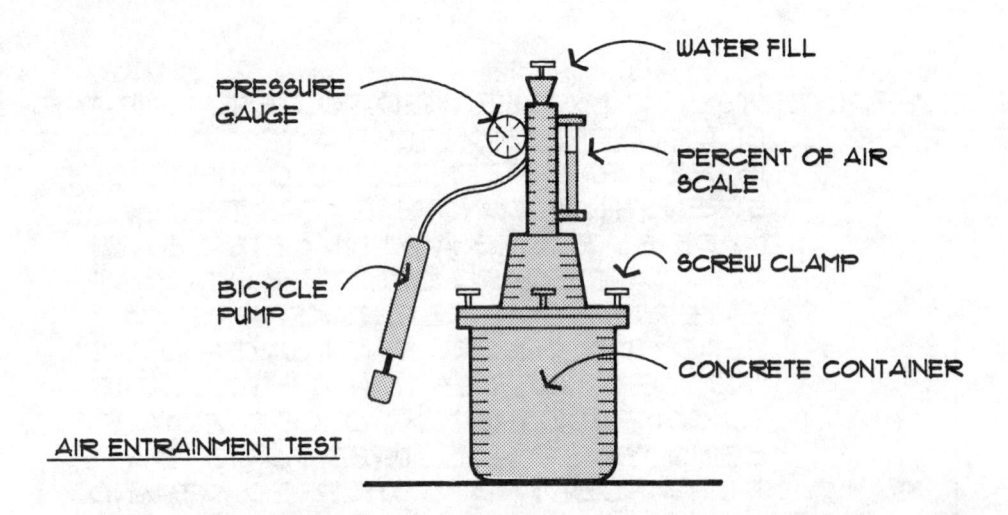

AIR ENTRAINMENT TEST

(Diagram labels: PRESSURE GAUGE, WATER FILL, PERCENT OF AIR SCALE, SCREW CLAMP, BICYCLE PUMP, CONCRETE CONTAINER)

AIR ENTRAINMENT IS A TEST TO MEASURE THE PERCENT OF AIR IN CONCRETE. AIR-ENTRAINED CONCRETE IS OBTAINED BY ADDING AN ADMIXTURE TO THE CONCRETE AT THE READY MIX PLANT. (AN ADMIXTURE IS A CHEMICAL THAT WILL CHANGE THE PROPERTIES OF CONCRETE.) CONCRETE NORMALLY HAS 1% TO 2% AIR IN THE MIX, BUT THE ADDITION OF AN ADMIXTURE CAN INCREASE THE AMOUNT OF AIR TO 6%. THE ADDITIONAL AIR IMPROVES THE RESISTANCE THAT CONCRETE HAS TO FREEZING AND THAWING WEATHER, AND ACTS AS A SHOCK ABSORBER TO REDUCE THE FACE OF THE EXPOSED CONCRETE FROM SHEARING OFF (OR SPALLING). SPECIFICATIONS TYPICALLY REQUIRE THAT ALL CONCRETE EXPOSED TO THE WEATHER BE AIR ENTRAINED. THE AIR-ENTRAINMENT TEST IS MADE ON THE CONSTRUCTION SITE BY FILLING A CONTAINER WITH THREE LAYERS OF CONCRETE AND RODDING THEM. THE TOP OF THE TEST UNIT IS THEN CLAMPED TO THE CONTAINER, FILLED WITH WATER, AND PRESSURIZED WITH A BICYCLE PUMP. A DIRECT READING SCALE INDICATES THE PERCENT OF AIR IN THE MIX.

REPLAY
CIRCLE THE LETTER OF THE STATEMENT THAT CORRECTLY ANSWERS THE QUESTION.

1. IF, ON A 105° DAY, YOU WERE INSPECTING A JOB IN WHICH A 4" CONCRETE SLAB WAS BEING PLACED, WHICH OF THE FOLLOWING SHOULD YOU NOT APPROVE?

   A. REPLACING SOME OF THE WATER AT THE READY MIX PLANT WITH CHILLED WATER
   B. THE CONTRACTOR'S ADDING TWO GALLONS OF WATER PER SACK OF CEMENT TO COOL THE MIX
   C. ORDERING THE JOB TO BE CLOSED IF THE SLAB CAN'T BE COOLED
   D. SPRINKLING THE SLAB WITH WATER ONCE IT HAS INITIALLY SET

BUILDING MATERIALS   12-20

2. CONCRETE CURES BY
   A. CALCIFYING
   B. MAGIC
   C. DRYING
   D. HYDRATION

3. WHAT IS THE BEST WATER/CEMENT RATIO DESIGN MIX FOR A CONCRETE SLAB?
   A. ADD ENOUGH WATER TO MAKE THE CONCRETE "LOOK GOOD"
   B. 0.45
   C. 0.6
   D. 0.75

4. A RATHER COMMON PROPORTION MIX FOR CONCRETE IS 1:2:3. WHICH MATERIAL WOULD YOU EXPECT TO BE INDICATED BY THE 2?
   A. AGGREGATE
   B. CEMENT
   C. WATER
   D. SAND

5. WHAT WOULD BE A REASONABLE COMPRESSIVE STRENGTH TO SPECIFY FOR A RESIDENTIAL CONCRETE FOOTING?
   A. 1,500 PSI
   B. 3,500 PSI
   C. 5,500 PSI
   D. 7,500 PSI

6. WHY SHOULDN'T CONCRETE BE DROPPED MORE THAN THREE FEET WHEN IT IS BEING PLACED IN THE FORM?
   A. THE MORE DENSE AGGREGATE COULD DROP TO THE BOTTOM.
   B. DROPPING WILL COMPRESS THE GRAVEL SUBBASE.
   C. WATER WILL RISE TO THE TOP OF THE MIX.
   D. THE FORMS COULD SPREAD BECAUSE OF THE ADDED WEIGHT.

7. WHAT IS THE MAXIMUM SIZE AGGREGATE TYPICALLY USED IN CONCRETE?
   A. 2 1/2"
   B. 1 1/2"
   C. 1"
   D. 1/2"

BUILDING MATERIALS

8. WHICH TEST WILL DETERMINE THE WATER/CEMENT RATIO IN CONCRETE?

   A. PERCOLATION
   B. AIR ENTRAINMENT
   C. TEST CYLINDER
   D. SLUMP TEST

9. WHICH STATEMENT IS <u>INCORRECT</u>?

   A. WATER USED IN MAKING CONCRETE SHOULD BE POTABLE.
   B. SAND USED IN MAKING CONCRETE SHOULD BE FREE OF ORGANIC MATERIALS.
   C. <u>CEMENT</u> IS THE CORRECT TERM FOR MATERIAL DELIVERED TO THE SITE IN A READY MIX TRUCK.
   D. THE ROCK USED IN CONCRETE IS CALLED <u>AGGREGATE</u>.

10. WHICH STATEMENT IS CORRECT?

    A. USING TYPE I PORTLAND CEMENT IN FREEZING WEATHER WILL REDUCE THE TIME NECESSARY TO HEAT THE FORMS.
    B. THE COMPRESSIVE STRENGTH OF CONCRETE CAN BE INCREASED BY REDUCING THE WATER/CEMENT RATIO.
    C. A SACK OF CEMENT WEIGHS 100 POUNDS.
    D. THE COMPRESSIVE STRENGTH OF CONCRETE CAN BE INCREASED BY ADDING AIR-ENTRAINING AGENTS.

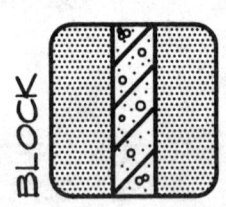

MASONRY

MASONRY CAN BE DIVIDED INTO TWO DISTINCT CATEGORIES: <u>BLOCK</u> AND <u>BRICK</u>. BOTH TYPES ARE BONDED TOGETHER WITH MORTAR TO PRODUCE WALLS. MASONRY CONSTRUCTION HAS SEVERAL ADVANTAGES OVER WOOD FRAME, INCLUDING THE FOLLOWING:

- LOAD-BEARING MASONRY IS CONSIDERABLY STRONGER THAN WOOD.
- MASONRY PROVIDES EXCELLENT FIRE PROTECTION.
- BRICK IS VERY WEATHER-RESISTANT.
- MASONRY CONSTRUCTION IS MUCH MORE DURABLE THAN WOOD.

<u>CONCRETE BLOCK</u>

CONCRETE BLOCK IS MANUFACTURED FROM CEMENT, SAND, WATER, AND AGGREGATE. THE AGGREGATE USED FOR BLOCK IS USUALLY LIMITED TO 3/8" TO 1/2" IN DIAMETER. THE CHART ON PAGE 12-23 SHOWS SOME OF THE SEVERAL HUNDRED BLOCK SIZES AVAILABLE.

BUILDING MATERIALS

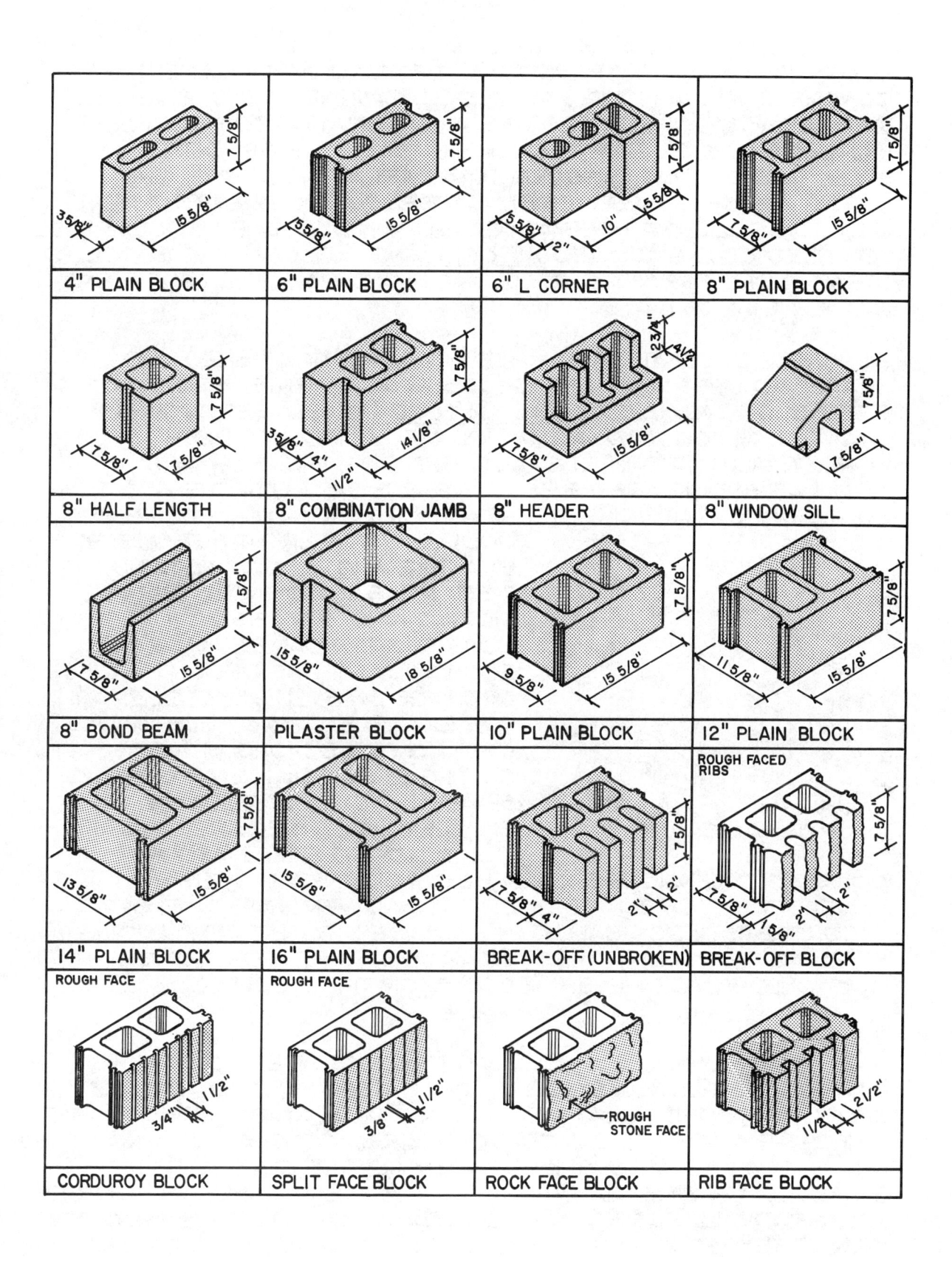

4" PLAIN BLOCK	6" PLAIN BLOCK	6" L CORNER	8" PLAIN BLOCK
8" HALF LENGTH	8" COMBINATION JAMB	8" HEADER	8" WINDOW SILL
8" BOND BEAM	PILASTER BLOCK	10" PLAIN BLOCK	12" PLAIN BLOCK
14" PLAIN BLOCK	16" PLAIN BLOCK	BREAK-OFF (UNBROKEN)	BREAK-OFF BLOCK
CORDUROY BLOCK	SPLIT FACE BLOCK	ROCK FACE BLOCK	RIB FACE BLOCK

BUILDING MATERIALS 12-23

BLOCK IS FORMED BY FORCING A VERY LOW-WATER/CEMENT-RATIO CONCRETE INTO A MOLD. THE BLOCK MACHINE FORMS SEVERAL UNITS AT A TIME USING PRESSURE AND VIBRATION TO PRODUCE A UNIFORM SHAPE. THE WET CONCRETE "BLANK" IS DEPOSITED ON A STEEL PALLET THAT IS MOVED TO AN AREA FOR CURING. THE CURING PROCESS INVOLVES PLACING BLOCK IN AN ENVIRONMENT WITH CONTROLLED TEMPERATURE AND HUMIDITY. ONE PROCESS USED TO SPEED CURING, CALLED AUTOCLAVING, SUBJECTS THE BLOCK TO STEAM UNDER PRESSURE, RESULTING IN A CURING TIME OF 8 HOURS RATHER THAN 28 DAYS.

CONCRETE BLOCK IS AVAILABLE IN A VARIETY OF SIZES AND SHAPES TO MEET A NUMBER OF JOB REQUIREMENTS. STANDARD SIZED BLOCK (CALLED MODULAR BLOCK) HAS A SET DIMENSION THAT WILL ALLOW IT TO ACCOMMODATE 8" MODULES BOTH HORIZONTALLY AND VERTICALLY. THE DIMENSIONS OF AN 8" MODULAR BLOCK ARE 7 5/8" x 7 5/8" x 15 5/8". WITH THE ADDITION OF A 3/8" MORTAR JOINT, THE HEIGHT OR LENGTH WILL FIT THE 8" MODULE. A DIFFERENT SIZE UNIT, FOR EXAMPLE A 10" BLOCK, RETAINS THE 7 5/8" x 15 5/8" DIMENSION, BUT THE WIDTH CHANGES TO 9 5/8". MASONRY CONSTRUCTION CAN BE MADE MORE ECONOMICAL IF THE DESIGN PLACES OPENINGS ON EVEN 8" MODULES. FOR EXAMPLE: A 4'-0" WIDE WINDOW OPENING CAN BE LAID WITHOUT CUTTING BLOCK, WHILE AN OPENING SEVERAL INCHES LARGER OR SMALLER WOULD REQUIRE CUTTING THE BLOCK TO SIZE. MASONRY COURSING DIMENSIONS SHOULD BE CONSIDERED IN THE DEVELOPMENT OF BOTH HORIZONTAL AND VERTICAL DIMENSIONS. A CONCRETE BLOCK WALL CAN BE MADE STRONGER BY ADDING STEEL REINFORCING IN THE MORTAR JOINTS. REINFORCING IS COMMONLY PLACED EVERY SECOND OR THIRD COURSE.

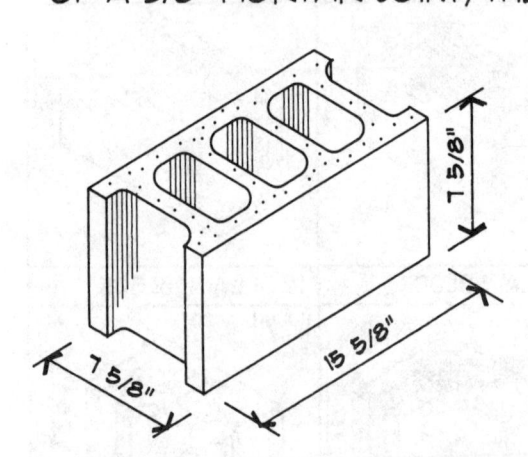

BRICK
LIKE BLOCK, BRICK IS A MODULAR PRODUCT SIZED TO FIT WITH OTHER CONSTRUCTION SYSTEMS. THE MATERIALS USED TO MAKE BRICK ARE SIMPLY CLAY AND WATER. ONCE CLAY DEPOSITS ARE MINED, THEY ARE GROUND TO THE DESIRED CONSISTENCY AND MIXED WITH WATER INTO A DOUGHLIKE MATERIAL. THE CLAY IS THEN EXTRUDED OR WIRE-CUT INTO THE PROPER BRICK SIZE. THE PIECES ARE GRADUALLY DRIED IN A LOW-HEAT OVEN AND THEN FIRED IN A KILN AT TEMPERATURES APPROACHING 2,000° F. THIS PROCESS

BUILDING MATERIALS

CHANGES THE CLAY INTO A GLASSLIKE MATERIAL THAT IS VERY HARD AND WILL RESIST WEATHER. ONCE THE BRICK HAS COOLED, IT IS STACKED ON WOODED PALLETS AND IS READY FOR USE. THE VARIETY OF COLORS IN BRICK IS DUE TO THE DIFFERENT TYPES OF CLAY USED AND THE VARIOUS TEMPERATURES AT WHICH IT IS FIRED. IN ADDITION, ELEMENTS SUCH AS IRON AND MANGANESE CAN BE MIXED INTO THE CLAY TO CHANGE THE FINAL COLOR. TEMPERATURE AND CLAY ALSO AFFECT THE HARDNESS OF BRICK. VERY HARD BRICKS, CALLED PAVERS, ARE USED FOR FLOORING. FACE BRICK IS USED FOR MOST EXTERIOR CONDITIONS, WHILE COMMON BRICK IS USED AS A BACK-UP MATERIAL.

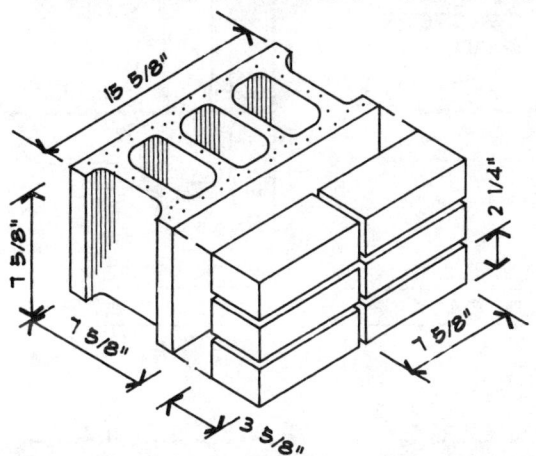

BRICK COMES IN A NUMBER OF SIZES: THE MOST COMMON PRODUCT IS CALLED MODULAR. THE SIZE OF A MODULAR BRICK IS 2 1/4" x 3 5/8" x 7 5/8". THOSE DIMENSIONS ALLOW A STACK OF BRICK THREE HIGH AND TWO WIDE (WHEN COMBINED WITH A 3/8" MORTAR JOINT) TO EQUAL THE SIZE OF A STANDARD CONCRETE BLOCK. THIS IS EXTREMELY IMPORTANT IN COMMERCIAL CONSTRUCTION WHERE BRICK AND BLOCK ARE USED TOGETHER. IT IS COMMON TO PLACE WIRE-TIE REINFORCING EVERY SECOND OR THIRD BLOCK COURSE TO TIE THE MORTAR JOINTS OF THE BRICK AND BLOCK TOGETHER.

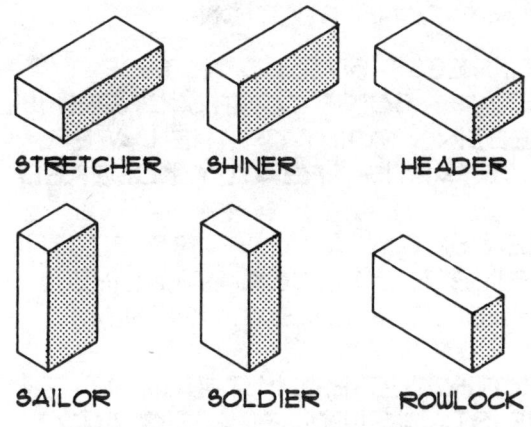

IT IS POSSIBLE FOR BRICK TO BE EXPOSED WITH SIX DIFFERENT SURFACES, OR FACES, SHOWING. EACH FACE IS IDENTIFIED WITH A DIFFERENT NAME AS ILLUSTRATED AT LEFT.

BRICK IS NOT USED AS A LOAD-BEARING MATERIAL. THAT MEANS THAT A BRICK WALL IS NOT USED TO SUPPORT FLOOR LOADS SUCH AS JOISTS AND BEAMS. INSTEAD, A BACK-UP WALL IS LOCATED BEHIND THE BRICK WALL TO SUPPORT THE STRUCTURE. RESIDENTIAL CONSTRUCTION TYPICALLY USES A STUD WALL FOR BACK-UP TO BRICK, WHILE COMMERCIAL BUILDING FREQUENTLY USES CONCRETE BLOCK OR A METAL STUD WALL. IN THIS TYPE OF CONSTRUCTION, THE BRICK WALL IS KNOWN AS A VENEER WALL. THREE WALL TYPES ARE ILLUSTRATED ON PAGE 12-26.

BUILDING MATERIALS

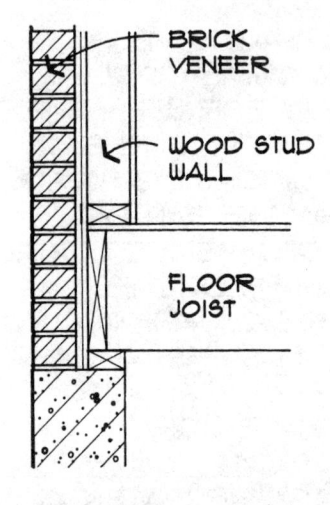

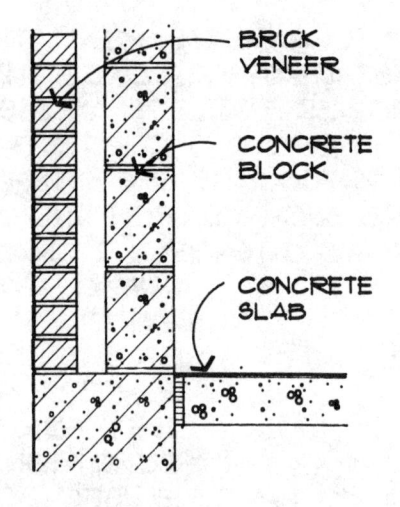

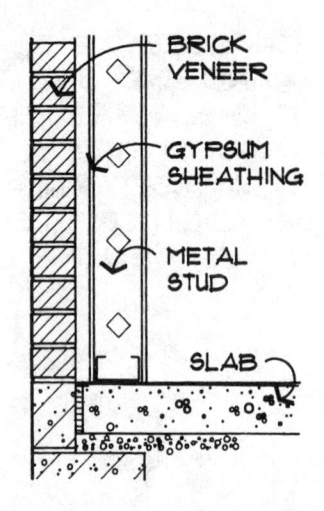

BRICK VENEER WALL WITH A WOOD STUD BACK-UP

BRICK VENEER WALL WITH A CONCRETE BLOCK BACK-UP

BRICK VENEER WALL WITH A METAL STUD BACK-UP

MORTAR

MORTAR IS USED TO BOND BRICK OR BLOCK INTO A SOLID WALL UNIT. THE MATERIAL IS TYPICALLY MADE FROM CEMENT, SAND, WATER, AND LIME. THE ADDITION OF LIME MAKES THE MORTAR STICK TO THE MASONRY WHEN IT IS LAID PLUS IT MAKES THE HARDENED PRODUCT MORE FLEXIBLE. A PRODUCT CALLED <u>MASONRY CEMENT</u> CONTAINS BOTH LIME AND PORTLAND CEMENT. MORTAR HAS THE SAME TEMPERATURE RESTRICTIONS AS CONCRETE; FREEZING WEATHER REQUIRES ENCLOSING AND HEATING THE SPACE AROUND THE MASONRY. SEVERAL OTHER PRECAUTIONS SHOULD ALSO BE FOLLOWED TO INSURE QUALITY MASONRY CONSTRUCTION:

- CALCIUM CHLORIDE (SALT) OR ANTIFREEZE SHOULD NOT BE PERMITTED TO BE ADDED TO MORTAR. SOME CONTRACTORS WILL TRY TO DO THIS TO LOWER THE FREEZING POINT OF THE WATER, BUT THE FINAL STRENGTH OF THE MORTAR IS GREATLY LOWERED IF THIS IS ALLOWED.
- ONCE A BRICK OR BLOCK HAS BEEN SET IN A MORTAR BED, THE UNIT SHOULD NOT BE MOVED. TAPPING THE BLOCK INTO LINE WITH A MASONRY HAMMER COULD RESULT IN BREAKING THE WEATHER-TIGHT MORTAR BOND.
- BRICK AND BLOCK SHOULD BE PROTECTED FROM THE WEATHER ON THE JOB SITE BY COVERING THE STACK WITH PLASTIC AND STORING IT ON DRY GROUND. BLOCK SHOULD NOT BE WETTED DOWN BEFORE IT IS LAID. ALLOWING THE MASON TO LAY WET BLOCK WEAKENS THE MASONRY BOND.
- MORTAR JOINTS SHOULD BE CONCAVE TO MAKE THEM WATERTIGHT; THIS IS CALLED <u>STRIKING THE JOINT</u>.

BUILDING MATERIALS

REPLAY

MARK (T) IF THE STATEMENT IS TRUE AND (F) IF THE STATEMENT IS FALSE.

_____ 1. THE STANDARD SIZE OF A MODULAR BLOCK IS 10" x 10" x 16".

_____ 2. AUTOCLAVE BLOCK IS CURED BY SUBJECTING IT TO STEAM UNDER PRESSURE.

_____ 3. BRICK IS MADE FROM CLAY, PORTLAND CEMENT, AND WATER.

_____ 4. THE STANDARD SIZE OF A MODULAR BRICK IS 2 1/4" x 3 5/8" x 7 5/8".

_____ 5. CONCRETE BLOCK IS MANUFACTURED FROM THE SAME MATERIAL AS POURED CONCRETE.

_____ 6. IF MORTAR IS GOING TO BE USED IN FREEZING WEATHER, THE MASON SHOULD ADD 5 POUNDS OF CALCIUM CHLORIDE PER SACK OF MASONRY CEMENT.

_____ 7. LIME IS ADDED TO MORTAR TO GIVE IT STRENGTH.

_____ 8. A PAVER IS A SOFT BRICK USED AS A BACK-UP MATERIAL FOR FACE BRICK.

_____ 9. THE TYPICAL WIDTH OF A MORTAR JOINT IS 3/8".

_____ 10. BRICK AND BLOCK SHOULD NOT BE MOVED AFTER THEY HAVE BEEN PLACED IN THE MORTAR BED.

INSULATION

THE ENERGY CONSUMPTION OF A BUILDING DEPENDS ON MANY FACTORS, BUT THE EASIEST TO CONTROL IS THE TYPE AND AMOUNT OF INSULATION USED IN THE EXTERIOR SHELL (THE ROOF, WALLS, AND FLOOR). HEAT AND COOLING ARE TRANSFERRED IN THREE WAYS:

1. <u>CONDUCTION</u> IS TRANSFER OF HEAT THROUGH A SOLID.
2. <u>CONVECTION</u> IS TRANSFER OF HEAT THROUGH A LIQUID OR A GAS.
3. <u>RADIATION</u> IS TRANSFER OF HEAT THROUGH WAVES SUCH AS ULTRAVIOLET RADIATION.

BUILDING MATERIALS | 12-27

INSULATION MATERIALS PREVENT THE TRANSFER OF HEAT BY SLOWING CONDUCTION, CONVECTION, AND RADIATION RATES. ONLY A FEW INSULATION PRODUCTS WORK TO REDUCE CONVECTION AND RADIATION HEAT TRANSFER. CONVECTION (HEAT FLOW THROUGH AIR) IS PRIMARILY REDUCED BY INSTALLING PLASTIC VAPOR BARRIERS ON THE WARM SIDE OF A WALL AND BY WEATHER-STRIPPING WINDOWS AND DOORS. RADIANT HEAT CAN ONLY BE REDUCED BY PLACING A REFLECTIVE SURFACE IN THE PATH OF HEAT TRANSFER. THIS IS ACCOMPLISHED BY USING ALUMINUM-FOIL-FACED INSULATION OR GYPSUM BOARD. IN THE REST OF THIS UNIT, WE WILL BE DISCUSSING CONDUCTION HEAT TRANSFER.

NOT ALL INSULATION HAS THE SAME EFFECTIVENESS. FOR EXAMPLE, 1" OF WOOD HAS 1/3 THE INSULATIVE VALUE OF 1" OF BLOWN CELLULOSE INSULATION. THE CONDUCTION INSULATIVE QUALITY OF A MATERIAL IS MEASURED IN UNITS CALLED R FACTORS. THE HIGHER THE R FACTOR, THE BETTER THE INSULATION. THE RECIPROCAL TO THE R FACTOR IS CALLED THE U FACTOR (U = 1/R). THE U FACTOR CAN BE USED TO CALCULATE HEAT LOSS THROUGH CONSTRUCTION MATERIALS. HEAT IS MEASURED IN BTU'S (BRITISH THERMAL UNITS). ONE BTU IS THE AMOUNT OF HEAT NECESSARY TO RAISE ONE POUND OF WATER ONE DEGREE FAHRENHEIT, ABOUT THE AMOUNT OF HEAT GIVEN OFF WHEN A WOOD MATCH BURNS. DEVICES USED FOR HEATING, SUCH AS FURNACES AND RADIATORS, ARE RATED IN BTU'S. THE FOLLOWING IS THE FORMULA USED TO CALCULATE HEAT LOSS:

$$Q = U \times A (T_1 - T_2)$$

Q IS THE TOTAL HEAT LOSS IN BTU'S PER HOUR
U IS THE SUM OF THE U FACTORS THAT MAKE UP THE WALL
A IS THE AREA OF THE WALL IN SQUARE FEET
T_1 IS THE INSIDE DESIGN TEMPERATURE IN F°
T_2 IS THE OUTSIDE DESIGN TEMPERATURE IN F°

FOR EXAMPLE, CALCULATE THE HEAT LOSS FOR 1,500 SQ FT OF THE WALL SHOWN BELOW. ASSUME THE INSIDE AIR TEMPERATURE TO BE 73° F AND THE OUTSIDE AIR TEMPERATURE TO BE 0° F.

(STEP 1) CALCULATE THE SUM OF THE R FACTORS IN THE WALL (SEE PAGE 12-29)

MATERIAL	R
OUTSIDE AIR FILM	.17
SIDING	.5
SHEATHING	.5
6" FIBERGLASS	19.0
GYP. BOARD	.5
INSIDE AIR FILM	.68
TOTAL R	21.35

(STEP 2) CALCULATE THE U FACTOR FROM THE SUM OF THE R FACTORS

U = 1/R
U = 1 / 21.35 = .047

(STEP 3) CALCULATE THE HEAT LOSS

$Q = U \times A (T_1 - T_2)$
Q = .047 × 1,500 (73° - 0°)
Q = 5,146 BTU/HOUR

THIS MEANS THAT 1,500 SQUARE FEET OF THE WALL WILL LOSE 5,146 BTU'S PER HOUR. THE TOTAL HEAT LOSS IS FIGURED BY ADDING THE LOSS FOR GLASS, ROOFING, DOORS, ETC.

BUILDING MATERIALS

INSULATION SELECTION SHOULD BE BASED ON PERFORMANCE AND COMPATABILITY WITH THE CONSTRUCTION SYSTEM. THE CHART BELOW LISTS SEVERAL COMMON CONSTRUCTION INSULATION PRODUCTS.

INSULATION MATERIALS			
MATERIAL	SECTION	R FACTOR	USE
FIBERGLASS		3.16 PER INCH	BLANKET OR RIGID BATTS BETWEEN STUDS OR JOISTS; THE MOST WIDELY USED INSULATION FOR RESIDENTIAL CONSTRUCTION
POLYURETHANE		6.2 PER INCH	RIGID BOARDS OR SPRAYED IN WALLS; URETHANE IS AN EXCELLENT INSULATION BUT QUITE EXPENSIVE
POLYSTYRENE		3.8 PER INCH	RIGID BOARDS GLUED TO WALLS; MAY BE USED BELOW GRADE; DEGRADES IN SUNLIGHT; EXTRUDED (STYROFOAM) OR MOLDED (BEAD-BOARD)
CONCRETE BLOCK (8")		1.1 FOR 8"	EXTERIOR AND FOUNDATION WALLS; THE LOW R FACTOR USUALLY REQUIRES ADDING INSULATION (VERMICULITE OR POLYURETHANE) TO THE BLOCK CORE
CELLULOSE		3.3 PER INCH	POURED OR BLOWN INTO ATTIC SPACE; MADE FROM PULVERIZED WOOD PRODUCTS; CELLULOSE MUST BE FIRE-PROOFED AT THE FACTORY
VERMICULITE		2.5 PER INCH	POURED LOOSE FILL INSULATION; MADE FROM EXPANDED MINERALS; CAN BE USED TO FILL CONCRETE BLOCK OR CAVITY STUD WALLS
GLASS		1 (SINGLE) 2 (DOUBLE) 3 (HP)	INSULATED GLASS HAS 2 OR 3 SHEETS; HIGH-PERFORMANCE (HP) GLASS HAS A METALLIC COATING BONDED TO INSIDE PANE AND IS FILLED WITH ARGON GAS
WOOD		1 PER INCH	WOOD SIDING AND SHEATHING
INSULATING CONCRETE		.85 PER INCH	POURED CONCRETE; SOME AGGREGATE IS REPLACED WITH LIGHTER WEIGHT MINERAL PRODUCTS SUCH AS VERMICULITE
GYPSUM BOARD		1 PER INCH	INTERIOR WALLS, ROOF, AND WALL SHEATHING
AIR FILM		.17 OUTSIDE AIR .68 INSIDE AIR	A THIN FILM OF AIR ADDS TO THE INSULATION VALUE OF A WALL (THE OUTSIDE WALL IS CALCULATED WITH A 15 MPH WIND)

BUILDING MATERIALS

INSULATION REQUIREMNETS VARY WITH THE CLIMATES IN WHICH A BUILDING MIGHT BE LOCATED. A ROOF IN A NORTHERN CLIMATE, FOR EXAMPLE, COULD REQUIRE AN R OF 38, WHILE A ROOF IN A WARMER LOCATION COULD REQUIRE ONLY AN R 19.

IN ADDITION TO INSULATION, IT IS NECESSARY TO PLACE A <u>VAPOR BARRIER</u> IN A WALL OR ROOF ASSEMBLY. A VAPOR BARRIER PREVENTS MOISTURE FROM ESCAPING FROM THE INTERIOR OF A BUILDING INTO THE INSULATION, WHERE IT COULD FREEZE; IT SHOULD BE PLACED ON THE "WARM" SIDE OF THE WALL, BETWEEN THE WALL- BOARD AND THE INSULATION. A COMMON VAPOR BARRIER IS 4 MIL (4 THOUSANDTHS OF AN INCH) POLYETHYLENE PLASTIC (COMMONLY CALLED "POLY").

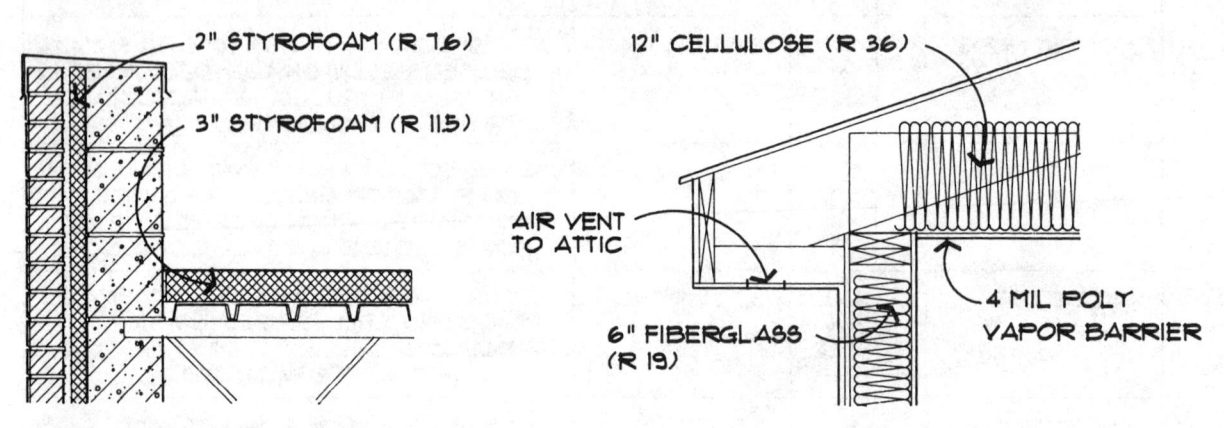

- 2" STYROFOAM (R 7.6)
- 3" STYROFOAM (R 11.5)
- 12" CELLULOSE (R 36)
- AIR VENT TO ATTIC
- 6" FIBERGLASS (R 19)
- 4 MIL POLY VAPOR BARRIER

REPLAY
MARK (T) IF THE STATEMENT IS TRUE. IF THE STATEMENT IS FALSE, MARK (F) AND CHANGE THE UNDERLINED WORD(S) AS NECESSARY TO MAKE THE STATEMENT TRUE.

_____ ( )1. <u>2"</u> OF INSULATION WITH AN R 2.5 PER INCH IS BETTER THAN 1" OF INSULATION WITH AN R OF 7.

_____ ( )2. A ROOF IN A NORTHERN CLIMATE WITH AN R FACTOR OF 15 IS <u>NOT WELL</u> INSULATED.

_____ ( )3. A SINGLE SHEET OF GLASS HAS AN R OF <u>1</u>.

_____ ( )4. THE ONLY WAY <u>CONVECTION</u> HEAT FLOW CAN BE REDUCED IS WITH A SHINY MIRRORED SURFACE.

_____ ( )5. BASED ON THE TABLE ON INSULATION MATERIALS ON PAGE 12-29, IT WOULD TAKE <u>FIVE</u> 8" CONCRETE BLOCK WALLS TO EQUAL 2" OF POLYURETHANE INSULATION.

BUILDING MATERIALS 12-30

_____ ( ) 6. A U FACTOR IS THE <u>SAME AS</u> THE R FACTOR.

_____ ( ) 7. HIGH-PERFORMANCE GLASS HAS NEARLY <u>TWICE</u> THE INSULATION VALUE OF A SINGLE PANE OF GLASS.

8-10. USE THE SPACE BELOW RIGHT TO CALCULATE THE HEAT LOSS IN BTU'S. USE A 72° F INSIDE DESIGN TEMPERATURE AND A -10° F OUTSIDE TEMPERATURE.

- 280 SQ FT 6" FIBERGLASS (R 19)
- 25 SQ FT 1" INSULATED GLASS (R 2)
- 280 SQ FT STUCCO (R 1)
- 56 SQ FT HIGH-PERFORMANCE GLASS DOOR (R 3)
- 280 SQ FT 1/2" GYPSUM BD. (R 5) (INTERIOR WALL)
- 280 SQ FT INTERIOR AIR (R .68) OUTSIDE AIR (R .17)

BTU'S PER HOUR HEAT LOSS = _____

ROOFING

ROOFING MATERIALS RANGE FROM WOOD AND METAL TO PETROLEUM-BASED PRODUCTS. ONE OF THE MOST COMMON IS ASPHALT, WHICH IS DISTILLED FROM PETROLEUM. THE RESULTING BLACK MATERIAL IS USED IN A VARIETY OF PRODUCTS IN WHICH MOISTURE-RESISTANCE AND DURABILITY ARE REQUIRED. ASPHALT-BASED ROOFING CAN BE DIVIDED INTO TWO CATEGORIES: <u>FLAT</u> AND <u>PITCHED</u>. A FLAT ROOF REQUIRES ONE COMPLETE MEMBRANE THAT IS WATERTIGHT, WHILE A PITCHED ROOF IS MADE FROM SHINGLES DESIGNED TO SHED WATER IN ONE DIRECTION.

MOST ASPHALT ROOFING PRODUCTS START WITH A MATERIAL CALLED

BUILDING MATERIALS 12-31

ROOFING FELT (ALSO CALLED TAR PAPER). ROOFING FELT IS MADE BY IMPREGNATING RAG FELT WITH ASPHALT; IT IS CUT IN 36" WIDTHS AND ROLLED FOR USE IN ROOFING. ROOFING PRODUCTS ARE MEASURED BY THEIR WEIGHT IN 100 SQ FT UNITS (CALLED SQUARES). THE TERM 30-POUND FELT MEANS THAT A 10' × 10' PIECE OF FELT WOULD WEIGH 30 POUNDS.

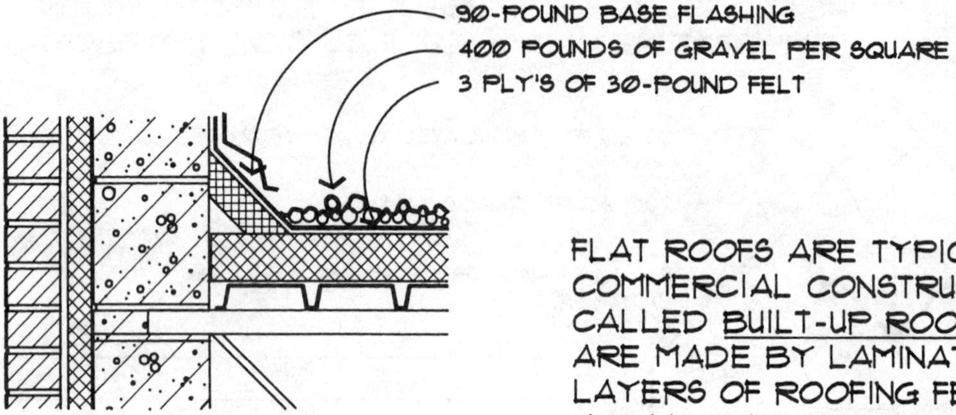

90-POUND BASE FLASHING
400 POUNDS OF GRAVEL PER SQUARE
3 PLY'S OF 30-POUND FELT

BUILT-UP ROOF AND WALL INTERSECTION

FLAT ROOFS ARE TYPICAL IN COMMERCIAL CONSTRUCTION. CALLED BUILT-UP ROOFS, THEY ARE MADE BY LAMINATING LAYERS OF ROOFING FELT WITH HOT MOPPED ASPHALT. THE ROOF CONSTRUCTION IS BEGUN WITH A ROOF DECK (CALLED A SUBSTRATE). ONCE RIGID INSULATION HAS BEEN SECURED TO THE DECK, LAYERS OF ROOFING FELT ARE LAMINATED TO THE DECK WITH HOT ASPHALT. ONCE THE FINAL SHEET HAS BEEN ROLLED, A COAT OF ASPHALT IS MOPPED ON THE SURFACE AND A GRAVEL WEAR SURFACE IS APPLIED.

A POPULAR ALTERNATIVE TO A BUILT-UP ROOF IS CALLED AN EPDM (THIS STANDS FOR ETHYLENE PROPYLENE DIENE MONOMER). THIS TYPE OF ROOF CONSISTS OF A THIN RUBBERLIKE SHEET THAT RESEMBLES A TIRE INNERTUBE. A ONE-PIECE EPDM ROOF IS LAID LOOSE OVER THE INSULATION AND MASTIC IS APPLIED (GLUED) AT THE EDGES. ROOF SEAMS ARE SEALED BY USING MASTIC TO LAP TWO EPDM SHEETS TOGETHER. THE LOOSE ROOF SHEET MUST BE SECURED TO THE DECK TO PREVENT IT FROM BLOWING OFF IN SHEAR WINDS. THIS IS USUALLY DONE BY COVERING THE DECK WITH 3" OF LOOSE WASHED GRAVEL (CALLED BALLAST) OR BY USING A CAP FASTENER, THE BOTTOM OF WHICH IS ATTACHED TO THE DECK WHILE THE TOP IS SNAPPED OVER THE EPDM SHEET WITHOUT CUTTING IT.

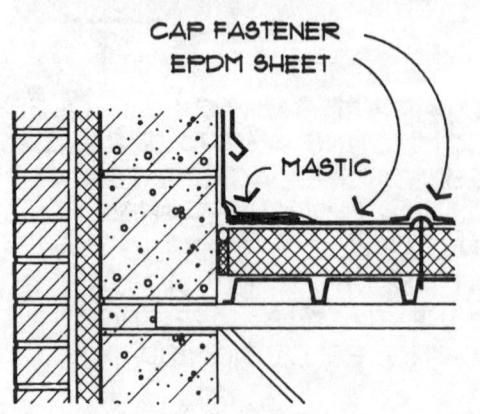

CAP FASTENER
EPDM SHEET
MASTIC

EPDM ROOF AND WALL INTERSECTION

BUILDING MATERIALS

SHINGLES

ASPHALT SHINGLES ARE MADE WITH A HEAVY BASE OF ASPHALT-SATURATED FELT. HOT ASPHALT IS SPREAD OVER THE SURFACE AND MINERAL GRANUALS ARE ROLLED ON TO GIVE THE SHINGLE COLOR, TEXTURE, AND A WEARING SURFACE. MOST SHINGLES ARE 36" LONG AND 12" HIGH. ONE SHINGLE IS LAPPED OVER THE NEXT TO EXPOSE 5" OF THE 12" WIDTH (THIS IS CALLED THE WEATHER OF THE SHINGLE). SHINGLES ARE CUT TO SIZE AND STACKED IN PACKAGES CALLED BUNDLES; USUALLY IT TAKES TWO OR THREE BUNDLES TO COVER A SQUARE OF ROOFING. ASPHALT SHINGLES ARE MEASURED BY THEIR WEIGHT PER SQUARE. THE MOST TYPICAL WEIGHT IS 240 POUNDS PER SQUARE, BUT 340-POUND LAMINATED TAB SHINGLES ARE POPULAR. MOST SHINGLES REQUIRE A MINIMUM ROOF PITCH OF 4/12 (ABOUT 18°) TO PROPERLY REPEL WATER. A SEAL-DOWN TAB SHINGLE HAS A SPOT OF ASPHALT ON THE BACKSIDE. HEAT FROM THE SUN MELTS THE TAB OF ASPHALT, GIVING THE SHINGLE ADDED RESISTANCE TO FLAPPING IN HIGH WINDS.

WOOD SHINGLES ARE COMMONLY MADE FROM RED CEDAR. THE NATURAL PRESERVATIVE QUALITY OF THIS TYPE OF WOOD ALLOWS THESE SHINGLES TO LAST FOR 25 YEARS OR MORE. CEDAR SHINGLES ARE AVAILABLE IN HANDSPLIT (ROUGH SURFACE) AND TAPER SPLIT (SMOOTH SURFACE). WOOD SHINGLES ARE AVAILABLE IN THREE GRADES: BLUE (1#), RED (2#), AND BLACK (3#). CEDAR SHINGLES SHOULD BE USED ON A MINIMUM 4/12 ROOF PITCH WITH A 30# FELT UNDERLAYMENT. SOME LOCAL CODES LIMIT WOOD SHINGLE USE DUE TO FIRE CONCERNS.

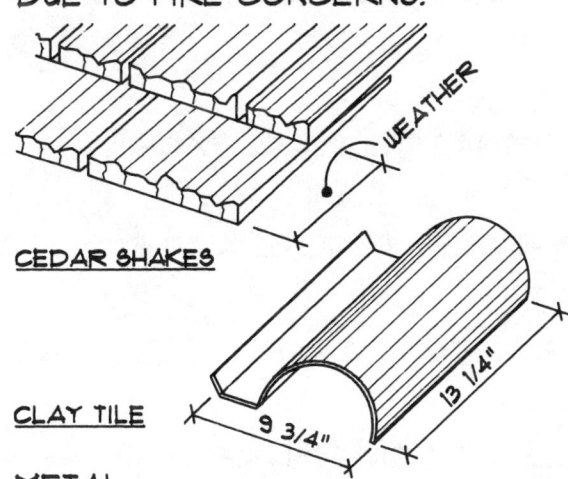

CLAY TILE ROOFING IS AVAILABLE IN THE HALF-ROUND PROFILE SHOWN IN THE ILLUSTRATION OR IN FLAT INTERLOCKING SHAPES. NONCORROSIVE NAILS SHOULD BE USED WITH PREDRILLED TILE. THE MINIMUM PITCH IS 3/12 FOR FLAT TILE AND 4/12 FOR THE "SPANISH" TILE ILLUSTRATED. 45# FELT SHOULD BE USED FOR UNDERLAYMENT. THE 800# WEIGHT OF CLAY TILE IS OVER THREE TIMES THAT OF OTHER SHINGLES.

METAL

METAL ROOFING INVOLVES ATTACHING METAL SHEETS TO THE SUBSTRATE WITH BRACKETS. TRADITIONAL METALS SUCH AS COPPER AND LEAD HAVE BECOME EXPENSIVE, MAKING TERNE METAL AND ALUMINUM THE MOST FREQUENTLY USED MATERIALS FOR METAL ROOFING. TERNE IS A COATING THAT IS APPLIED TO

BUILDING MATERIALS

SHEET STEEL. THE COATING, WHICH IS SIMILAR TO PEWTER, CONTAINS ELEMENTS SUCH AS LEAD, ZINC, AND TITANIUM. THE WIDTH OF THE ROOF PANELS (CALLED PANS) RANGE FROM 20" TO 28"; THEY ARE FASTENED WITH STANDING OR BATTEN SEAMS. FABRICATION STARTS BY ATTACHING BRACKETS TO THE ROOF DECK. THE PANS OF THE METAL DECK ARE THEN FOLDED AROUND THE BRACKET. BATTEN SEAM ROOFING CAN BE APPLIED TO ROOF SLOPES GREATER THAN 3/12. BRACKETS CAN BE NAILED TO WOOD DECKS OR BOLTED TO METAL SURFACES.

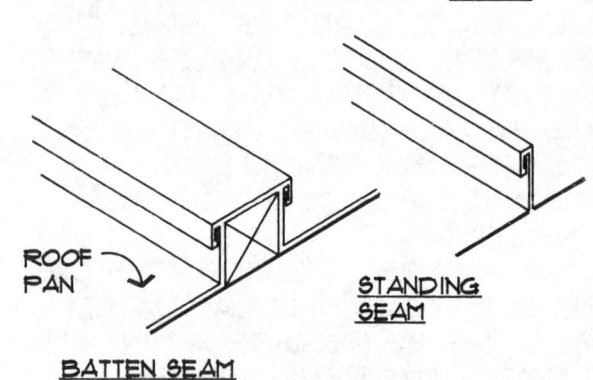

ALUMINUM ROOFING IS FABRICATED IN SHEETS APPROXIMATELY 3'-6" WIDE AND UP TO 39'-0" LONG (DEPENDING ON THE FABRICATOR). SHEETS ARE GIVEN AN ANODIZED COLOR FINISH COMMONLY IN THE BLACK AND BROWN RANGE. THE SHEETS ARE USUALLY CLIPPED TO A PLYWOOD DECK. MOST METAL DECKS ARE DESIGNED TO HAVE INTERLOCKING EDGES TO REDUCE POSSIBLE WATER LEAKAGE. DEPENDING ON THE DESIGN, THE MINIMUM SLOPE CAN BE 3/12 OR 2/12.

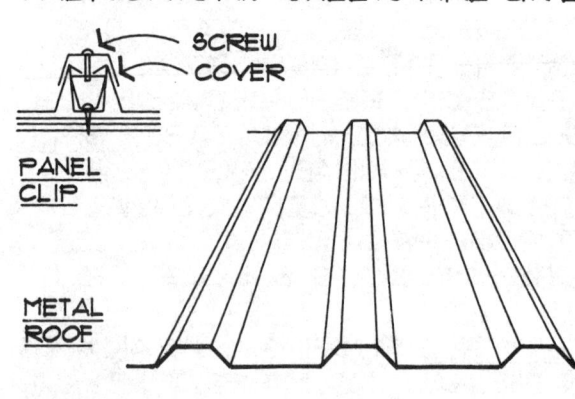

REPLAY
FILL IN THE BLANK WITH THE WORD(S) THAT WILL MAKE EACH STATEMENT CORRECT.

_____ 1. MOST ASPHALT SHINGLES REQUIRE A MINIMUM _____ ROOF PITCH.

_____ 2. ONE SQUARE OF ROOFING EQUALS _____ SQUARE FEET.

_____ 3. THE STANDARD WEIGHT PER SQUARE OF AN ASPHALT SHINGLE ROOF IS _____ POUNDS.

_____ 4. ANOTHER NAME FOR A FLAT ROOF THAT HAS LAMINATIONS OF ASPHALT AND ROOFING FELT IS A _____ ROOF.

BUILDING MATERIALS

_____ 5. BUILDING PAPER IS MADE BY IMPREGNATING TAR INTO _____.

_____ 6. CAP FASTENERS OR _____ IS USED TO PREVENT AN EPDM ROOF FROM BLOWING OFF THE DECK.

_____ 7. THE EXPOSED SURFACE OF A SHINGLE IS CALLED THE _____.

_____ 8. THE MINIMUM SLOPE FOR A STANDING BATTEN SEAM METAL ROOF IS _____.

9-10. SKETCH AND LABEL THE ROOFING CONDITION SHOWING AN EPDM ROOF. USE A GRAVEL BALLAST TO SECURE THE MEMBRANE.

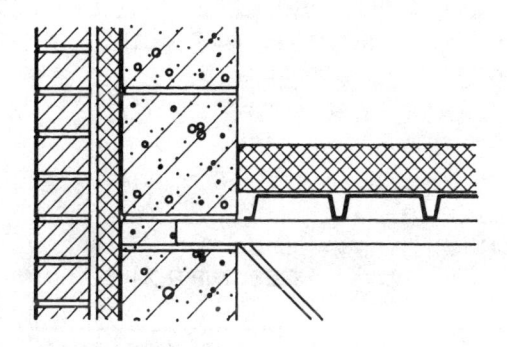

GYPSUM

GYPSUM IS A WHITE ROCKLIKE MINERAL CHEMICALLY CALLED HYDROUS CALCIUM SULFATE. ONCE GYPSUM HAS BEEN MINED, IT IS CLEANED AND CRUSHED TO A FINE POWDER. THIS MATERIAL IS THEN FED INTO A ROTARY OVEN WHERE THE 350° F TEMPERATURE DRIVES AWAY MUCH OF THE MOISTURE NATURALLY FOUND IN GYPSUM. THE PRODUCT AT THIS STAGE IS PLASTER OF PARIS, WHICH HARDENS WHEN MIXED WITH WATER. MOST GYPSUM MIXTURES ARE CARRIED ONE STEP BEYOND PLASTER OF PARIS BY ADDING MATERIALS THAT CONTROL HARDENING TIME AND STRENGTH. GYPSUM PRODUCTS ARE EITHER PLACED IN BAGS FOR MIXING ON THE JOB SITE OR FORMED INTO BOARDS AT THE FACTORY.

| BUILDING MATERIALS | 12-35 |

GYPSUM HAS SEVERAL PROPERTIES THAT MAKE IT AN EXCELLENT CHOICE FOR WALL MATERIAL. GYPSUM CONTAINS ABOUT 20% TRAPPED MOISTURE. A GYPSUM WALL SUBJECTED TO THE HIGH HEAT OF A FIRE WILL TURN THIS TRAPPED MOISTURE INTO STEAM WHICH WILL THEN SERVE TO COOL THE SURFACE OF THE WALL AND ACT AS A FIRE BARRIER. BUILDING CODES SET FIRE STANDARDS FOR SEPARATING SPACES IN A BUILDING AND FOR ISOLATING THE STRUCTURAL COMPONENTS. THESE STANDARDS ARE BASED ON THE <u>HOURLY FIRE SEPARATION</u>, OR THE TIME A FIRE WOULD BE CONTAINED; A TWO-HOUR SEPARATION FOR AN ENCLOSED EXIT STAIR OR A FOUR-HOUR RATING FOR A STEEL COLUMN MIGHT BE REQUIRED, FOR EXAMPLE. THE CHART BELOW SHOWS THE HOURLY FIRE SEPARATION FOR SEVERAL WALL SYSTEMS. THE CHART ALSO SHOWS THE SOUND SEPARATION PROPERTIES FOR GYPSUM WALLS. SOUND VOLUME IS MEASURED IN A UNIT CALLED A <u>DECIBEL</u> (ABBREVIATED dB). A SPEAKING VOICE IS RATED AT 60 dB, A SYMPHONY IS 100 dB, AND THE SOUND IN A PRIVATE OFFICE IS 40 dB. WALL SOUND REDUCTION IS MEASURED IN A UNIT CALLED <u>SOUND TRANSMISSION CLASS</u> (STC). A WALL WITH AN STC OF 50 WOULD REDUCE THE SOUND BY 50 dB'S AS THE SOUND WAVES PASSED THROUGH THE WALL. FOR EXAMPLE, BUILDING CODES MAY REQUIRE APARTMENT UNITS TO BE SEPARATED WITH AN STC OF 50 WHILE A DOCTOR'S OFFICE COULD REQUIRE AN STC OF 60.

SECTION	FIRE / STC	WALL DESCRIPTION	SECTION	FIRE / STC	WALL DESCRIPTION
	1 HR / STC 30	1 LAYER OF 1/2" TYPE X GYP. BD. NAILED TO 2" x 4" STUDS AT 16" O.C. (EACH SIDE)		2 HR / STC 35	1 LAYER OF 1/2" TYPE X GYP. BD. OVER 1" T AND G GYPSUM COREBOARD
	1 HR / STC 50	1 LAYER OF 5/8" GYP. BD. (1 SIDE ON CHANNELS) W/ 1 1/2" MINERAL INSULATION		2 HR / STC 50	2 LAYERS OF 1/2" TYPE X GYP. BD. ON 1 5/8" STUDS W/ FIBERGLASS
	2 HR / STC 50	2 LAYERS OF 5/8" TYPE X GYP. BD. ON STAGGERED 2" x 4" STUDS		2 HR / STC 40	2 LAYERS OF 5/8" TYPE X GYP. BD. SCREWED TO 2 1/2" METAL STUDS
	1 HR / STC 30	1 LAYER OF 5/8" TYPE X GYP. BD. SCREWED TO 1 5/8" CHANNELS AT 16" O.C.		3 HR / STC 40	2 LAYERS OF 5/8" TYPE X GYP. BD. ON 2 LAYERS OF 2" GYP. COREBOARD
	1 HR / STC 40	1 LAYER OF 5/8" TYPE X GYP. BD. SCREWED TO 3 5/8" METAL STUDS		4 HR / STC 40	2 LAYERS OF GYP. COREBOARD W/ 5/8" TYPE X GYP. BD. ON FURRING CHANNELS

BUILDING MATERIALS

GYPSUM BOARD PRODUCTS (COMMONLY CALLED BY THE TRADE NAMES "SHEET ROCK" AND "DRY WALL") ARE MADE BY MIXING GYPSUM AND WATER ON A CONVEYOR BELT AND SANDWICHING THE MIXTURE BETWEEN TWO SHEETS OF PAPER. GYPSUM BOARD IS USUALLY 4'-0" WIDE AND 8'-0" OR 12'-0" LONG. THICKNESS OF THE BOARD RANGES FROM 1/4" TO 1"; THE MOST COMMON UNITS ARE 1/2" AND 5/8" THICK. <u>TYPE X</u> GYPSUM BOARD HAS SPECIAL FIRE-RESISTANT ADDITIVES TO GIVE IT A HIGHER FIRE RATING. WATER-RESISTANT GYPSUM BOARD (CALLED <u>WR</u>) SHOULD BE USED IN AREAS WHERE IT COULD COME IN CONTACT WITH WATER, SUCH AS BATHROOMS. THE SURFACE PAPER ON WR GYPSUM BOARD IS TYPICALLY COLORED GREEN, WHICH IS THE REASON IT IS FREQUENTLY REFERRED TO AS "GREEN ROCK."

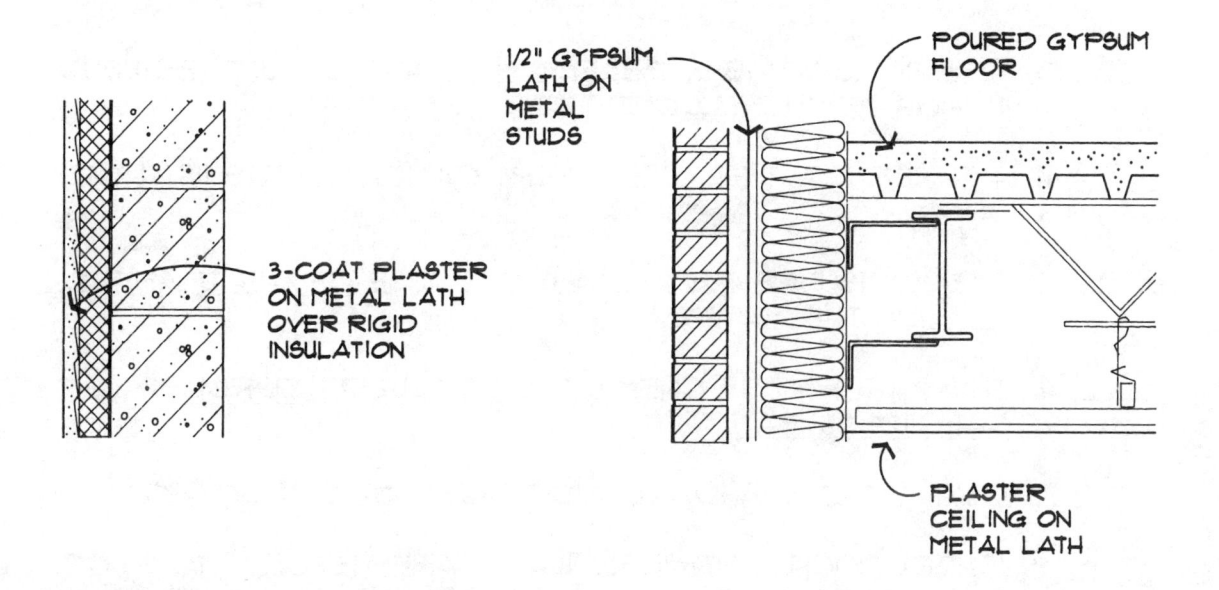

THERE ARE ADDITIONAL GYPSUM PRODUCTS AVAILABLE RANGING FROM A FLOOR-LEVELING MATERIAL TO PLASTER. POURED FLOOR PRODUCTS (SUCH AS "GYP-CRETE") CONSIST OF A THICK GYPSUM SLURRY THAT IS SPREAD OVER WOOD OR CONCRETE DECKING. THIS PRODUCT IS PLACED AT A THICKNESS OF 3/4" OR MORE AND CAN BE WALKED ON THE DAY AFTER IT IS APPLIED. IT NOT ONLY SMOOTHS AND LEVELS THE FLOOR BUT IT INCREASES THE STC AND FIRE RATINGS. <u>PLASTER</u> IS A MIX OF LIME, CEMENT, AND AGGREGATE (SUCH AS SAND OR VERMICULITE). WHEN MIXED WITH WATER, PLASTER FORMS A PLASTIC MASS THAT SETS AND HARDENS WHEN IT IS APPLIED TO A SURFACE. PLASTER IS APPLIED TO A METAL SCREEN, CALLED <u>LATH</u>, WHICH IS FASTENED TO STUDS. PLASTER IS TYPICALLY APPLIED IN THREE COATS: (1) "SCRATCH COAT," (2) "BROWN COAT," AND (3) "FINISH COAT."

BUILDING MATERIALS

REPLAY
MATCH EACH TERM WITH ITS CORRESPONDING STATEMENT BELOW.

A. GYPSUM   F. FIREPROOF   K. MOISTURE
B. SPACKLE   G. TYPE X   L. GYP-CRETE
C. LATH   H. WP   M. SAND
D. GYPSUM BOARD   I. BAGGED   N. 36"
E. WATERPROOF   J. SCRATCH   O. 48"

_____ 1. THIS GYPSUM BOARD IS DESIGNED TO MEET BUILDING CODE REQUIREMENTS FOR FIRE SEPARATION.

_____ 2. GYPSUM PRODUCTS CAN GENERALLY BE GROUPED INTO TWO CATEGORIES, GYPSUM BOARD AND _____ MATERIAL.

_____ 3. "GREEN ROCK" IS LABELED _____ AND SHOULD BE USED IN HIGH-MOISTURE CONDITIONS.

_____ 4. A THREE-COAT PLASTER APPLICATION STARTS WITH THIS LAYER.

_____ 5. GYPSUM IS FIRE-RETARDANT BECAUSE OF THE TRAPPED _____ IN THE MATERIAL.

_____ 6. THIS MATERIAL IS CHEMICALLY CALLED <u>HYDROUS CALCIUM SULFATE</u>.

_____ 7. WHAT IS THE STANDARD WIDTH FOR GYPSUM BOARD?

_____ 8. "SHEET ROCK" AND "DRY WALL" ARE TRADE NAMES FOR THIS PRODUCT.

_____ 9. THIS IS A TRADE NAME FOR A GYPSUM PRODUCT THAT CAN BE USED TO LEVEL FLOORS.

_____ 10. THIS PRODUCT IS FREQUENTLY MIXED WITH PLASTER.

GLASS

GLASS IS PRODUCED BY MELTING A SPECIAL GRADE OF SAND WITH SODA ASH AT TEMPERATURES OF 2,000° F. THE MOLTEN GLASS IS THEN FORMED INTO SHEETS WITH A UNIFORM THICKNESS. THE LEAST

BUILDING MATERIALS   12-38

EXPENSIVE RESIDENTIAL GLASS IS CALLED <u>SHEET GLASS</u>. IT IS FORMED BY POURING MOLTEN GLASS ON A SHEET AND SIMPLY ALLOWING IT TO COOL. SHEET GLASS IS THE MATERIAL AVAILABLE AT LUMBER YARDS OR HARDWARE STORES FOR REPLACEMENT WINDOWS. THIS TYPE OF GLASS CONTAINS SLIGHT OPTICAL FLAWS IN THE SHEET THAT CAN DISTORT VISION.

MOST GLASS USED IN NEW CONSTRUCTION IS EITHER <u>FLOAT GLASS</u> OR <u>POLISHED PLATE GLASS</u>. THE NAMES OF BOTH OF THESE PRODUCTS REFER TO THE WAY THE GLASS IS PREPARED AFTER RAW MATERIALS HAVE BEEN MOLDED. FLOAT GLASS IS PRODUCED BY PASSING A CONTINUOUS SHEET OF GLASS OVER MOLTEN TIN. THE SHEET OF GLASS IS THEN REHEATED (THIS PROCESS IS CALLED <u>ANNEALING</u>) TO PRODUCE AN OPTICALLY DISTORTION-FREE PRODUCT. POLISHED PLATE GLASS IS A SIMILAR-QUALITY MATERIAL PRODUCED BY GRINDING BOTH ITS SURFACES OPTICALLY SMOOTH.

GLASS IS FIT INTO FRAMES USING MATERIALS CALLED <u>GLAZING COMPOUNDS</u>. THESE CAN RANGE FROM SILICONE TO POLYBUTENE TAPE. THE ILLUSTRATION BELOW SHOWS SEVERAL FRAME CONDITIONS.

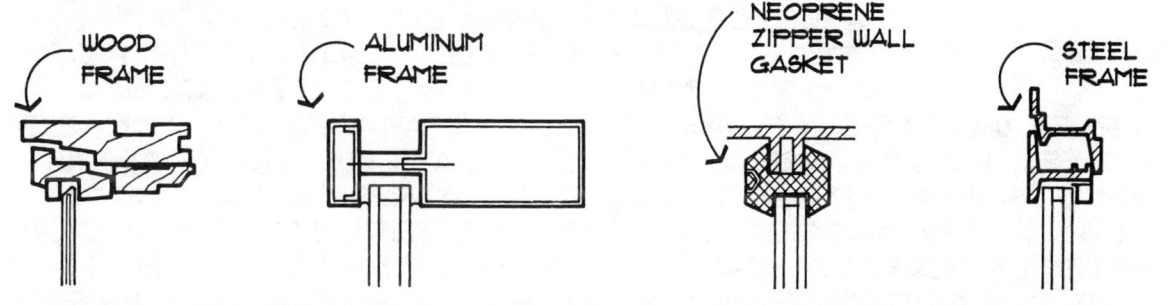

- WOOD FRAME
- ALUMINUM FRAME
- NEOPRENE ZIPPER WALL GASKET
- STEEL FRAME

SEVERAL GLASS PRODUCTS ARE FABRICATED TO PROVIDE SPECIAL PROTECTION. <u>TEMPERED GLASS</u> IS PRODUCED BY CUTTING THE GLASS TO SIZE AND PLACING IT IN AN ANNEALING FURNACE. THE RED-HOT SHEET IS THEN RAPIDLY COOLED TO PRODUCE SURFACE TENSION. TEMPERED GLASS HAS TWO UNIQUE PROPERTIES: (1) THE MATERIAL IS FOUR TO FIVE TIMES STRONGER THAN FLOAT GLASS, AND (2) THE GLASS BREAKS INTO SMALL CUBELIKE FRAGMENTS RATHER THAN JAGGED PIECES. FOR THESE REASONS, TEMPERED GLASS IS FREQUENTLY REQUIRED BY BUILDING CODE FOR GLASS DOORS AND CORRIDOR WINDOWS. <u>SAFETY GLASS</u> IS MADE BY SANDWICHING TWO SHEETS OF GLASS AROUND A SHEET OF CLEAR PLASTIC. THE INNER CORE OF PLASTIC BONDS THE GLASS TOGETHER IF THE SHEET IS BROKEN. SAFETY GLASS IS USED FOR THE FRONT WINDSHIELD OF A CAR AND FOR SKYLIGHTS, WHERE FALLING PIECES OF BROKEN GLASS ARE A CONCERN. <u>WIRE GLASS</u> IS PRODUCED BY

BUILDING MATERIALS

MELTING THE GLASS AROUND PATTERNED WIRE. SOME WIRE GLASS PATTERNS MAY BE USED WHERE SAFETY GLAZING IS REQUIRED IN CORRIDORS OR SKYLIGHTS.

SEVERAL TYPES OF GLASS ARE PRODUCED TO REDUCE THE HEAT BUILDUP INSIDE A BUILDING. ONE COMMON PRODUCT, CALLED <u>HEAT REDUCING GLASS</u>, IS TINTED LIKE THE LENSES IN SUNGLASSES. A PORTION OF THE SUNLIGHT THAT STRIKES THE GLASS (AROUND 10% TO 15%) IS THERBY REFLECTED TO THE OUTSIDE. <u>REFLECTIVE GLASS</u> IS FABRICATED BY PLATING A THIN METALLIC COATING ON THE INSIDE SURFACE ON A SHEET OF INSULATED GLASS. THIS MIRRORED SURFACE ACTS TO REFLECT HEAT GENERATED BY SUNLIGHT TO THE OUTSIDE WHILE THE VIEW REMAINS CLEAR. MIRRORED GLASS IS AVAILABLE IN SILVER, GOLD, AND SEVERAL OTHER SHADES.

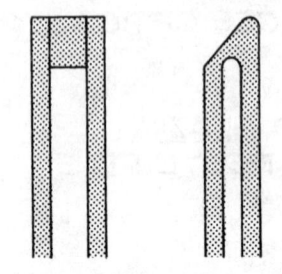

THE SECTION ON INSULATION POINTED OUT THAT GLASS HAS AN EXTREMELY LOW INSULATION VALUE. A SINGLE SHEET OF FLOAT GLASS, FOR EXAMPLE, HAS AN R VALUE OF 1. SEVERAL GLASS PRODUCTS, THEREFORE, ARE FABRICATED TO REDUCE THE HEAT LOSS THROUGH THE MATERIAL. <u>INSULATING GLASS</u> IS PRODUCED BY SPACING TWO OR THREE SHEETS OF GLASS INTO A UNIT. THE CAVITY BETWEEN SHEETS IS SEALED AND FILLED WITH DRY AIR (TO ELIMINATE MOISTURE CONDENSATION). LARGER UNITS OF GLASS ARE USUALLY SEPARATED WITH A SPACER AND SEALED WITH AN ELASTOMERIC SEALANT. <u>WELDED GLASS</u> IS USED FOR SMALLER GLASS SIZES (USUALLY RESIDENTIAL WINDOW UNITS). IT IS FABRICATED BY MELTING THE PERIMETER EDGES OF TWO PIECES OF GLASS TOGETHER. TWO SHEETS OF INSULATING GLASS CAN HAVE AN R FACTOR OF 2, WHILE TRIPLE GLAZING CAN HAVE AN R OF 2.5. <u>LOW E GLASS</u> (ALSO CALLED <u>HIGH-PERFORMANCE GLASS</u>) IS MADE BY PLATING A METALLIC SURFACE ON THE INTERIOR SHEET OF DOUBLE INSULATING GLASS AND FILLING THE CAVITY SPACE WITH ARGON GAS. LOW E GLASS HAS AN R FACTOR OF NEARLY 3.5.

INSULATED   WELDED

REPLAY
FILL IN THE BLANK WITH A WORD THAT WILL MAKE THE STATEMENT CORRECT.

_____ 1. FLOAT GLASS IS PRODUCED BY PASSING SHEETS OVER MOLTEN _____.

_____ 2. TEMPERED GLASS IS _____ TIMES STRONGER THAN STANDARD FLOAT GLASS.

BUILDING MATERIALS   12-40

_____ 3. THE TYPE OF GLASS MOST FREQUENTLY FOUND IN LUMBER YARDS AS A REPLACEMENT FOR WINDOWS IS _____ GLASS.

_____ 4. TRIPLE INSULATED GLASS HAS AN R FACTOR OF _____.

_____ 5. THE GLASS COMMONLY REQUIRED FOR A SLIDING GLASS DOOR IS _____ GLASS.

_____ 6. THE GLASS COMMONLY REQUIRED FOR A SKYLIGHT IS _____ GLASS.

_____ 7. THE GLASS PRODUCT THAT WOULD BE SPECIFIED TO LOWER THE AMOUNT OF SUMMER SUN HEAT BUILDUP WOULD BE _____ GLASS.

_____ 8. TWO GLASS PRODUCTS THAT ARE FREE OF OPTICAL DISTORTION ARE POLISHED PLATE GLASS AND _____ GLASS.

_____ 9. STANDARD INSULATED GLASS IS FILLED WITH _____ BETWEEN THE TWO SHEETS.

_____ 10. THIS GLASS HAS THE HIGHEST R VALUE OF ANY DOUBLE INSULATED GLASS UNIT: _____.

NONFERROUS METALS

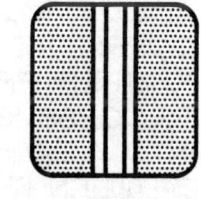

THE TERM <u>NONFERROUS METAL</u> APPLIES TO ALL METALS USED ON THE JOB THAT DO NOT CONTAIN IRON. MOST OF THESE METALS HAVE A COMMON CHARACTERISTIC OF BEING MORE RESISTANT TO CORROSION THAN IRON. NONFERROUS METALS USUALLY COST MORE THAN IRON, SO THEIR USE IS GENERALLY LIMITED TO AREAS WHERE FERROUS METALS ARE UNACCEPTABLE. SOME OF THE MORE COMMON METALS IN THIS GROUP ARE ALUMINUM, COPPER, ZINC, BRASS, AND BRONZE.

ALUMINUM
ALUMINUM HAS A WIDE NUMBER OF USES RANGING FROM WINDOWS TO NAILS. THE PRODUCTION OF ALUMINUM IS QUITE COSTLY AND USES

BUILDING MATERIALS | 12-41

SUBSTANTIAL AMOUNTS OF ENERGY. BAUXITE ORE IS MINED AND MIXED WITH SODA ASH AND QUICK LIME TO PRODUCE A MATERIAL CALLED <u>ALUMINA</u>. IT TAKES 8,000 POUNDS OF BAUXITE, 3,000 POUNDS OF COAL, 1,300 POUNDS OF CARBON, AND 20,000 KILOWATT HOURS OF ELECTRICITY TO PRODUCE 2,000 POUNDS OF ALUMINUM. MOST ALUMINUM PRODUCTS ARE FORMED THROUGH A PROCESS CALLED <u>EXTRUSION</u>. A STEEL DIE IS MACHINED TO THE DESIRED PATTERN OF THE EXTRUSION. THE DIE IS THEN LOCKED INTO A CASTING MACHINE AND A HEATED PIECE OF ALUMINUM IS HYDRAULICALLY PRESSED THROUGH. THE RESULTING FORM IS A PERFECT DUPLICATE OF THE DIE PATTERN IN LENGTHS OF UP TO 30 FEET. ALUMINUM EXTRUSIONS ARE USED IN A NUMBER OF CONDITIONS, RANGING FROM WINDOW UNITS TO ROOF FLASHING. ALUMINUM SHEETS ARE USUALLY MEASURED BY THIER THICKNESS IN INCHES. A TYPICAL SHEET SIZE IS .019".

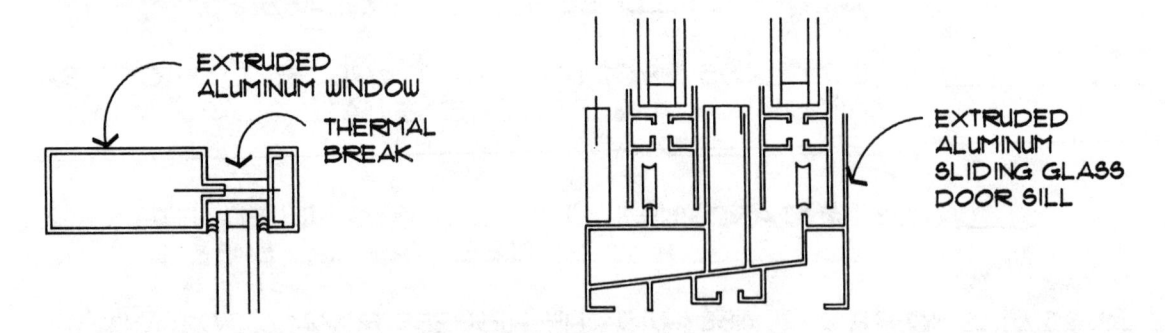

ALUMINUM RESISTS CORROSION BY FORMING A PROTECTIVE OXIDE COATING OVER THE OUTSIDE SURFACE. WHILE THIS COATING IS ONLY ABOUT 1/10,000" THICK, IT PROTECTS THE ALUMINUM FROM BEING CORRODED IN THE AIR. MOST ALUMINUM USED IN ARCHITECTURE IS FURTHER PROTECTED BY GIVING IT AN <u>ANODIZED</u> FINISH. THIS PROCESS IS ACCOMPLISHED BY SUBMERGING A PIECE OF ALUMINUM INTO A TANK OF ACID AND PASSING A DIRECT ELECTRICAL CURRENT BETWEEN IT AND THE ACID. THE RESULTING COAT OF OXIDE IS NOT ONLY THICKER BUT IT CAN BE GIVEN AN EXTREMELY DURABLE COLOR FINISH. THE CORROSION-RESISTANCE OF ALUMINUM MAKES IT AN EXCELLENT CHOICE FOR PRODUCTS FROM NAILS TO ROOFING SHEETS.

ALUMINUM IS A VERY ACTIVE ELEMENT, WHICH MEANS THAT IT MUST A PROTECTED FROM COMING IN CONTACT WITH OTHER METALS SUCH AS IRON OR COPPER. IF THE TWO DISSIMILAR METALS ARE IN DIRECT CONTACT IN THE PRESENCE OF WATER, A WEAK BATTERY ACTION (CALLED <u>GALVANIC ACTION</u>) WILL CAUSE ONE OF THE TWO METALS TO CORRODE. A SIMPLE SOLUTION TO THIS PROBLEM WOULD BE TO PAINT THE CONTACT AREA WITH BITUMINOUS PAINT.

BUILDING MATERIALS   12-42

COPPER

COPPER IS PERHAPS THE MOST VERSATILE METAL USED IN CONSTRUCTION. IT IS THE PRINCIPAL METAL USED IN PLUMBING AND ELECTRICAL WIRING, PLUS IT IS USED FOR ROOFING AND WALL FLASHING. THE MAJOR DISADVANTAGE OF COPPER IS ITS HIGH COST. COPPER IS REFINED BY MELTING ORE AND DRAWING OFF THE IMPURITIES. DEPENDING ON ITS INTENDED USE, THE METAL IS THEN EITHER ROLLED INTO SHEETS OR DRAWN INTO WIRE OR TUBE STOCK. COPPER HAS SEVERAL QUALITIES WHICH MAKE IT AN EXCELLENT BUILDING MATERIAL:

1. COPPER IS A VERY GOOD CONDUCTOR OF ELECTRICITY, WHICH MAKES IT ABOUT THE ONLY MATERIAL THAT IS USED FOR COMMERCIAL AND RESIDENTIAL WIRING.
2. COPPER CAN BE EASILY FASTENED TOGETHER USING SOLDER; THIS MAKES IT A GOOD CHOICE FOR WATERPIPES AND ROOF FLASHING.
3. COPPER RESISTS CORROSION BY FORMING A PROTECTIVE OXIDE ON THE SURFACE (IT APPEARS AS A GREEN COLOR CALLED PATINA). THIS MAKES IT A GOOD CHOICE FOR ROOFING.

THE ILLUSTRATIONS BELOW SHOW FLASHING CONDITIONS THAT COULD USE COPPER.

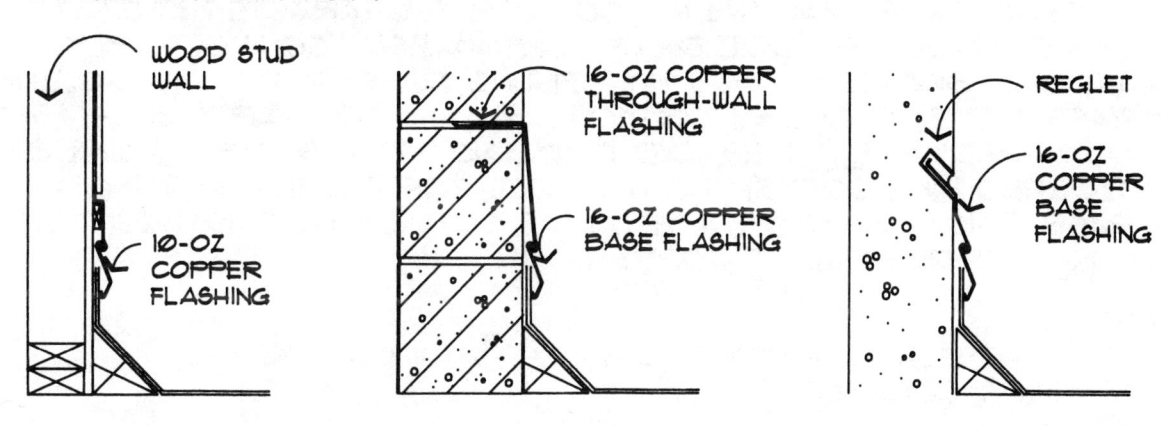

CORROSION-RESISTANCE AND THE EASE OF BENDING SHEETS MAKE COPPER A PREMIUM ROOFING MATERIAL. ITS HIGH COST HAS MADE IT AN EXPENSIVE CHOICE, HOWEVER. COPPER FLASHING IS MEASURED BY ITS WEIGHT IN OUNCES PER SQUARE FOOT. FOR EXAMPLE, THE NOTE "16 OZ COPPER" INDICATES THAT A 12" x 12" SQUARE WOULD WEIGH 16 OUNCES.

LIKE ALUMINUM, COPPER IS AN ACTIVE ELEMENT THAT MUST BE PROTECTED FROM COMING IN CONTACT WITH OTHER METALS. THE GREATEST GALVANIC ACTION OCCURS WHEN COPPER COMES IN CONTACT WITH ALUMINUM, FERROUS METAL, AND ZINC.

BUILDING MATERIALS

ZINC

ZINC IS A SILVER-GRAY-COLORED METAL THAT IS USED AS A PROTECTIVE COATING OVER METALS (USUALLY IRON) TO PREVENT CORROSION. ZINC PLATING ON IRON IS CALLED <u>GALVANIZED IRON</u> (IT IS ABBREVIATED G.I.). THE MOST COMMON METHOD OF PROVIDING A GALVANIZED FINISH IS TO COAT SHEET METAL OR NAILS WITH MOLTEN ZINC. HOT-DIPPED GALVANIZED PRODUCTS ARE INTENDED FOR OUTDOOR WEATHER CONDITIONS. IN A SECOND METHOD, CALLED <u>ELECTROGALVANIZING</u>, A THIN COAT OF ZINC IS APPLIED BY ELECTRICALLY PLATING IT ON IRON PRODUCTS SUCH AS NAILS. NAILS TREATED THIS WAY ARE INTENDED FOR INTERIOR USE WHERE THEY COULD COME IN CONTACT WITH A SLIGHT AMOUNT OF MOISTURE, SUCH AS WET LATEX PAINT. ZINC SHOULD NOT COME IN CONTACT WITH BRASS, BRONZE, OR IRON BECAUSE OF GALVANIC CORROSION.

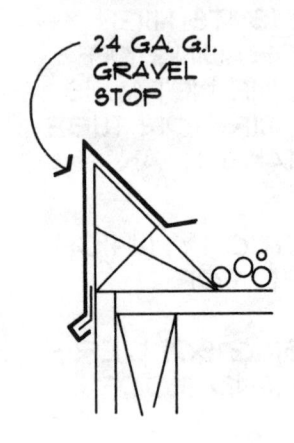

24 GA. G.I. GRAVEL STOP

BRASS AND BRONZE

BRASS IS A MAN-MADE METAL PRODUCED BY MELTING COPPER AND ZINC. BRASS HAS THE NONCORROSIVE CHARACTERISTICS OF COPPER, WHILE THE ADDITION OF ZINC MAKES IT CONSIDERABLY HARDER. BRONZE IS MADE BY MELTING COPPER AND TIN TOGETHER. BRASS AND BRONZE ARE COMMONLY CAST INTO SHAPES SUCH AS DOOR HARDWARE, HINGES, AND PLUMBING FITTINGS. BRASS CAN BE SOLDERED LIKE COPPER, SO IT IS USED FOR PLUMBING FITTINGS. BRASS IS NOT AS ACTIVE A METAL AS COPPER, SO IT IS USED TO CONNECT IRON PIPES TO COPPER.

REPLAY

FILL IN THE BLANK WITH THE WORD(S) THAT WILL MAKE THE STATEMENT CORRECT.

_____ 1. <u>NONFERROUS METAL</u> IS A TERM THAT COVERS ALL METAL IN CONSTRUCTION EXCEPT _____.

_____ 2. ALUMINUM IS FORMED INTO SHAPES BY PRESSING IT THROUGH A DIE IN A PROCESS CALLED _____.

_____ 3. THE PROCESS THAT GIVES ALUMINUM A COLOR FINISH IS CALLED _____.

_____ 4. _____ IS A METAL THAT CAN BE USED FOR WIRING, ROOF FLASHING, AND PLUMBING PIPE.

BUILDING MATERIALS | 12-44

_____ 5. A METAL THAT IS PRODUCED BY MELTING ZINC AND COPPER TOGETHER IS CALLED _____.

_____ 6. IF TWO DISSIMILAR METALS, SUCH AS ALUMINUM AND COPPER, COME IN CONTACT WITH EACH OTHER IN THE PRESENCE OF WATER, CORROSION WILL OCCUR THROUGH A PROCESS CALLED _____.

_____ 7. IRON IS DIPPED INTO MELTED _____ TO PROVIDE A RUST-RESISTANT COATING.

_____ 8. ALUMINUM RESISTS CORROSION BY FORMING A PROTECTIVE _____ COATING OVER THE SURFACE.

_____ 9. WHILE ALUMINUM IS MEASURED BY ITS THICKNESS IN INCHES, COPPER IS MEASURED BY _____.

_____ 10. MISCELLANEOUS METALS SUCH AS ALUMINUM, ZINC, AND COPPER HAVE THE COMMON CHARACTERISTIC OF _____ RESISTANCE.

SEALANTS

THE TERM <u>SEALANT</u> APPLIES TO A SPREADABLE PRODUCT USED TO BRIDGE A SPACE BETWEEN CONSTRUCTION MATERIALS. ONCE A SEALANT HAS BEEN APPLIED, IT USUALLY CURES TO A FLEXIBLE SEAL BETWEEN THE MATERIALS. MOST SEALANT IS PACKAGED IN CARTRIDGES THAT FIT INTO A CALKING GUN, BUT LARGE APPLICATIONS ARE FED THROUGH PRESSURE HOSES. SEALANTS HAVE BECOME VERY SOPHISTICATED IN THE LAST 30 YEARS. PRIOR TO THAT TIME, ABOUT THE ONLY PRODUCT AVAILABLE WAS PUTTY. THAT MATERIAL WAS MADE BY MIXING LINSEED OIL AND CALCIUM CARBONATE. PUTTY MUST BE COATED WITH PAINT OR IT WILL BECOME DRY AND BRITTLE. THERE ARE MANY DIFFERENT SEALANTS AVAILABLE IN ARCHITECTURE NOW, INCLUDING OIL-BASED, ACRYLIC, SILICONE, AND POLYURETHANE PRODUCTS. THESE MATERIALS HAVE SPECIFIC PROPERTIES WHICH NECESSITATE CARE IN MATCHING THE PRODUCT TO THE JOB.

BUILDING MATERIALS | 12-45

SEALANT TYPE	APPLICATION TEMPERATURE	COST	PRIMER REQUIRED	SUGGESTED USES AND PRECAUTIONS
LATEX	60-100° F	$	NO	RESIDENTIAL APPLICATIONS; 7-10 YEAR LIFE; WATER SOLUBLE WHILE CURING
ACRYLIC	40-130° F	$	NO	15-20 YEAR LIFE; ALLOWS 30% JOINT MOVEMENT; GOOD RESIDENTIAL SEALANT
POLYSULFIDE (ONE-PART)	60-100° F	$$	YES	GOOD COMMERCIAL SEALANT; STRONG ODOR; CURES WITH CHEMICAL REACTION WITH AIR
POLYSULFIDE (TWO-PART)	40-100° F	$$	YES	MIXED WITH CURING AGENT TO ACTIVATE CURE; WIDE RANGE OF COMMERCIAL APPLICATIONS; ALLOWS 75% JOINT MOVEMENT
POLYURETHANE (ONE-PART)	40-100° F	$$$	YES	GOOD COMMERCIAL SEALANT; BONDS WELL TO CONCRETE; AVAILABLE IN AEROSOL CANS; CURES WITH AIR CONTACT
POLYURETHANE (TWO-PART)	40-120° F	$$$	YES	SETS RAPIDLY WHEN MIXED WITH PRIMER; GOOD SEALANT WITH CONCRETE AND TRAFFIC AREAS
SILICONE	0-120° F	$$$$	NO	CURES WHEN EXPOSED TO AIR; ALLOWS 100% JOINT MOVEMENT; 50 YEAR LIFE; CAN'T BE PAINTED; NOT RECOMMENDED FOR CONCRETE APPLICATION

SEVERAL POINTS TO CONSIDER WHEN SELECTING SEALANTS ARE THE FOLLOWING:

- USE A PRODUCT THAT IS DESIGNED FOR THE CONSTRUCTION MATERIAL TO BE SEALED. FOR EXAMPLE, IT IS QUITE POSSIBLE THAT THE SEALANT USED TO CONNECT TWO PIECES OF SHEET METAL WOULD NOT BE RECOMMENDED TO SEAL GLASS OR WOOD.
- TEMPERATURE AND HUMIDITY LEVELS DURING APPLICATION SHOULD BE CONSIDERED. SILICONE CAN BE APPLIED AT BELOW 32° F, BUT A ONE-PART POLYSULFIDE MUST BE USED AT ROOM TEMPERATURE.
- CONSIDER THE COLOR OF THE SEALANT; SOME ARE AVAILABLE IN WHITE, BROWN, AND BLACK RANGES, WHILE OTHERS CAN BE PAINTED AFTER APPLICATION.
- THERE IS A WIDE RANGE OF LIFE EXPECTANCY FOR SEALANTS. SOME WILL LAST 5 YEARS, WHILE OTHERS WILL LAST 50 YEARS.
- SEALANT DESIGN SHOULD INVOLVE EXPECTED MOVEMENT; SOME PRODUCTS PERMIT A GREAT DEAL MORE MOVEMENT THAN OTHERS.
- THE COST OF THE MOST EXPENSIVE SEALANT CAN BE TEN TIMES GREATER THAN THE CHEAPEST.

BUILDING MATERIALS

SEALANTS ARE USED TO PROVIDE A FLEXIBLE WATERPROOF CONNECTION BETWEEN CONSTRUCTION MATERIALS. THE MAJOR COMPONENTS OF A GOOD JOINT SEAL ARE (1) THE SUBSTRATE, (2) THE PRIMER, (3) THE JOINT FILLER, AND (4) THE SEALANT.

SUBSTRATES IS THE TERM APPLIED TO THE BUILDING MATERIALS TO BE BRIDGED WITH THE SEALANT. SUBSTRATES CAN CONSIST OF WOOD, MASONRY, CONCRETE, GLASS, OR METAL. EACH MATERIAL POSES A UNIQUE CONDITION FOR SEALANT SELECTION. SUBSTRATES CAN GENERALLY BE PLACED IN TWO CATEGORIES: POROUS AND NON-POROUS. WOOD IS A POROUS SUBSTRATE WHILE GLASS IS NON-POROUS. SEALANTS MUST BE APPLIED TO SUBSTRATES THAT ARE CLEAN, DRY, AND FREE OF OIL.

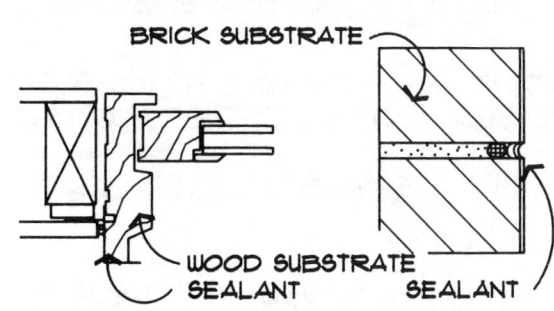

IN SOME CASES, A PRIMER MUST BE APPLIED TO THE SUBSTRATE BEFORE THE SEALANT. A PRIMER IS PARTICULARLY NECESSARY FOR CONCRETE AND MASONRY IN ORDER TO IMPROVE THE ADHESION BETWEEN THE TWO SUBSTRATES, AND IT IS USUALLY APPLIED WITH A THIN BRUSH COAT OR SPRAY. IT IS BEST TO REFER TO THE APPLICATION DIRECTIONS FROM THE SEALANT MANUFACTURER BEFORE USE.

A JOINT FILLER IS USED TO CONTROL THE DEPTH OF THE SEALANT JOINT BY PROVIDING A BACK-UP. IF THE JOINT TO BE FILLED IS TOO DEEP, SQUEEZING SEALANT INTO THE JOINT IS WASTEFUL AND OF POOR DESIGN. MOST JOINT FILLERS COME IN A ROPE FORM THAT IS "TOOLED" INTO THE JOINT CAVITY. A COMMONLY USED PRODUCT IS A URETHANE FOAM ROPE (CALLED ETHAFOAM). THE DIAMETER OF THE ROPE SHOULD BE GREATER THAN THE JOINT SPACE TO ASSURE A TIGHT FIT.

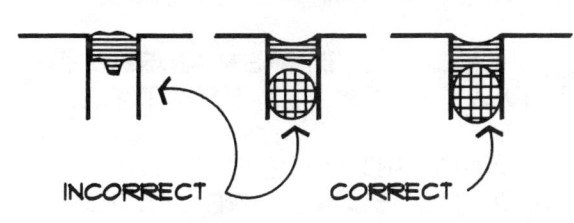

SEALANT MATERIALS ARE DEFINED IN THE CHART ON PAGE 12-46. NOTE THAT SEVERAL PRODUCTS ARE CALLED "TWO-PART"; THIS MEANS THAT THOSE SEALANTS ARE MIXED WITH A CATALYST TO CAUSE THEM TO CURE. MOST ONE-PART SEALANTS (SUCH AS SILICONE) USE MOISTURE IN THE AIR AS A CATALYST FOR CURING. SEALANTS SUCH AS ACRYLIC AND OIL-BASED RELEASE SOME OF THE SOLVENT CONTAINED IN THE SEALANT TO CAUSE THEM TO CURE. THE PROPORTIONS OF A SEALANT JOINT (WIDTH AND DEPTH) ARE IMPORTANT FOR GOOD DESIGN. REFER TO THE ABOVE ILLUSTRATION

BUILDING MATERIALS

FOR RECOMMENDED PROPORTIONS. ARCHITECT'S SPECIFICATIONS FREQUENTLY REQUIRE THE CONTRACTOR TO "TOOL" THE SEALANT TO FORCE IT INTO THE JOINT, ELIMINATING AIR POCKETS AND ENSURING CONTACT OF THE SEALANT WITH THE SIDES OF THE JOINT. THE JOINT SHOULD BE CONCAVE OR "FLUSH" (STRAIGHT ACROSS).

REPLAY

MARK (T) IF THE STATEMENT IS TRUE AND (F) IF THE STATEMENT IS FALSE.

_____ 1. TO ENSURE A PROPER BOND, IT IS IMPORTANT TO MOISTEN A JOINT WITH WATER BEFORE SEALANT IS APPLIED.

_____ 2. SOME ONE-PART SEALANTS USE THE MOISTURE IN THE AIR TO CAUSE THEM TO CURE.

_____ 3. THE SUBSTRATE OF A JOINT IS THE MATERIAL ON WHICH THE SEALANT IS APPLIED.

_____ 4. SILICONE WOULD BE A POOR SEALANT CHOICE IF THE JOINT HAD TO BE PAINTED TO MATCH A WINDOW FRAME.

_____ 5. THE MOST EXPENSIVE SEALANT IS ALMOST ALWAYS THE BEST CHOICE FOR THE JOB.

_____ 6. PUTTY IS A POOR CHOICE FOR SEALANT BECAUSE IT BECOMES BRITTLE AND HARD IF IT IS EXPOSED TO AIR.

_____ 7. A PRIMER IS A CHEMICAL APPLIED TO THE JOINT TO CAUSE THE SEALANT TO CURE PROPERLY.

_____ 8. SOME SEALANTS CAN BE APPLIED AT TEMPERATURES OF 0° F, BUT MOST MUST BE USED AT ROOM TEMPERATURE.

_____ 9. INSTALL SEALANTS IN STRICT ACCORDANCE WITH THE MANUFACTURER'S RECOMMENDATIONS AND PRECAUTIONS.

_____ 10. ONE PRODUCT THAT COULD BE USED AS A JOINT FILLER IS A URETHANE FOAM ROPE CALLED ETHAFOAM.

11-12. CIRCLE THE LETTER(S) THAT CORRESPOND TO THE SEALANT DETAILS THAT INDICATE A PROPER DESIGN.

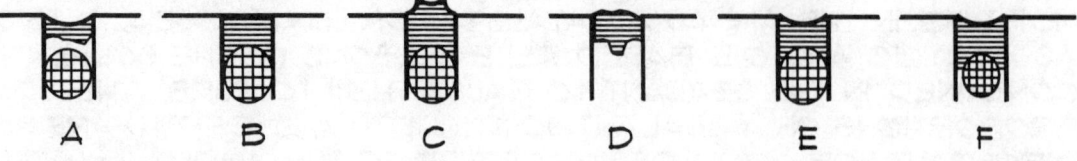

A   B   C   D   E   F

BUILDING MATERIALS   12-48

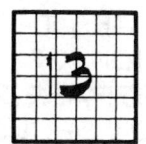

SITE PLANS AND SITE DETAILS

A WORKING DRAWING PACKAGE STARTS WITH A DRAWING SHOWING THE PROPERTY. A SITE PLAN TYPICALLY SHOWS THE CONTRACTOR THE COMPLETED CONDITION OF A PROJECT. A WAY TO VISUALIZE THIS IS TO PICTURE FLYING OVER THE SITE AFTER ALL WORK HAS BEEN COMPLETED. IN THIS UNIT, WE WILL COVER TOPICS RANGING FROM PARKING TO CHANGING THE GRADE OF A SITE. MOST RESIDENTIAL AND SMALL COMMERCIAL PROJECTS INCLUDE ALL SITE DATA ON ONE SHEET; LARGER COMMERCIAL PROJECTS CAN HAVE A "BEFORE" PLAN AND AN "AFTER" PLAN, THE FIRST DRAWING SHOWING EXISTING SITE CONDITIONS AND THE SECOND SHOWING ALL SITE IMPROVEMENTS.

IT IS ESSENTIAL THAT ALL SITE DATA IS RECEIVED BEFORE A PROJECT IS STARTED. SOME OF THIS INFORMATION IS NOTED BELOW.

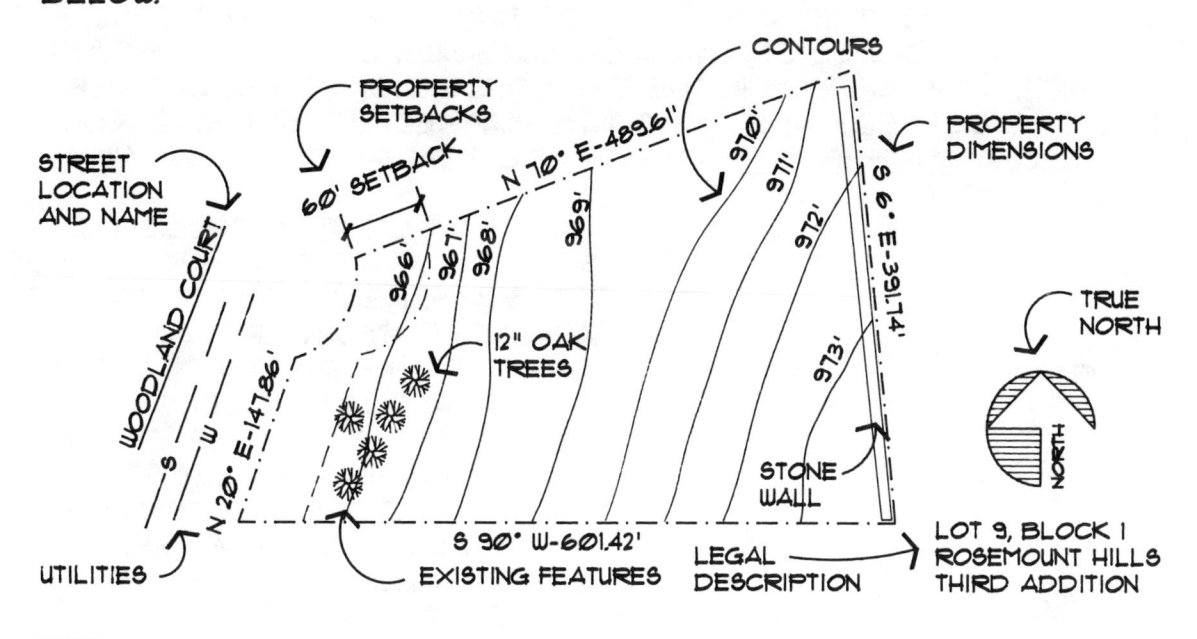

SITE PLAN AND DETAILS   13-1

THE CONTRACT BETWEEN AN ARCHITECT AND AN OWNER STATES THAT THE OWNER SHALL FURNISH ALL NECESSARY SITE INFORMATION. IT IS TYPICALLY THE LAW THAT SITE INFORMATION MUST BE PREPARED BY A LICENSED LAND SURVEYOR. THE ILLUSTRATION BELOW SHOWS SURVEY DATA FOR THE SITE. NOTE THAT EACH SIDE OF THE PROPERTY IS DEFINED WITH A BEARING DIRECTION AND LENGTH (GIVEN IN UNITS OF ONE-HUNDREDTH OF A FOOT). WHILE THE BEARING OF A LINE APPEARS COMPLEX AT FIRST GLANCE, IT IS ACTUALLY QUITE EASY TO UNDERSTAND. A LINE ALWAYS STARTS IN A TRUE NORTH OR SOUTH DIRECTION; THE ANGLE (OR <u>DEVIATION</u>) TO THE EAST OR WEST IS THEN GIVEN IN DEGREES, MINUTES, AND SECONDS.

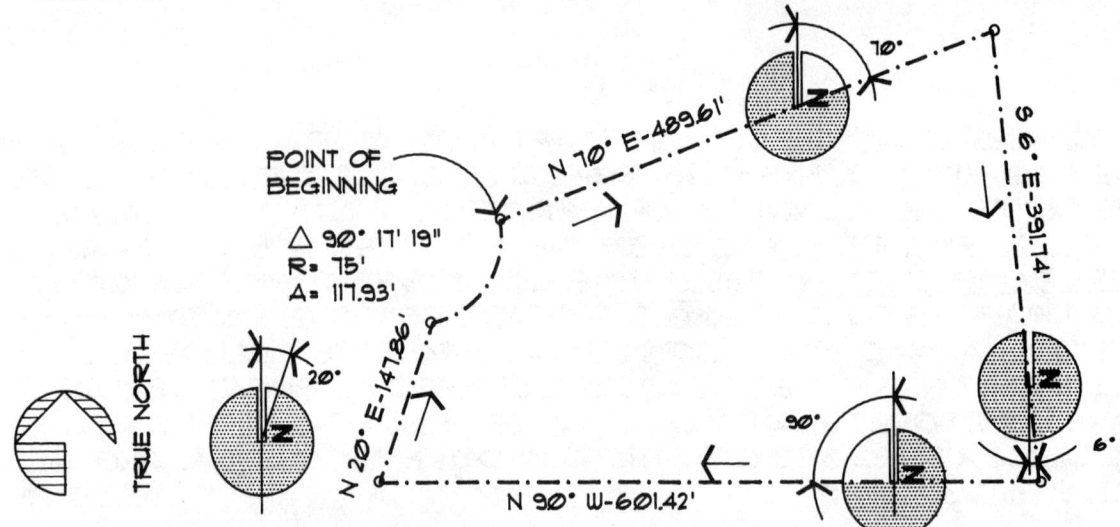

FOR EXAMPLE, THE PROPERTY LINE STARTING AT THE SPOT MARKED "POINT OF BEGINNING" SHOWS THAT THE LINE IS 70° EAST OF TRUE NORTH (N 70° E) AND ITS LENGTH IS 489.61'. A PROPERTY SURVEY STARTS FROM A POINT OF BEGINNING AND ROTATES IN EITHER A CLOCKWISE OR COUNTERCLOCKWISE DIRECTION AROUND THE SITE. (THE ARROWS IN THE EXAMPLE INDICATE A CLOCKWISE SURVEY.) CORNERS ARE TYPICALLY MARKED WITH A METAL ROD (CALLED A <u>PROPERTY PIN</u>), WHICH ARE INDICATED ON A DRAWING WITH A CIRCLE.

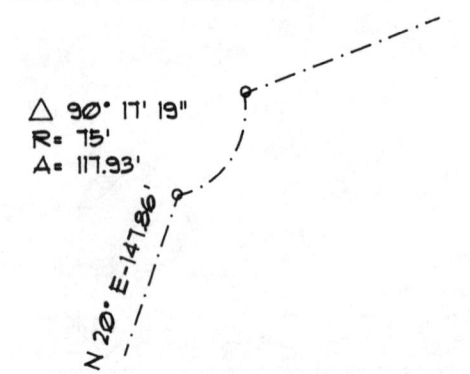

THE EXAMPLE ALSO SHOWS THE SURVEY DATA FOR AN ARC. THREE ITEMS ARE REQUIRED TO INDICATE A PORTION OF AN ARC: (1) THE ANGLE, (2) THE RADIUS OF THE CIRCLE, AND (3) THE LENGTH OF THE ARC. THE ANGLE OF THE ARC (Δ) IS 90 DEGREES, 17 MINUTES, AND 19 SECONDS, WHILE THE ACTUAL LENGTH OF THE ARC IS 117.93' (ABOUT 117'-11 1/8").

SITE PLANS AND DETAILS

THE NEXT ITEM ON THE PLAN DEFINES THE SLOPE OF THE SITE; THIS IS CALLED THE <u>TOPOGRAPHY</u>. A TOPOGRAPHIC SURVEY FOR A SMALL SITE IS ACCOMPLISHED BY FIRST MARKING A GRID ON THE LAND (50' OR 100' SPACING IS COMMON) AND THEN USING A LEVEL TO DETERMINE GRADE AT EACH POINT ON THE GRID. A SURVEY IS STARTED FROM A KNOWN POINT OF ELEVATION, CALLED THE BENCH MARK (B. M.). THE BENCH MARK IS GIVEN IN FEET ABOVE SEA LEVEL; FIRE HYDRANTS ARE FREQUENTLY USED BY CITIES IN RECORDING THIS DATA. THE EXAMPLE BELOW SHOWS HOW A SPECIFIC ELEVATION IS DETERMINED USING THIS METHOD.

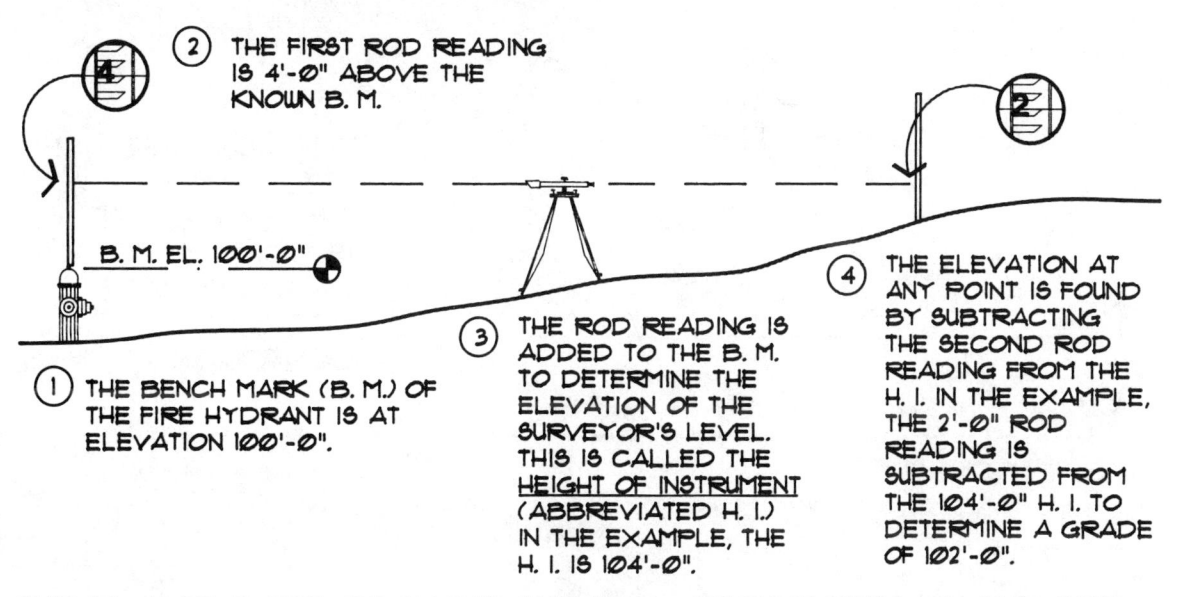

② THE FIRST ROD READING IS 4'-0" ABOVE THE KNOWN B. M.

B. M. EL. 100'-0"

① THE BENCH MARK (B. M.) OF THE FIRE HYDRANT IS AT ELEVATION 100'-0".

③ THE ROD READING IS ADDED TO THE B. M. TO DETERMINE THE ELEVATION OF THE SURVEYOR'S LEVEL. THIS IS CALLED THE <u>HEIGHT OF INSTRUMENT</u> (ABBREVIATED H. I.) IN THE EXAMPLE, THE H. I. IS 104'-0".

④ THE ELEVATION AT ANY POINT IS FOUND BY SUBTRACTING THE SECOND ROD READING FROM THE H. I. IN THE EXAMPLE, THE 2'-0" ROD READING IS SUBTRACTED FROM THE 104'-0" H. I. TO DETERMINE A GRADE OF 102'-0".

THE EXAMPLE BELOW SHOWS THE ELEVATION POINTS ON THE SITE.

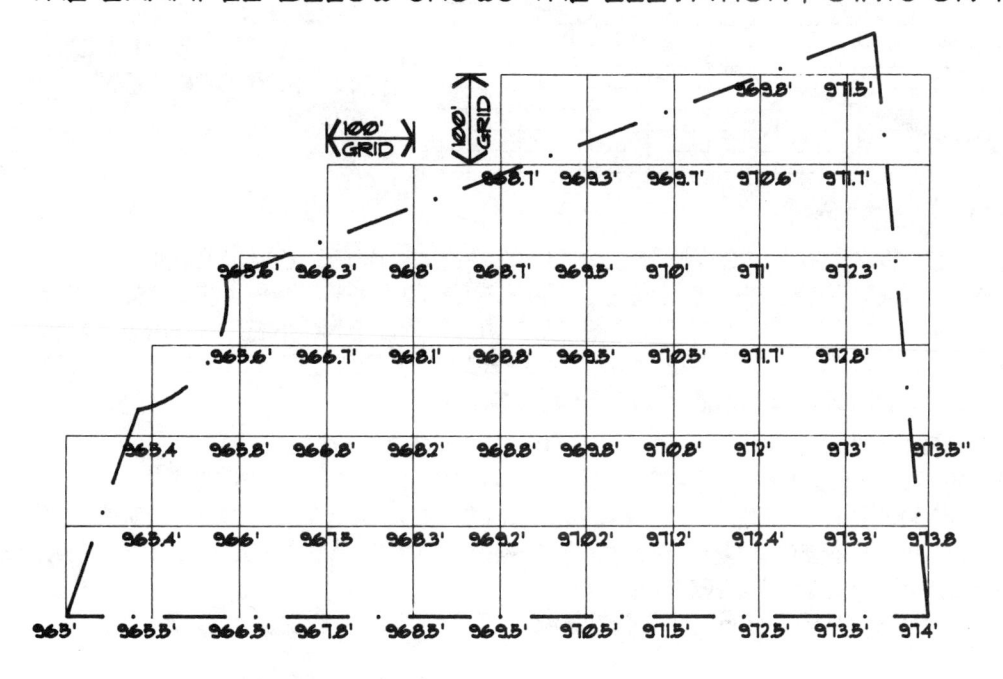

SITE PLANS AND DETAILS   13-3

THE NEXT STEP INVOLVES TRANSLATING THE DATA INTO CONTOUR LINES (ALSO CALLED <u>TOPOGRAPHIC CONTOURS</u>). THE LINES ARE GENERATED BY CONNECTING EVEN FOOT MARKS ON THE GRID INTO A SMOOTH CURVE. A WAY TO VISUALIZE THIS IS TO CONSTRUCT A CARDBOARD MODEL OF THE SITE WITH EACH CONTOUR MAKING UP A SEPARATE LAYER. THE RESULTING MODEL WOULD SHOW THE SLOPE OF THE HILL. THE ILLUSTRATION BELOW SHOWS THE TOPOGRAPHIC SITE PLAN. THE SECTION MARKED "A-A" SHOWS A CROSS SECTION CUT THROUGH THE SITE.

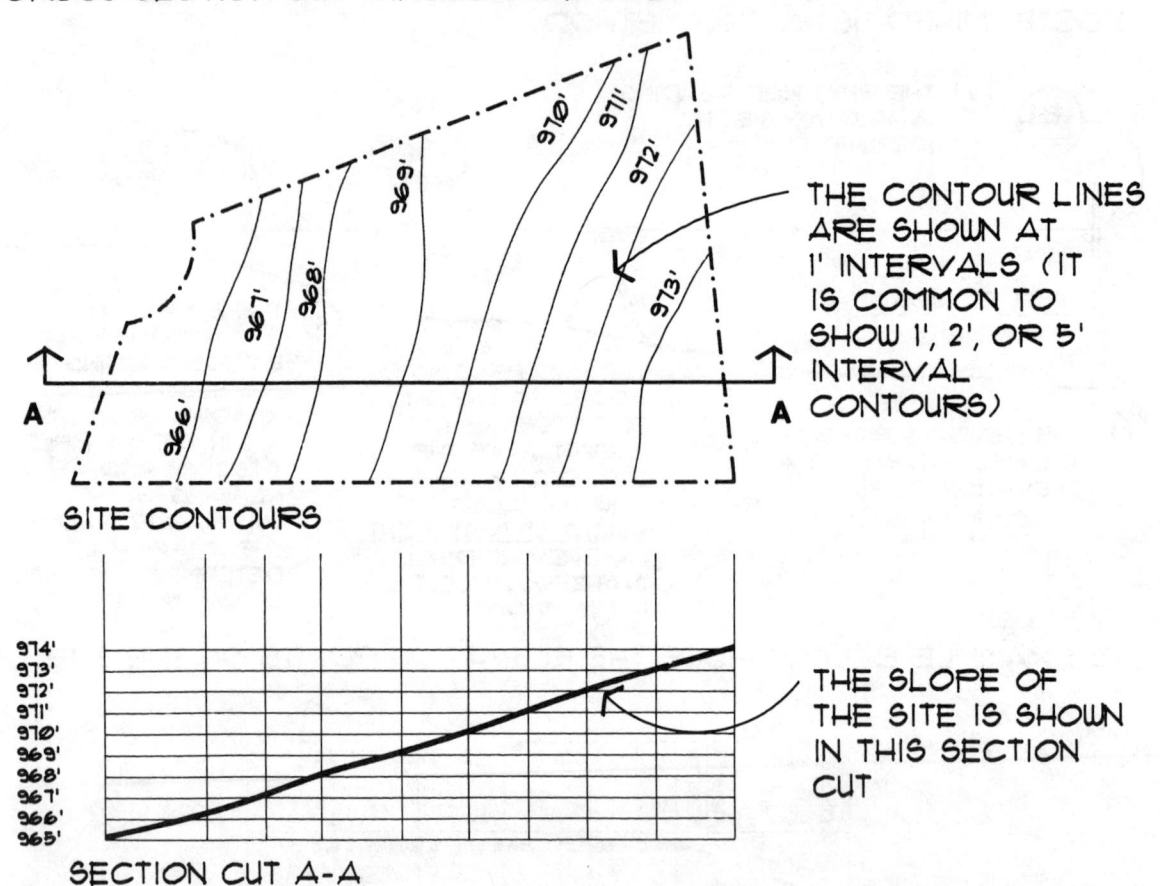

THE CONTOUR LINES ARE SHOWN AT 1' INTERVALS (IT IS COMMON TO SHOW 1', 2', OR 5' INTERVAL CONTOURS)

SITE CONTOURS

THE SLOPE OF THE SITE IS SHOWN IN THIS SECTION CUT

SECTION CUT A-A

A COMMON CONDITION IN SITE PLANNING REQUIRES CHANGING TOPOGRAPHIC CONTOURS TO MEET THE NEEDS OF THE NEW BUILDING. SITE GRADING IS TYPICALLY DONE BY A CIVIL ENGINEER HIRED BY THE ARCHITECT. SOME OF THE MAJOR POINTS TO BE CONSIDERED IN CHANGING CONTOURS ARE THE FOLLOWING:

1. MOVING EARTH ON OR OFF A SITE IS COSTLY; IT IS LESS EXPENSIVE TO "SCULPT" THE SITE WITH FILL AVAILABLE.
2. THE SITE (PARTICULARLY PARKING AREAS) MUST DRAIN TO SEWERS.
3. TOPOGRAPHIC LINES MUST REMAIN THE SAME AT PROPERTY LINES.
4. CONTOUR LINES CAN'T CROSS.
5. CONTOUR LINES MUST BE IN ORDER (970' MUST FOLLOW 969').

SITE PLANS AND DETAILS

THE SITE PLAN BELOW ILLUSTRATES SEVERAL SOLUTIONS FOR THE FIRE STATION PROJECT. EXISTING CONTOURS ARE SHOWN AS DASHED LINES, WHILE CHANGES IN TOPOGRAPHY ARE ILLUSTRATED AS SOLID LINES. NOTE THAT CONTOURS START AND STOP AT THE SAME POINTS ALONG THE PROPERTY LINE.

A REVIEW OF THE SITE SHOWS THAT GRADE RISES FROM 721' AT THE SOUTH ENTRANCE TO 723' ON THE NORTH SIDE OF THE PROPOSED BUILDING. THE DESIGN REQUIRES TWO ENTRANCES FOR THE FIRE TRUCKS THAT MUST BE AT THE SAME GRADE. THIS REQUIREMENT SUGGESTS THAT THE BUILDING SHOULD BE PLACED ON A LEVEL PLATEAU AT ELEVATION 722'-6". THE REMAINDER OF THE BUILDING IS PLACED 6" HIGHER AT ELEVATION 723'-0". NOTE HOW CONTOUR 722' IS WRAPPED AROUND THE BUILDING TO ALLOW FORMATION OF THE PLATEAU. GRADE CONDITIONS AT THE BERM (A SLOPED HILL) ALONG THE EAST PARKING LOT ARE SOLVED BY BUILDING A RETAINING WALL. ONCE ROUGH TOPOGRAPHY IS DETERMINED, IT IS NECESSARY TO REVIEW SPECIFIC CONCERNS, SUCH AS WATER DRAINAGE, IN THE PARKING LOT. THIS CAN BE DONE BY NOTING NECESSARY ELEVATION POINTS ON A SKETCH OF THE PARKING AREA.

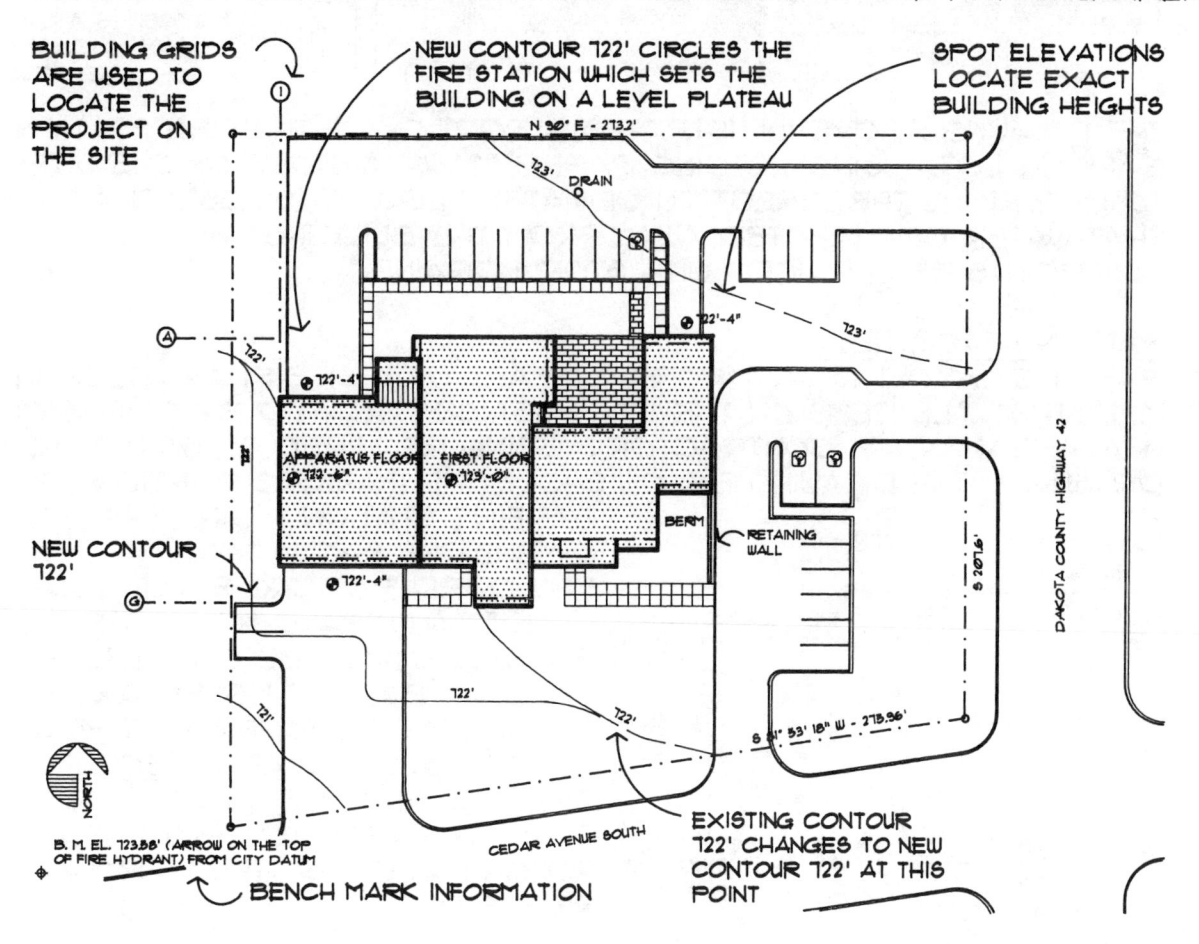

SITE PLANS AND DETAILS   13-5

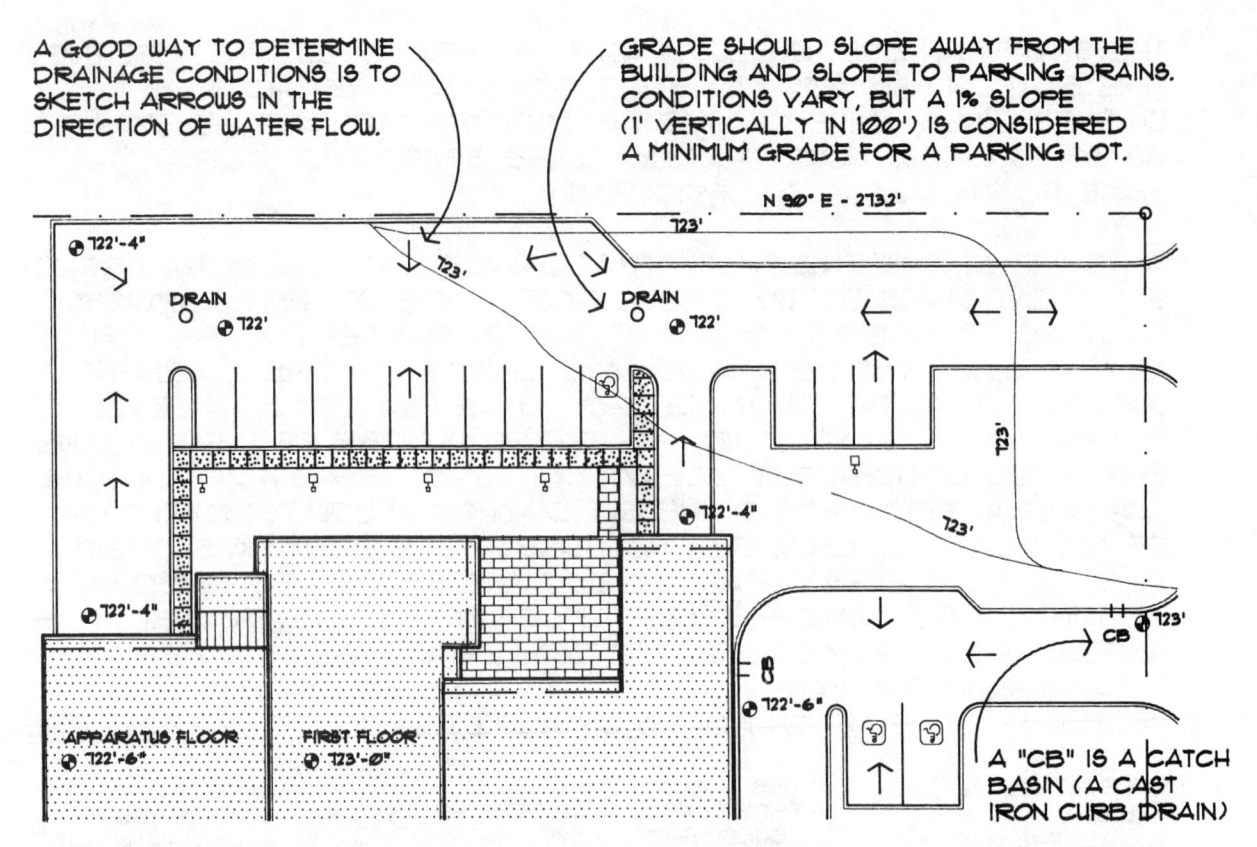

A GOOD WAY TO DETERMINE DRAINAGE CONDITIONS IS TO SKETCH ARROWS IN THE DIRECTION OF WATER FLOW.

GRADE SHOULD SLOPE AWAY FROM THE BUILDING AND SLOPE TO PARKING DRAINS. CONDITIONS VARY, BUT A 1% SLOPE (1" VERTICALLY IN 100') IS CONSIDERED A MINIMUM GRADE FOR A PARKING LOT.

A "CB" IS A CATCH BASIN (A CAST IRON CURB DRAIN)

THE DRAWING ABOVE ILLUSTRATES A PORTION OF THE FIRE STATION PARKING LOT. USING TRACING PAPER, MARK ARROWS ON THE SITE TO DETERMINE THE DIRECTION OF WATER FLOW. IT IS ESSENTIAL THAT WATER BE DIRECTED AWAY FROM THE BUILDING AND THAT LOW POINTS BE SERVICED WITH STORM DRAINS.

PARKING FACILITIES

PARKING LAYOUT IS AN IMPORTANT PART OF A SITE PLAN. KEEP IN MIND THAT ALL ITEMS ON THE SITE MUST BE LOCATED BY DIMENSION (RATHER THAN THE CONTRACTOR'S BEING REQUIRED TO SCALE THE DRAWING). THE DRAWING BELOW SHOWS THE PARKING PORTION OF THE FIRE STATION PLAN. THE DIMENSIONS SHOWN FOR A STANDARD PARKING STALL, TWO-LANE TRAFFIC, AND HANDICAP PARKING COULD BE CONSIDERED TYPICAL (BUT NOT NECESSARILY THE RULE). CONSULT A REFERENCE SOURCE, SUCH AS ARCHITECTURAL GRAPHIC STANDARDS, AND USE TRACING PAPER TO PRODUCE A ROUGH LAYOUT OF THE PARKING REQUIREMENTS.

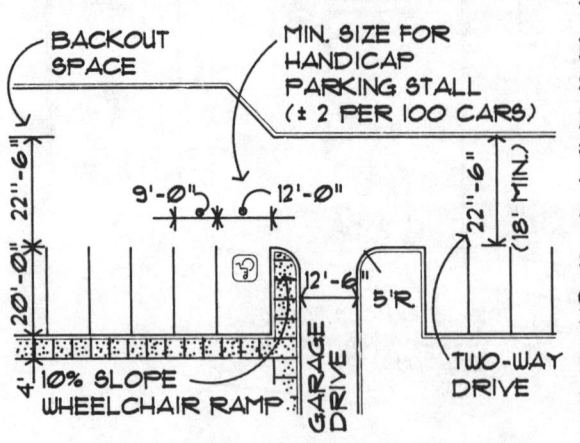

SITE PLANS AND DETAILS   13-6

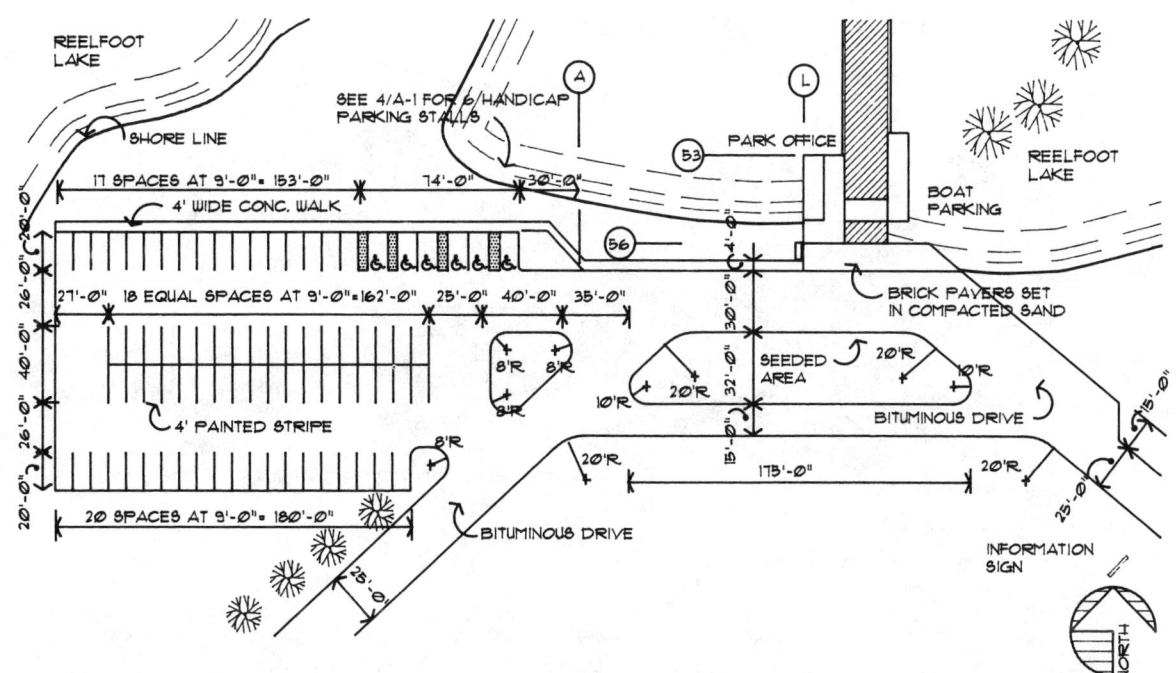

THE SITE PLAN ABOVE ILLUSTRATES A PARKING SOLUTION FOR THE REELFOOT LAKE RESTAURANT PROJECT. THE ENTRY TO THE SITE IS FROM THE SOUTHEAST AND TRAFFIC TRAVELS IN A COUNTER-CLOCKWISE PATTERN. THE DESIGN ALLOWS A SEPARATE DROP-OFF DRIVE FOR THE MOTEL AND RESTAURANT ENTRY; THE 30' ROAD WIDTH ALLOWS TEMPORARY PARKING FOR CHECK-IN. THE NARROW ROAD TO THE SOUTH PERMITS DIRECT ACCESS TO THE PARKING LOT. THE LOT PROVIDES PARKING FOR 73 STANDARD STALLS AND 5 HANDICAP SPACES. PARKING IS SET AT 90° – THIS REQUIRES A GREATER TRAFFIC CORRIDOR WIDTH BUT ALLOWS ACCESS FROM EITHER DIRECTION. THE ILLUSTRATION BELOW SHOWS A BLOW-UP OF A PORTION OF THE PARKING. IT IS IMPORTANT TO STUDY THE DESIGN FOR VEHICLE TRAFFIC. THIS TYPICALLY REQUIRES DEVELOPING (ON TRACING PAPER) SEVERAL SCHEMES THAT REFLECT DIFFERENT CONCEPTS. A GOOD APPROACH IS TO MAKE NOTES ON EACH DRAWING POINTING OUT THE STRONG AND WEAK CONDITIONS OF THE SOLUTION. THE REELFOOT SITE SOLUTION SEEMS TO WORK WELL IN ALLOWING A VIEW OF THE BUILDING AND LAKE TO A DRIVER DRIVING INTO THE SITE.

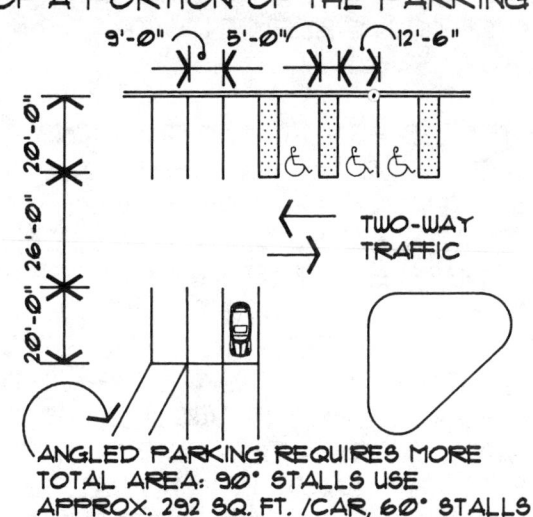

ANGLED PARKING REQUIRES MORE TOTAL AREA: 90° STALLS USE APPROX. 292 SQ. FT./CAR, 60° STALLS REQUIRES APPROX. 347 SQ. FT./CAR

SITE PLANS AND DETAILS   13-7

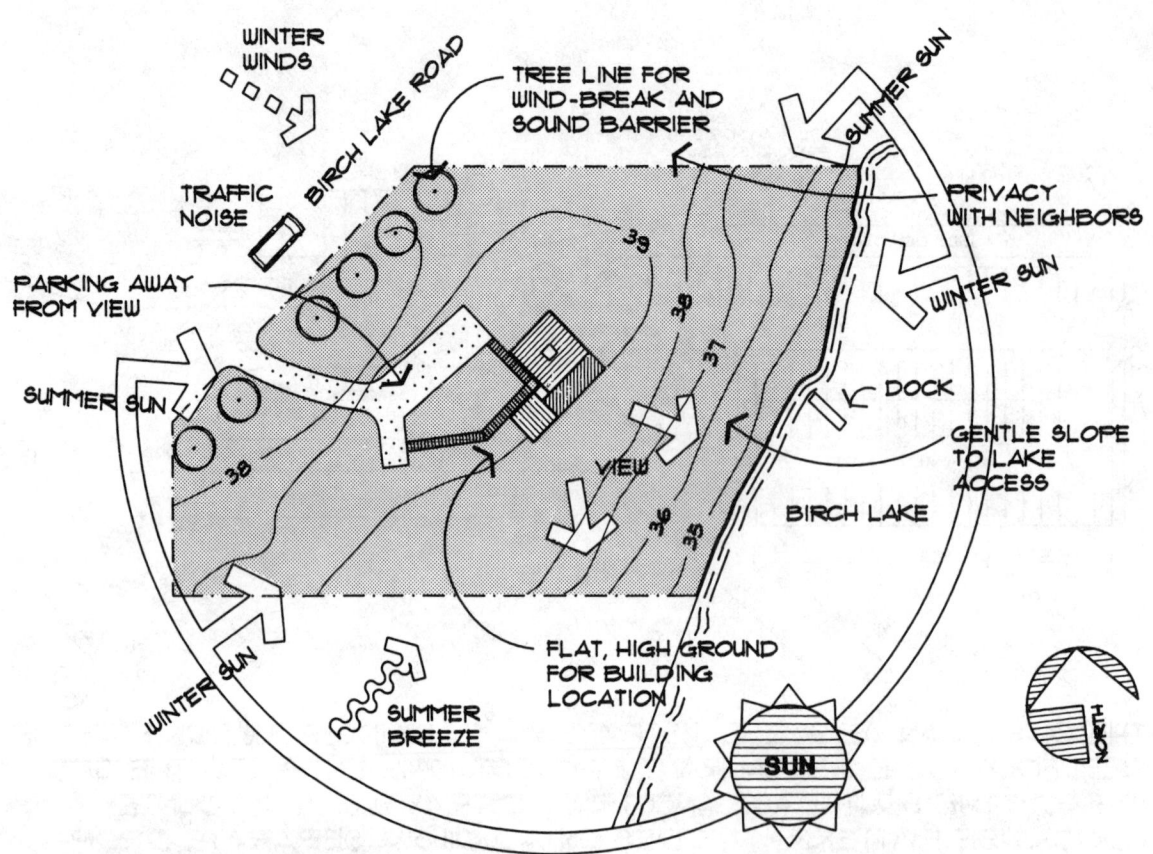

SITE DESIGN

IN THIS SECTION WE WILL REVIEW SOME OF THE CONCERNS THAT SHOULD BE ADDRESSED IN DETERMINING SITE DESIGN. DECISIONS REGARDING THE LOCATION OF PARKING AND THE BUILDING ARE MADE ON THE BASIS OF THE FOLLOWING: PHYSICAL ANALYSIS AND DESIGN CRITERIA. IN THE FIRST SECTION OF THIS UNIT WE CONSIDERED SEVERAL PHYSICAL CONCERNS SUCH AS GRADE, THE SIZE OF A SITE, AND VEHICLE REQUIREMENTS. AS YOU CAN SEE, SITE PLANNING REQUIRES THE STUDY OF MANY ELEMENTS THAT WON'T BE FOUND ON A SITE SURVEY.

THE SITE PLAN SHOWN ABOVE ILLUSTRATES SEVERAL CONCERNS THAT SHOULD BE ADDRESSED BEFORE BUILDING AND PARKING LOCATIONS ARE FINALIZED. NOTES ON THE CABIN SITE PLAN RELATE TO ELEMENTS SUCH AS THE BEST VIEW, SUMMER BREEZES, AND TRAFFIC NOISE. WHILE NONE OF THESE ELEMENTS WILL APPEAR ON THE FINAL WORKING DRAWINGS, IT WOULD BE QUITE EASY TO ARGUE THAT THE SUCCESS OF THE PROJECT IS TIED TO THEIR STUDY. LET'S CONSIDER AN ELEMENT AS SIMPLE AS THE PREVAILING WINDS IN THE SUMMER. THE LOCATION OF A SCREEN PORCH WOULD PROVE MORE SUCCESSFUL IF THIS FEATURE WERE ACCOUNTED FOR IN THE DESIGN. A GOOD WAY TO BEGIN A SITE DESIGN STUDY WOULD BE TO MAKE A TRACING PAPER SKETCH OF THE SITE AND ADD NOTES

SITE PLANS AND DETAILS   13-8

SPECIFIC TO SITE DESIGN.

BELOW ARE LISTED SEVERAL CRITERIA THAT MAY BE USED TO EVALUATE AND DESIGN SITE CONDITIONS. WE WILL USE THE EXAMPLE OF THE "SKYWAY HOUSE" (UNIT 23) TO ILLUSTRATE THESE CRITERIA. THE SITE HAS SOME EXTREMELY GOOD FEATURES (FOR EXAMPLE, A HIGH RIVER BLUFF VIEW), AND SOME VERY DIFFICULT CONDITIONS (SUCH AS A FREEWAY TO THE WEST AND A SIZE OF UNDER 5,000 SQ FT). KEEP IN MIND THAT THE FOLLOWING CHECKLIST CAN BE USED TO EVALUATE ANY SITE.

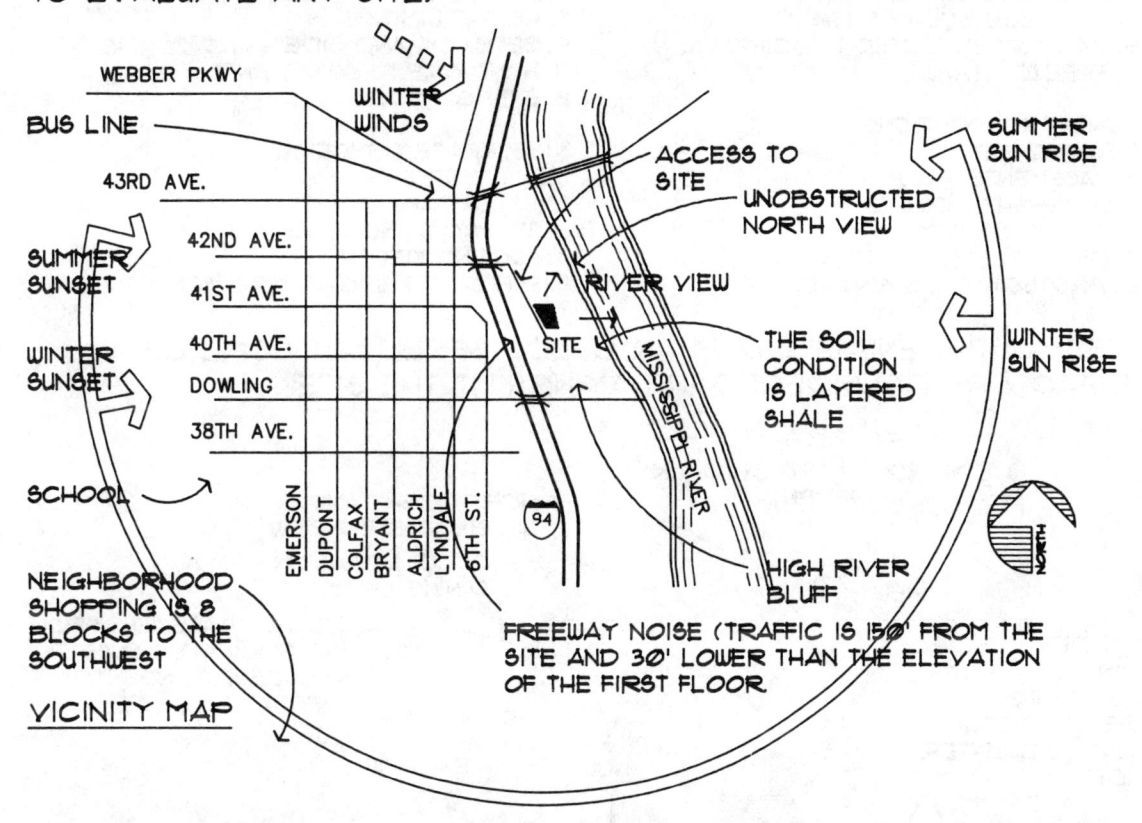

VICINITY MAP

SITE ANALYSIS CHECK LIST   (USE THIS LIST TO DETERMINE THE STRONG AND WEAK FEATURES OF A SITE)

A. LAND USE
　1. EXISTING TREES
　2. EXISTING WET LANDS
　3. HISTORICAL VALUE
　4. NATURE AND WILDLIFE
　5. WATERWAYS

B. UTILITIES AND TRANSPORTATION
　1. EXISTING WATER, SEWER AND GAS
　2. HIGHWAY ACCESS
　3. ACCESS TO PUBLIC TRANSPORTATION
　4. PROPOSED SITE DENSITY
　　(I. C., HOUSING PER ACRE)
　5. MUNICIPAL SERVICES (I. C., FIRE)

C. COMMUNITY SERVICES
　1. SCHOOLS
　2. SHOPPING
　3. LIBRARIES
　4. POST OFFICE
　5. MEDICAL
　6. RECREATION

D. IMPACT ON TRAFFIC
　1. RELATIONSHIP TO AREA TRAFFIC
　2. COMMUNITY ACCESS TO SITE
　3. RELATIONSHIP TO ADJACENT BUILDINGS
　4. SECURITY
　5. IMPACT ON URBAN FABRIC

SITE PLANS AND DETAILS

SITE ANALYSIS CHECKLIST (CONTINUED)

E. PHYSICAL CHARACTERISTICS
1. EXISTING CONTOURS
2. WATERSHED THROUGH SITE
3. EXISTING FEATURES (I. C., ROCK, WALLS, POWER LINES)
4. EXISTING ROADS AND LOGICAL ACCESS

F. CLIMATE
1. SOLAR ANGLES
2. SITE ORIENTATION
3. ANNUAL RAIN AND SNOW
4. POSSIBLE SOLAR ENERGY
5. MAXIMUM EXPECTED PRECIPITATION
6. FREEZE / THAW

G. ZONING RESTRICTIONS
1. ZONING USE
2. EASEMENTS
3. WATERSHED RIGHTS
4. RIGHTS OF WAY
5. DEED RESTRICTIONS
6. PROTECTIVE COVENANTS

H. HUMAN CONSIDERATIONS
1. PUBLIC VS. PRIVATE SPACE
2. RELATIONSHIP OF DESIGNED SPACES
3. LIFESTYLES OF PEOPLE USING SITE
4. COMMUNITY ESTEEM AND VALUES

I. LEGAL
1. OCCUPANCY REQUIREMENTS
2. CONSTRUCTION TYPE
3. STRUCTURAL TYPE
4. FIRE PROTECTION
5. HEIGHT LIMITS
6. SETBACK AND SIDE YARD ZONING
7. HANDICAP REQUIREMENTS
8. ENERGY CODES

J. SUBSURFACE CONCERNS
1. SOIL TYPES
2. WATER TABLE
3. SEISMIC CONDITIONS
4. FOOTING DEPTH
5. EFFECT ON NEIGHBORING STRUCTURES

NOTES ON THE ENLARGED PLAN BELOW SPELL OUT SOME OF THE FACTORS CONSIDERED IN LAYING OUT THE SITE.

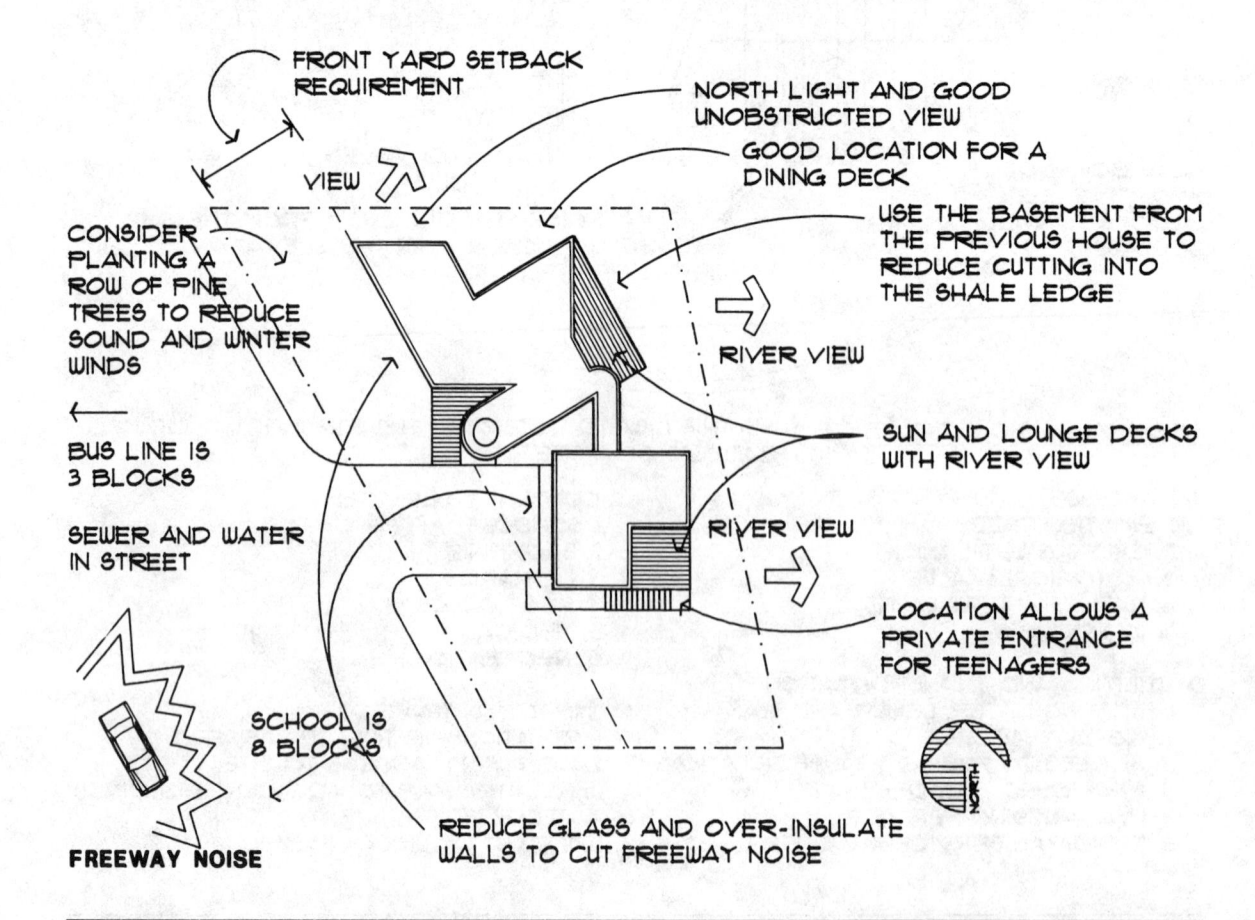

- FRONT YARD SETBACK REQUIREMENT
- VIEW
- NORTH LIGHT AND GOOD UNOBSTRUCTED VIEW
- GOOD LOCATION FOR A DINING DECK
- CONSIDER PLANTING A ROW OF PINE TREES TO REDUCE SOUND AND WINTER WINDS
- USE THE BASEMENT FROM THE PREVIOUS HOUSE TO REDUCE CUTTING INTO THE SHALE LEDGE
- RIVER VIEW
- BUS LINE IS 3 BLOCKS
- SEWER AND WATER IN STREET
- SUN AND LOUNGE DECKS WITH RIVER VIEW
- RIVER VIEW
- LOCATION ALLOWS A PRIVATE ENTRANCE FOR TEENAGERS
- SCHOOL IS 8 BLOCKS
- FREEWAY NOISE
- REDUCE GLASS AND OVER-INSULATE WALLS TO CUT FREEWAY NOISE

SITE PLANS AND DETAILS | 13-10

THE FOLLOWING SECTION WILL REVIEW THE STEP-BY-STEP ASSEMBLY OF A SITE DRAWING. IN ORGANIZING A DRAWING YOU SHOULD START WITH THE LARGEST PART OF THE SITE (THE BORDER) AND WORK YOUR WAY TO THE FINE DETAIL. IT IS IMPORTANT TO SOLVE CONDITIONS, SUCH AS TOPOGRAPHIC CHANGES, BEFORE STARTING THE WORKING DRAWING; THE SITE PLAN SHOULD REFLECT ALL CHANGES THAT ARE TO BE MADE ON THE PROJECT.

SITE WORK IS FREQUENTLY CONSTRUCTED BY A SEPARATE CONTRACTOR. FOR THAT REASON, IT IS IMPORTANT TO LOCATE ALL EXTERIOR DIMENSIONS AND MATERIALS ON THE SITE SHEET. DIMENSION STRINGS SHOULD INCLUDE THE RADIUS OF CURBS AND WIDTH OF ROADS. WHEN MAKING A FINAL CHECK OF THE SITE DRAWING, REMEMBER THAT THE CONTRACTOR SHOULD NOT BE REQUIRED TO SCALE THE DRAWING TO LOCATE ITEMS.

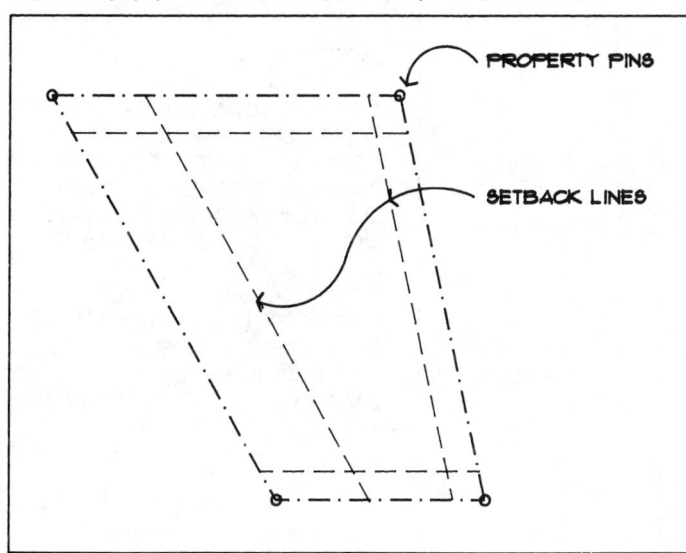

BOUNDARY LINES

START THE SITE PLAN BY LOCATING THE PROPERTY LINES. SITE DRAWINGS ARE COMMONLY DRAWN AT AN ENGINEER'S SCALE (I. C., 1"=20' TO 1"=50'). SELECT THE LARGEST SCALE THAT WILL WORK WITH THE SHEET LAYOUT. USE A DASH-DOT LINE TO DELINEATE THE PROPERTY AND DRAW A CIRCLE FOR EACH PROPERTY PIN. TYPICALLY, NORTH SHOULD POINT TO THE TOP OF THE DRAWING.

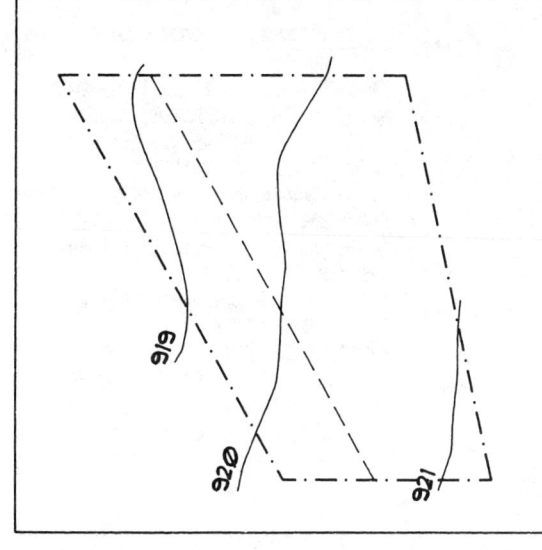

CONTOUR LINES

THE NEXT STEP IS TO LOCATE THE CONTOUR LINES ON THE SITE. EXISTING CONTOURS ARE DRAWN AS DASHED LINES; CHANGES IN CONTOURS ARE SHOWN AS SOLID LINES.

SITE PLANS AND DETAILS   13-11

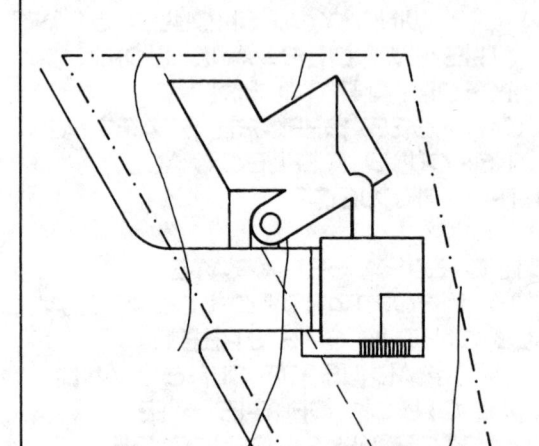

LOCATE BUILDING

IN THIS STEP THE BUILDING IS DRAWN ON THE SITE. KEEP IN MIND THAT THE BUILDING MUST BE DRAWN AT THE SAME SCALE AS THE SITE. A WAY TO SPEED THE BUILDING DRAWING PROCESS IS TO TRACE A REDUCED COPY OF THE ARCHITECTURAL PLAN. ALSO IN THIS STEP CURBS, DRIVES, AND WALKS ARE LOCATED ON THE SITE.

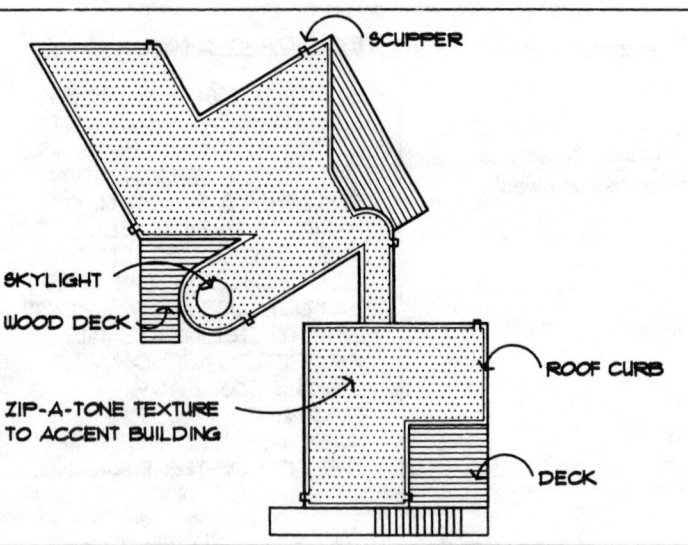

ROOF DETAIL

THIS DRAWING SHOWS AN ENLARGED VIEW OF THE PROJECT ROOF. THE SITE PLAN SHOULD SHOW ROOF DETAILS SUCH AS DRAINS, SKYLIGHTS, AND DECKS. IT IS COMMON TO USE A DOT-TEXTURE FILM (ONE PRODUCT IS ZIP-A-TONE) TO ACCENT THE BUILDING. THE FILM IS STUCK TO THE DRAWING AND CUT TO SIZE WITH A MAT KNIFE.

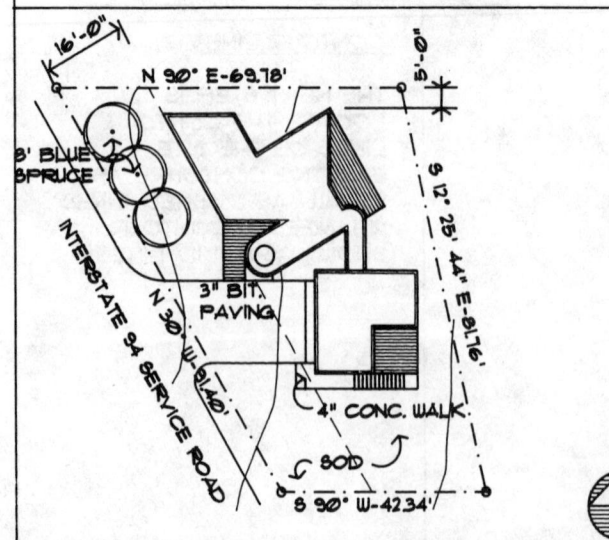

NOTES AND DIMENSIONS

THE FINAL STEP IS TO ADD NOTES, DIMENSIONS, AND DETAILS TO THE SITE. ORGANIZE DIMENSION STRINGS USING TRACING PAPER AND A FELT PEN. SITE NOTES SHOULD DEFINE OBJECTS SUCH AS WALK THICKNESS AND MATERIAL, TREE SPECIES, AND LOCATION OR DETAILS (FLAG POLE, BENCH, STEPS, ETC.). A NORTH ARROW SHOULD BE SHOWN.

SITE PLANS AND DETAILS   13-12

THE FOLLOWING IS A GENERAL CHECKLIST FOR ITEMS THAT SHOULD BE SHOWN ON WORKING DRAWING SITE PLANS.

SITE PLAN CHECKLIST

- ☐ NORTH ARROW
- ☐ TOPOGRAPHY (EXISTING)
- ☐ TOPOGRAPHY (CHANGES)
- ☐ STREET NAMES
- ☐ PROPERTY DIMENSIONS
- ☐ PROPERTY PINS
- ☐ CURB RADIUS
- ☐ BENCH MARKS
- ☐ SOD & SEED AREAS
- ☐ DRAWING TITLE / SCALE
- ☐ SITE DETAIL LOCATIONS
- ☐ FINISH FLOOR ELEVS.
- ☐ HANDICAP PARKING
- ☐ NEW LANDSCAPE
- ☐ EXT. LIGHT FIXTURES
- ☐ BUILDING LOCATION
- ☐ UTILITY LINES
- ☐ PAVING MATERIAL
- ☐ SIDEWALKS
- ☐ FENCES
- ☐ EXISTING STRUCTURES
- ☐ TREES & SHRUBS
- ☐ CONSTRUCTION LIMITS
- ☐ SOIL BORING LOCATIONS
- ☐ TEMPORARY FACILITIES
- ☐ ROOF DRAINS & SCUPPER
- ☐ CATCH BASINS & DRAINS
- ☐ GRADE ELEVATIONS
- ☐ OUTLINE PATIOS & DECKS
- ☐ LEGAL DESCRIPTION

SITE DETAILS

IT IS COMMON TO DRAW DETAILS ASSOCIATED WITH THE SITE ON THE SITE PLAN SHEET. THESE COULD INCLUDE THE FOLLOWING: HANDICAP PARKING STALLS, FLAGPOLES, OR BENCHES. SOME OF THE CONSTRUCTION DETAILS ASSOCIATED WITH SITE PLANS ARE SHOWN IN THE FOLLOWING ILLUSTRATIONS:

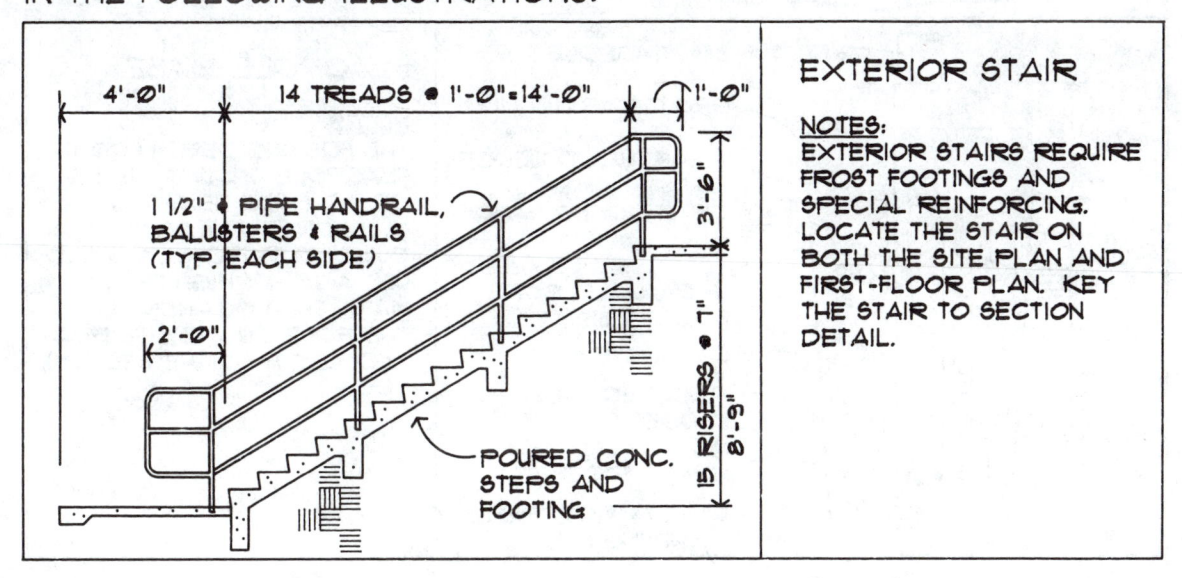

EXTERIOR STAIR

NOTES:
EXTERIOR STAIRS REQUIRE FROST FOOTINGS AND SPECIAL REINFORCING. LOCATE THE STAIR ON BOTH THE SITE PLAN AND FIRST-FLOOR PLAN. KEY THE STAIR TO SECTION DETAIL.

SITE PLANS AND DETAILS

WOOD BENCH

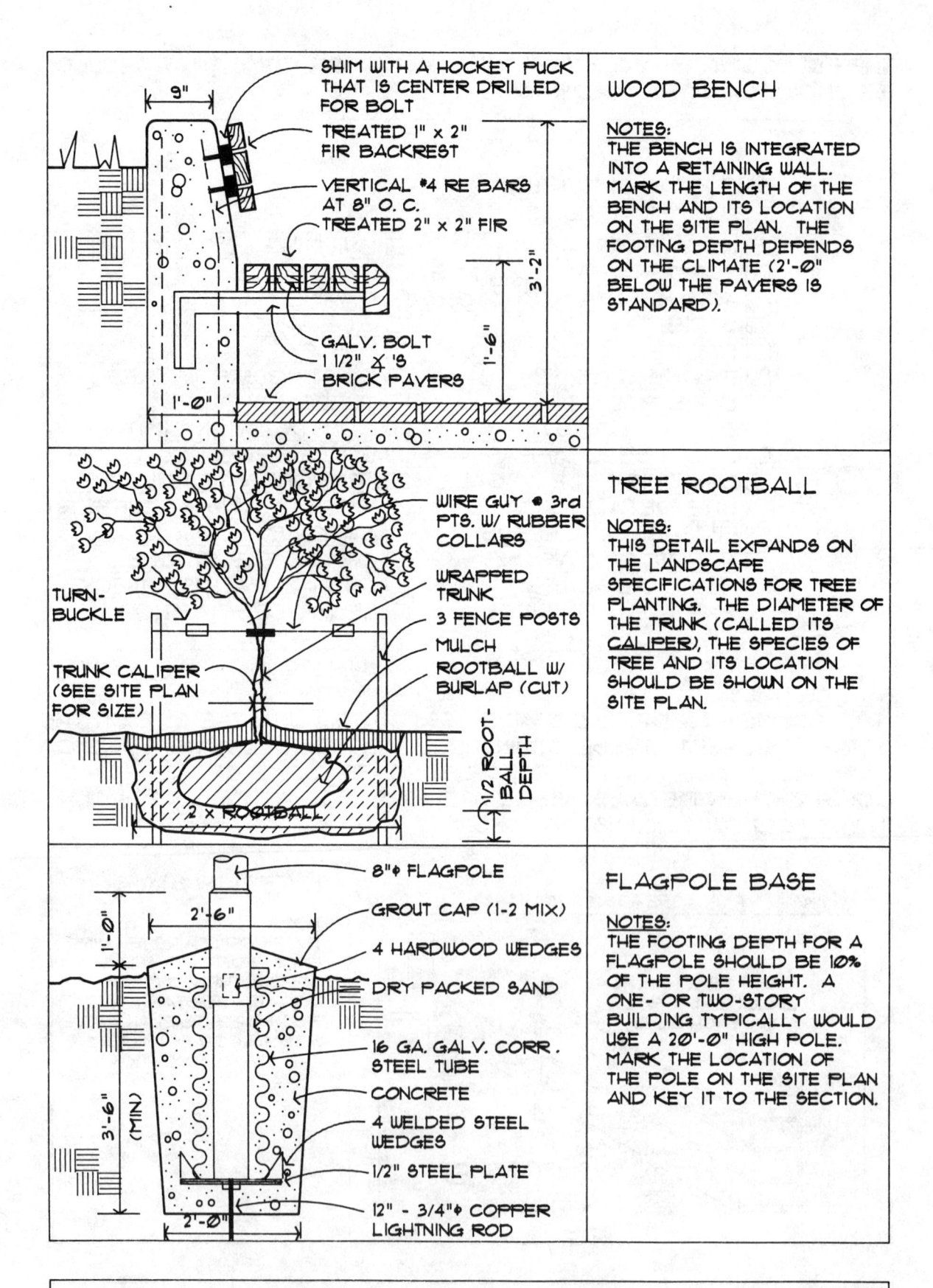

NOTES:
THE BENCH IS INTEGRATED INTO A RETAINING WALL. MARK THE LENGTH OF THE BENCH AND ITS LOCATION ON THE SITE PLAN. THE FOOTING DEPTH DEPENDS ON THE CLIMATE (2'-0" BELOW THE PAVERS IS STANDARD).

Labels:
- 9"
- SHIM WITH A HOCKEY PUCK THAT IS CENTER DRILLED FOR BOLT
- TREATED 1" x 2" FIR BACKREST
- VERTICAL #4 RE BARS AT 8" O.C.
- TREATED 2" x 2" FIR
- 3'-2"
- 1'-6"
- GALV. BOLT 1 1/2" x 'S
- BRICK PAVERS
- 1'-0"

TREE ROOTBALL

NOTES:
THIS DETAIL EXPANDS ON THE LANDSCAPE SPECIFICATIONS FOR TREE PLANTING. THE DIAMETER OF THE TRUNK (CALLED ITS CALIPER), THE SPECIES OF TREE AND ITS LOCATION SHOULD BE SHOWN ON THE SITE PLAN.

Labels:
- WIRE GUY @ 3rd PTS. W/ RUBBER COLLARS
- WRAPPED TRUNK
- 3 FENCE POSTS
- MULCH
- ROOTBALL W/ BURLAP (CUT)
- TURNBUCKLE
- TRUNK CALIPER (SEE SITE PLAN FOR SIZE)
- 1/2 ROOTBALL DEPTH
- 2 x ROOTBALL

FLAGPOLE BASE

NOTES:
THE FOOTING DEPTH FOR A FLAGPOLE SHOULD BE 10% OF THE POLE HEIGHT. A ONE- OR TWO-STORY BUILDING TYPICALLY WOULD USE A 20'-0" HIGH POLE. MARK THE LOCATION OF THE POLE ON THE SITE PLAN AND KEY IT TO THE SECTION.

Labels:
- 8"⌀ FLAGPOLE
- GROUT CAP (1-2 MIX)
- 4 HARDWOOD WEDGES
- DRY PACKED SAND
- 16 GA. GALV. CORR. STEEL TUBE
- CONCRETE
- 4 WELDED STEEL WEDGES
- 1/2" STEEL PLATE
- 12" - 3/4"⌀ COPPER LIGHTNING ROD
- 1'-0"
- 2'-6"
- 3'-6" (MIN)
- 2'-0"

SITE PLAN AND DETAILS

13-14

TRASH RECEPTACLE

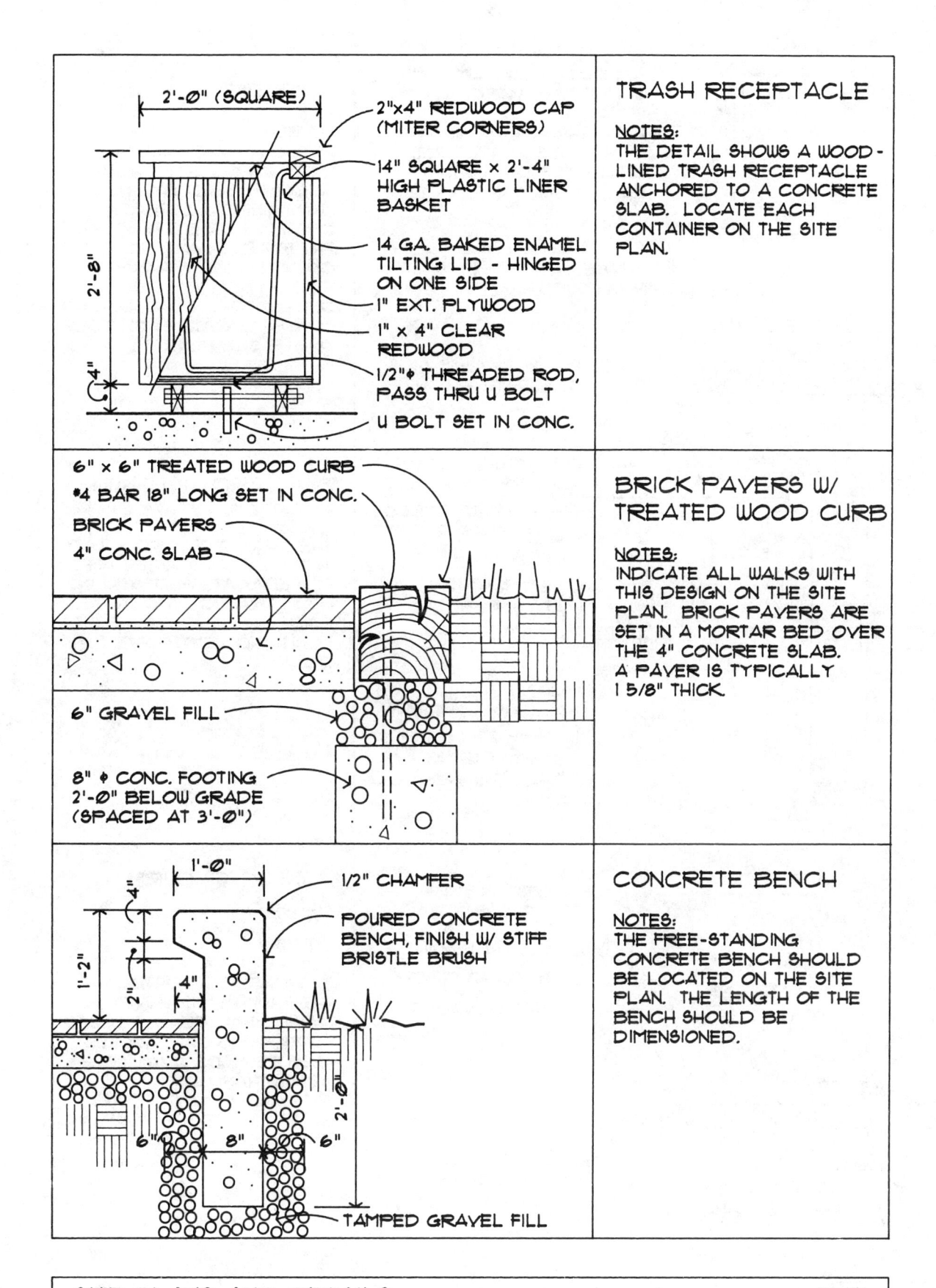

NOTES:
THE DETAIL SHOWS A WOOD-LINED TRASH RECEPTACLE ANCHORED TO A CONCRETE SLAB. LOCATE EACH CONTAINER ON THE SITE PLAN.

Labels (detail drawing):
- 2'-0" (SQUARE)
- 2'-8"
- 4"
- 2"x4" REDWOOD CAP (MITER CORNERS)
- 14" SQUARE x 2'-4" HIGH PLASTIC LINER BASKET
- 14 GA. BAKED ENAMEL TILTING LID - HINGED ON ONE SIDE
- 1" EXT. PLYWOOD
- 1" x 4" CLEAR REDWOOD
- 1/2"∅ THREADED ROD, PASS THRU U BOLT
- U BOLT SET IN CONC.

BRICK PAVERS W/ TREATED WOOD CURB

NOTES:
INDICATE ALL WALKS WITH THIS DESIGN ON THE SITE PLAN. BRICK PAVERS ARE SET IN A MORTAR BED OVER THE 4" CONCRETE SLAB. A PAVER IS TYPICALLY 1 5/8" THICK.

Labels (detail drawing):
- 6" x 6" TREATED WOOD CURB
- #4 BAR 18" LONG SET IN CONC.
- BRICK PAVERS
- 4" CONC. SLAB
- 6" GRAVEL FILL
- 8" ∅ CONC. FOOTING 2'-0" BELOW GRADE (SPACED AT 3'-0")

CONCRETE BENCH

NOTES:
THE FREE-STANDING CONCRETE BENCH SHOULD BE LOCATED ON THE SITE PLAN. THE LENGTH OF THE BENCH SHOULD BE DIMENSIONED.

Labels (detail drawing):
- 1'-0"
- 4"
- 1'-2"
- 2"
- 4"
- 8"
- 6"
- 2'-0"
- 6"
- 1/2" CHAMFER
- POURED CONCRETE BENCH, FINISH W/ STIFF BRISTLE BRUSH
- TAMPED GRAVEL FILL

SITE PLANS AND DETAILS   13-15

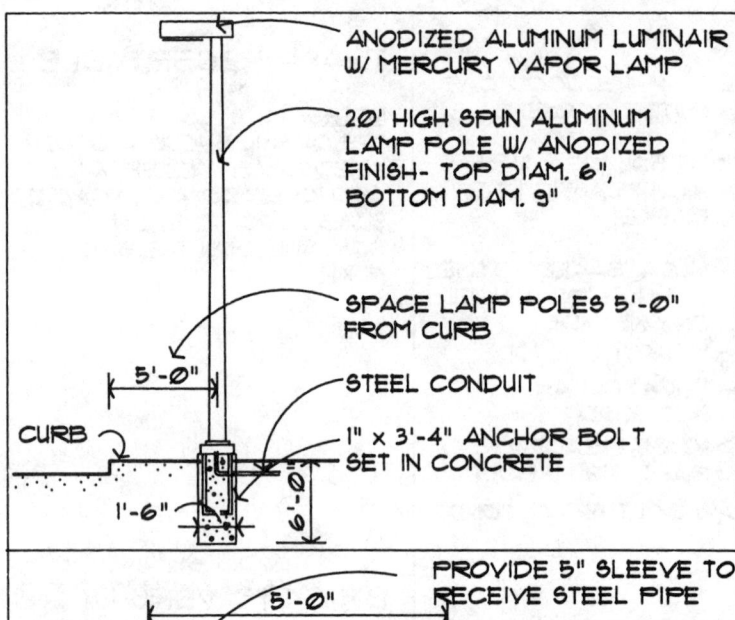

PARKING LOT LIGHT

Anodized aluminum luminair w/ mercury vapor lamp

20' high spun aluminum lamp pole w/ anodized finish- top diam. 6", bottom diam. 9"

Space lamp poles 5'-0" from curb

Steel conduit

1" x 3'-4" anchor bolt set in concrete

Curb — 5'-0" — 1'-6" — 6'-0"

NOTES:
Protect parking lights from cars. This can be accomplished by maintaining a setback distance or by placing the pole on a concrete column. Lights range in height from 10' to 30' depending on lot use and scale. Locate each pole on the site plan.

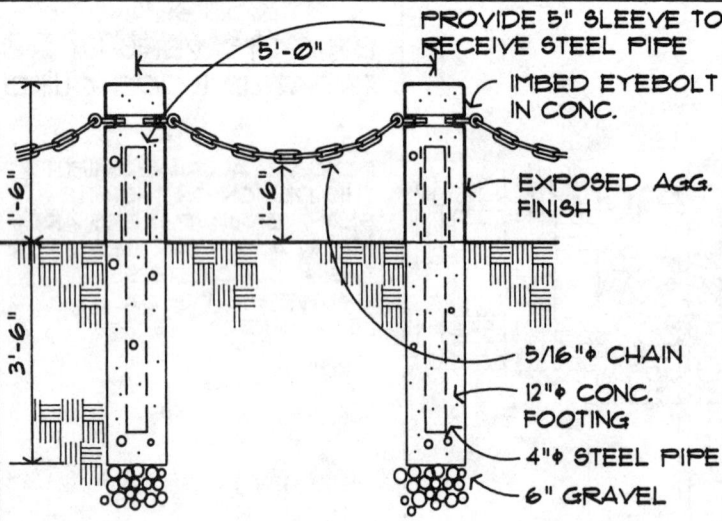

BOLLARD W/ CHAIN

Provide 5" sleeve to receive steel pipe

Imbed eyebolt in conc.

Exposed agg. finish

5/16"⌀ chain

12"⌀ conc. footing

4"⌀ steel pipe

6" gravel

5'-0", 1'-6", 1'-6", 3'-6"

NOTES:
The chain bollard shown in the detail can be used to separate pedestrians from traffic. Locate each bollard on the site plan and key to the detail.

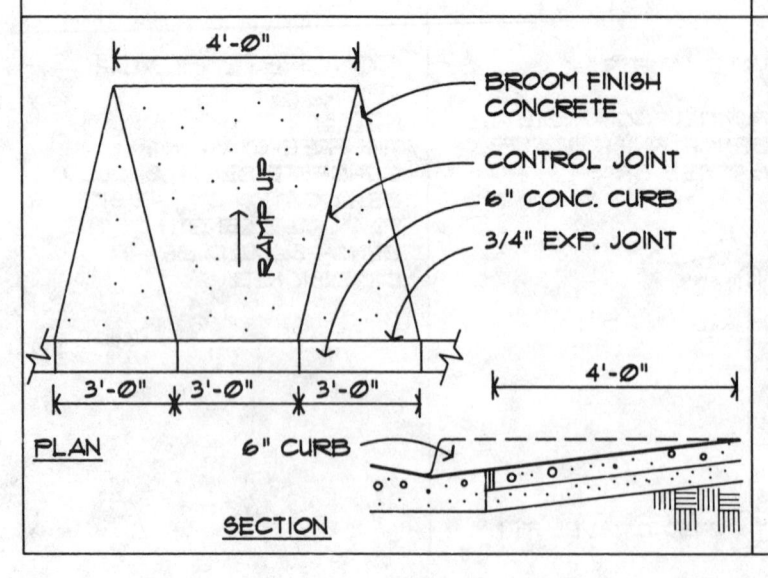

HANDICAP CURB ACCESS

4'-0"

Broom finish concrete

Control joint

6" conc. curb

3/4" exp. joint

RAMP UP

3'-0" | 3'-0" | 3'-0"   4'-0"

PLAN   6" CURB

SECTION

NOTES:
Consult handicap standards to determine the minimum width and maximum allowable slope for a curb cut. Access must be made available at all handicap entrances. Locate the ramp on the site plan and key to the detail.

SITE PLANS AND DETAILS   13-16

REPLAY
1. CALCULATE THE ELEVATION OF POINT "B" USING THE SURVEY ROD READINGS SHOWN BELOW IN THE ILLUSTRATION.

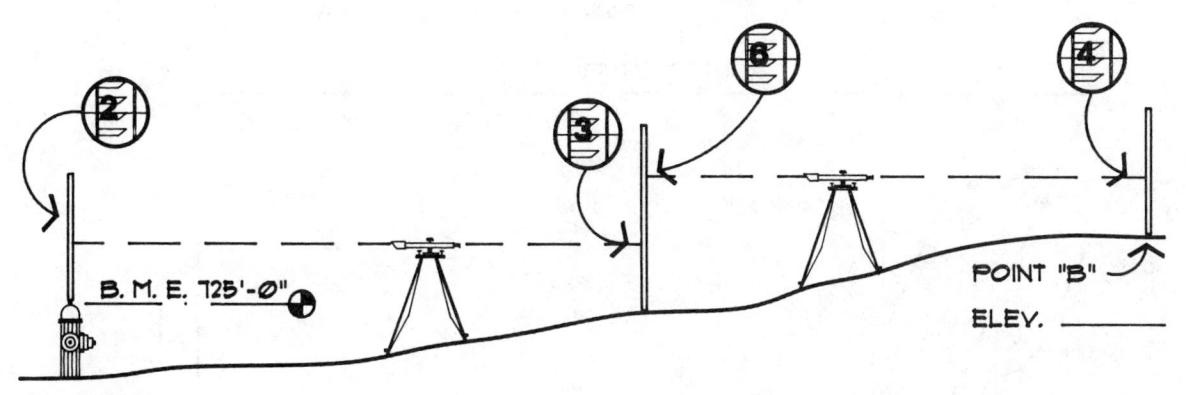

B.M.E. 725'-0"

POINT "A"

POINT "B" ELEV. _____

2. DRAW TOPOGRAPHIC CONTOURS AT 2' INTERVALS USING THE SURVEY DATA SHOWN ON THE SITE PLAN BELOW.

75'	77.5'	79'	79.5'	81'	84'	84'	87'	90'	90'
76'	79'	80.5'	81'	81.5'	83.8'	86.2'	88.5'	90'	90'
78'	80.5'	83'	85'	85.5'	86'	87.2'	87.2'	88'	90'
79'	82.5'	85'	87'	88.5'	89.5'	90'	90.5'	91'	91.5'
81'	84'	87.5'	90'	90.5'	91'	91.5'	92'	92'	92.6'
82.5'	86.5'	90'	91'	91.5'	91.8'	91.5'	91'	91'	93'
			91'	92'	91'	91'	90'	90'	91.5'
			92'	91'	90'	90.5'	91'	92'	

SITE PLANS AND DETAILS   13-17

3. WRITE THE BEARING DIRECTION AND LENGTH ALONG EACH SIDE OF THE PROPERTY ILLUSTRATED BELOW.

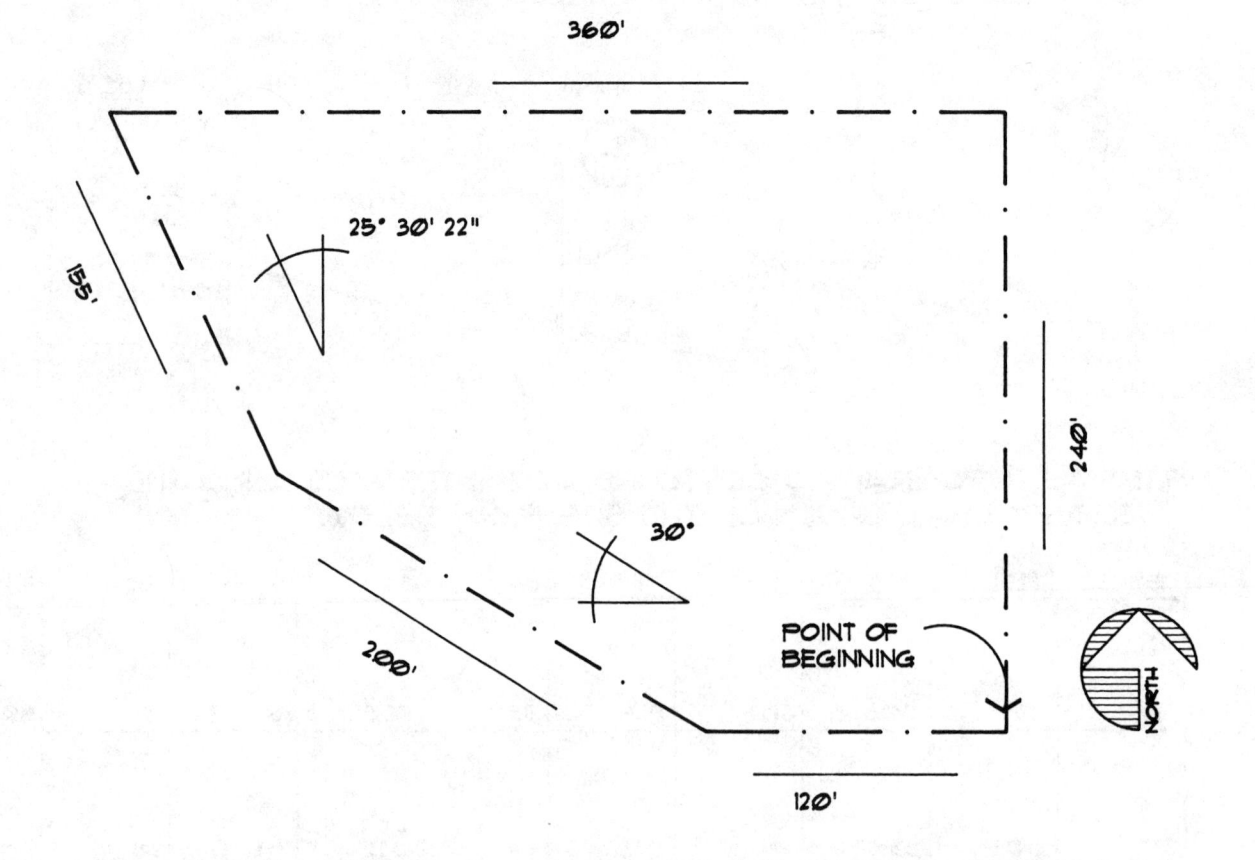

4. WRITE THE ACCEPTED MINIMUM DIMENSION FOR EACH SPACE SHOWN ON THE PARKING PLAN BELOW.

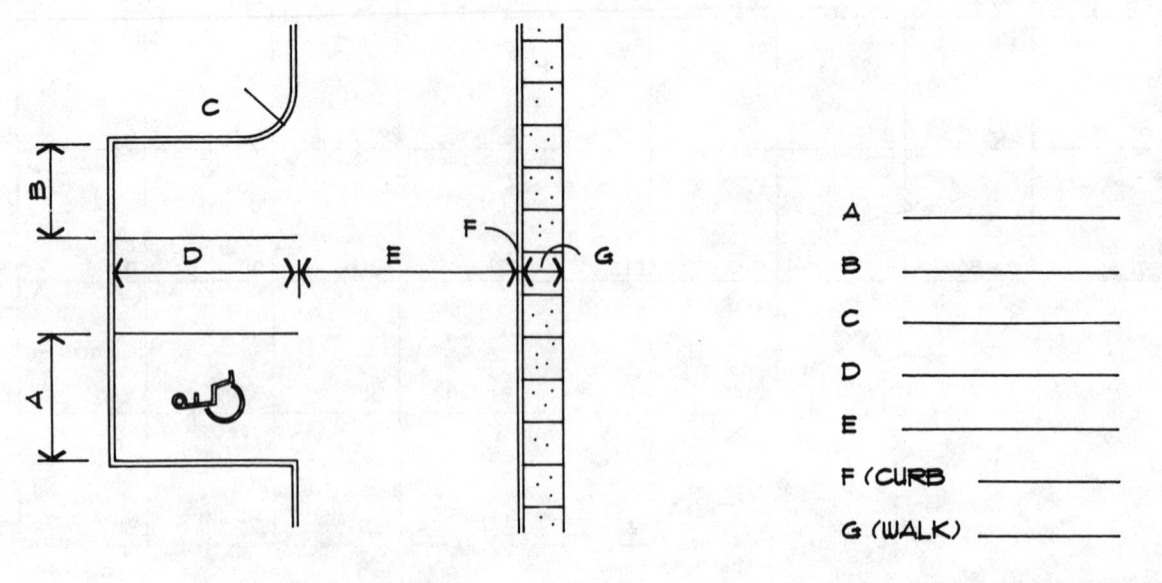

A _____
B _____
C _____
D _____
E _____
F (CURB) _____
G (WALK) _____

SITE PLANS AND DETAILS

14 FLOOR PLANS

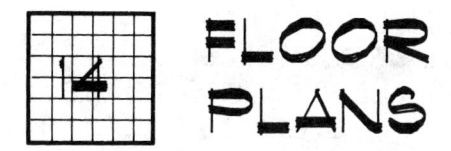

A FLOOR PLAN IS THE MOST IMPORTANT PART OF A DRAWING PACKAGE. DECISIONS MADE ON THE FLOOR PLAN DETERMINE NEARLY ALL OTHER ASPECTS OF THE WORKING DRAWINGS. IN THE FIRST PORTION OF OUR DISCUSSION ON FLOOR PLANS, WE WILL REFER TO THE EXAMPLE SHOWN BELOW.

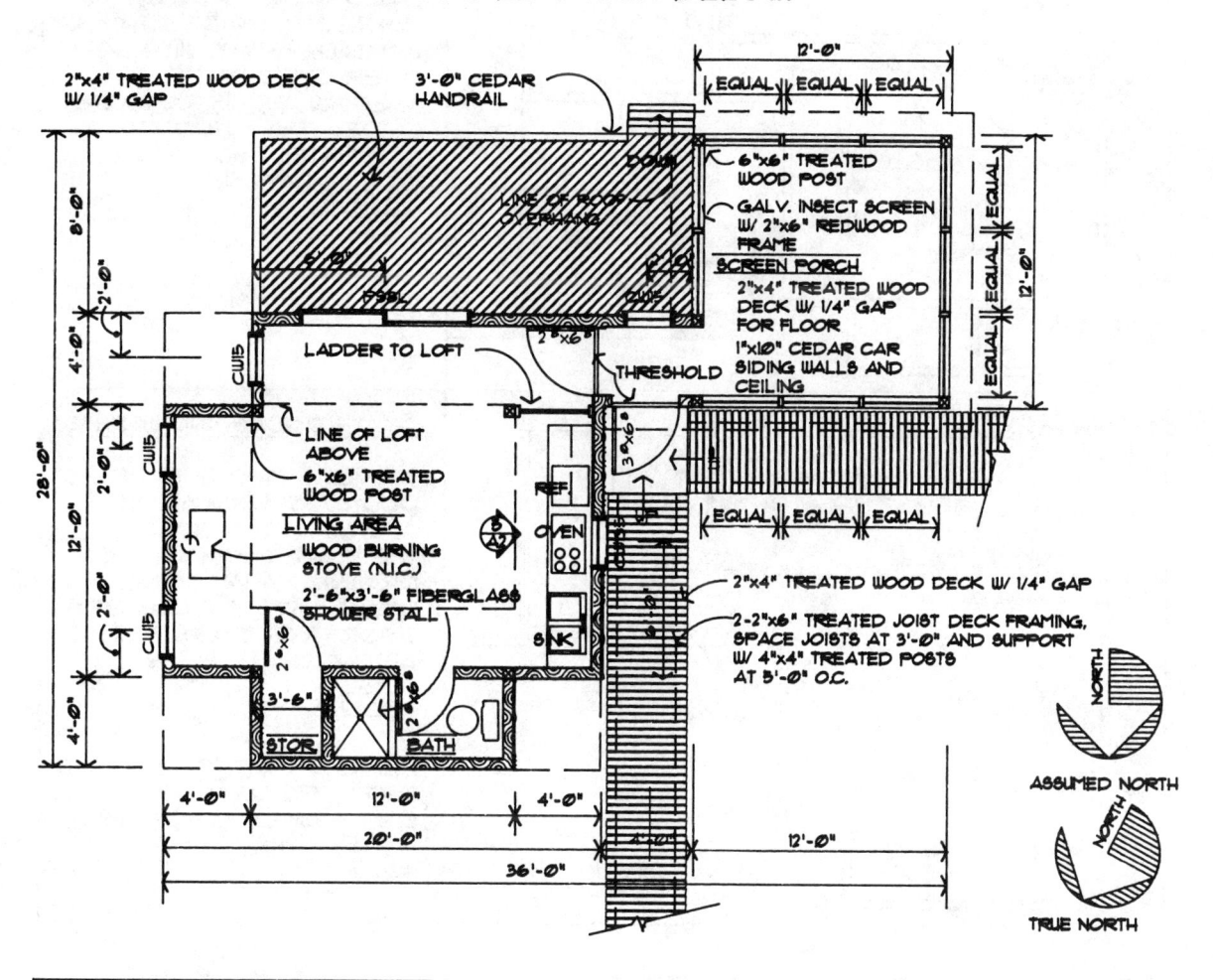

FLOOR PLANS — 14-1

ON THE NEXT SEVERAL PAGES WE WILL FOLLOW THE STEP-BY-STEP ASSEMBLY OF THE CABIN FLOOR PLAN. THE SEQUENCE SHOULD BEGIN WITH A SHEET LAYOUT THAT LOCATES ALL OBJECTS TO BE DRAWN. ONCE THE PLAN LOCATION HAS BEEN DETERMINED, START BY DRAWING THE OVERALL BUILDING USING LIGHT LINES. EVERY PROJECT WILL PRESENT A UNIQUE SET OF CONDITIONS, BUT THE GOAL IS TO START WITH A BROAD PICTURE AND WORK TO FINE DETAILS.

UNIT 6 PRESENTED THE CONCEPT THAT A WORKING DRAWING SHOULD BE ASSEMBLED IN THREE SEPARATE LAYERS: (1) THE ACTUAL DRAWING, (2) DIMENSION STRINGS, AND (3) NOTES. WE WILL NOW EXPAND ON THAT IDEA BY REVIEWING THE STEPS USED TO BUILD A PLAN.

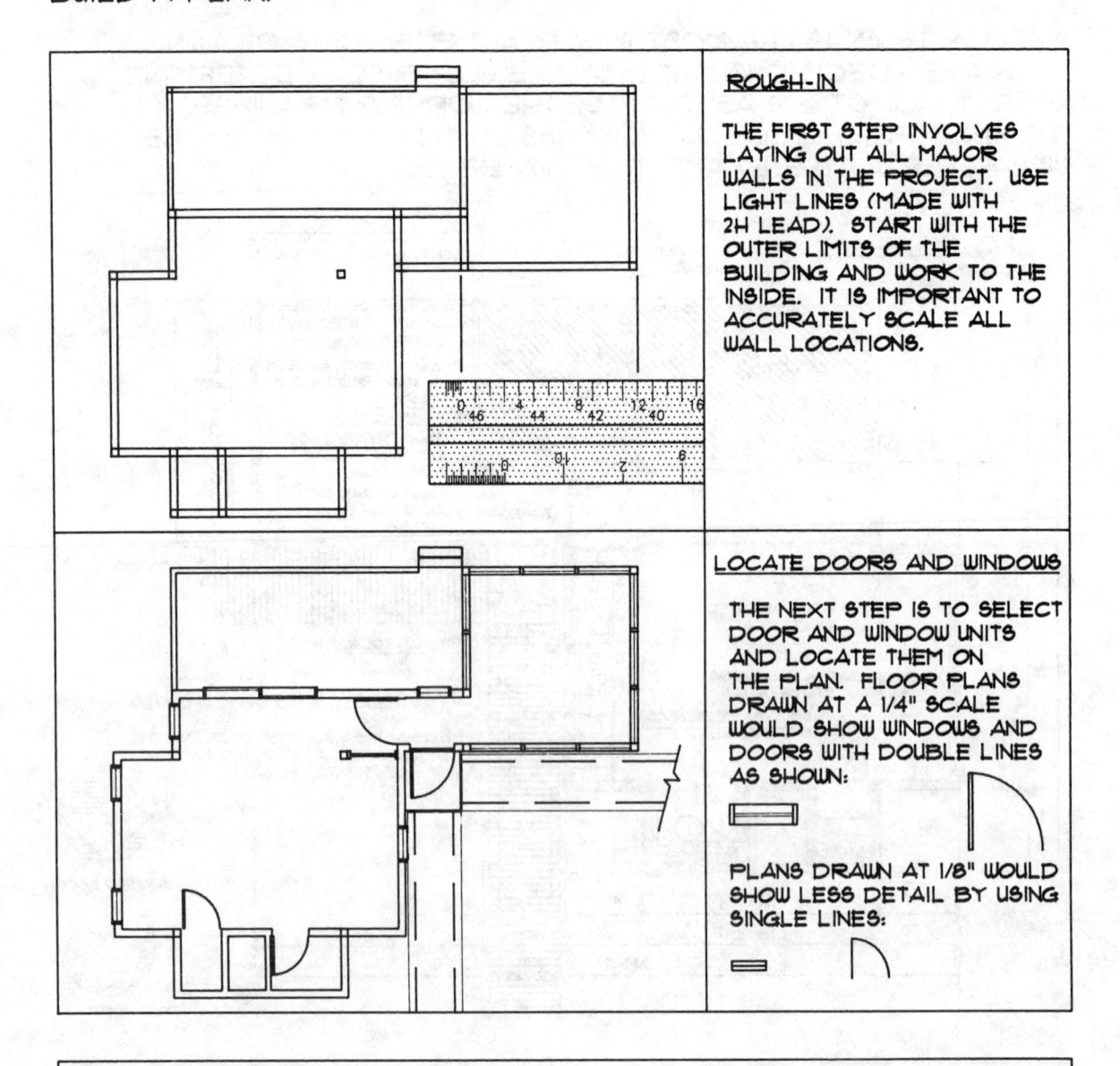

ROUGH-IN

THE FIRST STEP INVOLVES LAYING OUT ALL MAJOR WALLS IN THE PROJECT. USE LIGHT LINES (MADE WITH 2H LEAD). START WITH THE OUTER LIMITS OF THE BUILDING AND WORK TO THE INSIDE. IT IS IMPORTANT TO ACCURATELY SCALE ALL WALL LOCATIONS.

LOCATE DOORS AND WINDOWS

THE NEXT STEP IS TO SELECT DOOR AND WINDOW UNITS AND LOCATE THEM ON THE PLAN. FLOOR PLANS DRAWN AT A 1/4" SCALE WOULD SHOW WINDOWS AND DOORS WITH DOUBLE LINES AS SHOWN:

PLANS DRAWN AT 1/8" WOULD SHOW LESS DETAIL BY USING SINGLE LINES:

FLOOR PLANS   14-2

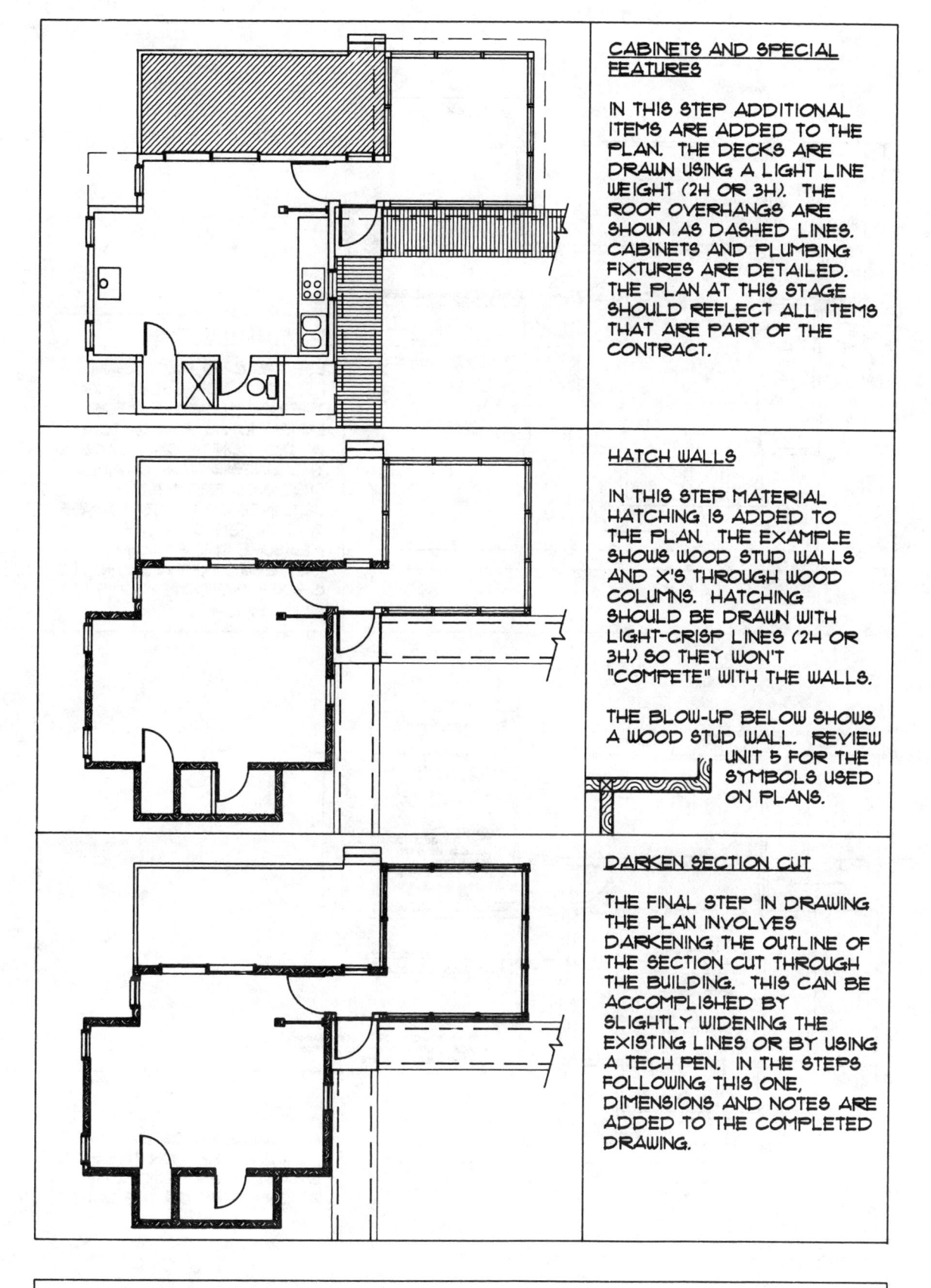

CABINETS AND SPECIAL FEATURES

IN THIS STEP ADDITIONAL ITEMS ARE ADDED TO THE PLAN. THE DECKS ARE DRAWN USING A LIGHT LINE WEIGHT (2H OR 3H). THE ROOF OVERHANGS ARE SHOWN AS DASHED LINES. CABINETS AND PLUMBING FIXTURES ARE DETAILED. THE PLAN AT THIS STAGE SHOULD REFLECT ALL ITEMS THAT ARE PART OF THE CONTRACT.

HATCH WALLS

IN THIS STEP MATERIAL HATCHING IS ADDED TO THE PLAN. THE EXAMPLE SHOWS WOOD STUD WALLS AND X'S THROUGH WOOD COLUMNS. HATCHING SHOULD BE DRAWN WITH LIGHT-CRISP LINES (2H OR 3H) SO THEY WON'T "COMPETE" WITH THE WALLS.

THE BLOW-UP BELOW SHOWS A WOOD STUD WALL. REVIEW UNIT 5 FOR THE SYMBOLS USED ON PLANS.

DARKEN SECTION CUT

THE FINAL STEP IN DRAWING THE PLAN INVOLVES DARKENING THE OUTLINE OF THE SECTION CUT THROUGH THE BUILDING. THIS CAN BE ACCOMPLISHED BY SLIGHTLY WIDENING THE EXISTING LINES OR BY USING A TECH PEN. IN THE STEPS FOLLOWING THIS ONE, DIMENSIONS AND NOTES ARE ADDED TO THE COMPLETED DRAWING.

FLOOR PLANS   14-3

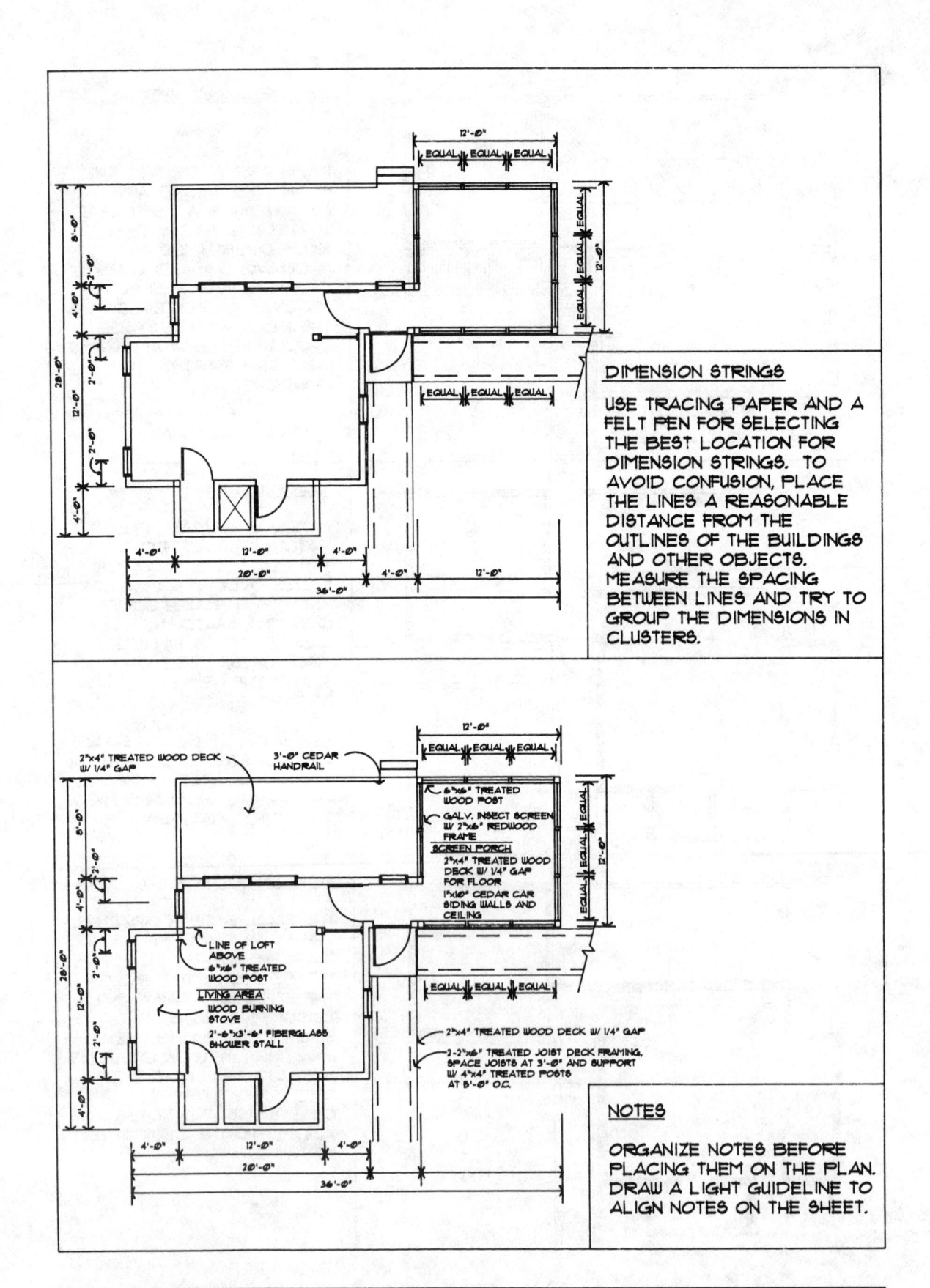

DIMENSION STRINGS

USE TRACING PAPER AND A FELT PEN FOR SELECTING THE BEST LOCATION FOR DIMENSION STRINGS. TO AVOID CONFUSION, PLACE THE LINES A REASONABLE DISTANCE FROM THE OUTLINES OF THE BUILDINGS AND OTHER OBJECTS. MEASURE THE SPACING BETWEEN LINES AND TRY TO GROUP THE DIMENSIONS IN CLUSTERS.

NOTES

ORGANIZE NOTES BEFORE PLACING THEM ON THE PLAN. DRAW A LIGHT GUIDELINE TO ALIGN NOTES ON THE SHEET.

FLOOR PLANS 14-4

THE STEPS IN THE ASSEMBLY OF A COMMERCIAL PROJECT ARE SIMILAR TO THOSE OF A RESIDENTIAL PROJECT, WITH SEVERAL EXCEPTIONS. HOUSE PLANS ARE DRAWN WITH SUFFICIENT DETAIL. WHICH ALLOWS MOST ITEMS TO BE DRAW WITH SUFFICIENT DETAIL. COMMERCIAL PLANS, ON THE OTHER HAND, ARE TYPICALLY DRAWN AT A 1/8"=1'-0" SCALE. THIS SMALL SCALE REQUIRES BLOW-UPS OF AREAS SUCH AS STAIRS AND TOILETS. A SECOND DIFFERENCE INVOLVES THE ORGANIZATION OF THE STRUCTURAL DESIGN OF A COMMERCIAL PROJECT. ALTHOUGH MOST HOUSES HAVE LOAD-BEARING WALLS, LEADING TO A FAIRLY RANDOM STRUCTURAL PATTERN, COMMERCIAL PROJECTS TYPICALLY HAVE MORE ORDERED FRAMING REQUIRING UNIFORM COLUMN AND BEAM LAYOUTS. FOR THAT REASON, MOST COMMERCIAL PLANS BEGIN WITH A SYSTEM OF GRID LINES THAT DEFINE THE LOCATION OF THE STRUCTURE. LET'S USE THE MOTEL/RESTAURANT SHOWN BELOW AS AN EXAMPLE.

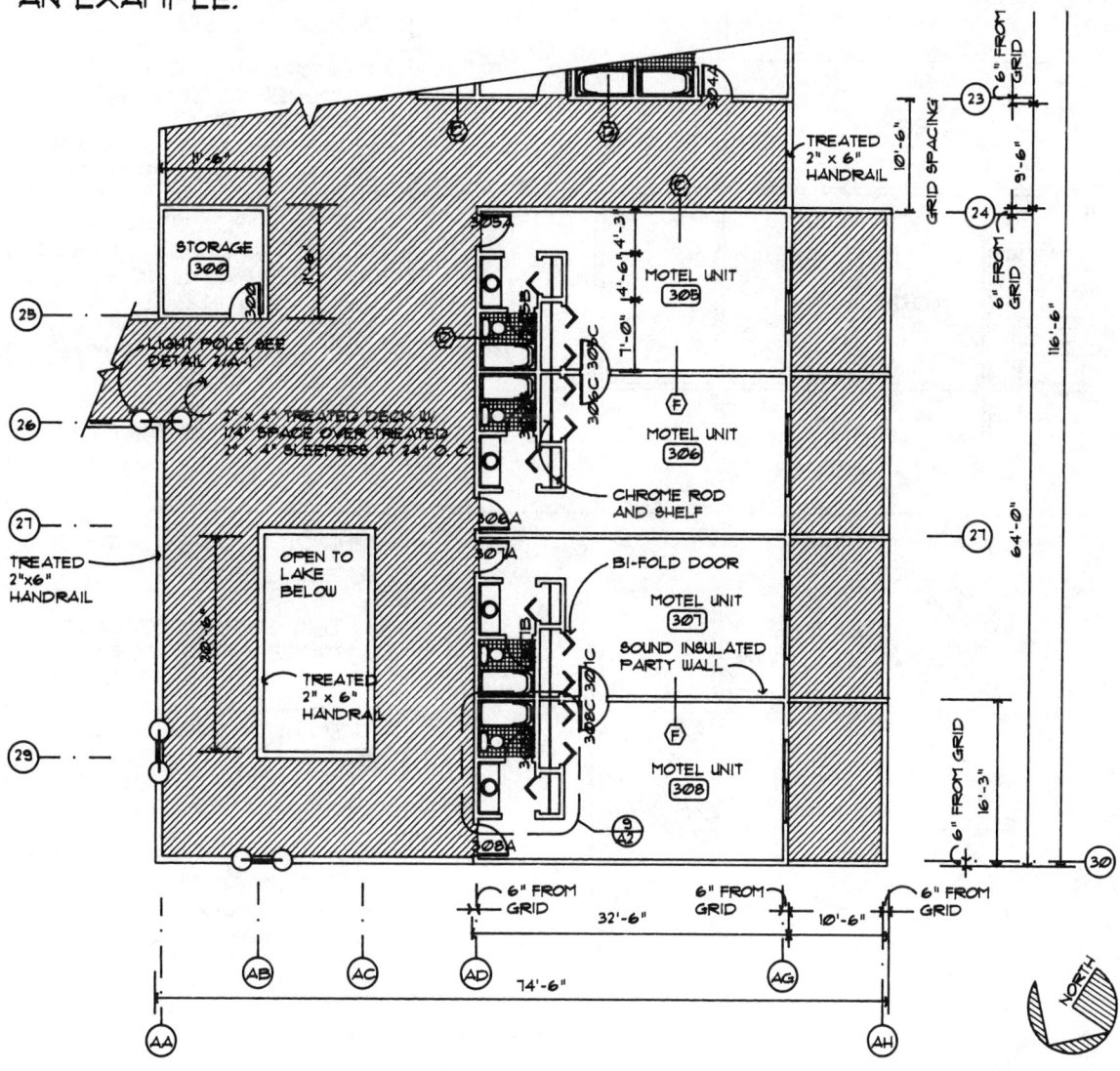

FLOOR PLANS 14-5

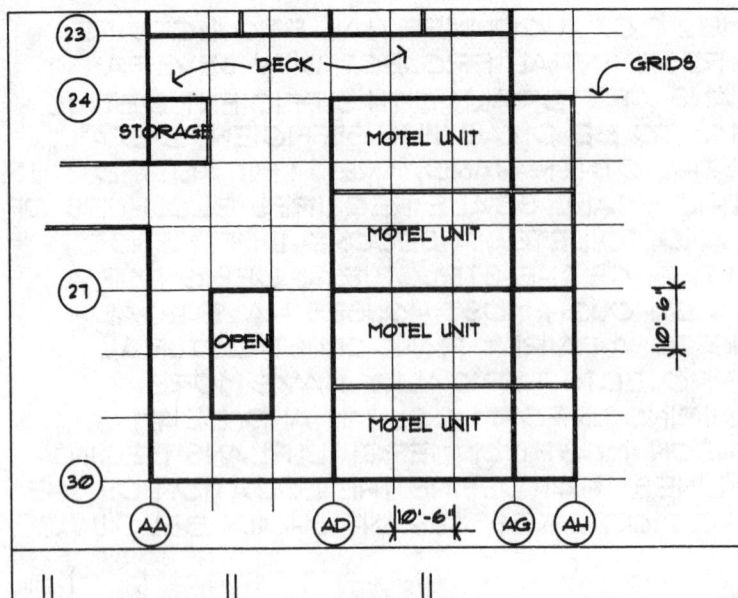

GRID LAYOUT

COMMERCIAL PROJECTS TYPICALLY START WITH A STRUCTURAL GRID. IT IS COMMON FOR COLUMNS TO BE LOCATED AT THE INTERSECTION OF GRID LINES (BUT THAT ISN'T ALWAYS THE RULE). START BY SKETCHING COLUMNS IN WALLS.

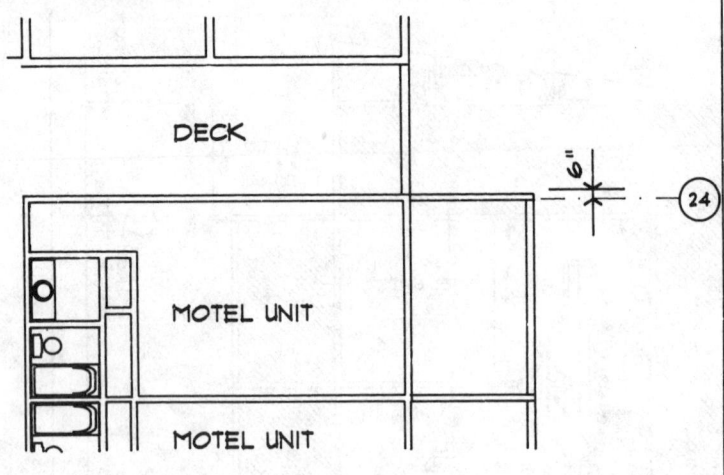

ROUGH-IN WALLS

THE ROUGH-IN STEP INVOLVES SETTING THE LOCATION OF ALL WALLS IN THE PROJECT. BEGIN BY MEASURING THE MAIN WALLS ON THE PLAN (IN THE EXAMPLE, DRAW THE OUTSIDE WALLS AND WALLS THAT SEPARATE MOTEL UNITS). CONTINUE THE PLAN BY DRAWING "SECONDARY" WALLS, SUCH AS CLOSETS. USE LIGHT LINES AND DISREGARD WINDOW AND DOOR LOCATIONS AT THIS STEP.

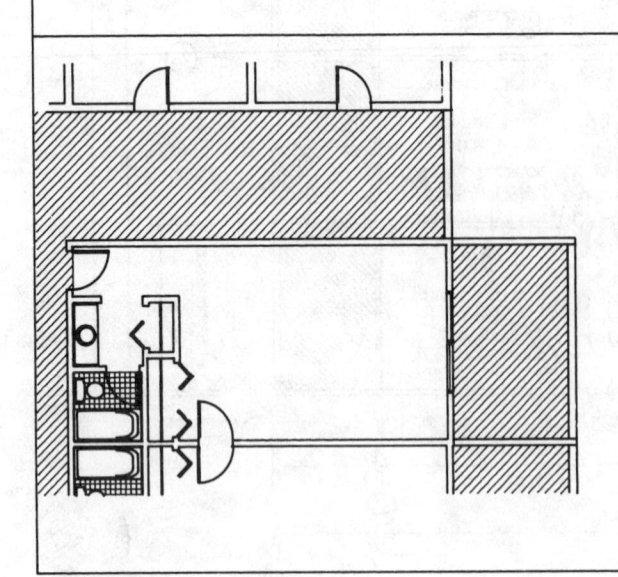

WINDOWS, DOORS, AND SPECIAL FEATURES

IN THIS STEP DOORS AND WINDOWS ARE ADDED TO THE PLAN. DRAW THE UNITS TO SCALE AND LOCATE THEM (WITH DIMENSION STRINGS) FROM WALL INTERSECTIONS OR GRID LINES.

THE EXAMPLE SHOWS THE ADDITION OF PLUMBING FIXTURES, FLOOR TILE, AND THE EXTERIOR DECKS. MOST SPECIAL FEATURES SHOULD BE DRAWN WITH A LIGHTER LINE WEIGHT.

FLOOR PLANS   14-6

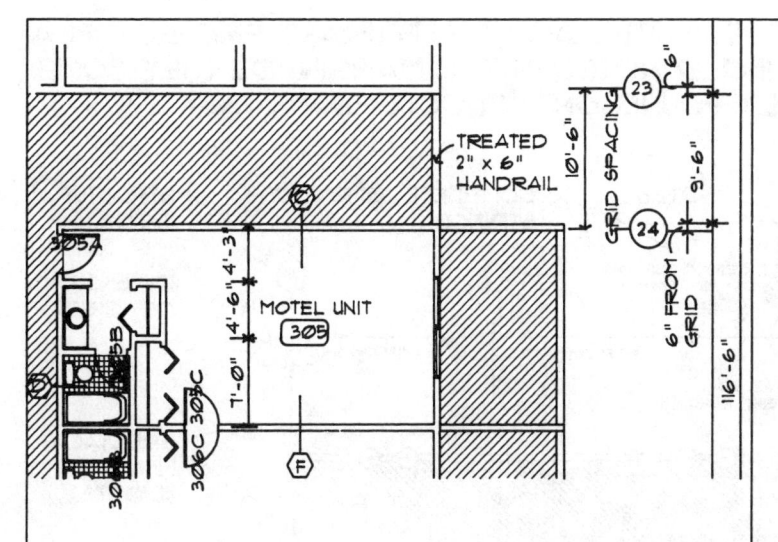

DIMENSIONS AND NOTES

IN THE FINAL STEP NOTES AND DIMENSION STRINGS ARE ADDED TO THE PLAN. SKETCH THEIR LOCATION ON TRACING PAPER BEFORE PLACING THEM ON THE PLAN. GRID LINES MAY BE USED TO DIMENSION WALL AND DOOR LOCATIONS. IN THE MOTEL EXAMPLE, IT IS ASSUMED THAT DIMENSIONS SHOWN ON ONE UNIT APPLY TO ALL UNITS (UNLESS OTHERWISE NOTED).

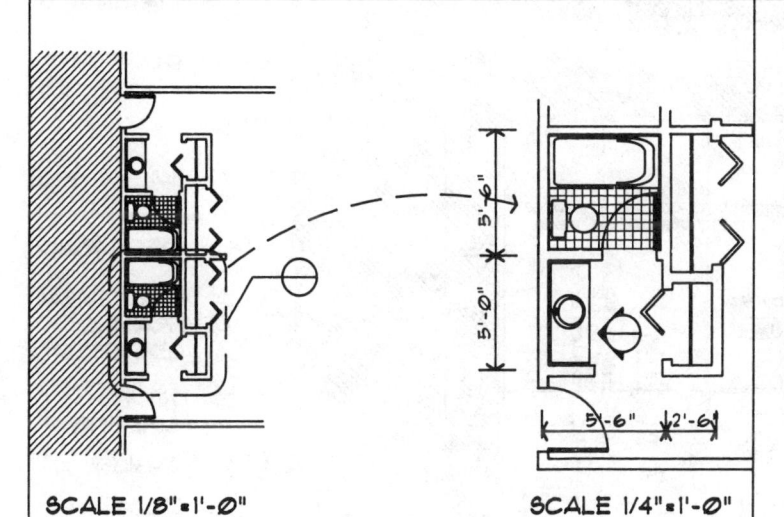

PLAN BLOW-UPS

A 1/8"=1'-0" FLOOR PLAN IS TOO SMALL TO SHOW MUCH DETAIL, ESPECIALLY IN TIGHT AREAS SUCH AS TOILETS AND STAIRS. FOR THAT REASON, 1/4" BLOW-UPS ARE MADE TO ALLOW FOR DIMENSIONS AND NOTES. PLACE DIMENSION STRINGS ON THE LARGER DETAIL AND NOT ON THE SMALLER SCALE PLAN.

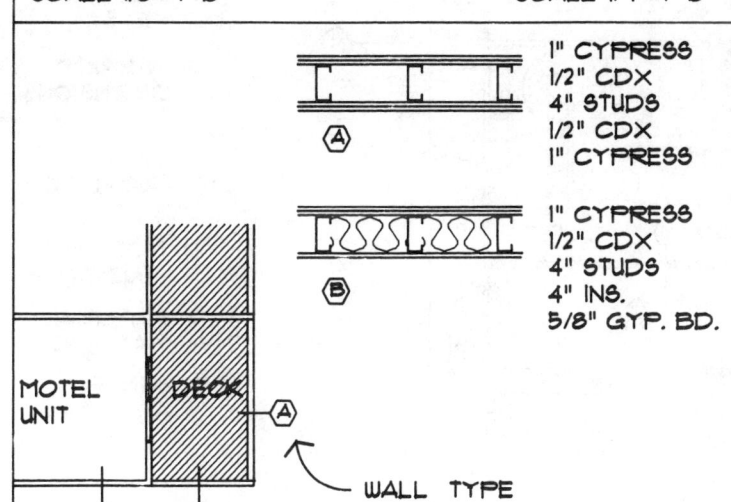

WALL TYPES

WALL TYPES ARE DIFFICULT TO INDICATE ON COMMERCIAL PLANS BECAUSE OF THE SMALL SCALE. ONE SOLUTION IS TO LABEL EACH CONDITION WITH A LETTER "TAG." THE TAG IS THEN KEYED TO A LARGE-SCALE DETAIL WHICH SHOWS THE CONSTRUCTION.

FLOOR PLANS 14-7

ANOTHER PORTION OF THE MOTEL AND RESTAURANT PROJECT PLAN IS SHOWN BELOW. THE BOLD NOTES IN THE MARGIN IDENTIFY SOME OF THE ITEMS TYPICALLY FOUND ON A FLOOR PLAN.

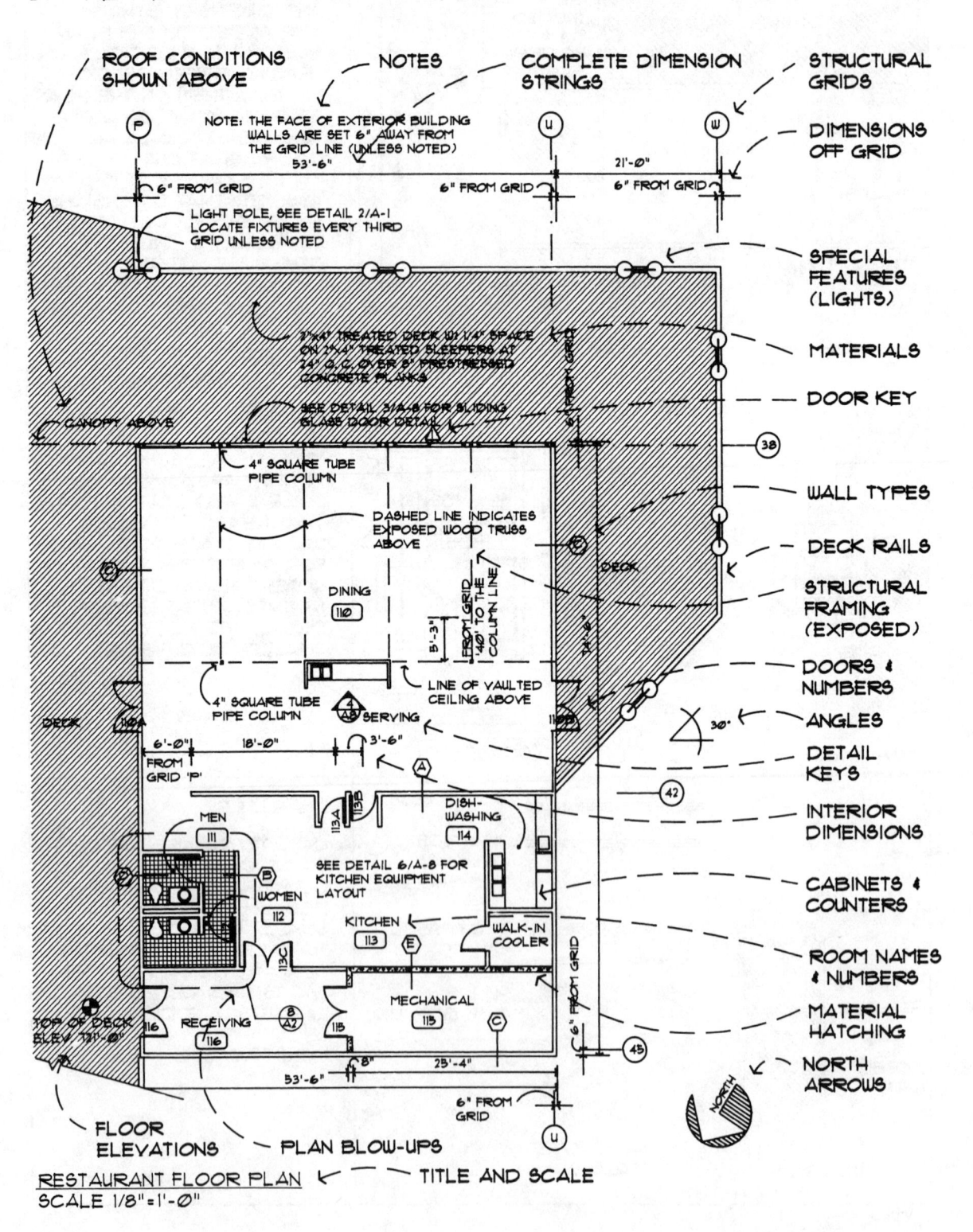

ROOF CONDITIONS SHOWN ABOVE — **NOTES** — **COMPLETE DIMENSION STRINGS** — **STRUCTURAL GRIDS** — **DIMENSIONS OFF GRID** — **SPECIAL FEATURES (LIGHTS)** — **MATERIALS** — **DOOR KEY** — **WALL TYPES** — **DECK RAILS** — **STRUCTURAL FRAMING (EXPOSED)** — **DOORS & NUMBERS** — **ANGLES** — **DETAIL KEYS** — **INTERIOR DIMENSIONS** — **CABINETS & COUNTERS** — **ROOM NAMES & NUMBERS** — **MATERIAL HATCHING** — **NORTH ARROWS**

FLOOR ELEVATIONS — **PLAN BLOW-UPS** — **TITLE AND SCALE**

RESTAURANT FLOOR PLAN
SCALE 1/8" = 1'-0"

FLOOR PLANS — 14-8

A GENERAL CHECKLIST FOR ITEMS THAT SHOULD BE SHOWN ON WORKING DRAWING FLOOR PLANS IS SHOWN BELOW.

FLOOR PLAN CHECKLIST

- ☐ COORDINATE DIMENSIONS
- ☐ OVERALL BUILDING DIM.
- ☐ GRIDS
- ☐ ROOM NAME & NUMBER
- ☐ DOOR NUMBERS
- ☐ FLOOR ELEVATIONS
- ☐ RAMP & STAIR DIRECTION
- ☐ WALL MATERIALS
- ☐ CEILING HEIGHT
- ☐ NORTH
- ☐ DOOR THRESHOLDS
- ☐ PLUMBING FIXTURES
- ☐ STAIR DIMENSIONS
- ☐ FOLDING PARTITIONS
- ☐ EXPANSION JOINTS
- ☐ CABINETS (BASE & TOP)
- ☐ RECESSED FLOOR MATS
- ☐ FIRE EXTINGUISHERS
- ☐ DRINKING FOUNTAINS
- ☐ LADDERS
- ☐ CHALKBOARDS
- ☐ FLOOR PATTERNS
- ☐ EXTERIOR WALK & PATIO
- ☐ FIREPLACE
- ☐ CLOSET ROD & SHELF
- ☐ WINDOW TAGS
- ☐ WALL TYPES
- ☐ WALL HATCHING
- ☐ HANDRAILS
- ☐ COLUMNS
- ☐ DASH ITEMS ABOVE
- ☐ RECESSED EQUIPMENT
- ☐ KEY PLAN BLOW-UPS
- ☐ FLOOR DRAINS
- ☐ STAIR DIRECTION ARROW

FLOOR PLAN DETAILS

IN THIS SECTION WE WILL REVIEW THE TECHNIQUES USED TO DRAW A VARIETY OF ITEMS ON A FLOOR PLAN.

THESE FOUR STEPS ILLUSTRATE THE SEQUENCE OF DRAWING, FROM ROUGHING-IN THE PLAN TO ADDING DETAIL.

1. STEP 1 (ROUGH-IN)
2. STEP 2 (WINDOWS AND DOORS)
3. STEP 3 (HATCHING)
4. STEP 4 (NOTES AND DIMENSIONS)

FLOOR PLANS   14-9

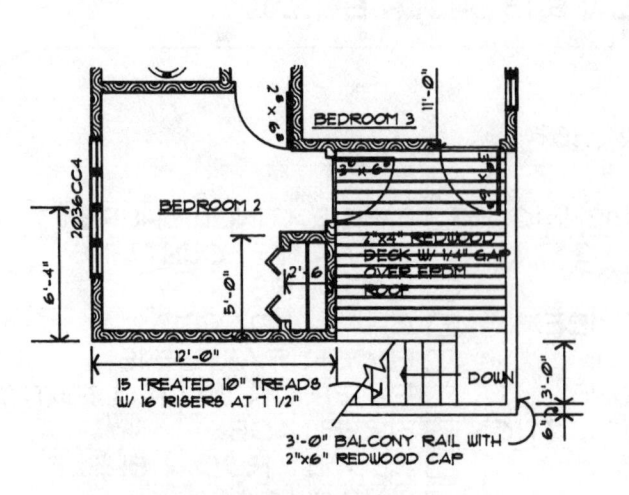

DECK

THE ILLUSTRATION SHOWS A SECOND-FLOOR DECK IN PLAN; NOTES ON THE PLAN SPECIFY THE MATERIAL AND DIMENSIONS OF THE DECK CONSTRUCTION. THE SECTION CUT SHOWS A PORTION OF THE STAIR. THE NOTE THERE SPECIFIES THE NUMBER OF TREADS AND RISERS ALONG WITH THEIR DIMENSIONS.

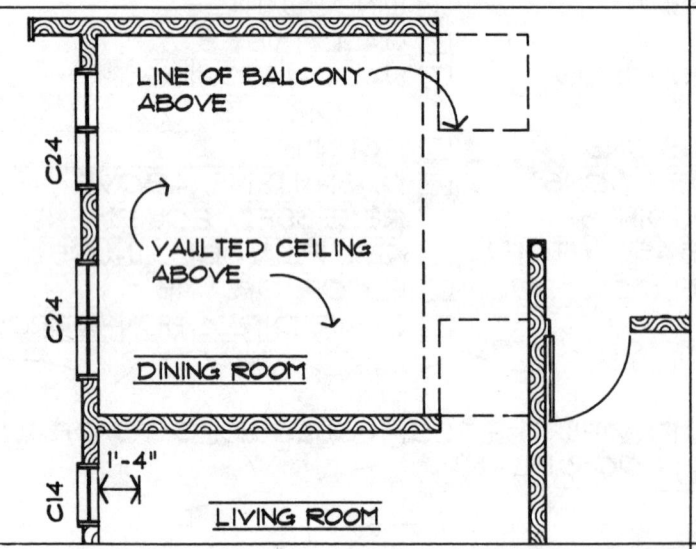

OVERHEAD CONDITIONS

FLOOR PLANS ARE GENERATED BY CUTTING A HORIZONTAL PLANE THROUGH THE BUILDING ROUGHLY 3'-0" ABOVE THE FLOOR AND THEN LOOKING DOWN. ITEMS THAT OCCUR ABOVE THE "CUT PLANE" ARE NOTED OR INDICATED BY DASHED LINES. THE ILLUSTRATION SHOWS THE SILHOUETTE OF A SECOND-FLOOR BALCONY AS A DASHED LINE. THE NOTE "VAULTED CEILING ABOVE" INDICATES THAT THE CEILING ABOVE THE DINING ROOM IS SLOPED.

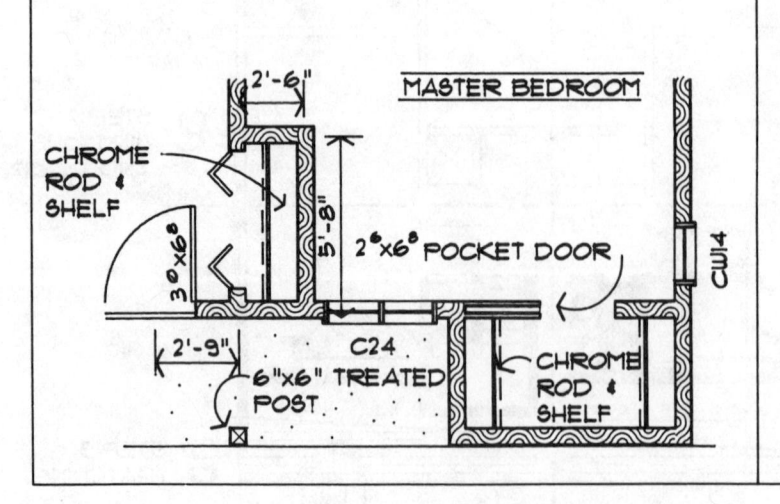

CLOSETS

THE ILLUSTRATION SHOWS CLOSET DOOR CONDITIONS WITH A POCKET DOOR AND BI-FOLD DOORS. IT IS COMMON TO NOTE A ROD AND SHELF.

FLOOR PLANS   14-10

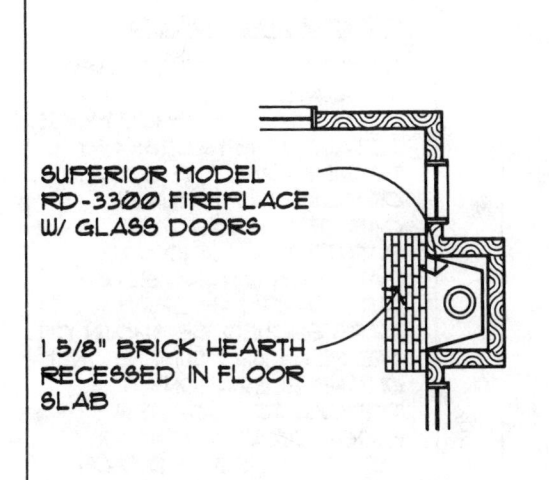

FIREPLACE

THE PLAN OF A FIREPLACE IS ILLUSTRATED BY CUTTING A SECTION THROUGH THE PORTION OF THE SLOPED WALL. THE CIRCLE REPRESENTS THE FLUE ABOVE. REFER TO THE MANUFACTURER'S DATA FOR THE SIZE OF THE FIREPROOF HEARTH. (THE MODEL AND MANUFACTURER SHOULD BE NOTED ON THE PLAN.)

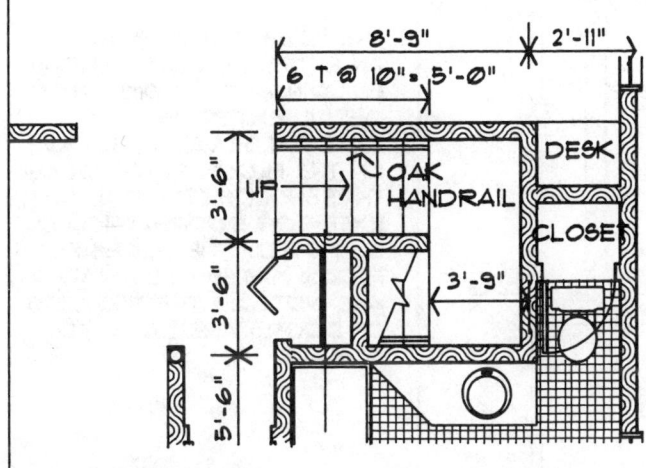

(Labels on drawing: SUPERIOR MODEL RD-3300 FIREPLACE W/ GLASS DOORS; 1 5/8" BRICK HEARTH RECESSED IN FLOOR SLAB)

STAIR

STAIRS PRESENT UNIQUE PROBLEMS IN WORKING DRAWING ASSEMBLY. THE NUMBER AND DIMENSION OF EACH TREAD SHOULD BE SHOWN ON THE PLAN. IT IS NECESSARY TO INDICATE THE DIRECTION OF TRAVEL (UP OR DOWN) ON THE PLAN. THE ENTIRE "RUN" OF THE PLAN CAN'T BE SHOWN DUE TO THE SECTION CUT. FOR THAT REASON, A CUT LINE MUST BE INDICATED ON THE PLAN.

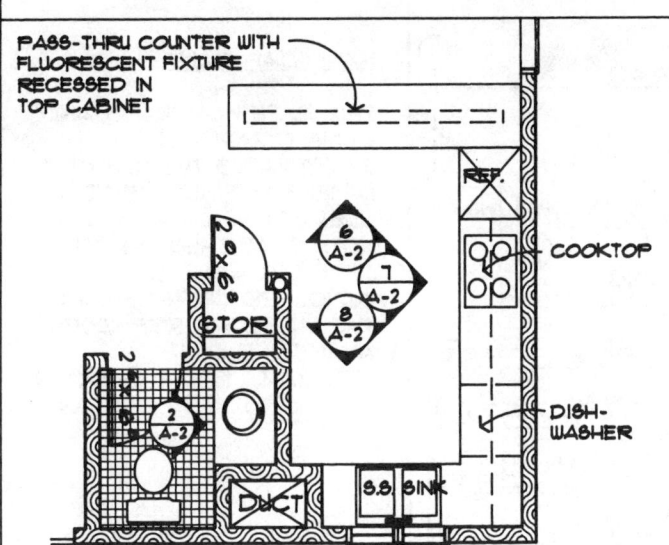

(Labels on drawing: 8'-9"; 2'-11"; 6 T @ 10" = 5'-0"; 3'-6"; 3'-6"; 5'-6"; UP; OAK HANDRAIL; DESK; CLOSE; 3'-9"; CUT LINE)

KITCHEN CABINETS

THE ILLUSTRATION SHOWS A KITCHEN LAYOUT. APPLIANCES SHOULD BE NOTED ON THE PLAN. TOP CABINETS (TYPICALLY 13" DEEP) ARE SHOWN ON THE PLAN AS DASHED LINES. THE ELEVATION BUBBLES KEY (OR REFERENCE) TO CABINET ELEVATION DETAILS. CABINETS ARE TYPICALLY DIMENSIONED ON THE ELEVATIONS WHERE THERE IS MORE ROOM. IN THE EXAMPLE, CABINET ELEVATIONS ARE KEYED TO DETAILS 6, 7, AND 8 ON SHEET A-2.

(Labels on drawing: PASS-THRU COUNTER WITH FLUORESCENT FIXTURE RECESSED IN TOP CABINET; 2x6; 2x6; STOR.; REF.; COOKTOP; DISHWASHER; DUCT; S.S. SINK; 6/A-2; 7/A-2; 8/A-2; 2/A-2)

FLOOR PLANS   14-11

COMMERCIAL TOILETS

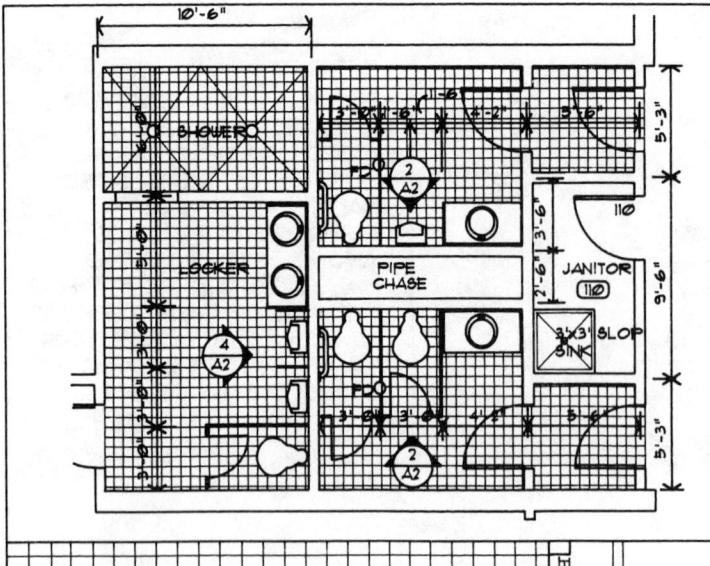

COMMERCIAL TOILETS ARE TYPICALLY BLOWN UP TO A 1/4" SCALE TO SHOW MORE DETAIL. IT IS NECESSARY TO DIMENSION THE LOCATION OF PLUMBING FIXTURES, CABINETS, AND TOILET PARTITIONS. HANDICAP PARTITION DOORS SWING OUT. HANDICAP GRAB BARS SHOULD BE SHOWN ON THE PLAN AND DIMENSIONED ON THE ELEVATION. IT IS TYPICAL TO LOCATE A FLOOR DRAIN (ABBREVIATED "F. D.") ON THE PLAN.

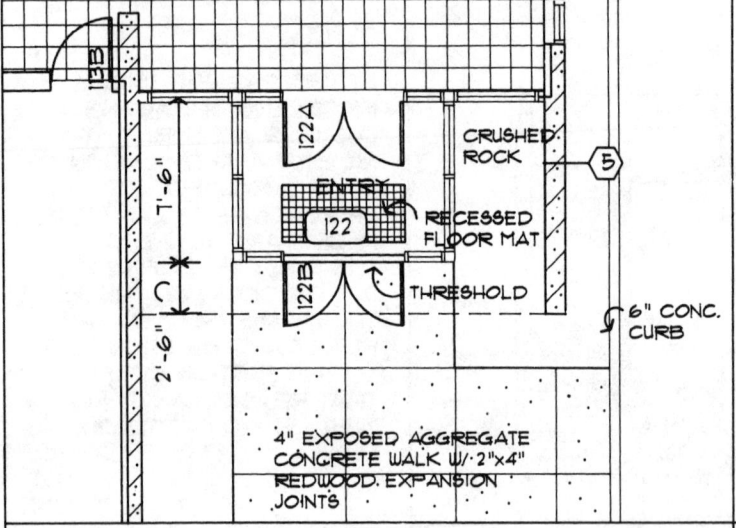

ENTRY

THE ILLUSTRATION SHOWS AN ENTRY IN A COMMERCIAL BUILDING. IT IS COMMON TO DETAIL EXTERIOR MATERIALS (WALKS, ROCK) ON THE FLOOR PLAN. DOOR THRESHOLDS (TYPICAL ON EXTERIOR DOORS) SHOULD BE NOTED. THE RECESSED FLOOR MAT IS ILLUSTRATED AND NOTED. THE TWO SETS OF DOORS ARE LABELED 122A AND 122B.

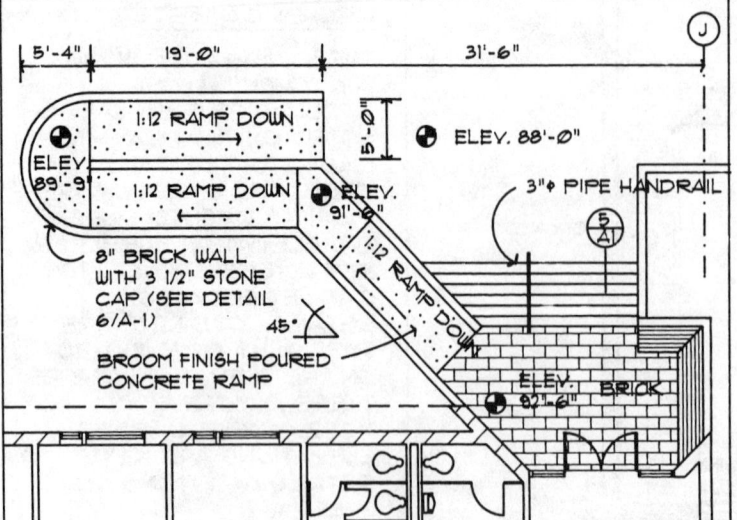

HANDICAP RAMP

THIS EXTERIOR RAMP AND STAIR CONDITION ILLUSTRATES THE USE OF DIMENSIONS AND SPOT ELEVATIONS ON A PLAN. NOTE THAT THE DIRECTION OF SLOPE ON THE RAMP IS INDICATED ON THE PLAN. THE 1:12 SLOPE REPRESENTS AN INCLINE OF 1" VERTICALLY FOR EVERY 12" IN A HORIZONTAL DISTANCE.

FLOOR PLANS

14-12

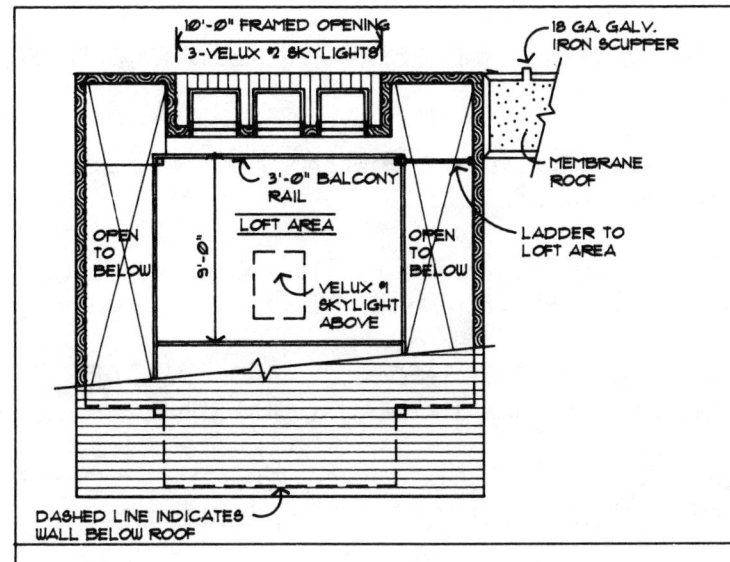

SECOND-FLOOR LOFT

THE SECOND-FLOOR PLAN ILLUSTRATED SHOWS THAT A TWO-STORY SPACE IS INDICATED WITH AN X. THE SLOPED ROOF IS MARKED WITH A SLASH LINE WHERE IT IS CUT THROUGH WITH A PLANE.

A DASHED BOX INDICATES THAT A SKYLIGHT IS LOCATED DIRECTLY ABOVE. THE DASHED LINE BELOW THE ROOF REPRESENTS THE OUTLINE OF THE BUILDING BELOW THE ROOF.

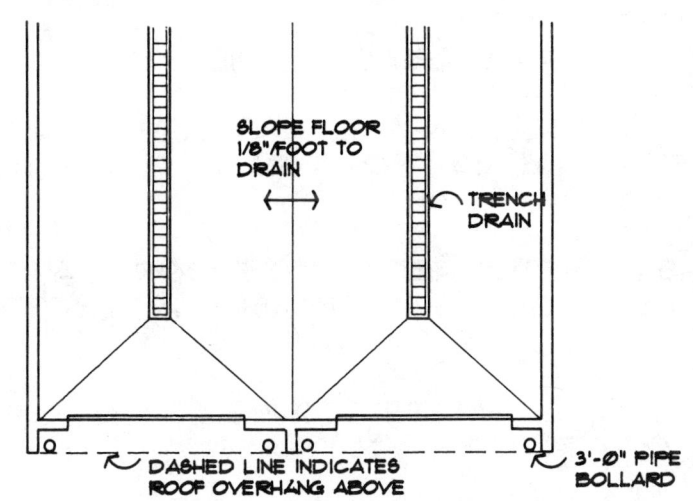

SLOPED FLOOR

A SLOPED FLOOR IS DETAILED BY DRAWING LIGHT LINES FROM THE HIGH POINT OF THE FLOOR TO THE DRAIN. IT IS NECESSARY TO NOTE THE SLOPE PER FOOT (TYPICALLY 1/8" PER FOOT).

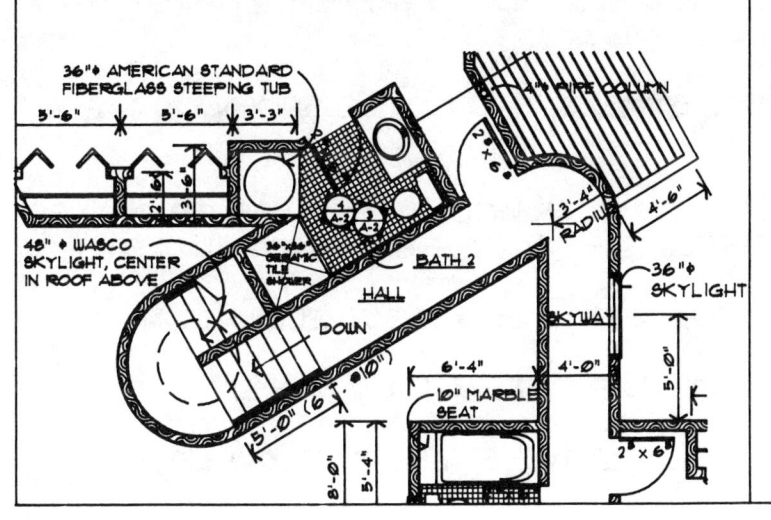

STAIR/SKYWAY DETAIL

THE SECOND-FLOOR PLAN ILLUSTRATES A VARIETY OF CONDITIONS RANGING FROM A STAIR WITH A CIRCULAR LANDING TO A SKYWAY LINK IN THE MASTER BATH AN ARRANGEMENT OF FOUR PLUMBING FIXTURES IS SHOWN. THE SIZE AND DESCRIPTION OF THE SHOWER AND TUB ARE NOTED ON THE PLAN.

FLOOR PLANS 14-13

REPLAY
CIRCLE (T) IF THE STATEMENT IS TRUE AND (F) IF THE STATEMENT IS FALSE.

T F 1. BEGIN A FLOOR PLAN BY DRAWING HEAVY-DARK LINES TO SHOW THE MAJOR WALLS.

T F 2. IT IS NECESSARY TO SHOW THE DIRECTION OF TRAVEL (UP OR DOWN) ON A STAIR DRAWN IN PLAN.

T F 3. THE PLAN VIEW OF THE TOP UNIT FOR A KITCHEN CABINET WOULD BE DRAWN WITH A LIGHT CONTINUOUS LINE.

T F 4. MATERIAL HATCHING (SUCH AS WOOD STUDS) SHOULD BE DRAWN WITH A HEAVY LINE TO MATCH THE WALL LINE.

T F 5. IT IS TYPICAL TO ENLARGE A TOILET PLAN TO A 1/4"=1'-0" SCALE WHEN DRAWING A COMMERCIAL BUILDING.

T F 6. A SLOPED FLOOR IS DRAWN IN A PLAN VIEW BY DRAWING DASHED LINES FROM THE HIGH POINT ON THE FLOOR TO THE LOW POINT.

T F 7. AN ITEMS THAT IS DIRECTLY ABOVE THE FLOOR PLAN VIEW (SUCH AS A SKYLIGHT) IS DRAWN USING A DASHED LINE.

T F 8. SPOT ELEVATIONS WOULD BE USED TO IDENTIFY DIFFERENT FLOOR HEIGHTS ON A FLOOR PLAN.

T F 9. A FLOOR PLAN CHECKLIST ITEM WOULD BE TO DRAW BUILDING SECTION CUT SYMBOLS (REFER TO PAGE 5-6) ON THE PLAN VIEW.

T F 10. A NORTH ARROW SYMBOL SHOULD BE SHOWN ON THE FLOOR PLAN.

T F 11. COMMERCIAL FLOOR PLANS COMMONLY USE GRID LINES TO IDENTIFY THE OUTER FACE OF EXTERIOR WALLS.

T F 12. ⊕ THIS SYMBOL IDENTIFIES A SPOT ELEVATION.

T F 13. Ⓔ THIS SYMBOL IDENTIFIES A WALL TYPE.

T F 14. ③/A-3 THIS SYMBOL IDENTIFIES A PLAN BLOW-UP.

FLOOR PLANS

EXTERIOR ELEVATIONS

EXTERIOR ELEVATIONS DISPLAY THE ORTHOGRAPHIC (TWO-DIMENSIONAL) VIEW OF THE OUTSIDE OF A BUILDING. KEEP IN MIND THAT ELEVATIONS SHOW THE HEIGHT AND WIDTH OF A PROJECT- DEPTH IS SHOWN ON THE FLOOR PLAN. COMBINING THE ELEVATIONS AND PLAN RESULTS IN A THREE-DIMENSIONAL MODEL.

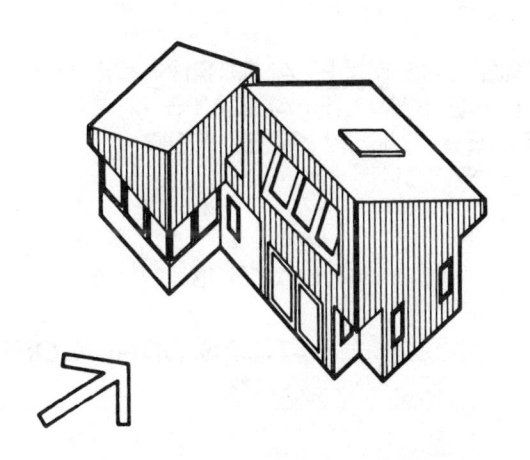

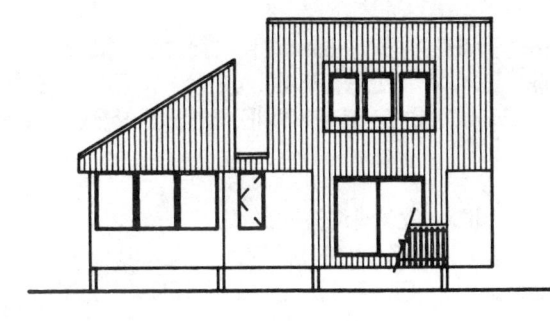

THE VIEW TO THE LEFT SHOWS AN ISOMETRIC OF THE CABIN PROJECT. THE ARROW INDICATES THE DIRECTION OF THE ELEVATION. COMPARE THIS DRAWING WITH THE ELEVATION VIEW SHOWN BELOW.

NOTE THAT SEVERAL FEATURES THAT ARE VISIBLE IN THE ISOMETRIC VIEW CAN'T BE SEEN IN THE ELEVATION. THE SCREEN PORCH TO THE LEFT OF THE CABIN AND THE NOTCH ON THE RIGHT SIDE, FOR EXAMPLE, APPEAR AS FLAT SURFACES IN THE ORTHOGRAPHIC VIEW. ALSO, THE SLOPED WINDOW ON THE SECOND FLOOR IS NOT APPARENT WHEN IT IS VIEWED IN ELEVATION. IT IS NECESSARY TO COMBINE SEVERAL DRAWINGS (PLANS, ELEVATIONS, AND SECTIONS) TO PRODUCE A COMPLETE VIEW OF THE BUILDING.

EXTERIOR ELEVATIONS 15-1

ELEVATION VIEWS TYPICALLY CONCENTRATE ON SHOWING EXTERIOR MATERIALS AND VERTICAL DIMENSIONS (THE REMAINING DIMENSIONS ARE SHOWN ON THE FLOOR PLANS). THE ELEVATION BELOW DISPLAYS MOST HEIGHTS WITH A "BULL'S-EYE" ELEVATION MARKER: ———⊕. THE MARK IS USED TO INDICATE MAJOR POINTS ON THE BUILDING THAT THE CONTRACTOR CAN USE IN FRAMING.

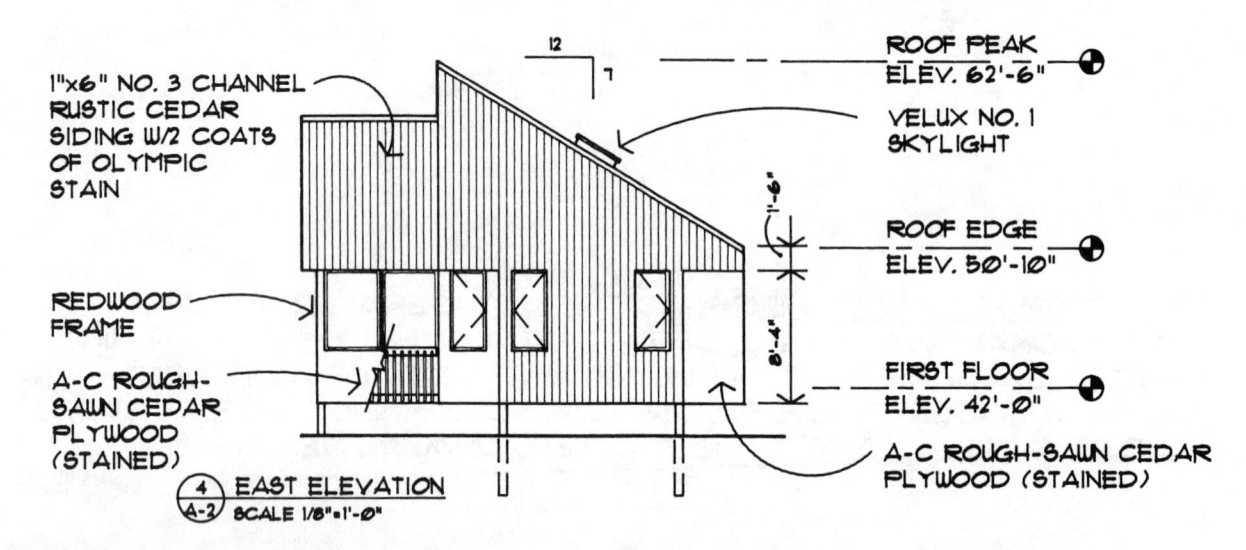

ROOF PITCH IS INDICATED BY SHOWING THE RISE AND RUN OF THE SLOPE. THE HORIZONTAL DISTANCE (THE RUN) IS ALWAYS 12; THE VERTICAL DIMENSION (THE RISE) DEFINES THE ANGLE. FOR EXAMPLE, THE CABIN HAS A 7:12 ROOF PITCH:

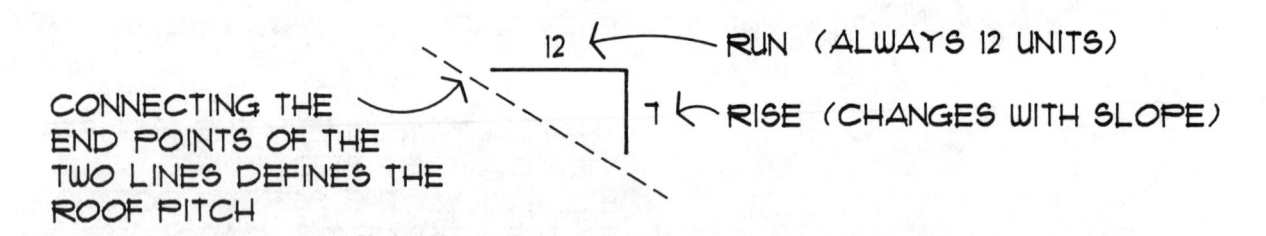

THE TITLE OF AN ELEVATION IS DETERMINED BY WHICH COMPASS SIDE OF THE BUILDING IS SHOWN. FOR EXAMPLE, THE VIEW ABOVE IS CALLED THE "EAST ELEVATION" — THIS WOULD BE THE VIEW SEEN ON THE EAST SIDE OF THE BUILDING.

HERE WE WILL PRESENT RESIDENTIAL AND COMMERCIAL ELEVATIONS AT A 1/8"=1'-0" SCALE. IT IS POSSIBLE TO DRAW RESIDENTIAL ELEVATIONS AT A 1/4" SCALE, BUT IT IS GENERALLY UNNECESSARY. KEEP IN MIND THAT ELEVATIONS SHOW MATERIALS AND DIMENSIONS; THERE IS NO NEED TO TAKE UP THE ADDED SPACE OF 1/4" ELEVATIONS IN THE DRAWING PACKAGE.

EXTERIOR ELEVATIONS

GENERALLY SPEAKING, AN ELEVATION IS RELATIVELY EASY TO DRAW: IT IS THE VIEW THAT YOU WOULD SEE BY TAKING A PICTURE OF THE OUTSIDE OF THE COMPLETED BUILDING. THE ORTHOGRAPHIC VIEW CAN GET A BIT COMPLICATED, HOWEVER, WHEN TWO SLOPED SURFACES INTERSECT (SUCH AS IN A ROOF CONDITION). THE BEST WAY TO APPROACH THIS SITUATION IS TO CONSTRUCT A STUDY MODEL OF THE PROJECT IN ORDER TO DETERMINE THE ANGLE OF INTERSECTION BEFORE YOU BEGIN THE ELEVATION.

THE STEP-BY-STEP ASSEMBLY OF THE CABIN SOUTH ELEVATION IS SHOWN BELOW. A GOOD WAY TO BEGIN IS TO MAKE A PRINT OF THE FLOOR PLAN TO USE AS A GUIDE. (IN THIS EXAMPLE, THE PLAN WAS REDUCED IN A COPY MACHINE BY 50% TO PRODUCE A 1/8" SCALE DRAWING.) SIMPLY ROTATE THE PLAN BY 90° IN ORDER TO CONSTRUCT EACH SUCCEEDING VIEW.

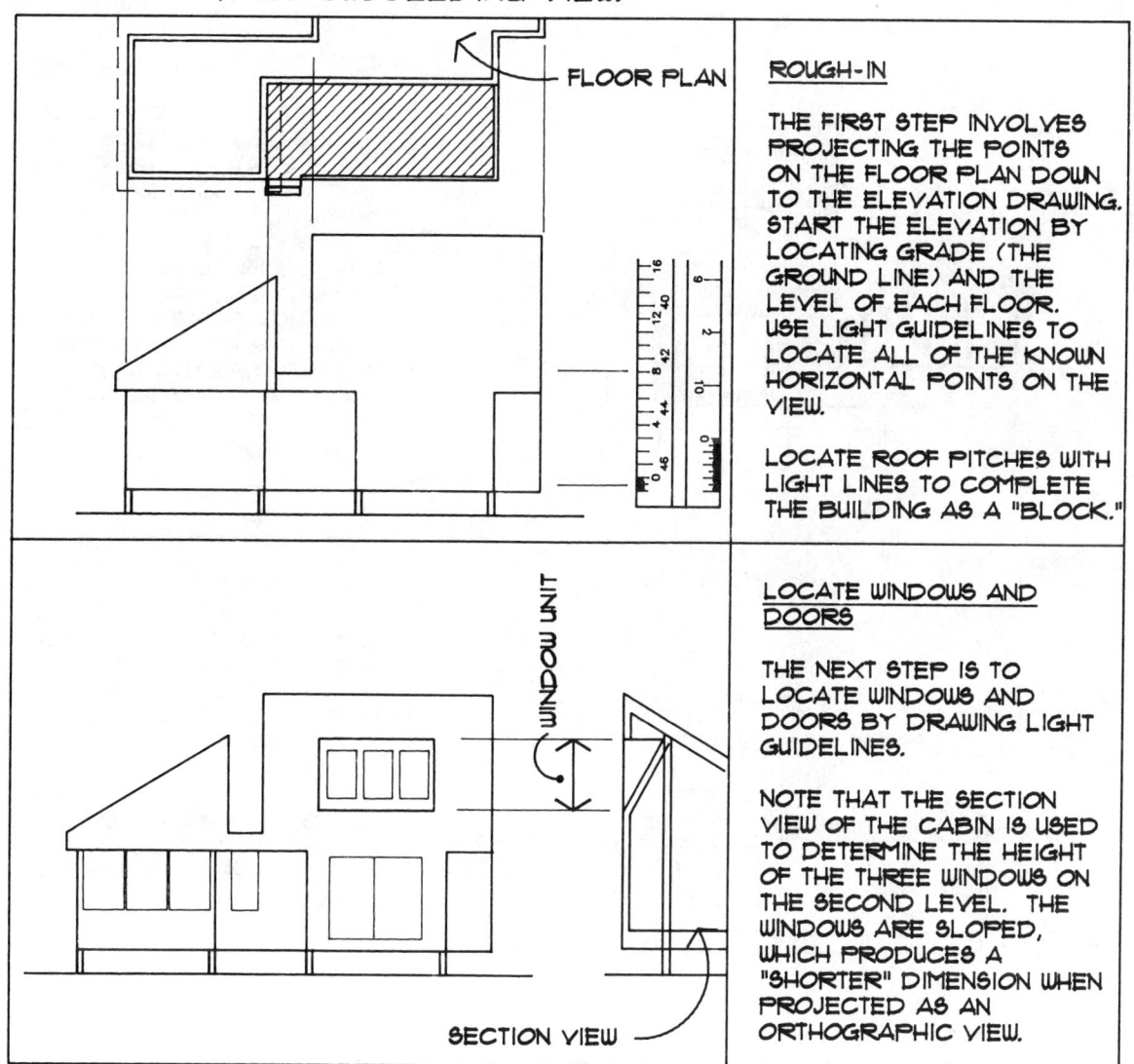

ROUGH-IN

THE FIRST STEP INVOLVES PROJECTING THE POINTS ON THE FLOOR PLAN DOWN TO THE ELEVATION DRAWING. START THE ELEVATION BY LOCATING GRADE (THE GROUND LINE) AND THE LEVEL OF EACH FLOOR. USE LIGHT GUIDELINES TO LOCATE ALL OF THE KNOWN HORIZONTAL POINTS ON THE VIEW.

LOCATE ROOF PITCHES WITH LIGHT LINES TO COMPLETE THE BUILDING AS A "BLOCK."

LOCATE WINDOWS AND DOORS

THE NEXT STEP IS TO LOCATE WINDOWS AND DOORS BY DRAWING LIGHT GUIDELINES.

NOTE THAT THE SECTION VIEW OF THE CABIN IS USED TO DETERMINE THE HEIGHT OF THE THREE WINDOWS ON THE SECOND LEVEL. THE WINDOWS ARE SLOPED, WHICH PRODUCES A "SHORTER" DIMENSION WHEN PROJECTED AS AN ORTHOGRAPHIC VIEW.

EXTERIOR ELEVATIONS   15-3

DARKEN THE SILHOUETTE AROUND THE VIEW

FINALIZE THE OUTLINE

IN THE NEXT STEP, DETAIL IS ADDED TO THE ELEVATION. CONSTRUCTION LINES ARE ERASED AND THE VIEW IS DARKENED. IT IS COMMON TO DRAW WINDOW FRAMES WITH DOUBLE LINES FOR ACCENT.

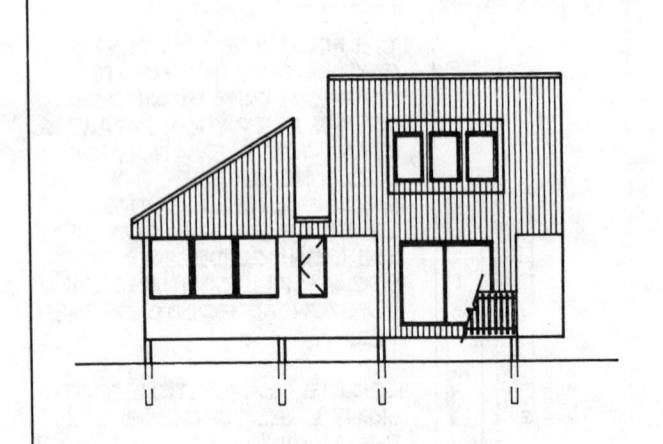

WINDOW FRAMES

ADD MATERIAL INDICATIONS

IN THIS STEP, CONSTRUCTION MATERIALS ARE ADDED TO THE ELEVATION. THE VERTICAL SIDING IS DRAWN WITH A "LIGHT-CRISP" LINE THAT SHOULDN'T COMPETE WITH THE BUILDING OUTLINE. DASHED LINES ARE USED TO INDICATE THE POSTS SET IN THE GROUND TO SUPPORT THE BUILDING (DASHED LINES ARE ALSO USED FOR FOOTINGS AND FOUNDATIONS).

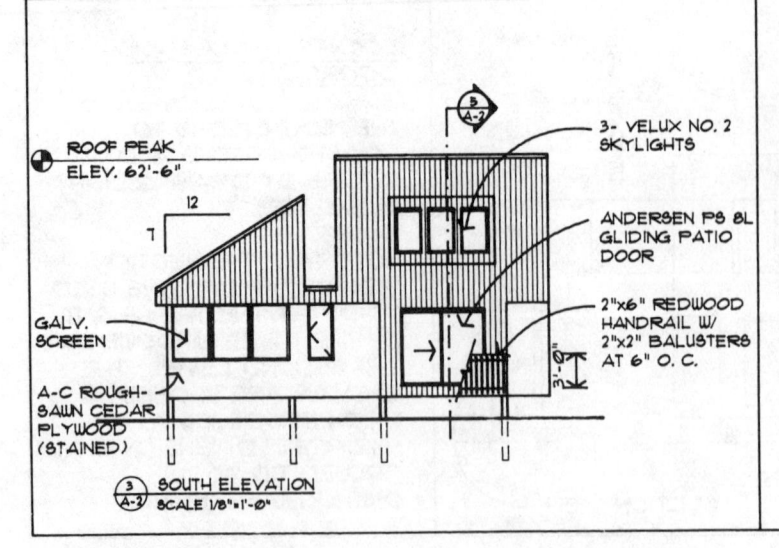

ROOF PEAK ELEV. 62'-6"

3- VELUX NO. 2 SKYLIGHTS

ANDERSEN PS 8L GLIDING PATIO DOOR

GALV. SCREEN

2"x6" REDWOOD HANDRAIL W/ 2"x2" BALUSTERS AT 6" O.C.

A-C ROUGH-SAWN CEDAR PLYWOOD (STAINED)

3 SOUTH ELEVATION
A-2 SCALE 1/8"=1'-0"

FINAL STEP

THE LAST STEP IN DRAWING THE ELEVATION IS TO ADD NOTES AND DIMENSIONS. NOTES SHOULD BE ALIGNED AND GROUPED TO "BALANCE" THE DETAIL. ONE PRACTICE IS TO PLACE NOTES ON ONE SIDE OF THE ELEVATION AND BULL'S-EYES ON THE OPPOSITE SIDE.

EXTERIOR ELEVATIONS 15-4

THE ASSEMBLY OF COMMERCIAL ELEVATIONS IS SIMILAR TO THE ASSEMBLY OF RESIDENTIAL ELEVATIONS IN EVERY RESPECT. IN OUR DISCUSSION OF COMMERCIAL ELEVATIONS, WE WILL USE THE STUDENT LIBRARY AS AN EXAMPLE. THE BUILDING SITS ON A SLOPED SITE THAT IS VISIBLE ON THE ELEVATION BELOW.

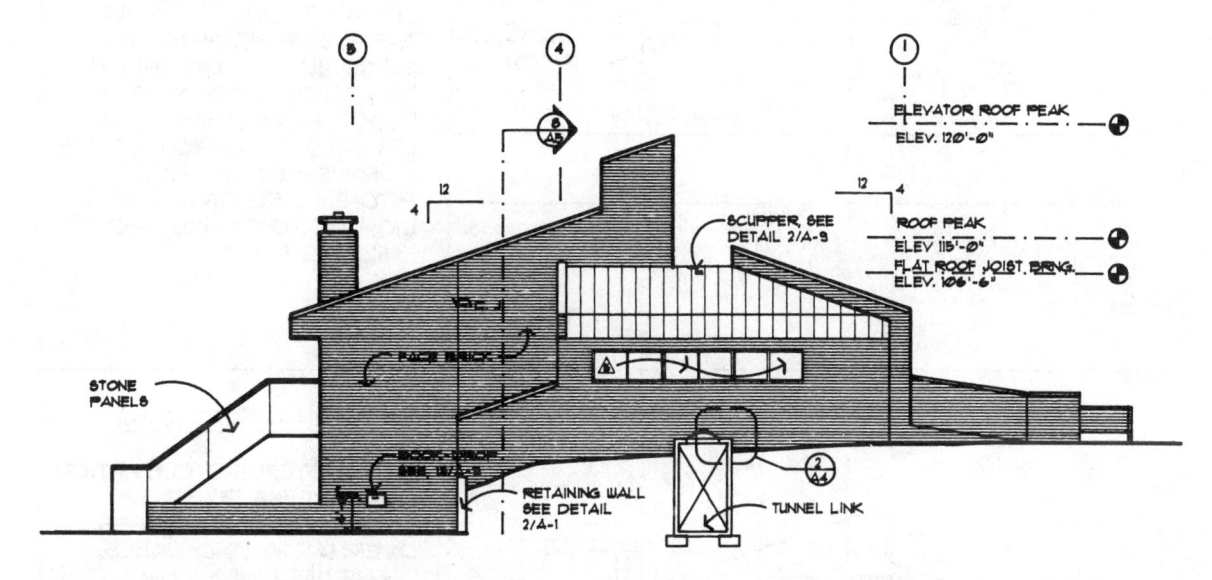

NOTE THAT THE ROOF PITCHES ARE VISIBLE ON THE ELEVATION ABOVE (THE EAST ELEVATION), WHILE IT IS NOT POSSIBLE TO SEE THAT THE BUILDING HAS A SLOPED ROOF ON THE NORTH ELEVATION (SHOWN BELOW). IN ORDER TO ASSEMBLE A COMPLETE MODEL OF THE PROJECT, ALL FOUR ELEVATIONS AND THE FLOOR PLAN WILL BE USED. JUST AS IN RESIDENTIAL ELEVATION VIEWS, THE PRIMARY FUNCTION OF COMMERCIAL ELEVATIONS IS TO SHOW: (1) BUILDING FORM, (2) MATERIALS, (3) WINDOWS AND DOORS, AND (4) FLOOR HEIGHTS.

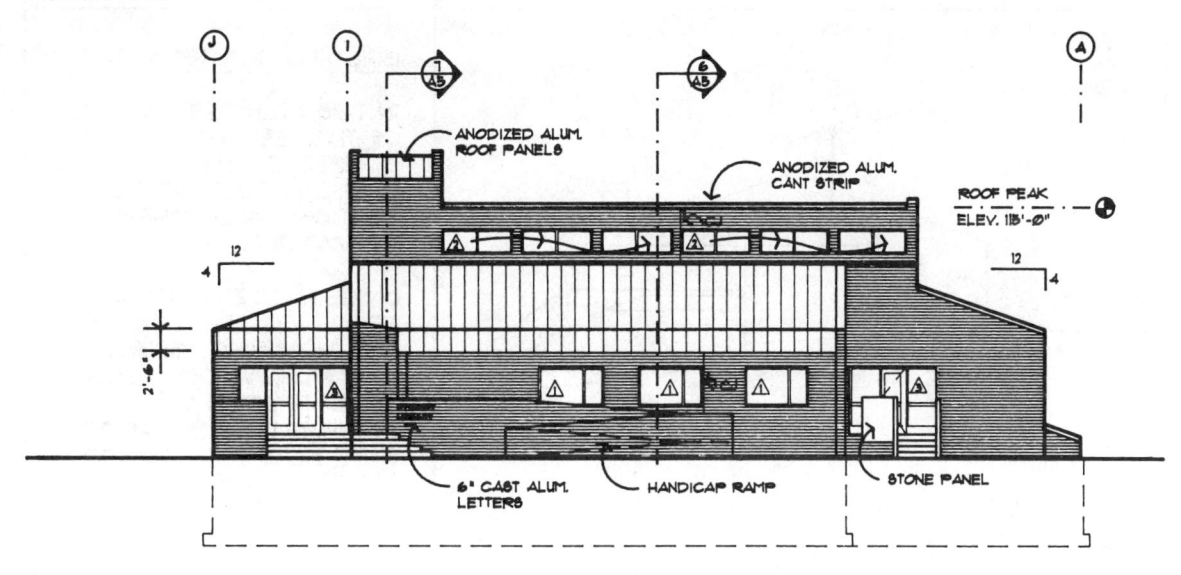

EXTERIOR ELEVATIONS   15-5

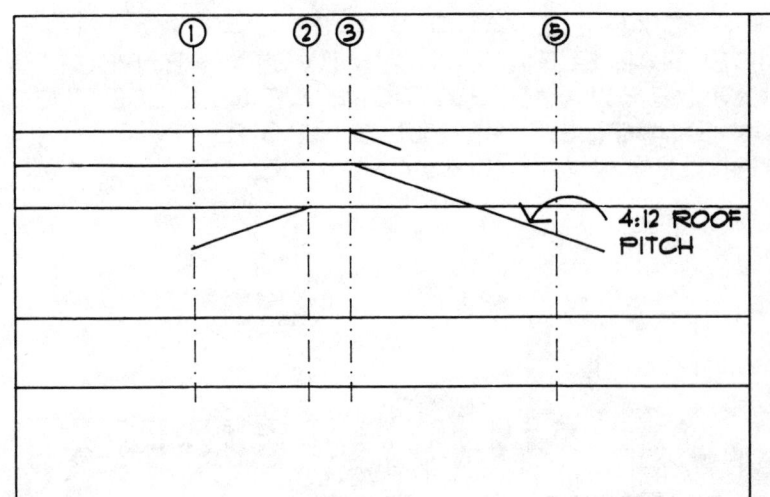

LOCATE GRIDS AND FLOORS

THE ASSEMBLY OF THIS RATHER COMPLICATED ELEVATION IS BEGUN BY LOCATING THE GRIDS AND THE FLOOR HEIGHTS. A GOOD WAY TO DO THIS IS TO PLACE A COPY OF THE FLOOR PLAN ABOVE THE DRAWING AND PROJECT THE CORNERS DOWN. ROOF PITCHES ARE DRAWN IN LIGHTLY TO DEFINE THE BUILDING FORM.

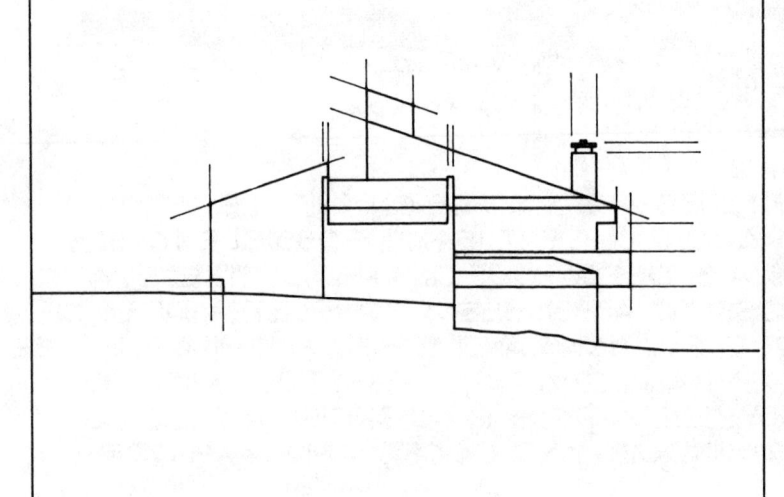

4:12 ROOF PITCH

ROUGH-IN THE BUILDING

IN THIS STEP THE ELEVATION IS FURTHER REFINED BY LOCATING ROOF PITCHES, OVERHANGS, AND WALLS. DRAW THE LINES LIGHTLY INITIALLY, THEN DARKEN THE ONES THAT WILL REMAIN ON THE FINAL DRAWING.

USE THE FLOOR ELEVATIONS ALREADY ESTABLISHED AS POINTS OF MEASURE. REMEMBER THAT IT IS IMPORTANT TO DEVELOP AN ACCURATELY SCALED DRAWING.

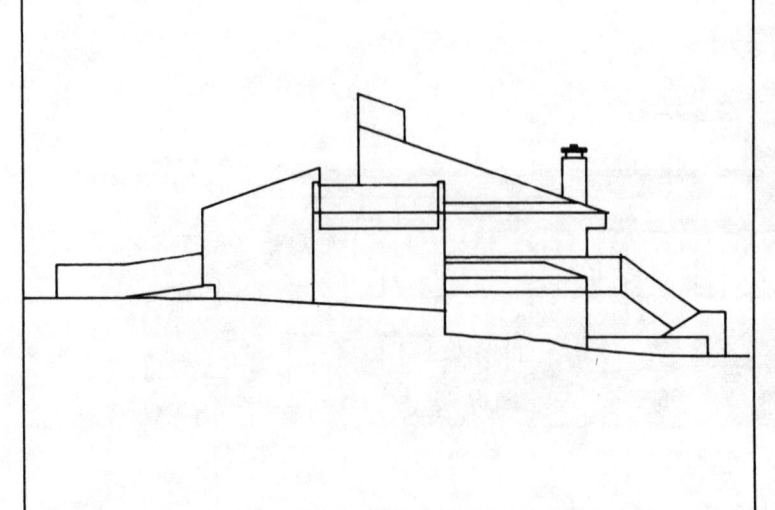

BUILDING OUTLINE

IN THIS STEP, THE OUTLINE OF THE ELEVATION IS COMPLETED BY COORDINATING THE PLANS, SECTIONS, AND OTHER ELEVATIONS.

ONCE AN ELEVATION IS RESOLVED, USE IT TO DRAW THE REMAINING VIEWS. FOR EXAMPLE, A ROOF HEIGHT DEVELOPED IN ONE DRAWING MUST BE AT THE SAME HEIGHT ON ALL OTHER VIEWS.

EXTERIOR ELEVATIONS

LOCATE DOORS AND WINDOWS

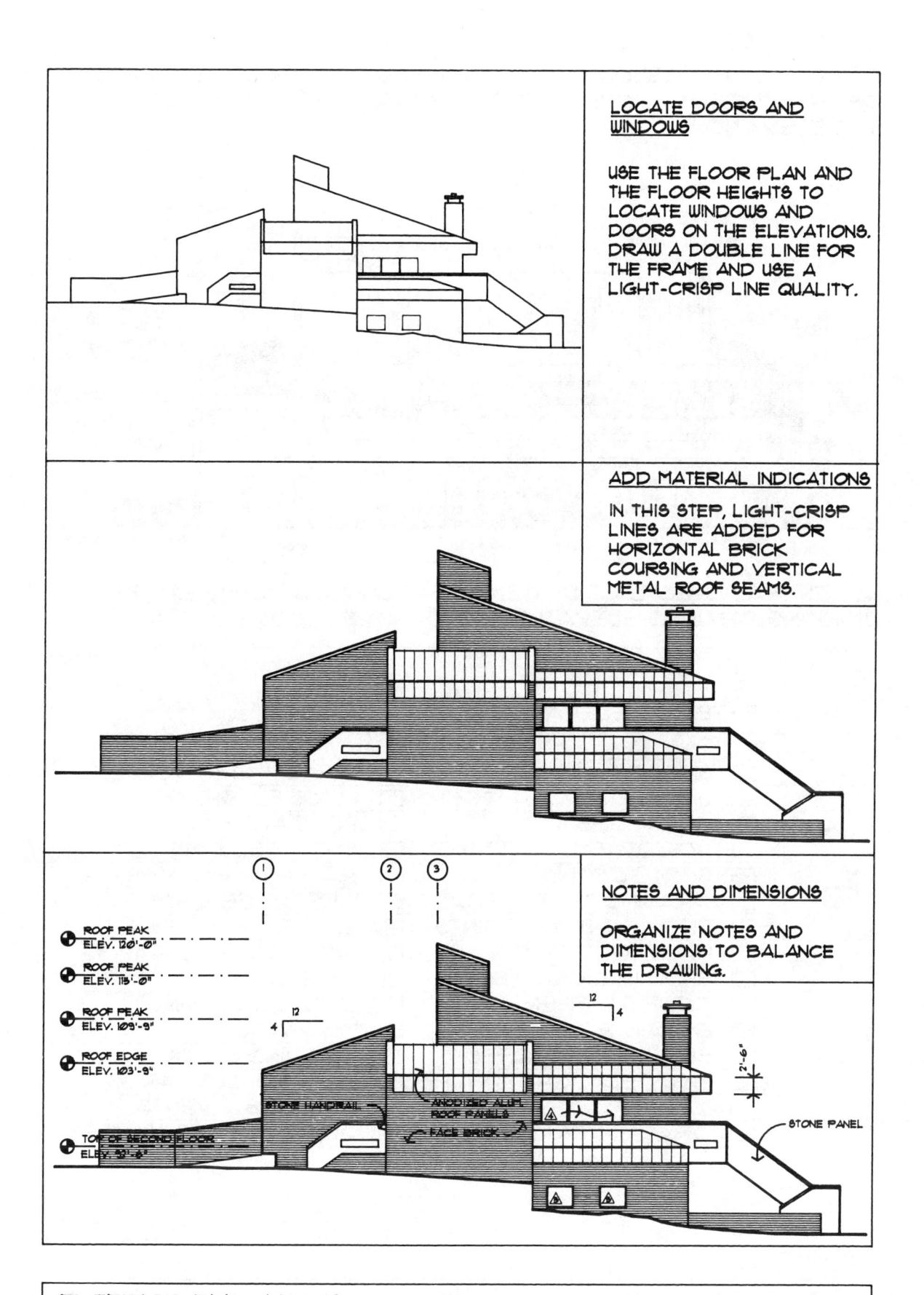

USE THE FLOOR PLAN AND THE FLOOR HEIGHTS TO LOCATE WINDOWS AND DOORS ON THE ELEVATIONS. DRAW A DOUBLE LINE FOR THE FRAME AND USE A LIGHT-CRISP LINE QUALITY.

ADD MATERIAL INDICATIONS

IN THIS STEP, LIGHT-CRISP LINES ARE ADDED FOR HORIZONTAL BRICK COURSING AND VERTICAL METAL ROOF SEAMS.

NOTES AND DIMENSIONS

ORGANIZE NOTES AND DIMENSIONS TO BALANCE THE DRAWING.

ROOF PEAK ELEV. 120'-0"
ROOF PEAK ELEV. 115'-0"
ROOF PEAK ELEV. 109'-9"
ROOF EDGE ELEV. 103'-9"
TOP OF SECOND FLOOR ELEV. 92'-6"

STONE HANDRAIL
ANODIZED ALUM. ROOF PANELS
FACE BRICK
STONE PANEL

EXTERIOR ELEVATIONS 15-7

THE ELEVATION BELOW SHOWS THE FINAL VIEW (SOUTH ELEVATION) OF THE LIBRARY. NOTE THAT TWO SECTION VIEWS ARE SHOWN ON THE ELEVATION.

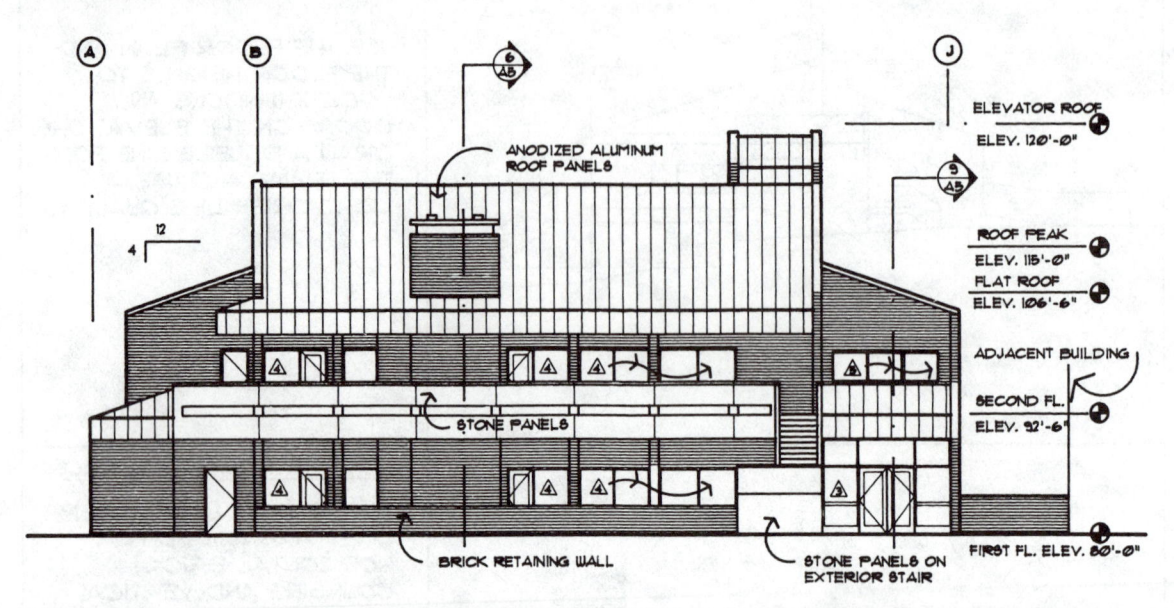

(Elevation drawing showing the South Elevation of the library, with callouts for: ANODIZED ALUMINUM ROOF PANELS, STONE PANELS, BRICK RETAINING WALL, STONE PANELS ON EXTERIOR STAIR, ADJACENT BUILDING. Elevations noted: ELEVATOR ROOF ELEV. 120'-0", ROOF PEAK ELEV. 115'-0", FLAT ROOF ELEV. 106'-6", SECOND FL. ELEV. 92'-6", FIRST FL. ELEV. 80'-0". Grid lines A, B, J. Roof slope 4:12.)

A GENERAL CHECKLIST OF ITEMS THAT SHOULD BE SHOWN ON WORKING DRAWING ELEVATIONS IS SHOWN BELOW.

EXTERIOR ELEVATION CHECKLIST

- ☐ SHOW FLOOR ELEVATION
- ☐ SHOW WINDOWS & DOORS
- ☐ GRID LINES
- ☐ HORIZONTAL DIMENSIONS
- ☐ SHOW FOOTINGS
- ☐ DRAWING TITLE & SCALE
- ☐ SHOW CONTROL JOINTS
- ☐ WALL SECTION CUT LINES
- ☐ SHOW WINDOW TYPES
- ☐ ROOF SCUPPERS
- ☐ DETAIL ROOF CURBS
- ☐ SHOW ROOF SLOPES
- ☐ MOUNTED LIGHT FIXTURES
- ☐ LADDERS
- ☐ DRAW EXTERIOR GRADE
- ☐ DRAW MATERIALS
- ☐ ROOF FLASHING
- ☐ INDICATE SIGNS
- ☐ SHOW COLUMNS
- ☐ RAILINGS & RAMPS
- ☐ FIREPLACE CHIMNEYS
- ☐ EXTERIOR STEPS
- ☐ HOSE BIBS & DRAINS
- ☐ SKYLIGHTS
- ☐ BRICK COURSING
- ☐ MECHANICAL EQUIPMENT
- ☐ LOADING DOCKS
- ☐ POSTS & BOLLARDS
- ☐ LOUVERS & VENTS
- ☐ ADJACENT STRUCTURES

EXTERIOR ELEVATIONS   15-8

EXTERIOR ELEVATION DETAILS

IN THIS SECTION WE WILL REVIEW THE TECHNIQUES USED TO DRAW A VARIETY OF ITEMS ON EXTERIOR ELEVATIONS. BUILDING MATERIALS DRAWN IN ELEVATION ARE NOT CROSSHATCHED (AS SHOWN IN UNIT 5). INSTEAD, THEY ARE DRAWN TO LOOK SIMILAR TO THE WAY THEY WOULD APPEAR IN A PICTURE. FOR EXAMPLE:

BRICK IS CROSSHATCHED THIS WAY.

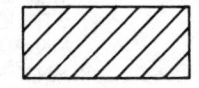

BRICK IS SHOWN THIS WAY IN ELEVATION.

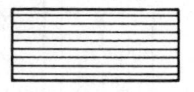

BUILDING MATERIALS SHOULD BE DRAWN WITH A LIGHT-CRISP LINE QUALITY. THE INTENT IS TO SHOW THE "FABRIC" OF A BUILDING; THE MATERIAL SHOULDN'T COMPETE WITH THE MAJOR LINES OF THE ELEVATION.

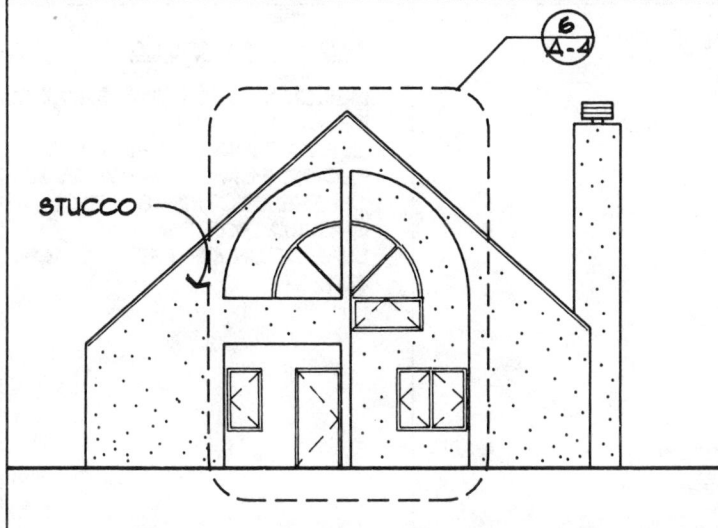

MATERIALS (STUCCO)

BUILDING MATERIALS ARE TYPICALLY DRAWN THE WAY THEY WOULD APPEAR WHEN CONSTRUCTED. THE VIEW TO THE LEFT SHOWS A STUCCO WALL. STUCCO CAN EITHER BE SHOWN AS STIPPLED (DOTTED) OR AS A PLAIN SURFACE WITH A NOTE.

THE DASHED DETAIL NOTE INDICATES THAT AN ENLARGED DETAIL OF THE ENTRY IS DRAWN ON DETAIL 6 ON SHEET A-4.

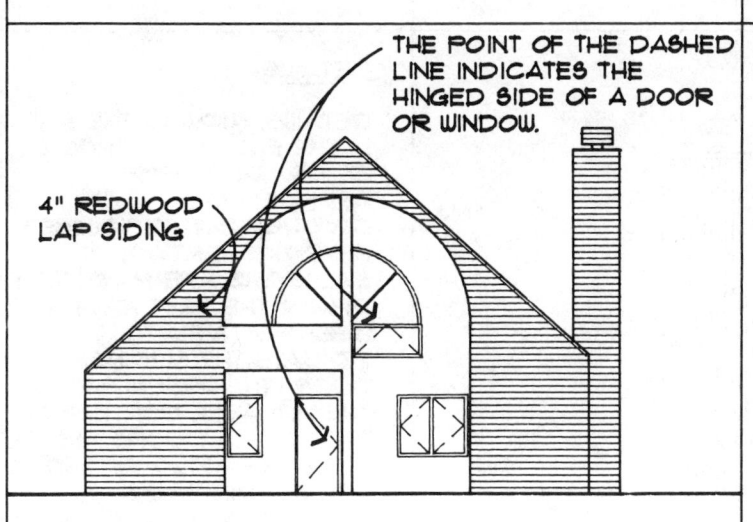

THE POINT OF THE DASHED LINE INDICATES THE HINGED SIDE OF A DOOR OR WINDOW.

4" REDWOOD LAP SIDING

MATERIALS (LAP SIDING)

THE SAME ELEVATION IS SHOWN HERE WITH 4" LAP SIDING. THE SIDING IS DRAWN WITH A LIGHT-CRISP LINE WEIGHT. USE A 1/16" ARCHITECT'S SCALE TO MEASURE THE SPACING. MATERIALS ON SMALL-SCALE ELEVATIONS DON'T TYPICALLY REQUIRE PRECISION MEASUREMENT, BUT MAINTAINING UNIFORM SPACING IS IMPORTANT. DASHED LINES ARE USED ON DOORS AND WINDOWS TO INDICATE THE DIRECTION OF SWING.

EXTERIOR ELEVATIONS 15-9

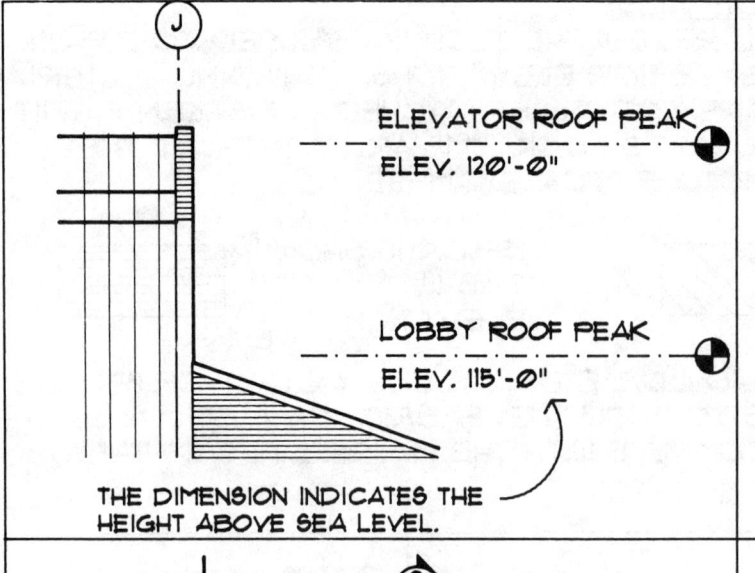

ELEVATION POINTS AND GRIDS

IN THIS VIEW, ELEVATION POINT SYMBOLS ARE SHOWN. ELEVATIONS TYPICALLY LOCATE MEASURABLE POINTS ON THE BUILDING SUCH AS STRUCTURAL BEAMS, FINISHED FLOOR HEIGHTS, AND ROOF PEAKS. A BUILDING GRID IS MARKED WITH THE GRID LETTER ENCLOSED IN A CIRCLE. IT IS COMMON TO SHOW GRIDS ONLY AT MAJOR POINTS ON THE ELEVATION (SUCH AS BUILDING CORNERS).

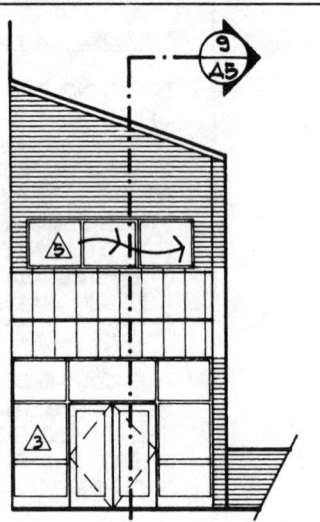

ELEVATOR ROOF PEAK
ELEV. 120'-0"

LOBBY ROOF PEAK
ELEV. 115'-0"

THE DIMENSION INDICATES THE HEIGHT ABOVE SEA LEVEL.

SECTION SYMBOLS

BUILDING SECTIONS SHOULD BE SHOWN ON THE ELEVATIONS (NOT ON THE FLOOR PLAN). THE ARROW ON THE SECTION SYMBOL SHOULD POINT IN THE DIRECTION OF THE SECTION CUT.

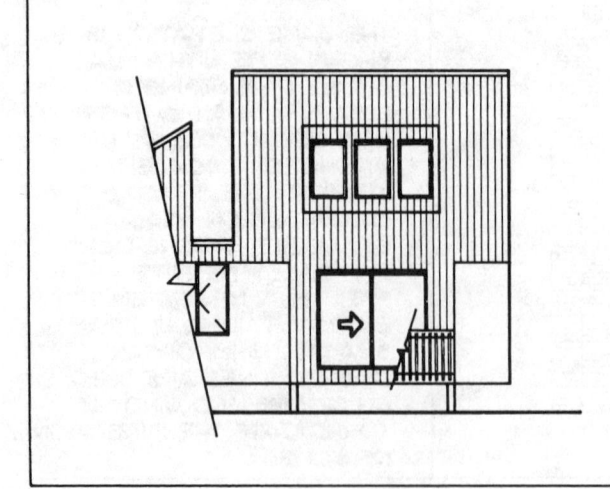

DETAILS

DETAILS, SUCH AS THE RAIL IN THE ELEVATION, SHOULD BE DRAWN TO SHOW APPROPRIATE CONSTRUCTION TECHNIQUES. HERE THE VERTICAL BALUSTERS ARE PARTIALLY DRAWN, THE REST HAVING BEEN REMOVED TO INDICATE THE SLIDING DOOR (THE ARROW SHOWS THE MOVABLE PORTION OF THE DOOR). DOORS AND WINDOWS SHOULD BE SHOWN WITH DOUBLE LINES (SPACED AT 2" IN SCALE) INDICATING THE FRAMES.

EXTERIOR ELEVATIONS 15-10

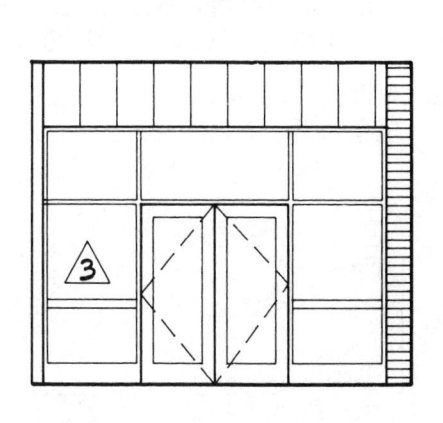

WINDOW TAGS

WINDOWS ARE INDICATED WITH A TRIANGULAR NUMBERED "TAG" THAT IS KEYED TO A LARGER-SCALE DETAIL. IDENTICAL WINDOWS WOULD BE IDENTIFIED WITH THE SAME NUMBER.

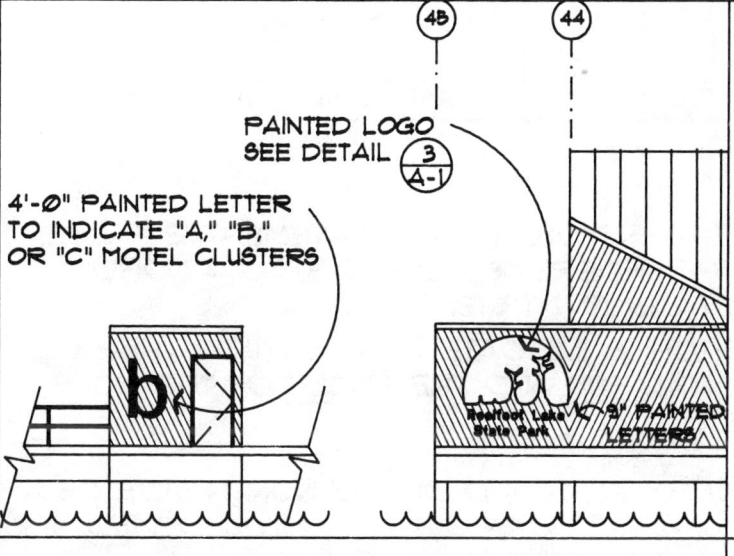

SPECIAL DETAILS

THE ELEVATIONS SHOW TWO SPECIAL PAINTED CONDITIONS ON THE BUILDING. THE LOGO IS TOO SMALL (AT A 1/8" SCALE) TO SHOW SUFFICIENT DETAIL SO IT IS KEYED TO A LARGER-SCALE DETAIL (3/A-1).

NOTE THAT THE WATERLINE IN THE ELEVATION IS SHOWN AS A SERIES OF ARCS DEPICTING WAVES.

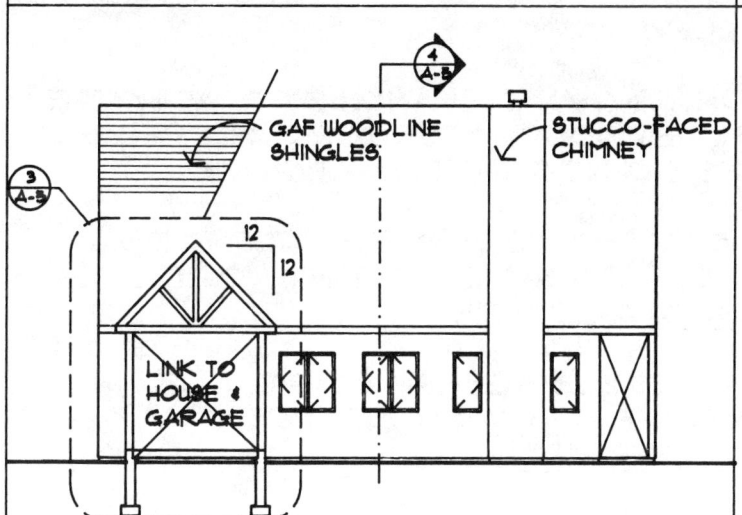

COMBINED SECTIONS AND ELEVATIONS

THE ELEVATION SHOWN TO THE LEFT CONTAINS A PARTIAL SECTION CUT THROUGH THE LINK. THIS ALLOWS A PORTION OF THE BUILDING TO BE REMOVED IN ORDER TO SHOW THE ENTIRE ELEVATION. PART OF THE SHINGLES ARE SHOWN WITH A SECTION CUT LINE.

NOTE THAT IT IS COMMON TO SHOW A GRADE LINE THAT EXTENDS BEYOND THE ELEVATION.

EXTERIOR ELEVATIONS   15-11

REPLAY
CALCULATE THE FOUR NUMBERED ELEVATION POINTS INDICATED ON THE ELEVATION BELOW (THE FIRST-FLOOR ELEVATION IS 100'-0").

1. SECOND FLOOR _____   3. ARC RADIUS _____
2. ROOF EDGE _____   4. TOP OF ROOF _____

MARK (T) IF THE STATEMENT IS TRUE. IF THE STATEMENT IS FALSE, MARK (F) AND CHANGE THE UNDERLINED WORD(S) TO A WORD THAT WOULD MAKE THE STATEMENT TRUE.

_____ ( ) 5. ROOF PITCH IS INDICATED BY SHOWING THE HORIZONTAL <u>RUN</u> AND THE <u>ANGLE</u> OF THE ROOF SLOPE.

_____ ( ) 6. IF YOU WERE TO STAND ON THE NORTH SIDE OF A BUILDING AND LOOK SOUTH, YOU WOULD VIEW THE <u>NORTH</u> ELEVATION.

_____ ( ) 7. BEGIN DRAWING AN ELEVATION BY PLACING THE <u>SECTION</u> VIEW ABOVE YOUR WORK AND PROJECT THE LINES DOWN TO THE ELEVATION VIEW.

_____ ( ) 8. BUILDING MATERIALS IN AN ELEVATION VIEW SHOULD BE DRAWN THE WAY THEY WOULD LOOK IN A <u>CROSSHATCHED</u> VIEW.

_____ ( ) 9. SECTION VIEW BUBBLES SHOULD BE SHOWN ON THE <u>ELEVATION</u> VIEW, NOT ON THE <u>FLOOR PLAN</u>.

_____ ( ) 10. ELEVATION VIEWS SHOW <u>HEIGHT</u> AND <u>DEPTH</u>.

EXTERIOR ELEVATIONS   15-12

16 BUILDING SECTIONS

A SET OF ARCHITECTURAL DRAWINGS IS COMPRISED OF THREE ORTHOGRAPHIC VIEWS— PLANS, ELEVATIONS, AND SECTIONS. THE SECTION VIEW, WHICH IS GENERATED BY CUTTING A VERTICAL PLANE THROUGH THE BUILDING, IS PERHAPS THE MOST DIFFICULT TO DRAW, BUT IT CONVEYS THE GREATEST AMOUNT OF INFORMATION ABOUT THE BUILDING. AS DISCUSSED IN UNIT 17, THERE IS A STRONG LINK BETWEEN BUILDING SECTIONS AND WALL SECTIONS. BUILDING SECTIONS ARE CUT THROUGH THE ENTIRE PROJECT AND ARE DRAWN AT A SMALL SCALE; THESE DRAWINGS THEN ACT AS AN INDEX FOR THE LARGER-SCALE WALL SECTIONS.

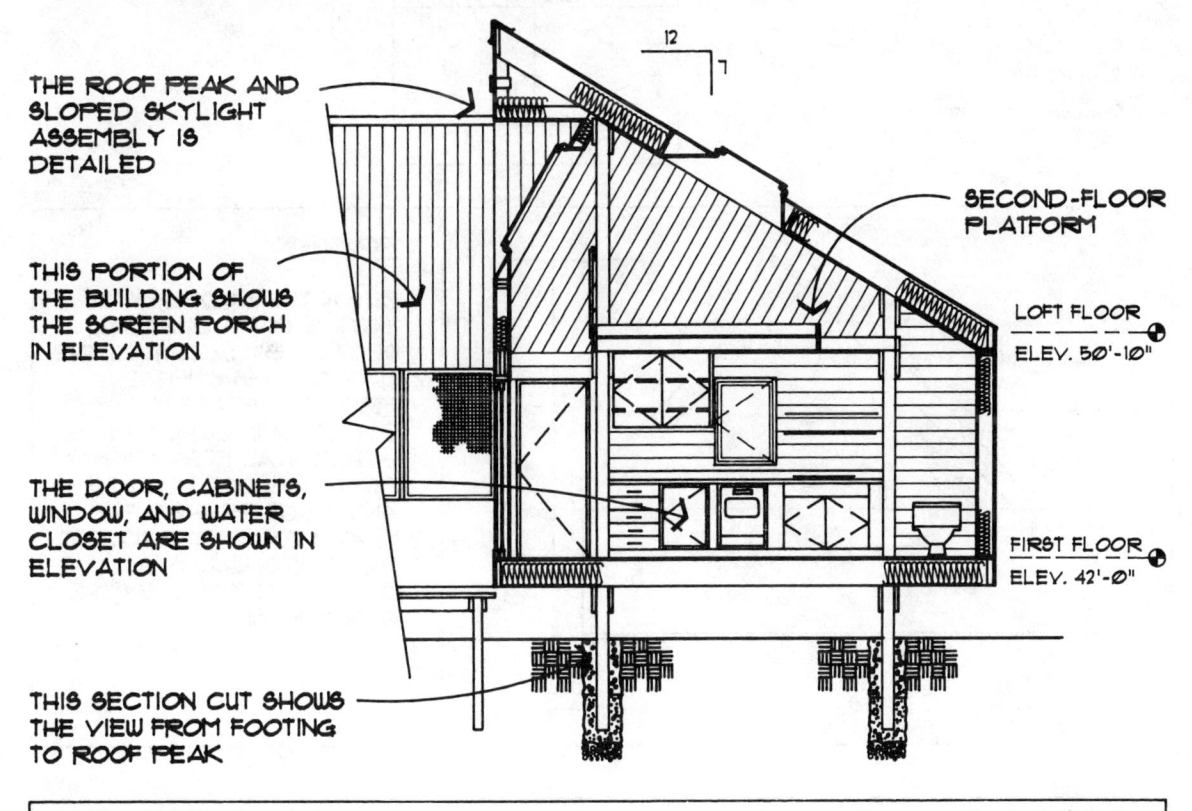

- THE ROOF PEAK AND SLOPED SKYLIGHT ASSEMBLY IS DETAILED
- THIS PORTION OF THE BUILDING SHOWS THE SCREEN PORCH IN ELEVATION
- THE DOOR, CABINETS, WINDOW, AND WATER CLOSET ARE SHOWN IN ELEVATION
- THIS SECTION CUT SHOWS THE VIEW FROM FOOTING TO ROOF PEAK
- SECOND-FLOOR PLATFORM
- LOFT FLOOR ELEV. 50'-10"
- FIRST FLOOR ELEV. 42'-0"

| BUILDING SECTIONS | 16-1 |

IF THERE IS A RULE OF THUMB FOR LOCATING A BUILDING SECTION, IT WOULD BE TO MAKE THE CUT THROUGH THE MOST COMPLEX PART OF A BUILDING. A SECOND RULE WOULD BE TO CUT SECTIONS THROUGH EVERY UNIQUE CONDITION IN THE PROJECT- THIS WOULD INCLUDE TWO-STORY SPACES, ROOF OVERHANGS, AND BALCONIES. FOLLOWING THESE RULES WILL HELP TO ASSURE A BETTER UNDERSTANDING OF THE PROJECT FOR THOSE USING YOUR BUILDING SECTIONS.

BUILDING SECTIONS ARE GENERATED BY FIRST SELECTING THE CUTS ON THE FLOOR PLAN. THE PLAN BELOW SHOWS THREE SECTION PLANE CUTS THROUGH THE HOUSE. SECTION A-A IS CUT THROUGH THE GARAGE AND SHOWS THE TRUSS. SECTION B-B CUTS THROUGH THE LINK BETWEEN THE HOUSE AND GARAGE. SECTION C-C DEVELOPS A PLANE THROUGH THE VAULTED DINING ROOM AND STAIR; BELOW WE WILL EXAMINE THE STEPS IN DEVELOPINT THAT CUT.

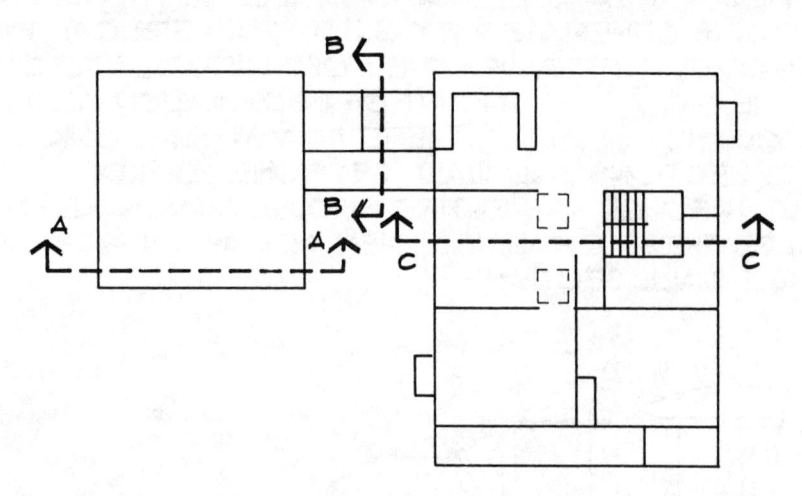

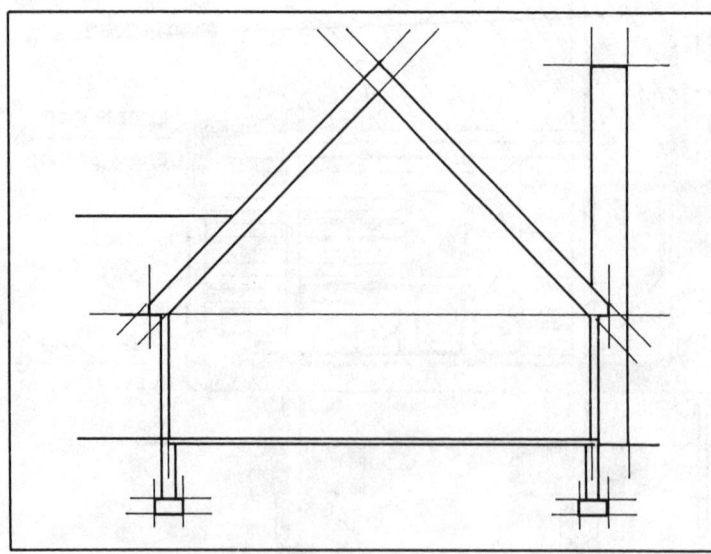

ROUGH-IN

BEGIN THE PROCESS OF LAYING OUT A BUILDING SECTION BY LOCATING THE MAJOR LINES ON THE PROJECT. START BY ESTABLISHING THE HORIZONTAL ELEVATION POINTS (FLOOR HEIGHTS AND ROOF PEAKS). THE NEXT STEP IS TO PROJECT THE GRIDS, WALLS, AND COLUMNS DOWN FROM THE FLOOR PLAN.

BUILDING SECTIONS　　　　　16-2

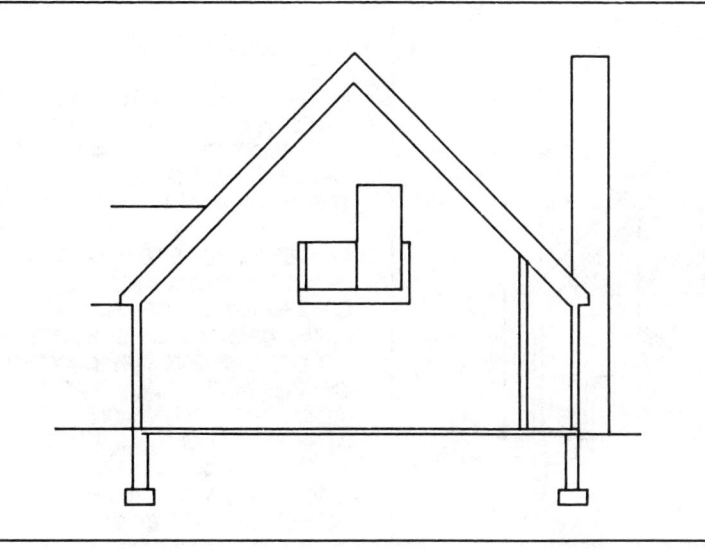

REFINE WALL LAYOUT

NEXT, ALL MAJOR OBJECTS ARE LOCATED ON THE SECTION. OBJECTS SUCH AS THE FLOOR SLAB, SECOND FLOOR, AND WALLS ARE PLACED.

USE CRISP LINES FOR FINAL OUTLINES OF THE OBJECTS ON THE SECTION.

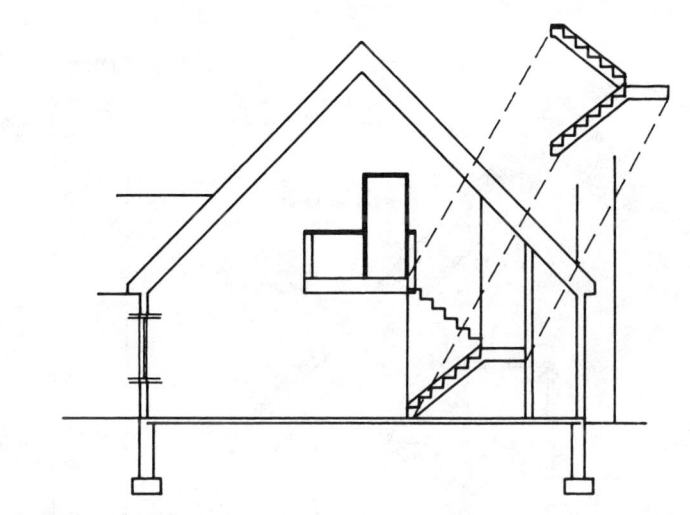

DETAIL LAYOUT

IN THIS STEP, DETAILS ARE ADDED TO THE BUILDING SECTION. IN THE EXAMPLE, THE STAIR TREADS AND RISERS PLUS THE WINDOW HEAD AND SILL ARE LOCATED.

IT IS IMPORTANT TO DRAW THE BUILDING OUTLINE ACCURATELY SO THAT AN ITEM SUCH AS A STAIR WILL FIT CORRECTLY.

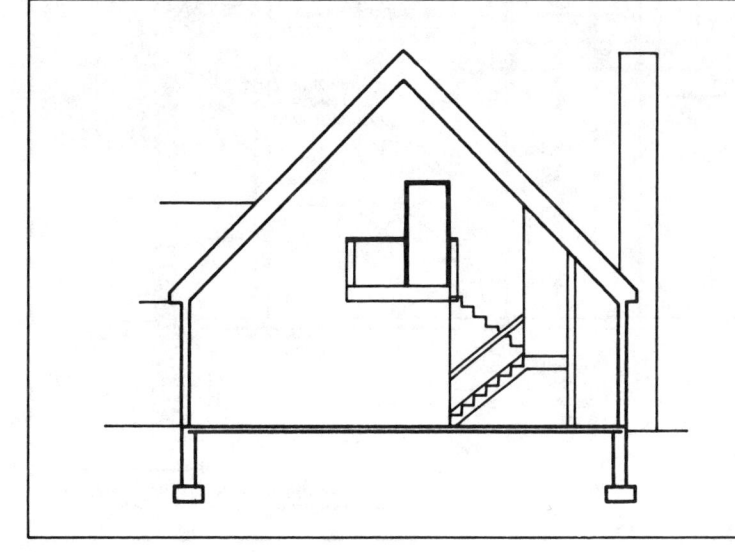

SECTION OUTLINE

ONCE THE DETAILS HAVE BEEN FINALIZED, THE CUT LINE THROUGH THE BUILDING IS DARKENED. ONE TECHNIQUE FOR DOING THIS IS TO USE A TECH PEN TO INK THE SILHOUETTE.

BUILDING SECTIONS   16-3

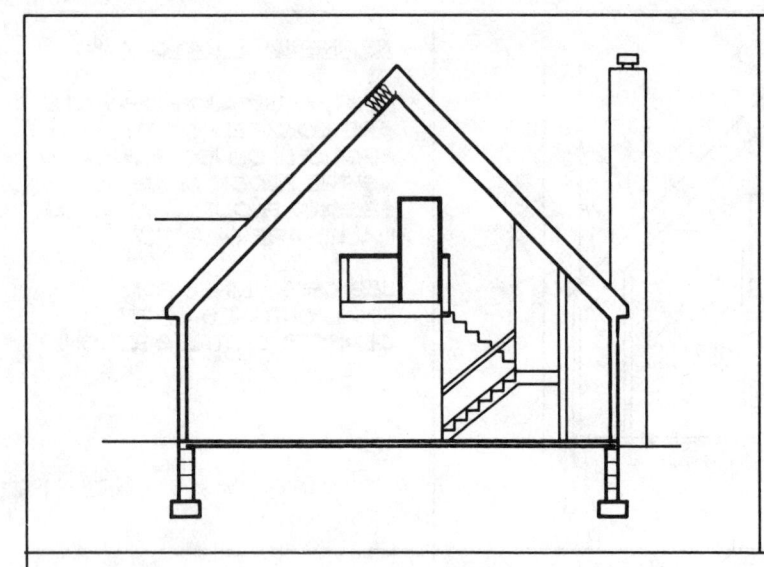

MATERIAL INDICATIONS

IN THIS STEP, MATERIAL HATCHING IS ADDED TO THE SECTION. USE A LIGHT-CRISP LINE TO INDICATE THE MATERIALS.

IN THE FINAL STEP, SHOWN BELOW, NOTES AND DIMENSIONS ARE ADDED. FIRST USE TRACING PAPER TO DETERMINE THE LAYOUT OF THE MATERIAL. THEN ADD THE DIMENSION STRINGS, AND FINALLY THE NOTES. DRAW LIGHT GUIDELINES TO ALIGN NOTES ON THE DRAWING.

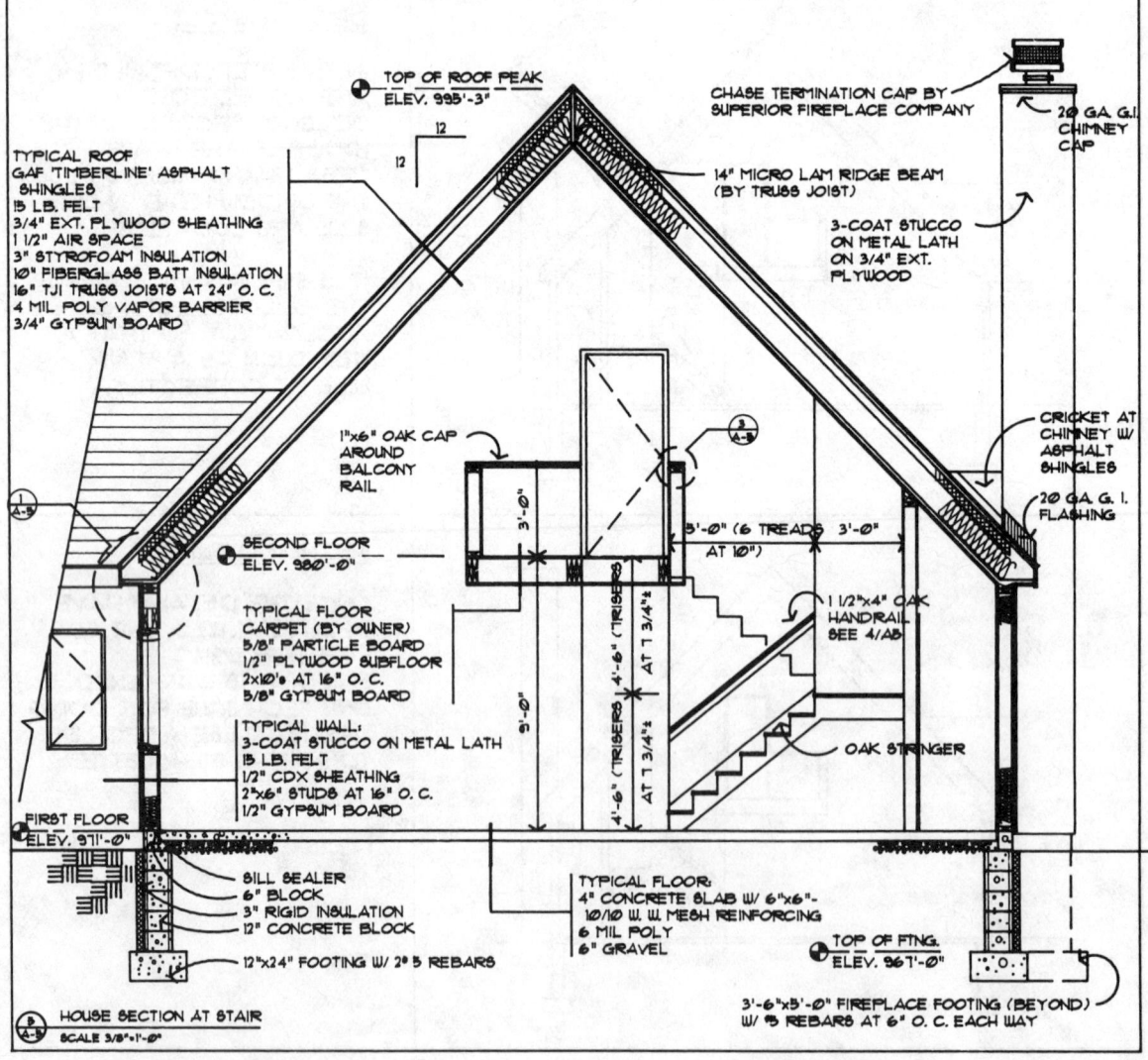

TOP OF ROOF PEAK
ELEV. 993'-3"

CHASE TERMINATION CAP BY SUPERIOR FIREPLACE COMPANY

20 GA G.I. CHIMNEY CAP

TYPICAL ROOF
GAF 'TIMBERLINE' ASPHALT SHINGLES
15 LB. FELT
3/4" EXT. PLYWOOD SHEATHING
1 1/2" AIR SPACE
3" STYROFOAM INSULATION
10" FIBERGLASS BATT INSULATION
16" TJI TRUSS JOISTS AT 24" O.C.
4 MIL POLY VAPOR BARRIER
3/4" GYPSUM BOARD

14" MICRO LAM RIDGE BEAM (BY TRUSS JOIST)

3-COAT STUCCO ON METAL LATH ON 3/4" EXT. PLYWOOD

1"x6" OAK CAP AROUND BALCONY RAIL

CRICKET AT CHIMNEY W/ ASPHALT SHINGLES

20 GA G.I. FLASHING

SECOND FLOOR
ELEV. 980'-0"

3'-0" (6 TREADS AT 10") 3'-0"

1 1/2"x4" OAK HANDRAIL SEE 4/A8

TYPICAL FLOOR
CARPET (BY OWNER)
5/8" PARTICLE BOARD
1/2" PLYWOOD SUBFLOOR
2x10's AT 16" O.C.
5/8" GYPSUM BOARD

4'-6" (7 RISERS AT 7 3/4"±)

OAK STRINGER

TYPICAL WALL
3-COAT STUCCO ON METAL LATH
15 LB. FELT
1/2" CDX SHEATHING
2"x6" STUDS AT 16" O.C.
1/2" GYPSUM BOARD

FIRST FLOOR
ELEV. 971'-0"

SILL SEALER
6" BLOCK
3" RIGID INSULATION
12" CONCRETE BLOCK

TYPICAL FLOOR
4" CONCRETE SLAB W/ 6"x6"- 10/10 W.W. MESH REINFORCING
6 MIL POLY
6" GRAVEL

TOP OF FTNG.
ELEV. 967'-0"

12"x24" FOOTING W/ 2 #5 REBARS

3'-6"x5'-0" FIREPLACE FOOTING (BEYOND) W/ #5 REBARS AT 6" O.C. EACH WAY

HOUSE SECTION AT STAIR
SCALE 3/8"=1'-0"

BUILDING SECTIONS

16-4

WE WILL USE THE FIRE STATION TO EXAMINE THE STEPS IN THE ASSEMBLY OF COMMERCIAL BUILDING SECTIONS. BEGIN THE PROCESS BY MAKING SECTION CUTS THROUGH PARTS OF THE PROJECT THAT HAVE DIFFERENT CONSTRUCTION SYSTEMS. USE THE FLOOR PLAN AS A GUIDE TO MARK THE LOCATION OF EACH PROPOSED CUT. THE POINT IS TO MARK ALL CUTS IN THE BUILDING THAT SHOW UNIQUE CONSTRUCTION.

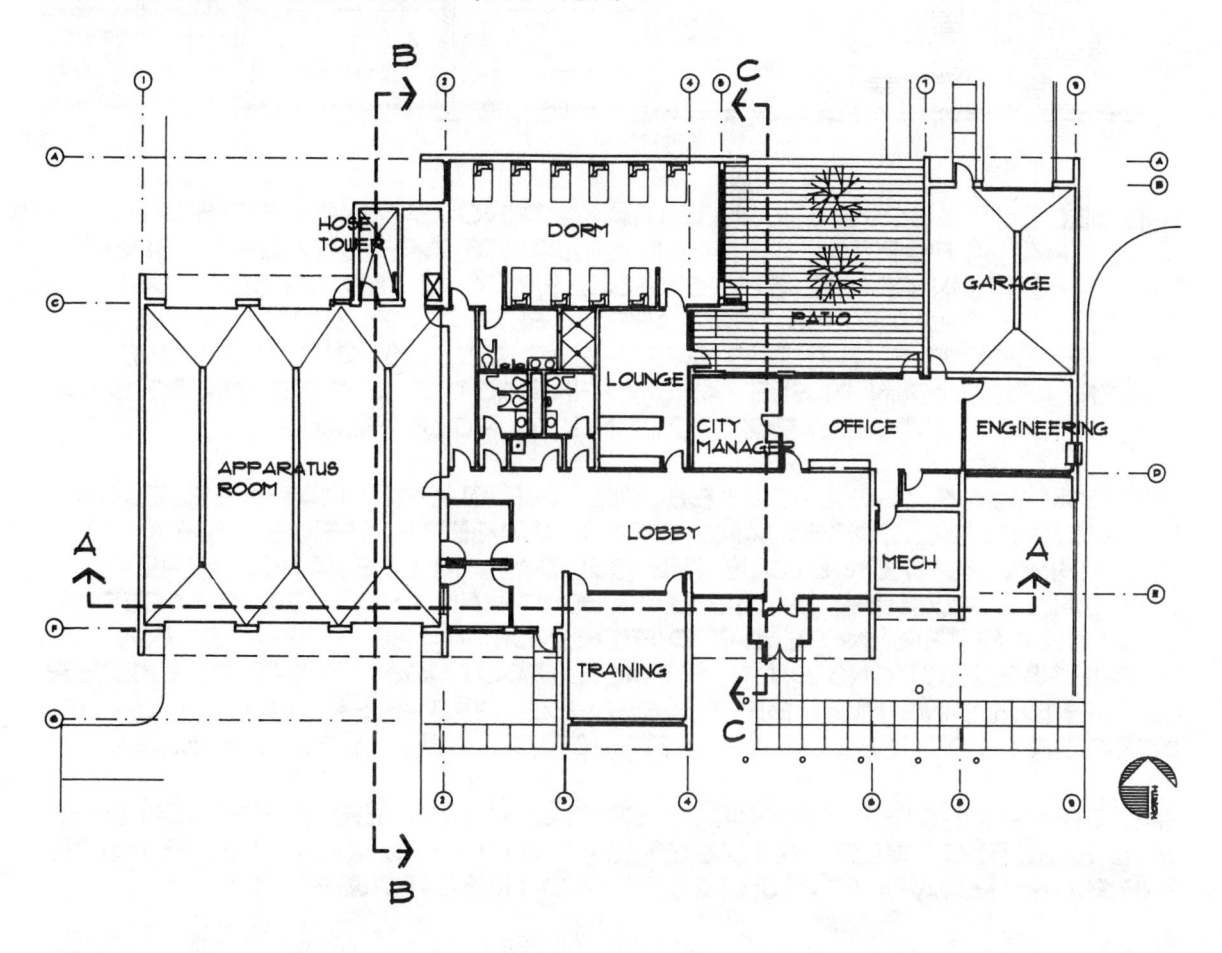

SECTION A-A CUTS THROUGH THE APPARATUS ROOM, THE TRAINING AREA, AND THE ENTRY. THE CUT IS CALLED A **LONGITUDINAL** SECTION BECAUSE IT IS CUT THROUGH THE LONG AXIS OF THE BUILDING. SECTIONS B-B AND C-C ARE CALLED **TRANSVERSE** CUTS BECAUSE THEY ARE CUT THROUGH THE SHORT AXIS.

THE ILLUSTRATION ABOVE SHOWS STRAIGHT SECTION CUTS THROUGH THE BUILDING. IN SOME SITUATIONS, HOWEVER, IT MIGHT BE A GOOD DECISION TO OFFSET THE CUT LINES IN ORDER TO SHOW MORE OF THE PROJECT. KEEP IN MIND THAT SECTION CUTS ARE GENERATED ON THE PLAN VIEW. THE SECTION SYMBOLS SHOULD BE SHOWN ON THE EXTERIOR ELEVATIONS, NOT ON THE PLAN.

BUILDING SECTIONS   16-5

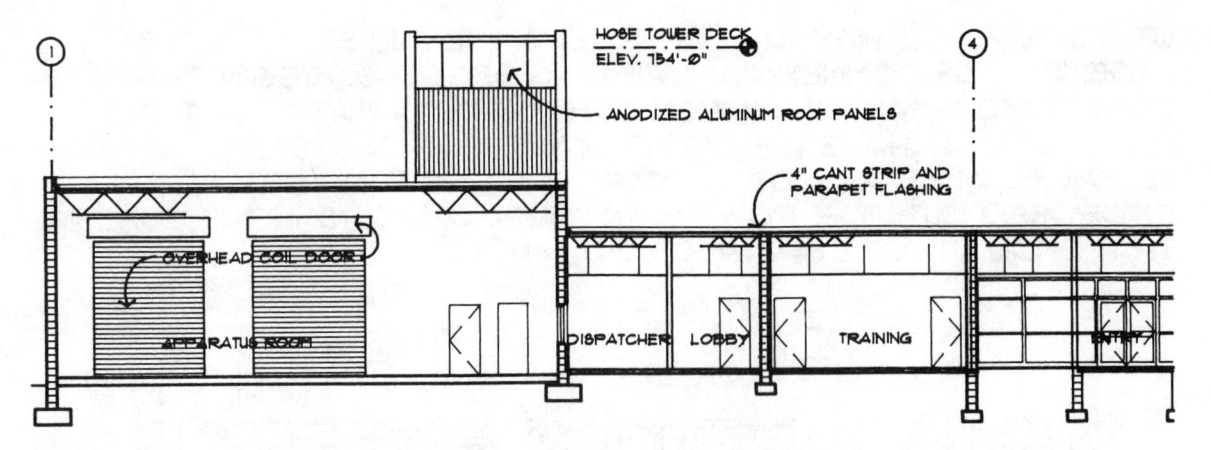

THE SECTION ABOVE SHOWS CUT A-A THROUGH THE FIRE STATION. NOTE THAT A PORTION OF THE BAR JOISTS ARE DRAWN TO SHOW THE DIRECTION OF THE STRUCTURAL SPAN. BUILDING SECTIONS TYPICALLY SHOW ITEMS THAT ARE IN ELEVATION BEYOND THE CUT. (IN THIS EXAMPLE, THE TWO OVERHEAD DOORS AND THE HOSE TOWER ARE SHOWN IN ELEVATION.) IN FACT, IT IS COMMON TO SHOW THE ENTIRE SECTION (FROM FOOTING TO ROOF PEAK).

SECTION CUT C-C IS SHOWN BELOW. THE SHORT TRANSVERSE CUT IS THROUGH THE LOBBY AND CITY MANAGER'S OFFICE. THE REMAINING PORTION SHOWS THE BUILDING IN ELEVATION. THE BUILDING STRUCTURE SHOWS BAR JOISTS (IN END VIEW) SPACED AT 2'-0" ON CENTER. NOTE THE DIFFERENCE IN THE DEPTH OF FOOTINGS IN THE TWO SECTIONS ON THIS PAGE. FOOTINGS AT THE PERIMETER OF THE BUILDING MUST BE PLACED BELOW THE FROST LINE, WHILE INTERIOR FOOTINGS CAN BE SET JUST BELOW THE FLOOR SLAB.

THE STEP-BY-STEP ASSEMBLY OF THE TRANSVERSE SECTION B-B WILL BE DESCRIBED ON PAGES 16-7 AND 16-8. THAT CUT IS MADE THROUGH THE APPARATUS ROOM AND HOSE TOWER.

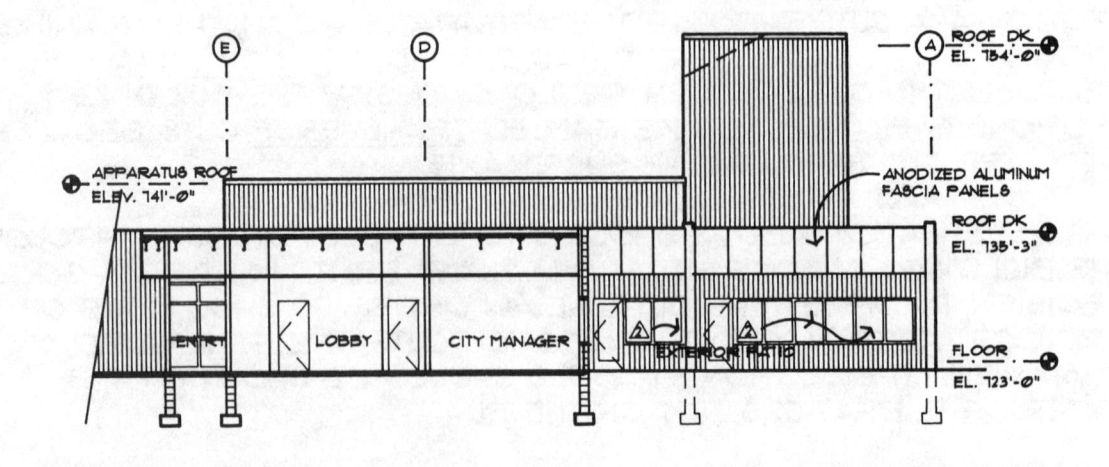

BUILDING SECTIONS

LOCATE THE GRIDS, WALLS, AND FLOORS

THE FIRST STEP INVOLVES LOCATING FLOOR HEIGHTS AND GRIDS ON THE SECTION. USE THE CUT LINES ON THE FLOOR PLAN TO PROJECT WALLS DOWN TO THE SECTION.

ROUGH-IN

IN THIS STEP, DETAILS SUCH AS WALL WIDTHS ARE ADDED TO THE SECTION. USE LIGHT GUIDELINES TO ROUGH-IN THE BUILDING OUTLINE.

SECTION OUTLINE

IN THIS STEP, THE SECTION CUT LINE IS DARKENED TO ACCENT THE BUILDING. REFINE THE DETAIL BY ERASING UNNECESSARY GUIDELINES.

BUILDING SECTIONS 16-7

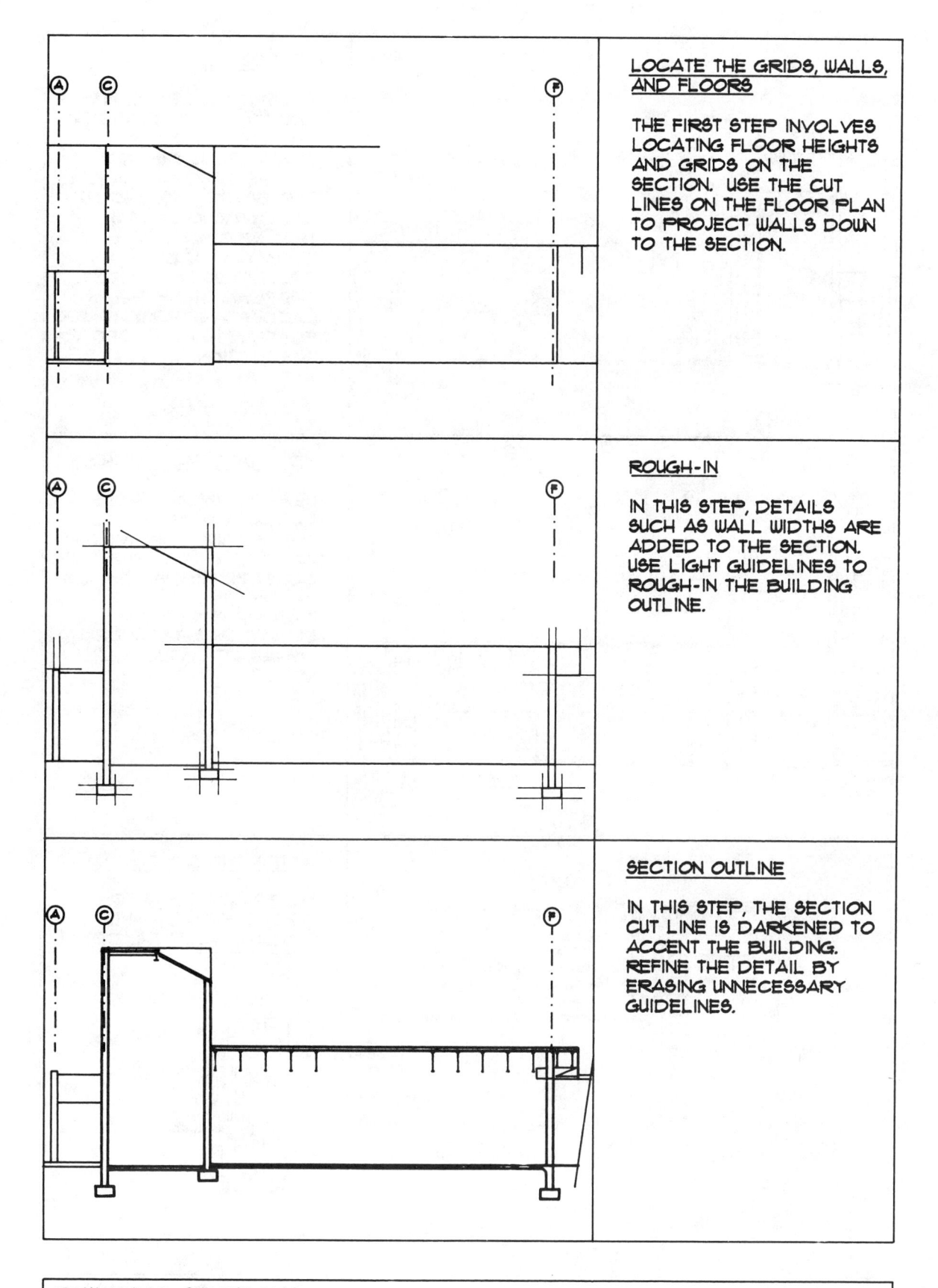

ADD DETAILS

ADDITIONAL DETAIL IS ADDED TO THE SECTION IN THIS STEP, AND THE STRUCTURE IS DEFINED (IN THIS CASE, BAR JOISTS AND BEAMS ARE SHOWN). WINDOWS AND DOORS THAT APPEAR IN ELEVATION ARE PROJECTED DOWN FROM THE PLAN. HERE THE LADDER AND HOSE TOWER PLATFORM ARE ADDED TO THE SECTION.

ADD MATERIAL HATCHING

NEXT, MATERIAL CROSS-HATCHING IS ADDED TO THE SECTION. USE A LIGHT-CRISP LINE TO DEFINE THE CONSTRUCTION MATERIALS.

MATERIALS SHOWN IN ELEVATION SHOULD BE DRAWN WITH A LIGHT LINE WEIGHT.

NOTES AND DIMENSIONS

THE FINAL STEP IS TO ORGANIZE NOTES AND DIMENSIONS ON THE DETAIL.

BUILDING SECTIONS   16-8

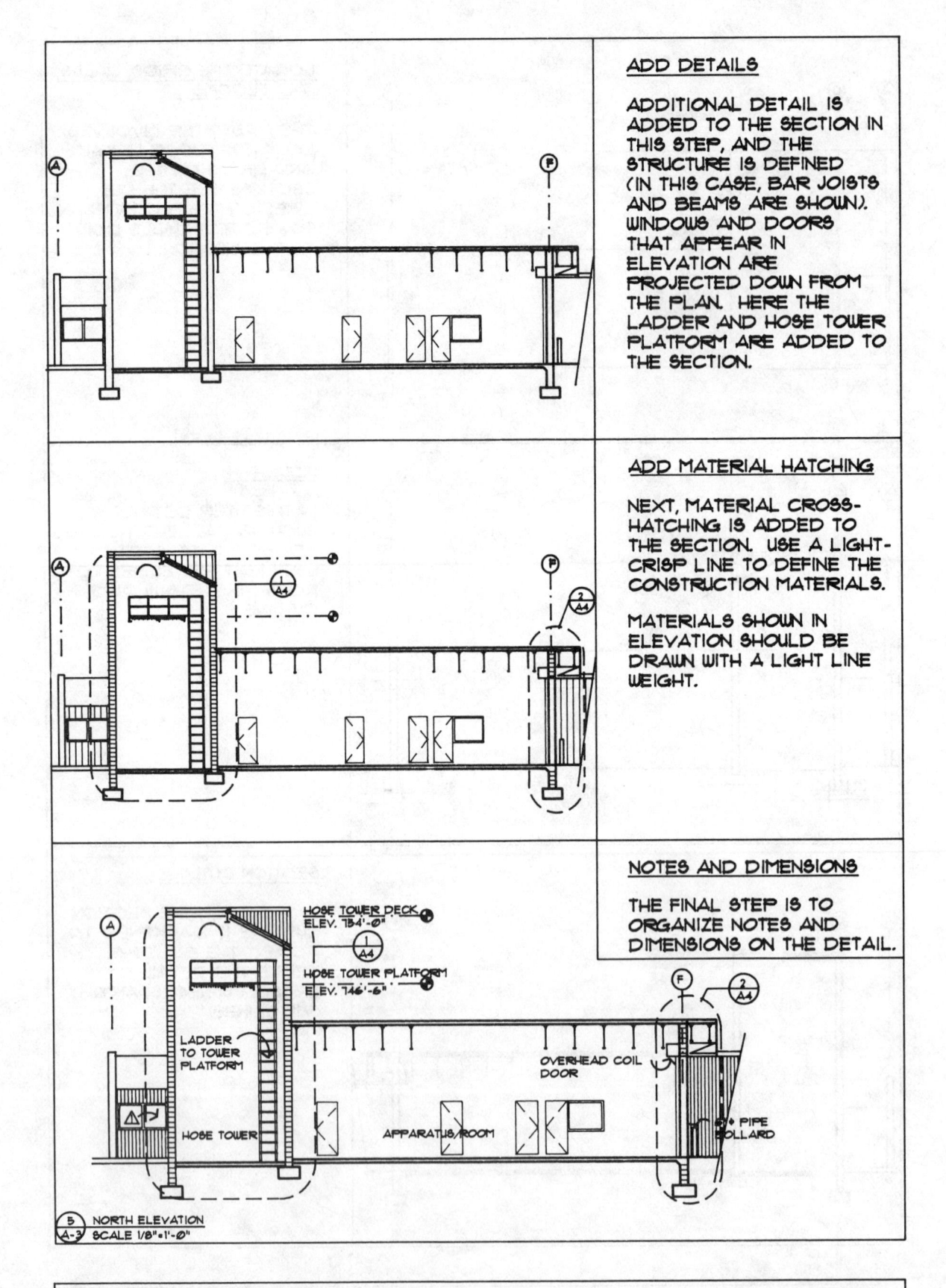

A GENERAL CHECKLIST FOR ITEMS THAT SHOULD BE INCLUDED ON WORKING DRAWING BUILDING SECTIONS IS SHOWN BELOW.

BUILDING SECTION CHECKLIST

- ☐ SHOW FLOOR ELEVATIONS
- ☐ ROOF ELEV BULL'S-EYES
- ☐ INDICATE ROOM NAME
- ☐ STRUCTURAL FRAMING
- ☐ HATCH MATERIALS
- ☐ VERTICAL DIMENSIONS
- ☐ KEY TO WALL SECTIONS
- ☐ MASONRY COURSING
- ☐ SHOW ITEMS IN ELEVATION
- ☐ PROVIDE A SECTION FOR ALL UNIQUE WALL TYPES
- ☐ SHOW MAJOR GRID LINES
- ☐ FOOTINGS & FOUNDATIONS
- ☐ CRAWL SPACE
- ☐ CEILINGS
- ☐ WALL CONSTRUCTION
- ☐ COLUMNS
- ☐ ROOF SLOPES
- ☐ STAIRS
- ☐ PARAPET CAPS
- ☐ ROOF INTERSECTION FLASHING
- ☐ GENERAL NOTES

BUILDING SECTION DETAILS

THE FOLLOWING SECTION WILL REVIEW THE TECHNIQUES USED TO DRAW A VARIETY OF ITEMS ON A BUILDING SECTION. BUILDING SECTIONS SHOULD BE SHOWN AT A SCALE THAT IS APPROPRIATE TO THE WORKING DRAWING PACKAGE. RESIDENTIAL EXAMPLES IN THIS PRESENTATION ARE DRAWN AT 3/8"=1'-0"; COMMERCIAL EXAMPLES ARE DRAWN AT A 1/8"=1'-0" SCALE.

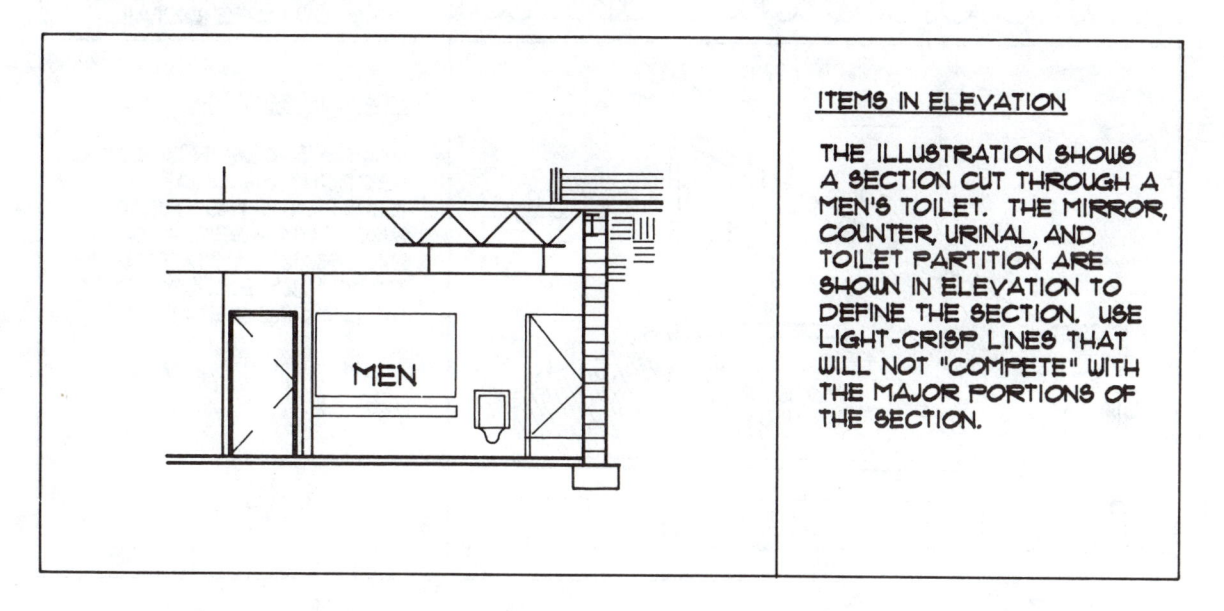

ITEMS IN ELEVATION

THE ILLUSTRATION SHOWS A SECTION CUT THROUGH A MEN'S TOILET. THE MIRROR, COUNTER, URINAL, AND TOILET PARTITION ARE SHOWN IN ELEVATION TO DEFINE THE SECTION. USE LIGHT-CRISP LINES THAT WILL NOT "COMPETE" WITH THE MAJOR PORTIONS OF THE SECTION.

BUILDING SECTIONS

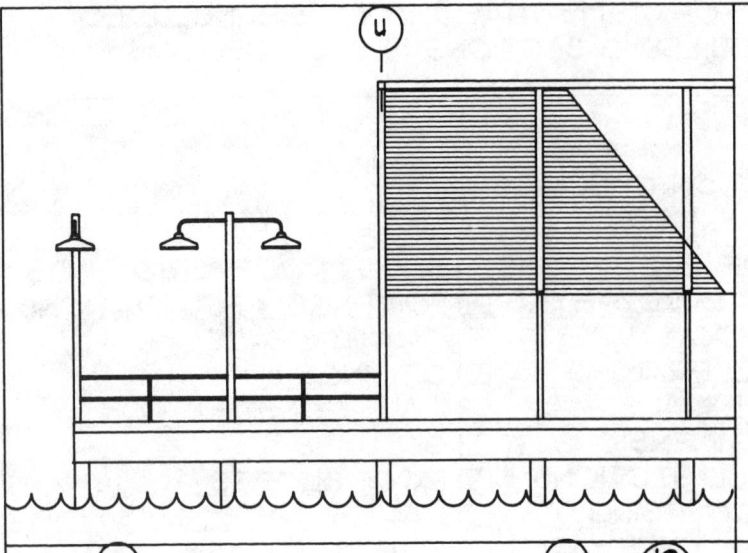

ELEMENTS PERPENDICULAR TO THE ROOF SLOPE

HERE A PERPENDICULAR SECTION IS CUT THROUGH A TRUSS AND WOOD DECK ROOF. A CUT MADE IN THIS DIRECTION DOESN'T SHOW MUCH OF THE BUILDING CONSTRUCTION AND SHOULD THEREFORE BE AVOIDED UNLESS IT DEFINES A PORTION OF THE BUILDING THAT CAN'T BE SHOWN ANY OTHER WAY.

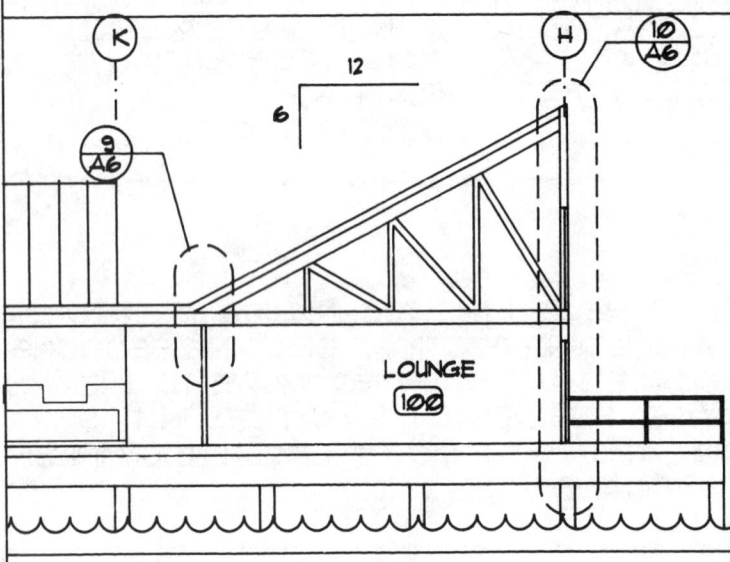

TRUSS SECTION

THIS SECTION ILLUSTRATES A 90° CUT THROUGH THE SAME BUILDING SHOWN ABOVE, BUT IT SHOWS MUCH MORE OF THE CONSTRUCTION THAN THE PERPENDICULAR SECTION. NOTE THAT BUILDING SECTIONS ARE NOT INTENDED TO SHOW DETAILED CONSTRUCTION; THE SCALE IS TOO SMALL. TWO WALL SECTIONS ARE INDICATED ON THE DETAIL. THESE WILL BE ENLARGED TO SHOW MORE DETAIL.

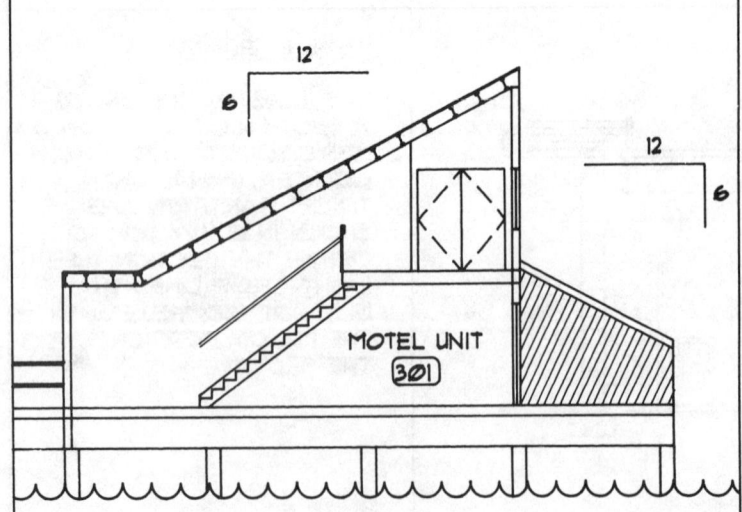

STAIR IN SECTION

STAIRS SHOWN IN BUILDING SECTIONS SHOULD ILLUSTRATE THE TREAD, RISER, STRINGER, AND HANDRAIL. A STAIR IS TYPICALLY ENLARGED TO SHOW MORE DETAIL.

BUILDING SECTIONS 16-10

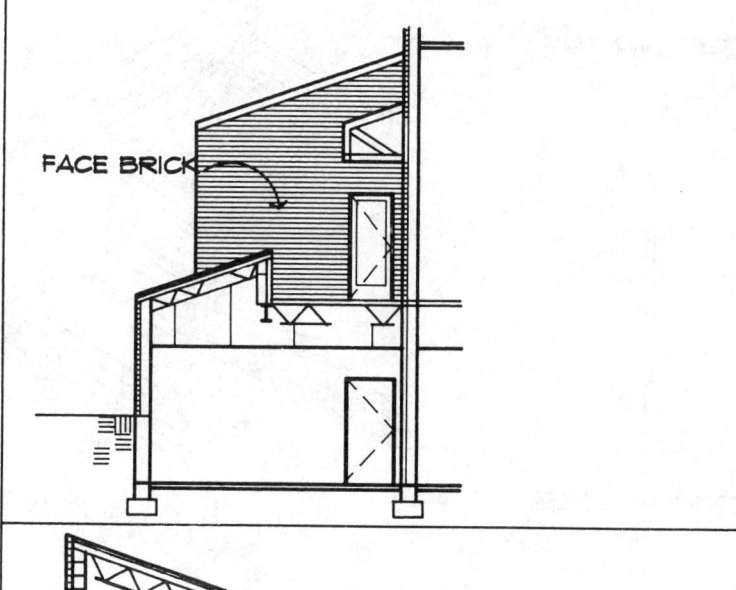

ELEMENTS PARALLEL TO THE SECTION CUT

THIS SECTION ILLUSTRATES A CUT THROUGH A SECOND-FLOOR BALCONY. THE SLOPED ROOF AND DECK ARE SUPPORTED BY STEEL BAR JOISTS.

BUILDING SECTIONS USUALLY START FROM THE FOOTINGS AND RUN TO THE ROOF PEAK. THE SECOND-FLOOR BRICK WALL IS SHOWN IN ELEVATION TO COMPLETE THE DETAIL.

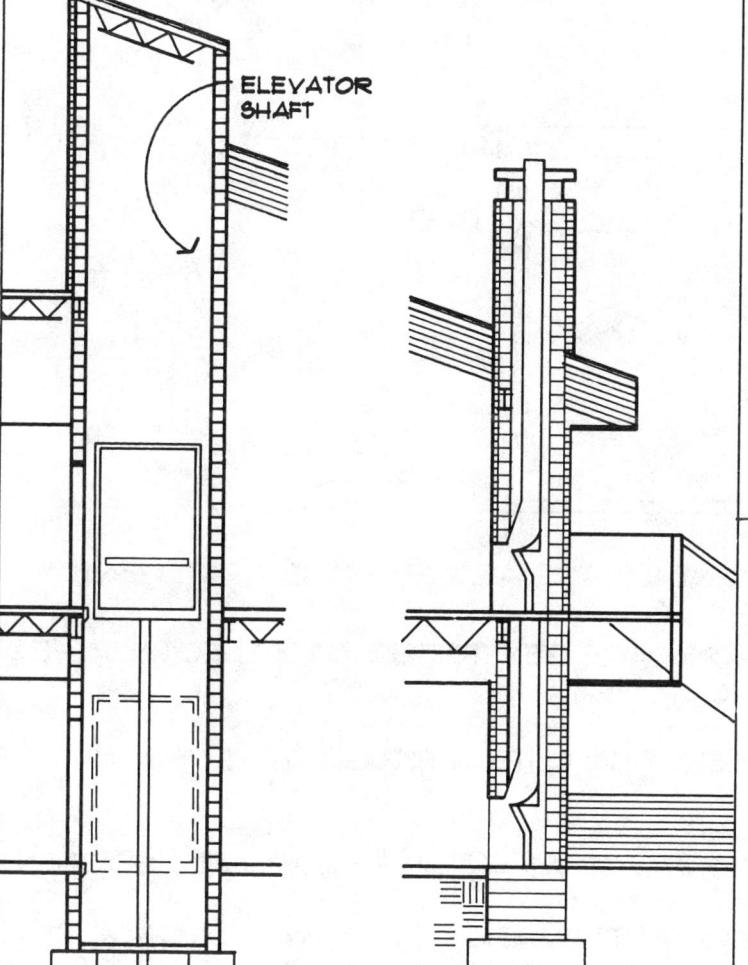

FACE BRICK

ELEVATOR

THE BUILDING DETAIL ON THE LEFT SHOWS A SECTION CUT THROUGH AN ELEVATOR SHAFT. NOTE THAT MASONRY COURSING IS TYPICALLY SHOWN IN BUILDING SECTIONS TO DEFINE THE BEARING HEIGHTS OF FLOORS AND ROOFS. SECTIONS SHOULD BE ACCURATELY DRAWN; THE INTENT IS TO SHOW THE OVERALL BUILDING (THE SCALE IS TOO SMALL TO SHOW PRECISE DETAIL).

ELEVATOR SHAFT

FIREPLACE

THE BUILDING SECTION ON THE RIGHT ILLUSTRATES A CUT THROUGH FIREPLACES ON TWO FLOORS. THE SECTION STARTS WITH A FOOTING AND RUNS TO THE CHIMNEY CAP. THE PURPOSE OF THE SECTION IS TO ILLUSTRATE GENERAL CONSTRUCTION. LARGER SCALE BLOW-UPS WILL SHOW GREATER DETAIL.

BUILDING SECTIONS   16-11

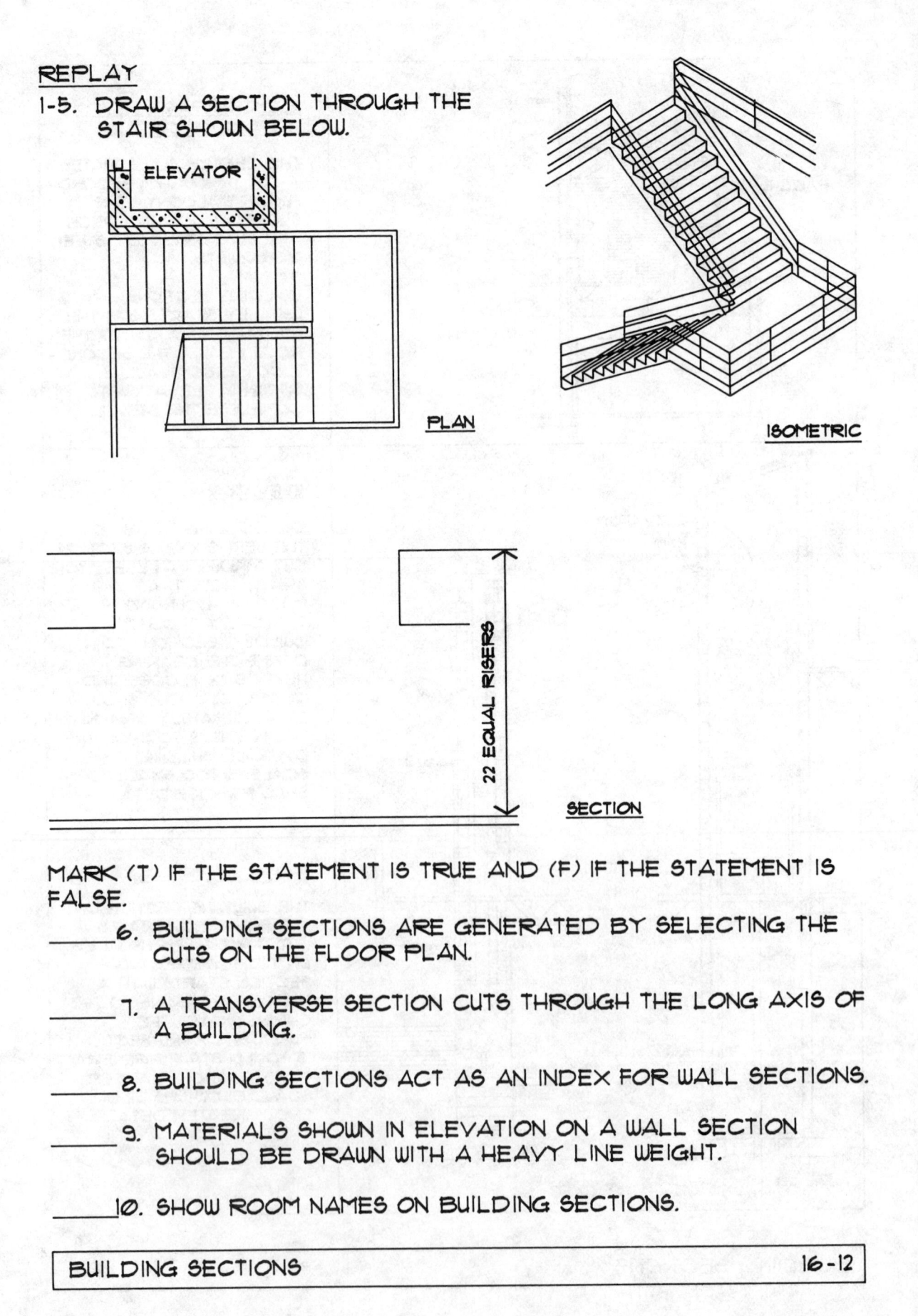

REPLAY

1-5. DRAW A SECTION THROUGH THE STAIR SHOWN BELOW.

ELEVATOR

PLAN

ISOMETRIC

22 EQUAL RISERS

SECTION

MARK (T) IF THE STATEMENT IS TRUE AND (F) IF THE STATEMENT IS FALSE.

_____ 6. BUILDING SECTIONS ARE GENERATED BY SELECTING THE CUTS ON THE FLOOR PLAN.

_____ 7. A TRANSVERSE SECTION CUTS THROUGH THE LONG AXIS OF A BUILDING.

_____ 8. BUILDING SECTIONS ACT AS AN INDEX FOR WALL SECTIONS.

_____ 9. MATERIALS SHOWN IN ELEVATION ON A WALL SECTION SHOULD BE DRAWN WITH A HEAVY LINE WEIGHT.

_____ 10. SHOW ROOM NAMES ON BUILDING SECTIONS.

BUILDING SECTIONS   16-12

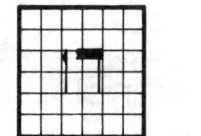

WALL SECTIONS

WALL SECTIONS ARE GENERATED BY FIRST MAKING A VERTICAL CUT THROUGH A PORTION OF A BUILDING. THEY DIFFER FROM BUILDING SECTIONS ONLY IN SCALE. WHILE A BUILDING SECTION (UNIT 16) IS INTENDED TO PROVIDE AN OVERALL VIEW OF A BUILDING, A WALL SECTION SHOWS ONLY AN ENLARGED PORTION OF ONE WALL. BUILDING SECTIONS ACT AS AN INDEX FOR WALL SECTIONS.

THE ISOMETRIC BELOW SHOWS THE SKYWAY HOUSE WITH FIVE PLANES CUTTING THROUGH WALLS. (WE WILL EXAMINE THE SECTIONS CREATED BY THESE CUTS IN THE FIRST PART OF THIS UNIT.) EVERY UNIQUE WALL CONDITION SHOULD BE SHOWN IN SECTION - REMEMBER THAT IT IS MUCH EASIER TO SOLVE A CONDITION ON PAPER THAN WHEN IT IS ACTUALLY UNDER CONSTRUCTION. IT IS A COMMON PRACTICE TO DRAW THE ENTIRE SECTION FROM FOOTING TO ROOF PEAK IN ORDER TO DETERMINE THE TOTAL BUILDING SYSTEM.

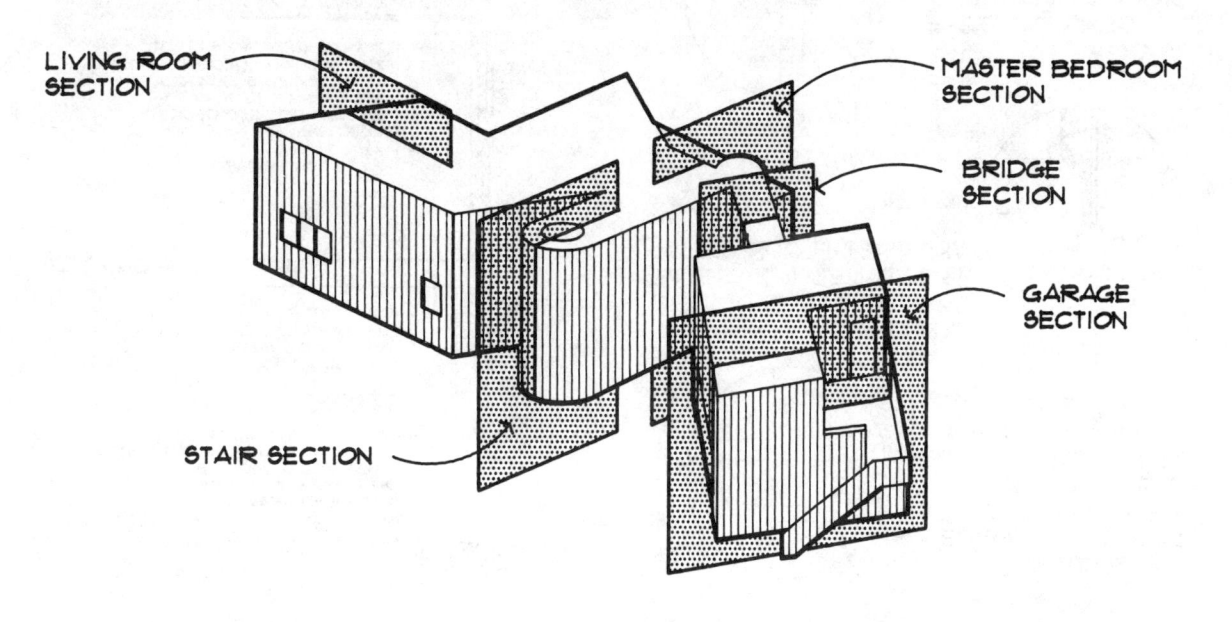

WALL SECTIONS 17-1

THE SCALE USED TO DRAW WALL SECTIONS VARIES: TYPICALLY A 3/8" = 1'-0" OR 1/2" = 1'-0" SCALE IS USED FOR RESIDENTIAL PROJECTS, WHILE A 1/2" = 1'-0" OR 3/4" = 1'-0" SCALE IS USED FOR COMMERCIAL WORKING DRAWINGS. SELECTION OF THE SCALE FOR A WALL SECTION DEPENDS ON THE AMOUNT OF DETAIL THAT IS TO BE SHOWN. RESIDENTIAL WALL SECTIONS SHOULD INDICATE ITEMS SUCH AS STUDS, JOISTS, INSULATION, AND WINDOW FRAMES.

THE WALL SECTION SHOWN BELOW CUTS THROUGH THE MASTER BEDROOM, KITCHEN, AND BASEMENT. THIS IS AN IMPORTANT DETAIL BECAUSE IT SHOWS THE SECOND-FLOOR DECK CONDITION. THE NOTES TO THE LEFT WILL IDENTIFY ITEMS TYPICALLY FOUND ON A RESIDENTIAL WALL SECTION.

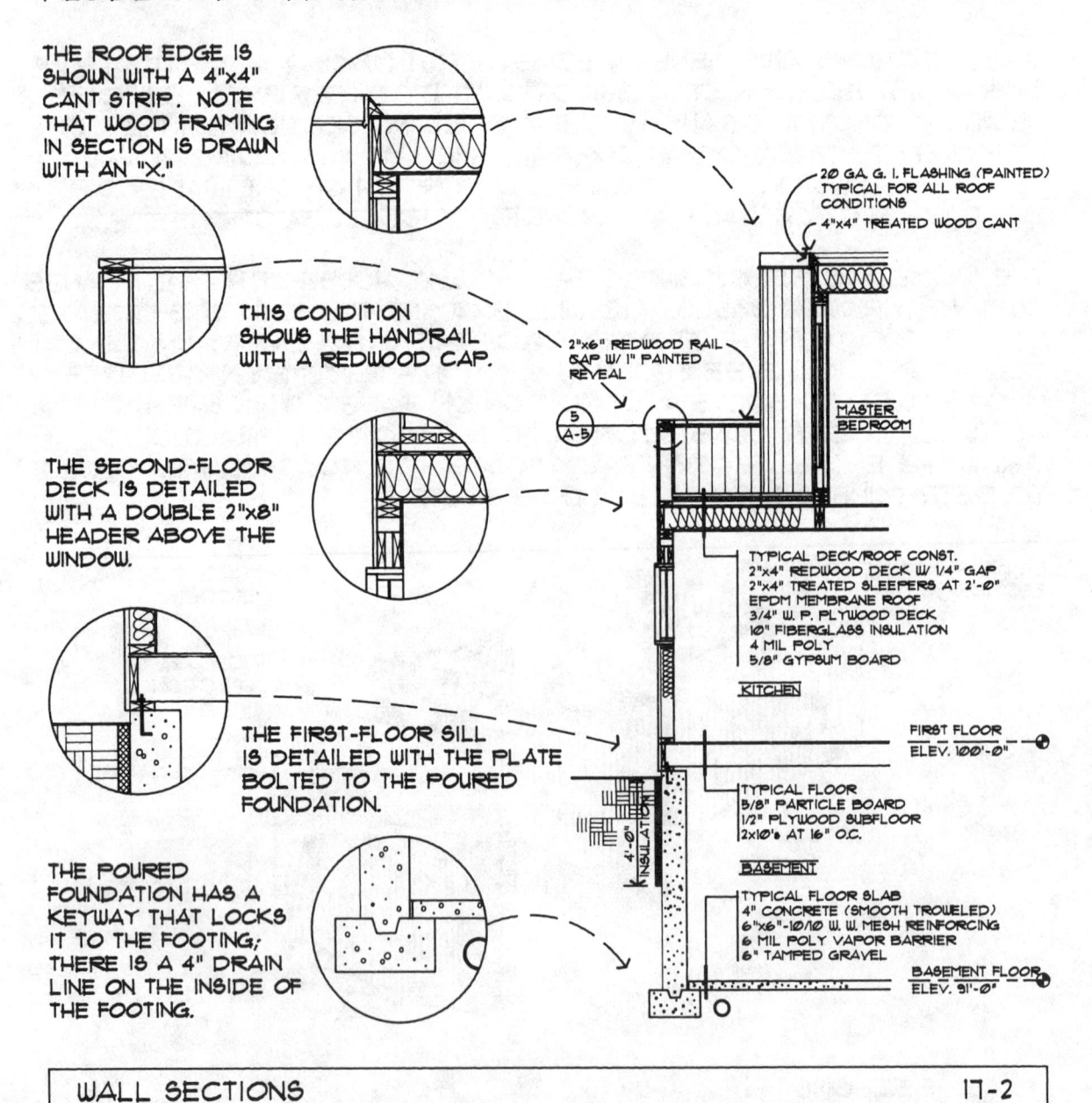

THE ROOF EDGE IS SHOWN WITH A 4"x4" CANT STRIP. NOTE THAT WOOD FRAMING IN SECTION IS DRAWN WITH AN "X."

THIS CONDITION SHOWS THE HANDRAIL WITH A REDWOOD CAP.

THE SECOND-FLOOR DECK IS DETAILED WITH A DOUBLE 2"x8" HEADER ABOVE THE WINDOW.

THE FIRST-FLOOR SILL IS DETAILED WITH THE PLATE BOLTED TO THE POURED FOUNDATION.

THE POURED FOUNDATION HAS A KEYWAY THAT LOCKS IT TO THE FOOTING; THERE IS A 4" DRAIN LINE ON THE INSIDE OF THE FOOTING.

20 GA. G.I. FLASHING (PAINTED) TYPICAL FOR ALL ROOF CONDITIONS
4"x4" TREATED WOOD CANT
2"x6" REDWOOD RAIL CAP W/ 1" PAINTED REVEAL

MASTER BEDROOM

TYPICAL DECK/ROOF CONST.
2"x4" REDWOOD DECK W/ 1/4" GAP
2"x4" TREATED SLEEPERS AT 2'-0"
EPDM MEMBRANE ROOF
3/4" W.P. PLYWOOD DECK
10" FIBERGLASS INSULATION
4 MIL POLY
5/8" GYPSUM BOARD

KITCHEN

FIRST FLOOR ELEV. 100'-0"

TYPICAL FLOOR
5/8" PARTICLE BOARD
1/2" PLYWOOD SUBFLOOR
2x10's AT 16" O.C.

BASEMENT

TYPICAL FLOOR SLAB
4" CONCRETE (SMOOTH TROWELED)
6"x6"-10/10 W.W. MESH REINFORCING
6 MIL POLY VAPOR BARRIER
6" TAMPED GRAVEL

BASEMENT FLOOR ELEV. 91'-0"

WALL SECTIONS   17-2

THE "NUTS-AND-BOLTS" ASSEMBLY OF A PROJECT IS SPELLED OUT ON WALL SECTIONS, ESPECIALLY THE INTERSECTION OF FLOORS AND ROOFS WITH THE WALL. BEGIN CONSTRUCTING A SECTION BY MAKING A SKETCH ON TRACING PAPER THAT YOU CAN USE TO "SOLVE" EACH CONDITION.

THE WALL SECTION SHOWN BELOW CUTS THROUGH THE CENTER OF THE STAIR TOWER. THIS DETAIL IS ESSENTIAL TO THE CONSTRUCTION OF THE STAIR AND SKYLIGHT IN THE ROOF. THE DETAILS SHOWN IN BUBBLES TO THE LEFT PROVIDE ENLARGED VIEWS OF IMPORTANT PORTIONS OF THE SECTION.

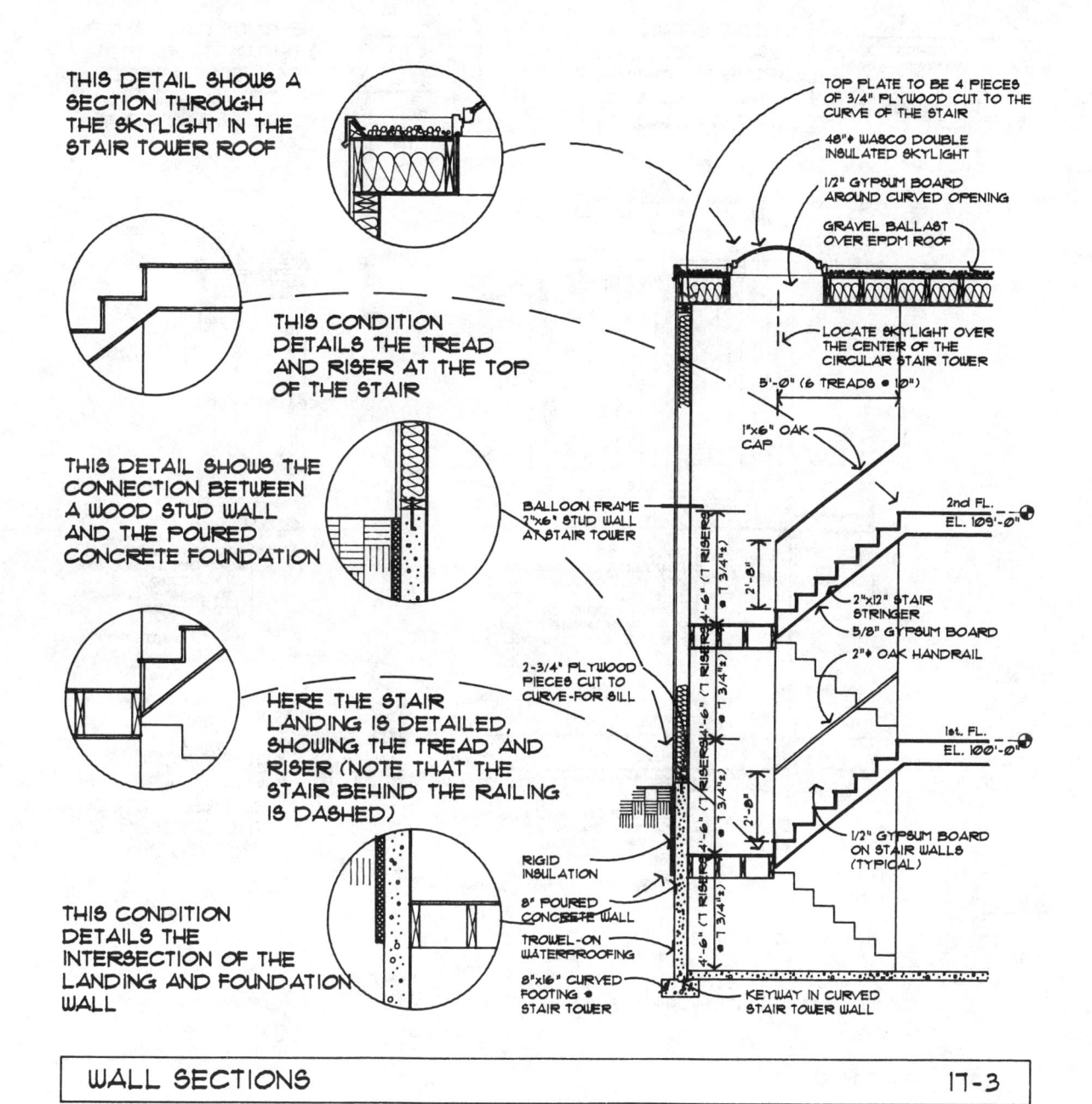

THIS DETAIL SHOWS A SECTION THROUGH THE SKYLIGHT IN THE STAIR TOWER ROOF

THIS CONDITION DETAILS THE TREAD AND RISER AT THE TOP OF THE STAIR

THIS DETAIL SHOWS THE CONNECTION BETWEEN A WOOD STUD WALL AND THE POURED CONCRETE FOUNDATION

HERE THE STAIR LANDING IS DETAILED, SHOWING THE TREAD AND RISER (NOTE THAT THE STAIR BEHIND THE RAILING IS DASHED)

THIS CONDITION DETAILS THE INTERSECTION OF THE LANDING AND FOUNDATION WALL

TOP PLATE TO BE 4 PIECES OF 3/4" PLYWOOD CUT TO THE CURVE OF THE STAIR

48"⌀ WASCO DOUBLE INSULATED SKYLIGHT

1/2" GYPSUM BOARD AROUND CURVED OPENING

GRAVEL BALLAST OVER EPDM ROOF

LOCATE SKYLIGHT OVER THE CENTER OF THE CIRCULAR STAIR TOWER

5'-0" (6 TREADS @ 10")

1"x6" OAK CAP

BALLOON FRAME 2"x6" STUD WALL AT STAIR TOWER

2"x12" STAIR STRINGER

5/8" GYPSUM BOARD

2"⌀ OAK HANDRAIL

2-3/4" PLYWOOD PIECES CUT TO CURVE-FOR SILL

1/2" GYPSUM BOARD ON STAIR WALLS (TYPICAL)

RIGID INSULATION

8" POURED CONCRETE WALL

TROWEL-ON WATERPROOFING

8"x16" CURVED FOOTING @ STAIR TOWER

KEYWAY IN CURVED STAIR TOWER WALL

2nd FL. EL. 109'-0"

1st. FL. EL. 100'-0"

WALL SECTIONS   17-3

TWO WALL SECTIONS ARE SHOWN ON THIS PAGE. THE DETAIL TO THE LEFT CUTS THROUGH THE SECOND-FLOOR DECK ABOVE THE GARAGE AND SHOWS THE STAIR IN ELEVATION. THE SECTION TO THE RIGHT DETAILS THE BRIDGE THAT CONNECTS THE HOUSE AND GARAGE.

NOTES THAT ACCOMPANY WALL SECTIONS SHOULD DEFINE THE ENTIRE ASSEMBLY OF THE WALL OR ROOF. IN THE EXAMPLE BELOW, NOTES FOR THE DECK ABOVE THE GARAGE AND THE BRIDGE FLOOR ARE PLACED IN THE ORDER OF CONSTRUCTION (BEGINNING WITH THE TOP DECK AND PROGRESSING DOWN THROUGH THE LAYERS OF BUILDING MATERIALS).

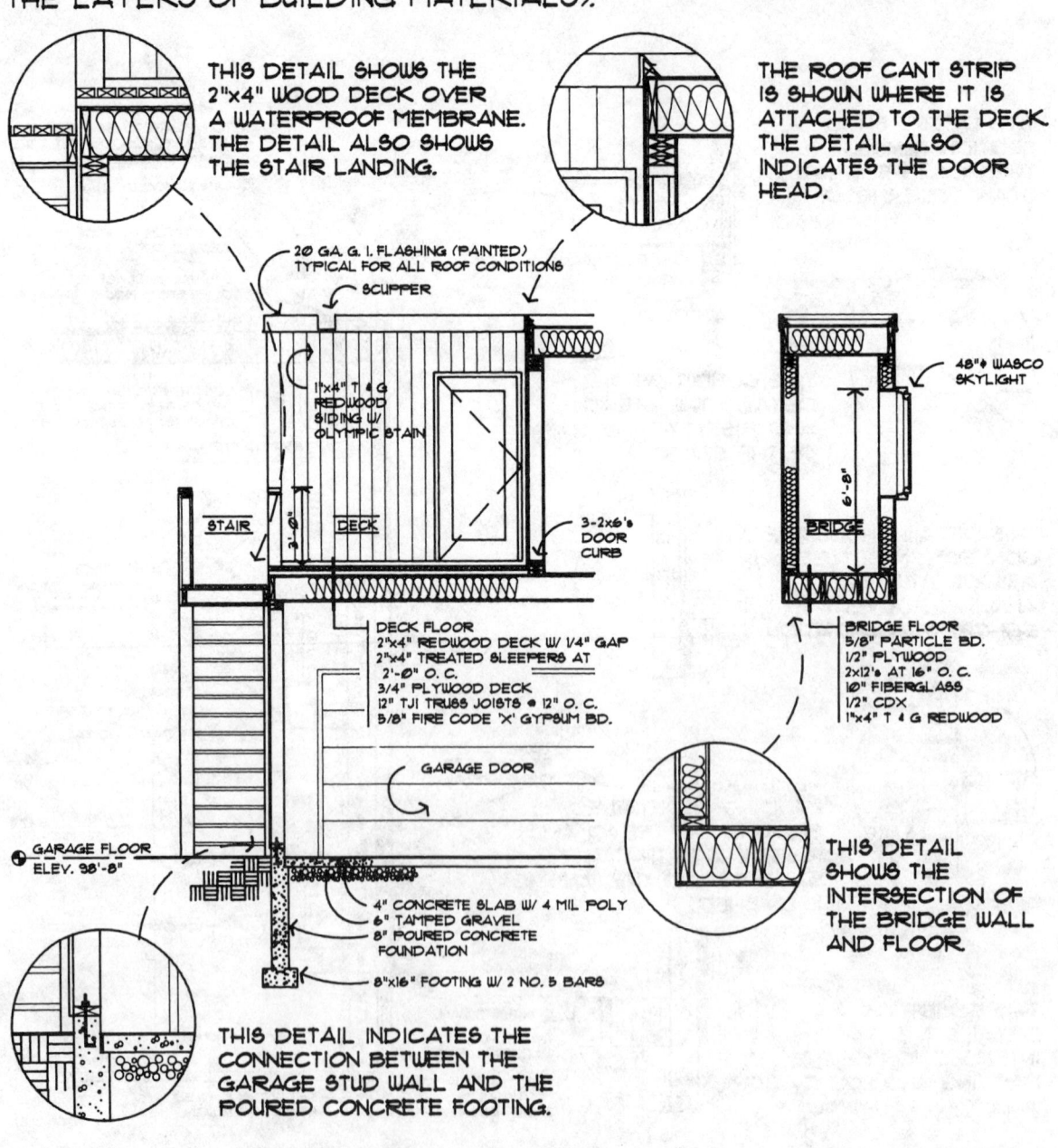

THIS DETAIL SHOWS THE 2"x4" WOOD DECK OVER A WATERPROOF MEMBRANE. THE DETAIL ALSO SHOWS THE STAIR LANDING.

THE ROOF CANT STRIP IS SHOWN WHERE IT IS ATTACHED TO THE DECK. THE DETAIL ALSO INDICATES THE DOOR HEAD.

20 GA. G. I. FLASHING (PAINTED) TYPICAL FOR ALL ROOF CONDITIONS
SCUPPER
1"x4" T & G REDWOOD SIDING W/ OLYMPIC STAIN
STAIR
DECK
3-2x6's DOOR CURB

48"⌀ WASCO SKYLIGHT
BRIDGE

DECK FLOOR
2"x4" REDWOOD DECK W/ 1/4" GAP
2"x4" TREATED SLEEPERS AT 2'-0" O. C.
3/4" PLYWOOD DECK
12" TJI TRUSS JOISTS @ 12" O. C.
5/8" FIRE CODE 'X' GYPSUM BD.

GARAGE DOOR

BRIDGE FLOOR
5/8" PARTICLE BD.
1/2" PLYWOOD
2x12's AT 16" O. C.
10" FIBERGLASS
1/2" CDX
1"x4" T & G REDWOOD

GARAGE FLOOR ELEV. 98'-8"
4" CONCRETE SLAB W/ 4 MIL POLY
6" TAMPED GRAVEL
8" POURED CONCRETE FOUNDATION
8"x16" FOOTING W/ 2 NO. 5 BARS

THIS DETAIL SHOWS THE INTERSECTION OF THE BRIDGE WALL AND FLOOR

THIS DETAIL INDICATES THE CONNECTION BETWEEN THE GARAGE STUD WALL AND THE POURED CONCRETE FOOTING.

WALL SECTIONS

17-4

ON PAGES 17-5 AND 17-6, WE WILL EXAMINE THE ASSEMBLY OF A WALL SECTION CUT THROUGH THE LIVING ROOM. THIS SECTION IS OF PARTICULAR IMPORTANCE BECAUSE IT DISPLAYS THE SECOND-FLOOR MASTER BEDROOM BALCONY.

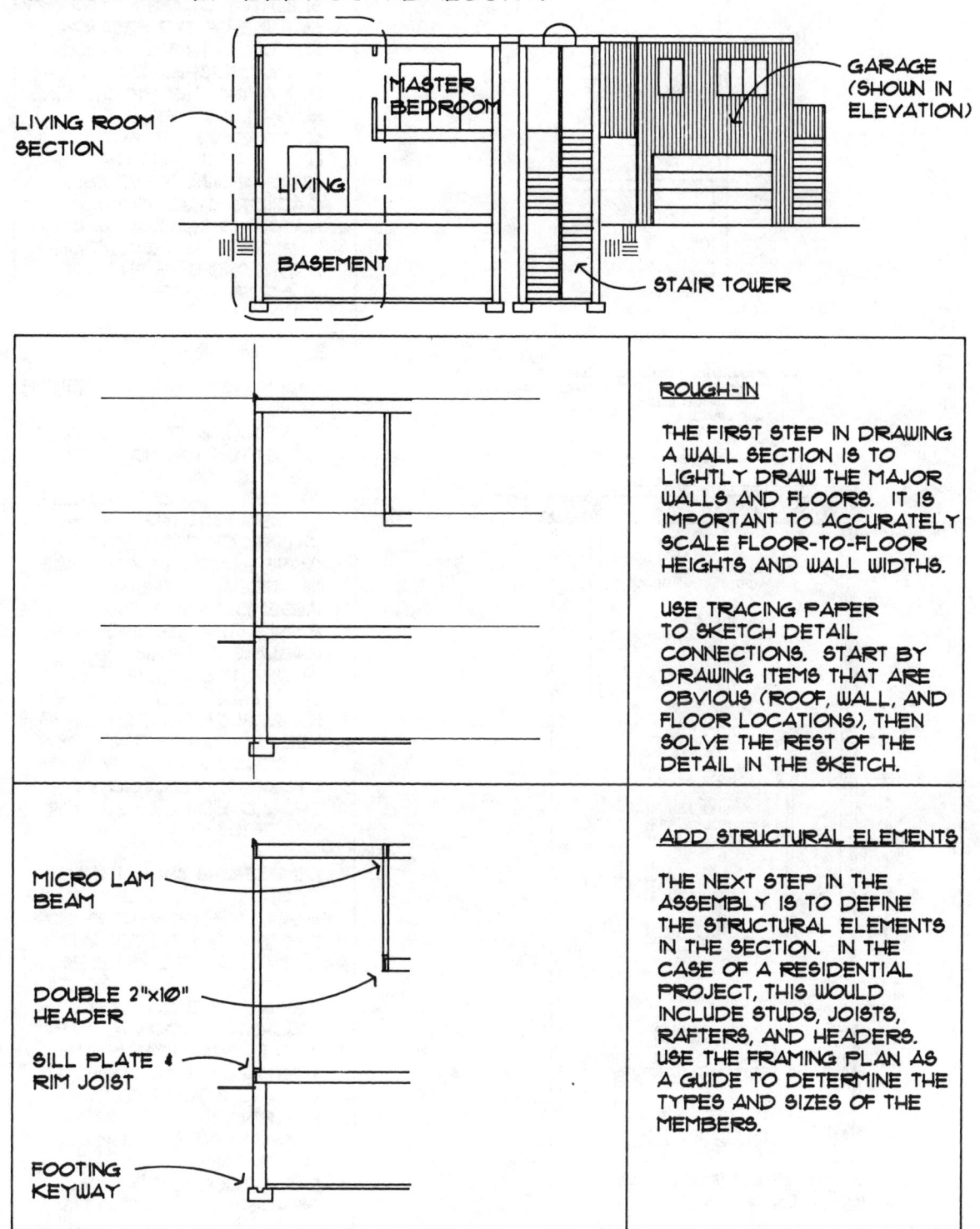

- LIVING ROOM SECTION
- MASTER BEDROOM
- LIVING
- BASEMENT
- GARAGE (SHOWN IN ELEVATION)
- STAIR TOWER

ROUGH-IN

THE FIRST STEP IN DRAWING A WALL SECTION IS TO LIGHTLY DRAW THE MAJOR WALLS AND FLOORS. IT IS IMPORTANT TO ACCURATELY SCALE FLOOR-TO-FLOOR HEIGHTS AND WALL WIDTHS.

USE TRACING PAPER TO SKETCH DETAIL CONNECTIONS. START BY DRAWING ITEMS THAT ARE OBVIOUS (ROOF, WALL, AND FLOOR LOCATIONS), THEN SOLVE THE REST OF THE DETAIL IN THE SKETCH.

ADD STRUCTURAL ELEMENTS

THE NEXT STEP IN THE ASSEMBLY IS TO DEFINE THE STRUCTURAL ELEMENTS IN THE SECTION. IN THE CASE OF A RESIDENTIAL PROJECT, THIS WOULD INCLUDE STUDS, JOISTS, RAFTERS, AND HEADERS. USE THE FRAMING PLAN AS A GUIDE TO DETERMINE THE TYPES AND SIZES OF THE MEMBERS.

- MICRO LAM BEAM
- DOUBLE 2"x10" HEADER
- SILL PLATE & RIM JOIST
- FOOTING KEYWAY

WALL SECTIONS

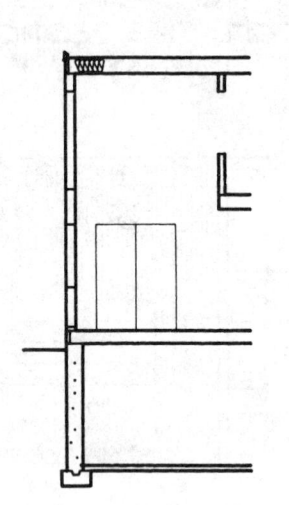

DARKEN THE SECTION CUT

THE NEXT STEP IS TO SLIGHTLY DARKEN THE OUTLINE OF THE SECTION CUT LINE. THIS CAN BE ACCOMPLISHED BY (1) MAKING THE PENCIL LINE SLIGHTLY WIDER, (2) TRACING THE OUTLINE WITH A TECH PEN, OR (3) CHANGING PENS ON A CAD DRAWING. CROSS-HATCHING INDICATING SUCH ELEMENTS AS INSULATION AND CONCRETE SHOULD ALSO BE ADDED IN THIS STEP.

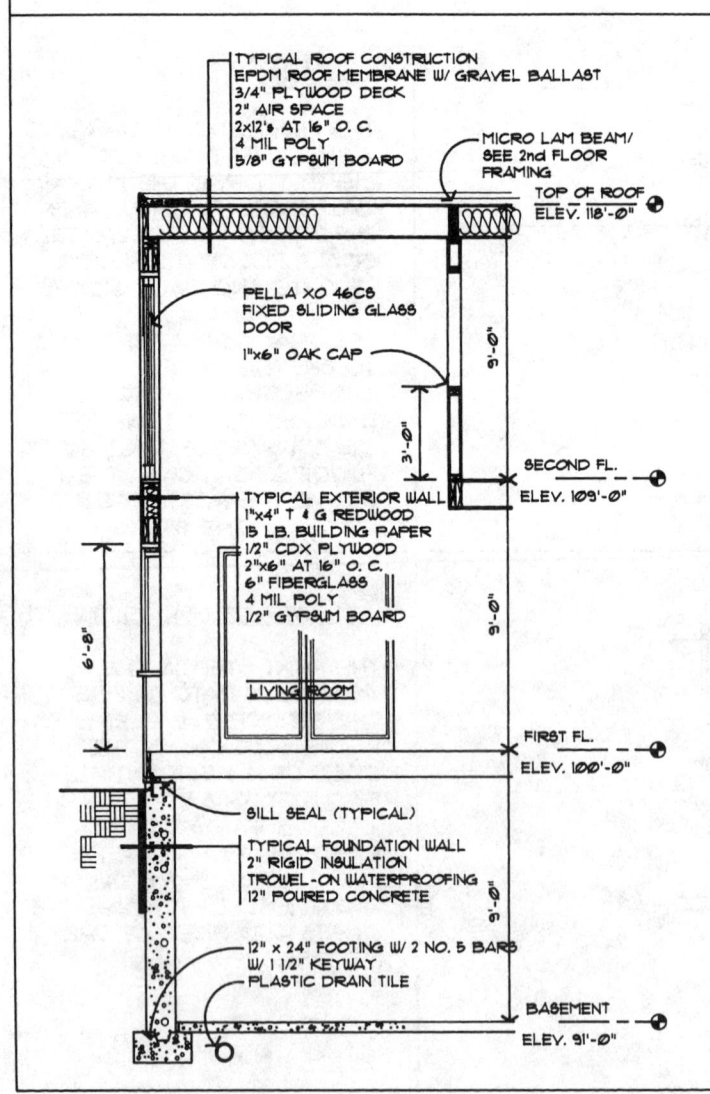

ADD NOTES AND DIMENSIONS

THE FINAL STEP IS TO ADD CONSTRUCTION NOTES TO THE SECTION. IN THE EXAMPLE, A NOTE SYSTEM IS USED FOR THE WALLS AND ROOF THAT LISTS CONSTRUCTION MATERIALS IN ORDER OF THEIR ASSEMBLY AND USES A SINGLE LEADER LINE FOR CALLING OUT THIS INFORMATION. THIS TECHNIQUE MINIMIZES THE NUMBER OF LEADER LINES NEEDED, WHICH TENDS TO PRODUCE A NEATER DRAWING. ALSO, NOTES SHOULD BE ALIGNED FOR NEATNESS.

DIMENSIONS ON A WALL SECTION GENERALLY INVOLVE FLOOR-TO-FLOOR DIMENSION STRINGS AND ELEVATION BULL'S-EYES. DIMENSION STRINGS SHOULD DEFINE VERTICAL HEIGHTS (SUCH AS WINDOW HEADS AND FLOOR MEASUREMENTS). THE BULL'S-EYE SHOULD LOCATE STRUCTURAL BEARING POINTS. NOTES AND DIMENSIONS SHOULD BE ORGANIZED SO THEY DON'T "COMPETE" FOR SPACE ON THE DRAWING.

WALL SECTIONS

17-6

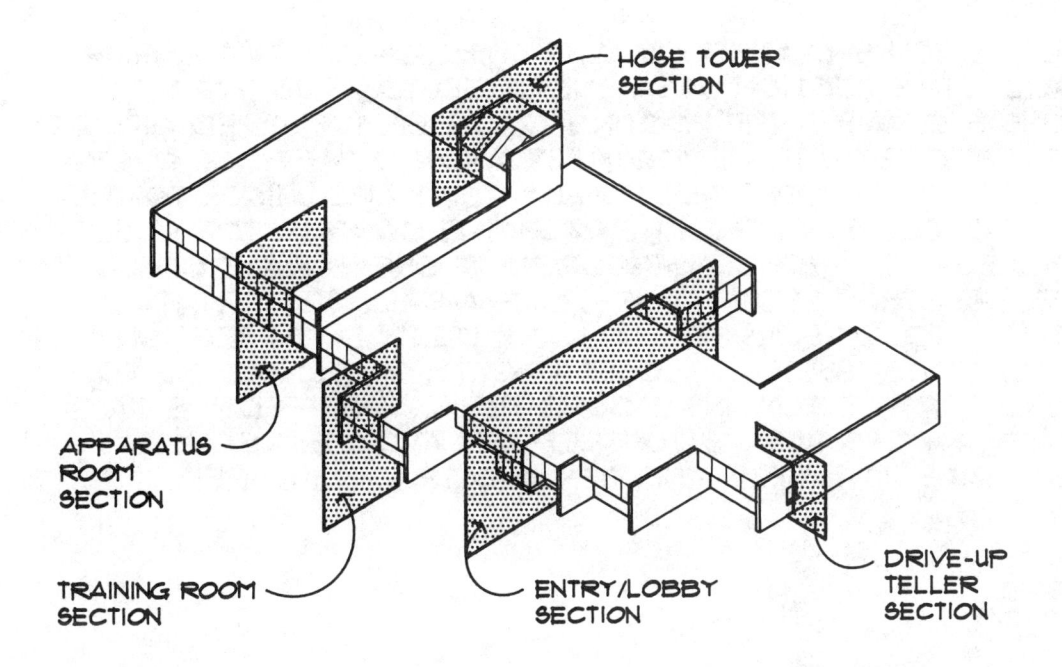

IN THIS PORTION OF THE UNIT WE WILL EXAMINE WALL SECTIONS FOR THE FIRE STATION. THE ISOMETRIC ABOVE SHOWS FIVE PLANE CUTS THROUGH THE BUILDING. BEGIN THE WALL SECTION BY REVIEWING THE BUILDING SECTIONS THAT WERE DEVELOPED FOR THE FIRE STATION IN UNIT 16. THE SMALL-SCALE SECTION ACTS AS AN INDEX TO DEVELOP LARGER-SCALE WALL SECTIONS.

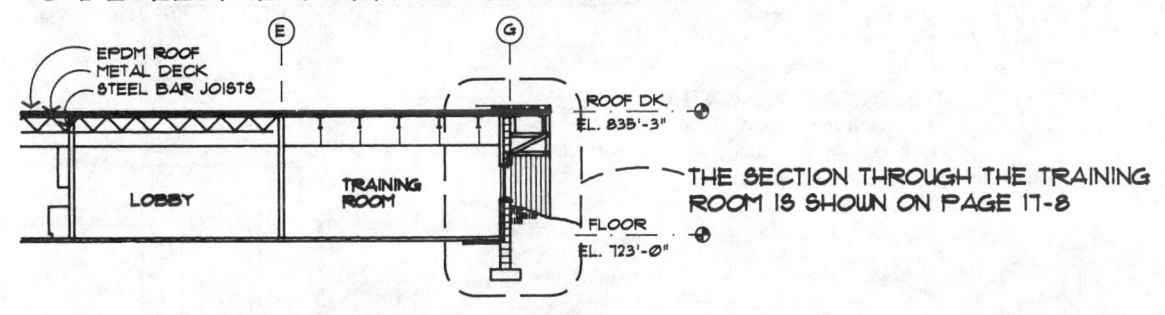

WALL SECTIONS SHOULD DO MORE THAN MAGNIFY THE CONSTRUCTION CONDITIONS IN A BUILDING SECTION; THEY SHOULD ACCURATELY SHOW ALL ELEMENTS. FOR EXAMPLE, CONCRETE BLOCK SHOULD BE DRAWN WITH A 3/8" MORTAR JOINT AND THE HEAD-TO-SILL DIMENSION OF A WINDOW UNIT MUST BE EXACT. ALSO, THE LOCATION OF A WINDOW IN A MASONRY WALL SHOULD BE DRAWN USING 8" MODULAR COURSING (ELIMINATING THE NEED TO CUT THE BLOCK). ALTHOUGH FLOOR PLANS ARE THE MOST "IMPORTANT" DRAWINGS IN THE CONSTRUCTION SET, IT COULD BE ARGUED THAT WALL SECTIONS ARE THE MOST DIFFICULT TO DRAW. THEIR CAREFUL ASSEMBLY, HOWEVER, WILL PROVIDE A COMPREHENSIVE PICTURE OF THE BUILDING.

WALL SECTIONS

THE WALL SECTION SHOWN BELOW CUTS THROUGH THE TRAINING ROOM WALL. THIS SECTION WAS GENERATED TO ILLUSTRATE CONDITIONS SUCH AS (1) THE FOOTING, (2) A BERM (SLOPED GROUND ON THE EXTERIOR), (3) THE WINDOW UNIT, AND (4) THE ROOF OVERHANG. ALL OF THESE CONSTRUCTION SYSTEMS ARE UNIQUE TO THIS DETAIL; IF THIS SECTION WEREN'T DRAWN, THE CONTRACTOR WOULD HAVE TO GUESS AT THEIR CONSTRUCTION. IF ONE PHRASE COULD DESCRIBE THE STEPS USED TO DEVELOP A WALL SECTION, IT WOULD BE "PROBLEM SOLVING." ALWAYS BEGIN EACH SECTION WITH "KNOWN" ELEMENTS (SUCH AS FLOOR HEIGHTS, GRIDS, AND BEAMS), THEN SOLVE FOR THE REMAINING CONDITIONS. AN EFFECTIVE WAY TO ACCOMPLISH THIS TASK IS TO PREPARE AND USE DETAILED SKETCHES MADE WITH A FELT-TIP PEN AND TRACING PAPER.

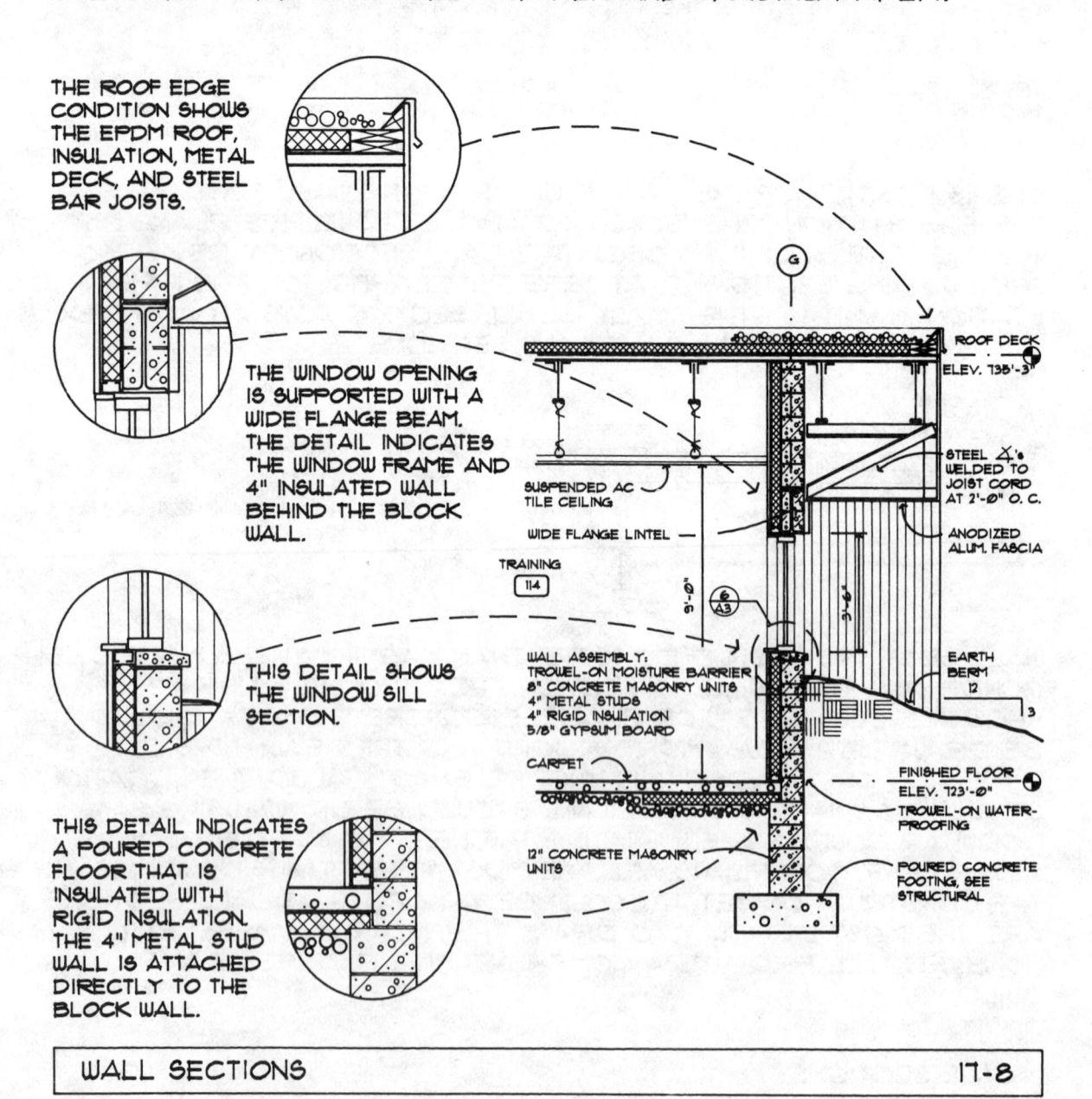

THE ROOF EDGE CONDITION SHOWS THE EPDM ROOF, INSULATION, METAL DECK, AND STEEL BAR JOISTS.

THE WINDOW OPENING IS SUPPORTED WITH A WIDE FLANGE BEAM. THE DETAIL INDICATES THE WINDOW FRAME AND 4" INSULATED WALL BEHIND THE BLOCK WALL.

THIS DETAIL SHOWS THE WINDOW SILL SECTION.

THIS DETAIL INDICATES A POURED CONCRETE FLOOR THAT IS INSULATED WITH RIGID INSULATION. THE 4" METAL STUD WALL IS ATTACHED DIRECTLY TO THE BLOCK WALL.

SUSPENDED AC TILE CEILING
WIDE FLANGE LINTEL
TRAINING 114
WALL ASSEMBLY:
TROWEL-ON MOISTURE BARRIER
8" CONCRETE MASONRY UNITS
4" METAL STUDS
4" RIGID INSULATION
5/8" GYPSUM BOARD
CARPET
12" CONCRETE MASONRY UNITS

ROOF DECK ELEV. 735'-3"
STEEL ∠'s WELDED TO JOIST CORD AT 2'-0" O.C.
ANODIZED ALUM. FASCIA
EARTH BERM
FINISHED FLOOR ELEV. 723'-0"
TROWEL-ON WATERPROOFING
POURED CONCRETE FOOTING, SEE STRUCTURAL

WALL SECTIONS | 17-8

WALL SECTIONS SHOULD BE DRAWN WITH A BALANCE BETWEEN LINES, NOTES, AND DIMENSIONS. THE EXAMPLE BELOW SHOWS THE ORGANIZATION OF THESE THREE ELEMENTS. AS WITH OTHER DRAWINGS, THE LINE DRAWING SHOULD BE COMPLETED FIRST AND THEN NOTES SHOULD BE ADDED. NOTES SHOULD BE PLACED CLOSE TO RELATED OBJECTS AND SHOULD BE ORGANIZED TO ELIMINATE THE NEED TO CROSS LEADER LINES. THE EXAMPLE BELOW SHOWS TWO VERTICAL COLUMNS OF NOTES THAT ACT TO BALANCE THE DRAWING. DIMENSIONS ARE SHOWN TWO WAYS ON WALL SECTIONS: (1) USING VERTICAL DIMENSION STRINGS, AND (2) USING BULL'S-EYES THAT INDICATE FLOORS, ROOFS, AND STRUCTURAL BEARING POINTS.

THIS WALL SECTION INDICATES A CUT THROUGH THE DRIVE-UP TELLER WINWOW.

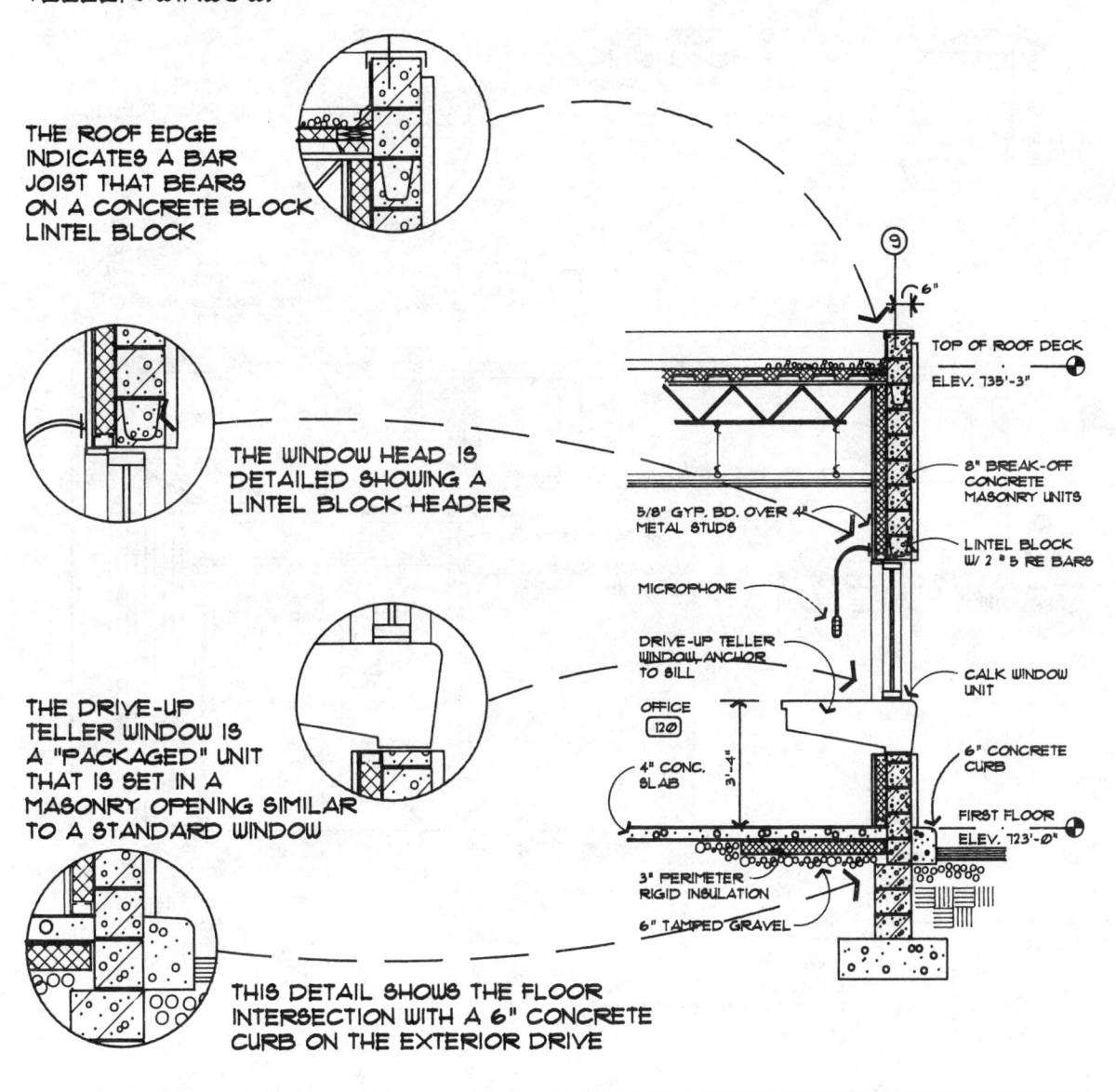

THE ROOF EDGE INDICATES A BAR JOIST THAT BEARS ON A CONCRETE BLOCK LINTEL BLOCK

THE WINDOW HEAD IS DETAILED SHOWING A LINTEL BLOCK HEADER

THE DRIVE-UP TELLER WINDOW IS A "PACKAGED" UNIT THAT IS SET IN A MASONRY OPENING SIMILAR TO A STANDARD WINDOW

THIS DETAIL SHOWS THE FLOOR INTERSECTION WITH A 6" CONCRETE CURB ON THE EXTERIOR DRIVE

TOP OF ROOF DECK ELEV. 735'-3"

8" BREAK-OFF CONCRETE MASONRY UNITS

5/8" GYP. BD. OVER 4" METAL STUDS

LINTEL BLOCK W/ 2 #5 RE BARS

MICROPHONE

DRIVE-UP TELLER WINDOW, ANCHOR TO SILL

CALK WINDOW UNIT

OFFICE 120

4" CONC. SLAB

6" CONCRETE CURB

FIRST FLOOR ELEV. 723'-0"

3" PERIMETER RIGID INSULATION

6" TAMPED GRAVEL

| WALL SECTIONS | 17-9 |

WALL SECTIONS SHOULD BE ORGANIZED ON THE DRAWING SHEET USING SEVERAL RULES:

1. FLOOR AND ROOF ELEVATION POINTS SHOULD LINE UP ON EACH DRAWING.
2. WALL SECTIONS ON THE SHEET SHOULD BE SPACED EVENLY. (THE TECHNIQUE DISCUSSED IN UNIT 7 BREAKS A 24" x 36" SHEET INTO FIVE EQUAL VERTICAL UNITS.)
3. IT ISN'T NECESSARY TO REPEAT THE SAME NOTE ON SIMILAR SECTIONS ON A SHEET; INSTEAD USE "SIMILAR TO DETAIL A-4."
4. IF THERE IS ROOM ON THE SHEET, WALL SECTIONS SHOULD BE SHOWN FROM FOOTING TO ROOF PEAK WITHOUT CUTTING THE DETAIL.

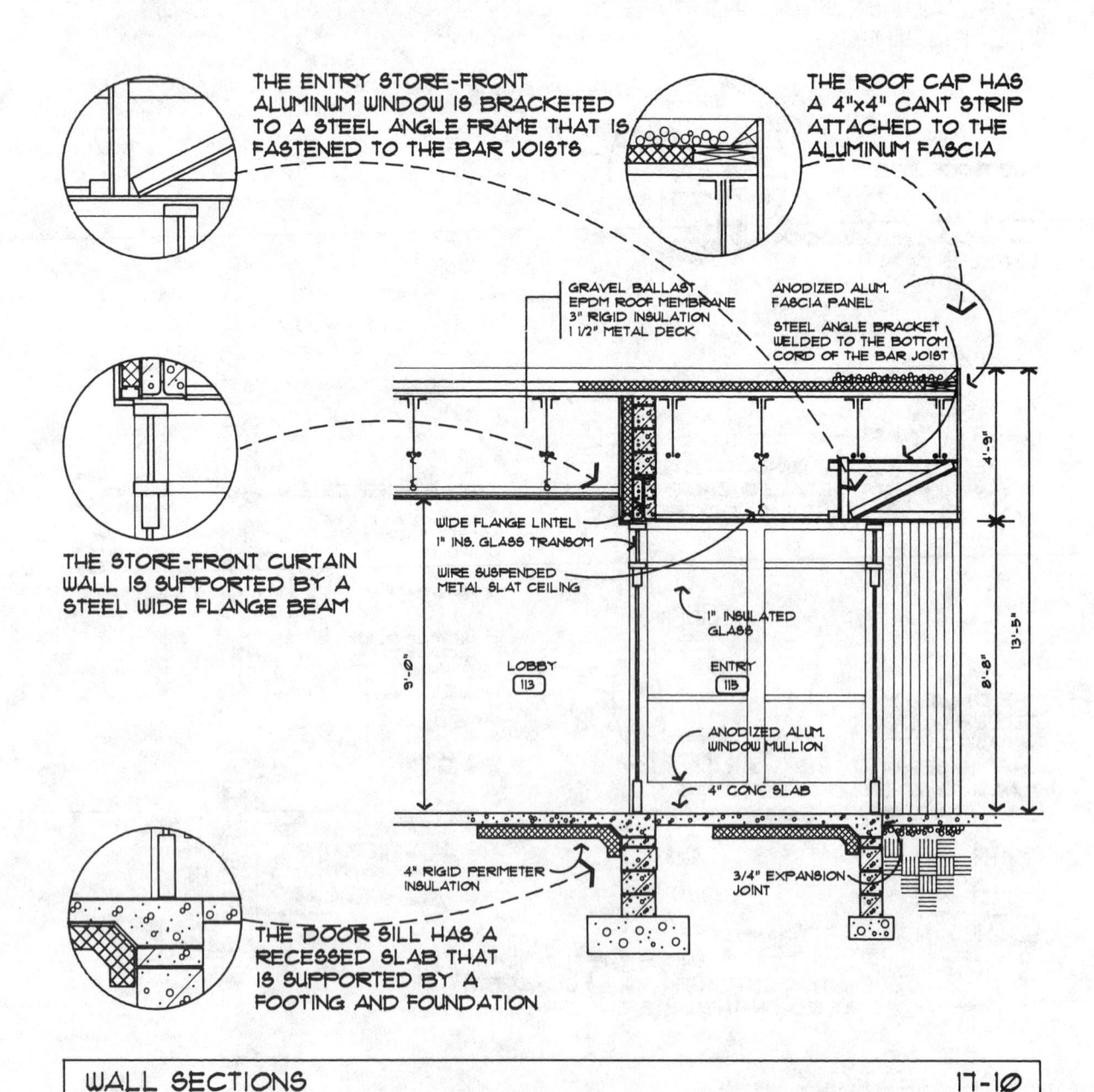

THE ENTRY STORE-FRONT ALUMINUM WINDOW IS BRACKETED TO A STEEL ANGLE FRAME THAT IS FASTENED TO THE BAR JOISTS

THE ROOF CAP HAS A 4"x4" CANT STRIP ATTACHED TO THE ALUMINUM FASCIA

GRAVEL BALLAST
EPDM ROOF MEMBRANE
3" RIGID INSULATION
1 1/2" METAL DECK

ANODIZED ALUM. FASCIA PANEL

STEEL ANGLE BRACKET WELDED TO THE BOTTOM CORD OF THE BAR JOIST

THE STORE-FRONT CURTAIN WALL IS SUPPORTED BY A STEEL WIDE FLANGE BEAM

WIDE FLANGE LINTEL
1" INS. GLASS TRANSOM
WIRE SUSPENDED METAL SLAT CEILING

1" INSULATED GLASS

LOBBY
113

ENTRY
115

ANODIZED ALUM. WINDOW MULLION

4" CONC SLAB

4" RIGID PERIMETER INSULATION

3/4" EXPANSION JOINT

THE DOOR SILL HAS A RECESSED SLAB THAT IS SUPPORTED BY A FOOTING AND FOUNDATION

WALL SECTIONS   17-10

WALL SECTIONS

THE WALL SECTION ON THIS PAGE IS CUT THROUGH THE HOSE TOWER.

THIS DETAIL SHOWS THE INTERSECTION OF THE FLAT AND SLOPED ROOFS

THE HOSE TOWER PLATFORM IS BRACKETED USING A STEEL CHANNEL

THE HOSE TOWER FLOOR SHOWS A 6" CURB

- 4" METAL DECK SUPPORTED BY 3 1/2"x3 1/2"x1/4" ANGLES
- ANODIZED ALUM. ROOF CAP
- TOP OF DECK ELEV. 754'-0"
- HOSE TRACK PULLEY
- HOSE RACK WELDED TO 8" CHANNEL
- 4" METAL DECK
- 1 1/2"Ø PIPE RAIL
- METAL GRATING FLOOR
- 1 1/4" SPACING
- C 12 x 21 AT PERIMETER W/ 1 1/2" x 3 1/2" x 1/4"
- 8'-0"
- 2'-8"
- HOSE TOWER PLATFORM ELEV. 746'-9"
- 12" BREAK-OFF CONCRETE BLOCK
- FLASHING & COUNTER-FLASHING
- 4" x 4" TREATED CANT STRIP W/ 2 TREATED 2 x 4'S BOLTED TO DECK
- PROVIDE BLOCK-CORE INSULATION IN CONCRETE MASONRY UNITS EXPOSED TO THE EXTERIOR (TYPE 'I' WALL)
- PROVIDE LADDER-TIE BLOCK REINFORCEMENT EVERY 2nd COURSE
- 2'-0"
- 12" RUNGS
- 3/4"Ø STEEL BAR RUNGS EXTENDED THRU STRINGER AND WELD
- 2" x 3/8" VERTICAL STEEL BAR STRINGER
- 12" CONCRETE MASONRY UNITS W/ INSULATED CORE
- HOSE TOWER 101
- THIS DETAIL SHOWS THE ROOF/WALL INTERSECTION
- 12" CONCRETE MASONRY UNITS
- LINTEL BLOCK AT DOOR HEADER
- BRACKET LADDER TO FLOOR W/ 5/8"Ø BOLTS
- 6" CONCRETE FLOOR W/ 6"x6"/10-10 WIRE MESH REINFORCING OVER 6 MIL POLY VAPOR BARRIER
- SLOPE FLOOR TO DRAIN
- 4" STEP DOWN
- 6" CONCRETE SLAB W/ 6"x 6"/ 10-10 WIRE REINFORCING
- 6 MIL POLY REINFORCING
- 6" TAMPED GRAVEL
- POURED CONCRETE FOOTING
- DRAIN

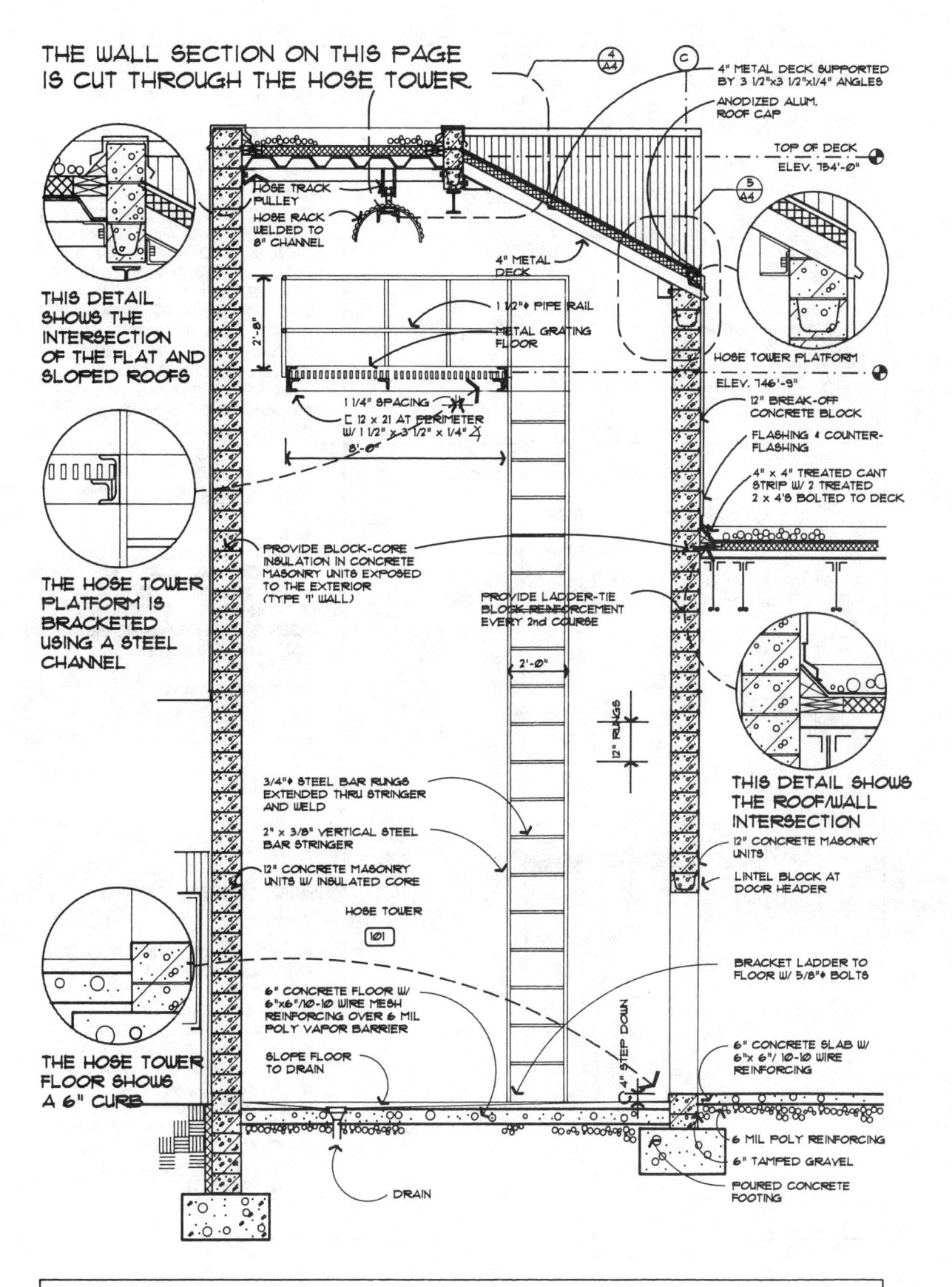

17-11

ROOF HEIGHT

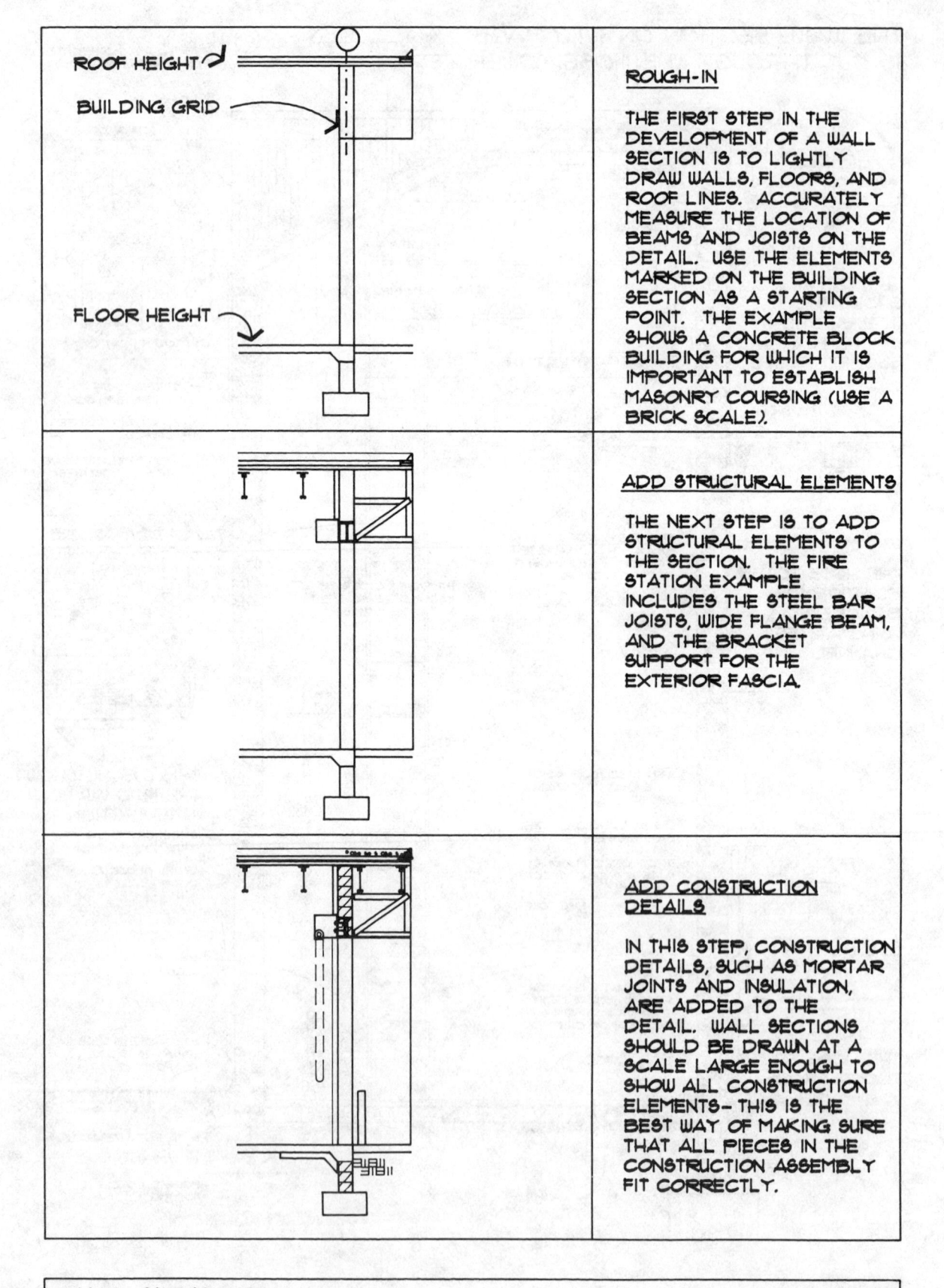

BUILDING GRID

FLOOR HEIGHT

ROUGH-IN

THE FIRST STEP IN THE DEVELOPMENT OF A WALL SECTION IS TO LIGHTLY DRAW WALLS, FLOORS, AND ROOF LINES. ACCURATELY MEASURE THE LOCATION OF BEAMS AND JOISTS ON THE DETAIL. USE THE ELEMENTS MARKED ON THE BUILDING SECTION AS A STARTING POINT. THE EXAMPLE SHOWS A CONCRETE BLOCK BUILDING FOR WHICH IT IS IMPORTANT TO ESTABLISH MASONRY COURSING (USE A BRICK SCALE).

ADD STRUCTURAL ELEMENTS

THE NEXT STEP IS TO ADD STRUCTURAL ELEMENTS TO THE SECTION. THE FIRE STATION EXAMPLE INCLUDES THE STEEL BAR JOISTS, WIDE FLANGE BEAM, AND THE BRACKET SUPPORT FOR THE EXTERIOR FASCIA.

ADD CONSTRUCTION DETAILS

IN THIS STEP, CONSTRUCTION DETAILS, SUCH AS MORTAR JOINTS AND INSULATION, ARE ADDED TO THE DETAIL. WALL SECTIONS SHOULD BE DRAWN AT A SCALE LARGE ENOUGH TO SHOW ALL CONSTRUCTION ELEMENTS – THIS IS THE BEST WAY OF MAKING SURE THAT ALL PIECES IN THE CONSTRUCTION ASSEMBLY FIT CORRECTLY.

WALL SECTIONS

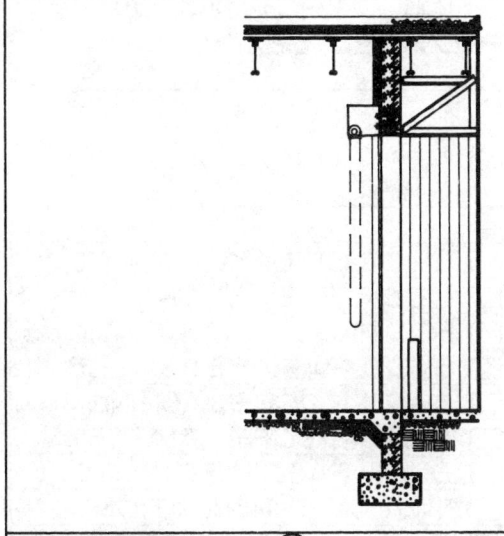

DARKEN THE SECTION CUT

THE NEXT STEP IS TO DARKEN THE OUTLINE OF THE SECTION CUT. THIS STEP ALSO INCLUDES CROSSHATCHING ALL CONSTRUCTION MATERIALS.

THE ILLUSTRATION SHOWS THE RIB-FACE CONCRETE BLOCK IN ELEVATION.

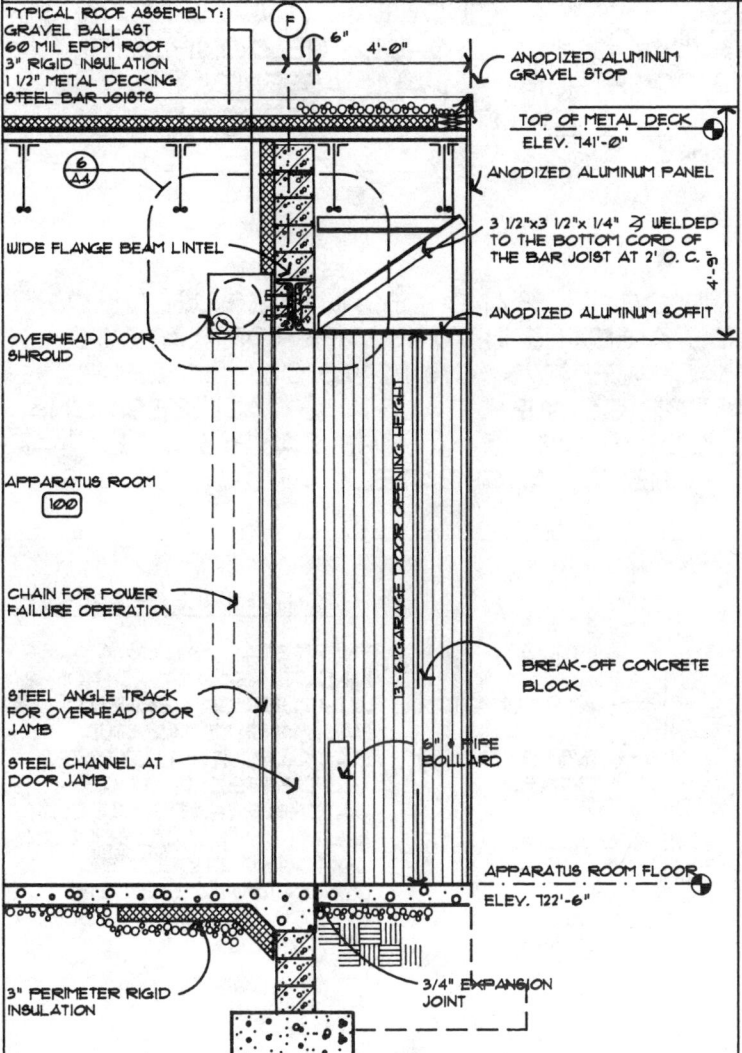

NOTES AND DIMENSIONS

THE FINAL STEP IS TO ADD CONSTRUCTION NOTES AND DIMENSION STRINGS. NOTES SHOULD BE ALIGNED IN A WAY THAT BALANCES THE DRAWING.

CONSTRUCTION NOTES SHOULD BE COMBINED WITH MATERIAL HATCHING TO FULLY EXPLAIN ALL ITEMS IN THE SECTION. KEEP IN MIND THAT THE ASSEMBLY OF THE WALL MUST BE MADE VERY CLEAR TO THE CONTRACTOR.

DIMENSION STRINGS SHOULD BE LIMITED TO ITEMS THAT ARE NOT SHOWN ON THE FLOOR PLAN. IT IS COMMON TO SHOW VERTICAL HEIGHTS (SUCH AS CEILING HEIGHTS AND FASCIA DIMENSIONS) ON THE SECTION.

Labels on drawing:
- TYPICAL ROOF ASSEMBLY: GRAVEL BALLAST / 60 MIL EPDM ROOF / 3" RIGID INSULATION / 1 1/2" METAL DECKING / STEEL BAR JOISTS
- ANODIZED ALUMINUM GRAVEL STOP
- TOP OF METAL DECK ELEV. 741'-0"
- ANODIZED ALUMINUM PANEL
- 3 1/2"x3 1/2"x 1/4" ∠ WELDED TO THE BOTTOM CORD OF THE BAR JOIST AT 2' O.C.
- ANODIZED ALUMINUM SOFFIT
- WIDE FLANGE BEAM LINTEL
- OVERHEAD DOOR SHROUD
- APPARATUS ROOM 100
- CHAIN FOR POWER FAILURE OPERATION
- STEEL ANGLE TRACK FOR OVERHEAD DOOR JAMB
- STEEL CHANNEL AT DOOR JAMB
- 13'-6" GARAGE DOOR OPENING HEIGHT
- BREAK-OFF CONCRETE BLOCK
- 6" ∅ PIPE BOLLARD
- APPARATUS ROOM FLOOR ELEV. 722'-6"
- 3/4" EXPANSION JOINT
- 3" PERIMETER RIGID INSULATION

WALL SECTIONS 17-13

A GENERAL CHECKLIST OF ITEMS THAT SHOULD BE SHOWN ON WORKING DRAWING WALL SECTIONS IS PROVIDED BELOW.

WALL SECTION CHECKLIST

- ☐ SHOW FLOOR ELEVATIONS
- ☐ SHOW ROOF PITCHES
- ☐ SHOW BEAMS AND JOISTS
- ☐ SHOW INTERIOR FEATURES
- ☐ HATCH MATERIALS
- ☐ OUTLINE SECTION CUTS
- ☐ INDICATE GRID LINES
- ☐ CALL OUT ROOM NAMES
- ☐ KEY DETAILS
- ☐ TIE MAJOR BUILDING COMPONENTS TOGETHER
- ☐ SHOW CEILING HEIGHTS
- ☐ DECK ELEVATIONS
- ☐ FOOTINGS & FOUNDATIONS
- ☐ SHOW PARAPET WALLS
- ☐ SHOW ROOF FLASHING
- ☐ DETAIL SOFFIT MATERIALS
- ☐ SHOW FASCIA FRAMING
- ☐ INDICATE INSULATION
- ☐ DETAIL WINDOW FRAMES
- ☐ SHOW THE COMPLETE WALL ASSEMBLY
- ☐ NOTE WATERPROOFING

WALL SECTION DETAILS

THIS SECTION WILL EXAMINE DETAILS AND TECHNIQUES USED TO DRAW WALL SECTIONS. USE A SCALE THAT IS APPROPRIATE TO THE WORKING DRAWING PACKAGE: 3/8" OR 1/2" IS COMMON FOR RESIDENTIAL, 1/2" OR 3/4" FOR COMMERCIAL. ALL WALL SECTIONS IN THE DRAWING SET SHOULD BE DRAWN AT THE SAME SCALE. TAKE CARE TO DRAW ALL COMPONENTS ACCURATELY AND TO SCALE.

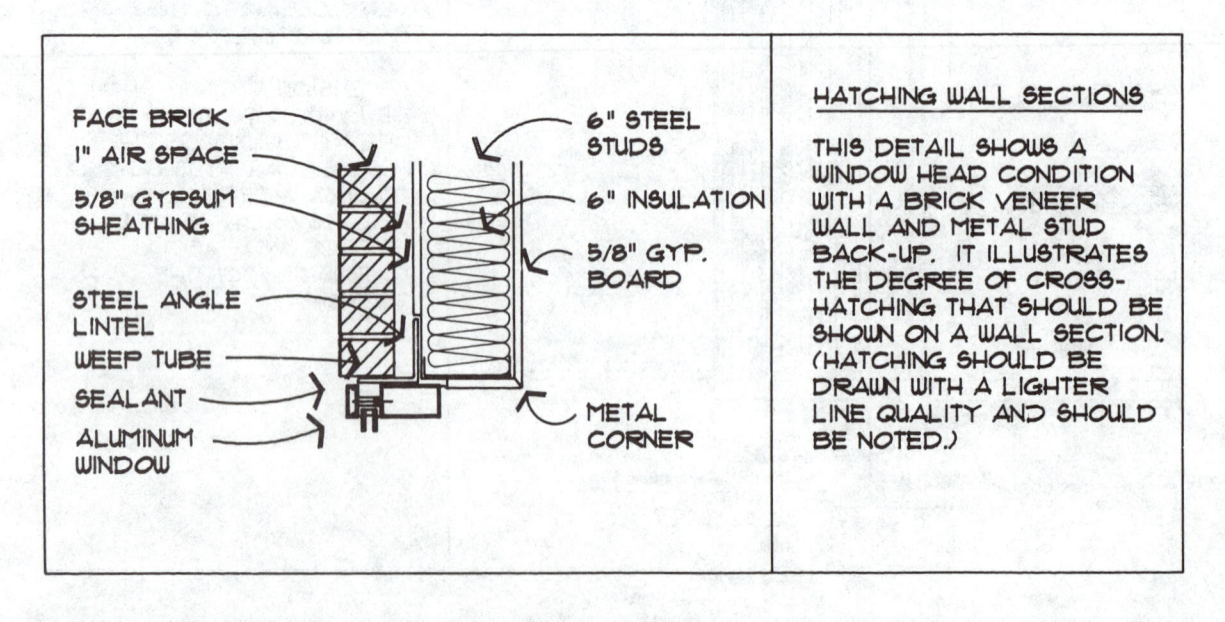

HATCHING WALL SECTIONS

THIS DETAIL SHOWS A WINDOW HEAD CONDITION WITH A BRICK VENEER WALL AND METAL STUD BACK-UP. IT ILLUSTRATES THE DEGREE OF CROSS-HATCHING THAT SHOULD BE SHOWN ON A WALL SECTION. (HATCHING SHOULD BE DRAWN WITH A LIGHTER LINE QUALITY AND SHOULD BE NOTED.)

Detail labels: FACE BRICK, 1" AIR SPACE, 5/8" GYPSUM SHEATHING, STEEL ANGLE LINTEL, WEEP TUBE, SEALANT, ALUMINUM WINDOW, 6" STEEL STUDS, 6" INSULATION, 5/8" GYP. BOARD, METAL CORNER

WALL SECTIONS

SLOPED GLAZING

THIS WALL SECTION ILLUSTRATES A CUT THROUGH A SECOND-FLOOR BALCONY WITH A SLOPED SKYLIGHT. CROSSHATCHING ON THE SECTION SHOWS FIBERGLASS INSULATION CUTS THROUGH WOOD JOISTS. THE LIGHTER DIAGONAL LINES INDICATE CEDAR SIDING SHOWN IN ELEVATION BEYOND THE SECTION CUT.

HANDRAIL SIM. TO DETAIL ON 3/A-2

ROOF INTERSECTION

THIS SECTION SHOWS A WIDE FLANGE BEAM SUPPORTING BAR JOISTS AND METAL DECKING. THE DETAIL SHOWS A MASONRY WALL ABOVE THE BEAM WITH A WINDOW SILL.

THIS IS A GOOD EXAMPLE OF THE AMOUNT OF DETAIL THAT SHOULD BE INCLUDED ON A WALL SECTION.

THRU-WALL FLASHING W/ WEEPS AT 32" O.C.

3 1/2"x3 1/2"x1/4" SHELF ANGLE

EPDM MEMBRANE ROOF

1 1/2" METAL DECK

BAR JOISTS

ROOF EDGE

THIS SECTION CUTS THROUGH A WINDOW HEAD AND ROOF PEAK. THE STEEL BRACKET WELDED TO THE WIDE FLANGE BEAM SUPPORTS THE SLOPED WOOD LAMINATED BEAM (TO THE RIGHT).

THE EXAMPLE SHOWS THE DARKER OUTLINE OF THE SECTION CUT, WITH LIGHTER LINES INDICATING "LESS IMPORTANT" ITEMS SUCH AS HATCHING AND THE WOOD LAMINATIONS.

ANODIZED ALUM. FLASHING STRIP

KEEPER NAILED TO MASONRY

LAM BEAM BRACKET WELDED TO WIDE FLANGE

THRU-WALL FLASHING

1/4" STEEL PLATE BRICK LEDGE WELDED TO BEAM

ALUM. WINDOW FRAME

SET FLASHING IN WATER CUT-OFF MASTIC

WALL SECTIONS   17-15

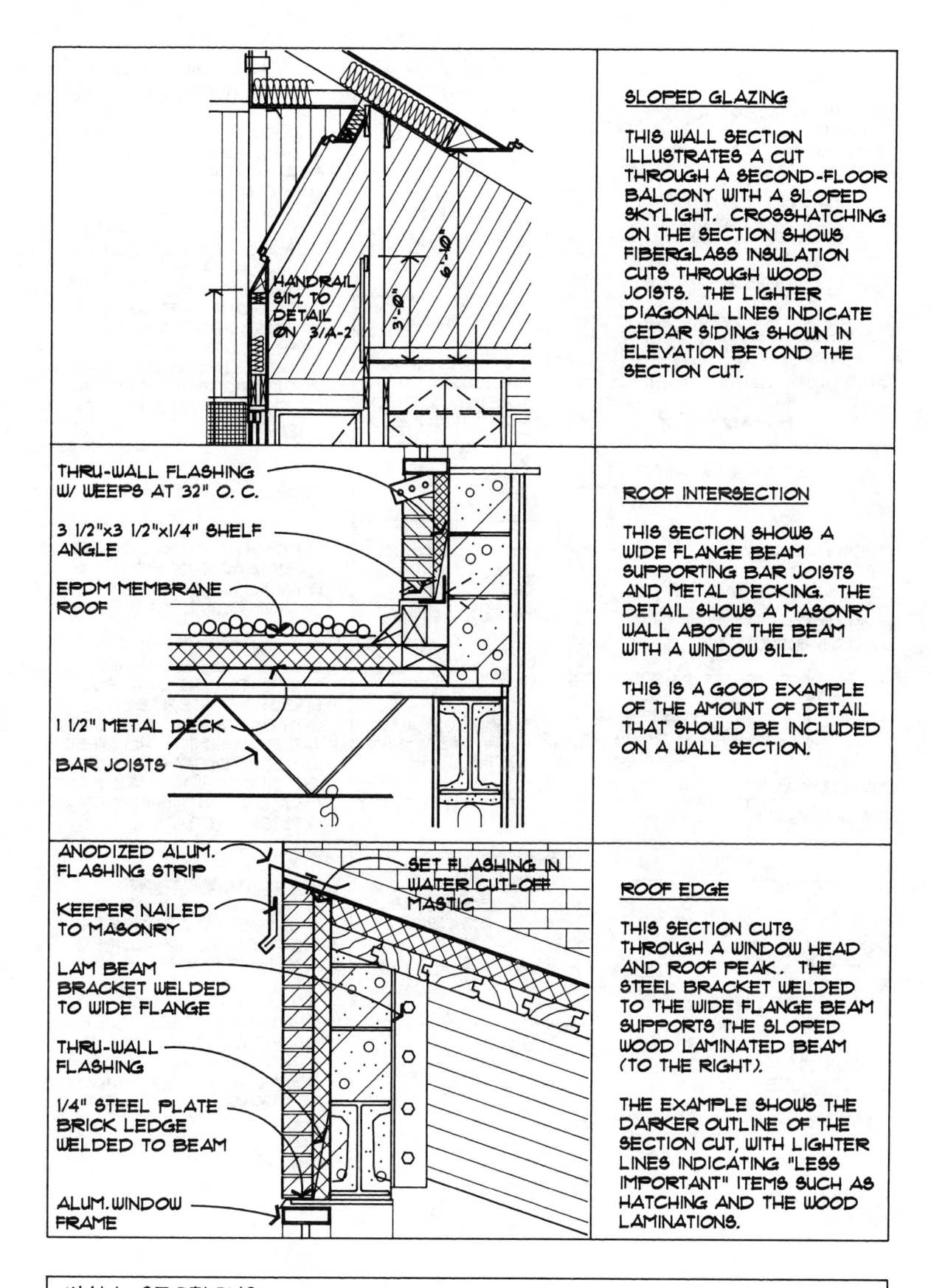

ROOF EDGE DETAIL

THIS WALL SECTION SHOWS A CUT THROUGH A LOAD-BEARING WALL THAT IS SUPPORTING STEEL BAR JOISTS.

IT IS A GOOD EXAMPLE OF BALANCE BETWEEN THE DRAWING, NOTES, AND DIMENSIONS. THE DETAIL WAS DRAWN FIRST; NOTES WERE ADDED (IN AN ORGANIZED MANNER); AND THEN IMPORTANT VERTICAL DIMENSIONS WERE ADDED.

Labels on drawing: 4"x4" CANT STRIP; ALUM. CAP FLASHING; GRAVEL BALLAST; EPDM ROOF MEMBRANE; 3" RIGID INS.; TOP OF DECK ELEV. 735'-3"; 1'-2"; 1 1/2" METAL DECK; LINTEL BLOCK W/2 #5 BARS; 8" BREAK-OFF BLOCK; 4" METAL STUDS; 4" RIGID INS.; STEEL BAR JOISTS; 5/8" GYP. BOARD

OVERHEAD DOOR

THIS WALL SECTION IS CUT THROUGH A MOTOR-DRIVEN OVERHEAD DOOR THAT IS BRACKETED TO A WIDE FLANGE BEAM.

WALL SECTIONS SHOULD DEFINE ALL STRUCTURAL ELEMENTS. THE EXAMPLE SHOWS THE STEEL BEAM WITH BOLTS THAT SUPPORT THE DOOR UNIT. THE STEEL ANGLES TO THE RIGHT OF THE BLOCK WALL ARE PART OF A BRACKET SUPPORTING A ROOF OVERHANG.

Labels on drawing: OVERHEAD DOOR THRU-BOLTED TO WIDE FLANGE BEAM; OVERHEAD DOOR SHROUD; MOTOR; 3 1/2"x3 1/2"x1/4" ∠ WELDED TO BAR JOISTS; ANODIZED ALUM. SOFFIT FASTENED TO BRACKET

ROOF INTERSECTION

THIS SECTION DETAILS THE INTERSECTION OF SLOPED AND FLAT ROOFS.

WALL SECTIONS SHOULD ILLUSTRATE STEEL ANGLES, ROOF DECKS, AND BRACKETS. ONCE THE DETAIL HAS BEEN DRAWN, USE TRACING PAPER AND A FELT PEN TO ORGANIZE NOTES AND DIMENSIONS ON THE DRAWING.

Labels on drawing: ANODIZED ALUM. CAP; ANODIZED ALUM. ROOF PANEL BONDED TO PLYWOOD; 3" RIGID INSULATION TOP OF DECK ELEV. 754'-0"; 3 1/2"x3 1/2"x1/4" SHELF ANGLE; LINTEL BLOCK; WIDE FLANGE BEAM; 4"x12"x1/4" ∠ W/ 1/4" STEEL ℞ BOLTED TO BLOCK; 4" METAL DECK

WALL SECTIONS

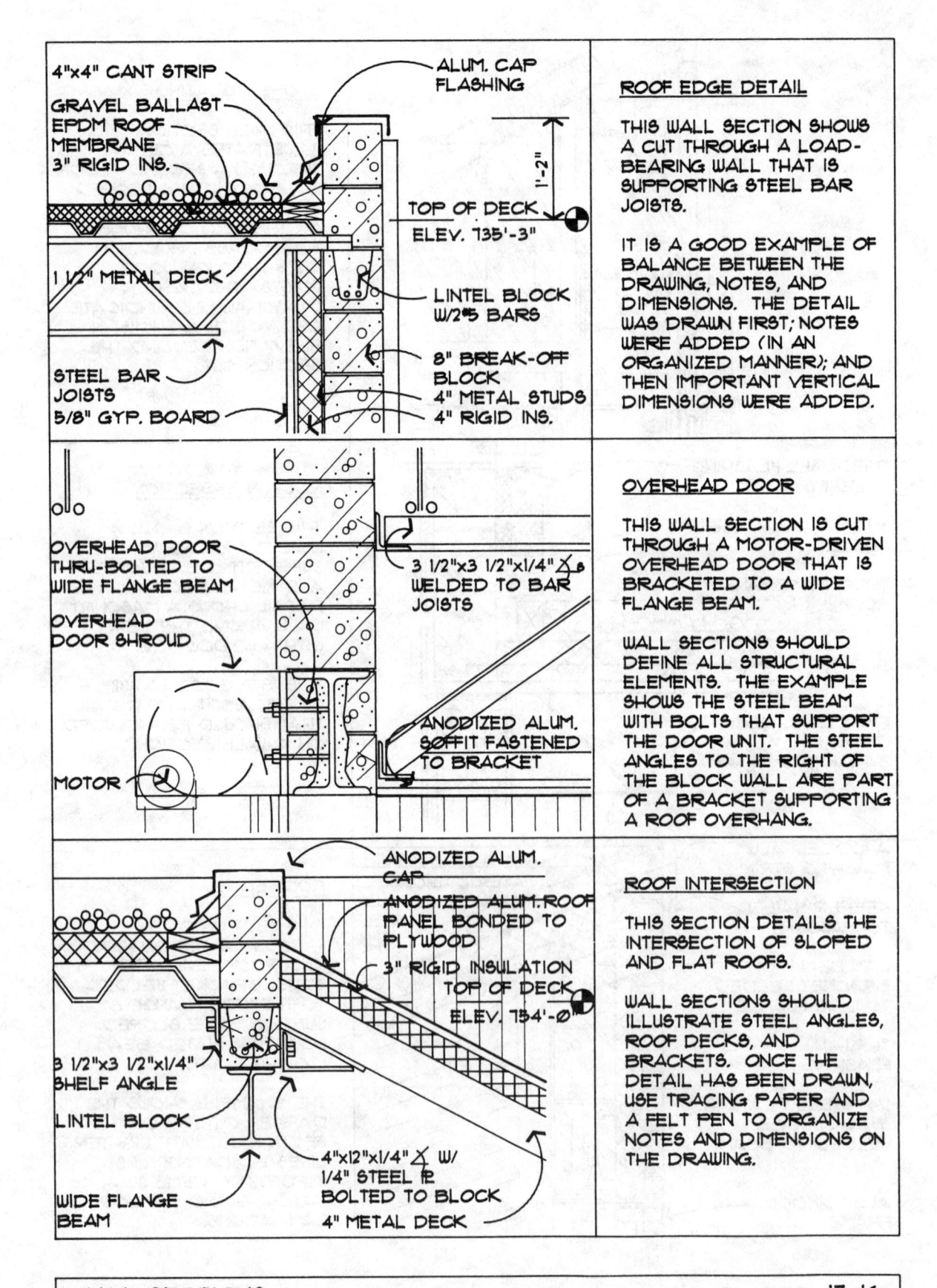

17-16

THE WALL SECTION ON THIS PAGE IS CUT THROUGH A BRICK VENEER WALL WITH A STEEL STUD BACKUP.

- TOP OF MASONRY
  ELEV. 127'-4"

- JOIST BEARING
  ELEV. 125'-4"

TYPICAL CURTAIN WALL
 4" FACE BRICK
 AIR SPACE W/ 15# FELT
 5/8" GYPSUM SHEATHING
 6" METAL STUDS
 6" BATT INSULATION
 VAPOR BARRIER

- BOTTOM OF ANGLE
  ELEV. 120'-0"

PRECAST CONC. SILL

4" ROCK-FACE CONCRETE BLOCK

- TOP OF CONCRETE SLAB
  ELEV. 112'-8"

FABRIC FLASHING OVER ANGLE W/ ROPE WICKS AT 24" O.C.

- BOTTOM OF ANGLE
  ELEV. 109'-4"

PAINT BOTTOM OF ANGLE

7/8" STUCCO- FLOAT FINISH OVER GALV. METAL LATH & 3/4" FURRING CHANNELS AT 12" O.C. & 3 5/8" 18 GA. STEEL STUDS AT 16" O.C.

1" HEAT-REDUCING INSULATED GLASS SET IN 1 3/4" x 4 1/2" ALUM. FRAME

- TOP OF CONCRETE SLAB
  ELEV. 100'-0"

TYPICAL CONST. BELOW WINDOWS
 12" ROCK-FACE BLOCK
 1 1/2" FURRING AT 24" O.C.
 1 1/2" EXTRUDED POLYSTYRENE INSULATION
 5/8" GYPSUM BOARD

GRID

TYPICAL ROOF CONSTRUCTION
 4-PLY ASPHALT BUILT-UP ROOFING
 3/4" FIBERBOARD INSULATION
 2 1/2" ISOCYANURATE INSULATION
 5/8" GYPSUM SHEATHING
 STEEL DECK

5/8" GYP. BD. OVER SOFFIT TO 6" ABOVE A.C. TILE CLNG.

3/4" RED OAK SILL W/ EASED EDGES

5/8" GYP. BD.

3" CONCRETE OVER STEEL DECK

6" BATT INSULATION

A.C. TILE

CALK BOTH SIDES OF FRAME

WOOD SILL

EXPANSION JOINT

WALL SECTIONS

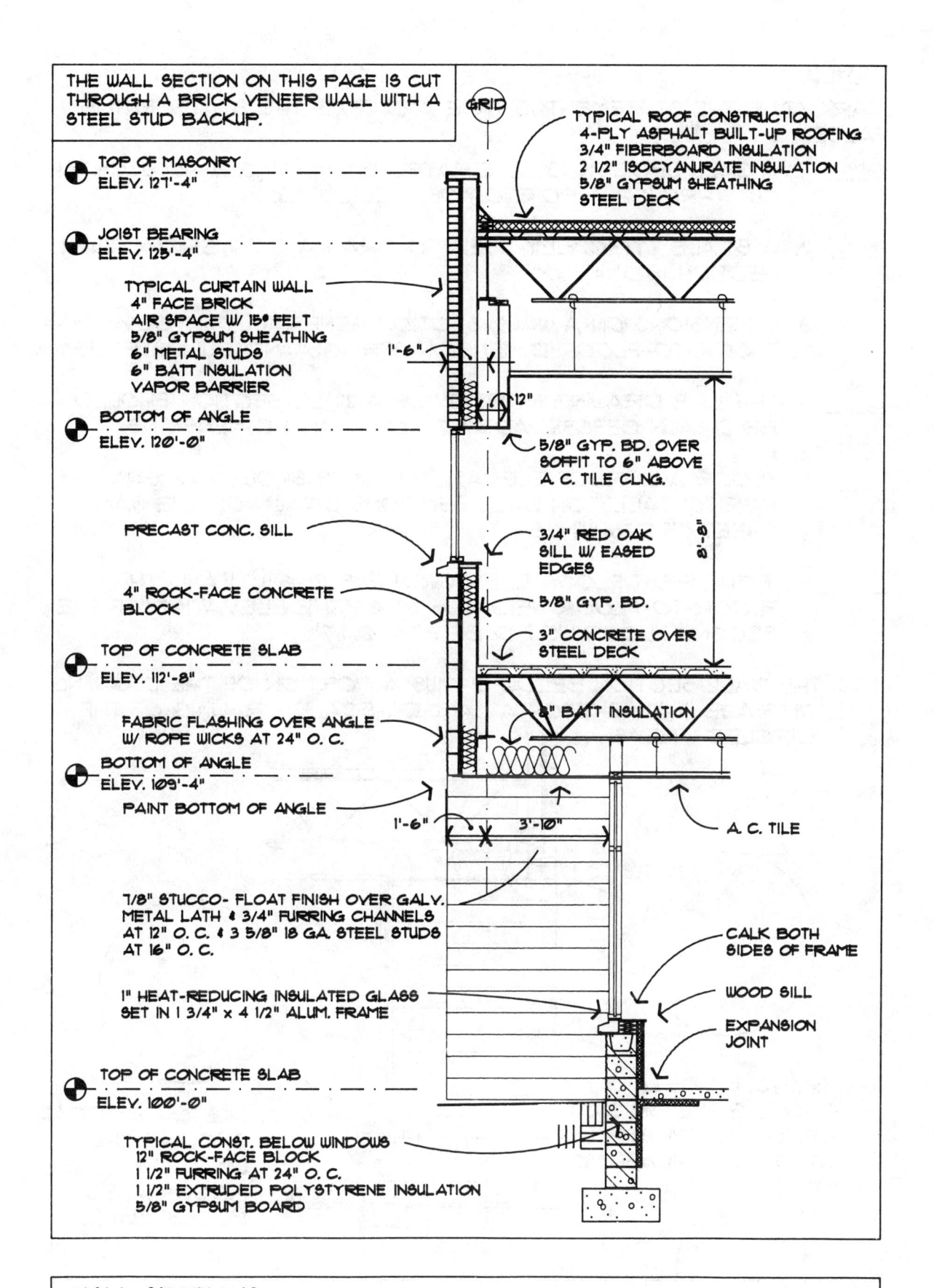

17-17

REPLAY
MARK (T) IF THE STATEMENT IS TRUE AND (F) IF THE STATEMENT IS FALSE.

_____ 1. A WALL SECTION IS GENERATED BY MAKING A HORIZONTAL CUT THROUGH A PORTION OF A BUILDING.

_____ 2. A SCALE TYPICALLY USED TO DRAW A COMMERCIAL WALL SECTION IS 3" = 1'-0".

_____ 3. DIMENSIONS ON A WALL SECTION GENERALLY INVOLVE FLOOR-TO-FLOOR DIMENSION STRINGS AND BULL'S-EYES.

_____ 4. THE LINE DRAWING PORTION OF A WALL SECTION SHOULD BE DRAWN BEFORE ADDING NOTES AND DIMENSIONS.

_____ 5. FLOOR AND ROOF ELEVATION POINTS SHOULD ALIGN HORIZONTALLY ON WALL SECTIONS DRAWN ON THE SAME SHEET OF DRAWINGS.

_____ 6. IF THE FIRST FLOOR ELEVATION IS 522'-6 1/2" AND THE FLOOR-TO-FLOOR HEIGHT IS 12'-6", THE ELEVATION OF THE SECOND FLOOR WOULD BE 534'-0 1/2".

7-10. THE WALL SECTION BELOW SHOWS A PORTION OF THE DRAWING ON PAGE 17-17. SKETCH A LARGER-SCALE DRAWING OF THE CIRCLED AREAS.

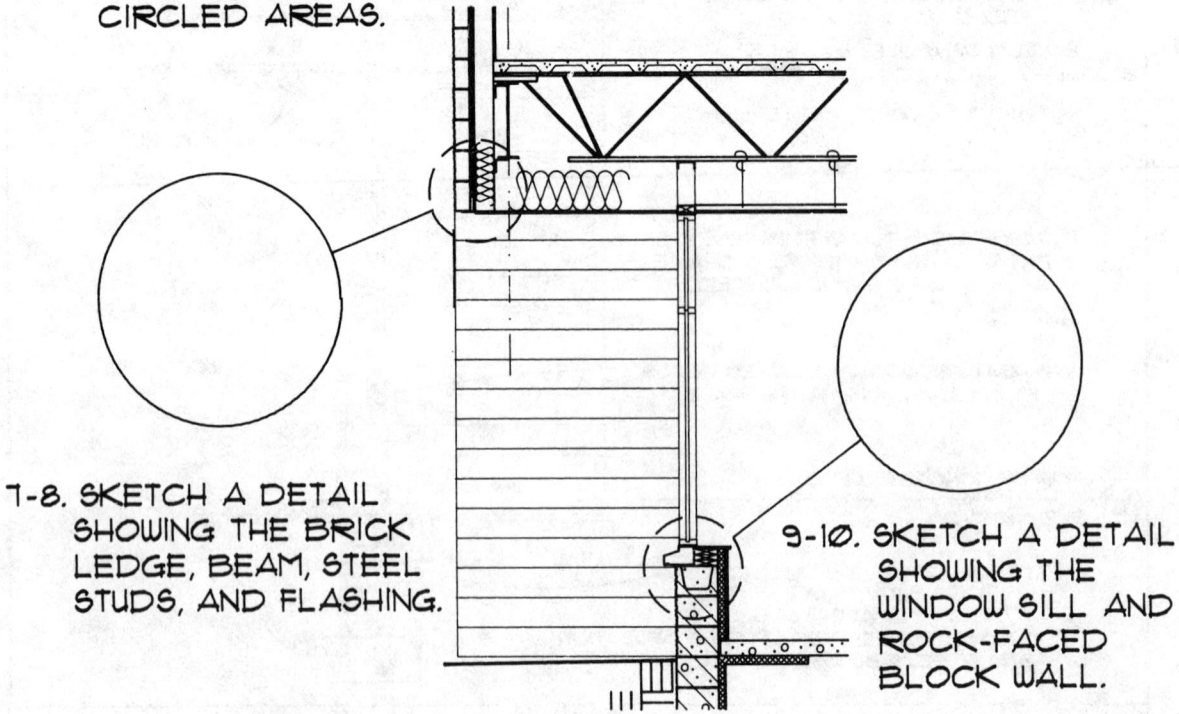

7-8. SKETCH A DETAIL SHOWING THE BRICK LEDGE, BEAM, STEEL STUDS, AND FLASHING.

9-10. SKETCH A DETAIL SHOWING THE WINDOW SILL AND ROCK-FACED BLOCK WALL.

WALL SECTIONS

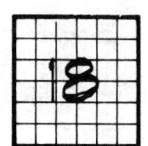

STAIRS AND ELEVATORS

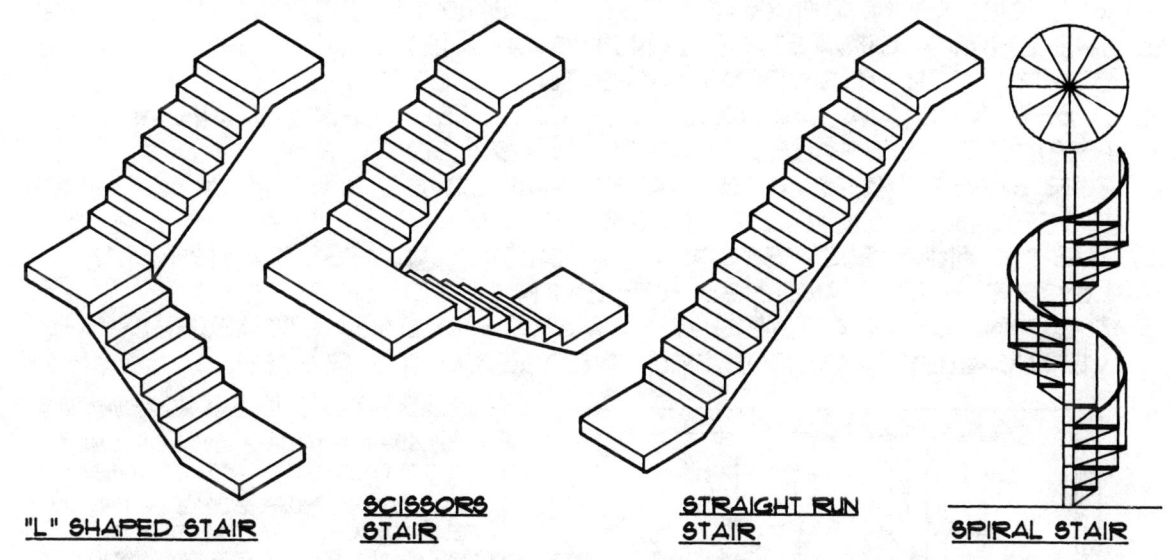

"L" SHAPED STAIR   SCISSORS STAIR   STRAIGHT RUN STAIR   SPIRAL STAIR

STAIR DESIGN AND LAYOUT POSE A UNIQUE SET OF PROBLEMS IN THE DEVELOPMENT OF A WORKING DRAWING PACKAGE. STAIRS NOT ONLY AFFECT THE CIRCULATION PATTERN IN A DESIGN, BUT A NUMBER OF BUILDING CODE REQUIREMENTS CONTROL SIZE AND PLACEMENT OF STAIRS. THE FOLLOWING LIST COVERS SOME TYPICAL CODE REQUIREMENTS (BE SURE TO CHECK LOCAL CODES):

1. THE MINIMUM WIDTH FOR A RESIDENTIAL STAIR IS 2'-8" (3'-0" IS COMMON).
2. THE MINIMUM WIDTH FOR A COMMERCIAL STAIR SERVING FEWER THAN 50 PEOPLE IS 3'-0", FOR MORE THAN 50 PEOPLE, 3'-8".
3. DOORS ENTERING COMMERCIAL STAIRS MUST SWING IN THE DIRECTION OF EXIT.
4. THERE IS A MAXIMUM HEIGHT OF 12'-0" BETWEEN STAIR LANDINGS.
5. A HANDRAIL MUST BE 2'-6" TO 2'-10" FROM THE STAIR NOSING.
6. COMMERCIAL STAIRS 3'-8" AND WIDER MUST HAVE HANDRAILS ON BOTH SIDES; THE RAIL MUST EXTEND 6" FROM THE LAST TREAD.

TREAD (T) — 1" NOSING
(1 1/2" IS MAX)
RISER (R)

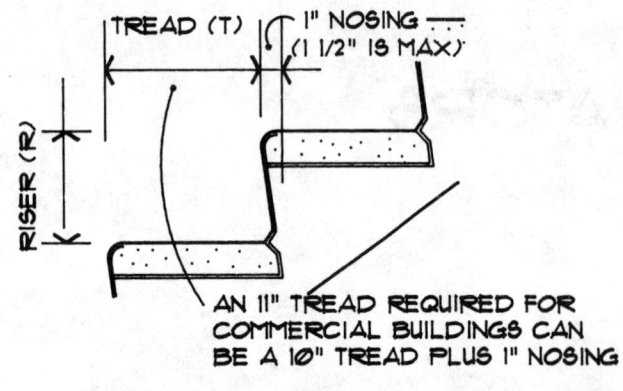

AN 11" TREAD REQUIRED FOR COMMERCIAL BUILDINGS CAN BE A 10" TREAD PLUS 1" NOSING

7. THE MAXIMUM RISER HEIGHT FOR A COMMERCIAL STAIR IS 7" (8" FOR RESIDENTIAL). USE ONE OF THESE THREE FORMULAS TO DETERMINE THE TREAD SIZE:
   - T + R = 17" (or) 17 1/2"
   - 2R + T = 24" (or) 25"
   - R × T = 70" (to) 75"

USING THE FORMULA, THE SELECTION OF A 7" RISER WOULD RESULT IN A 10" TREAD. NOTE THAT THE NOSING IS INCLUDED IN THE TREAD DIMENSION.

8. ALL RISERS IN A FLIGHT OF STAIRS SHOULD BE THE SAME HEIGHT.
9. THE LENGTH OF A STAIR LANDING SHOULD BE THE SAME AS THE STAIR WIDTH (IT DOESN'T HAVE TO EXCEED 4'-0").
10. A SPIRAL STAIR CAN ONLY BE USED AS AN EXIT STAIR IN RESIDENTIAL SPACES LESS THAN 400 SQ FT.
11. FOR SAFETY PURPOSES, THERE SHOULD BE A MINIMUM OF THREE RISERS IN A FLIGHT OF STAIRS.
12. THE MAXIMUM SLOPE FOR A HANDICAP ACCESS RAMP IS 1:12. LOCATE 5'-0" LANDINGS FOR EVERY 5'-0" OF RISE.
13. THE MINIMUM HEAD HEIGHT IN A STAIR IS 6'-8" (MEASURED VERTICALLY FROM THE FRONT EDGE OF THE RISER).

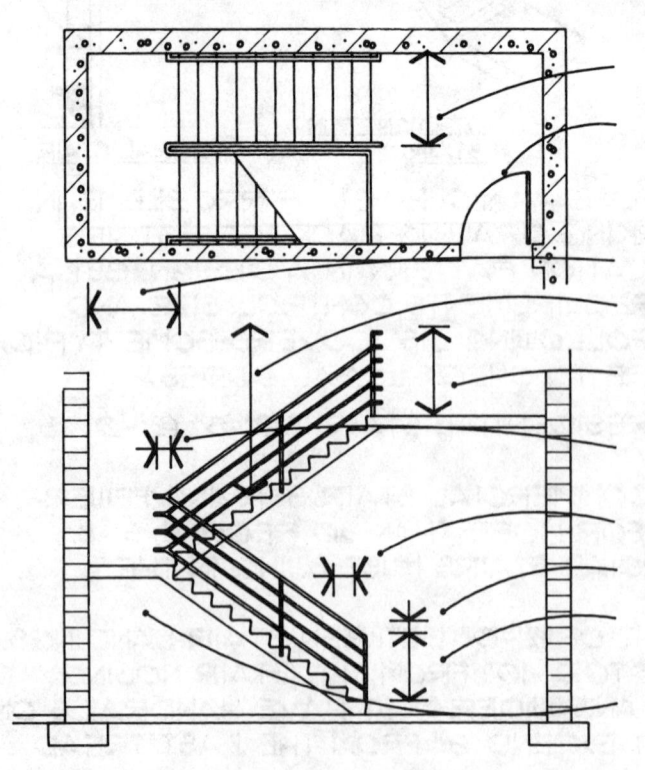

COMMERCIAL STAIR REQUIREMENTS

MIN. STAIR WIDTH IS 3'-0" FOR LESS THAN 50 PEOPLE (44" FOR OVER 50)

STAIR DOORS MUST SWING IN THE DIRECTION OF EXIT; THE DOOR SWING CAN'T REDUCE THE LANDING WIDTH TO LESS THAN 1/2 OF ITS REQUIRED WIDTH

THE LANDING MUST BE THE SAME WIDTH AS THE STAIR (4'-0" MAX.)

MINIMUM HEAD HEIGHT IS 6'-8"

THE MINIMUM HEIGHT FOR A BALCONY RAIL IS 3'-6"

THE HANDRAIL MUST EXTEND 6" BEYOND THE STAIR NOSING

MINIMUM TREAD IS 10"

MAXIMUM RISER HEIGHT IS 7"

THE HEIGHT OF A HANDRAIL MUST BE BETWEEN 2'-6" AND 2'-10"

THE MAXIMUM STAIR RISE IS 12'-0" WITHOUT A LANDING

STAIRS AND ELEVATORS

TERMS USED IN STAIR DESIGN ARE DEFINED IN THE ILLUSTRATION BELOW.

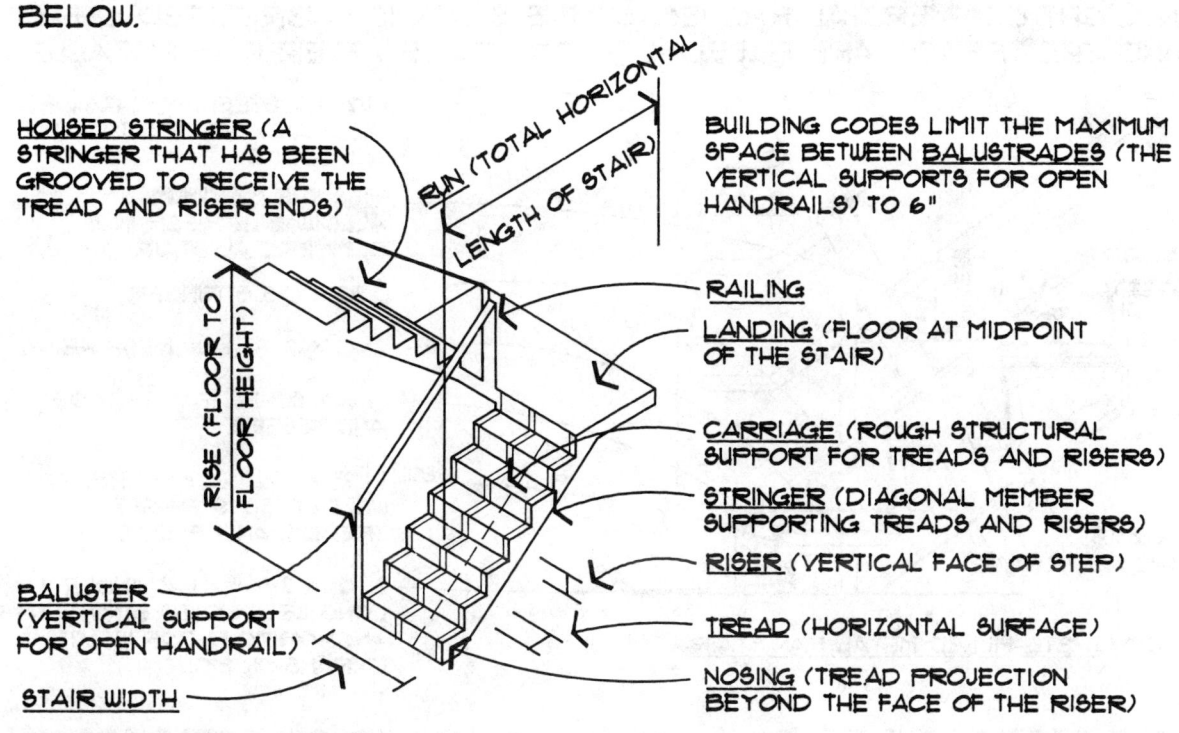

HOUSED STRINGER (A STRINGER THAT HAS BEEN GROOVED TO RECEIVE THE TREAD AND RISER ENDS)

RUN (TOTAL HORIZONTAL LENGTH OF STAIR)

BUILDING CODES LIMIT THE MAXIMUM SPACE BETWEEN BALUSTRADES (THE VERTICAL SUPPORTS FOR OPEN HANDRAILS) TO 6"

RAILING

LANDING (FLOOR AT MIDPOINT OF THE STAIR)

RISE (FLOOR TO FLOOR HEIGHT)

CARRIAGE (ROUGH STRUCTURAL SUPPORT FOR TREADS AND RISERS)

STRINGER (DIAGONAL MEMBER SUPPORTING TREADS AND RISERS)

RISER (VERTICAL FACE OF STEP)

BALUSTER (VERTICAL SUPPORT FOR OPEN HANDRAIL)

TREAD (HORIZONTAL SURFACE)

STAIR WIDTH

NOSING (TREAD PROJECTION BEYOND THE FACE OF THE RISER)

STAIR MATERIALS

THE TYPE OF MATERIAL USED TO BUILD A STAIR IS DETERMINED BY THE OCCUPANCY; RESIDENTIAL PROJECTS ARE TYPICALLY CONSTRUCTED OF WOOD, WHILE COMMERCIAL STAIRS ARE USUALLY MADE OF CONCRETE OR STEEL. IN THIS SECTION WE WILL REVIEW THE TECHNIQUES USED FOR WOOD, STEEL, AND CONCRETE STAIR DESIGN.

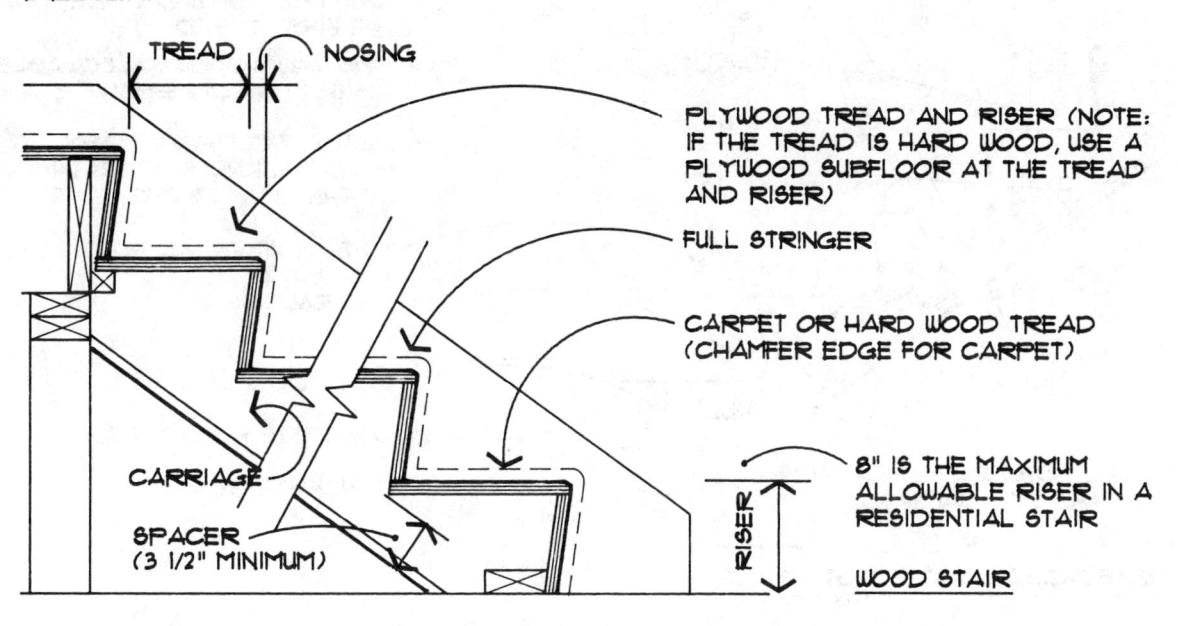

TREAD | NOSING

PLYWOOD TREAD AND RISER (NOTE: IF THE TREAD IS HARD WOOD, USE A PLYWOOD SUBFLOOR AT THE TREAD AND RISER)

FULL STRINGER

CARPET OR HARD WOOD TREAD (CHAMFER EDGE FOR CARPET)

CARRIAGE

SPACER (3 1/2" MINIMUM)

RISER

8" IS THE MAXIMUM ALLOWABLE RISER IN A RESIDENTIAL STAIR

WOOD STAIR

STAIRS AND ELEVATORS

THE DETAIL BELOW ILLUSTRATES A METAL PAN STAIR FREQUENTLY USED IN LIGHT COMMERCIAL PROJECTS. THE STAIR IS FABRICATED OFF-SITE AND THE TREADS ARE FILLED WITH CONCRETE AFTER IT IS INSTALLED.

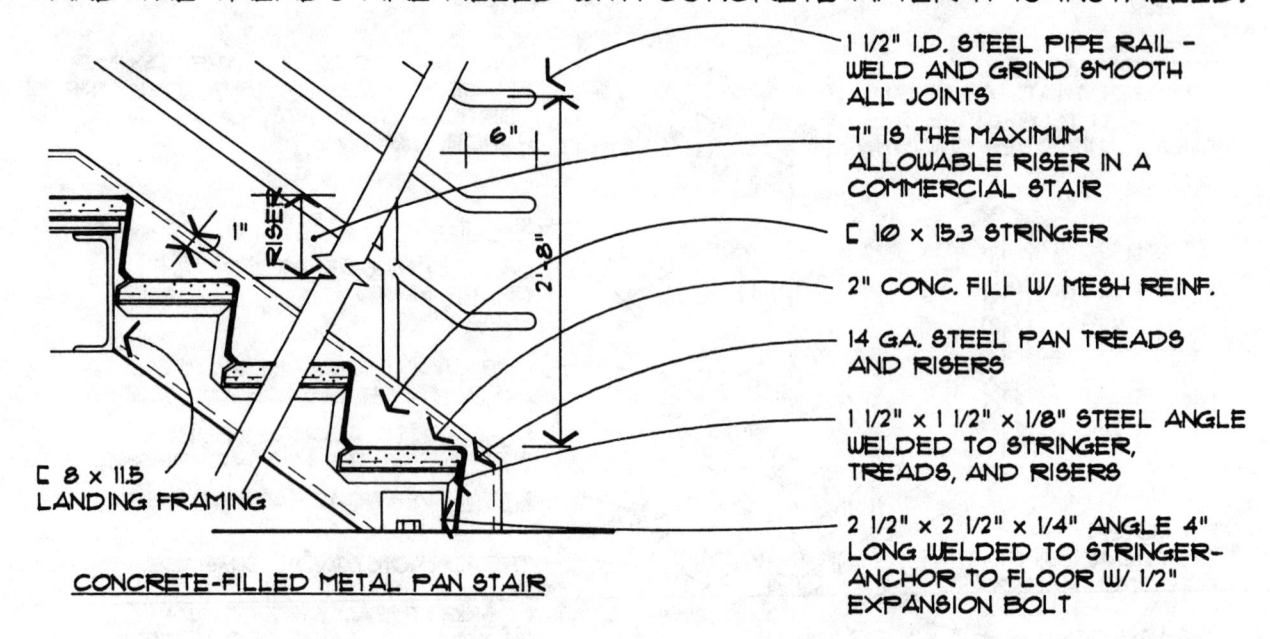

- 1 1/2" I.D. STEEL PIPE RAIL - WELD AND GRIND SMOOTH ALL JOINTS
- 7" IS THE MAXIMUM ALLOWABLE RISER IN A COMMERCIAL STAIR
- C 10 x 15.3 STRINGER
- 2" CONC. FILL W/ MESH REINF.
- 14 GA. STEEL PAN TREADS AND RISERS
- 1 1/2" x 1 1/2" x 1/8" STEEL ANGLE WELDED TO STRINGER, TREADS, AND RISERS
- 2 1/2" x 2 1/2" x 1/4" ANGLE 4" LONG WELDED TO STRINGER - ANCHOR TO FLOOR W/ 1/2" EXPANSION BOLT
- C 8 x 11.5 LANDING FRAMING

CONCRETE-FILLED METAL PAN STAIR

THE SECTION CUT BELOW IS THROUGH A POURED CONCRETE STAIR. THE STAIR IS STRUCTURED USING STEEL REINFORCING (DOWELS). A PRELIMINARY DESIGN RULE IS THAT THE SMALLEST THICKNESS OF THE CONCRETE STAIR SHOULD BE 1/26th OF THE SPAN.

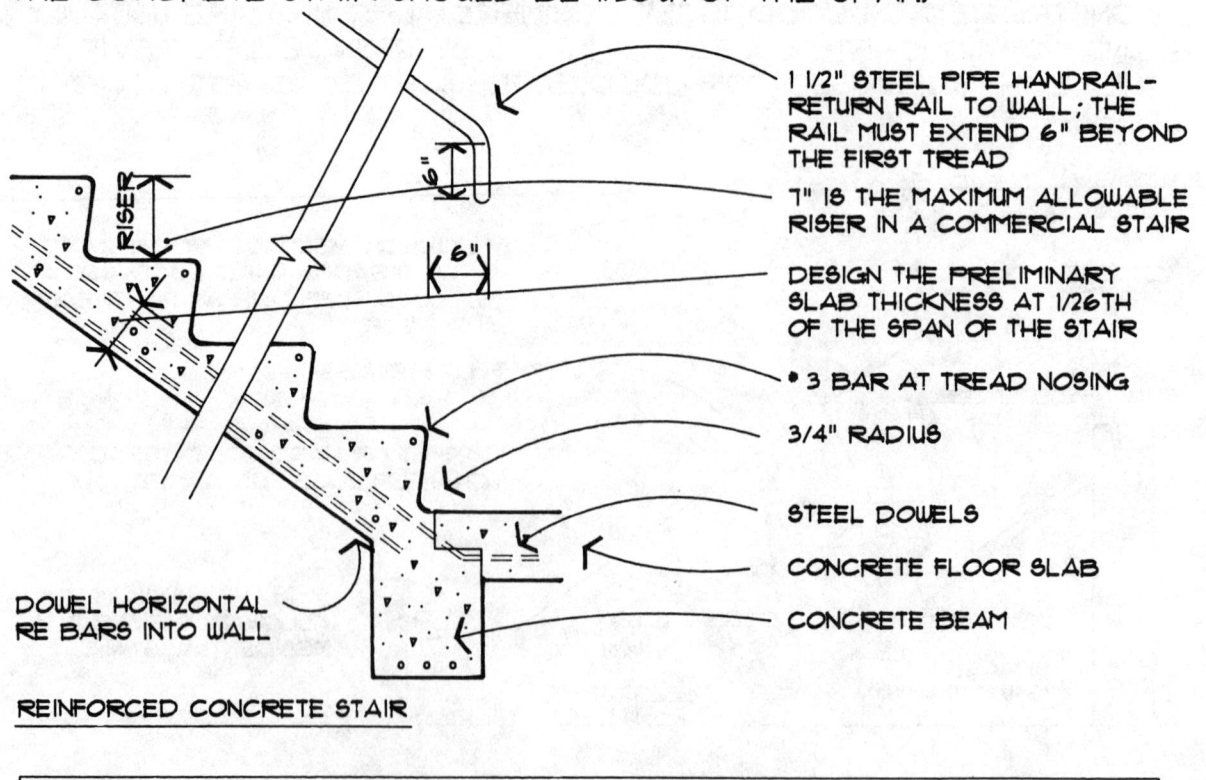

- 1 1/2" STEEL PIPE HANDRAIL - RETURN RAIL TO WALL; THE RAIL MUST EXTEND 6" BEYOND THE FIRST TREAD
- 7" IS THE MAXIMUM ALLOWABLE RISER IN A COMMERCIAL STAIR
- DESIGN THE PRELIMINARY SLAB THICKNESS AT 1/26th OF THE SPAN OF THE STAIR
- #3 BAR AT TREAD NOSING
- 3/4" RADIUS
- STEEL DOWELS
- CONCRETE FLOOR SLAB
- CONCRETE BEAM
- DOWEL HORIZONTAL RE BARS INTO WALL

REINFORCED CONCRETE STAIR

STAIRS AND ELEVATORS   18-4

THE FIRST STEP IN STAIR DESIGN AND LAYOUT IS TO DETERMINE THE FLOOR-TO-FLOOR HEIGHT. THE NEXT STEP IS TO REVIEW THE BUILDING CODE REQUIREMENTS THAT WILL GOVERN THE STAIR DESIGN. CODES ARE ESTABLISHED TO PROTECT THE OCCUPANTS OF A BUILDING; THERE ARE SEVERAL DIFFERENT BUILDING CODES IN THE COUNTRY AND A NUMBER OF OCCUPANT REQUIREMENTS WITHIN EACH CODE. FOR EXAMPLE, THE <u>UNIFORM BUILDING CODE</u> REQUIREMENTS FOR A HOUSE WOULD BE QUITE DIFFERENT FROM THOSE FOR A SCHOOL. IT IS NECESSARY TO SHOW EVERY STAIR IN PLAN AND SECTION TO FULLY DETAIL ITS CONSTRUCTION. BOTH THE PLAN AND SECTION VIEWS ARE TYPICALLY DRAWN AT A 1/4" = 1'-0" SCALE.

ON PAGES 18-5 THROUGH 18-7 WE WILL REVIEW THE DESIGN OF A RESIDENTIAL STAIR THAT IS A 180° RETURN SCISSORS STAIR WITH A LANDING AT MIDLEVEL.

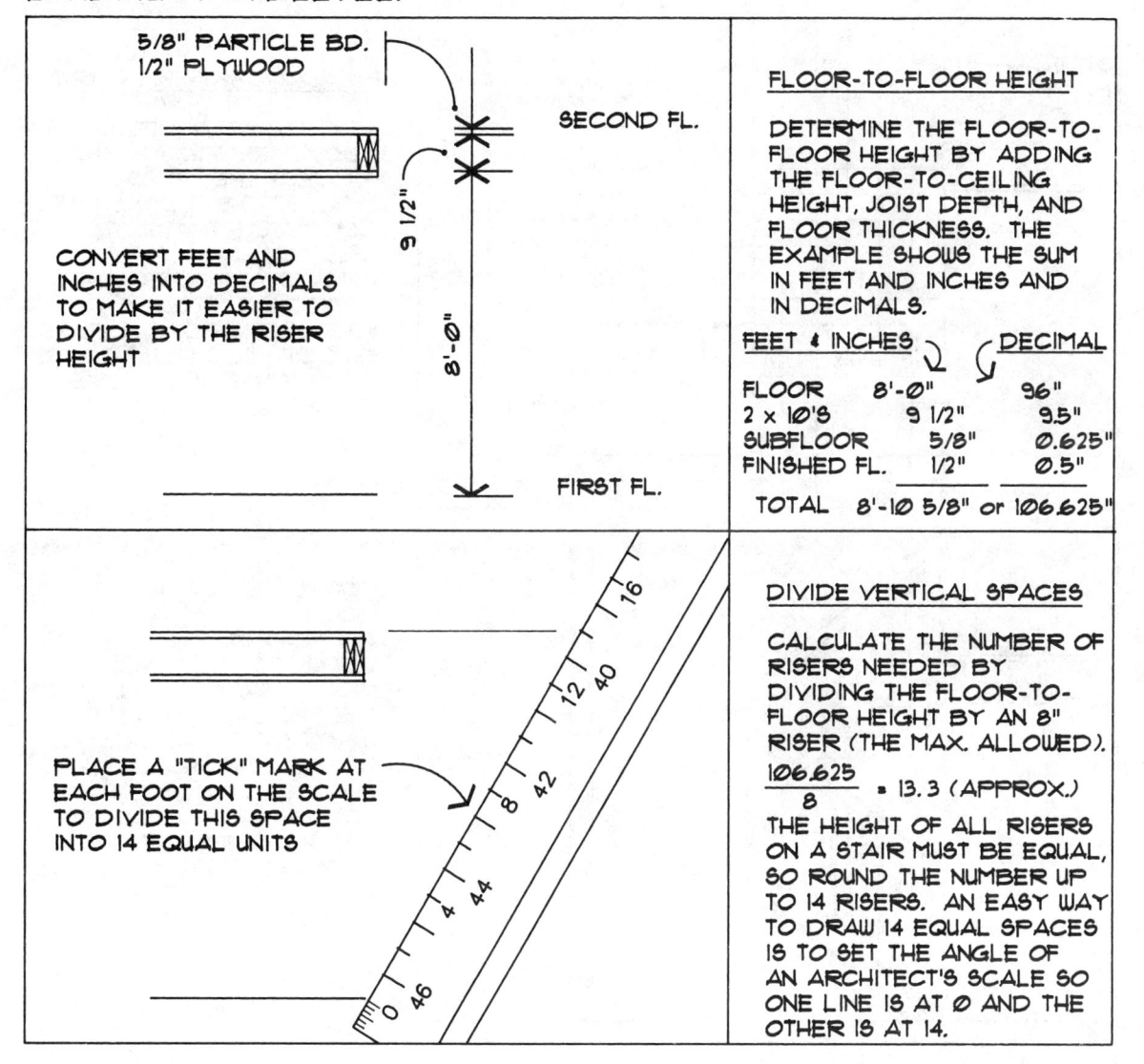

5/8" PARTICLE BD.
1/2" PLYWOOD

SECOND FL.

9 1/2"

8'-0"

FIRST FL.

CONVERT FEET AND INCHES INTO DECIMALS TO MAKE IT EASIER TO DIVIDE BY THE RISER HEIGHT

FLOOR-TO-FLOOR HEIGHT

DETERMINE THE FLOOR-TO-FLOOR HEIGHT BY ADDING THE FLOOR-TO-CEILING HEIGHT, JOIST DEPTH, AND FLOOR THICKNESS. THE EXAMPLE SHOWS THE SUM IN FEET AND INCHES AND IN DECIMALS.

FEET & INCHES		DECIMAL
FLOOR	8'-0"	96"
2 x 10'S	9 1/2"	9.5"
SUBFLOOR	5/8"	0.625"
FINISHED FL.	1/2"	0.5"
TOTAL	8'-10 5/8" or	106.625"

PLACE A "TICK" MARK AT EACH FOOT ON THE SCALE TO DIVIDE THIS SPACE INTO 14 EQUAL UNITS

DIVIDE VERTICAL SPACES

CALCULATE THE NUMBER OF RISERS NEEDED BY DIVIDING THE FLOOR-TO-FLOOR HEIGHT BY AN 8" RISER (THE MAX. ALLOWED).

$$\frac{106.625}{8} = 13.3 \text{ (APPROX.)}$$

THE HEIGHT OF ALL RISERS ON A STAIR MUST BE EQUAL, SO ROUND THE NUMBER UP TO 14 RISERS. AN EASY WAY TO DRAW 14 EQUAL SPACES IS TO SET THE ANGLE OF AN ARCHITECT'S SCALE SO ONE LINE IS AT 0 AND THE OTHER IS AT 14.

STAIRS AND ELEVATORS

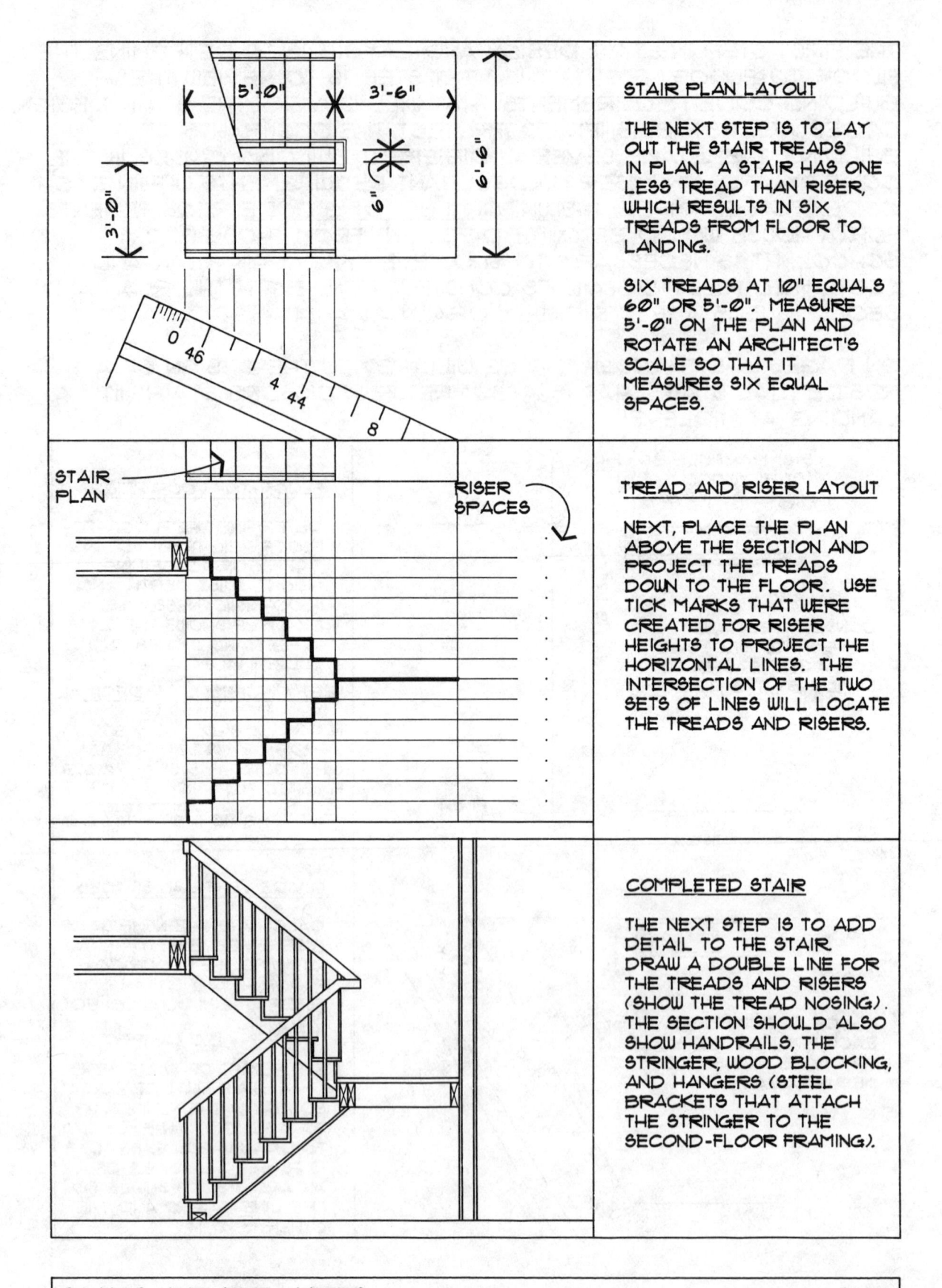

STAIR PLAN LAYOUT

THE NEXT STEP IS TO LAY OUT THE STAIR TREADS IN PLAN. A STAIR HAS ONE LESS TREAD THAN RISER, WHICH RESULTS IN SIX TREADS FROM FLOOR TO LANDING.

SIX TREADS AT 10" EQUALS 60" OR 5'-0". MEASURE 5'-0" ON THE PLAN AND ROTATE AN ARCHITECT'S SCALE SO THAT IT MEASURES SIX EQUAL SPACES.

TREAD AND RISER LAYOUT

NEXT, PLACE THE PLAN ABOVE THE SECTION AND PROJECT THE TREADS DOWN TO THE FLOOR. USE TICK MARKS THAT WERE CREATED FOR RISER HEIGHTS TO PROJECT THE HORIZONTAL LINES. THE INTERSECTION OF THE TWO SETS OF LINES WILL LOCATE THE TREADS AND RISERS.

COMPLETED STAIR

THE NEXT STEP IS TO ADD DETAIL TO THE STAIR. DRAW A DOUBLE LINE FOR THE TREADS AND RISERS (SHOW THE TREAD NOSING). THE SECTION SHOULD ALSO SHOW HANDRAILS, THE STRINGER, WOOD BLOCKING, AND HANGERS (STEEL BRACKETS THAT ATTACH THE STRINGER TO THE SECOND-FLOOR FRAMING).

STAIRS AND ELEVATORS 18-6

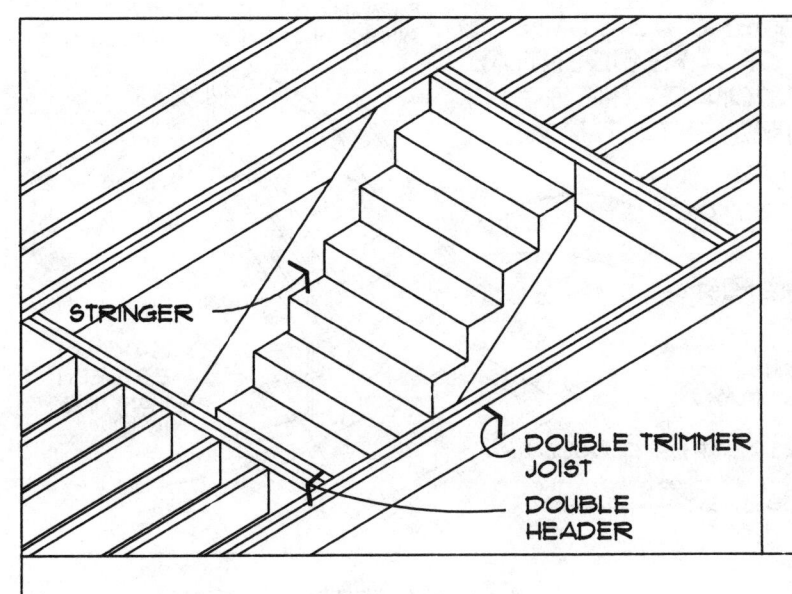

STAIRWELL FRAMING

WOOD FRAMING FOR A RESIDENTIAL STAIR REQUIRES THAT ONE OR MORE JOISTS MUST BE CUT. THE ILLUSTRATION SHOWS A STAIRWELL THAT RUNS PARALLEL TO THE JOIST SPAN. A COMMON WAY TO SOLVE THE FRAMING IS TO DOUBLE THE PARALLEL JOISTS (CALLED <u>TRIMMERS</u>) AND HEAD (SUPPORT WITH A BEAM) EACH END WITH A DOUBLE HEADER.

- STRINGER
- DOUBLE TRIMMER JOIST
- DOUBLE HEADER

COMPLETED WOOD STAIR

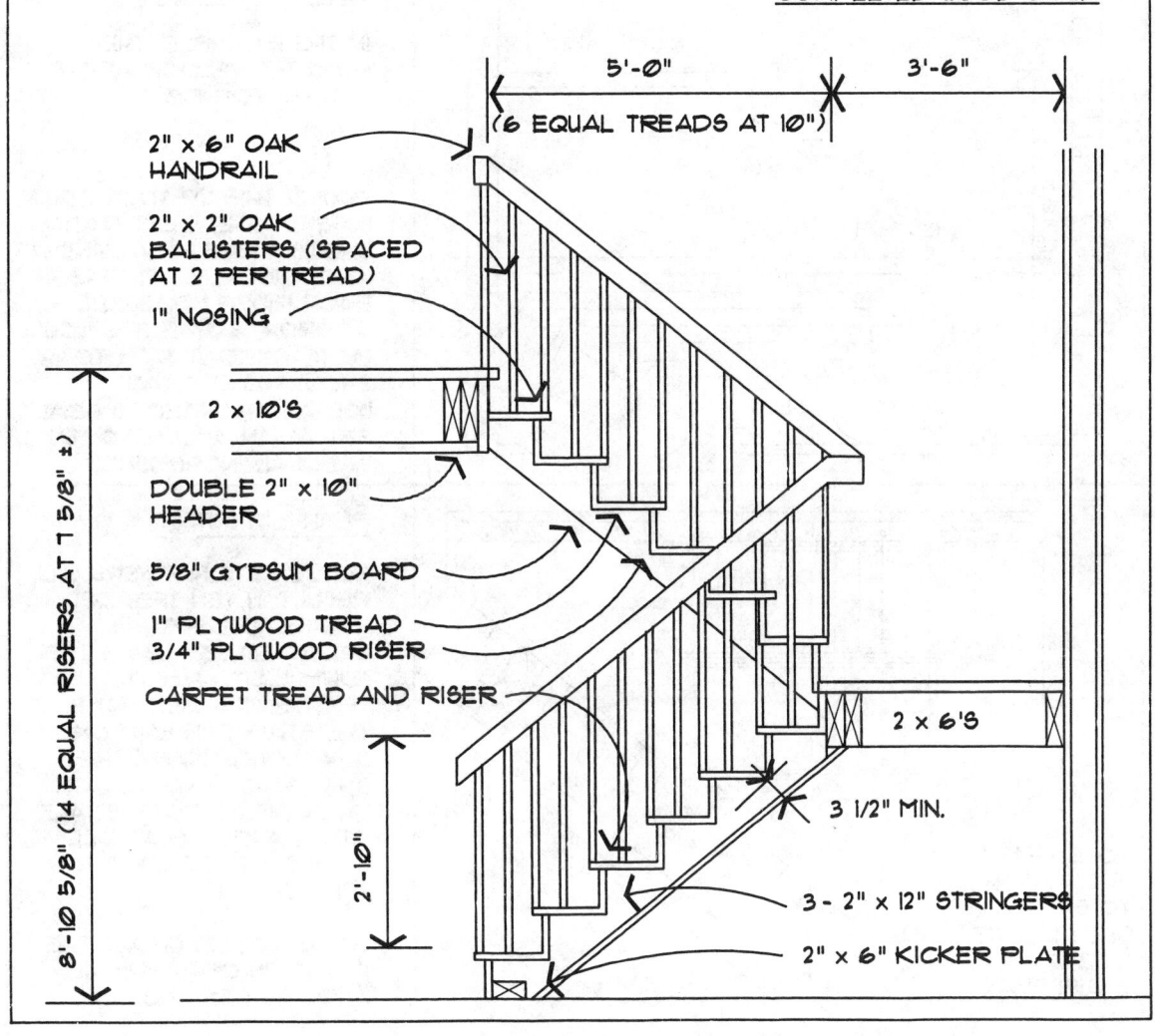

5'-0" (6 EQUAL TREADS AT 10") | 3'-6"

- 2" x 6" OAK HANDRAIL
- 2" x 2" OAK BALUSTERS (SPACED AT 2 PER TREAD)
- 1" NOSING
- 2 x 10'S
- DOUBLE 2" x 10" HEADER
- 5/8" GYPSUM BOARD
- 1" PLYWOOD TREAD
- 3/4" PLYWOOD RISER
- CARPET TREAD AND RISER
- 2 x 6'S
- 3 1/2" MIN.
- 3 - 2" x 12" STRINGERS
- 2" x 6" KICKER PLATE

8'-10 5/8" (14 EQUAL RISERS AT 7 5/8" ±)

2'-10"

STAIRS AND ELEVATORS   18-7

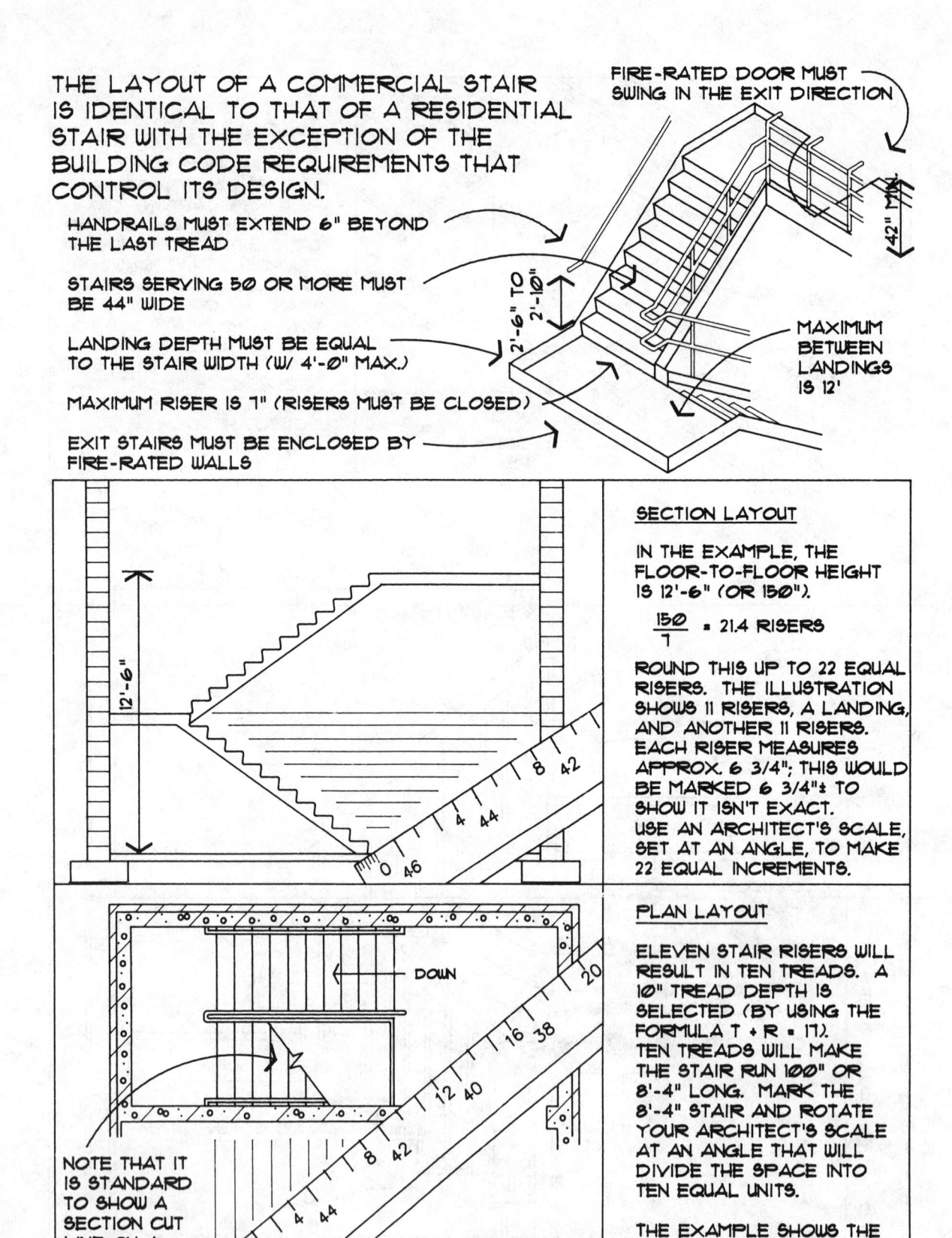

THE LAYOUT OF A COMMERCIAL STAIR IS IDENTICAL TO THAT OF A RESIDENTIAL STAIR WITH THE EXCEPTION OF THE BUILDING CODE REQUIREMENTS THAT CONTROL ITS DESIGN.

- HANDRAILS MUST EXTEND 6" BEYOND THE LAST TREAD
- STAIRS SERVING 50 OR MORE MUST BE 44" WIDE
- LANDING DEPTH MUST BE EQUAL TO THE STAIR WIDTH (W/ 4'-0" MAX.)
- MAXIMUM RISER IS 7" (RISERS MUST BE CLOSED)
- EXIT STAIRS MUST BE ENCLOSED BY FIRE-RATED WALLS

FIRE-RATED DOOR MUST SWING IN THE EXIT DIRECTION

42" MIN.

2'-6" TO 2'-10"

MAXIMUM BETWEEN LANDINGS IS 12'

SECTION LAYOUT

IN THE EXAMPLE, THE FLOOR-TO-FLOOR HEIGHT IS 12'-6" (OR 150").

$$\frac{150}{7} = 21.4 \text{ RISERS}$$

ROUND THIS UP TO 22 EQUAL RISERS. THE ILLUSTRATION SHOWS 11 RISERS, A LANDING, AND ANOTHER 11 RISERS. EACH RISER MEASURES APPROX. 6 3/4"; THIS WOULD BE MARKED 6 3/4"± TO SHOW IT ISN'T EXACT. USE AN ARCHITECT'S SCALE, SET AT AN ANGLE, TO MAKE 22 EQUAL INCREMENTS.

PLAN LAYOUT

ELEVEN STAIR RISERS WILL RESULT IN TEN TREADS. A 10" TREAD DEPTH IS SELECTED (BY USING THE FORMULA T + R = 17). TEN TREADS WILL MAKE THE STAIR RUN 100" OR 8'-4" LONG. MARK THE 8'-4" STAIR AND ROTATE YOUR ARCHITECT'S SCALE AT AN ANGLE THAT WILL DIVIDE THE SPACE INTO TEN EQUAL UNITS.

THE EXAMPLE SHOWS THE ADDITION OF HANDRAILS AND THE LANDING.

NOTE THAT IT IS STANDARD TO SHOW A SECTION CUT LINE ON A STAIR PLAN

STAIRS AND ELEVATORS   18-8

COMPLETED STAIR

THE PLAN AND SECTION SHOWN BELOW DETAIL A COMPLETED COMMERCIAL STAIR. NOTE THAT IT IS NECESSARY TO INDICATE THE STAIR DIRECTION (DOWN OR UP). IT IS COMMON TO INDICATE EACH STAIR BY A LETTER ("STAIR A") RATHER THAN BY THE NUMBERS THAT ARE USED FOR ROOMS. THE REASON IS THAT THE STAIR SHOULD HAVE IDENTICAL MARKS ON EACH FLOOR. THE LANDING ELEVATION IS INDICATED (ELEV. 86'-3") TO DEFINE THE EXACT HEIGHT.

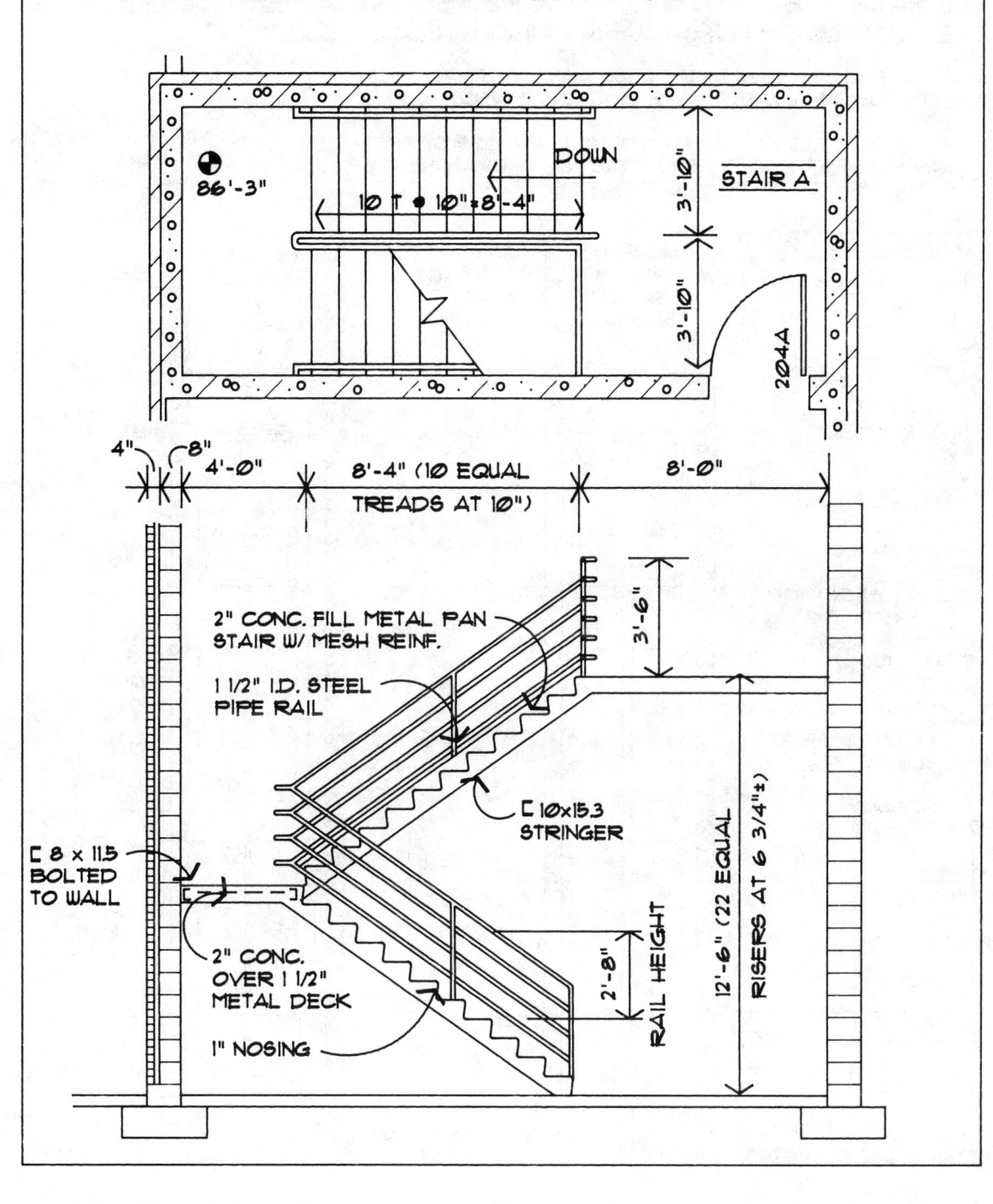

STAIRS AND ELEVATORS 18-9

ELEVATORS

THE TWO MAJOR CATEGORIES OF ELEVATORS ARE HYDRAULIC AND TRACTION (ALSO CALLED ELECTRIC). HYDRAULIC ELEVATORS USE A PISTON, SIMILAR TO A SERVICE STATION HOIST, TO RAISE AND LOWER THE CAB. TRACTION ELEVATORS USE AN ELECTRIC MOTOR TO MOVE THE CAB (THE CAB IS BALANCED WITH COUNTERWEIGHTS IN THE SHAFT). ELECTRIC ELEVATORS REQUIRE A PENTHOUSE ABOVE THE TOP FLOOR FOR HOUSING MECHANICAL EQUIPMENT.

1. A HYDRAULIC ELEVATOR IS LESS COSTLY TO INSTALL.
2. HYDRAULIC ELEVATORS ARE LIMITED TO ABOUT 60 FEET VERTICALLY.
3. HYDRAULIC ELEVATORS HAVE SPEED RANGES OF FROM 75 TO 200 FEET PER MINUTE (FPM); TRACTION ELEVATORS HAVE RATED SPEEDS OF 500 TO 1,200 FPM.

CAPACITY	A	B
2,000 LBS	6'-0"	5'-0"
2,500 LBS	7'-0"	5'-0"
3,000 LBS	7'-0"	5'-6"
3,500 LBS	7'-0"	6'-2"

ELEVATOR PLAN

2-HOUR RATED FIRE WALL (TYPICALLY 8" CONC. BLOCK OR 2 LAYERS OF 5/8" GYP. BOARD ON METAL STUDS)

LOCATE EQUIP. RM. A MAX. OF 70' FROM THE ELEVATOR

MECH. EQUIP. RM. (MIN. 7'-6"x5')

ELEVATOR PIT (MIN. 4'-0" BELOW THE BOTTOM FLOOR)

HYDRAULIC ELEVATOR

PISTON DEPTH EQUALS THE ELEVATOR TRAVEL

HOISTWAY EQUIPMENT ROOM (SAME SIZE AS THE SHAFT AND 7'-6" HIGH)

HOISTING BEAM

MACHINE BEAM

GUIDERAIL

COUNTER-WEIGHT

SHOCK-ABSORBER

TRACTION ELEVATOR

STAIRS AND ELEVATORS | 18-10

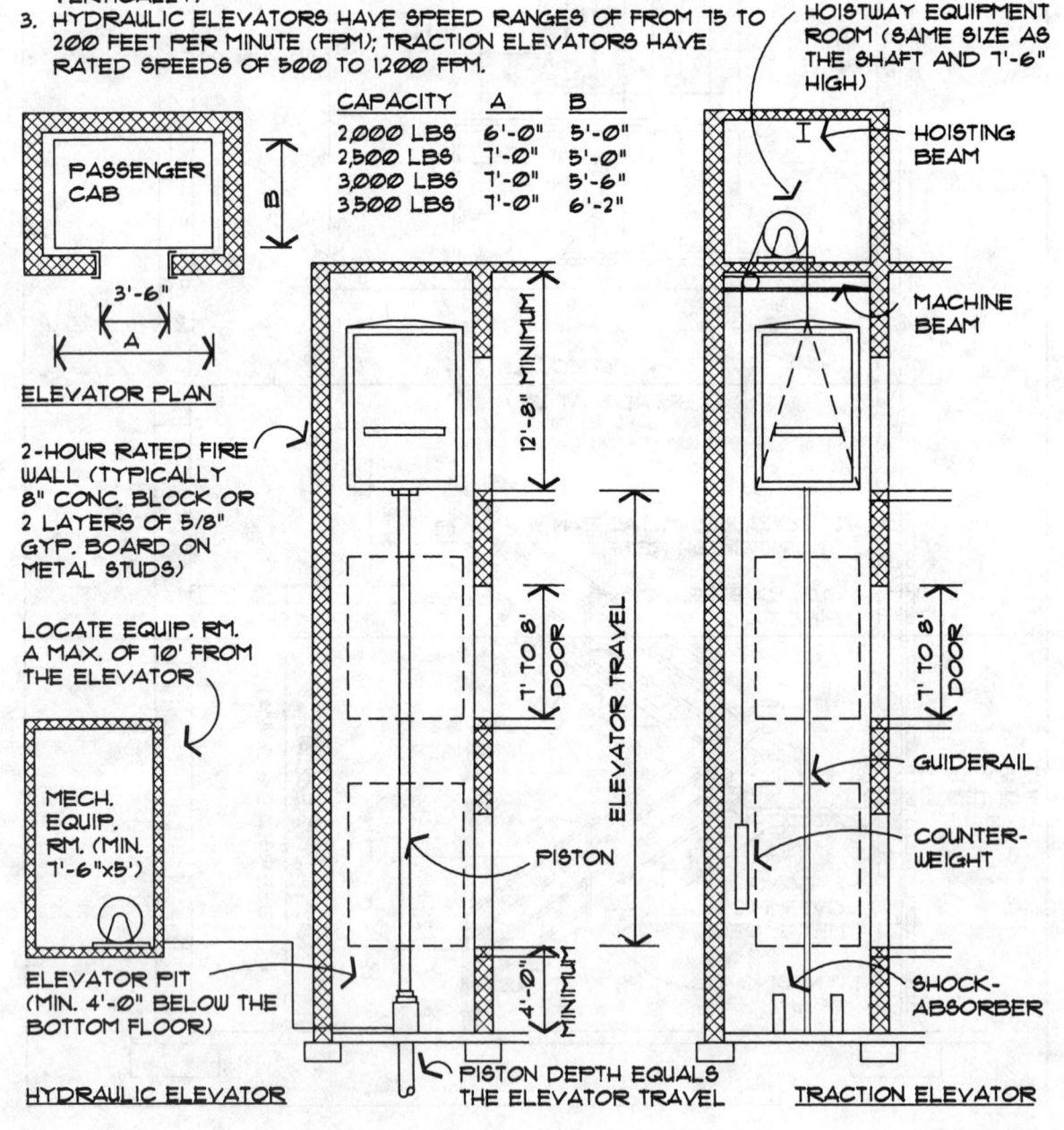

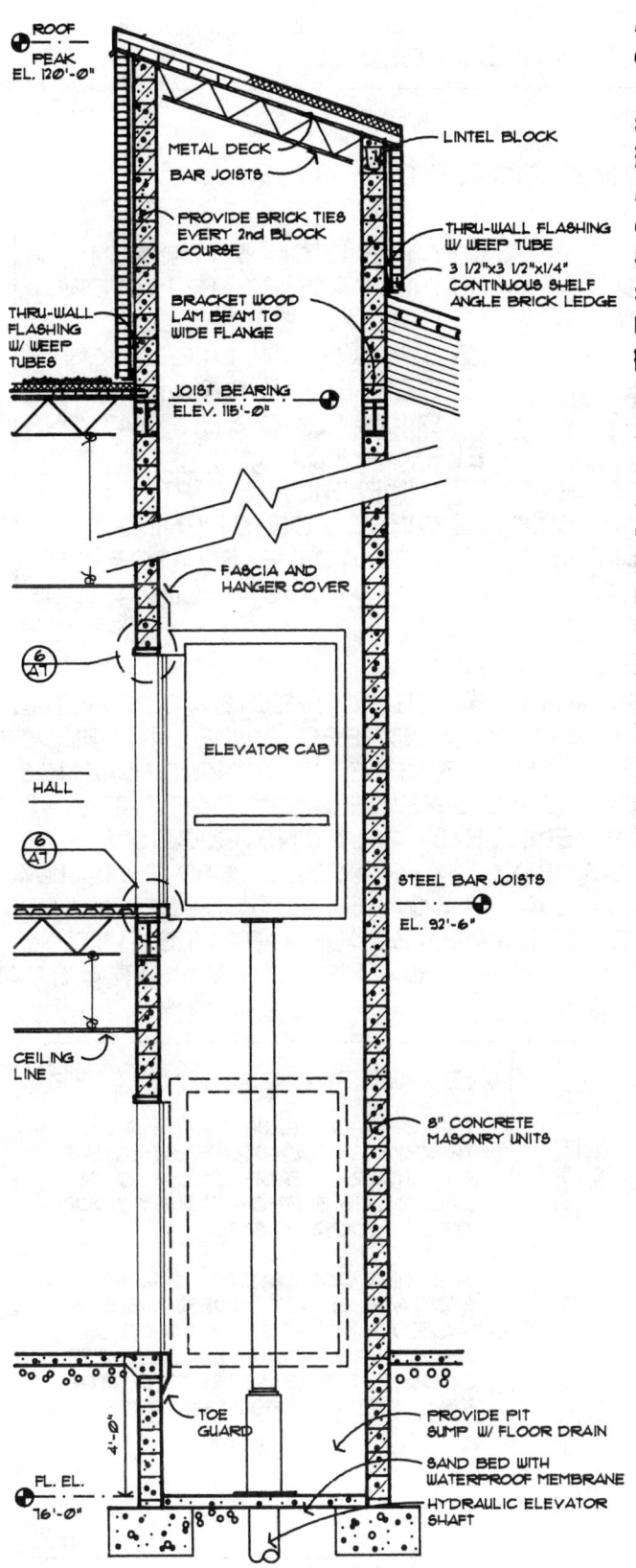

A SECTION AND PLAN VIEW OF A HYDRAULIC ELEVATOR IN THE STUDENT LIBRARY ARE SHOWN HERE. THE MECHANICAL EQUIPMENT ROOM IS LOCATED APPROXIMATELY 25 FEET AWAY ON THE FIRST FLOOR. A HYDRAULIC ELEVATOR WAS SELECTED OVER AN ELECTRIC UNIT BECAUSE OF THE ONE-FLOOR TRAVEL AND THE LOWER COST. THE SHAFT ABOVE THE SECOND FLOOR IS A DESIGN ELEMENT; IT ISN'T ACTUALLY NECESSARY TO THE OPERATION OF A HYDRAULIC ELEVATOR. IF AN ELECTRIC UNIT WERE SELECTED, A PENTHOUSE FLOOR WOULD BE LOCATED APPROXIMATELY 15 FEET ABOVE THE HEIGHT OF THE SECOND FLOOR. THE TWO TYPES OF ELEVATORS ARE DRAWN IN A SIMILAR WAY IN PLAN AND SECTION VIEWS.

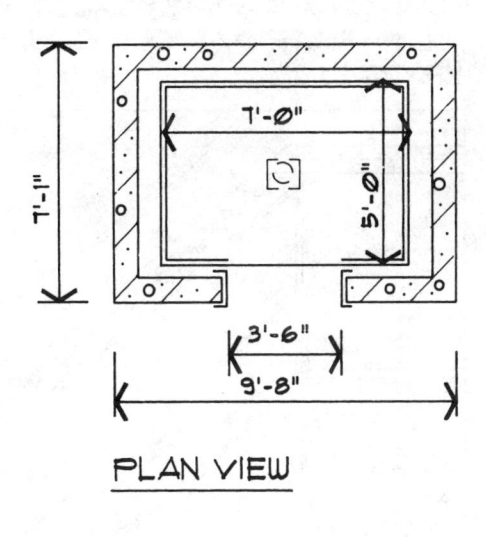

PLAN VIEW

SECTION VIEW

STAIRS AND ELEVATORS

18-11

A GENERAL CHECKLIST FOR ITEMS THAT SHOULD BE INCLUDED ON STAIR AND ELEVATOR DETAILS IS SHOWN BELOW.

STAIR AND ELEVATOR CHECKLIST

STAIRS
- [ ] CHECK STAIR CODE FOR:
- [ ] MAX. RISER HEIGHT
- [ ] MIN. TREAD DEPTH
- [ ] STAIR WIDTH
- [ ] EXIT DOOR SWINGS
- [ ] HANDRAIL HEIGHT
- [ ] BALUSTER SPACING
- [ ] LANDING REQUIREMENTS
- [ ] TREAD/RISER DIMENSIONS
- [ ] VERTICAL DIMENSIONS
- [ ] DIMENSION STAIR RUN
- [ ] INDICATE STAIR MATERIAL
- [ ] CHECK HEADROOM
- [ ] SHOW STAIR DIRECTION
- [ ] DETAIL HANDRAILS
- [ ] SHOW FLOOR ELEVATIONS

ELEVATORS
- [ ] DIMENSION SHAFT
- [ ] DIM. DOOR OPENINGS
- [ ] PROVIDE ELEVATOR PIT
- [ ] SHOW FLOOR ELEVATIONS

STAIR AND ELEVATOR DETAILS

STAIR AND ELEVATOR CONDITIONS MUST BE SOLVED EARLY IN THE DESIGN PROCESS. IT IS IMPORTANT TO ADDRESS CODE AND FLOOR PLAN CIRCULATION CONDITIONS LONG BEFORE WORKING DRAWINGS ARE STARTED. IN THIS SECTION WE WILL REVIEW SOME OF THE DETAILS THAT ARE USED TO ASSEMBLE STAIR CONSTRUCTION DRAWINGS. THREE TYPES OF DRAWINGS ARE NEEDED TO DETAIL A STAIR: (1) A PLAN VIEW (TYPICALLY 1/4" SCALE), (2) A SECTION VIEW (DRAWN AT A 1/4" SCALE), AND (3) LARGE-SCALE DETAILS THAT ILLUSTRATE VARIOUS CONDITIONS (THESE CAN BE DRAWN AT A SCALE UP TO 1 1/2").

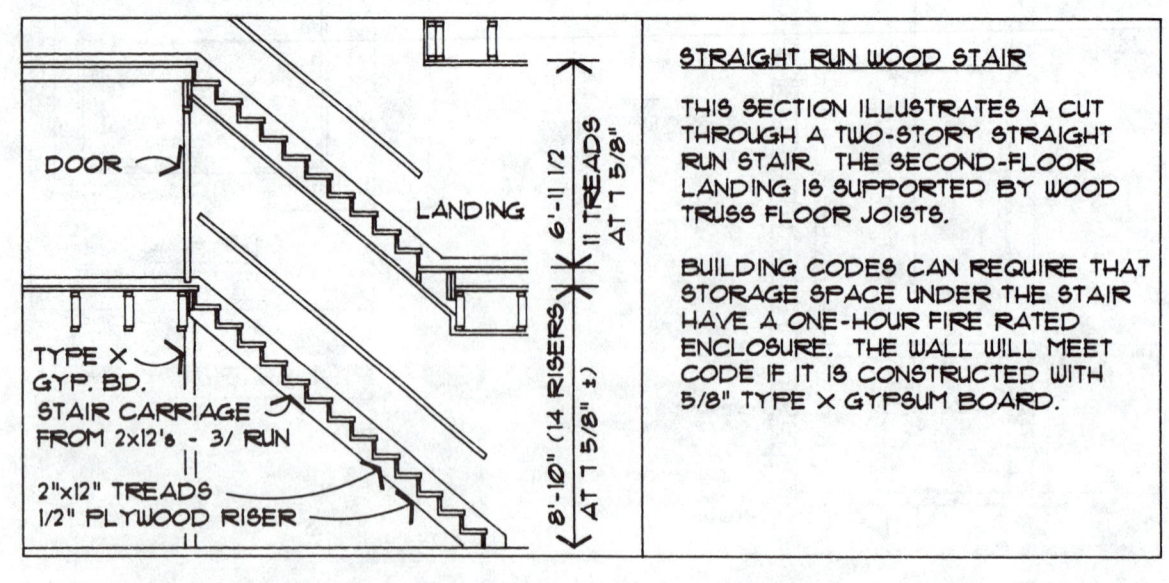

STRAIGHT RUN WOOD STAIR

THIS SECTION ILLUSTRATES A CUT THROUGH A TWO-STORY STRAIGHT RUN STAIR. THE SECOND-FLOOR LANDING IS SUPPORTED BY WOOD TRUSS FLOOR JOISTS.

BUILDING CODES CAN REQUIRE THAT STORAGE SPACE UNDER THE STAIR HAVE A ONE-HOUR FIRE RATED ENCLOSURE. THE WALL WILL MEET CODE IF IT IS CONSTRUCTED WITH 5/8" TYPE X GYPSUM BOARD.

Section labels: DOOR; LANDING; TYPE X GYP. BD.; STAIR CARRIAGE FROM 2x12's - 3/ RUN; 2"x12" TREADS; 1/2" PLYWOOD RISER; 6'-11 1/2" (11 TREADS AT 7 5/8"); 8'-10" (14 RISERS AT 7 5/8" ±)

STAIRS AND ELEVATORS 18-12

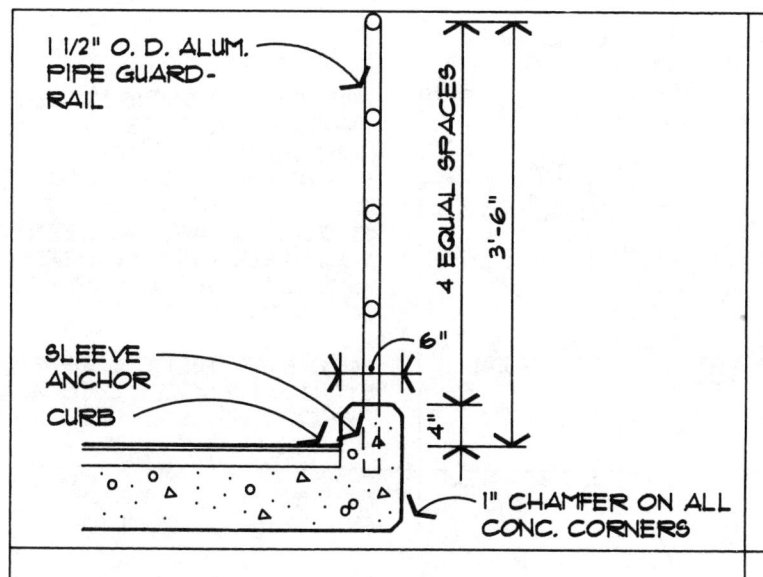

BALCONY RAIL

THIS DETAIL SHOWS A SECTION CUT THROUGH A BALCONY RAIL SET IN A CONCRETE FLOOR SLAB. A PIPE SLEEVE WHICH RECEIVES THE 1 1/2" ALUMINUM GUARDRAIL, IS PLACED IN THE SLAB.

THE RAIL MEETS THE BUILDING CODE REQUIREMENTS OF A 3'-6" HEIGHT AND A 4" CURB.

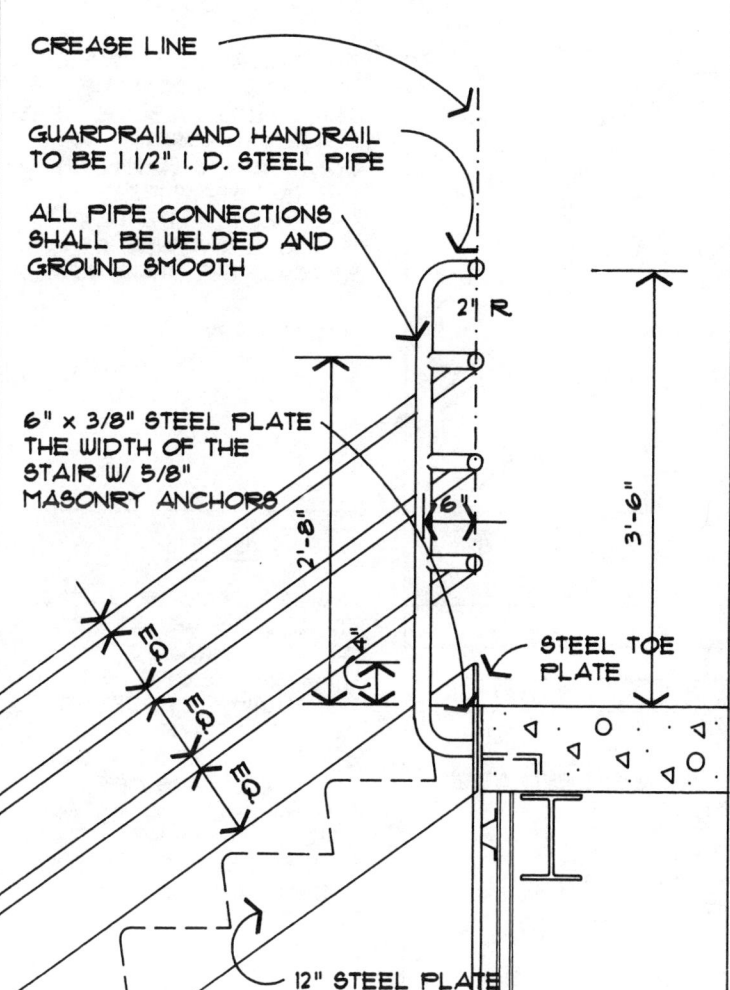

Labels on drawing:
- 1 1/2" O.D. ALUM. PIPE GUARDRAIL
- 4 EQUAL SPACES
- 3'-6"
- 6"
- 4"
- SLEEVE ANCHOR CURB
- 1" CHAMFER ON ALL CONC. CORNERS

STAIR HANDRAIL

THIS DETAIL IS CUT THROUGH THE TOP HANDRAIL OF A STAIR. THE CURVED GUARDRAIL IS WELDED TO A STEEL PLATE THAT IS ANCHORED TO THE CONCRETE SLAB. NOTE THAT THE GUARDRAIL IS 3'-6" ABOVE THE FLOOR AND THE HANDRAIL IS 2'-8" FROM THE FRONT EDGE OF THE STAIR TREAD.

THE LINES INDICATING THE TREADS AND RISERS ARE DASHED BECAUSE THE SECTION CUT IS MADE IN FRONT OF THE STAIR RUN.

Labels on drawing:
- CREASE LINE
- GUARDRAIL AND HANDRAIL TO BE 1 1/2" I.D. STEEL PIPE
- ALL PIPE CONNECTIONS SHALL BE WELDED AND GROUND SMOOTH
- 2" R
- 6" x 3/8" STEEL PLATE THE WIDTH OF THE STAIR W/ 5/8" MASONRY ANCHORS
- 2'-8"
- 6"
- 4"
- 3'-6"
- EQ, EQ, EQ
- STEEL TOE PLATE
- 12" STEEL PLATE STRINGER

STAIRS AND ELEVATORS   18-13

1 1/2" I.D. STEEL PIPE RAIL

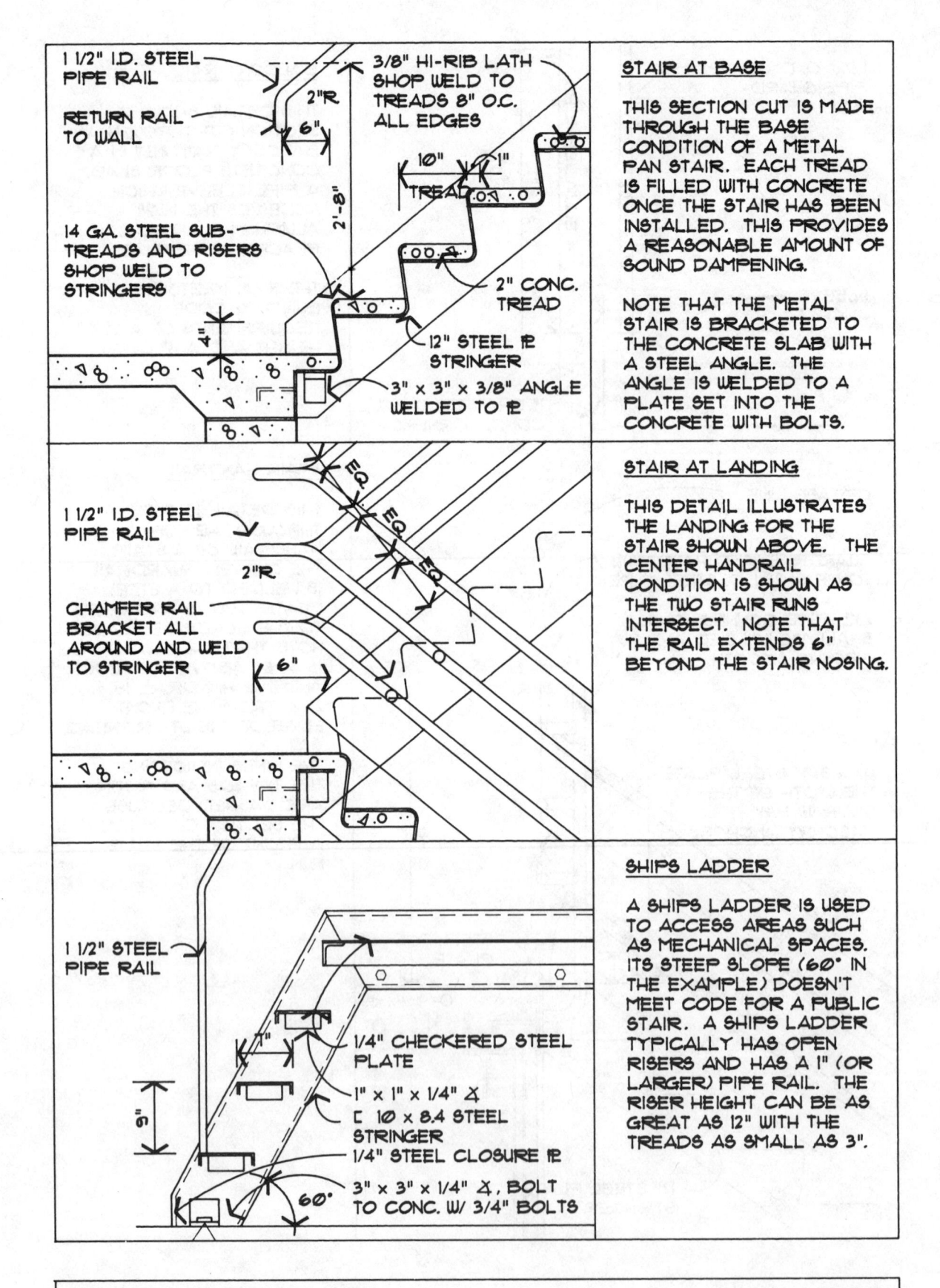

RETURN RAIL TO WALL

3/8" HI-RIB LATH SHOP WELD TO TREADS 8" O.C. ALL EDGES

2"R
6"
2'-8"
10" 1"
TREAD
2" CONC. TREAD

14 GA. STEEL SUB-TREADS AND RISERS SHOP WELD TO STRINGERS

4"

12" STEEL ℔ STRINGER

3" x 3" x 3/8" ANGLE WELDED TO ℔

STAIR AT BASE

THIS SECTION CUT IS MADE THROUGH THE BASE CONDITION OF A METAL PAN STAIR. EACH TREAD IS FILLED WITH CONCRETE ONCE THE STAIR HAS BEEN INSTALLED. THIS PROVIDES A REASONABLE AMOUNT OF SOUND DAMPENING.

NOTE THAT THE METAL STAIR IS BRACKETED TO THE CONCRETE SLAB WITH A STEEL ANGLE. THE ANGLE IS WELDED TO A PLATE SET INTO THE CONCRETE WITH BOLTS.

1 1/2" I.D. STEEL PIPE RAIL

2"R

EQ. EQ. EQ.

CHAMFER RAIL BRACKET ALL AROUND AND WELD TO STRINGER

6"

STAIR AT LANDING

THIS DETAIL ILLUSTRATES THE LANDING FOR THE STAIR SHOWN ABOVE. THE CENTER HANDRAIL CONDITION IS SHOWN AS THE TWO STAIR RUNS INTERSECT. NOTE THAT THE RAIL EXTENDS 6" BEYOND THE STAIR NOSING.

1 1/2" STEEL PIPE RAIL

7"
9"

1/4" CHECKERED STEEL PLATE

1" x 1" x 1/4" ⌐

C 10 x 8.4 STEEL STRINGER

1/4" STEEL CLOSURE ℔

3" x 3" x 1/4" ⌐, BOLT TO CONC. W/ 3/4" BOLTS

60°

SHIPS LADDER

A SHIPS LADDER IS USED TO ACCESS AREAS SUCH AS MECHANICAL SPACES. ITS STEEP SLOPE (60° IN THE EXAMPLE) DOESN'T MEET CODE FOR A PUBLIC STAIR. A SHIPS LADDER TYPICALLY HAS OPEN RISERS AND HAS A 1" (OR LARGER) PIPE RAIL. THE RISER HEIGHT CAN BE AS GREAT AS 12" WITH THE TREADS AS SMALL AS 3".

STAIRS AND ELEVATORS   18-14

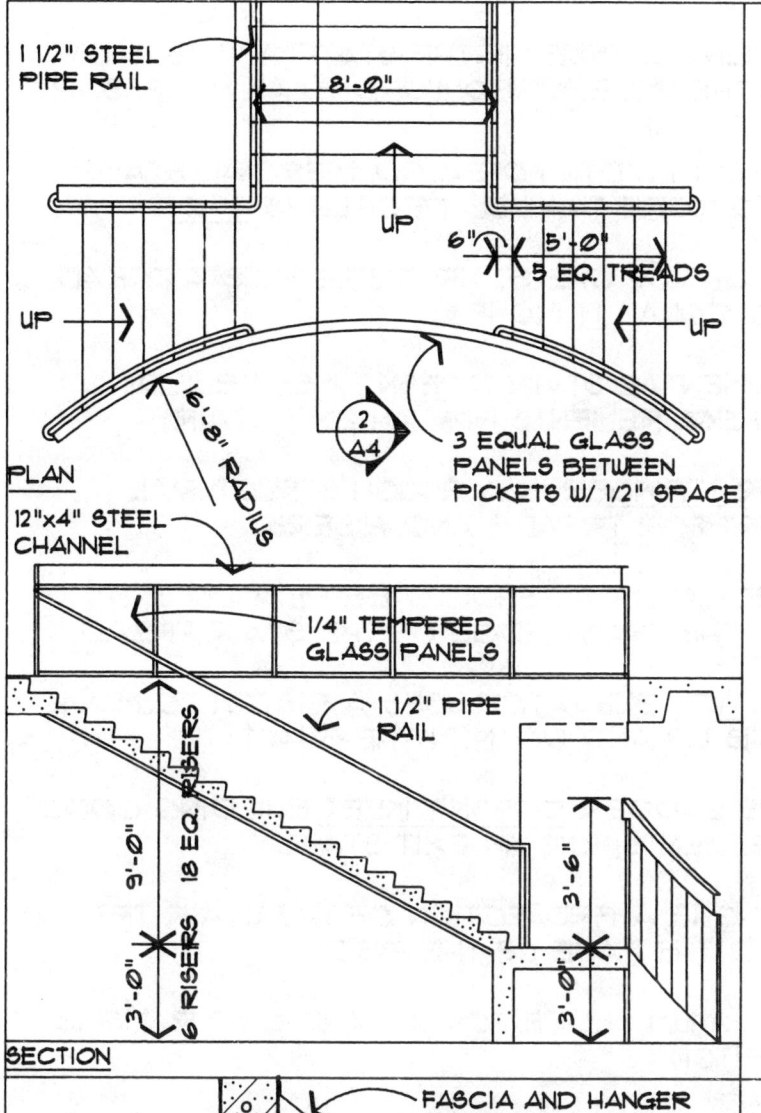

MONUMENTAL STAIR

THIS ILLUSTRATION SHOWS A PLAN AND SECTION VIEW OF A MONUMENTAL STAIR. THIS STAIR IS TYPICALLY INTENDED TO BE THE "GRAND" STAIR IN A BUILDING. SINCE IT DOESN'T MEET THE BUILDING CODE REQUIREMENTS FOR AN ENCLOSED EXIT STAIR, OTHER STAIRS (THAT MEET CODE) MUST BE PROVIDED.

THIS STAIR HAS SEVERAL DETAILS THAT MAKE IT UNIQUE. THE LAST FIVE TREADS ARE FLARED TO GIVE THE STAIR MORE "IMPORTANCE." THE HANDRAIL IS A 4" x 12" STEEL CHANNEL WITH TEMPERED GLASS BELOW. NOTE THAT THE RISER HEIGHT IS 6", WHILE THE TREADS ARE 12".

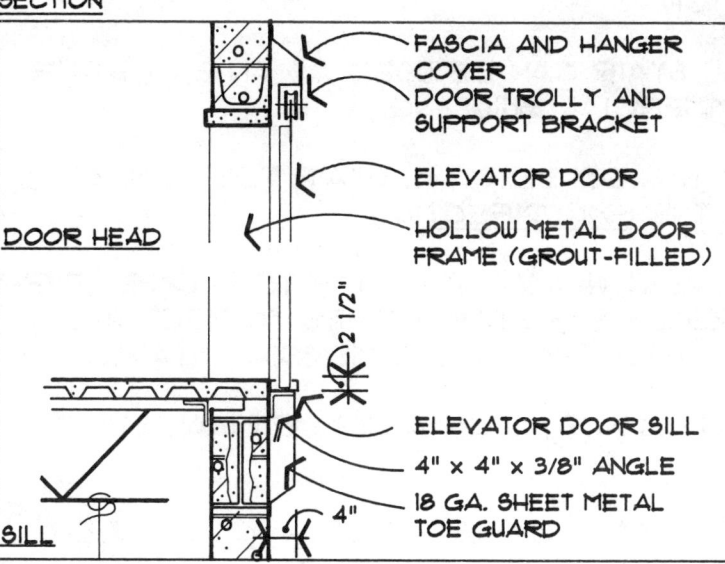

ELEVATOR FRAME DETAILS

THESE DETAILS SHOW THE HEAD AND SILL CONDITIONS FOR THE HYDRAULIC ELEVATOR ON PAGE 18-11. ARCHITECTURAL PLANS ARE TYPICALLY LIMITED TO THE PLAN VIEW OF THE SHAFT AND THE DOOR DETAILS. ADDITIONAL CONDITIONS ARE DEFINED IN THE ARCHITECT'S SPECIFICATIONS AND DETAILED DRAWINGS SUBMITTED BY THE MANUFACTURER IN THE FORM OF SHOP DRAWINGS.

STAIRS AND ELEVATORS | 18-15

REPLAY

MARK (T) IF THE STATEMENT IS TRUE. IF THE STATEMENT IS FALSE, MARK (F) AND CHANGE THE UNDERLINED WORD(S) AS NECESSARY TO MAKE THE STATEMENT TRUE.

_____ ( ) 1. THE MINIMUM WIDTH FOR A COMMERCIAL STAIR SERVING MORE THAN 50 PEOPLE IS <u>4'-0"</u>.

_____ ( ) 2. THE HEIGHT OF ONE STAIR RISER PLUS A TREAD SHOULD EQUAL <u>17</u> INCHES.

_____ ( ) 3. A MONUMENTAL STAIR <u>DOESN'T MEET</u> BUILDING CODE REQUIREMENTS FOR AN EXIT STAIR.

_____ ( ) 4. A STAIR <u>STRINGER</u> IS A ROUGH STRUCTURAL SUPPORT FOR TREADS AND RISERS.

_____ ( ) 5. A STAIR HANDRAIL SHOULD BE PLACED <u>2'-8"</u> ABOVE THE FRONT EDGE OF THE STAIR TREAD.

_____ ( ) 6. A <u>TRACTION</u> ELEVATOR USES A PISTON TO MOVE THE CAB UP AND DOWN IN THE SHAFT.

_____ ( ) 7. A SHIPS LADDER <u>DOESN'T MEET</u> BUILDING CODE REQUIREMENTS FOR AN EXIT STAIR.

_____ ( ) 8. A <u>NOSING</u> IS A PROJECTION OF THE STAIR TREAD BEYOND THE FACE OF THE RISER.

_____ ( ) 9. THE MAXIMUM SLOPE FOR A HANDICAP RAMP IS A <u>1:10</u> PITCH.

_____ ( ) 10. A SPIRAL STAIR <u>CAN</u> BE USED AS AN EXIT STAIR IN A COMMERCIAL BUILDING.

_____ ( ) 11. A DOOR IN A COMMERCIAL STAIR TOWER MUST SWING IN THE <u>EXIT DIRECTION</u>.

_____ ( ) 12. A BUILDING WITH A 10'-4" FLOOR-TO-FLOOR HEIGHT WOULD REQUIRE <u>16</u> STAIR RISERS TO MEET THE MAXIMUM HEIGHT FOR A COMMERCIAL STAIR.

_____ ( ) 13. THE MAXIMUM NOSING ON A COMMERICAL STAIR IS <u>1 1/2"</u>.

_____ ( ) 14. THERE IS A MAXIMUM HEIGHT OF <u>14'-0"</u> BETWEEN STAIR LANDINGS FOR A COMMERCIAL STAIR.

| STAIRS AND ELEVATORS | 18-16 |

SCHEDULES

A SCHEDULE IS AN ORGANIZED SOURCE OF INFORMATION REGARDING THE VARIOUS ELEMENTS FOUND IN A CONSTRUCTION DRAWING PACKAGE. ITS PURPOSE IS TO REDUCE THE NEED FOR NOTES ON FLOOR PLANS AND ELEVATIONS BY CONCENTRATING THE INFORMATION THEY CONVEY AND TRANSFERRING IT TO ANOTHER SPACE. THE MOST FREQUENTLY USED SCHEDULES ON ARCHITECTURAL PLANS INCLUDE THE FOLLOWING:

- ROOM FINISHES
- DOOR REQUIREMENTS
- KITCHEN EQUIPMENT REQUIREMENTS
- WINDOW TYPES
- WALL TYPES

ENGINEERING DRAWINGS ALSO USE SCHEDULES, RANGING FROM THOSE FOR BEAM AND COLUMN TYPES TO THOSE FOR LIGHTING FIXTURES.

OFFICE STANDARDS VARY GREATLY WHEN IT COMES TO SCHEDULES. SOME FIRMS PRINT SCHEDULES IN THE SPECIFICATION, WHILE OTHERS INCLUDE THEM ON THE WORKING DRAWING SHEET. THIS UNIT WILL REVIEW SEVERAL DIFFERENT SCHEDULE FORMATS.

ROOM FINISH SCHEDULE								
ROOM NAME	ROOM NUMBER	FLOOR		BASE	WALL		CEILING	REMARKS
		MAT.	FINISH		MAT.	FINISH	MAT.	

A ROOM FINISH SCHEDULE IS FOUND IN MOST CONSTRUCTION DRAWING SETS. IT PROVIDES THE CONTRACTOR WITH FLOOR, WALL, AND CEILING INFORMATION ON EVERY ROOM IN THE PROJECT. THE FIRST STEP IN ORGANIZING THE SCHEDULE IS NUMBERING THE ROOMS. NUMBERS ARE ASSIGNED ON THE FLOOR PLAN FROM LEFT TO RIGHT, STARTING WITH THE UPPER LEFT ROOM (SIMILAR TO THE WAY YOU WOULD READ A BOOK). FIRST-FLOOR ROOMS ARE GIVEN NUMBERS IN THE 100'S, SECOND-FLOOR ROOM NUMBERS IN THE 200'S, ETC.

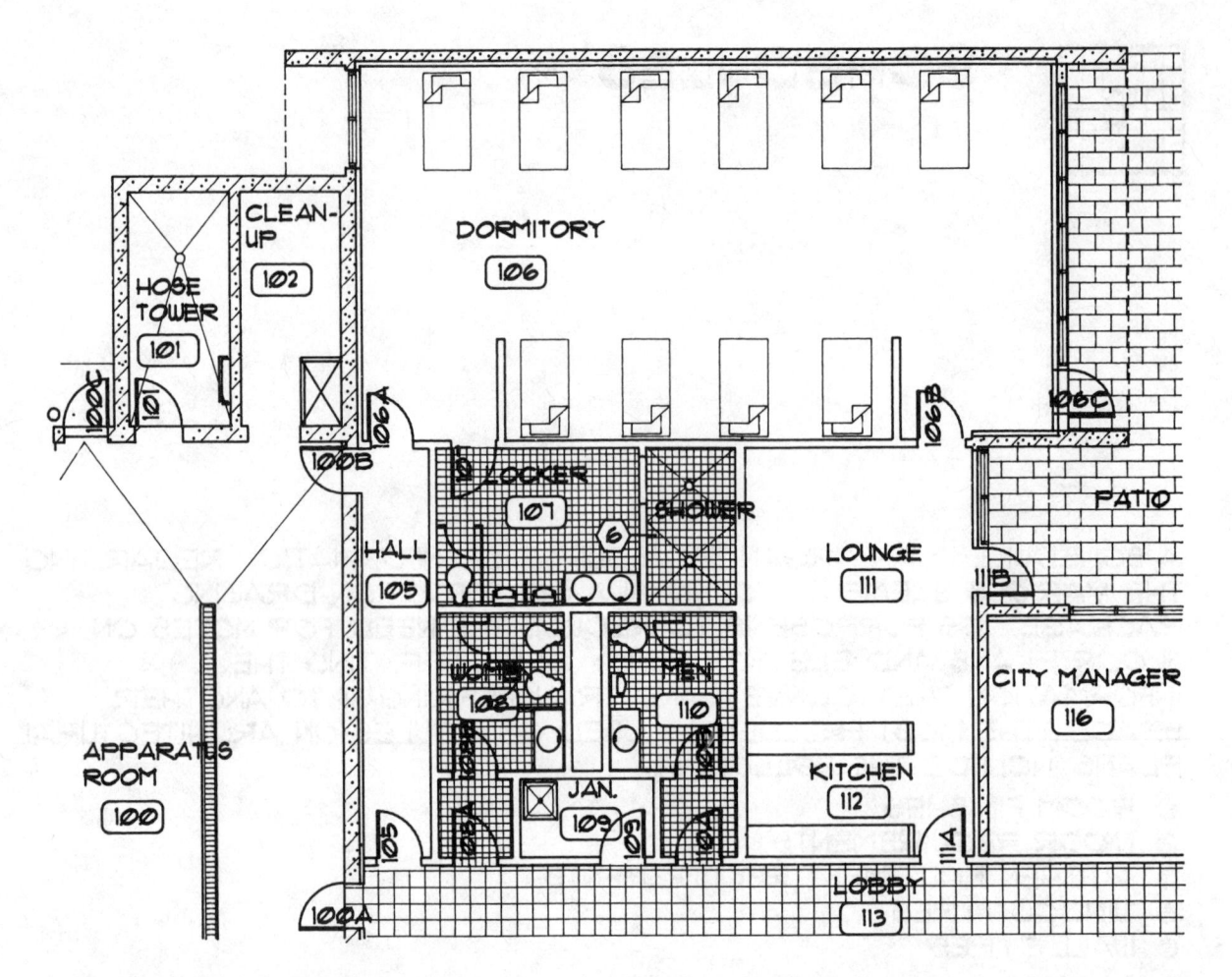

ROOM FINISH SCHEDULES

WE WILL USE THE PORTION OF THE FIRE STATION PLAN SHOWN ABOVE TO DEVELOP ROOM, DOOR, AND WALL SCHEDULES. OUR DISCUSSION WILL BEGIN WITH THE ASSEMBLY OF A ROOM FINISH SCHEDULE. IN THIS TYPE OF SCHEDULE, THE CONTRACTOR IS GIVEN INFORMATION CONCERNING THE FLOOR, BASE (THE NARROW STRIP ALONG THE WALL WHERE IT INTERSECTS WITH THE FLOOR), WALL, AND CEILING. THE SCHEDULE BELOW DETAILS THE ROOMS SHOWN ON THE PLAN.

ROOM FINISH SCHEDULE								
ROOM NAME	ROOM NUMBER	FLOOR		BASE	WALL		CEILING	REMARKS
		MAT.	FINISH		MAT.	FINISH		
APPARATUS	100	CONC.	EXP.	VINYL	BLOCK	PAINT	EXP.	PAINT EXP. JOISTS
HOSE TOWER	101	CONC.	EXP.	NONE	BLOCK	PAINT	EXP.	
CLEAN-UP	102	CONC.	EXP.	NONE	BLOCK	PAINT	EXP.	
HALL	105	CONC.	CARPET	VINYL	GYP. BD.	VINYL	AC TILE	
DORMITORY	106	CONC.	CARPET	VINYL	GYP. BD.	PAINT	AC TILE	
LOCKER	107	CONC.	C. TILE	C. TILE	W.P. GYP.	C. TILE	W.P. GYP.	PAINT CEILING

NOTE THAT IT IS A STANDARD PRACTICE TO IDENTIFY EACH ROOM WITH A ROOM NAME AND ROOM NUMBER.

SCHEDULES   19-2

THE ROOM FINISH SCHEDULE SHOWN HERE ILLUSTRATES A SLIGHTLY DIFFERENT FORMAT. "BULLETS" ARE USED TO IDENTIFY MATERIALS, THEREBY REDUCING THE AMOUNT OF HAND PRINTING REQUIRED TO COMPLETE THE SCHEDULE. WITH THIS FORMAT IT IS IMPORTANT TO MAKE SURE THAT BULLETS ARE PLACED IN THE CORRECT BOXES.

ROOM FINISH SCHEDULE		FLOOR					BASE			WALL			FINISH			CEILING			REMARKS
ROOM NAME	ROOM NUMBER	MAT.		FINISH			MAT.			MAT.			FINISH						
		CONC.	EXPOSED	CARPET	C. TILE	VINYL	VINYL	EXPOSED	C. TILE	BLOCK	GYP. BD.	W.P. GYP.	PAINT	VINYL	C. TILE	EXPOSED	AC. TILE	W.P. GYP.	
APPARATUS	100	●		●			●			●			●			●			PAINT EXP. JOISTS
HOSE TOWER	101	●		●			●			●			●			●			
CLEAN-UP	102	●					●			●			●			●			
HALL	105	●			●					●				●			●		
DORMITORY	106	●			●		●				●		●				●		
LOCKER	107					●			●			●			●			●	PAINT GYP. CEILING

THE NEXT SCHEDULE INDICATES THE MATERIAL AND FINISH FOR EACH COMPASS POINT IN A ROOM. FOR EXAMPLE, THE SOUTH WALL OF THE DORMITORY IS MADE OF PAINTED GYPSUM BOARD. BECAUSE OF THE INCREASED AMOUNT OF INFORMATION CONTAINED ON THIS SCHEDULE, A KEY FOR MATERIALS AND FINISHES IS NEEDED.

ROOM FINISH SCHEDULE																	
ROOM NAME	ROOM NUMBER	FLOOR		BASE		N. WALL		E. WALL		S. WALL		W. WALL		CEILING		REMARKS
		MAT	FIN	MAT	FIN	MAT	FIN	MAT	FIN	MAT	FIN	MAT	FIN	MAT	FIN	
APPARATUS	100	A	1	G	1	F	2	F	2	F	2	F	2	G	2	PAINT JOISTS
HOSE TOWER	101	A	1	G	1	F	2	F	2	F	2	F	2	G	2	
CLEAN-UP	102	A	1	G	1	F	2	F	2	F	2	F	2	G	2	
HALL	105	A	6	C	4	F	5	D	5	F	5	F	5	H	4	
DORMITORY	106	A	6	C	4	F	2	F	2	D	2	D	2	H	4	
LOCKER	107	A	3	J	4	J	4	J	4	J	4	J	4	E	4	PAINT CEILING

MATERIAL AND FINISH KEY	
MATERIAL LIST	MATERIAL FINISH
A. CONCRETE	1. EXPOSED
B. VINYL TILE	2. PAINT
C. VINYL BASE	3. VARNISH
D. GYPSUM BOARD	4. FACTORY FINISH
E. WATERPROOF GYPSUM BOARD	5. VINYL WALL COVERING
F. CONCRETE BLOCK	6. CARPET
G. EXPOSED STRUCTURE	
H. LAY-IN AC TILE	
J. CERAMIC TILE	

DOOR SCHEDULES

A DOOR SCHEDULE COORDINATES INFORMATION SUCH AS DOOR SIZE, FRAME SIZE, JAMB DETAILS, AND TYPE OF HARDWARE REQUIRED FOR ALL DOORS SHOWN ON THE PLAN. DOORS ARE ASSIGNED THE SAME NUMBER AS THE ROOM. IF THERE IS MORE THAN ONE DOOR IN A ROOM, LETTERS ARE ALSO USED (FOR EXAMPLE, 102A AND 102B).

SCHEDULES

THE SCHEDULE BELOW DIVIDES DOOR INFORMATION INTO THREE CATEGORIES: (1) DOOR TYPE, (2) FRAME TYPE, AND (3) TABULAR DATA. THE DOOR AND FRAME TYPES ARE DRAWN IN ELEVATION (TYPICALLY AT A 1/4"=1'-0" SCALE). THE TABULAR DATA INCLUDES INFORMATION SUCH AS THE CODE FIRE RATING OF THE DOOR AND THE HARDWARE GROUP. (A HARDWARE GROUP IDENTIFIES ITEMS SUCH AS HINGES, CLOSERS, LOCKS, AND KICK PLATES - SPECIFIC INFORMATION REGARDING THESE ITEMS IS TYPICALLY FOUND IN THE SPECIFICATIONS.)

AS AN EXAMPLE, REFER TO DOOR 100C IN THE SCHEDULE. THE DOOR IS 3'-0" WIDE, 6'-10" HIGH, AND 1 3/4" THICK. IT IS A "TYPE A" DOOR AND IS MADE FROM HOLLOW METAL. THE DOOR HAS A 3'-4" x 7'-0" HOLLOW METAL FRAME (REFER TO THE FRAME TYPE) AND IS IN HARDWARE GROUP 4. THE DOOR ALSO HAS A THRESHOLD (A WEATHERPROOF METAL STRIP AT THE SILL).

DOOR SCHEDULE							
DOOR NUMBER	DOOR SIZE	DOOR TYPE	MATERIAL	LABEL	FRAME	HDWR	REMARKS
100A	3'-0" x 6'-10" x 1 3/4"	D	H.M.	B	1	2	
100B	3'-0" x 6'-10" x 1 3/4"	D	H.M.	B	1	2	
100C	3'-0" x 6'-10" x 1 3/4"	A	H.M.		1	4	THRESHOLD
101	3'-0" x 6'-10" x 1 3/4"	A	H.M.		1	3	
105	3'-0" x 6'-10" x 1 3/4"	D	P. LAM.		1	2	
106A	3'-0" x 6'-10" x 1 3/4"	A	P. LAM.		1	2	
106B	3'-0" x 6'-10" x 1 3/4"	A	P. LAM.		1	2	
106C	3'-0" x 6'-10" x 1 3/4"	C	ALUM.		1	6	
107	3'-0" x 6'-10" x 1 3/4"	A	P. LAM.		1	2	
108A	3'-0" x 6'-10" x 1 3/4"	A	P. LAM.		1	2	

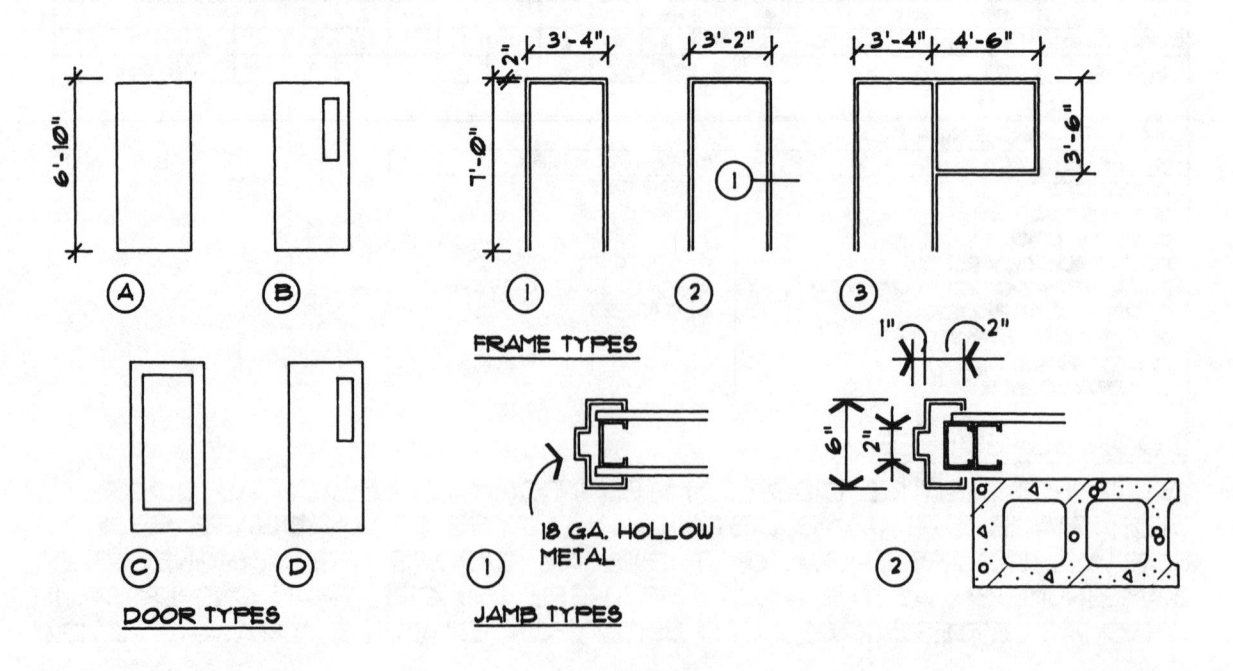

FRAME TYPES

DOOR TYPES

JAMB TYPES

SCHEDULES

19-4

WALL TYPES

A WALL TYPE SCHEDULE INCLUDES INFORMATION ON THE ASSEMBLY OF EVERY WALL IN THE PROJECT. WALL CONDITIONS ARE INDICATED ON THE FLOOR PLAN BY USING A NUMBERED HEXAGON. THIS IS THEN KEYED TO DETAIL BLOW-UPS THAT SHOW THE WALL CONSTRUCTION. THE KEY SHOULD BE USED AT EVERY POINT ON THE PLAN IN WHICH IT IS NECESSARY TO DEFINE THE WALL. IN THE PORTION OF THE FIRE STATION PLAN SHOWN BELOW, TWO WALL TYPE CONDITIONS ARE IDENTIFIED AND KEYED TO WALL DETAILS.

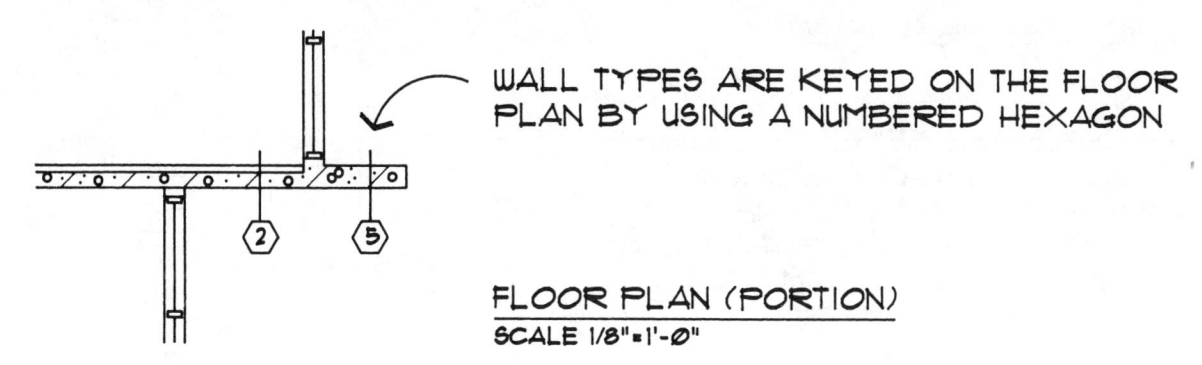

WALL TYPES ARE KEYED ON THE FLOOR PLAN BY USING A NUMBERED HEXAGON

FLOOR PLAN (PORTION)
SCALE 1/8"=1'-0"

THE SIX DETAILS SHOWN BELOW ILLUSTRATE POSSIBLE WALL TYPES. (WALL TYPES ARE TYPICALLY DRAWN AT A SCALE OF 3/4"=1'-0" OR LARGER.)

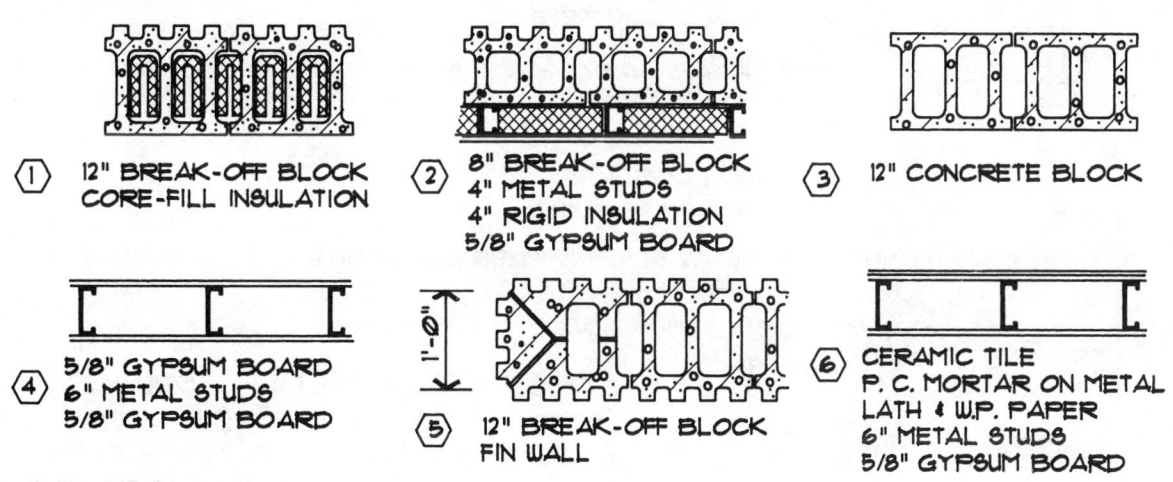

1. 12" BREAK-OFF BLOCK
   CORE-FILL INSULATION

2. 8" BREAK-OFF BLOCK
   4" METAL STUDS
   4" RIGID INSULATION
   5/8" GYPSUM BOARD

3. 12" CONCRETE BLOCK

4. 5/8" GYPSUM BOARD
   6" METAL STUDS
   5/8" GYPSUM BOARD

5. 12" BREAK-OFF BLOCK
   FIN WALL

6. CERAMIC TILE
   P. C. MORTAR ON METAL LATH & W.P. PAPER
   6" METAL STUDS
   5/8" GYPSUM BOARD

WINDOW TYPES

A WINDOW TYPE SCHEDULE INCLUDES INFORMATION ON THE SIZE AND FRAME DETAIL OF WINDOWS DRAWN ON THE EXTERIOR BUILDING ELEVATIONS. THE SMALL DRAWING SCALE USED FOR ELEVATION VIEWS MAKES IT DIFFICULT TO PLACE DIMENSION STRINGS AROUND EACH WINDOW UNIT. A WINDOW SCHEDULE "KEYS" WINDOWS (BY USING A DELTA SYMBOL △) TO LARGER-SCALE ELEVATION VIEWS OF THE WINDOW FRAMES.

SCHEDULES

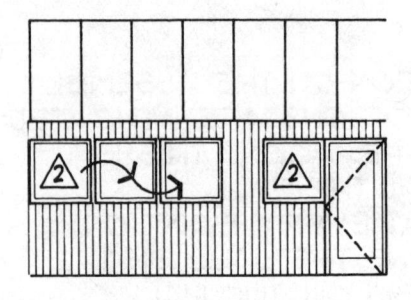

THE FIRST STEP IN ORGANIZING A WINDOW SCHEDULE IS IDENTIFYING EVERY WINDOW UNIT WITH A DELTA SYMBOL. NOTE THAT MORE THAN ONE IDENTICAL WINDOW IS IDENTIFIED BY A CURVED LEADER LINE AND ARROWS FROM ONE KEY NOTE.

PARTIAL BUILDING ELEVATION

WINDOWS ARE KEYED TO LARGER-SCALE ELEVATIONS (TYPICALLY DRAWN AT 1/4"=1'-0"). THE ELEVATIONS PROVIDE A DRAWING LARGE ENOUGH TO DIMENSION THE FRAME HEIGHT AND WIDTH.

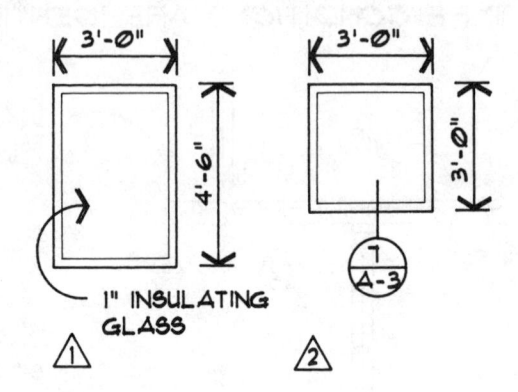

WINDOW TYPES

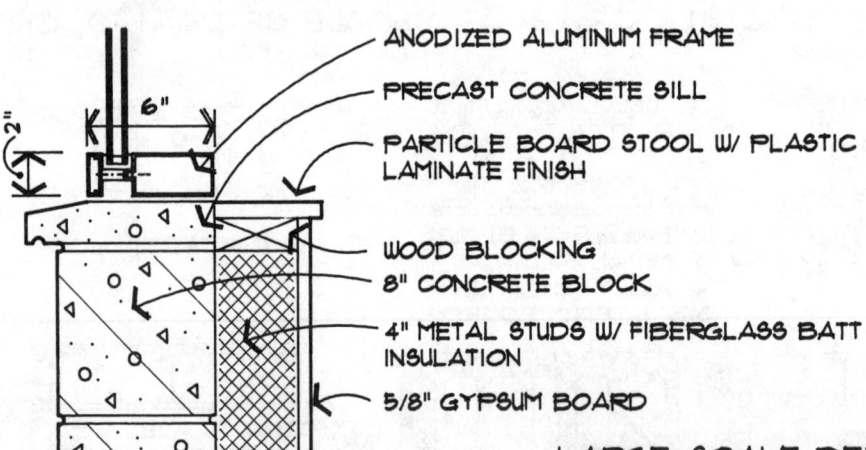

- ANODIZED ALUMINUM FRAME
- PRECAST CONCRETE SILL
- PARTICLE BOARD STOOL W/ PLASTIC LAMINATE FINISH
- WOOD BLOCKING
- 8" CONCRETE BLOCK
- 4" METAL STUDS W/ FIBERGLASS BATT INSULATION
- 5/8" GYPSUM BOARD

7/A-3 WINDOW SILL DETAIL

LARGE-SCALE DETAILS ARE KEYED FROM THE WINDOW TYPES. CARE SHOULD BE TAKEN TO MAKE SURE THAT THE SILL CONDITION DETAIL IS COMMON TO ALL WINDOWS IDENTIFIED AS THE SAME TYPE. WINDOW FRAME TYPE SCHEDULES AREN'T TRUE SCHEDULES AS ROOM AND DOOR SCHEDULES ARE. INSTEAD, THEY ARE A SERIES OF ELEVATIONS THAT ARE KEYED TO THE EXTERIOR VIEWS OF THE BUILDING, ELIMINATING THE NEED FOR DIMENSION STRINGS AND NOTES FOR EACH INDIVIDUAL FRAME. (EVERY WINDOW THAT IS UNIQUE SHOULD BE ASSIGNED A DIFFERENT FRAME NUMBER.)

SCHEDULES

KITCHEN EQUIPMENT SCHEDULE

THE PLAN BELOW SHOWS THE KITCHEN IN THE MOTEL/RESTAURANT PROJECT. NOTE THAT THE 20 PIECES OF KITCHEN EQUIPMENT ARE NUMBERED AND KEYED TO AN EQUIPMENT SCHEDULE.

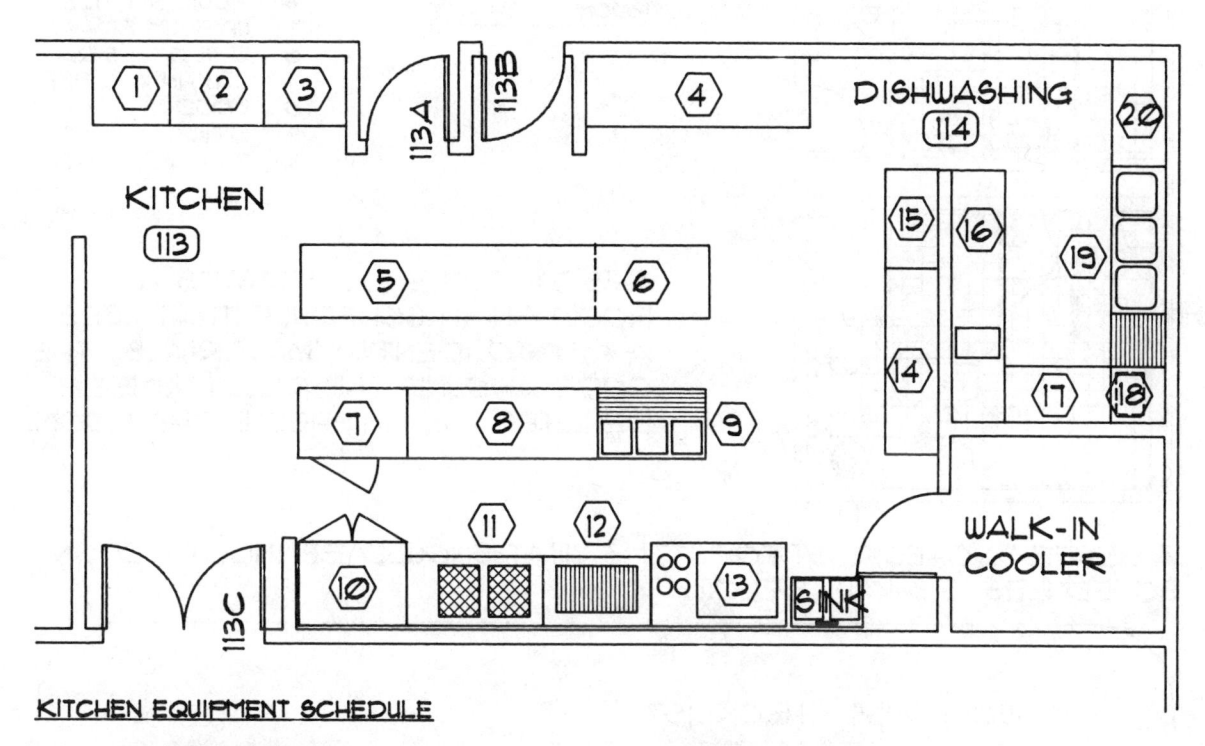

KITCHEN EQUIPMENT SCHEDULE

1. MILK DISPENSER
2. COFFEE MAKER
3. ICE CREAM CABINET
4. CLEAN PLATE STORAGE
5. HOT SERVING TABLE
6. SALAD PREPARATION
7. REFRIGERATOR
8. WORK TABLE
9. 3-SECTION HOT FOOD TABLE
10. FREEZER
11. FRYERS (2)
12. CHAR-GAS GRILLE
13. RANGE
14. WORK TABLE
15. ICE MAKER
16. CLEAN DISH TABLE
17. DISHWASHER
18. BOOSTER
19. 3-COMPARTMENT SINK
20. SOILED DISH TABLE

AS WITH OTHER SCHEDULES, AN EQUIPMENT SCHEDULE REDUCES THE NUMBER OF NOTES NEEDED ON THE ARCHITECTURAL PLANS AND CONCENTRATES THE INFORMATION. THIS TYPE OF SCHEDULE IS QUITE BRIEF; IT IS NECESSARY TO REFER THE CONTRACTOR TO THE SPECIFICATIONS TO OBTAIN ADDITIONAL INFORMATION ABOUT EACH PIECE OF EQUIPMENT. FOR EXAMPLE, THE RANGE IDENTIFIED AS ITEM 13 WOULD REQUIRE THE FOLLOWING DATA:

KEY	NAME	SIZE	MATERIAL	POWER	CAPACITY	REMARKS	MFGR/MODEL
13	RANGE	28"x42"x30"	STAINLESS STEEL	GAS	4-BURNER 36" GRILL 2 OVENS	OVEN SIZE 20"x24"x24"	HOBART #4230

SCHEDULES 19-7

ROOM FINISH KEY

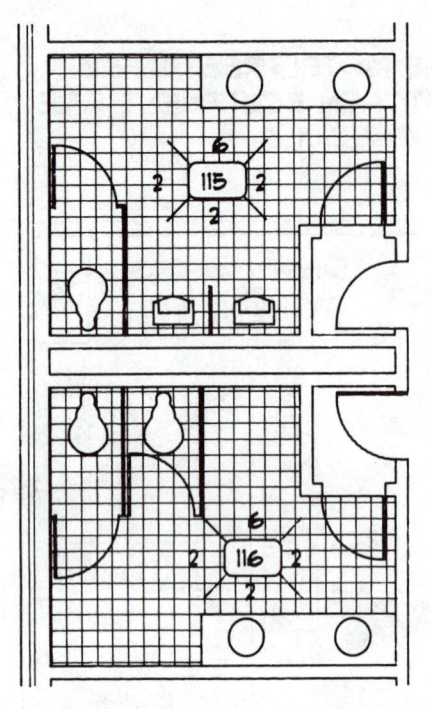

CEILING
WALL [100] BASE
FLOOR

FINISHES

0 NONE
1 VINYL
2 CERAMIC TILE
3 CARPET
4 RESILIENT TILE
5 GYPSUM BOARD
6 W. P. GYP. BD.
7 LAY-IN A C TILE
8 WOOD
9 BRICK
10 PAINTED BLOCK

THIS EXAMPLE ILLUSTRATES A ROOM FINISH SCHEDULE THAT USES A KEY TO IDENTIFY MATERIALS. THE CODE AROUND THE ROOM NUMBER DENOTES THE FINISHES IN THE ROOM.

A GENERAL CHECKLIST FOR ITEMS THAT SHOULD BE INCLUDED ON SCHEDULES IS SHOWN BELOW.

SCHEDULE CHECKLIST

ROOM FINISH
- ☐ ROOM NAME
- ☐ ROOM NUMBER
- ☐ FLOOR MATERIAL/FINISH
- ☐ BASE MATERIAL/FINISH
- ☐ WALL MATERIAL/FINISH
- ☐ CEILING MATERIAL/FINISH
- ☐ NOTES AND REMARKS

WINDOWS
- ☐ KEY TO PLANS
- ☐ DIMENSION ELEVATIONS
- ☐ HEAD/JAMB/SILL DETAIL

DOORS
- ☐ PANEL ELEVATIONS
- ☐ FRAME ELEVATIONS
- ☐ DOOR SIZE
- ☐ DOOR THICKNESS
- ☐ FIRE RATING
- ☐ HARDWARE GROUP
- ☐ KEY DOORS TO PLAN

FIXTURES
- ☐ FIXTURE SYMBOL
- ☐ MODEL
- ☐ SIZE

CONSIDER USING A SCHEDULE ANY TIME INFORMATION ON THE PLANS REQUIRES A GREAT NUMBER OF NOTES. IN ADDITION TO ROOM FINISH AND DOOR SCHEDULES, IT IS NOT UNCOMMON TO USE NAILING SCHEDULES, PLUMBING SCHEDULES, AND KITCHEN APPLIANCE SCHEDULES.

SCHEDULES

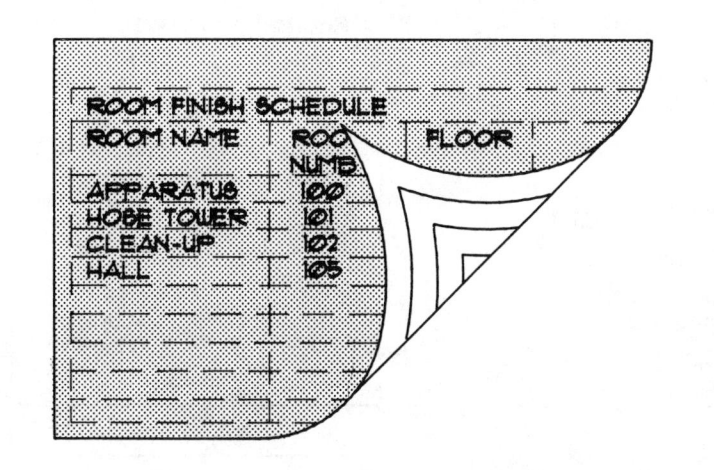

DRAFTING A SCHEDULE

ITEMS ON A SCHEDULE TEND TO CHANGE FREQUENTLY IN THE WORKING DRAWING STAGE. A WAY TO REDUCE THE MESS CAUSED BY ERASING CHANGES IS TO DRAW THE LINES FOR THE SCHEDULE ON THE BACK-SIDE OF THE DRAFTING SHEET. THAT WAY, ERASING PRINTING ON THE FACE OF THE SHEET WON'T AFFECT THE LINES ON THE SCHEDULE.

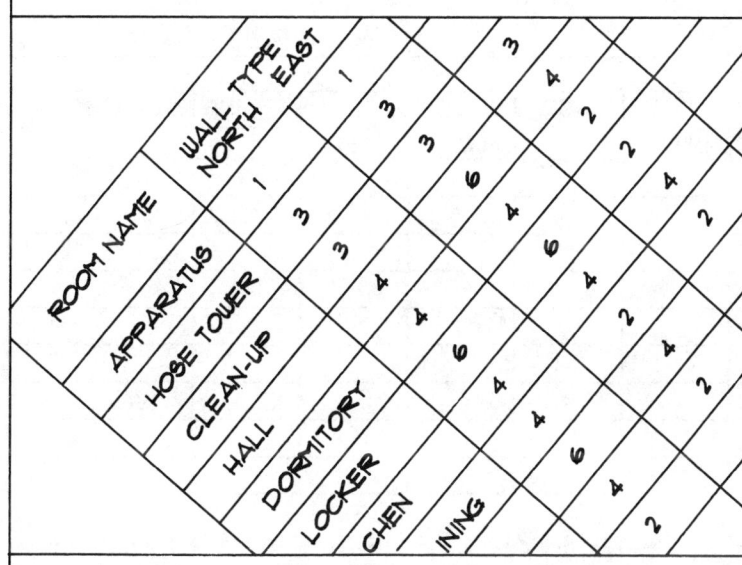

SCHEDULE MOCK-UP

AN IMPORTANT STEP IN THE ASSEMBLY OF ANY SCHEDULE IS THE CAREFUL PLANNING OF THE INFORMATION BEFORE IT IS PLACED ON THE DRAWINGS SHEET. DO THIS BY MAKING NOTES ON A SEPARATE SHEET OF PAPER WHILE YOU ARE IN THE STAGE OF DRAFTING THE FLOOR PLAN. ALLOW 10% TO 15% ADDITIONAL SPACE ON THE SCHEDULE FOR ANY ADDED ITEMS THAT YOU MIGHT WISH TO ADD LATER.

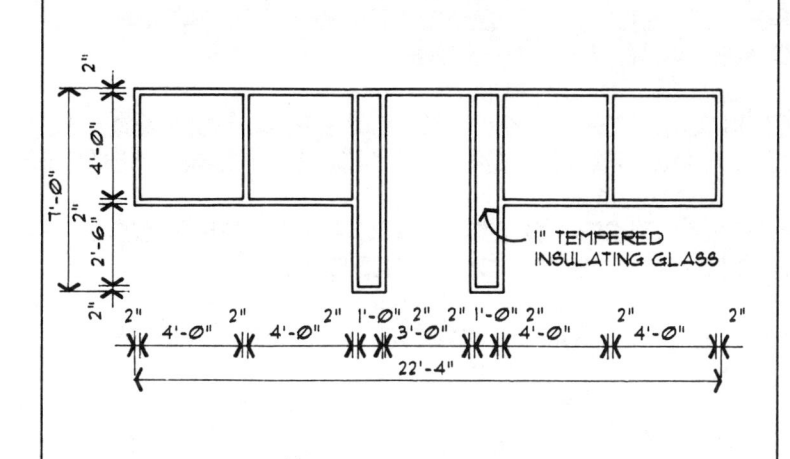

SCHEDULE LOCATION

A SCHEDULE SHOULD BE LOCATED IN THE DRAWING PACKAGE NEAR THE AREA WHERE IT WILL BE USED. FOR EXAMPLE, A WINDOW TYPE SCHEDULE SHOULD BE PLACED NEAR THE SHEET DETAILING THE EXTERIOR ELEVATIONS, WHILE WALL TYPES ARE BEST LOCATED ON THE FLOOR PLAN SHEET.

SCHEDULES 19-9

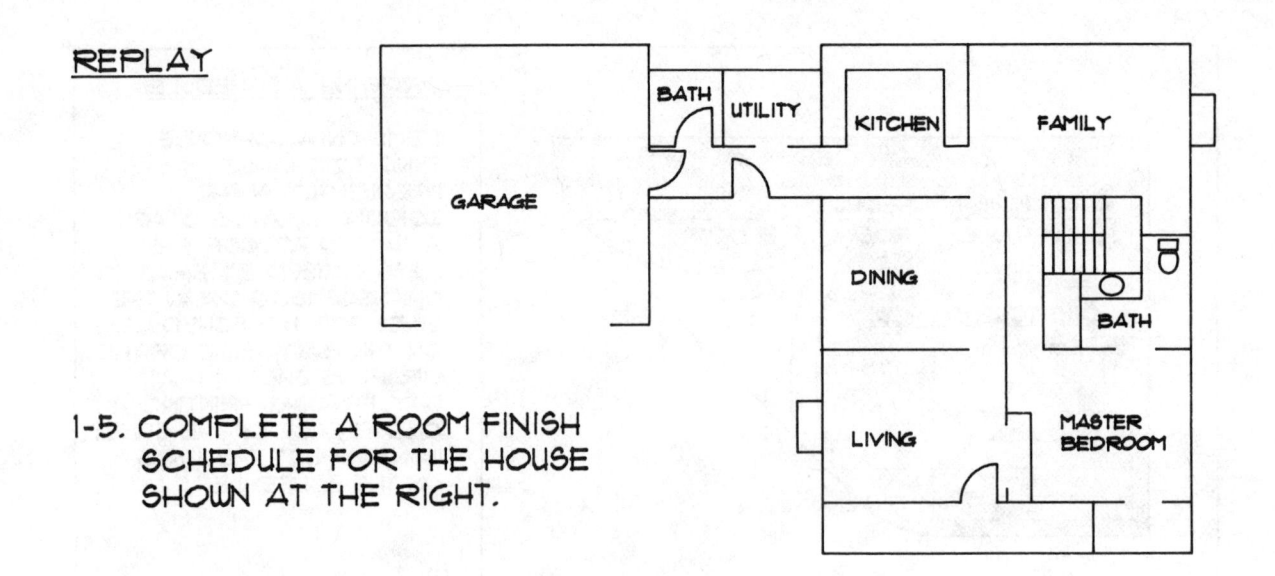

REPLAY

1-5. COMPLETE A ROOM FINISH SCHEDULE FOR THE HOUSE SHOWN AT THE RIGHT.

ROOM FINISH SCHEDULE								
ROOM NAME	ROOM NUMBER	FLOOR		BASE	WALL		CEILING	REMARKS
		MAT.	FINISH		MAT.	FINISH		

MARK (T) IF THE STATEMENT IS TRUE AND (F) IF THE STATEMENT IS FALSE.

_____ 6. WALL TYPES ARE KEYED ON THE BUILDING ELEVATIONS WITH NUMBERED HEXAGONS.

_____ 7. GYPSUM BOARD WOULD BE A GOOD MATERIAL CHOICE FOR A "BASE" IN THE LIVING ROOM OF THE HOUSE PLAN ABOVE.

_____ 8. IT IS A COMMON PRACTICE TO INDICATE THE FIRE CODE RATING OF A DOOR ON THE DOOR SCHEDULE.

_____ 9. A ROOM FINISH SCHEDULE SHOULD IDENTIFY ROOMS BY ROOM NAME AND ROOM NUMBER.

_____ 10. BASED ON THE FIRE STATION PLAN ON PAGE 19-2, THE DORMITORY HAS A CERAMIC TILE FLOOR FINISH.

SCHEDULES

DETAIL ASSEMBLY

DETAIL ASSEMBLY IS THE FINAL STEP OF A PROCESS THAT BEGAN WITH DESIGN AND WAS DEVELOPED THROUGH PLANS, ELEVATIONS, AND SECTIONS. WHILE DETAILS ARE THE LAST THING TO DRAW, THEY CAN ALSO BE THE MOST DIFFICULT TO ASSEMBLE. DETAILS ARE DRAWN AT A SCALE LARGE ENOUGH TO LITERALLY SHOW "NUTS AND BOLTS"- THIS IS THE STEP IN WHICH ALL OF THE PARTS MUST "FIT" AND "WORK."

WHILE THERE ISN'T ANY SECRET TO DETAIL ASSEMBLY, THERE ARE SEVERAL KEY FACTORS THAT ARE ESSENTIAL TO SUCCESS:
1. RESEARCH THE MANUFACTURERS' CATALOGS TO DETERMINE HOW A PRODUCT CAN BE INCORPORATED INTO THE DETAIL.
2. SKETCH THE DETAIL (USING TRACING PAPER) TO DETERMINE THE WAY MATERIALS WORK TOGETHER.
3. DRAW THE PART OF THE DETAIL THAT YOU KNOW (SUCH AS WALLS AND ROOFS), AND SOLVE FOR THE OTHER CONDITIONS.
4. USE BUILDING AND WALL SECTIONS AS A POINT OF BEGINNING TO GENERATE DETAILS.
5. "REDLINE" THE DRAWING FREQUENTLY- THAT IS, RUN A PRINT OF THE DRAWING AND USE A FELT-TIP PEN TO REFINE THE DETAIL.
6. REVIEW OTHER SETS OF DRAWINGS WITH SIMILAR CONDITIONS.

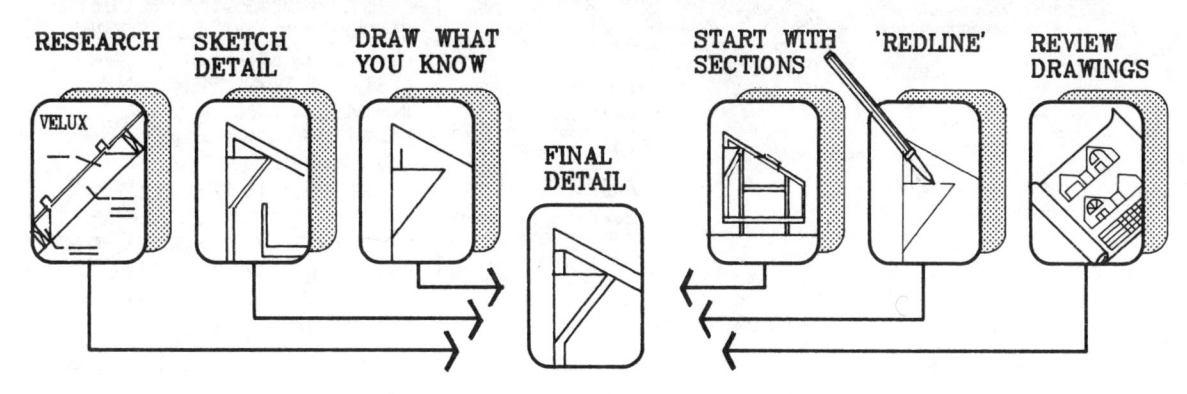

DETAIL ASSEMBLY 20-1

START A DETAIL BY SELECTING POINTS ON THE BUILDING SECTION THAT NEED MORE DEFINITION. (DETAILS ARE TYPICALLY DRAWN AT A 1"=1'-0" OR 1 1/2"=1'-0" SCALE TO SHOW ALL OF THE ELEMENTS IN CONSTRUCTION.) THE CABIN WALL SECTION BELOW ILLUSTRATES FOUR AREAS THAT COULD BE ENLARGED IN A DETAIL. A GOOD QUESTION TO ASK IS: DOES THE CONTRACTOR HAVE ENOUGH INFORMATION TO BUILD THIS PORTION OF THE PROJECT? IF THE ANSWER IS NO, THE SECTION SHOULD BE ENLARGED. THE DECISION OF WHAT TO DETAIL IS A MATTER OF POLICY WITH MOST ARCHITECTS. SOME OFFICES WILL DRAW DETAIL BOOKS THAT ARE SEVERAL HUNDRED PAGES LONG, WHILE OTHER FIRMS HOLD DETAILS TO A MINIMUM. A GOOD POLICY TO FOLLOW IS TO SOLVE CONSTRUCTION CONDITIONS ON THE WORKING DRAWINGS RATHER THAN TO WAIT FOR PROBLEMS TO SHOW UP DURING CONSTRUCTION.

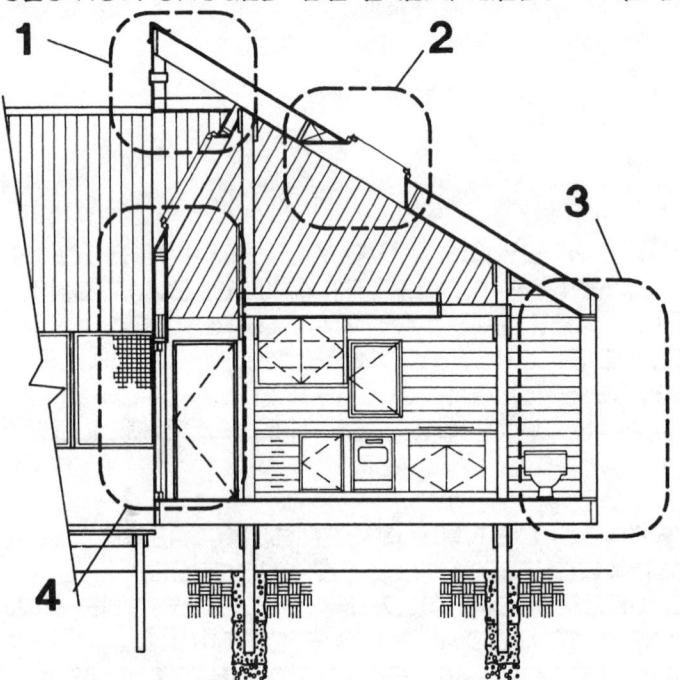

THIS UNIT WILL REVIEW THE DEVELOPMENT OF A SERIES OF DETAILS FOR THE PROJECTS WE ARE USING AS EXAMPLES IN THE TEXT. THE INFORMATION GIVEN REGARDING THE STEP-BY-STEP ASSEMBLY OF THE DETAILS CAN BE APPLIED TO DRAWING OTHER CONDITIONS.

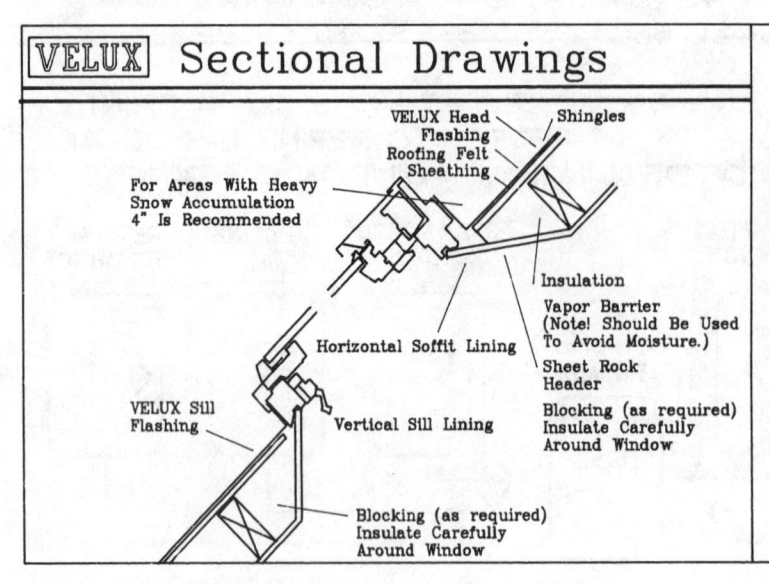

THE FIRST EXAMPLE REVIEWS THE RESEARCH NEEDED TO PLACE SEVERAL ROOF WINDOWS IN THE CABIN SHOWN ABOVE (DETAILS 1 AND 2). THE DRAWING AT THE LEFT SHOWS A MANUFACTURERS' CATALOG WITH NOTES AND DETAILS THAT PERTAIN TO INSTALLATION. A VITAL PART OF ACHIEVING SUCCESSFUL DETAIL ASSEMBLY IS DEVELOPING AN ABILITY TO TRANSFER PRODUCT INFORMATION FROM MANUFACTURERS' CATALOGS TO THE CONSTRUCTION DETAIL.

DETAIL ASSEMBLY   20-2

VELUX # 1
(30 5/8" x 38 1/2")

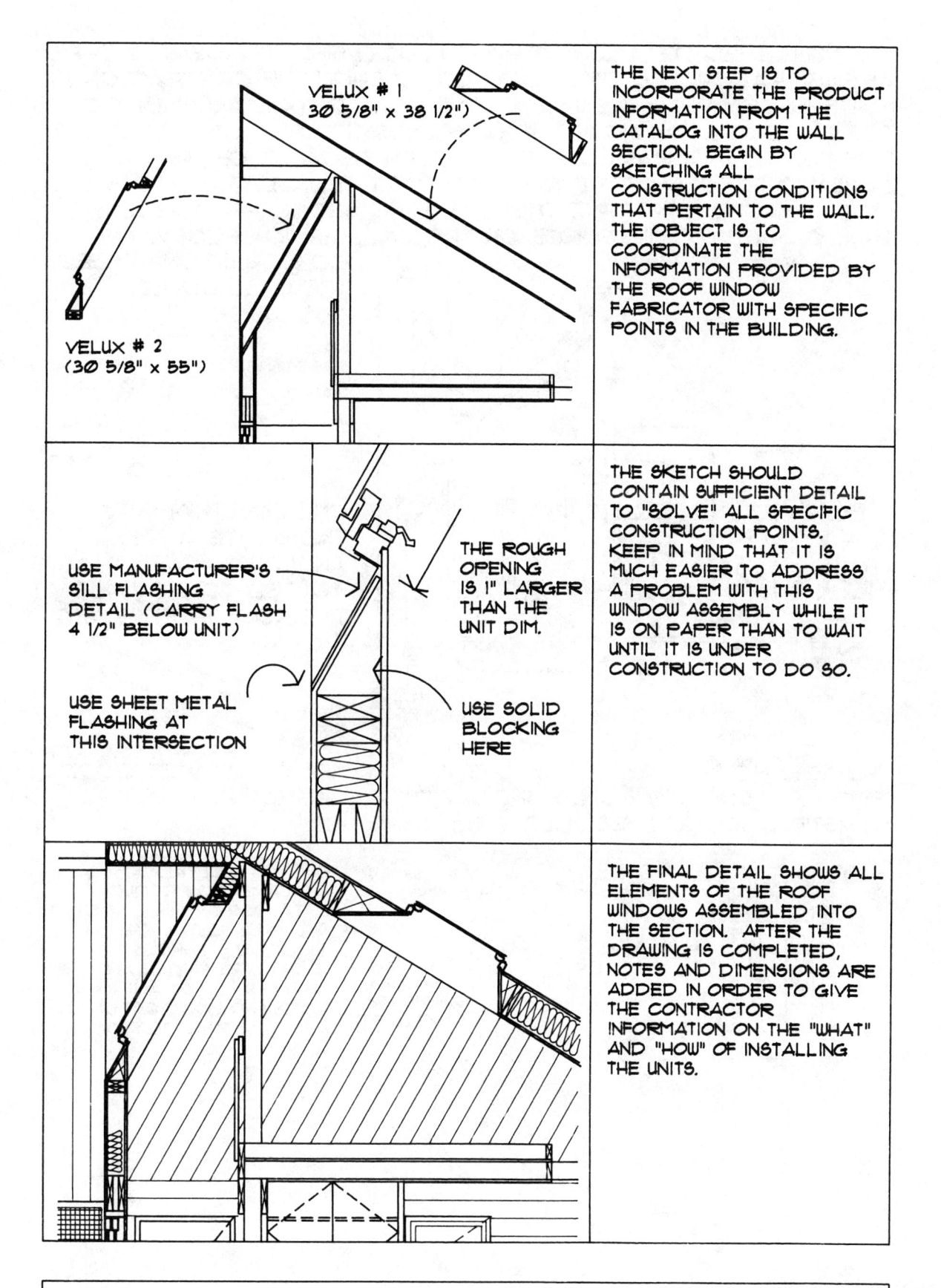

VELUX # 2
(30 5/8" x 55")

THE NEXT STEP IS TO INCORPORATE THE PRODUCT INFORMATION FROM THE CATALOG INTO THE WALL SECTION. BEGIN BY SKETCHING ALL CONSTRUCTION CONDITIONS THAT PERTAIN TO THE WALL. THE OBJECT IS TO COORDINATE THE INFORMATION PROVIDED BY THE ROOF WINDOW FABRICATOR WITH SPECIFIC POINTS IN THE BUILDING.

USE MANUFACTURER'S SILL FLASHING DETAIL (CARRY FLASH 4 1/2" BELOW UNIT)

USE SHEET METAL FLASHING AT THIS INTERSECTION

THE ROUGH OPENING IS 1" LARGER THAN THE UNIT DIM.

USE SOLID BLOCKING HERE

THE SKETCH SHOULD CONTAIN SUFFICIENT DETAIL TO "SOLVE" ALL SPECIFIC CONSTRUCTION POINTS. KEEP IN MIND THAT IT IS MUCH EASIER TO ADDRESS A PROBLEM WITH THIS WINDOW ASSEMBLY WHILE IT IS ON PAPER THAN TO WAIT UNTIL IT IS UNDER CONSTRUCTION TO DO SO.

THE FINAL DETAIL SHOWS ALL ELEMENTS OF THE ROOF WINDOWS ASSEMBLED INTO THE SECTION. AFTER THE DRAWING IS COMPLETED, NOTES AND DIMENSIONS ARE ADDED IN ORDER TO GIVE THE CONTRACTOR INFORMATION ON THE "WHAT" AND "HOW" OF INSTALLING THE UNITS.

DETAIL ASSEMBLY   20-3

THE NUMBERED DETAILS ON THIS BUILDING SECTION IDENTIFY THREE AREAS THAT SHOULD BE ENLARGED TO SHOW THE CONTRACTOR MORE INFORMATION. WE WILL EXAMINE THE DETAIL ASSEMBLY OF THE WINDOW HEAD AND ROOF EAVE (MARKED "1" ON THE SECTION). THIS DETAIL IS A PARTICULAR CONCERN BECAUSE OF THE WAY OUTWARD FORCES OF THE ROOF AFFECT THE WALL. THE TWO-STORY OPEN SPACE MEANS THAT THERE ARE NO SECOND-FLOOR JOISTS THAT CAN RESIST THE FORCE ON THE WALL. IF NO SPECIAL CONSTRUCTION IS USED, THE WALL COULD COLLAPSE.

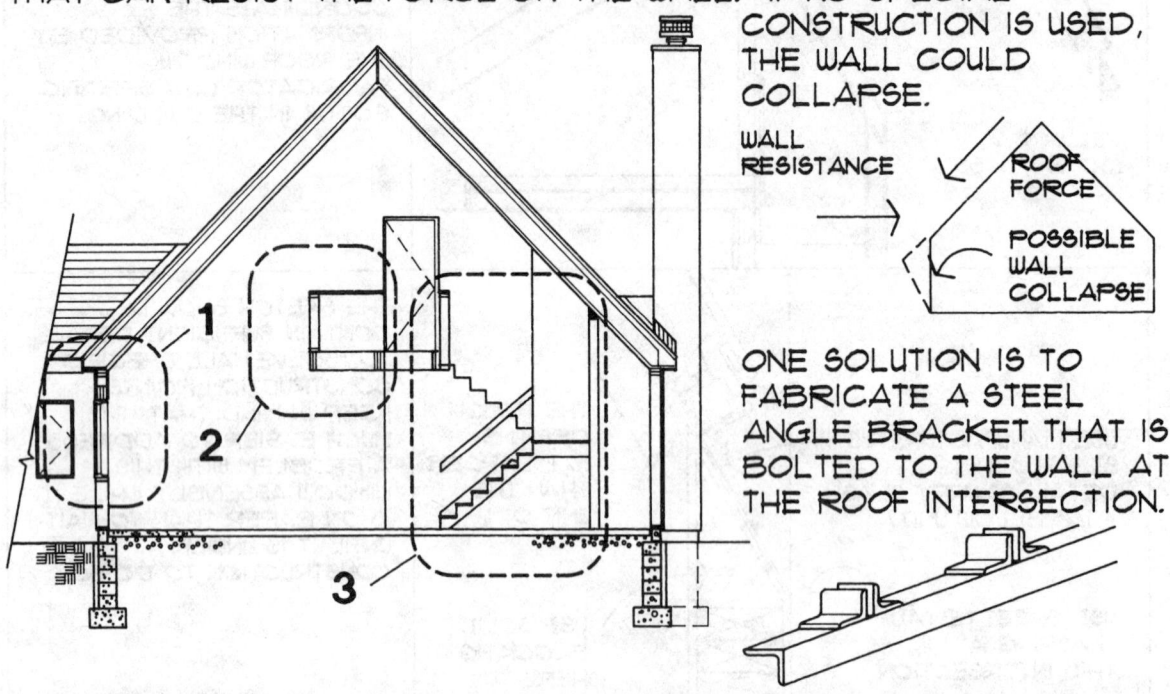

WALL RESISTANCE
ROOF FORCE
POSSIBLE WALL COLLAPSE

ONE SOLUTION IS TO FABRICATE A STEEL ANGLE BRACKET THAT IS BOLTED TO THE WALL AT THE ROOF INTERSECTION.

THERE IS NO "QUICK FIX" FOR DETAIL ASSEMBLY. IT TAKES GOOD PROBLEM-SOLVING SKILLS AND A FIRM BACKGROUND IN CONSTRUCTION TO ASSEMBLE A BUILDING.

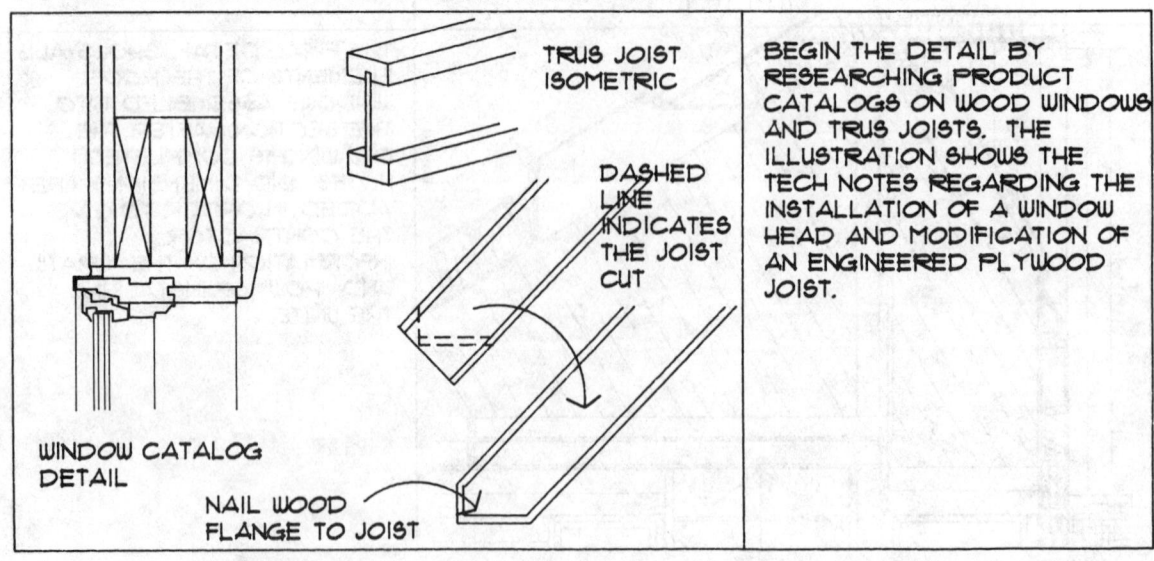

TRUS JOIST ISOMETRIC

DASHED LINE INDICATES THE JOIST CUT

WINDOW CATALOG DETAIL

NAIL WOOD FLANGE TO JOIST

BEGIN THE DETAIL BY RESEARCHING PRODUCT CATALOGS ON WOOD WINDOWS AND TRUS JOISTS. THE ILLUSTRATION SHOWS THE TECH NOTES REGARDING THE INSTALLATION OF A WINDOW HEAD AND MODIFICATION OF AN ENGINEERED PLYWOOD JOIST.

DETAIL ASSEMBLY 20-4

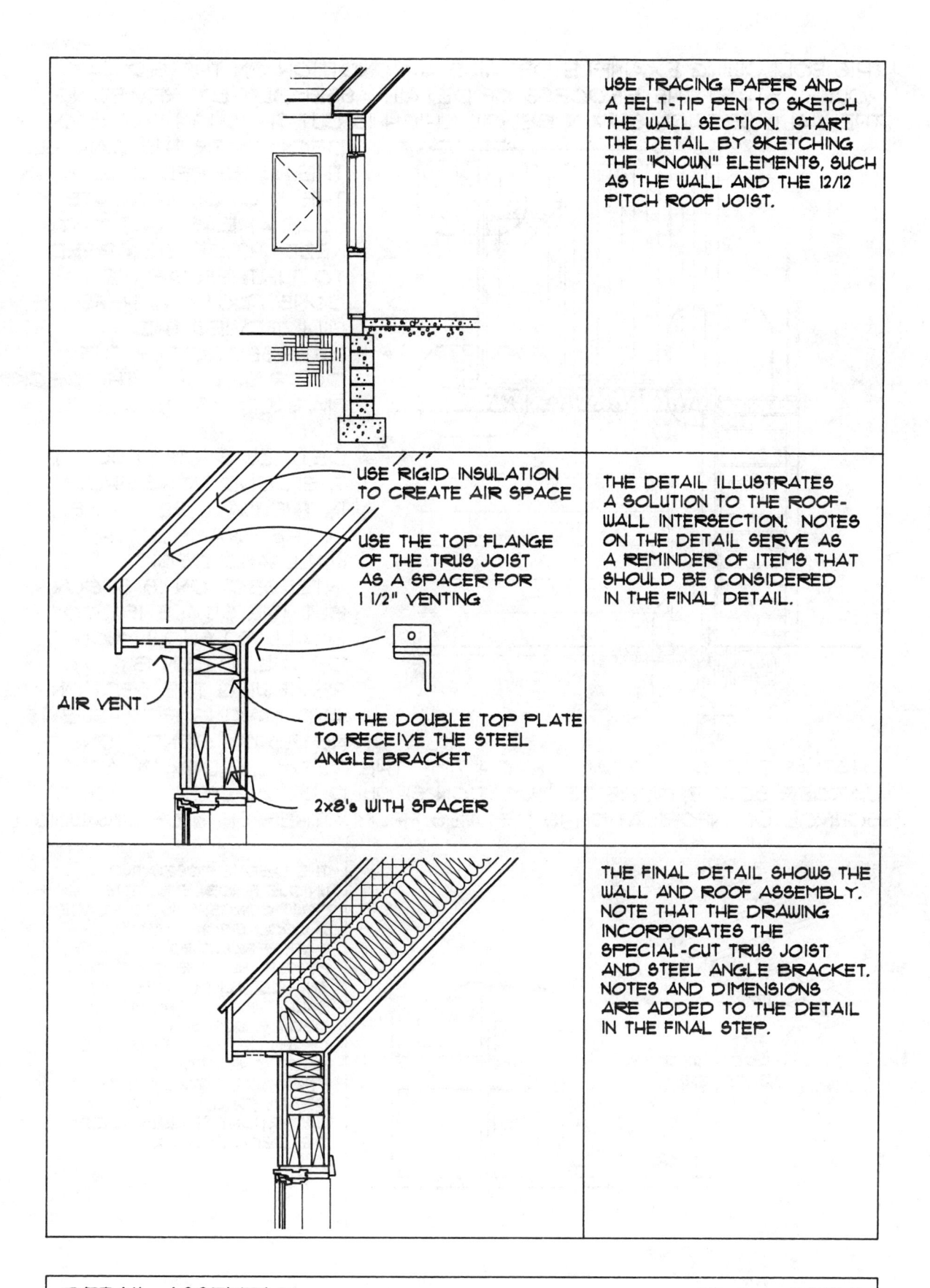

USE TRACING PAPER AND A FELT-TIP PEN TO SKETCH THE WALL SECTION. START THE DETAIL BY SKETCHING THE "KNOWN" ELEMENTS, SUCH AS THE WALL AND THE 12/12 PITCH ROOF JOIST.

USE RIGID INSULATION TO CREATE AIR SPACE

USE THE TOP FLANGE OF THE TRUS JOIST AS A SPACER FOR 1 1/2" VENTING

AIR VENT

CUT THE DOUBLE TOP PLATE TO RECEIVE THE STEEL ANGLE BRACKET

2x8's WITH SPACER

THE DETAIL ILLUSTRATES A SOLUTION TO THE ROOF-WALL INTERSECTION. NOTES ON THE DETAIL SERVE AS A REMINDER OF ITEMS THAT SHOULD BE CONSIDERED IN THE FINAL DETAIL.

THE FINAL DETAIL SHOWS THE WALL AND ROOF ASSEMBLY. NOTE THAT THE DRAWING INCORPORATES THE SPECIAL-CUT TRUS JOIST AND STEEL ANGLE BRACKET. NOTES AND DIMENSIONS ARE ADDED TO THE DETAIL IN THE FINAL STEP.

DETAIL ASSEMBLY 20-5

THIS FOLLOWING EXAMPLE DETAILS A CONDITION ON THE SKYWAY HOUSE. START THE PROCESS OF DETAIL ASSEMBLY BY REVIEWING THE WALL SECTION SHOWN BELOW, WHICH IS CUT THROUGH THE WOOD DECK OVER THE GARAGE. THE NUMBERED AREAS ON THE SECTION INDICATE FOUR AREAS THAT MAY NEED TO BE ENLARGED TO FURTHER DEFINE CONSTRUCTION. HERE WE WILL REVIEW THE INTERSECTION OF THE DOOR SILL WITH THE DECK MARKED AS DETAIL "3."

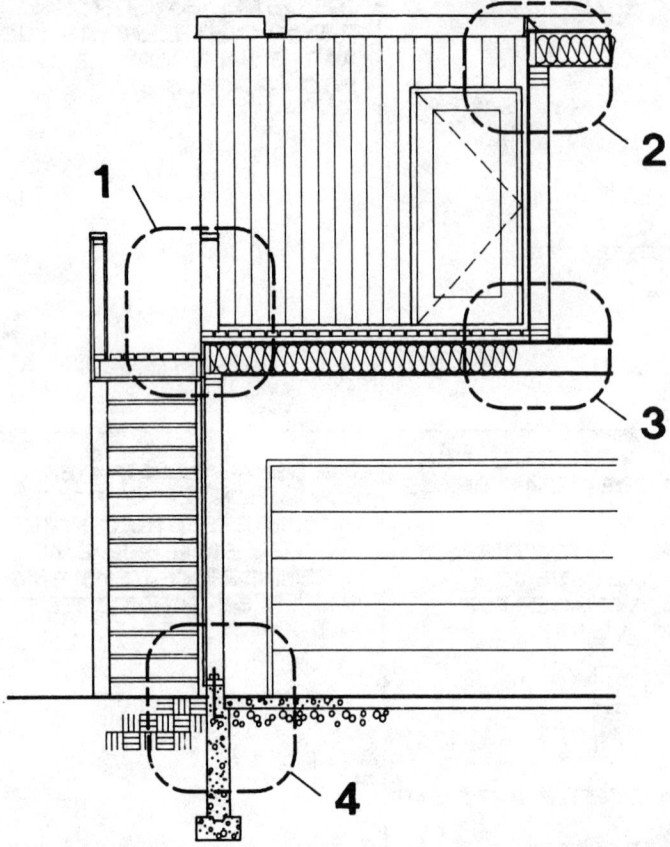

DETAILS SHOULD SOLVE THE CONDITIONS SHOWN IN THE WALL SECTIONS. IN THE EXAMPLE, THE WALL AND DECK INTERSECTION IS SHOWN, BUT THE SCALE IS TOO SMALL TO SHOW MUCH DETAIL. BEGIN BY REVIEWING THE SECTION AND MAKING RED-LINE NOTES ON CONDITIONS THAT AFFECT THE DETAIL. EACH TIME THE DETAIL IS DRAWN AT A LARGER SCALE, MORE INFORMATION SHOULD BE ADDED. A GOOD SOURCE OF INFORMATION IS DETAILS FROM OTHER SETS OF DRAWINGS.

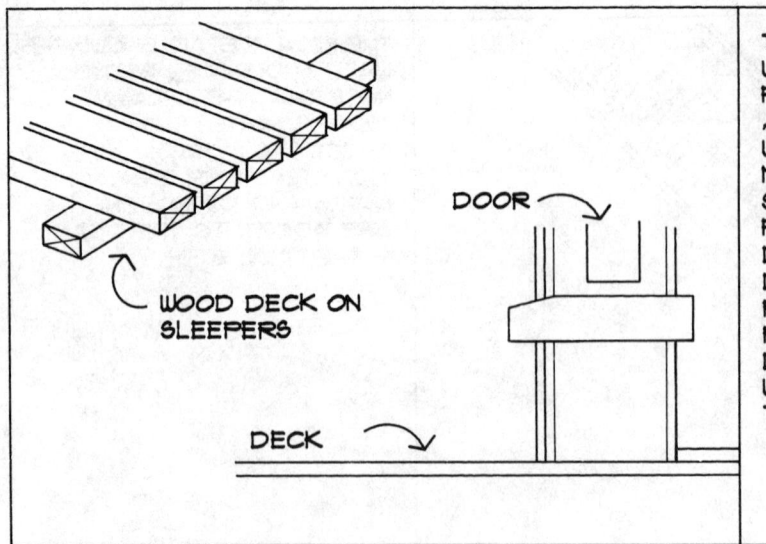

THE DETAIL POSES TWO UNIQUE PROBLEMS. THE FIRST CONCERN IS TO PLACE A WOOD DECK OVER A WATERPROOF ROOF MEMBRANE. THE CONDITION SHOULD ALLOW WATER TO FALL THROUGH THE WOOD DECK FLOOR SLATS AND DRAIN OFF THE MEMBRANE ROOF. THE SECOND PROBLEM IS TO DRAW A DETAIL THAT WILL MAKE A WATERTIGHT SEAL BETWEEN THE DECK AND WALL.

DETAIL ASSEMBLY   20-6

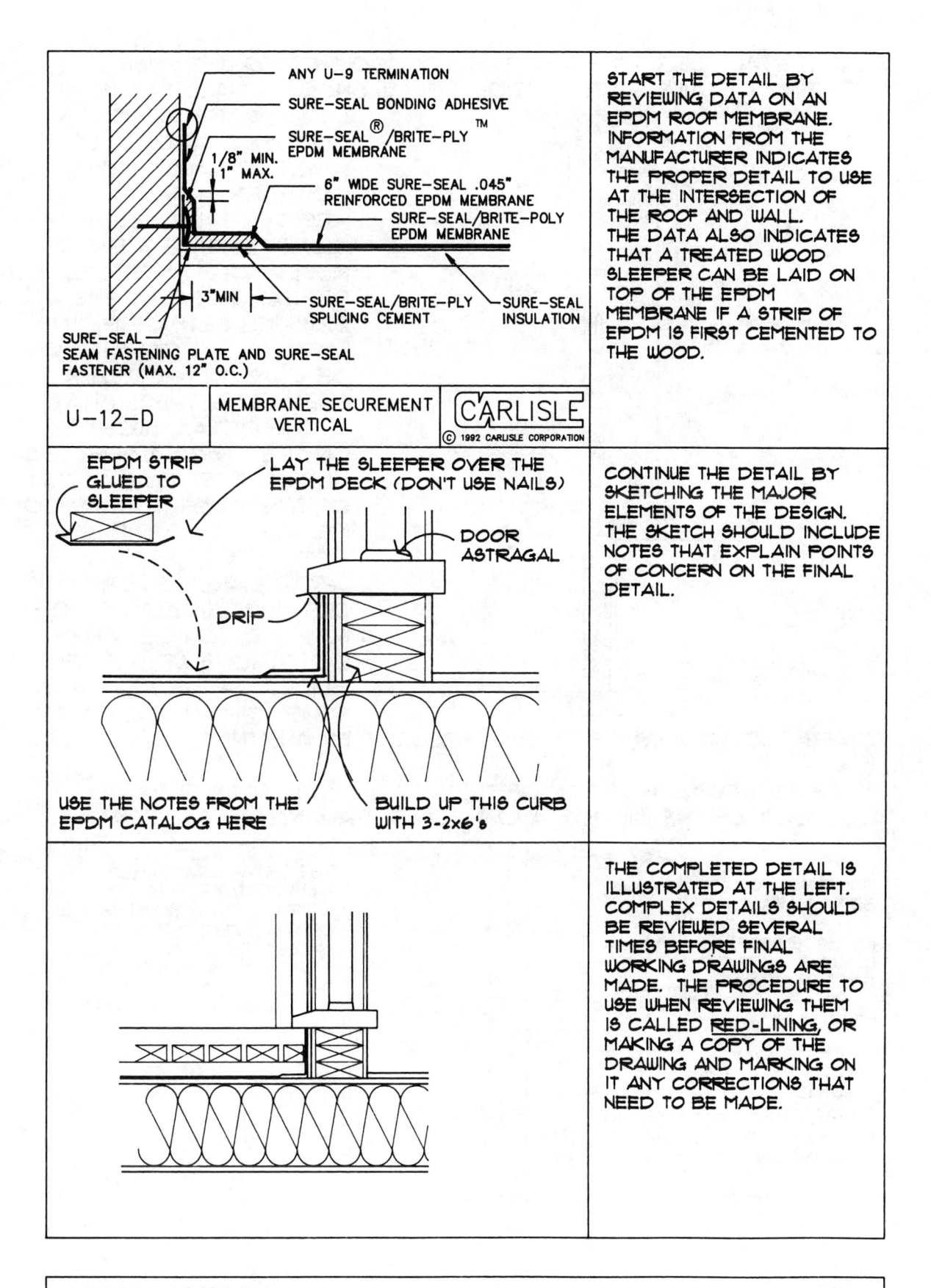

Panel 1 (U-12-D: MEMBRANE SECUREMENT VERTICAL — CARLISLE © 1992 CARLISLE CORPORATION)

- ANY U-9 TERMINATION
- SURE-SEAL BONDING ADHESIVE
- SURE-SEAL®/BRITE-PLY™ EPDM MEMBRANE
- 1/8" MIN. 1" MAX.
- 6" WIDE SURE-SEAL .045" REINFORCED EPDM MEMBRANE
- SURE-SEAL/BRITE-POLY EPDM MEMBRANE
- 3" MIN
- SURE-SEAL/BRITE-PLY SPLICING CEMENT
- SURE-SEAL INSULATION
- SURE-SEAL SEAM FASTENING PLATE AND SURE-SEAL FASTENER (MAX. 12" O.C.)

START THE DETAIL BY REVIEWING DATA ON AN EPDM ROOF MEMBRANE. INFORMATION FROM THE MANUFACTURER INDICATES THE PROPER DETAIL TO USE AT THE INTERSECTION OF THE ROOF AND WALL. THE DATA ALSO INDICATES THAT A TREATED WOOD SLEEPER CAN BE LAID ON TOP OF THE EPDM MEMBRANE IF A STRIP OF EPDM IS FIRST CEMENTED TO THE WOOD.

Panel 2

- EPDM STRIP GLUED TO SLEEPER
- LAY THE SLEEPER OVER THE EPDM DECK (DON'T USE NAILS)
- DOOR ASTRAGAL
- DRIP
- USE THE NOTES FROM THE EPDM CATALOG HERE
- BUILD UP THIS CURB WITH 3-2x6's

CONTINUE THE DETAIL BY SKETCHING THE MAJOR ELEMENTS OF THE DESIGN. THE SKETCH SHOULD INCLUDE NOTES THAT EXPLAIN POINTS OF CONCERN ON THE FINAL DETAIL.

Panel 3

THE COMPLETED DETAIL IS ILLUSTRATED AT THE LEFT. COMPLEX DETAILS SHOULD BE REVIEWED SEVERAL TIMES BEFORE FINAL WORKING DRAWINGS ARE MADE. THE PROCEDURE TO USE WHEN REVIEWING THEM IS CALLED RED-LINING, OR MAKING A COPY OF THE DRAWING AND MARKING ON IT ANY CORRECTIONS THAT NEED TO BE MADE.

DETAIL ASSEMBLY

SMALL-SCALE SECTIONS ARE THE BEST SOURCE TO USE WHEN CREATING DETAILS. THE SECTION BELOW SHOWS A WALL IN THE LIBRARY PROJECT. COMMERCIAL DETAILS ARE TYPICALLY MORE COMPLEX THAN RESIDENTIAL ONES AND REQUIRE QUITE A BIT OF RESEARCH. AN EXCELLENT RESEARCH SOURCE IS EXISTING SETS OF PLANS FOR SIMILAR CONDITIONS. BE CAREFUL, HOWEVER, WHEN USING THESE THAT (1) THE DETAIL "WORKED" ON THE ORIGINAL PROJECT, AND (2) THE TECHNOLOGY OF THE ORIGINAL PROJECT TRANSFERS TO THE NEW WORK. KEEP IN MIND THAT NEARLY EVERY DETAIL WILL NEED TO BE REVISED TO MEET THE CONDITIONS OF THE NEW BUILDING— THE KEY IS TO DEVELOP AN ABILITY TO ADAPT TECHNOLOGY FROM ONE PROJECT TO ANOTHER.

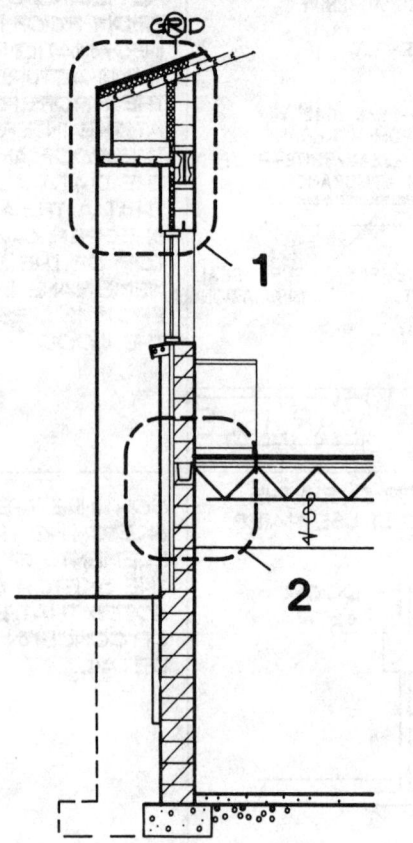

IN THE FOLLOWING PORTION OF THE UNIT, WE WILL ADDRESS THE ASSEMBLY OF THE WINDOW AND ROOF OVERHANG (DETAIL "1").

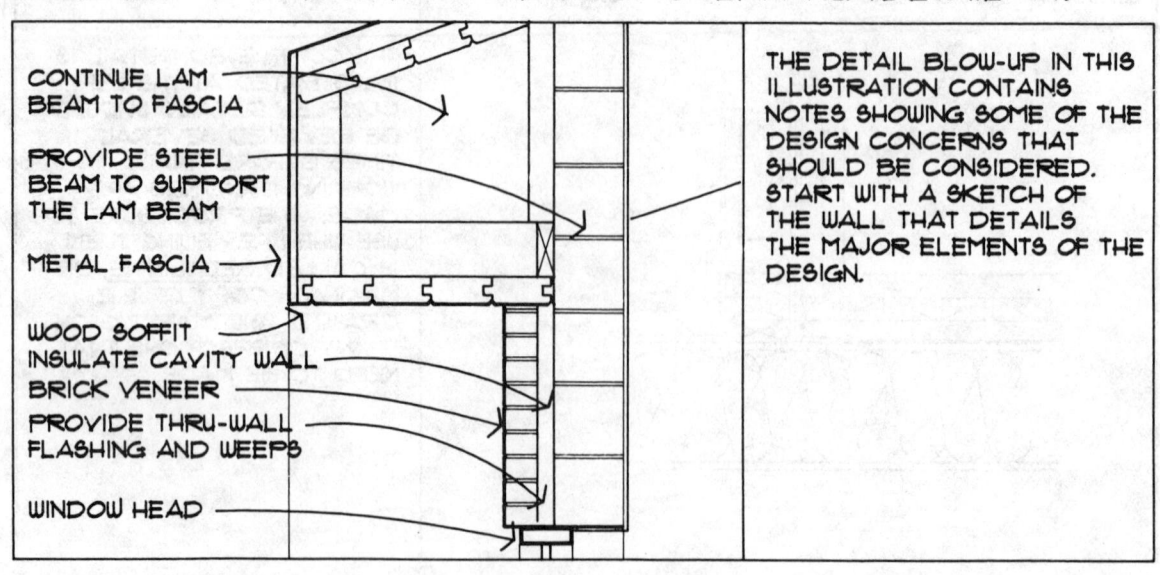

- CONTINUE LAM BEAM TO FASCIA
- PROVIDE STEEL BEAM TO SUPPORT THE LAM BEAM
- METAL FASCIA
- WOOD SOFFIT
- INSULATE CAVITY WALL
- BRICK VENEER
- PROVIDE THRU-WALL FLASHING AND WEEPS
- WINDOW HEAD

THE DETAIL BLOW-UP IN THIS ILLUSTRATION CONTAINS NOTES SHOWING SOME OF THE DESIGN CONCERNS THAT SHOULD BE CONSIDERED. START WITH A SKETCH OF THE WALL THAT DETAILS THE MAJOR ELEMENTS OF THE DESIGN.

DETAIL ASSEMBLY   20-8

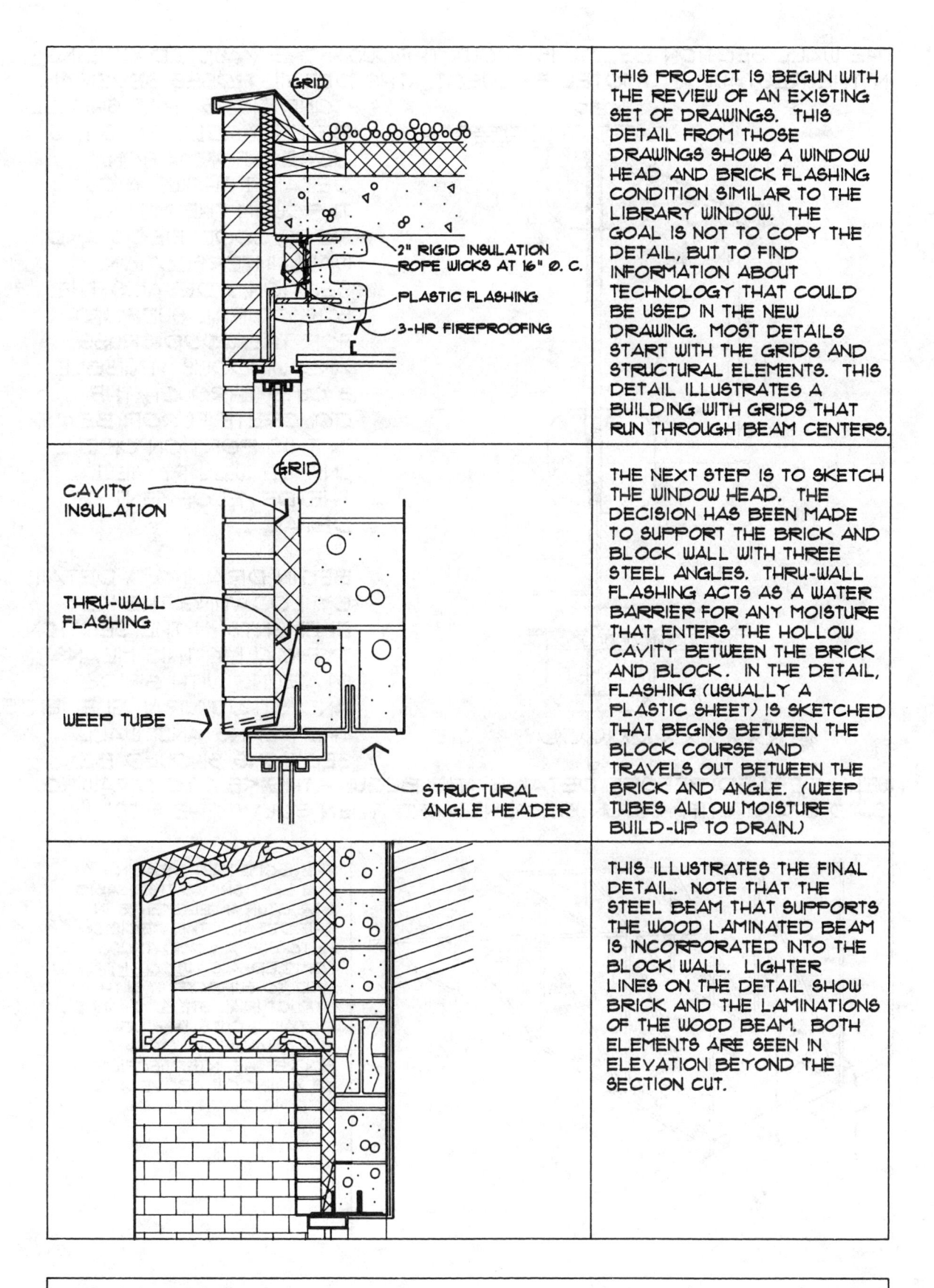

(detail drawing with labels: GRID, 2" RIGID INSULATION ROPE WICKS AT 16" O.C., PLASTIC FLASHING, 3-HR FIREPROOFING)	THIS PROJECT IS BEGUN WITH THE REVIEW OF AN EXISTING SET OF DRAWINGS. THIS DETAIL FROM THOSE DRAWINGS SHOWS A WINDOW HEAD AND BRICK FLASHING CONDITION SIMILAR TO THE LIBRARY WINDOW. THE GOAL IS NOT TO COPY THE DETAIL, BUT TO FIND INFORMATION ABOUT TECHNOLOGY THAT COULD BE USED IN THE NEW DRAWING. MOST DETAILS START WITH THE GRIDS AND STRUCTURAL ELEMENTS. THIS DETAIL ILLUSTRATES A BUILDING WITH GRIDS THAT RUN THROUGH BEAM CENTERS.
(detail drawing with labels: GRID, CAVITY INSULATION, THRU-WALL FLASHING, WEEP TUBE, STRUCTURAL ANGLE HEADER)	THE NEXT STEP IS TO SKETCH THE WINDOW HEAD. THE DECISION HAS BEEN MADE TO SUPPORT THE BRICK AND BLOCK WALL WITH THREE STEEL ANGLES. THRU-WALL FLASHING ACTS AS A WATER BARRIER FOR ANY MOISTURE THAT ENTERS THE HOLLOW CAVITY BETWEEN THE BRICK AND BLOCK. IN THE DETAIL, FLASHING (USUALLY A PLASTIC SHEET) IS SKETCHED THAT BEGINS BETWEEN THE BLOCK COURSE AND TRAVELS OUT BETWEEN THE BRICK AND ANGLE. (WEEP TUBES ALLOW MOISTURE BUILD-UP TO DRAIN.)
(final detail drawing)	THIS ILLUSTRATES THE FINAL DETAIL. NOTE THAT THE STEEL BEAM THAT SUPPORTS THE WOOD LAMINATED BEAM IS INCORPORATED INTO THE BLOCK WALL. LIGHTER LINES ON THE DETAIL SHOW BRICK AND THE LAMINATIONS OF THE WOOD BEAM. BOTH ELEMENTS ARE SEEN IN ELEVATION BEYOND THE SECTION CUT.

DETAIL ASSEMBLY

THE WALL SECTION BELOW IS A CUT THROUGH THE VAULTED CEILING IN THE RESTAURANT/MOTEL PROJECT. THE DETAIL POSES SEVERAL CONDITIONS THAT SHOULD BE ENLARGED TO SHOW MORE INFORMATION. DETAIL 1 SHOWS A CUT THROUGH THE METAL ROOF, WOOD DECK, AND WALL INTERSECTION. SECTION 2 DETAILS THE STRUCTURAL SUPPORT FOR THE WOOD TRUSS AND WINDOWS. BUBBLE 3 CUTS THROUGH THE CONCRETE FLOOR BEAM. IN THIS PORTION OF THE UNIT WE WILL REVIEW THE DEVELOPMENT OF DETAIL 2.

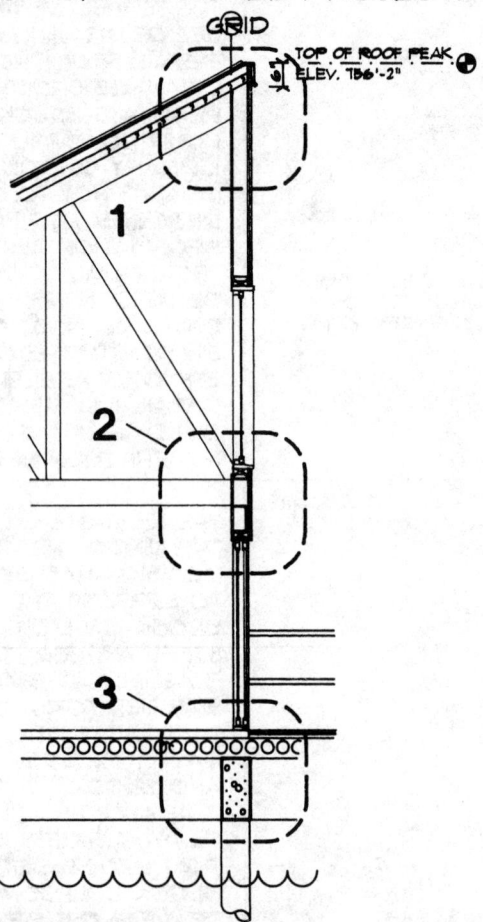

BEGIN DRAWING A DETAIL BY LOCATING THE KEY ELEMENTS IN THE SECTION. TYPICALLY, THIS MEANS STARTING WITH GRIDS AND STRUCTURAL ELEMENTS. THE PLANS AND WALL SECTIONS SHOULD BE WELL DEFINED BEFORE DETAILS ARE BEGUN— THE KEY TO DRAWING IS TO START WITH KNOWN ELEMENTS AND THEN SOLVE THE REST.

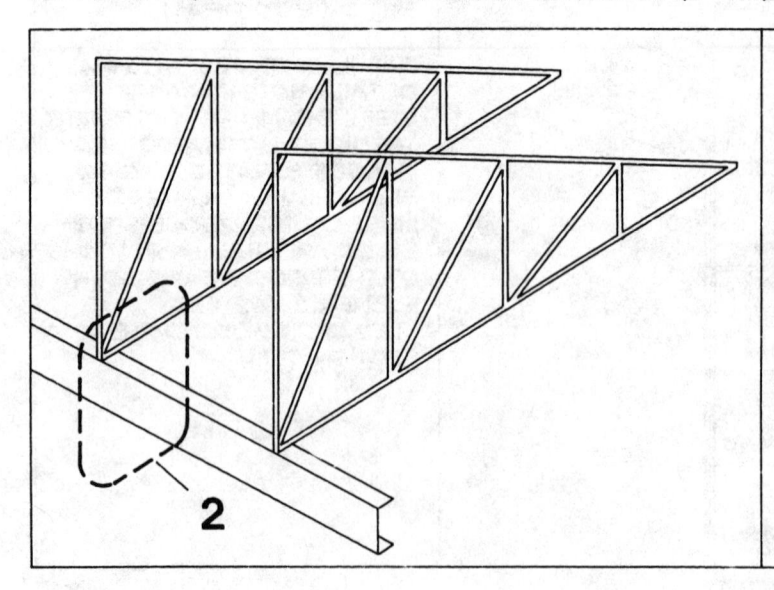

THE ISOMETRIC DRAWING AT THE LEFT SHOWS THE BASIC STRUCTURAL ELEMENTS IN THE DETAIL. THE DECISION IS TO USE A WOOD TRUSS (CALLED A SAWTOOTH TRUSS) AND TO SUPPORT IT WITH A STRUCTURAL STEEL CHANNEL. DETAIL 2 CUTS THROUGH THE CHANNEL AND MUST SOLVE THE INTERSECTION OF A WINDOW ABOVE AND SLIDING DOOR BELOW.

DETAIL ASSEMBLY   20-10

DOUBLE STEEL ANGLE BRACKET TO ATTACH WOOD TRUSS

STRUCTURAL STEEL CHANNEL

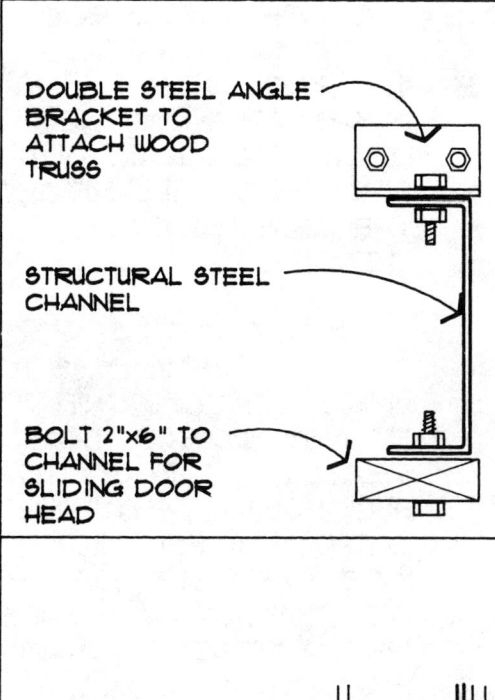

BOLT 2"x6" TO CHANNEL FOR SLIDING DOOR HEAD

THE FIRST STEP IS TO SKETCH THE STRUCTURAL COMPONENTS USED TO SUPPORT THE TRUSS. NOTES INDICATE THAT TWO ANGLE BRACKETS ARE TO BE BOLTED TO THE CHANNEL. (THE BRACKETS WILL BE USED TO ATTACH EACH WOOD TRUSS.) THE 2"x6" BOLTED TO THE BOTTOM OF THE CHANNEL WILL BE USED TO FASTEN THE SLIDING DOOR.

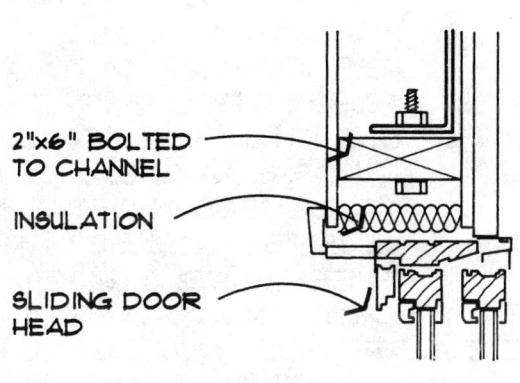

2"x6" BOLTED TO CHANNEL

INSULATION

SLIDING DOOR HEAD

THE NEXT STEP IS TO REVIEW THE DOOR MANUFACTURER'S CATALOG TO DETERMINE THE DIMENSION AND "FIT" OF THE UNIT. A GOOD WAY TO SOLVE THE DETAIL WOULD BE TO MAKE A TRACING PAPER SKETCH OVER THE RELEVANT SECTION IN THE CATALOG.

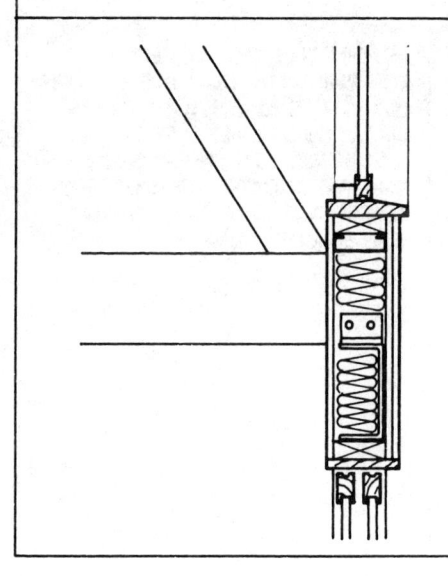

THE FINAL DETAIL SHOWS THE TRUSS SUPPORTED BY A STRUCTURAL STEEL CHANNEL. THE EXTERIOR WALL IS FABRICATED FROM STEEL STUDS, INSULATION, AND PLYWOOD SHEATHING. NOTE THAT THE WINDOW IS FRAMED WITH A WOOD ROUGH SILL AND THE SLIDING DOOR HAS A WOOD HEADER.

DETAIL ASSEMBLY 20-11

THE WALL SECTION BELOW IS CUT THROUGH THE APPARATUS ROOM DOOR IN THE FIRE STATION. DETAILS 1 AND 2 CUT THROUGH THE ROOF DECK AND DOOR HEAD, WHILE DETAIL 3 PROVIDES INFORMATION ON THE FOUNDATION WALL. IN THIS SECTION WE WILL REVIEW THE ASSEMBLY OF DETAIL 1.

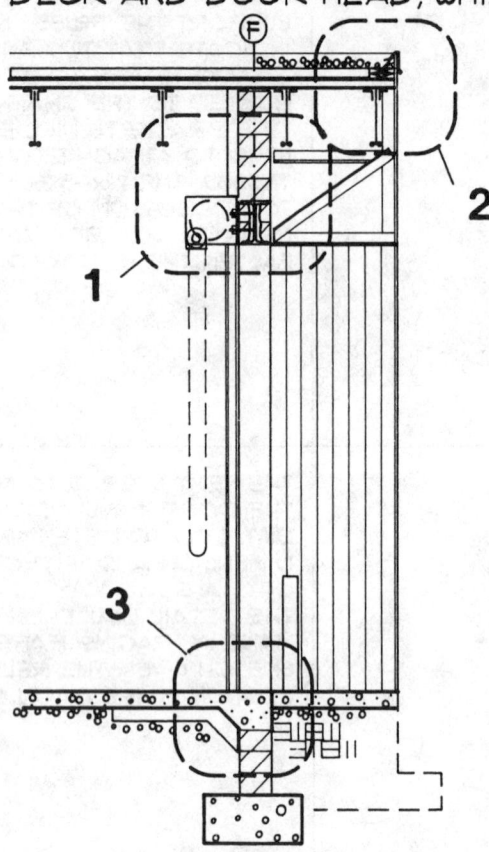

AN IMPORTANT TASK IN DETAIL ASSEMBLY IS TO MAKE THE COMPONENTS FIT AND "WORK." THAT REALLY IS THE KEY TO SUCCESSFUL DETAILING, BUT IT IS ALSO ONE OF THE MOST DIFFICULT JOBS TO ACCOMPLISH. A BUILDING ISN'T A PRODUCTION-LINE PRODUCT THAT WILL BE REPRODUCED MANY TIMES— THERE IS ONLY ONE CHANCE TO MAKE IT WORK. A GREAT DEAL OF SUCCESS IN DETAIL ASSEMBLY COMES WITH EXPERIENCE; A GOOD RULE TO FOLLOW, HOWEVER, BOTH AS A STUDENT AND AS A PROFESSIONAL, IS TO HAVE SOMEONE ELSE REVIEW YOUR DETAILS IN ORDER TO DETECT ANY POINTS THAT MAY NEED REVISION.

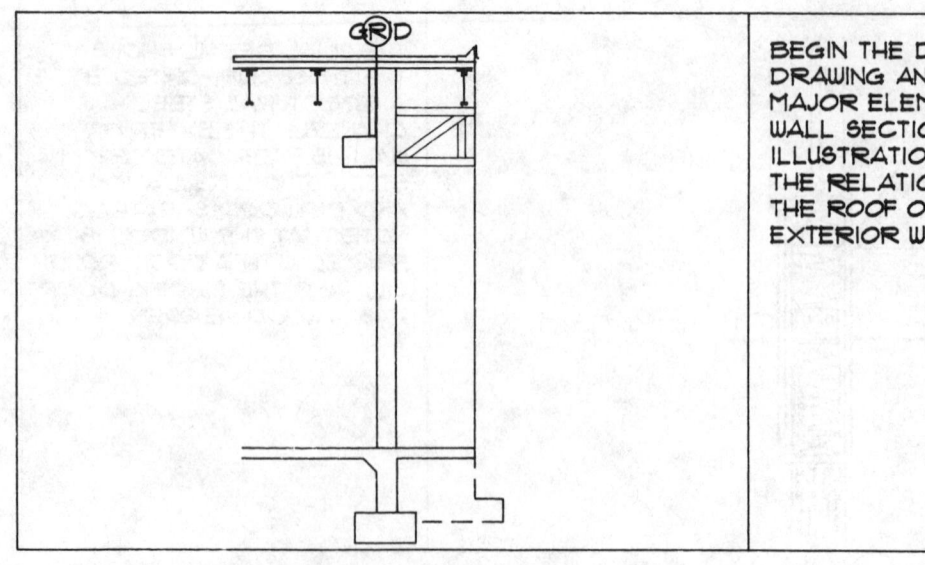

BEGIN THE DETAIL BY DRAWING AN OUTLINE OF THE MAJOR ELEMENTS IN THE WALL SECTION. THE ILLUSTRATION HERE SHOWS THE RELATIONSHIP BETWEEN THE ROOF OVERHANG AND EXTERIOR WALL.

DETAIL ASSEMBLY 20-12

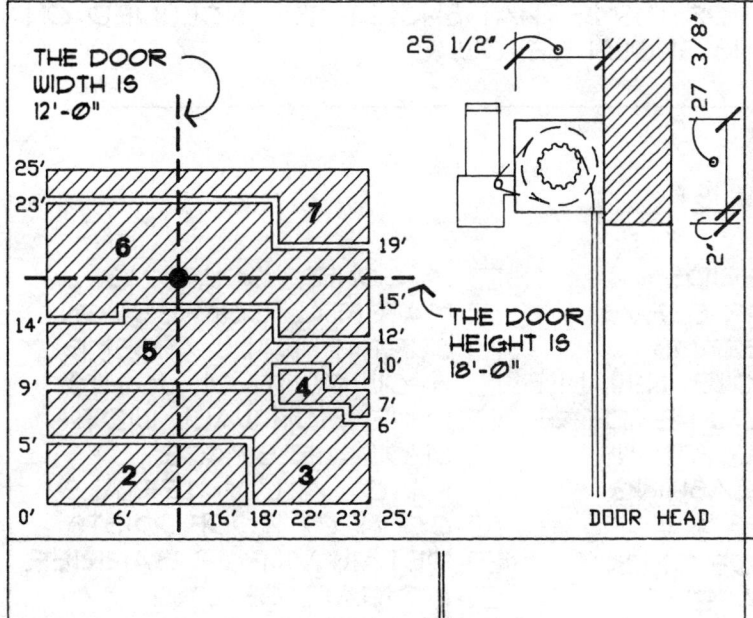

THESE TWO DRAWINGS ARE "CLIPS" TAKEN FROM A MANUFACTURER'S CATALOG ON ROLLING SERVICE DOORS. ENTER THE HEIGHT AND WIDTH OF THE DOOR OPENING IN THE CHART AT THE LEFT. THE INTERSECTION OF THE TWO DIMENSIONS INDICATES AN "AREA NUMBER" (6) THAT IS SPECIFIC TO THIS COMPANY. THE AREA NUMBER IS ENTERED INTO A CHART TO INDICATE THAT THE ROLLING DOOR IS 25 ½" WIDE AND 27 ⅜" HIGH. THE DOOR HEAD SECTION SHOWS THE DIMENSIONS FOR THE DOOR HOUSING AND MOTOR.

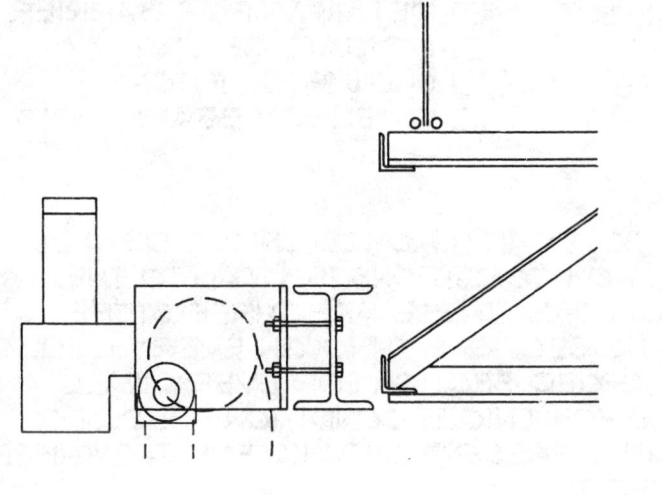

THIS ILLUSTRATES THE STRUCTURAL ELEMENTS IN THE DETAIL. THE SKETCH STARTS WITH THE STEEL WIDE FLANGE BEAM. (THE BLOCK WALL HAS BEEN ELIMINATED TO DEFINE THE STRUCTURE.) THE ROLLING DOOR IS BOLTED (THROUGH THE BLOCK) TO THE BEAM. THE "Z" STRUCTURE FOR THE ROOF OVERHANG IS FABRICATED FROM STEEL ANGLES. THE FRAME IS WELDED TO THE BAR JOISTS AND FASTENED TO THE BLOCK WALL WITH TWO ANGLES.

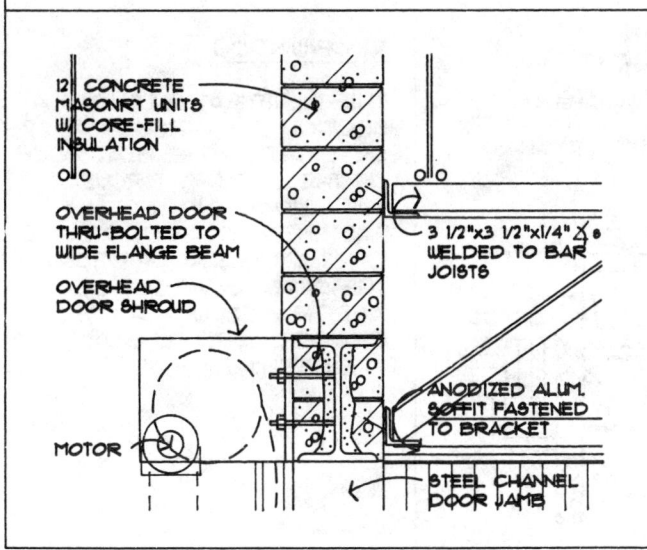

THIS ILLUSTRATES THE FINAL DETAIL, COMPLETE WITH NOTES. IT IS IMPORTANT TO DRAW ITEMS, SUCH AS BLOCK COURSING, ACCURATELY TO DETERMINE THE SIZE AND FIT OF ALL BUILDING MATERIALS.

DETAIL ASSEMBLY　　　20-13

A GENERAL CHECKLIST FOR ITEMS THAT SHOULD BE INCLUDED ON LARGE-SCALE DETAILS IS SHOWN BELOW.

DETAIL CHECKLIST

- ☐ INDICATE GRIDS
- ☐ SHOW FLOOR ELEVS.
- ☐ INDICATE BEAMS
- ☐ SHOW WINDOWS IN WALLS
- ☐ SHOW WINDOW HEADERS
- ☐ DETAIL INSULATION
- ☐ INDICATE FLASHING
- ☐ SHOW WEEPS & WICKS
- ☐ DETAIL ROOF DECKS
- ☐ SHOW PARAPETS
- ☐ INDICATE FASCIAS
- ☐ MASONRY COURSING
- ☐ MATERIAL CONNECTION
- ☐ CURTAIN WALL ASSEMBLY
- ☐ SHOW CONTROL JOINTS
- ☐ DIMENSION WALL WIDTH
- ☐ SHOW AIR SPACE
- ☐ HATCH ALL MATERIALS
- ☐ CONNECT ROOF JOISTS
- ☐ DETAIL VAPOR BARRIER
- ☐ INDICATE CEILING
- ☐ SHOW ROOF PITCH
- ☐ DIMENISON BEARING PTS.

DETAIL EXAMPLES

A PROJECT COULD REQUIRE SEVERAL HUNDRED UNIQUE DETAILS. SOLVING SPECIFIC CONSTRUCTION CONDITIONS IS VITAL TO THE PROPER ASSEMBLY OF A BUILDING. THERE ARE THREE STEPS IN THE PROCESS: (1) CUT BUILDING SECTIONS THROUGH EVERY UNIQUE CONDITION, (2) DRAW AN ENLARGED SECTION FOR EVERY WALL CONDITION, (3) DRAW DETAILS FOR UNIQUE CONDITIONS SHOWN ON WALL SECTIONS. BELOW WE WILL PRESENT DETAILS FOR THE THREE COMMERCIAL PROJECTS IN THE TEXT.

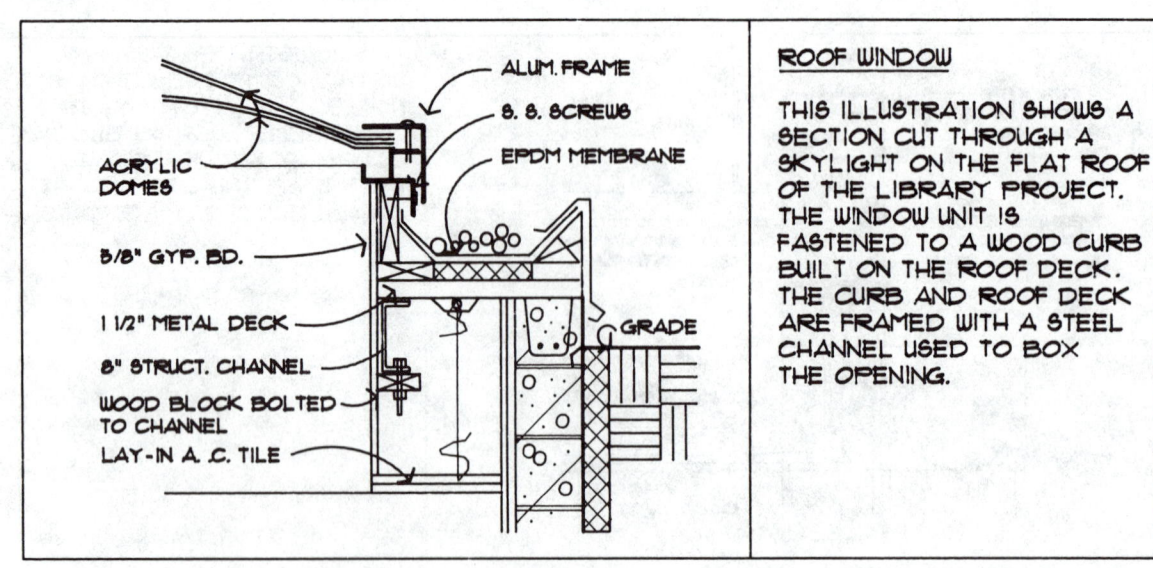

ROOF WINDOW

THIS ILLUSTRATION SHOWS A SECTION CUT THROUGH A SKYLIGHT ON THE FLAT ROOF OF THE LIBRARY PROJECT. THE WINDOW UNIT IS FASTENED TO A WOOD CURB BUILT ON THE ROOF DECK. THE CURB AND ROOF DECK ARE FRAMED WITH A STEEL CHANNEL USED TO BOX THE OPENING.

Labels: ACRYLIC DOMES, ALUM. FRAME, S.S. SCREWS, EPDM MEMBRANE, 5/8" GYP. BD., 1 1/2" METAL DECK, 8" STRUCT. CHANNEL, WOOD BLOCK BOLTED TO CHANNEL, LAY-IN A.C. TILE, GRADE

DETAIL ASSEMBLY 20-14

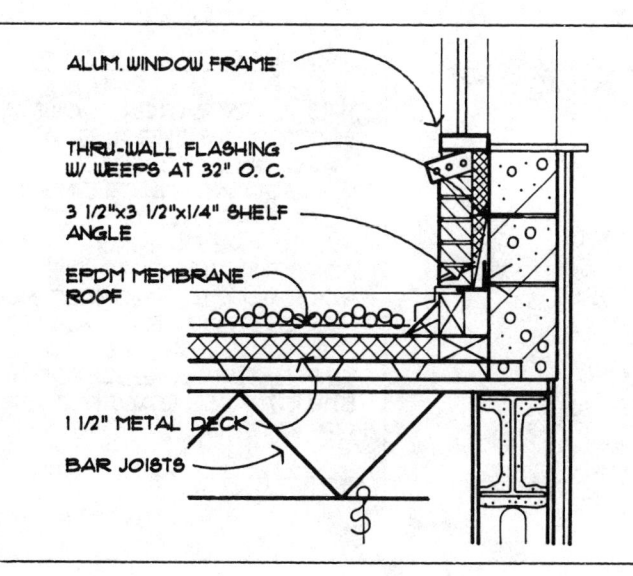

CLERE STORY WINDOW

A HIGH WINDOW IN THE TWO-STORY SPACE (CALLED A CLERE STORY) IS FIT INTO A BRICK AND BLOCK WALL. STRUCTURAL SUPPORT FOR THE ROOF DECK AND WALL IS PROVIDED BY A STEEL WIDE FLANGE BEAM. NOTE THAT STRUCTURAL STEEL MUST BE PROTECTED WITH A SPRAY-ON FIREPROOFING MATERIAL. THE THRU-WALL FLASHING DETAIL IS SIMILAR TO OTHER EXAMPLES IN THIS UNIT.

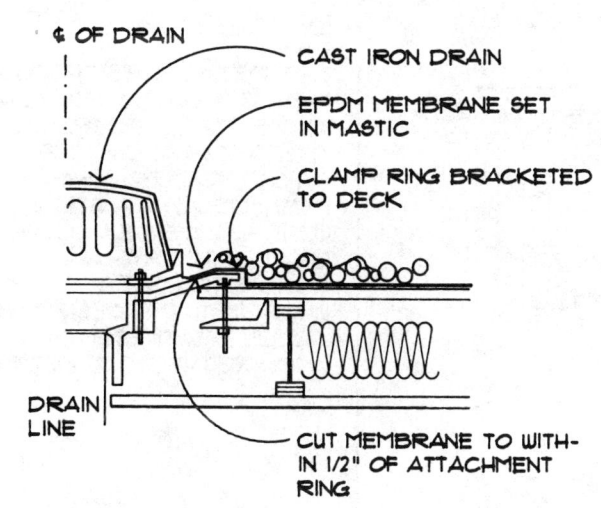

Labels: ALUM. WINDOW FRAME; THRU-WALL FLASHING W/ WEEPS AT 32" O.C.; 3 1/2"x3 1/2"x1/4" SHELF ANGLE; EPDM MEMBRANE ROOF; 1 1/2" METAL DECK; BAR JOISTS

ROOF DRAIN

THIS DETAIL CUTS THROUGH A ROOF DRAIN ON THE MOTEL/RESTAURANT PROJECT. THE PURPOSE OF THE SECTION IS TO SHOW THE CONNECTION BETWEEN THE MANUFACTURED DRAIN AND THE ROOF ASSEMBLY.

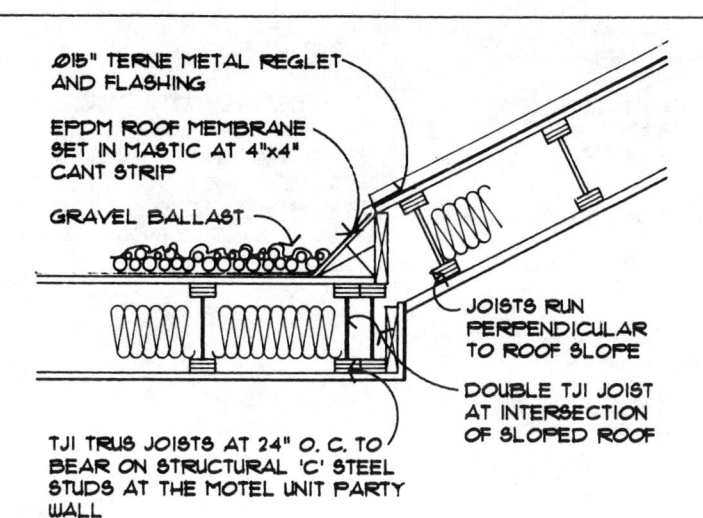

Labels: ¢ OF DRAIN; CAST IRON DRAIN; EPDM MEMBRANE SET IN MASTIC; CLAMP RING BRACKETED TO DECK; DRAIN LINE; CUT MEMBRANE TO WITHIN 1/2" OF ATTACHMENT RING

ROOF INTERSECTION

THIS DETAIL SHOWS THE INTERSECTION OF FLAT AND PITCHED ROOFS ON THE MOTEL PROJECT. NOTE THAT TJI JOISTS ARE DOUBLED TO PROVIDE SUPPORT AT THE INTERSECTION. THE PITCHED ROOF IS METAL CLAD WITH TERNE (A COATED SHEET METAL). THE DETAIL IS IMPORTANT BECAUSE IT SHOWS THE FLASHING BETWEEN THE METAL AND MEMBRANE ROOF.

Labels: Ø15" TERNE METAL REGLET AND FLASHING; EPDM ROOF MEMBRANE SET IN MASTIC AT 4"x4" CANT STRIP; GRAVEL BALLAST; JOISTS RUN PERPENDICULAR TO ROOF SLOPE; DOUBLE TJI JOIST AT INTERSECTION OF SLOPED ROOF; TJI TRUS JOISTS AT 24" O.C. TO BEAR ON STRUCTURAL 'C' STEEL STUDS AT THE MOTEL UNIT PARTY WALL

DETAIL ASSEMBLY 20-15

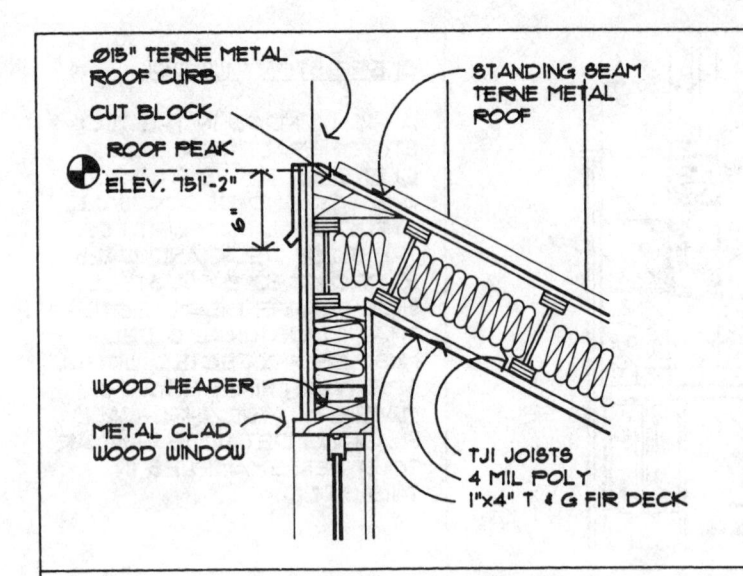

WINDOW HEAD AT ROOF PEAK

THIS ILLUSTRATION SHOWS A SECTION CUT THROUGH A FIXED WINDOW ON THE VAULTED MOTEL CEILING. NOTE THAT THE TJI ROOF JOISTS ARE RUNNING PERPENDICULAR TO THE ROOF SLOPE. THIS DECISION HAS BEEN MADE TO REDUCE THE ROOF SPAN AND TO ELIMINATE THE NEED FOR A STRUCTURAL HEADER OVER THE WINDOWS.

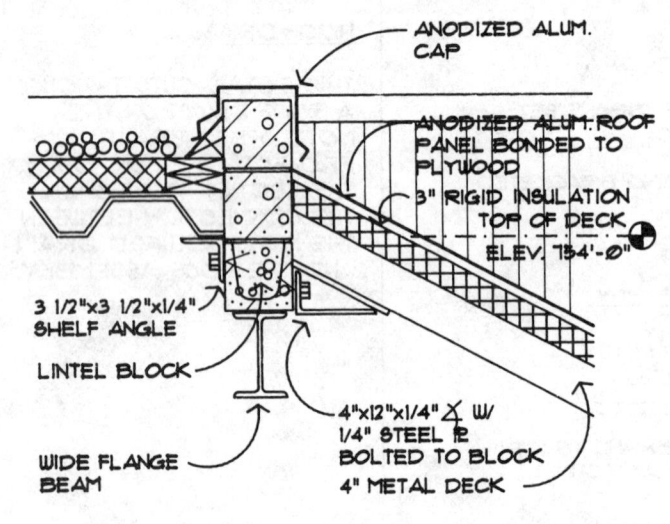

Labels on detail:
- .015" TERNE METAL ROOF CURB
- CUT BLOCK
- ROOF PEAK ELEV. 751'-2"
- STANDING SEAM TERNE METAL ROOF
- WOOD HEADER
- METAL CLAD WOOD WINDOW
- TJI JOISTS
- 4 MIL POLY
- 1"x4" T & G FIR DECK

ROOF EDGE

THIS DETAIL CUTS THROUGH THE INTERSECTION OF FLAT AND PITCHED ROOFS ON THE FIRE STATION. THE STRUCTURAL FRAMING IS PROVIDED BY A STEEL WIDE FLANGE BEAM. THE BEAM SUPPORTS A CONCRETE LINTEL BLOCK, WHICH IN TURN HOLDS TWO ANGLE BRACKETS TO ANCHOR THE ROOF DECKS.

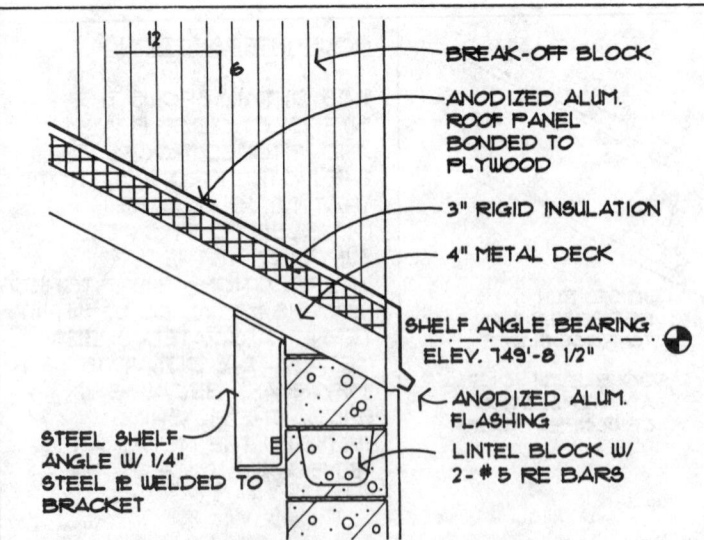

Labels on detail:
- ANODIZED ALUM. CAP
- ANODIZED ALUM. ROOF PANEL BONDED TO PLYWOOD
- 3" RIGID INSULATION TOP OF DECK ELEV. 754'-0"
- 3 1/2"x3 1/2"x1/4" SHELF ANGLE
- LINTEL BLOCK
- 4"x12"x1/4" ∠ W/ 1/4" STEEL ℞ BOLTED TO BLOCK
- 4" METAL DECK
- WIDE FLANGE BEAM

ROOF FASCIA

THIS DETAIL CUTS THROUGH THE BOTTOM EDGE OF THE ROOF SHOWN IN THE DRAWING ABOVE. THE ROOF DECK IS SUPPORTED BY A SHELF ANGLE THAT IS BOLTED TO THE LINTEL BLOCK.

Labels on detail:
- BREAK-OFF BLOCK
- ANODIZED ALUM. ROOF PANEL BONDED TO PLYWOOD
- 3" RIGID INSULATION
- 4" METAL DECK
- SHELF ANGLE BEARING ELEV. 749'-8 1/2"
- ANODIZED ALUM. FLASHING
- LINTEL BLOCK W/ 2-#5 RE BARS
- STEEL SHELF ANGLE W/ 1/4" STEEL ℞ WELDED TO BRACKET

DETAIL ASSEMBLY 20-16

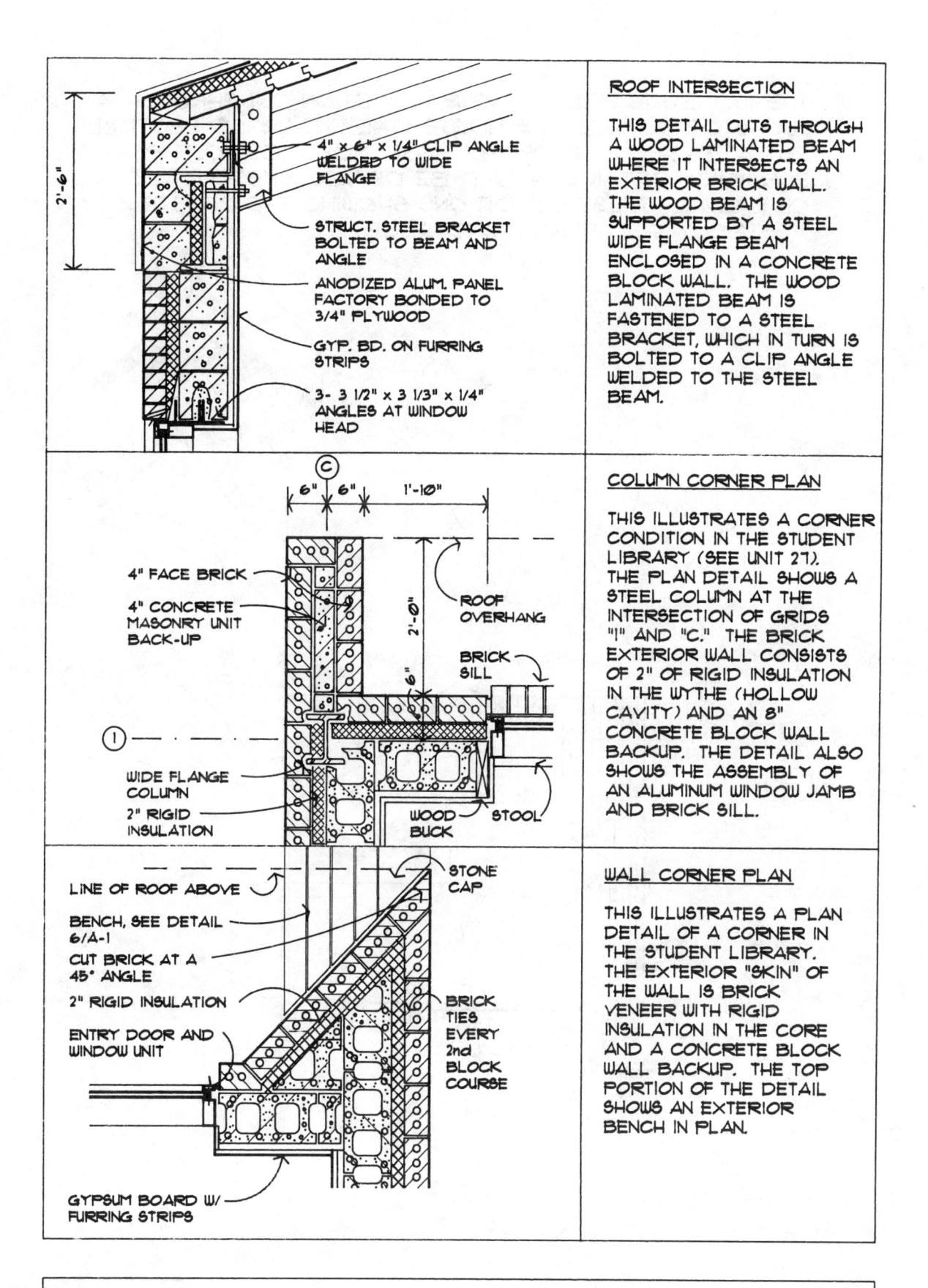

ROOF INTERSECTION

THIS DETAIL CUTS THROUGH A WOOD LAMINATED BEAM WHERE IT INTERSECTS AN EXTERIOR BRICK WALL. THE WOOD BEAM IS SUPPORTED BY A STEEL WIDE FLANGE BEAM ENCLOSED IN A CONCRETE BLOCK WALL. THE WOOD LAMINATED BEAM IS FASTENED TO A STEEL BRACKET, WHICH IN TURN IS BOLTED TO A CLIP ANGLE WELDED TO THE STEEL BEAM.

Labels on drawing:
- 4" x 6" x 1/4" CLIP ANGLE WELDED TO WIDE FLANGE
- STRUCT. STEEL BRACKET BOLTED TO BEAM AND ANGLE
- ANODIZED ALUM. PANEL FACTORY BONDED TO 3/4" PLYWOOD
- GYP. BD. ON FURRING STRIPS
- 3- 3 1/2" x 3 1/3" x 1/4" ANGLES AT WINDOW HEAD
- 2'-6"

COLUMN CORNER PLAN

THIS ILLUSTRATES A CORNER CONDITION IN THE STUDENT LIBRARY (SEE UNIT 27). THE PLAN DETAIL SHOWS A STEEL COLUMN AT THE INTERSECTION OF GRIDS "1" AND "C." THE BRICK EXTERIOR WALL CONSISTS OF 2" OF RIGID INSULATION IN THE WYTHE (HOLLOW CAVITY) AND AN 8" CONCRETE BLOCK WALL BACKUP. THE DETAIL ALSO SHOWS THE ASSEMBLY OF AN ALUMINUM WINDOW JAMB AND BRICK SILL.

Labels on drawing:
- 4" FACE BRICK
- 4" CONCRETE MASONRY UNIT BACK-UP
- WIDE FLANGE COLUMN
- 2" RIGID INSULATION
- ROOF OVERHANG
- BRICK SILL
- WOOD BUCK
- STOOL
- 6", 6", 1'-10"
- 2'-0", 6"

WALL CORNER PLAN

THIS ILLUSTRATES A PLAN DETAIL OF A CORNER IN THE STUDENT LIBRARY. THE EXTERIOR "SKIN" OF THE WALL IS BRICK VENEER WITH RIGID INSULATION IN THE CORE AND A CONCRETE BLOCK WALL BACKUP. THE TOP PORTION OF THE DETAIL SHOWS AN EXTERIOR BENCH IN PLAN.

Labels on drawing:
- LINE OF ROOF ABOVE
- BENCH, SEE DETAIL 6/A-1
- CUT BRICK AT A 45° ANGLE
- 2" RIGID INSULATION
- ENTRY DOOR AND WINDOW UNIT
- STONE CAP
- BRICK TIES EVERY 2nd BLOCK COURSE
- GYPSUM BOARD W/ FURRING STRIPS

DETAIL ASSEMBLY   20-17

REPLAY

1-10. THE ISOMETRIC BELOW SHOWS A SECTION CUT THROUGH A TWO-STORY SPACE IN A HOUSE. THE ENLARGED SECTION CUT AT THE BOTTOM OF THE PAGE INDICATES FOUR POINTS FOR WHICH DETAILS SHOULD BE DRAWN. SKETCH A DETAIL OF EACH OF THESE CONDITIONS SHOWING THE CONSTRUCTION ASSEMBLY OF THE WALL AND ROOF.

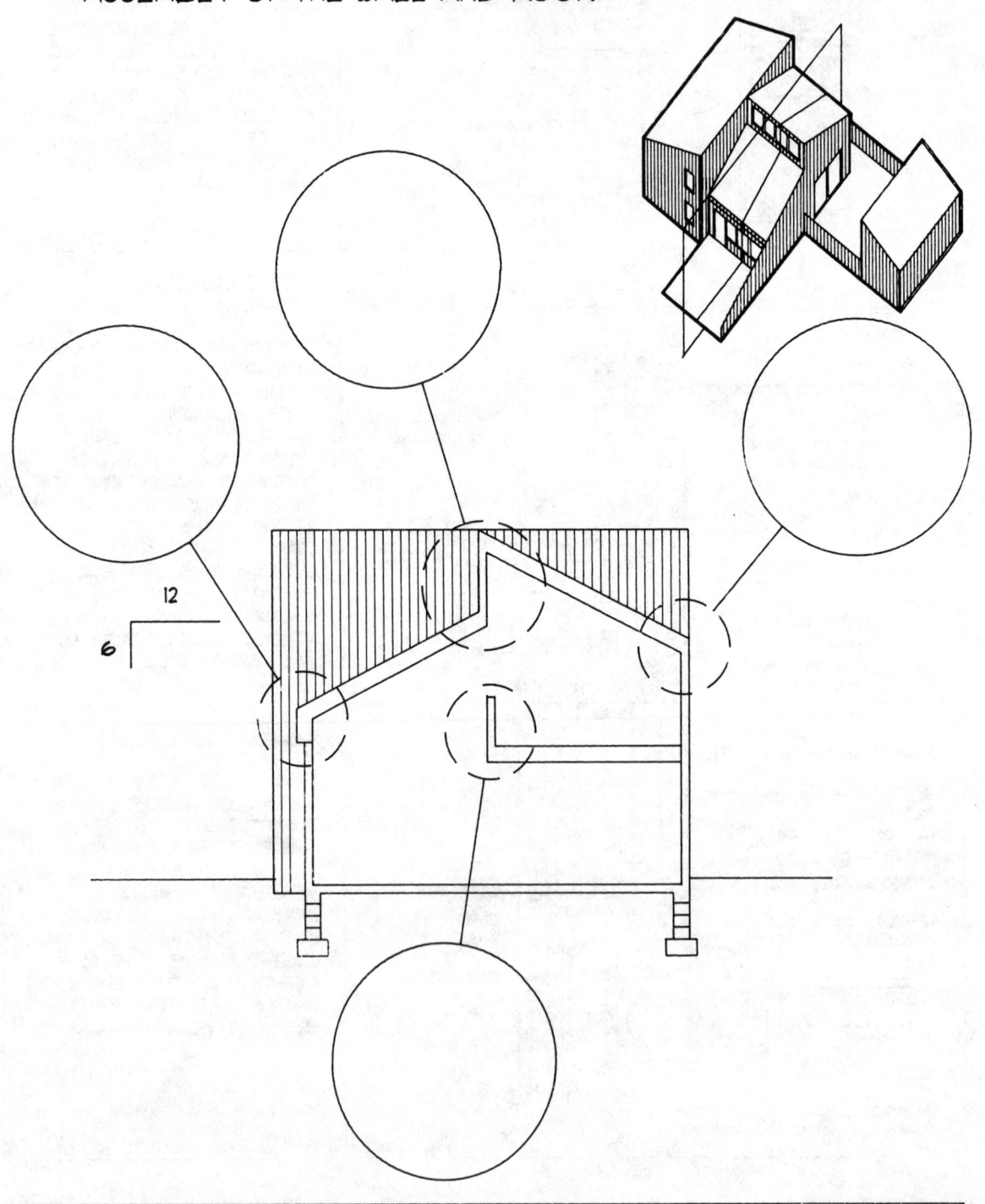

DETAIL ASSEMBLY 20-18

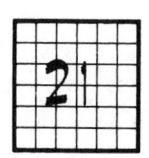

BIRCH LAKE CABIN

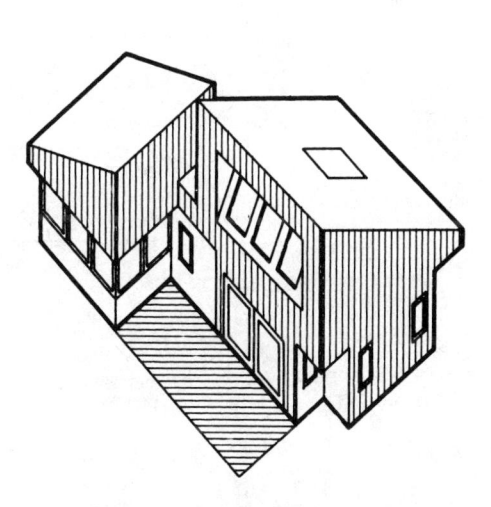

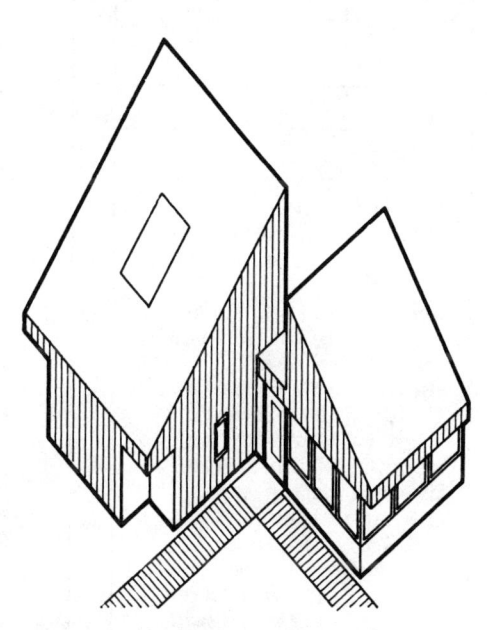

THIS UNIT PRESENTS THE CONSTRUCTION DRAWINGS FOR A SMALL CABIN. THIS BUILDING IS UNUSUAL BECAUSE IT IS SUPPORTED BY EIGHT POSTS SET IN CONCRETE (SIMILAR TO THE WAY A DOCK IS SUPPORTED IN A LAKE SHORE). THE POSTS CARRY THE WEIGHT OF THE FIRST AND SECOND FLOORS PLUS THE WEIGHT OF THE ROOF. THE SPACING FOR POSTS ON EACH BUILDING IS 12'-0" ON CENTER. THE MAIN CABIN SIZE HAS BEEN EXTENDED TO 20'-0" BY ALLOWING THE FLOOR JOISTS TO OVERHANG, OR CANTILEVER, 4'-0" BEYOND THE LINE OF EACH POST. THE FLOOR PLAN IS VERY SIMPLE; THE MAIN CABIN CONSISTS OF A LIVING AREA WITH A SMALL KITCHEN AND BATH. A LADDER CONNECTS THE LIVING AREA TO A 9' x 12" SLEEPING LOFT. THE OPEN TWO-STORY LOFT AND SKYLIGHTS GIVE THE CABIN AN ARCHITECTURAL "VOLUME." THE ATTACHED SCREEN PORCH HAS A TREATED 2" x 4" FLOOR; A 1/4" SPACE BETWEEN THE DECK ALLOWS DRAINAGE. THE CABIN IS INSULATED AND HEATED WITH A WOOD-BURNING STOVE.

BIRCH LAKE CABIN

Site Plan and Floor Plans/A-1

Sheet A-1 contains the site plan, floor plans, and framing plans. The site plan gives the location of roads and the cabin using dimension strings. The first-floor plan shows decks and walks around the building perimeter. Windows are located by dimensioning to the center of the unit; on the plan they are identified by the manufacturer's catalog numbers.

Note that the second-floor plan cuts through the roof and shows the shingles in elevation. The plan blow-up of the front entry shown below illustrates the amount of detail that should be used. The section cut through the building is drawn with a slightly heavier line weight, while a lighter line weight is used for the wood deck and hatching. A door schedule was eliminated by placing door sizes directly on the plan.

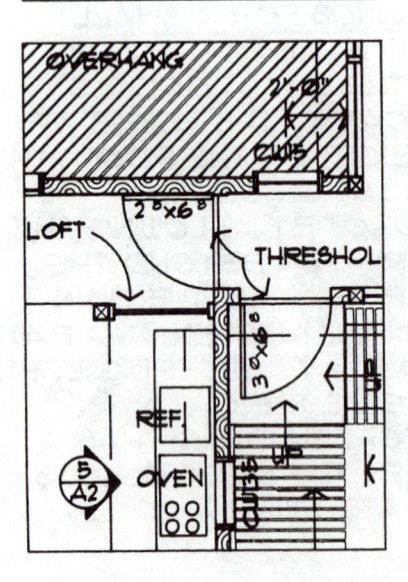

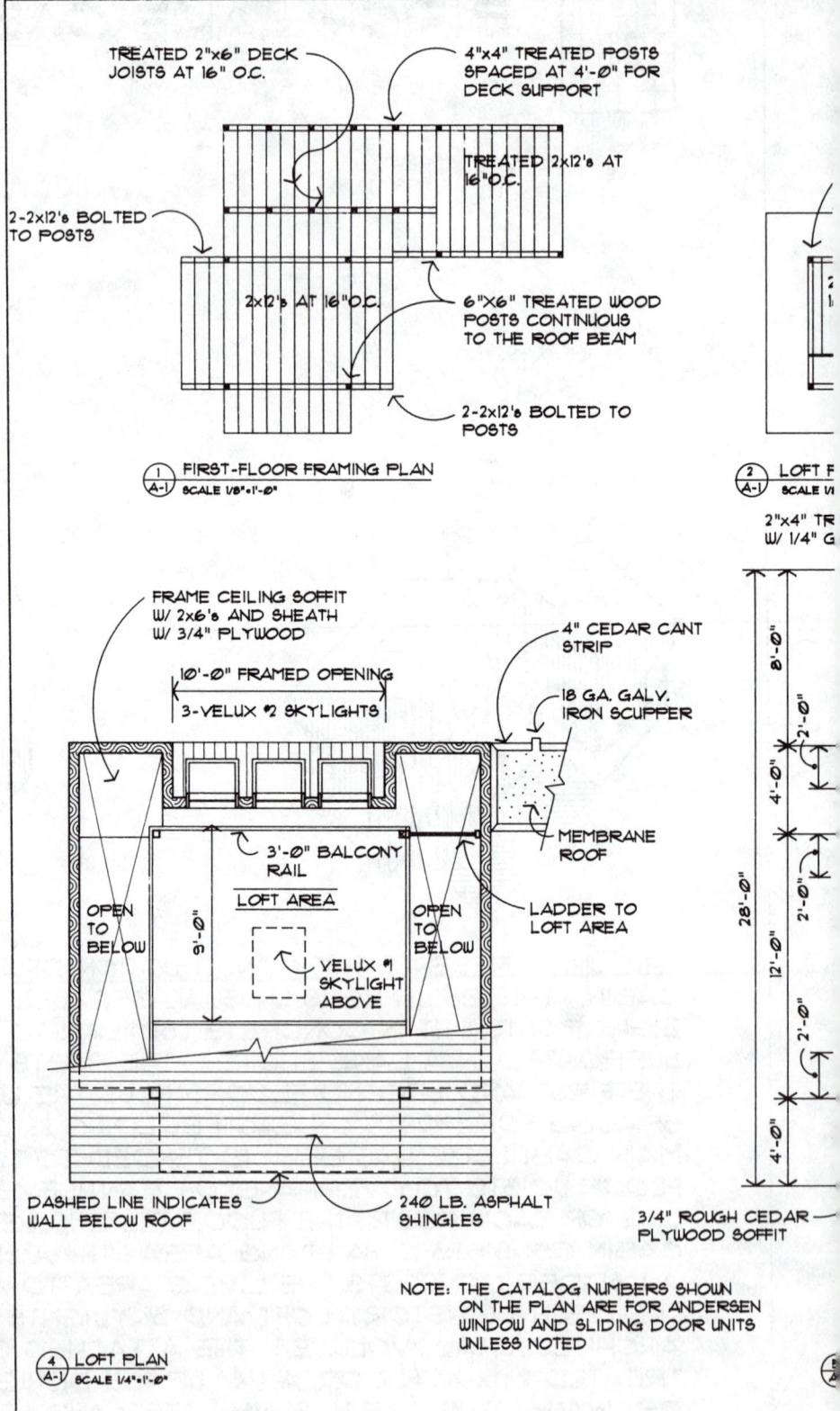

FIRST-FLOOR FRAMING PLAN — 1/A-1, SCALE 1/8"=1'-0"
- TREATED 2"x6" DECK JOISTS AT 16" O.C.
- 4"x4" TREATED POSTS SPACED AT 4'-0" FOR DECK SUPPORT
- TREATED 2x12's AT 16" O.C.
- 2-2x12's BOLTED TO POSTS
- 2x12's AT 16" O.C.
- 6"x6" TREATED WOOD POSTS CONTINUOUS TO THE ROOF BEAM
- 2-2x12's BOLTED TO POSTS

LOFT PLAN — 4/A-1, SCALE 1/4"=1'-0"
- FRAME CEILING SOFFIT W/ 2x6's AND SHEATH W/ 3/4" PLYWOOD
- 4" CEDAR CANT STRIP
- 10'-0" FRAMED OPENING, 3-VELUX #2 SKYLIGHTS
- 18 GA. GALV. IRON SCUPPER
- 3'-0" BALCONY RAIL
- LOFT AREA, 9'-0"
- OPEN TO BELOW
- VELUX #1 SKYLIGHT ABOVE
- MEMBRANE ROOF
- LADDER TO LOFT AREA
- DASHED LINE INDICATES WALL BELOW ROOF
- 240 LB. ASPHALT SHINGLES
- 3/4" ROUGH CEDAR PLYWOOD SOFFIT

NOTE: THE CATALOG NUMBERS SHOWN ON THE PLAN ARE FOR ANDERSEN WINDOW AND SLIDING DOOR UNITS UNLESS NOTED

BIRCH LAKE CABIN 21-2

LOFT FRAMING PLAN
SCALE 1/8" = 1'-0"

- 6"x6" TREATED POSTS
- DOUBLE 2x12's
- 2x6's AT 16" O.C.
- 2-2x12's BOLTED TO 6"x6" POSTS
- DOUBLE 2x12's

SITE PLAN
A-1   SCALE 1"= 40'

BIRCH LAKE ROAD
160'
125'
45'
60'
190'
50'-0"
38, 39, 37, 36, 35
4" GRAVEL DRIVE
2"x4" WOOD WALK
DOCK
BIRCH LAKE
NORTH

FIRST-FLOOR PLAN
A-1   SCALE 1/4" = 1'-0"

- 2"x4" TREATED WOOD DECK W/ 1/4" GAP
- 3'-0" CEDAR HANDRAIL
- LINE OF ROOF OVERHANG
- 6"x6" TREATED WOOD POST
- GALV. INSECT SCREEN W/ 2"x6" REDWOOD FRAME
- **SCREEN PORCH**
- 2"x4" TREATED WOOD DECK W/ 1/4" GAP FOR FLOOR
- 1"x10" CEDAR CAR SIDING WALLS AND CEILING
- LADDER TO LOFT
- THRESHOLD
- LINE OF LOFT ABOVE
- 6"x6" TREATED WOOD POST
- **LIVING AREA**
- WOOD BURNING STOVE (N.I.C.)
- 2'-6"x3'-6" FIBERGLASS SHOWER STALL
- REF
- OVEN
- SNK
- STOR
- BATH
- 2"x4" TREATED WOOD DECK W/ 1/4" GAP
- 2-2"x6" TREATED JOIST DECK FRAMING, SPACE JOISTS AT 3'-0" AND SUPPORT W/ 4"x4" TREATED POSTS AT 5'-0" O.C.
- CEDAR SOFFIT

12'-0" EQUAL EQUAL EQUAL
12'-0" EQUAL EQUAL EQUAL
4'-0" 12'-0" 4'-0"
20'-0"
36'-0"
12'-0"

ASSUMED NORTH
TRUE NORTH

BIRCH LAKE CABIN — SITE PLAN, FLOOR PLANS AND FRAMING PLANS

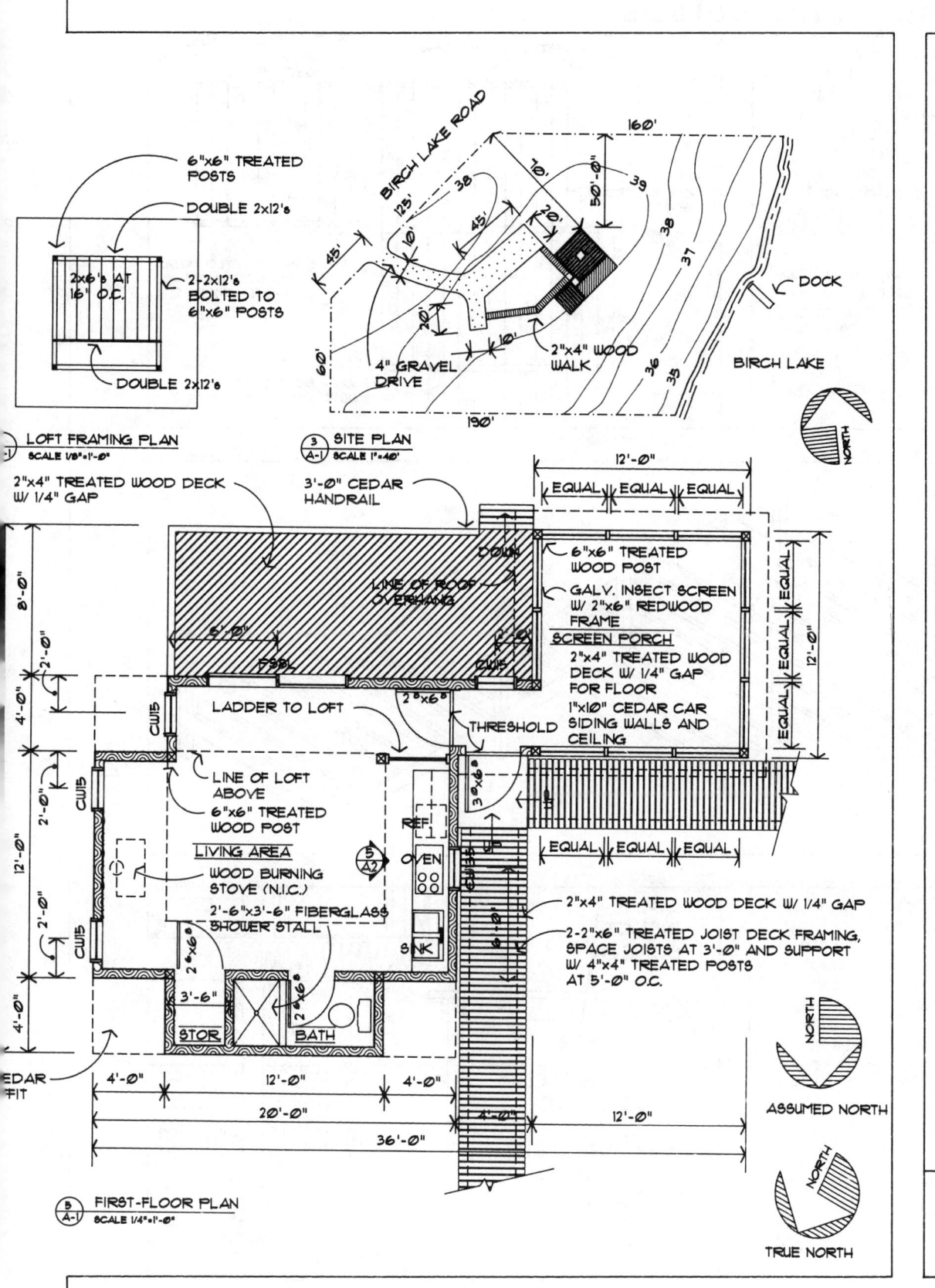

A1

BIRCH LAKE CABIN   21-3

Framing and Details

Structural framing is an integral part of a building design. The construction drawing phase of a project must give the contractor information on the location and size of all structural components. The cabin is unique in that it is structured with eight treated posts (rather than with footings and foundations). The four posts for the main cabin support the first floor, second floor, and roof.

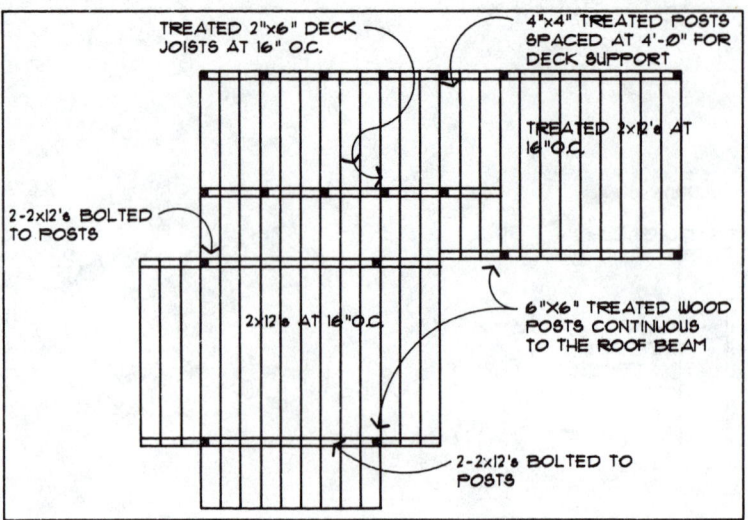

Framing plan detail:
- TREATED 2"x6" DECK JOISTS AT 16" O.C.
- 4"x4" TREATED POSTS SPACED AT 4'-0" FOR DECK SUPPORT
- TREATED 2x12's AT 16" O.C.
- 2-2x12's BOLTED TO POSTS
- 2x12's AT 16" O.C.
- 6"x6" TREATED WOOD POSTS CONTINUOUS TO THE ROOF BEAM
- 2-2x12's BOLTED TO POSTS

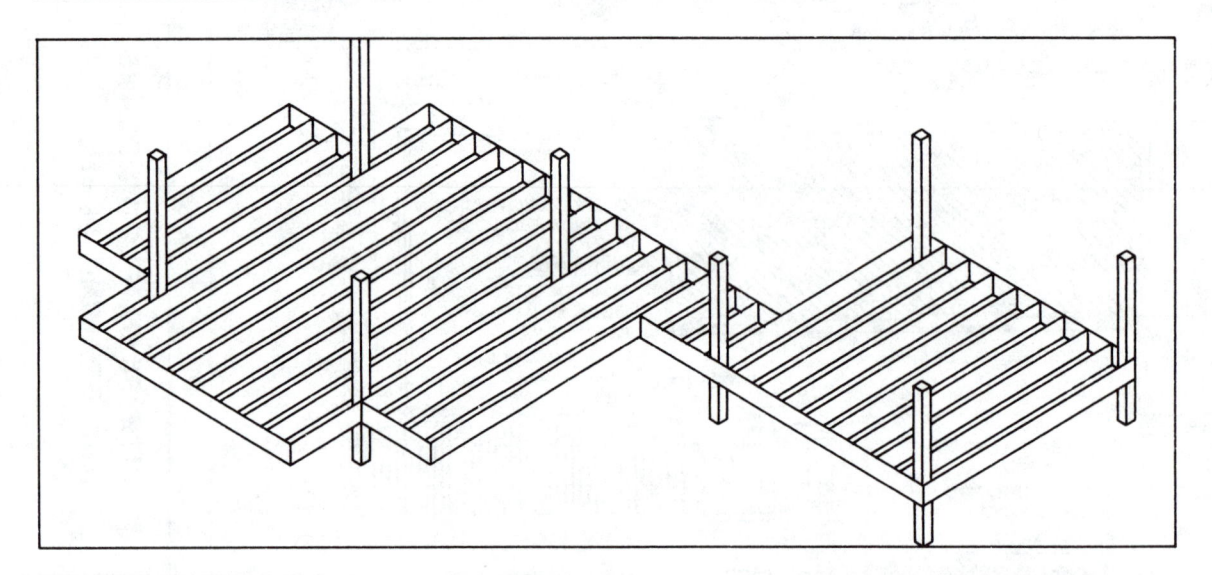

The isometric drawing above shows the first-floor framing. Both the main cabin and screen porch are supported with wood posts spaced at 12'. The cabin differs from the porch, however, in that its joists have an overhang of 4' (this is called a <u>cantilever</u>). The detail at the right shows a portion of the cantilevered floor joists as well as a support post 3'-6" below grade and set in concrete.

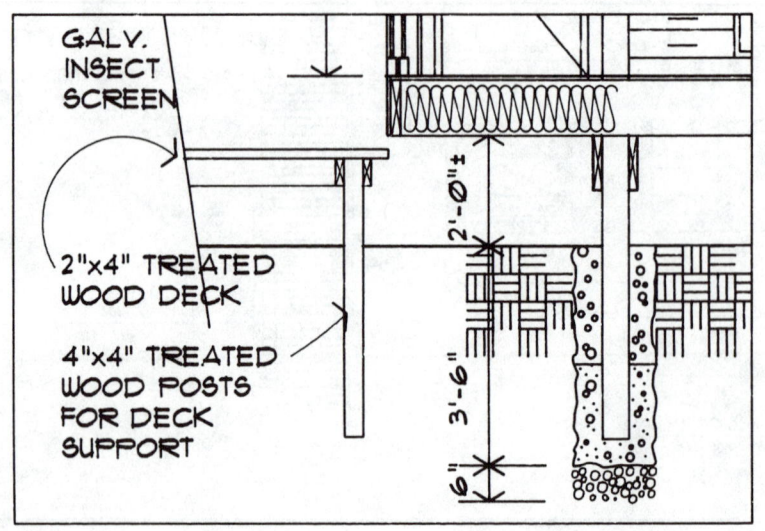

Section detail:
- GALV. INSECT SCREEN
- 2"x4" TREATED WOOD DECK
- 4"x4" TREATED WOOD POSTS FOR DECK SUPPORT
- 2'-0"±
- 3'-6"
- 6"

BIRCH LAKE CABIN   21-4

Framing and Details

The detail at the right shows a blow-up of the roof/skylight detail. Framing for the roof is supplied by 2-2 x 12's that are bolted to the top of the post. The two skylights are framed into the roof and wall using details supplied by the roof window manufacturer. The isometric below shows the same detail with the joists, studs, and headers that are part of the building frame.

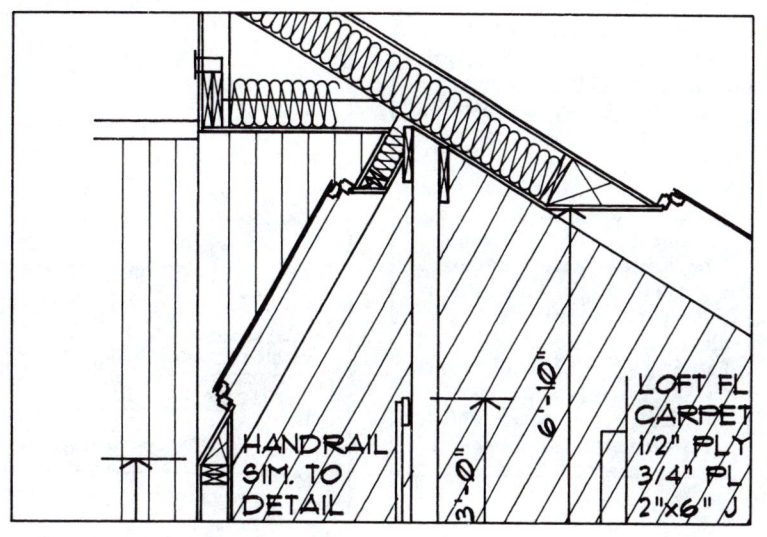

The isometric at the right shows the first-floor joists and roof rafters for the project. A drawing like this is used to study the project during design. The three orthographic framing plans on the construction drawings provide the contractor with the information needed to build the project. Note that the sloped roof skylight is framed by doubling the joists on each side of the opening.

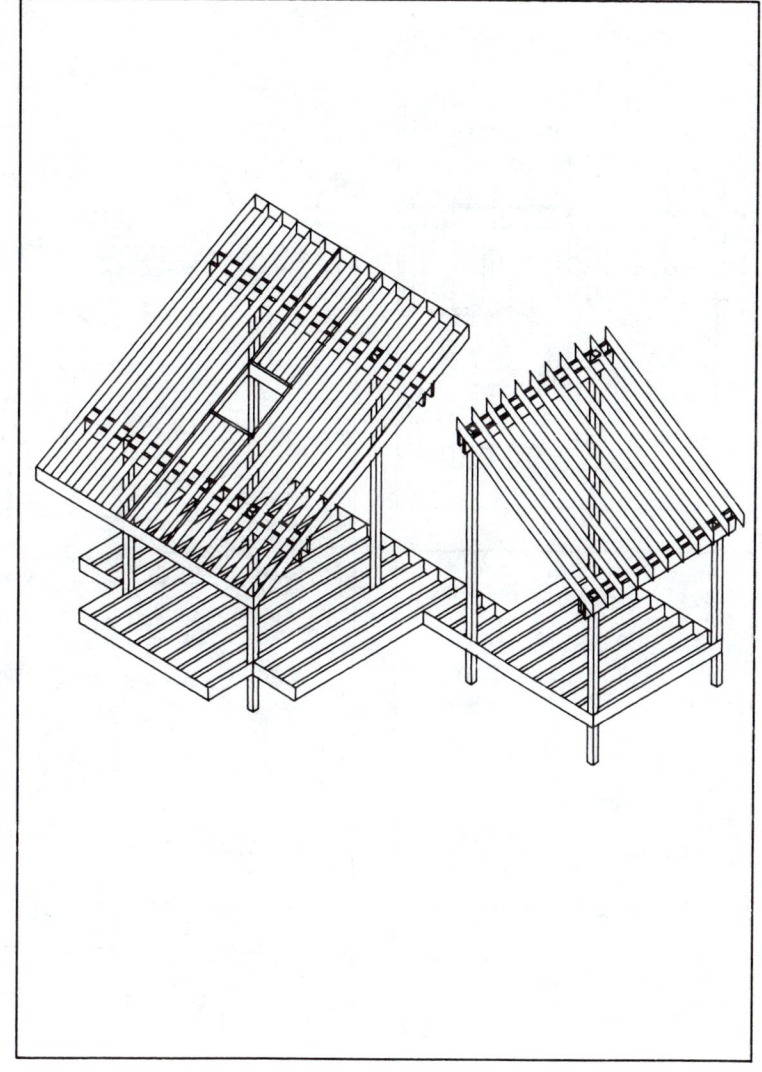

BIRCH LAKE CABIN

Elevations and Building Section/A-2

Sheet A-2 illustrates the exterior elevations and a building section. The sheet layout placed the center of each elevation on an axis along the left side; the section was then positioned to balance the sheet. The section cuts through the main cabin to detail the skylights, roof, and footings. A major reason for drawing a section is to show the connections between walls, floors, and roofs.

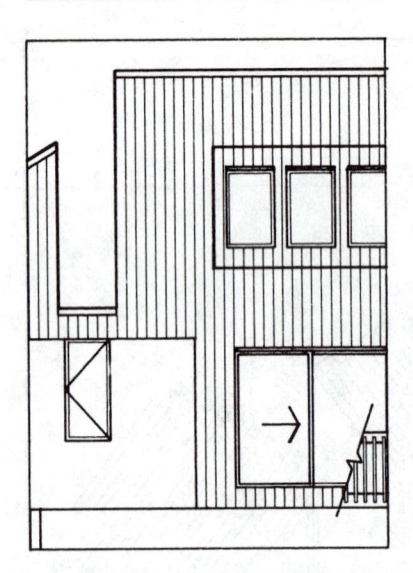

Above is a partial blow-up of an elevation view. On the 1/8" = 1'-0" drawing, window and door frames are drawn with double lines. The cedar siding is drawn using a lighter line weight so it won't "overpower" the major lines on the elevation. A portion of the handrail is detailed, but it was cut to allow the sliding door to be shown. Note that the sloped window appears flat in the elevation view.

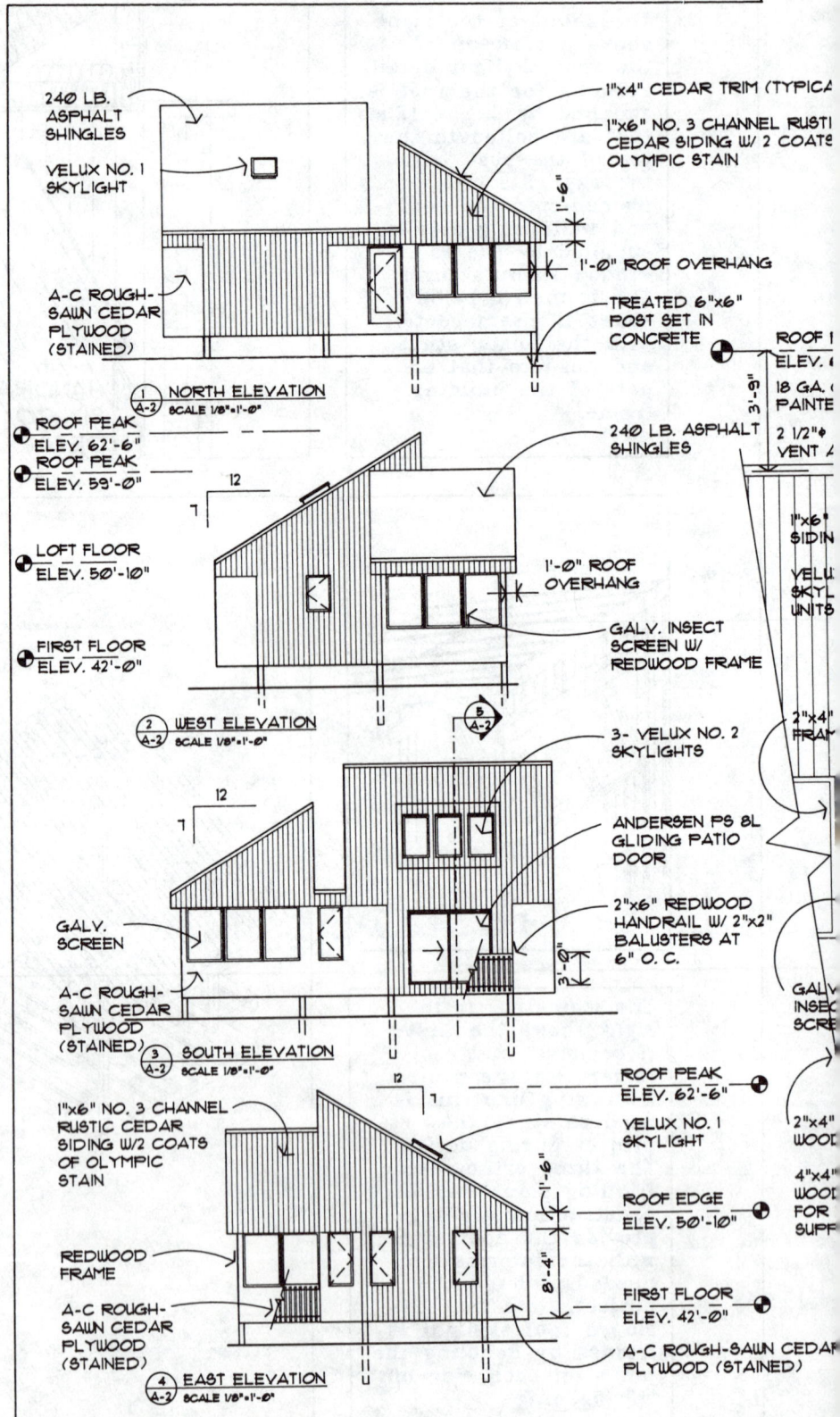

North Elevation (1/A-2, Scale 1/8"=1'-0")
- 240 LB. ASPHALT SHINGLES
- VELUX NO. 1 SKYLIGHT
- A-C ROUGH-SAWN CEDAR PLYWOOD (STAINED)
- 1"x4" CEDAR TRIM (TYPICAL)
- 1"x6" NO. 3 CHANNEL RUSTIC CEDAR SIDING W/ 2 COATS OLYMPIC STAIN
- 1'-0" ROOF OVERHANG
- TREATED 6"x6" POST SET IN CONCRETE

West Elevation (2/A-2, Scale 1/8"=1'-0")
- ROOF PEAK ELEV. 62'-6"
- ROOF PEAK ELEV. 59'-0"
- LOFT FLOOR ELEV. 50'-10"
- FIRST FLOOR ELEV. 42'-0"
- 240 LB. ASPHALT SHINGLES
- 1'-0" ROOF OVERHANG
- GALV. INSECT SCREEN W/ REDWOOD FRAME

South Elevation (3/A-2, Scale 1/8"=1'-0")
- 3- VELUX NO. 2 SKYLIGHTS
- ANDERSEN PS 8L GLIDING PATIO DOOR
- 2"x6" REDWOOD HANDRAIL W/ 2"x2" BALUSTERS AT 6" O.C.
- GALV. SCREEN
- A-C ROUGH-SAWN CEDAR PLYWOOD (STAINED)

East Elevation (4/A-2, Scale 1/8"=1'-0")
- 1"x6" NO. 3 CHANNEL RUSTIC CEDAR SIDING W/2 COATS OF OLYMPIC STAIN
- REDWOOD FRAME
- A-C ROUGH-SAWN CEDAR PLYWOOD (STAINED)
- ROOF PEAK ELEV. 62'-6"
- VELUX NO. 1 SKYLIGHT
- ROOF EDGE ELEV. 50'-10"
- FIRST FLOOR ELEV. 42'-0"
- A-C ROUGH-SAWN CEDAR PLYWOOD (STAINED)

Building Section callouts:
- ROOF ELEV.
- 18 GA. PAINTED
- 2 1/2"Ø VENT
- 1"x6" SIDING
- VELUX SKYLIGHT UNITS
- 2"x4" FRAMING
- GALV. INSECT SCREEN
- 2"x4" WOOD
- 4"x4" WOOD FOR SUPPORT

BIRCH LAKE CABIN

21-6

BIRCH LAKE CABIN — ELEVATIONS AND BUILDING SECTION

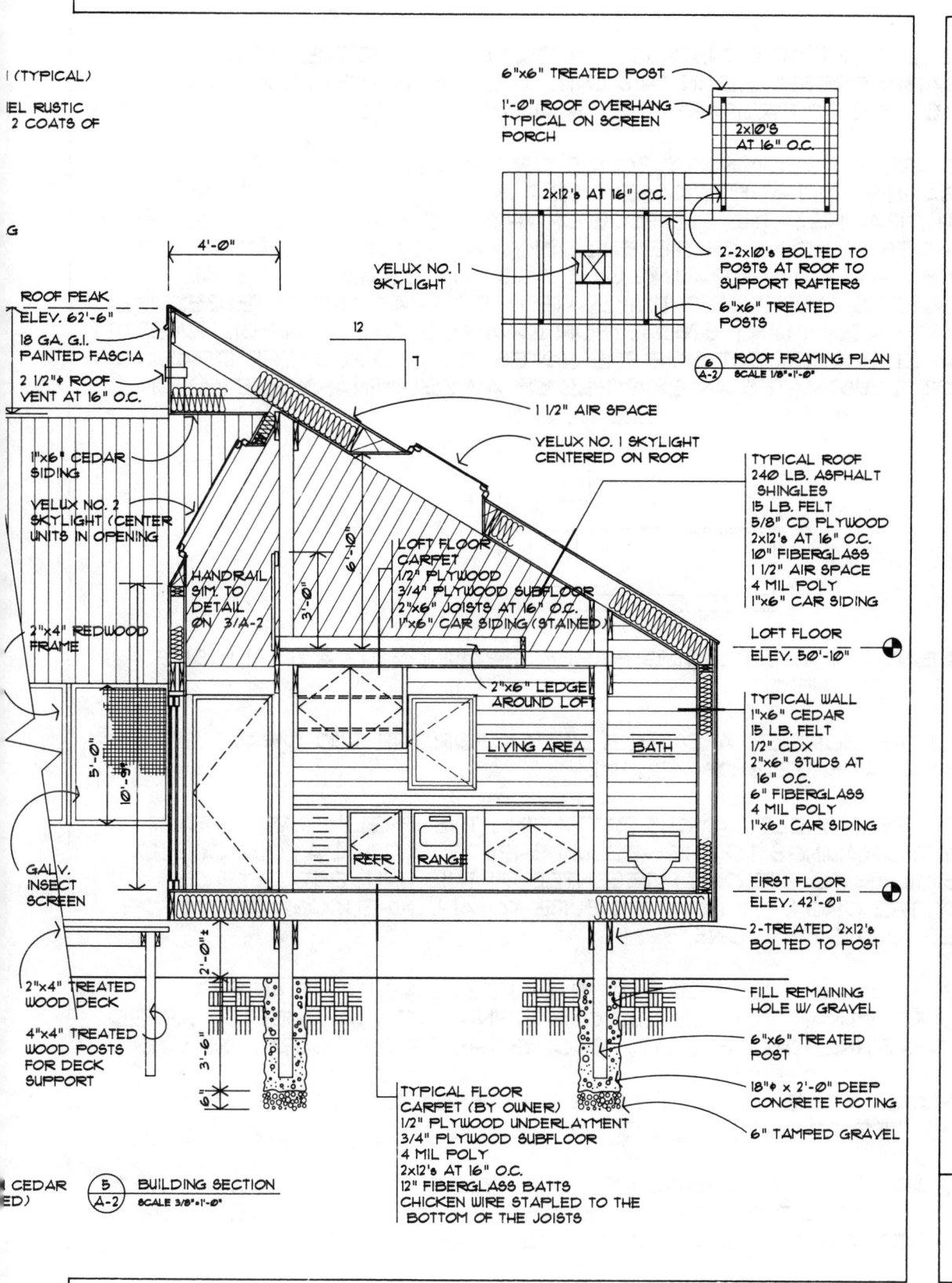

Roof Framing Plan (6/A-2, Scale 1/8"=1'-0")

- 6"x6" TREATED POST
- 1'-0" ROOF OVERHANG TYPICAL ON SCREEN PORCH
- 2x10'S AT 16" O.C.
- 2x12's AT 16" O.C.
- VELUX NO. 1 SKYLIGHT
- 2-2x10's BOLTED TO POSTS AT ROOF TO SUPPORT RAFTERS
- 6"x6" TREATED POSTS

Building Section (5/A-2, Scale 3/8"=1'-0")

- (TYPICAL)
- IEL RUSTIC 2 COATS OF
- ROOF PEAK ELEV. 62'-6"
- 18 GA. G.I. PAINTED FASCIA
- 2 1/2" Ø ROOF VENT AT 16" O.C.
- 4'-0"
- 1"x6" CEDAR SIDING
- VELUX NO. 2 SKYLIGHT (CENTER UNITS IN OPENING)
- 2"x4" REDWOOD FRAME
- GALV. INSECT SCREEN
- 2"x4" TREATED WOOD DECK
- 4"x4" TREATED WOOD POSTS FOR DECK SUPPORT
- CEDAR ED)
- 1 1/2" AIR SPACE
- VELUX NO. 1 SKYLIGHT CENTERED ON ROOF
- HANDRAIL SIM. TO DETAIL ON 3/A-2
- LOFT FLOOR CARPET / 1/2" PLYWOOD / 3/4" PLYWOOD SUBFLOOR / 2"x6" JOISTS AT 16" O.C. / 1"x6" CAR SIDING (STAINED)
- 2"x6" LEDGE AROUND LOFT
- LIVING AREA
- BATH
- REFR
- RANGE
- TYPICAL ROOF: 240 LB. ASPHALT SHINGLES / 15 LB. FELT / 5/8" CD PLYWOOD / 2x12's AT 16" O.C. / 10" FIBERGLASS / 1 1/2" AIR SPACE / 4 MIL POLY / 1"x6" CAR SIDING
- LOFT FLOOR ELEV. 50'-10"
- TYPICAL WALL: 1"x6" CEDAR / 15 LB. FELT / 1/2" CDX / 2"x6" STUDS AT 16" O.C. / 6" FIBERGLASS / 4 MIL POLY / 1"x6" CAR SIDING
- FIRST FLOOR ELEV. 42'-0"
- 2-TREATED 2x12's BOLTED TO POST
- FILL REMAINING HOLE W/ GRAVEL
- 6"x6" TREATED POST
- 18"Ø x 2'-0" DEEP CONCRETE FOOTING
- 6" TAMPED GRAVEL
- TYPICAL FLOOR: CARPET (BY OWNER) / 1/2" PLYWOOD UNDERLAYMENT / 3/4" PLYWOOD SUBFLOOR / 4 MIL POLY / 2x12's AT 16" O.C. / 12" FIBERGLASS BATTS / CHICKEN WIRE STAPLED TO THE BOTTOM OF THE JOISTS

A2

BIRCH LAKE CABIN   21-7

REPLAY

ASSEMBLE A SET OF CONSTRUCTION DRAWINGS FOR THE BIRCH LAKE CABIN PRESENTED IN THIS UNIT. USE THE INSTRUCTIONS LISTED BELOW TO PREPARE THE DRAWING PACKAGE.

1. PREPARE A PRELIMINARY SCALE DRAWING FOR EACH OF THE 11 DRAWINGS IN THE PACKAGE (USE THE SCALE NOTED BELOW EACH DRAWING). THE PURPOSE OF THIS EXERCISE IS (1) TO GAIN AN UNDERSTANDING OF THE BUILDING, AND (2) TO DETERMINE THE SPACE THAT EACH DRAWING WILL OCCUPY. DRAW THE DETAILS ON TRACING PAPER AND ELIMINATE LINES THAT AREN'T "ESSENTIAL" TO THE PRELIMINARY STUDY. (FOR EXAMPLE, DRAW THE SILHOUETTE OF AN ELEVATION BUT SKIP THE NOTES AND SIDING.) THE DRAWING BELOW ILLUSTRATES AN EXAMPLE OF A PRELIMINARY ELEVATION.

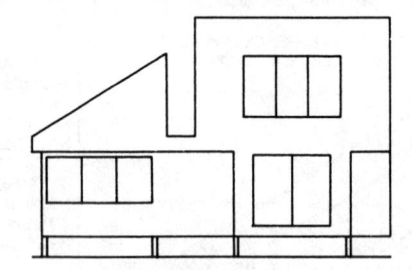

2. TRIM EACH OF THE TRACING PAPER DRAWINGS TO A SMALL SIZE AND LABEL THEM.

3. DRAW THE BORDER AND TITLE BLOCK FOR THE TWO DRAWINGS ON 18" x 24" SHEETS OF VELLUM.

4. PREPARE A SHEET LAYOUT BY TAPING THE PRELIMINARY TRACING PAPER DRAWINGS TO THE VELLUM SHEETS. YOUR LAYOUT COULD BE SIMILAR TO THE ONE PRESENTED IN THIS UNIT, BUT TRY TO VARY THE ORGANIZATION. BE SURE TO ALLOW ENOUGH ROOM FOR NOTES AND DIMENSIONS.

5. ONCE YOU ARE SATISFIED WITH THE SHEET LAYOUT, TRANSFER THE PRELIMINARY DRAWINGS TO THE FINAL VELLUM SHEETS. SPEED THE DRAFTING PROCESS BY TRACING THE PRELIMINARY DRAWING.

6. PREPARE A TIME SCHEDULE FOR THE ASSEMBLY OF THE DRAWING SET (REFER TO UNIT 11, "PROBLEM SOLVING").

7. PREPARE A SET OF PRINTS OF YOUR PROJECT AT APPROXIMATELY 50% AND 75% COMPLETION. USE A FELT-TIP PEN TO MAKE CORRECTIONS AND CHANGES IN YOUR WORK.

| BIRCH LAKE CABIN | 21-8 |

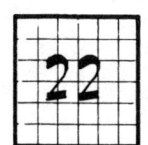

22 12/12 PITCH ROOF HOUSE

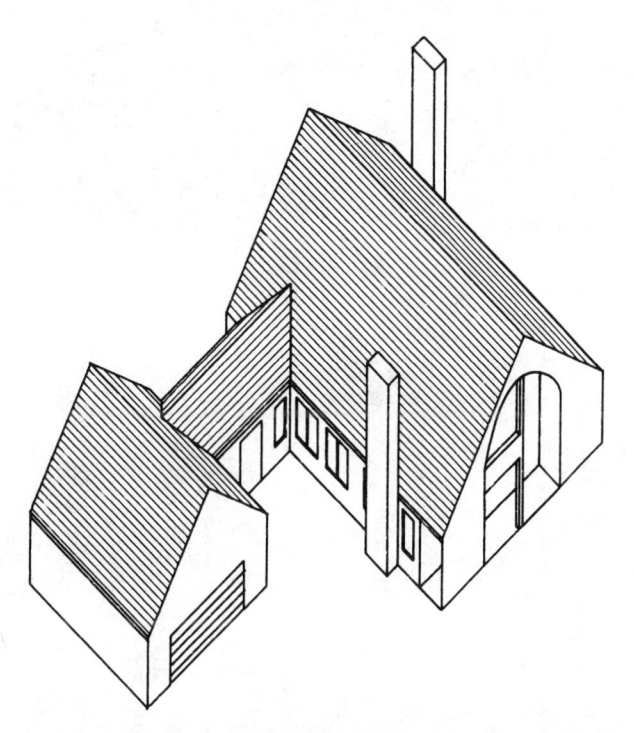

THIS UNIT EXAMINES THE CONSTRUCTION DRAWINGS FOR A THREE-BEDROOM HOUSE. UNIQUE FEATURES OF THIS PROJECT INCLUDE VAULTED CEILINGS IN THE DINING ROOM AND BEDROOMS AND TWO CIRCLE-TOP WINDOWS. THE HOUSE AND GARAGE HAVE 12/12 PITCH ROOFS (A 45° ANGLE) THAT COMBINE WITH THE HALF-ROUND ARC OVER THE FRONT DOOR TO FORM A GEOMETRIC HOUSE DESIGN. THE MAIN PORTION OF THE HOUSE USES "I"-SHAPED PLYWOOD ROOF RAFTERS THAT SPAN FROM THE RIDGE TO THE EXTERIOR WALL. THE FLOOR JOISTS ACT AS THE THIRD LEG OF A TRIANGLE TO MAKE THE ROOF A RIGID STRUCTURE. THE GARAGE AND CONNECTING LINK USE PRE-ENGINEERED TRUSSES FOR ROOF SUPPORT. THE ENTIRE BUILDING USES A CONCRETE SLAB-ON-GRADE FOR THE FIRST FLOOR. FOUNDATION WALLS ON THE HOUSE HAVE 3" RIGID INSULATION AROUND THE PERIMETER TO REDUCE HEAT LOSS. THE EXTERIOR "SKIN" ON THE HOUSE IS STUCCO APPLIED TO PLYWOOD SHEATHING.

12/12 PITCH ROOF HOUSE

Site Plan/A-1

This project is located on a large (3 1/2 acre) site. The plan shows the legal description, property dimensions, and topography. Contours 971' and 972' have been cut slightly into the hill to provide a flat plateau for the house. Note that the center line of the road is dimensioned from the property corner. The house is located with dimension strings from the south and west property corners.

An enlarged portion of the site plan is shown below. The house is detailed with closely spaced parallel lines in the direction of the shingles. This was done to "highlight" the building on the site. Walks and roads (defined with a dot pattern) are located with dimension strings. The brick patio, dimensioned on this plan, is also drawn and noted on the floor plan.

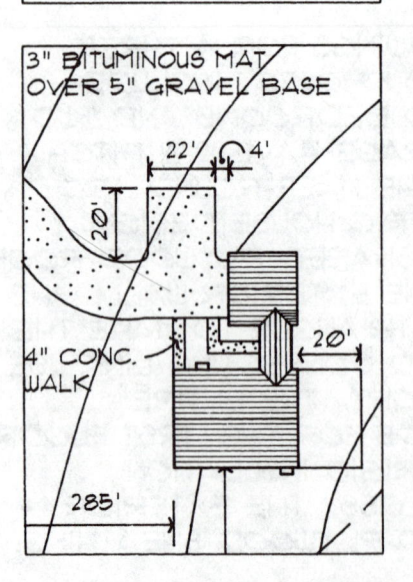

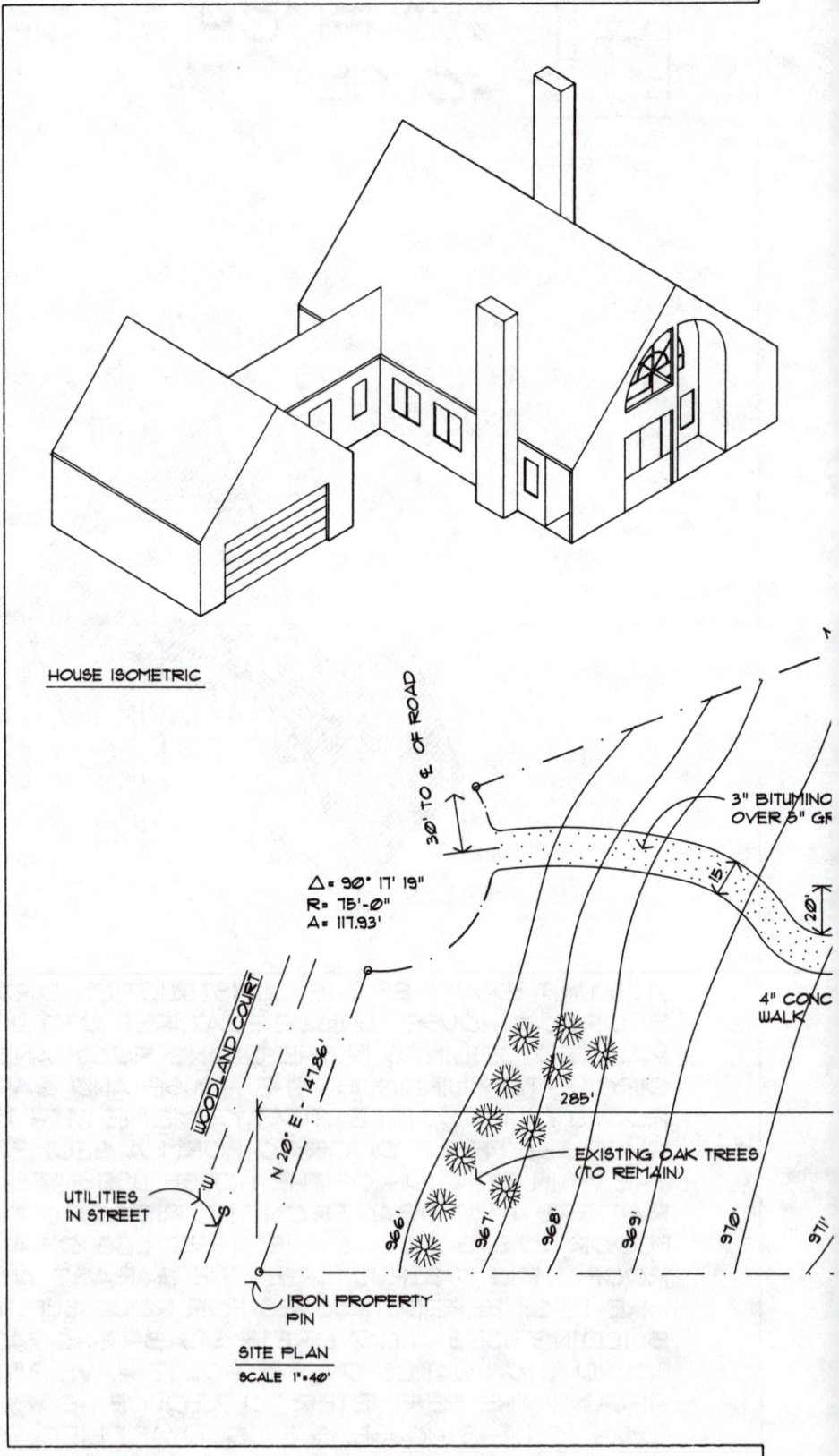

HOUSE ISOMETRIC

Δ = 90° 17' 19"
R = 75'-0"
A = 117.93'

SITE PLAN
SCALE 1" = 40'

12/12 PITCH ROOF HOUSE   22-2

12/12 PITCH ROOF HOUSE
SHEET INDEX

SHEET	DRAWING
A-1	SITE PLAN
A-2	FIRST-FLOOR PLAN AND FRAMING
A-3	SECOND-FLOOR PLAN AND FRAMING
A-4	ELEVATIONS
A-5	BUILDING SECTIONS

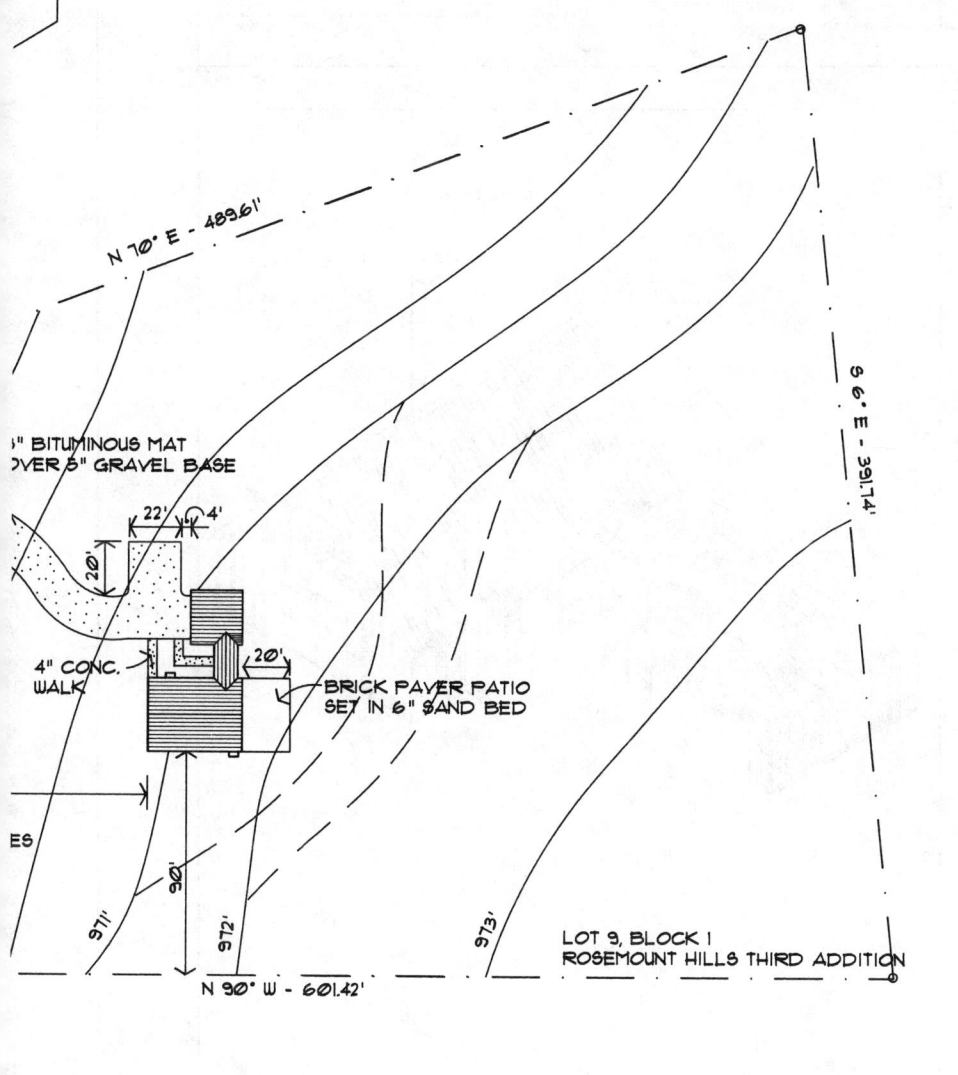

N 70° E - 489.61'

S 6° E - 391.74'

5" BITUMINOUS MAT OVER 6" GRAVEL BASE

22' 4'
20'
20'

4" CONC. WALK

BRICK PAVER PATIO SET IN 6" SAND BED

90'

97.1' 97.2' 97.3'

LOT 9, BLOCK 1
ROSEMOUNT HILLS THIRD ADDITION

N 90° W - 601.42'

NORTH

12/12 PITCH ROOF HOUSE — SITE PLAN

A1

12/12 PITCH ROOF HOUSE

22-3

Framing and Details

The structural framing used on the project is illustrated on this page. The drawing to the right defines the size and spacing for wood roof joists and trusses. The two drawings below show the framing used to install the half-round windows on the end elevations. The architectural package typically wouldn't contain the window framing shown below, however, since these decisions would be left to the contractor.

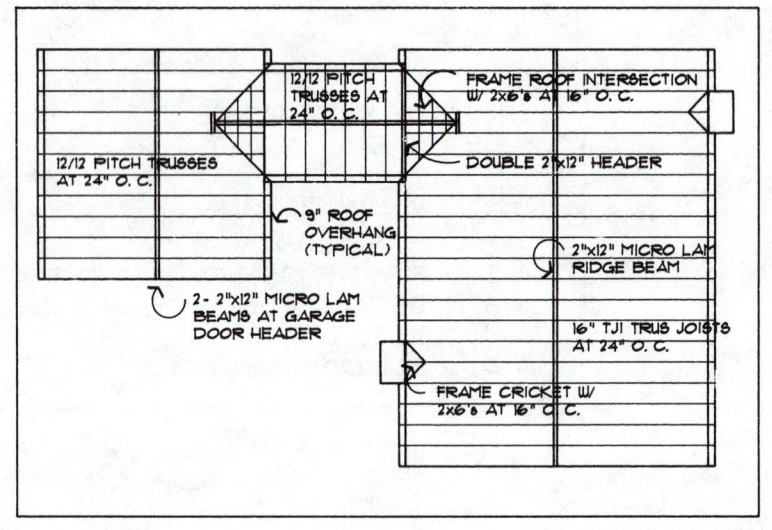

- 12/12 PITCH TRUSSES AT 24" O.C.
- 12/12 PITCH TRUSSES AT 24" O.C.
- FRAME ROOF INTERSECTION W/ 2x6's AT 16" O.C.
- DOUBLE 2"x12" HEADER
- 9" ROOF OVERHANG (TYPICAL)
- 2"x12" MICRO LAM RIDGE BEAM
- 2 - 2"x12" MICRO LAM BEAMS AT GARAGE DOOR HEADER
- 16" TJI TRUS JOISTS AT 24" O.C.
- FRAME CRICKET W/ 2x6's AT 16" O.C.

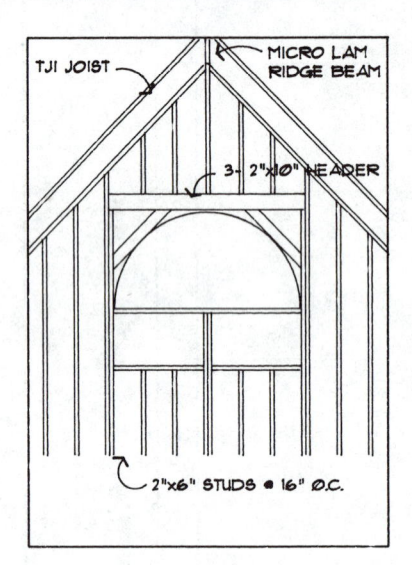

- TJI JOIST
- MICRO LAM RIDGE BEAM
- 3 - 2"x10" HEADER
- 2"x6" STUDS @ 16" O.C.

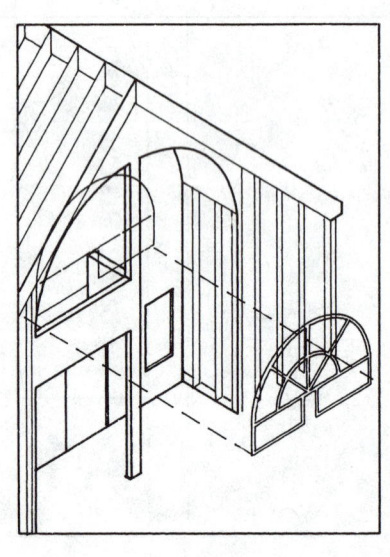

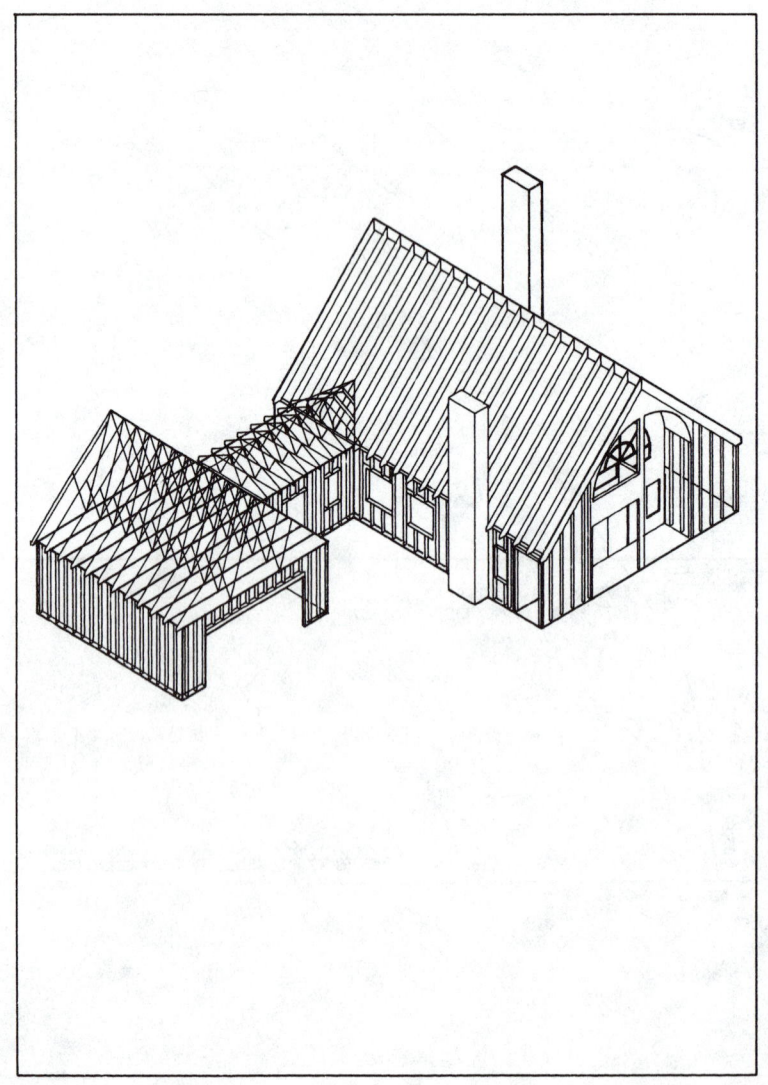

12/12 PITCH ROOF HOUSE 22-4

Framing and Details

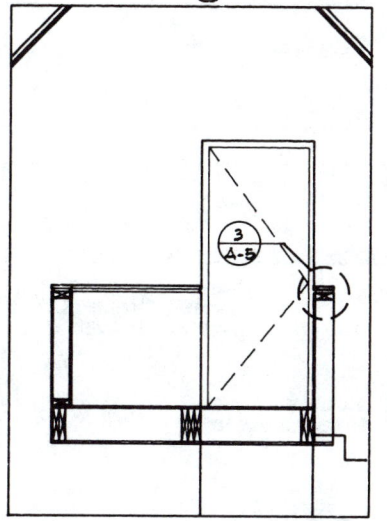

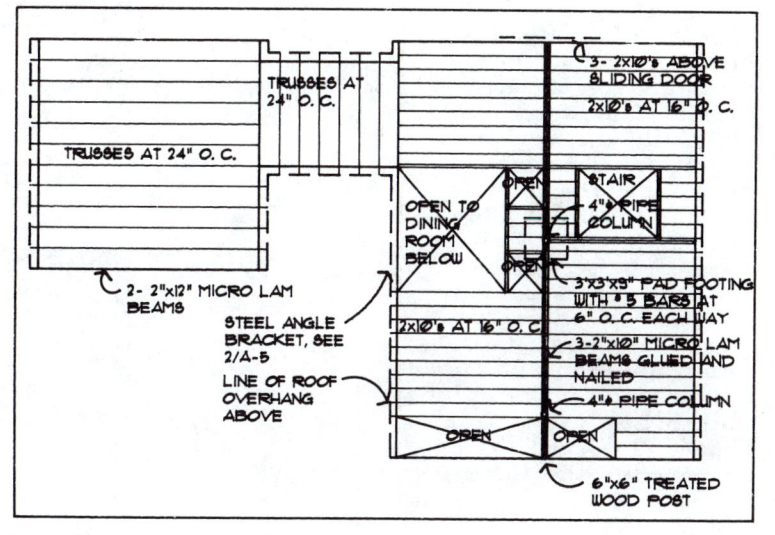

The drawings on this page show second-floor framing details. The plan at the upper right defines the structural members used to support the floor. The X's at the stair, entry, and dining room indicate that these areas are open to the first floor (and are not framed). The dashed square in the center of the house indicates a pad footing used to support a column. The detail above shows a balcony section cut.

The isometric view at the right shows a cut-away drawing of the second-floor balcony and stair. The detail shows TJI roof joists spanning from the ridge beam to the outside load-bearing wall. The balcony is supported by a beam that is tied to double floor joists at both bedrooms. Floor joists span from the exterior wall to a micro lam beam that runs along the center axis of the house.

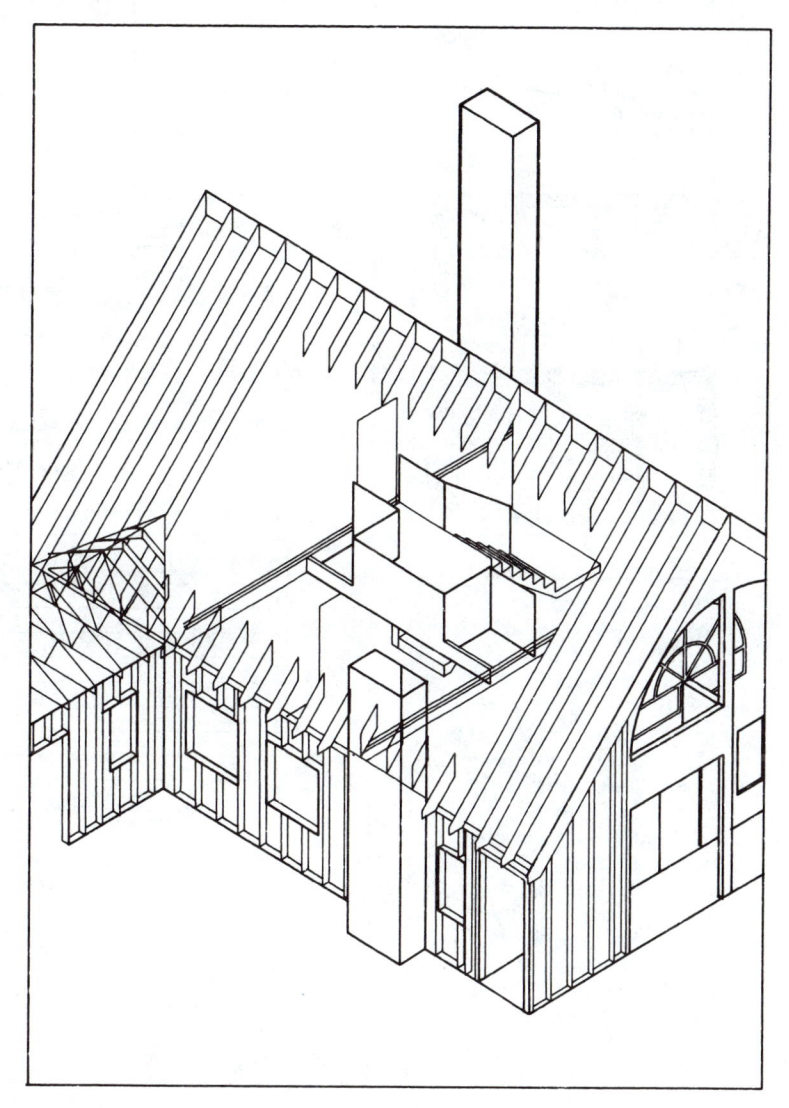

12/12 PITCH ROOF HOUSE   22-5

First-Floor Plan/A-2

Sheet A-2 contains the first-floor plan and framing for the house. Floor plans are typically the beginning point for construction drawings. The drawing below illustrates the three "layers" of a project (discussed in Unit 6). Layer one consists of the actual drawing—doors, stairs, windows, etc.; notes and dimensions make up the other two layers. This sheet is a good example of making the three layers "fit."

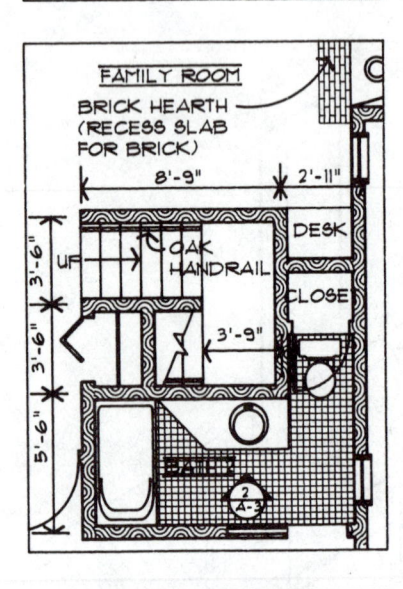

Above is shown an enlarged portion of the floor plan, illustrating the amount of detail to use on a 1/4" = 1'-0" drawing. The walls are drawn with a slightly darker line weight to indicate the section plane cut. Lighter lines illustrate the ceramic tile in the bath, and crosshatching is used for wood stud walls. Window frames are drawn with double lines to indicate jamb widths.

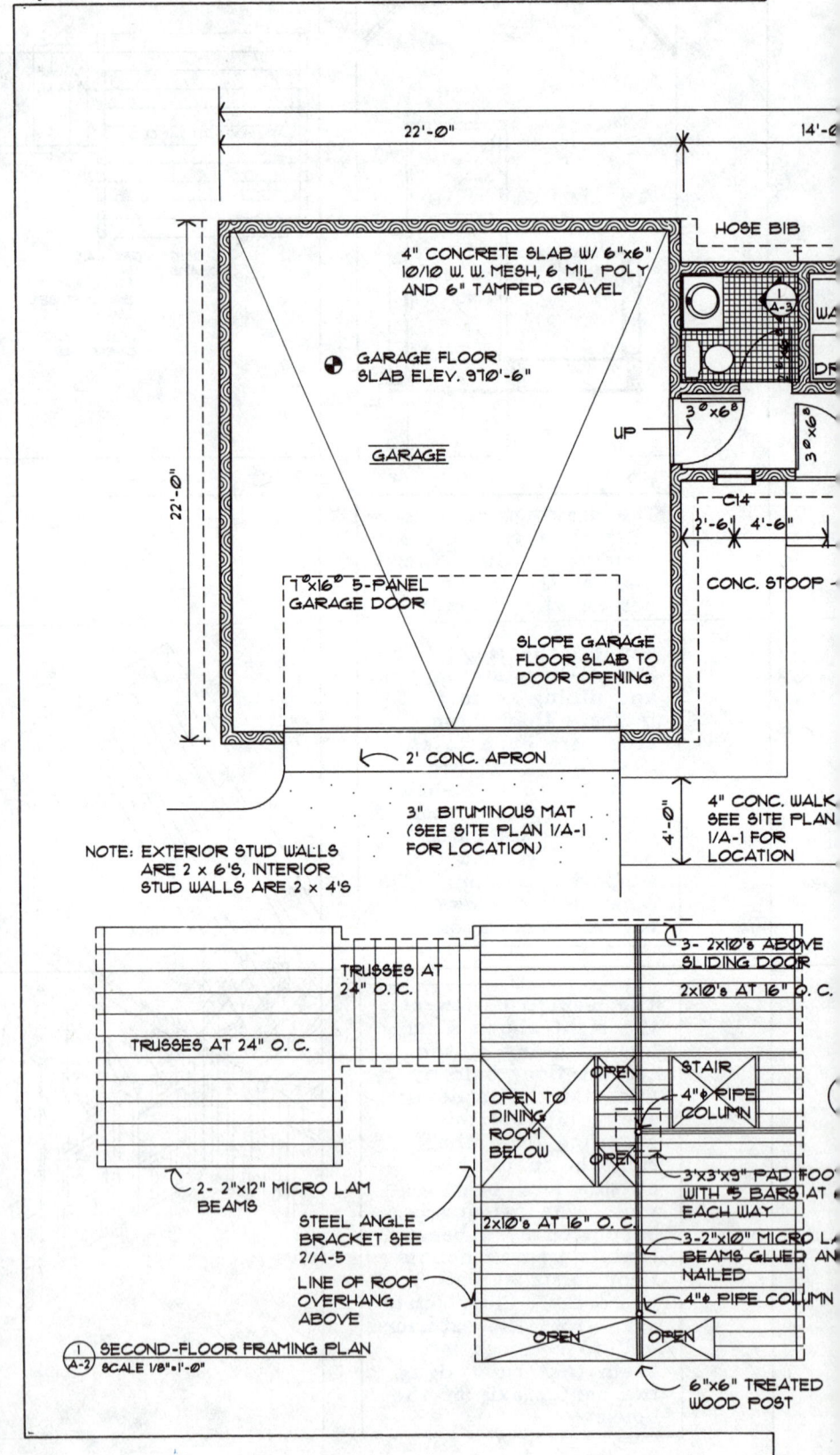

12/12 PITCH ROOF HOUSE   22-6

12/12 PITCH ROOF HOUSE — FIRST-FLOOR PLAN AND FRAMING

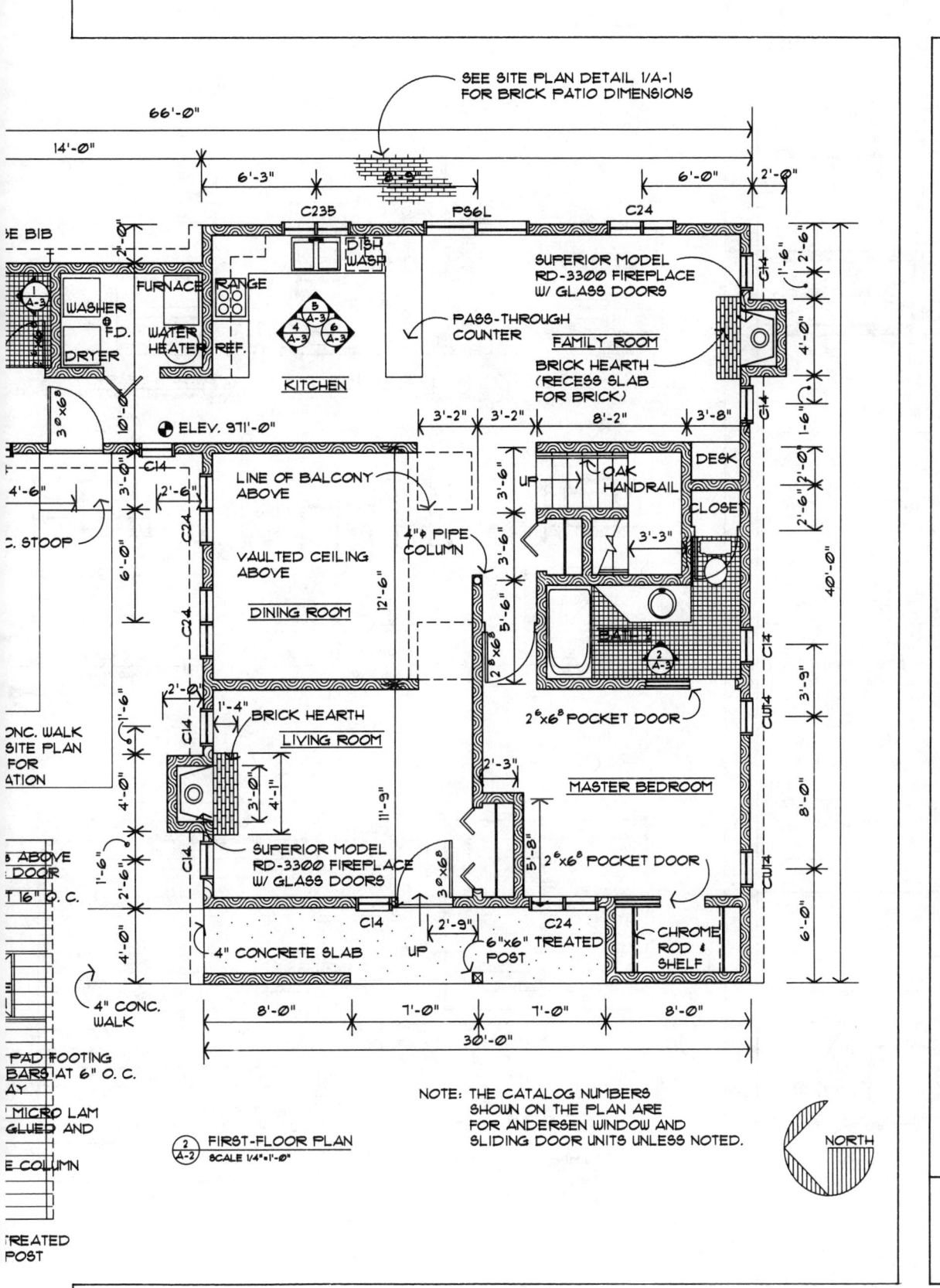

Sheet A2

12/12 PITCH ROOF HOUSE — 22-7

Note: The catalog numbers shown on the plan are for Andersen window and sliding door units unless noted.

Rooms and features labeled on plan:
- Kitchen (with Furnace, Water Heater, Range, Ref., Dish Wash)
- Washer/Dryer, F.D.
- Family Room — Superior Model RD-3300 Fireplace w/ Glass Doors, Brick Hearth (Recess Slab for Brick), Pass-Through Counter
- Dining Room — Line of Balcony Above, Vaulted Ceiling Above, 4"⌀ Pipe Column
- Living Room — Brick Hearth, Superior Model RD-3300 Fireplace w/ Glass Doors
- Bath — Oak Handrail, Desk, Closet, 2⁶×6⁸ Pocket Door
- Master Bedroom — 2⁶×6⁸ Pocket Door, Chrome Rod & Shelf
- Conc. Stoop, Conc. Walk, 4" Concrete Slab, 4" Conc. Walk
- 6"×6" Treated Post
- Elev. 971'-0"
- See Site Plan Detail 1/A-1 for Brick Patio Dimensions

Key dimensions: 66'-0" overall width; 40'-0" overall depth; 30'-0", 14'-0", 8'-0", 7'-0", 6'-3", 6'-0", etc.

Window/door callouts: C235, PS6L, C24, C14, CW14

First-Floor Plan — Scale 1/4" = 1'-0" (2/A-2)

NORTH arrow indicated.

Second-Floor Plan/A-3

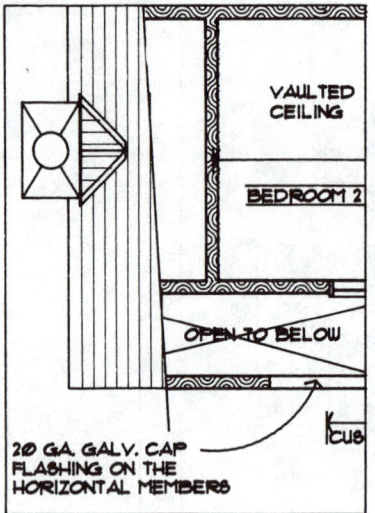

VAULTED CEILING

BEDROOM 2

OPEN TO BELOW

20 GA. GALV. CAP FLASHING ON THE HORIZONTAL MEMBERS

Sheet A-3 contains the second-floor plan, roof framing, and cabinet elevations. The floor plans and framing plans have been placed in identical positions on sheets A-2 and A-3 to improve sheet layout. Note that the second-floor section cut plane shows the roof shingles in elevation below the cut. The drawings above and below show portions of the plan and cabinet elevation and illustrate the amount of drafting detail to use.

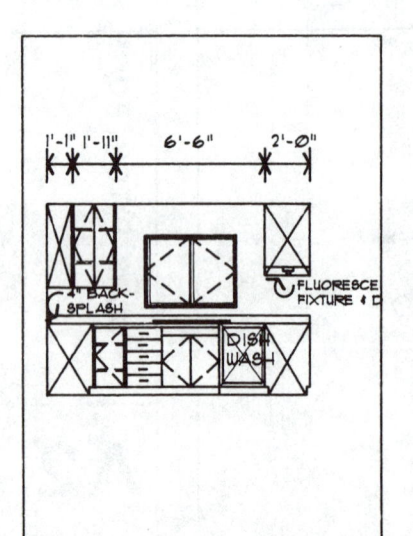

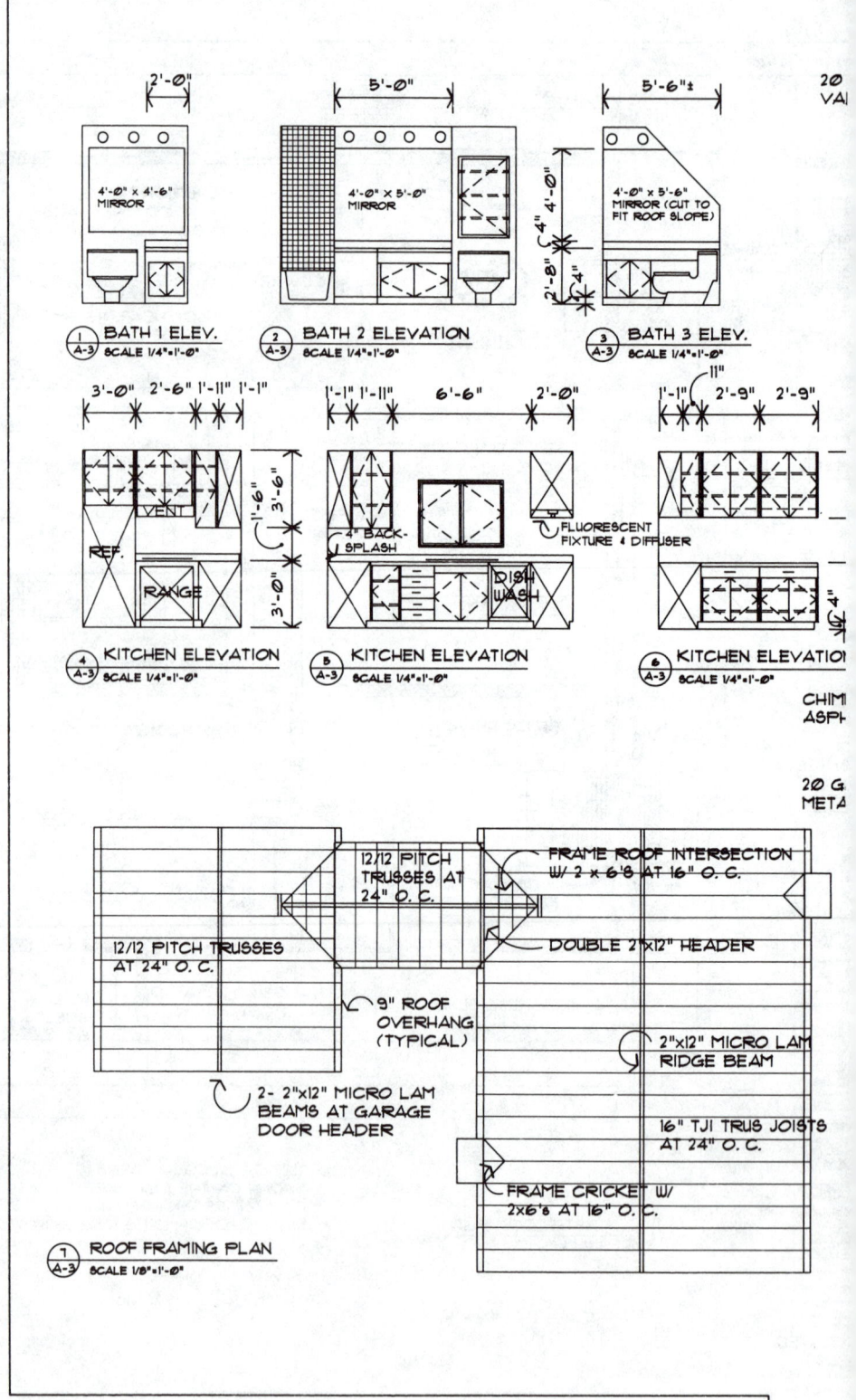

4'-0" x 4'-6" MIRROR

1 BATH 1 ELEV.
A-3 SCALE 1/4"=1'-0"

4'-0" x 5'-0" MIRROR

2 BATH 2 ELEVATION
A-3 SCALE 1/4"=1'-0"

4'-0" x 5'-6" MIRROR (CUT TO FIT ROOF SLOPE)

3 BATH 3 ELEV.
A-3 SCALE 1/4"=1'-0"

VENT
REF.
4" BACK SPLASH
RANGE

4 KITCHEN ELEVATION
A-3 SCALE 1/4"=1'-0"

4" BACK SPLASH
DISH WASH

5 KITCHEN ELEVATION
A-3 SCALE 1/4"=1'-0"

FLUORESCENT FIXTURE & DIFFUSER

6 KITCHEN ELEVATION
A-3 SCALE 1/4"=1'-0"

4" BACK SPLASH
DISH WASH
FLUORESCENT FIXTURE & D

12/12 PITCH TRUSSES AT 24" O.C.

12/12 PITCH TRUSSES AT 24" O.C.

FRAME ROOF INTERSECTION W/ 2 x 6'S AT 16" O.C.

DOUBLE 2 x 12" HEADER

9" ROOF OVERHANG (TYPICAL)

2 - 2"x12" MICRO LAM BEAMS AT GARAGE DOOR HEADER

2"x12" MICRO LAM RIDGE BEAM

16" TJI TRUS JOISTS AT 24" O.C.

FRAME CRICKET W/ 2x6'S AT 16" O.C.

1 ROOF FRAMING PLAN
A-3 SCALE 1/8"=1'-0"

12/12 PITCH ROOF HOUSE   22-8

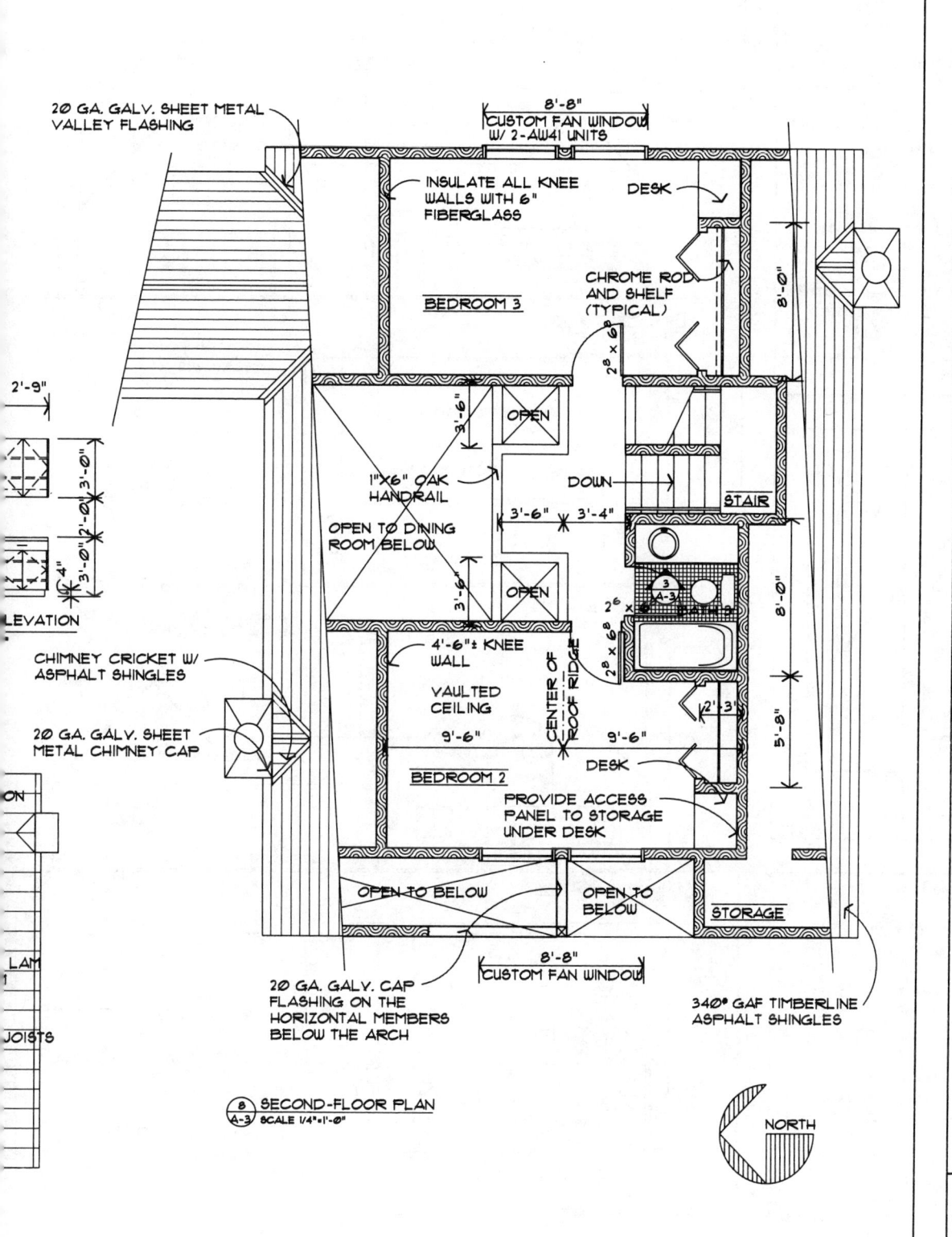

Second-Floor Plan Annotations

- 20 GA. GALV. SHEET METAL VALLEY FLASHING
- 8'-8" CUSTOM FAN WINDOW W/ 2-AW41 UNITS
- INSULATE ALL KNEE WALLS WITH 6" FIBERGLASS
- DESK
- BEDROOM 3
- CHROME ROD AND SHELF (TYPICAL)
- 8'-0"
- 2'-9"
- 3'-0" 2'-0" 3'-0"
- 4" 3'-0" 2'-0" 3'-0"
- ELEVATION
- $2^8 \times 6^8$
- OPEN
- 3'-6"
- 1"×6" OAK HANDRAIL
- OPEN TO DINING ROOM BELOW
- DOWN
- STAIR
- 3'-6" 3'-4"
- 3'-6"
- OPEN
- $2^6 \times 6^8$ BATH
- CHIMNEY CRICKET W/ ASPHALT SHINGLES
- 4'-6"± KNEE WALL
- VAULTED CEILING
- CENTER OF ROOF RIDGE
- 20 GA. GALV. SHEET METAL CHIMNEY CAP
- $2^8 \times 6^8$
- 8'-0"
- 9'-6"   9'-6"
- BEDROOM 2
- DESK
- 2'-3"
- 5'-8"
- PROVIDE ACCESS PANEL TO STORAGE UNDER DESK
- OPEN TO BELOW
- OPEN TO BELOW
- STORAGE
- 8'-8" CUSTOM FAN WINDOW
- 20 GA. GALV. CAP FLASHING ON THE HORIZONTAL MEMBERS BELOW THE ARCH
- 340# GAF TIMBERLINE ASPHALT SHINGLES
- LAM
- JOISTS

8 / A-3 SECOND-FLOOR PLAN SCALE 1/4"=1'-0"

NORTH

12/12 PITCH ROOF HOUSE — SECOND-FLOOR PLAN AND FRAMING

A3

12/12 PITCH ROOF HOUSE

22-9

Elevations/A-4

Sheet A-4 contains the building elevations, door details, and room finish schedule. The half-round opening at the entry is enlarged (to a 1/4" = 1'-0" scale) to allow room for dimension strings. The end elevations contain a custom-made fan window combined with two awning windows. This unit is enlarged to show the design and important dimensions. Door sizes and materials are identified in the "door type" elevations.

An enlarged portion of the west elevation is illustrated above. Dashed lines on the door and windows indicate the direction of swing (the pointed side of the triangle shows the hinge). A slightly darker line weight is used around the silhouette of the elevation in order to "accent" the detail. Note that the grade line is extended beyond the house to visually "tie" it to the ground.

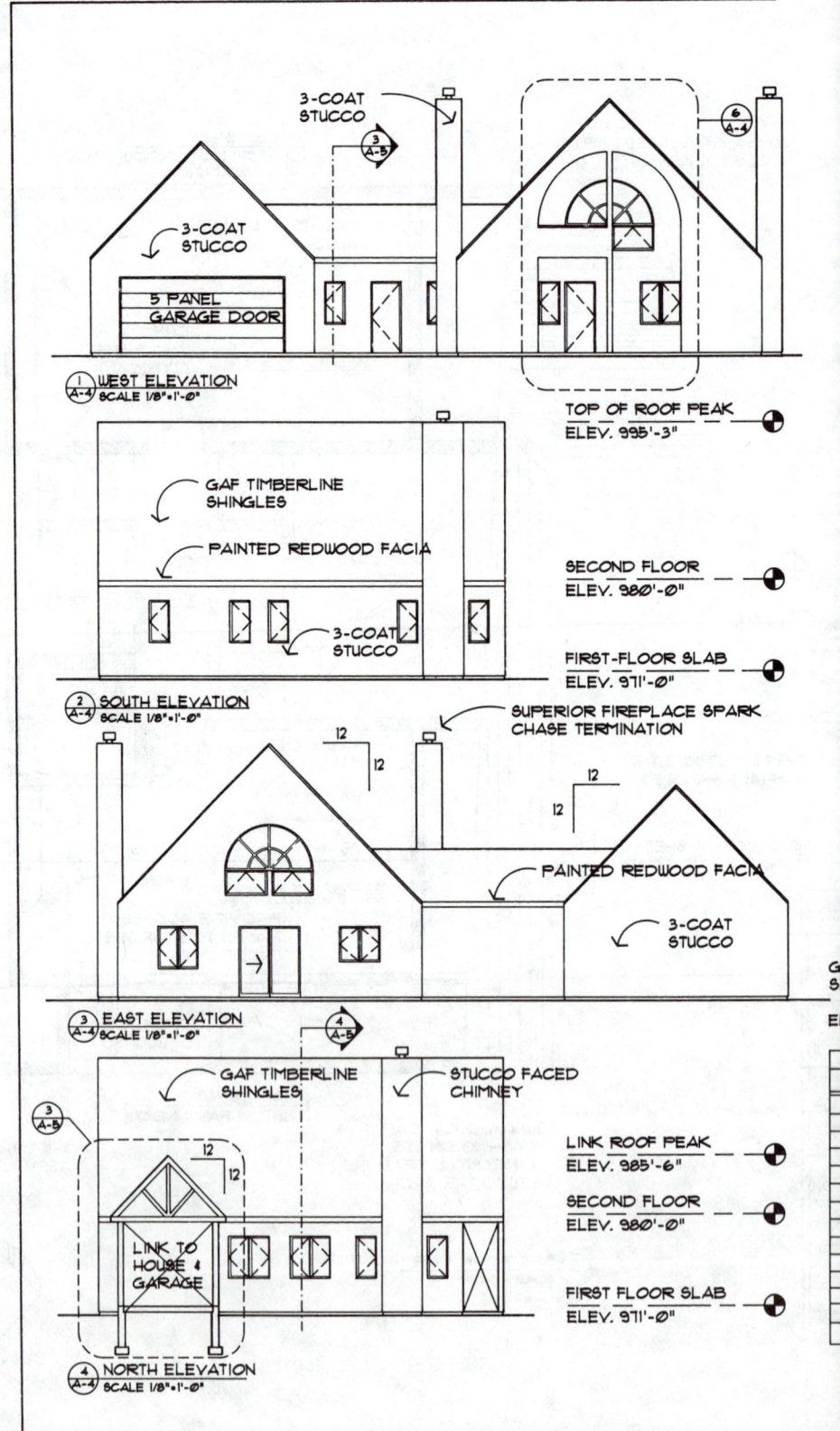

12/12 PITCH ROOF HOUSE

22-10

12/12 PITCH ROOF HOUSE ELEVATIONS

A4

12/12 PITCH ROOF HOUSE — 22-11

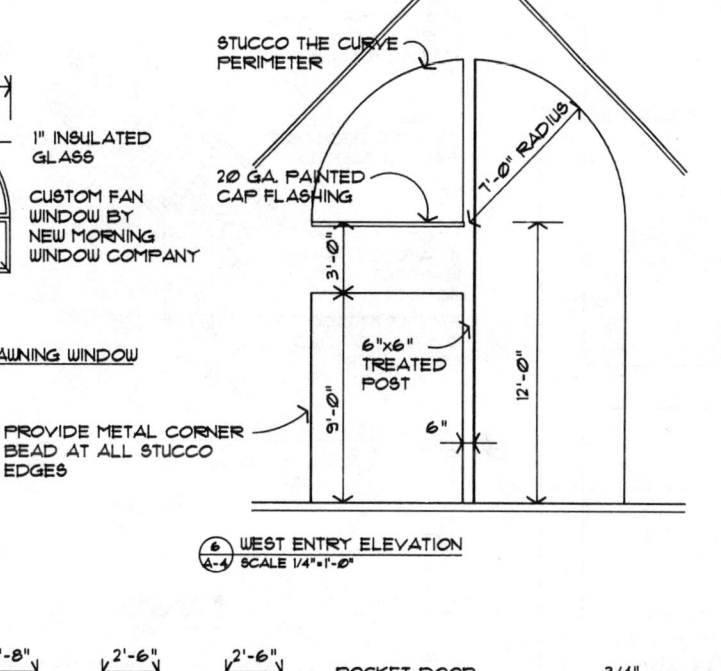

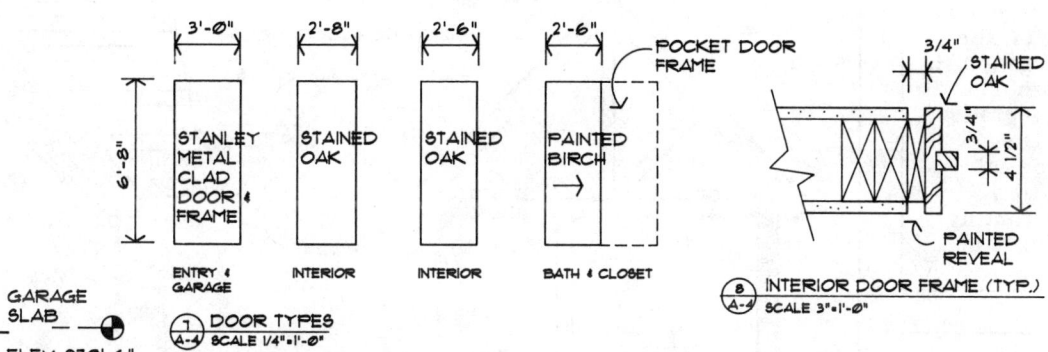

Combination Fan/Awning Window
5 / A-4 SCALE 1/4"=1'-0"

- 8'-8" wide
- 1" INSULATED GLASS
- CUSTOM FAN WINDOW BY NEW MORNING WINDOW COMPANY
- AW41 / AW41
- 8"

West Entry Elevation
6 / A-4 SCALE 1/4"=1'-0"

- STUCCO THE CURVE PERIMETER
- 20 GA. PAINTED CAP FLASHING
- 7'-0" RADIUS
- 3'-0"
- 6"x6" TREATED POST
- 9'-0"
- 12'-0"
- 6"
- PROVIDE METAL CORNER BEAD AT ALL STUCCO EDGES

Door Types
7 / A-4 SCALE 1/4"=1'-0"

Door	Width	Description	Use
1	3'-0"	STANLEY METAL CLAD DOOR & FRAME	ENTRY & GARAGE
2	2'-8"	STAINED OAK	INTERIOR
3	2'-6"	STAINED OAK	INTERIOR
4	2'-6"	PAINTED BIRCH (POCKET DOOR FRAME)	BATH & CLOSET

All doors 6'-8" height.

Interior Door Frame (Typ.)
8 / A-4 SCALE 3"=1'-0"

- 3/4" STAINED OAK
- 3/4"
- 4 1/2"
- PAINTED REVEAL

GARAGE SLAB ELEV. 970'-6"

Room Finish Schedule

ROOM NAME	FLOOR	BASE	WALL	FINISH	CEILING	FINISH	REMARKS
BATH 1	C.T.	C.T.	W.P. GYP.	C.T.	W.P. GYP.	PAINT	
LAUNDRY/UTILITY	VINYL	VINYL	GYP. BD.	PAINT	GYP. BD.	PAINT	
KITCHEN	VINYL	VINYL	GYP. BD.	PAINT	GYP. BD.	PAINT	
FAMILY ROOM	CARPET	WOOD	GYP. BD.	PAINT	GYP. BD.	PAINT	
DINING ROOM	Q TILE	WOOD	GYP. BD.	PAINT	GYP. BD.	PAINT	VAULTED CLNG.
HALL	CARPET	WOOD	GYP. BD.	PAINT	GYP. BD.	PAINT	
MASTER BEDROOM	CARPET	WOOD	GYP. BD.	PAINT	GYP. BD.	PAINT	
LIVING ROOM	CARPET	WOOD	GYP. BD.	PAINT	GYP. BD.	PAINT	
STAIR	CARPET	WOOD	GYP. BD.	PAINT	GYP. BD.	PAINT	
BATH 2	C.T.	C.T.	W.P. GYP.	C.T.	W.P. GYP.	PAINT	
BEDROOM 2	CARPET	WOOD	GYP. BD.	PAINT	GYP. BD.	PAINT	VAULTED CLNG.
BATH 3	C.T.	C.T.	W.P. GYP.	C.T.	W.P. GYP.	PAINT	VAULTED CLNG.
BEDROOM 3	CARPET	WOOD	GYP. BD.	PAINT	GYP. BD.	PAINT	VAULTED CLNG.
GARAGE	CONC.	NONE	EXPOSED	NONE	EXPOSED	NONE	

Building Sections/A-5

Sheet A-5 illustrates sections and details for the project. The main section cut through the house shows the stair and balcony construction. Building sections should detail all unusual conditions in a building; here a triangular roof called a cricket, designed to divert ice and water at the intersection of the roof and chimney, is detailed.

The enlarged section below shows the footing and foundation for the house. Note that the 12" foundation wall is reduced at the top block course to provide space for the "floating" concrete slab. The perimeter of the house is insulated with 3" of rigid foam board that runs from grade to the top of the footing. The detail indicates elevation points for the footing and top of floor slab.

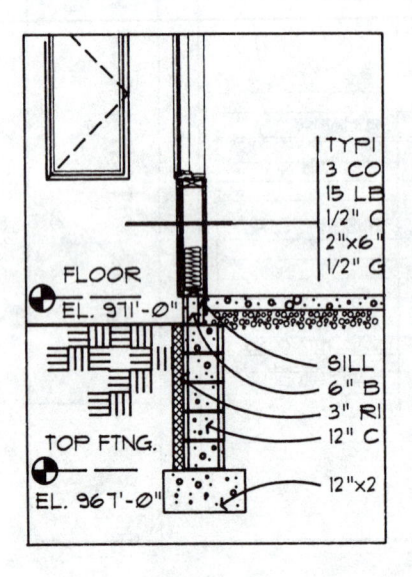

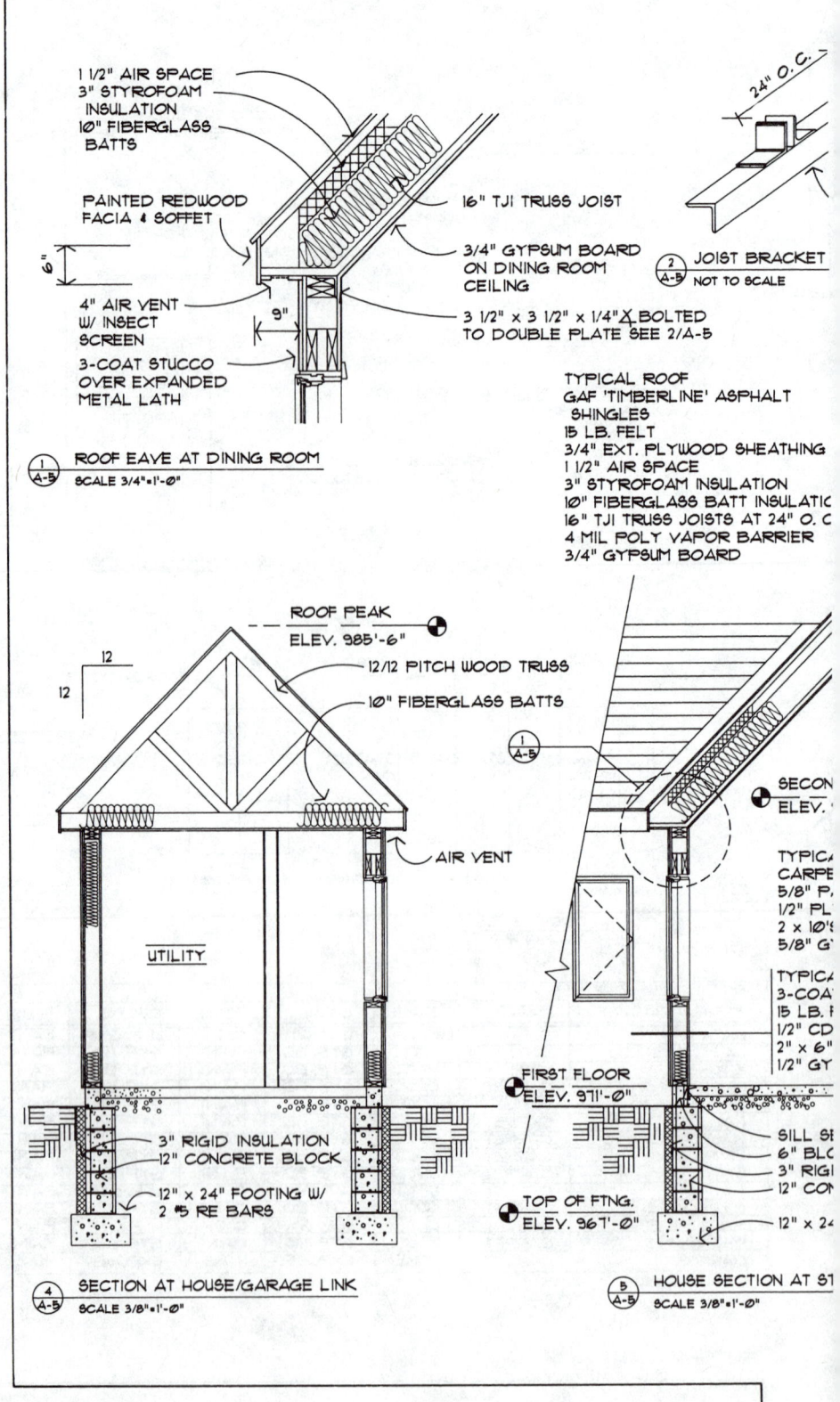

Roof Eave at Dining Room (1/A-5, scale 3/4"=1'-0")
- 1 1/2" AIR SPACE
- 3" STYROFOAM INSULATION
- 10" FIBERGLASS BATTS
- PAINTED REDWOOD FACIA & SOFFET
- 4" AIR VENT W/ INSECT SCREEN
- 3-COAT STUCCO OVER EXPANDED METAL LATH
- 16" TJI TRUSS JOIST
- 3/4" GYPSUM BOARD ON DINING ROOM CEILING
- 3 1/2" x 3 1/2" x 1/4" L BOLTED TO DOUBLE PLATE SEE 2/A-5

Joist Bracket (2/A-5, not to scale) — 24" O.C.

Typical Roof
- GAF 'TIMBERLINE' ASPHALT SHINGLES
- 15 LB. FELT
- 3/4" EXT. PLYWOOD SHEATHING
- 1 1/2" AIR SPACE
- 3" STYROFOAM INSULATION
- 10" FIBERGLASS BATT INSULATION
- 16" TJI TRUSS JOISTS AT 24" O.C.
- 4 MIL POLY VAPOR BARRIER
- 3/4" GYPSUM BOARD

Section at House/Garage Link (4/A-5, scale 3/8"=1'-0")
- ROOF PEAK ELEV. 985'-6"
- 12/12 PITCH WOOD TRUSS
- 10" FIBERGLASS BATTS
- AIR VENT
- UTILITY
- 3" RIGID INSULATION
- 12" CONCRETE BLOCK
- 12" x 24" FOOTING W/ 2 #5 RE BARS

House Section at S... (5/A-5, scale 3/8"=1'-0")
- FIRST FLOOR ELEV. 971'-0"
- TOP OF FTNG. ELEV. 967'-0"
- SILL S...
- 6" BLO...
- 3" RIGI...
- 12" CO...
- 12" x 2...

FLOOR EL. 971'-0"
TOP FTNG. EL. 967'-0"
- SILL
- 6" B...
- 3" RI...
- 12" C...
- 12"x2...

12/12 PITCH ROOF HOUSE   22-12

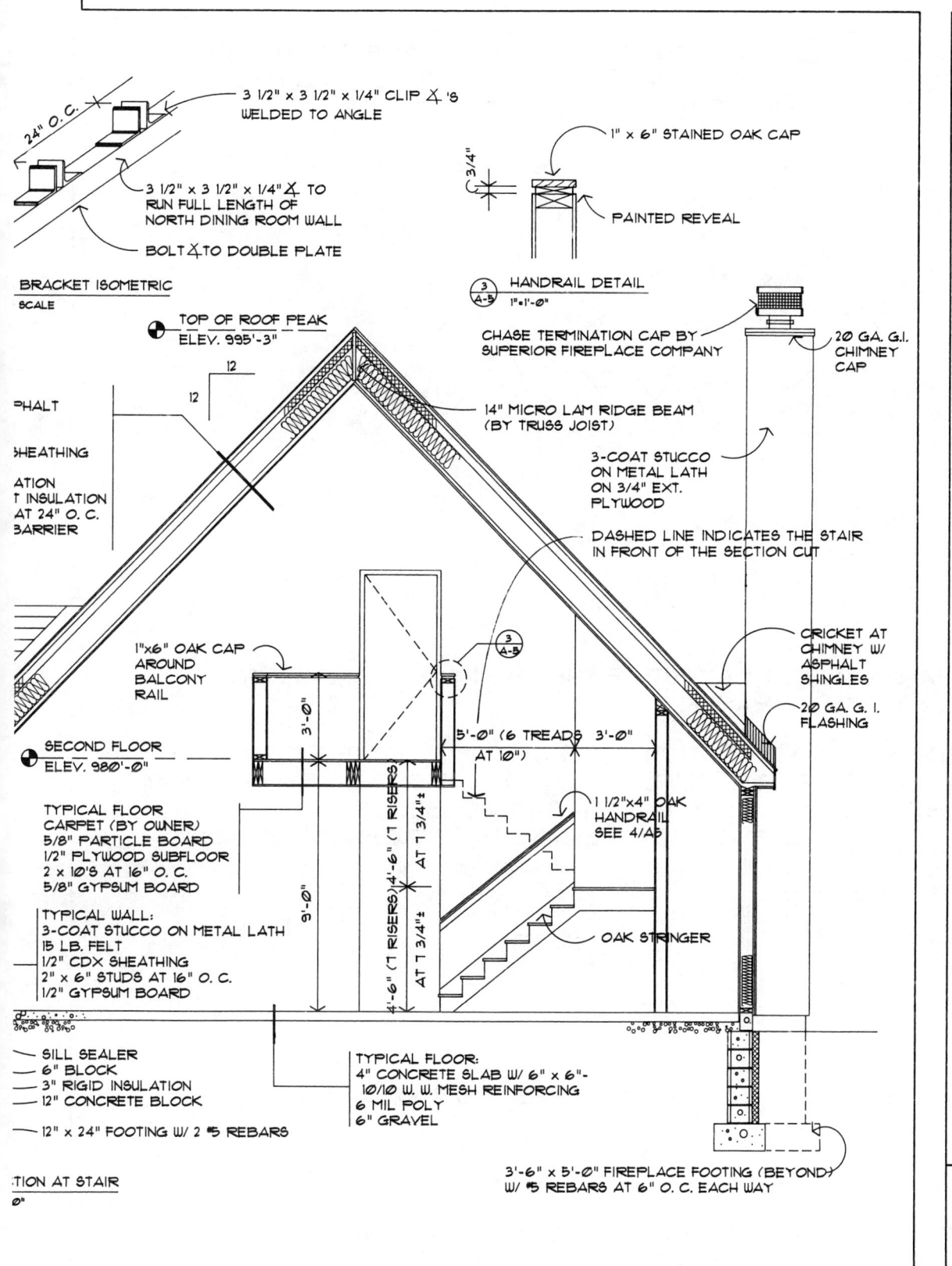

BRACKET ISOMETRIC
SCALE

- 24" O.C.
- 3 1/2" x 3 1/2" x 1/4" CLIP ∠ 'S WELDED TO ANGLE
- 3 1/2" x 3 1/2" x 1/4" ∠ TO RUN FULL LENGTH OF NORTH DINING ROOM WALL
- BOLT ∠ TO DOUBLE PLATE

3/A-5 HANDRAIL DETAIL 1"=1'-0"
- 1" x 6" STAINED OAK CAP
- 3/4"
- PAINTED REVEAL

- TOP OF ROOF PEAK ELEV. 995'-3"
- 12 / 12
- CHASE TERMINATION CAP BY SUPERIOR FIREPLACE COMPANY
- 20 GA. G.I. CHIMNEY CAP
- 14" MICRO LAM RIDGE BEAM (BY TRUSS JOIST)
- 3-COAT STUCCO ON METAL LATH ON 3/4" EXT. PLYWOOD
- ASPHALT
- SHEATHING
- ATION
- T INSULATION AT 24" O.C.
- BARRIER
- DASHED LINE INDICATES THE STAIR IN FRONT OF THE SECTION CUT
- 1"x6" OAK CAP AROUND BALCONY RAIL
- CRICKET AT CHIMNEY W/ ASPHALT SHINGLES
- 20 GA. G.I. FLASHING
- SECOND FLOOR ELEV. 980'-0"
- 3'-0" 5'-0" (6 TREADS AT 10") 3'-0"
- 1 1/2"x4" OAK HANDRAIL SEE 4/A5
- TYPICAL FLOOR:
  CARPET (BY OWNER)
  5/8" PARTICLE BOARD
  1/2" PLYWOOD SUBFLOOR
  2 x 10'S AT 16" O.C.
  5/8" GYPSUM BOARD
- 4'-6" (7 RISERS) AT 7 3/4"±
- 4'-6" (7 RISERS) AT 7 3/4"±
- 9'-0"
- OAK STRINGER
- TYPICAL WALL:
  3-COAT STUCCO ON METAL LATH
  15 LB. FELT
  1/2" CDX SHEATHING
  2" x 6" STUDS AT 16" O.C.
  1/2" GYPSUM BOARD
- SILL SEALER
- 6" BLOCK
- 3" RIGID INSULATION
- 12" CONCRETE BLOCK
- 12" x 24" FOOTING W/ 2 #5 REBARS
- TYPICAL FLOOR:
  4" CONCRETE SLAB W/ 6" x 6" - 10/10 W.W. MESH REINFORCING
  6 MIL POLY
  6" GRAVEL
- TION AT STAIR
- 3'-6" x 5'-0" FIREPLACE FOOTING (BEYOND) W/ #5 REBARS AT 6" O.C. EACH WAY

12/12 PITCH ROOF HOUSE — BUILDING SECTIONS

A5

12/12 PITCH ROOF HOUSE   22-13

REPLAY
ASSEMBLE A SET OF CONSTRUCTION DRAWINGS FOR THE 12/12 PITCH ROOF HOUSE PRESENTED IN THIS UNIT. USE THE INSTRUCTIONS LISTED BELOW TO PREPARE THE DRAWING PACKAGE.

1. ASSEMBLE A STUDY MODEL OF THE HOUSE.

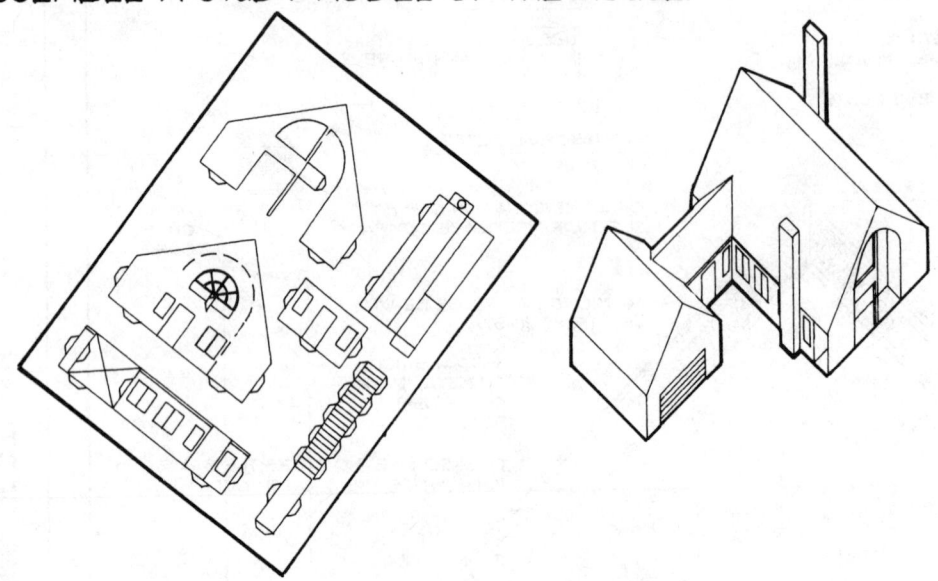

2. PREPARE A SHEET LAYOUT OF THE DRAWING PACKAGE ON 8 1/2" x 11" TYPING PAPER.

3. SKETCH PLAN AND SECTION VIEWS OF COMPLICATED PORTIONS OF THE HOUSE, FOR EXAMPLE, THE STAIR, FRONT ENTRY, KITCHEN, AND BATHROOMS. YOUR SKETCH SHOULD BE USED TO DETERMINE CONSTRUCTION TOLERANCES BETWEEN MATERIALS.

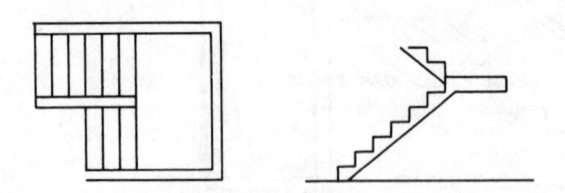

4. PREPARE A TIME SCHEDULE FOR THE ASSEMBLY OF THE DRAWING SET.

5. ASSEMBLE A WORKING DRAWING PACKAGE FOR THE HOUSE.

6. REVIEW A CHECK-SET OF THE PROJECT AT APPROXIMATELY 50% AND 75% OF COMPLETION.

12/12 PITCH ROOF HOUSE

23 SKYWAY HOUSE

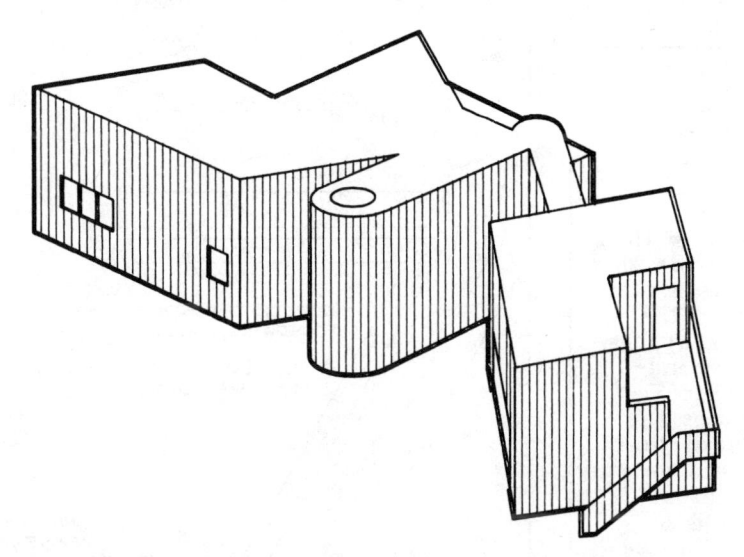

THIS UNIT PRESENTS THE CONSTRUCTION DRAWINGS FOR A HOUSE ON A VERY UNIQUE SITE. THE PROJECT SITS ON A SMALL (4,400 SQ FT) CITY LOT WITH A FREEWAY VIEW TO THE WEST AND A RIVER VIEW TO THE EAST. THE CITY ZONING ORDINANCE REQUIRES A 16' FRONT YARD SETBACK AND A 5' SETBACK FOR SIDE AND BACK YARDS. THE LOT IS ON A HILL THAT IS 200' FROM THE FREEWAY AND 300' FROM THE RIVER. THE DESIGN PLACES THE EMPHASIS OF THE HOUSE ON THE RIVER VIEW SIDE. WINDOWS ALONG THE FREEWAY SIDE OF THE HOUSE HAVE BEEN HELD TO A MINIMUM. THE ROUND STAIR TOWER ACTS AS A CENTER OF THE DESIGN. TWO BEDROOMS (FOR TEENAGERS) HAVE BEEN PLACED OVER THE GARAGE AND HAVE A PRIVATE STAIR AND DECK. THESE BEDROOMS ARE CONNECTED WITH THE REST OF THE HOUSE BY A SECOND-FLOOR SKYWAY. THE TWO-STORY LIVING ROOM COMBINES WITH AN OPEN KITCHEN AND DINING ROOM TO MAKE THE HOUSE SEEM LARGER THAN ITS 1,700 SQ FT. THE MASTER BEDROOM IS OPEN TO THE LIVING ROOM AND HAS A PRIVATE DECK WITH A RIVER VIEW.

| SKYWAY HOUSE | 23-1 |

Site Plan and Basement Plan/A-1

Sheet A-1 illustrates the site plan, framing plan, and basement plan. On all three plans north faces up on the sheet. The basement footing is indicated with a dashed line that runs around the perimeter of the foundation wall. The dashed square in the basement represents a poured concrete footing that supports a 4" pipe column. The basement walls have hollow beam pockets to support the first-floor beams.

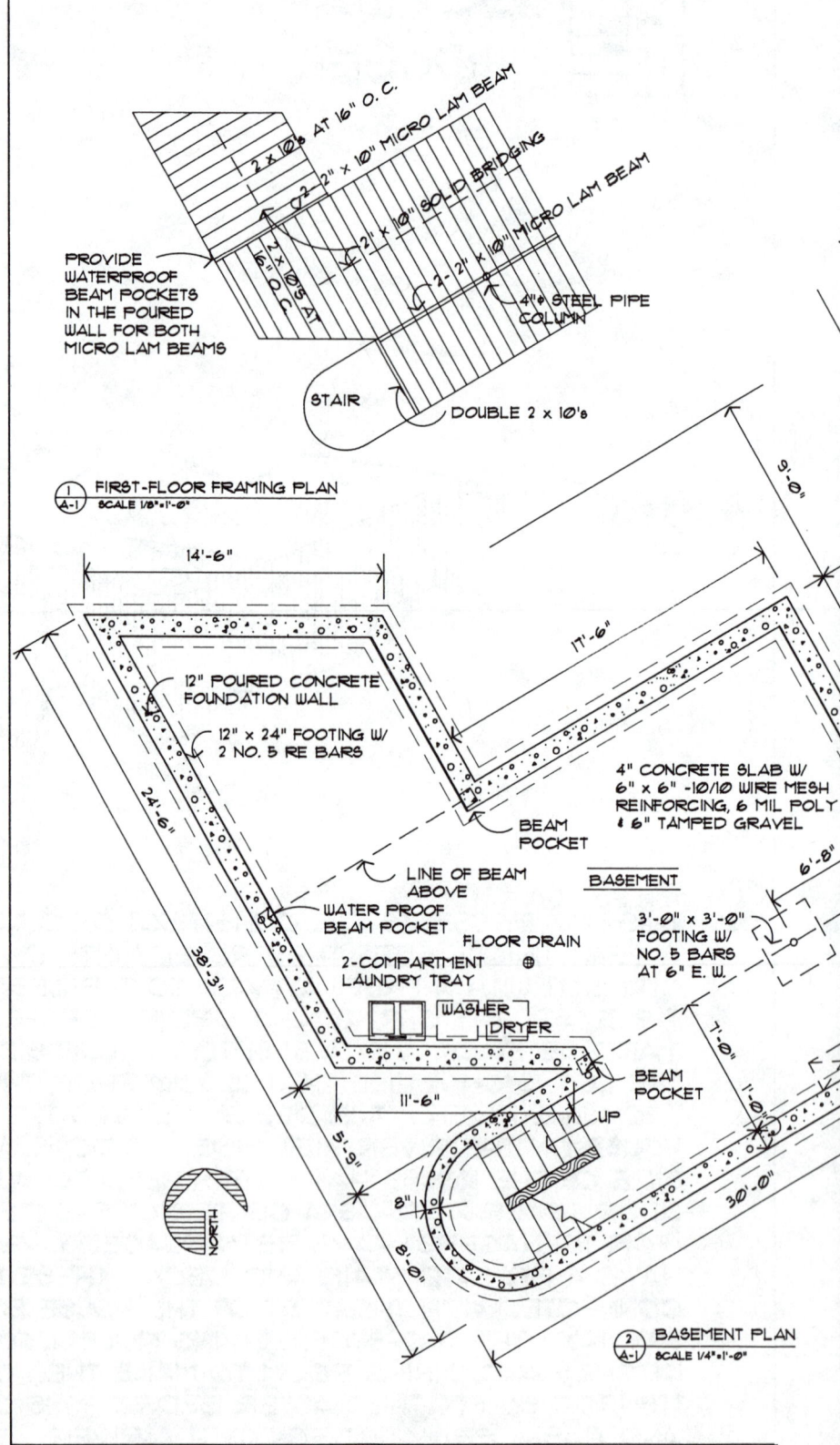

A portion of the site plan is illustrated below. The house is drawn with a double line around the perimeter to show the 4" cant strip. The site plan doubles as a roof plan by showing the skylight, roof scuppers, and the two second-floor decks. The drawing indicates the amount of detail that should be shown on the plan. Note that all materials should be identified and located with dimension strings.

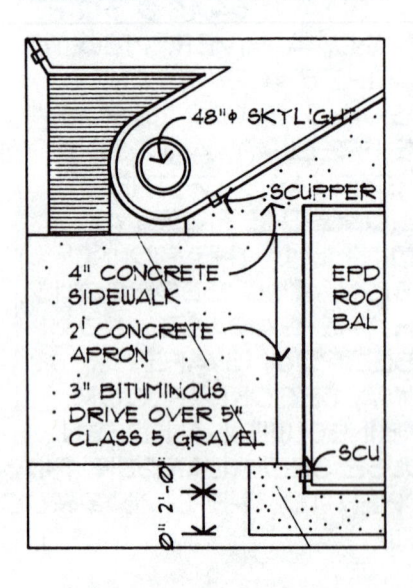

SKYWAY HOUSE — 23-2

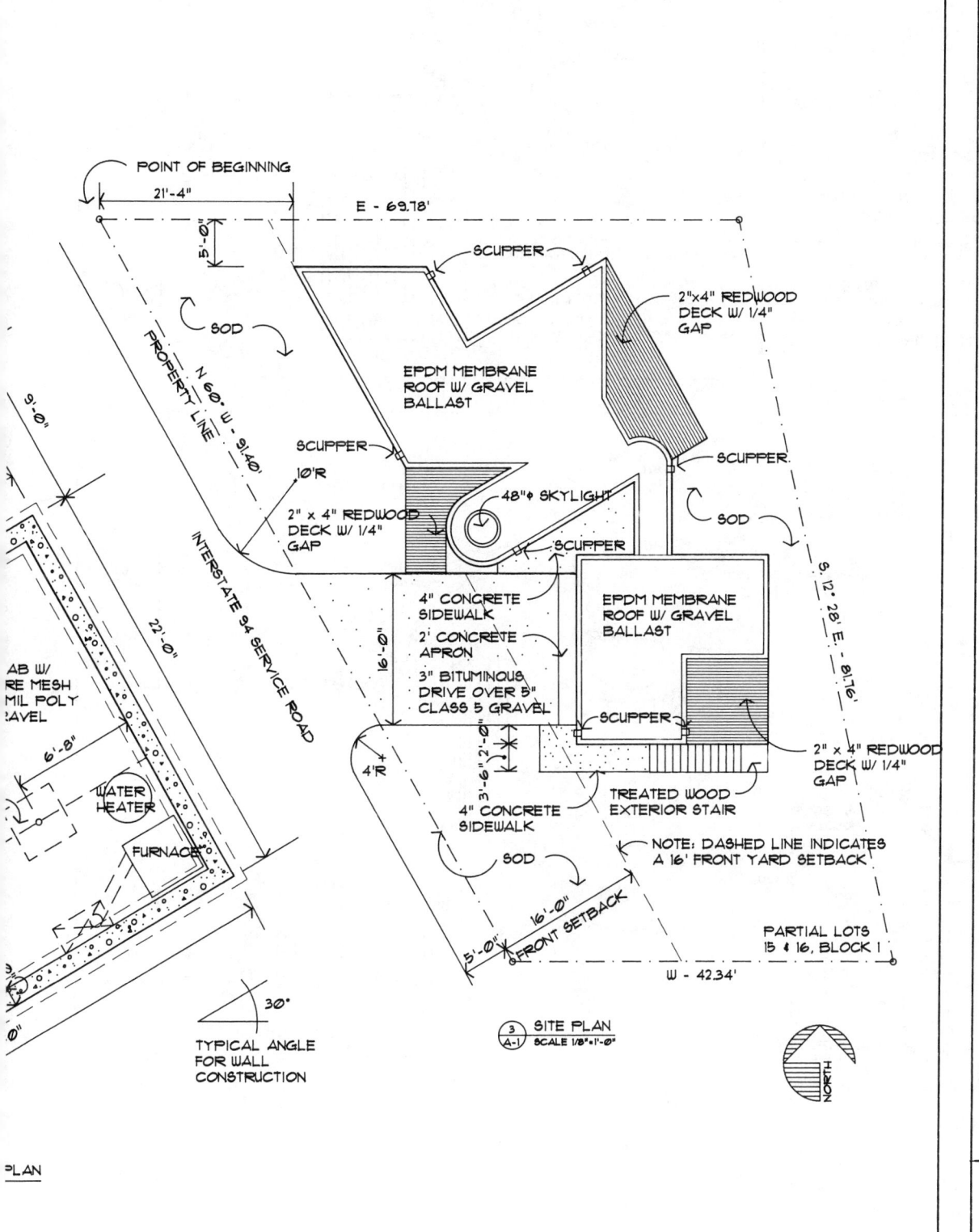

SKYWAY HOUSE — SITE PLAN AND BASEMENT PLAN

Site Plan Annotations:

- POINT OF BEGINNING
- 21'-4"
- E - 69.78'
- 5'-0"
- SCUPPER
- 2"x4" REDWOOD DECK W/ 1/4" GAP
- SOD
- N 60° W - 91.40'
- PROPERTY LINE
- INTERSTATE 94 SERVICE ROAD
- EPDM MEMBRANE ROOF W/ GRAVEL BALLAST
- SCUPPER
- 10' R
- 2" x 4" REDWOOD DECK W/ 1/4" GAP
- 48"⌀ SKYLIGHT
- SCUPPER
- SOD
- S 12° 28' E - 81.76'
- 4" CONCRETE SIDEWALK
- 2' CONCRETE APRON
- 3" BITUMINOUS DRIVE OVER 5" CLASS 5 GRAVEL
- 16'-0"
- EPDM MEMBRANE ROOF W/ GRAVEL BALLAST
- SCUPPER
- 2"x 4" REDWOOD DECK W/ 1/4" GAP
- TREATED WOOD EXTERIOR STAIR
- 3'-6" 2'-0"
- 4' R
- 4" CONCRETE SIDEWALK
- SOD
- NOTE: DASHED LINE INDICATES A 16' FRONT YARD SETBACK
- 5'-0" 16'-0" FRONT SETBACK
- PARTIAL LOTS 15 & 16, BLOCK 1
- W - 42.34'
- 22'-0"
- 9'-0"
- 6'-8"
- SLAB W/ WIRE MESH MIL POLY GRAVEL
- WATER HEATER
- FURNACE
- 30° TYPICAL ANGLE FOR WALL CONSTRUCTION

3 / A-1 — SITE PLAN
SCALE 1/8" = 1'-0"

NORTH

SKYWAY HOUSE

A1

SKYWAY HOUSE 23-3

Framing and Details

This sheet contains drawings that show second-floor framing and stair details. The framing plan details the size and spacing of all structural members. Giving dimensions isn't necessary since they are given on the floor plan. The isometric below shows a cut-away drawing of the stair tower that illustrates the half-round landing and scissors stair. The stair section is shown below.

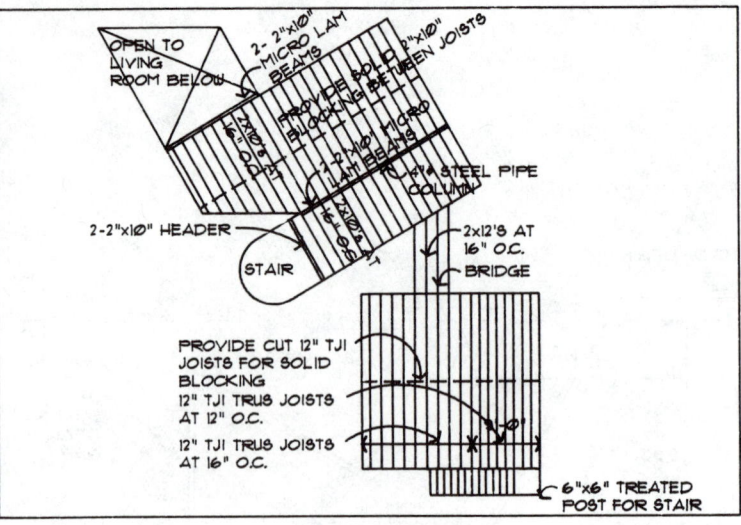

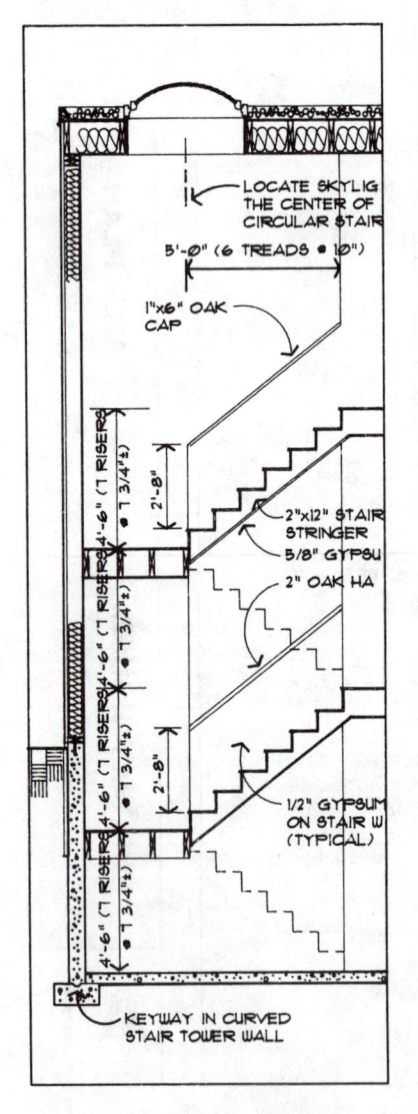

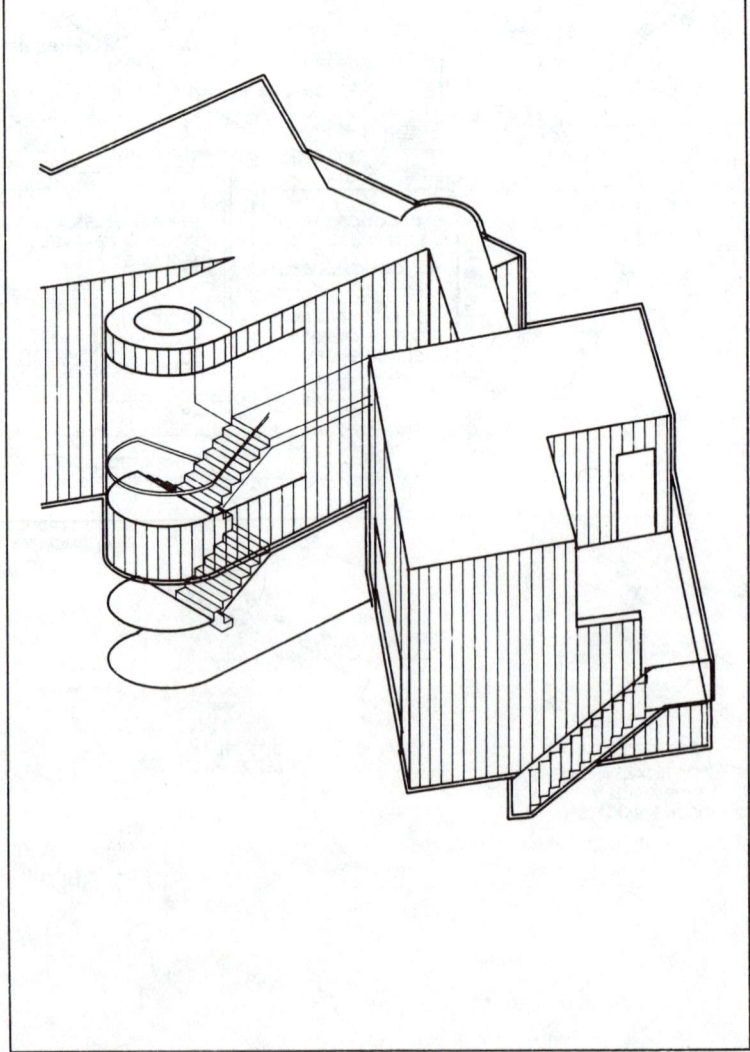

SKYWAY HOUSE

23-4

Framing and Details

The drawings on this page show roof details for the house. The framing plan at the right uses two plywood micro lam beams to reduce the roof joist span. One end of the beam (near the master bedroom deck) is supported by a 4" pipe column. This column runs all the way to the basement footing. The two drawings below show the roof framing as an isometric and a wall section.

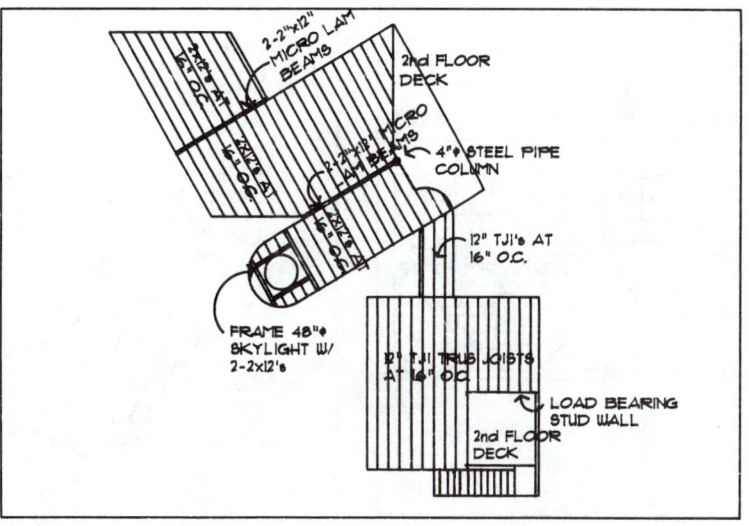

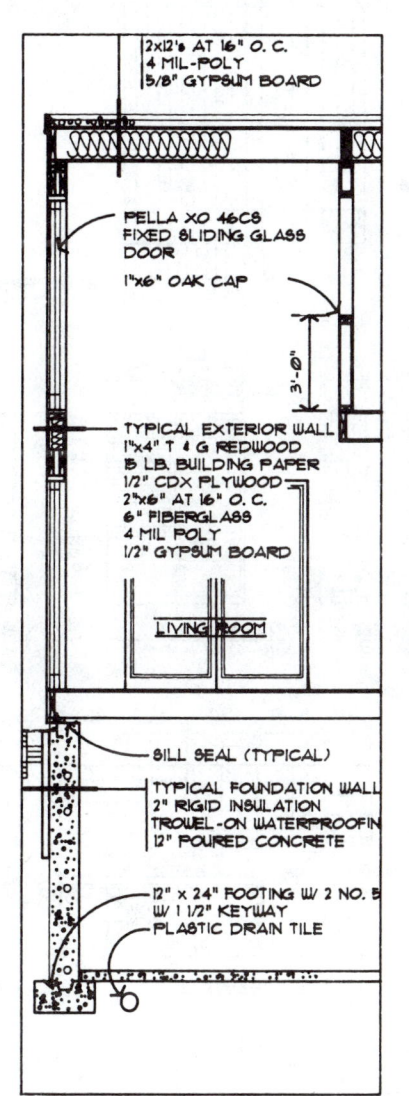

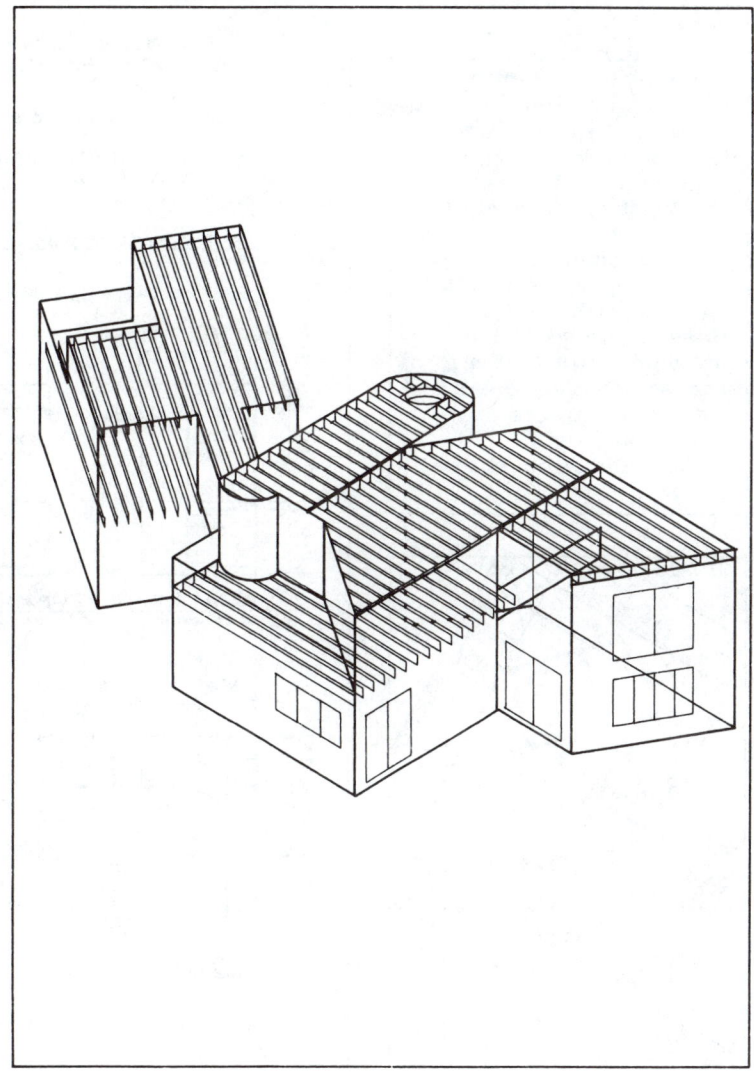

SKYWAY HOUSE

First-Floor Plan/A-2

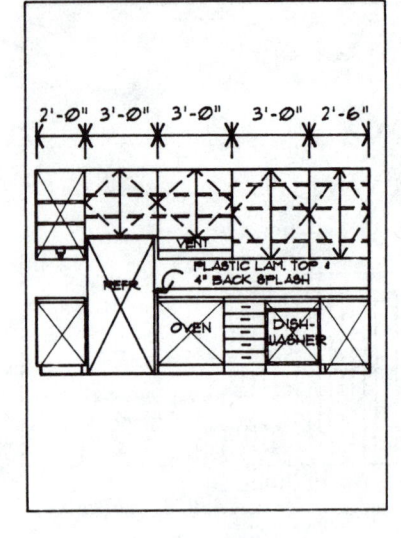

Sheet A-2 shows the first-floor plan and second-floor framing and cabinet details. The elevation above shows the amount of detail that should be used for kitchen cabinets. The drawing indicates cabinet sizes, shows door hinges, and details shelves with dashed lines. The plan blow-up below illustrates the amount of detail to use when drawing cabinets. Detail 7/A-2 is the elevation shown above.

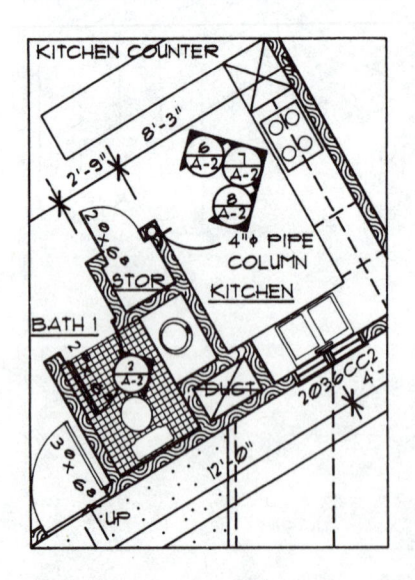

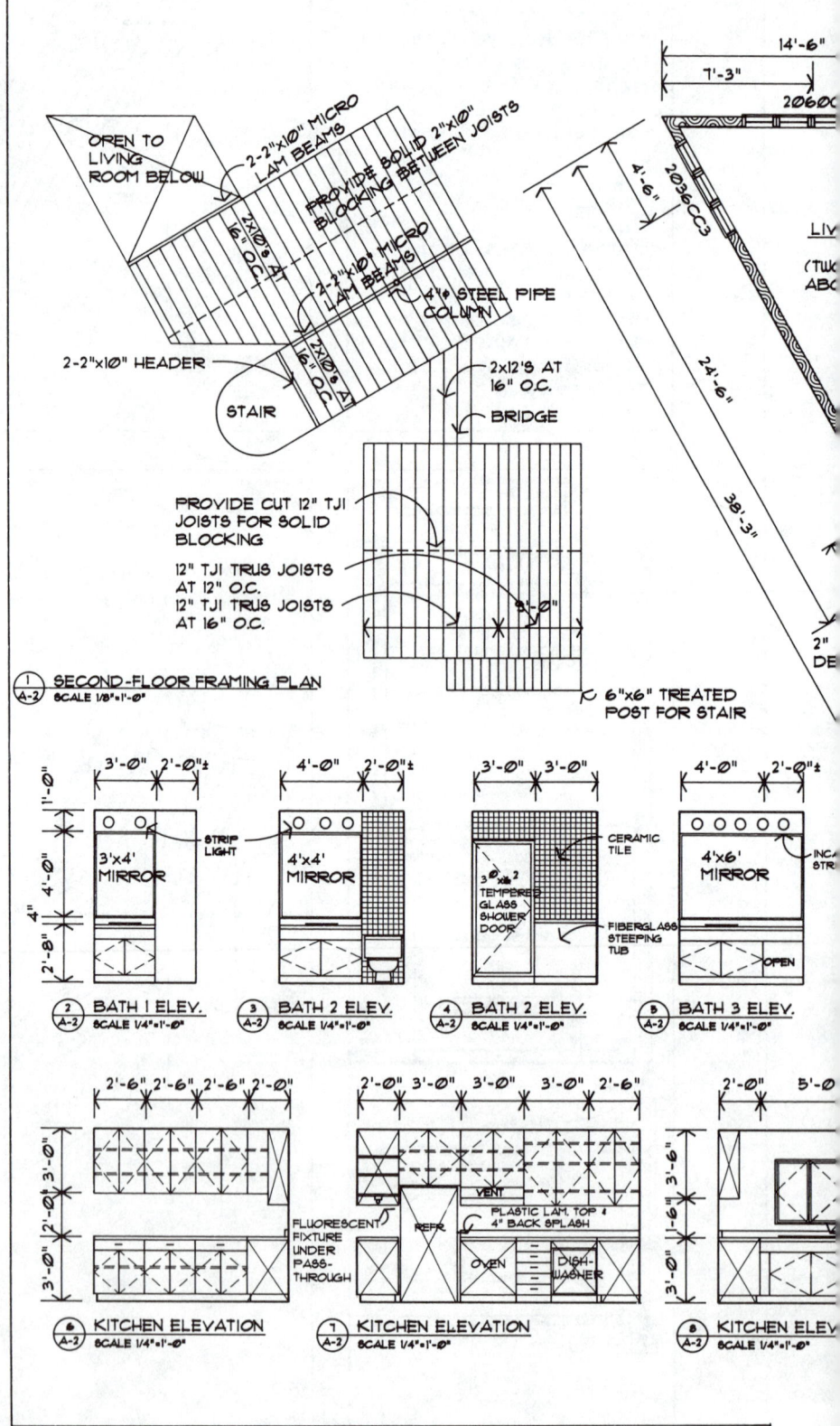

SKYWAY HOUSE
23-6

FIRST-FLOOR PLAN

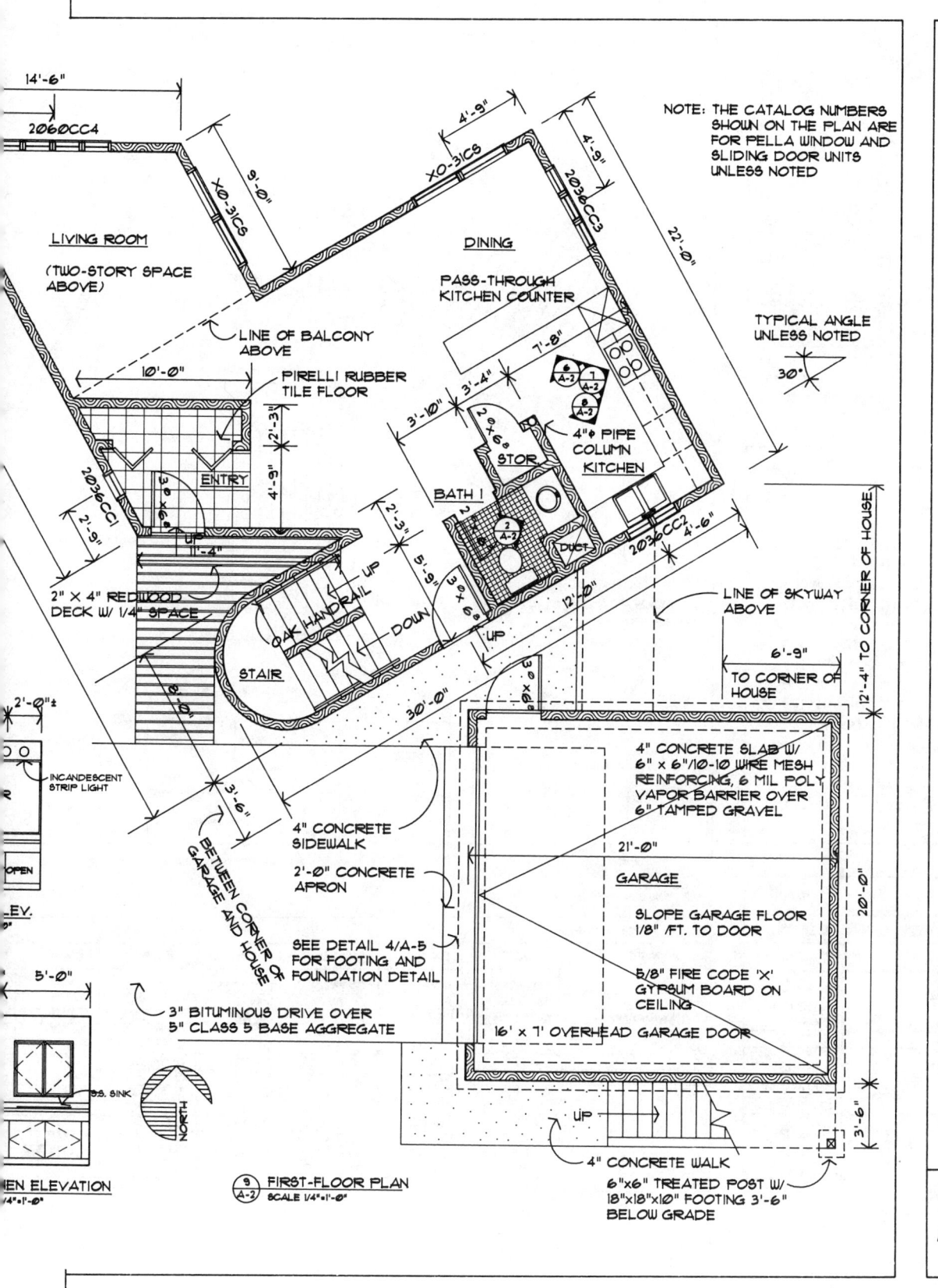

SKYWAY HOUSE

A2

SKYWAY HOUSE   23-7

Second-Floor Plan/A-3

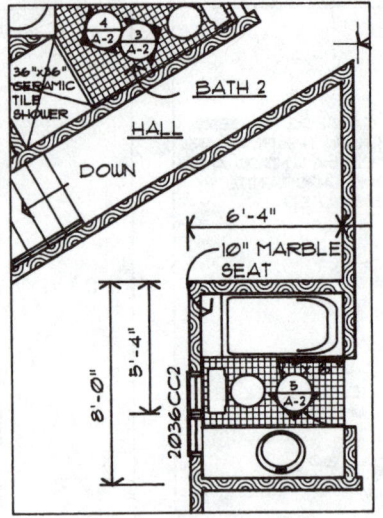

Sheet A-3 contains the second-floor plan and roof framing plan. The plans are placed at a location identical to the layout on sheet A-2. The decks are drawn with lines to illustrate the direction of the 2 x 4's. The two-story living room is noted and drawn with an "X" from corner to corner. The drawing above shows a portion of two baths and the skyway. The schedule below includes every room in the project.

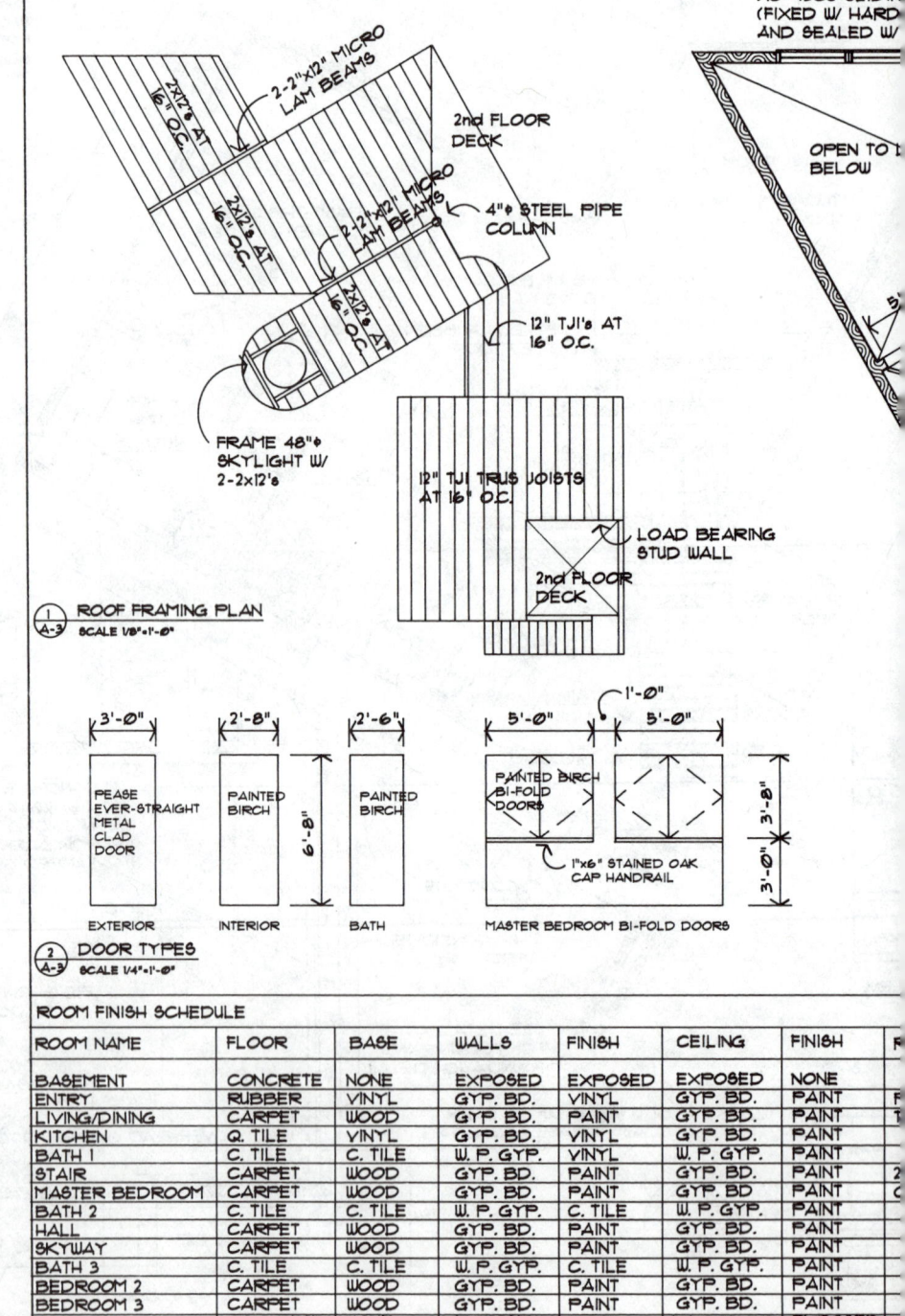

ROOM FINISH SCHEDULE

ROOM NAME	FLOOR
BASEMENT	CONCRETE
ENTRY	RUBBER
LIVING/DINING	CARPET
KITCHEN	Q. TILE
BATH 1	C. TILE
STAIR	CARPET
MASTER BEDROOM	CARPET
BATH 2	C. TILE
HALL	CARPET
SKYWAY	CARPET
BATH 3	C. TILE
BEDROOM 2	CARPET
BEDROOM 3	CARPET
GARAGE	CONCRETE

ROOM FINISH SCHEDULE

ROOM NAME	FLOOR	BASE	WALLS	FINISH	CEILING	FINISH
BASEMENT	CONCRETE	NONE	EXPOSED	EXPOSED	EXPOSED	NONE
ENTRY	RUBBER	VINYL	GYP. BD.	VINYL	GYP. BD.	PAINT
LIVING/DINING	CARPET	WOOD	GYP. BD.	PAINT	GYP. BD.	PAINT
KITCHEN	Q. TILE	VINYL	GYP. BD.	VINYL	GYP. BD.	PAINT
BATH 1	C. TILE	C. TILE	W. P. GYP.	VINYL	W. P. GYP.	PAINT
STAIR	CARPET	WOOD	GYP. BD.	PAINT	GYP. BD.	PAINT
MASTER BEDROOM	CARPET	WOOD	GYP. BD.	PAINT	GYP. BD	PAINT
BATH 2	C. TILE	C. TILE	W. P. GYP.	C. TILE	W. P. GYP.	PAINT
HALL	CARPET	WOOD	GYP. BD.	PAINT	GYP. BD.	PAINT
SKYWAY	CARPET	WOOD	GYP. BD.	PAINT	GYP. BD.	PAINT
BATH 3	C. TILE	C. TILE	W. P. GYP.	C. TILE	W. P. GYP.	PAINT
BEDROOM 2	CARPET	WOOD	GYP. BD.	PAINT	GYP. BD.	PAINT
BEDROOM 3	CARPET	WOOD	GYP. BD.	PAINT	GYP. BD.	PAINT
GARAGE	CONCRETE	NONE	EXPOSED	NONE	'X' GYP. BD.	EXPOSED

SKYWAY HOUSE

23-8

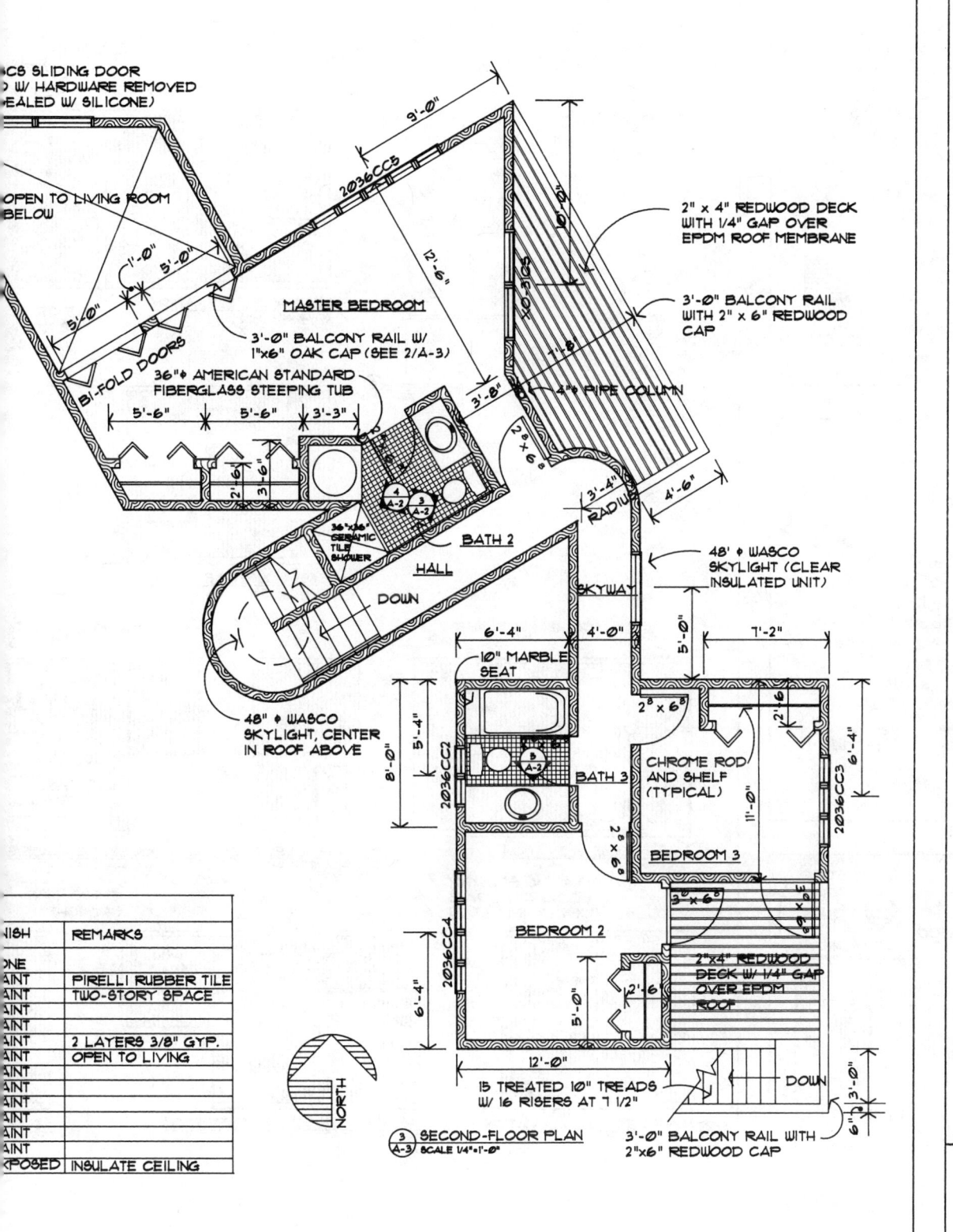

SKYWAY HOUSE — SECOND-FLOOR PLAN

Sheet A3 — 23-9

Annotations on plan:

- CS SLIDING DOOR W/ HARDWARE REMOVED (SEALED W/ SILICONE)
- OPEN TO LIVING ROOM BELOW
- BI-FOLD DOORS
- MASTER BEDROOM
- 2036CC5
- 2" x 4" REDWOOD DECK WITH 1/4" GAP OVER EPDM ROOF MEMBRANE
- 3'-0" BALCONY RAIL WITH 2" x 6" REDWOOD CAP
- 3'-0" BALCONY RAIL W/ 1"x 6" OAK CAP (SEE 2/A-3)
- 36"⌀ AMERICAN STANDARD FIBERGLASS STEEPING TUB
- 4"⌀ PIPE COLUMN
- 36"x36" CERAMIC TILE SHOWER
- BATH 2
- HALL / DOWN
- 48"⌀ WASCO SKYLIGHT, CENTER IN ROOF ABOVE
- 48"⌀ WASCO SKYLIGHT (CLEAR INSULATED UNIT)
- SKYWAY
- 10" MARBLE SEAT
- 2036CC2
- BATH 3
- CHROME ROD AND SHELF (TYPICAL)
- BEDROOM 3
- 2036CC3
- BEDROOM 2
- 2036CC4
- 2" x 4" REDWOOD DECK W/ 1/4" GAP OVER EPDM ROOF
- 15 TREATED 10" TREADS W/ 16 RISERS AT 7 1/2"
- DOWN
- 3'-0" BALCONY RAIL WITH 2" x 6" REDWOOD CAP
- NORTH

3 / A-3 SECOND-FLOOR PLAN SCALE 1/4" = 1'-0"

Finish schedule (partial, left margin):

NISH	REMARKS
ONE	
AINT	PIRELLI RUBBER TILE
AINT	TWO-STORY SPACE
AINT	
AINT	
AINT	2 LAYERS 3/8" GYP.
AINT	OPEN TO LIVING
AINT	
AINT	
AINT	
AINT	
POSED	INSULATE CEILING

SKYWAY HOUSE

Elevations/A-4

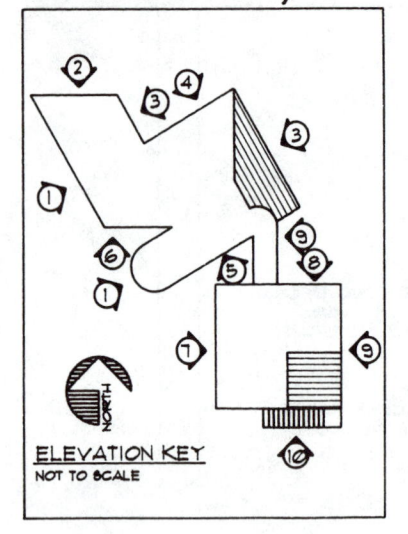

ELEVATION KEY
NOT TO SCALE

Sheet A-4 illustrates exterior elevations and a section cut through the stair tower. An orthographic drawing of the entire house would produce a distorted view of some parts, so instead a key plan (shown above) is used to illustrate a true view of each part. Note that wall sections are keyed from the elevation. The blow-up below shows the detail drafting used on the west elevation.

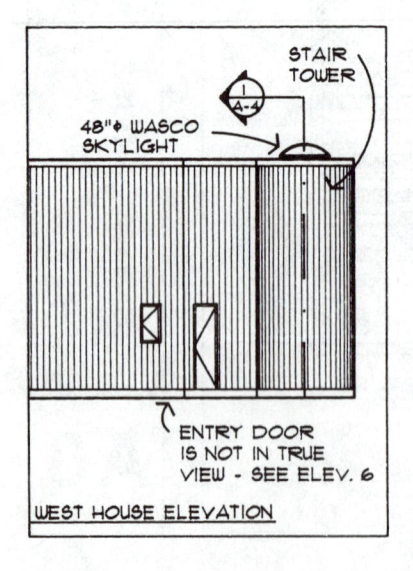

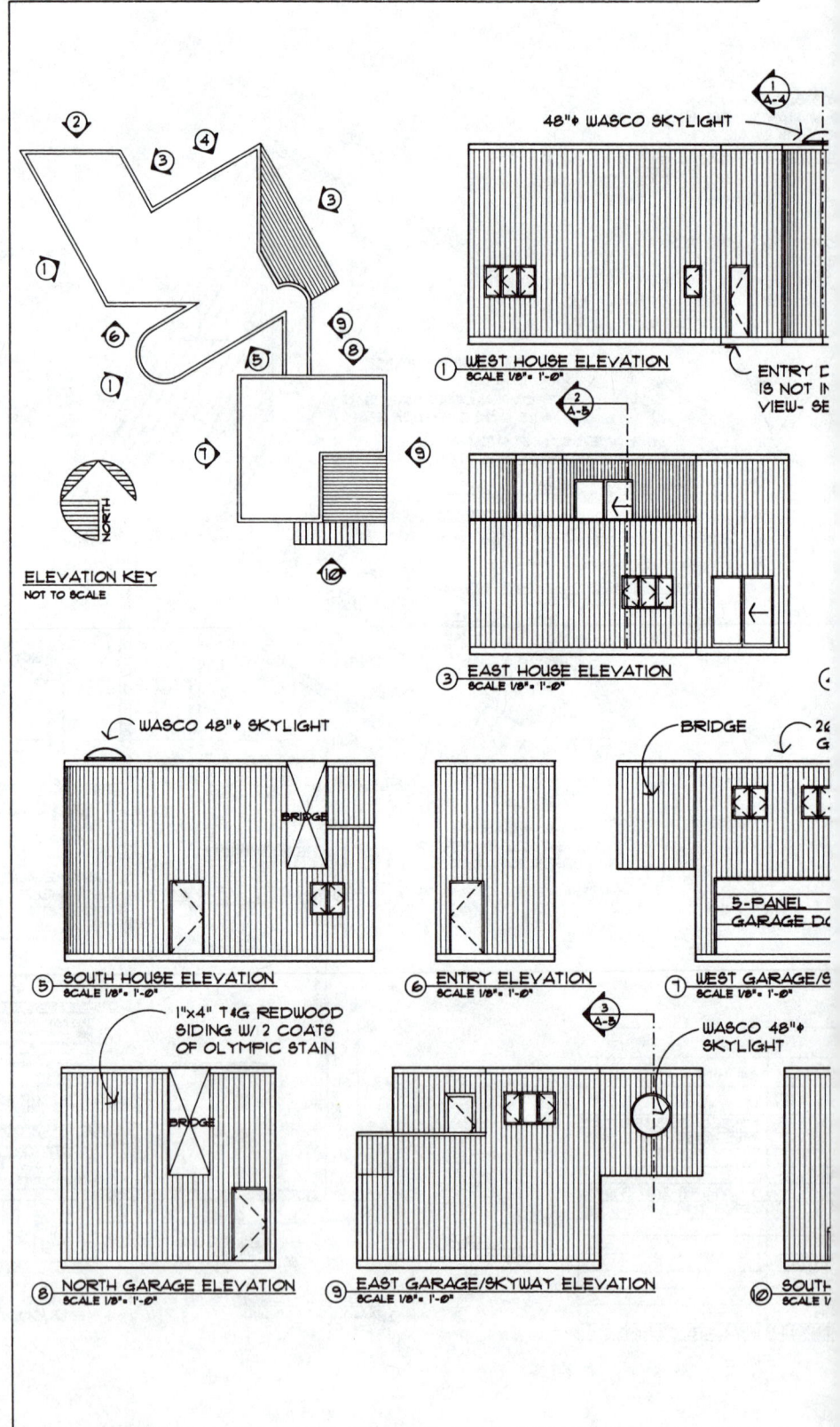

STAIR TOWER
48"⌀ WASCO SKYLIGHT
ENTRY DOOR IS NOT IN TRUE VIEW - SEE ELEV. 6
WEST HOUSE ELEVATION

ELEVATION KEY
NOT TO SCALE

48"⌀ WASCO SKYLIGHT

① **WEST HOUSE ELEVATION**
SCALE 1/8"= 1'-0"

ENTRY DOOR IS NOT IN VIEW- SE

③ **EAST HOUSE ELEVATION**
SCALE 1/8"= 1'-0"

WASCO 48"⌀ SKYLIGHT
BRIDGE

⑤ **SOUTH HOUSE ELEVATION**
SCALE 1/8"= 1'-0"

⑥ **ENTRY ELEVATION**
SCALE 1/8"= 1'-0"

BRIDGE
5-PANEL GARAGE DO

⑦ **WEST GARAGE/S**
SCALE 1/8"= 1'-0"

1"x4" T&G REDWOOD SIDING W/ 2 COATS OF OLYMPIC STAIN

WASCO 48"⌀ SKYLIGHT

⑧ **NORTH GARAGE ELEVATION**
SCALE 1/8"= 1'-0"

⑨ **EAST GARAGE/SKYWAY ELEVATION**
SCALE 1/8"= 1'-0"

⑩ **SOUTH**
SCALE 1/

SKYWAY HOUSE   23-10

SKYWAY HOUSE — ELEVATIONS

Sheet A4

Elevations (left side)

- **Stair Tower** — reference 1/A-4
- Entry door is not in true view — see Elev. 6
- **② North House Elevation** — Scale 1/8" = 1'-0"
  - Top of Roof Deck, Elev. 118'-0"
  - Pella fixed sliding door unit
  - Second Floor, Elev. 109'-0"
  - First Floor, Elev. 100'-0"
- **④ North House Elevation** — Scale 1/8" = 1'-0"
  - 1"x4" T&G redwood siding w/ 2 coats of Olympic stain
  - Top of Roof Deck, Elev. 118'-0"
  - Second Floor, Elev. 109'-0"
  - First Floor, Elev. 100'-0"
- **Garage/Skyway Elevation** — Scale 1/8" = 1'-0"
  - 20 ga. G.I. painted gravel stop
  - Top of Roof Deck, Elev. 118'-0"
  - Second Floor, Elev. 109'-0"
  - 2-3/4" plywood pieces cut to curve — for sill plate
  - Garage Floor, Elev. 98'-8"
  - 16-panel garage door
- **⑩ South Garage Elevation** — Scale 1/8" = 1'-0"
  - Wasco 48"⌀ skylight

① Section at Stair Tower — Scale 3/8" = 1'-0"

- Top plate to be 4 pieces of 3/4" plywood cut to the curve of the stair
- 48"⌀ Wasco double insulated skylight
- 1/2" gypsum board around curved opening
- Gravel ballast over EPDM roof
- Locate skylight over the center of the circular stair tower
- 5'-0" (6 treads @ 10")
- 1"x6" oak cap
- Balloon frame 2"x6" stud wall at stair tower
- 4'-6" (7 risers @ 7 3/4"±), 2'-8"
- 2"x12" stair stringer
- 5/8" gypsum board
- 2"⌀ oak handrail
- 2nd Fl. El. 109'-0"
- 1st Fl. El. 100'-0"
- 1/2" gypsum board on stair walls (typical)
- 2" rigid insulation
- 8" poured concrete wall
- Trowel-on waterproofing
- 8"x16" curved footing @ stair tower
- Keyway in curved stair tower wall

SKYWAY HOUSE 23-11

Wall Sections/A-5

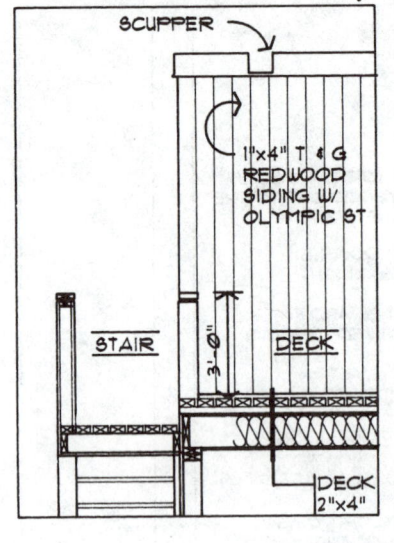

SCUPPER
1"x4" T & G REDWOOD SIDING W/ OLYMPIC ST
STAIR
DECK
DECK 2"x4"

Sheet A-5 contains wall sections cut through various parts of the house. Section cuts should be determined by defining every unique condition in the project. A good way to do this is to use a 3-dimensional study model. Move around the model building, marking each condition that requires definition. The drawings above and below show drafting detail that is necessary to use when assembling a wall section.

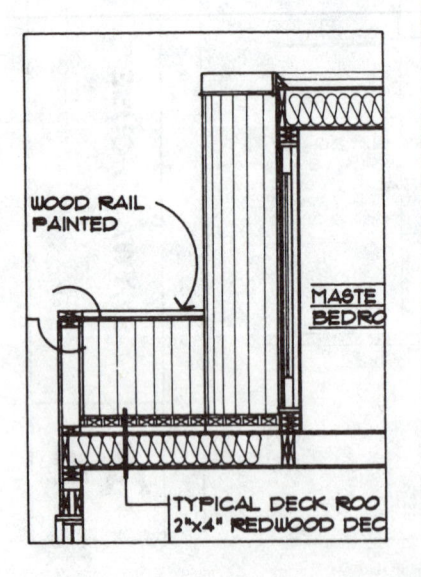

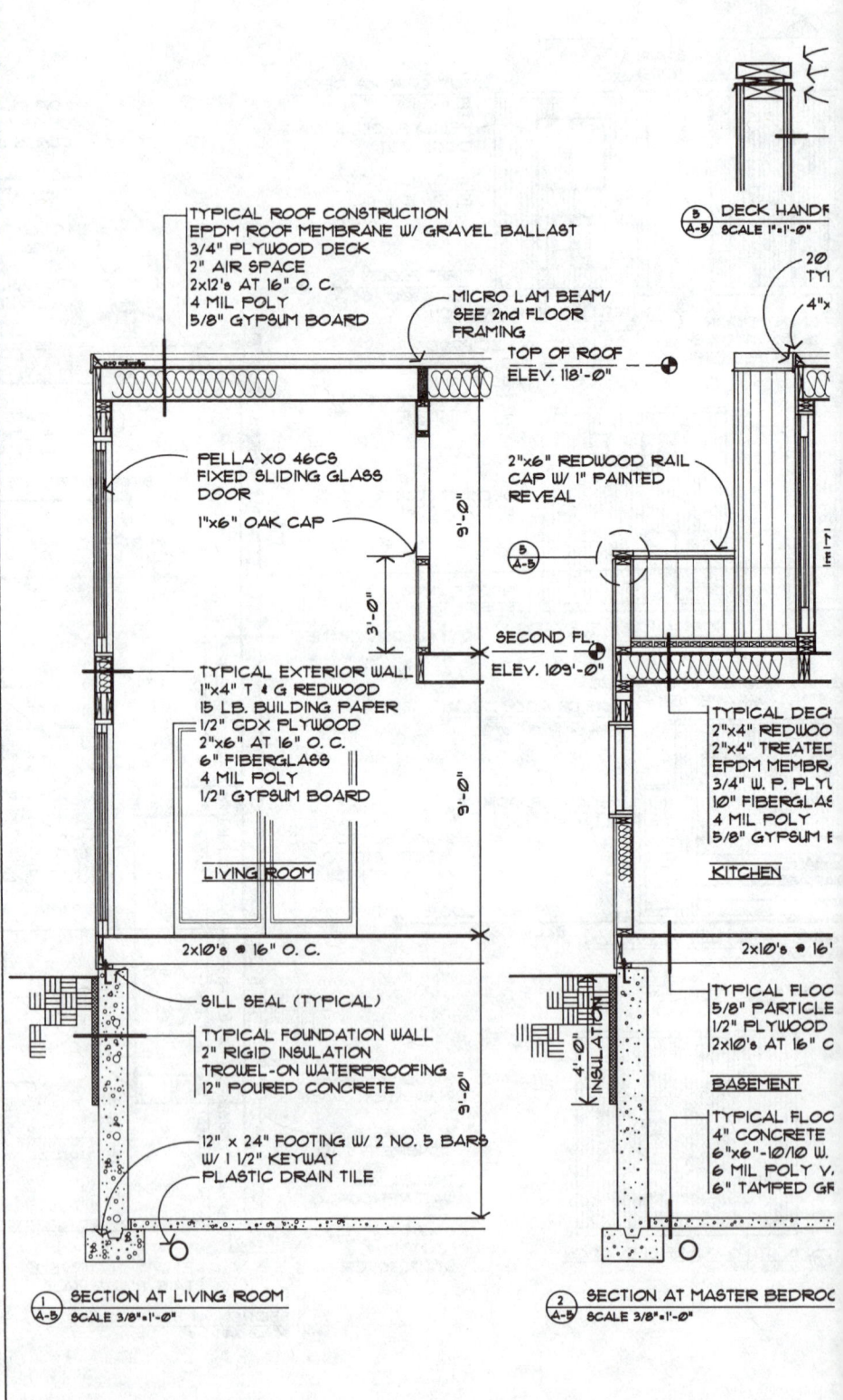

WOOD RAIL PAINTED
MASTER BEDROOM
TYPICAL DECK ROO
2"x4" REDWOOD DEC

TYPICAL ROOF CONSTRUCTION
EPDM ROOF MEMBRANE W/ GRAVEL BALLAST
3/4" PLYWOOD DECK
2" AIR SPACE
2x12's AT 16" O.C.
4 MIL POLY
5/8" GYPSUM BOARD

MICRO LAM BEAM/ SEE 2nd FLOOR FRAMING

TOP OF ROOF ELEV. 118'-0"

PELLA XO 46CS FIXED SLIDING GLASS DOOR
1"x6" OAK CAP

2"x6" REDWOOD RAIL CAP W/ 1" PAINTED REVEAL

SECOND FL. ELEV. 109'-0"

TYPICAL EXTERIOR WALL
1"x4" T & G REDWOOD
15 LB. BUILDING PAPER
1/2" CDX PLYWOOD
2"x6" AT 16" O.C.
6" FIBERGLASS
4 MIL POLY
1/2" GYPSUM BOARD

LIVING ROOM

TYPICAL DECK
2"x4" REDWOO
2"x4" TREATED
EPDM MEMBR
3/4" W.P. PLY
10" FIBERGLAS
4 MIL POLY
5/8" GYPSUM B

KITCHEN

2x10's @ 16" O.C.

SILL SEAL (TYPICAL)
TYPICAL FOUNDATION WALL
2" RIGID INSULATION
TROWEL-ON WATERPROOFING
12" POURED CONCRETE

12" x 24" FOOTING W/ 2 NO. 5 BARS W/ 1 1/2" KEYWAY
PLASTIC DRAIN TILE

2x10's @ 16"
TYPICAL FLOO
5/8" PARTICLE
1/2" PLYWOOD
2x10's AT 16" O

BASEMENT

TYPICAL FLOO
4" CONCRETE
6"x6"-10/10 W.
6 MIL POLY V.
6" TAMPED GR

DECK HANDR
SCALE 1"=1'-0"

① SECTION AT LIVING ROOM
A-5 SCALE 3/8"=1'-0"

② SECTION AT MASTER BEDROO
A-5 SCALE 3/8"=1'-0"

SKYWAY HOUSE   23-12

Deck Handrail Detail

- 2"x6" REDWOOD RAIL CAP
- 1"x4" TREATED REVEAL (PAINTED)
- 20 GA. G. I. CAP FLASHING
- TREATED 2x4's
- 1/2" EXT. PLYWOOD
- 1"x4" T & G REDWOOD SIDING

DECK HANDRAIL DETAIL
SCALE 1"=1'-0"

Scupper Isometric

- 20 GA. G. I. SCUPPER
- BUILDING LINE
- 4"
- 6"
- 4" 8"
- 3-SIDE OPEN FACE DOWNSPOUT

NOTE: REFER TO THE ROOF PLAN ON SHEET A-1 FOR SCUPPER LOCATIONS

6 SCUPPER ISOMETRIC
A-5 NOT TO SCALE

Section at Bridge

- 20 GA. G. I. FLASHING (PAINTED) TYPICAL FOR ALL ROOF CONDITIONS
- 4"x4" TREATED WOOD CANT
- 48"Ø WASCO SKYLIGHT

MASTER BEDROOM

BRIDGE 6'-8"

TYPICAL DECK/ROOF CONST.
- 2"x4" REDWOOD DECK W/ 1/4" GAP
- 2"x4" TREATED SLEEPERS AT 2'-0"
- EPDM MEMBRANE ROOF
- 3/4" W. P. PLYWOOD DECK
- FIBERGLASS INSULATION
- 4 MIL POLY
- 5/8" GYPSUM BOARD

KITCHEN

BRIDGE FLOOR
- 5/8" PARTICLE BD.
- 1/2" PLYWOOD
- 2x12's AT 16" O.C.
- 10" FIBERGLASS
- 1/2" CDX
- 1"x4" T & G REDWOOD

3 SECTION AT BRIDGE
A-5 SCALE 3/8"=1'-0"

Section at Garage and Deck

- 20 GA. G. I. FLASHING (PAINTED) TYPICAL FOR ALL ROOF CONDITIONS
- SCUPPER
- 1"x4" T & G REDWOOD SIDING W/ OLYMPIC STAIN

STAIR   DECK

3'-0"

3-2x6's DOOR CURB

DECK FLOOR
- 2"x4" REDWOOD DECK W/ 1/4" GAP
- 2"x4" TREATED SLEEPERS AT 2'-0" O.C.
- 3/4" PLYWOOD DECK
- 12" TJI TRUSS JOISTS @ 12" O.C.
- 5/8" FIRE CODE 'X' GYPSUM BD.

GARAGE DOOR

FIRST FLOOR ELEV. 100'-0"
GARAGE FLOOR ELEV. 98'-8"

2x10's @ 16" O.C.

TYPICAL FLOOR
- 5/8" PARTICLE BOARD
- 1/2" PLYWOOD SUBFLOOR
- 2x10's AT 16" O.C.

BASEMENT

TYPICAL FLOOR SLAB
- 4" CONCRETE (SMOOTH TROWELED)
- 6x6-10/10 W. W. MESH REINFORCING
- 4 MIL POLY VAPOR BARRIER
- 6" TAMPED GRAVEL

BASEMENT FLOOR ELEV. 91'-0"

MASTER BEDROOM DECK

- 4" CONCRETE SLAB W/ 4 MIL POLY
- 6" TAMPED GRAVEL
- 8" POURED CONCRETE FOUNDATION
- 8"x16" FOOTING W/ 2 NO. 5 BARS

4 SECTION AT GARAGE AND DECK
A-5 SCALE 3/8"=1'-0"

WALL SECTIONS

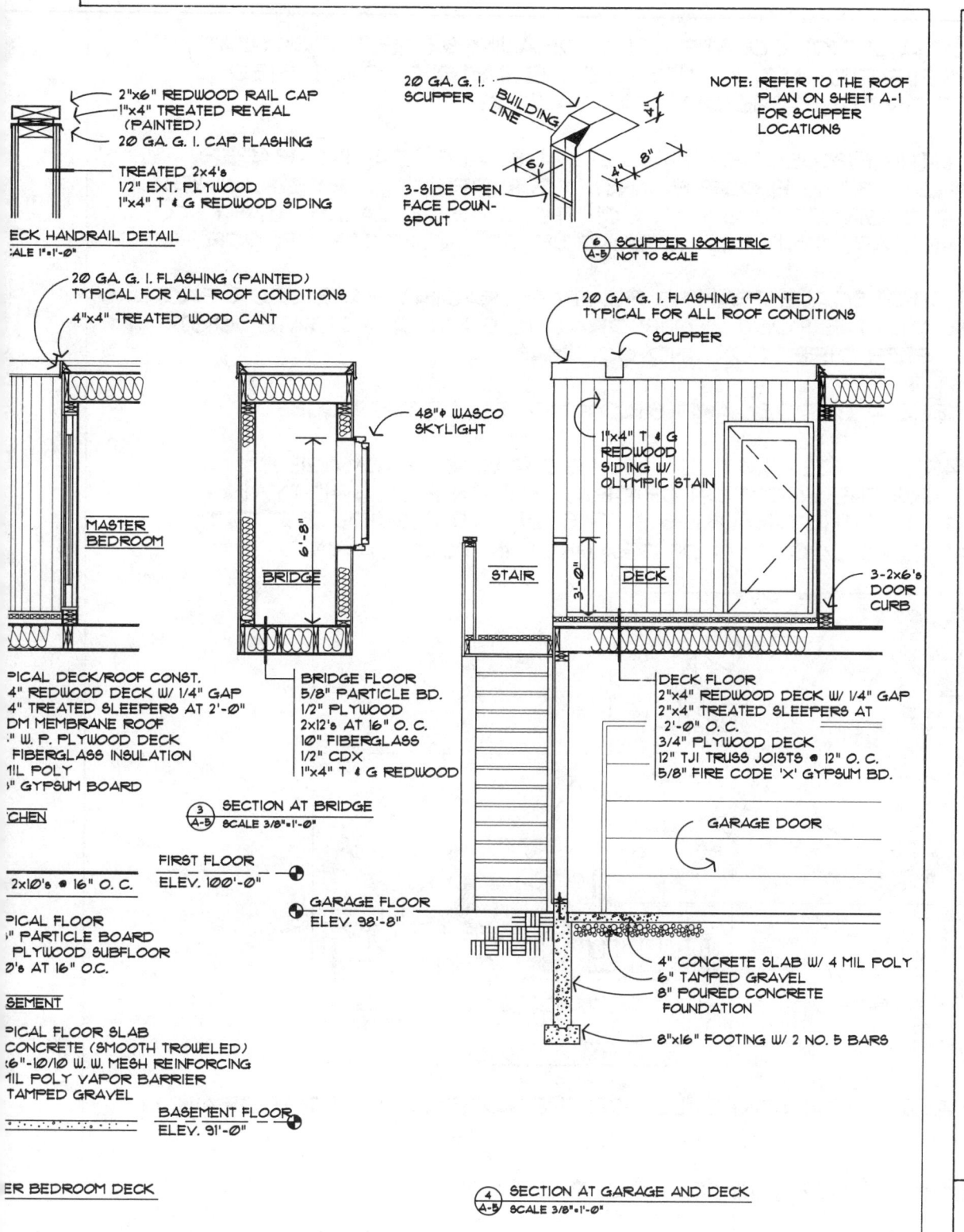

SKYWAY HOUSE

A5

SKYWAY HOUSE — 23-13

REPLAY

ASSEMBLE A SET OF CONSTRUCTION DRAWINGS FOR THE SKYWAY HOUSE PRESENTED IN THIS UNIT. USE THE INSTRUCTIONS LISTED BELOW TO PREPARE THE DRAWING PACKAGE.

1. REVIEW THE PROJECT BY MAKING 1/4" SCALE TRACING-PAPER DRAWINGS OF THE FLOOR PLANS. YOUR PRELIMINARY DRAWINGS SHOULD BEGIN WITH A LAYOUT OF THE OUTSIDE WALLS, STARTING WITH THE BASEMENT AND WORKING UP TO THE SECOND FLOOR.

2. DRAW A 1/8" SCALE FRAMING PLAN ON TRACING PAPER FOR EACH FLOOR AND THE ROOF. YOUR DRAWING SHOULD INDICATE JOIST AND RAFTER DIRECTION AND COLUMNS.

3. ASSEMBLE A CARDBOARD STUDY MODEL OF THE HOUSE.

4. PREPARE A SHEET LAYOUT OF THE DRAWING PACKAGE BY SKETCHING THE LOCATION OF DRAWINGS ON 8 1/2" x 11" TYPING PAPER. USE THE DRAWINGS IN THIS UNIT AS A GUIDE, BUT TRY TO VARY THE LOCATION OF DRAWINGS IN YOUR LAYOUT.

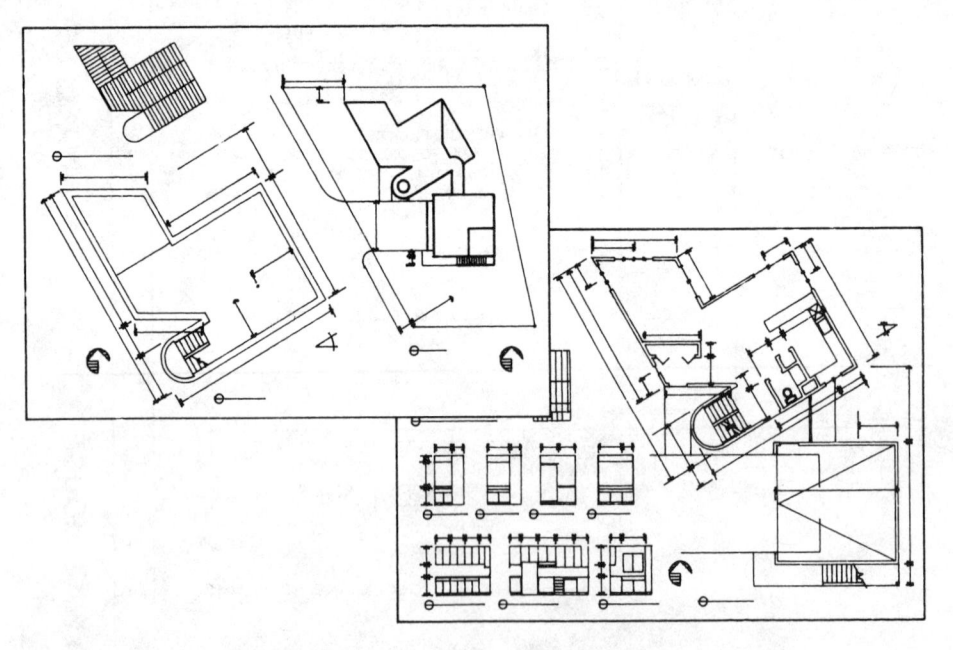

5. PREPARE A TIME SCHEDULE FOR THE ASSEMBLY OF THE DRAWING PACKAGE.

6. ASSEMBLE A WORKING DRAWING PACKAGE FOR THE HOUSE.

7. REVIEW A CHECK-SET OF THE PROJECT AT APPROXIMATELY 50% AMD 75% OF COMPLETION.

SKYWAY HOUSE

24 PROJECT DESIGN

ARCHITECTURAL DESIGN GROWS OUT OF A STEP-BY-STEP ANALYSIS OF CONDITIONS THAT AFFECT THE FORM AND FUNCTION OF A BUILDING. THESE STEPS PROVIDE INFORMATION THAT WILL ENABLE YOU TO MAKE DECISIONS ABOUT THE SIZE, THE STYLE, THE LOCATION, AND THE VOLUME OF A BUILDING. THE MATERIAL IN THIS UNIT WILL PROVIDE YOU WITH A VOCABULARY TO USE WHEN DESIGNING YOUR BUILDING. DESIGN INVOLVES ORGANIZING THE FLOOR PLAN, THE INTERIOR SPACE, AND THE EXTERIOR SPACE INTO A FUNCTIONAL AND AESTHETICALLY PLEASING STATEMENT. THIS UNIT IS DIVIDED INTO TWO SECTIONS: (1) ELEMENTARY INFORMATION REGARDING PROJECT ASSEMBLY, AND (2) SEVERAL EXAMPLES OF PROJECTS IN THEIR PRELIMINARY DESIGN PHASE. IT TAKES CONSIDERABLE TIME, SKILL, AND UNDERSTANDING TO DESIGN A QUALITY PROJECT. A TYPICAL ARCHITECT'S CONTRACT DEVOTES ROUGHLY 35% OF THE TOTAL PROJECT TIME TO DESIGN (WORKING DRAWINGS ACCOUNT FOR AN ADDITIONAL 40% AND THE CONSTRUCTION PHASE USES APPROXIMATELY 25%). OUR DISCUSSION OF DESIGN WILL BE DIVIDED INTO SIX SECTIONS:

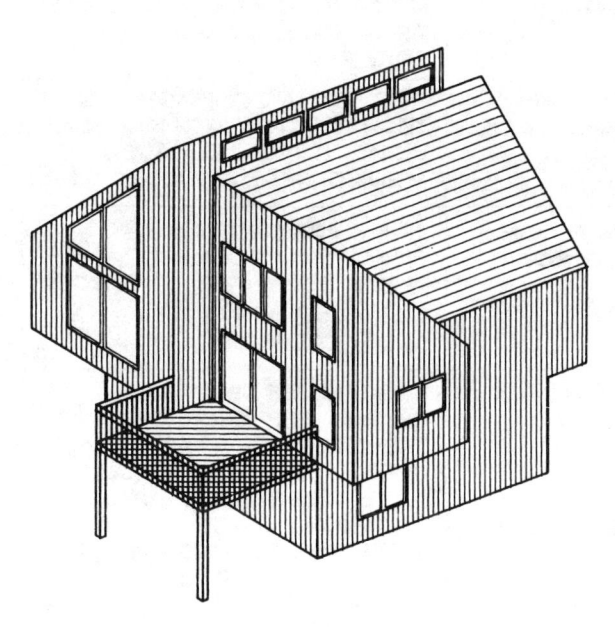

- PROGRAMMING
- ANALYSIS
- ORGANIZATION AND PLANNING
- DESIGN FACTORS
- MASSING
- STUDY MODELS

PROJECT DESIGN 24-1

PROGRAMMING

THE DESIGN PROCESS IS BEGUN BY WRITING A PROGRAM FOR THE PROJECT. A <u>PROGRAM</u> IS A STATEMENT THAT DEFINES EVERY SPACE IN THE BUILDING BY SIZE, USE, VOLUME, RELATIONSHIP WITH OTHER SPACES, FURNITURE IT WOULD CONTAIN, AND SPECIAL FEATURES. THIS IS THE POINT AT WHICH YOUR CLIENT HAS SOME OF HIS OR HER GREATEST INPUT IN THE DESIGN OF THE PROJECT. THE PROGRAM WOULD REFLECT THIS INPUT BY INCLUDING SUCH ITEMS AS THE TYPE OF ENTERTAINING DONE IN A HOUSE, WHETHER IT WILL CONTAIN A MUSIC ROOM (WITH SPECIAL SOUND REDUCTION BETWEEN ROOMS), THE AMOUNT OF NATURAL LIGHT THAT WOULD ENTER EACH ROOM, AND WHAT VIEWS ARE DESIRED.

THIS UNIT WILL USE A THREE-BEDROOM HOUSE LOCATED ON A SITE WITH A LAKE VIEW AS AN EXAMPLE. INFORMATION THAT WOULD BE USED TO FORM A CONCEPT FOR THE DESIGN IS PRESENTED IN THE PROGRAM BELOW.

ROOM NAME	ROOM SIZE	ROOM RELATIONSHIPS	SPECIAL FEATURES
LIVING ROOM	16' x 16'	THE LIVING AREA SHOULD OPEN TO THE DINING SPACE FOR PARTIES. LOCATE NEAR THE KITCHEN THE OFFICE/LOFT SHOULD OPEN TO THIS AREA.	THIS WILL BE THE CENTER OF THE HOUSE. PROVIDE HIGH CEILINGS WITH LOTS OF GLASS AND A LAKE VIEW. THE ROOM SHOULD HAVE A FIREPLACE AND 120 SQ FT OF SHELIVNG.
DINING (EXTERIOR DECK)	8' x 12' (DECK IS 12' x 12')	PLACE THE DINING AREA ADJACENT TO THE KITCHEN. PLACE NEXT TO LIVING ROOM FOR EXPANDED PARTIES.	THIS SPACE SHOULD SERVE FAMILY DINING AND FORMAL PARTIES. PROVIDE A WALL THAT SEPARATES IT FROM THE KITCHEN. THE DECK WILL ACT AS AN EXTENSION OF THIS SPACE.
KITCHEN	8' x 12'	LOCATE NEXT TO THE DINING ROOM AND DECK. PLACE NEAR THE ENTRY FOR GROCERIES.	PROVIDE A COMPACT "HIGH TECH" KITCHEN WITH NATURAL LIGHT. IT SHOULD HAVE A VIEW TO THE BACKYARD.
STUDY	9' x 12'	PLACE ON MAIN FLOOR NEAR THE LIVING ROOM.	THIS SHOULD BE A QUIET SPACE WITH BOOKSHELVES AND A COMPUTER. THE ROOM WILL ALSO SERVE AS A GUEST BEDROOM.
FAMILY	11' x 11'	PLACE AWAY FROM THE LIVING ROOM (ON A DIFFERENT LEVEL, IF POSSIBLE). LOCATE NEAR CHILDREN'S BEDROOMS.	THIS WILL BE USED FOR GAMES, TELEVISION AND FOR THE CHILDREN TO ENTERTAIN GUESTS. THE ROOM SHOULD HAVE A SEPARATE ENTRANCE AND SMALL PATIO. ISOLATE THE STEREO SOUND FROM THE MAIN LIVING AREAS.

PROJECT DESIGN

HOUSE PROGRAM (CONTINUED)

ROOM NAME	ROOM SIZE	ROOM RELATIONSHIPS	SPECIAL FEATURES
BOY'S BEDROOM	9' x 12'	PLACE AWAY FROM MASTER BEDROOM. SEPARATE OUTSIDE ENTRY. PLACE CLOSE TO FAMILY ROOM.	PROVIDE QUITE STUDY SPACE. ISOLATE STEREO SOUND FROM OTHER LIVING AREAS. PROVIDE A LAKE VIEW.
GIRL'S BEDROOM	11' x 12'	LOCATE AWAY FROM THE MASTER BEDROOM AND CLOSE TO FAMILY ROOM.	THIS ROOM HAS FEATURES SIMILAR TO BOY'S BEDROOM. PROVIDE 10' OF CLOSET.
LOFT/OFFICE	12' x 13'	PROVIDE EASY ACCESS TO THE FRONT ENTRY FOR OCCASIONAL OFFICE USE.	THIS SPACE SHOULD BE OPEN WITH A LAKE VIEW AND NATURAL LIGHT. PROVIDE FOR A COMPUTER AND DRAFTING BOARD. THE SPACE SHOULD HAVE 50 SQ FT OF SHELVING.
MASTER BEDROOM	8' x 16'	PLACE CLOSE TO MASTER BATH. LOCATE NEAR LOFT.	PROVIDE A VAULTED CEILING AND A LAKE VIEW. THIS SPACE SHOULD BE BRIGHT AND SUNNY.
BATH(S)	6' x 8' (6' x 5' HALF-BATH)	PROVIDE: (1) MASTER BATH, (2) CHILDREN'S BATH, AND (3) HALF-BATH ON MAIN FLOOR.	THE MASTER-BATH SHOULD HAVE A WHIRLPOOL BATHTUB. THE CHILDREN'S BATH SHOULD HAVE A SHOWER.

A PROGRAM IS A WRITTEN DESCRIPTION OF THE NEEDS OF A CLIENT. IT SHOULD BE POSSIBLE TO RETURN TO THE PROGRAM, ONCE THE FINAL DESIGN IS COMPLETE, AND VERIFY THAT ALL OF THE PROGRAM STATEMENTS HAVE BEEN MET. YOU MIGHT CONSIDER EXPANDING THE PROGRAM BY ADDING A SMALL SKETCH OF EACH ROOM CONTAINING ITEMS SUCH AS FURNITURE AND VIEWS THAT WOULD AID IN VISUALIZING THE DESIGN.

ANALYSIS

DESIGN ANALYSIS INVOLVES REVIEWING THE FACTORS THAT AFFECT THE ORGANIZATION OF THE PROJECT. A GOOD TOOL TO USE IN ACCOMPLISHING THIS TASK IS A SKETCH OF CONDITIONS MADE WITH A FELT-TIP PEN ON TRACING PAPER. YOUR SKETCH-ANALYSIS SHOULD CONTAIN NOTES THAT WILL HELP YOU IN THE DESIGN PROCESS. SOME TIPS TO REMEMBER WHEN ADDING YOUR NOTES ARE THE FOLLOWING:

- MARK THE BEST VIEWS ON THE SITE.
- LOCATE GOOD POINTS FOR DRIVES, WALKS, AND PARKING.
- CONSIDER TRAFFIC NOISE AND PRIVACY FROM NEIGHBORS.
- LOCATE GOOD SUMMER AND WINTER SOLAR ANGLES.
- REVIEW THE SITE CONTOURS TO DETERMINE ENTRY LOCATIONS.
- EXAMINE CONSTRUCTION MATERIALS THAT WILL FIT THE PROJECT.
- REVIEW THE CONSTRUCTION BUDGET.
- MARK SITE FEATURES (TREES, WATER, FENCES, ETC.) THAT WILL AFFECT THE DESIGN.

PROJECT DESIGN

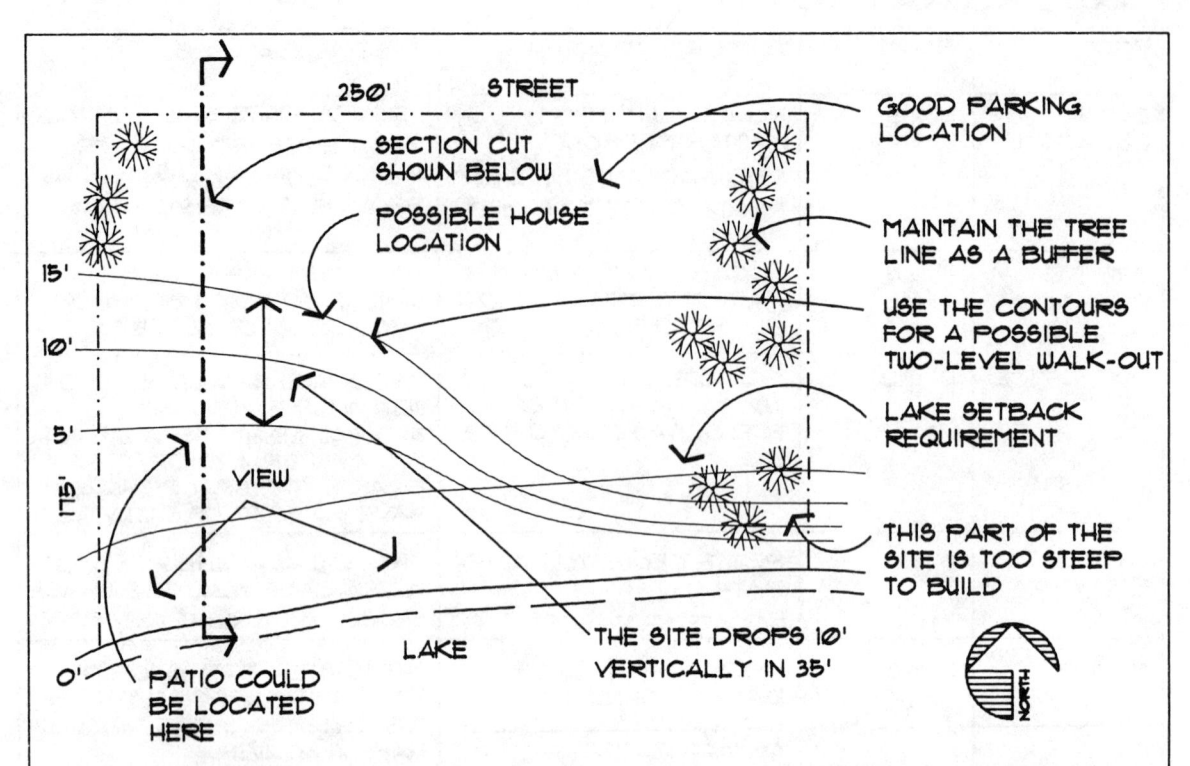

[Site plan with labels:]
- 250' STREET
- SECTION CUT SHOWN BELOW
- GOOD PARKING LOCATION
- POSSIBLE HOUSE LOCATION
- MAINTAIN THE TREE LINE AS A BUFFER
- USE THE CONTOURS FOR A POSSIBLE TWO-LEVEL WALK-OUT
- LAKE SETBACK REQUIREMENT
- THIS PART OF THE SITE IS TOO STEEP TO BUILD
- 15', 10', 5', 0'
- 175'
- VIEW
- LAKE
- THE SITE DROPS 10' VERTICALLY IN 35'
- PATIO COULD BE LOCATED HERE
- NORTH

BEGIN DESIGN ANALYSIS WITH THE SITE. ON THE PLAN ABOVE NOTES ARE SHOWN THAT DEFINE SOME OF THE CONSIDERATIONS THAT ARE PART OF THE ANALYSIS FOR THE HOUSE. THE STRONGEST FEATURE OF THE SITE IS THE LAKE VIEW; IT WILL DETERMINE MANY OF THE MAJOR DESIGN DECISIONS. A SECOND FEATURE IS THE RATHER STEEP CHANGE IN GRADE; THIS COULD INDICATE A SPLIT-LEVEL DESIGN. DON'T ENTER THE ANALYSIS PHASE OF DESIGN WITH A PRECONCEIVED IDEA— LET YOUR PROGRAM AND ANALYSIS DIRECT YOUR DESIGN CONCEPT.

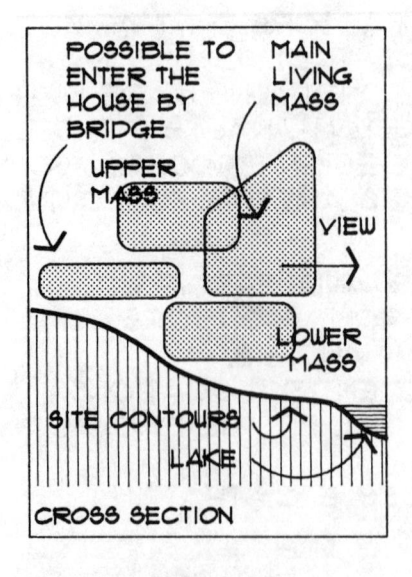

[Cross section diagram labels:]
- POSSIBLE TO ENTER THE HOUSE BY BRIDGE
- MAIN LIVING MASS
- UPPER MASS
- VIEW
- LOWER MASS
- SITE CONTOURS
- LAKE
- CROSS SECTION

THE DRAWING AT THE LEFT SHOWS A "BUBBLE DIAGRAM" OF THE BUILDING IN A CROSS SECTION OF THE SITE. IT DOESN'T SHOW ROOMS; INSTEAD, IT INDICATES A CONCEPT OF "MASSING" FOR THE DESIGN THAT COULD FIT THE SITE. THIS IS ONE OF MANY SKETCHES THAT WILL BE GENERATED TO STUDY THE PROJECT. MAKE NOTES TO YOURSELF CONCERNING FEATURES THAT YOU LIKE AND ITEMS THAT NEED FURTHER REFINEMENT. DON'T TRY TO RUSH THE DESIGN PROCESS— IT TAKES TIME AND A GREAT DEAL OF STUDY.

PROJECT DESIGN

ORGANIZATION AND PLANNING

TO THIS POINT, THE DESIGN PROCESS HAS INVOLVED FORMING A CONCEPT BY USING PROBLEM-SOLVING TECHNIQUES. IN THE ORGANIZATION AND PLANNING STEP, WE WILL BEGIN TO DRAW A FLOOR PLAN. ARCHITECTS USE SEVERAL DIFFERENT TECHNIQUES TO DETERMINE PLAN LAYOUT; WE WILL USE A SIMPLE PROCESS THAT INVOLVES CUTTING THE PROGRAM SPACES OUT OF PAPER AND THEN MANIPULATING THEM INTO A DESIGN. FIRST, WE WILL NEED TO USE AN ARCHITECT'S SCALE TO MARK EACH AREA TO THE SIZE DETERMINED IN THE PROGRAM. USE A DISPOSABLE PAPER, SUCH AS TYPING PAPER, AND DRAW THE ROOMS TO AN 1/8" = 1'-0" SCALE. LABEL THE ROOM NAMES AND IMPORTANT DESIGN CONCERNS (E.G., "LAKE VIEW," "FIREPLACE," OR "LOCATE NEXT TO KITCHEN"). A FURTHER STEP THAT AIDS IN THE DESIGN PROCESS IS TO USE COLORED PAPER FOR INDICATING THE DIFFERENT FUNCTIONS OF SPACES. FOR EXAMPLE, THE HOUSE PROGRAM (PAGES 24-2 AND 24-3) STATES THAT THE TWO CHILDREN'S BEDROOMS, THE FAMILY ROOM, AND A BATH SHOULD BE LOCATED NEXT TO ONE ANOTHER. USING THE SAME COLOR PAPER FOR THESE ROOMS WOULD MAKE THE PLANNING PROCESS EASIER BY IDENTIFYING THEIR ASSOCIATION BY COLOR. ONE SOLUTION FOR THE HOUSE IS SHOWN BELOW.

THE PROGRAM WAS USED TO DETERMINE THAT THESE ROOMS WOULD WORK TOGETHER. USE THE SAME COLOR PAPER TO IDENTIFY THEIR ASSOCIATION.

THIS SCHEME SHOWS THE LOWER LEVEL OF THE HOUSE. THE DESIGN IS TIED TO THE IDEA THAT THE PROJECT COULD WORK WITH A THREE LEVEL HOUSE. A BRIDGE WOULD BE USED TO ENTER AT MID-LEVEL (THIS WOULD WORK WELL WITH THE CONTOURS).

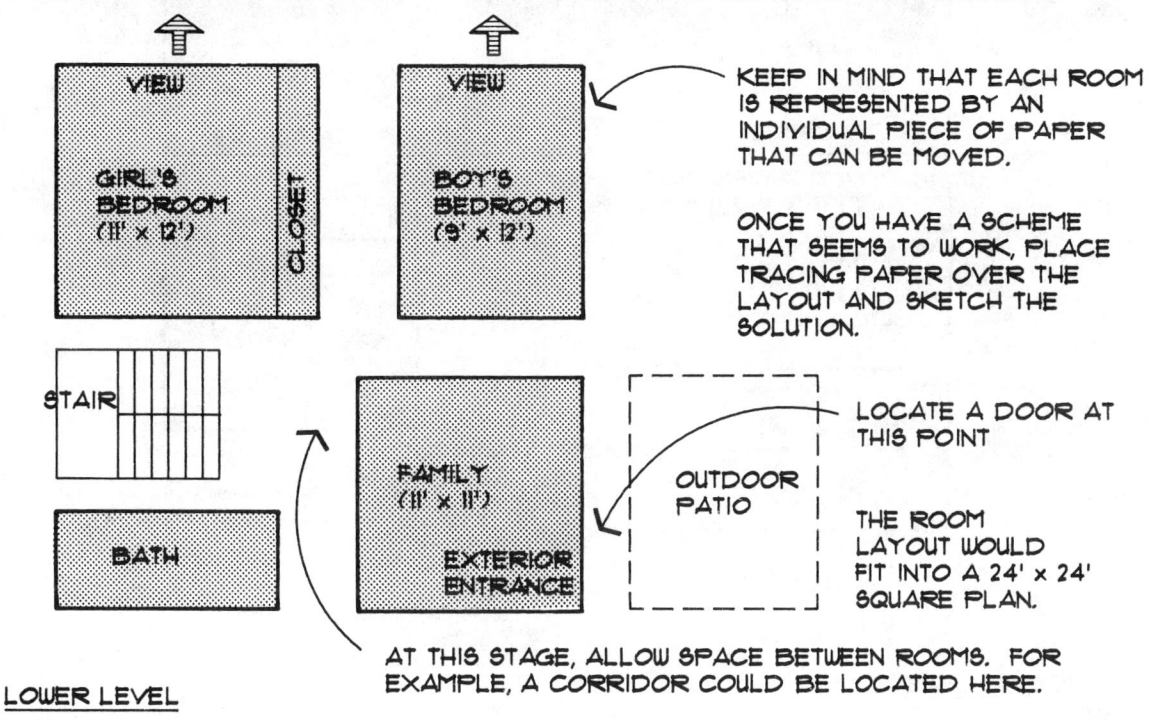

VIEW

GIRL'S BEDROOM (11' x 12') CLOSET

VIEW

BOY'S BEDROOM (9' x 12')

KEEP IN MIND THAT EACH ROOM IS REPRESENTED BY AN INDIVIDUAL PIECE OF PAPER THAT CAN BE MOVED.

ONCE YOU HAVE A SCHEME THAT SEEMS TO WORK, PLACE TRACING PAPER OVER THE LAYOUT AND SKETCH THE SOLUTION.

STAIR

BATH

FAMILY (11' x 11') EXTERIOR ENTRANCE

OUTDOOR PATIO

LOCATE A DOOR AT THIS POINT

THE ROOM LAYOUT WOULD FIT INTO A 24' x 24' SQUARE PLAN.

AT THIS STAGE, ALLOW SPACE BETWEEN ROOMS. FOR EXAMPLE, A CORRIDOR COULD BE LOCATED HERE.

LOWER LEVEL

PROJECT DESIGN

A SOLUTION TO THE MAIN FLOOR PLAN IS ILLUSTRATED BELOW. THE PROGRAM INDICATES A RELATIONSHIP BETWEEN THE LIVING ROOM, DINING ROOM, KITCHEN, AND STUDY THAT WOULD PLACE THEM CLOSE TOGETHER. AN ADVANTAGE TO USING THE PAPER CUT-OUT PLANNING PROCESS IS THE FLEXIBILITY THAT IT ALLOWS: A DESIGN CHANGE IS MADE BY SIMPLY RELOCATING A PAPER ROOM PIECE. IT ALSO PROVIDES YOU WITH THE ABILITY TO CRITICIZE THE RELATIONSHIPS BETWEEN SPACES, AN IMPORTANT FACTOR IN DESIGN. ONCE YOU HAVE A DESIGN THAT YOU LIKE, MAKE A SKETCH OF THE LAYOUT ON TRACING PAPER AND LABEL IT "SCHEME 1." WHEN YOU HAVE THREE (OR MORE) SCHEMES, CRITICIZE YOUR SKETCHES BY LISTING THE STRONG (AND WEAK) POINTS OF EACH DESIGN. THE NEXT STEP IS TO INCORPORATE THE STRONG POINTS OF EACH DESIGN INTO YOUR FINAL SOLUTION.

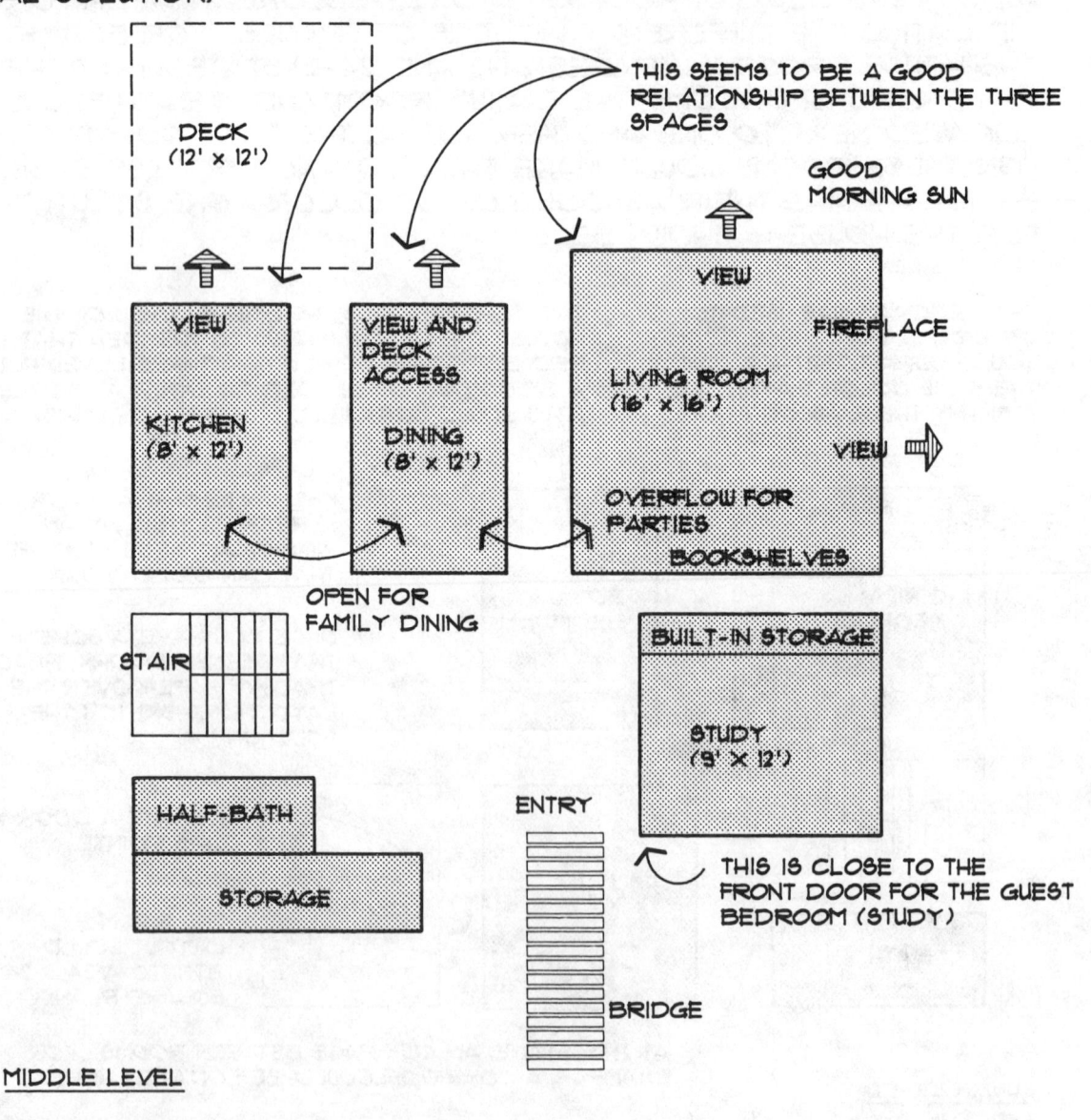

DECK (12' x 12')

THIS SEEMS TO BE A GOOD RELATIONSHIP BETWEEN THE THREE SPACES

GOOD MORNING SUN

VIEW

KITCHEN (8' x 12')

VIEW AND DECK ACCESS

DINING (8' x 12')

VIEW

LIVING ROOM (16' x 16')

FIREPLACE

VIEW

OVERFLOW FOR PARTIES

BOOKSHELVES

OPEN FOR FAMILY DINING

STAIR

BUILT-IN STORAGE

STUDY (9' x 12')

HALF-BATH

STORAGE

ENTRY

THIS IS CLOSE TO THE FRONT DOOR FOR THE GUEST BEDROOM (STUDY)

BRIDGE

MIDDLE LEVEL

PROJECT DESIGN 24-6

THE UPPER LEVEL OF THE HOUSE PLAN IS SHOWN BELOW. THE PROGRAM DIRECTS THE RELATIONSHIP BETWEEN SPACES HERE AS IT DID FOR THE FIRST TWO FLOORS. THE NEXT STEP IN ORGANIZING AND PLANNING INVOLVES REFINEMENT OF THE SCHEMATIC PLANS INTO A FLOOR PLAN WITH WALLS AND WINDOWS.

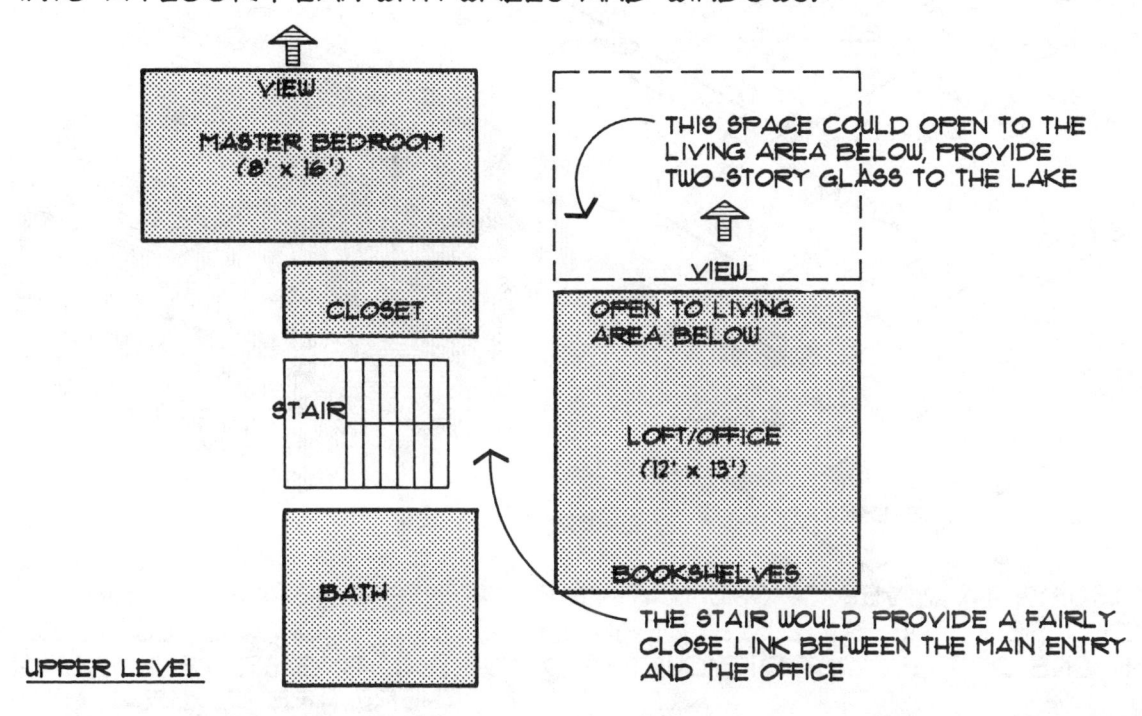

MASTER BEDROOM (8' x 16'), VIEW

THIS SPACE COULD OPEN TO THE LIVING AREA BELOW, PROVIDE TWO-STORY GLASS TO THE LAKE

VIEW

CLOSET

OPEN TO LIVING AREA BELOW

STAIR

LOFT/OFFICE (12' x 13')

BOOKSHELVES

BATH

THE STAIR WOULD PROVIDE A FAIRLY CLOSE LINK BETWEEN THE MAIN ENTRY AND THE OFFICE

UPPER LEVEL

A KEY ELEMENT IN THE SUCCESS OF THIS DESIGN, OR ANY OTHER, IS TO CONCENTRATE ON PRODUCING A WELL-ORGANIZED FLOOR PLAN BEFORE MOVING TO A THREE-DIMENSIONAL FORM. A GOOD DESIGN WILL ALLOW THE FLOOR PLAN TO DIRECT THE BUILDING VOLUME.

DESIGN FACTORS

ONCE YOU ARE SATISFIED WITH A SCHEMATIC FLOOR PLAN, YOUR NEXT STEP IS TO BEGIN TO DEVELOP IT INTO A THREE-DIMENSIONAL FORM (ARCHITECTS COMMONLY CALL THIS <u>MASSING</u>). THIS STEP TYPICALLY CAUSES PROBLEMS FOR A BEGINNING DESIGNER BECAUSE IT IS DIFFICULT TO LEARN HOW TO "GET AN IDEA." THERE ARE TWO WAYS OF APPROACHING DESIGN DEVELOPMENT THAT YOU SHOULD FIND HELPFUL, HOWEVER: (1) USE THE ANALYSIS THAT YOU HAVE ALREADY PREPARED FOR THE PROJECT, AND (2) RESEARCH ARCHITECTURAL PROJECTS FOR DESIGN SOLUTIONS. YOU MIGHT BEGIN YOUR RESEARCH, FOR EXAMPLE, BY REVIEWING THREE MONTHLY MAGAZINES: <u>ARCHITECTURAL RECORD</u>, <u>PROGRESSIVE ARCHITECTURE</u>, AND <u>ARCHITECTURE</u>. THEY PROVIDE PROBABLY THE BEST SOURCE FOR NEW DESIGN FORMS IN THE PROFESSION. KEEP IN MIND THAT THE OBJECT OF RESEARCHING OTHER PROJECTS IS TO GAIN IDEAS IN FORM AND MASS RELATIONSHIPS, NOT TO COPY.

PROJECT DESIGN

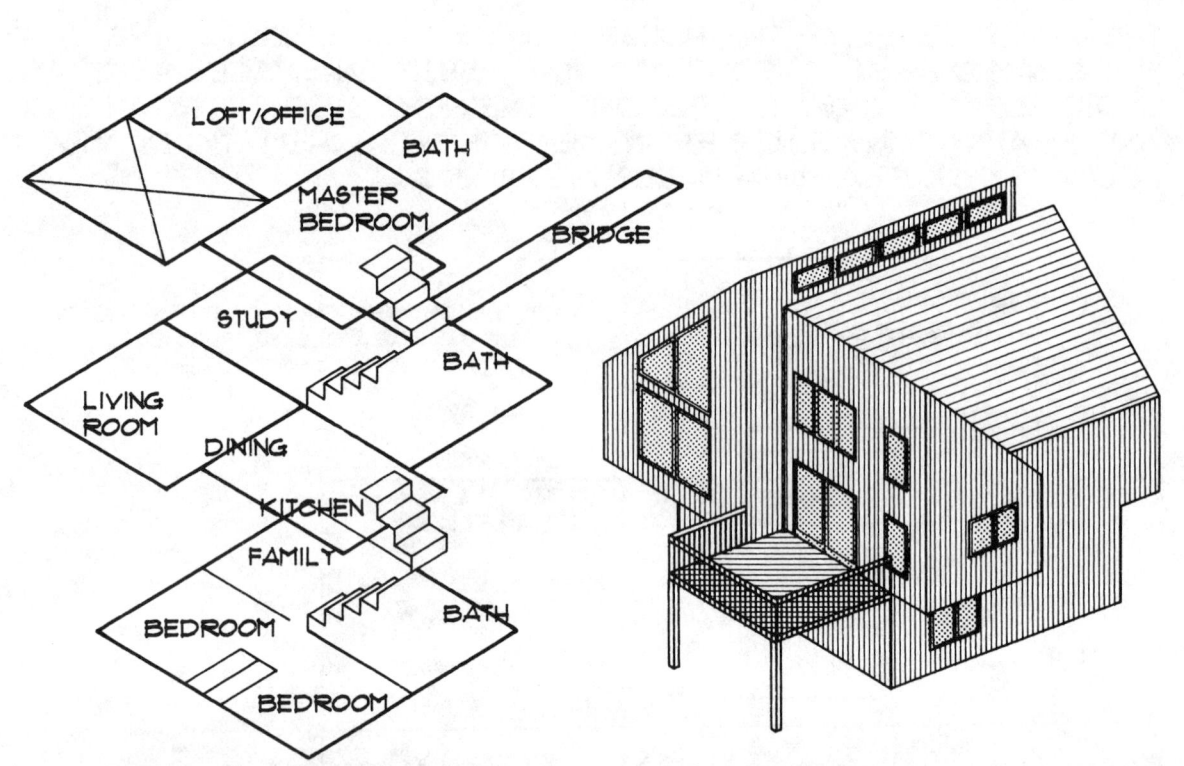

MASSING INVOLVES COORDINATING BOTH INTERIOR AND EXTERIOR VOLUMES IN THE BUILDING. DEFINING THE SHAPE OF A BUILDING CAN BE ONE OF THE MOST DIFFICULT AND YET EXCITING STEPS IN DESIGN. THERE ARE SEVERAL STEPS THAT SHOULD BE TAKEN WHEN MAKING DECISIONS ABOUT THE FORM A BUILDING TAKES. ONE IS TO STUDY THE PROJECT IN MODEL FORM: CONSTRUCT A MODEL SO THAT THE PROPORTIONS OF THE BUILDING CAN BE EVALUATED. A SECOND IS TO REVIEW DESIGN PRINCIPLES IN ARCHITECTURAL MAGAZINES; MAGAZINES SUCH AS <u>ARCHITECTURAL RECORD</u>, <u>PROGRESSIVE ARCHITECTURE</u>, AND <u>ARCHITECTURE</u> CAN PROVIDE INFORMATION REGARDING THE FORM AND MATERIALS USED IN QUALITY ARCHITECTURE. A THIRD STEP IS TO MAKE SURE THAT DECISIONS MADE IN THE PROGRAM AND FLOOR PLAN LAYOUT ARE FOLLOWED IN THE BUILDING MASSING STAGE.

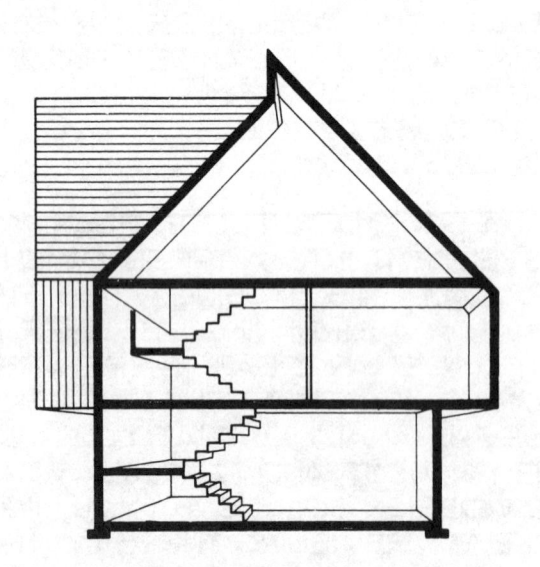

| PROJECT DESIGN | 24-8 |

A BUILDING DESIGN INVOLVES THE COMBINATION OF SEVERAL SHAPES INTO A VOLUME. THE RELATIONSHIP BETWEEN SHAPES DEFINES THE INTERIOR AND EXTERIOR FORM OF THE BUILDING. THIS FORM, ALONG WITH THE TEXTURE OF THE MATERIALS, DETERMINES THE QUALITY OF DESIGN. FRANK LLOYD WRIGHT'S 1930S HOUSE, CALLED "FALLING WATER," IS A SERIES OF CONCRETE, GLASS, AND STONE FORMS BUILT OVER A WATERFALL. THE PROJECT, VOTED THE BEST PIECE OF 20TH CENTURY ARCHITECTURE IN A READER SURVEY DONE BY <u>ARCHITECTURAL RECORD</u>, IS AN EXCELLENT EXAMPLE OF A BUILDING WITH SIMPLE SHAPES THAT FORM A BOND WITH THE SITE. CONTRAST THAT WITH A SMALL STORE IN LONG ISLAND THAT WAS BUILT IN THE FORM OF A DUCK. WHILE BOTH BUILDINGS HAVE SHAPE, ONE HARMONIZES WITH THE SITE - THE OTHER "FIGHTS" WITH IT.

BUILDINGS TAKE MANY SHAPES. THE ILLUSTRATION BELOW SHOWS SOME COMMON ROOF FORMS THAT INFLUENCE DESIGN. MANY DESIGNS, LIKE "FALLING WATER," COMBINE SHAPES TO PRODUCE A UNIQUE BUILDING FORM.

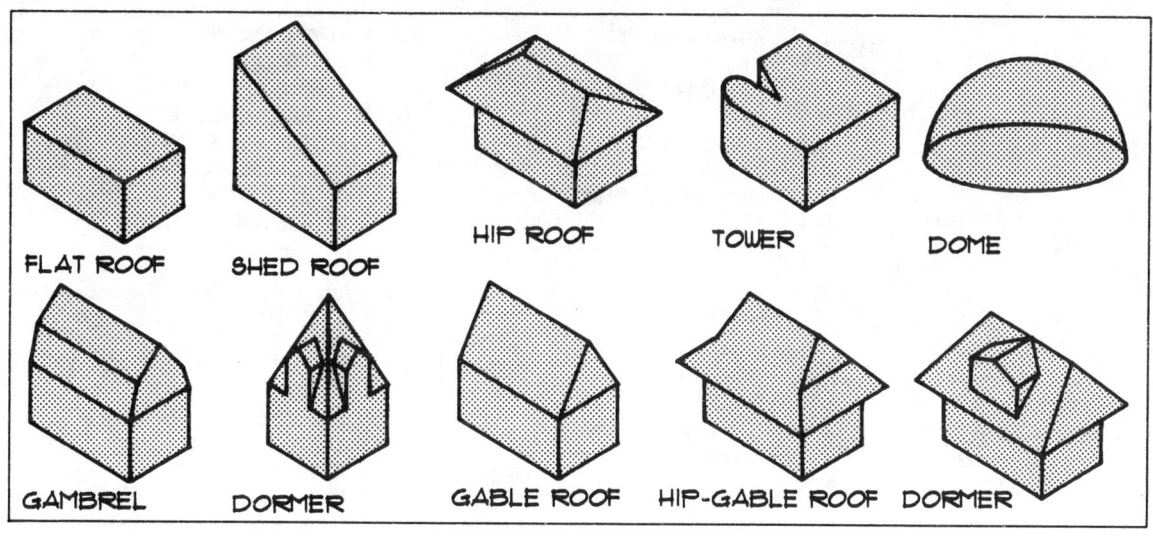

FRANK LLOYD WRIGHT'S FALLING WATER

DOOR

LONG ISLAND DUCK SHOP

FLAT ROOF • SHED ROOF • HIP ROOF • TOWER • DOME

GAMBREL • DORMER • GABLE ROOF • HIP-GABLE ROOF • DORMER

PROJECT DESIGN

24-9

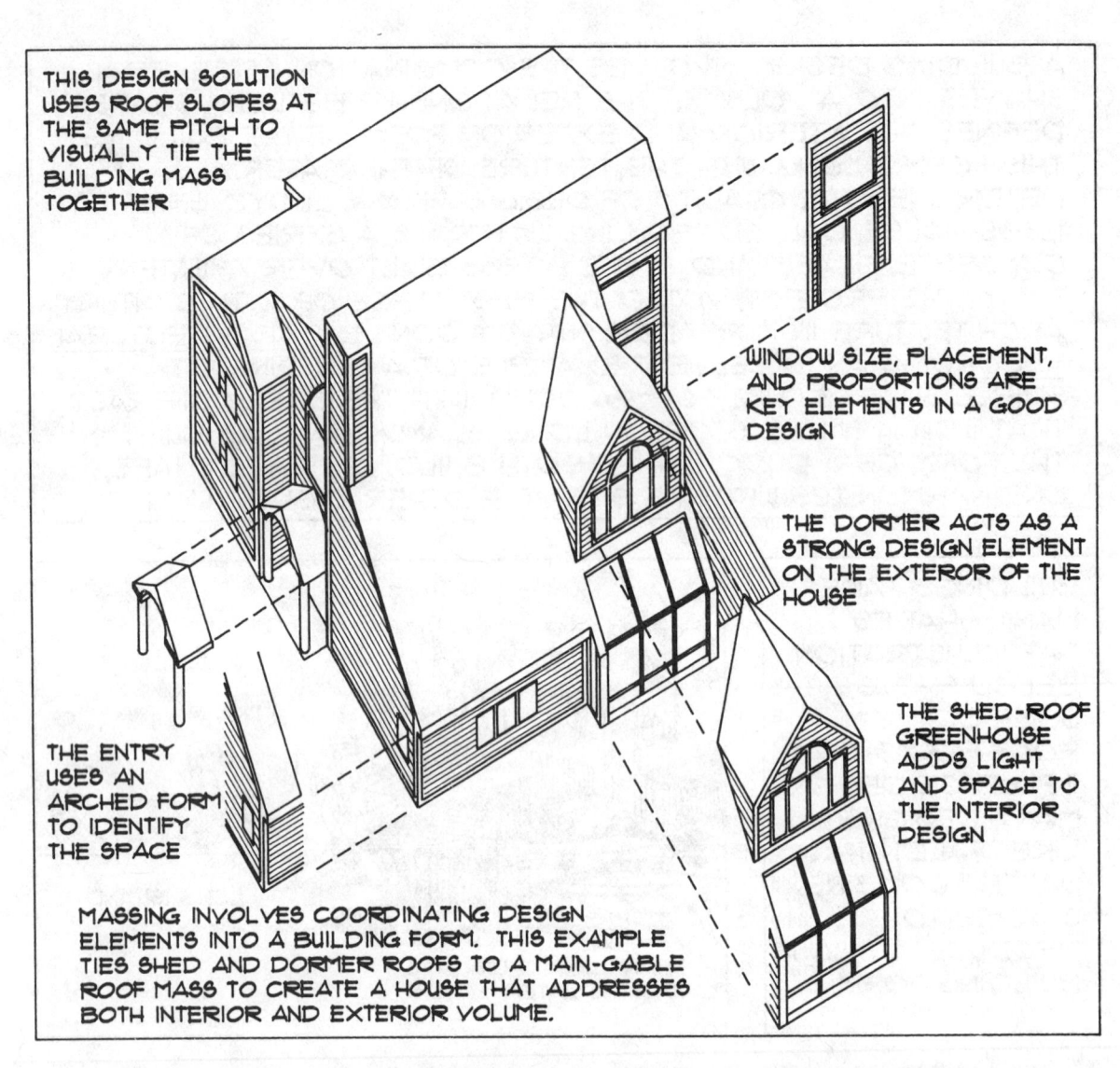

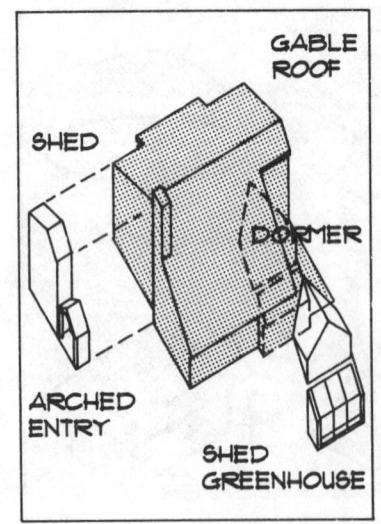

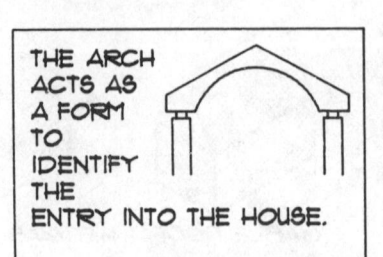

THIS DESIGN SOLUTION USES ROOF SLOPES AT THE SAME PITCH TO VISUALLY TIE THE BUILDING MASS TOGETHER

WINDOW SIZE, PLACEMENT, AND PROPORTIONS ARE KEY ELEMENTS IN A GOOD DESIGN

THE DORMER ACTS AS A STRONG DESIGN ELEMENT ON THE EXTERIOR OF THE HOUSE

THE SHED-ROOF GREENHOUSE ADDS LIGHT AND SPACE TO THE INTERIOR DESIGN

THE ENTRY USES AN ARCHED FORM TO IDENTIFY THE SPACE

MASSING INVOLVES COORDINATING DESIGN ELEMENTS INTO A BUILDING FORM. THIS EXAMPLE TIES SHED AND DORMER ROOFS TO A MAIN-GABLE ROOF MASS TO CREATE A HOUSE THAT ADDRESSES BOTH INTERIOR AND EXTERIOR VOLUME.

GABLE ROOF
SHED
DORMER
ARCHED ENTRY
SHED GREENHOUSE

THE ROUND FORM OF THE WINDOW REPEATS THE ARC OVER THE FRONT ENTRY.

THE DORMER ACTS TO BALANCE THE LARGE GABLE ROOF, PLUS IT CREATES AN INTERESTING INTERIOR SPACE.

THE ARCH ACTS AS A FORM TO IDENTIFY THE ENTRY INTO THE HOUSE.

THE SHED GREENHOUSE FOLLOWS THE DORMER PROPORTIONS TO BALANCE THE BUILDING MASS.

PROJECT DESIGN   24-10

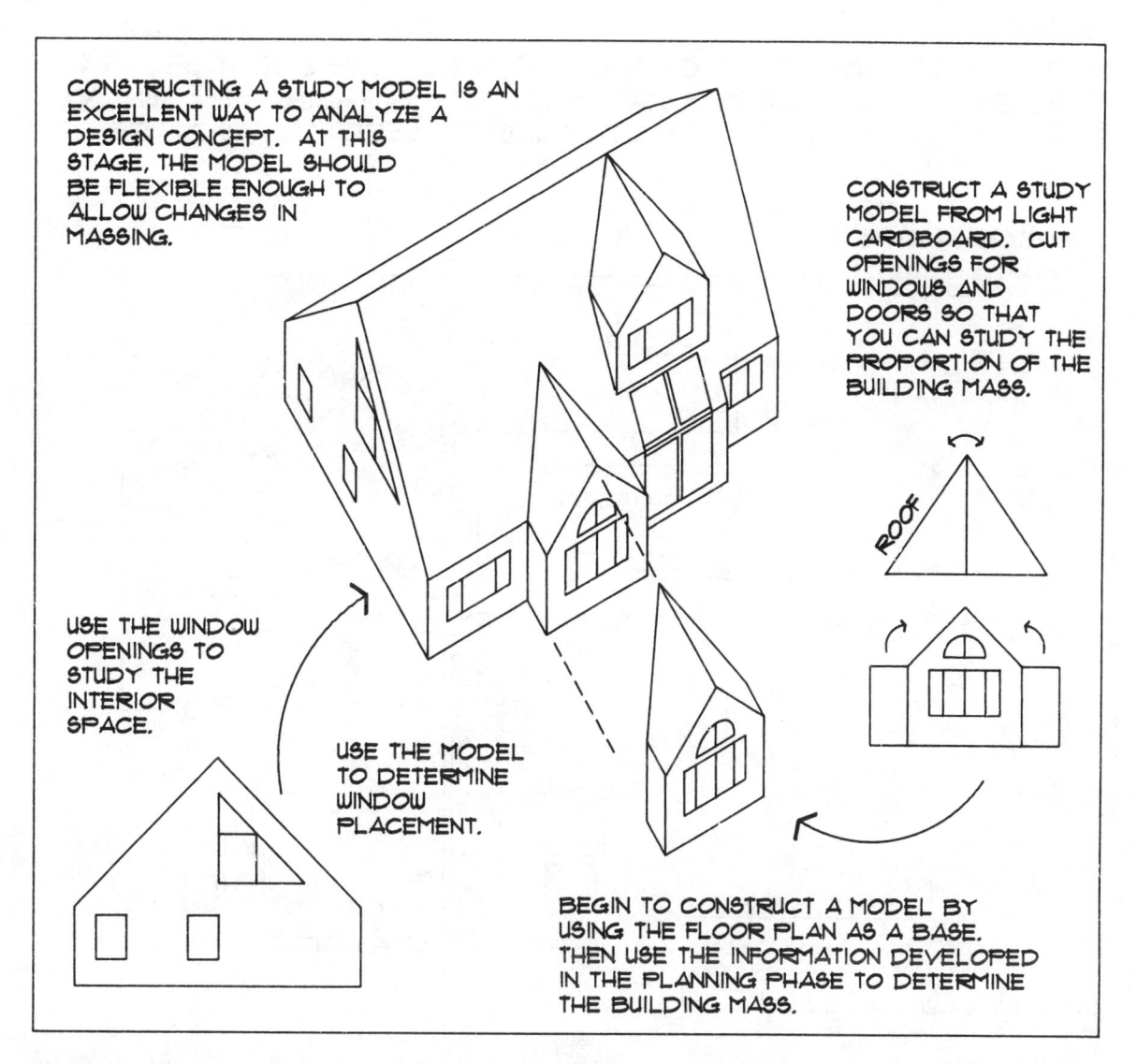

CONSTRUCTING A STUDY MODEL IS AN EXCELLENT WAY TO ANALYZE A DESIGN CONCEPT. AT THIS STAGE, THE MODEL SHOULD BE FLEXIBLE ENOUGH TO ALLOW CHANGES IN MASSING.

CONSTRUCT A STUDY MODEL FROM LIGHT CARDBOARD. CUT OPENINGS FOR WINDOWS AND DOORS SO THAT YOU CAN STUDY THE PROPORTION OF THE BUILDING MASS.

USE THE WINDOW OPENINGS TO STUDY THE INTERIOR SPACE.

USE THE MODEL TO DETERMINE WINDOW PLACEMENT.

BEGIN TO CONSTRUCT A MODEL BY USING THE FLOOR PLAN AS A BASE. THEN USE THE INFORMATION DEVELOPED IN THE PLANNING PHASE TO DETERMINE THE BUILDING MASS.

A STUDY MODEL IS A DESIGN TOOL THAT ALLOWS AN ARCHITECT TO REVIEW THE EXTERIOR AND INTERIOR VOLUMES IN A THREE-DIMENSIONAL VIEW. (INTERIOR VOLUMES CAN BE STUDIED BY CONSTRUCTING ROOF SLOPES, BALCONY RAILS, AND STAIRS.) IF PROBLEMS ARISE WHILE PUTTING A CARDBOARD MODEL TOGETHER, IT'S CERTAIN THERE WILL BE PROBLEMS IN ASSEMBLING THE WORKING DRAWING PACKAGE. KEEP IN MIND THAT A STUDY MODEL IS INTENDED TO PROVIDE THE ARCHITECT WITH INFORMATION; DON'T HESITATE TO MAKE CHANGES THAT WILL IMPROVE THE PROPORTIONS OF THE BUILDING. BE SURE TO VIEW THE MODEL FROM DIFFERENT ANGLES TO CRITIQUE THE DESIGN.

USE THE FLOOR PLAN AS A BASE FOR THE MODEL. GLUE THE WALLS TO THE BASE AND ADD THE ROOF. USE AN 1/8" SCALE FOR HOUSES AND A 1/16" SCALE FOR COMMERCIAL PROJECTS.

PROJECT DESIGN

REPLAY

IN THE REMAINING PAGES OF THIS UNIT, WE WILL PRESENT SEVERAL RESIDENTIAL AND COMMERCIAL PROJECTS IN THEIR PRELIMINARY DESIGN PHASE. THIS MATERIAL COULD BE USED AS A SOURCE FOR WORKING DRAWING PROJECTS FOR YOU TO ASSEMBLE.

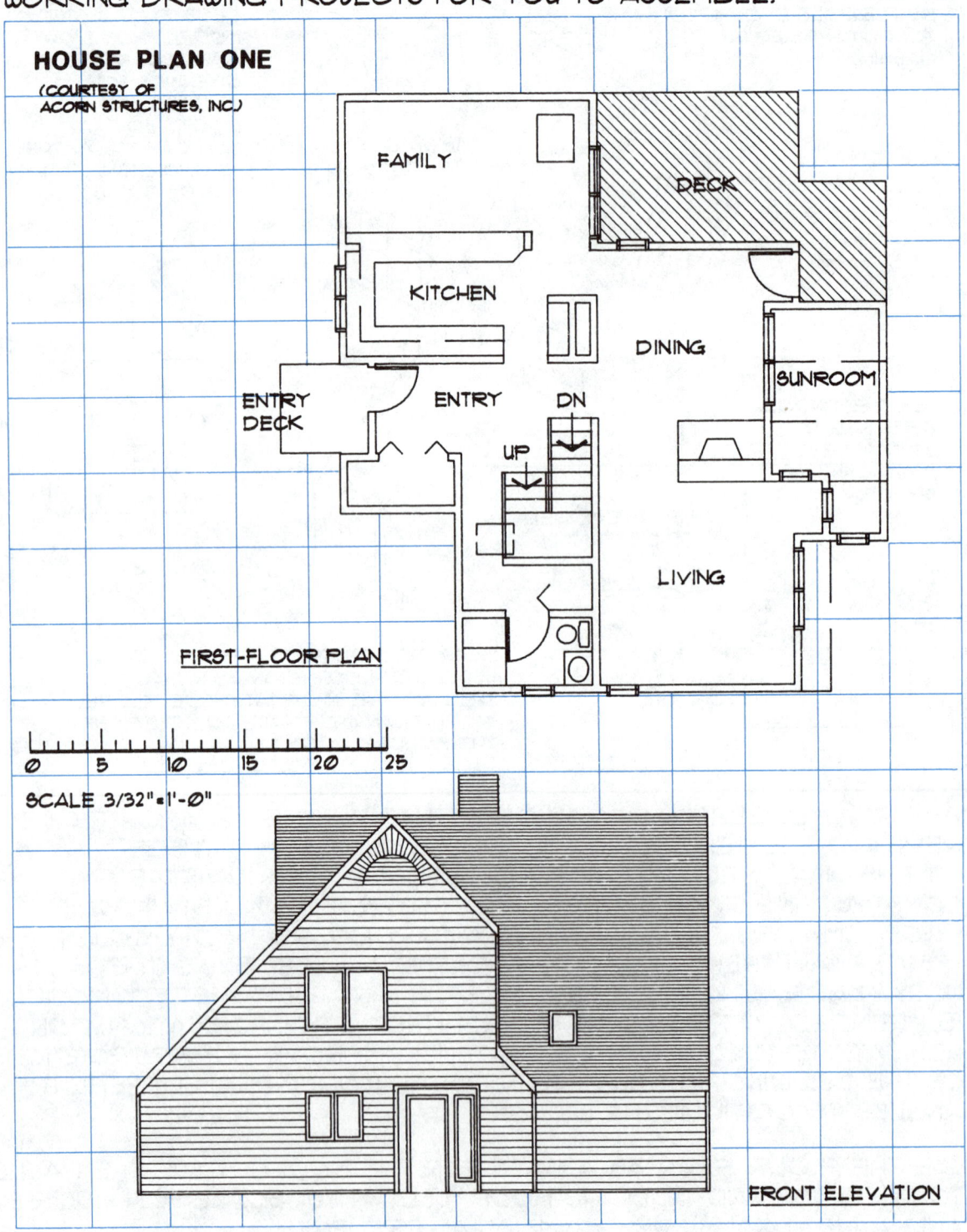

HOUSE PLAN ONE
(COURTESY OF ACORN STRUCTURES, INC.)

FAMILY — DECK — KITCHEN — DINING — SUNROOM — ENTRY DECK — ENTRY — DN — UP — LIVING

FIRST-FLOOR PLAN

0   5   10   15   20   25

SCALE 3/32" = 1'-0"

FRONT ELEVATION

PROJECT DESIGN 24-12

HOUSE PLAN ONE

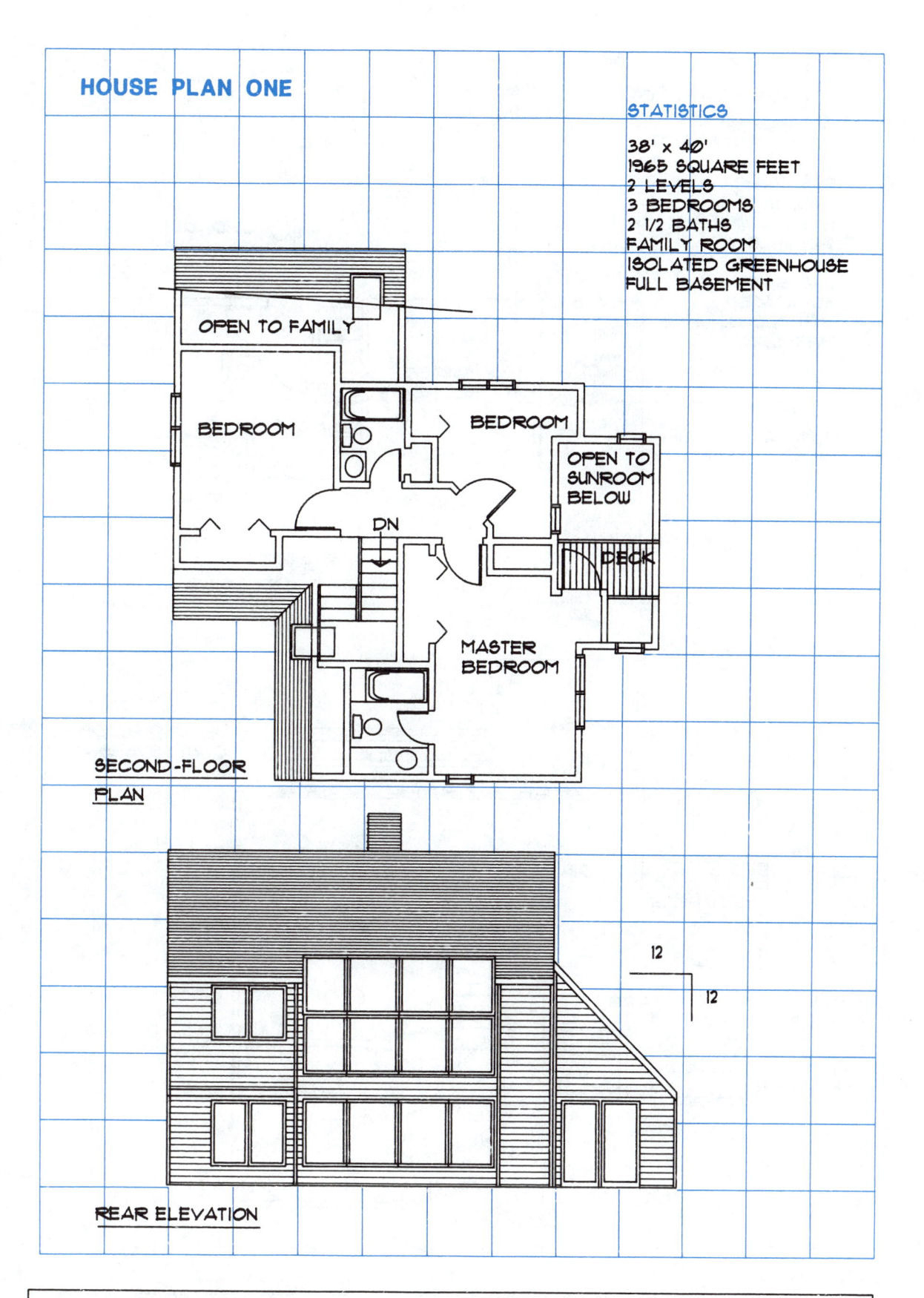

STATISTICS

38' x 40'
1965 SQUARE FEET
2 LEVELS
3 BEDROOMS
2 1/2 BATHS
FAMILY ROOM
ISOLATED GREENHOUSE
FULL BASEMENT

SECOND-FLOOR PLAN

REAR ELEVATION

PROJECT DESIGN 24-13

HOUSE PLAN TWO

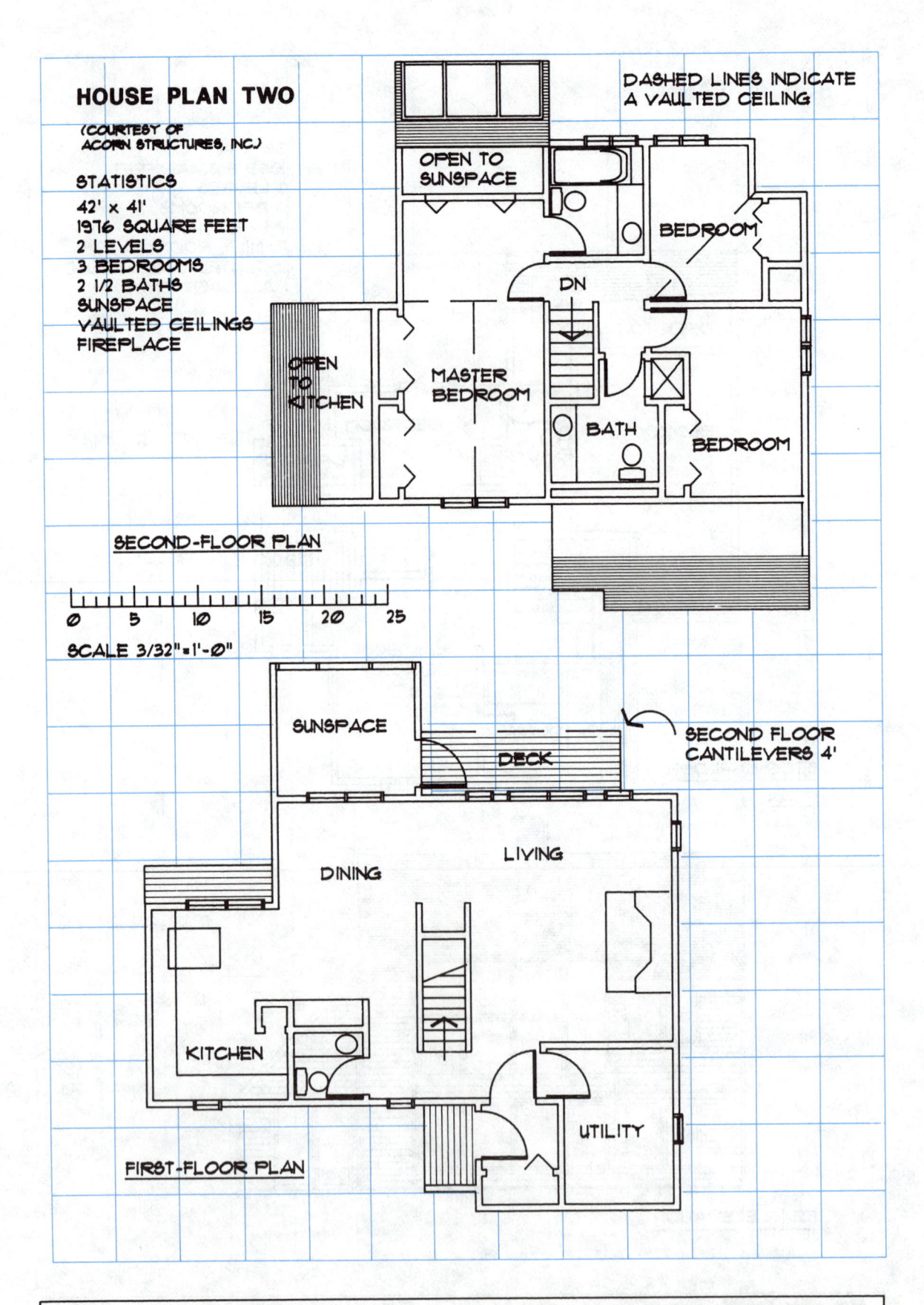

(COURTESY OF ACORN STRUCTURES, INC.)

STATISTICS
42' x 41'
1976 SQUARE FEET
2 LEVELS
3 BEDROOMS
2 1/2 BATHS
SUNSPACE
VAULTED CEILINGS
FIREPLACE

DASHED LINES INDICATE A VAULTED CEILING

SECOND-FLOOR PLAN

SCALE 3/32" = 1'-0"

SECOND FLOOR CANTILEVERS 4'

FIRST-FLOOR PLAN

PROJECT DESIGN

24-14

HOUSE PLAN TWO

12 / 12

REAR ELEVATION

PROJECT DESIGN | 24-15

COMMUNITY CENTER

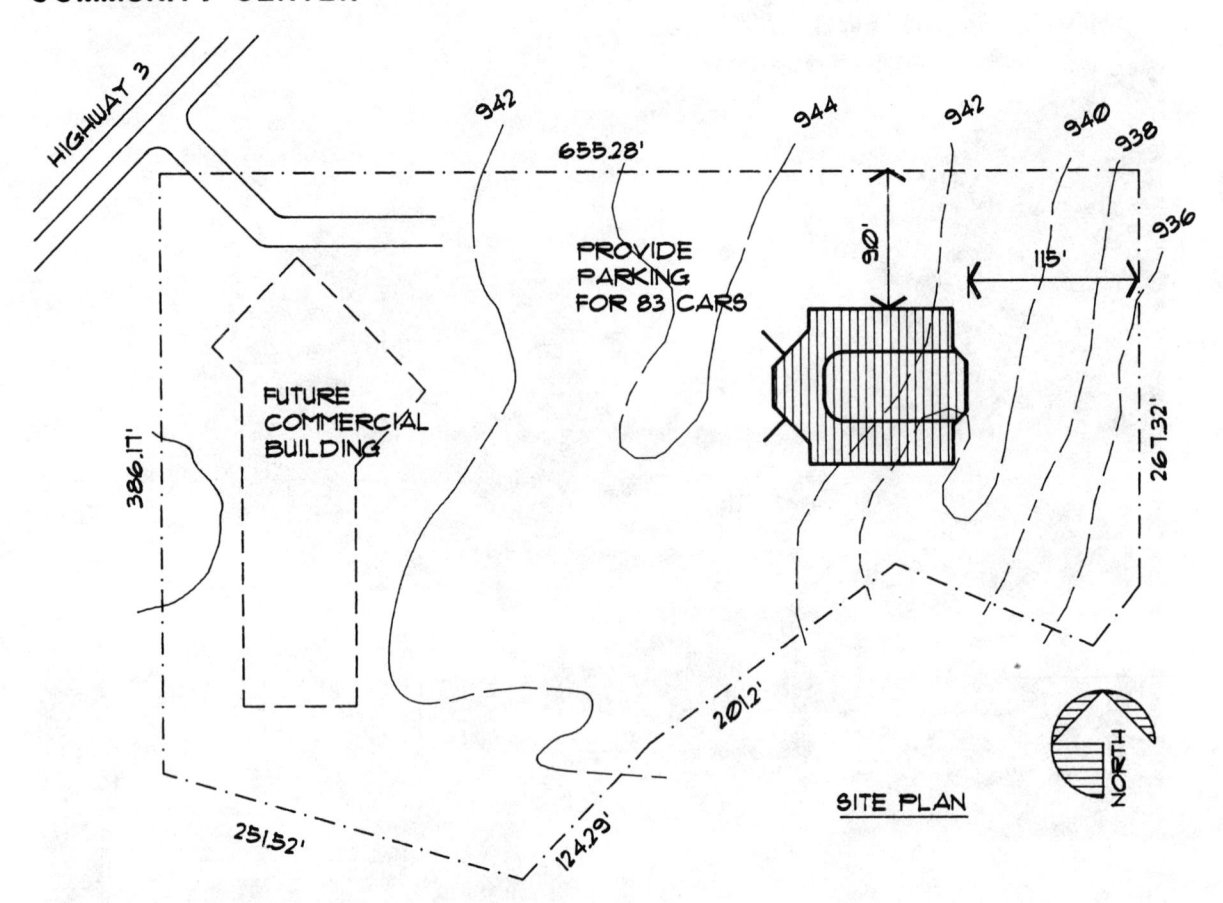

SITE PLAN

A SUBURBAN COMMUNITY IS PLANNING TO BUILD A SOCIAL CENTER THAT WILL BE USED FOR COMMUNITY EVENTS. THE BRICK AND BLOCK BUILDING HAS A DANCE FLOOR SURROUNDED BY FIXED-BOOTH SEATING. THE BUILDING ALSO HAS A RAISED STAGE, FOOD SERVICE AREA, COAT CHECK ROOM, AND OFFICE. THE CENTER'S LOCATION IS INDICATED ON THE FIVE-ACRE SITE SHOWN ABOVE. YOUR REPLAY ASSIGNMENT IS TO DEVELOP A WORKING DRAWING PACKAGE FOR THE BUILDING. YOUR DESIGN SOLUTION SHOULD INCLUDE ON-SITE PARKING FOR 83 CARS.

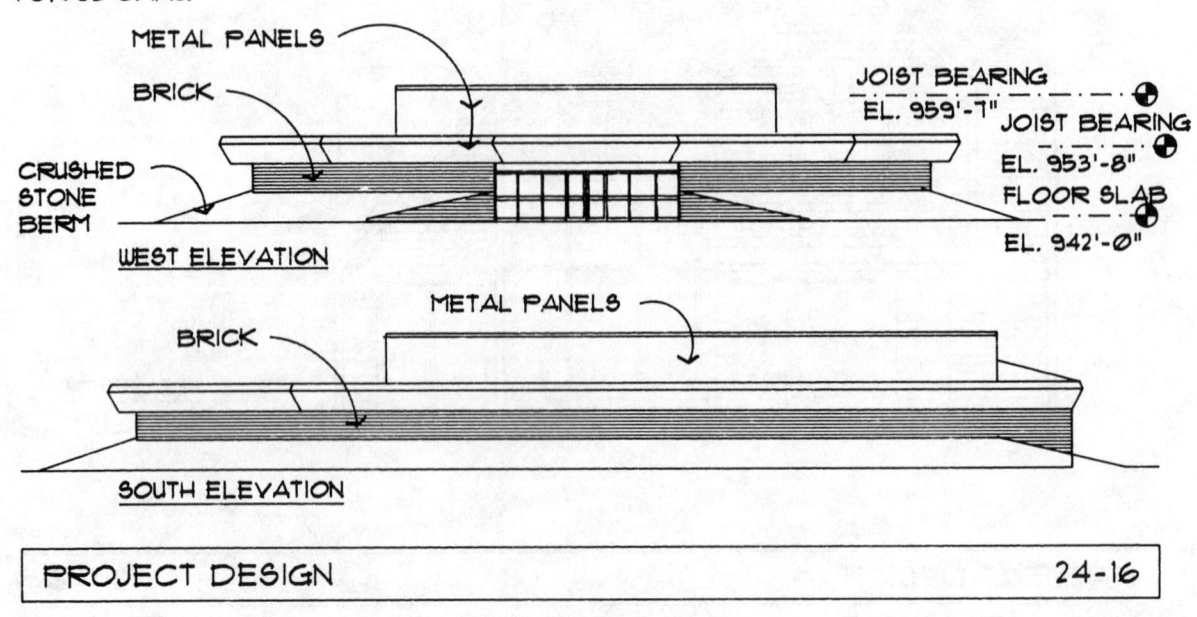

WEST ELEVATION

- METAL PANELS
- BRICK
- CRUSHED STONE BERM
- JOIST BEARING EL. 959'-7"
- JOIST BEARING EL. 953'-8"
- FLOOR SLAB EL. 942'-0"

SOUTH ELEVATION

- BRICK
- METAL PANELS

PROJECT DESIGN 24-16

PROJECT DESIGN   24-17

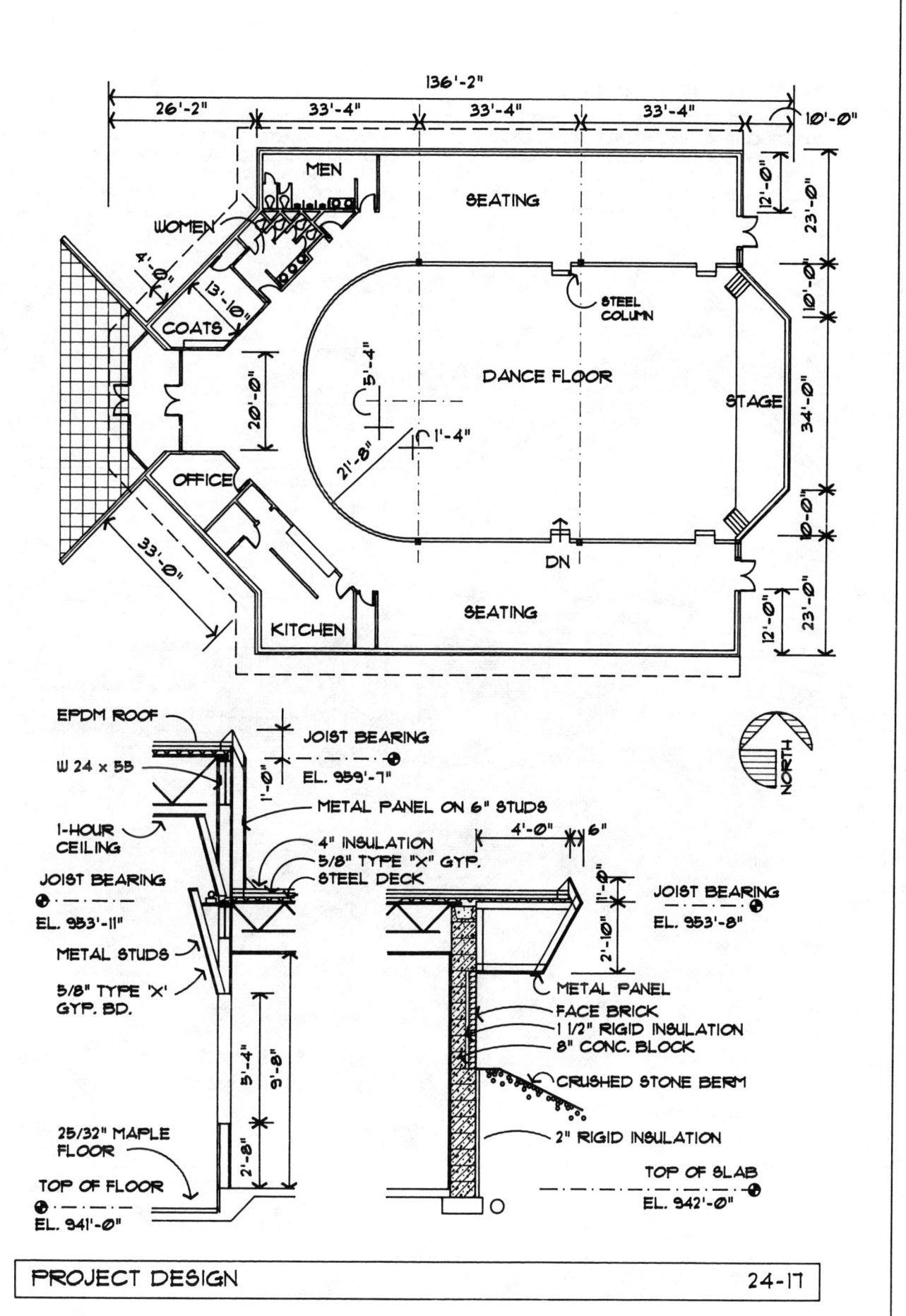

RESTAURANT COMPLEX

THIS PROJECT CONSISTS OF FOUR BUILDINGS BUILT ON A CITY LAKE. THE LARGEST BUILDING IS A TWO-STORY RESTAURANT WITH A DECK FOR OUTDOOR DINING. THE SECOND BUILDING IS A FAST-FOOD RESTAURANT. (THIS RESTAURANT WOULD ALSO SERVE AS A WINTER ICE-RINK WARMING HOUSE WITH THE ADDITION OF RUBBER FLOOR MATS.) THE THIRD BUILDING IS A RENTAL SHOP FOR SPORTS EQUIPMENT (SKATES, SKIS, AND CANOES). THE TROLLEY STATION CONNECTS THE RESTAURANT COMPLEX TO A SECOND LAKE THREE MILES AWAY.

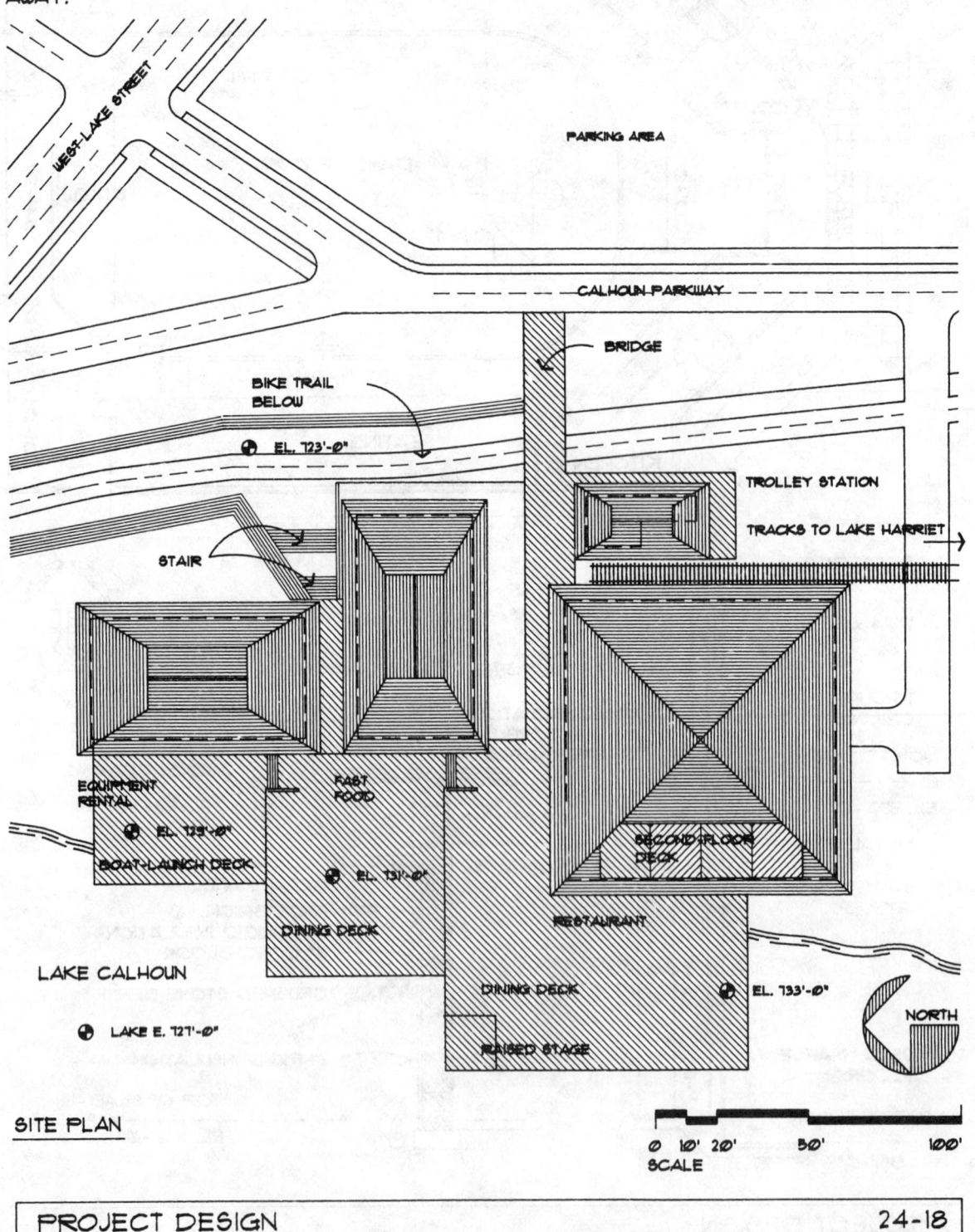

SITE PLAN

PROJECT DESIGN 24-18

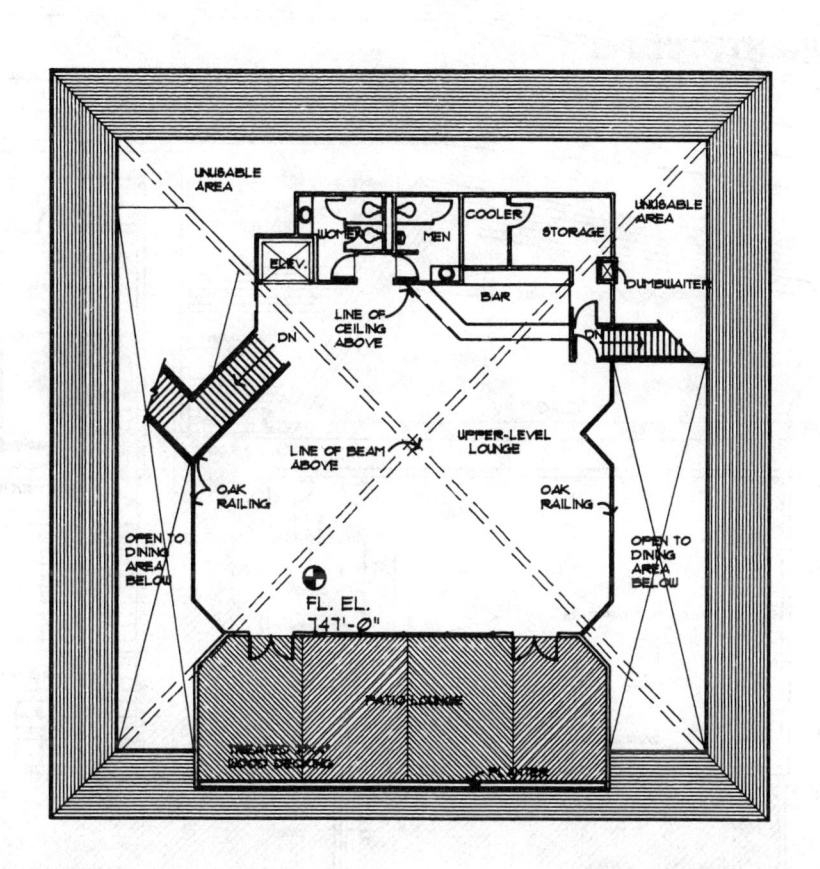

SECOND-FLOOR RESTAURANT PLAN

THE SECOND-LEVEL RESTAURANT PLAN IS SHOWN ABOVE. THE PLAN OPENS TO A DECK WITH A VIEW TO THE LAKE. THE BUILDING STRUCTURE CONSISTS OF WOOD LAMINATED BEAMS WITH A TIMBER DECK. THE WEST ELEVATION VIEW SHOWN BELOW INDICATES THE PROJECT DESIGN. THE EXTERIOR BUILDING MATERIALS USED ARE CUT LIMESTONE, HEAT-REDUCING GLASS, AND HAND-SPLIT CEDAR SHINGLES.

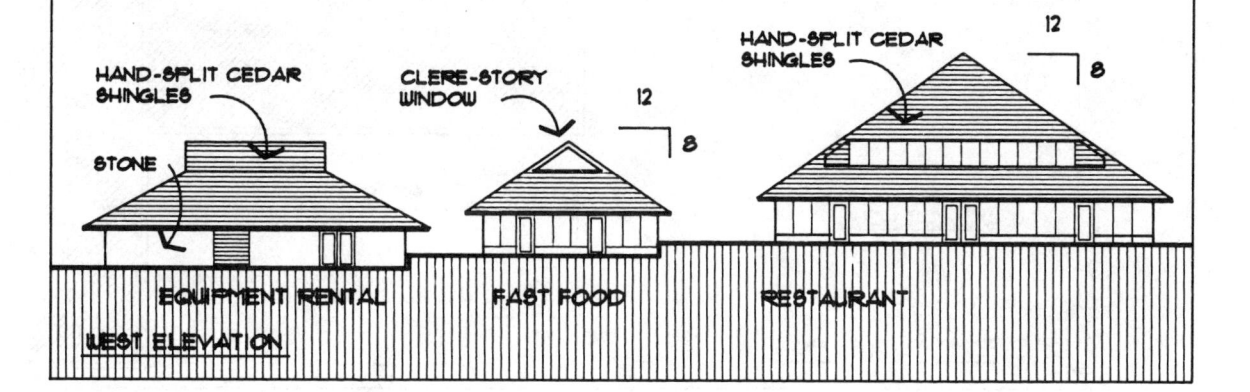

PROJECT DESIGN

24-19

RESTAURANT COMPLEX

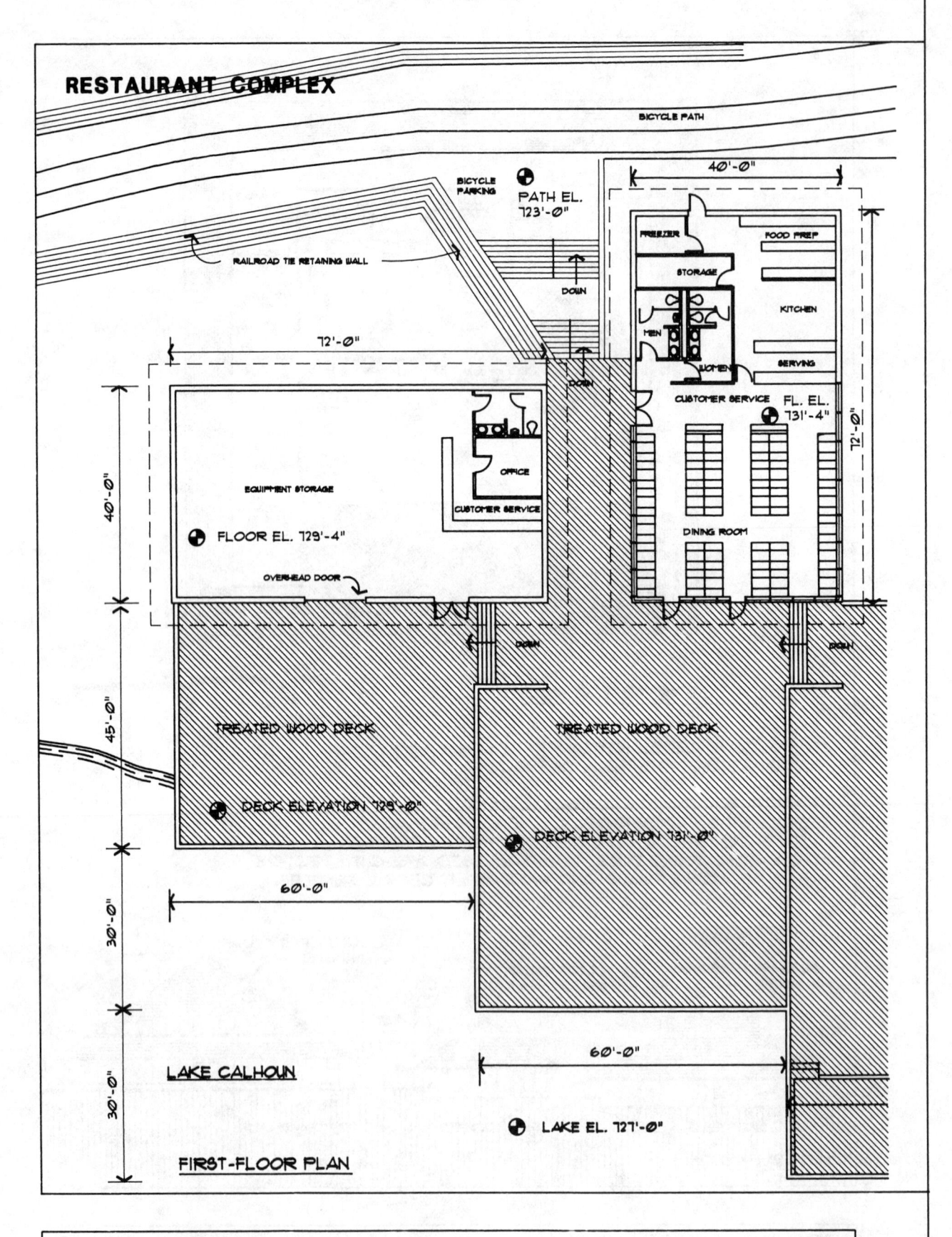

FIRST-FLOOR PLAN

- BICYCLE PATH
- PATH EL. 723'-0"
- BICYCLE PARKING
- RAILROAD TIE RETAINING WALL
- FREEZER
- STORAGE
- FOOD PREP
- KITCHEN
- MEN
- WOMEN
- SERVING
- CUSTOMER SERVICE
- FL. EL. 731'-4"
- DINING ROOM
- EQUIPMENT STORAGE
- FLOOR EL. 729'-4"
- OFFICE
- CUSTOMER SERVICE
- OVERHEAD DOOR
- DOWN
- TREATED WOOD DECK
- DECK ELEVATION 729'-0"
- TREATED WOOD DECK
- DECK ELEVATION 731'-0"
- LAKE CALHOUN
- LAKE EL. 727'-0"

Dimensions: 40'-0", 72'-0", 72'-0", 40'-0", 45'-0", 30'-0", 30'-0", 60'-0", 60'-0"

PROJECT DESIGN 24-20

PROJECT DESIGN | 24-21

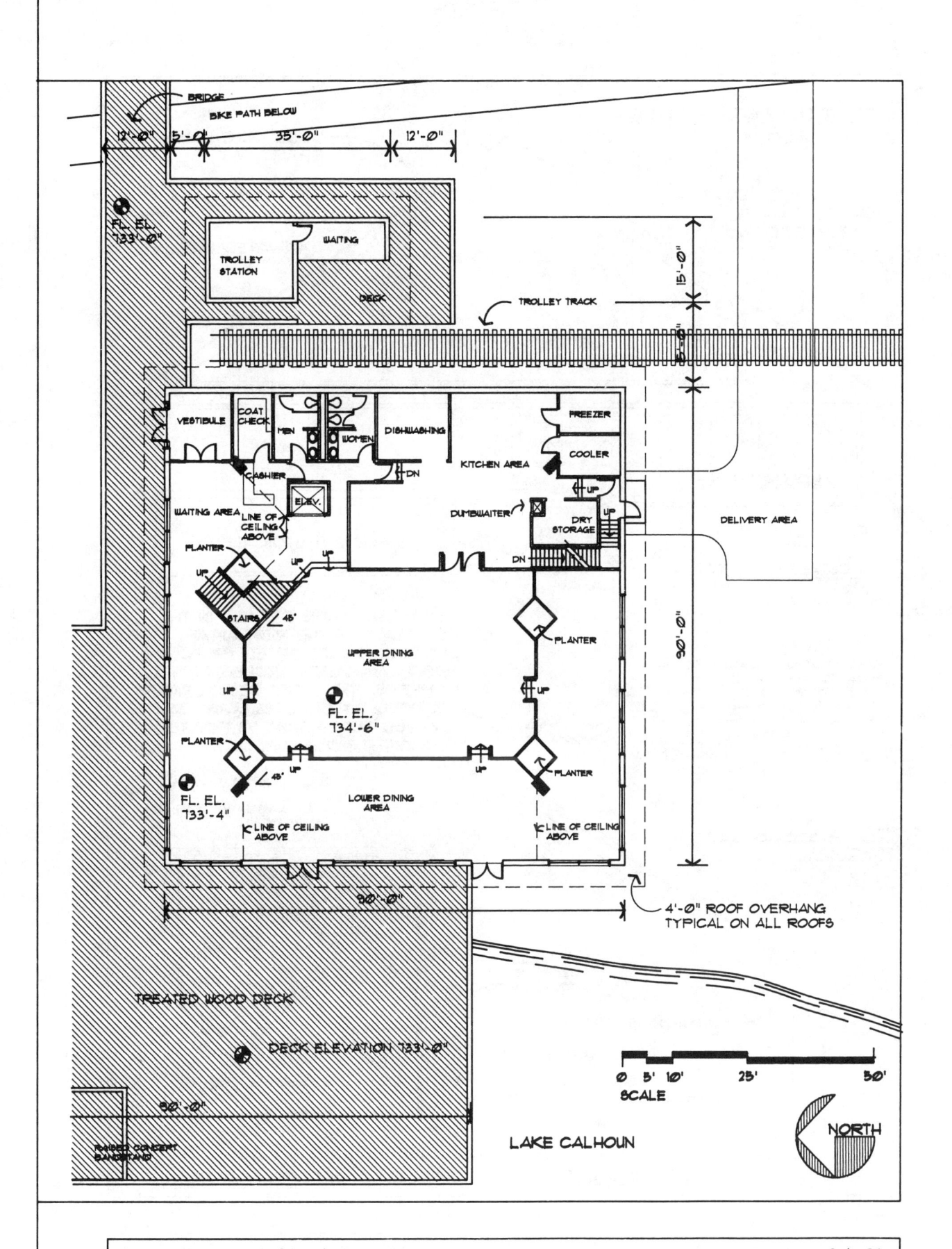

RESTAURANT COMPLEX

RESTAURANT SECTION

Labels:
- HAND-SPLIT CEDAR SHINGLES OVER TIMBER DECKING
- WOOD GLUE LAMINATED BEAM
- 12 / 8
- LAMINATED PURLIN
- DECK
- SECOND-FLOOR RESTAURANT
- LOWER DINING
- UPPER DINING
- KITCHEN
- PRESTRESSED CONCRETE PLANK
- BASEMENT STORAGE

RESTAURANT ROOF SECTION

- HAND-SPLIT CEDAR SHINGLES
- 15 LB. FELT
- 3/4" PLYWOOD
- 1 1/2" AIR SPACE
- TREATED 2 x 10'S
- 8" FOAM INSULATION
- 2 1/2" TIMBER DECK

THIS PAGE SHOWS DETAILS IN THE ASSEMBLY OF THE RESTAURANT. THE BUILDING IS SUPPORTED BY FOUR WOOD LAMINATED ARCHES AT THE CORNERS. THE ROOF DECK SPAN IS REDUCED BY PLACING WOOD BEAMS (CALLED <u>PURLINS</u>) AT 1/3 POINTS ALONG THE ROOF SUPPORT.

RESTAURANT WOOD LAMINATED ARCH

- WOOD LAMINATED ARCH

RESTAURANT ROOF FRAMING PLAN

- WOOD LAMINATED ARCH
- WOOD LAMINATED PURLINS (AT 1/3 POINTS)
- 2 1/2" TIMBER TONGUE AND GROOVE DECKING
- WOOD LAMINATED COLLAR BEAM (AROUND PERIMETER OF EXTERIOR WALL)

PROJECT DESIGN

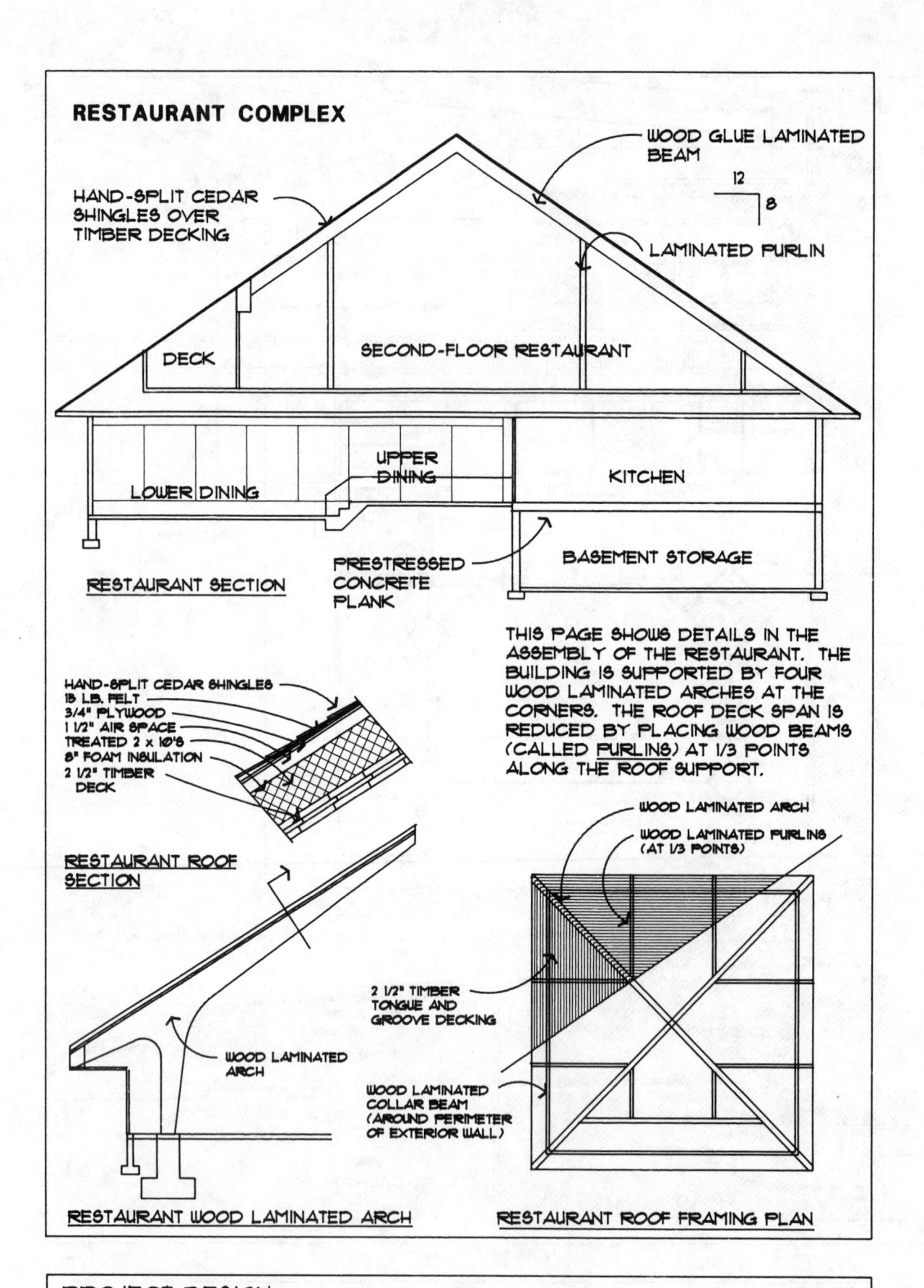

24-22

25 FIRE STATION

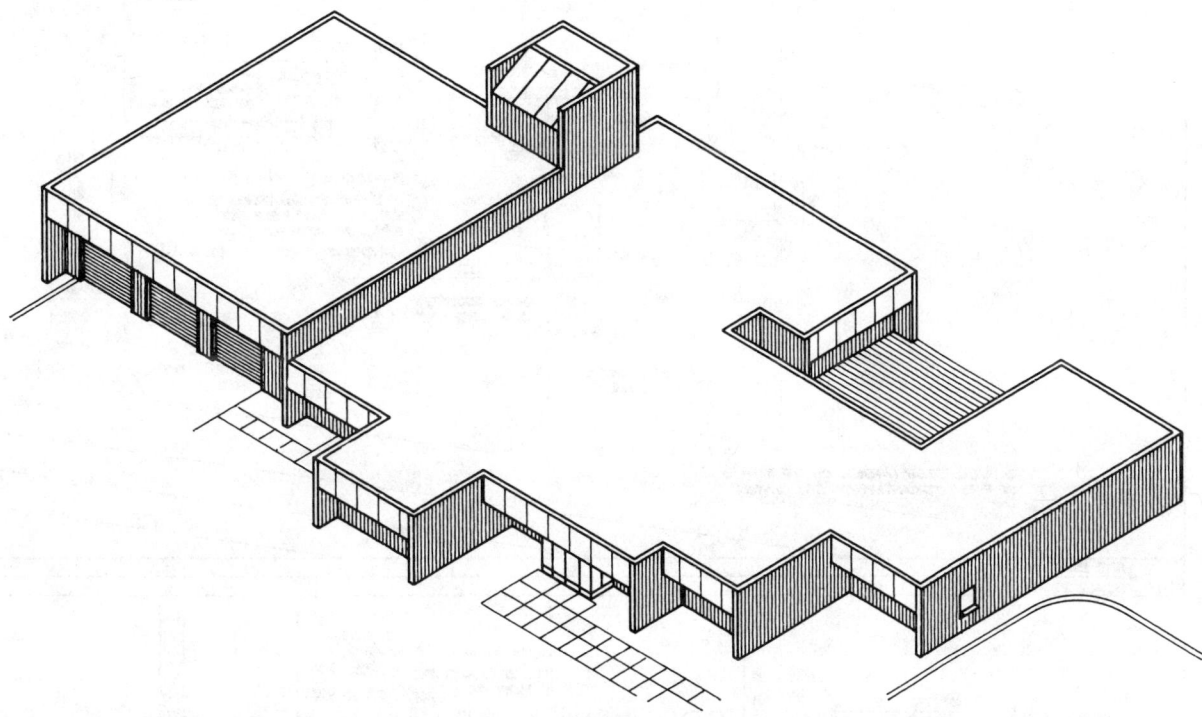

THIS UNIT CONTAINS THE CONSTRUCTION DRAWING PACKAGE FOR THE FIRE STATION. THE EXTERIOR WALL OF THE BUILDING IS 8" BREAK-OFF BLOCK WITH 4" INSULATED METAL STUDS. THE PROJECT IS STRUCTURED USING STEEL BAR JOISTS THAT ARE SUPPORTED WITH LOAD-BEARING BLOCK WALLS. THE PROJECT HAS A 30' HOSE TOWER USED TO HANG HOSES TO DRY. IN ADDITION TO STORAGE FOR FIRE TRUCKS, THE BUILDING CONTAINS DORMITORY SPACE FOR FIRE FIGHTERS AND CITY OFFICES.

| FIRE STATION | 25-1 |

Site Plan/A-1

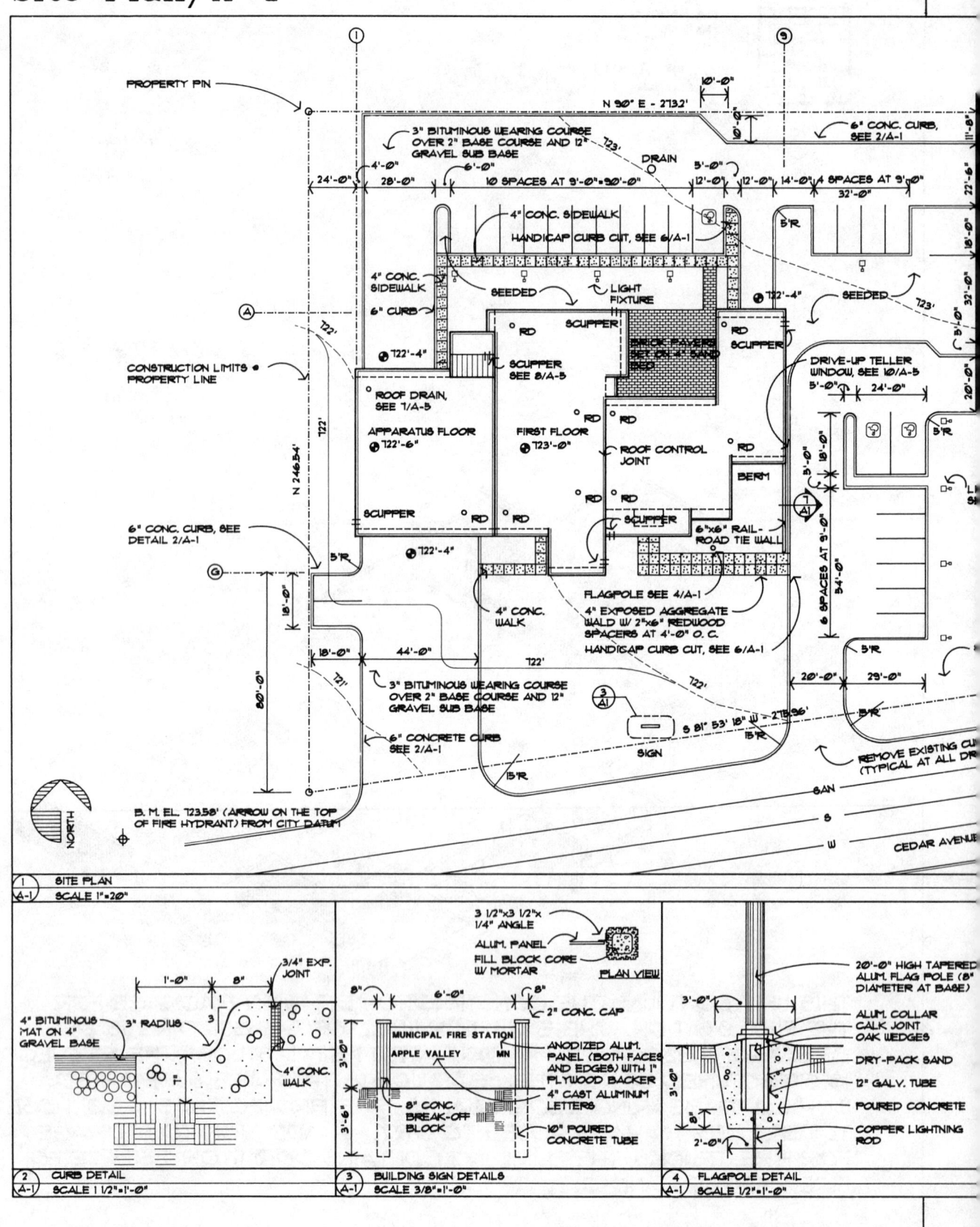

1. SITE PLAN
SCALE 1" = 20'

2. CURB DETAIL
SCALE 1 1/2" = 1'-0"

3. BUILDING SIGN DETAILS
SCALE 3/8" = 1'-0"

4. FLAGPOLE DETAIL
SCALE 1/2" = 1'-0"

FIRE STATION

25-2

MUNICIPAL FIRE STATION
APPLE VALLEY   MN

INDEX

SHEET	DRAWING
A1	SITE PLAN
A2	FLOOR PLAN
A3	ELEVATIONS & BUILDING SECTIONS
A4	WALL SECTIONS & DETAILS
A5	MISCELLANEOUS DETAILS & REFLECTED CEILING PLAN

8 EXTERIOR LIGHT FIXTURES
A-1 SCALE 1/2"=1'-0"

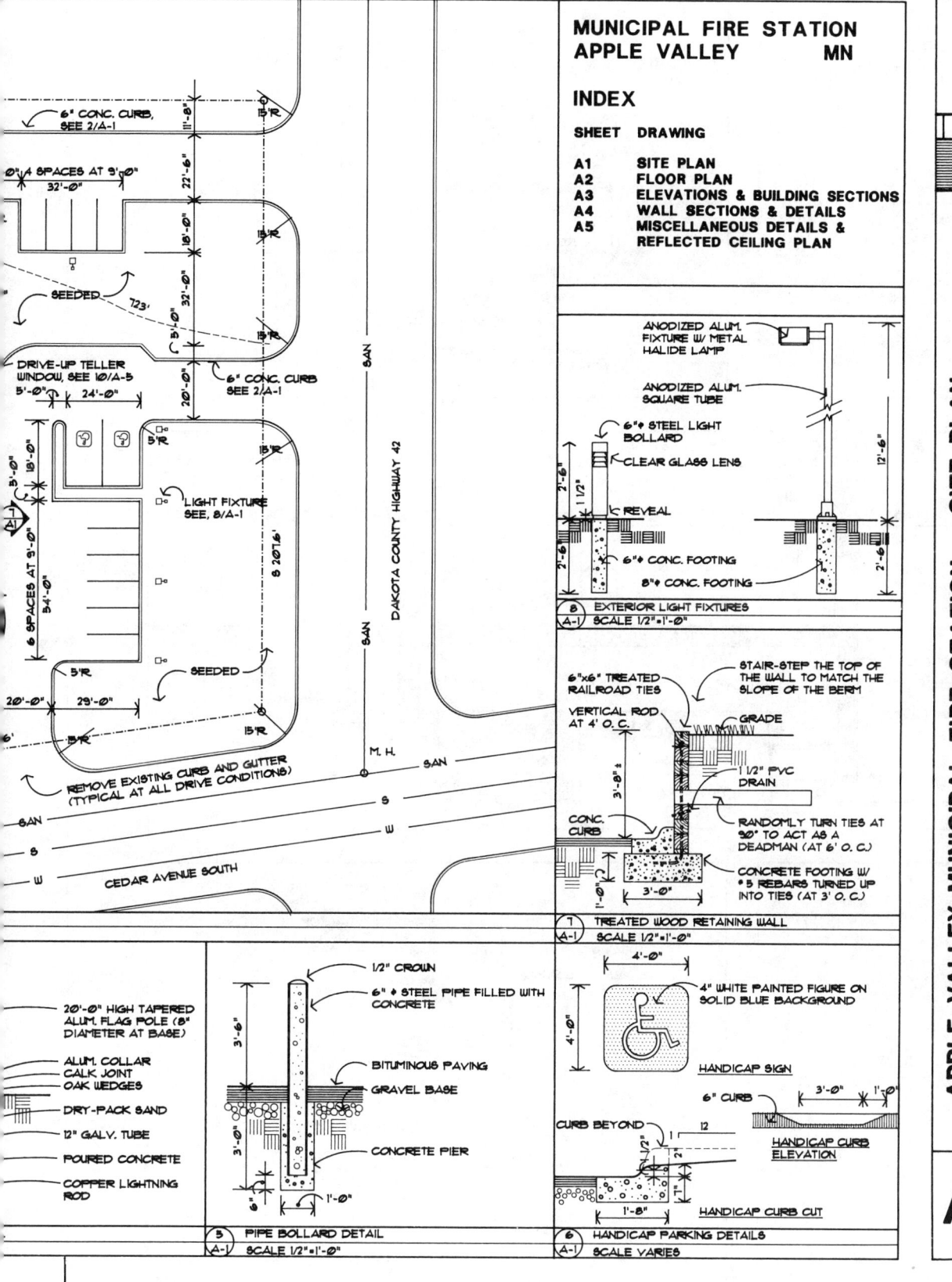

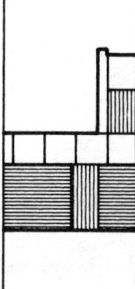

- ANODIZED ALUM. FIXTURE W/ METAL HALIDE LAMP
- ANODIZED ALUM. SQUARE TUBE
- 6"⌀ STEEL LIGHT BOLLARD
- CLEAR GLASS LENS
- REVEAL
- 6"⌀ CONC. FOOTING
- 8"⌀ CONC. FOOTING

7 TREATED WOOD RETAINING WALL
A-1 SCALE 1/2"=1'-0"

- 6"x6" TREATED RAILROAD TIES
- STAIR-STEP THE TOP OF THE WALL TO MATCH THE SLOPE OF THE BERM
- VERTICAL ROD AT 4' O.C.
- GRADE
- 1 1/2" PVC DRAIN
- CONC. CURB
- RANDOMLY TURN TIES AT 90° TO ACT AS A DEADMAN (AT 6' O.C.)
- CONCRETE FOOTING W/ #5 REBARS TURNED UP INTO TIES (AT 3' O.C.)

5 PIPE BOLLARD DETAIL
A-1 SCALE 1/2"=1'-0"

- 1/2" CROWN
- 6"⌀ STEEL PIPE FILLED WITH CONCRETE
- BITUMINOUS PAVING
- GRAVEL BASE
- CONCRETE PIER
- 20'-0" HIGH TAPERED ALUM. FLAG POLE (8" DIAMETER AT BASE)
- ALUM. COLLAR
- CALK JOINT
- OAK WEDGES
- DRY-PACK SAND
- 12" GALV. TUBE
- POURED CONCRETE
- COPPER LIGHTNING ROD

6 HANDICAP PARKING DETAILS
A-1 SCALE VARIES

- 4" WHITE PAINTED FIGURE ON SOLID BLUE BACKGROUND
- HANDICAP SIGN
- 6" CURB
- CURB BEYOND
- HANDICAP CURB ELEVATION
- HANDICAP CURB CUT

APPLE VALLEY MUNICIPAL FIRE STATION   SITE PLAN
14550 CEDAR AVENUE SOUTH
APPLE VALLEY, MN

A1

FIRE STATION   25-3

Site Plan/A-1

The detail to the right illustrates two light fixtures on the project. Details pertaining to the site are commonly located on the site plan sheet. The details should be "keyed" to the site for reference.

The detail below shows a portion of the site parking. It is essential to locate all site items by dimension; walks and brick pavers have been noted and located here by dimension string.

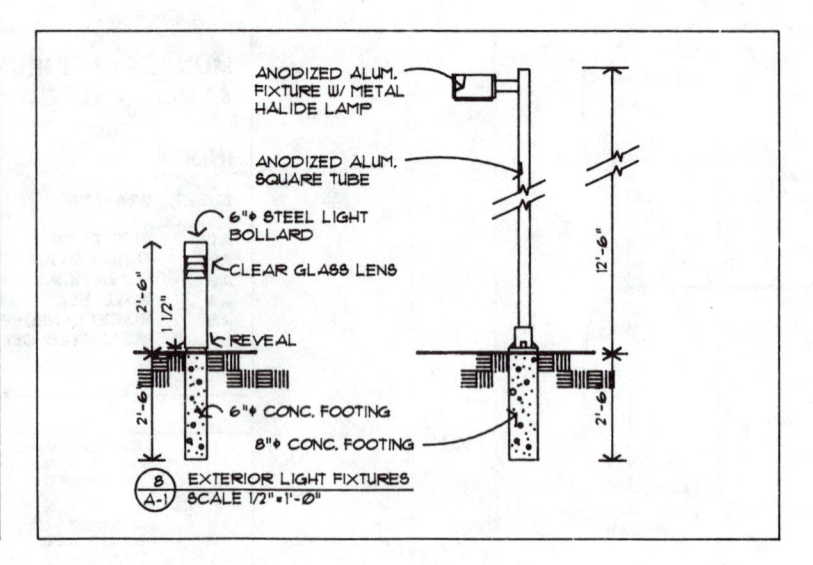

ANODIZED ALUM. FIXTURE W/ METAL HALIDE LAMP
ANODIZED ALUM. SQUARE TUBE
6"⌀ STEEL LIGHT BOLLARD
CLEAR GLASS LENS
REVEAL
6"⌀ CONC. FOOTING
8"⌀ CONC. FOOTING
2'-6"
1 1/2"
2'-6"
12'-6"
2'-6"

8/A-1 EXTERIOR LIGHT FIXTURES
SCALE 1/2"=1'-0"

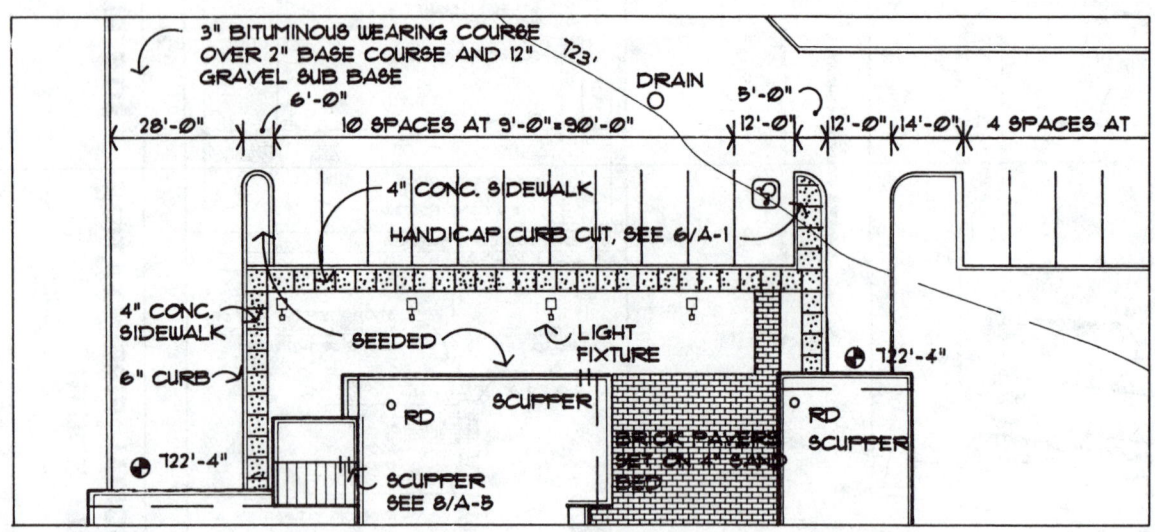

3" BITUMINOUS WEARING COURSE OVER 2" BASE COURSE AND 12" GRAVEL SUB BASE
DRAIN
28'-0" 6'-0" 10 SPACES AT 9'-0"=90'-0" 5'-0" 12'-0" 12'-0" 14'-0" 4 SPACES AT
4" CONC. SIDEWALK
HANDICAP CURB CUT, SEE 6/A-1
4" CONC. SIDEWALK
6" CURB
722'-4"
SEEDED
LIGHT FIXTURE
RD
SCUPPER
SCUPPER SEE 8/A-5
BRICK PAVERS SET ON 4" SAND BED
RD SCUPPER
722'-4"

Site details must address all features that are to be changed. The detail at the right shows a railroad-tie retaining wall along the parking lot edge of the site. Details should indicate the materials, dimensions, and construction techniques necessary to build the object. In this example, detail 7/A-1 is marked on the site plan and noted to be a 6"x 6" railroad-tie retaining wall.

6"x6" TREATED RAILROAD TIES
STAIR-STEP THE TOP OF THE WALL TO MATCH THE SLOPE OF THE BERM
VERTICAL ROD AT 4' O.C.
GRADE
1 1/2" PVC DRAIN
CONC. CURB
RANDOMLY TURN TIES AT 90° TO ACT AS A DEADMAN (AT 6' O.C.)
CONCRETE FOOTING W/ #5 REBARS TURNED UP INTO TIES (AT 3' O.C.)
3'-8"±
1'-0"
3'-0"

7/A-1 TREATED WOOD RETAINING WALL
SCALE 1/2"=1'-0"

FIRE STATION

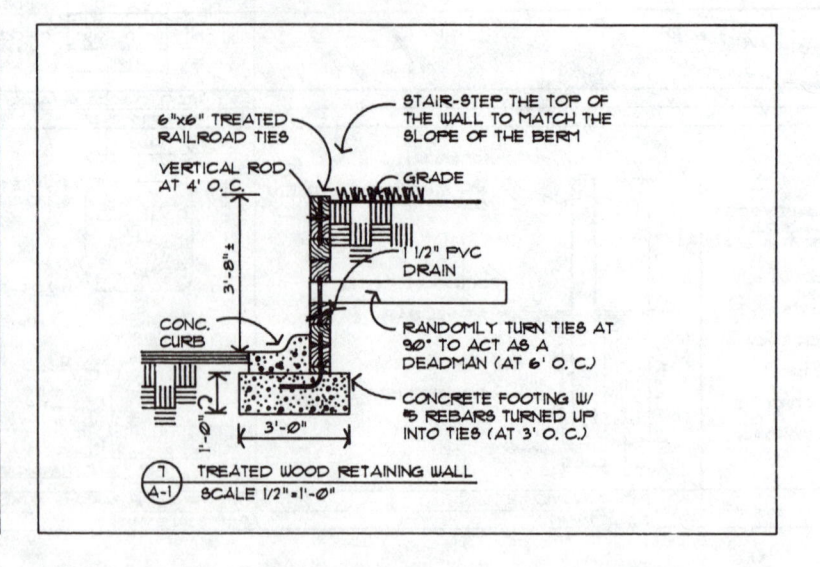

Site Plan/A-1

These two details, the curb detail (2/A-1) and the handicap parking detail (6/A-1), identify additional site conditions. Details should provide exact data on construction assembly; specifications would indicate product quality. This project was "red-lined" (corrections were made on a print with a felt-tip pen) at about 90% of its completion in order to coordinate conditions on the site with the details.

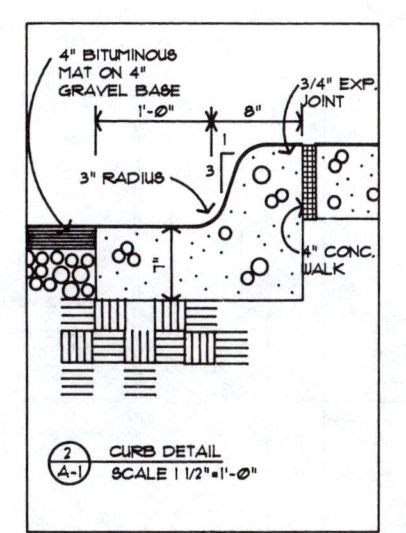

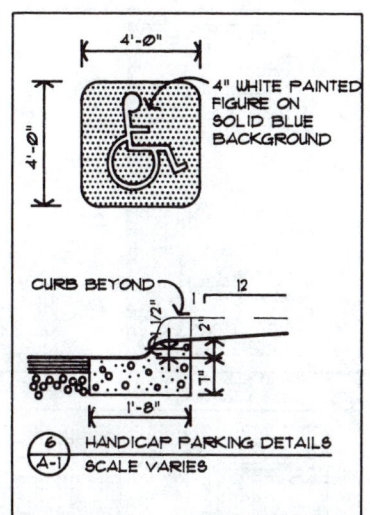

This portion of the site plan shows topographic contours and "spot" elevations (in which the exact height is crucial). Note that the existing contours are shown dashed while changes are marked with solid lines.

The building location and site features are dimensioned from the property line. Here the south and east lines are illustrated. Note that curb radii are given (e.g., 15' R).

This detail illustrates a section cut through the flagpole base. This type of section cut is necessary for the proper design of an item such as the flagpole that is to be selected from a catalog (much of the material on the footing size would be supplied by the company that fabricates the pole). The detail location is also marked on the site plan.

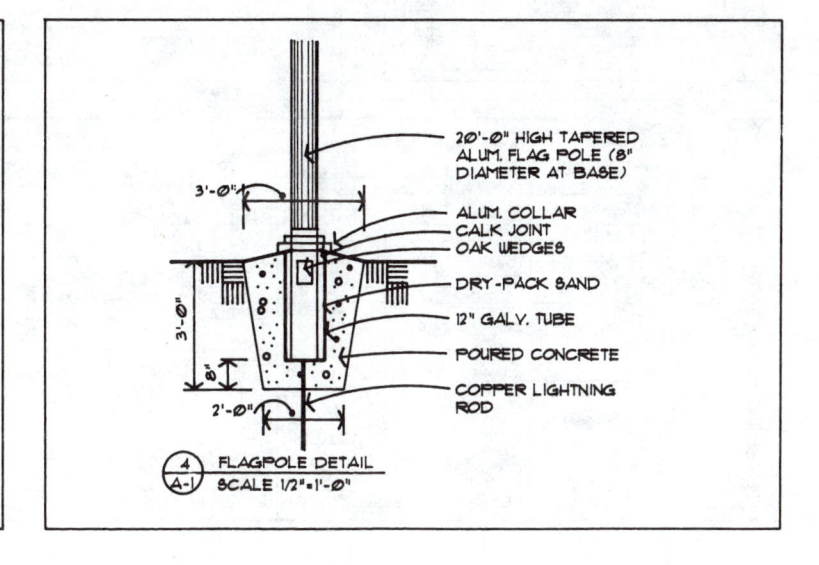

FIRE STATION

25-5

Floor Plan/A-2

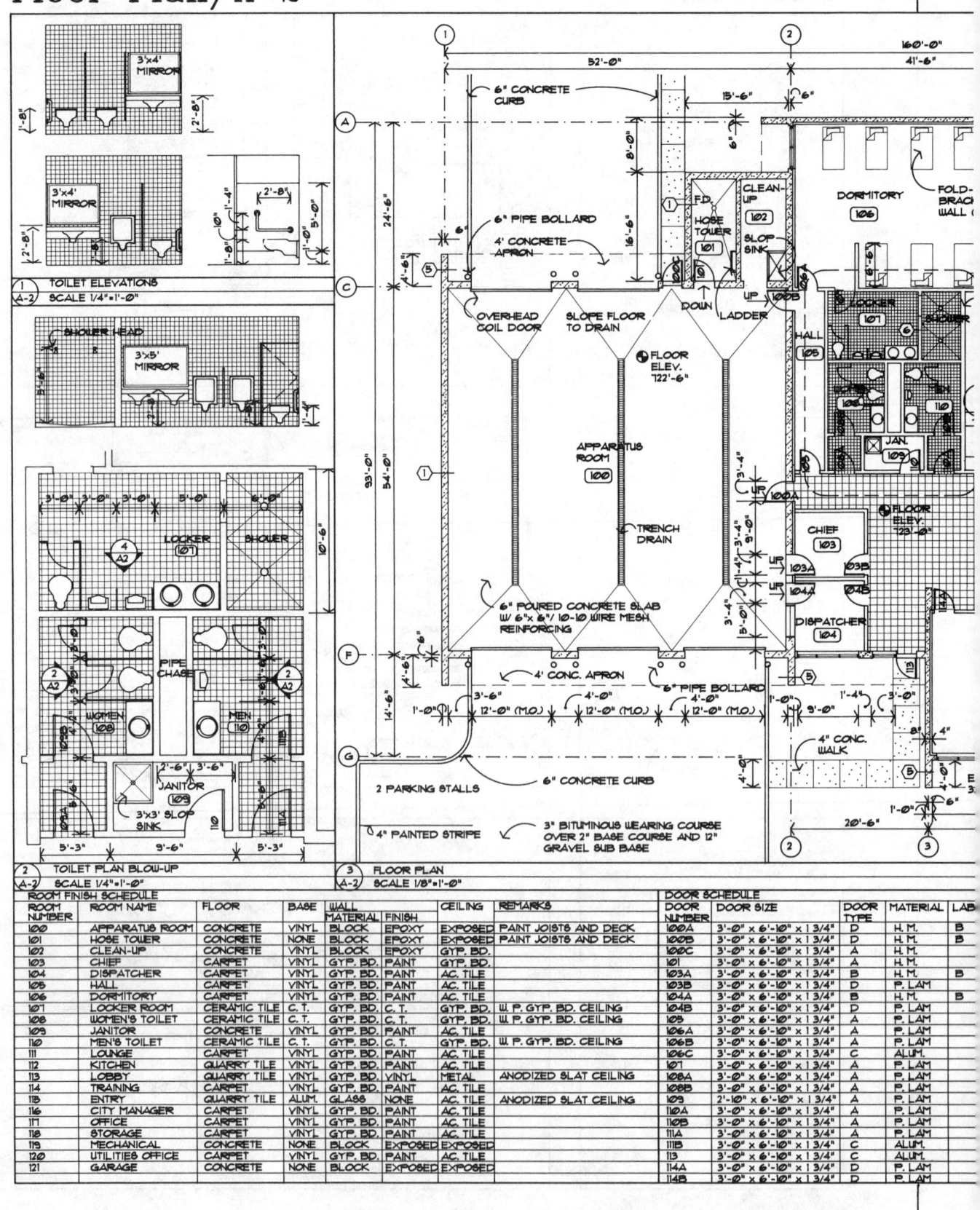

FIRE STATION

25-6

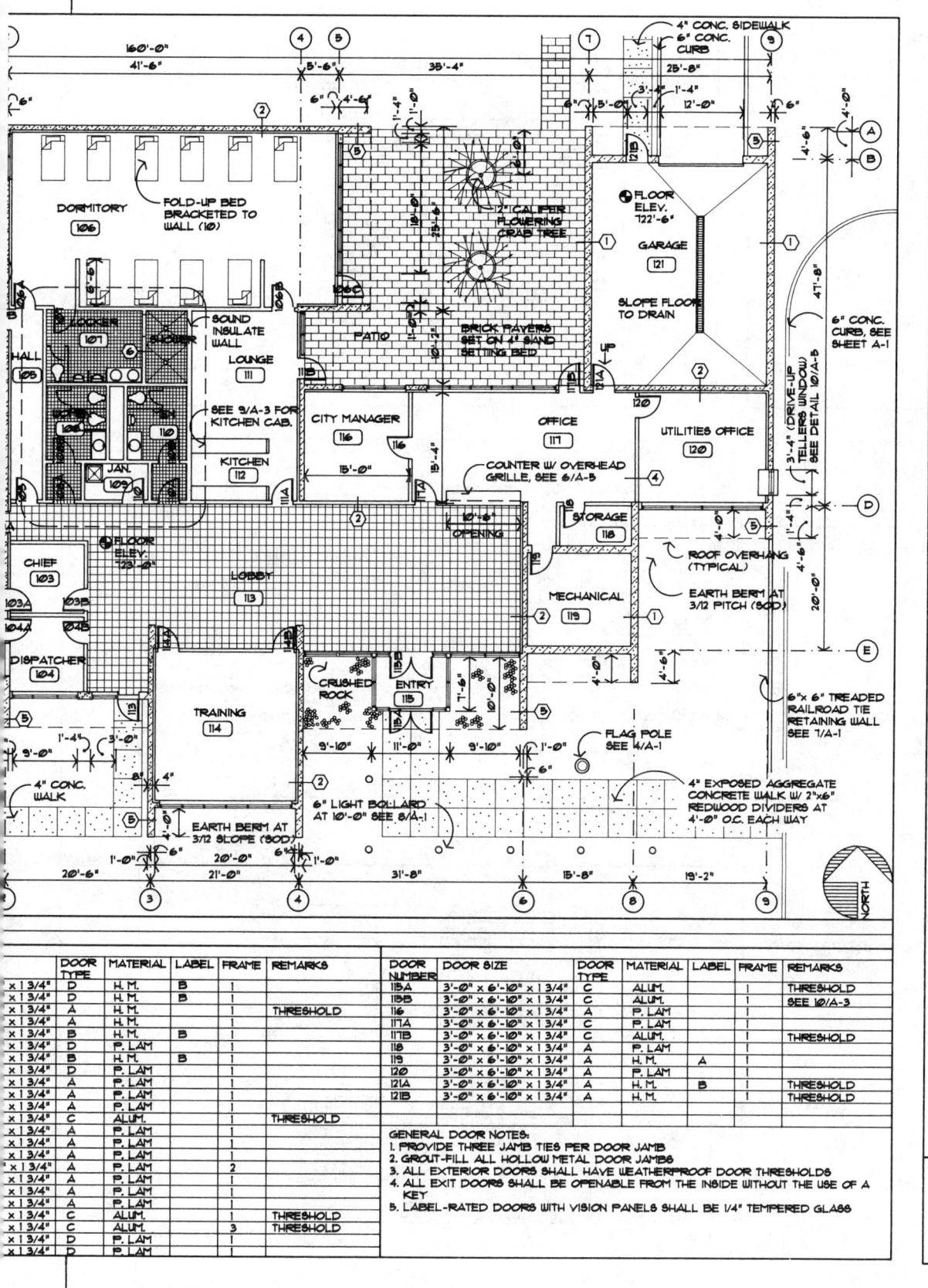

APPLE VALLEY MUNICIPAL FIRE STATION FLOOR PLAN
14550 CEDAR AVENUE SOUTH
APPLE VALLEY, MN

Sheet A2

FIRE STATION 25-7

Rooms
- DORMITORY 106
- LOUNGE 111
- KITCHEN 112
- JAN. 109
- HALL 105
- CHIEF 103
- DISPATCHER 104
- LOBBY 113
- TRAINING 114
- ENTRY 115
- CITY MANAGER 116
- OFFICE 117
- MECHANICAL 119
- STORAGE 118
- UTILITIES OFFICE 120
- GARAGE 121
- PATIO

Notes on plan
- FOLD-UP BED BRACKETED TO WALL (10)
- SOUND INSULATE WALL
- SEE 9/A-3 FOR KITCHEN CAB.
- 1" CALIPER FLOWERING CRAB TREE
- BRICK PAVERS SET ON 4" SAND SETTING BED
- FLOOR ELEV. 722'-6"
- FLOOR ELEV. 723'-0"
- SLOPE FLOOR TO DRAIN
- 4" CONC. SIDEWALK
- 6" CONC. CURB
- 3'-4" (DRIVE-UP TELLERS WINDOW) SEE DETAIL 10/A-5
- 6" CONC. CURB, SEE SHEET A-1
- COUNTER W/ OVERHEAD GRILLE, SEE 6/A-5
- ROOF OVERHANG (TYPICAL)
- EARTH BERM AT 3/12 PITCH (SOD)
- 6"x 6" TREATED RAILROAD TIE RETAINING WALL SEE 7/A-1
- FLAG POLE SEE 4/A-1
- 4" EXPOSED AGGREGATE CONCRETE WALK W/ 2"x6" REDWOOD DIVIDERS AT 4'-0" O.C. EACH WAY
- 6" LIGHT BOLLARD AT 10'-0" SEE 8/A-1
- EARTH BERM AT 3/12 SLOPE (SOD)
- 4" CONC. WALK
- CRUSHED ROCK

Door Schedule

	DOOR TYPE	MATERIAL	LABEL	FRAME	REMARKS
x 1 3/4"	D	H.M.	B	1	
x 1 3/4"	D	H.M.	B	1	
x 1 3/4"	A	H.M.		1	THRESHOLD
x 1 3/4"	A	H.M.		1	
x 1 3/4"	B	H.M.	B	1	
x 1 3/4"	D	P. LAM		1	
x 1 3/4"	B	H.M.	B	1	
x 1 3/4"	D	P. LAM		1	
x 1 3/4"	A	P. LAM		1	
x 1 3/4"	A	P. LAM		1	
x 1 3/4"	C	ALUM.		1	THRESHOLD
x 1 3/4"	A	P. LAM		1	
x 1 3/4"	A	P. LAM		2	
x 1 3/4"	A	P. LAM		1	
x 1 3/4"	A	P. LAM		1	
x 1 3/4"	C	ALUM.		1	THRESHOLD
x 1 3/4"	C	ALUM.		3	THRESHOLD
x 1 3/4"	D	P. LAM		1	
x 1 3/4"	D	P. LAM		1	

DOOR NUMBER	DOOR SIZE	DOOR TYPE	MATERIAL	LABEL	FRAME	REMARKS
115A	3'-0" x 6'-10" x 1 3/4"	C	ALUM.		1	THRESHOLD
115B	3'-0" x 6'-10" x 1 3/4"	C	ALUM.		1	SEE 10/A-3
116	3'-0" x 6'-10" x 1 3/4"	A	P. LAM			
117A	3'-0" x 6'-10" x 1 3/4"	C	P. LAM			
117B	3'-0" x 6'-10" x 1 3/4"	C	ALUM.			THRESHOLD
118	3'-0" x 6'-10" x 1 3/4"	A	P. LAM			
119	3'-0" x 6'-10" x 1 3/4"	A	H.M.	A		
120	3'-0" x 6'-10" x 1 3/4"	A	P. LAM			
121A	3'-0" x 6'-10" x 1 3/4"	A	H.M.	B		THRESHOLD
121B	3'-0" x 6'-10" x 1 3/4"	A	H.M.			THRESHOLD

GENERAL DOOR NOTES:
1. PROVIDE THREE JAMB TIES PER DOOR JAMB
2. GROUT-FILL ALL HOLLOW METAL DOOR JAMBS
3. ALL EXTERIOR DOORS SHALL HAVE WEATHERPROOF DOOR THRESHOLDS
4. ALL EXIT DOORS SHALL BE OPENABLE FROM THE INSIDE WITHOUT THE USE OF A KEY
5. LABEL-RATED DOORS WITH VISION PANELS SHALL BE 1/4" TEMPERED GLASS

Floor Plan/A-2

A portion of the toilet plan blow-up is shown to the right. It is common to enlarge commercial toilet plans (to a 1/4" = 1'-0" scale) to show detail and dimension strings. The plan indicates the size of items such as toilet partitions and spacing between fixtures. The bubbles are used to indicate wall elevations that show mounting heights.

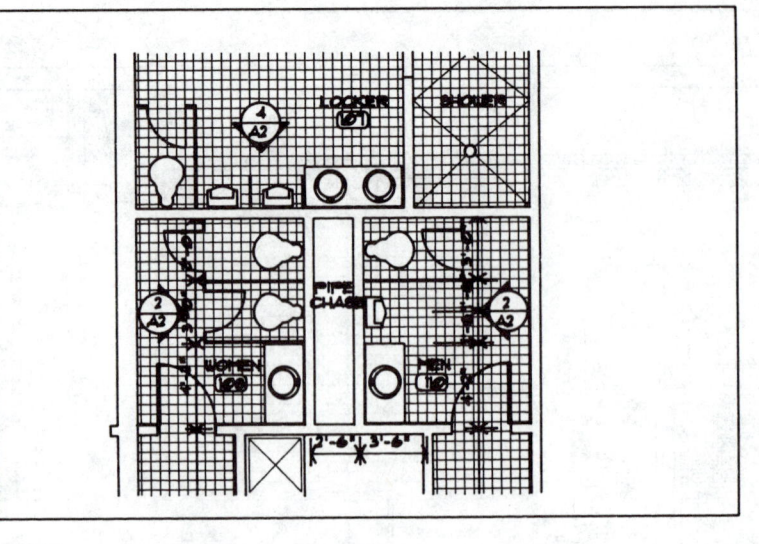

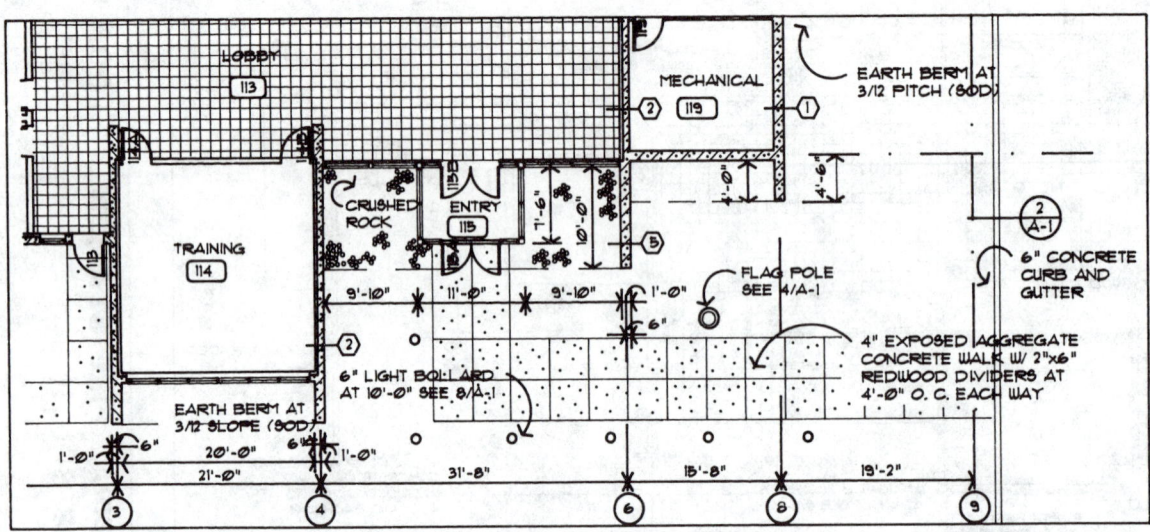

A portion of the floor plan at the entry is shown above. Wall types (shown in hexagons) are keyed to plan blow-ups. Grids are shown along the bottom of the drawing. Note that much of the building is dimensioned from the grids. Exterior items, such as walks and lights, are drawn using a lighter line weight so they don't compete with lines drawn for building walls.

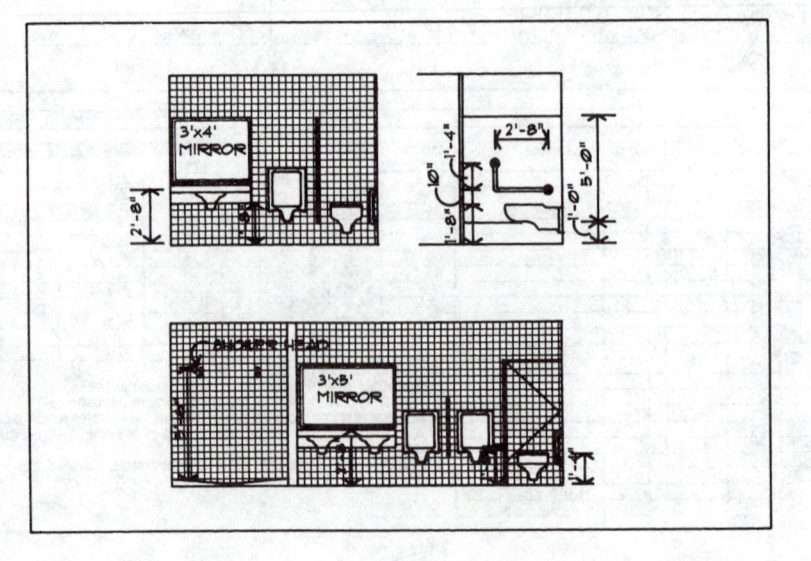

FIRE STATION — 25-8

Floor Plan/A-2

This is a portion of the floor plan at the entrance to the fire truck apparatus room. Door openings are dimensioned with a masonry opening (M.O.). The single-step rise from the apparatus floor to the chief and dispatcher's room is marked with an arrow and the word up. Interior dimensions for the office doors and windows are positioned out of the way of notes.

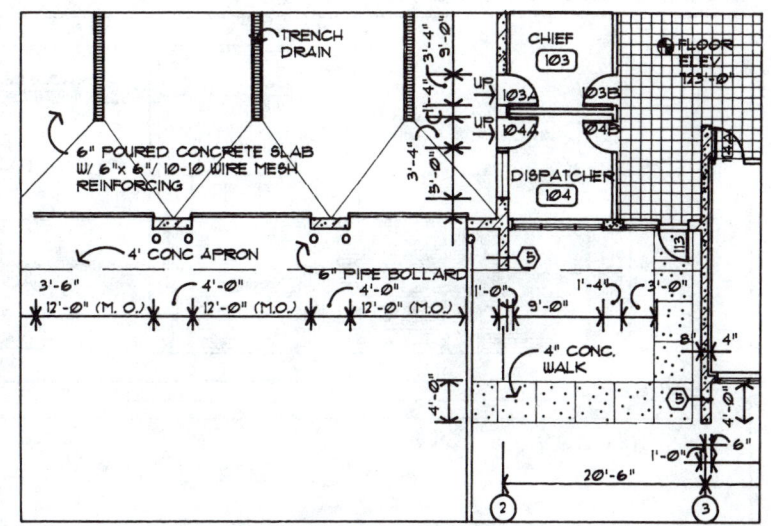

A room finish schedule provides information for every room on the plan. It is a good practice to place a schedule on the same sheet as the plan.

The partial plan below shows the area around the court yard. Grids on the plan define the center of load-bearing block walls. Note that doors and walls are dimensioned from the closest grid line.

ROOM FINISH SCHEDULE

ROOM NUMBER	ROOM NAME	FLOOR	BASE	WALL MATERIAL	FINISH
100	APPARATUS ROOM	CONCRETE	VINYL	BLOCK	EPOXY
101	HOSE TOWER	CONCRETE	NONE	BLOCK	EPOXY
102	CLEAN-UP	CONCRETE	VINYL	BLOCK	EPOXY
103	CHIEF	CARPET	VINYL	GYP. BD.	PAINT
104	DISPATCHER	CARPET	VINYL	GYP. BD.	PAINT
105	HALL	CARPET	VINYL	GYP. BD.	PAINT
106	DORMITORY	CARPET	VINYL	GYP. BD.	PAINT
107	LOCKER ROOM	CERAMIC TILE	C.T.	GYP. BD.	C.T.
108	WOMEN'S TOILET	CERAMIC TILE	C.T.	GYP. BD.	C.T.
109	JANITOR	CONCRETE	VINYL	GYP. BD.	PAINT
110	MEN'S TOILET	CERAMIC TILE	C.T.	GYP. BD.	C.T.
111	LOUNGE	CARPET	VINYL	GYP. BD.	PAINT
112	KITCHEN	QUARRY TILE	VINYL	GYP. BD.	PAINT
113	LOBBY	QUARRY TILE	VINYL	GYP. BD.	VINYL
114	TRAINING	CARPET	VINYL	GYP. BD.	PAINT
115	ENTRY	QUARRY TILE	ALUM.	GLASS	NONE

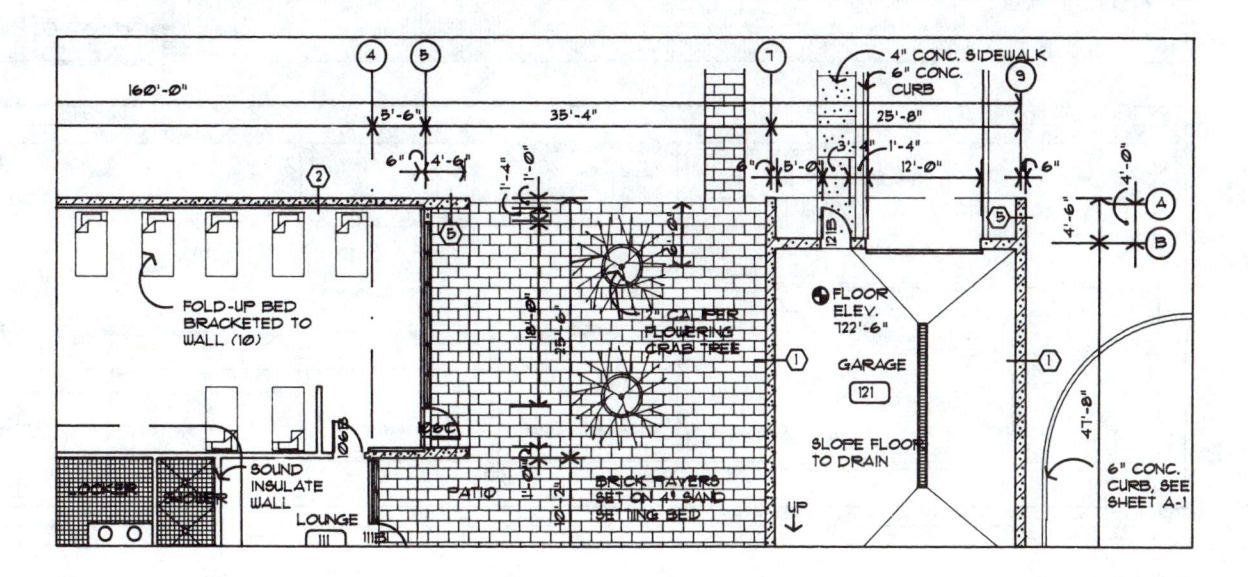

FIRE STATION   25-9

Elevations/A-3

① SOUTH ELEVATION
A-3 SCALE 1/8"=1'-0"

HOSE TOWER DECK ELEV. 754'-0"
LOWER ROOF BEARING ELEV. 749'-8 1/2"
APPARATUS RM. DECK ELEV. 741'-0"

- ANODIZED ALUMINUM FASCIA PANELS
- OVERHEAD COIL DOOR
- 6"⌀ PIPE BOLLARD
- SLOPED EARTH BERM

② NORTH ELEVATION
A-3 SCALE 1/4"=1'-0"

- OVERHEAD COIL DOOR
- ANODIZED ALUMINUM FASCIA PANELS
- BREAK-OFF BLOCK

③ WEST ELEVATION
A-3 SCALE 1/8"=1'-0"

- LINE OF SLOPED HOSE TOWER ROOF
- ANODIZED ALUMINUM CAP
- BREAK-OFF BLOCK
- LADDER TO TOWER PLATFORM
- HOSE TOWER

⑤ NORTH ELEVATION
A-3 SCALE 1/8"=1'-0"

HOSE TOWER DECK ELEV. 754'-0"
HOSE TOWER PLAT. ELEV. 746'-6"

⑤ BUILDING SECTION THRU APPARATUS AND OFFICE AREA
A-3 SCALE 1/8"=1'-0"

HOSE TOWER DECK ELEV. 754'-0"

- ANODIZED ALUMINUM ROOF PANELS
- 4" CANT STRIP AND PARAPET FLASHING
- OVERHEAD COIL DOOR
- APPARATUS ROOM
- DISPATCHER
- LOBBY
- TRAINING
- ENTRY
- MECHANICAL

FIRE STATION 25-10

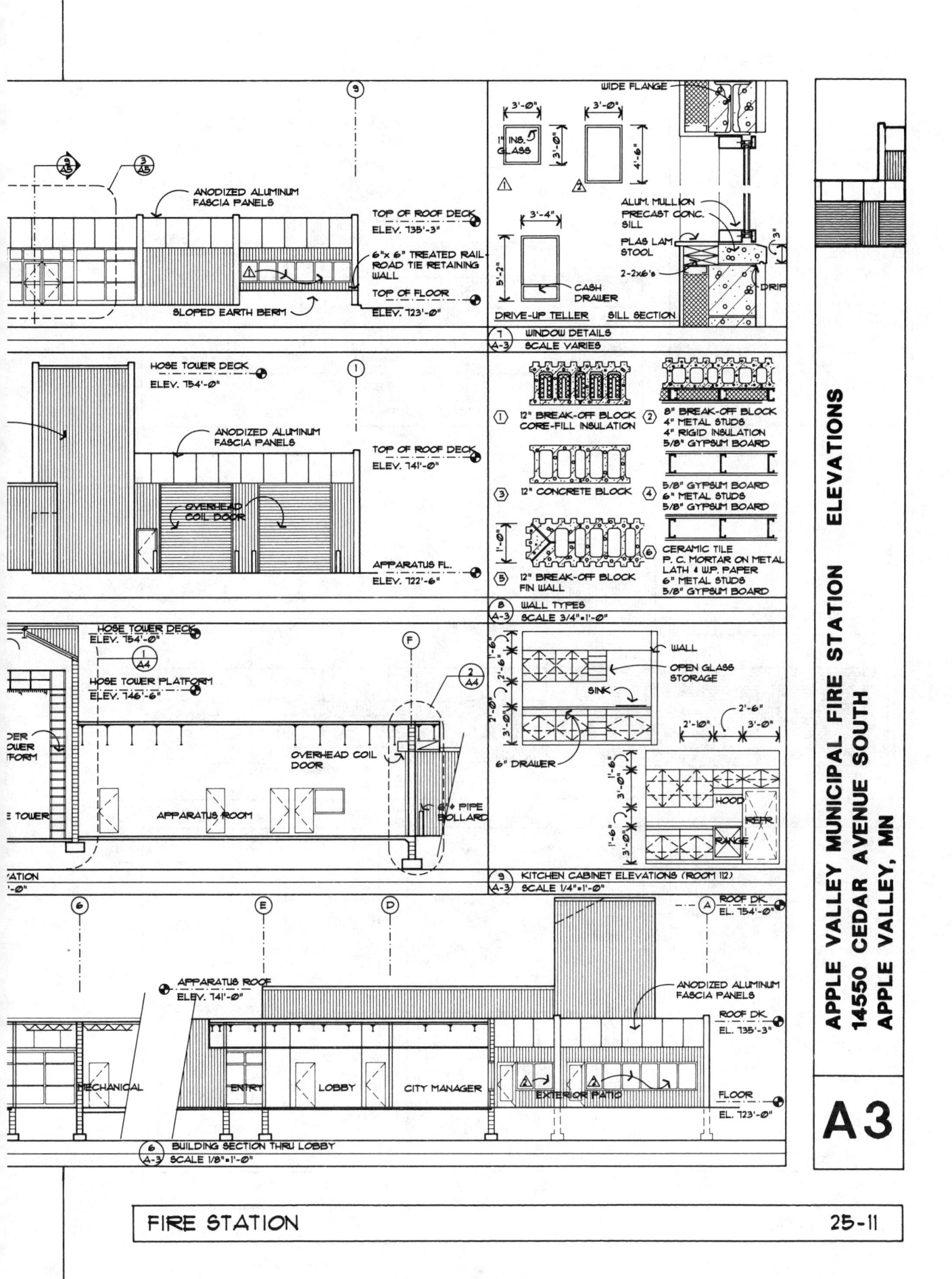

APPLE VALLEY MUNICIPAL FIRE STATION ELEVATIONS
14550 CEDAR AVENUE SOUTH
APPLE VALLEY, MN

A3

FIRE STATION 25-11

Elevations/A-3

The drawing at the right shows a building section cut and an elevation of the west patio wall. Elevations should show materials as they appear in the orthographic view. In this example, the break-off block is represented by vertical lines and the metal panels are drawn as rectangles.

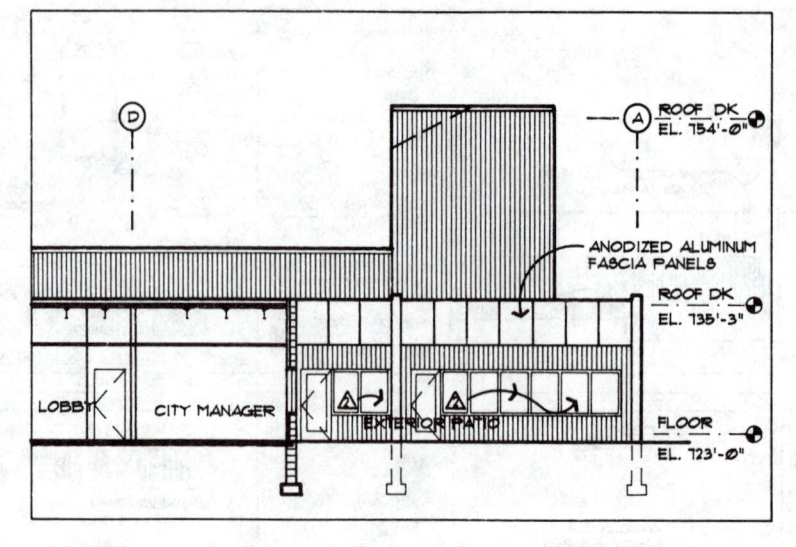

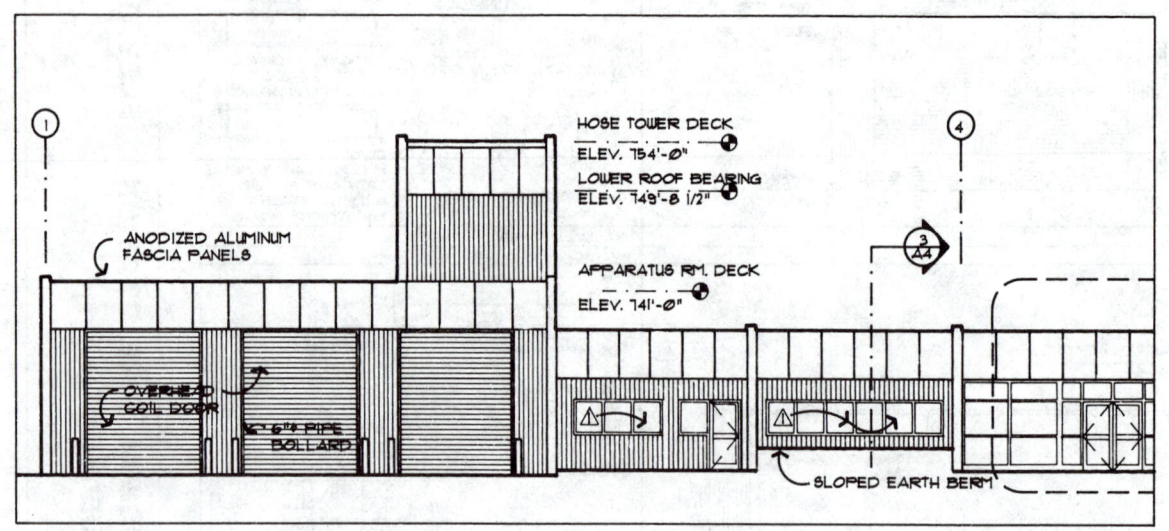

The south elevation shown above illustrates the amount of detail found in a typical elevation. Window and door frames should be drawn with double lines. Grids should be drawn at major points on the building.

The drawings at the right illustrate the entry and east end of the building. Elevation points on the project should be shown with a bull's-eye and the height above grade.

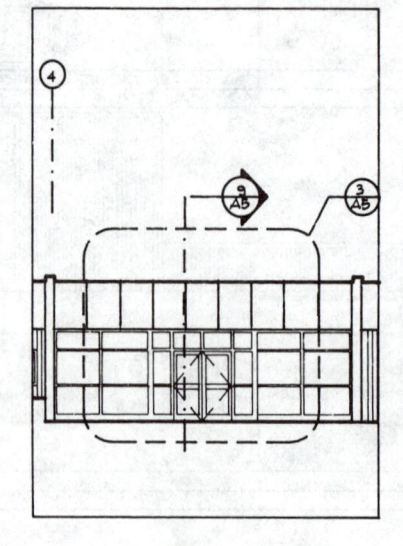

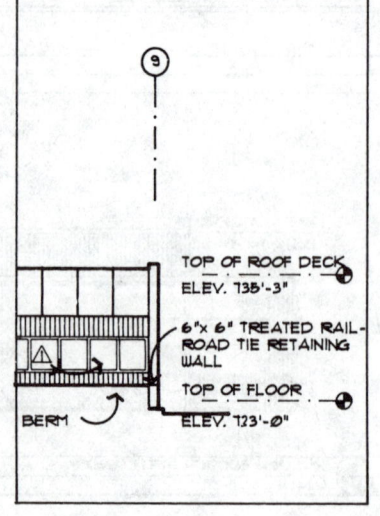

FIRE STATION 25-12

Elevations/A-3

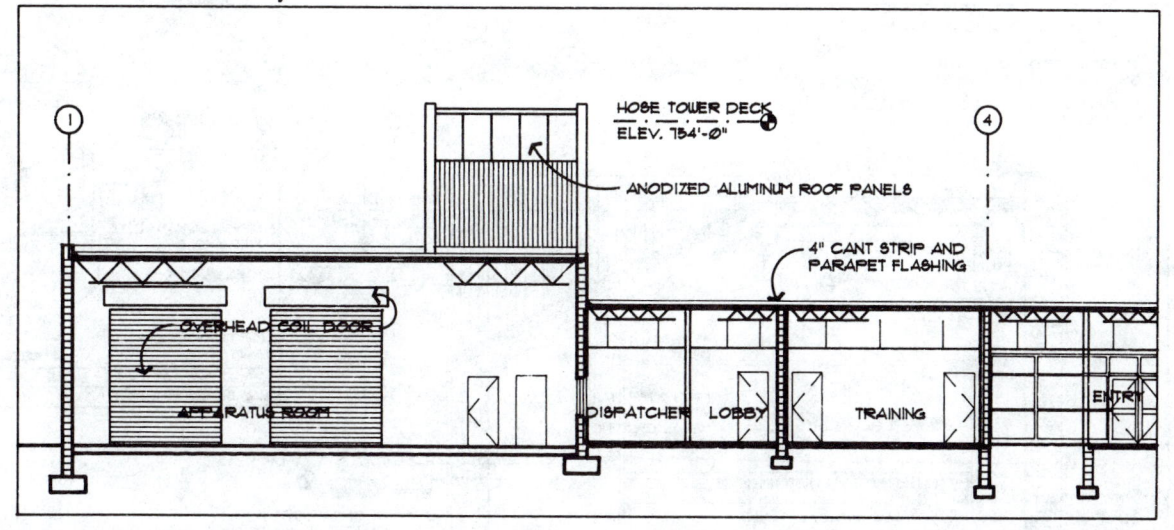

The section cut above illustrates the amount of detail that should be shown, including items such as room names, structural elements, and doors beyond the section. The hose tower is seen in elevation beyond the section plane.

Wall types illustrated to the right include every wall assembly in the building. Walls on the plan should be keyed to these wall types using a hexagonal bubble.

1. 12" BREAK-OFF BLOCK CORE-FILL INSULATION
2. 8" BREAK-OFF BLOCK / 4" METAL STUDS / 4" RIGID INSULATION / 5/8" GYPSUM BOARD
3. 12" CONCRETE BLOCK
4. 5/8" GYPSUM BOARD / 6" METAL STUDS / 5/8" GYPSUM BOARD
5. 12" BREAK-OFF BLOCK FIN WALL
6. CERAMIC TILE / P.C. MORTAR ON METAL LATH & W.P. PAPER / 6" METAL STUDS / 5/8" GYPSUM BOARD

This detail illustrates the window types in the projects. Windows are drawn at a larger scale (1/4" = 1'-0") to allow space for dimension strings. Frame types are identified by numbers in deltas. /3\ The same tags are used on the building elevations to specify frame sizes. The window frame head and sill section is drawn to show installation. Note that the window sill is made of precast concrete.

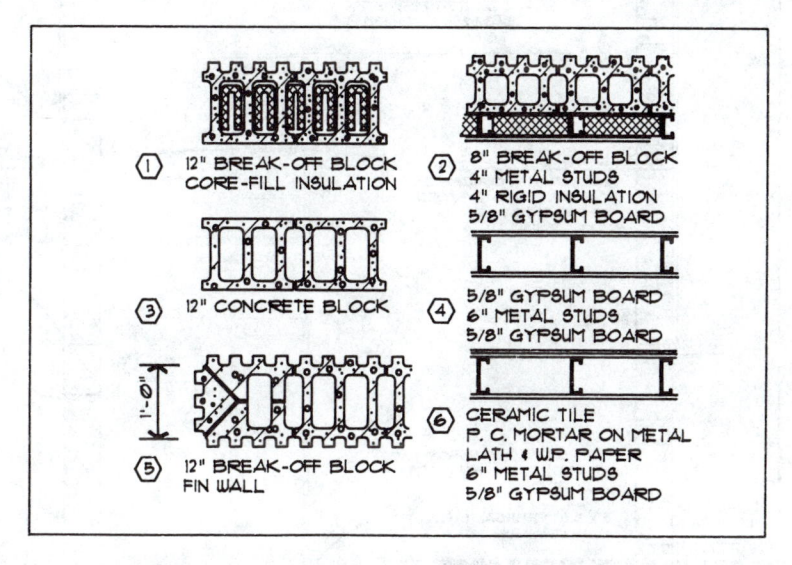

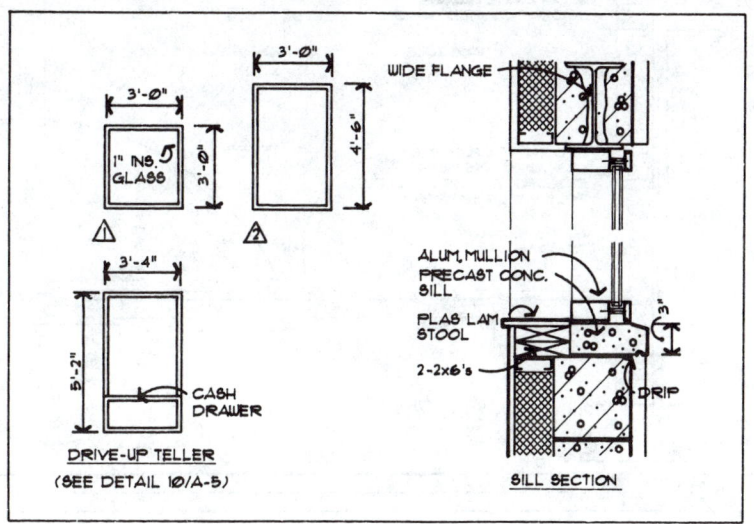

FIRE STATION 25-13

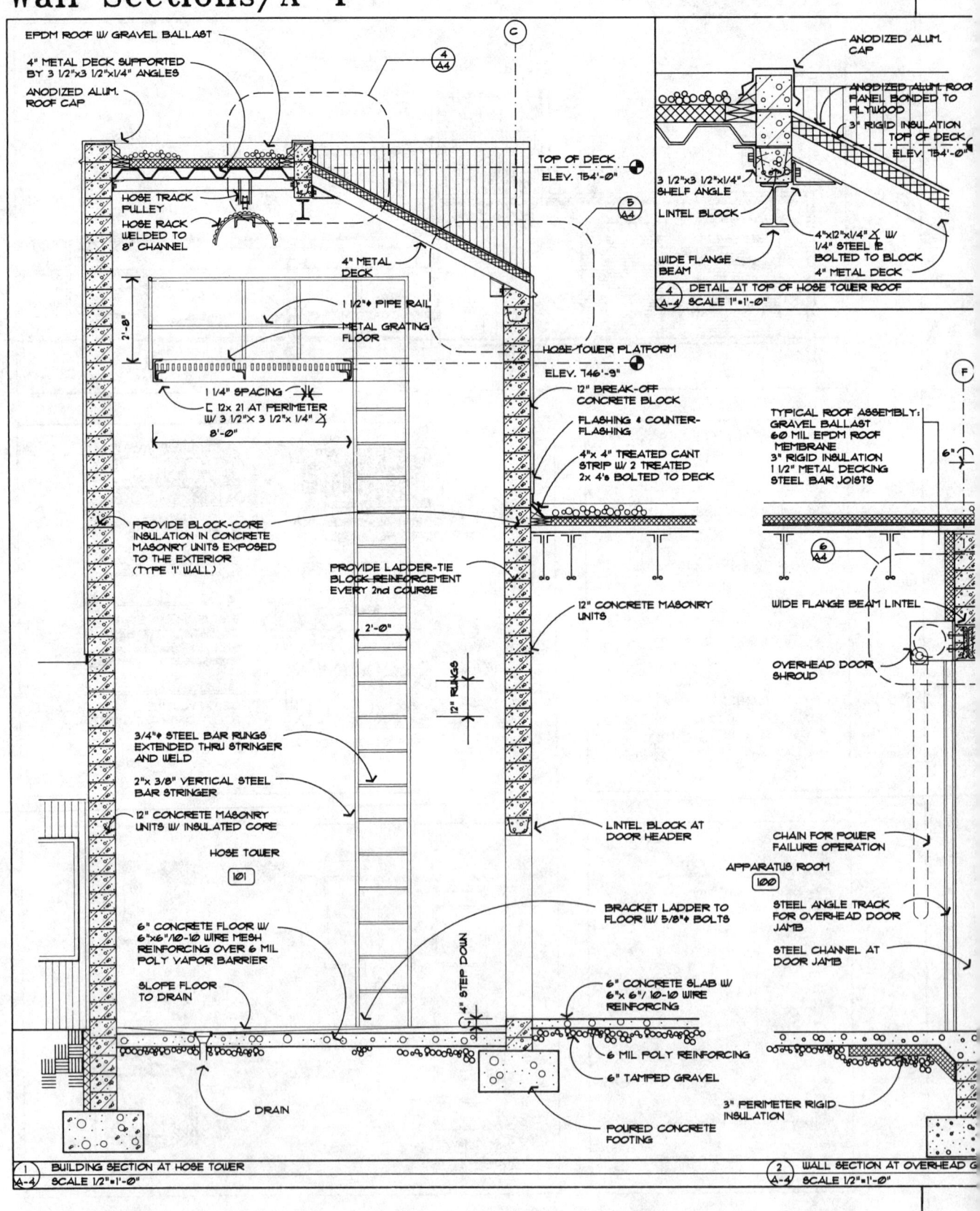

Wall Sections/A-4

Building Section at Hose Tower

- EPDM ROOF W/ GRAVEL BALLAST
- 4" METAL DECK SUPPORTED BY 3 1/2"x 3 1/2"x1/4" ANGLES
- ANODIZED ALUM. ROOF CAP
- HOSE TRACK PULLEY
- HOSE RACK WELDED TO 8" CHANNEL
- 4" METAL DECK
- 1 1/2"⌀ PIPE RAIL
- METAL GRATING FLOOR
- 1 1/4" SPACING
- C 12x 21 AT PERIMETER W/ 3 1/2"x 3 1/2"x 1/4"
- TOP OF DECK ELEV. 754'-0"
- HOSE TOWER PLATFORM ELEV. 746'-9"
- 12" BREAK-OFF CONCRETE BLOCK
- FLASHING & COUNTER-FLASHING
- 4"x 4" TREATED CANT STRIP W/ 2 TREATED 2x 4's BOLTED TO DECK
- PROVIDE BLOCK-CORE INSULATION IN CONCRETE MASONRY UNITS EXPOSED TO THE EXTERIOR (TYPE '1' WALL)
- PROVIDE LADDER-TIE BLOCK REINFORCEMENT EVERY 2nd COURSE
- 12" CONCRETE MASONRY UNITS
- 3/4"⌀ STEEL BAR RUNGS EXTENDED THRU STRINGER AND WELD
- 2"x 3/8" VERTICAL STEEL BAR STRINGER
- 12" CONCRETE MASONRY UNITS W/ INSULATED CORE
- HOSE TOWER 101
- LINTEL BLOCK AT DOOR HEADER
- BRACKET LADDER TO FLOOR W/ 5/8"⌀ BOLTS
- 6" CONCRETE FLOOR W/ 6"x6"/10-10 WIRE MESH REINFORCING OVER 6 MIL POLY VAPOR BARRIER
- SLOPE FLOOR TO DRAIN
- 6" CONCRETE SLAB W/ 6"x 6"/ 10-10 WIRE REINFORCING
- 6 MIL POLY REINFORCING
- 6" TAMPED GRAVEL
- POURED CONCRETE FOOTING
- 12" RINGS
- 2'-0"
- 4" STEP DOWN

1 / BUILDING SECTION AT HOSE TOWER
A-4 / SCALE 1/2"=1'-0"

Detail at Top of Hose Tower Roof

- ANODIZED ALUM. CAP
- ANODIZED ALUM. ROOF PANEL BONDED TO PLYWOOD
- 3" RIGID INSULATION TOP OF DECK ELEV. 754'-0"
- 3 1/2"x 3 1/2"x1/4" SHELF ANGLE
- LINTEL BLOCK
- WIDE FLANGE BEAM
- 4"x 12"x1/4" W/ 1/4" STEEL R BOLTED TO BLOCK
- 4" METAL DECK

4 / DETAIL AT TOP OF HOSE TOWER ROOF
A-4 / SCALE 1"=1'-0"

Wall Section at Overhead

- TYPICAL ROOF ASSEMBLY: GRAVEL BALLAST 60 MIL EPDM ROOF MEMBRANE 3" RIGID INSULATION 1 1/2" METAL DECKING STEEL BAR JOISTS
- WIDE FLANGE BEAM LINTEL
- OVERHEAD DOOR SHROUD
- CHAIN FOR POWER FAILURE OPERATION
- APPARATUS ROOM 100
- STEEL ANGLE TRACK FOR OVERHEAD DOOR JAMB
- STEEL CHANNEL AT DOOR JAMB
- 3" PERIMETER RIGID INSULATION

2 / WALL SECTION AT OVERHEAD
A-4 / SCALE 1/2"=1'-0"

FIRE STATION   25-14

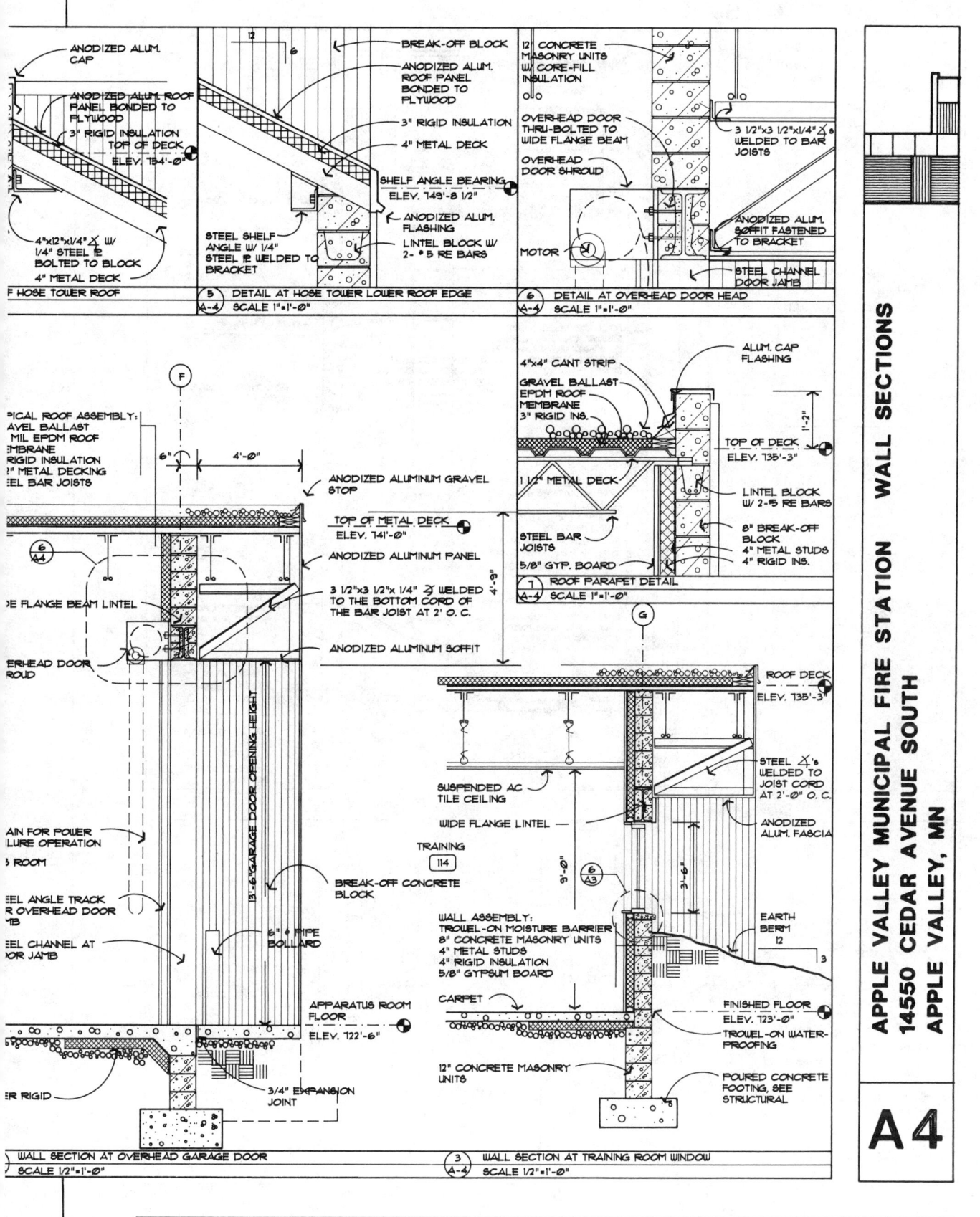

APPLE VALLEY MUNICIPAL FIRE STATION WALL SECTIONS
14550 CEDAR AVENUE SOUTH
APPLE VALLEY, MN

A4

FIRE STATION   25-15

Wall Sections/A-4

This wall section cuts through the hose tower. At this scale, it is possible to show items such as masonry coursing and structural members. (Materials are drawn at an accurate scale to make sure that all "pieces" of the building fit.) The wall section to the right is also important because it shows the ladder and platform construction.

Two blow-ups of the hose tower roof edge are shown at the bottom of the page. These details have been generated from wall sections, by first locating structural beams and walls, in order to further define assembly procedures. Determining the appropriate metal flashing at the intersection of the roof and wall is an important factor in completing these details.

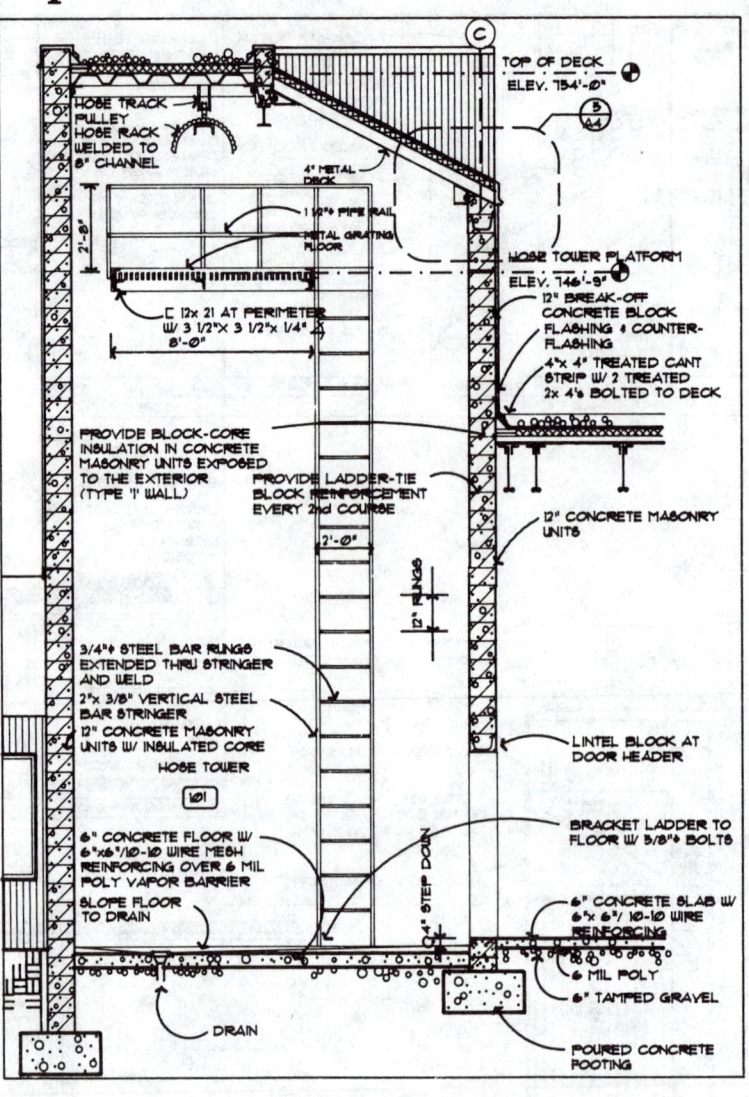

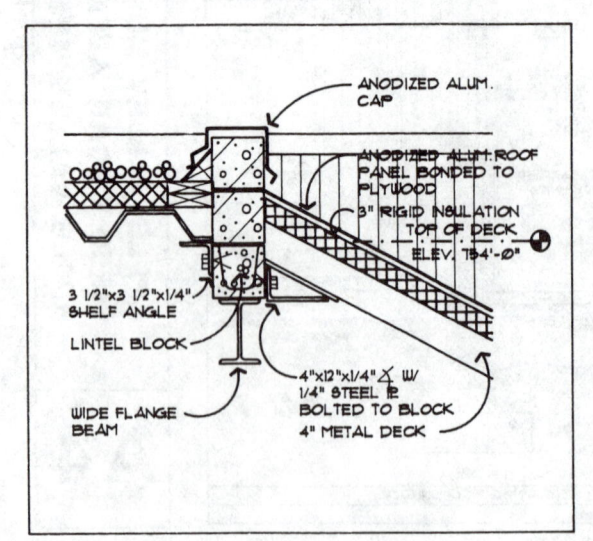

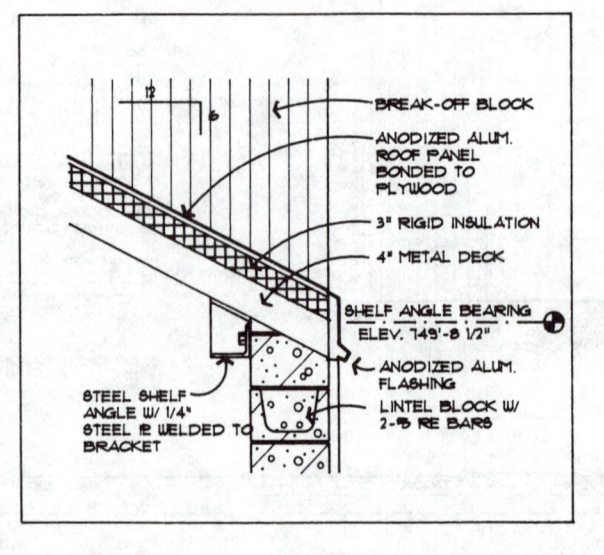

FIRE STATION

25-16

Wall Sections/A-4

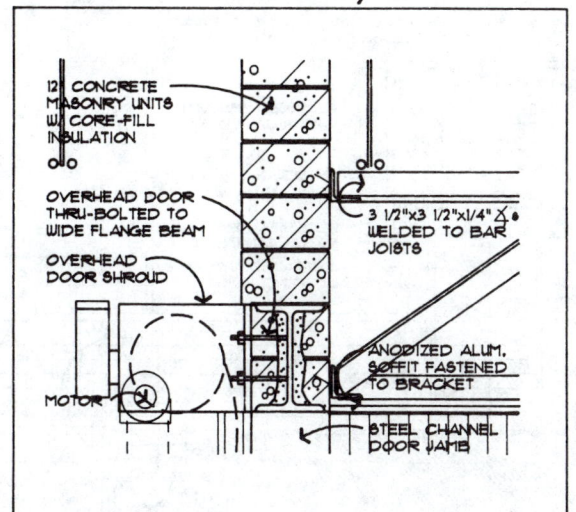

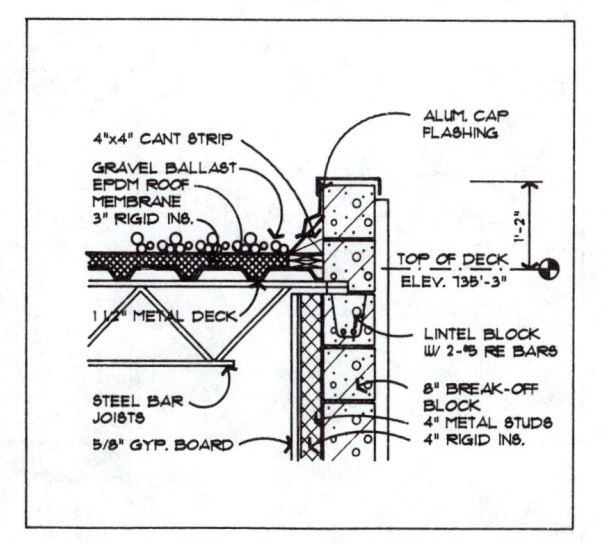

The details above show sections cut through the apparatus room door and a typical roof edge. Details require a thorough knowledge of the building assembly. Here beams, roof decking, bar joists, and the rolling door must all be accurately drawn and fit into the system. The resulting details are a combination of catalog data on the components (e.g., bar joists, masonry) and known information on the wall assembly.

The section on the right cuts through a window unit in the training room. It shows a wide flange steel beam at the window head with a 4'-0" fascia beyond the wall. This section is important because it details the sloped earth berm and the structure for the roof overhang.

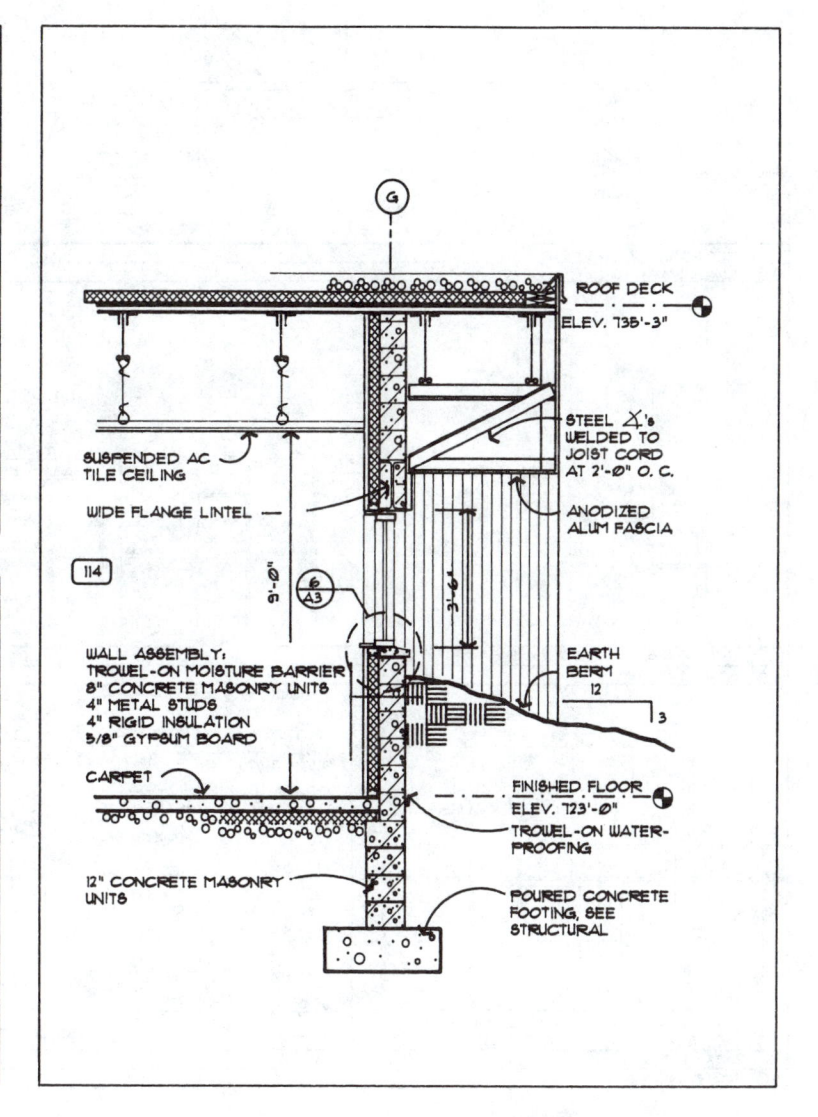

FIRE STATION   25-17

Wall Sections/A-5

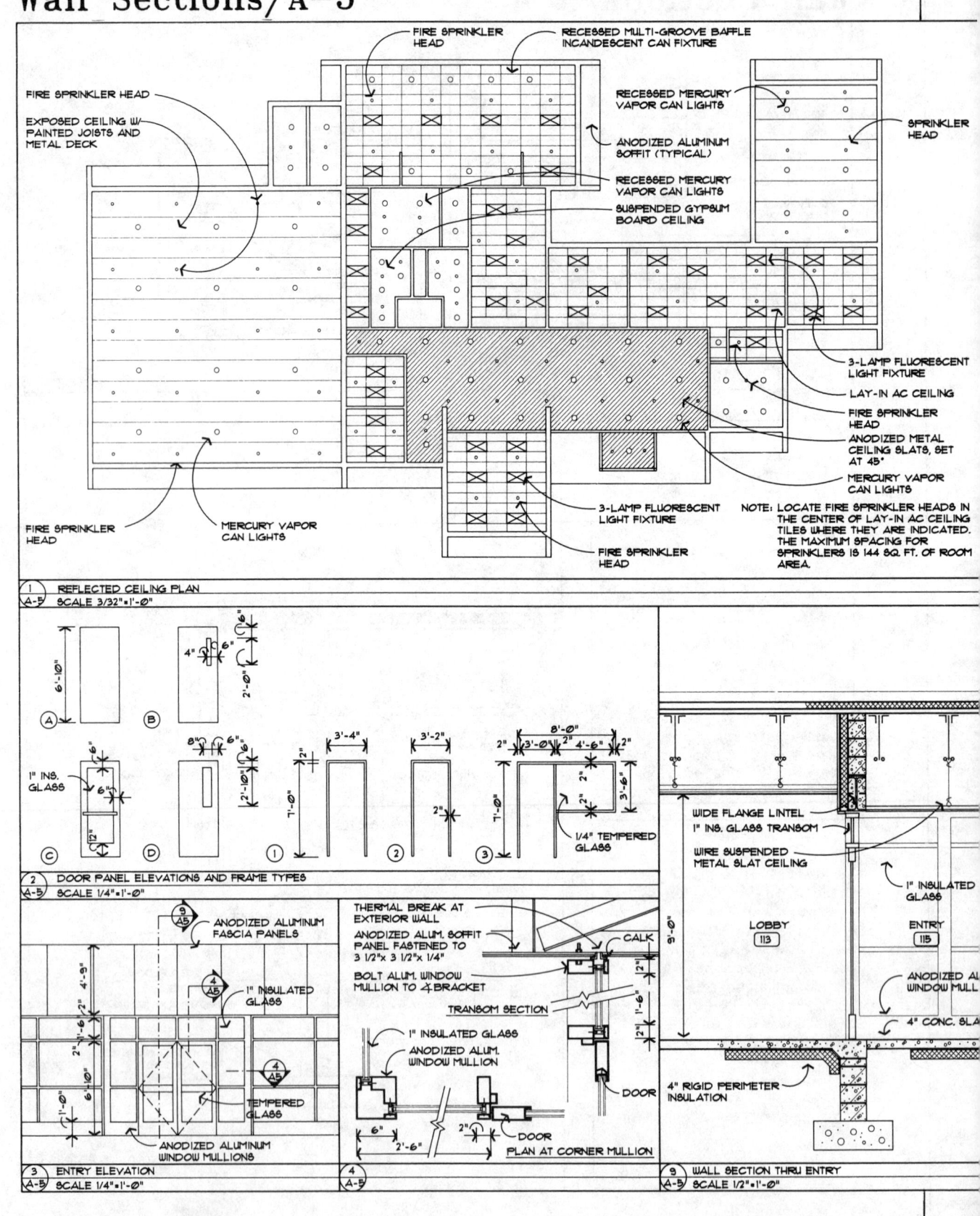

FIRE STATION

25-18

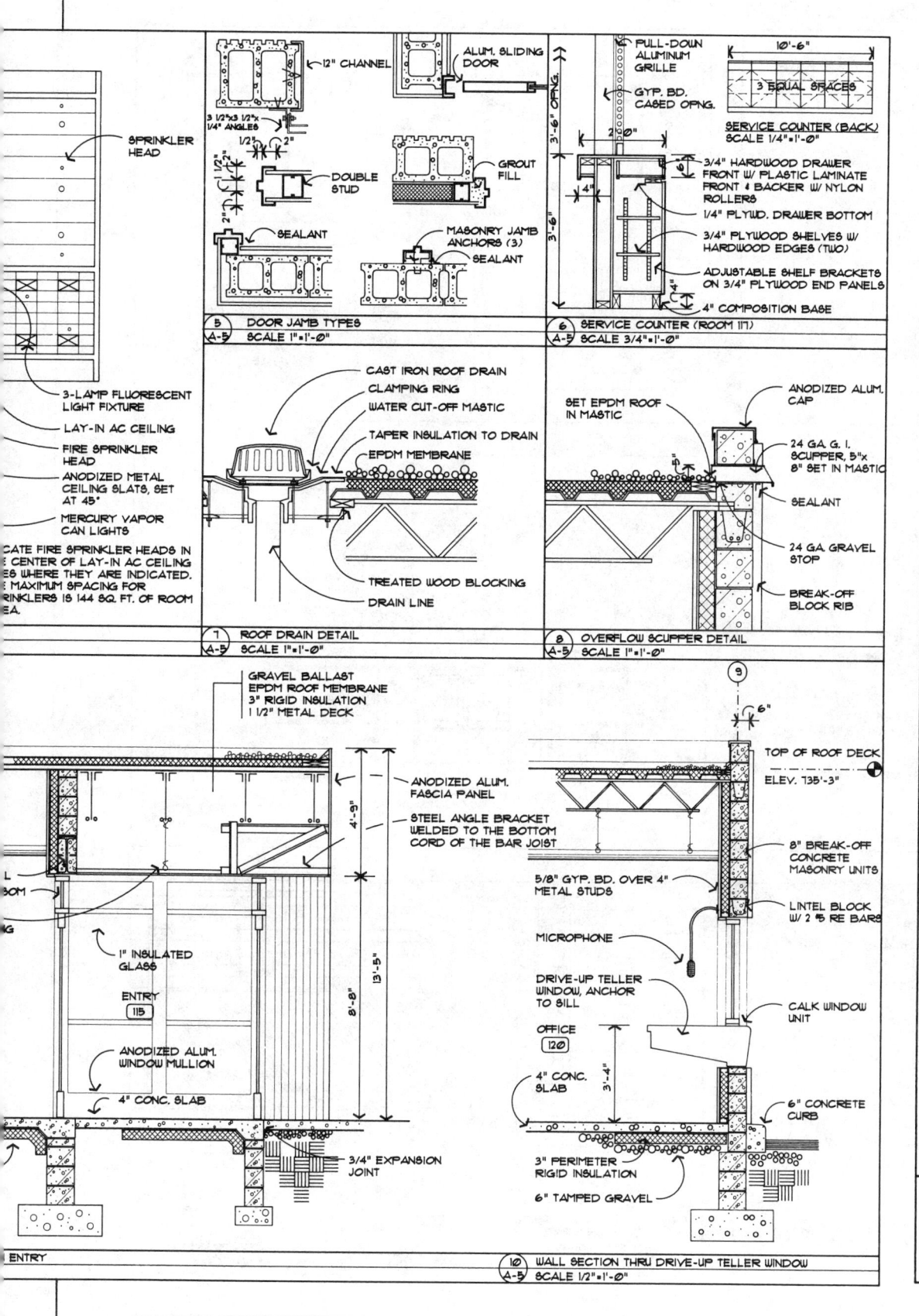

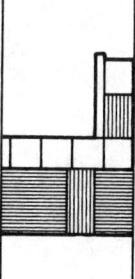

APPLE VALLEY MUNICIPAL FIRE STATION — WALL SECTIONS
14550 CEDAR AVENUE SOUTH, APPLE VALLEY, MN

Sheet A5 — FIRE STATION — 25-19

---

5 / A-5 — DOOR JAMB TYPES
Scale: 1" = 1'-0"

- 12" CHANNEL
- ALUM. SLIDING DOOR
- 3 1/2" x 3 1/2" x 1/4" ANGLES
- DOUBLE STUD
- GROUT FILL
- SEALANT
- MASONRY JAMB ANCHORS (3)
- SEALANT

6 / A-5 — SERVICE COUNTER (ROOM 117)
Scale: 3/4" = 1'-0"

- PULL-DOWN ALUMINUM GRILLE
- GYP. BD. CASED OPNG.
- 3'-6" OPNG.
- 2'-0"
- SERVICE COUNTER (BACK) — Scale 1/4" = 1'-0"
- 10'-6", 3 EQUAL SPACES
- 3/4" HARDWOOD DRAWER FRONT W/ PLASTIC LAMINATE FRONT & BACKER W/ NYLON ROLLERS
- 1/4" PLYWD. DRAWER BOTTOM
- 3/4" PLYWOOD SHELVES W/ HARDWOOD EDGES (TWO)
- ADJUSTABLE SHELF BRACKETS ON 3/4" PLYWOOD END PANELS
- 4" COMPOSITION BASE

(left column notes)
- SPRINKLER HEAD
- 3-LAMP FLUORESCENT LIGHT FIXTURE
- LAY-IN AC CEILING
- FIRE SPRINKLER HEAD
- ANODIZED METAL CEILING SLATS, SET AT 45°
- MERCURY VAPOR CAN LIGHTS
- [LO]CATE FIRE SPRINKLER HEADS IN [TH]E CENTER OF LAY-IN AC CEILING [TIL]ES WHERE THEY ARE INDICATED. [TH]E MAXIMUM SPACING FOR [SP]RINKLERS IS 144 SQ. FT. OF ROOM [AR]EA.

7 / A-5 — ROOF DRAIN DETAIL
Scale: 1" = 1'-0"

- CAST IRON ROOF DRAIN
- CLAMPING RING
- WATER CUT-OFF MASTIC
- TAPER INSULATION TO DRAIN
- EPDM MEMBRANE
- TREATED WOOD BLOCKING
- DRAIN LINE

8 / A-5 — OVERFLOW SCUPPER DETAIL
Scale: 1" = 1'-0"

- SET EPDM ROOF IN MASTIC
- ANODIZED ALUM. CAP
- 24 GA. G.I. SCUPPER, 5" x 8" SET IN MASTIC
- SEALANT
- 24 GA. GRAVEL STOP
- BREAK-OFF BLOCK RIB

---

10 / A-5 — WALL SECTION THRU DRIVE-UP TELLER WINDOW
Scale: 1/2" = 1'-0"

- GRAVEL BALLAST
- EPDM ROOF MEMBRANE
- 3" RIGID INSULATION
- 1 1/2" METAL DECK
- ANODIZED ALUM. FASCIA PANEL
- STEEL ANGLE BRACKET WELDED TO THE BOTTOM CORD OF THE BAR JOIST
- 5/8" GYP. BD. OVER 4" METAL STUDS
- TOP OF ROOF DECK ELEV. 735'-3"
- 8" BREAK-OFF CONCRETE MASONRY UNITS
- LINTEL BLOCK W/ 2 #5 RE BARS
- MICROPHONE
- DRIVE-UP TELLER WINDOW, ANCHOR TO SILL
- CALK WINDOW UNIT
- 1" INSULATED GLASS
- ENTRY 115
- ANODIZED ALUM. WINDOW MULLION
- 4" CONC. SLAB
- OFFICE 120
- 4" CONC. SLAB
- 6" CONCRETE CURB
- 3/4" EXPANSION JOINT
- 3" PERIMETER RIGID INSULATION
- 6" TAMPED GRAVEL
- 4'-9", 8'-8", 13'-5", 3'-4"

Wall Sections/A-5

This drawing illustrates door panel and frame types. A panel view is a front elevation of the door, while the frame view is an elevation of the door frame. The two views are "keyed" to the door schedule.

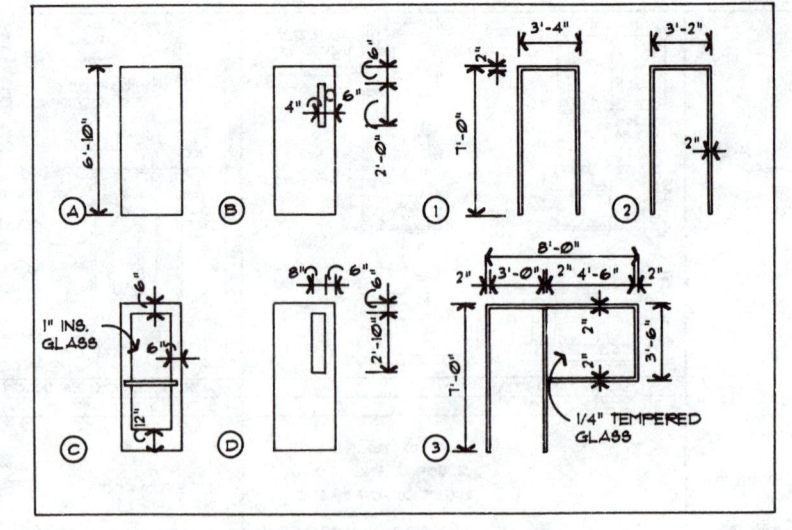

Areas of a project that need more definition can be blown up to allow for dimensions and detail. The example to the right shows a 1/4" = 1'-0" scale elevation of the front entry. The aluminum window frame, called a store front, provides the contractor with notes and dimensions that couldn't be included on the smaller scale building elevation.

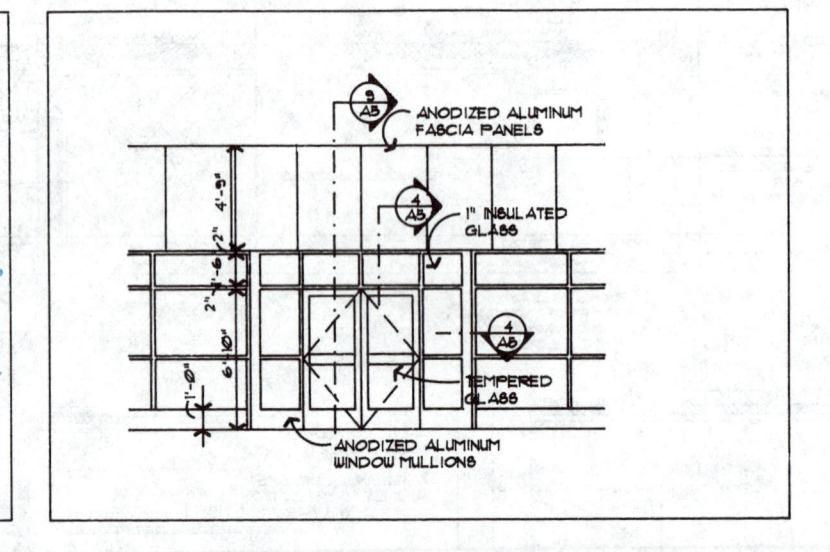

At the right is a portion of the reflected ceiling plan showing a "footprint" of the floor plan with a pattern of items fixed to the ceiling. Such a plan usually includes light fixtures, speakers, sprinklers, mechanical ducts, and ceiling tile. Items on the plan are drawn and indicated by note. In rooms with ceiling tile, the 2' x 4' grid pattern of the A.C. tile is used to position light fixtures and sprinkler heads.

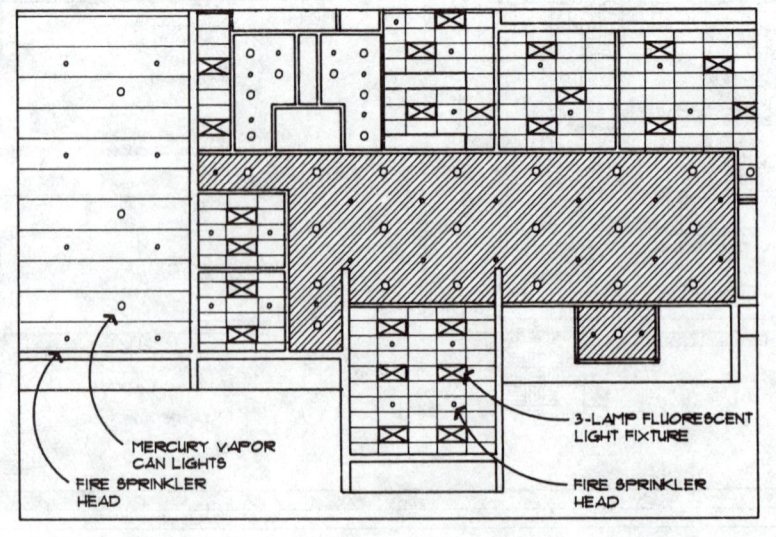

FIRE STATION

25-20

Wall Sections/A-5

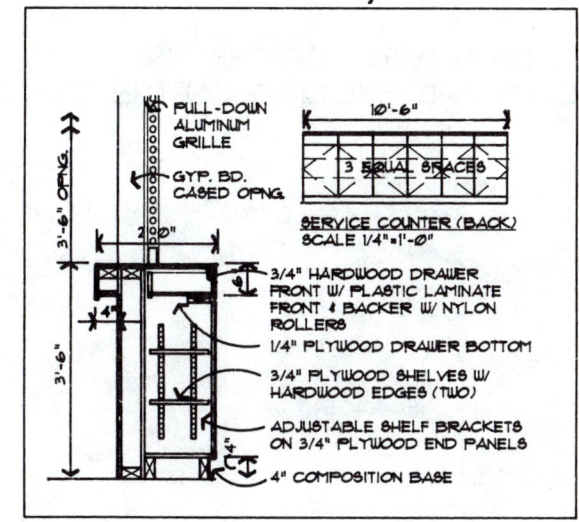

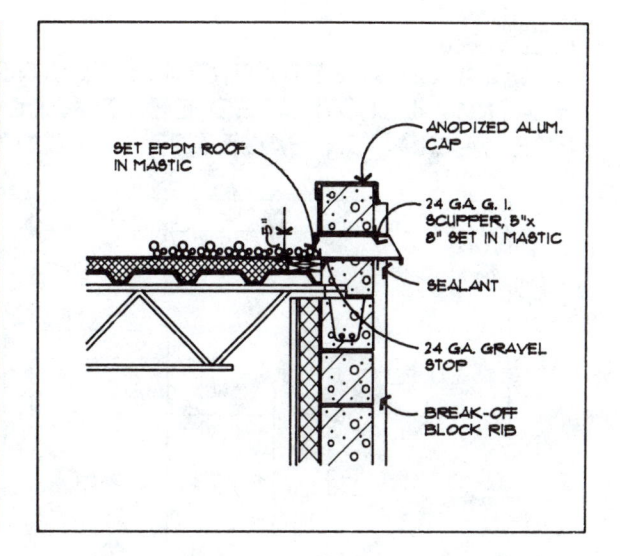

The drawings above show additional details in the project. The drawing to the left is a section cut through a service counter in the office. It shows a pull-down grille over a 3'-6" high counter.

The detail to the right cuts through an overflow scupper on the roof. A scupper allows water to run off the roof if roof drains should become clogged.

The wall section in the drawing at the right is cut through a drive-up teller window (used for paying city bills). The detail is identical to other wall sections with a teller's window inserted into the opening. A U-shaped lintel block is used as a header above the unit. a product catalog detail has been used to determine the appropriate size and fastening technique for the teller window.

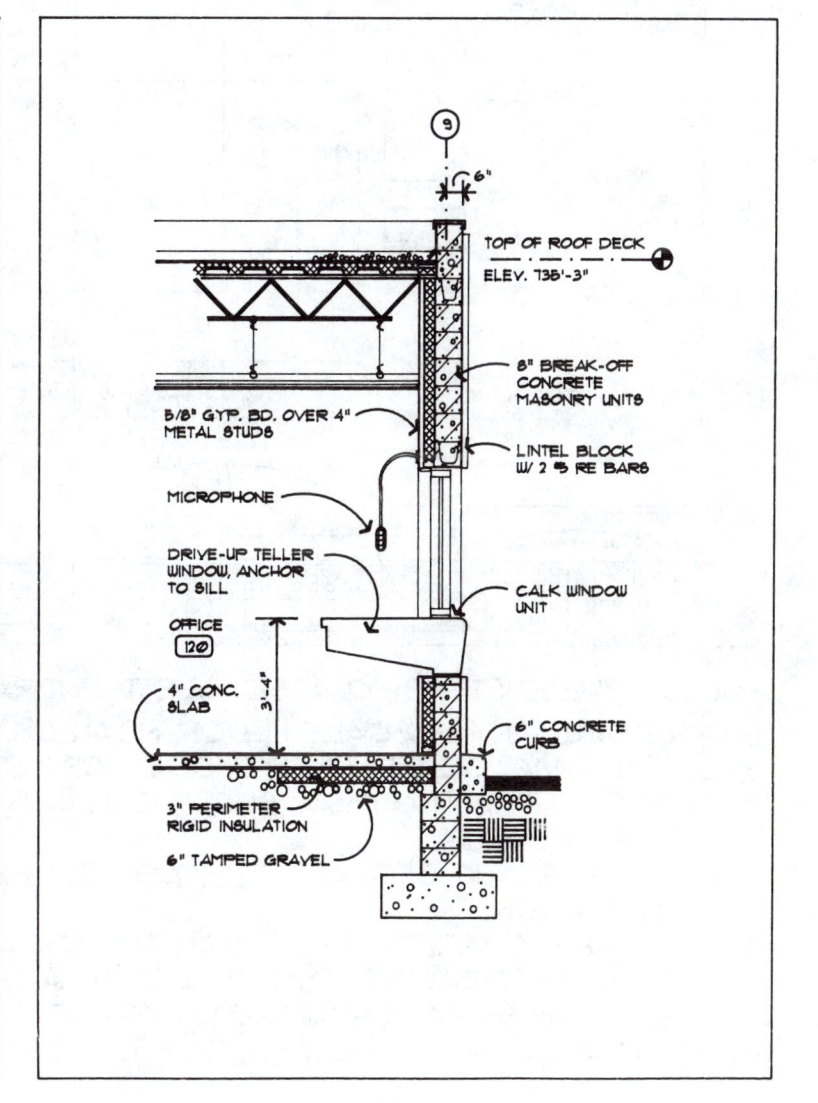

FIRE STATION   25-21

REPLAY

ASSEMBLE A SET OF CONSTRUCTION DRAWINGS FOR THE FIRE STATION ILLUSTRATED BELOW. LOCATE THE BUILDING ON THE SITE SHOWN ON PAGES 25-2 AND 25-3.

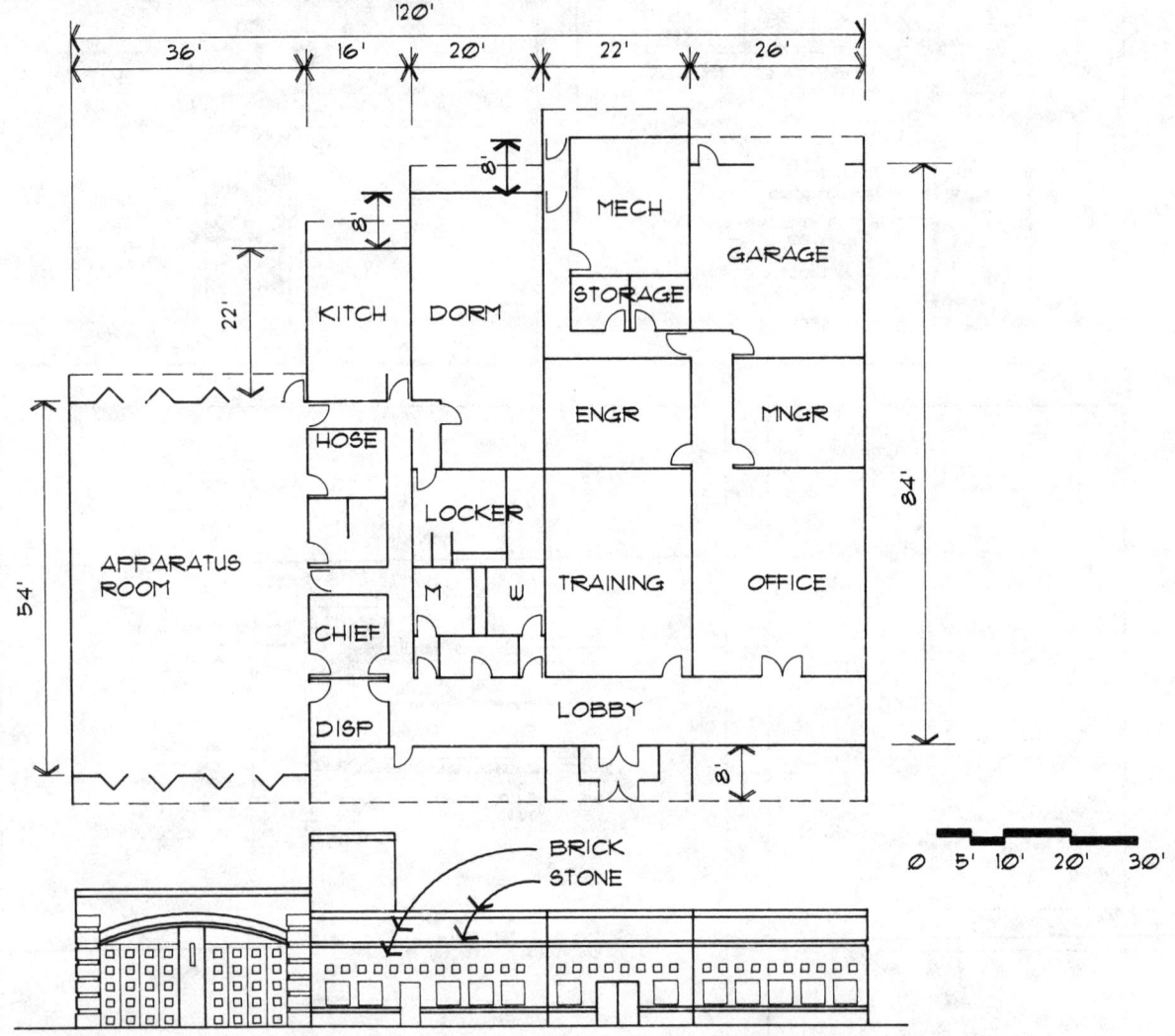

FOLLOW THESE STEPS TO ASSEMBLE THE DRAWING PACKAGE:
1. PREPARE AN 1/8" SCALE FLOOR PLAN ON TRACING PAPER.
2. BUILD A 1/16" SCALE STUDY MODEL OF YOUR PROJECT.
3. SKETCH A FRAMING PLAN SHOWING JOISTS, BEAMS, AND LOAD-BEARING WALLS.
4. DRAW BUILDING SECTIONS THROUGH SEVERAL PLACES IN THE FIRE STATION.
5. PREPARE A SHEET LAYOUT FOR THE DRAWING PACKAGE. USE THE SET OF DRAWINGS IN THIS UNIT AS A GUIDE TO DETERMINE THE DETAILS THAT SHOULD BE INCLUDED.
6. PREPARE A TIME SCHEDULE FOR THE DRAWINGS.

FIRE STATION

26 MOTEL AND RESTAURANT

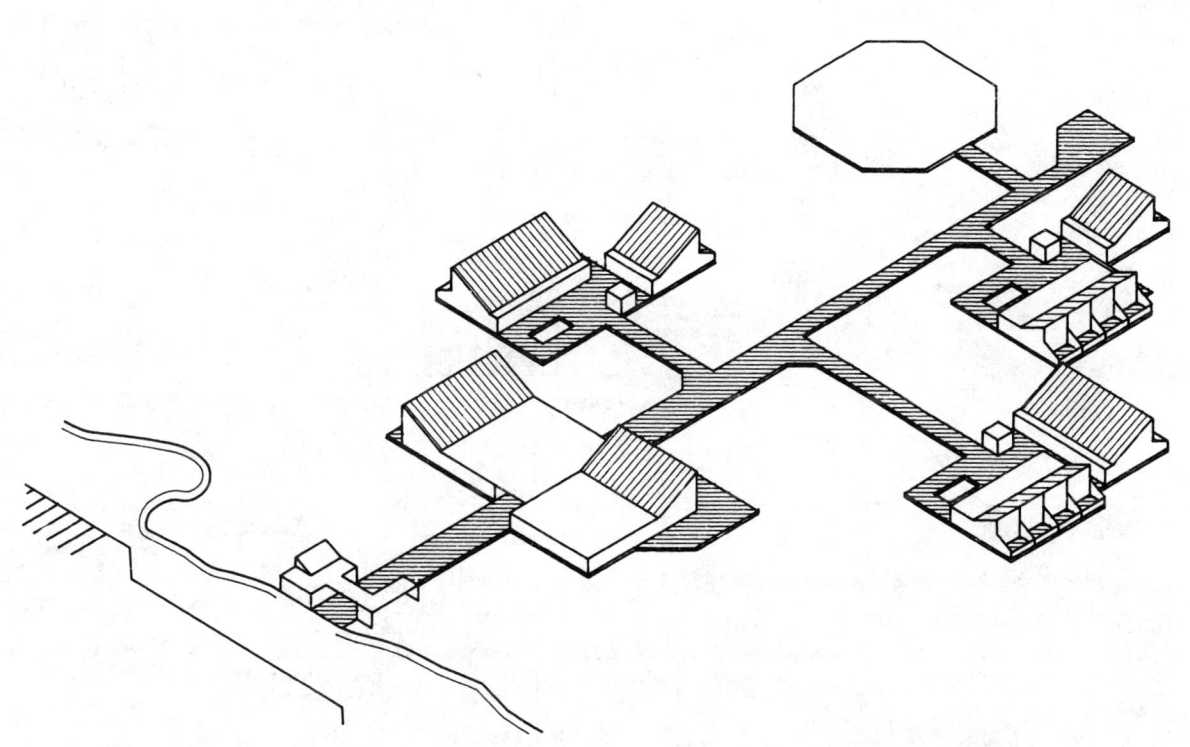

THIS UNIT PRESENTS A VERY UNIQUE PROJECT: FOUR CLUSTERS OF BUILDINGS LOCATED OVER A LAKE TO MAKE A RESTAURANT AND MOTEL COMPLEX. THE TWO-CITY-BLOCK-LONG SERIES OF BUILDINGS IS SUPPORTED BY CONCRETE PILINGS DRIVEN INTO THE LAKE BED, AND THE PARK ATMOSPHERE OF THE PROJECT IS ACCENTED BY PLACING BUILDINGS AROUND CYPRESS TREES GROWING IN THE LAKE. THE RESTAURANT, LOUNGE, AND ALL MOTEL UNITS HAVE DECKS THAT TIE THE BUILDINGS TO THEIR NATURAL SURROUNDINGS.

| MOTEL AND RESTAURANT | 26-1 |

Site Plan/A-1

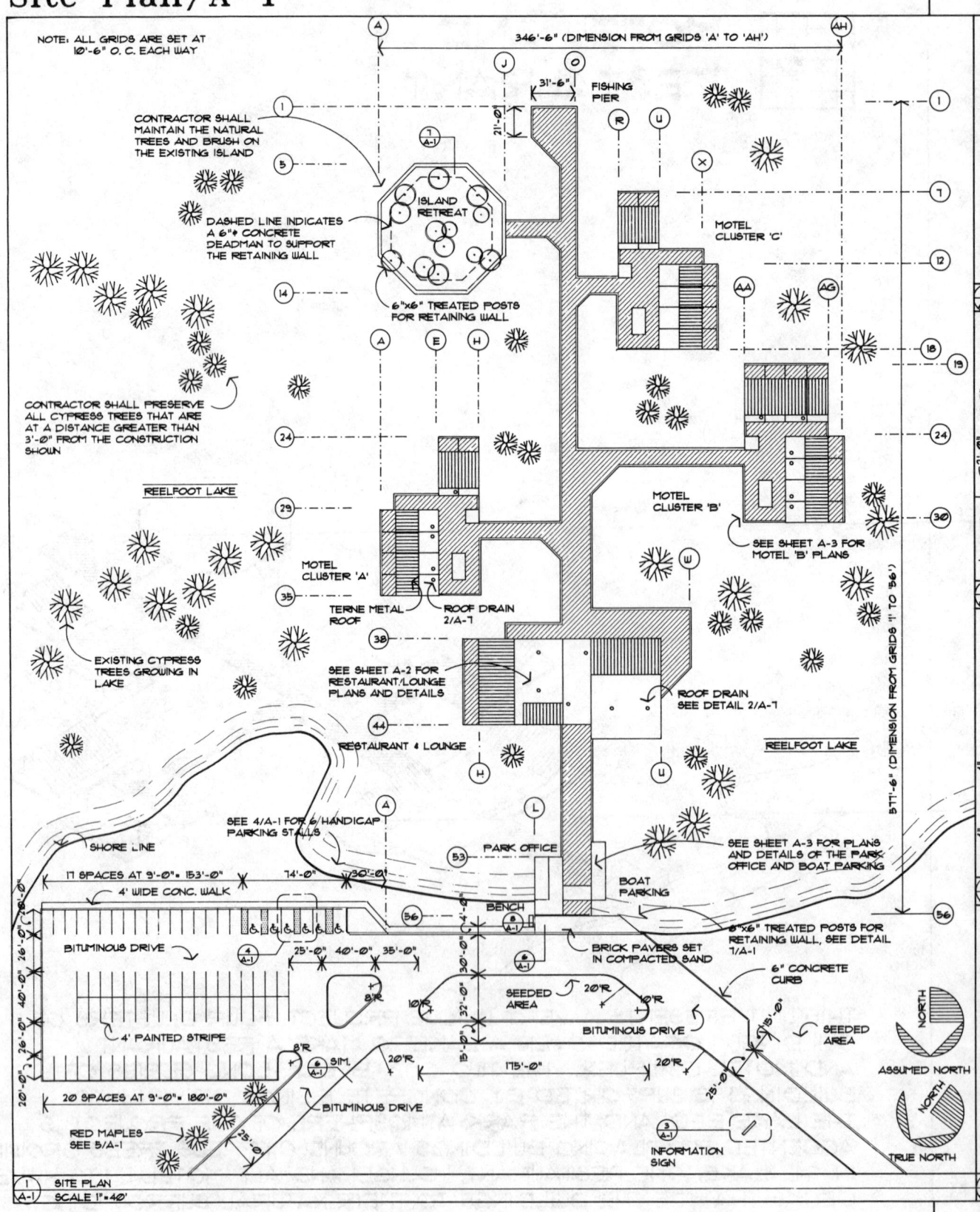

MOTEL AND RESTAURANT

26-2

Reelfoot Lake State Park
Tiptonville, Tn

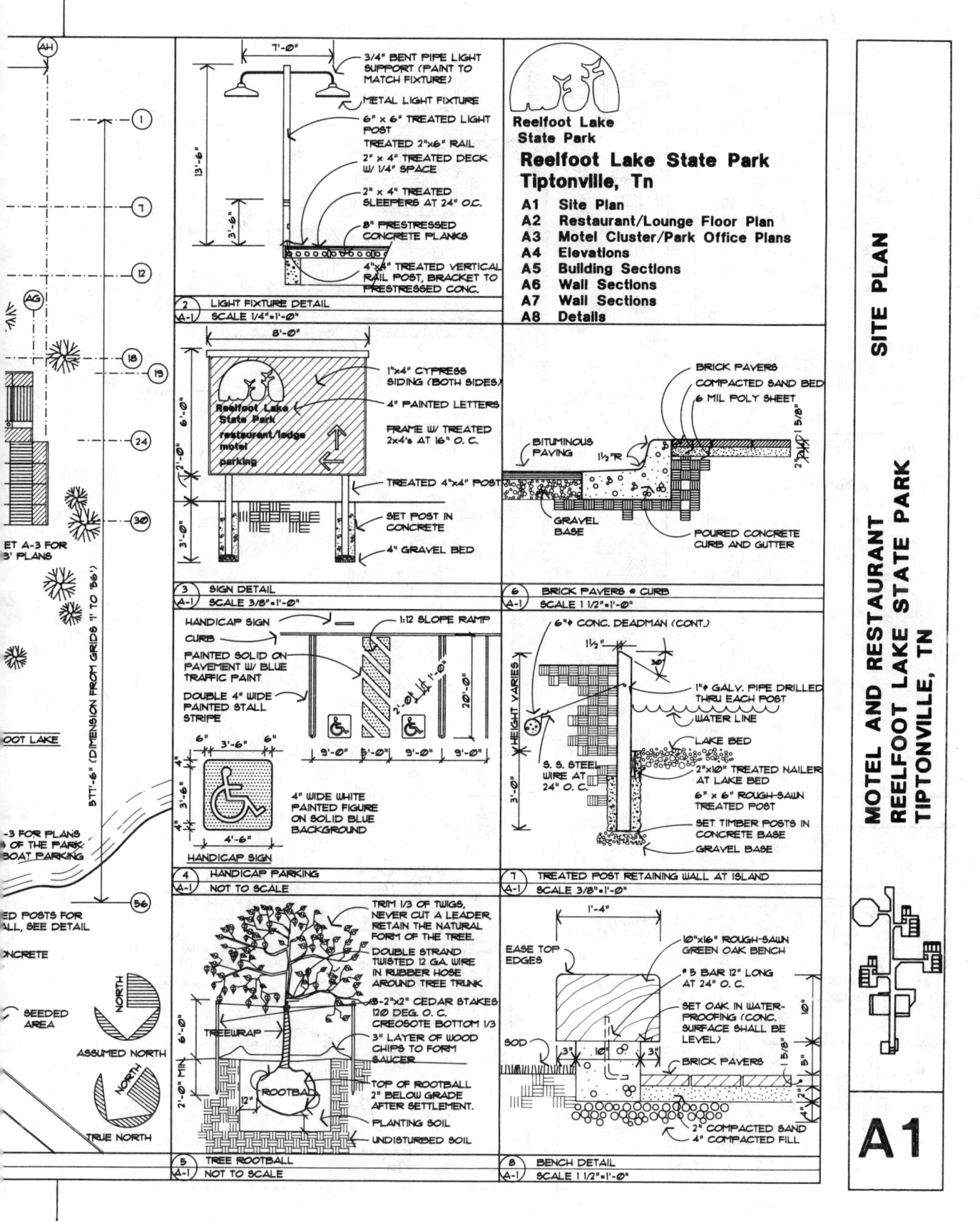

- A1 Site Plan
- A2 Restaurant/Lounge Floor Plan
- A3 Motel Cluster/Park Office Plans
- A4 Elevations
- A5 Building Sections
- A6 Wall Sections
- A7 Wall Sections
- A8 Details

SITE PLAN

MOTEL AND RESTAURANT
REELFOOT LAKE STATE PARK
TIPTONVILLE, TN

A1

MOTEL AND RESTAURANT   26-3

Site Plan/A-1

The entire project is organized around a 10'-6" structural grid. Intersections of each grid mark the location of a concrete piling driven into the lake bed. These pilings support concrete beams that carry precast concrete decking. The site plan shows the location of major grids (mainly the corners) to coordinate dimensioning of each building in the complex. The project is 33 grids wide and 55 grids north to south.

The details for an information sign and a tree on the site are shown below. The 6'x 8' sign is constructed from diagonal cypress; its location is marked on the site plan. The tree section details planting specifications.

Site details are typically located on the site sheet (rather than with the building details). Key all details back to the site plan.

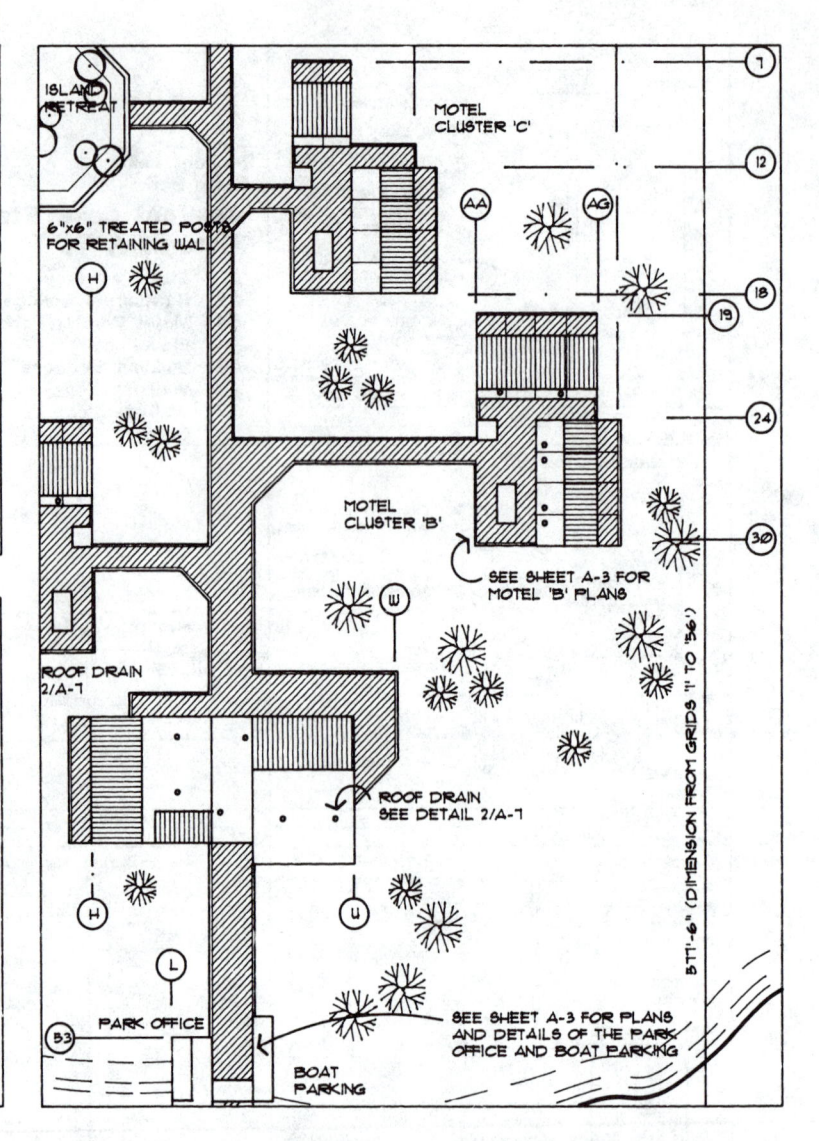

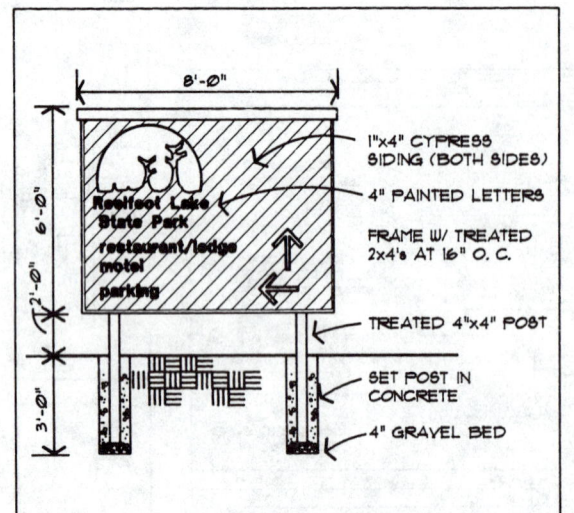

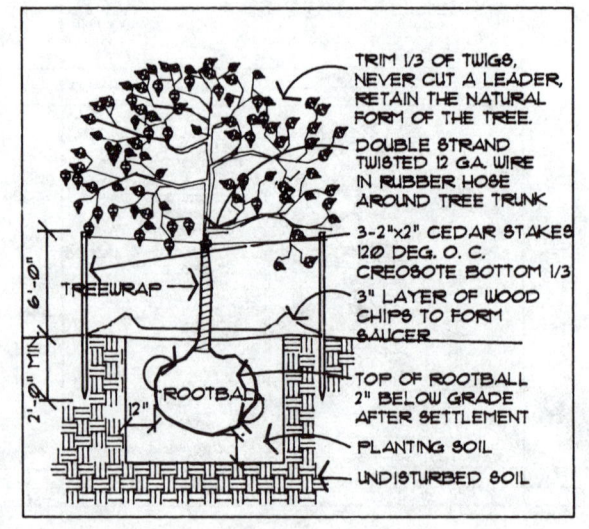

MOTEL AND RESTAURANT

26-4

Site Plan/A-1

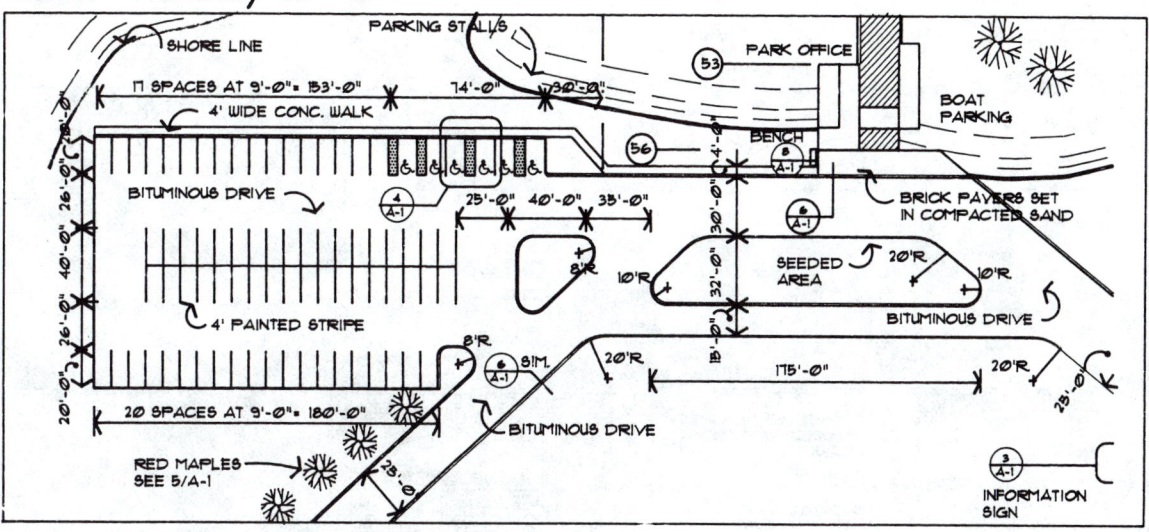

The parking lot layout is shown above. Parking should be tied to the building by a dimension string (in this example, grid "A"). The plan also contains information on stall size, materials, curbs, and drainage. Note that all items on the site plan must be located by dimension (e.g., 17 spaces at 9'-0"). Handicap parking stalls are noted on the plan and keyed to a larger-scale detail.

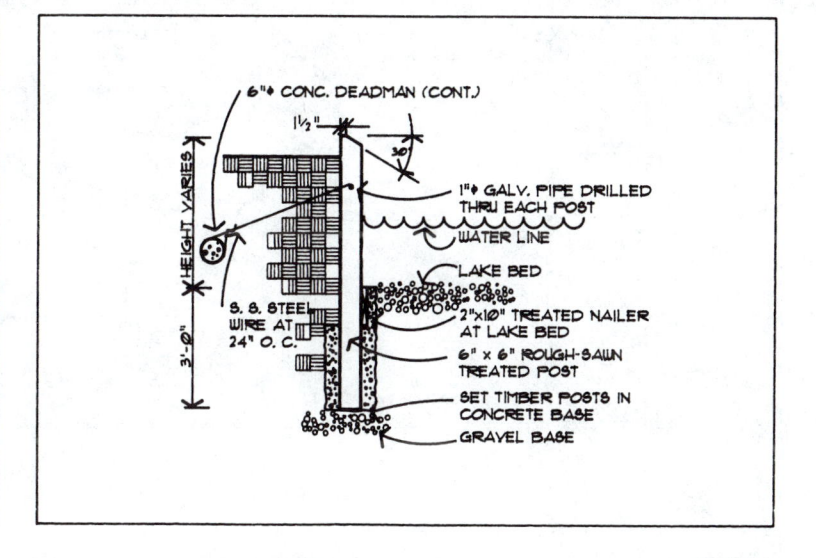

The drawings to the right illustrate site details that must be enlarged to show construction assembly. The 6" x 6" treated-post retaining wall is located along the shore and at the perimeter of the island retreat. The top detail shows a post set in concrete that is anchored with a stainless steel wire tied to a buried concrete support (called a <u>deadman</u>). The bench shown in the bottom detail is keyed to the site plan.

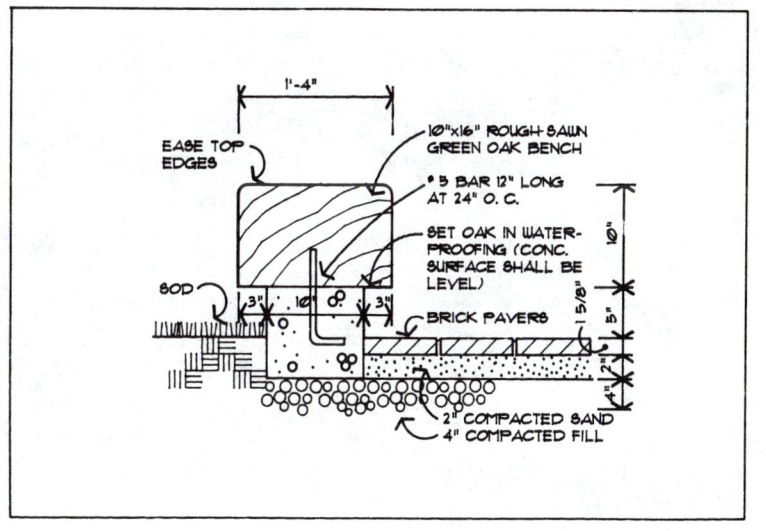

MOTEL AND RESTAURANT 26-5

Restaurant Plan/A-2

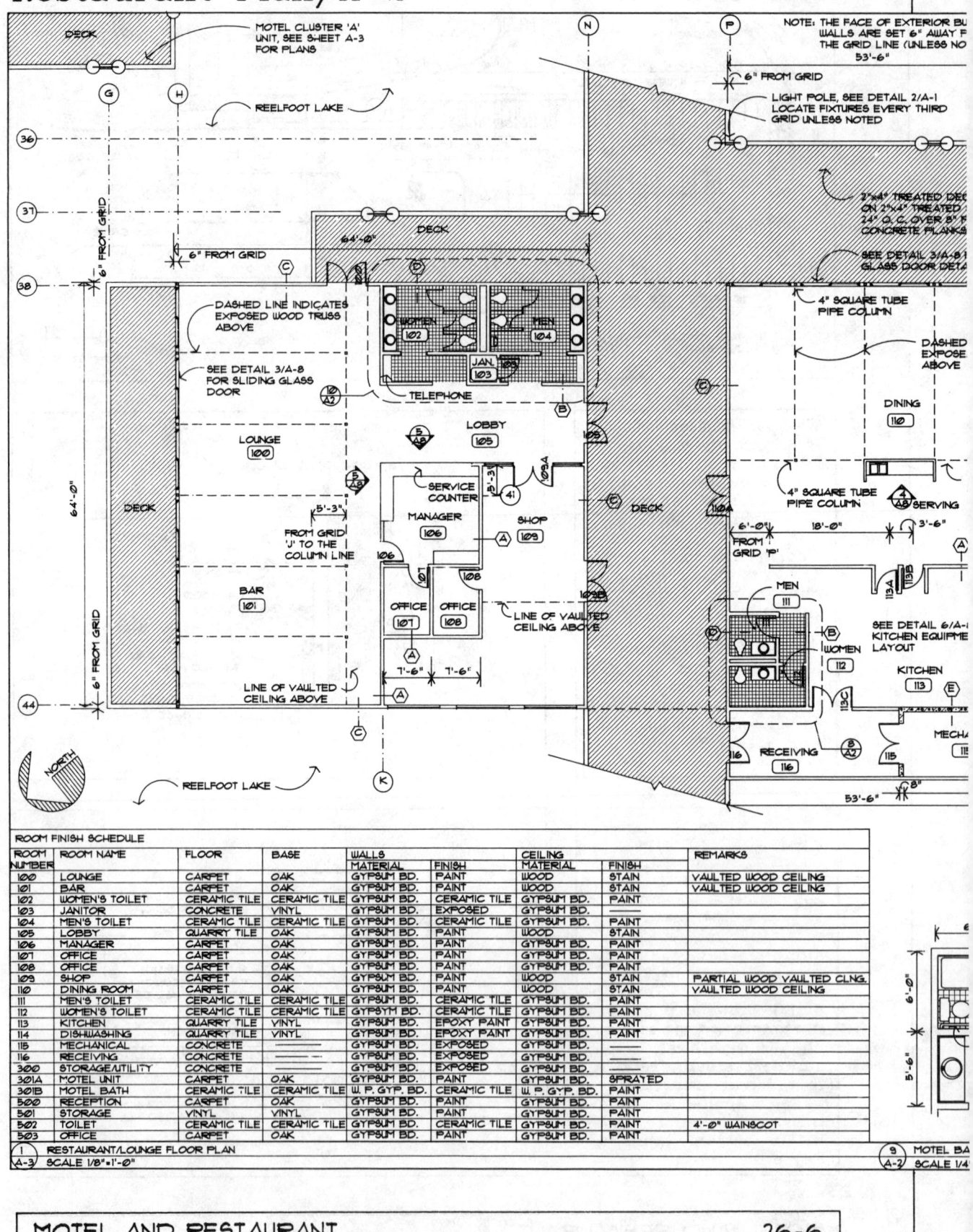

NOTE: THE FACE OF EXTERIOR BU[ILDING]
WALLS ARE SET 6" AWAY F[ROM]
THE GRID LINE (UNLESS NO[TED])

MOTEL CLUSTER 'A' UNIT, SEE SHEET A-3 FOR PLANS

REELFOOT LAKE

LIGHT POLE, SEE DETAIL 2/A-1 LOCATE FIXTURES EVERY THIRD GRID UNLESS NOTED

2"x4" TREATED DEC[K]
ON 2"x4" TREATED
24" O.C. OVER 8" [ ]
CONCRETE PLANKS
SEE DETAIL 3/A-8 [ ]
GLASS DOOR DETA[IL]

DECK

6" FROM GRID

4" SQUARE TUBE PIPE COLUMN

DASHED LINE INDICATES EXPOSED WOOD TRUSS ABOVE

SEE DETAIL 3/A-8 FOR SLIDING GLASS DOOR

DASHED [LINE]
EXPOSE[D]
ABOVE

WOMEN 102
MEN 104
JAN. 103
TELEPHONE

DINING 110

LOUNGE 100

LOBBY 105

4" SQUARE TUBE PIPE COLUMN

SERVING

DECK

SERVICE COUNTER

MANAGER 106
SHOP 109

5'-3" FROM GRID 'J' TO THE COLUMN LINE

MEN 111

BAR 101

OFFICE 107
OFFICE 108

SEE DETAIL 6/A-1 KITCHEN EQUIPME[NT] LAYOUT

WOMEN 112

LINE OF VAULTED CEILING ABOVE

KITCHEN 113

7'-6" 7'-6"

LINE OF VAULTED CEILING ABOVE

MECHA[NICAL]

RECEIVING 116

115

NORTH

REELFOOT LAKE

53'-6"

| ROOM FINISH SCHEDULE |
ROOM NUMBER	ROOM NAME	FLOOR	BASE	WALLS MATERIAL	FINISH	CEILING MATERIAL	FINISH	REMARKS
100	LOUNGE	CARPET	OAK	GYPSUM BD.	PAINT	WOOD	STAIN	VAULTED WOOD CEILING
101	BAR	CARPET	OAK	GYPSUM BD.	PAINT	WOOD	STAIN	VAULTED WOOD CEILING
102	WOMEN'S TOILET	CERAMIC TILE	CERAMIC TILE	GYPSUM BD.	CERAMIC TILE	GYPSUM BD.	PAINT	
103	JANITOR	CONCRETE	VINYL	GYPSUM BD.	EXPOSED	GYPSUM BD.		
104	MEN'S TOILET	CERAMIC TILE	CERAMIC TILE	GYPSUM BD.	CERAMIC TILE	GYPSUM BD.	PAINT	
105	LOBBY	QUARRY TILE	OAK	GYPSUM BD.	PAINT	WOOD	STAIN	
106	MANAGER	CARPET	OAK	GYPSUM BD.	PAINT	GYPSUM BD.	PAINT	
107	OFFICE	CARPET	OAK	GYPSUM BD.	PAINT	GYPSUM BD.	PAINT	
108	OFFICE	CARPET	OAK	GYPSUM BD.	PAINT	GYPSUM BD.	PAINT	
109	SHOP	CARPET	OAK	GYPSUM BD.	PAINT	WOOD	STAIN	PARTIAL WOOD VAULTED CLNG.
110	DINING ROOM	CARPET	OAK	GYPSUM BD.	PAINT	WOOD	STAIN	VAULTED WOOD CEILING
111	MEN'S TOILET	CERAMIC TILE	CERAMIC TILE	GYPSUM BD.	CERAMIC TILE	GYPSUM BD.	PAINT	
112	WOMEN'S TOILET	CERAMIC TILE	CERAMIC TILE	GYPSYM BD.	CERAMIC TILE	GYPSUM BD.	PAINT	
113	KITCHEN	QUARRY TILE	VINYL	GYPSUM BD.	EPOXY PAINT	GYPSUM BD.	PAINT	
114	DISHWASHING	QUARRY TILE	VINYL	GYPSUM BD.	EPOXY PAINT	GYPSUM BD.	PAINT	
115	MECHANICAL	CONCRETE	———	GYPSUM BD.	EXPOSED	GYPSUM BD.	———	
116	RECEIVING	CONCRETE	———	GYPSUM BD.	EXPOSED	GYPSUM BD.	———	
300	STORAGE/UTILITY	CONCRETE	———	GYPSUM BD.	EXPOSED	GYPSUM BD.	———	
301A	MOTEL UNIT	CARPET	OAK	GYPSUM BD.	PAINT	GYPSUM BD.	SPRAYED	
301B	MOTEL BATH	CERAMIC TILE	CERAMIC TILE	W.P. GYP. BD.	CERAMIC TILE	W.P. GYP. BD.	PAINT	
500	RECEPTION	CARPET	OAK	GYPSUM BD.	PAINT	GYPSUM BD.	PAINT	
501	STORAGE	VINYL	VINYL	GYPSUM BD.	PAINT	GYPSUM BD.	PAINT	
502	TOILET	CERAMIC TILE	CERAMIC TILE	GYPSUM BD.	PAINT	GYPSUM BD.	PAINT	4'-0" WAINSCOT
503	OFFICE	CARPET	OAK	GYPSUM BD.	PAINT	GYPSUM BD.	PAINT	

1 / A-3 RESTAURANT/LOUNGE FLOOR PLAN SCALE 1/8"=1'-0"

9 / A-2 MOTEL BA[TH] SCALE 1/4["=1'-0"]

MOTEL AND RESTAURANT

26-6

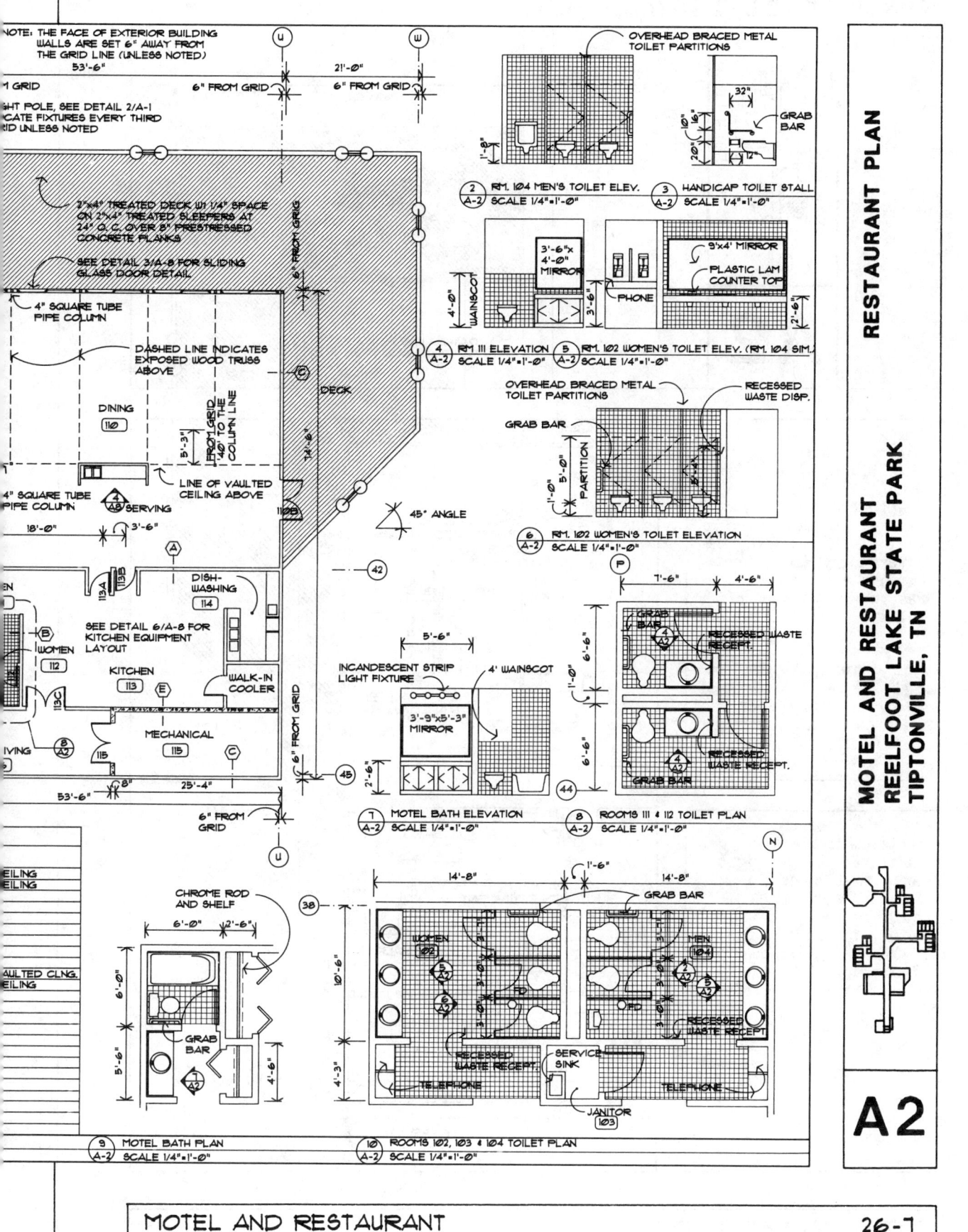

MOTEL AND RESTAURANT
REELFOOT LAKE STATE PARK
TIPTONVILLE, TN

RESTAURANT PLAN

A2

MOTEL AND RESTAURANT   26-7

Restaurant Plan/A-2

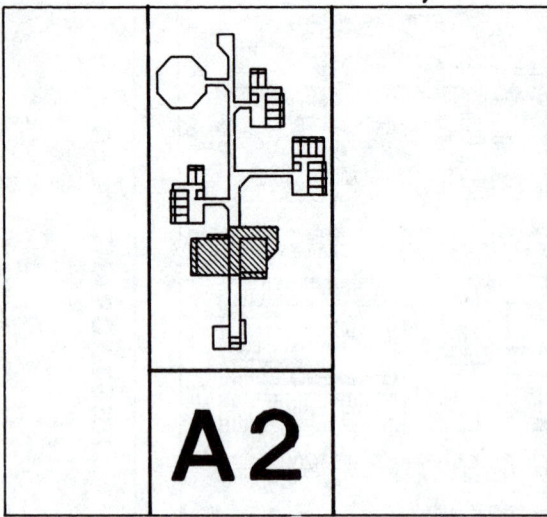

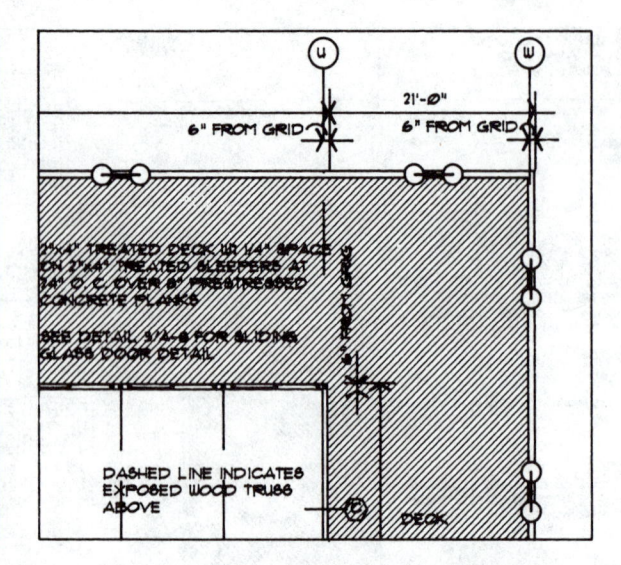

A2

The drawing above shows a portion of the title block with a "key" plan. The small-scale graphic of the project is used to show what part of the building is covered on each sheet. In this case, the restaurant section of sheet A-2 is indicated by crosshatching.

The drawing at the top right shows a corner of the restaurant deck. Note that the building and deck are located with grid bubbles.

A portion of the restaurant plan is displayed at the right. Note that walls are located using the building grid; they are either on one of the 10'-6" grids or are dimensioned to the closest grid line. Every room in the plan has a name and number. Doors are identified using the room number. Walls in the project are indicated with the hexagonal numbered symbols.

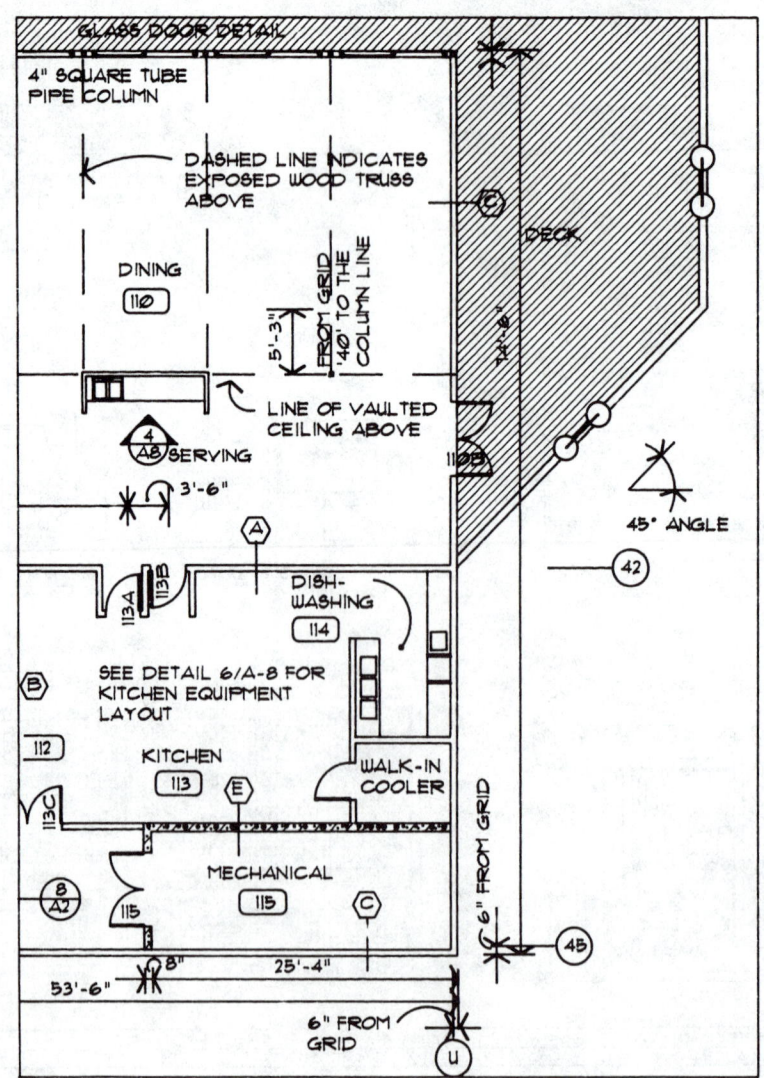

MOTEL AND RESTAURANT

26-8

Lounge Plan/A-2

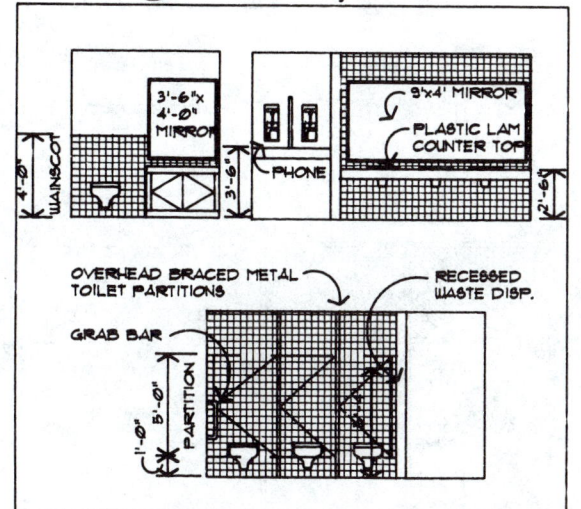

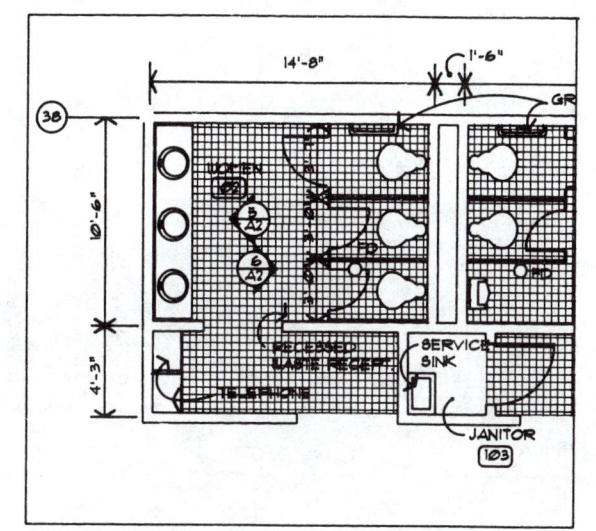

The two drawings above illustrate elevation and plan views of the toilets in the lounge building. Small spaces, such as toilets, are typically enlarged to allow room for dimension strings and notes. Note that handicap toilet partitions are wider, have doors that swing out, have grab bars, and must provide space to maneuver in front of the door.

The partial plan of the lounge at the right illustrates the detail that should be shown on a 1/8" scale plan. Doors and windows are defined, columns are located, and items, such as the motel counter, are indicated. The dashed lines show the trusses in the vaulted ceiling above. Columns and walls are located with grids on the plan. The motel cluster is located in the upper left corner of the plan.

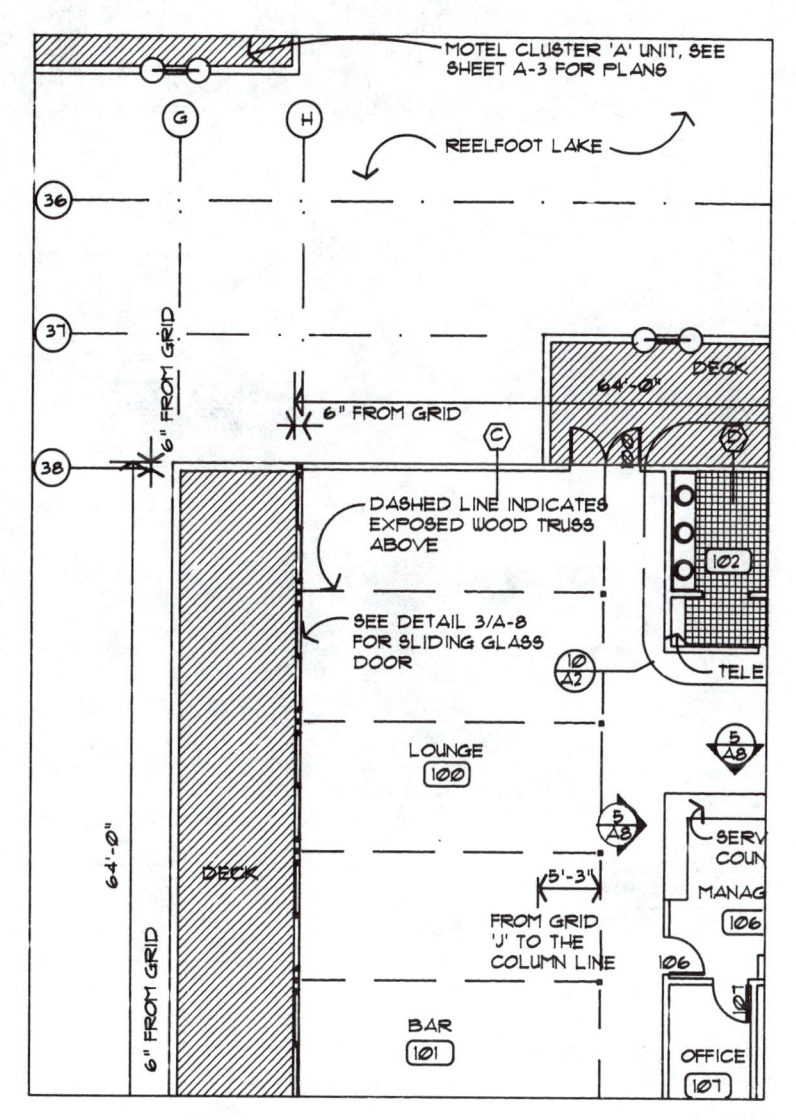

MOTEL AND RESTAURANT 26-9

Motel Plans/A-3

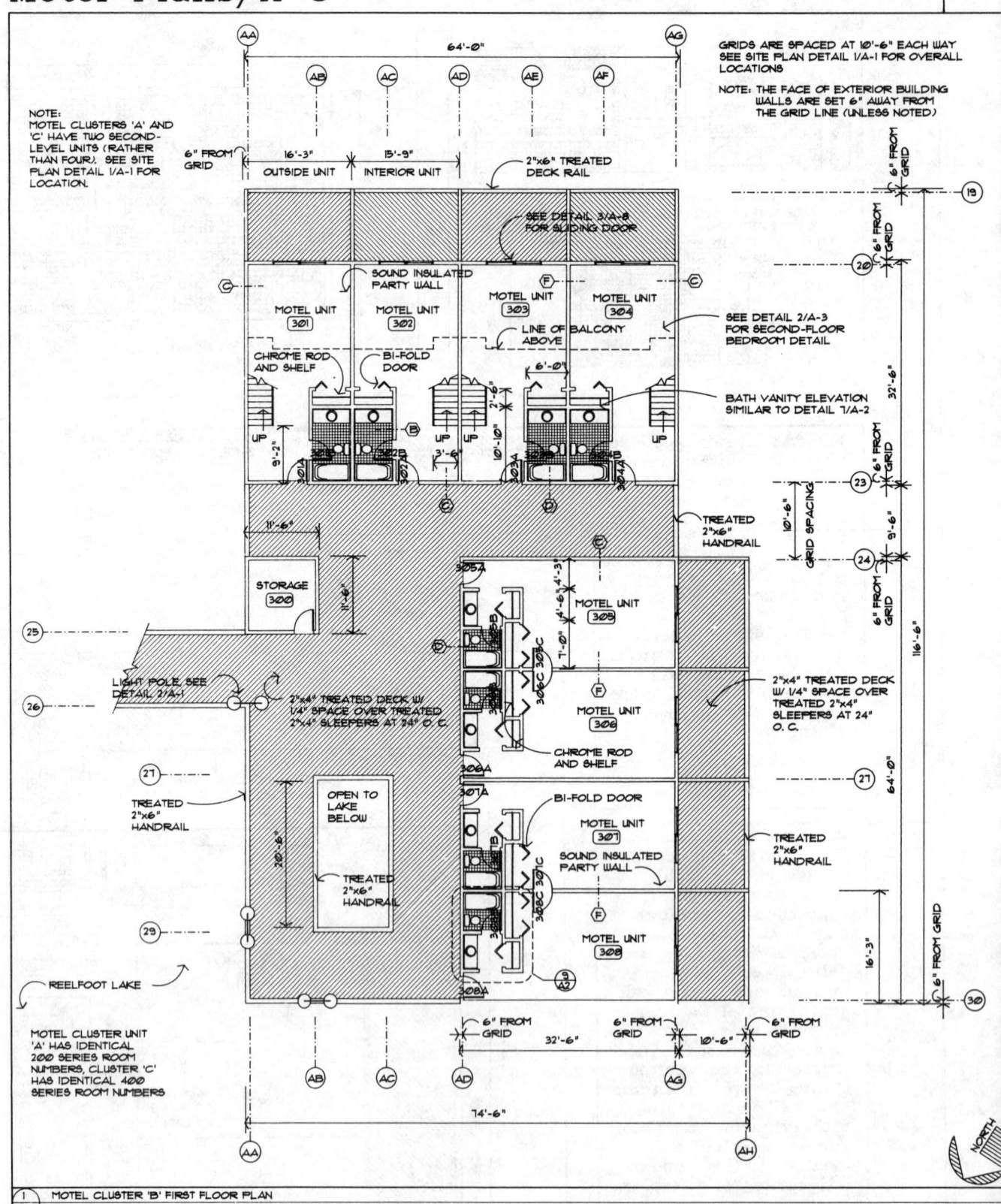

MOTEL AND RESTAURANT

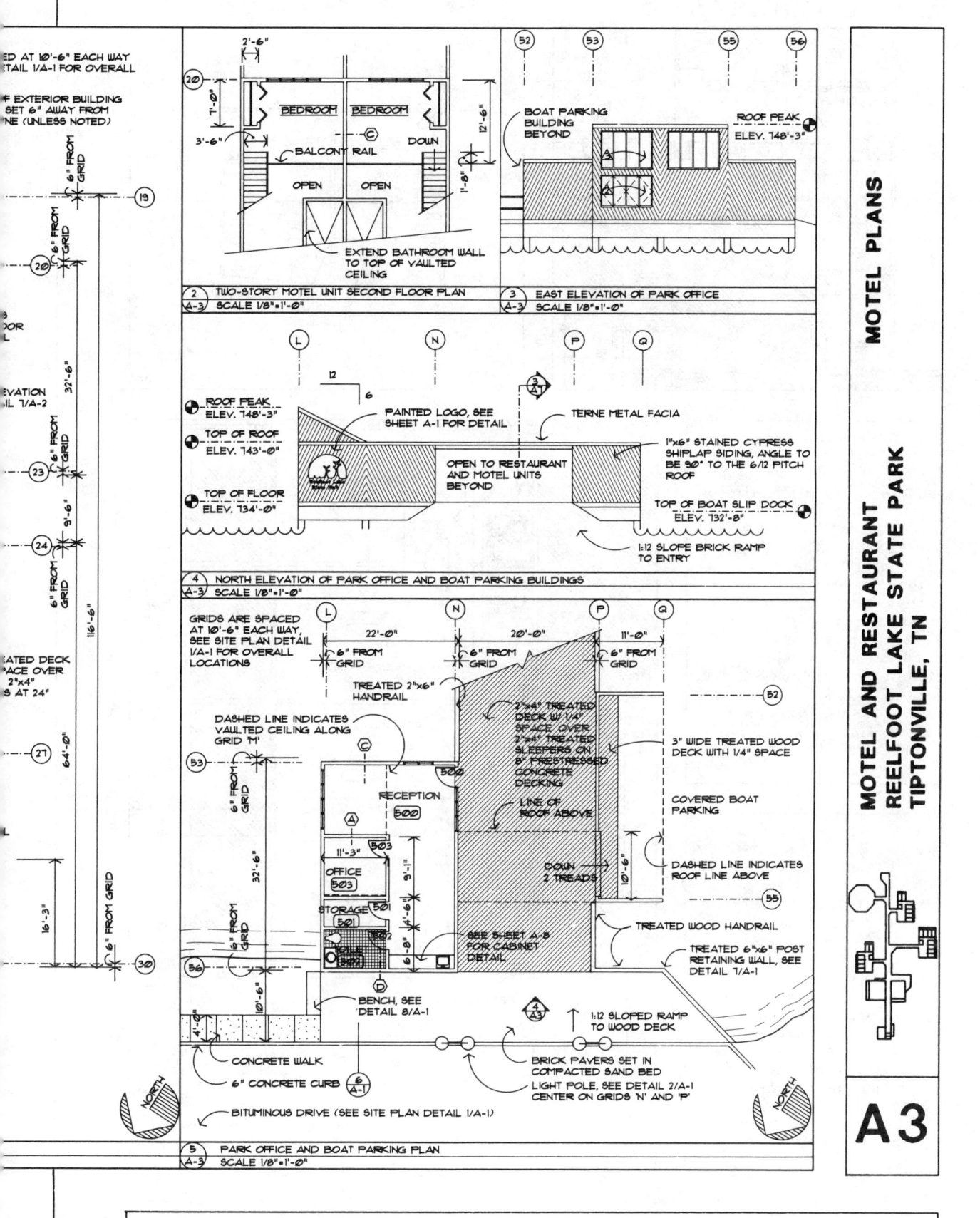

MOTEL PLANS

MOTEL AND RESTAURANT
REELFOOT LAKE STATE PARK
TIPTONVILLE, TN

A3

26-11

MOTEL AND RESTAURANT

Motel Plans/A-3

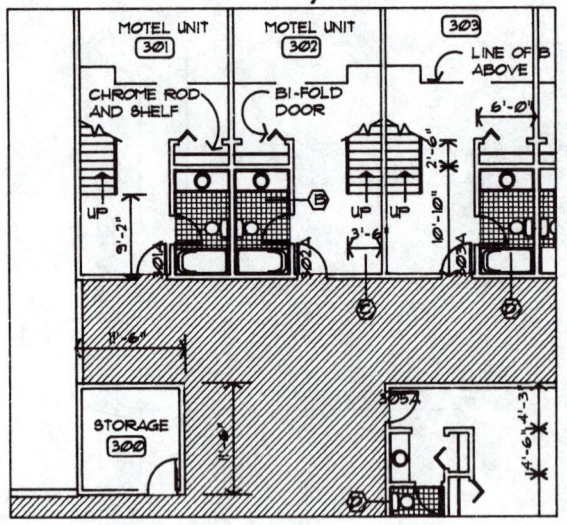

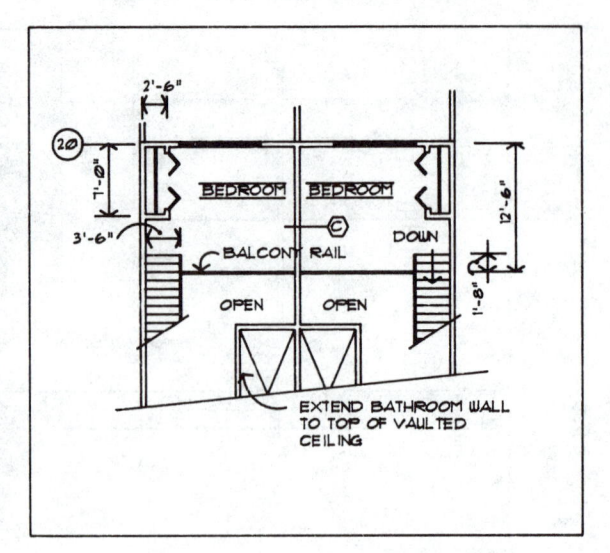

The plans above show the first and second floors of the two-story motel unit. The first-floor plan details a portion of the deck area and the storage building. There are three motel clusters that have similar floor plans. (Unit "B" is the only cluster drawn; notes on the plan indicate the differences in clusters "A" and "C".) The dashed line on the first-floor plan shows the balcony above.

The floor plan at the right details a portion of the one-story model unit. The building grid used to center the pilings and concrete floor beams is also used to locate the steel stud walls. Exterior walls are 6" from the grid; walls between motel units are centered on the grid. Bathroom dimensions can be found on the 1/4" plan blow-up. Note that each unit has a private wood deck.

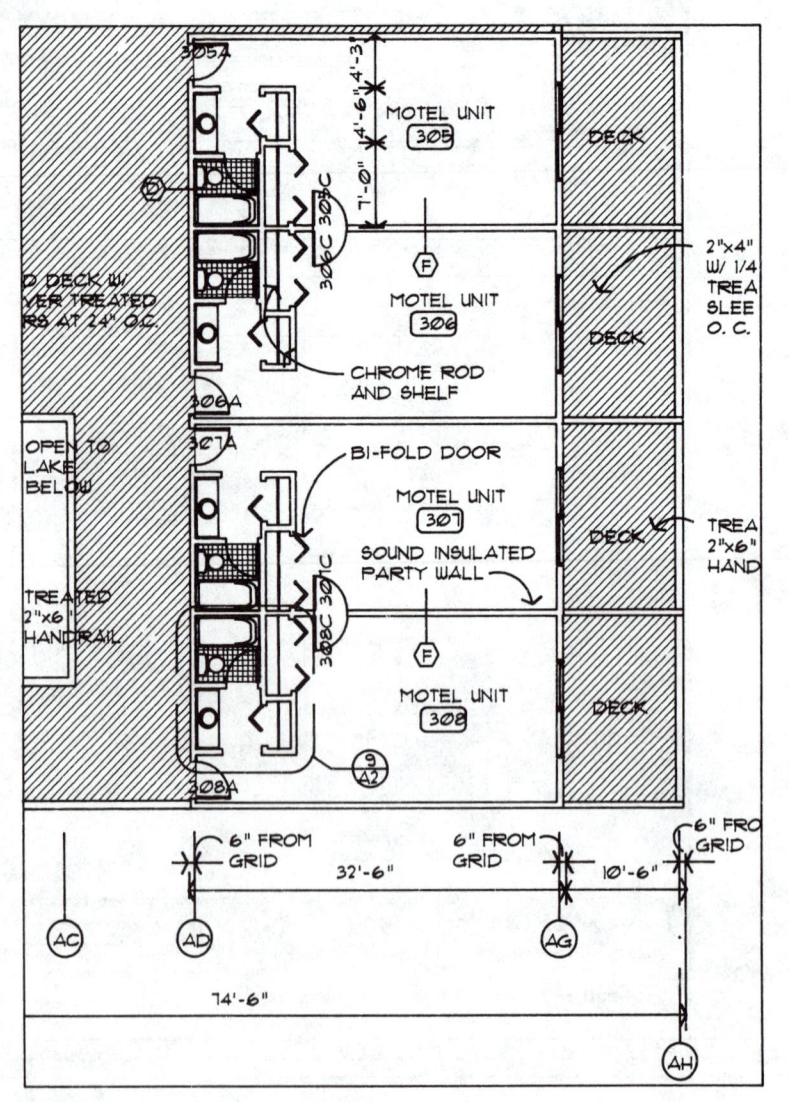

MOTEL AND RESTAURANT   26-12

Park Office Plans and Elevations/A-3

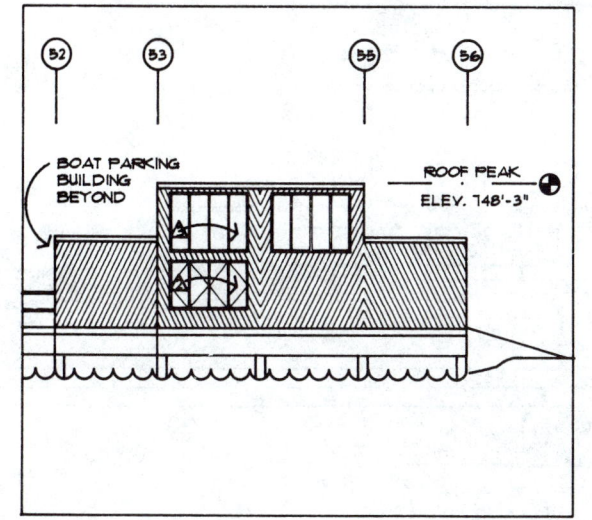

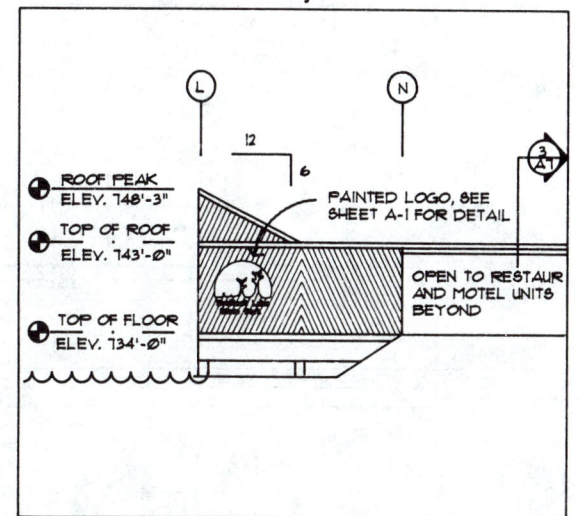

The park office, located at the shore line, is elevated in the views above. Major points of the building are located with the project grids. Windows are keyed to the schedule with a delta and unit number. The major bearing points for the walls and roof are located with a bull's-eye and the elevation above the bench mark. The diagonal siding is drawn with light lines and noted to be at 90° to the roof pitch.

The park office and covered boat parking plans are illustrated at the right. The plans and elevations for this portion of the project are located by using grids developed for the entire complex. The exterior wooden decks and brick pavers are added to the plan to provide a complete building assembly. Details on this plan should be coordinated with the site plan.

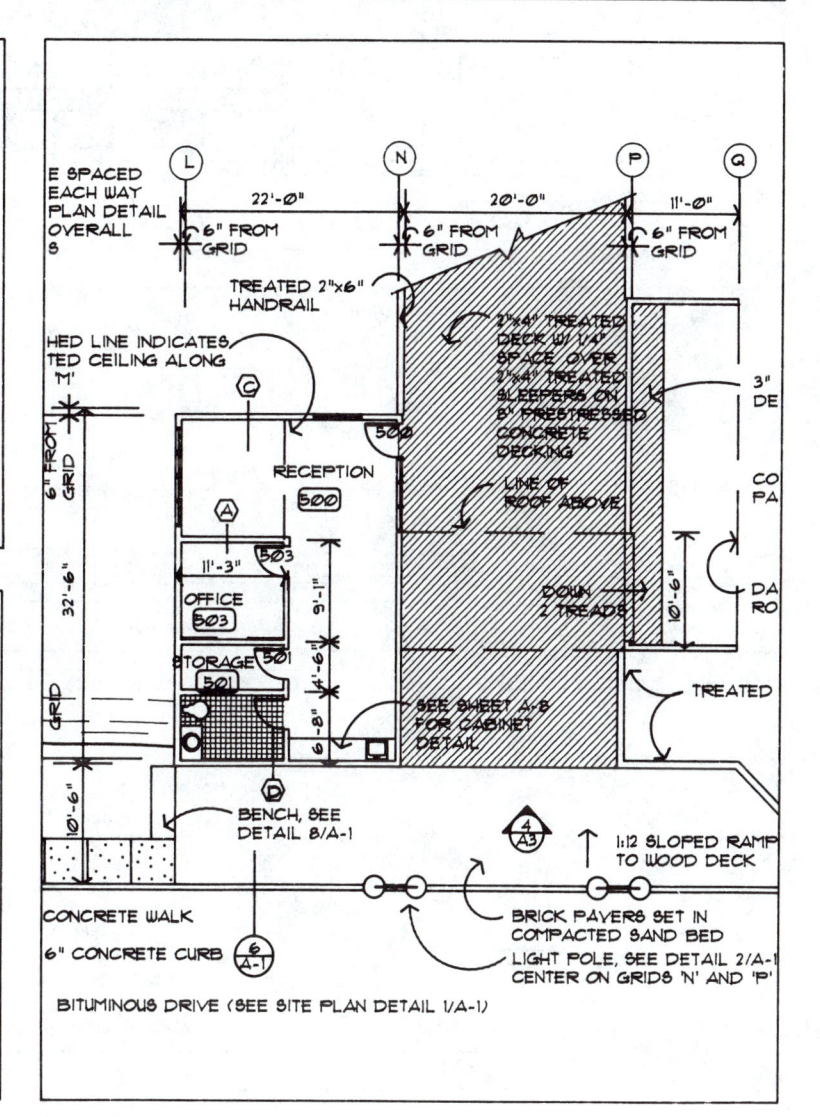

MOTEL AND RESTAURANT   26-13

Elevations/A-4

1 EAST ELEVATION RESTAURANT / LOUNGE
SCALE 1/8"=1'-0"

- TOP OF ROOF PEAK ELEV. 756'-2"
- TERNE METAL FLASHING
- TOP OF R ELEV. 756
- TOP OF R ELEV. 743
- TOP OF FLOOR ELEV. 734'-0"
- PRECAST CONCRETE PANELS OVER BUTT ENDS OF FLOOR DECK
- TOP OF FL ELEV. 734
- LAKE ELEVATION 730'-0"±

4 SOUTH ELEVATION RESTAURANT / LOUNGE
SCALE 1/8"=1'-0"

- TERNE METAL FLASHING SEE DETAIL 2/A-6
- 16" HELVETICA PAINTED LETTERS
- STANDING SEAM TERNE METAL ROOF
- restaurant
- TERNE METAL FLASHING
- OPEN TO MOTEL UNITS BEYOND

5 WEST ELEVATION RESTAURANT / LOUNGE
SCALE 1/8"=1'-0"

- TOP OF ROOF PEAK ELEV. 756'-2"
- TOP OF GIFT SHOP ROOF PEAK ELEV. 751'-2"
- PAINTED LOGO SEE 3/A-1
- TOP OF ROOF DECK ELEV. 743'-0"
- STANDING SEAM TERNE METAL ROOF
- STAINED CYPRESS SHIPLAP SIDING AT 90° TO THE ROOF SLOPE
- TOP OF FLOOR EL. 734'-0"
- Reelfoot Lake State Park / 9" PAINTED LETTERS
- PRECAST CONCRETE PIERS

8 NORTH ELEVATION RESTAURANT / LOUNGE
SCALE 1/8"=1'-0"

- TOP OF ROOF PEAK ELEV. 756'-2"
- 12 / 6
- ROOF PEAK ELEV. 751'-2"
- ROOF PEAK ELEV. 751'-2"
- OPEN TO MOTEL UNITS BEYOND
- TOP OF FLOOR ELEV. 734'-0"
- LAKE ELEVATION ELEV. 730'-0"

MOTEL AND RESTAURANT 26-14

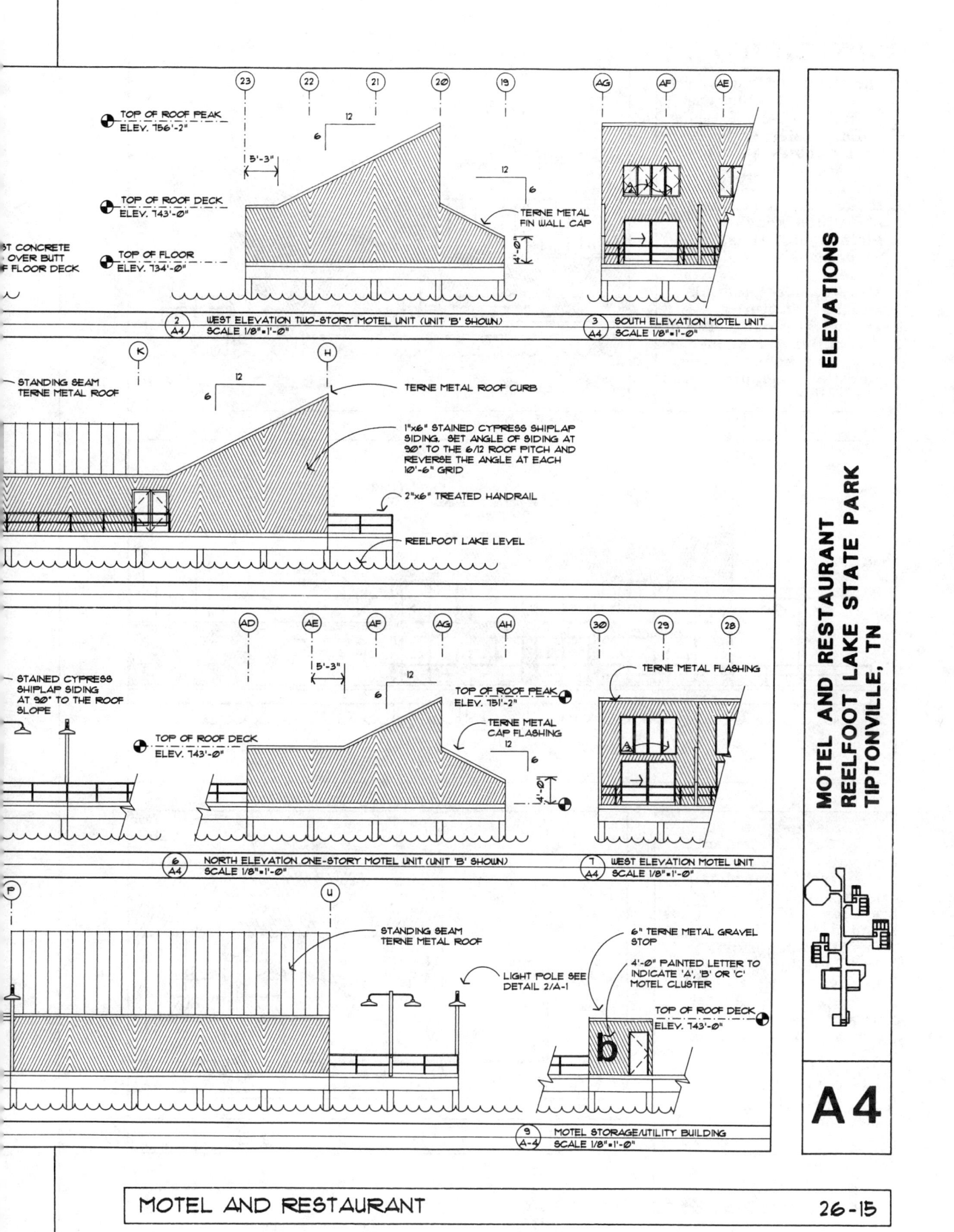

ELEVATIONS

MOTEL AND RESTAURANT
REELFOOT LAKE STATE PARK
TIPTONVILLE, TN

A4

MOTEL AND RESTAURANT   26-15

2/A4 — WEST ELEVATION TWO-STORY MOTEL UNIT (UNIT 'B' SHOWN)
SCALE 1/8" = 1'-0"

- TOP OF ROOF PEAK ELEV. 756'-2"
- TOP OF ROOF DECK ELEV. 743'-0"
- TOP OF FLOOR ELEV. 734'-0"
- 5'-3"
- 12 / 6
- ST CONCRETE OVER BUTT F FLOOR DECK

3/A4 — SOUTH ELEVATION MOTEL UNIT
SCALE 1/8" = 1'-0"

- TERNE METAL FIN WALL CAP

(unlabeled elevation)
- STANDING SEAM TERNE METAL ROOF
- TERNE METAL ROOF CURB
- 1"x6" STAINED CYPRESS SHIPLAP SIDING. SET ANGLE OF SIDING AT 90° TO THE 6/12 ROOF PITCH AND REVERSE THE ANGLE AT EACH 10'-6" GRID
- 2"x6" TREATED HANDRAIL
- REELFOOT LAKE LEVEL

6/A4 — NORTH ELEVATION ONE-STORY MOTEL UNIT (UNIT 'B' SHOWN)
SCALE 1/8" = 1'-0"

- STAINED CYPRESS SHIPLAP SIDING AT 90° TO THE ROOF SLOPE
- TOP OF ROOF DECK ELEV. 743'-0"
- 5'-3"
- 12 / 6

7/A4 — WEST ELEVATION MOTEL UNIT
SCALE 1/8" = 1'-0"

- TERNE METAL FLASHING
- TOP OF ROOF PEAK ELEV. 751'-2"
- TERNE METAL CAP FLASHING
- 4'-0"

9/A-4 — MOTEL STORAGE/UTILITY BUILDING
SCALE 1/8" = 1'-0"

- STANDING SEAM TERNE METAL ROOF
- LIGHT POLE SEE DETAIL 2/A-1
- 6" TERNE METAL GRAVEL STOP
- 4'-0" PAINTED LETTER TO INDICATE 'A', 'B' OR 'C' MOTEL CLUSTER
- TOP OF ROOF DECK ELEV. 743'-0"

Elevations/A-4

The drawings below and to the right illustrate portions of the exterior building elevations. Grid bubbles at the corners of each building make it easy to identify locations. Elevations should include materials, windows, and roof slopes. These drawings also include handrails and light fixtures around the perimeter of the building. Rippled lines are added to the elevation to indicate the water line.

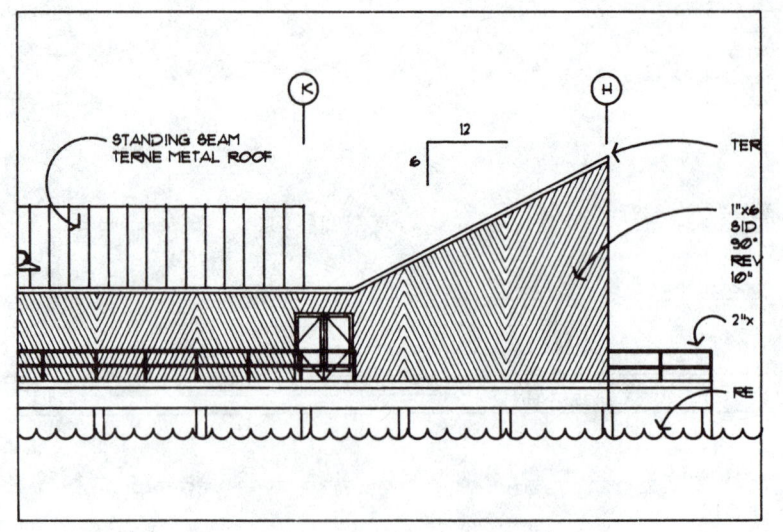

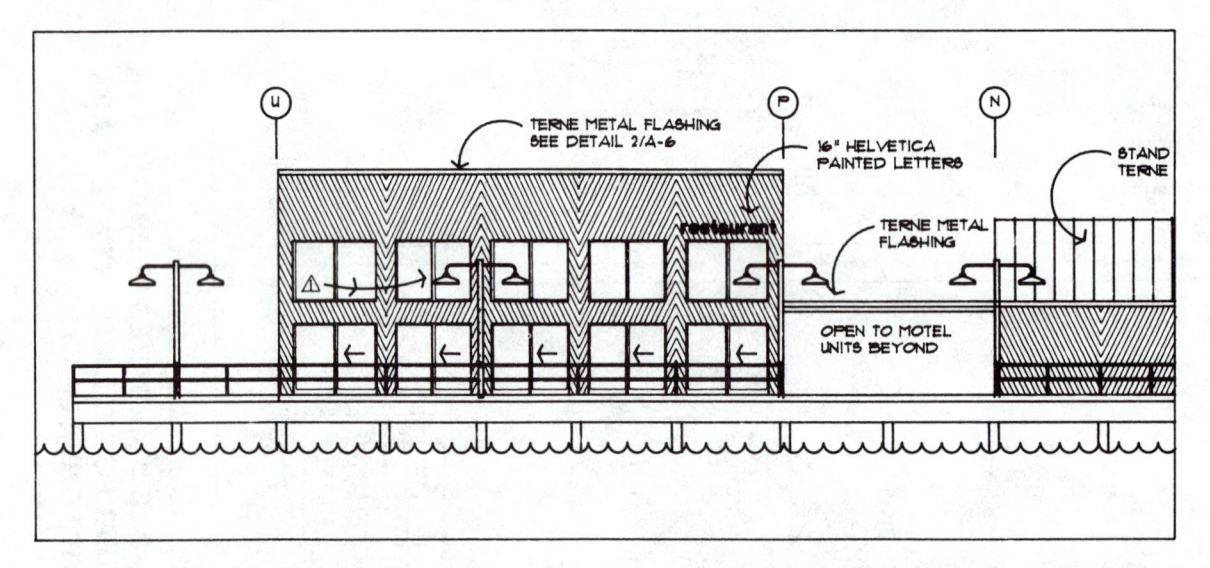

An enlarged portion of the south restaurant elevation is shown to the right. The detail uses double lines for window and door frames and defines the pattern for the wood siding. The building silhouette is drawn with a slightly darker line quality to accent the elevation. Arrows on the sliding doors indicate the panels that are operable. The windows are keyed to an elevation schedule.

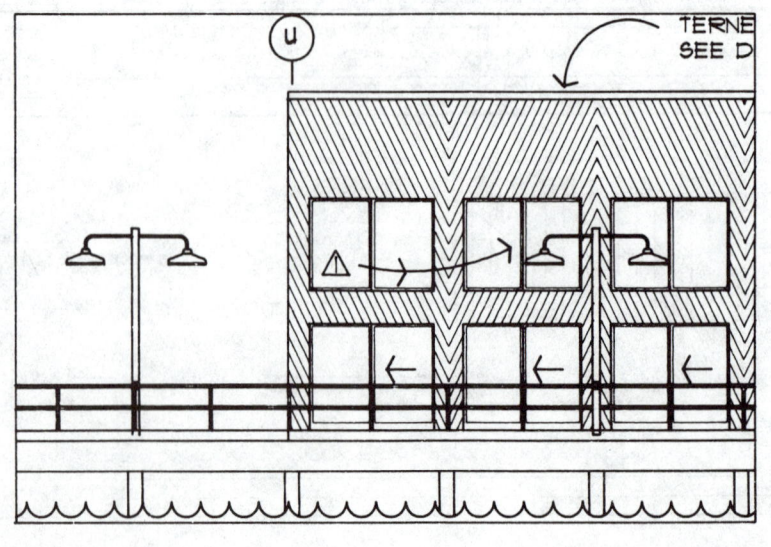

MOTEL AND RESTAURANT 26-16

Elevations/A-4

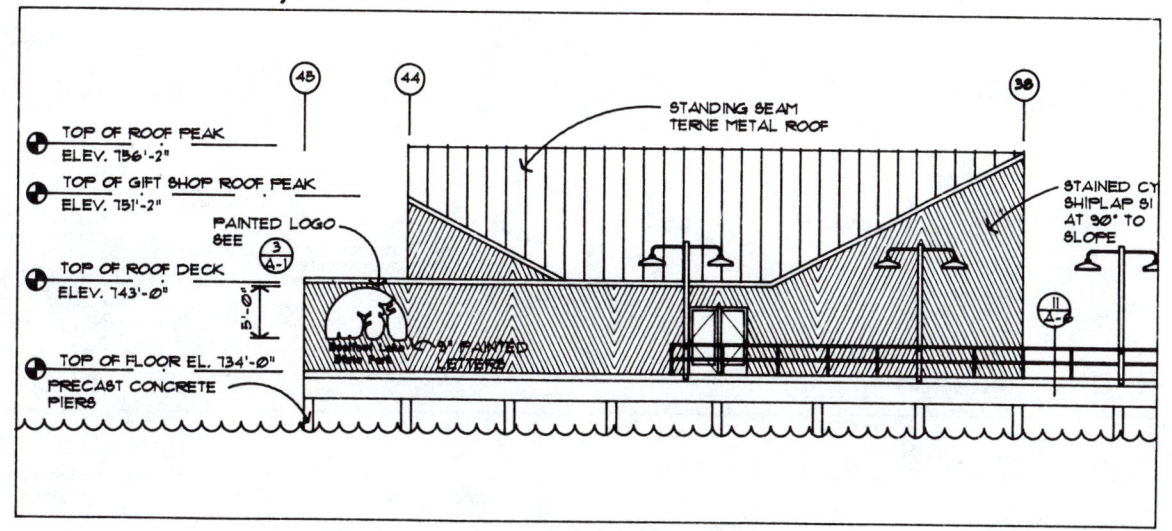

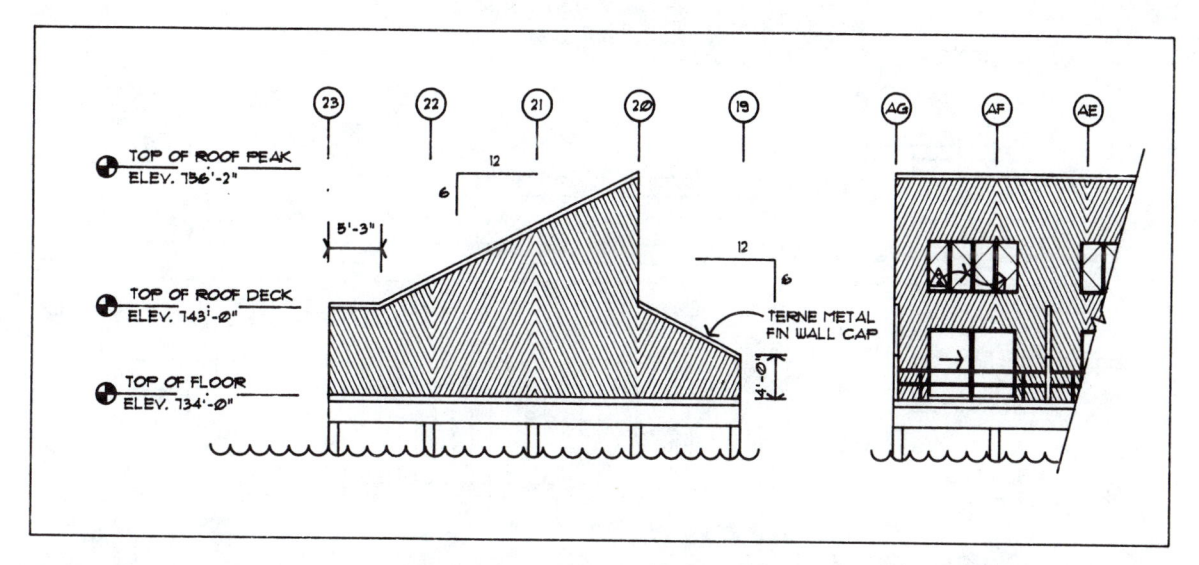

The west restaurant elevation is shown at the top of the page. The front orthographic view of the roof includes the ribs of the terne metal roof. Note that the painted logo is dimensioned and keyed to a detail on the first sheet.

The middle and bottom drawings illustrate elevations of the motel. The enlarged elevation to the right shows the amount of detail used for a typical elevation.

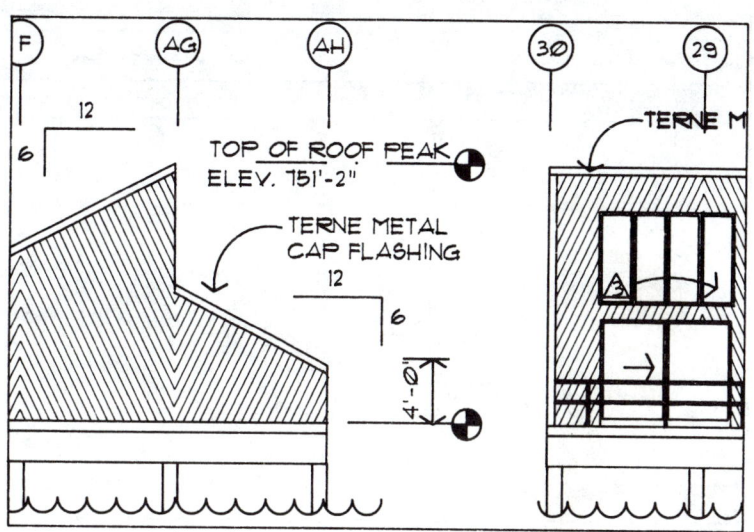

MOTEL AND RESTAURANT | 26-17

Building Sections/A-5

TOP OF ROOF PEAK ELEV. 751'-2"
TOP OF ROOF DECK ELEV. 743'-0"
TOP OF FLOOR SLAB ELEV. 734'-0"

TJI TRUSS JOISTS RUNNING PERPENDICULAR TO THE ROOF SLOPE AT 24" O.C.

FIN WALL W/ 1"x6" CYPRESS SIDING ON BOTH SIDES

TREATED 2x4's W/ 1/4" SPACE OVER TREATED 2x4's AT 24" O.C. ON 8" PRECAST CONC. DECKING

MOTEL UNIT 301
MOTEL UNIT 308

1/A-5 SECTION THROUGH TWO-STORY MOTEL UNIT SCALE 1/8"=1'-0"
2/A-5 SECTION THROUGH SINGLE-STORY MOTEL UNIT SCALE 1/8"=1'-0"

3"x6" T & G FIR DECK
WOOD TRUSSES AT 10'-6" O.C.
STANDING SEAM TERNE METAL ROOF

DINING 110
OPEN WALK-WAY TO MOTEL CLUSTERS
SHOP 109

4/A-5 SECTION THROUGH DINING AND LOUNGE SCALE 1/8"=1'-0"

TOP OF ROOF PEAK ELEV. 756'-2"
GIFT SHOP ROOF PEAK ELEV. 751'-2"
TOP OF ROOF DECK ELEV. 743'-0"
TOP OF FLOOR ELEV. 734'-0"
PRECAST CONCRETE PIERS

STANDING SEAM TERNE METAL ROOF
KITCHEN 113
DINING 110

4/A-5 SECTION THROUGH KITCHEN AND DINING ROOM SCALE 1/8"=1'-0"

TOP OF ROOF PEAK ELEV. 756'-2"
EXPOSED WOOD TRUSS SPACED AT 10'-6" O.C.
WOOD DECK CEILING
TOP OF FLOOR ELEV. 734'-0"

LOUNGE 100
SHOP 109
OPEN WALKWAY TO MOTEL CLUSTERS

6/A-5 SECTION THROUGH LOUNGE-GIFT SHOP AND KITCHEN SCALE 1/8"=1'-0"

MOTEL AND RESTAURANT   26-18

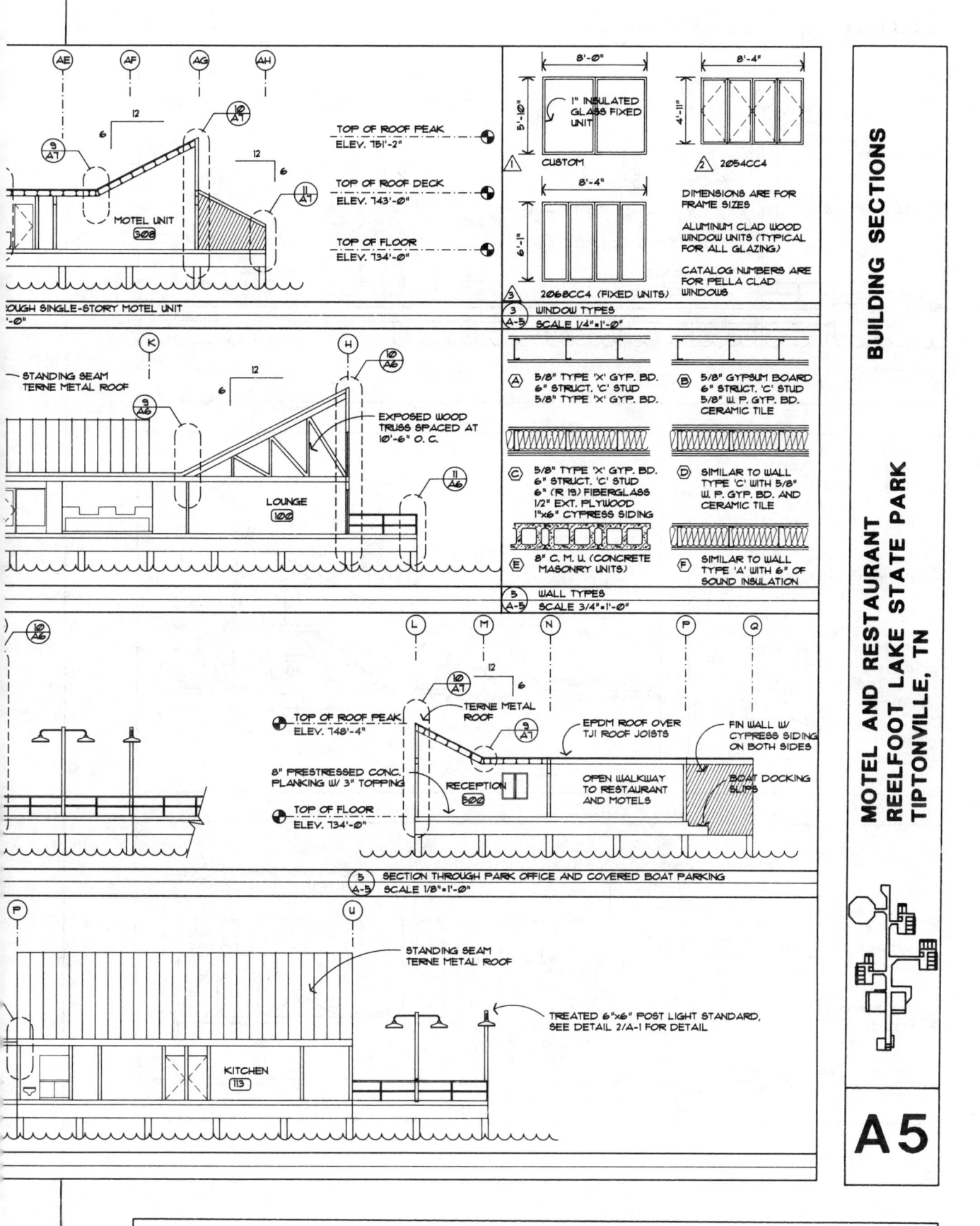

BUILDING SECTIONS

Window Types (3 / A-5, Scale 1/4" = 1'-0")

- CUSTOM — 8'-0" × 5'-10", 1" INSULATED GLASS FIXED UNIT
- 2054CC4 — 8'-4" × 4'-11"
- 2068CC4 (FIXED UNITS) — 8'-4" × 6'-1"

DIMENSIONS ARE FOR FRAME SIZES

ALUMINUM CLAD WOOD WINDOW UNITS (TYPICAL FOR ALL GLAZING)

CATALOG NUMBERS ARE FOR PELLA CLAD WINDOWS

Wall Types (5 / A-5, Scale 3/4" = 1'-0")

- A: 5/8" TYPE 'X' GYP. BD. / 6" STRUCT. 'C' STUD / 5/8" TYPE 'X' GYP. BD.
- B: 5/8" GYPSUM BOARD / 6" STRUCT. 'C' STUD / 5/8" W. P. GYP. BD. / CERAMIC TILE
- C: 5/8" TYPE 'X' GYP. BD. / 6" STRUCT. 'C' STUD / 6" (R 19) FIBERGLASS / 1/2" EXT. PLYWOOD / 1"×6" CYPRESS SIDING
- D: SIMILAR TO WALL TYPE 'C' WITH 5/8" W. P. GYP. BD. AND CERAMIC TILE
- E: 8" C. M. U. (CONCRETE MASONRY UNITS)
- F: SIMILAR TO WALL TYPE 'A' WITH 6" OF SOUND INSULATION

Section Through Single-Story Motel Unit

- TOP OF ROOF PEAK ELEV. 751'-2"
- TOP OF ROOF DECK ELEV. 743'-0"
- TOP OF FLOOR ELEV. 734'-0"
- MOTEL UNIT 508

Section (Lounge)

- STANDING SEAM TERNE METAL ROOF
- EXPOSED WOOD TRUSS SPACED AT 10'-6" O.C.
- LOUNGE 100

Section Through Park Office and Covered Boat Parking (5 / A-5, Scale 1/8" = 1'-0")

- TOP OF ROOF PEAK ELEV. 748'-4"
- 8" PRESTRESSED CONC. PLANKING W/ 3" TOPPING
- TOP OF FLOOR ELEV. 734'-0"
- TERNE METAL ROOF
- EPDM ROOF OVER TJI ROOF JOISTS
- FIN WALL W/ CYPRESS SIDING ON BOTH SIDES
- RECEPTION 500
- OPEN WALKWAY TO RESTAURANT AND MOTELS
- BOAT DOCKING SLIPS

Kitchen Elevation

- STANDING SEAM TERNE METAL ROOF
- TREATED 6"×6" POST LIGHT STANDARD, SEE DETAIL 2/A-1 FOR DETAIL
- KITCHEN 113

MOTEL AND RESTAURANT
REELFOOT LAKE STATE PARK
TIPTONVILLE, TN

A5

MOTEL AND RESTAURANT   26-19

Building Sections/A-5

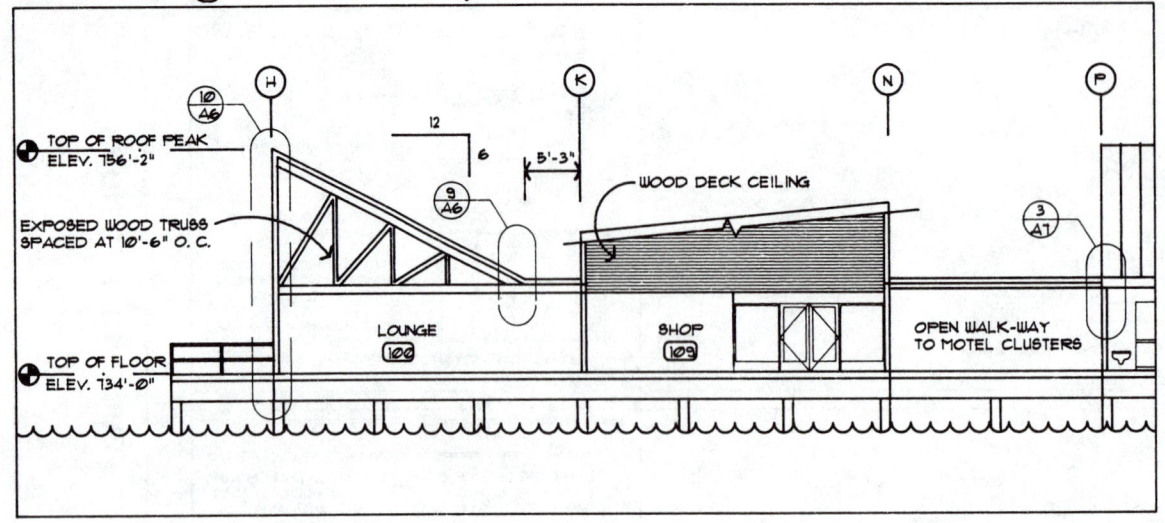

These three drawings show section cuts through portions of the project. The section above is cut parallel to the gift shop roof deck and is drawn using a diagonal line at the roof. The parallel lines indicate the timber deck in elevation. The motel section at the right cuts through the stair. The bottom section indicates the dining truss. Building sections are used as a key to index the larger-scale wall sections.

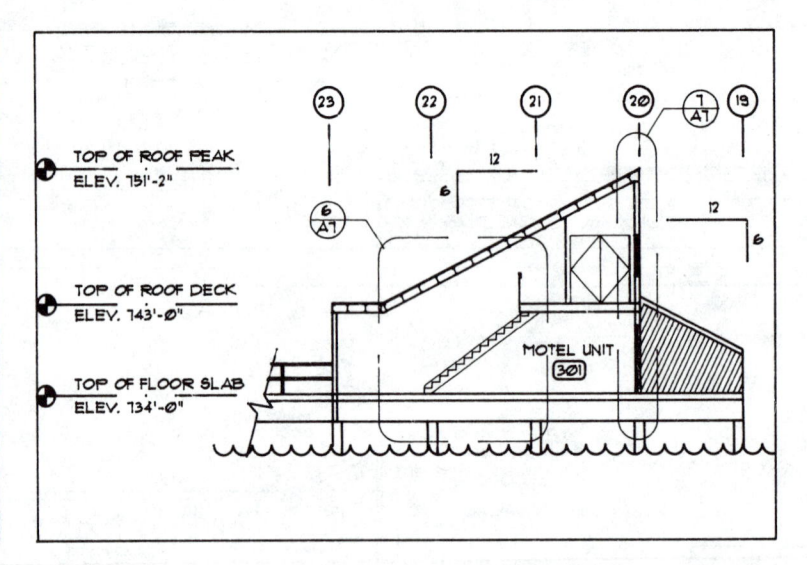

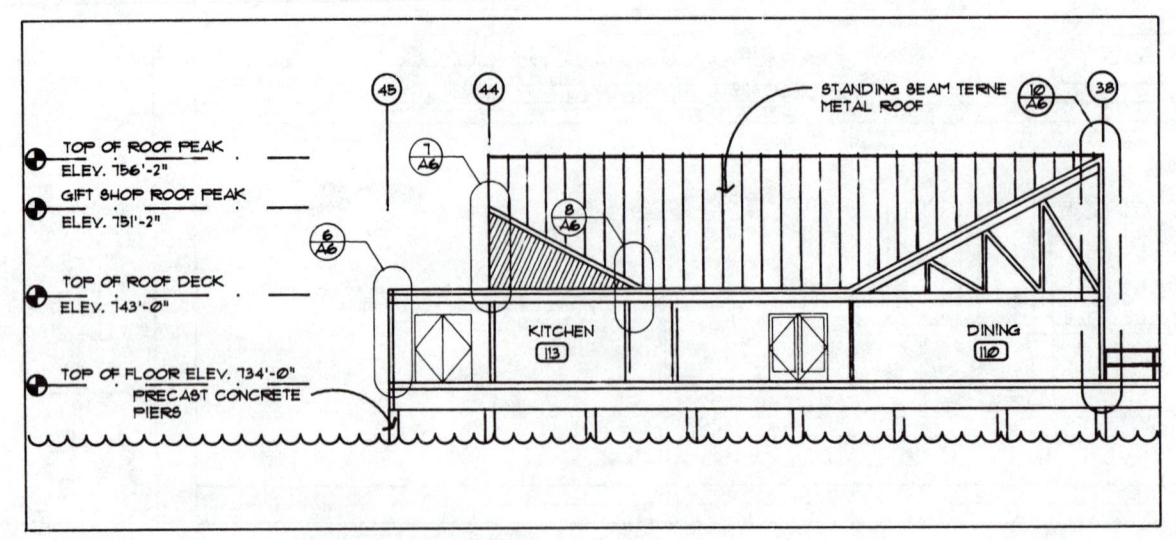

MOTEL AND RESTAURANT

26-20

Building Sections/A-5

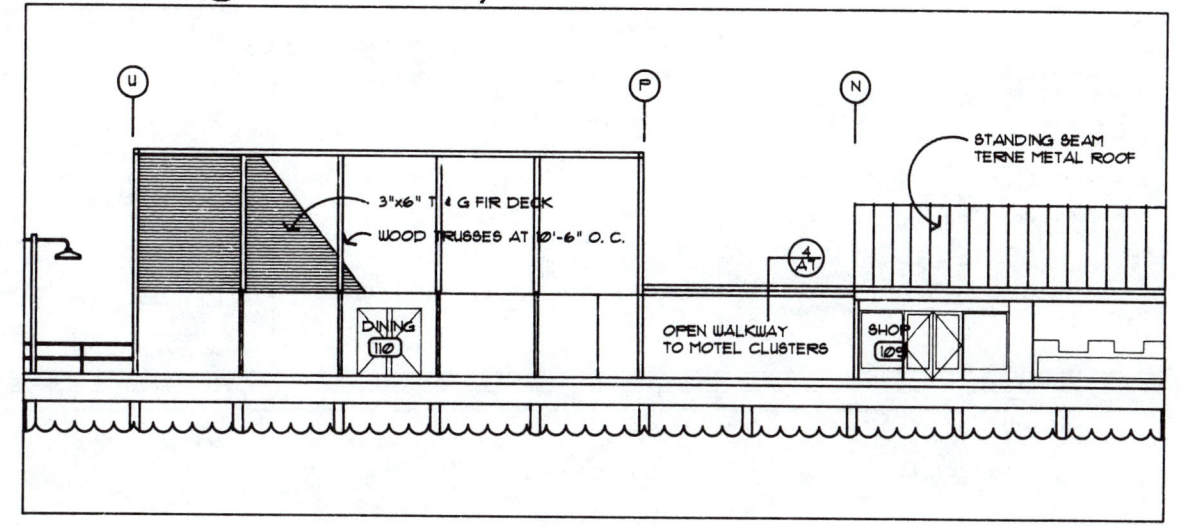

The longitudinal building section above cuts through the restaurant and lounge. The cut in the dining room shows an end view of the wood trusses (spaced at the 10'-6" grid). The truss is tied to a steel beam which is supported by columns at the grids. The floor system for the project consists of prestressed concrete decking with a 3" poured concrete topping.

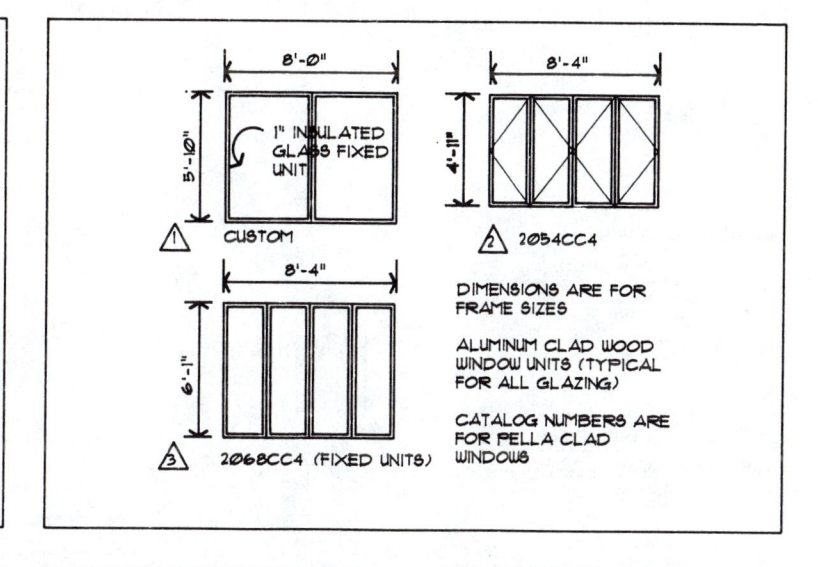

DIMENSIONS ARE FOR FRAME SIZES

ALUMINUM CLAD WOOD WINDOW UNITS (TYPICAL FOR ALL GLAZING)

CATALOG NUMBERS ARE FOR PELLA CLAD WINDOWS

The two drawings at the right illustrate some miscellaneous details on the project. The top drawing shows the window types used in the complex. Delta symbols on building elevations are keyed to this detail. Wall types for the project range from 8" concrete block to 6" metal studs with plywood sheathing. The hexagonal symbols on the floor plans are keyed to this detail.

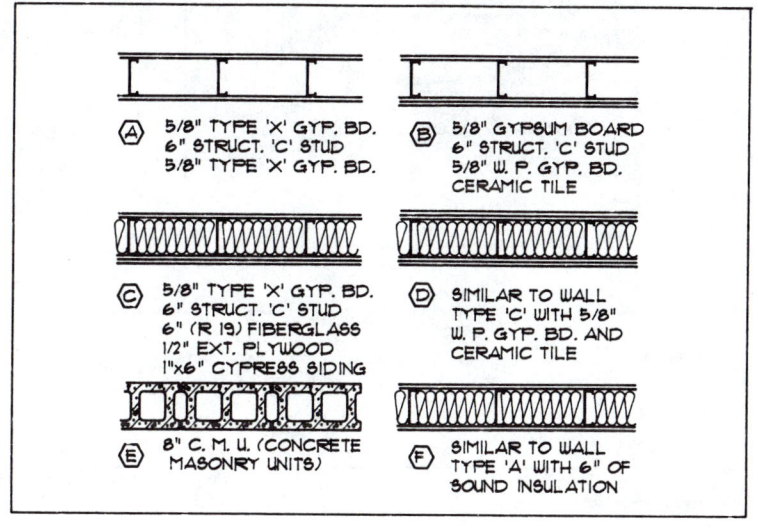

A) 5/8" TYPE 'X' GYP. BD.
6" STRUCT. 'C' STUD
5/8" TYPE 'X' GYP. BD.

B) 5/8" GYPSUM BOARD
6" STRUCT. 'C' STUD
5/8" W. P. GYP. BD.
CERAMIC TILE

C) 5/8" TYPE 'X' GYP. BD.
6" STRUCT. 'C' STUD
6" (R 19) FIBERGLASS
1/2" EXT. PLYWOOD
1"x6" CYPRESS SIDING

D) SIMILAR TO WALL TYPE 'C' WITH 5/8" W. P. GYP. BD. AND CERAMIC TILE

E) 8" C. M. U. (CONCRETE MASONRY UNITS)

F) SIMILAR TO WALL TYPE 'A' WITH 6" OF SOUND INSULATION

MOTEL AND RESTAURANT

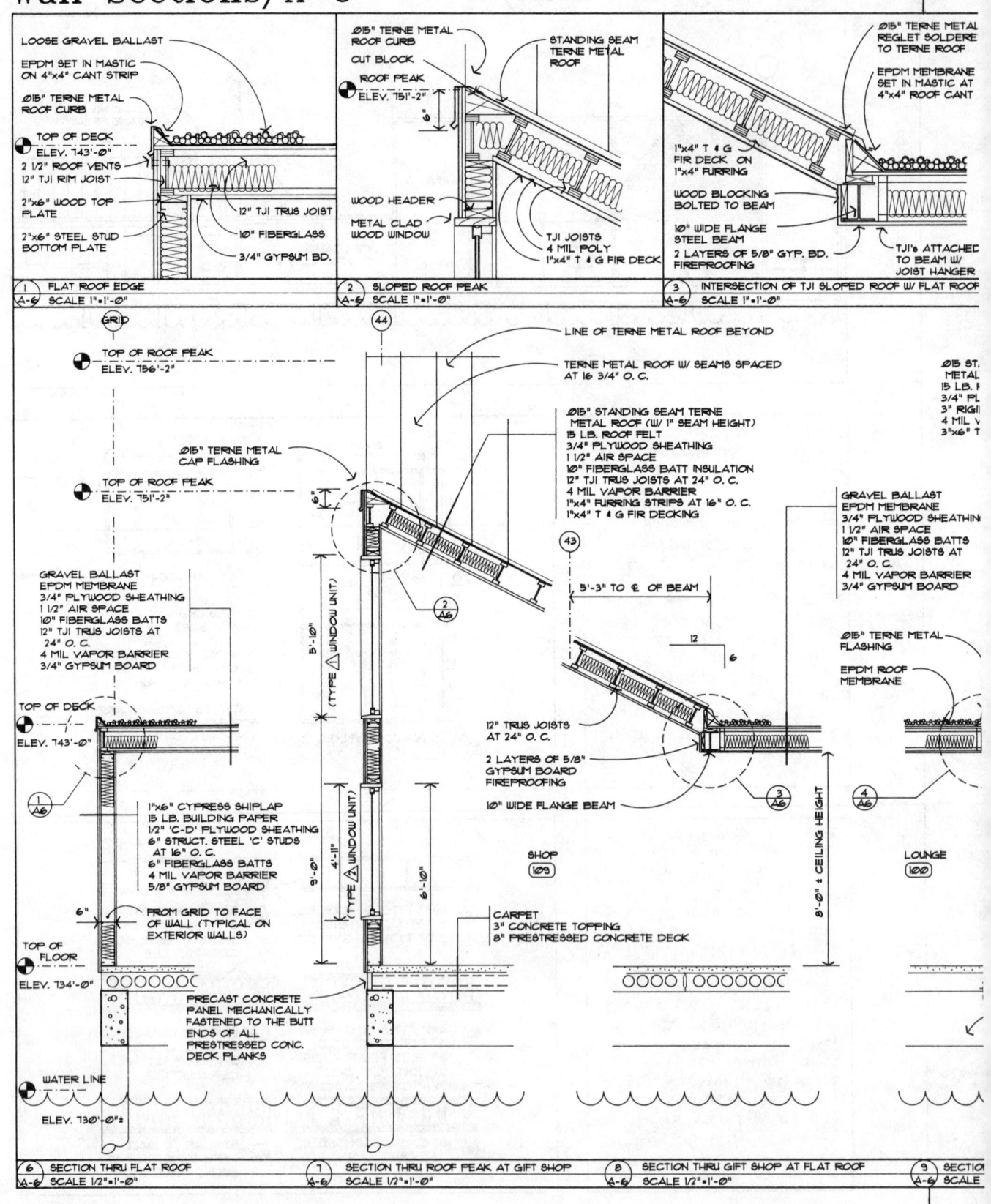

Wall Sections/A-6

Detail 1 — Flat Roof Edge (Scale 1"=1'-0")
- LOOSE GRAVEL BALLAST
- EPDM SET IN MASTIC ON 4"x4" CANT STRIP
- Ø15" TERNE METAL ROOF CURB
- TOP OF DECK ELEV. 743'-0"
- 2 1/2" ROOF VENTS
- 12" TJI RIM JOIST
- 2"x6" WOOD TOP PLATE
- 2"x6" STEEL STUD BOTTOM PLATE
- 12" TJI TRUS JOIST
- 10" FIBERGLASS
- 3/4" GYPSUM BD.

Detail 2 — Sloped Roof Peak (Scale 1"=1'-0")
- Ø15" TERNE METAL ROOF CURB
- CUT BLOCK
- ROOF PEAK ELEV. 751'-2"
- STANDING SEAM TERNE METAL ROOF
- WOOD HEADER
- METAL CLAD WOOD WINDOW
- TJI JOISTS
- 4 MIL POLY
- 1"x4" T & G FIR DECK

Detail 3 — Intersection of TJI Sloped Roof w/ Flat Roof (Scale 1"=1'-0")
- Ø15" TERNE METAL REGLET SOLDERED TO TERNE ROOF
- EPDM MEMBRANE SET IN MASTIC AT 4"x4" ROOF CANT
- 1"x4" T & G FIR DECK ON 1"x4" FURRING
- WOOD BLOCKING BOLTED TO BEAM
- 10" WIDE FLANGE STEEL BEAM
- 2 LAYERS OF 5/8" GYP. BD. FIREPROOFING
- TJI's ATTACHED TO BEAM W/ JOIST HANGER

Detail 6 — Section Thru Flat Roof (Scale 1/2"=1'-0")
- TOP OF ROOF PEAK ELEV. 756'-2"
- TOP OF ROOF PEAK ELEV. 751'-2"
- GRAVEL BALLAST
- EPDM MEMBRANE
- 3/4" PLYWOOD SHEATHING
- 1 1/2" AIR SPACE
- 10" FIBERGLASS BATTS
- 12" TJI TRUS JOISTS AT 24" O.C.
- 4 MIL VAPOR BARRIER
- 3/4" GYPSUM BOARD
- TOP OF DECK ELEV. 743'-0"
- 1"x6" CYPRESS SHIPLAP
- 15 LB. BUILDING PAPER
- 1/2" 'C-D' PLYWOOD SHEATHING
- 6" STRUCT. STEEL 'C' STUDS AT 16" O.C.
- 6" FIBERGLASS BATTS
- 4 MIL VAPOR BARRIER
- 5/8" GYPSUM BOARD
- 6" FROM GRID TO FACE OF WALL (TYPICAL ON EXTERIOR WALLS)
- TOP OF FLOOR ELEV. 734'-0"
- PRECAST CONCRETE PANEL MECHANICALLY FASTENED TO THE BUTT ENDS OF ALL PRESTRESSED CONC. DECK PLANKS
- WATER LINE ELEV. 730'-0"±

Detail 7 — Section Thru Roof Peak at Gift Shop (Scale 1/2"=1'-0")
- GRID
- LINE OF TERNE METAL ROOF BEYOND
- TERNE METAL ROOF W/ SEAMS SPACED AT 16 3/4" O.C.
- Ø15" STANDING SEAM TERNE METAL ROOF (W/ 1" SEAM HEIGHT)
- 15 LB. ROOF FELT
- 3/4" PLYWOOD SHEATHING
- 1 1/2" AIR SPACE
- 10" FIBERGLASS BATT INSULATION
- 12" TJI TRUS JOISTS AT 24" O.C.
- 4 MIL VAPOR BARRIER
- 1"x4" FURRING STRIPS AT 16" O.C.
- 1"x4" T & G FIR DECKING
- Ø15" TERNE METAL CAP FLASHING
- (TYPE A WINDOW UNIT) 5'-10"
- (TYPE A WINDOW UNIT) 4'-11"
- 3'-0"
- 6'-10"

Detail 8 — Section Thru Gift Shop at Flat Roof (Scale 1/2"=1'-0")
- 5'-3" TO ₵ OF BEAM
- 12 / 6
- 12" TRUS JOISTS AT 24" O.C.
- 2 LAYERS OF 5/8" GYPSUM BOARD FIREPROOFING
- 10" WIDE FLANGE BEAM
- SHOP 109
- CARPET
- 3" CONCRETE TOPPING
- 8" PRESTRESSED CONCRETE DECK
- 8'-0" ± CEILING HEIGHT

Detail 9 — Section (partial)
- Ø15 ST. METAL
- 15 LB. R
- 3/4" PL
- 3" RIGI
- 4 MIL V
- 3"x6" T
- GRAVEL BALLAST
- EPDM MEMBRANE
- 3/4" PLYWOOD SHEATHING
- 1 1/2" AIR SPACE
- 10" FIBERGLASS BATTS
- 12" TJI TRUS JOISTS AT 24" O.C.
- 4 MIL VAPOR BARRIER
- 3/4" GYPSUM BOARD
- Ø15" TERNE METAL FLASHING
- EPDM ROOF MEMBRANE
- LOUNGE 100

MOTEL AND RESTAURANT   26-22

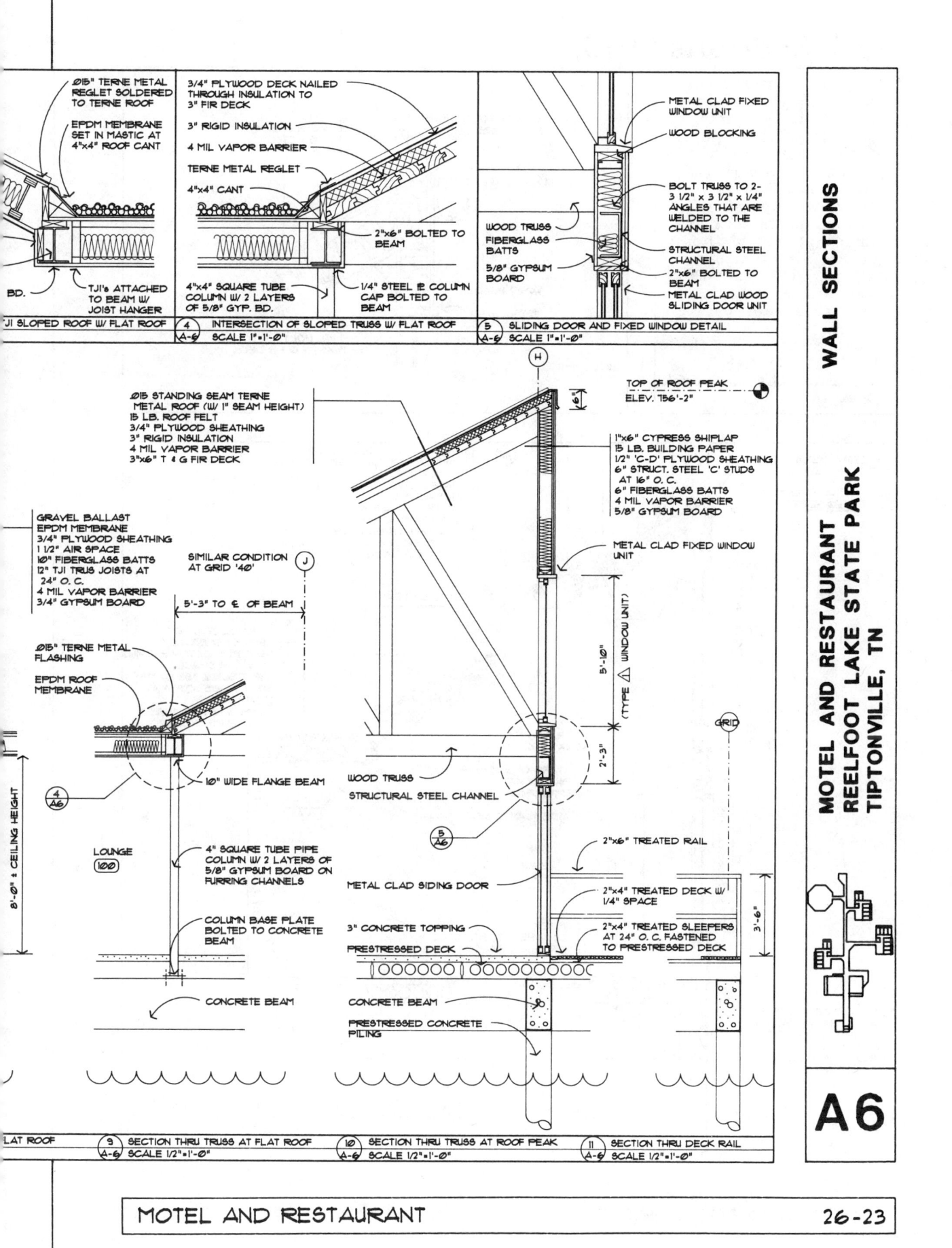

Detail 4 — Intersection of Sloped Truss w/ Flat Roof
Scale: 1" = 1'-0"

- .015" TERNE METAL REGLET SOLDERED TO TERNE ROOF
- 3/4" PLYWOOD DECK NAILED THROUGH INSULATION TO 3" FIR DECK
- EPDM MEMBRANE SET IN MASTIC AT 4"x4" ROOF CANT
- 3" RIGID INSULATION
- 4 MIL VAPOR BARRIER
- TERNE METAL REGLET
- 4"x4" CANT
- 2"x6" BOLTED TO BEAM
- TJI's ATTACHED TO BEAM W/ JOIST HANGER
- 4"x4" SQUARE TUBE COLUMN W/ 2 LAYERS OF 5/8" GYP. BD.
- 1/4" STEEL ℀ COLUMN CAP BOLTED TO BEAM

Detail 5 — Sliding Door and Fixed Window Detail
Scale: 1" = 1'-0"

- METAL CLAD FIXED WINDOW UNIT
- WOOD BLOCKING
- BOLT TRUSS TO 2- 3 1/2" x 3 1/2" x 1/4" ANGLES THAT ARE WELDED TO THE CHANNEL
- WOOD TRUSS
- FIBERGLASS BATTS
- 5/8" GYPSUM BOARD
- STRUCTURAL STEEL CHANNEL
- 2"x6" BOLTED TO BEAM
- METAL CLAD WOOD SLIDING DOOR UNIT

Detail 9 — Section Thru Truss at Flat Roof
Scale: 1/2" = 1'-0"

- GRAVEL BALLAST
- EPDM MEMBRANE
- 3/4" PLYWOOD SHEATHING
- 1 1/2" AIR SPACE
- 10" FIBERGLASS BATTS
- 12" TJI TRUS JOISTS AT 24" O.C.
- 4 MIL VAPOR BARRIER
- 3/4" GYPSUM BOARD
- .015" TERNE METAL FLASHING
- EPDM ROOF MEMBRANE
- 10" WIDE FLANGE BEAM
- 4" SQUARE TUBE PIPE COLUMN W/ 2 LAYERS OF 5/8" GYPSUM BOARD ON FURRING CHANNELS
- COLUMN BASE PLATE BOLTED TO CONCRETE BEAM
- CONCRETE BEAM
- LOUNGE 100
- 8'-0" ± CEILING HEIGHT

Detail 10 — Section Thru Truss at Roof Peak
Scale: 1/2" = 1'-0"

- TOP OF ROOF PEAK ELEV. 756'-2"
- .015 STANDING SEAM TERNE METAL ROOF (W/ 1" SEAM HEIGHT)
- 15 LB. ROOF FELT
- 3/4" PLYWOOD SHEATHING
- 3" RIGID INSULATION
- 4 MIL VAPOR BARRIER
- 3"x6" T & G FIR DECK
- 1"x6" CYPRESS SHIPLAP
- 15 LB. BUILDING PAPER
- 1/2" 'C-D' PLYWOOD SHEATHING
- 6" STRUCT. STEEL 'C' STUDS AT 16" O.C.
- 6" FIBERGLASS BATTS
- 4 MIL VAPOR BARRIER
- 5/8" GYPSUM BOARD
- METAL CLAD FIXED WINDOW UNIT
- SIMILAR CONDITION AT GRID '40'
- 5'-3" TO ℄ OF BEAM
- 5'-10" (TYPE △ WINDOW UNIT)
- 2'-3"
- WOOD TRUSS
- STRUCTURAL STEEL CHANNEL
- METAL CLAD SLIDING DOOR
- 3" CONCRETE TOPPING
- PRESTRESSED DECK
- CONCRETE BEAM

Detail 11 — Section Thru Deck Rail
Scale: 1/2" = 1'-0"

- 2"x6" TREATED RAIL
- 2"x4" TREATED DECK W/ 1/4" SPACE
- 2"x4" TREATED SLEEPERS AT 24" O.C. FASTENED TO PRESTRESSED DECK
- 3'-6"
- PRESTRESSED CONCRETE PILING

MOTEL AND RESTAURANT
REELFOOT LAKE STATE PARK
TIPTONVILLE, TN

WALL SECTIONS

A6

MOTEL AND RESTAURANT · 26-23

Wall Sections/A-6

The wall section below cuts through the sloped roof at the gift shop, starting with the piling at the water line and running to the roof peak. The roof is structured by using TJI plywood joists that are turned at 90° to the normal direction of roof rafters. This cuts the span and allows the steel stud walls between the motel units to support the roof. The detail at the right illustrates the roof peak blow-up.

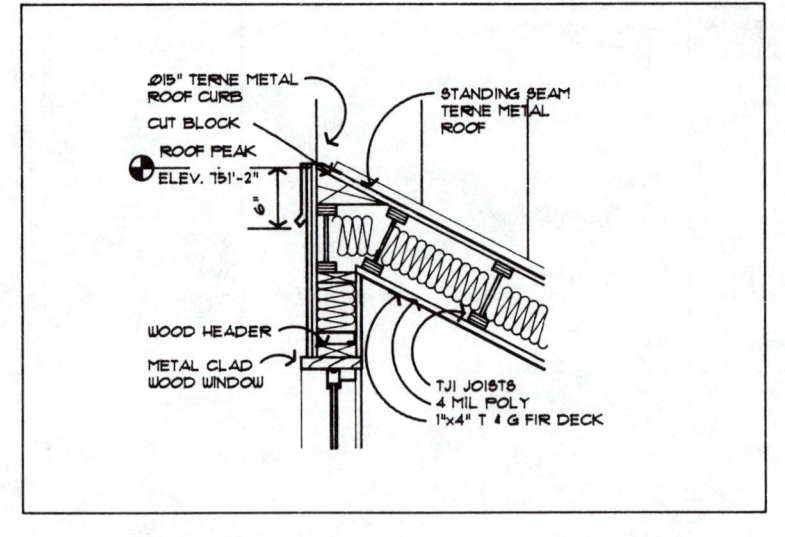

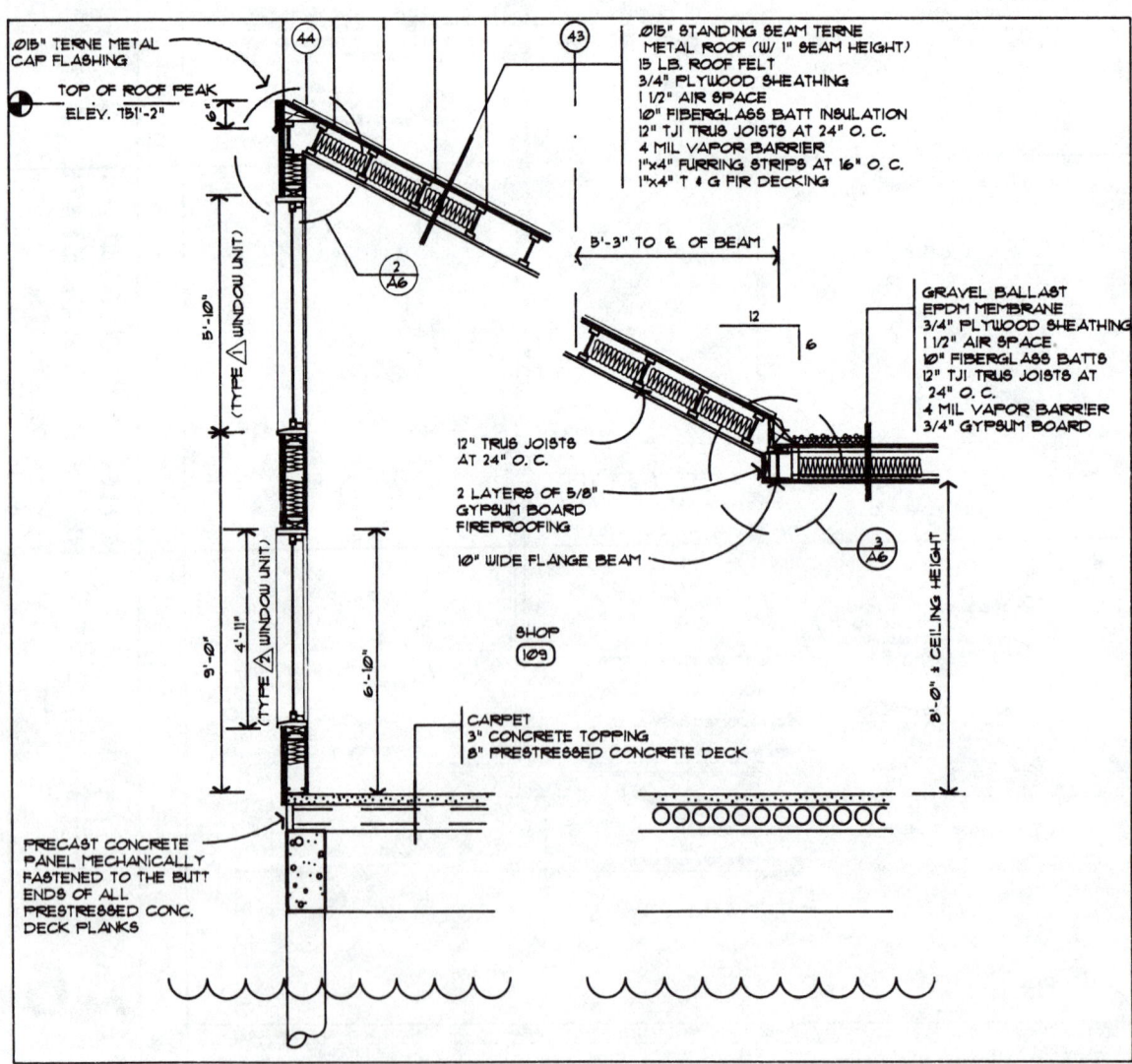

Roof peak detail (upper right):
- Ø15" TERNE METAL ROOF CURB
- STANDING SEAM TERNE METAL ROOF
- CUT BLOCK
- ROOF PEAK ELEV. 751'-2"
- 6"
- WOOD HEADER
- METAL CLAD WOOD WINDOW
- TJI JOISTS
- 4 MIL POLY
- 1"x4" T & G FIR DECK

Wall section (lower):
- Ø15" TERNE METAL CAP FLASHING
- TOP OF ROOF PEAK ELEV. 751'-2"
- Ø15" STANDING SEAM TERNE METAL ROOF (W/ 1" SEAM HEIGHT)
- 15 LB. ROOF FELT
- 3/4" PLYWOOD SHEATHING
- 1 1/2" AIR SPACE
- 10" FIBERGLASS BATT INSULATION
- 12" TJI TRUS JOISTS AT 24" O.C.
- 4 MIL VAPOR BARRIER
- 1"x4" FURRING STRIPS AT 16" O.C.
- 1"x4" T & G FIR DECKING
- 5'-3" TO ℄ OF BEAM
- GRAVEL BALLAST
- EPDM MEMBRANE
- 3/4" PLYWOOD SHEATHING
- 1 1/2" AIR SPACE
- 10" FIBERGLASS BATTS
- 12" TJI TRUS JOISTS AT 24" O.C.
- 4 MIL VAPOR BARRIER
- 3/4" GYPSUM BOARD
- 12" TRUS JOISTS AT 24" O.C.
- 2 LAYERS OF 5/8" GYPSUM BOARD FIREPROOFING
- 10" WIDE FLANGE BEAM
- SHOP 109
- CARPET
- 3" CONCRETE TOPPING
- 8" PRESTRESSED CONCRETE DECK
- PRECAST CONCRETE PANEL MECHANICALLY FASTENED TO THE BUTT ENDS OF ALL PRESTRESSED CONC. DECK PLANKS
- 5'-10" (TYPE A WINDOW UNIT)
- 4'-11" (TYPE A WINDOW UNIT)
- 9'-0"
- 6'-10"
- 8'-0" ± CEILING HEIGHT

MOTEL AND RESTAURANT 26-24

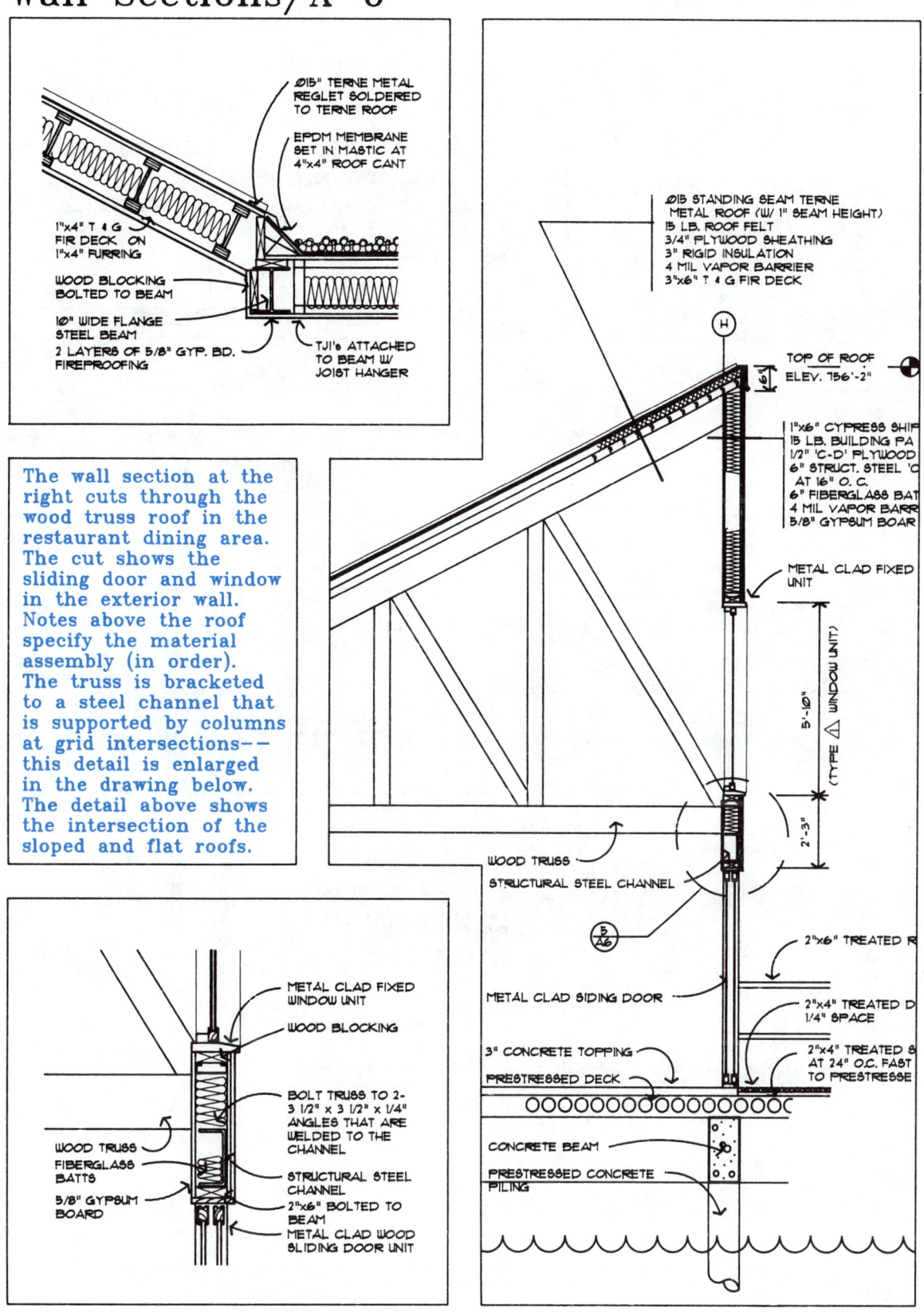

Wall Sections/A-6

Upper-left detail callouts:
- Ø15" TERNE METAL REGLET SOLDERED TO TERNE ROOF
- EPDM MEMBRANE SET IN MASTIC AT 4"x4" ROOF CANT
- 1"x4" T & G FIR DECK ON 1"x4" FURRING
- WOOD BLOCKING BOLTED TO BEAM
- 10" WIDE FLANGE STEEL BEAM
- 2 LAYERS OF 5/8" GYP. BD. FIREPROOFING
- TJI's ATTACHED TO BEAM W/ JOIST HANGER

Commentary (blue text):

The wall section at the right cuts through the wood truss roof in the restaurant dining area. The cut shows the sliding door and window in the exterior wall. Notes above the roof specify the material assembly (in order). The truss is bracketed to a steel channel that is supported by columns at grid intersections-- this detail is enlarged in the drawing below. The detail above shows the intersection of the sloped and flat roofs.

Lower-left detail callouts:
- METAL CLAD FIXED WINDOW UNIT
- WOOD BLOCKING
- BOLT TRUSS TO 2- 3 1/2" x 3 1/2" x 1/4" ANGLES THAT ARE WELDED TO THE CHANNEL
- WOOD TRUSS
- FIBERGLASS BATTS
- 5/8" GYPSUM BOARD
- STRUCTURAL STEEL CHANNEL
- 2"x6" BOLTED TO BEAM
- METAL CLAD WOOD SLIDING DOOR UNIT

Right wall section callouts:
- Ø15 STANDING SEAM TERNE METAL ROOF (W/ 1" SEAM HEIGHT)
- 15 LB. ROOF FELT
- 3/4" PLYWOOD SHEATHING
- 3" RIGID INSULATION
- 4 MIL VAPOR BARRIER
- 3"x6" T & G FIR DECK
- TOP OF ROOF ELEV. 756'-2"
- 1"x6" CYPRESS SHIP[LAP]
- 15 LB. BUILDING PA[PER]
- 1/2" C-D PLYWOOD
- 6" STRUCT. STEEL 'C' AT 16" O.C.
- 6" FIBERGLASS BAT[TS]
- 4 MIL VAPOR BARR[IER]
- 5/8" GYPSUM BOAR[D]
- METAL CLAD FIXED UNIT
- (TYPE A WINDOW UNIT) 5'-10"
- 2'-3"
- WOOD TRUSS
- STRUCTURAL STEEL CHANNEL
- 5/A6
- METAL CLAD SIDING DOOR
- 3" CONCRETE TOPPING
- PRESTRESSED DECK
- 2"x6" TREATED R[...]
- 2"x4" TREATED D[...] 1/4" SPACE
- 2"x4" TREATED S[...] AT 24" O.C. FAST[ENED] TO PRESTRESSE[D]
- CONCRETE BEAM
- PRESTRESSED CONCRETE PILING

MOTEL AND RESTAURANT

Wall Sections/A-7

1 — STAIR AT MOTEL SECOND FLOOR
SCALE 1"=1'-0"

- 2"x6" OAK HANDRAIL
- 3/4" x 3/4" SQ. STEEL TUBE BALLUSTERS SPACED AT 5" O.C.
- 10" TREAD
- 3'-6"
- 6 3/4" RISE
- 1" NOSING
- OAK STRINGER
- 5/8" GYPSUM BD.

2 — ROOF DRAIN
SCALE 1"=1'-0"

- ¢ OF DRAIN
- CAST IRON DRAIN
- EPDM MEMBRANE SET IN MASTIC
- CLAMP RING BRACKETED TO DECK
- DRAIN LINE
- CUT MEMBRANE TO WITHIN 1/2" OF ATTACHMENT RING

3 — ROOF CANOPY AT WALL INTERSECTION
SCALE 1"=1'-0"

- GRAVEL STOP BEYOND
- EPDM MEMBRANE
- 3/4" PLYWOOD
- 12" TJI's AT 12" O.C.
- Ø15" TERNE METAL FLASHING, CARRIED UNDER SIDING
- 10" WIDE FLANGE
- 1"x4" T & G FIR DECK
- TJI JOIST HANGER

6 — SECTION AT TWO-STORY MOTEL UNIT STAIR
SCALE 1/2"=1'-0"

- CUT BLOCK AT ROOF PEAK
- TERNE METAL ROOF W/ SEAMS SPACED AT 16 3/4" O.C.
- 12'-6" (15 TREADS AT 10")
- Ø15" STANDING SEAM TERNE METAL ROOF (W/ 1" STANDING SEAM)
- 15 LB. ROOF FELT
- 3/4" PLYWOOD SHEATHING
- 1 1/2" AIR SPACE
- 10" FIBERGLASS BATT INSULATION
- 12" TJI TRUS JOISTS AT 24" O.C.
- 4 MIL VAPOR BARRIER
- 3/4" GYPSUM BOARD
- BALCONY EXTENDS 1'-8" BEYOND THE NOSING OF THE TOP STAIR TREAD (SEE 2/A-3)
- CARPET
- 5/8" PARTICLE BOARD
- 1/2" PLYWOOD SUBFLOOR
- 12" TJI TRUS JOISTS AT 16" O.C.
- 3/4" GYPSUM BOARD
- TOP OF SECOND FLOOR ELEV. 743'-0"
- 2"x6" OAK HANDRAIL
- 5/8" GYPSUM BOARD UNDER STAIR
- 3/4"x 3/4" SQUARE STEEL TUBE BALLUSTERS SPACED AT 5" O.C.
- 2"x12" OAK STRINGER AT BOTH SIDES OF STAIR
- MOTEL UNIT 301
- CARPET
- 3" CONCRETE TOPPING
- 8" PRESTRESSED DECK
- 9'-0" (16 RISERS AT 6 3/4")
- 2'-8"
- TOP OF FLOOR ELEV. 734'-0"
- WATER LINE ELEV. 730'-0"±

7 — SECTION AT TWO-STORY MOTEL ROOF PEAK
SCALE 1/2"=1'-0"

- TOP OF ROOF PEAK ELEV. 756'-2"
- Ø15" TERNE METAL FLASHING
- 1"x6" CYPRESS SHIPLAP
- 15 LB. BUILDING PAPER
- 1/2" 'C-D' PLYWOOD SHEATHING
- 6" STRUCTURAL STEEL 'C' STUDS AT 16" O.C.
- 6" FIBERGLASS BATTS
- 4 MIL VAPOR BARRIER
- 5/8" GYPSUM BOARD
- (TYPE A CASEMENT WINDOW)
- 6'-8"
- 4'-11"
- Ø15" TERNE METAL CAP FLASHING
- 9'-0" (FLOOR TO FLOOR)
- 4'-0 1/8"
- 6'-8 1/8" (FRAME SIZE)
- METAL CLAD WOOD SLIDING GLASS DOOR

8 — SECTION THRU MOTEL
SCALE 1/2"=1'-0"

- 2"x6" TREATED FIR HANDRAIL
- 8'-0" ± CEILING HEIGHT
- THRESHOLD

MOTEL AND RESTAURANT

26-26

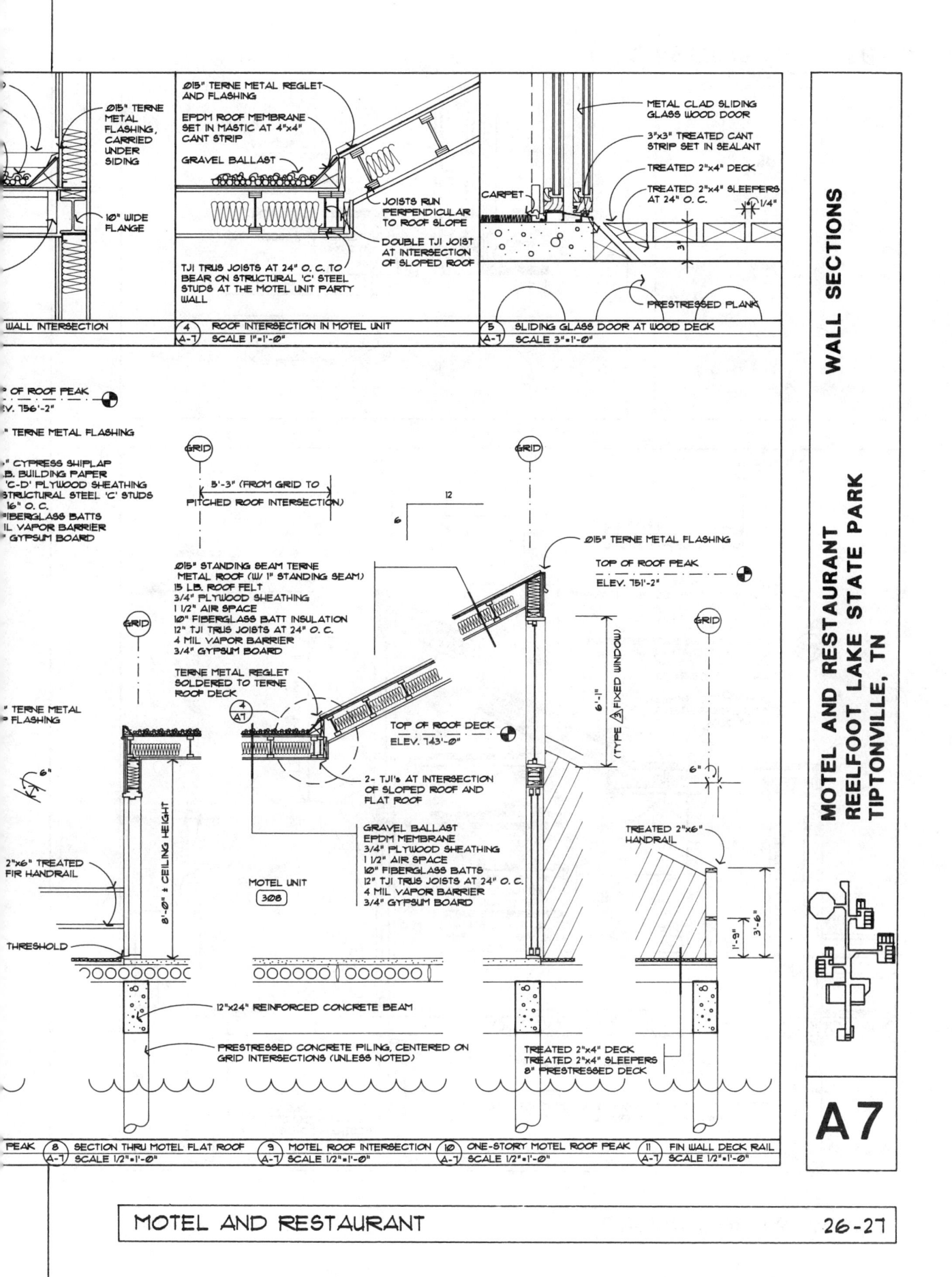

WALL SECTIONS

MOTEL AND RESTAURANT
REELFOOT LAKE STATE PARK
TIPTONVILLE, TN

A7

Drawing details include:

Detail 4 — ROOF INTERSECTION IN MOTEL UNIT (Scale 1"=1'-0")
- .015" TERNE METAL REGLET AND FLASHING
- EPDM ROOF MEMBRANE SET IN MASTIC AT 4"x4" CANT STRIP
- GRAVEL BALLAST
- .015" TERNE METAL FLASHING, CARRIED UNDER SIDING
- 10" WIDE FLANGE
- JOISTS RUN PERPENDICULAR TO ROOF SLOPE
- DOUBLE TJI JOIST AT INTERSECTION OF SLOPED ROOF
- TJI TRUS JOISTS AT 24" O.C. TO BEAR ON STRUCTURAL 'C' STEEL STUDS AT THE MOTEL UNIT PARTY WALL

Detail 5 — SLIDING GLASS DOOR AT WOOD DECK (Scale 3"=1'-0")
- METAL CLAD SLIDING GLASS WOOD DOOR
- 3"x3" TREATED CANT STRIP SET IN SEALANT
- TREATED 2"x4" DECK
- TREATED 2"x4" SLEEPERS AT 24" O.C.
- CARPET
- PRESTRESSED PLANK

Wall assembly notes:
- TOP OF ROOF PEAK ELEV. 756'-2"
- TERNE METAL FLASHING
- CYPRESS SHIPLAP
- B. BUILDING PAPER
- 'C-D' PLYWOOD SHEATHING
- STRUCTURAL STEEL 'C' STUDS 16" O.C.
- FIBERGLASS BATTS
- MIL VAPOR BARRIER
- GYPSUM BOARD

Detail 8 — SECTION THRU MOTEL FLAT ROOF (Scale 1/2"=1'-0")
- TERNE METAL FLASHING
- 2"x6" TREATED FIR HANDRAIL
- THRESHOLD
- 8'-0" ± CEILING HEIGHT
- 12"x24" REINFORCED CONCRETE BEAM
- PRESTRESSED CONCRETE PILING, CENTERED ON GRID INTERSECTIONS (UNLESS NOTED)

Detail 9 — MOTEL ROOF INTERSECTION (Scale 1/2"=1'-0")
- 5'-3" (FROM GRID TO PITCHED ROOF INTERSECTION)
- .015" STANDING SEAM TERNE METAL ROOF (W/ 1" STANDING SEAM)
- 15 LB. ROOF FELT
- 3/4" PLYWOOD SHEATHING
- 1 1/2" AIR SPACE
- 10" FIBERGLASS BATT INSULATION
- 12" TJI TRUS JOISTS AT 24" O.C.
- 4 MIL VAPOR BARRIER
- 3/4" GYPSUM BOARD
- TERNE METAL REGLET SOLDERED TO TERNE ROOF DECK
- TOP OF ROOF DECK ELEV. 743'-0"
- 2- TJI's AT INTERSECTION OF SLOPED ROOF AND FLAT ROOF
- GRAVEL BALLAST
- EPDM MEMBRANE
- 3/4" PLYWOOD SHEATHING
- 1 1/2" AIR SPACE
- 10" FIBERGLASS BATTS
- 12" TJI TRUS JOISTS AT 24" O.C.
- 4 MIL VAPOR BARRIER
- 3/4" GYPSUM BOARD
- MOTEL UNIT 308

Detail 10 — ONE-STORY MOTEL ROOF PEAK (Scale 1/2"=1'-0")
- .015" TERNE METAL FLASHING
- TOP OF ROOF PEAK ELEV. 751'-2"
- 6'-1" (TYPE A FIXED WINDOW)

Detail 11 — FIN WALL DECK RAIL (Scale 1/2"=1'-0")
- TREATED 2"x6" HANDRAIL
- TREATED 2"x4" DECK
- TREATED 2"x4" SLEEPERS
- 8" PRESTRESSED DECK
- 3'-6", 1'-9"

MOTEL AND RESTAURANT 26-27

Wall Sections/A-7

The detail below is a section cut through the one-story motel. The cut shows the vaulted ceiling and the clere story window above the sliding door. Note that the wall section is cut into four parts to reduce the size of the drawing. The detail to the right shows a blow-up of the sliding door sill as it intersects with the exterior wood deck. The interior floor has a 3" concrete topping.

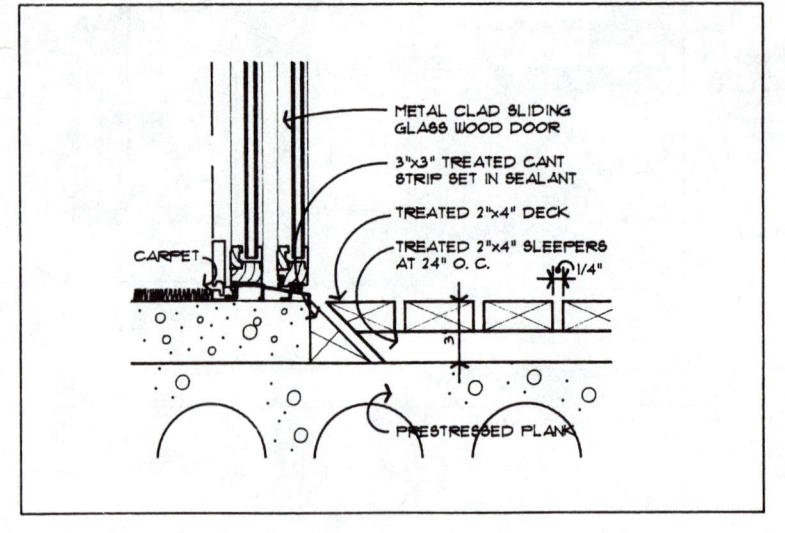

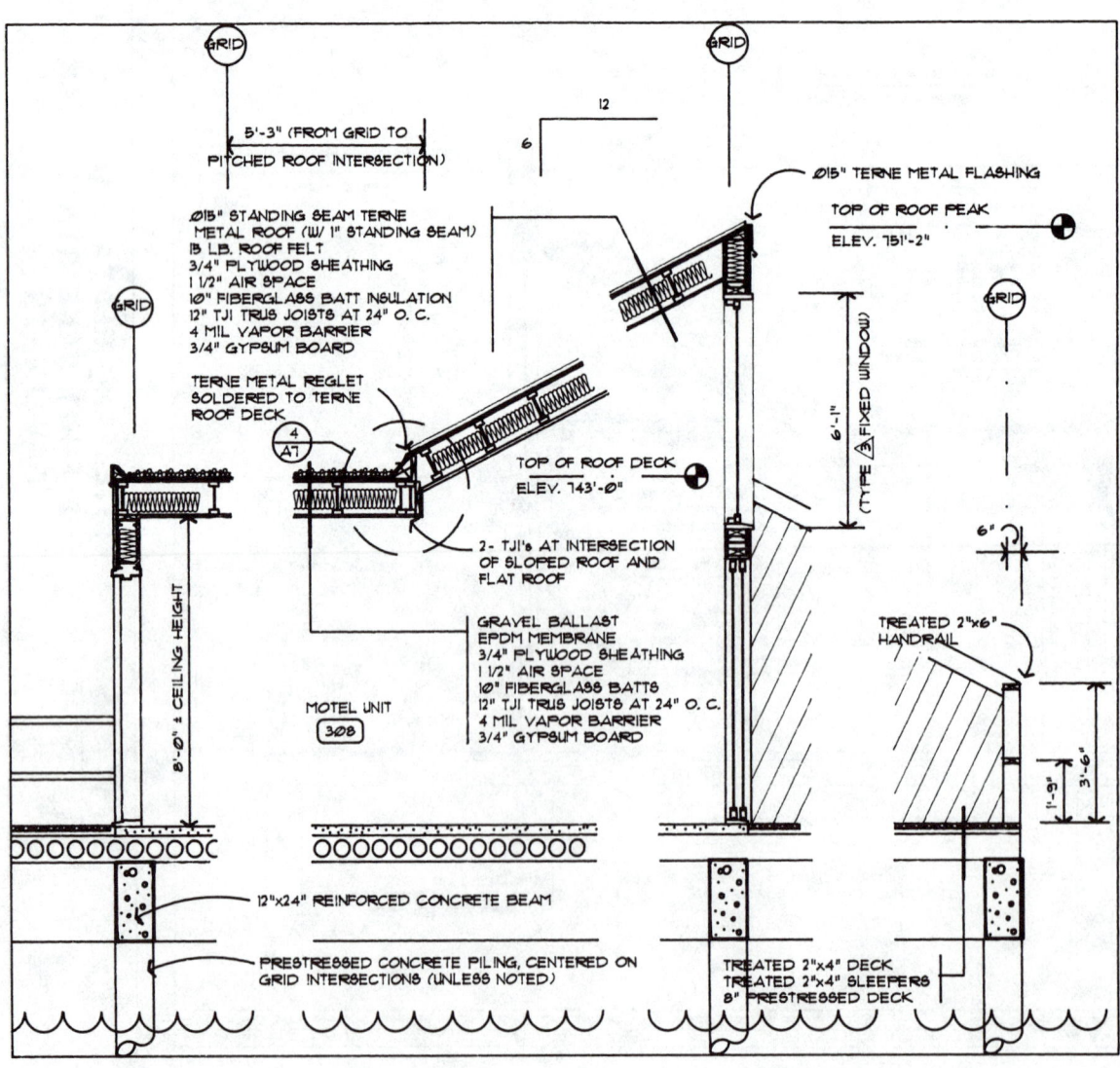

Sliding door sill detail:
- METAL CLAD SLIDING GLASS WOOD DOOR
- 3"x3" TREATED CANT STRIP SET IN SEALANT
- TREATED 2"x4" DECK
- TREATED 2"x4" SLEEPERS AT 24" O.C.
- CARPET
- PRESTRESSED PLANK

Wall section:
- 5'-3" (FROM GRID TO PITCHED ROOF INTERSECTION)
- Roof slope 6:12
- Ø15" STANDING SEAM TERNE METAL ROOF (W/ 1" STANDING SEAM)
- 15 LB. ROOF FELT
- 3/4" PLYWOOD SHEATHING
- 1 1/2" AIR SPACE
- 10" FIBERGLASS BATT INSULATION
- 12" TJI TRUS JOISTS AT 24" O.C.
- 4 MIL VAPOR BARRIER
- 3/4" GYPSUM BOARD
- TERNE METAL REGLET SOLDERED TO TERNE ROOF DECK
- 4/A7
- Ø15" TERNE METAL FLASHING
- TOP OF ROOF PEAK ELEV. 751'-2"
- TOP OF ROOF DECK ELEV. 743'-0"
- 2-TJI'S AT INTERSECTION OF SLOPED ROOF AND FLAT ROOF
- (TYPE A FIXED WINDOW) 6'-1"
- GRAVEL BALLAST
- EPDM MEMBRANE
- 3/4" PLYWOOD SHEATHING
- 1 1/2" AIR SPACE
- 10" FIBERGLASS BATTS
- 12" TJI TRUS JOISTS AT 24" O.C.
- 4 MIL VAPOR BARRIER
- 3/4" GYPSUM BOARD
- MOTEL UNIT 308
- 8'-0" ± CEILING HEIGHT
- TREATED 2"x6" HANDRAIL
- 6"
- 3'-6"
- 1'-9"
- 12"x24" REINFORCED CONCRETE BEAM
- PRESTRESSED CONCRETE PILING, CENTERED ON GRID INTERSECTIONS (UNLESS NOTED)
- TREATED 2"x4" DECK
- TREATED 2"x4" SLEEPERS
- 8" PRESTRESSED DECK

MOTEL AND RESTAURANT 26-28

Wall Sections/A-7

The wall section below is cut through the two-story motel. In addition to showing the floor and roof deck, this section cut details the stair assembly. It also includes items such as floor-to-floor height and materials. The detail blow-up at the right indicates specific points such as tread size and the handrail assembly. Note that the second floor and roof are framed with TJI joists.

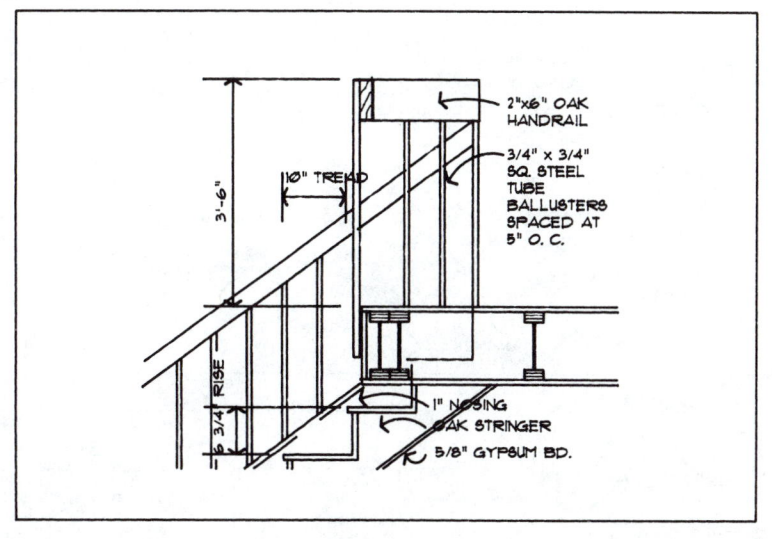

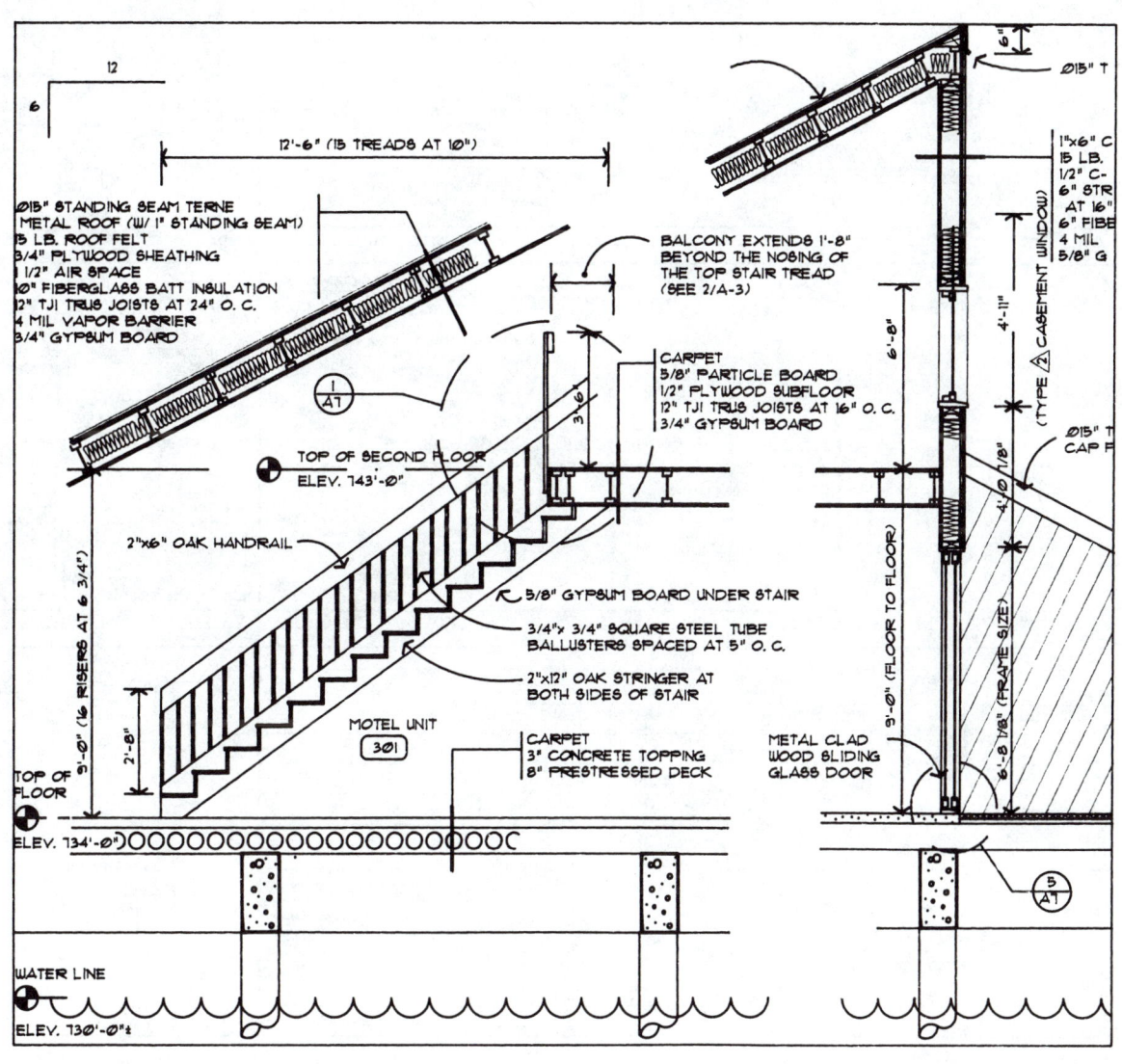

MOTEL AND RESTAURANT

26-29

Miscellaneous Details/A-8

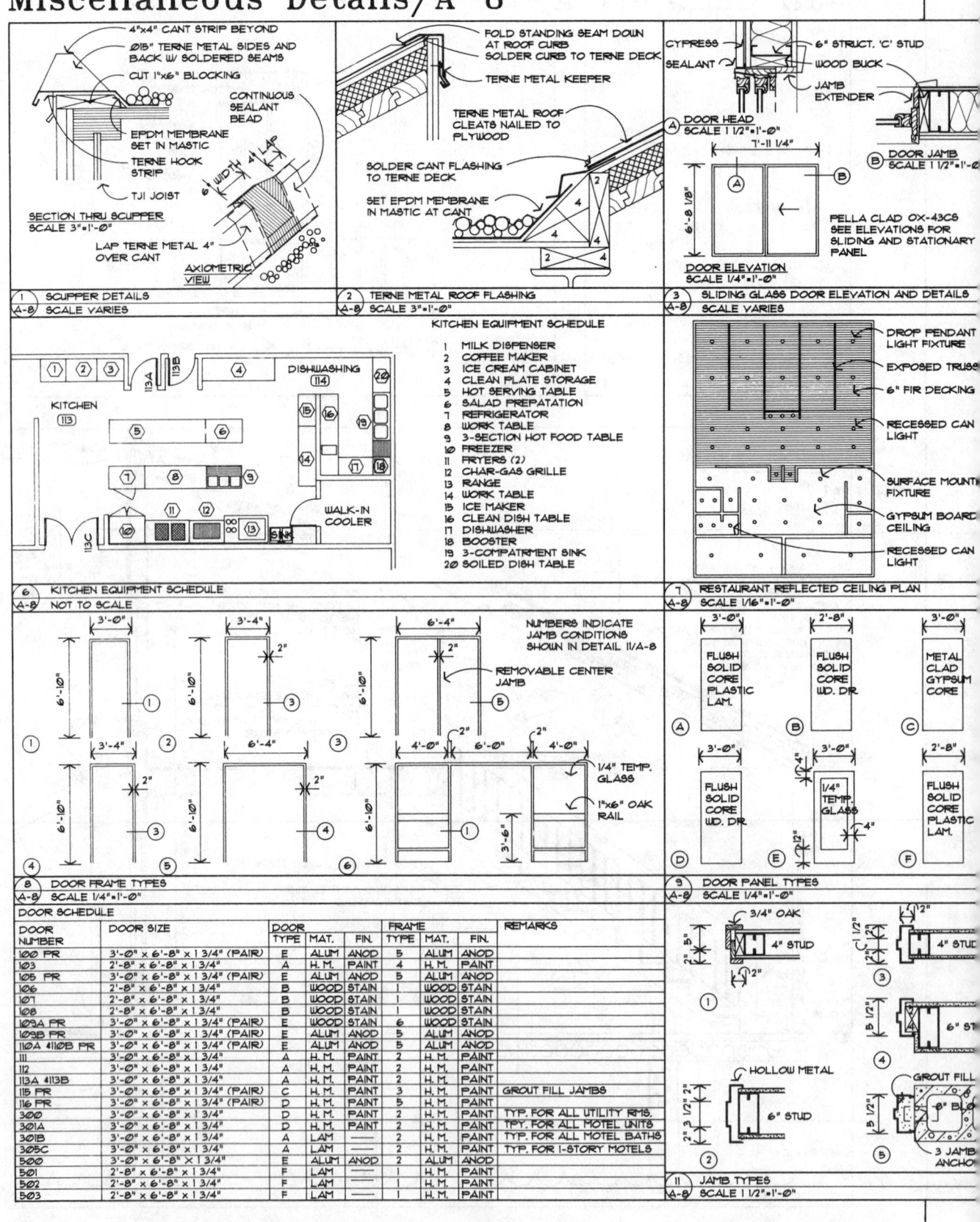

1 - Scupper Details (Scale Varies)

- 4"x4" CANT STRIP BEYOND
- Ø15" TERNE METAL SIDES AND BACK W/ SOLDERED SEAMS
- CUT 1"x6" BLOCKING
- CONTINUOUS SEALANT BEAD
- EPDM MEMBRANE SET IN MASTIC
- TERNE HOOK STRIP
- TJI JOIST
- LAP TERNE METAL 4" OVER CANT

SECTION THRU SCUPPER — SCALE 3"=1'-0"
AXIOMETRIC VIEW

2 - Terne Metal Roof Flashing (Scale 3"=1'-0")

- FOLD STANDING SEAM DOWN AT ROOF CURB
- SOLDER CURB TO TERNE DECK
- TERNE METAL KEEPER
- TERNE METAL ROOF
- CLEATS NAILED TO PLYWOOD
- SOLDER CANT FLASHING TO TERNE DECK
- SET EPDM MEMBRANE IN MASTIC AT CANT

3 - Sliding Glass Door Elevation and Details (Scale Varies)

- CYPRESS
- SEALANT
- 6" STRUCT. 'C' STUD
- WOOD BUCK
- JAMB EXTENDER

A DOOR HEAD — SCALE 1 1/2"=1'-0"
B DOOR JAMB — SCALE 1 1/2"=1'-0"

DOOR ELEVATION — SCALE 1/4"=1'-0"
7'-11 1/4" x 6'-8 1/8"

PELLA CLAD OX-43CS
SEE ELEVATIONS FOR SLIDING AND STATIONARY PANEL

6 - Kitchen Equipment Schedule (Not To Scale)

KITCHEN [113], DISHWASHING [114], WALK-IN COOLER

KITCHEN EQUIPMENT SCHEDULE:
1. MILK DISPENSER
2. COFFEE MAKER
3. ICE CREAM CABINET
4. CLEAN PLATE STORAGE
5. HOT SERVING TABLE
6. SALAD PREPARATION
7. REFRIGERATOR
8. WORK TABLE
9. 3-SECTION HOT FOOD TABLE
10. FREEZER
11. FRYERS (2)
12. CHAR-GAS GRILLE
13. RANGE
14. WORK TABLE
15. ICE MAKER
16. CLEAN DISH TABLE
17. DISHWASHER
18. BOOSTER
19. 3-COMPARTMENT SINK
20. SOILED DISH TABLE

7 - Restaurant Reflected Ceiling Plan (Scale 1/16"=1'-0")

- DROP PENDANT LIGHT FIXTURE
- EXPOSED TRUSS
- 6" FIR DECKING
- RECESSED CAN LIGHT
- SURFACE MOUNT FIXTURE
- GYPSUM BOARD CEILING
- RECESSED CAN LIGHT

8 - Door Frame Types (Scale 1/4"=1'-0")

Frame 1: 3'-0" x 6'-10"
Frame 2: 3'-4" x 6'-10", 2"
Frame 3: 6'-4" x 6'-10", 2" — NUMBERS INDICATE JAMB CONDITIONS SHOWN IN DETAIL 11/A-8; REMOVABLE CENTER JAMB
Frame 4: 3'-4" x 6'-10", 2"
Frame 5: 6'-4" x 6'-10", 2"
Frame 6: 4'-0" + 6'-0" + 4'-0" x 6'-10", 2" — 1/4" TEMP. GLASS; 1"x6" OAK RAIL; 3'-6"

9 - Door Panel Types (Scale 1/4"=1'-0")

A: 3'-0" FLUSH SOLID CORE PLASTIC LAM.
B: 2'-8" FLUSH SOLID CORE WD. DR.
C: 3'-0" METAL CLAD GYPSUM CORE
D: 3'-0" FLUSH SOLID CORE WD. DR.
E: 3'-0" 1/4" TEMP. GLASS (4")
F: 2'-8" FLUSH SOLID CORE PLASTIC LAM.

Door Schedule

DOOR NUMBER	DOOR SIZE	DOOR TYPE	MAT.	FIN.	FRAME TYPE	MAT.	FIN.	REMARKS
100 PR	3'-0" x 6'-8" x 1 3/4" (PAIR)	E	ALUM	ANOD	5	ALUM	ANOD	
103	2'-8" x 6'-8" x 1 3/4"	A	H.M.	PAINT	4	H.M.	PAINT	
105 PR	3'-0" x 6'-8" x 1 3/4" (PAIR)	E	ALUM	ANOD	5	ALUM	ANOD	
106	2'-8" x 6'-8" x 1 3/4"	B	WOOD	STAIN	1	WOOD	STAIN	
107	2'-8" x 6'-8" x 1 3/4"	B	WOOD	STAIN	1	WOOD	STAIN	
108	2'-8" x 6'-8" x 1 3/4"	B	WOOD	STAIN	1	WOOD	STAIN	
109A PR	3'-0" x 6'-8" x 1 3/4" (PAIR)	B	WOOD	STAIN	6	WOOD	STAIN	
109B PR	3'-0" x 6'-8" x 1 3/4" (PAIR)	E	ALUM	ANOD	5	ALUM	ANOD	
110A & 110B PR	3'-0" x 6'-8" x 1 3/4" (PAIR)	E	ALUM	ANOD	5	ALUM	ANOD	
111	3'-0" x 6'-8" x 1 3/4"	A	H.M.	PAINT	2	H.M.	PAINT	
112	3'-0" x 6'-8" x 1 3/4"	A	H.M.	PAINT	2	H.M.	PAINT	
113A & 113B	3'-0" x 6'-8" x 1 3/4"	A	H.M.	PAINT	2	H.M.	PAINT	
115 PR	3'-0" x 6'-8" x 1 3/4" (PAIR)	C	H.M.	PAINT	3	H.M.	PAINT	GROUT FILL JAMBS
116 PR	3'-0" x 6'-8" x 1 3/4" (PAIR)	D	H.M.	PAINT	5	H.M.	PAINT	
300	3'-0" x 6'-8" x 1 3/4"	D	H.M.	PAINT	2	H.M.	PAINT	TYP. FOR ALL UTILITY RMS.
301A	3'-0" x 6'-8" x 1 3/4"	D	H.M.	PAINT	2	H.M.	PAINT	TYP. FOR ALL MOTEL UNITS
301B	3'-0" x 6'-8" x 1 3/4"	A	LAM	—	2	H.M.	PAINT	TYP. FOR ALL MOTEL BATHS
305C	3'-0" x 6'-8" x 1 3/4"	A	LAM	—	2	H.M.	PAINT	TYP. FOR 1-STORY MOTELS
500	3'-0" x 6'-8" x 1 3/4"	E	ALUM	ANOD	2	ALUM	ANOD	
501	2'-8" x 6'-8" x 1 3/4"	F	LAM	—	1	H.M.	PAINT	
502	2'-8" x 6'-8" x 1 3/4"	F	LAM	—	1	H.M.	PAINT	
503	2'-8" x 6'-8" x 1 3/4"	F	LAM	—	1	H.M.	PAINT	

11 - Jamb Types (Scale 1 1/2"=1'-0")

1: 3/4" OAK, 4" STUD
2: HOLLOW METAL, 6" STUD
3: 4" STUD
4: 6" STUD
5: GROUT FILL, 8" BLOCK, 3 JAMB ANCHORS

MOTEL AND RESTAURANT — 26-30

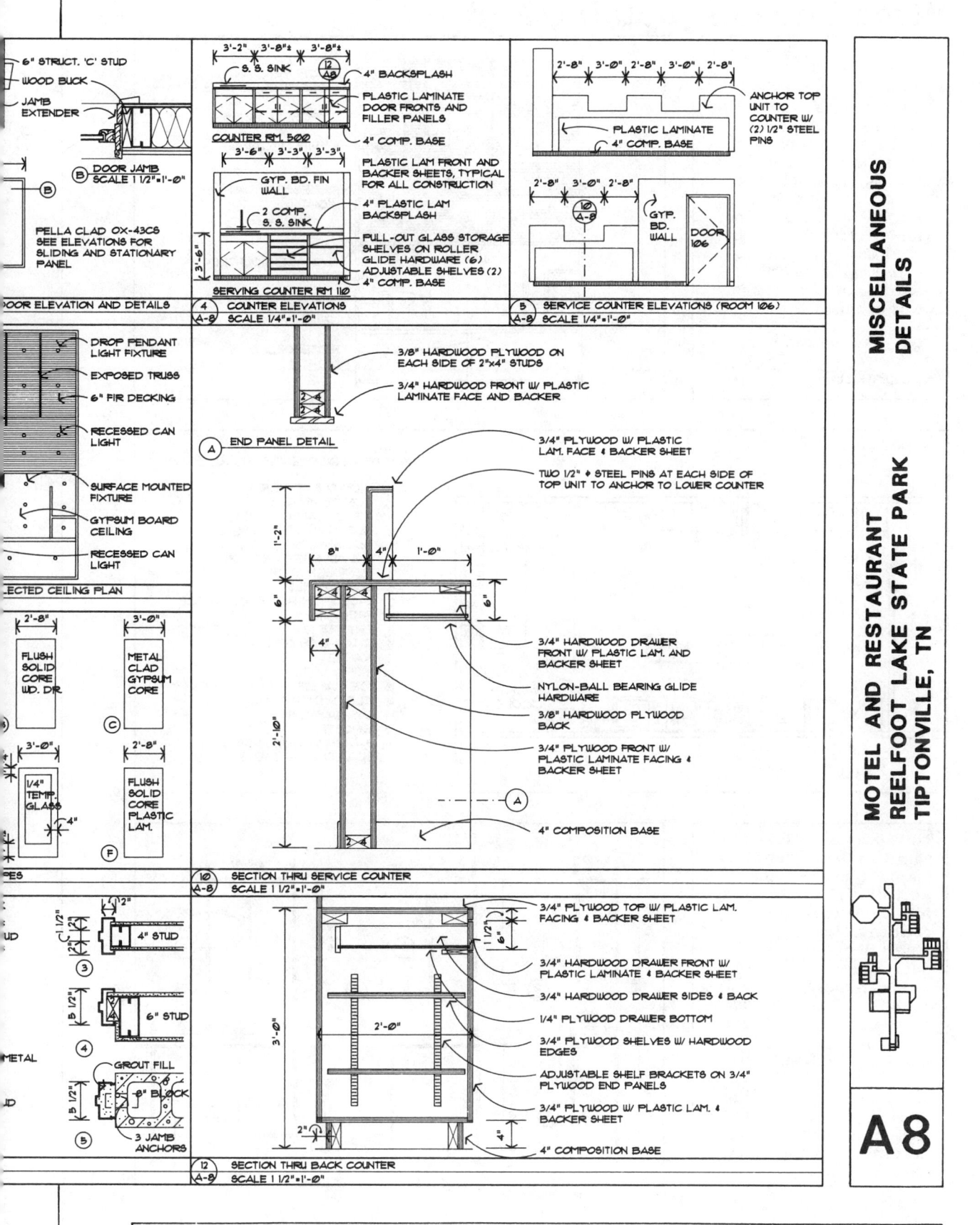

MISCELLANEOUS DETAILS

MOTEL AND RESTAURANT
REELFOOT LAKE STATE PARK
TIPTONVILLE, TN

A8

MOTEL AND RESTAURANT — 26-31

Door Jamb (B)
- 6" STRUCT. 'C' STUD
- WOOD BUCK
- JAMB EXTENDER
- PELLA CLAD OX-43CS SEE ELEVATIONS FOR SLIDING AND STATIONARY PANEL

SCALE 1 1/2"=1'-0"

Counter Elevations (4 / A-8)
SCALE 1/4"=1'-0"

COUNTER RM. 500
- 3'-2", 3'-8"±, 3'-8"±
- S.S. SINK
- 4" BACKSPLASH
- PLASTIC LAMINATE DOOR FRONTS AND FILLER PANELS
- 4" COMP. BASE

SERVING COUNTER RM. 110
- 3'-6", 3'-3", 3'-3"
- GYP. BD. FIN WALL
- 2 COMP. S.S. SINK
- 3'-6"
- PLASTIC LAM FRONT AND BACKER SHEETS, TYPICAL FOR ALL CONSTRUCTION
- 4" PLASTIC LAM BACKSPLASH
- PULL-OUT GLASS STORAGE SHELVES ON ROLLER GLIDE HARDWARE (6)
- ADJUSTABLE SHELVES (2)
- 4" COMP. BASE

Service Counter Elevations (Room 106) (5 / A-8)
SCALE 1/4"=1'-0"

- 2'-8", 3'-0", 2'-8", 3'-0", 2'-8"
- PLASTIC LAMINATE
- 4" COMP. BASE
- ANCHOR TOP UNIT TO COUNTER W/ (2) 1/2" STEEL PINS
- 2'-8", 3'-0", 2'-8"
- GYP. BD. WALL
- DOOR 106

Reflected Ceiling Plan
- DROP PENDANT LIGHT FIXTURE
- EXPOSED TRUSS
- 6" FIR DECKING
- RECESSED CAN LIGHT
- SURFACE MOUNTED FIXTURE
- GYPSUM BOARD CEILING
- RECESSED CAN LIGHT

Door Types
- (C) 2'-8" FLUSH SOLID CORE WD. DR.
- 3'-0" METAL CLAD GYPSUM CORE
- (F) 3'-0" 1/4" TEMP. GLASS
- 2'-8" FLUSH SOLID CORE PLASTIC LAM.

End Panel Detail (A)
- 3/8" HARDWOOD PLYWOOD ON EACH SIDE OF 2"x4" STUDS
- 3/4" HARDWOOD FRONT W/ PLASTIC LAMINATE FACE AND BACKER

Section Thru Service Counter (10 / A-8)
SCALE 1 1/2"=1'-0"

- 3/4" PLYWOOD W/ PLASTIC LAM. FACE & BACKER SHEET
- TWO 1/2" Ø STEEL PINS AT EACH SIDE OF TOP UNIT TO ANCHOR TO LOWER COUNTER
- 8", 4", 1'-0"
- 1'-2", 6", 6", 4", 2'-10"
- 3/4" HARDWOOD DRAWER FRONT W/ PLASTIC LAM. AND BACKER SHEET
- NYLON-BALL BEARING GLIDE HARDWARE
- 3/8" HARDWOOD PLYWOOD BACK
- 3/4" PLYWOOD FRONT W/ PLASTIC LAMINATE FACING & BACKER SHEET
- 4" COMPOSITION BASE

Wall Types
- (3) 4" STUD, 1/2", 1/2"
- (4) 6" STUD, 5 1/2"
- (5) 8" BLOCK, GROUT FILL, 5 1/2", 3 JAMB ANCHORS

Section Thru Back Counter (12 / A-8)
SCALE 1 1/2"=1'-0"

- 3/4" PLYWOOD TOP W/ PLASTIC LAM. FACING & BACKER SHEET
- 1 1/2", 6"
- 3/4" HARDWOOD DRAWER FRONT W/ PLASTIC LAMINATE & BACKER SHEET
- 3/4" HARDWOOD DRAWER SIDES & BACK
- 1/4" PLYWOOD DRAWER BOTTOM
- 3'-0", 2'-0"
- 3/4" PLYWOOD SHELVES W/ HARDWOOD EDGES
- ADJUSTABLE SHELF BRACKETS ON 3/4" PLYWOOD END PANELS
- 3/4" PLYWOOD W/ PLASTIC LAM. & BACKER SHEET
- 2", 4"
- 4" COMPOSITION BASE

Miscellaneous Details/A-8

The plan at the right illustrates the reflected ceiling in the kitchen and dining rooms. The solid lines in the dining room indicate the exposed wood trusses. The closely spaced parallel lines define the timber deck, and circles show light fixtures. The intent of this plan is to coordinate the design of the ceiling.

The plan below uses a key to locate kitchen equipment.

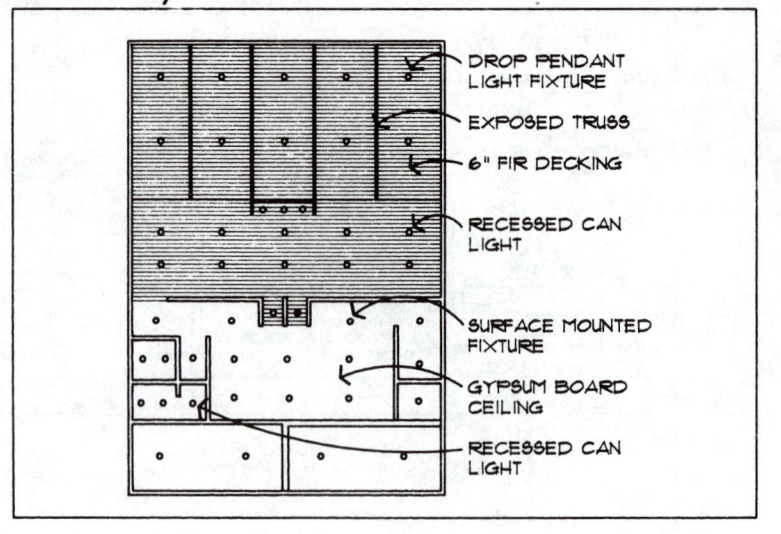

- DROP PENDANT LIGHT FIXTURE
- EXPOSED TRUSS
- 6" FIR DECKING
- RECESSED CAN LIGHT
- SURFACE MOUNTED FIXTURE
- GYPSUM BOARD CEILING
- RECESSED CAN LIGHT

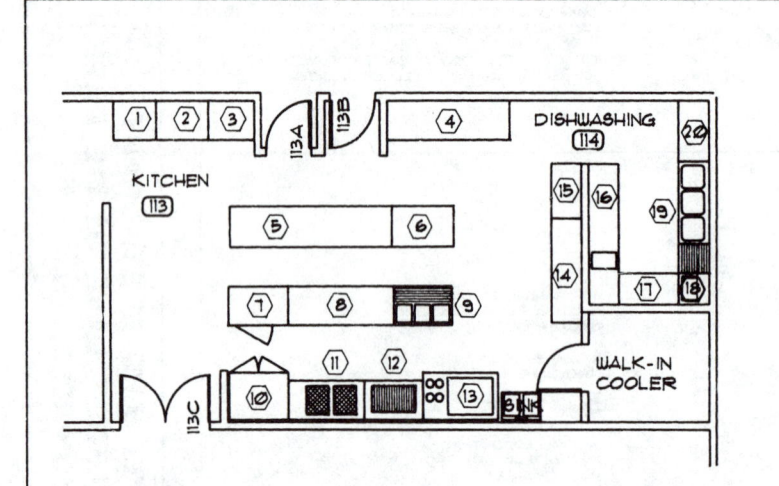

KITCHEN EQUIPMENT SCHEDULE

1. MILK DISPENSER
2. COFFEE MAKER
3. ICE CREAM CABINET
4. CLEAN PLATE STORAGE
5. HOT SERVING TABLE
6. SALAD PREPARATION
7. REFRIGERATOR
8. WORK TABLE
9. 3-SECTION HOT FOOD TABLE
10. FREEZER
11. FRYERS (2)
12. CHAR-GAS GRILLE
13. RANGE
14. WORK TABLE
15. ICE MAKER
16. CLEAN DISH TABLE
17. DISHWASHER
18. BOOSTER
19. 3-COMPARTMENT SINK
20. SOILED DISH TABLE

This drawing illustrates some of the door frame types on the project. (The frames for the entire job are concentrated in one detail located near the door schedule.) The jamb thickness is 2", which makes the width of the frame 4" wider than the door. In addition to frame sizes, the drawing indicates jamb conditions using circled numbers. Wood, hollow metal, and aluminum frames are used on this job.

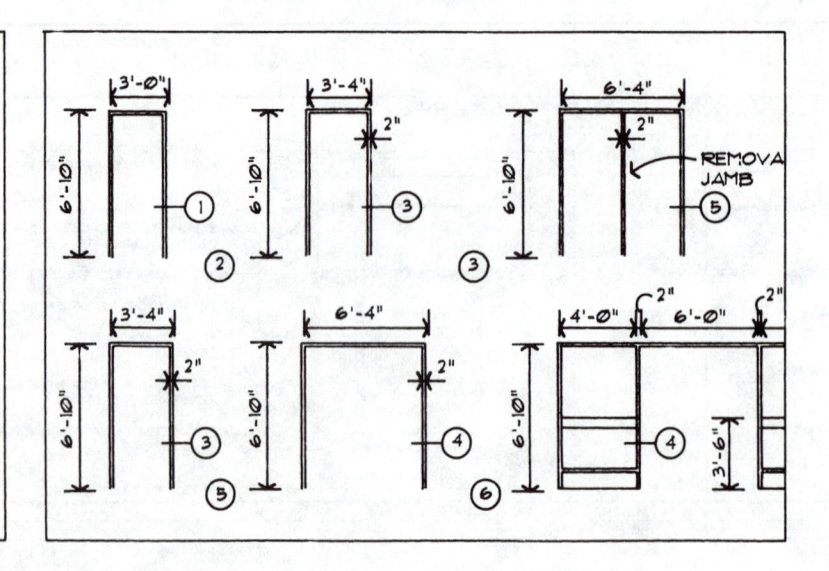

MOTEL AND RESTAURANT 26-32

Miscellaneous Details/A-8

The schedule at the right uses the door numbers on the floor plan to define the size, shape, and material used for all doors. (The schedule should be coordinated with the floor plan to determine the correct sizes and materials.) The door detail shown below cuts through each jamb as it intersects a wall. Jambs on the project consist of wood, hollow metal (bent sheet steel), or extruded aluminum.

DOOR SCHEDULE

DOOR NUMBER	DOOR SIZE	DOOR TYPE	MAT.	FIN.	FRAME TYPE	
100 PR	3'-0" x 6'-8" x 1 3/4" (PAIR)	E	ALUM	ANOD	5	A
103	2'-8" x 6'-8" x 1 3/4"	A	H. M.	PAINT	4	H
105 PR	3'-0" x 6'-8" x 1 3/4" (PAIR)	E	ALUM	ANOD	5	A
106	2'-8" x 6'-8" x 1 3/4"	B	WOOD	STAIN	1	W
107	2'-8" x 6'-8" x 1 3/4"	B	WOOD	STAIN	1	W
108	2'-8" x 6'-8" x 1 3/4"	B	WOOD	STAIN	1	W
109A PR	3'-0" x 6'-8" x 1 3/4" (PAIR)	E	WOOD	STAIN	6	W
109B PR	3'-0" x 6'-8" x 1 3/4" (PAIR)	E	ALUM	ANOD	5	A
110A & 110B PR	3'-0" x 6'-8" x 1 3/4" (PAIR)	E	ALUM	ANOD	5	A
111	3'-0" x 6'-8" x 1 3/4"	A	H. M.	PAINT	2	H
112	3'-0" x 6'-8" x 1 3/4"	A	H. M.	PAINT	2	H
113A & 113B	3'-0" x 6'-8" x 1 3/4"	A	H. M.	PAINT	2	H
115 PR	3'-0" x 6'-8" x 1 3/4" (PAIR)	C	H. M.	PAINT	3	H
116 PR	3'-0" x 6'-8" x 1 3/4" (PAIR)	D	H. M.	PAINT	5	H
300	3'-0" x 6'-8" x 1 3/4"	D	H. M.	PAINT	2	H
301A	3'-0" x 6'-8" x 1 3/4"	D	H. M.	PAINT	2	H
301B	3'-0" x 6'-8" x 1 3/4"	A	LAM	———	2	H
305C	3'-0" x 6'-8" x 1 3/4"	A	LAM	———	2	H
500	3'-0" x 6'-8" x 1 3/4"	E	ALUM	ANOD	2	A
501	2'-8" x 6'-8" x 1 3/4"	F	LAM	———	1	H
502	2'-8" x 6'-8" x 1 3/4"	F	LAM	———	1	H

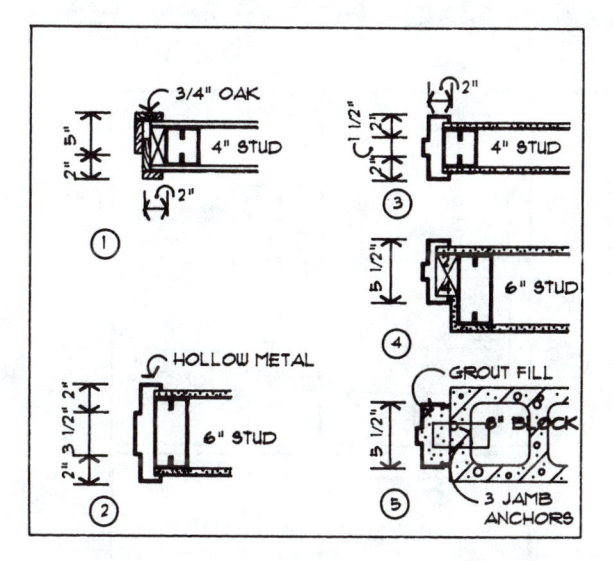

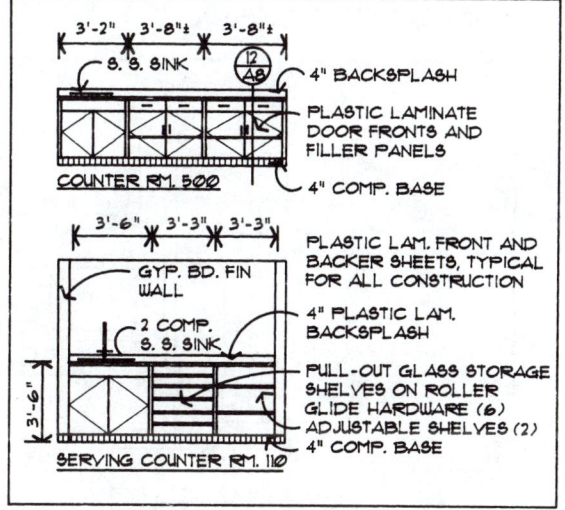

Midddle and lower right drawings illustrate cabinet details. A 1/4" = 1'-0" elevation view of a serving counter in the dining room (middle right) includes counter dimensions, locations of doors and drawers, and types of materials used. A larger-scale section cut through the cabinet (bottom right) provides the cabinet fabricator with information necessary to build the unit.

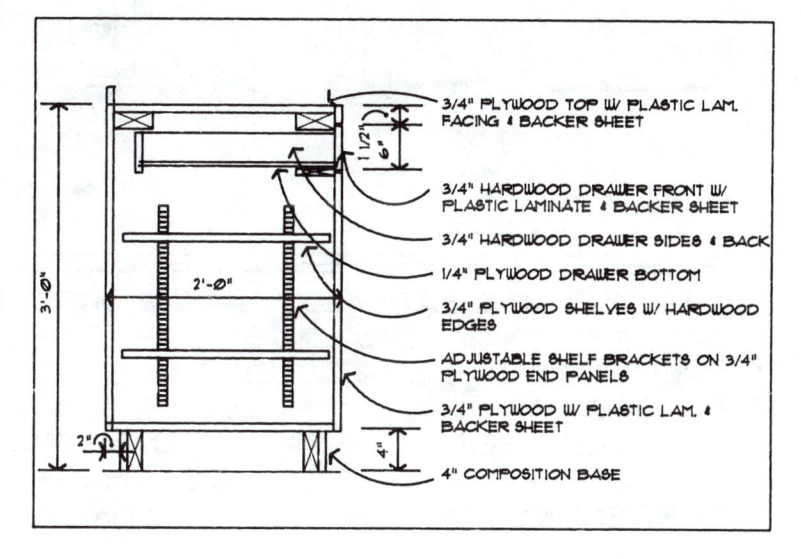

MOTEL AND RESTAURANT

26-33

REPLAY
ASSEMBLE A SET OF CONSTRUCTION DRAWINGS FOR THE MOTEL AND RESTAURANT PRESENTED IN THIS UNIT. USE THE INSTRUCTIONS LISTED BELOW TO PREPARE THE DRAWING PACKAGE.

1. PREPARE AN 1/8" SCALE FLOOR PLAN ON TRACING PAPER.
2. BUILD A 1/16" SCALE STUDY MODEL OF YOUR PROJECT (PAGES 29-18 THROUGH 29-24).
3. SKETCH A FRAMING PLAN SHOWING JOISTS, BEAMS, AND LOAD-BEARING WALLS.
4. DRAW BUILDING SECTIONS THROUGH SEVERAL PLACES IN THE MOTEL AND RESTAURANT BUILDINGS.
5. PREPARE A SHEET LAYOUT FOR THE DRAWING PACKAGE ON 8 1/2" x 11" TYPING PAPER. YOUR LAYOUT COULD BE SIMILAR TO ONE PRESENTED IN THIS UNIT, BUT TRY TO VARY THE ORGANIZATION. BE SURE TO ALLOW ENOUGH ROOM FOR NOTES AND DIMENSIONS.

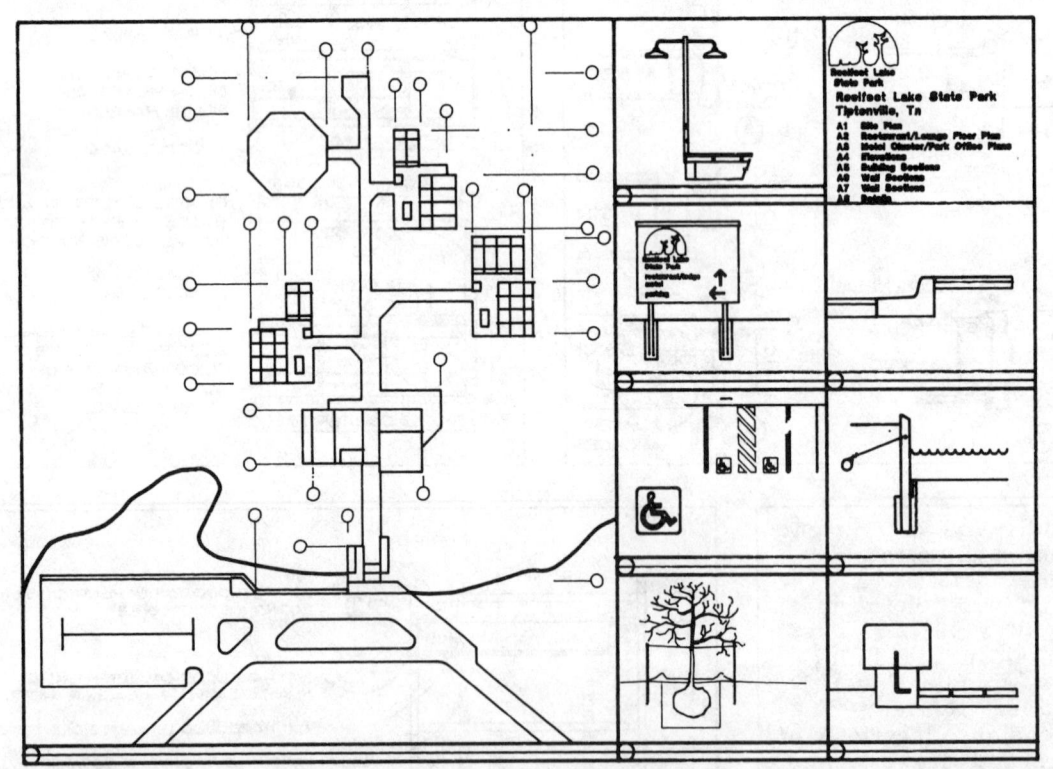

6. ONCE YOU ARE SATISFIED WITH THE SHEET LAYOUT, TRANSFER THE PRELIMINARY DRAWINGS TO THE FINAL VELLUM SHEETS.
7. PREPARE A TIME SCHEDULE FOR THE ASSEMBLY OF THE DRAWING SET (REFER TO UNIT 11, "PROBLEM SOLVING").
8. PREPARE A SET OF PRINTS OF YOUR PROJECT AT APPROXIMATELY 50% AND 75% COMPLETION. USE A FELT-TIP PEN TO MAKE CORRECTIONS AND CHANGES IN YOUR WORK.

MOTEL AND RESTAURANT

27 STUDENT LIBRARY

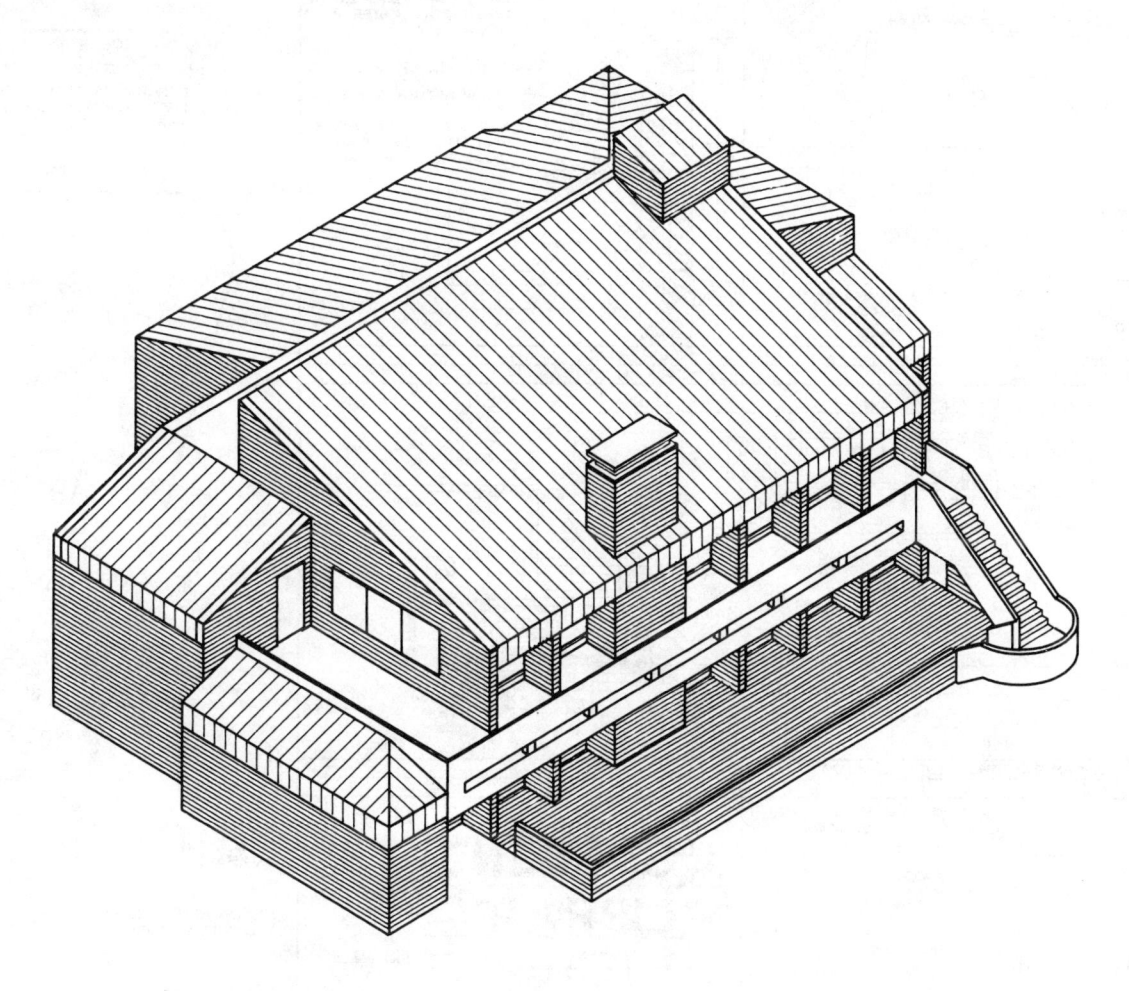

THIS UNIT PRESENTS THE WORKING DRAWINGS FOR THE COLLEGE LIBRARY PROJECT. THE TWO-STORY BRICK BUILDING IS ON A SLOPED SITE WITH A 10' CHANGE IN GRADE. THE READING ROOM HAS A VAULTED CEILING THAT IS STRUCTURED USING WOOD LAMINATED BEAMS AND TIMBER DECKING.

STUDENT LIBRARY   27-1

Site Plan/A-1

1 BICYCLE PARKING BOLLARDS — A-1 SCALE VARIES
- 1 1/2" × 30°
- 6"×6" ROUGH-SAWN TIMBER
- 2"Ø HOLE
- TREATED 2×10 W/ 16d GALV. NAILS
- SECTION 1/2"=1'-0"
- PLAN 1/4"=1'-0"
- SET BOLLARD IN AGGREGATE BASE
- ELEVATION 1/2"=1'-0"

2 BRICK RETAINING WALL — A-1 SCALE 1"=1'-0"
- 1 1/2"Ø PIPE RAIL
- 4" FACE BRICK
- 8" CONCRETE BLOCK
- 10 GA STAINLESS STEEL WIRE
- 2" PVC DRAIN AT 5'-0" O.C.
- 6"Ø CONCRETE DEADMAN

3 HANDICAP PARKING ZONE — A-1 SCALE 1/8"=1'-0"
- EXPOSED AGGREGATE CONCRETE
- SEE 1/A-1 FOR BIKE BOLLARD
- 6" CURB & GUTTER
- 5' SIDEWALK CONTROL JOINTS
- HANDICAP RAMP AT 1:12 SLOPE
- 4" STRIPE PAINTED W/ TRAFFIC PAINT
- 4" WIDE PAINTED FIGURE
- 12'-6", 12'-6", 20'-0", 4'-0"

5 EXTERIOR STAIR DETAIL — A-1 SCALE 1 1/2"=1'-0"
- BRICK PAVERS SET IN CONCRETE
- STIFF BRISTLE BROOM FINISH ACROSS TREAD
- 8" GRANULAR SUBBASE

6 BENCH DETAIL — A-1 SCALE 1"=1'-0"
- STONE CAP ANCHORED TO BRICK WITH 1"Ø STEEL PINS AT 2'-6" O.C.
- GROUT FILL BRICK CAVITY
- 2"×4" REDWOOD SLATS
- 3 1/2"×3 1/2"×1/4" ANGLES WELDED TOGETHER AND ANCHORED TO BRICK

7 HANDICAP RAMP/FRONT ENTRY BLOW-UP — A-1 SCALE 1/8"=1'-0"
- CONCRETE SIDEWALK
- 1:12 RAMP DOWN
- ELEV. 89'-9"
- ELEV. 88'-0"
- ELEV. 91'-3"
- 3"Ø PIPE HANDRAIL
- FLAGPOLE DETAIL SEE 4/A-1
- BRICK WALL
- 8" BRICK WALL WITH 3 1/2" STONE CAP (SEE DETAIL 6/A-1)
- BROOM FINISH POURED CONCRETE RAMP
- ELEV. 82'-6" BRICK
- 6 TREADS @ 10"
- BENCH DETAIL
- SODDED AREA

8 WALK LIGHT DETAIL — A-1 SCALE 1/4"=1'-0"
- MERCURY VAPOR LAMP IN ANODIZED ALUM. HOUSING
- ANODIZED ALUM. LIGHT POLE. TOP DIA. 3", BOTTOM DIA. 4"
- SPACE LIGHT POLES 4'-0" FROM SIDEWALK
- ANODIZED ALUM. COVER PLATE
- ANCHOR BOLTS (SUPPLIED BY LIGHT MANUFACTURER)
- POURED CONCRETE
- BURIED CONDUIT
- 12'-0", 4'-0"

9 ALUMINUM ENTRY LETTERS — A-1 SCALE VARIES
- STUDENT LIBRARY
- 6" CAST ALUM. LETTERS
- ELEVATION
- STONE CAP
- QUICK SETTING CEMENT
- SPACING COLLAR
- LETTER
- SECTION / MOUNTING DETAIL

10 SITE PLAN — A-1 SCALE 1/16"=1'-0"
- BENCH MARK ELEVATION 91.25' (ARROW ON TOP OF FIRE HYDRANT)
- SOD
- JOHN TYLER DRIVE
- 4'-0" HIGH BRICK RETAINING WALL AROUND TRASH DUMPSTER STORAGE
- REMOVE EXISTING CURB AND GUTTER AND PATCH OPENING
- 6" CONCRETE CURB AND GUTTER (TYPICAL)
- 3" CALIPER MAGNOLIA TREES (TYPICAL)

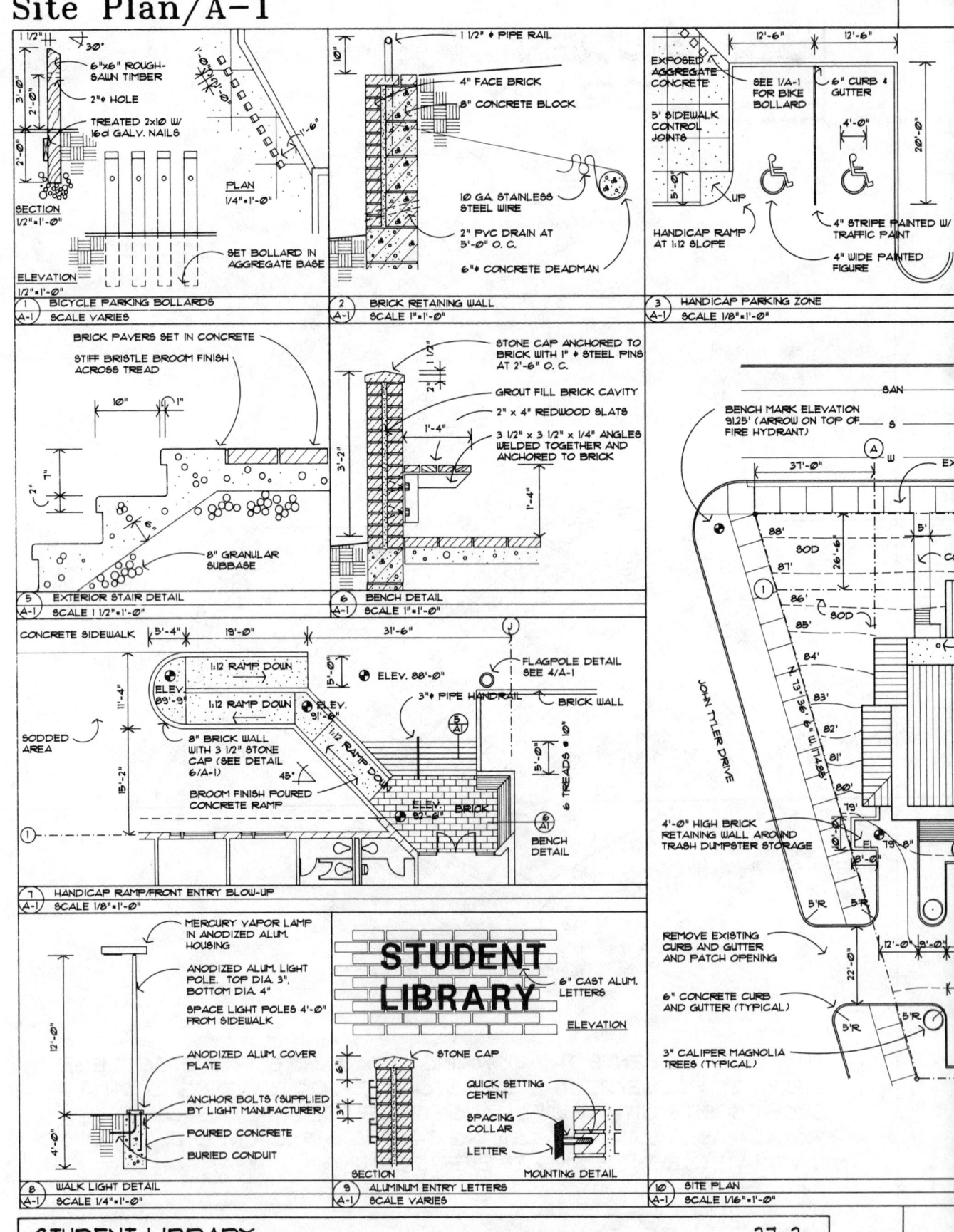

STUDENT LIBRARY

27-2

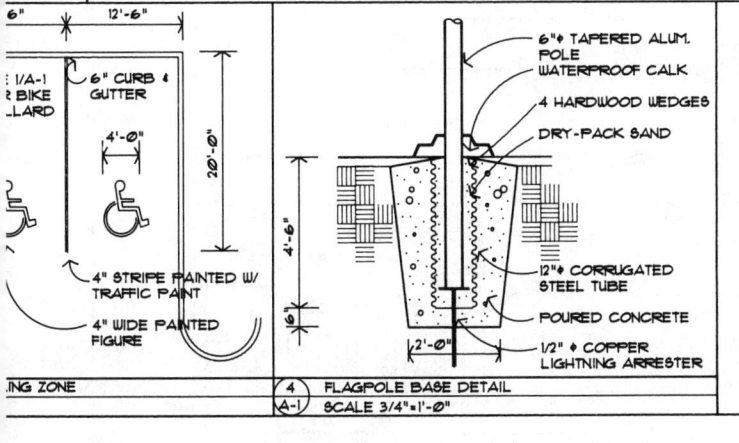

STUDENT LIBRARY
PEPPERDINE UNIVERSITY
MALIBU, CA

SHEET   DRAWINGS

- A-1   SITE PLAN
- A-2   FIRST-FLOOR PLAN
- A-3   SECOND-FLOOR PLAN
- A-4   ELEVATIONS
- A-5   BUILDING SECTIONS
- A-6   WALL SECTIONS
- A-7   WALL SECTIONS
- A-8   STAIR & CEILING DETAILS
- A-9   MISCELLANEOUS DETAILS

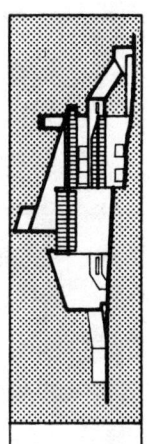

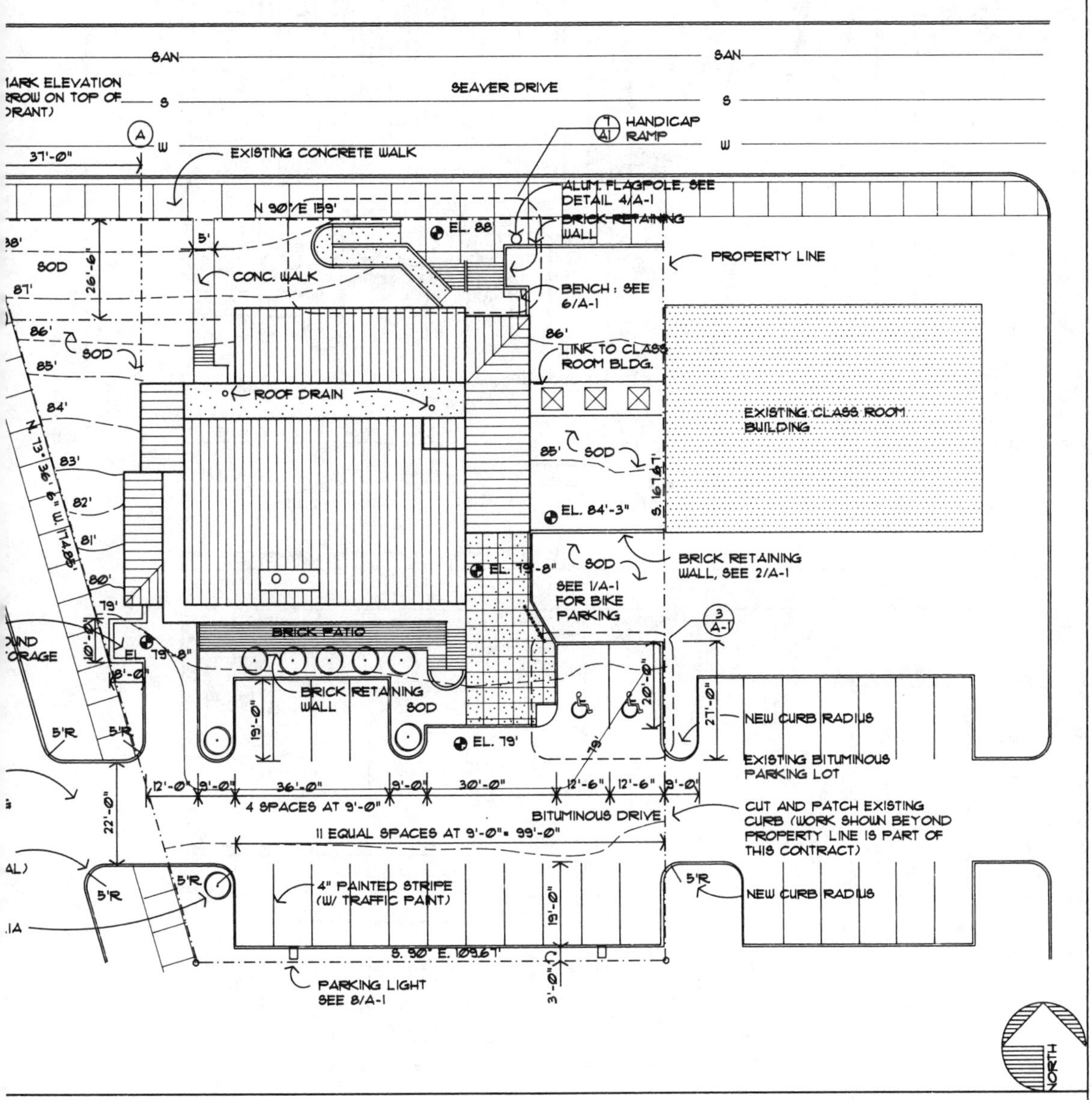

SITE PLAN

**STUDENT LIBRARY
PEPPERDINE UNIVERSITY
MALIBU, CA**

A1

STUDENT LIBRARY

27-3

Site Plan/A-1

A site plan must direct all construction changes on the exterior of the building. Topographic contours must match the entry heights; roads must be dimensioned and trees noted. The drawing at the right shows that building grids "A" and "1" are dimensioned from the property line. The bench mark on the fire hydrant indicates the source for vertical dimensions, and spot elevations are indicated at the building entries.

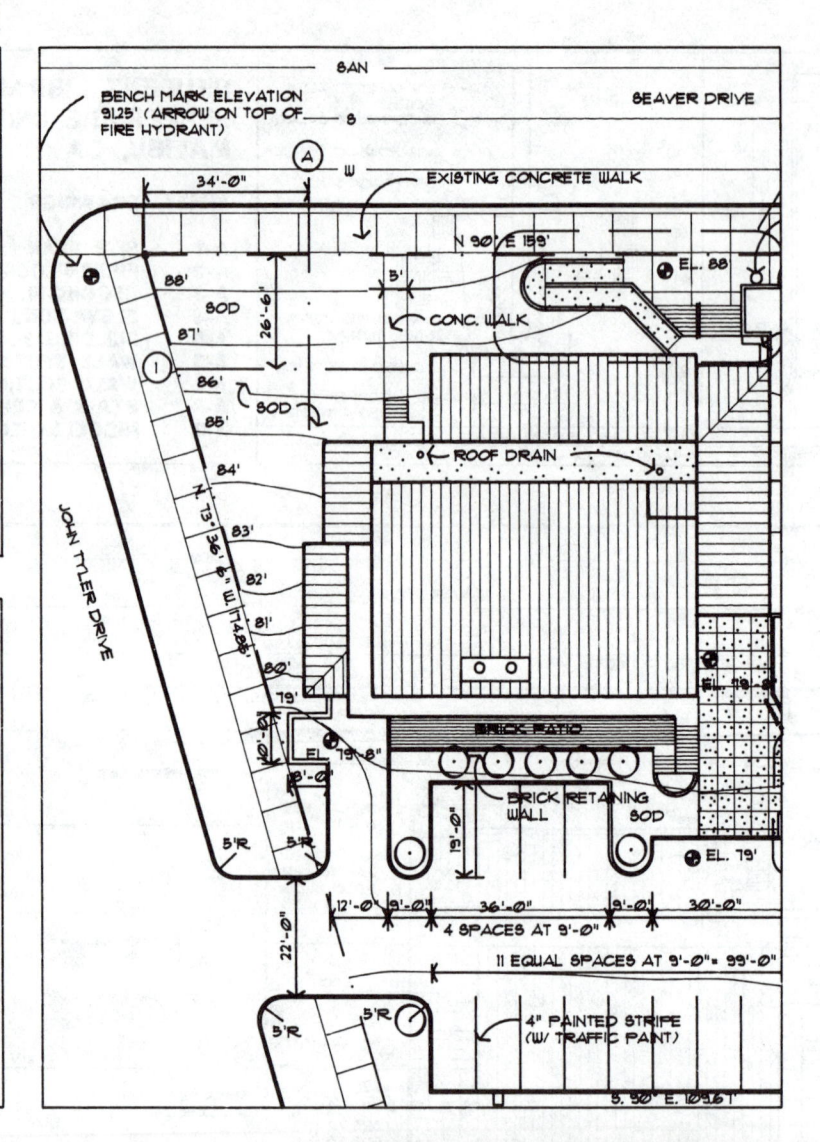

The detail at the lower left illustrates the dimensions and notes used to define two handicap parking stalls. Items such as the location of the ramp up to the walk and the size of the painted symbol are included. The detail at the right shows an enlarged portion of the parking lot. It is important to locate all parking spaces and curbs by dimension string (either from the grids or the property lines).

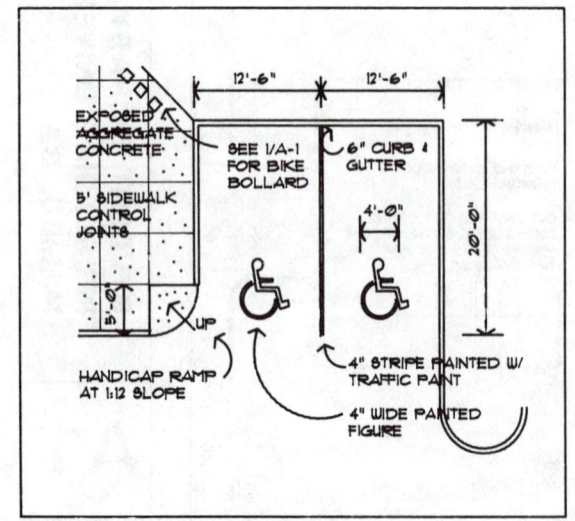

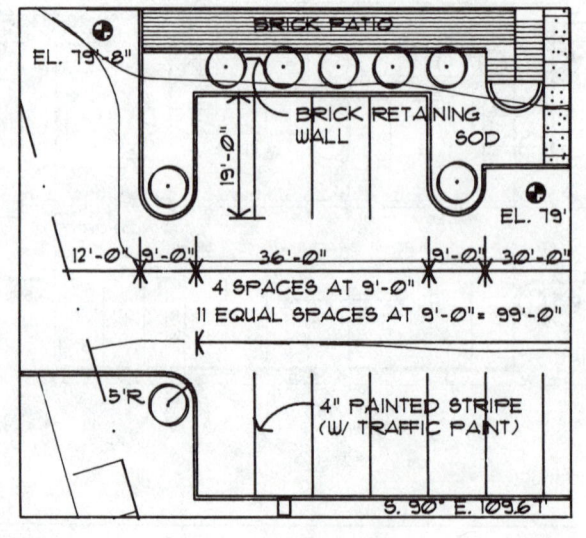

STUDENT LIBRARY

27-4

Site Plan/A-1

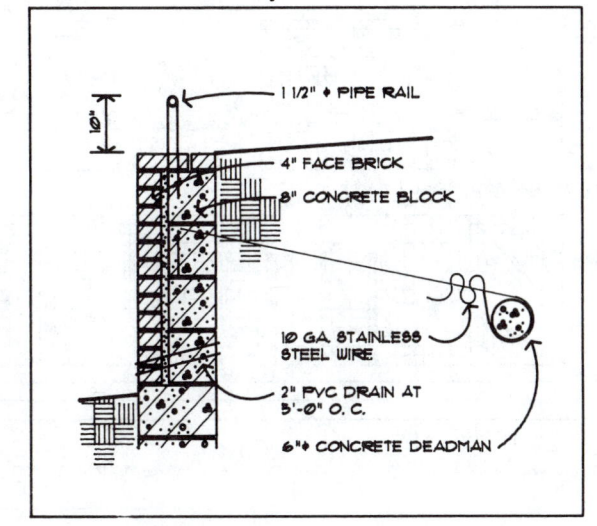

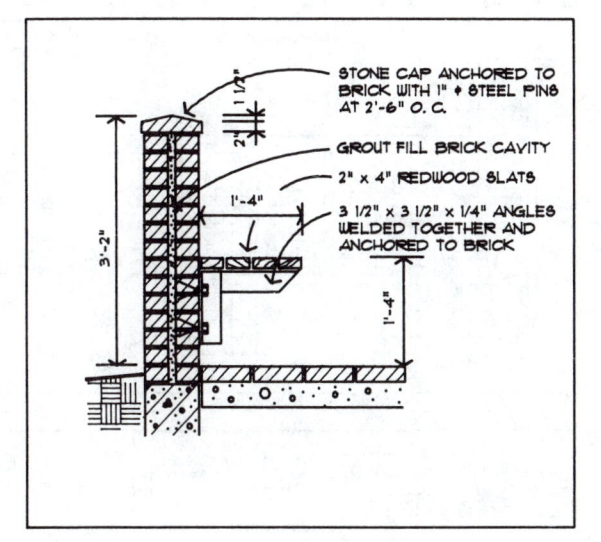

Site details should address all specific items to be built on the exterior of a project. These top four details define a wide range of construction on the site. The retaining wall shown above (top left) uses a concrete log (called a deadman) to counteract the weight of the earth. The bottom left detail illustrates a 6" wooden post design for locking bicycles. All details should be keyed to the site plan.

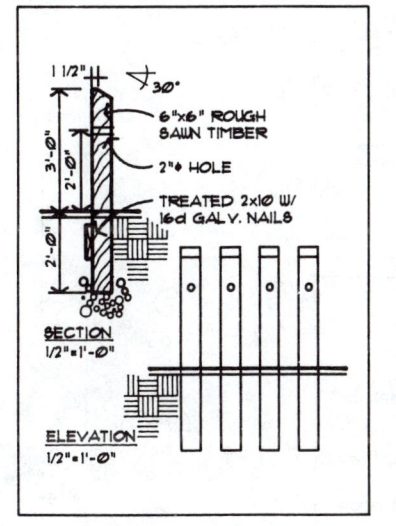

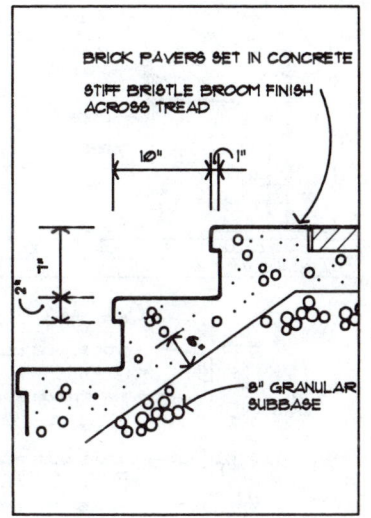

The handicap ramp at the right is enlarged to a 1/4" scale in order to define and dimension its construction. The location of the ramp is dimensioned from the building grids. The maximum ramp slope is shown on the detail (1' rise in a 12' length), and spot elevations are given at each landing. Note that the ramp is shown on the smaller-scale site plan and is keyed to this detail.

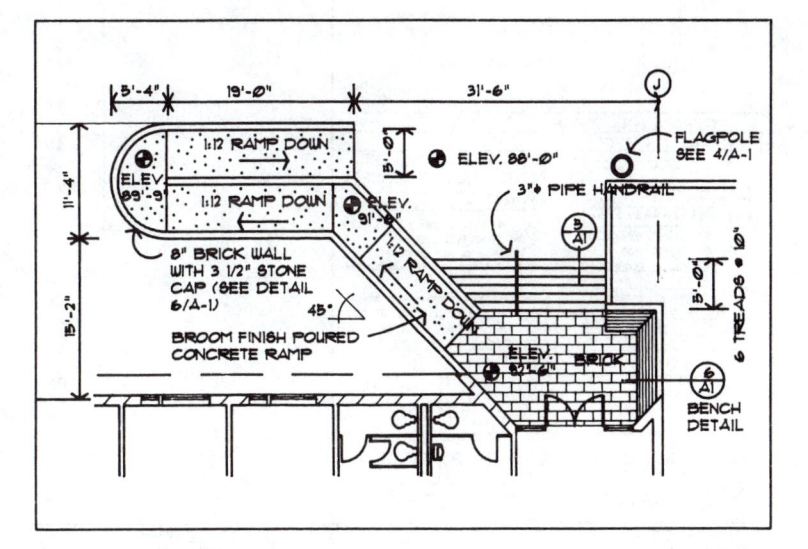

STUDENT LIBRARY

27-5

# First-Floor Plan/A-2

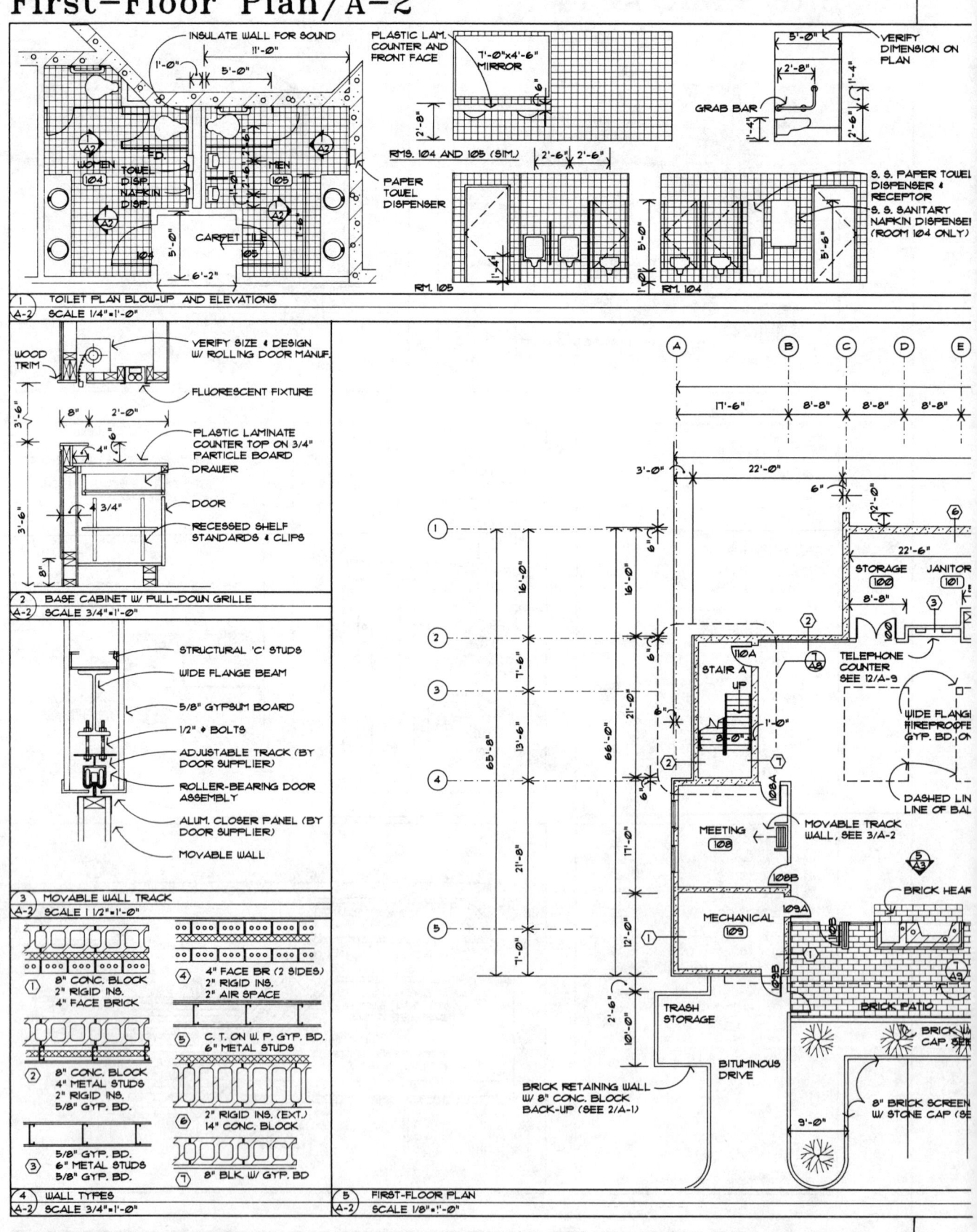

STUDENT LIBRARY

27-6

FIRST-FLOOR ROOM FINISH SCHEDULE

ROOM NUMBER	ROOM NAME	FLOOR	BASE	WALL MAT.	WALL FINISH	CEILING MAT.	REMARKS
100	STORAGE	VINYL TILE	VINYL	GYP. BD.	PAINT	A. C. TILE	
101	JANITOR	VINYL TILE	VINYL	GYP. BD.	PAINT	A. C. TILE	
102	LOUNGE	CARPET	VINYL	GYP. BD.	PAINT	A. C. TILE	(3)
103	CHECK-OUT	CARPET	VINYL	GYP. BD.	PAINT	A. C. TILE	
104	WOMEN	CERAMIC TILE	CERAMIC T.	GYP. BD.	CERAMIC T.	GYP. BD.	C. T. TO CLNG.
105	MEN	CERAMIC TILE	CERAMIC T.	GYP. BD.	CERAMIC T.	GYP. BD.	C. T. TO CLNG.
106	LINK	CARPET	VINYL	GYP. BD.	PAINT	METAL SLATS	(3)
107	FOYER	QUARRY TILE	BRICK	BRICK	EXPOSED	METAL SLATS	(2)
108	MEETING	CARPET	WOOD	GYP. BD.	PAINT	T & G FIR	(4)
109	MECHANICAL	CONCRETE	NONE	CONC. BLK	EXPOSED	GYP. BD.	(1)
110	READING	CARPET	WOOD	BRICK	EXPOSED	T & G FIR	(2)

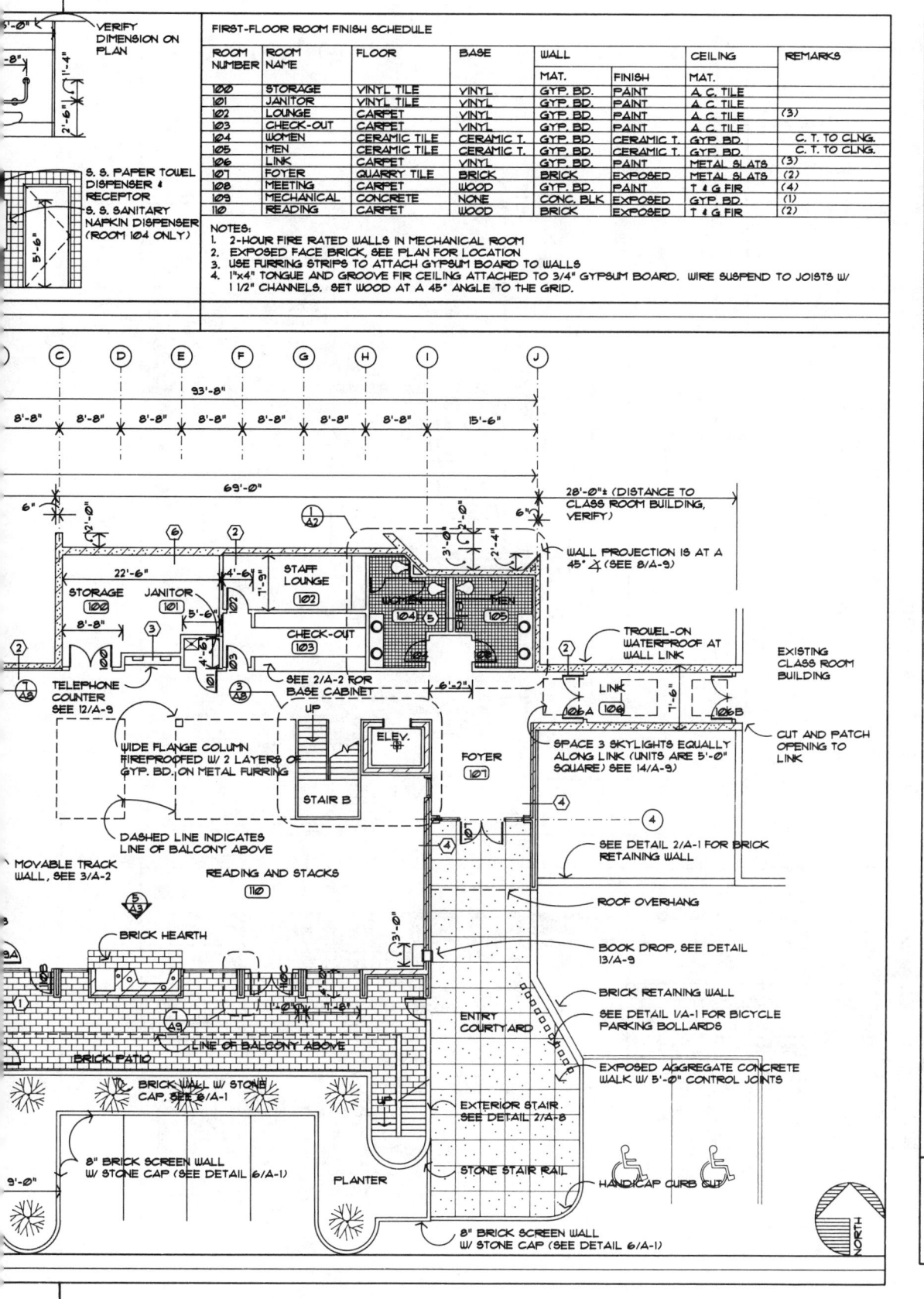

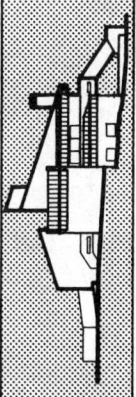

NOTES:
1. 2-HOUR FIRE RATED WALLS IN MECHANICAL ROOM
2. EXPOSED FACE BRICK, SEE PLAN FOR LOCATION
3. USE FURRING STRIPS TO ATTACH GYPSUM BOARD TO WALLS
4. 1"x4" TONGUE AND GROOVE FIR CEILING ATTACHED TO 3/4" GYPSUM BOARD. WIRE SUSPEND TO JOISTS W/ 1 1/2" CHANNELS. SET WOOD AT A 45° ANGLE TO THE GRID.

FIRST-FLOOR PLAN

STUDENT LIBRARY
PEPPERDINE UNIVERSITY
MALIBU, CA

A2

STUDENT LIBRARY

27-7

First-Floor Plan/A-2

The partial first-floor plan at the right illustrates the amount of detail needed in a construction drawing. Locating structural grids is the first step in producing a plan. The next step is to draw exterior walls, which are offset from the grid lines. Note that construction details for interior and exterior walls are identified by hexagonal wall types. All walls are located by dimension string from the grid.

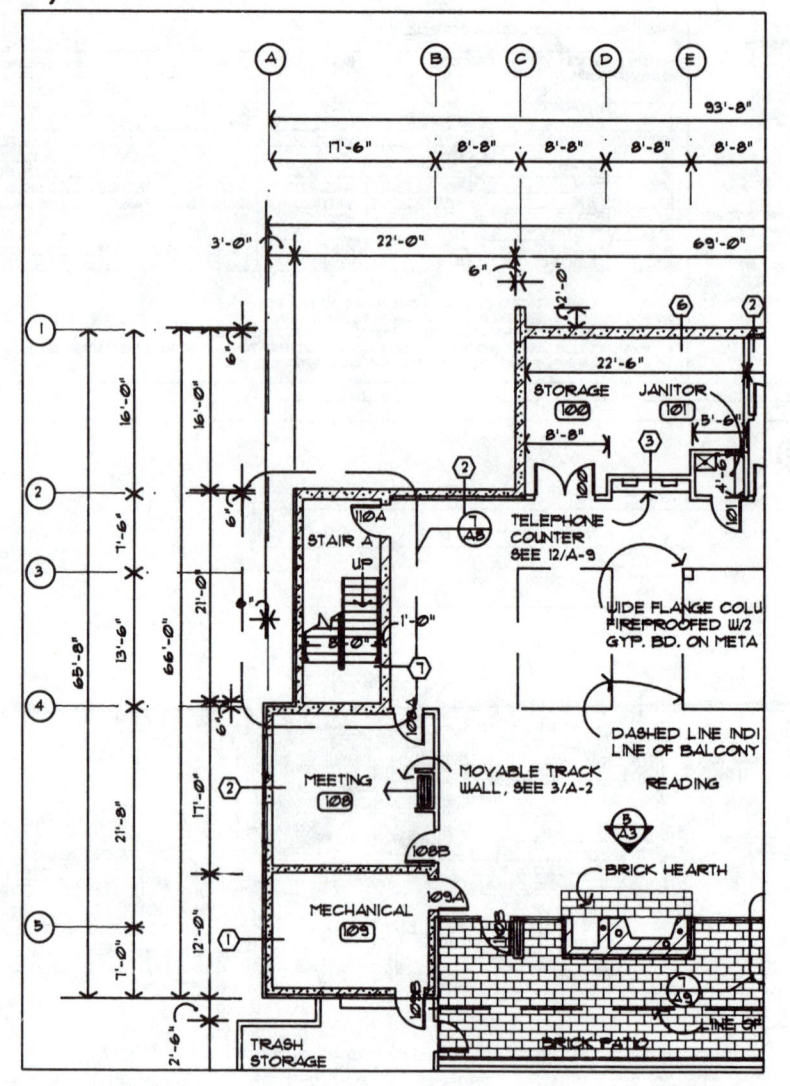

The detail below shows a blow-up of the first-floor toilet plan. The larger scale allows plumbing fixtures, floor drains, and grab bars to be drawn and located with dimension strings. Walls with plumbing fixtures should be shown in elevation in order to dimension the mounting height of fixtures and toilet partitions. Handicap stalls must be equipped with grab bars and have doors that swing out.

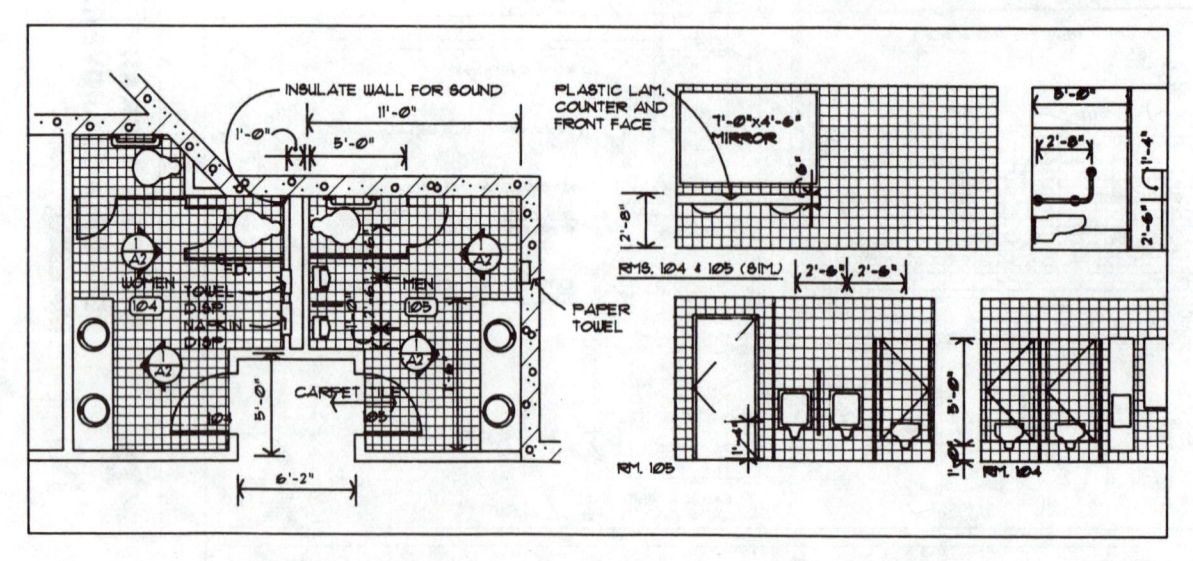

STUDENT LIBRARY

First-Floor Plan/A-2

A listing of wall types acts as a schedule for the assembly of wall construction in the building, eliminating the need to provide notes for all wall variations. The listing at the right provides a graphic detail of every wall in the library. The typical form of wall construction for the library is a brick exterior, an insulated cavity wall, and a concrete block back-up.

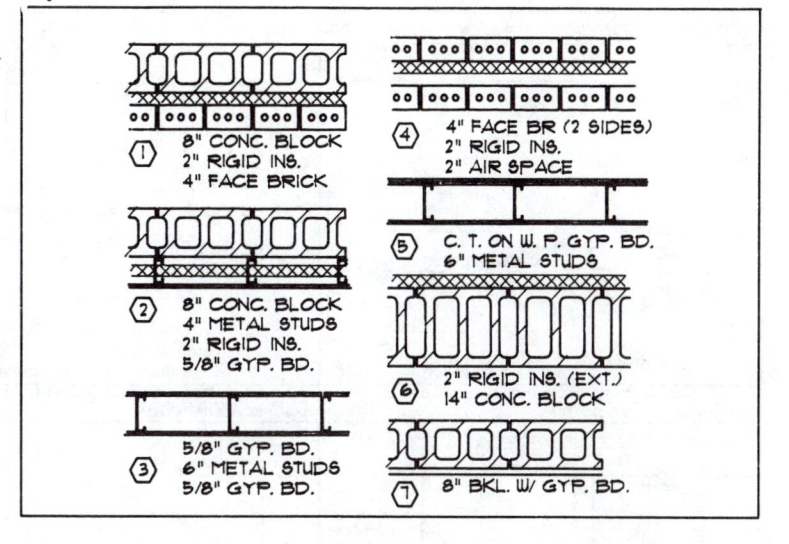

(1) 8" CONC. BLOCK / 2" RIGID INS. / 4" FACE BRICK

(2) 8" CONC. BLOCK / 4" METAL STUDS / 2" RIGID INS. / 5/8" GYP. BD.

(3) 5/8" GYP. BD. / 6" METAL STUDS / 5/8" GYP. BD.

(4) 4" FACE BR (2 SIDES) / 2" RIGID INS. / 2" AIR SPACE

(5) C. T. ON W. P. GYP. BD. / 6" METAL STUDS

(6) 2" RIGID INS. (EXT.) / 14" CONC. BLOCK

(7) 8" BKL. W/ GYP. BD.

FIRST-FLOOR ROOM FINISH SCHEDULE

ROOM NUMBER	ROOM NAME	FLOOR	BASE	WALL MAT.	WALL FINISH	CEILING MAT.	REMARKS
100	STORAGE	VINYL TILE	VINYL	GYP. BD.	PAINT	A. C. TILE	
101	JANITOR	VINYL TILE	VINYL	GYP. BD.	PAINT	A. C. TILE	
102	LOUNGE	CARPET	VINYL	GYP. BD.	PAINT	A. C. TILE	(3)
103	CHECK-OUT	CARPET	VINYL	GYP. BD.	PAINT	A. C. TILE	
104	WOMEN	CERAMIC TILE	CERAMIC T.	GYP. BD.	CERAMIC T.	GYP. BD.	C. T. TO CLNG.
105	MEN	CERAMIC TILE	CERAMIC T.	GYP. BD.	CERAMIC T.	GYP. BD.	C. T. TO CLNG.
106	LINK	CARPET	VINYL	GYP. BD.	PAINT	METAL SLATS	(3)
107	FOYER	QUARRY TILE	BRICK	BRICK	EXPOSED	METAL SLATS	(2)
108	MEETING	CARPET	WOOD	GYP. BD.	PAINT	T & G FIR	(4)
109	MECHANICAL	CONCRETE	NONE	CONC. BLK.	EXPOSED	GYP. BD.	(1)
110	READING	CARPET	WOOD	BRICK	EXPOSED	T & G FIR	(2)

NOTES:
1. 2-HOUR FIRE RATED WALLS IN MECHANICAL ROOM
2. EXPOSED FACE BRICK, SEE PLAN FOR LOCATION
3. USE FURRING STRIPS TO ATTACH GYPSUM BOARD TO WALLS
4. 1"x4" TONGUE AND GROOVE FIR CEILING ATTACHED TO 3/4" GYPSUM BOARD. WIRE SUSPEND TO JOISTS W/ 1 1/2" CHANNELS. SET WOOD AT A 45° ANGLE TO THE GRID.

A portion of the room finish schedule is shown above. Every room (including hallways and closets) should be included on the schedule.

A portion of the floor plan is shown to the right. The first step in producing the plan is to dimension walls and openings; notes, door numbers, and room names are then added. Make notes regarding items on the plan short and specific.

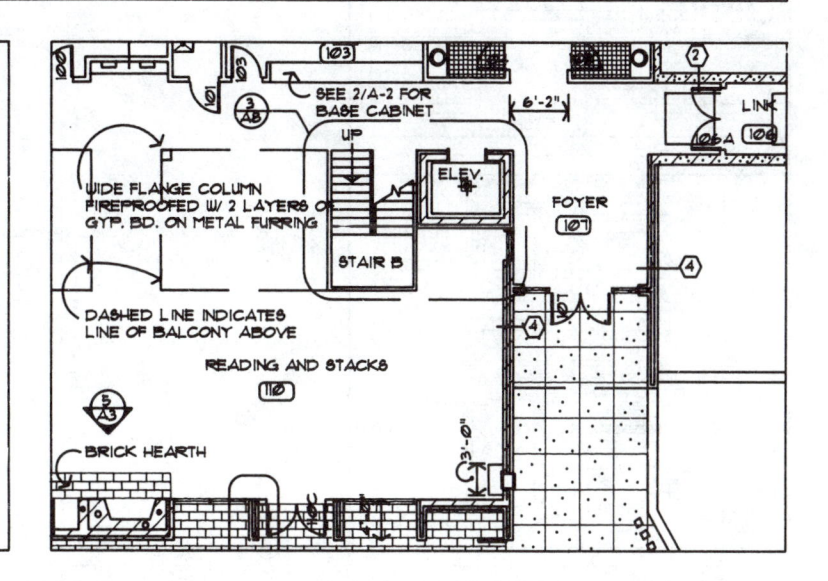

STUDENT LIBRARY 27-9

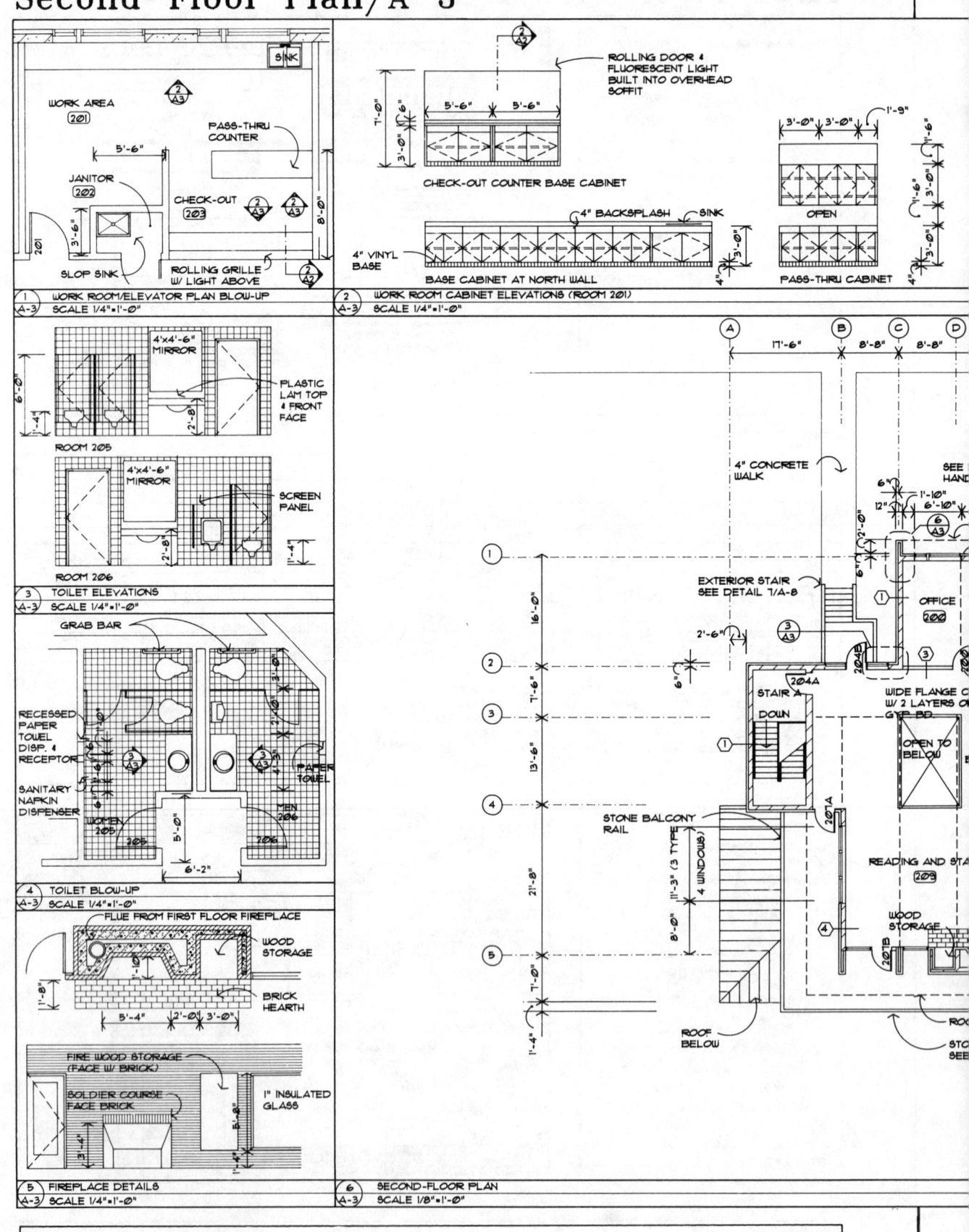

Second-Floor Plan/A-3

① WORK ROOM/ELEVATOR PLAN BLOW-UP
A-3 SCALE 1/4"=1'-0"

② WORK ROOM CABINET ELEVATIONS (ROOM 201)
A-3 SCALE 1/4"=1'-0"

③ TOILET ELEVATIONS
A-3 SCALE 1/4"=1'-0"

④ TOILET BLOW-UP
A-3 SCALE 1/4"=1'-0"

⑤ FIREPLACE DETAILS
A-3 SCALE 1/4"=1'-0"

⑥ SECOND-FLOOR PLAN
A-3 SCALE 1/8"=1'-0"

STUDENT LIBRARY 27-10

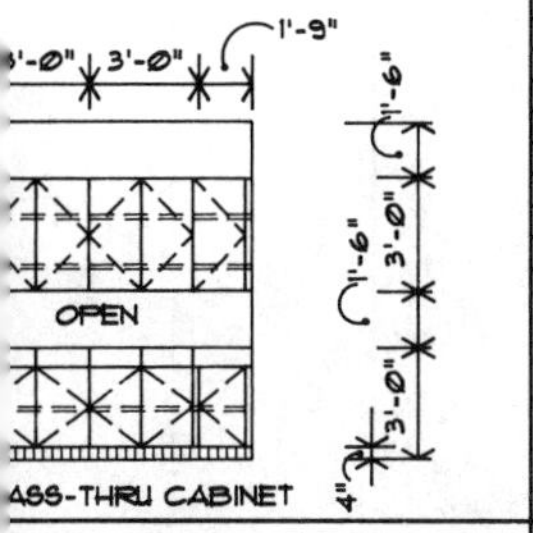

SECOND-FLOOR ROOM FINISH SCHEDULE

ROOM NUMBER	ROOM NAME	FLOOR	BASE	WALL MAT.	WALL FINISH	CEILING MAT.	REMARKS
200	OFFICE	CARPET	WOOD	GYP. BD.	PAINT	WOOD	(1) SLOPED CEILING
201	WORK AREA	CARPET	VINYL	GYP. BD.	PAINT	WOOD	(1) SLOPED CEILING
202	JANITOR	VINYL	VINYL	GYP. BD.	PAINT	A.C. TILE	
203	CHECK-OUT	CARPET	VINYL	GYP. BD.	PAINT	WOOD	(1) SLOPED CEILING
204	HALL	CARPET	WOOD	GYP. BD.	PAINT	MTL. SLATS	(3) SET SLATS @ 45°
205	WOMEN	CERAMIC TILE	CERAMIC T.	GYP. BD.	CERAMIC T.	GYP. BD.	(2)
206	MEN	CERAMIC T.	CERAMIC T.	GYP. BD.	CERAMIC T.	GYP. BD.	(2)
207	LOBBY	QUARRY TILE	BRICK	BRICK	BRICK	WOOD	(1) SLOPED CEILING
208	STUDY AREA	CARPET	BRICK	BRICK	BRICK	WOOD	(1) SLOPED CEILING
209	READING	CARPET	WOOD	BRICK	BRICK	WOOD	(1) SLOPED CEILING

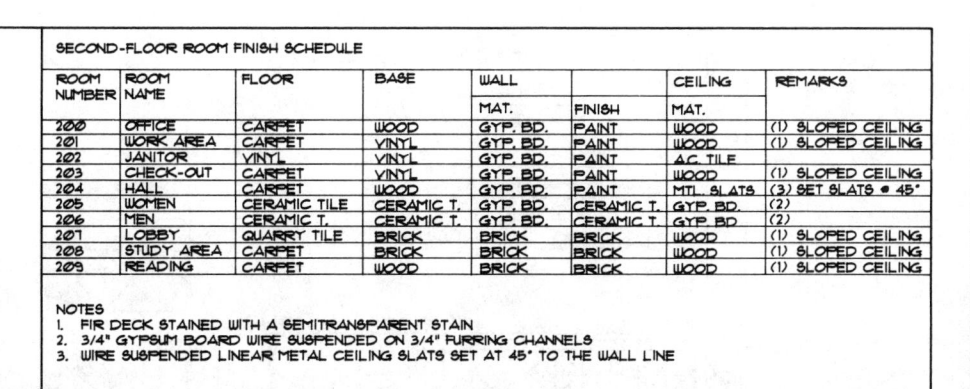

NOTES
1. FIR DECK STAINED WITH A SEMITRANSPARENT STAIN
2. 3/4" GYPSUM BOARD WIRE SUSPENDED ON 3/4" FURRING CHANNELS
3. WIRE SUSPENDED LINEAR METAL CEILING SLATS SET AT 45° TO THE WALL LINE

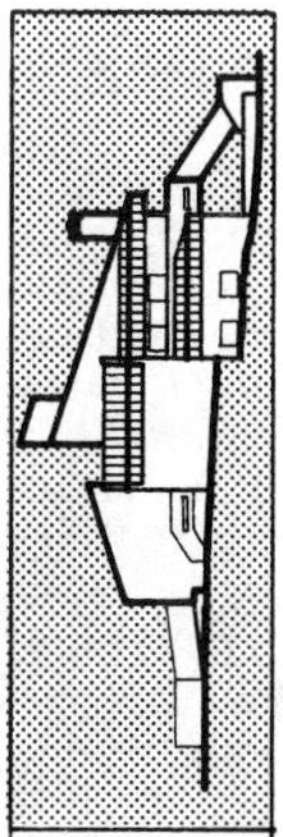

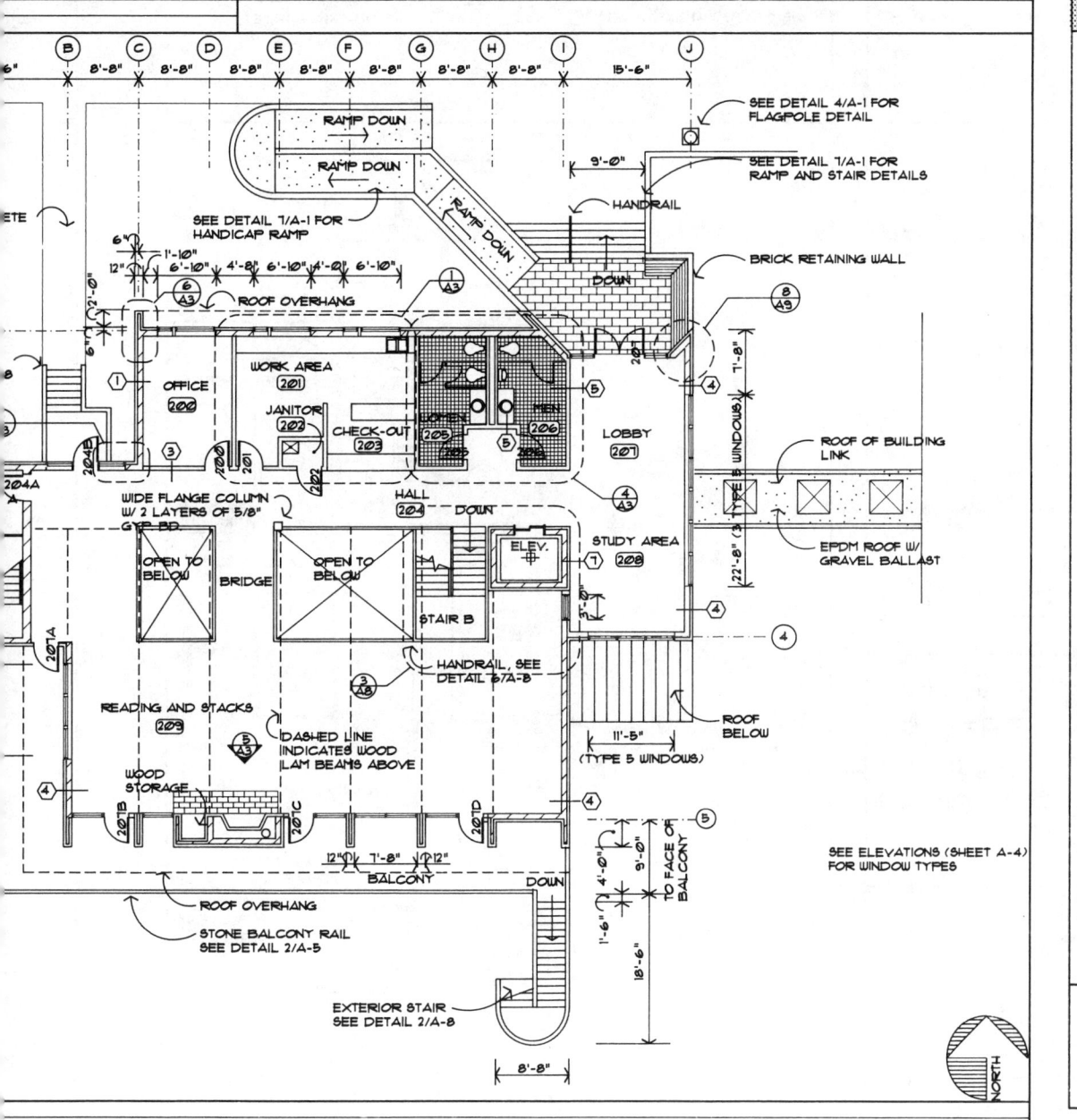

SECOND-FLOOR PLAN

STUDENT LIBRARY
PEPPERDINE UNIVERSITY
MALIBU, CA

A3

STUDENT LIBRARY

27-11

Second-Floor Plan/A-3

Specific items in the drawing package must be detailed to define construction. The illustration to the right elevates cabinets in the work room (room 201) and includes such items as door locations, dimensions, and finishes. This material, combined with data in the specifications, provides the contractor with information needed to build the units.

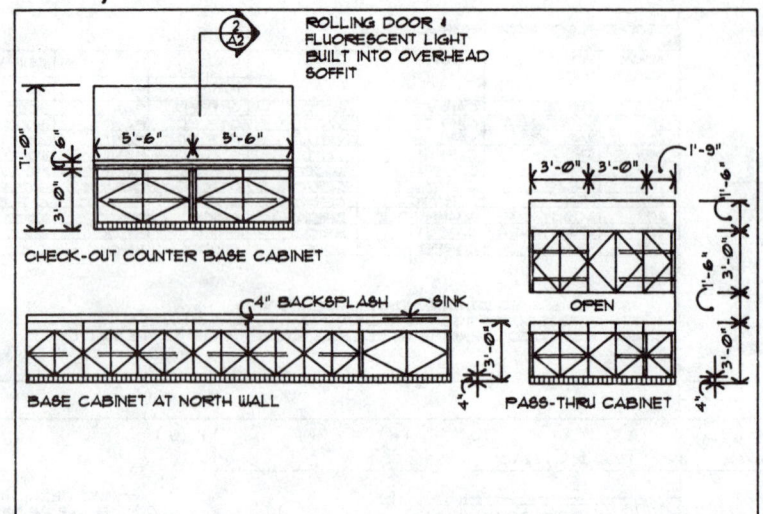

A portion of the second-floor plan is illustrated at the right. The open second-floor balcony is marked with an "X" and noted. The roof over the first-floor mechanical and meeting rooms (at grid "A" between grids "4" and "5") is drawn showing the ribs on the metal roof.

The enlarged drawing below shows two stairs. Note that 1/8" scale plans should detail treads and handrails.

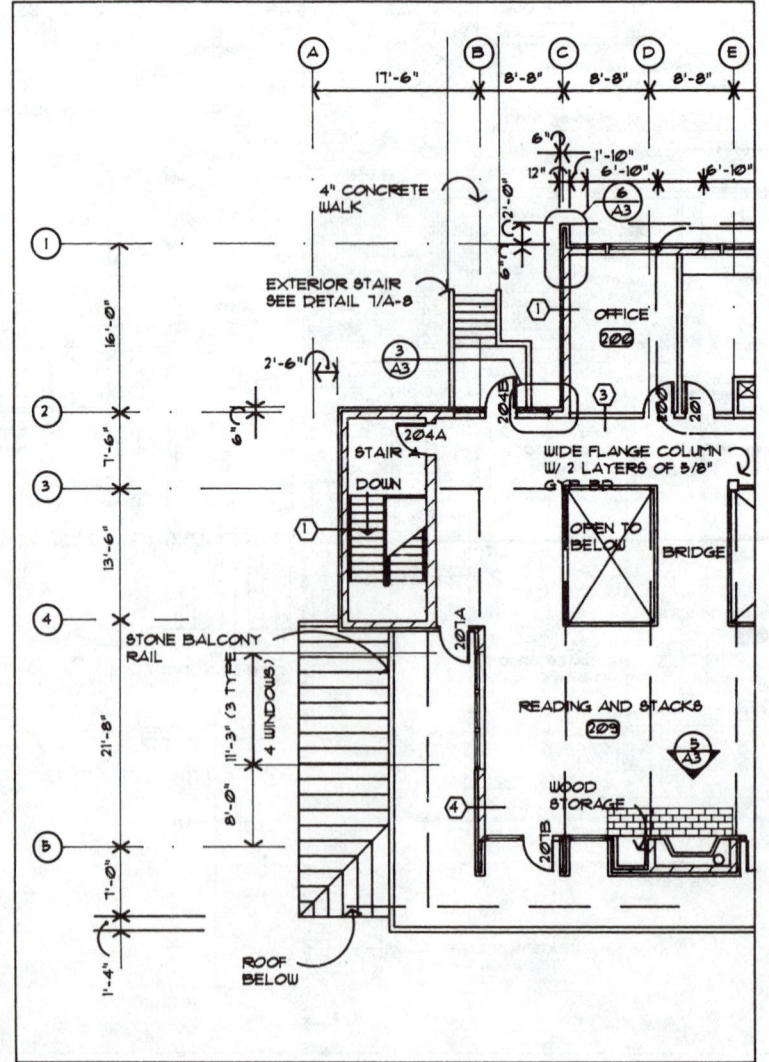

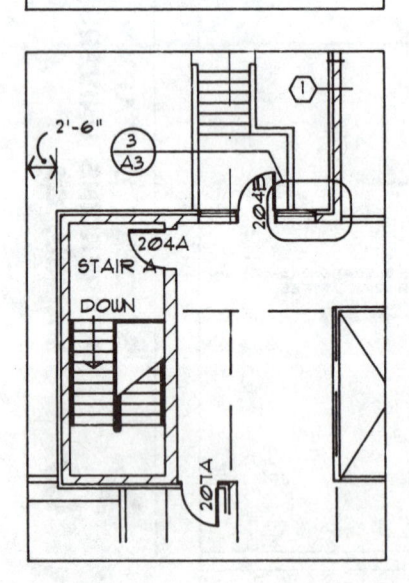

STUDENT LIBRARY

27-12

Second-Floor Plan/A-3

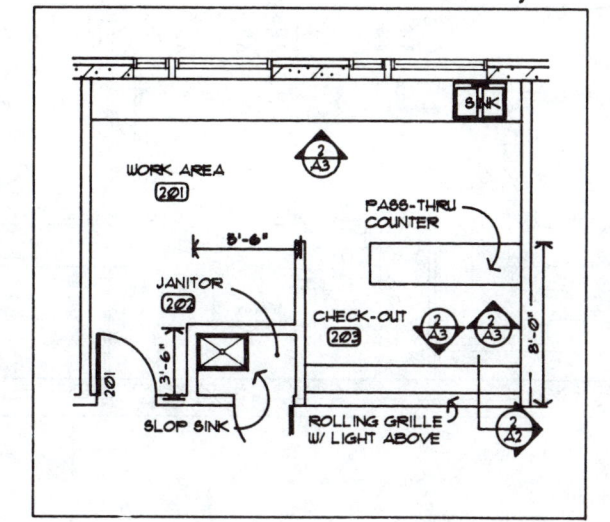

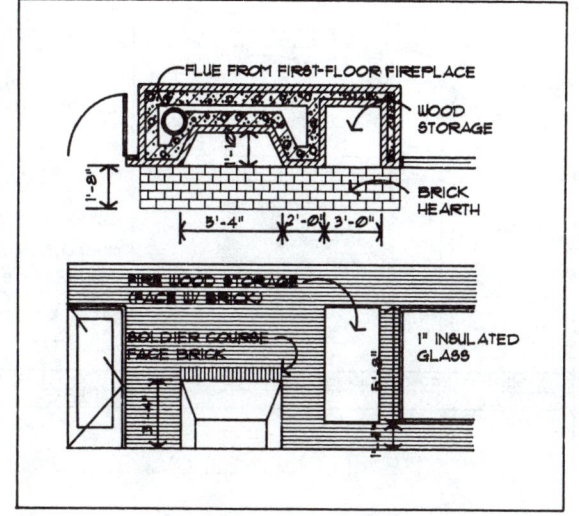

The detail above shows a 1/4" blow-up of the work room. The area was enlarged to allow space for section and elevation bubbles. It is common for the contractor to wait until walls are built before assembling shop drawings. These drawings, prepared by the cabinetmaker, show exact dimensions and details. The fireplace details (top right) show specific plan and elevation dimensions.

A portion of the second-floor plan is shown to the right. Note that two exterior stairs are drawn on the plan along with the interior stair and elevator. All of these items have been drawn at a 1/4" scale to show more detail. The dashed lines in the reading room represent the wood laminated beams on the ceiling. The three skylights in the link between the buildings are drawn in elevation.

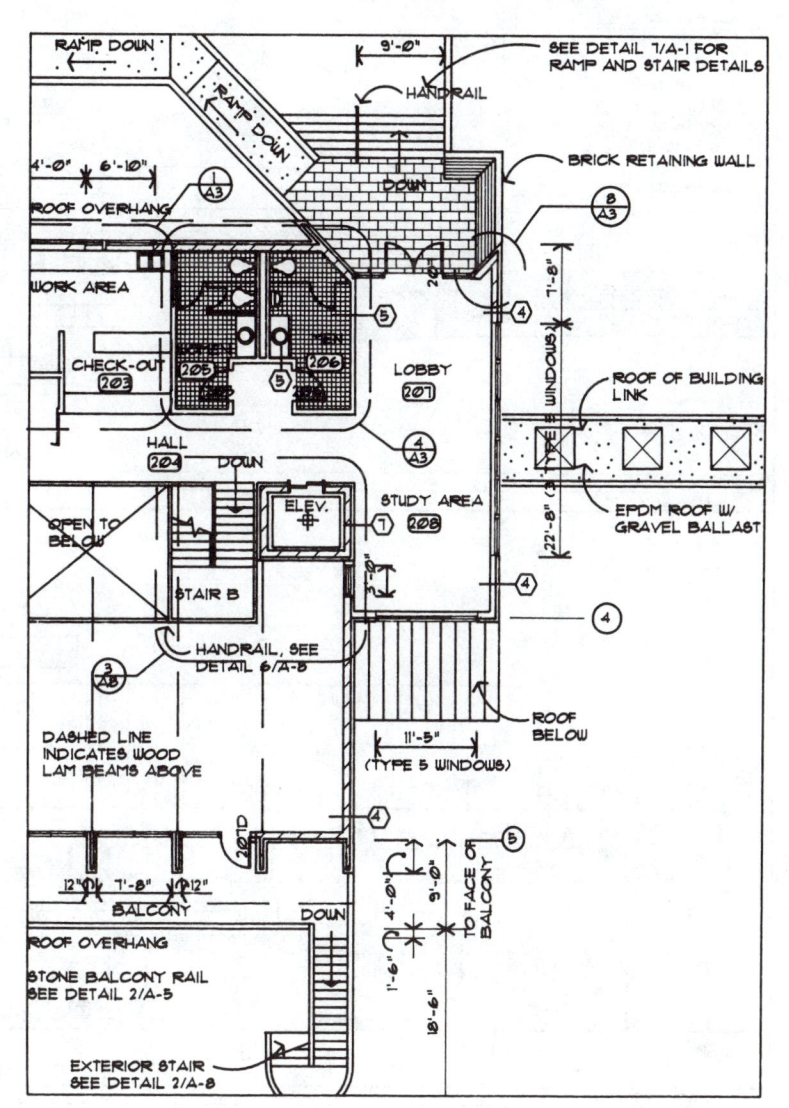

STUDENT LIBRARY   27-13

Elevations/A-4

1. SECOND FLOOR AT BEARING WALL
SCALE 1"=1'-0"

- 4" FACE BRICK
- 2" RIGID INSULATION
- 8" CONCRETE BLOCK
- 1" METAL FURRING STRIPS
- 5/8" GYPSUM BOARD
- 2" CONCRETE TOPPING
- EL. 92'-6"
- 1 1/2" METAL DECK
- LINTEL BLOCK W/ 2 #5 REBARS
- LADDER-TIE REINFORCEMENT (EVERY SECOND BLOCK COURSE)

2. SKYLIGHT AT TUNNEL
SCALE 1"=1'-0"

- ALUM. FRAME
- S. S. SCREWS
- EPDM MEMBRANE
- ACRYLIC DOMES
- 5/8" GYP. BD.
- 1 1/2" METAL DECK
- 8" STRUCT. CHANNEL
- WOOD BLOCK BOLTED TO CHANNEL
- LAY-IN A.C. TILE
- GRADE

3. FLAT ROOF INTERSECTION
SCALE 1"=1'-0"

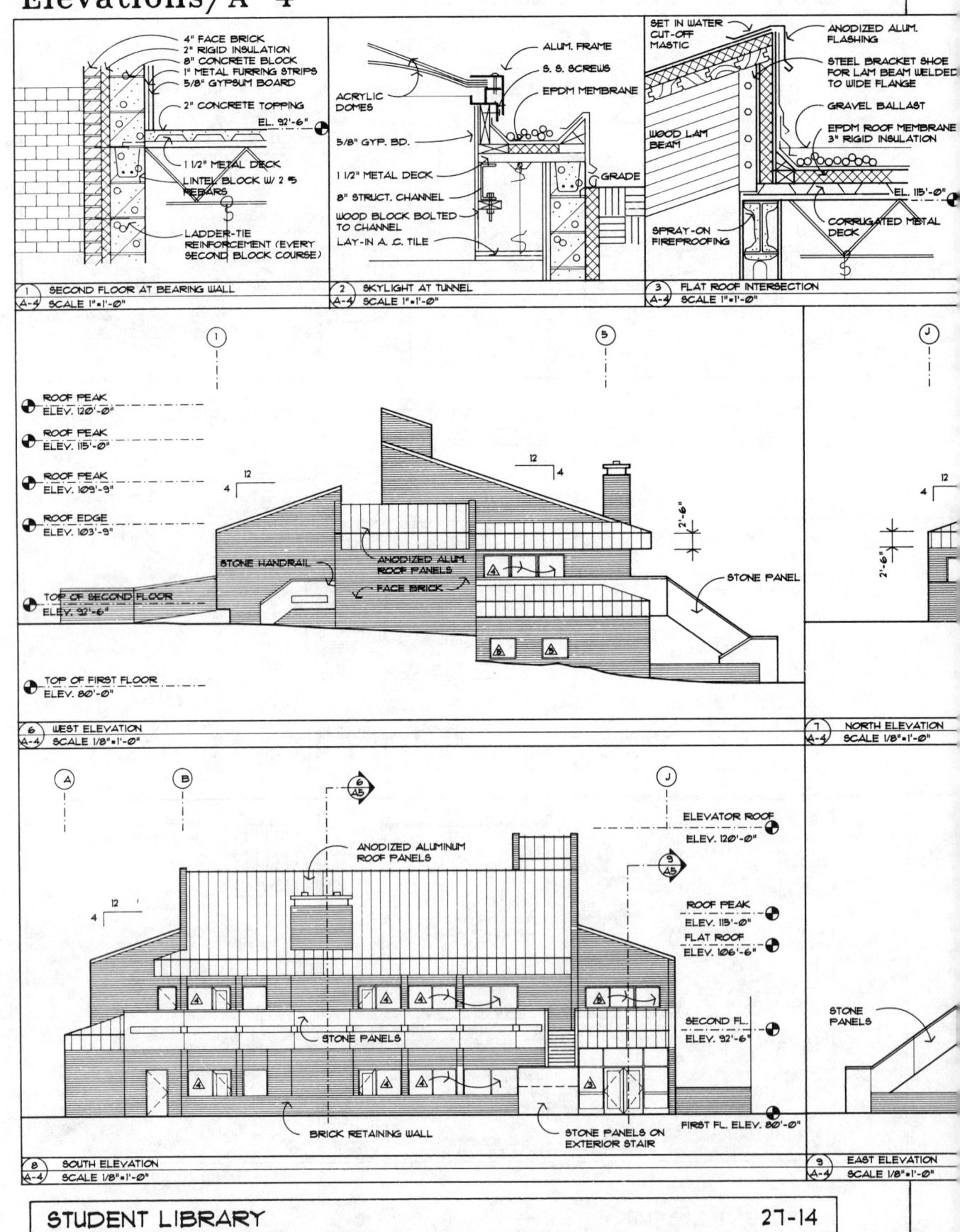

- SET IN WATER CUT-OFF MASTIC
- ANODIZED ALUM. FLASHING
- STEEL BRACKET SHOE FOR LAM BEAM WELDED TO WIDE FLANGE
- WOOD LAM BEAM
- GRAVEL BALLAST
- EPDM ROOF MEMBRANE
- 3" RIGID INSULATION
- EL. 115'-0"
- SPRAY-ON FIREPROOFING
- CORRUGATED METAL DECK

6. WEST ELEVATION
SCALE 1/8"=1'-0"

- ROOF PEAK ELEV. 120'-0"
- ROOF PEAK ELEV. 115'-0"
- ROOF PEAK ELEV. 109'-9"
- ROOF EDGE ELEV. 103'-9"
- TOP OF SECOND FLOOR ELEV. 92'-6"
- TOP OF FIRST FLOOR ELEV. 80'-0"
- STONE HANDRAIL
- ANODIZED ALUM. ROOF PANELS
- FACE BRICK
- STONE PANEL

7. NORTH ELEVATION
SCALE 1/8"=1'-0"

8. SOUTH ELEVATION
SCALE 1/8"=1'-0"

- ANODIZED ALUMINUM ROOF PANELS
- STONE PANELS
- BRICK RETAINING WALL
- STONE PANELS ON EXTERIOR STAIR
- ELEVATOR ROOF ELEV. 120'-0"
- ROOF PEAK ELEV. 115'-0"
- FLAT ROOF ELEV. 106'-6"
- SECOND FL. ELEV. 92'-6"
- FIRST FL. ELEV. 80'-0"

9. EAST ELEVATION
SCALE 1/8"=1'-0"

- STONE PANELS

STUDENT LIBRARY

27-14

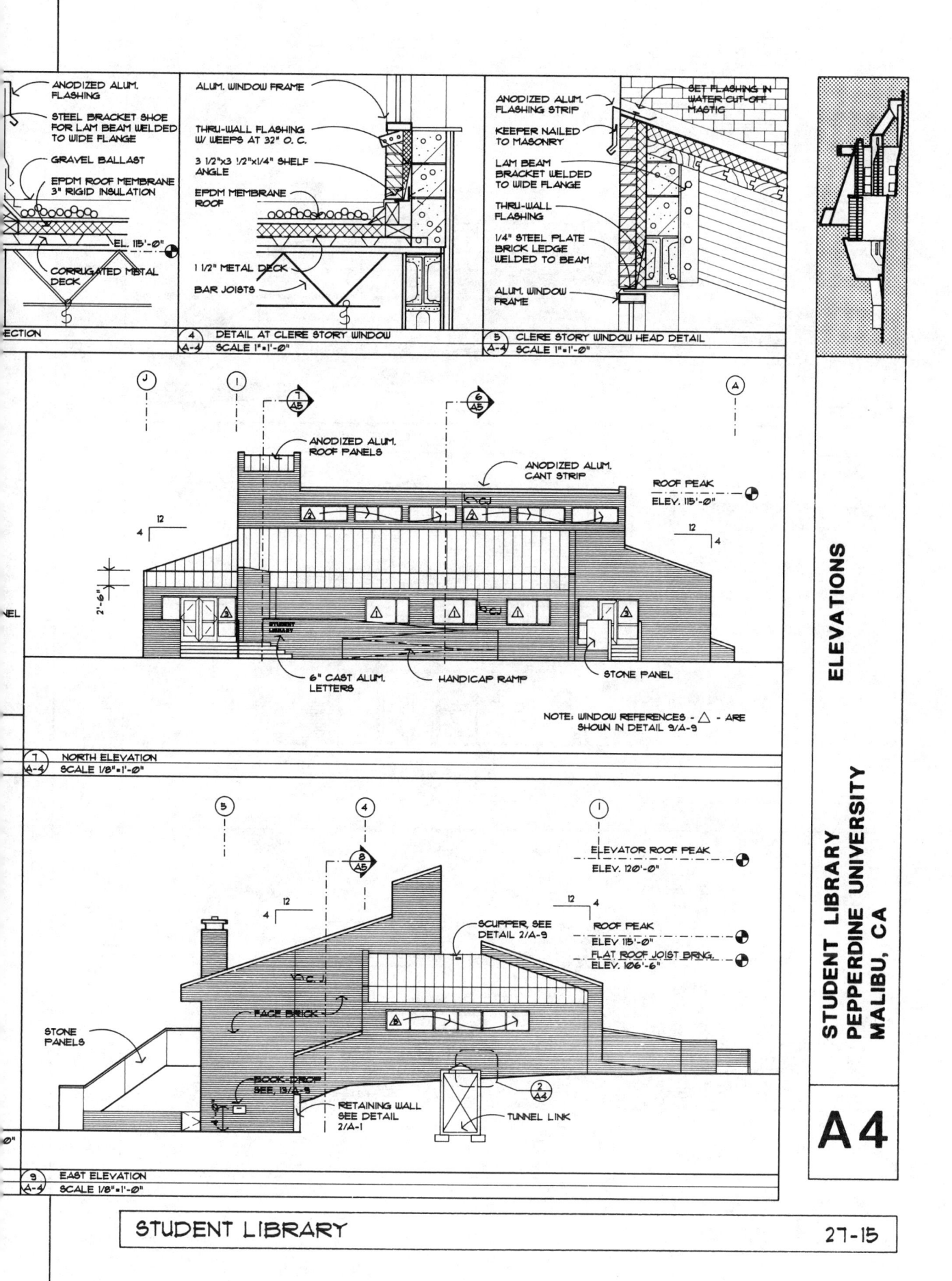

Detail 4: Detail at Clere Story Window
Scale: 1" = 1'-0"

- ANODIZED ALUM. FLASHING
- STEEL BRACKET SHOE FOR LAM BEAM WELDED TO WIDE FLANGE
- GRAVEL BALLAST
- EPDM ROOF MEMBRANE 3" RIGID INSULATION
- EL. 115'-0"
- CORRUGATED METAL DECK
- ALUM. WINDOW FRAME
- THRU-WALL FLASHING W/ WEEPS AT 32" O.C.
- 3 1/2"x3 1/2"x1/4" SHELF ANGLE
- EPDM MEMBRANE ROOF
- 1 1/2" METAL DECK
- BAR JOISTS

Detail 5: Clere Story Window Head Detail
Scale: 1" = 1'-0"

- ANODIZED ALUM. FLASHING STRIP
- KEEPER NAILED TO MASONRY
- LAM BEAM BRACKET WELDED TO WIDE FLANGE
- THRU-WALL FLASHING
- 1/4" STEEL PLATE BRICK LEDGE WELDED TO BEAM
- ALUM. WINDOW FRAME
- SET FLASHING IN WATER CUT-OFF MASTIC

North Elevation
Scale: 1/8" = 1'-0"

- ANODIZED ALUM. ROOF PANELS
- ANODIZED ALUM. CANT STRIP
- ROOF PEAK ELEV. 115'-0"
- 6" CAST ALUM. LETTERS
- HANDICAP RAMP
- STONE PANEL

NOTE: WINDOW REFERENCES - △ - ARE SHOWN IN DETAIL 9/A-9

East Elevation
Scale: 1/8" = 1'-0"

- ELEVATOR ROOF PEAK ELEV. 120'-0"
- ROOF PEAK ELEV. 115'-0"
- FLAT ROOF JOIST BRNG. ELEV. 106'-6"
- SCUPPER, SEE DETAIL 2/A-9
- FACE BRICK
- STONE PANELS
- BOOK DROP SEE 13/A-9
- RETAINING WALL SEE DETAIL 2/A-1
- TUNNEL LINK

STUDENT LIBRARY
PEPPERDINE UNIVERSITY
MALIBU, CA

ELEVATIONS

A4

STUDENT LIBRARY   27-15

Elevations/A-4

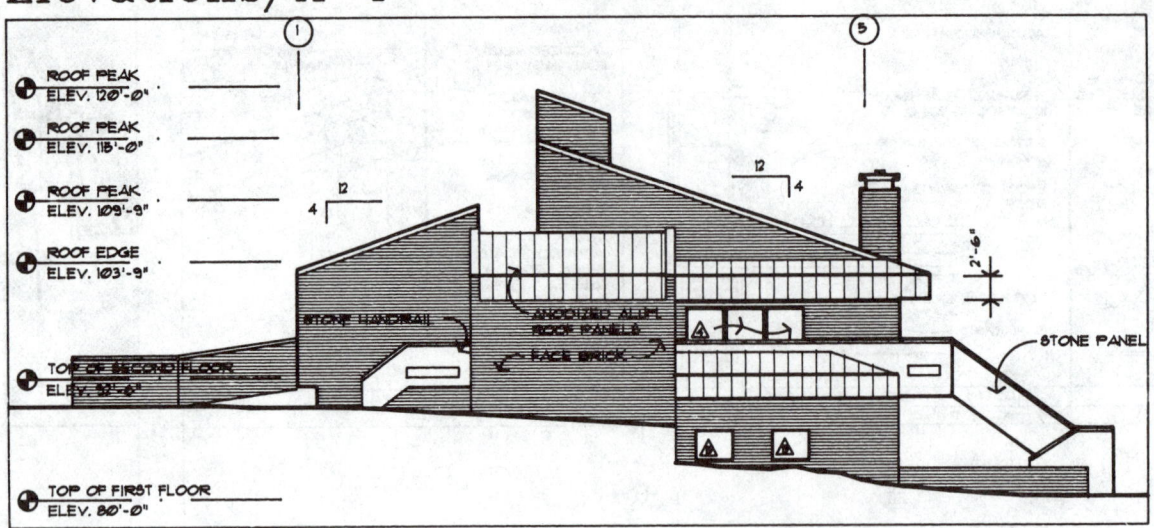

These drawings illustrate the amount of detail that should be shown on commercial elevations. Brick is shown with horizontal lines, the metal ribbed roof seams with vertical lines, and frames for windows and doors with double lines. Materials used on the building are noted, and window units are keyed with deltas. A roof pitch is shown for each slope.

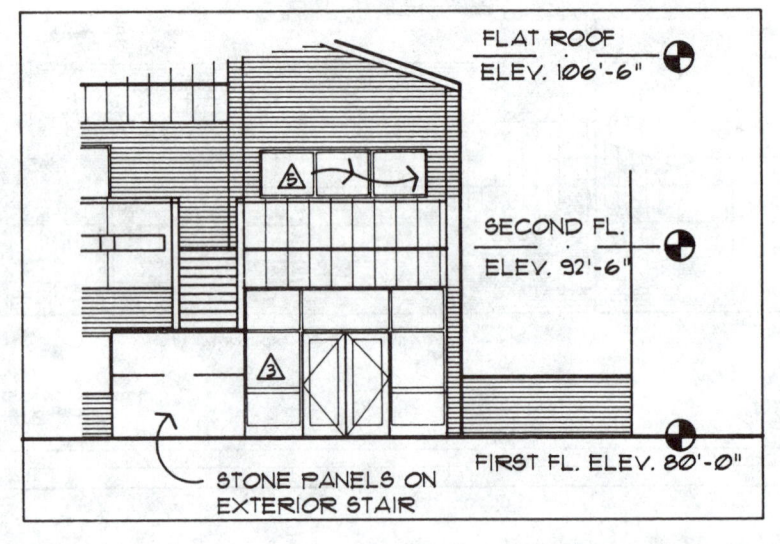

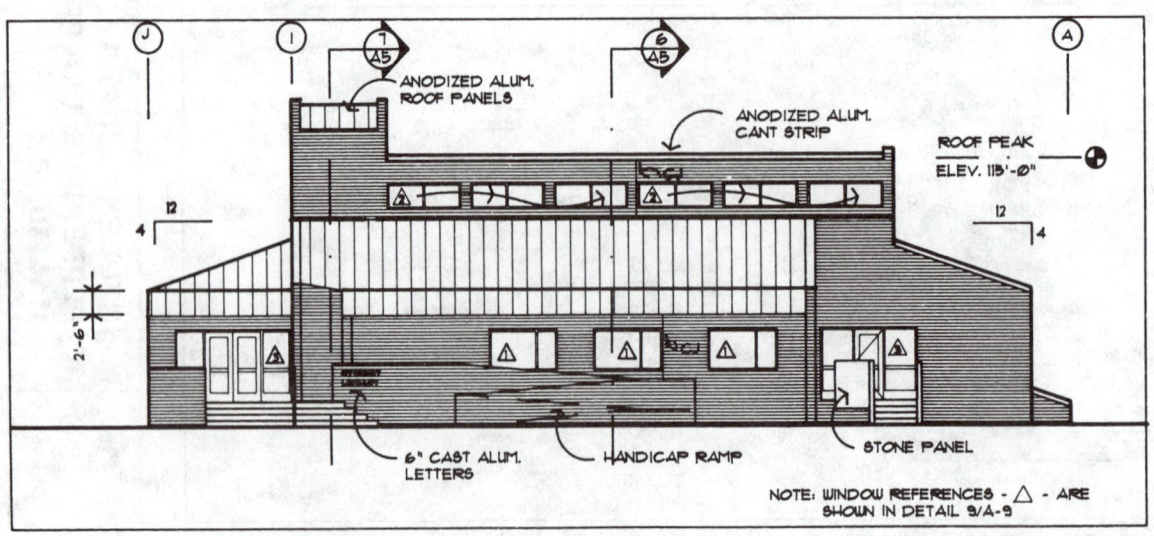

STUDENT LIBRARY

27-16

Elevations/A-4

Sheet A-4 contains several detail enlargements that are keyed to the wall sections. The detail at the right cuts through the second floor as it intersects a load-bearing wall. The floor is structured with steel bar joists and metal deck. The joists are supported by a concrete lintel block that runs along the perimeter of the wall. The U-shaped block is filled with concrete and acts as a beam.

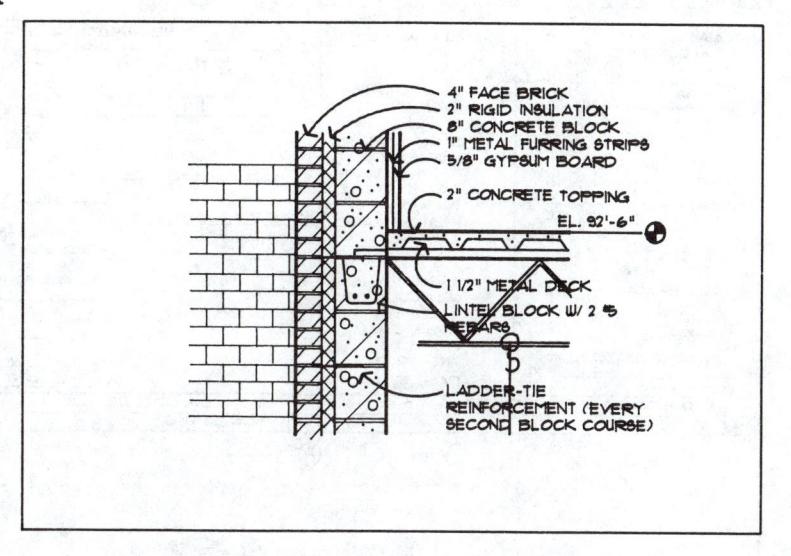

4" FACE BRICK
2" RIGID INSULATION
8" CONCRETE BLOCK
1" METAL FURRING STRIPS
5/8" GYPSUM BOARD
2" CONCRETE TOPPING
EL. 92'-6"
1 1/2" METAL DECK
LINTEL BLOCK W/ 2 #5 REBARS
LADDER-TIE REINFORCEMENT (EVERY SECOND BLOCK COURSE)

The elevation at the right details a section cut through the tunnel. The drawing is used to indicate a section detail blow-up showing the skylight in the roof (Detail 2/A-4). The two details below show blow-ups of roof conditions. They were developed by first drawing the steel beam used to support a wood laminated beam. The metal flashing is drawn at a large scale in order to define its assembly.

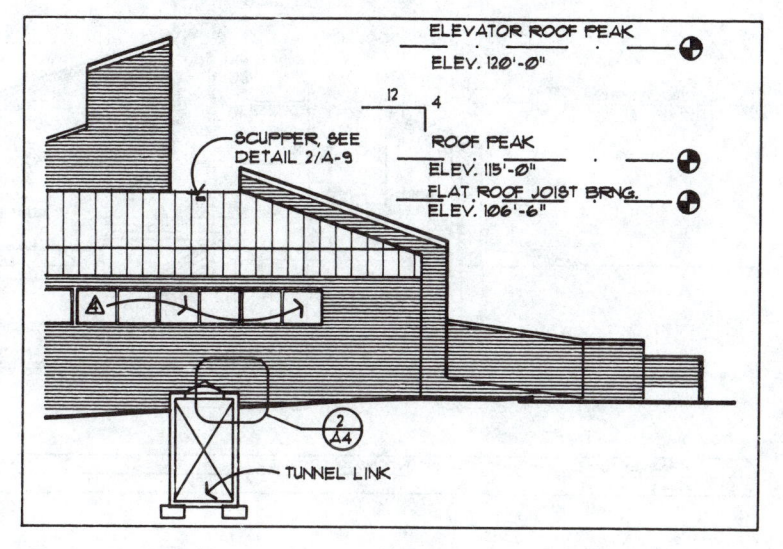

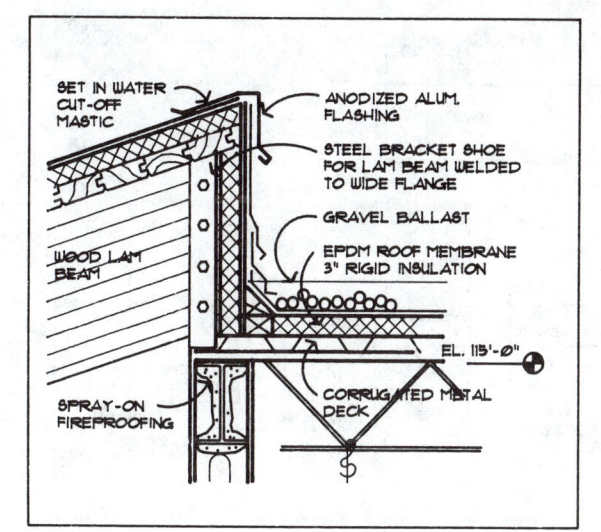

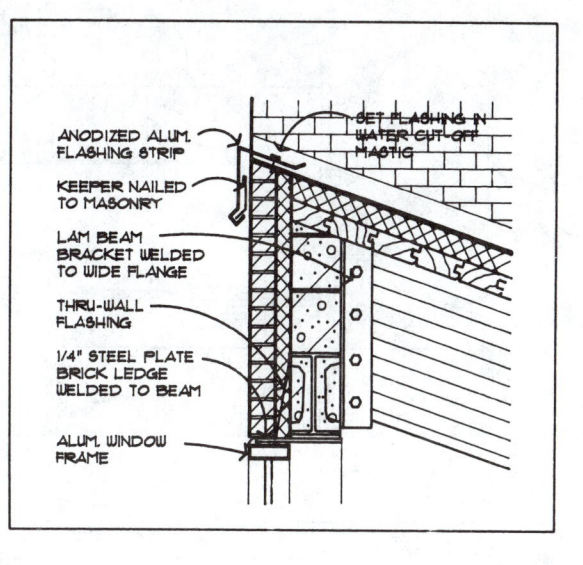

ELEVATOR ROOF PEAK
ELEV. 120'-0"
SCUPPER, SEE DETAIL 2/A-9
ROOF PEAK
ELEV. 115'-0"
FLAT ROOF JOIST BRNG.
ELEV. 106'-6"
TUNNEL LINK

SET IN WATER CUT-OFF MASTIC
ANODIZED ALUM. FLASHING
STEEL BRACKET SHOE FOR LAM BEAM WELDED TO WIDE FLANGE
GRAVEL BALLAST
EPDM ROOF MEMBRANE
3" RIGID INSULATION
WOOD LAM BEAM
EL. 115'-0"
SPRAY-ON FIREPROOFING
CORRUGATED METAL DECK

ANODIZED ALUM. FLASHING STRIP
SET FLASHING IN WATER CUT-OFF MASTIC
KEEPER NAILED TO MASONRY
LAM BEAM BRACKET WELDED TO WIDE FLANGE
THRU-WALL FLASHING
1/4" STEEL PLATE BRICK LEDGE WELDED TO BEAM
ALUM. WINDOW FRAME

STUDENT LIBRARY   27-17

Building Sections/A-5

1. STONE FASCIA AT SOUTH BALCONY
Scale: 1"=1'-0"

Labels: FLASHING REGLET SET IN CONCRETE; G.I. FLASHING; SEALANT W/ ROD BACK-UP; 4" CONC. TOPPING W/ 1/8" TEMPERED HARDBOARD, EPDM MEMBRANE AND 4" CONCRETE SLAB; WIDE FLANGE BEAM; 6" STONE PANEL; S.S. STRAP ANCHOR; 4" STEEL TUBE AT 2'-0" O.C.; 3 1/2"x3 1/2"x1/4" WELDED TO TUBE; 3 1/2"x5"x1/4" S.S. ANGLE W/ 3/4" S.S. STONE ANCHOR PIN; ANGLE BRACKET; WOOD SOFFIT; PAINT REVEAL

2. STONE BALCONY DETAILS
Scale: 1"=1'-0"

STONE PANEL ELEVATION, Scale 1/4"=1'-0"
HORIZONTAL SECTION AT CONTROL JOINT

Labels: SEE HORIZONTAL SECTION BELOW; CONTROL JOINT; ELEV. 92'-6" BALCONY FLOOR; STAINLESS STEEL SHELF ANGLE; 3" STAINLESS STEEL TUBE STONE ANCHOR; 1/2" S.S. PIN

3. ALUMINUM WINDOW SILL DETAIL
Scale: 1"=1'-0"

Labels: PLASTIC LAM. WINDOW STOOL; ALUM. WINDOW FRAME; BRICK SILL; THRU-WALL FLASHING; WEEP TUBES AT 32" O.C.; BRICK PAVERS; SAND SETTING BED; 2" RIGID INSULATION; GYP. BD.; FURRING; 6" GRAVEL

6. TRANSVERSE SECTION THRU READING ROOMS AND STAIR
Scale: 1/8"=1'-0"

Rooms: WORK AREA, HALL, READING, LOUNGE, CHECK-OUT, READING

Elevations: ROOF PEAK ELEV. 120'-0"; ROOF EDGE ELEV. 103'-10"; STONE RAIL; 2ND FLOOR ELEV. 92'-6"; FLAT ROOF BRNG. ELEV. 106'-6"

7. TRANSVERSE SECTION
Scale: 1/8"=1'-0"

Labels: SUSPENDED GYP. BD. CEILING ON METAL CHANNELS; HANDICAP RAMP SEE DETAIL 7/A-1

8. LONGITUDINAL SECTION THRU READING ROOMS AND STAIR
Scale: 1/8"=1'-0"

Rooms: MEETING, READING, BRIDGE, STAIR

Labels: ANODIZED ALUMINUM ROOF PANELS W/ STANDING SEAM; ELEVATOR ROOF ELEV. 120'-0"; ROOF PEAK ELEV. 115'-0"; FLAT ROOF BRNG. ELEV. 106'-6"; SECOND FL. ELEV. 92'-6"; BRICK RETAINING WALL; FIRST FL. ELEV. 80'-0"; STONE FACED EXTERIOR STAIR, SEE 2/A-8

9. TRANSVERSE SECTION
Scale: 1/8"=1'-0"

STUDENT LIBRARY   27-18

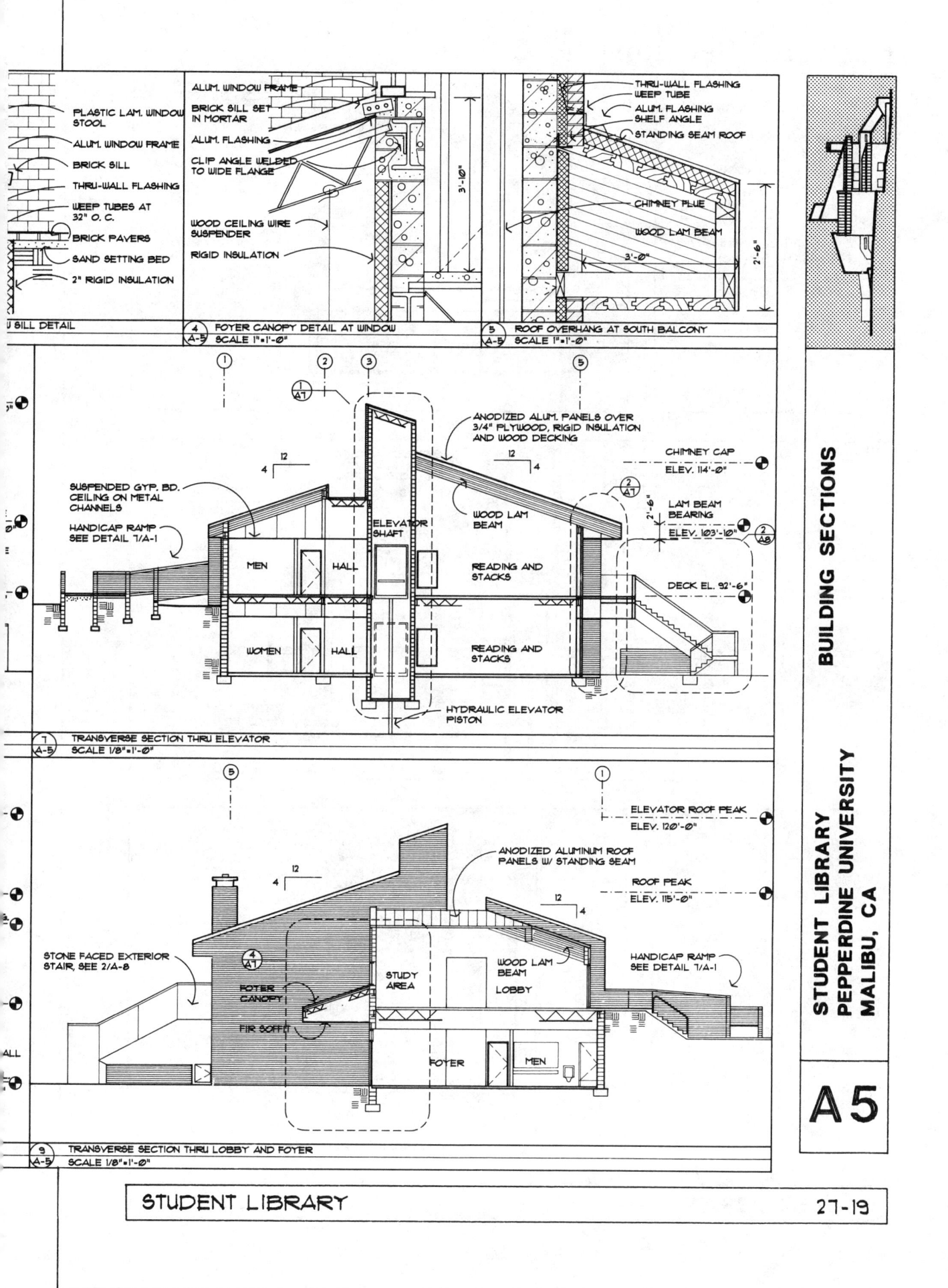

Sheet A5 — Building Sections

Sill Detail (partial)
- PLASTIC LAM. WINDOW STOOL
- ALUM. WINDOW FRAME
- BRICK SILL
- THRU-WALL FLASHING
- WEEP TUBES AT 32" O.C.
- BRICK PAVERS
- SAND SETTING BED
- 2" RIGID INSULATION

4/A-5 — Foyer Canopy Detail at Window
Scale 1" = 1'-0"
- ALUM. WINDOW FRAME
- BRICK SILL SET IN MORTAR
- ALUM. FLASHING
- CLIP ANGLE WELDED TO WIDE FLANGE
- WOOD CEILING WIRE SUSPENDER
- RIGID INSULATION
- 3'-10"

5/A-5 — Roof Overhang at South Balcony
Scale 1" = 1'-0"
- THRU-WALL FLASHING
- WEEP TUBE
- ALUM. FLASHING SHELF ANGLE
- STANDING SEAM ROOF
- CHIMNEY FLUE
- WOOD LAM BEAM
- 3'-0"
- 2'-6"

7/A-5 — Transverse Section Thru Elevator
Scale 1/8" = 1'-0"
- SUSPENDED GYP. BD. CEILING ON METAL CHANNELS
- HANDICAP RAMP SEE DETAIL 7/A-1
- ANODIZED ALUM. PANELS OVER 3/4" PLYWOOD, RIGID INSULATION AND WOOD DECKING
- CHIMNEY CAP ELEV. 114'-0"
- LAM BEAM BEARING ELEV. 103'-10"
- DECK EL. 92'-6"
- WOOD LAM BEAM
- ELEVATOR SHAFT
- MEN / HALL / READING AND STACKS
- WOMEN / HALL / READING AND STACKS
- HYDRAULIC ELEVATOR PISTON

9/A-5 — Transverse Section Thru Lobby and Foyer
Scale 1/8" = 1'-0"
- ELEVATOR ROOF PEAK ELEV. 120'-0"
- ANODIZED ALUMINUM ROOF PANELS W/ STANDING SEAM
- ROOF PEAK ELEV. 115'-0"
- STONE FACED EXTERIOR STAIR, SEE 2/A-8
- FOYER CANOPY
- FIR SOFFIT
- STUDY AREA
- WOOD LAM BEAM
- LOBBY
- HANDICAP RAMP SEE DETAIL 7/A-1
- FOYER
- MEN

STUDENT LIBRARY
PEPPERDINE UNIVERSITY
MALIBU, CA

BUILDING SECTIONS

A5

STUDENT LIBRARY — 27-19

Building Sections/A-5

A key to working drawing assembly involves cutting sections through all unique parts of the project. Building sections act as an index for wall sections, which in turn act as an index for details. The transverse section (cut on the short axis) to the right shows the construction of the first- and second-floor entries.

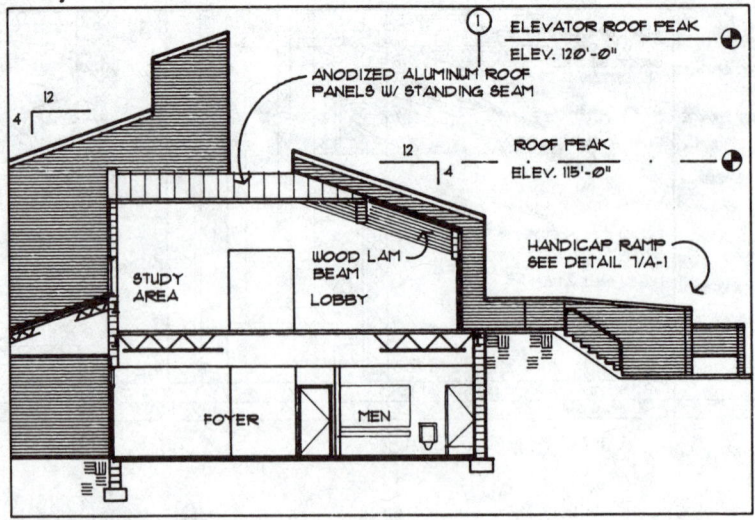

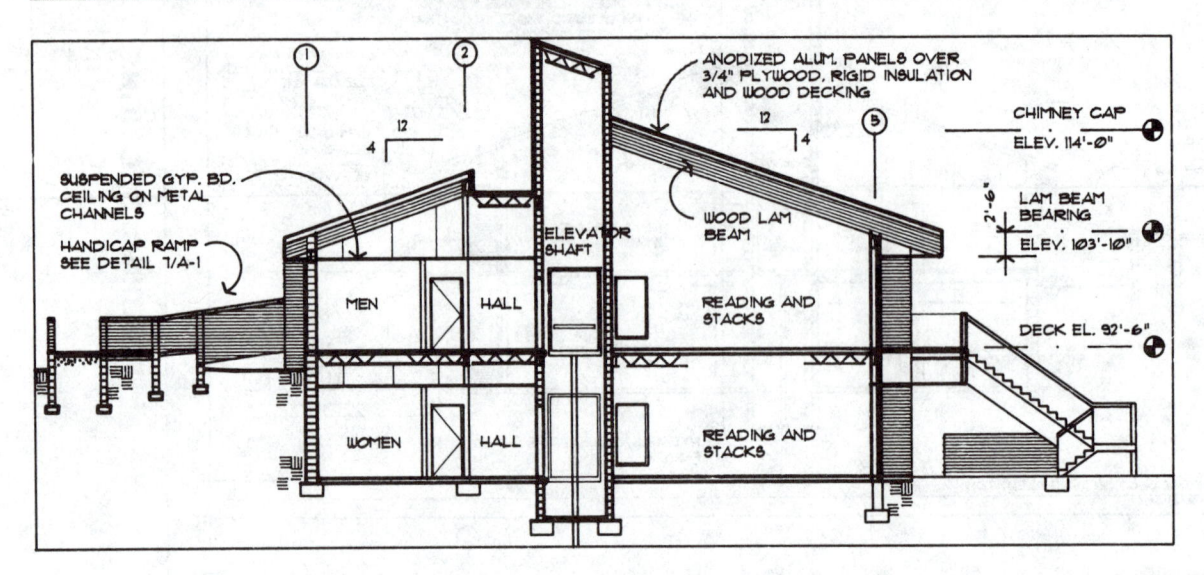

The transverse section shown above cuts through several major portions of the project. Cuts through the elevator shaft, vaulted reading room, and exterior stair are all enlarged in wall sections. Major grids and elevation bearing points should be shown on the section.

The detail at the right cuts through the roof overhang above the balcony.

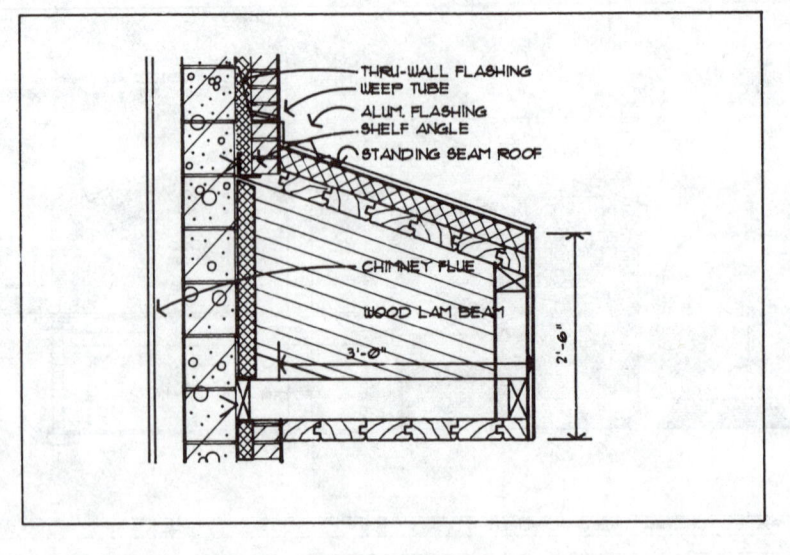

STUDENT LIBRARY   27-20

Building Sections/A-5

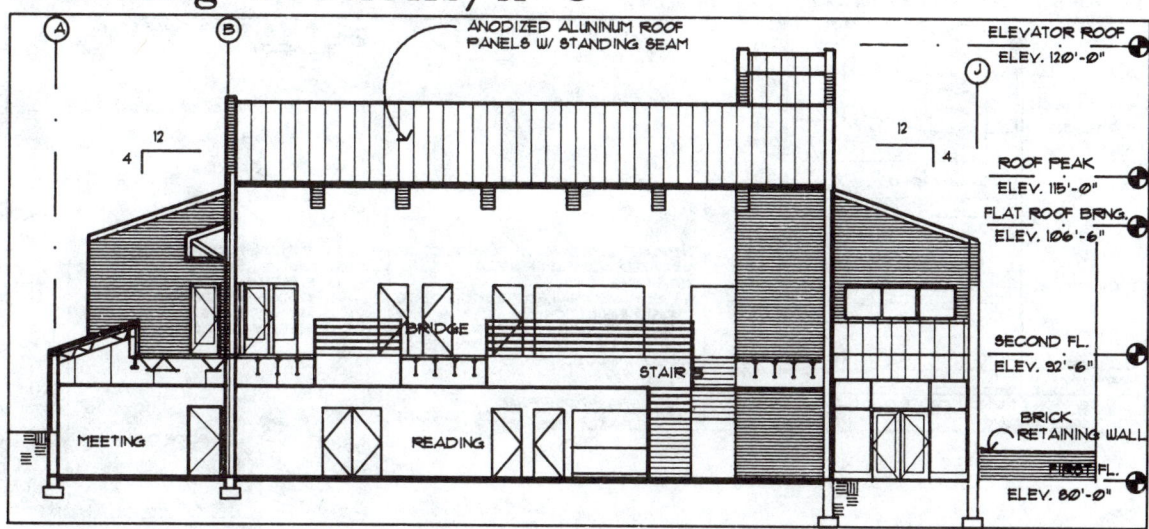

The longitudinal section shown above cuts through the vaulted reading room. The cut is perpendicular to the roof, showing each wood beam and the roof in elevation beyond the cut. The section below cuts through the major stair and fireplace. Both conditions are enlarged in order to show more detail.

The detail at the right cuts through the stone balcony.

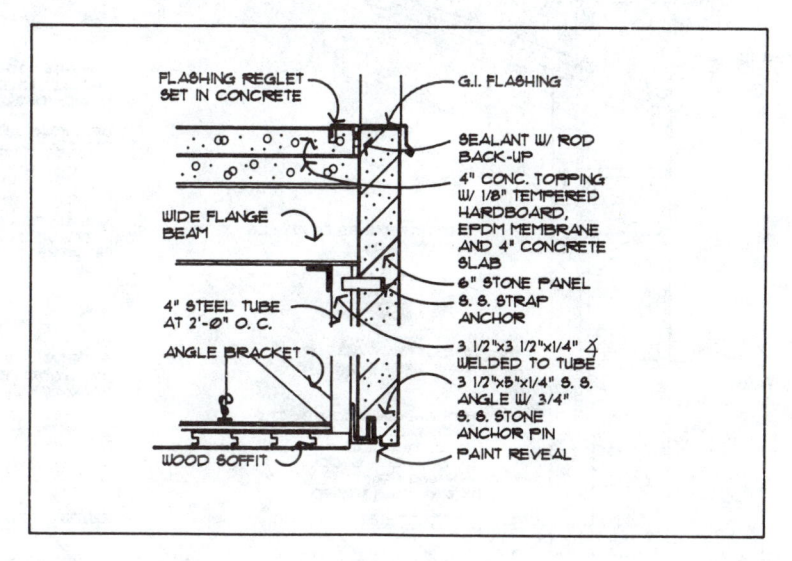

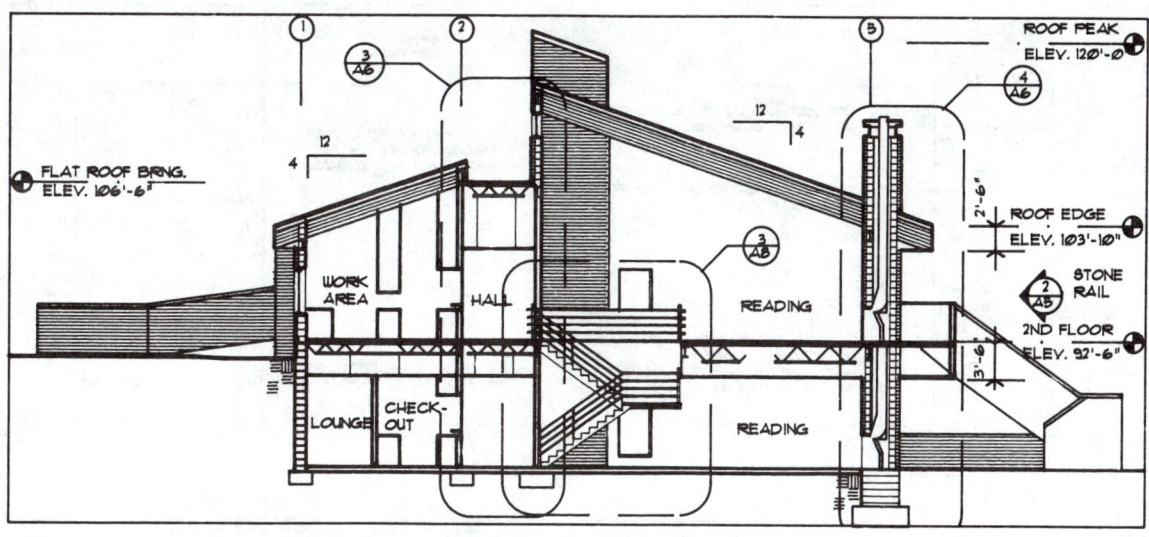

STUDENT LIBRARY 27-21

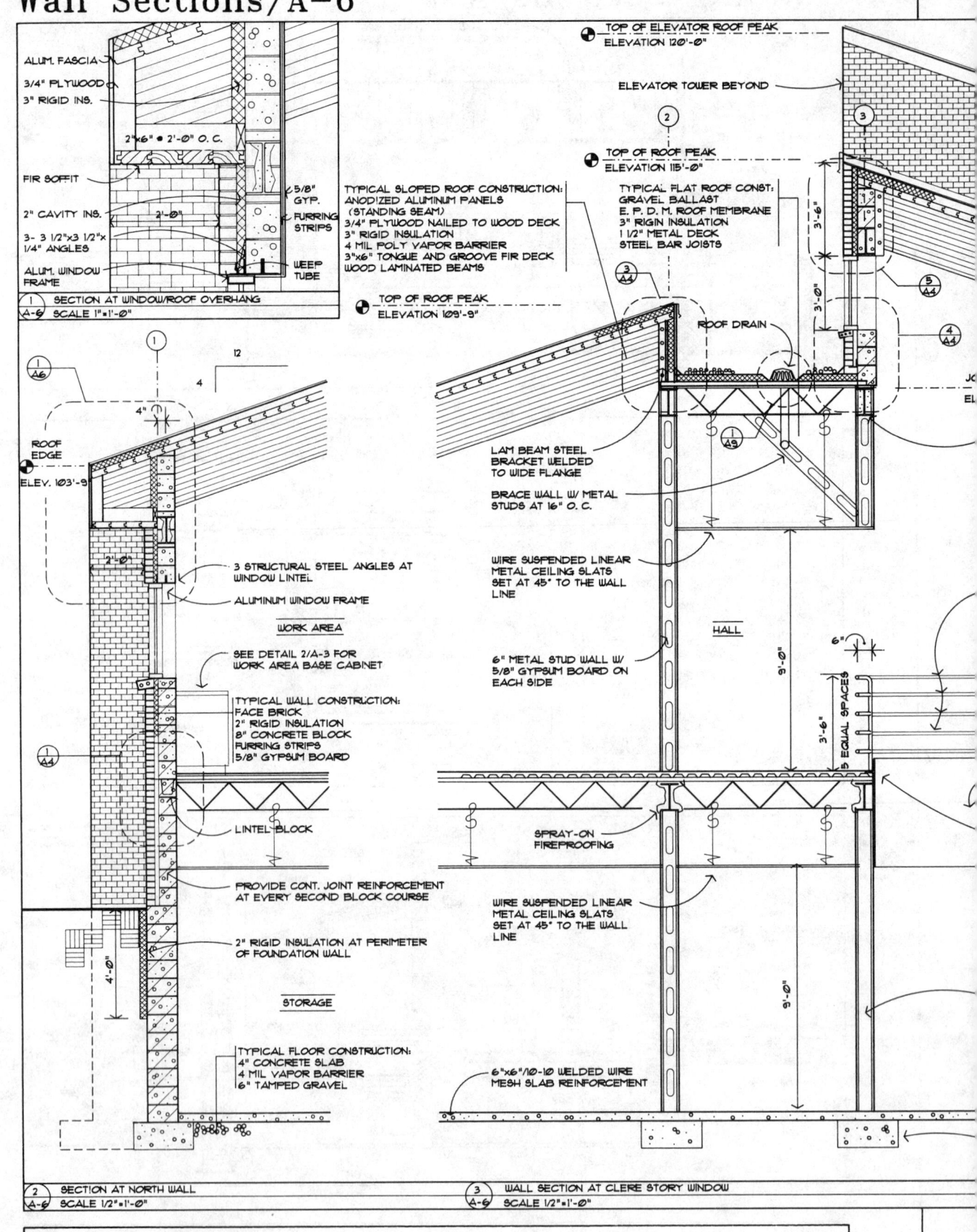

Wall Sections/A-6

Detail 1 — Section at Window/Roof Overhang (Scale 1"=1'-0")

Labels:
- ALUM. FASCIA
- 3/4" PLYWOOD
- 3" RIGID INS.
- 2"x6" @ 2'-0" O.C.
- FIR SOFFIT
- 2" CAVITY INS.
- 3 - 3 1/2"x3 1/2"x 1/4" ANGLES
- ALUM. WINDOW FRAME
- 5/8" GYP.
- FURRING STRIPS
- WEEP TUBE

TYPICAL SLOPED ROOF CONSTRUCTION:
ANODIZED ALUMINUM PANELS (STANDING SEAM)
3/4" PLYWOOD NAILED TO WOOD DECK
3" RIGID INSULATION
4 MIL POLY VAPOR BARRIER
3"x6" TONGUE AND GROOVE FIR DECK
WOOD LAMINATED BEAMS

TOP OF ELEVATOR ROOF PEAK ELEVATION 120'-0"

ELEVATOR TOWER BEYOND

TOP OF ROOF PEAK ELEVATION 115'-0"

TYPICAL FLAT ROOF CONST:
GRAVEL BALLAST
E.P.D.M. ROOF MEMBRANE
3" RIGID INSULATION
1 1/2" METAL DECK
STEEL BAR JOISTS

TOP OF ROOF PEAK ELEVATION 109'-9"

ROOF DRAIN

ROOF EDGE ELEV. 103'-9"

- 3 STRUCTURAL STEEL ANGLES AT WINDOW LINTEL
- ALUMINUM WINDOW FRAME
- WORK AREA
- SEE DETAIL 2/A-3 FOR WORK AREA BASE CABINET

TYPICAL WALL CONSTRUCTION:
FACE BRICK
2" RIGID INSULATION
8" CONCRETE BLOCK
FURRING STRIPS
5/8" GYPSUM BOARD

- LINTEL BLOCK
- PROVIDE CONT. JOINT REINFORCEMENT AT EVERY SECOND BLOCK COURSE
- 2" RIGID INSULATION AT PERIMETER OF FOUNDATION WALL
- STORAGE

TYPICAL FLOOR CONSTRUCTION:
4" CONCRETE SLAB
4 MIL VAPOR BARRIER
6" TAMPED GRAVEL

- LAM BEAM STEEL BRACKET WELDED TO WIDE FLANGE
- BRACE WALL W/ METAL STUDS AT 16" O.C.
- WIRE SUSPENDED LINEAR METAL CEILING SLATS SET AT 45° TO THE WALL LINE
- HALL
- 6" METAL STUD WALL W/ 5/8" GYPSUM BOARD ON EACH SIDE
- SPRAY-ON FIREPROOFING
- WIRE SUSPENDED LINEAR METAL CEILING SLATS SET AT 45° TO THE WALL LINE
- 6"x6"/10-10 WELDED WIRE MESH SLAB REINFORCEMENT

Detail 2 — Section at North Wall (Scale 1/2"=1'-0")

Detail 3 — Wall Section at Clere Story Window (Scale 1/2"=1'-0")

STUDENT LIBRARY

27-22

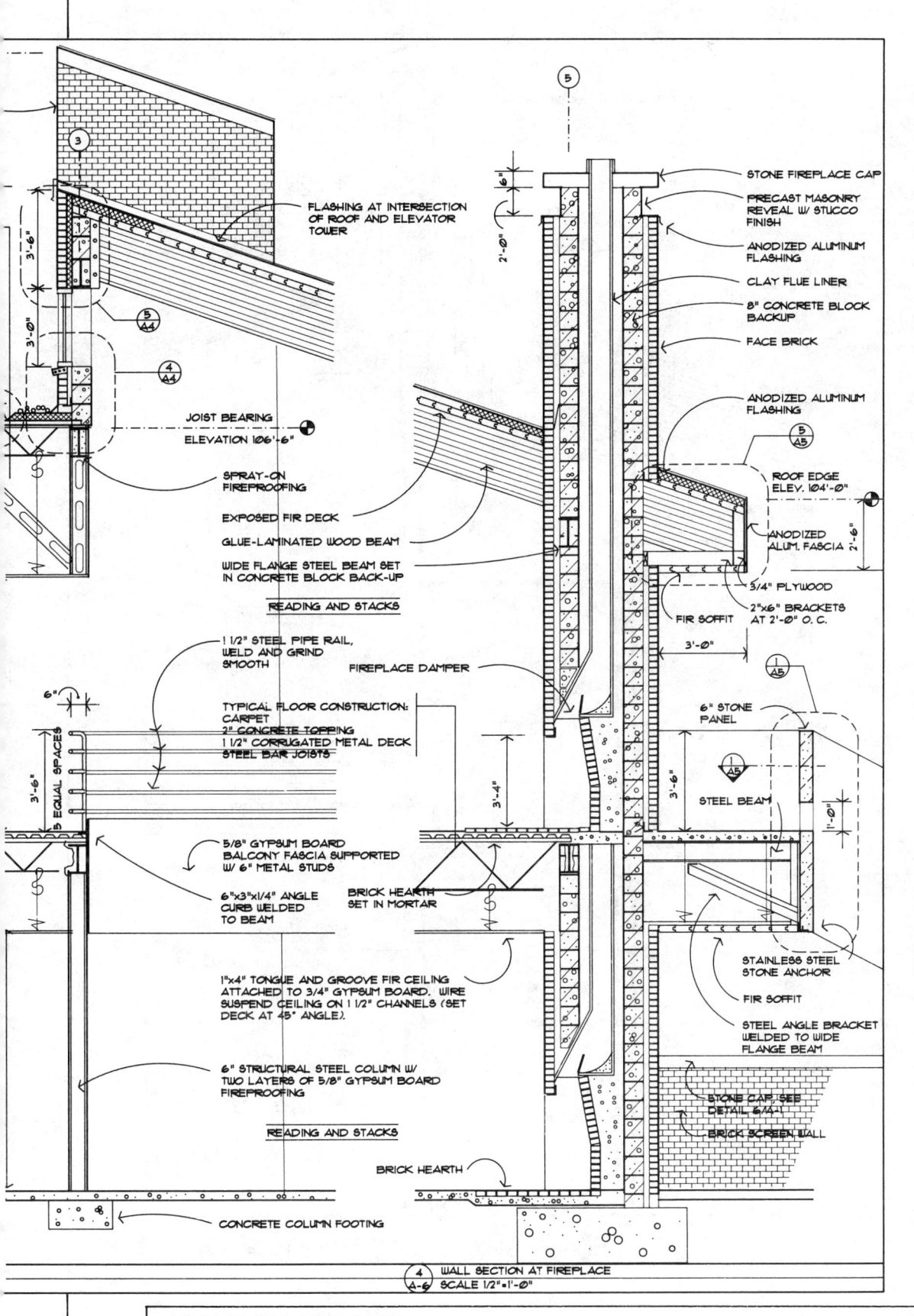

WALL SECTION AT FIREPLACE

STUDENT LIBRARY
PEPPERDINE UNIVERSITY
MALIBU, CA

WALL SECTIONS

A6

Labels (left section):
- FLASHING AT INTERSECTION OF ROOF AND ELEVATOR TOWER
- JOIST BEARING ELEVATION 106'-6"
- SPRAY-ON FIREPROOFING
- EXPOSED FIR DECK
- GLUE-LAMINATED WOOD BEAM
- WIDE FLANGE STEEL BEAM SET IN CONCRETE BLOCK BACK-UP
- READING AND STACKS
- 1 1/2" STEEL PIPE RAIL, WELD AND GRIND SMOOTH
- TYPICAL FLOOR CONSTRUCTION: CARPET / 2" CONCRETE TOPPING / 1 1/2" CORRUGATED METAL DECK / STEEL BAR JOISTS
- 5/8" GYPSUM BOARD BALCONY FASCIA SUPPORTED W/ 6" METAL STUDS
- 6"x3"x1/4" ANGLE CURB WELDED TO BEAM
- 1"x4" TONGUE AND GROOVE FIR CEILING ATTACHED TO 3/4" GYPSUM BOARD. WIRE SUSPEND CEILING ON 1 1/2" CHANNELS (SET DECK AT 45° ANGLE).
- 6" STRUCTURAL STEEL COLUMN W/ TWO LAYERS OF 5/8" GYPSUM BOARD FIREPROOFING
- READING AND STACKS
- BRICK HEARTH
- CONCRETE COLUMN FOOTING

Labels (right section):
- STONE FIREPLACE CAP
- PRECAST MASONRY REVEAL W/ STUCCO FINISH
- ANODIZED ALUMINUM FLASHING
- CLAY FLUE LINER
- 8" CONCRETE BLOCK BACKUP
- FACE BRICK
- ANODIZED ALUMINUM FLASHING
- ROOF EDGE ELEV. 104'-0"
- ANODIZED ALUM. FASCIA
- 3/4" PLYWOOD
- 2"x6" BRACKETS AT 2'-0" O.C.
- FIR SOFFIT
- 6" STONE PANEL
- STEEL BEAM
- FIREPLACE DAMPER
- BRICK HEARTH SET IN MORTAR
- STAINLESS STEEL STONE ANCHOR
- FIR SOFFIT
- STEEL ANGLE BRACKET WELDED TO WIDE FLANGE BEAM
- STONE CAP, SEE DETAIL 6/A-1
- BRICK SCREEN WALL
- BRICK HEARTH

4 WALL SECTION AT FIREPLACE
A-6   SCALE 1/2" = 1'-0"

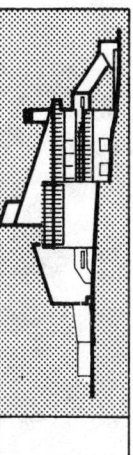

STUDENT LIBRARY

27-23

Wall Sections/A-6

TOP OF ELEVATOR ROOF PEAK
ELEVATION 120'-0"

ELEVATOR TOWER BEYOND

TOP OF ROOF PEAK
ELEVATION 115'-0"

TYPICAL SLOPED ROOF CONSTRUCTION:
ANODIZED ALUMINUM PANELS
(STANDING SEAM)
3/4" PLYWOOD NAILED TO WOOD DECK
3" RIGID INSULATION
4 MIL POLY VAPOR BARRIER
3"x6" TONGUE AND GROOVE FIR DECK
WOOD LAMINATED BEAMS

TYPICAL FLAT ROOF CONST:
GRAVEL BALLAST
EPDM ROOF MEMBRANE
3" RIGID INSULATION
1 1/2" METAL DECK
STEEL BAR JOISTS

TOP OF ROOF PEAK
ELEVATION 109'-9"

ROOF DRAIN

JOIST BEARING
ELEVATION 106'-6"

SPRAY-ON FIREPROOFING

LAM BEAM STEEL BRACKET WELDED TO WIDE FLANGE

BRACE WALL W/ METAL STUDS AT 16" O.C.

WIRE SUSPENDED LINEAR METAL CEILING SLATS SET AT 45° TO THE WALL LINE

HALL

READING AND STACKS

1 1/2" STEEL PIPE RAIL, WELD AND GRIND SMOOTH

6" METAL STUD WALL W/ 5/8" GYPSUM BOARD ON EACH SIDE

SPRAY-ON FIREPROOFING

5/8" GYPSUM BOARD BALCONY FASCIA SUPPORTED W/ 6" METAL STUDS

6"x3"x1/4" ANGLE CURB WELDED TO BEAM

WIRE SUSPENDED LINEAR METAL CEILING SLATS SET AT 45° TO THE WALL LINE

6" STRUCTURAL STEEL COLUMN W/ TWO LAYERS OF 5/8" GYPSUM BOARD FIREPROOFING

READING AND STACKS

6"x6"/10-10 WELDED WIRE MESH SLAB REINFORCEMENT

CONCRETE COLUMN FOOTING

This wall section cuts through the two-story vaulted ceiling in the reading room. The clere story window and flat roof are important elements in the wall assembly. Wide flange beams are used to bracket wood laminated beams for both sloped roofs. The steel beams also support bar joists on the flat roof. In addition, the section details the second-level balcony and handrail. All of these items will be blown up as details.

STUDENT LIBRARY

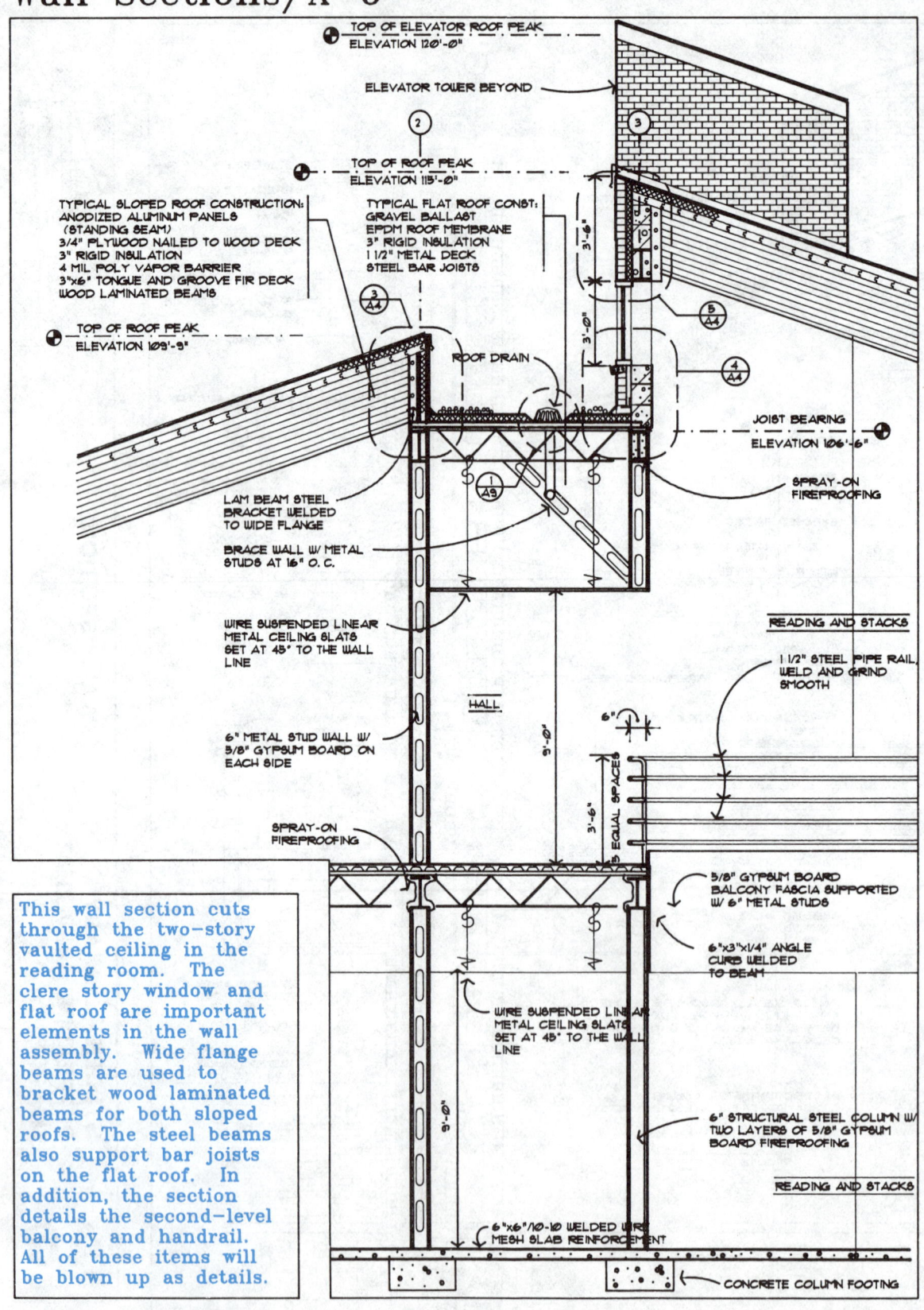

27-24

Wall Sections/A-6

Labels on drawing (top to bottom, right side):
- STONE FIREPLACE CAP
- PRECAST MASONRY REVEAL W/ STUCCO FINISH
- ANODIZED ALUMINUM FLASHING
- CLAY FLUE LINER
- 8" CONCRETE BLOCK BACK-UP
- FACE BRICK
- ANODIZED ALUMINUM FLASHING
- ROOF EDGE ELEV. 104'-0"
- ANODIZED ALUM. FASCIA
- 3/4" PLYWOOD
- FIR SOFFIT
- 2"x6" BRACKETS AT 2'-0" O.C.
- 6" STONE PANEL
- STEEL BEAM
- STAINLESS STEEL STONE ANCHOR
- FIR SOFFIT
- STEEL ANGLE BRACKET WELDED TO WIDE FLANGE BEAM
- STONE CAP SEE DETAIL 6/A.11
- BRICK SCREEN WALL

Labels on drawing (left side):
- EXPOSED FIR DECK
- GLUE-LAMINATED WOOD BEAM
- WIDE FLANGE STEEL BEAM SET IN CONCRETE BLOCK BACK-UP
- FIREPLACE DAMPER
- TYPICAL FLOOR CONSTRUCTION:
  CARPET
  2" CONCRETE TOPPING
  1 1/2" CORRUGATED METAL DECK
  STEEL BAR JOISTS
- BRICK HEARTH SET IN MORTAR
- BRICK HEARTH

Dimensions: 6", 2'-0", 3'-0", 3'-4", 3'-6", 2'-6", 1'-0"

This wall section details three elements: (1) the two levels of the fireplace, (2) the roof/fireplace intersection, and (3) the second-floor cantilevered balcony, the most complex of the three. Note that each column in the section supports a wide flange beam. The beam is used to support the stone handrail and concrete floor.

STUDENT LIBRARY   27-25

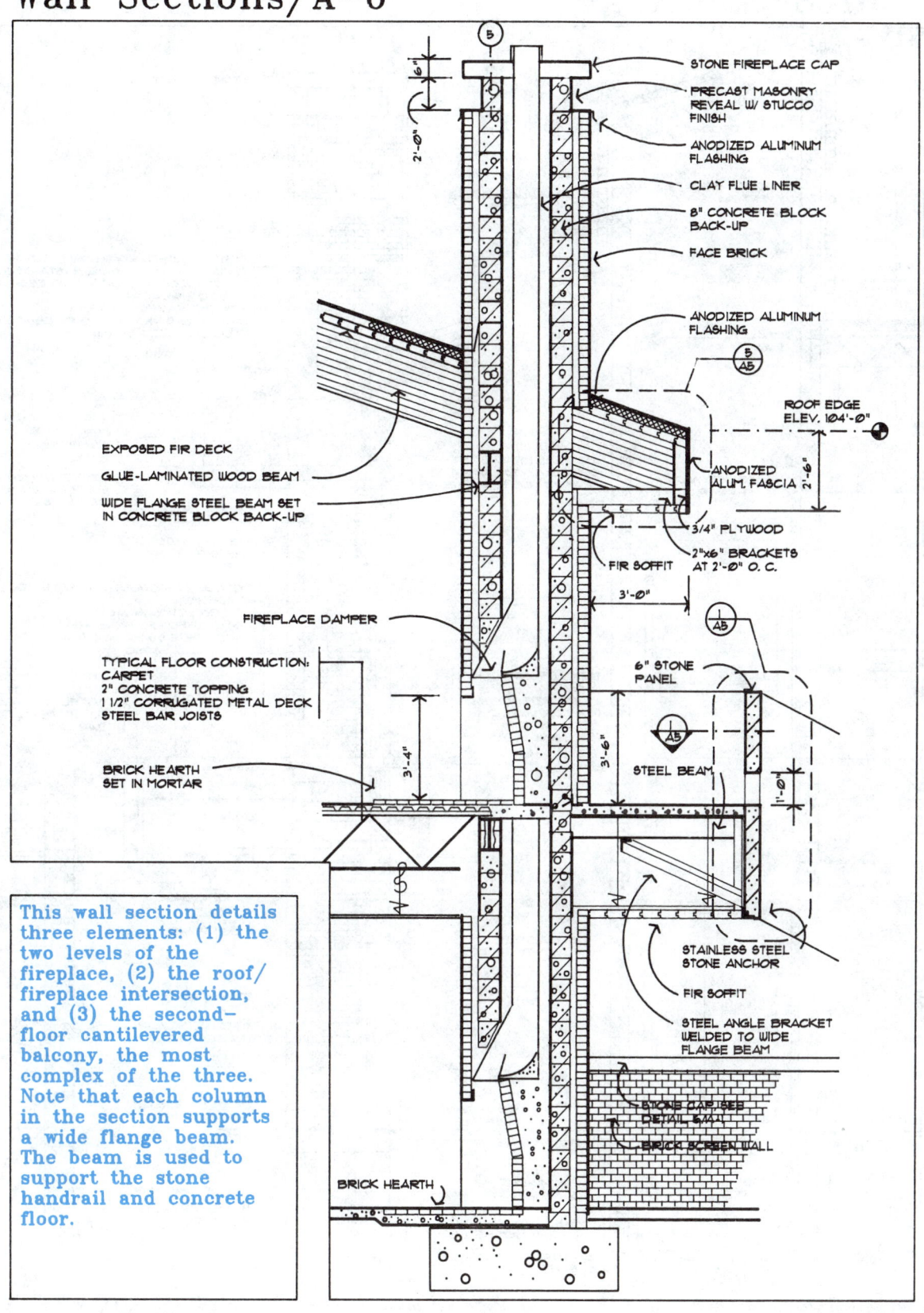

Wall Sections/A-7

STUDENT LIBRARY

Section 1 — SECTION THRU ELEVATOR SHAFT
SCALE 1/2"=1'-0"

- ROOF PEAK EL. 120'-0"
- METAL DECK BAR JOISTS
- LINTEL BLOCK
- PROVIDE BRICK TIES EVERY 2nd BLOCK COURSE
- THRU-WALL FLASHING W/ WEEP TUBE
- 3 1/2"x3 1/2"x1/4" CONTINUOUS SHELF ANGLE BRICK LEDGE
- THRU-WALL FLASHING W/ WEEP TUBES
- BRACKET WOOD LAM BEAM TO WIDE FLANGE
- JOIST BEARING ELEV. 115'-0"
- FASCIA AND HANGER COVER
- ELEVATOR CAB
- HALL
- CEILING LINE
- 8" CONCRETE MASONRY UNITS
- READING AND STACKS
- TOE GUARD
- FL. EL. 76'-0"
- PROVIDE PIT SUMP W/ FLOOR DRAIN
- SAND BED WITH WATERPROOF MEMBRANE
- HYDRAULIC ELEVATOR SHAFT

Section 2 — SECTION THRU BALCONY
SCALE 1/2"=1'-0"

- STONE CHIMNEY CAP
- TYPICAL SLOPED ROOF CONSTRUCTION:
  ANODIZED ALUMINUM PANELS (STANDING SEAM)
  3/4" PLYWOOD NAILED TO WOOD DECK
  3" RIGID INSULATION
  4 MIL POLY VAPOR BARRIER
  3"x6" TONGUE AND GROOVE FIR DECK
  WOOD LAMINATED BEAMS
- 1'-6" ROOF OVERHANG
- ANODIZED ALUMINUM FASCIA PANEL
- 3/4" PLYWOOD BACKUP
- TONGUE AND GROOVE FIR SOFFIT NAILED TO 2"x6" BRACKETS
- 2'-6" FASCIA
- USE STEEL BRACKET TO CONNECT WOOD LAMINATED BEAM TO WIDE FLANGE BEAM
- READING AND STACKS
- 9'-0" TO FACE OF BALCONY
- 3- 3 1/2" x 3 1/2" x 1/4" ANGLES FOR LINTEL SUPPORT
- TYPICAL EXTERIOR DECK CONSTRUCTION:
  4" CONCRETE
  1/8" PROTECTION BOARD
  1/16" UNCURED NEOPRENE SHEET
  4" CONCRETE STRUCTURAL SLAB
- TYPICAL FLOOR CONST:
  CARPET
  2" CONCRETE TOPPING
  1 1/2" CORRUGATED METAL DECK
  STEEL BAR JOISTS
- EL. 92'-6"
- 10'-0" HEAD HEIGHT (TYPICAL)
- 3'-6"
- STEEL BEAM
- STAINLESS STEEL STONE ANCHOR
- ANODIZED ALUM. FASCIA PANEL
- STONE CAP
- THRU-WALL FLASHING WITH WEEP TUBES
- ALUM. WINDOW FRAME
- PLASTIC LAM WINDOW STOOL
- THRU-WALL FLASHING W/ WEEP TUBE
- BRICK PAVERS SET IN 1" SAND BED
- 2" RIGID INSULATION
- TROWEL-ON WATERPROOFING
- 7'-0" TYPICAL HEAD HEIGHT

Section 3 — SECTION THRU MEETING ROOM AND...
SCALE 1/2"=1'-0"

- TYPICAL ROOF CONST:
  ANODIZED ALUM. PANELS
  3/4" PLYWOOD FASTENED TO 1 1/2" METAL DECK
  BAR JOISTS
- 92'-6"
- LINTEL BLOCK
- STEEL BEAM SUPPORT MOVABLE
- MOVABLE WALL
- 3- 3 1/2"x... ANGLES AT HEAD
- TYPE 5 W...
- PLASTIC
- 8" CONCRETE
- 2" RIGID
- 4" CONCRETE
- REINFORCED

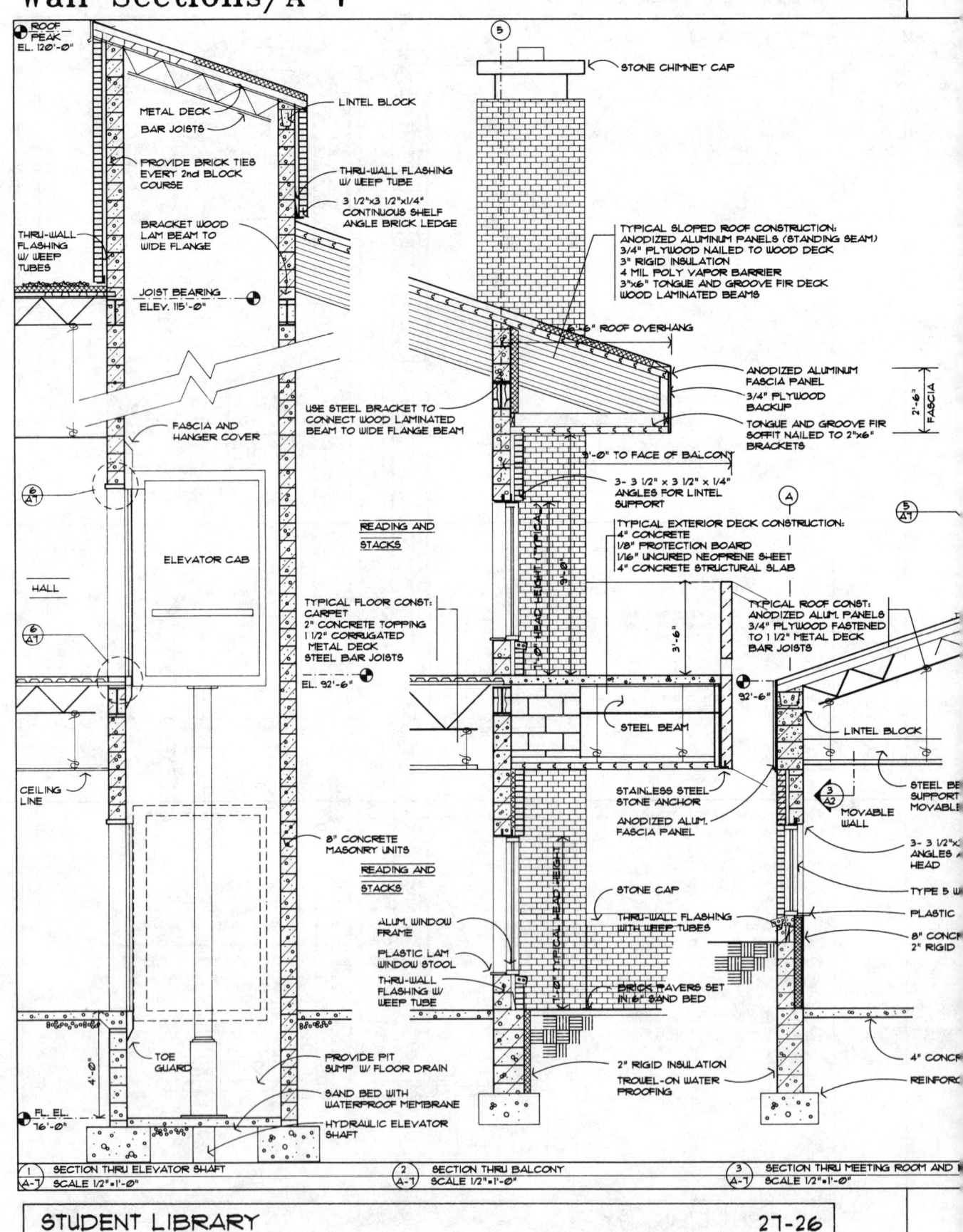

27-26

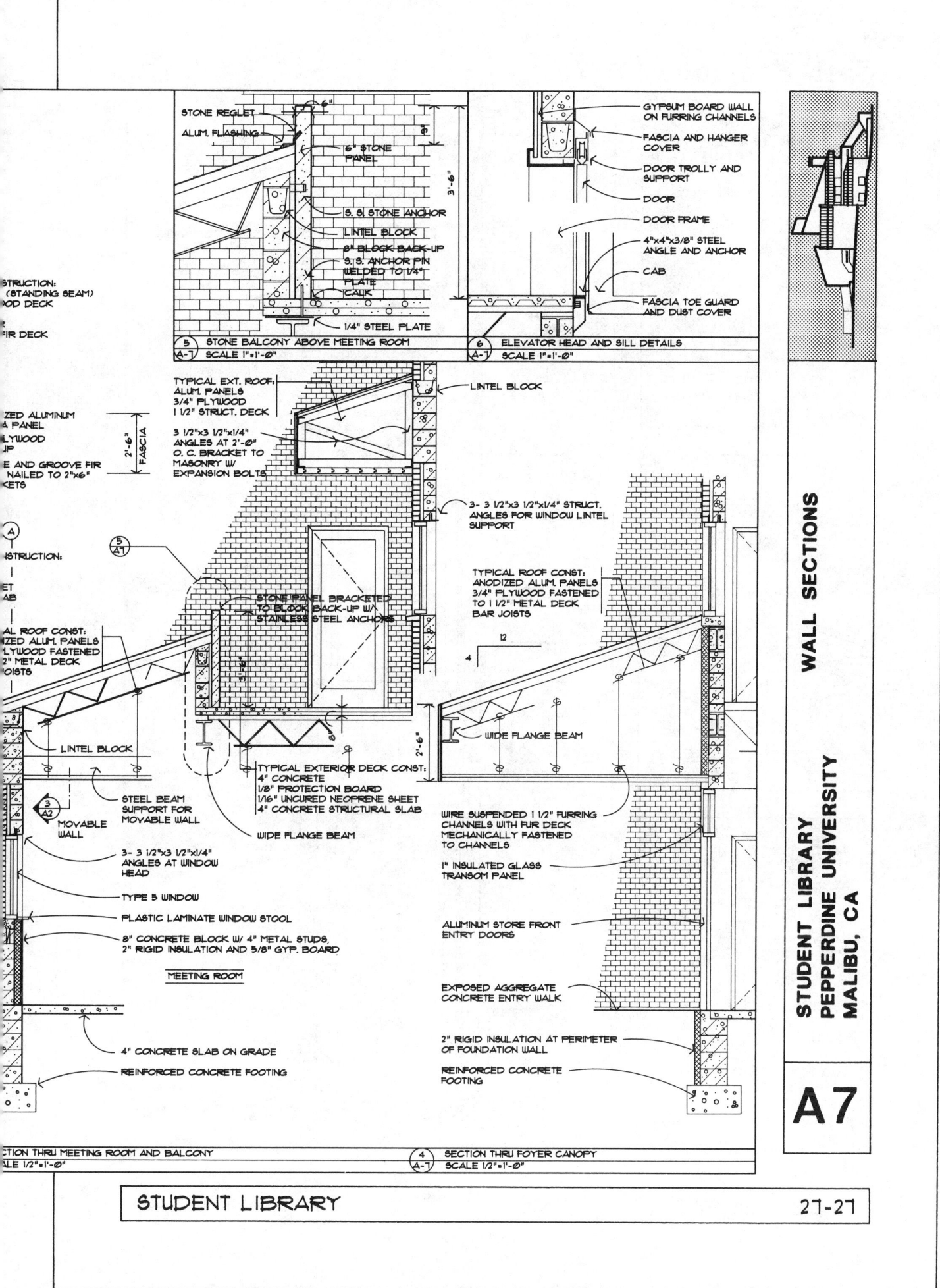

Detail 5 — Stone Balcony Above Meeting Room
Scale 1" = 1'-0"

- STONE REGLET
- ALUM. FLASHING
- 6" STONE PANEL
- S.S. STONE ANCHOR
- LINTEL BLOCK
- 8" BLOCK BACK-UP
- S.S. ANCHOR PIN WELDED TO 1/4" PLATE
- CAULK
- 1/4" STEEL PLATE

Detail 6 — Elevator Head and Sill Details
Scale 1" = 1'-0"

- GYPSUM BOARD WALL ON FURRING CHANNELS
- FASCIA AND HANGER COVER
- DOOR TROLLY AND SUPPORT
- DOOR
- DOOR FRAME
- 4"x4"x3/8" STEEL ANGLE AND ANCHOR
- CAB
- FASCIA TOE GUARD AND DUST COVER

Section Thru Meeting Room and Balcony
Scale 1/2" = 1'-0"

- TYPICAL EXT. ROOF:
  ALUM. PANELS
  3/4" PLYWOOD
  1 1/2" STRUCT. DECK
- 3 1/2"x3 1/2"x1/4" ANGLES AT 2'-0" O.C. BRACKET TO MASONRY W/ EXPANSION BOLTS
- 2'-6" FASCIA
- STONE PANEL BRACKETED TO BLOCK BACK-UP W/ STAINLESS STEEL ANCHORS
- LINTEL BLOCK
- STEEL BEAM SUPPORT FOR MOVABLE WALL
- MOVABLE WALL
- TYPICAL EXTERIOR DECK CONST:
  4" CONCRETE
  1/8" PROTECTION BOARD
  1/16" UNCURED NEOPRENE SHEET
  4" CONCRETE STRUCTURAL SLAB
- WIDE FLANGE BEAM
- 3- 3 1/2"x3 1/2"x1/4" ANGLES AT WINDOW HEAD
- TYPE 5 WINDOW
- PLASTIC LAMINATE WINDOW STOOL
- 8" CONCRETE BLOCK W/ 4" METAL STUDS, 2" RIGID INSULATION AND 5/8" GYP. BOARD
- MEETING ROOM
- 4" CONCRETE SLAB ON GRADE
- REINFORCED CONCRETE FOOTING

Section 4 — Section Thru Foyer Canopy
Scale 1/2" = 1'-0"

- LINTEL BLOCK
- 3- 3 1/2"x3 1/2"x1/4" STRUCT. ANGLES FOR WINDOW LINTEL SUPPORT
- TYPICAL ROOF CONST:
  ANODIZED ALUM. PANELS
  3/4" PLYWOOD FASTENED TO 1 1/2" METAL DECK BAR JOISTS
- 12 / 4
- WIDE FLANGE BEAM
- WIRE SUSPENDED 1 1/2" FURRING CHANNELS WITH FUR DECK MECHANICALLY FASTENED TO CHANNELS
- 1" INSULATED GLASS TRANSOM PANEL
- ALUMINUM STORE FRONT ENTRY DOORS
- EXPOSED AGGREGATE CONCRETE ENTRY WALK
- 2" RIGID INSULATION AT PERIMETER OF FOUNDATION WALL
- REINFORCED CONCRETE FOOTING

WALL SECTIONS

STUDENT LIBRARY
PEPPERDINE UNIVERSITY
MALIBU, CA

A7

STUDENT LIBRARY 27-27

Wall Sections/A-7

The detail below cuts through the canopy at the lower entry. The section shows two wide flange beams set into the concrete masonry wall. The upper beam supports the sloped bar joists of the canopy, while the lower beam holds the second floor and acts as a lintel for the entry door. Three steel angles above the second-floor window act as a header. The canopy ceiling is hung from wires tied to the sloped bar joists.

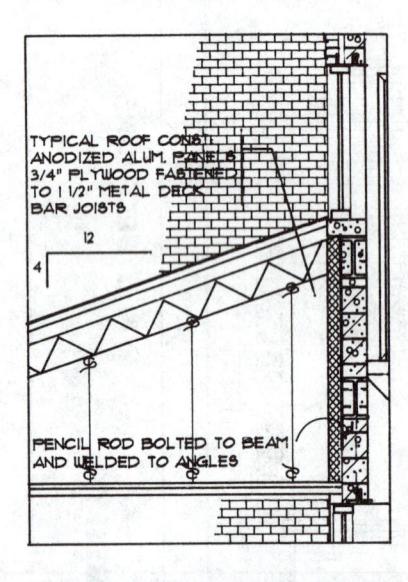

The wall section at the right shows a cut through the hydraulic elevator. (Note that the section was cut to fit the sheet.) This elevator uses a piston with a shaft that is drilled below the floor slab. It operates by pumping hydraulic fluid into the piston, causing it to rise. Most of the dimensions (including the pit size) are determined by reviewing elevator company specifications.

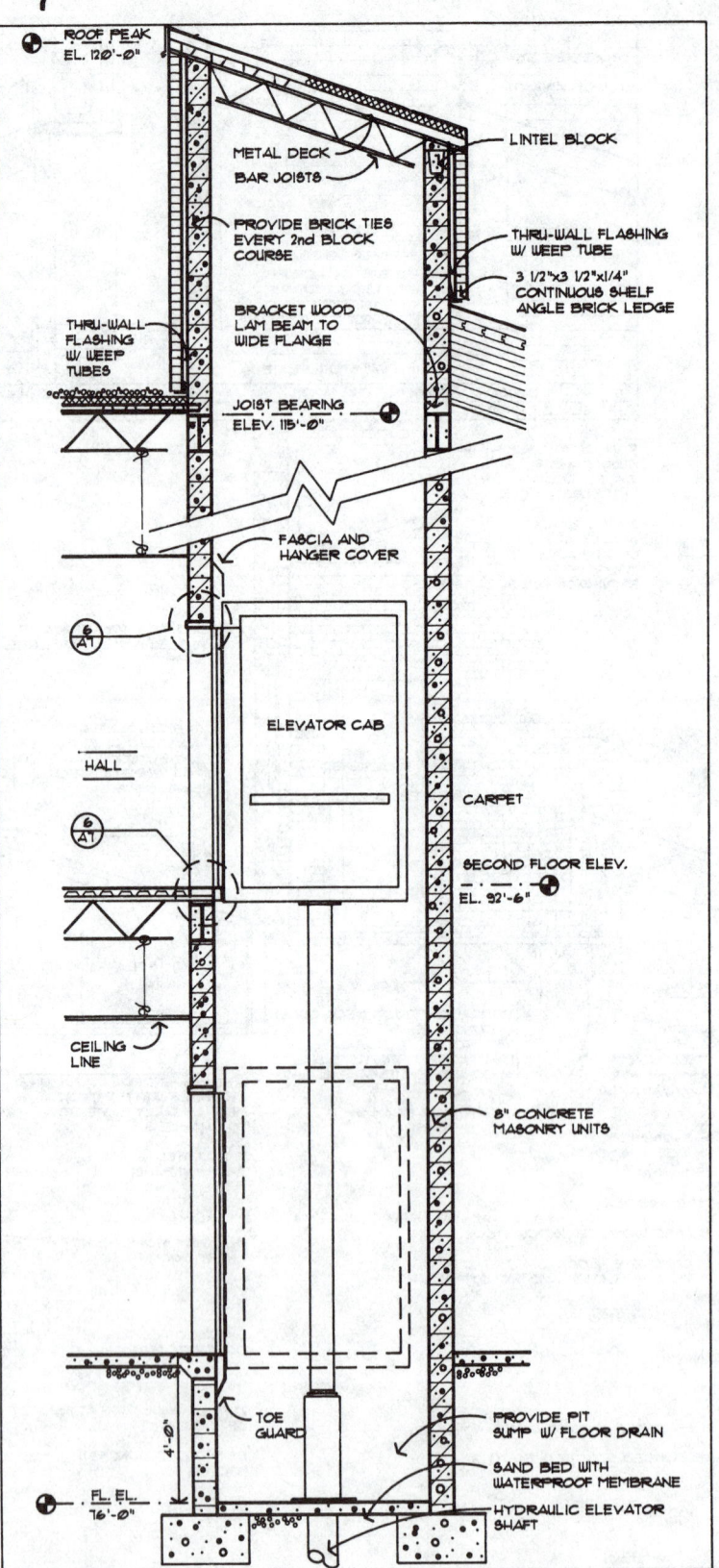

STUDENT LIBRARY   27-28

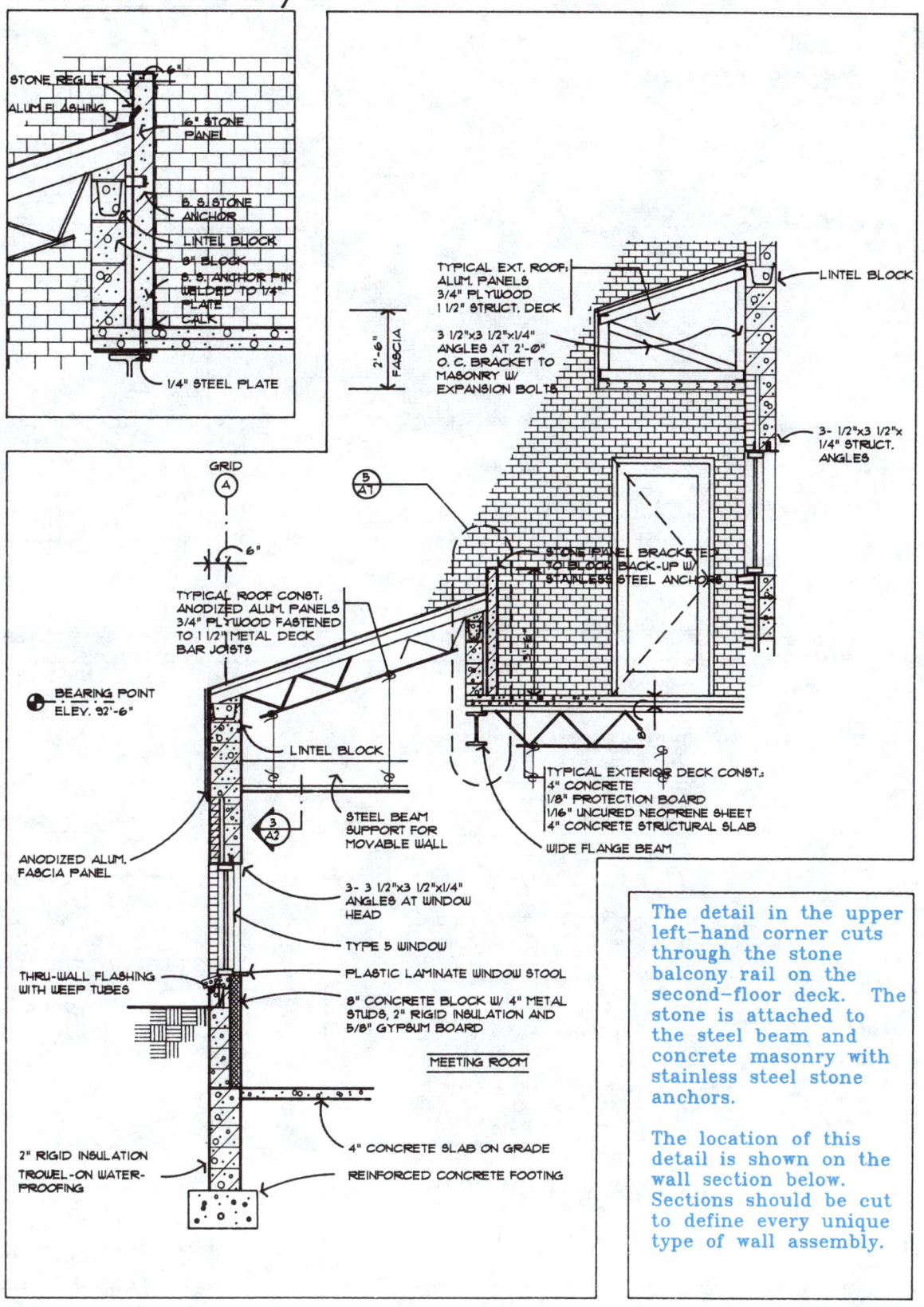

Wall Sections/A-7

Upper-left detail labels:
- STONE REGLET
- ALUM. FLASHING
- 6" STONE PANEL
- S. S. STONE ANCHOR
- LINTEL BLOCK
- 8" BLOCK
- S. S. ANCHOR PIN WELDED TO 1/4" PLATE
- CALK
- 1/4" STEEL PLATE

Right-side detail labels:
- TYPICAL EXT. ROOF: ALUM. PANELS, 3/4" PLYWOOD, 1 1/2" STRUCT. DECK
- 2'-6" FASCIA
- 3 1/2"x3 1/2"x1/4" ANGLES AT 2'-0" O.C. BRACKET TO MASONRY W/ EXPANSION BOLTS
- LINTEL BLOCK
- 3- 1/2"x3 1/2"x 1/4" STRUCT. ANGLES
- STONE PANEL BRACKETED TO BLOCK BACK-UP W/ STAINLESS STEEL ANCHORS
- TYPICAL EXTERIOR DECK CONST.: 4" CONCRETE, 1/8" PROTECTION BOARD, 1/16" UNCURED NEOPRENE SHEET, 4" CONCRETE STRUCTURAL SLAB
- WIDE FLANGE BEAM

Lower wall section labels:
- GRID A
- 6"
- TYPICAL ROOF CONST: ANODIZED ALUM. PANELS, 3/4" PLYWOOD FASTENED TO 1 1/2" METAL DECK, BAR JOISTS
- BEARING POINT ELEV. 92'-6"
- LINTEL BLOCK
- STEEL BEAM SUPPORT FOR MOVABLE WALL
- ANODIZED ALUM. FASCIA PANEL
- 3- 3 1/2"x3 1/2"x1/4" ANGLES AT WINDOW HEAD
- TYPE 5 WINDOW
- THRU-WALL FLASHING WITH WEEP TUBES
- PLASTIC LAMINATE WINDOW STOOL
- 8" CONCRETE BLOCK W/ 4" METAL STUDS, 2" RIGID INSULATION AND 5/8" GYPSUM BOARD
- MEETING ROOM
- 2" RIGID INSULATION TROWEL-ON WATERPROOFING
- 4" CONCRETE SLAB ON GRADE
- REINFORCED CONCRETE FOOTING

The detail in the upper left-hand corner cuts through the stone balcony rail on the second-floor deck. The stone is attached to the steel beam and concrete masonry with stainless steel stone anchors.

The location of this detail is shown on the wall section below. Sections should be cut to define every unique type of wall assembly.

STUDENT LIBRARY 27-29

Stairs and Reflected Ceilings/A-8

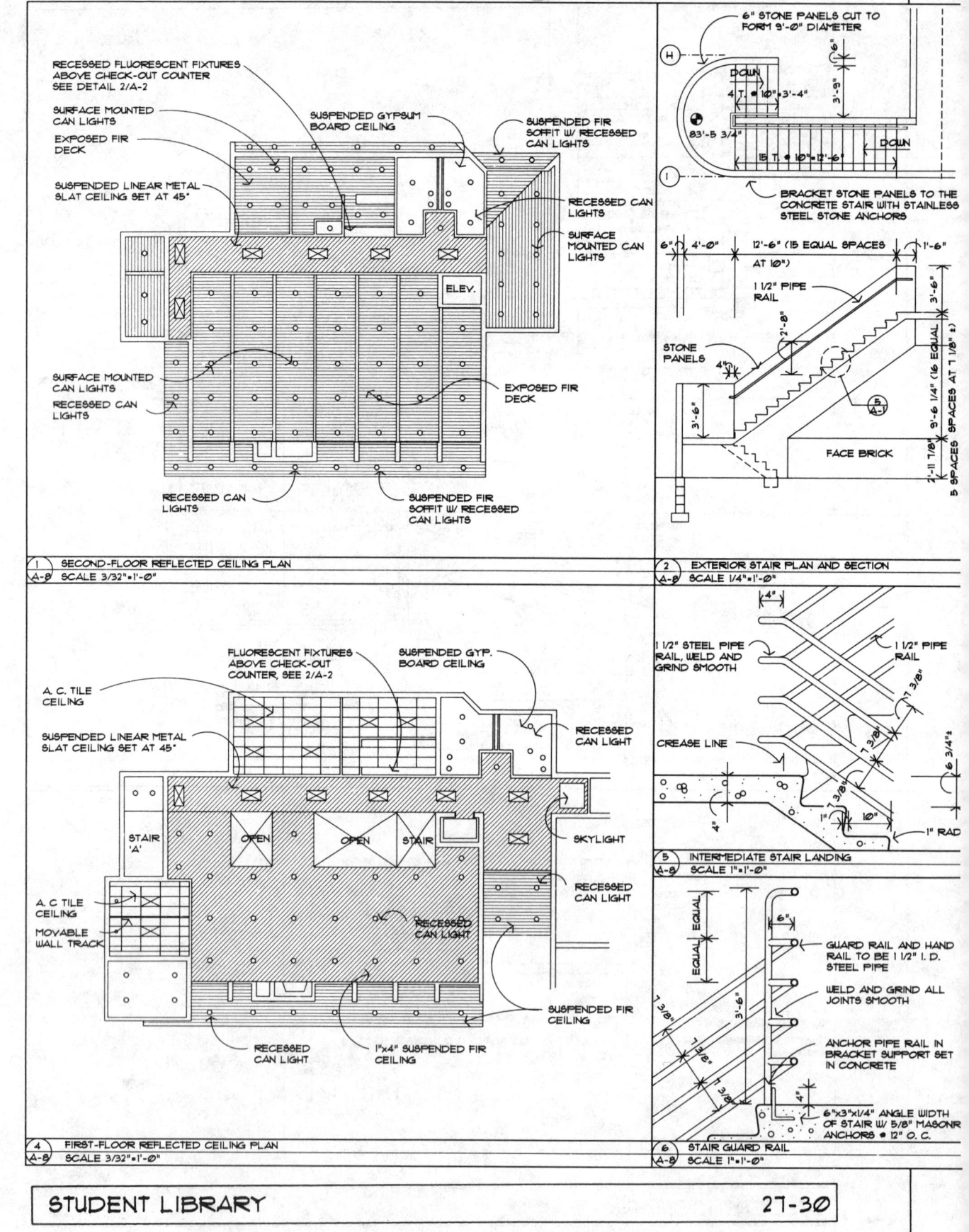

1 SECOND-FLOOR REFLECTED CEILING PLAN
A-8 SCALE 3/32"=1'-0"

Notes:
- RECESSED FLUORESCENT FIXTURES ABOVE CHECK-OUT COUNTER SEE DETAIL 2/A-2
- SURFACE MOUNTED CAN LIGHTS
- EXPOSED FIR DECK
- SUSPENDED LINEAR METAL SLAT CEILING SET AT 45°
- SUSPENDED GYPSUM BOARD CEILING
- SUSPENDED FIR SOFFIT W/ RECESSED CAN LIGHTS
- RECESSED CAN LIGHTS
- SURFACE MOUNTED CAN LIGHTS
- ELEV.
- SURFACE MOUNTED CAN LIGHTS
- RECESSED CAN LIGHTS
- EXPOSED FIR DECK
- RECESSED CAN LIGHTS
- SUSPENDED FIR SOFFIT W/ RECESSED CAN LIGHTS

2 EXTERIOR STAIR PLAN AND SECTION
A-8 SCALE 1/4"=1'-0"

- 6" STONE PANELS CUT TO FORM 9'-0" DIAMETER
- 4 T @ 10"=3'-4"
- 3'-9"
- 83'-5 3/4"
- 15 T @ 10"=12'-6"
- DOWN / DOWN
- BRACKET STONE PANELS TO THE CONCRETE STAIR WITH STAINLESS STEEL STONE ANCHORS
- 6", 4'-0", 12'-6" (15 EQUAL SPACES AT 10"), 1'-6"
- 1 1/2" PIPE RAIL
- 3'-6"
- 2'-8"
- STONE PANELS
- 4"
- 3'-6"
- 9'-6 1/4" (16 EQUAL SPACES AT 7 1/8" ±)
- 2'-11 7/8" / 5 SPACES
- FACE BRICK

4 FIRST-FLOOR REFLECTED CEILING PLAN
A-8 SCALE 3/32"=1'-0"

- FLUORESCENT FIXTURES ABOVE CHECK-OUT COUNTER, SEE 2/A-2
- SUSPENDED GYP. BOARD CEILING
- A.C. TILE CEILING
- SUSPENDED LINEAR METAL SLAT CEILING SET AT 45°
- RECESSED CAN LIGHT
- STAIR 'A'
- OPEN / OPEN / STAIR
- SKYLIGHT
- RECESSED CAN LIGHT
- A.C. TILE CEILING
- MOVABLE WALL TRACK
- RECESSED CAN LIGHT
- SUSPENDED FIR CEILING
- RECESSED CAN LIGHT
- 1"x4" SUSPENDED FIR CEILING

5 INTERMEDIATE STAIR LANDING
A-8 SCALE 1"=1'-0"

- 1 1/2" STEEL PIPE RAIL, WELD AND GRIND SMOOTH
- 1 1/2" PIPE RAIL
- CREASE LINE
- 4"
- 1 3/8"
- 6 3/4"
- 1"
- 10"
- 4"
- 1" RAD

6 STAIR GUARD RAIL
A-8 SCALE 1"=1'-0"

- GUARD RAIL AND HAND RAIL TO BE 1 1/2" I.D. STEEL PIPE
- WELD AND GRIND ALL JOINTS SMOOTH
- ANCHOR PIPE RAIL IN BRACKET SUPPORT SET IN CONCRETE
- 6"x3"x1/4" ANGLE WIDTH OF STAIR W/ 5/8" MASONRY ANCHORS @ 12" O.C.
- EQUAL / EQUAL
- 6"
- 3'-6"
- 4"

STUDENT LIBRARY 27-30

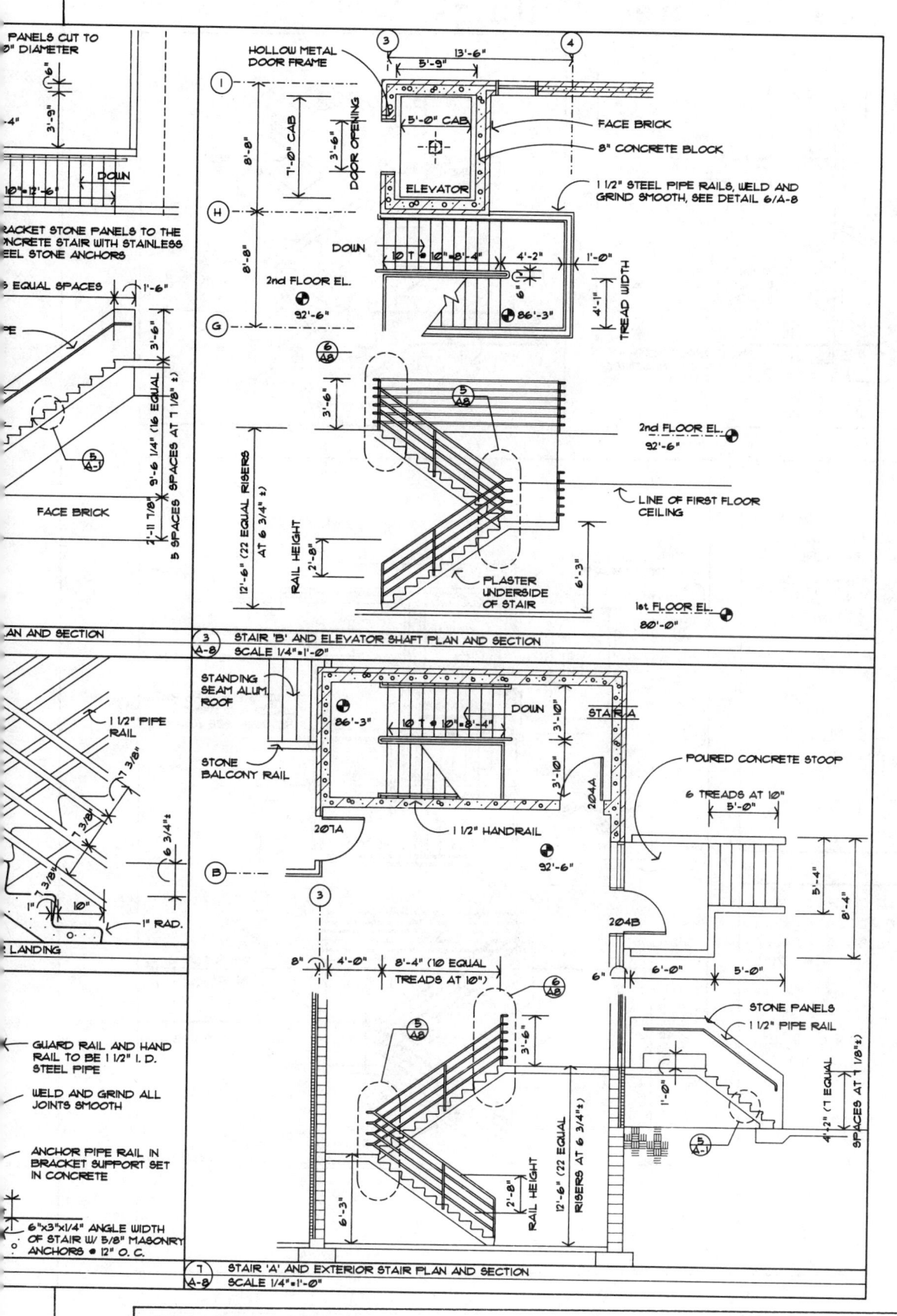

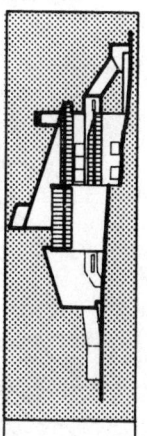

STAIRS AND REFLECTED CEILINGS

STUDENT LIBRARY
PEPPERDINE UNIVERSITY
MALIBU, CA

A8

Stair 'B' and Elevator Shaft Plan and Section
Scale 1/4" = 1'-0"

- Hollow Metal Door Frame
- 5'-0" CAB Elevator, 7'-0" CAB
- 3'-6" Door Opening
- Face Brick
- 8" Concrete Block
- 1 1/2" Steel Pipe Rails, weld and grind smooth, see detail 6/A-8
- DOWN, 10 T @ 10" = 8'-4"
- 4'-2" Tread Width, 1'-0"
- 2nd Floor El. 92'-6"
- 86'-3"
- 3'-6" Rail Height
- 12'-6" (22 Equal Risers at 6 3/4"±)
- 2'-8" Rail Height
- 2nd Floor El. 92'-6"
- Line of First Floor Ceiling
- Plaster Underside of Stair
- 6'-3"
- 1st Floor El. 80'-0"

Stair 'A' and Exterior Stair Plan and Section
Scale 1/4" = 1'-0"

- Standing Seam Alum. Roof
- Stone Balcony Rail
- 86'-3", 10 T @ 10" = 8'-4" DOWN
- Stair 'A'
- 1 1/2" Handrail
- 207A, 204A, 204B
- Poured Concrete Stoop
- 6 Treads at 10" = 5'-0"
- 5'-4", 8'-4"
- 92'-6"
- 6'-0", 5'-0"
- Stone Panels
- 1 1/2" Pipe Rail
- 8", 4'-0", 8'-4" (10 Equal Treads at 10")
- 3'-6"
- 12'-6" (22 Equal Risers at 6 3/4"±)
- 2'-8" Rail Height
- 6'-3"
- 4'-2" (7 Equal Spaces at 7 1/8"±)
- 1'-0"

Notes:
- Guard Rail and Hand Rail to be 1 1/2" I.D. Steel Pipe
- Weld and Grind all Joints Smooth
- Anchor Pipe Rail in Bracket Support set in Concrete
- 6"x3"x1/4" Angle width of stair w/ 5/8" Masonry Anchors @ 12" O.C.

STUDENT LIBRARY   27-31

Stairs and Reflected Ceilings/A-8

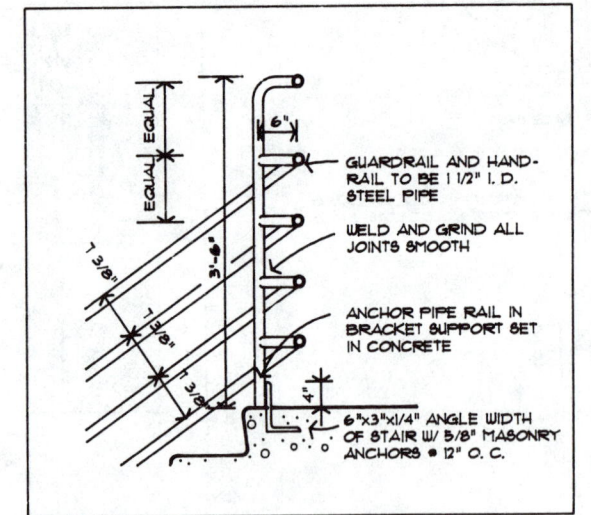

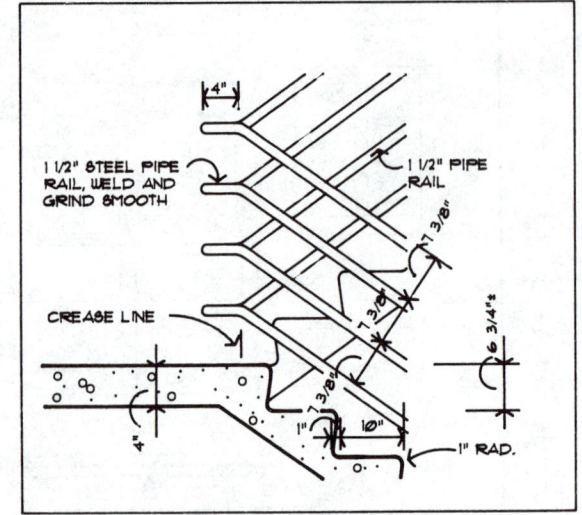

Stairs can present some unique detailing problems in a project. The two details shown above illustrate the railings at the top of the stair and at the landing. In preparing stair details, it is important to review local building code requirements in order to determine items such as tread and riser sizes, handrail heights, projections into the landings, and stair widths.

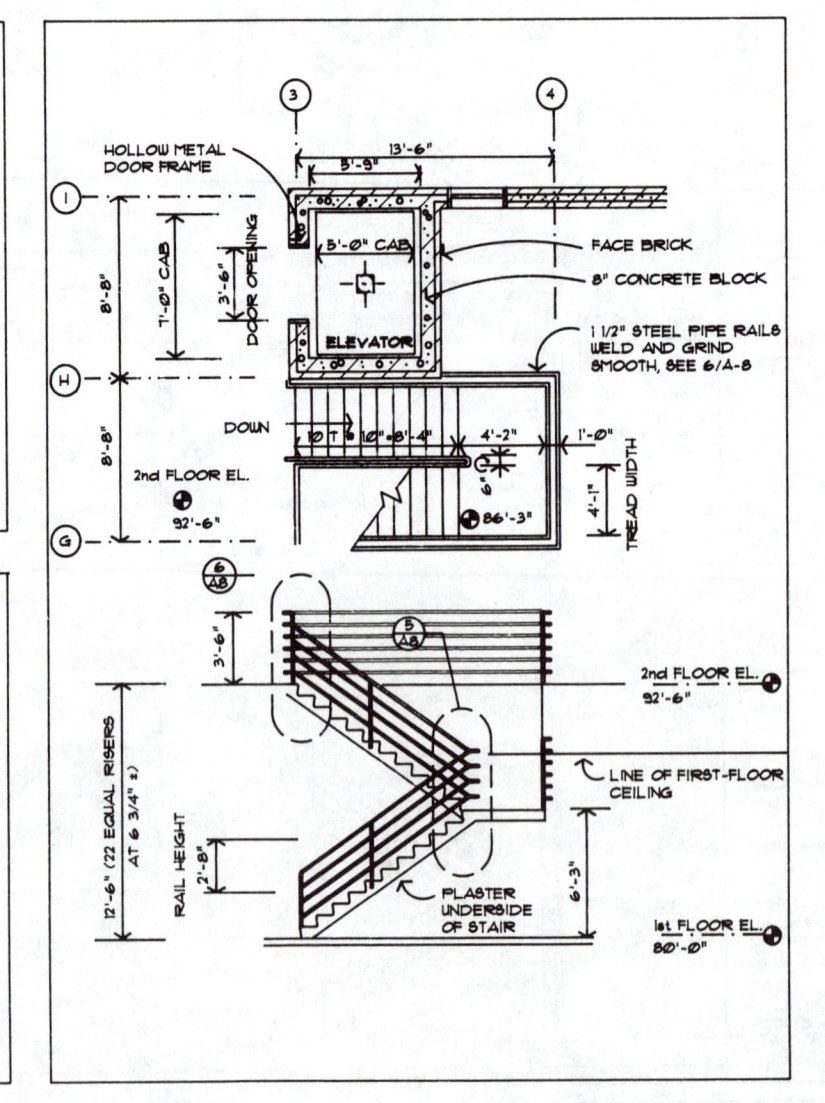

Commercial stairs are typically drawn in plan and section at a 1/4" scale in order to show the detail necessary to build these units. The stair illustrated to the right is the major stair in the reading room. It is called a <u>monumental stair</u> because it is open to the floor above. This type of stair may not be used as a code exit stair because it is not enclosed with fire-rated walls.

STUDENT LIBRARY

27-32

Stairs and Reflected Ceilings/A-8

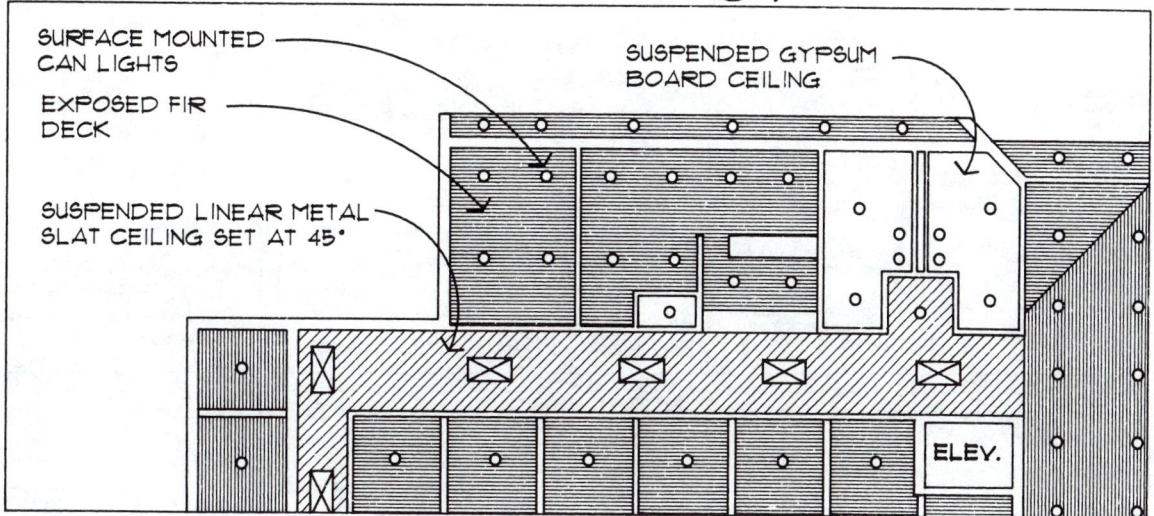

Labels on top drawing:
- SURFACE MOUNTED CAN LIGHTS
- EXPOSED FIR DECK
- SUSPENDED LINEAR METAL SLAT CEILING SET AT 45°
- SUSPENDED GYPSUM BOARD CEILING
- ELEV.

The drawing above shows a portion of the second-floor reflected ceiling plan. The plan is drawn with symbols that approximate the size and shape of the materials used: the circles indicate "can" light fixtures (round-surface mounted units), and the rectangles indicate fluorescent lights. The exposed beams and timber decking are drawn in rooms with vaulted ceilings.

The exterior stair is drawn in plan and section, as was the interior stair on page 27-32. The stair is constructed from poured concrete with stone panels attached to the structure with stainless steel pins and brackets. Detailing this stair requires more research than any other on the job. It would quite probably require meeting with a representative from a stone company to confirm the details.

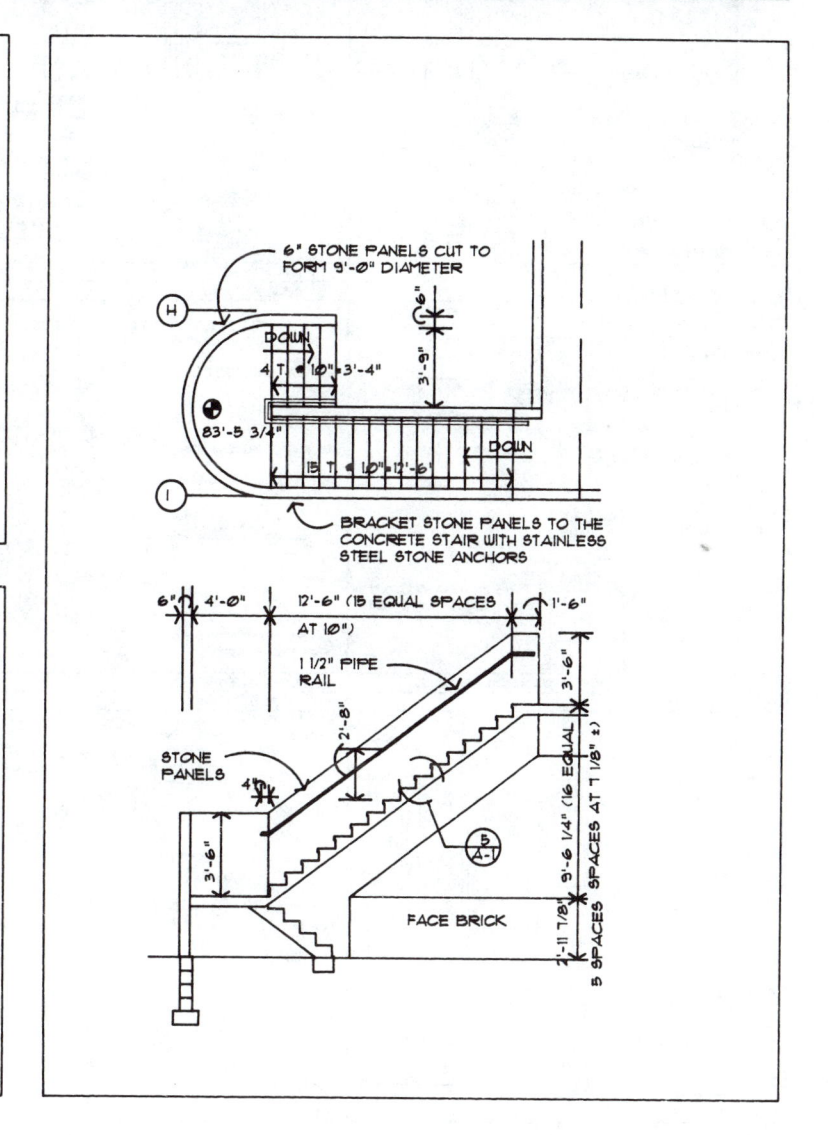

Labels on stair drawings:
- 6" STONE PANELS CUT TO FORM 9'-0" DIAMETER
- DOWN 4 T @ 10" = 3'-4"
- 83'-5 3/4"
- 15 T @ 10" = 12'-6" DOWN
- 3'-9"
- BRACKET STONE PANELS TO THE CONCRETE STAIR WITH STAINLESS STEEL STONE ANCHORS
- 6" 4'-0" 12'-6" (15 EQUAL SPACES AT 10") 1'-6"
- 1 1/2" PIPE RAIL
- 2'-8"
- 3'-6"
- STONE PANELS
- 3'-6"
- 9'-6 1/4" (16 EQUAL SPACES AT 7 1/8" ±)
- 2'-11 7/8" 5 SPACES
- FACE BRICK

STUDENT LIBRARY   27-33

Miscellaneous Details/A-9

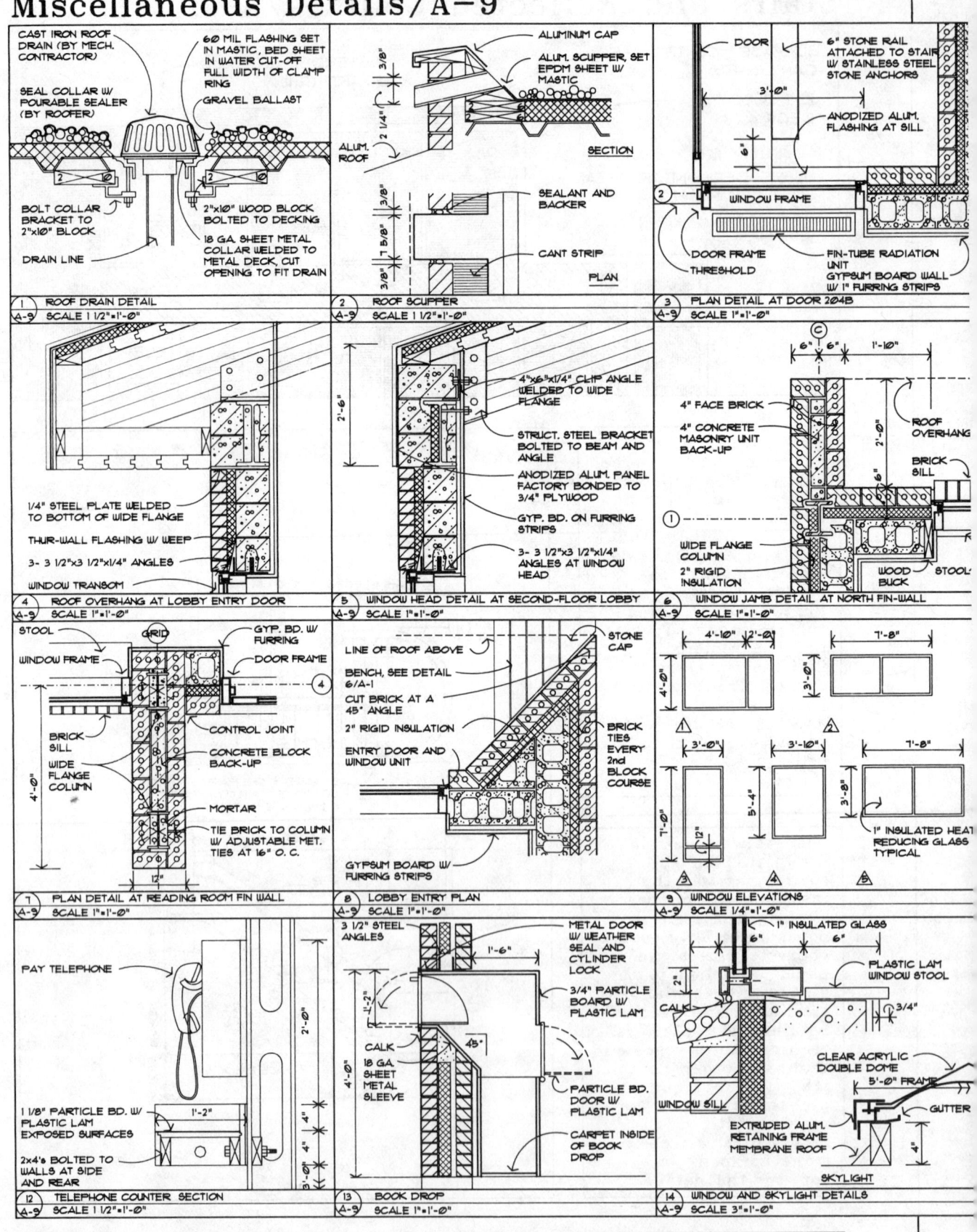

STUDENT LIBRARY 27-34

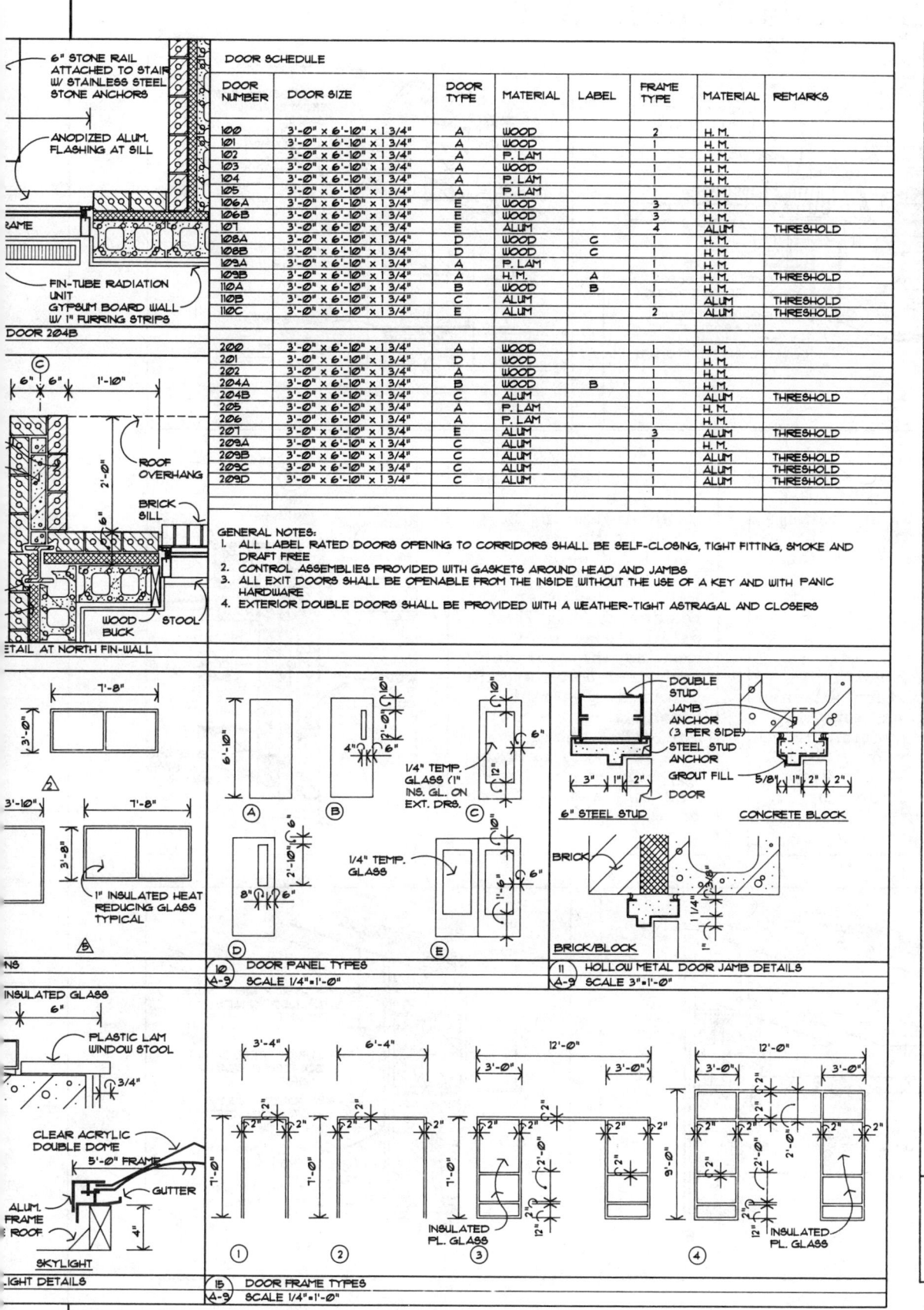

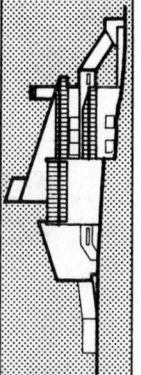

MISCELLANEOUS DETAILS

STUDENT LIBRARY
PEPPERDINE UNIVERSITY
MALIBU, CA

A9

DOOR SCHEDULE

DOOR NUMBER	DOOR SIZE	DOOR TYPE	MATERIAL	LABEL	FRAME TYPE	MATERIAL	REMARKS
100	3'-0" x 6'-10" x 1 3/4"	A	WOOD		2	H.M.	
101	3'-0" x 6'-10" x 1 3/4"	A	WOOD		1	H.M.	
102	3'-0" x 6'-10" x 1 3/4"	A	P. LAM		1	H.M.	
103	3'-0" x 6'-10" x 1 3/4"	A	WOOD		1	H.M.	
104	3'-0" x 6'-10" x 1 3/4"	A	P. LAM		1	H.M.	
105	3'-0" x 6'-10" x 1 3/4"	A	P. LAM		1	H.M.	
106A	3'-0" x 6'-10" x 1 3/4"	E	WOOD		3	H.M.	
106B	3'-0" x 6'-10" x 1 3/4"	E	WOOD		3	H.M.	
107	3'-0" x 6'-10" x 1 3/4"	E	ALUM		4	ALUM	THRESHOLD
108A	3'-0" x 6'-10" x 1 3/4"	D	WOOD	C	1	H.M.	
108B	3'-0" x 6'-10" x 1 3/4"	D	WOOD	C	1	H.M.	
109A	3'-0" x 6'-10" x 1 3/4"	A	P. LAM		1	H.M.	
109B	3'-0" x 6'-10" x 1 3/4"	A	H.M.	A	1	H.M.	THRESHOLD
110A	3'-0" x 6'-10" x 1 3/4"	B	WOOD	B	1	H.M.	
110B	3'-0" x 6'-10" x 1 3/4"	C	ALUM		1	ALUM	THRESHOLD
110C	3'-0" x 6'-10" x 1 3/4"	E	ALUM		2	ALUM	THRESHOLD
200	3'-0" x 6'-10" x 1 3/4"	A	WOOD		1	H.M.	
201	3'-0" x 6'-10" x 1 3/4"	D	WOOD		1	H.M.	
202	3'-0" x 6'-10" x 1 3/4"	A	WOOD		1	H.M.	
204A	3'-0" x 6'-10" x 1 3/4"	B	WOOD	B	1	H.M.	
204B	3'-0" x 6'-10" x 1 3/4"	C	ALUM		1	ALUM	THRESHOLD
205	3'-0" x 6'-10" x 1 3/4"	A	P. LAM		1	H.M.	
206	3'-0" x 6'-10" x 1 3/4"	A	P. LAM		1	H.M.	
207	3'-0" x 6'-10" x 1 3/4"	E	ALUM		3	ALUM	THRESHOLD
209A	3'-0" x 6'-10" x 1 3/4"	C	ALUM		1	H.M.	
209B	3'-0" x 6'-10" x 1 3/4"	C	ALUM		1	ALUM	THRESHOLD
209C	3'-0" x 6'-10" x 1 3/4"	C	ALUM		1	ALUM	THRESHOLD
209D	3'-0" x 6'-10" x 1 3/4"	C	ALUM		1	ALUM	THRESHOLD

GENERAL NOTES:
1. ALL LABEL RATED DOORS OPENING TO CORRIDORS SHALL BE SELF-CLOSING, TIGHT FITTING, SMOKE AND DRAFT FREE
2. CONTROL ASSEMBLIES PROVIDED WITH GASKETS AROUND HEAD AND JAMBS
3. ALL EXIT DOORS SHALL BE OPENABLE FROM THE INSIDE WITHOUT THE USE OF A KEY AND WITH PANIC HARDWARE
4. EXTERIOR DOUBLE DOORS SHALL BE PROVIDED WITH A WEATHER-TIGHT ASTRAGAL AND CLOSERS

---

10 DOOR PANEL TYPES — SCALE 1/4"=1'-0"

11 HOLLOW METAL DOOR JAMB DETAILS — SCALE 3"=1'-0"

15 DOOR FRAME TYPES — SCALE 1/4"=1'-0"

STUDENT LIBRARY 27-35

Miscellaneous Details/A-9

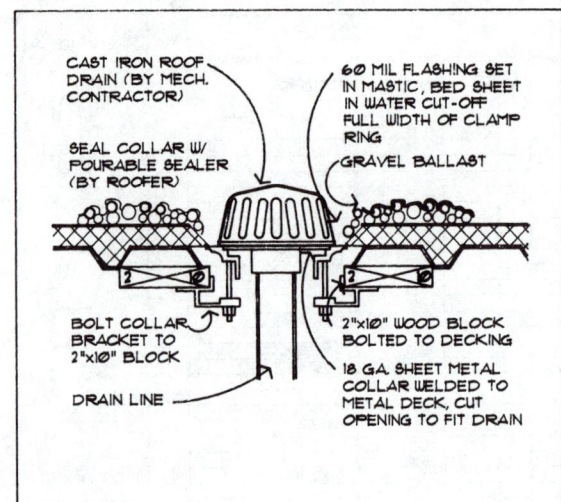

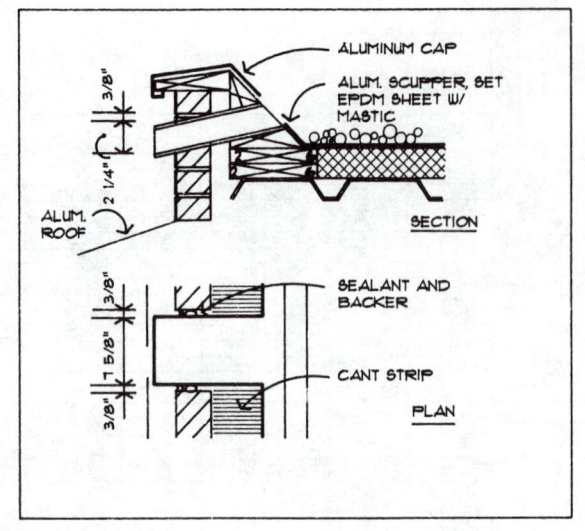

The two details above illustrate cuts through the roof water drainage system. The detail on the left shows the assembly of a cast iron roof drain. The unit is "flashed into" the EPDM flat roof. The drain is connected to an interior drain line that is in turn attached to the storm sewer. The second detail cuts through an overflow scupper. If the drain should become clogged, water runs off through the scupper.

The complexity of the building's wall system is illustrated in the detail at the right. The detail shows a plan view of a "fin wall" in the lower level reading room. The detail is begun by locating the grid line and steel columns (the columns support the second-floor balcony). The detail shows a window frame on the left side of the fin wall and a door frame on the right.

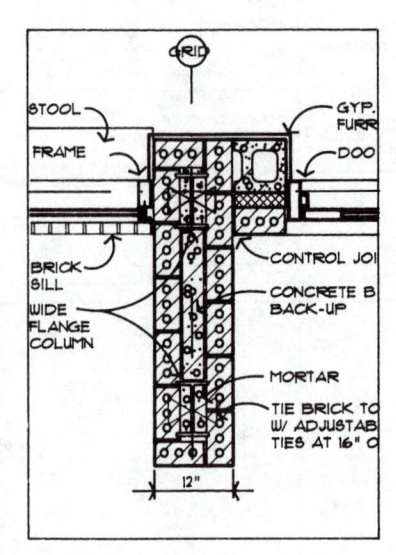

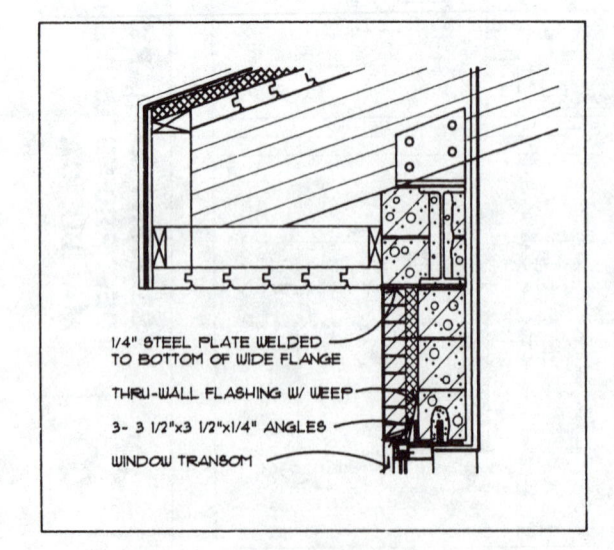

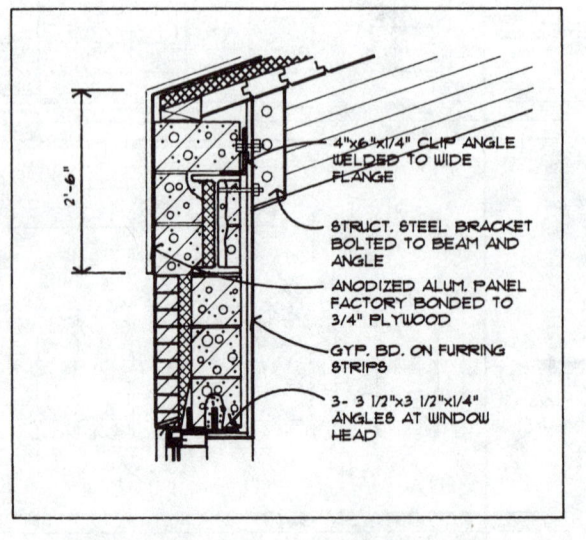

STUDENT LIBRARY

Miscellaneous Details/A-9

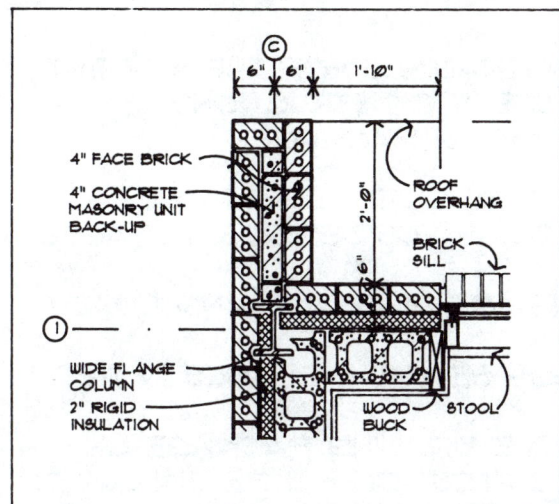

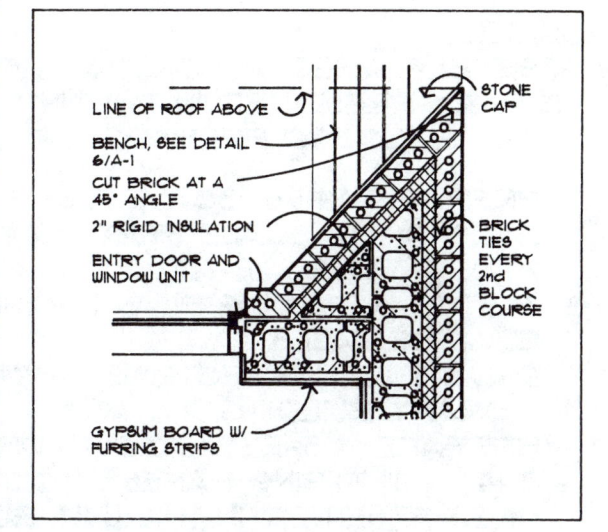

The plan details above illustrate two additional wall conditions. The detail top left cuts through the fin wall in the second-floor office. A wide flange column (at the intersection of grids "1" and "C" is incorporated into the concrete masonry back-up. The detail top right is cut through the 45° wall at the second-floor entry. The two drawings are drawn at a scale large enough to show every brick and block.

The detail at the right cuts through the book drop box at the lower floor entry. The detail shows the door opening through the brick wall and the particle board construction of the box.

The two details below illustrate a portion of the door schedule and the door frame elevations. Every door in the building is given a number and detailed by size and door type.

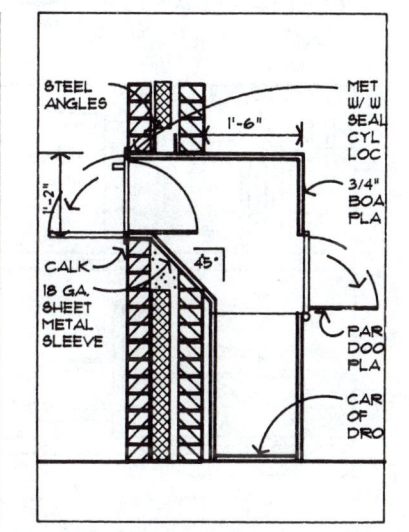

200	3'-0" x 6'-10" x 1 3/4"	A	WOOD
201	3'-0" x 6'-10" x 1 3/4"	D	WOOD
202	3'-0" x 6'-10" x 1 3/4"	A	WOOD
204A	3'-0" x 6'-10" x 1 3/4"	B	WOOD
204B	3'-0" x 6'-10" x 1 3/4"	C	ALUM
205	3'-0" x 6'-10" x 1 3/4"	A	P. LA
206	3'-0" x 6'-10" x 1 3/4"	A	P. LA
207	3'-0" x 6'-10" x 1 3/4"	E	ALUM
209A	3'-0" x 6'-10" x 1 3/4"	C	ALUM
209B	3'-0" x 6'-10" x 1 3/4"	C	ALUM
209C	3'-0" x 6'-10" x 1 3/4"	C	ALUM
209D	3'-0" x 6'-10" x 1 3/4"	C	ALUM

GENERAL NOTES:
1. ALL LABEL RATED DOORS OPENING TO CORRIDO
2. CONTROL ASSEMBLIES PROVIDED WITH GASKETS
3. ALL EXIT DOORS SHALL BE OPENABLE FROM THE HARDWARE
4. EXTERIOR DOUBLE DOORS SHALL BE PROVIDED

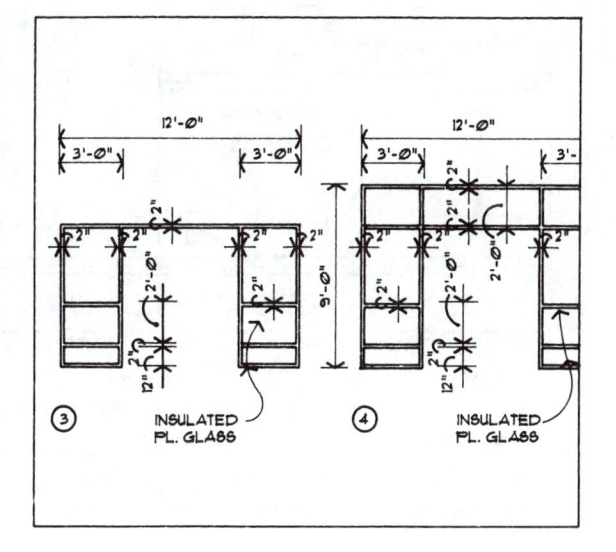

STUDENT LIBRARY   27-31

REPLAY

ASSEMBLE A SET OF CONSTRUCTION DRAWINGS FOR THE STUDENT LIBRARY PRESENTED IN THIS UNIT. USE THE INSTRUCTIONS LISTED BELOW TO PREPARE THE DRAWING PACKAGE.

1. PREPARE AN 1/8" SCALE FLOOR PLAN ON TRACING PAPER.
2. BUILD A 1/16" SCALE STUDY MODEL OF YOUR PROJECT (PAGES 29-25 THROUGH 29-30).
3. SKETCH A FRAMING PLAN SHOWING JOSITS, BEAMS, AND LOAD-BEARING WALLS.
4. DRAW BUILDING SECTIONS THROUGH SEVERAL PLACES IN THE LIBRARY BUILDING.
5. PREPARE A SHEET LAYOUT FOR THE DRAWING PACKAGE ON 8 1/2" x 11" TYPING PAPER. YOUR LAYOUT COULD BE SIMILAR TO ONE PRESENTED IN THIS UNIT, BUT TRY TO VARY THE ORGANIZATION. BE SURE TO ALLOW ENOUGH ROOM FOR NOTES AND DIMENSIONS.

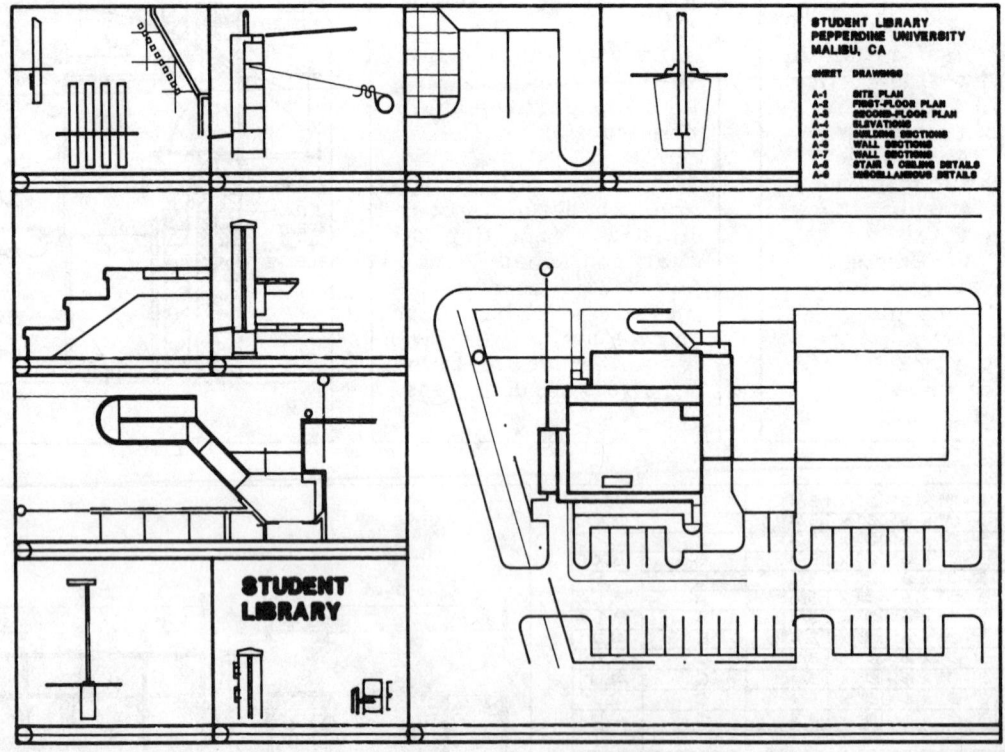

6. ONCE YOU ARE SATISFIED WITH THE SHEET LAYOUT, TRANSFER THE PRELIMINARY DRAWINGS TO THE FINAL VELLUM SHEETS.
7. PREPARE A TIME SCHEDULE FOR THE ASSEMBLY OF THE DRAWING SET (REFER TO UNIT 11, "PROBLEM SOLVING").
8. PREPARE A SET OF PRINTS OF YOUR PROJECT AT APPROXIMATELY 50% AND 75% COMPLETION. USE A FELT-TIP PEN TO MAKE CORRECTIONS AND CHANGES IN YOUR WORK

STUDENT LIBRARY

28 PRESENTATION DRAWINGS

A PRESENTATION DRAWING SHOWS A BUILDING IN ITS NATURAL SURROUNDINGS; IT IS INTENDED TO PROVIDE A CLIENT WITH A REALISTIC VIEW OF THE COMPLETED BUILDING. THE ADDITION OF TREES, CARS, AND PEOPLE TO THE DRAWING PROVIDES THE SCALE NEEDED SO THAT THE BUILDING CAN BE VISUALIZED WHILE IT IS STILL IN THE DESIGN PHASE. IN THIS STAGE, IT IS IMPORTANT TO GIVE YOUR CLIENT A VIEW OF THE PROJECT THAT HE OR SHE CAN UNDERSTAND, SO PRESENTATION DRAWINGS ARE USUALLY ASSEMBLED BEFORE WORKING DRAWINGS ARE PREPARED. THIS UNIT WILL PRESENT BASIC INFORMATION FOR DEVELOPING PRESENTATION ELEVATIONS, ISOMETRICS, AND PERSPECTIVE DRAWINGS.

ELEVATIONS

THE FIRST FORM OF PRESENTATION DRAWINGS WE WILL LOOK AT ARE ELEVATIONS WITH ADDED DETAILS. TYPICALLY, THIS MEANS ADDING TREES, MATERIAL HATCHING, AND PEOPLE TO A DRAWING THAT HAS ALREADY BEEN DEVELOPED IN THE PRELIMINARY DRAWING STAGE. TO THE LEFT IS SHOWN THE OUTLINE OF A CABIN THAT WAS DEVELOPED IN THE EARLY DESIGN STAGE. IN THE FOLLOWING STEPS, MATERIALS AND OTHER DETAILS WILL BE ADDED TO THE BASE ELEVATION. THE TECHNIQUES USED ARE QUITE SIMPLE; IT ISN'T NECESSARY TO HAVE A DEGREE IN ART TO "DRESS UP" A DRAWING IN A SIMPLE WAY.

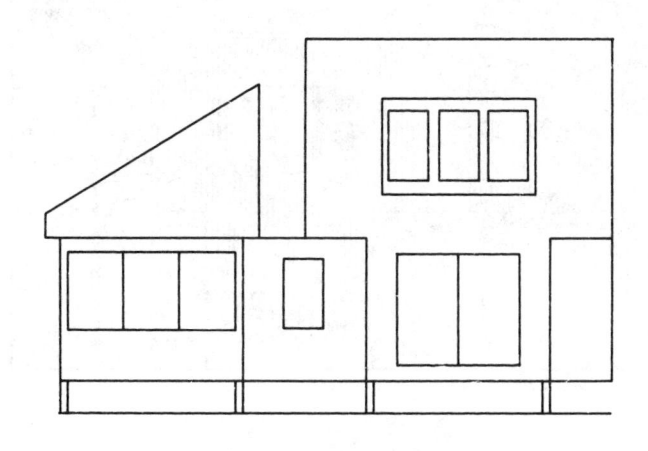

PRESENTATION DRAWINGS 28-1

IN THIS STEP SIDING AND WINDOW FRAMES ARE ADDED TO THE ELEVATION. USE A LIGHTER LINE QUALITY FOR ITEMS THAT ARE LESS IMPORTANT THAN THE BUILDING OUTLINE.

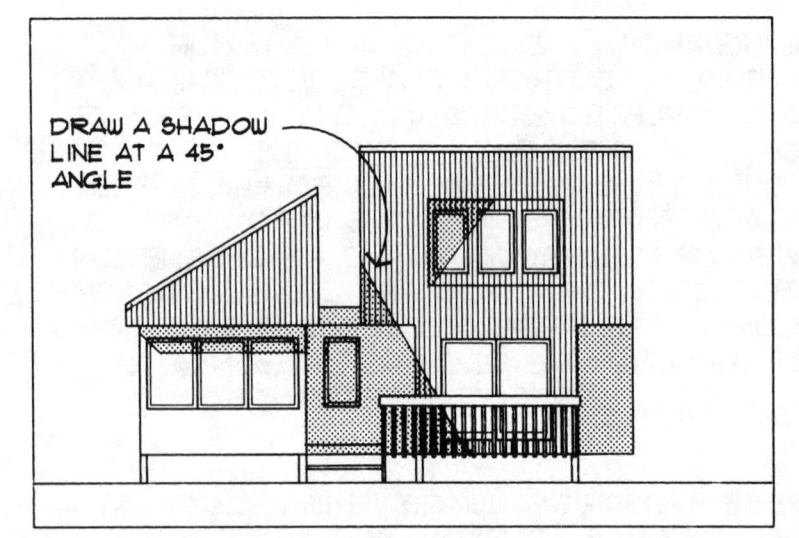

DRAW A SHADOW LINE AT A 45° ANGLE

IN THE NEXT STEP THE DECK RAIL, WINDOW SHADING, AND SHADOW LINES ARE ADDED TO THE ELEVATION. YOU CAN SAVE TIME BY USING A DRY-TRANSFER FILM (LIKE ZIP-A-TONE) FOR SHADING. THE SEMI-STICKY FILM HAS A DOT TEXTURE; IT IS APPLIED TO THE DRAWING AND TRIMMED WITH A MAT KNIFE. AN EASY WAY TO DETERMINE SHADOW LINES IS TO SHINE A BRIGHT LIGHT ON YOUR STUDY MODEL.

IN THE FINAL STEP TREES AND PEOPLE ARE ADDED TO THE ELEVATION. USE TRACING PAPER TO MAKE AN OVERLAY SKETCH OF THE PLACEMENT BEFORE YOU BEGIN THE DRAWING. FIGURES CAN BE ADDED TO THE DRAWING BY TRACING THEM FROM OTHER DRAWINGS, OR PRESS-ON TRANSFERS OF TREES AND PEOPLE CAN BE USED.

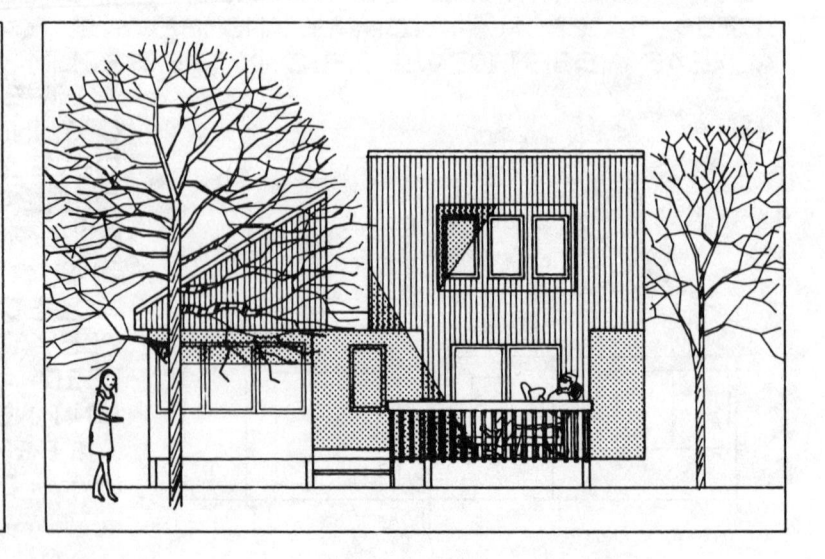

PRESENTATION DRAWINGS   28-2

ISOMETRICS

AN ISOMETRIC DRAWING IS THE EASIEST AND MOST POPULAR WAY OF DRAWING A THREE-DIMENSIONAL VIEW OF A BUILDING. THE VIEW IS GENERATED BY ROTATING THE FLOOR PLAN ON A 30° AXIS AND PROJECTING THE VERTICAL LINES UP. BY DEFINITION, AN ISOMETRIC VIEW USES THE SAME ANGLE OF PROJECTION ON EACH AXIS; A TRIMETRIC DRAWING IS DRAWN USING DIFFERENT ANGLES.

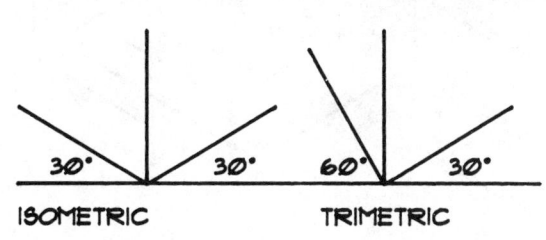

AN ISOMETRIC VIEW IS RELATIVELY EASY TO CONSTRUCT BECAUSE OBJECTS ALONG EACH OF THE THREE AXES ARE MEASURED IN TRUE LENGTH. THIS MEANS THAT A 10' LINE CAN BE SCALED AS 10' LONG ON ANY OF THE THREE AXIS LINES. CONSEQUENTLY, AN ISOMETRIC SHOWS TWO SIDES OF A BUILDING WITH THE SAME VIEW ANGLE; IN CONTRAST, A TRIMETRIC CAN BE USED WHEN ONE SIDE IS MORE IMPORTANT. THE STEEP ANGLE ON A TRIMETRIC DRAWING TENDS TO DISTORT THE BUILDING HEIGHT SO THAT IT IS REDUCED PROPORTIONATELY AS ILLUSTRATED BELOW. OBJECTS ALONG THE TWO DIAGONAL AXES ARE MEASURED IN TRUE LENGTH; THE VERTICAL HEIGHTS ARE MEASURED ALONG THE HORIZONTAL LINE AND THEN ARE PROJECTED TO THE VERTICAL HEIGHT USING A 30° ANGLE. THIS REDUCES THE HEIGHT, PRODUCING A BUILDING WITH LESS DISTORTION. FOLLOW THE STEPS BELOW TO CONSTRUCT ISOMETRIC AND TRIMETRIC VIEWS.

TO SHOW HEIGHT, MEASURE THE TRUE LENGTH (T. L.) ON THE HORIZONTAL AXIS AND PROJECT IT AT A 30° ANGLE

TRIMETRIC HEIGHT MEASURMENT

BEGIN THE ISOMETRIC BY LAYING OUT THE FLOOR PLAN ALONG TWO 30° AXES. USE AN ARCHITECT'S SCALE TO MEASURE THE TRUE LENGTH OF EACH LINE.

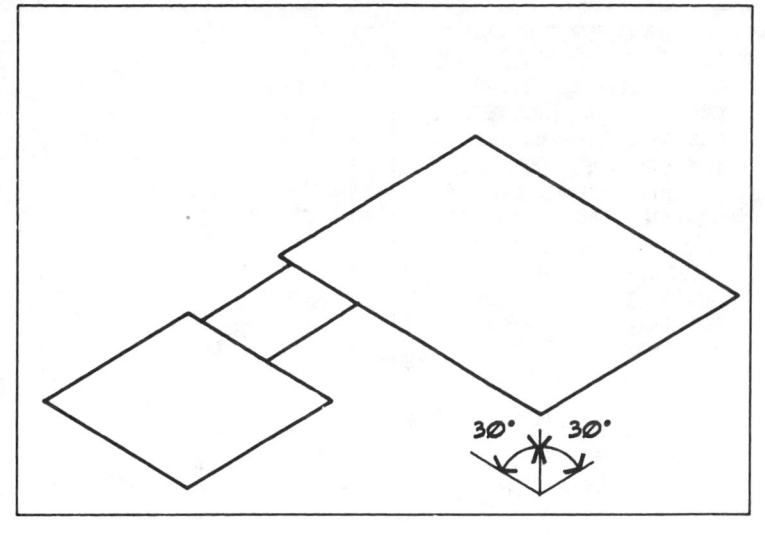

PRESENTATION DRAWINGS 28-3

IN THIS STEP THE VERTICAL HEIGHT IS ADDED TO THE BUILDING. THE LENGTH OF EACH VERTICAL LINE IS MEASURED USING AN ARCHITECT'S SCALE.

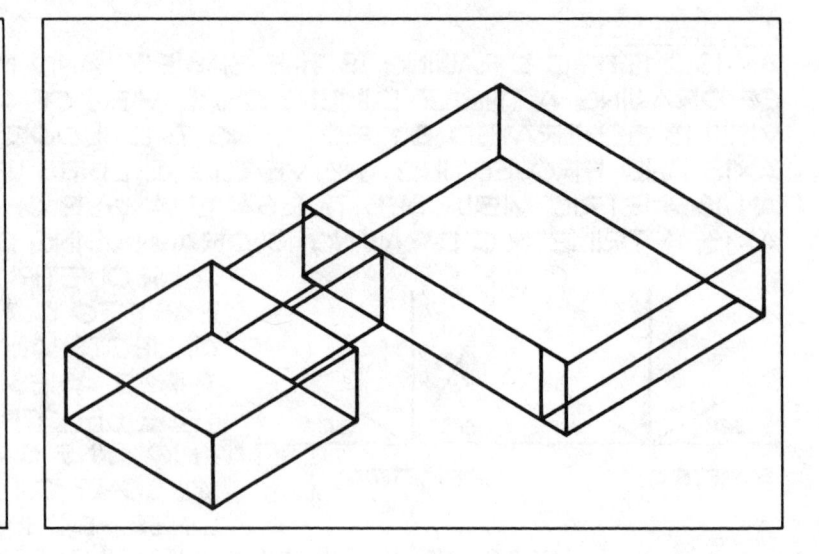

IN THE NEXT STEP THE ROOF PITCH IS LOCATED. CONSTRUCT AN ANGLE IN ISOMETRIC BY MEASURING THE RUN OF THE ROOF ALONG THE DIAGONAL AXIS AS WELL AS THE VERTICAL RISE. CONNECT THE TWO LINES TO DRAW THE ANGLE.

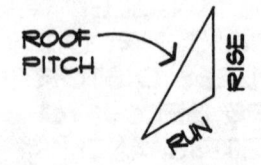

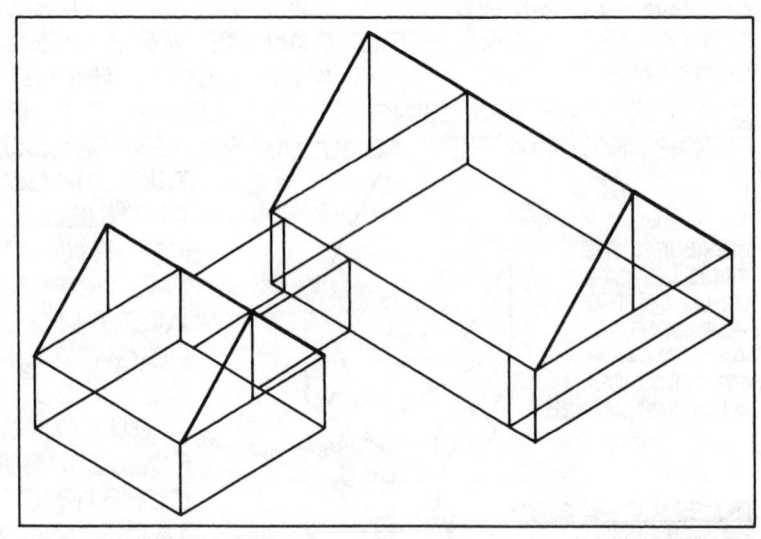

ROOF PITCH
RUN   RISE

IN THIS STEP THE HALF-CIRCLE IS CONSTRUCTED IN ISOMETRIC. START BY DRAWING AN ISOMETRIC SQUARE THAT WILL FIT THE CIRCLE. LOCATE THE MIDPOINTS ON THE SQUARE AND CONNECT THEM TO THE OPPOSITE CORNERS OF THE SQUARE. USE THE INTERSECTION OF THE LINES AS THE CENTER OF RADIUS "R1" AS SHOWN.

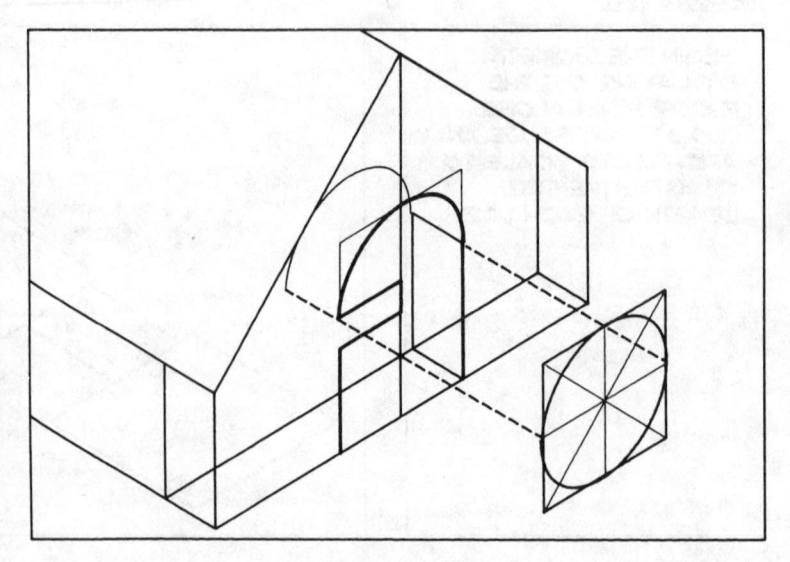

PRESENTATION DRAWINGS   28-4

THIS DRAWING ILLUSTRATES THE MAJOR LINES OF THE ISOMETRIC VIEW. THE NEXT STEP WOULD BE TO ADD ITEMS SUCH AS TREES, GROUND COVER, AND PEOPLE.

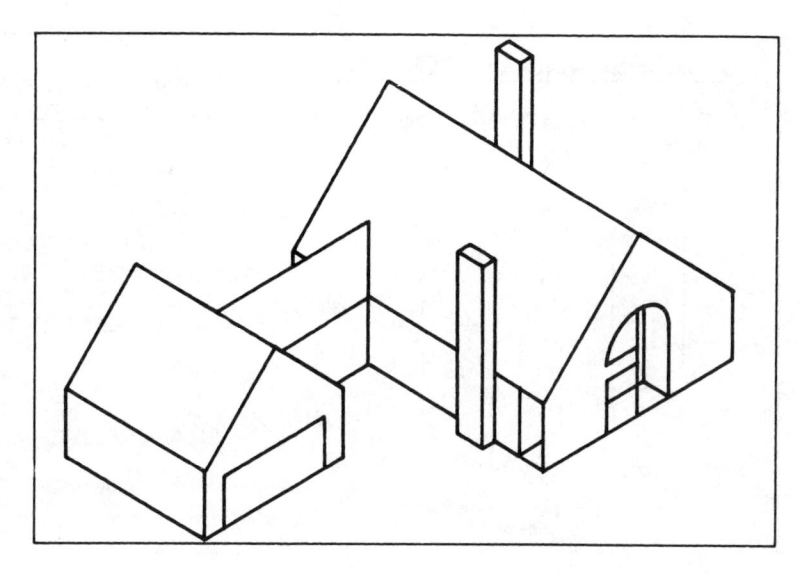

THIS DRAWING SHOWS THE SAME PROJECT AS SHOWN ABOVE IN A TRIMETRIC VIEW. THE DRAWING AXIS IS ROTATED TO 30° AND 60°. THE HORIZONTAL CONSTRUCTION LINE AT THE CORNER OF THE HOUSE IS USED TO MEASURE VERTICAL HEIGHTS. ONCE THE HEIGHTS ARE MARKED, THEY ARE PROJECTED AT A 30° ANGLE.

VERTICAL LINES ARE MEASURED ALONG THE BASE LINE AND PROJECTED AT A 30° ANGLE

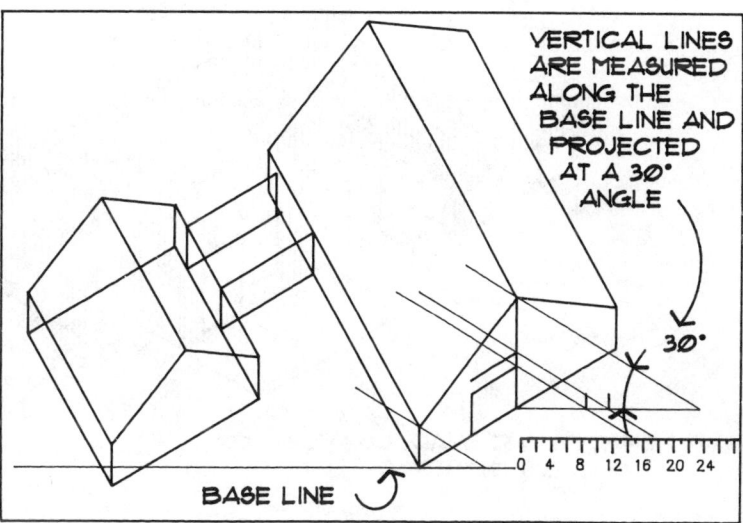

BASE LINE

AS AN OPTION TO USING THE HORIZONTAL CONSTRUCTION LINE METHOD, MULTIPLY THE HEIGHT BY THE TANGENT OF 30° (0.58). FOR EXAMPLE, A 10' LINE WOULD BE MEASURED AS 5.8' ON THE VERTICAL HEIGHT.

THE DRAWING AT THE RIGHT ILLUSTRATES THE FINAL TRIMETRIC VIEW. THE STEEPER AXIS SHOWS MORE OF THE ROOF THAN AN ISOMETRIC VIEW.

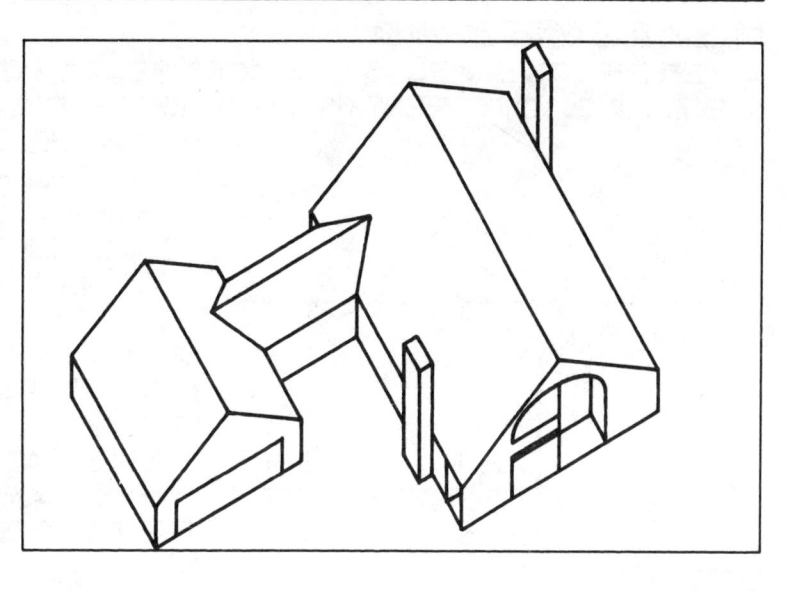

PRESENTATION DRAWINGS

28-5

SHADES AND SHADOWS

SHADES AND SHADOWS CAN BE CONSTRUCTED ON A BUILDING ISOMETRIC BY PROJECTING A LIGHT RAY LINE AT A 45° ANGLE FROM THE LIGHT SOURCE. SHADOW LINES ARE CONSTRUCTED BY DRAWING LINES AT ONE-HALF THE ANGLE OF THE ISOMETRIC AXIS (15° IN THE EXAMPLE). THE 15° SHADOW LINE IS PROJECTED FROM THE CORNER UNTIL IT INTERSECTS THE LIGHT RAY LINE.

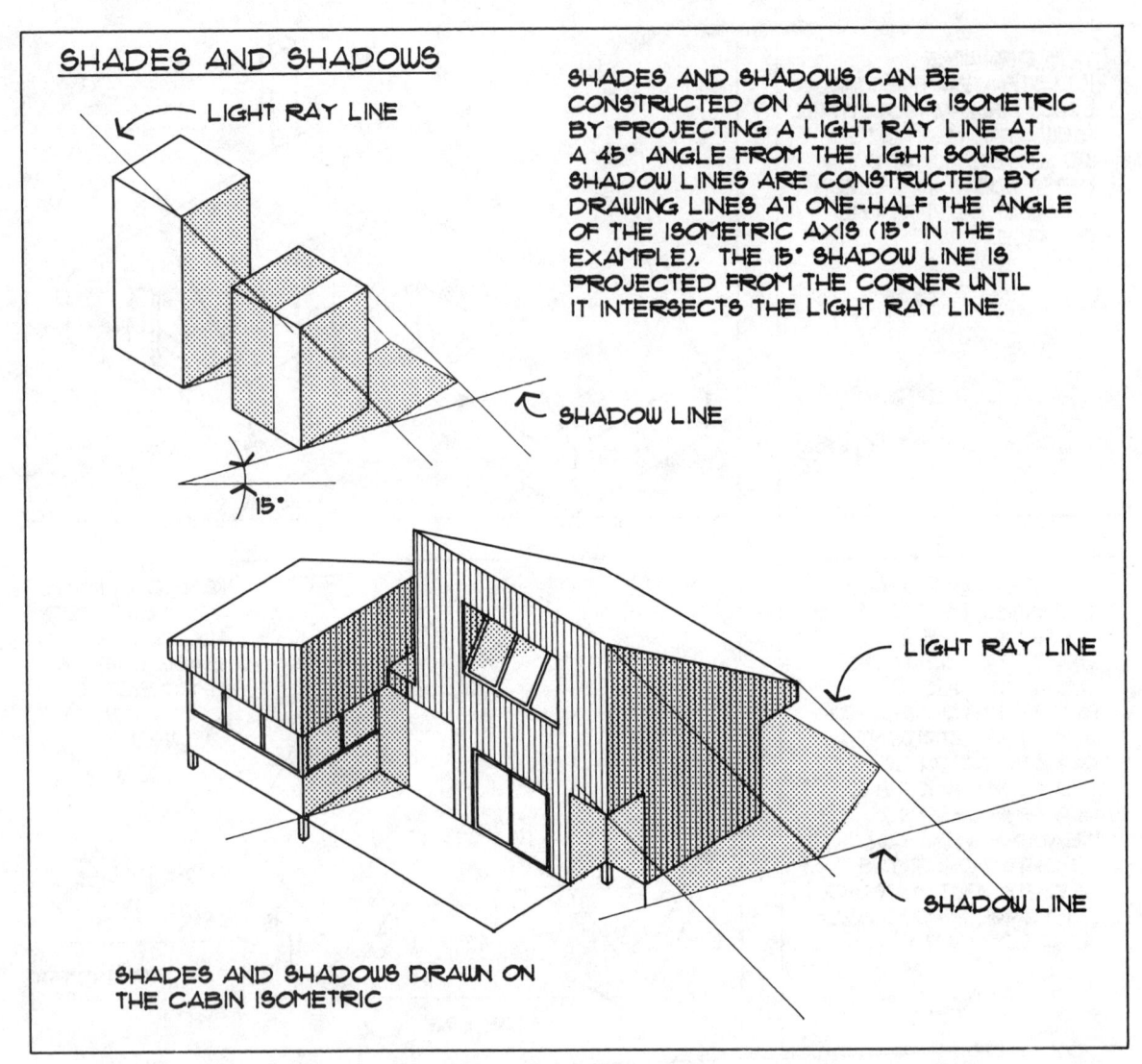

SHADES AND SHADOWS DRAWN ON THE CABIN ISOMETRIC

PERSPECTIVE DRAWING

A PERSPECTIVE VIEW IS THE MOST REALISTIC METHOD OF DRAWING A BUILDING. DIFFERENT FROM AN ISOMETRIC OR TRIMETRIC VIEW, PARALLEL LINES CONVERGE TO VANISHING POINTS IN A PERSPECTIVE VIEW. IN THIS SECTION WE WILL EXAMINE THE STEPS IN THE ASSEMBLY OF TWO-POINT PERSPECTIVES (LIKE THE ONE SHOWN AT THE LEFT) AND ONE-POINT PERSPECTIVES THAT ARE FREQUENTLY USED FOR INTERIOR PRESENTATIONS. THE ADDITION OF TREES, CARS, AND PEOPLE GIVES THE PERSPECTIVE VIEW SCALE AND REALISM.

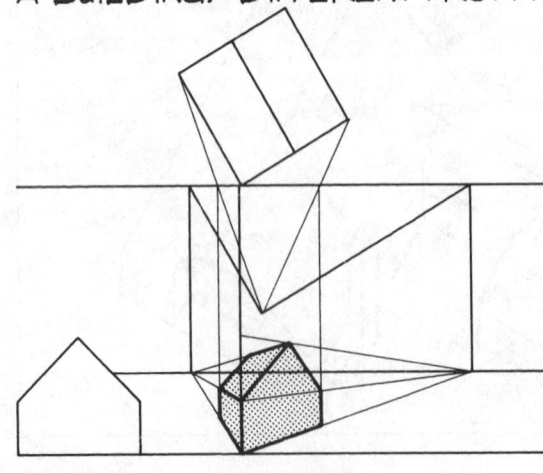

PRESENTATION DRAWINGS 28-6

FIRST, LET'S DEFINE THE ELEMENTS OF A TWO-POINT PERSPECTIVE.

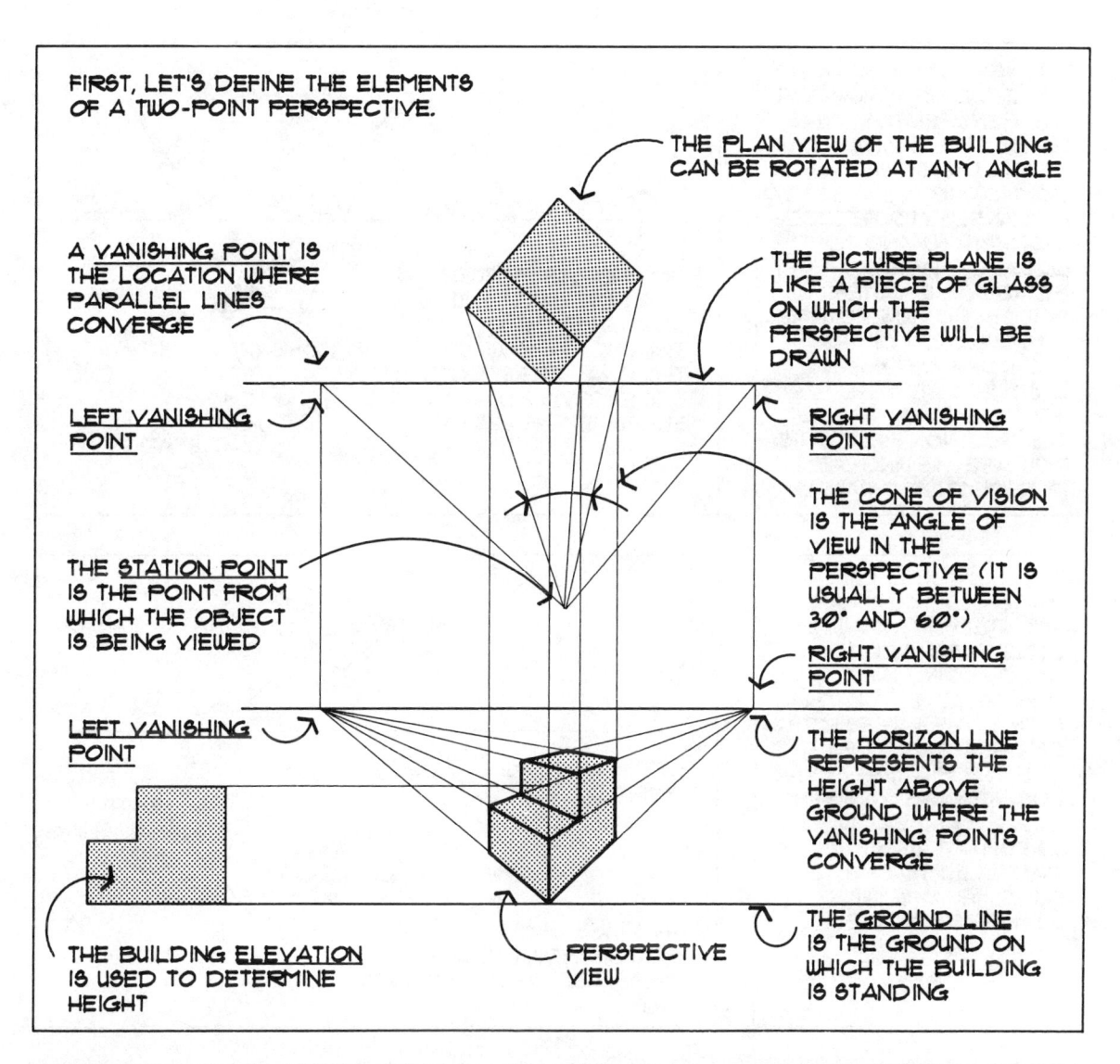

THE PLAN VIEW OF THE BUILDING CAN BE ROTATED AT ANY ANGLE

A VANISHING POINT IS THE LOCATION WHERE PARALLEL LINES CONVERGE

THE PICTURE PLANE IS LIKE A PIECE OF GLASS ON WHICH THE PERSPECTIVE WILL BE DRAWN

LEFT VANISHING POINT

RIGHT VANISHING POINT

THE CONE OF VISION IS THE ANGLE OF VIEW IN THE PERSPECTIVE (IT IS USUALLY BETWEEN 30° AND 60°)

THE STATION POINT IS THE POINT FROM WHICH THE OBJECT IS BEING VIEWED

RIGHT VANISHING POINT

LEFT VANISHING POINT

THE HORIZON LINE REPRESENTS THE HEIGHT ABOVE GROUND WHERE THE VANISHING POINTS CONVERGE

THE BUILDING ELEVATION IS USED TO DETERMINE HEIGHT

PERSPECTIVE VIEW

THE GROUND LINE IS THE GROUND ON WHICH THE BUILDING IS STANDING

BEGIN A PERSPECTIVE BY PLACING THE BUILDING PLAN ON THE DRAWING. THE PLAN SHOULD BE ROTATED TO PROVIDE THE DESIRED PERSPECTIVE VIEW. THE PICTURE PLANE IS THE FIRST OBJECT LOCATED ON THE DRAWING. THIS CAN BE VISUALIZED AS A PIECE OF GLASS ONTO WHICH THE PERSPECTIVE IS DRAWN. OBJECTS TOUCHING THE PICTURE PLANE MAY BE MEASURED IN TRUE HEIGHT.

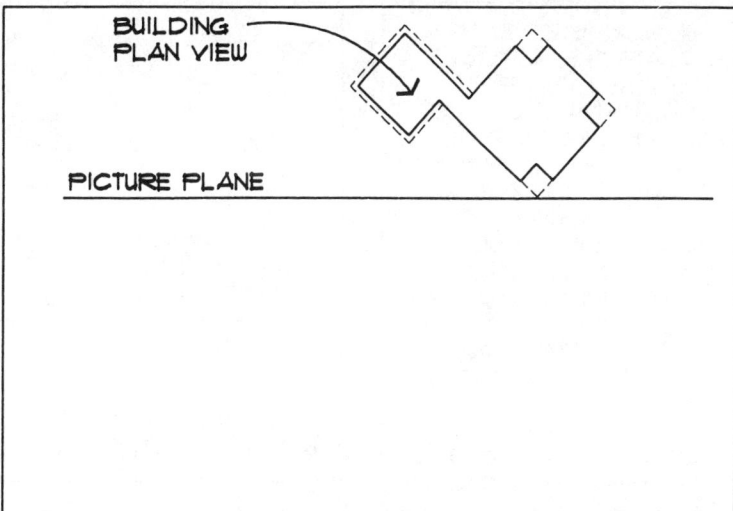

BUILDING PLAN VIEW

PICTURE PLANE

PRESENTATION DRAWINGS | 28-7

THE NEXT STEP LOCATES THE CONE OF VISION FOR THE PERSPECTIVE. THIS IS THE OUTER VIEW ANGLE OF THE DRAWING. IT IS COMMON TO USE A 30° TO 60° ANGLE (TO REDUCE DISTORTION) AND TO LOCATE IT MIDWAY BETWEEN THE OUTER BUILDING CORNERS. THE INTERSECTION OF THE TWO CONE-OF-VISION LINES LOCATES THE STATION POINT. THIS IS THE POSITION FROM WHICH YOU ARE VIEWING THE PERSPECTIVE DRAWING.

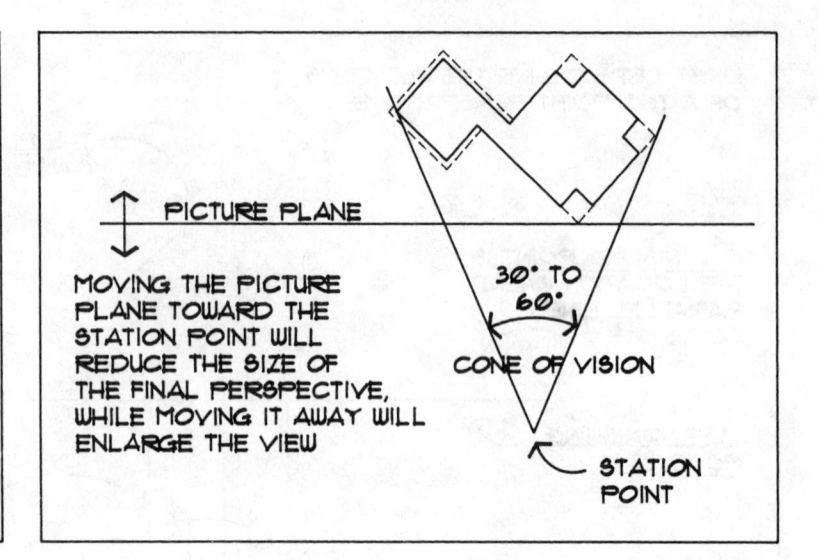

MOVING THE PICTURE PLANE TOWARD THE STATION POINT WILL REDUCE THE SIZE OF THE FINAL PERSPECTIVE, WHILE MOVING IT AWAY WILL ENLARGE THE VIEW

THE RIGHT AND LEFT VANISHING POINTS ARE LOCATED BY DRAWING LINES PARALLEL TO THE BUILDING AXIS THROUGH THE STATION POINT. THE INTERSECTION OF THESE TWO LINES WITH THE PICTURE PLANE LOCATES THE VANISHING POINTS. ALL BUILDING LINES THAT ARE PARALLEL TO THE BUILDING AXIS WILL CONVERGE AT THE VANISHING POINTS.

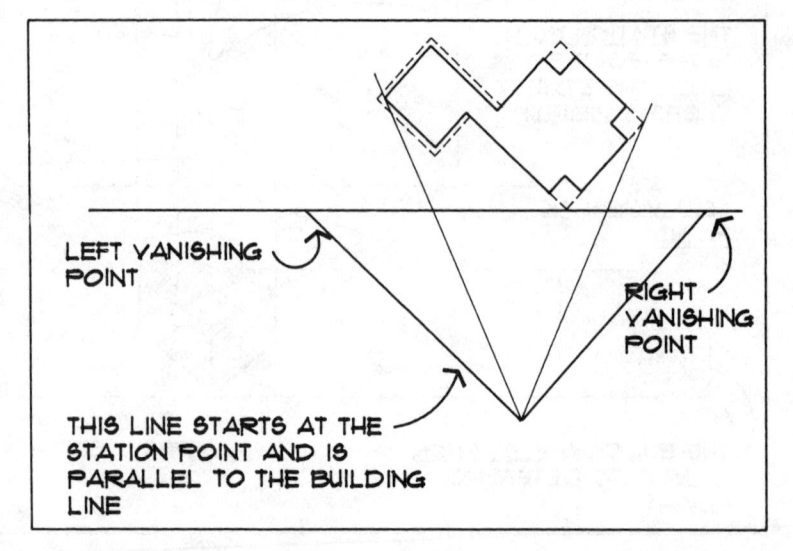

THIS LINE STARTS AT THE STATION POINT AND IS PARALLEL TO THE BUILDING LINE

THE NEXT STEP IS TO LOCATE THE HORIZON LINE. THIS IS THE HORIZONTAL DISTANCE ABOVE GROUND FOR THE STATION POINT. FOR EXAMPLE, A HORIZON LINE 50' ABOVE THE GROUND LINE WOULD SHOW A GREAT DEAL MORE OF THE ROOF THAN A 5' HIGH HORIZON LINE. START BY DRAWING AN ELEVATION VIEW (AT THE SAME SCALE AS THE PLAN). LOCATE THE HORIZON LINE AND DROP THE VANISHING POINTS.

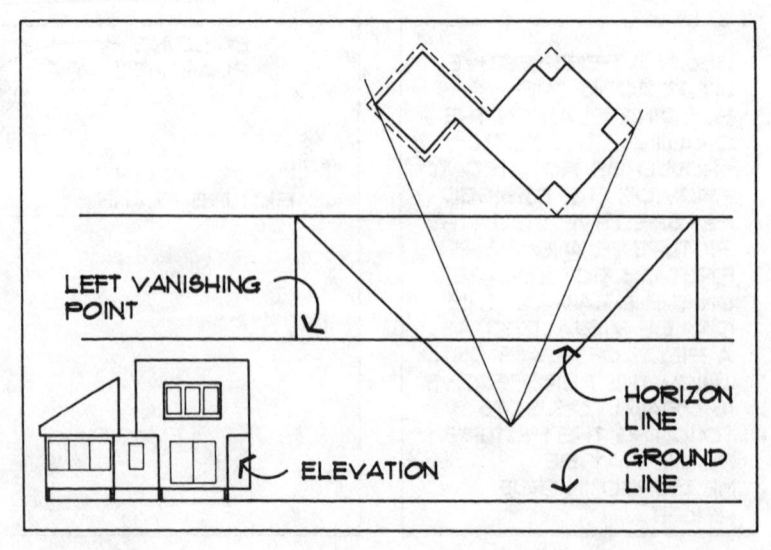

PRESENTATION DRAWINGS

28-8

BEGIN A PERSPECTIVE BY DRAWING A LINE FROM THE STATION POINT TO A BUILDING CORNER ON THE PLAN. THE CORNER WILL APPEAR ON THE PERSPECTIVE WHERE THE LINE CROSSES THE PICTURE PLANE. THE LINE IS THEN PROJECTED STRAIGHT DOWN TO THE PERSPECTIVE VIEW. THE NUMBERED STEPS TO THE RIGHT DEMONSTRATE THE CONSTRUCTION OF THE CORNERS OF THE MAIN CABIN WALL.

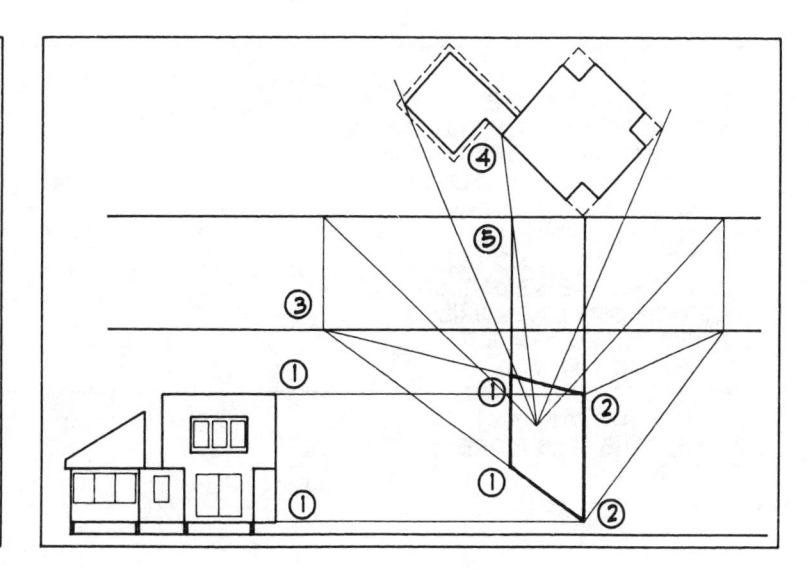

A LINE CAN ONLY BE MEASURED IN TRUE LENGTH IF IT TOUCHES THE PICTURE PLANE. THE STEPS ILLUSTRATE THE ASSEMBLY OF THE LEFT CORNER OF THE PORCH. STEP 1 LOCATES THE CORNER OF THE CABIN ON THE PICTURE PLANE. STEP 2 PROJECTS THE CORNER TO THE PICTURE PLANE ALONG EITHER AXIS OF THE BUILDING. STEP 3 MARKS THE TRUE HEIGHT. STEP 4 PROJECTS THE LINE TO THE VANISHING POINT.

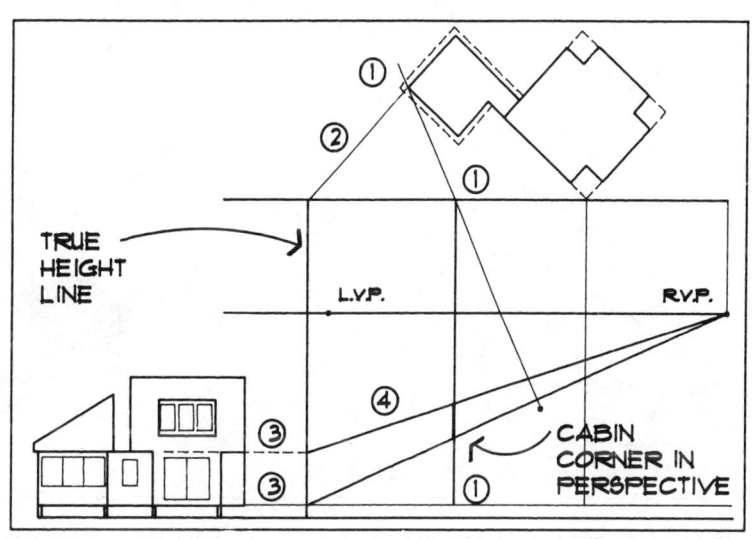

IN THIS STEP THE BACK CORNER OF THE CABIN ROOF IS LOCATED. ANGLES ARE CONSTRUCTED BY MARKING THE TWO ENDS OF THE LINE. STEP 1 LOCATES THE ROOF EDGE ON THE PICTURE PLANE. STEP 2 MARKS THE TOP AND BOTTOM ROOF POINTS ON THE TRUE LENGTH LINE THAT TOUCHES THE PICTURE PLANE. STEP 3 PROJECTS THE LOWER ROOF EDGE TO THE RIGHT VANISHING POINT.

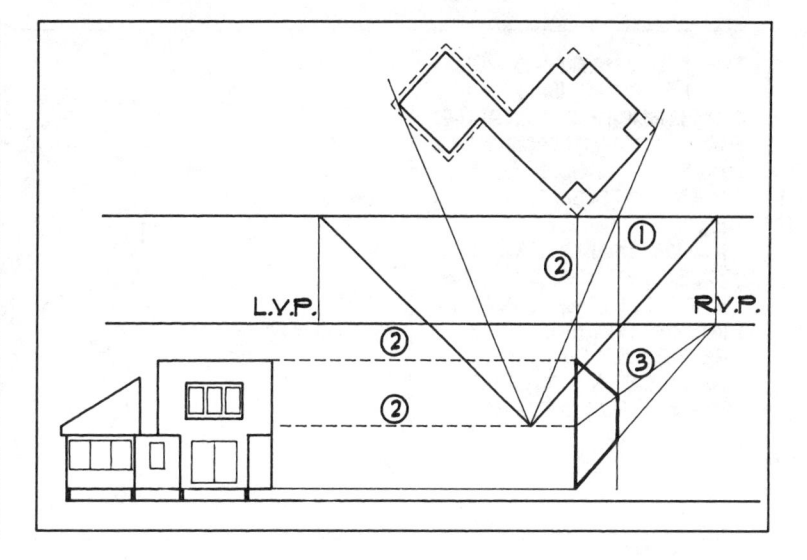

PRESENTATION DRAWINGS

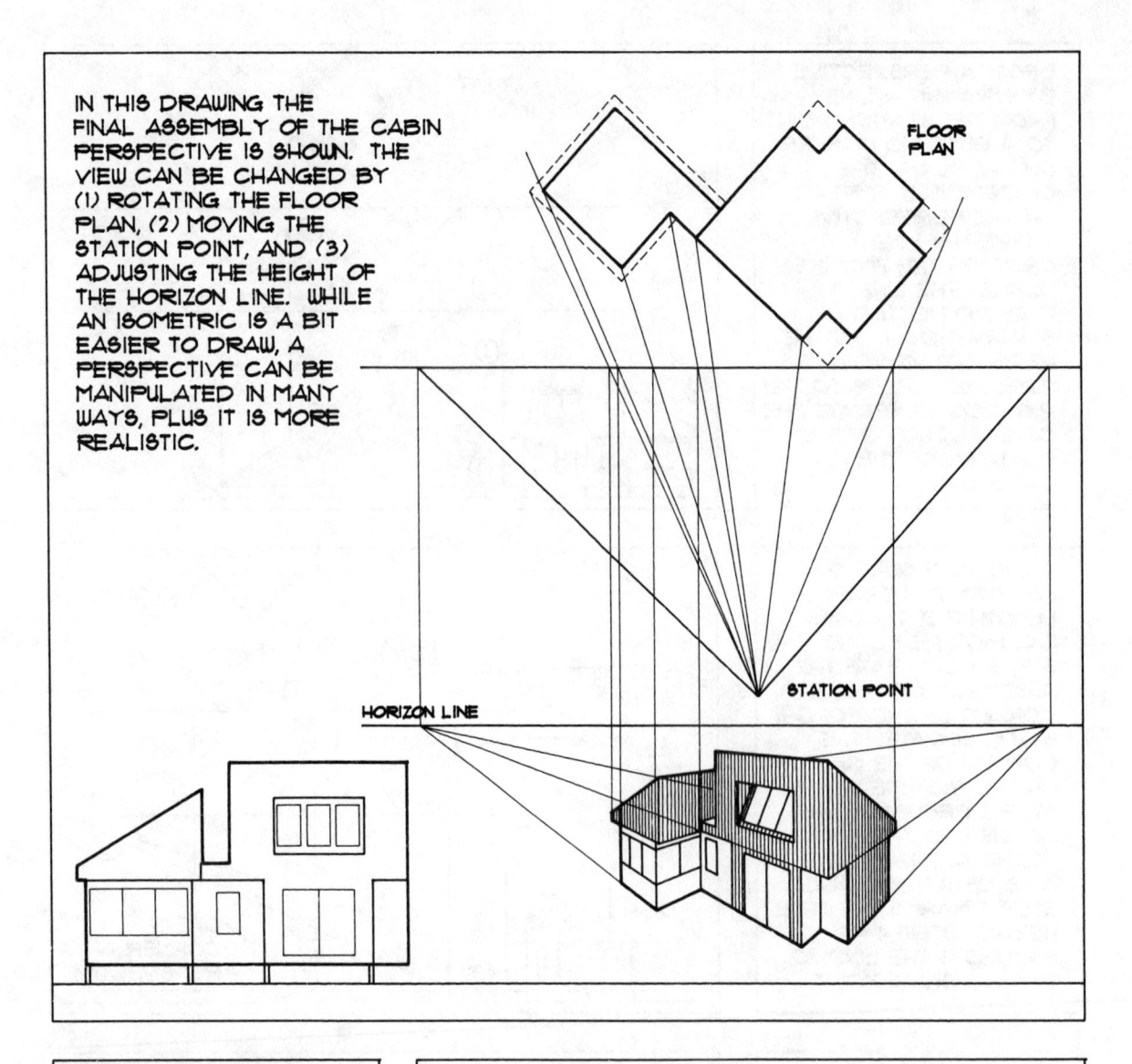

IN THIS DRAWING THE FINAL ASSEMBLY OF THE CABIN PERSPECTIVE IS SHOWN. THE VIEW CAN BE CHANGED BY (1) ROTATING THE FLOOR PLAN, (2) MOVING THE STATION POINT, AND (3) ADJUSTING THE HEIGHT OF THE HORIZON LINE. WHILE AN ISOMETRIC IS A BIT EASIER TO DRAW, A PERSPECTIVE CAN BE MANIPULATED IN MANY WAYS, PLUS IT IS MORE REALISTIC.

THE PERSPECTIVE VIEW TO THE RIGHT WAS CONSTRUCTED USING THE SAME STATION POINT AND BUILDING ANGLE AS THE PERSPECTIVE SHOWN ABOVE. THE ONLY CHANGE MADE WAS TO MOVE THE HORIZON LINE 75' ABOVE THE GROUND LINE OF THE BUILDING. THE RESULT WAS TO PRODUCE A DRAWING WITH A MUCH DIFFERENT ROOF VIEW.

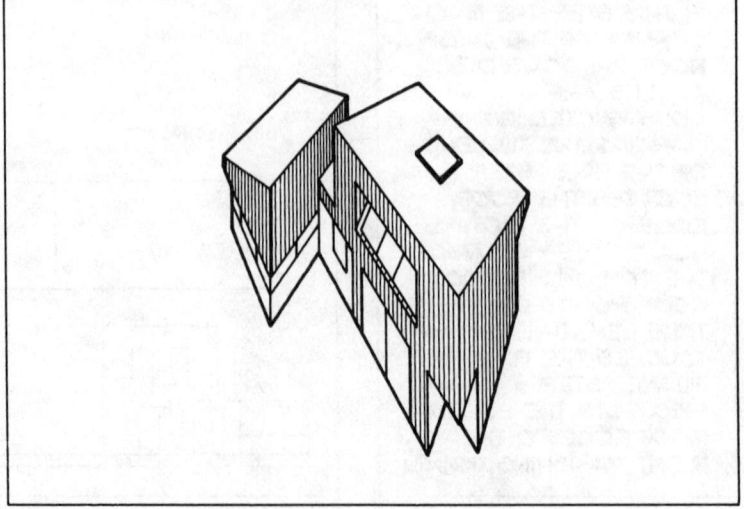

PRESENTATION DRAWINGS   28-10

ONE-POINT PERSPECTIVE

A ONE-POINT PERSPECTIVE IS EFFECTIVE IN PRESENTING INTERIOR SPACES. BEGIN BY LOCATING A VANISHING POINT WHERE ALL INTERIOR WALLS WILL CONVERGE. FOLLOW THE STEPS SHOWN BELOW TO DETERMINE THE DEPTH OF OBJECTS AS THEY DROP AWAY FROM THE SECTION CUT.

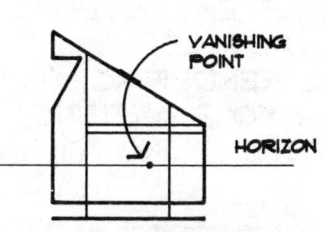

1. DRAW A BUILDING SECTION AND LOCATE A VANISHING POINT (5'-4" ABOVE THE FLOOR IS AT EYE LEVEL).

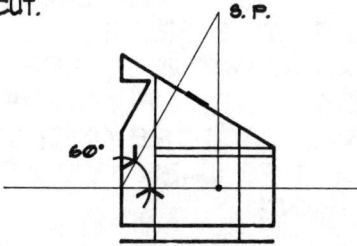

2. DRAW A LINE STRAIGHT UP FROM THE VANISHING POINT, THEN DRAW A SECOND LINE AT A 60° ANGLE FROM THE FARTHEST POINT AT WHICH THE DRAWING CROSSES THE HORIZON LINE. THE INTERSECTION OF THE TWO LINES IS THE STATION POINT (S. P.).

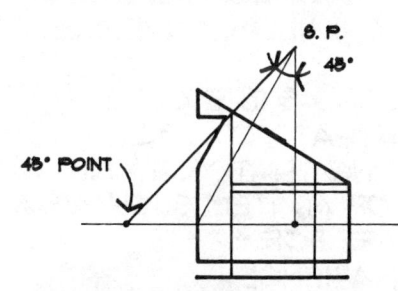

3. DRAW A 45° LINE FROM THE STATION POINT SO THAT IT CROSSES THE HORIZON LINE. THE INTERSECTION IS CALLED THE 45° POINT.

4. DRAW A LINE STRAIGHT DOWN FROM THE VANISHING POINT TO INTERSECT THE FLOOR LINE.

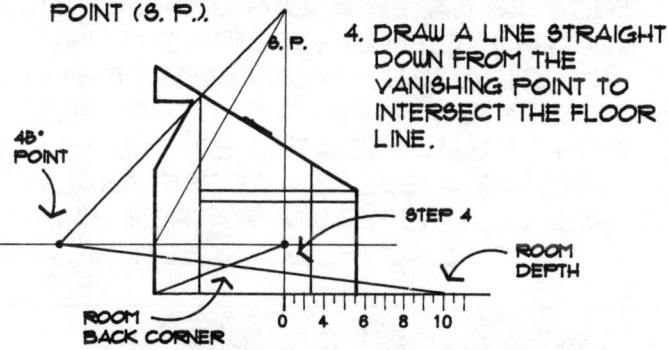

5. USE THE SAME SCALE AS USED IN THE SECTION TO MEASURE THE DEPTH OF THE ROOM (10' IN THE EXAMPLE ABOVE). DRAW A LINE FROM THE 45° POINT TO THE ROOM DEPTH. DRAW A SECOND LINE FROM THE LOWER LEFT CORNER OF THE SECTION TO THE VANISHING POINT. THE INTERSECTION OF THE LINES LOCATES THE BACK CORNER OF THE ROOM.

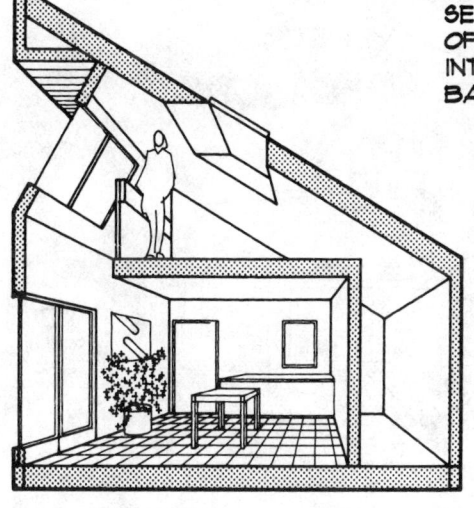

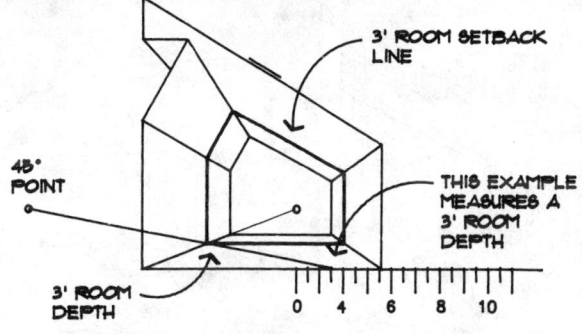

6. USE THE HORIZONTAL SCALE TO MEASURE ROOM DEPTH. DRAW A LINE FROM THE 45° POINT TO THE SCALE; THE DEPTH IS MARKED WHERE THIS LINE INTERSECTS THE LINE FROM THE ROOM CORNER TO THE VANISHING POINT.

COMPLETED ONE-POINT PERSPECTIVE

PRESENTATION DRAWINGS

PRESENTATION DRAWINGS

ONCE YOU HAVE DRAWN A BUILDING IN ISOMETRIC OR PERSPECTIVE, THE NEXT STEP IS TO ADD ITEMS SUCH AS TREES, CARS, AND PEOPLE TO GIVE THE DRAWING A SENSE OF REALISM AND SCALE. THIS SECTION WILL PRESENT SEVERAL PRESENTATION DRAWINGS (THESE ARE ALSO CALLED RENDERINGS). THE QUALITY OF YOUR FINAL RENDERING WILL DEPEND ON SEVERAL FACTORS (INCLUDING YOUR ARTISTIC TALENT). USE THESE TIPS WHEN YOU ARE ASSEMBLING A FINAL PRESENTATION DRAWING:

1. START WITH AN ACCURATE MECHANICAL PERSPECTIVE.
2. USE TRACING PAPER TO MAKE A MASTER SKETCH FOR LOCATING TREES, CARS, AND PEOPLE.
3. MARK THE VANISHING POINTS ON YOUR PERSPECTIVE; ITEMS SUCH AS WALLS AND GROUND TEXTURE SHOULD CONVERGE AT THE BUILDING VANISHING POINTS.
4. FOLLOW A WELL-DRAWN RENDERING (SUCH AS THE ONES PRESENTED HERE) AND COPY DETAILS THAT YOU LIKE.
5. DON'T BE INTIMIDATED BY THE RENDERING THAT YOU ARE USING AS A GUIDE; A CLOSE ANALYSIS OF AN ITEM SUCH AS A TREE WILL REVEAL A RATHER SIMPLE ART FORM.
6. A GOOD RENDERING TAKES TIME AND PATIENCE.

ACORN STRUCTURES, INC.

PRESENTATION DRAWINGS

THIS DRAWING ILLUSTRATES A LINE DRAWING OF A PERSPECTIVE. AT THE BOTTOM OF THE PAGE, TREES AND MATERIALS ARE ADDED TO THE DRAWING TO ILLUSTRATE A PRESENTATION-QUALITY PERSPECTIVE.

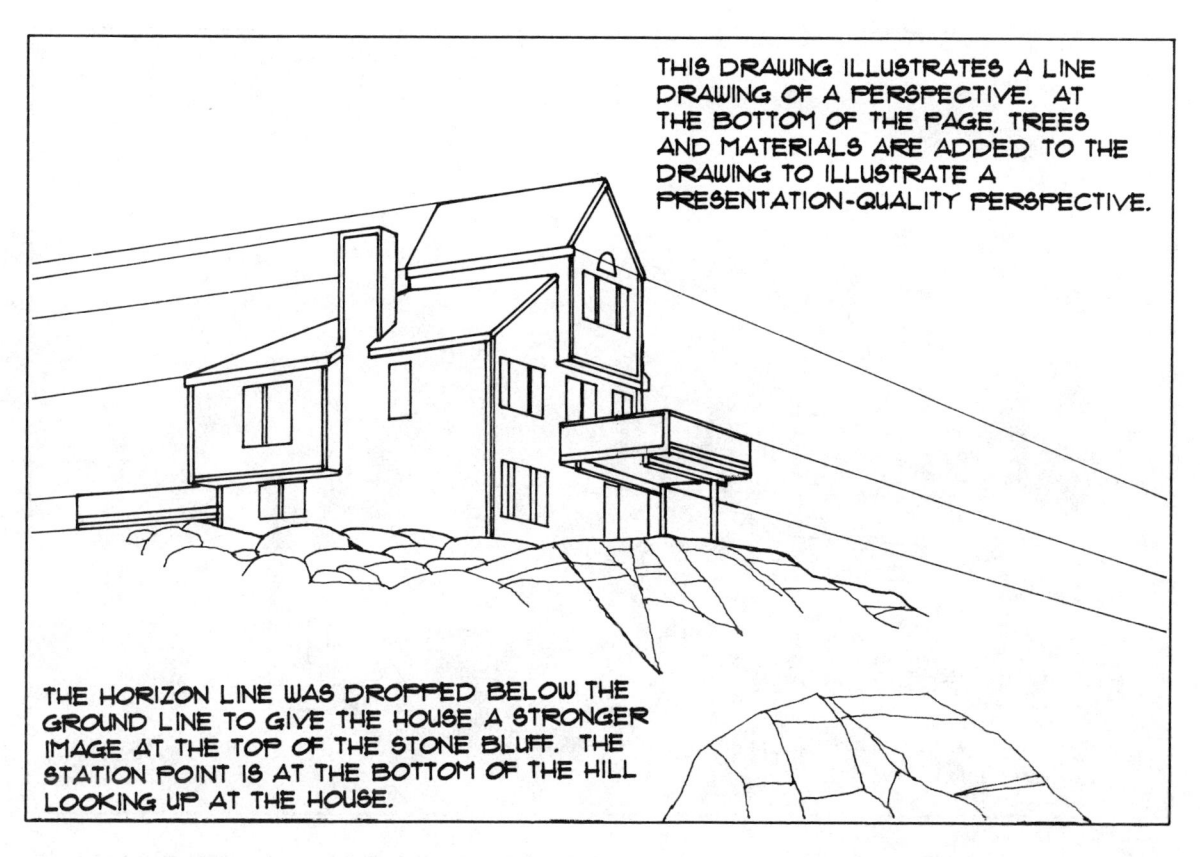

THE HORIZON LINE WAS DROPPED BELOW THE GROUND LINE TO GIVE THE HOUSE A STRONGER IMAGE AT THE TOP OF THE STONE BLUFF. THE STATION POINT IS AT THE BOTTOM OF THE HILL LOOKING UP AT THE HOUSE.

ACORN STRUCTURES, INC.

PRESENTATION DRAWINGS 28-13

ACORN STRUCTURES, INC.

ACORN STRUCTURES, INC.

PRESENTATION DRAWINGS 28-14

ACORN STRUCTURES, INC.

ACORN STRUCTURES, INC.

PRESENTATION DRAWINGS 28-15

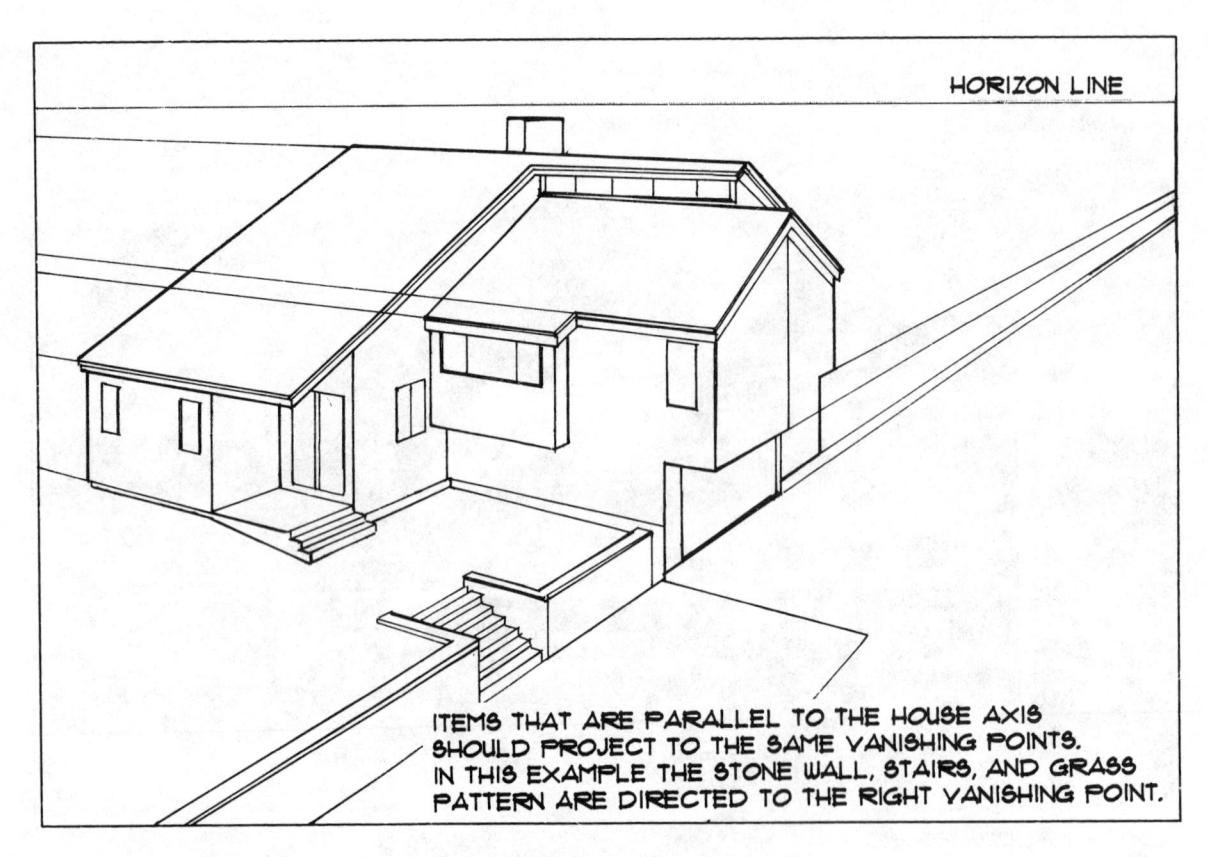

HORIZON LINE

ITEMS THAT ARE PARALLEL TO THE HOUSE AXIS SHOULD PROJECT TO THE SAME VANISHING POINTS. IN THIS EXAMPLE THE STONE WALL, STAIRS, AND GRASS PATTERN ARE DIRECTED TO THE RIGHT VANISHING POINT.

ACORN STRUCTURES, INC.

PRESENTATION DRAWINGS

28-16

ACORN STRUCTURES, INC.

ACORN STRUCTURES, INC.

PRESENTATION DRAWINGS

28-17

ACORN STRUCTURES, INC.

REPLAY

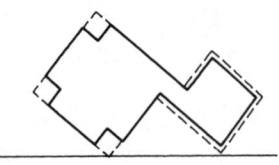

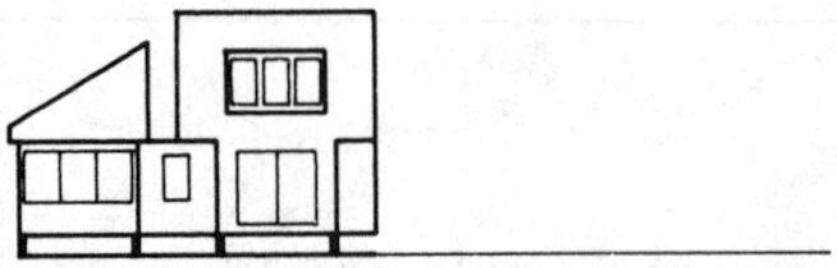

1. DRAW A PERSPECTIVE OF THE CABIN SIMILAR TO THE VIEW ON PAGE 28-10 BUT ROTATE THE PLAN 180° (AS SHOWN IN THE PLAN VIEW AT THE LEFT).

2. DRAW A PERSPECTIVE VIEW OF THE CABIN BY MOVING THE HORIZON LINE 10' BELOW THE GROUND LINE. RENDER THE PERSPECTIVE ON A ROCK BLUFF SIMILAR TO THE SITE ON PAGE 28-13.

3. INCREASE THE SIZE OF THE PERSPECTIVE VIEW DRAWN IN PROBLEM 1 BY PLACING THE PICTURE PLANE 5' BEYOND THE BACK CORNER OF THE CABIN.

4. DRAW A ONE-POINT PERSPECTIVE VIEW OF THE DINING ROOM FOR THE 12/12 PITCH ROOF HOUSE IN UNIT 22.

PRESENTATION DRAWINGS 28-18

29 STUDY MODELS

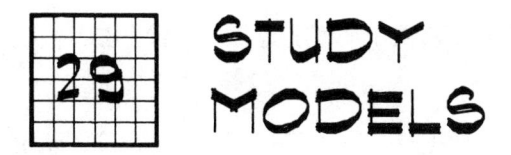

THIS UNIT PRESENTS STUDY MODELS FOR THE SIX PROJECTS IN THE TEXT. CONSTRUCTING A MODEL SHOULD BE ONE OF THE FIRST TASKS THAT YOU ACCOMPLISH DURING THE ASSEMBLY OF A SET OF CONSTRUCTION DRAWINGS.

YOU WILL NEED THREE TOOLS TO MAKE MODELS:

1. USE <u>WHITE GLUE</u> (NOT RUBBER CEMENT) TO FASTEN THE CARDBOARD MODEL PIECES TOGETHER. USE A THIN CONTINUOUS BEAD OF GLUE ALONG ONE EDGE OF THE CARDBOARD. SPREAD THE EDGE EVENLY WITH YOUR FINGER AND HOLD THE PIECES TOGETHER FOR SEVERAL SECONDS UNTIL THEY BOND.

2. SELECT A <u>METAL RULE</u> FOR A CUTTING EDGE (DON'T USE YOUR PLASTIC TRIANGLE). A GOOD CHOICE IS A 12" RULE WITH A CORK STRIP ON THE BACK WHICH WILL PREVENT SLIPPING.

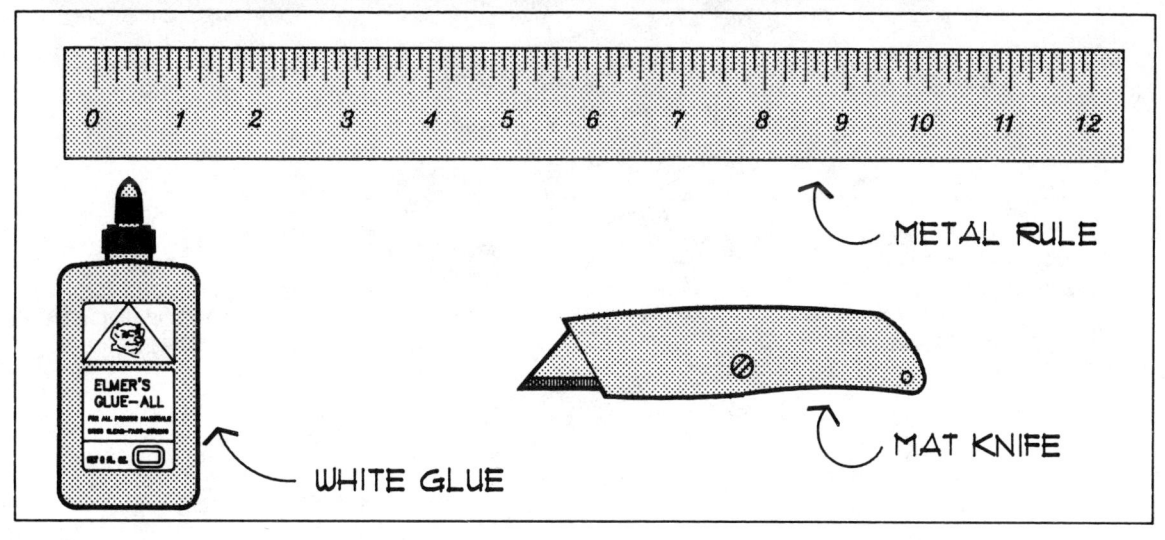

STUDY MODELS 29-1

3. USE A <u>MAT KNIFE</u> WITH A SHARP BLADE FOR MODEL BUILDING.

<u>TIPS</u>

- CUT AND ASSEMBLE MODEL PIECES IN THEIR NUMBERED ORDER.
- CUT ON A FLAT CARDBOARD SURFACE.
- CUT SMALL 90° CORNER BRACKETS TO BRACE CORNERS.
- CUT ONLY A FEW MODEL PIECES AT A TIME.
- MAKE PRECISE CUTS.
- FIT ONE PIECE AT A TIME.
- HOLD PIECES TOGETHER LONG ENOUGH FOR THE GLUE TO BOND.
- USE A LONG, THIN PIECE OF SCRAP CARDBOARD TO SPREAD GLUE ALONG THE INSIDE EDGES OF TWO PIECES.
- SPREAD GLUE ALONG ONE EDGE OF A MODEL PIECE WITH YOUR FINGER, MAKING SURE THAT THE GLUE BEAD IS UNIFORM.
- PRE-FIT PIECES IN TIGHT SPACES BEFORE GLUING.
- GLUE THE ROOF PIECE LAST, APPLYING A THIN BEAD OF GLUE TO THE PERIMETER OF THE ROOF PIECE (NOT TO THE WALL EDGE).
- WHITE GLUE IS WATER-BASED; USING TOO MUCH WILL TEND TO WARP THE CARDBOARD PIECES.
- PRACTICE MAKING SCORE-CUT LINES ON A PIECE OF CARDBOARD; THE TRICK IS TO MAKE A CUT THAT DOESN'T GO ALL THE WAY THROUGH.

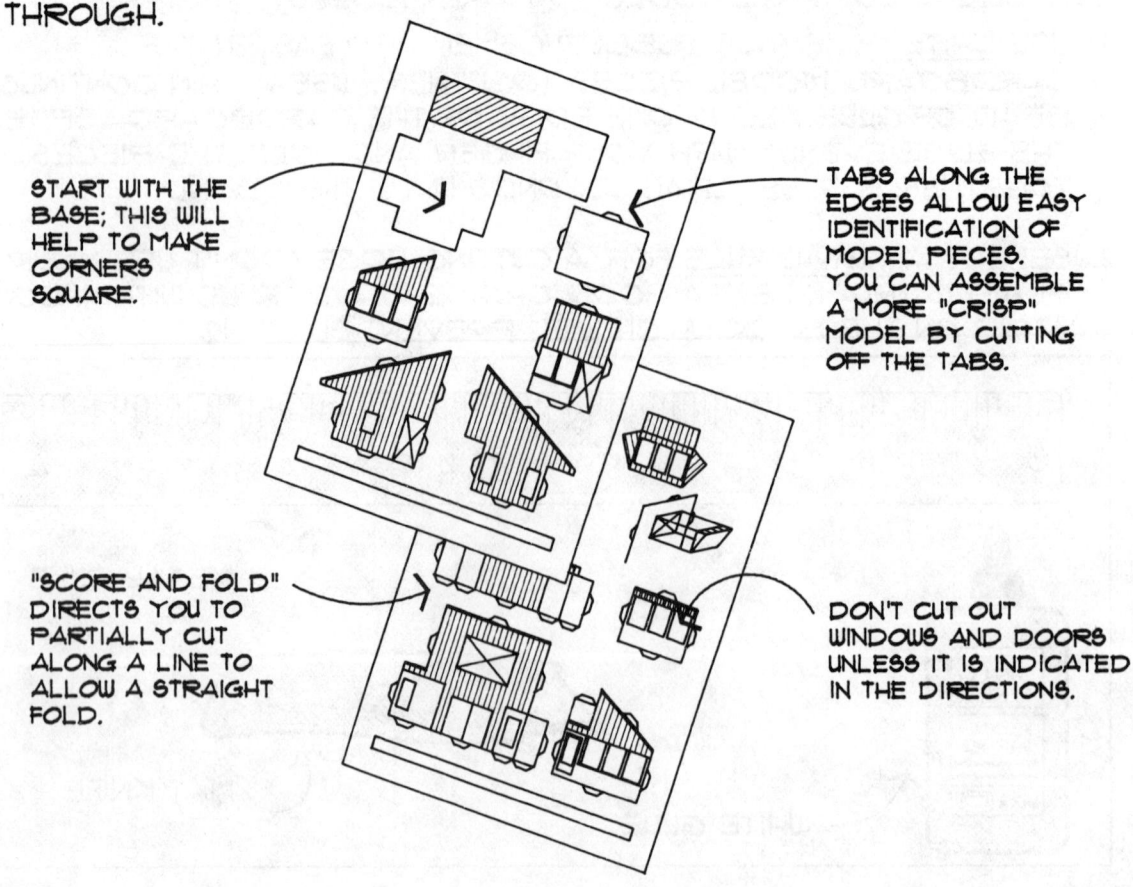

START WITH THE BASE; THIS WILL HELP TO MAKE CORNERS SQUARE.

TABS ALONG THE EDGES ALLOW EASY IDENTIFICATION OF MODEL PIECES. YOU CAN ASSEMBLE A MORE "CRISP" MODEL BY CUTTING OFF THE TABS.

"SCORE AND FOLD" DIRECTS YOU TO PARTIALLY CUT ALONG A LINE TO ALLOW A STRAIGHT FOLD.

DON'T CUT OUT WINDOWS AND DOORS UNLESS IT IS INDICATED IN THE DIRECTIONS.

STUDY MODELS

BIRCH LAKE CABIN STUDY MODEL (UNIT 21)   29-3

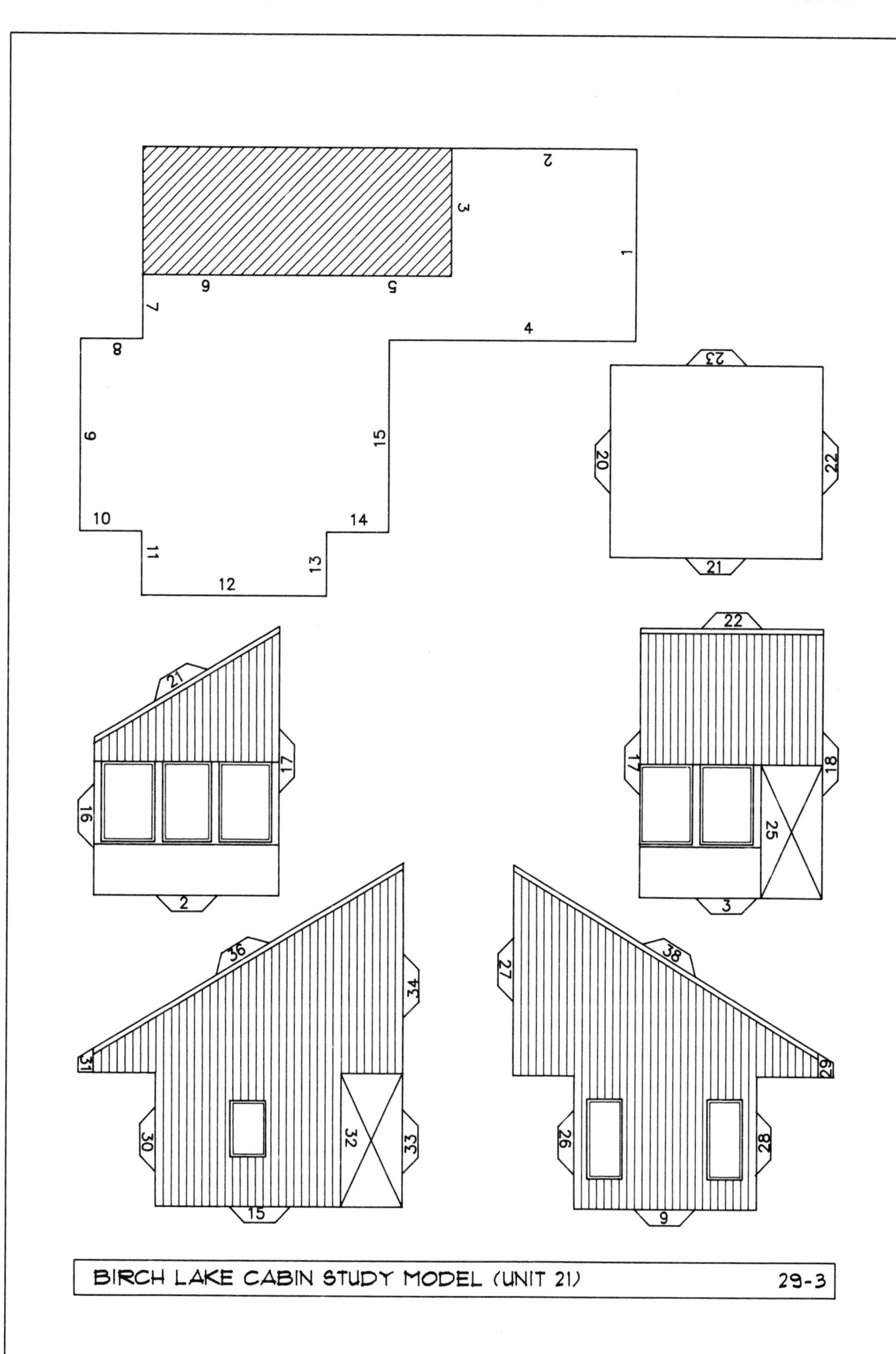

FOLD EDGES UP AND GLUE TOGETHER

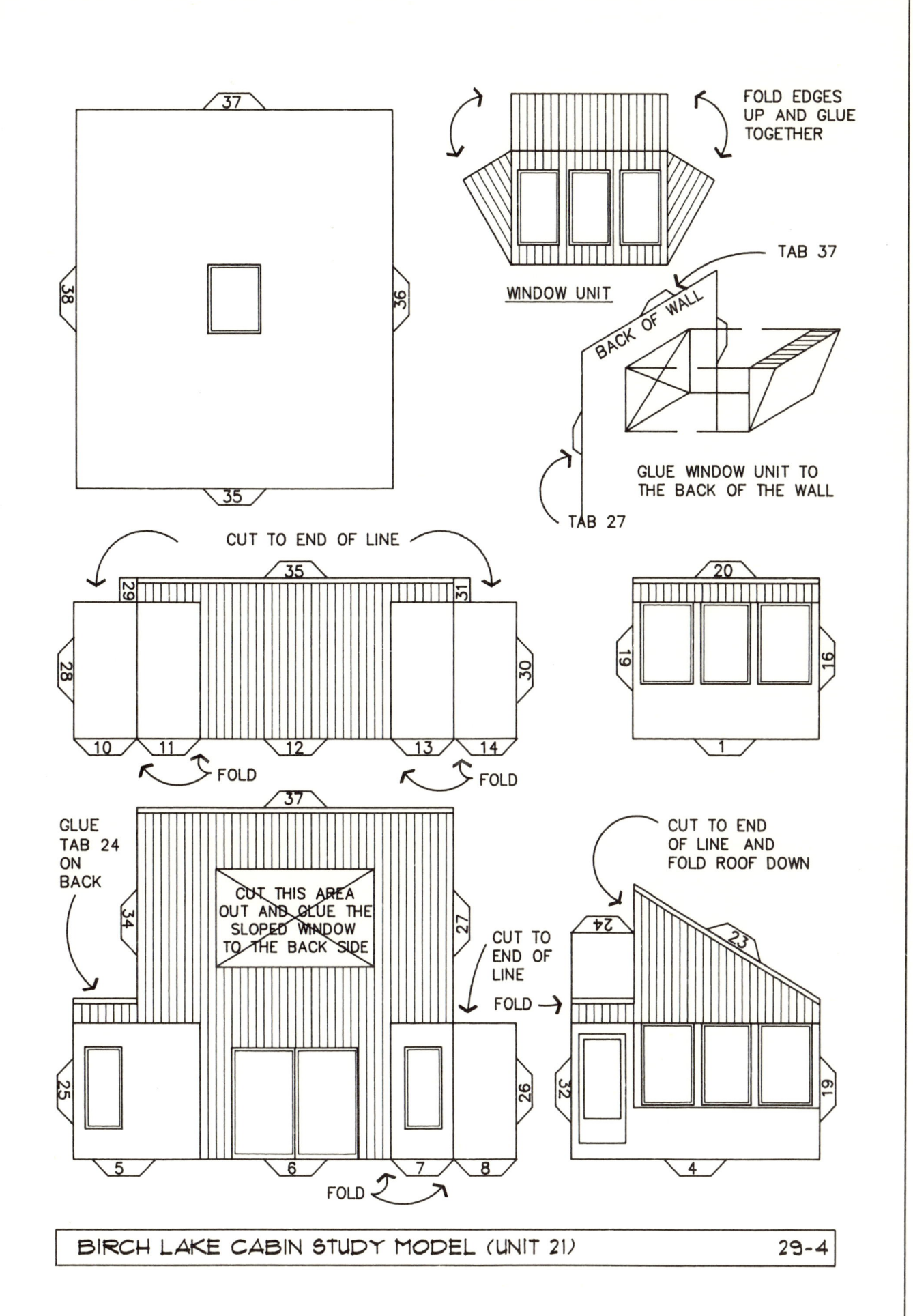

WINDOW UNIT

TAB 37

BACK OF WALL

GLUE WINDOW UNIT TO THE BACK OF THE WALL

TAB 27

CUT TO END OF LINE

FOLD

FOLD

GLUE TAB 24 ON BACK

CUT THIS AREA OUT AND GLUE THE SLOPED WINDOW TO THE BACK SIDE

CUT TO END OF LINE
FOLD

CUT TO END OF LINE AND FOLD ROOF DOWN

FOLD

BIRCH LAKE CABIN STUDY MODEL (UNIT 21)   29-4

12/12 PITCH ROOF HOUSE STUDY MODEL (UNIT 22)   29-5

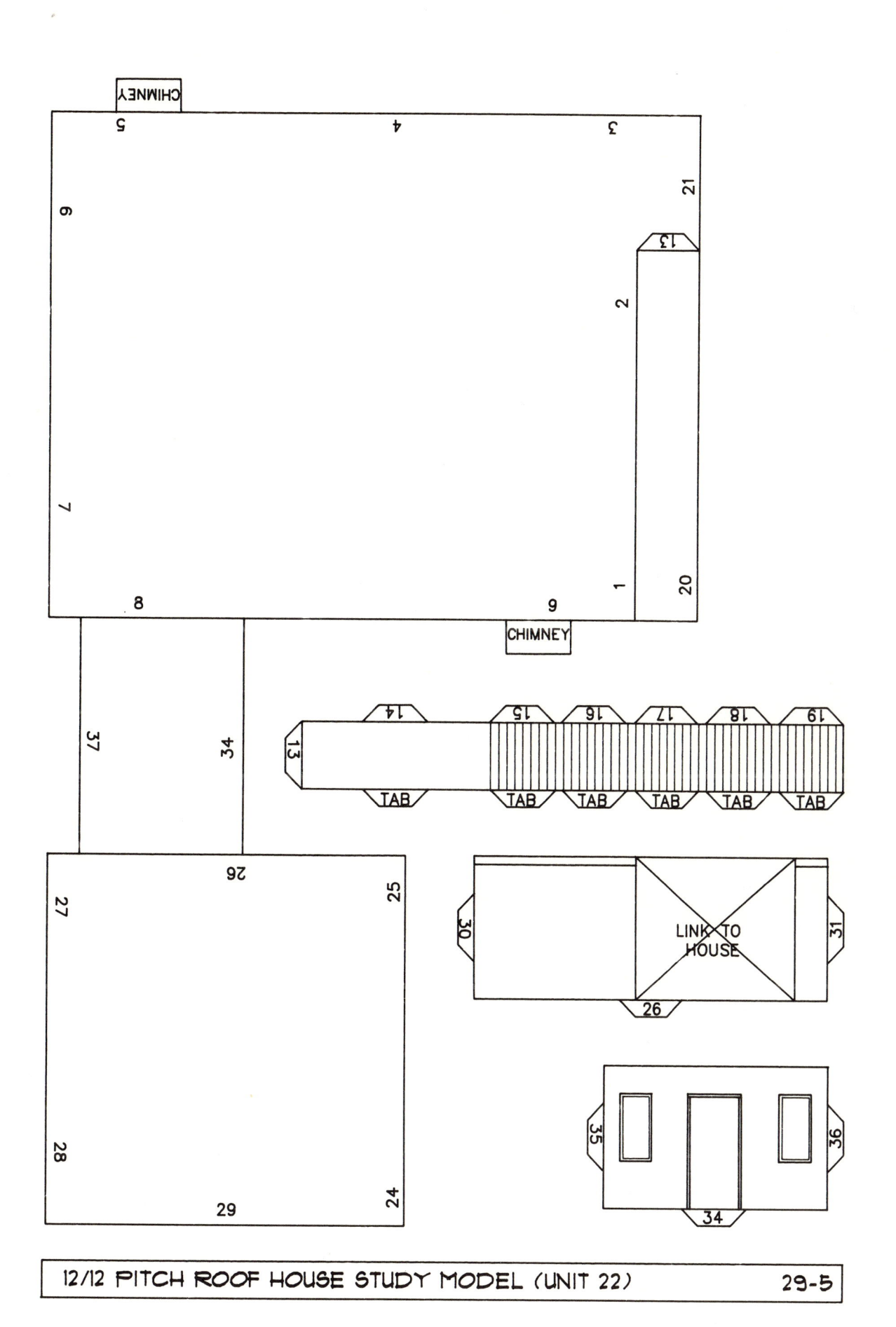

GLUE
LINK
ROOF ALONG
DASHED
LINE

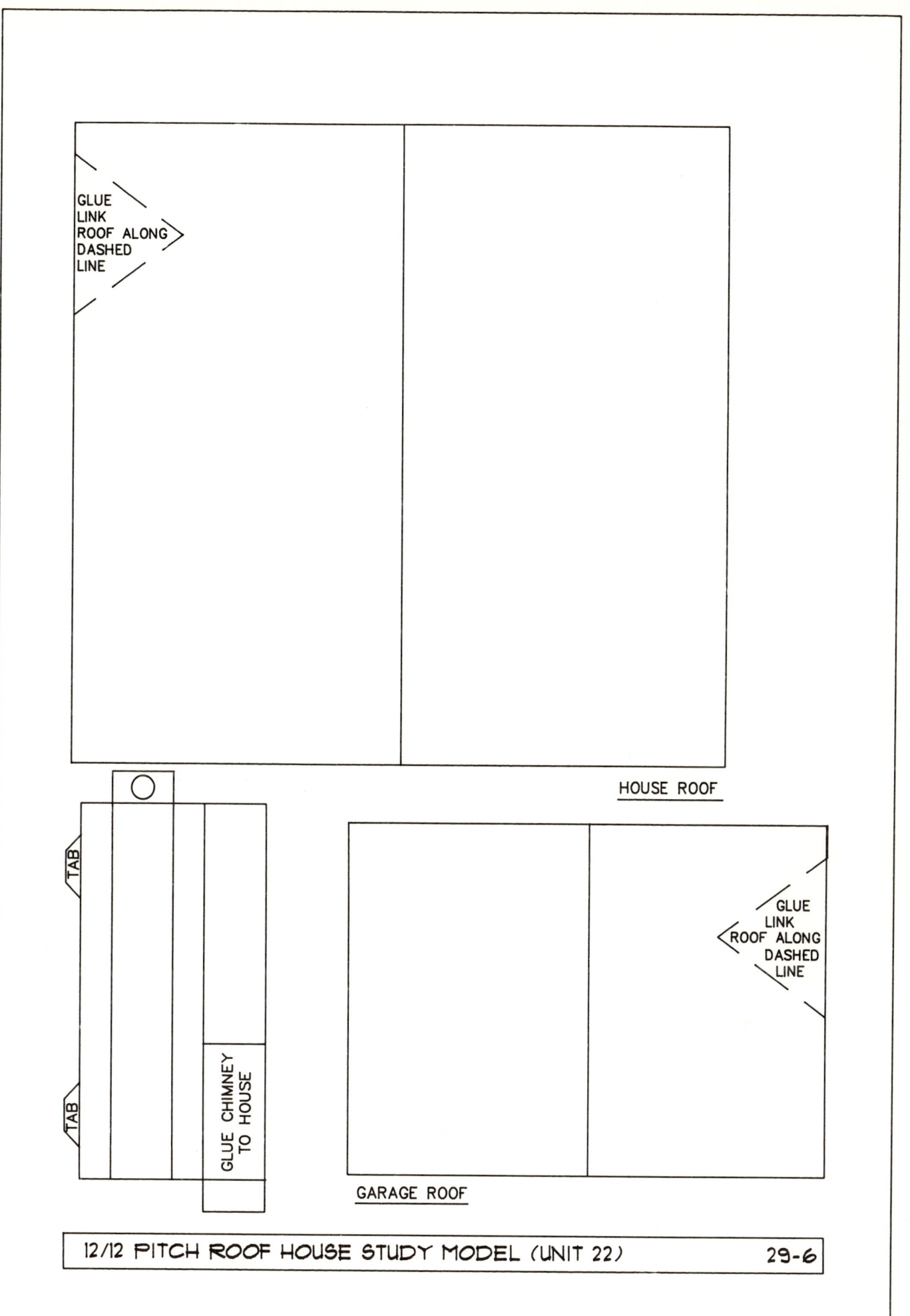

HOUSE ROOF

TAB

TAB

GLUE CHIMNEY TO HOUSE

GLUE
LINK
ROOF ALONG
DASHED
LINE

GARAGE ROOF

12/12 PITCH ROOF HOUSE STUDY MODEL (UNIT 22)

12/12 PITCH ROOF HOUSE STUDY MODEL (UNIT 22)   29-7

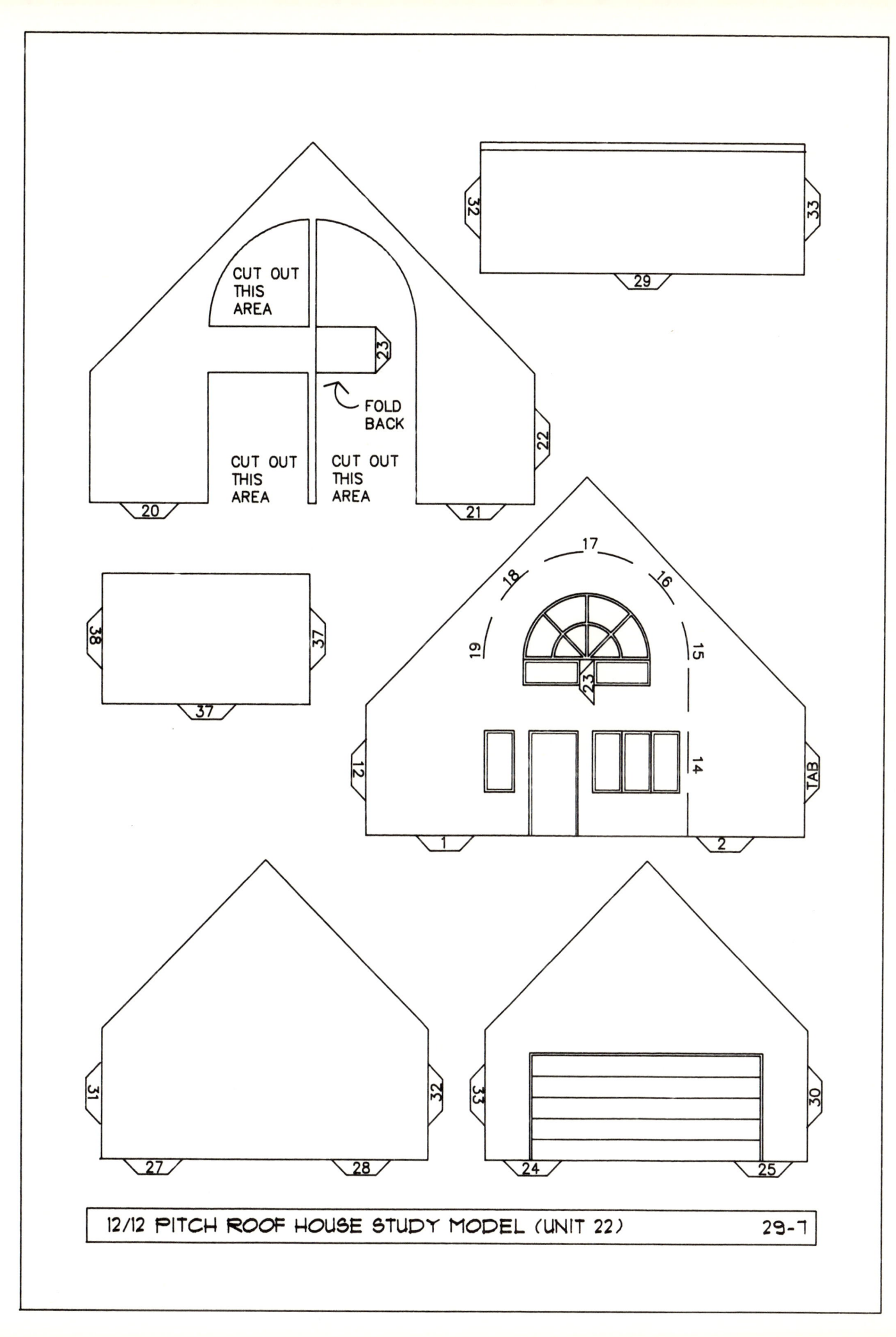

LINK ROOF

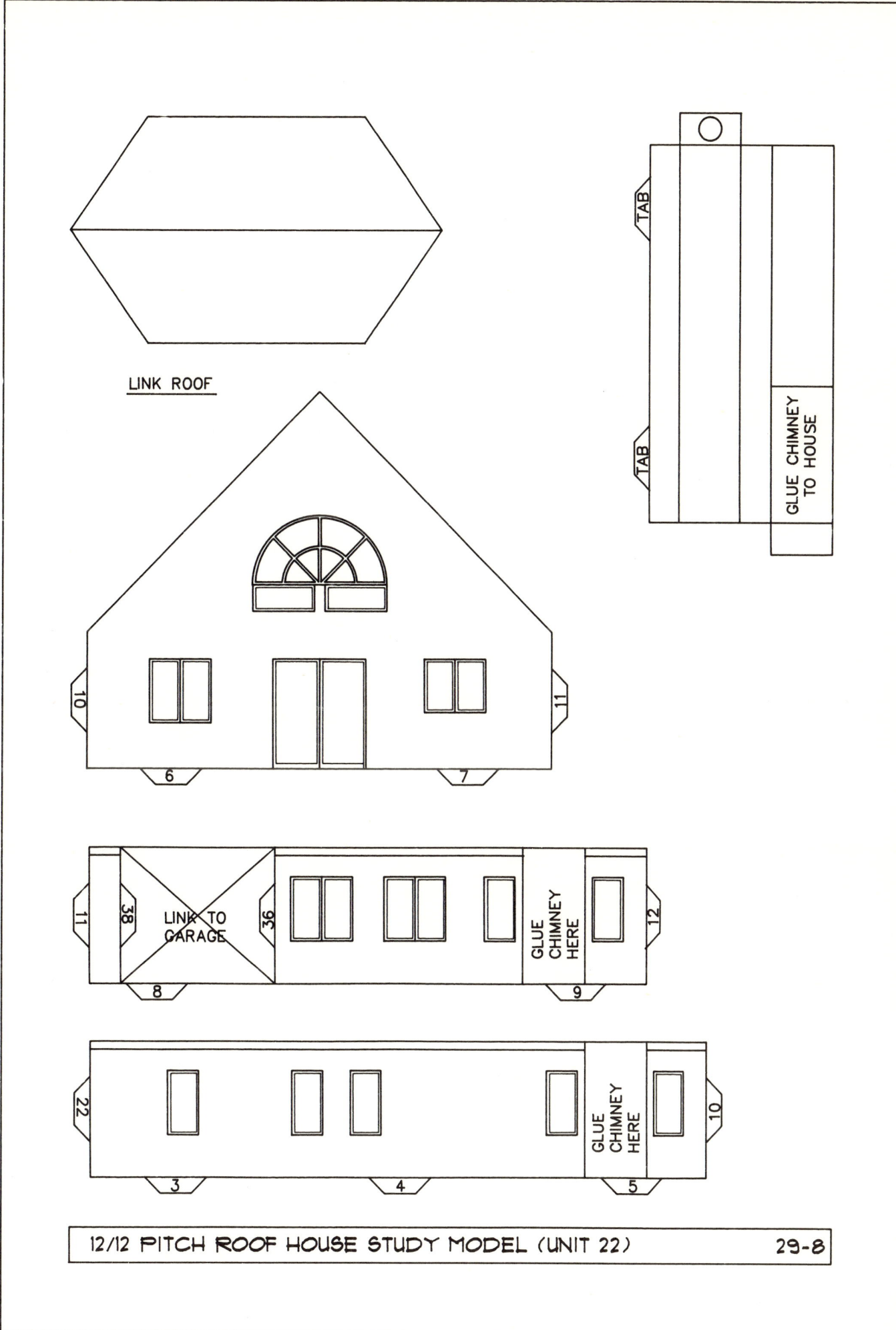

GLUE CHIMNEY TO HOUSE
TAB
TAB

10
11
6
7

11
38
LINK TO GARAGE
36
GLUE CHIMNEY HERE
12
8
9

22
GLUE CHIMNEY HERE
10
3
4
5

12/12 PITCH ROOF HOUSE STUDY MODEL (UNIT 22)   29-8

SKYWAY HOUSE STUDY MODEL (UNIT 23) 29-9

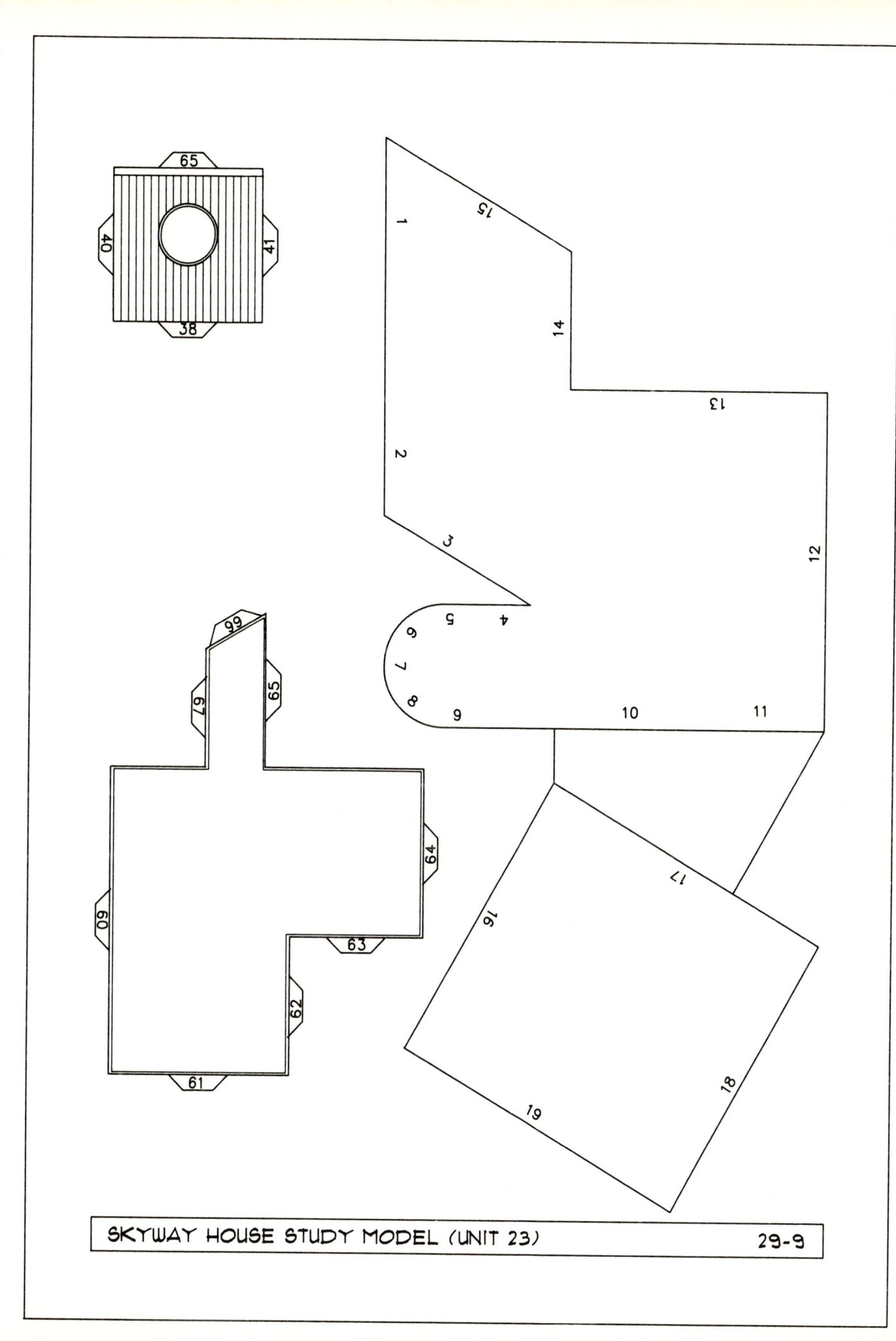

SKYWAY HOUSE STUDY MODEL (UNIT 23)   29-10

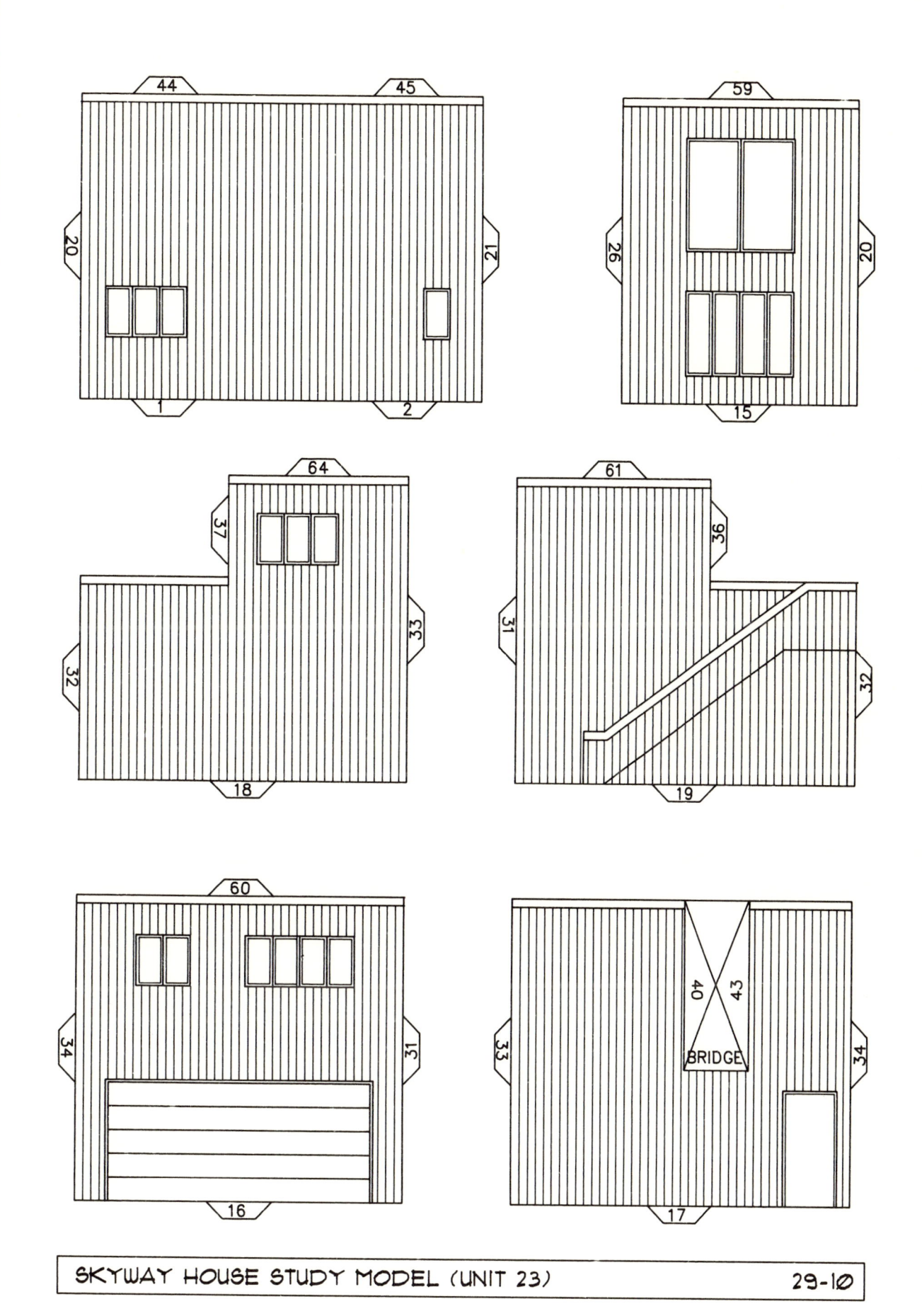

SKYWAY HOUSE STUDY MODEL (UNIT 23)   29-11

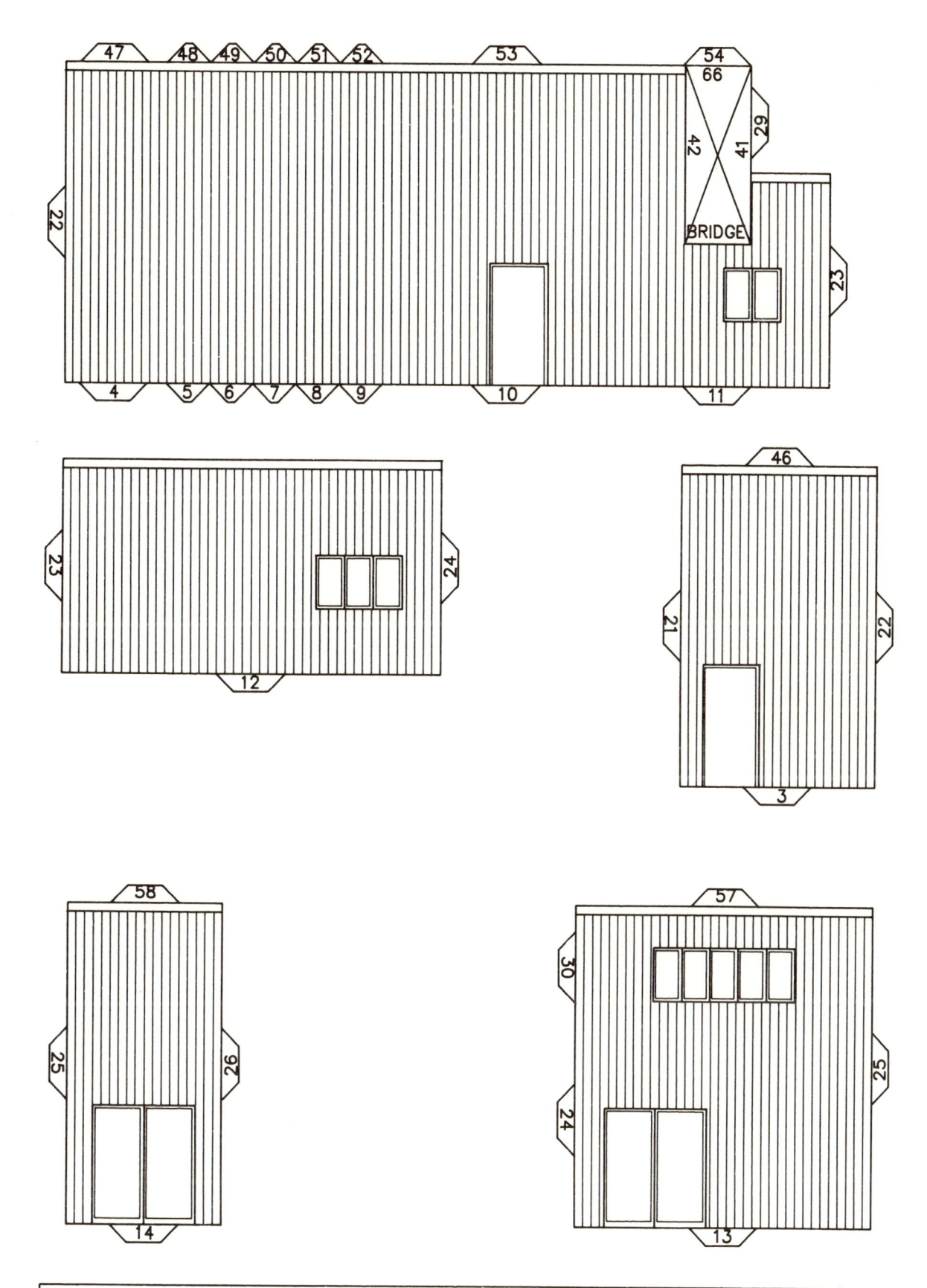

SKYWAY HOUSE STUDY MODEL (UNIT 23)   29-12

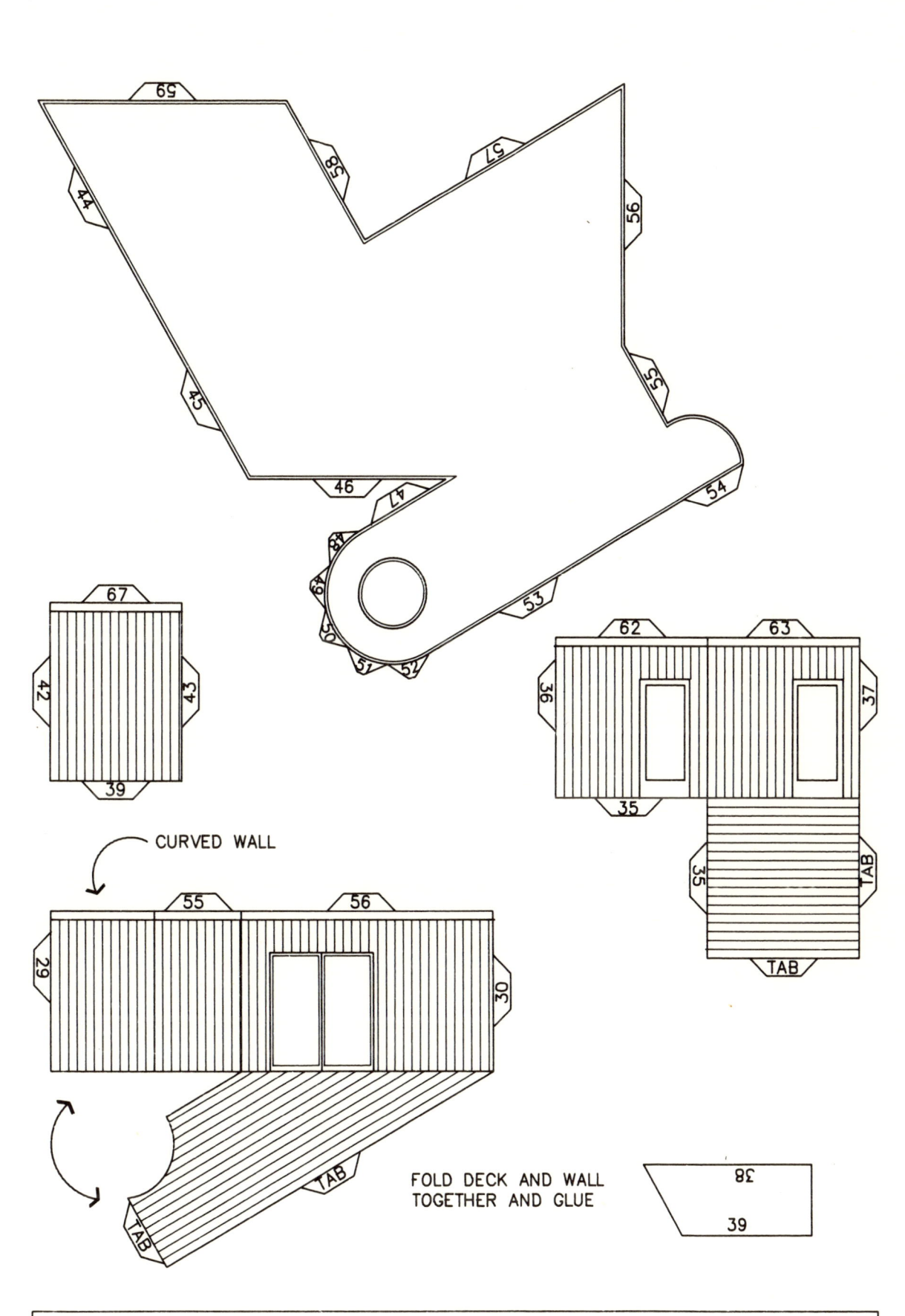

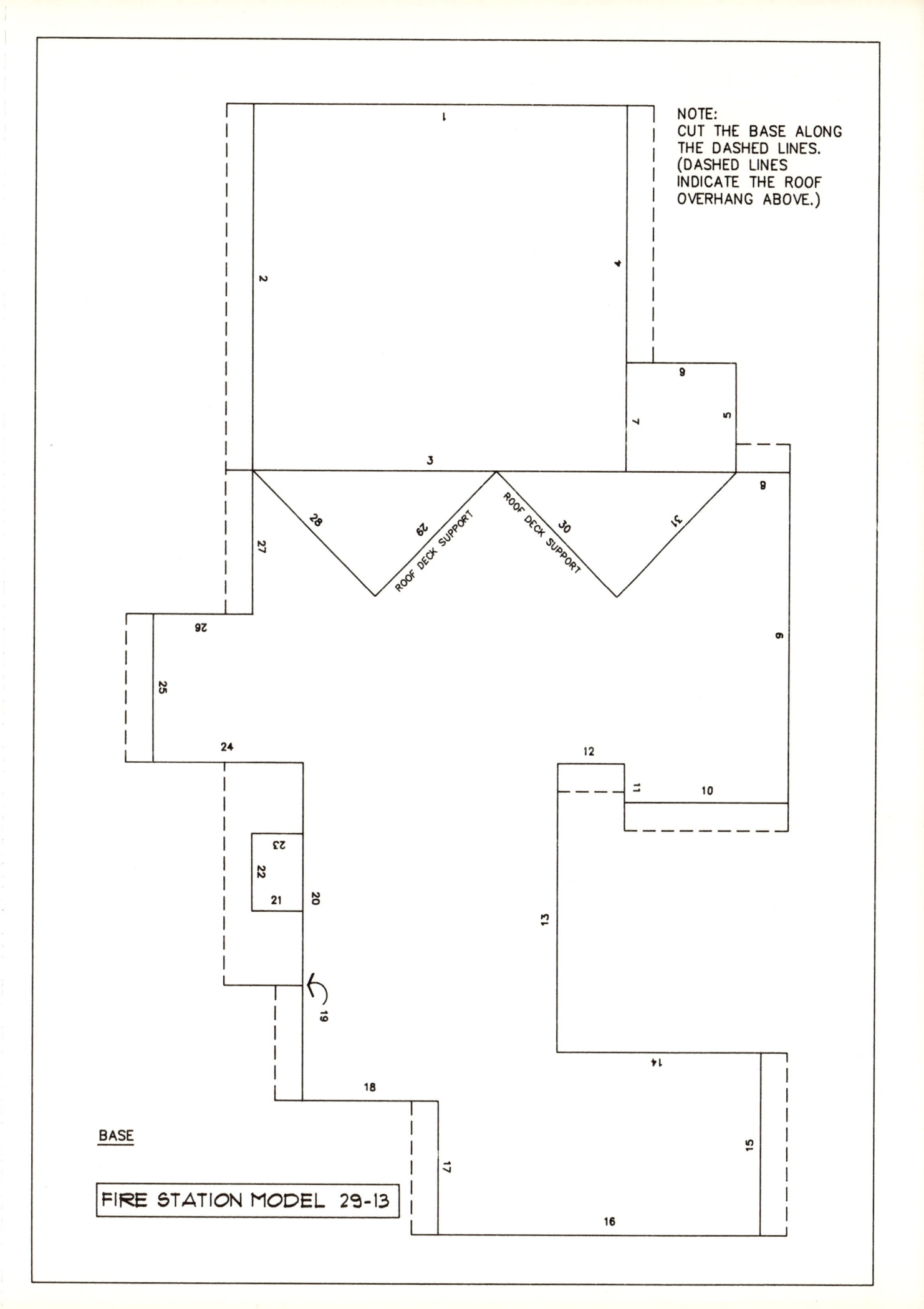

NOTE:
CUT THE BASE ALONG
THE DASHED LINES.
(DASHED LINES
INDICATE THE ROOF
OVERHANG ABOVE.)

ROOF DECK SUPPORT
ROOF DECK SUPPORT

BASE

FIRE STATION MODEL 29-13

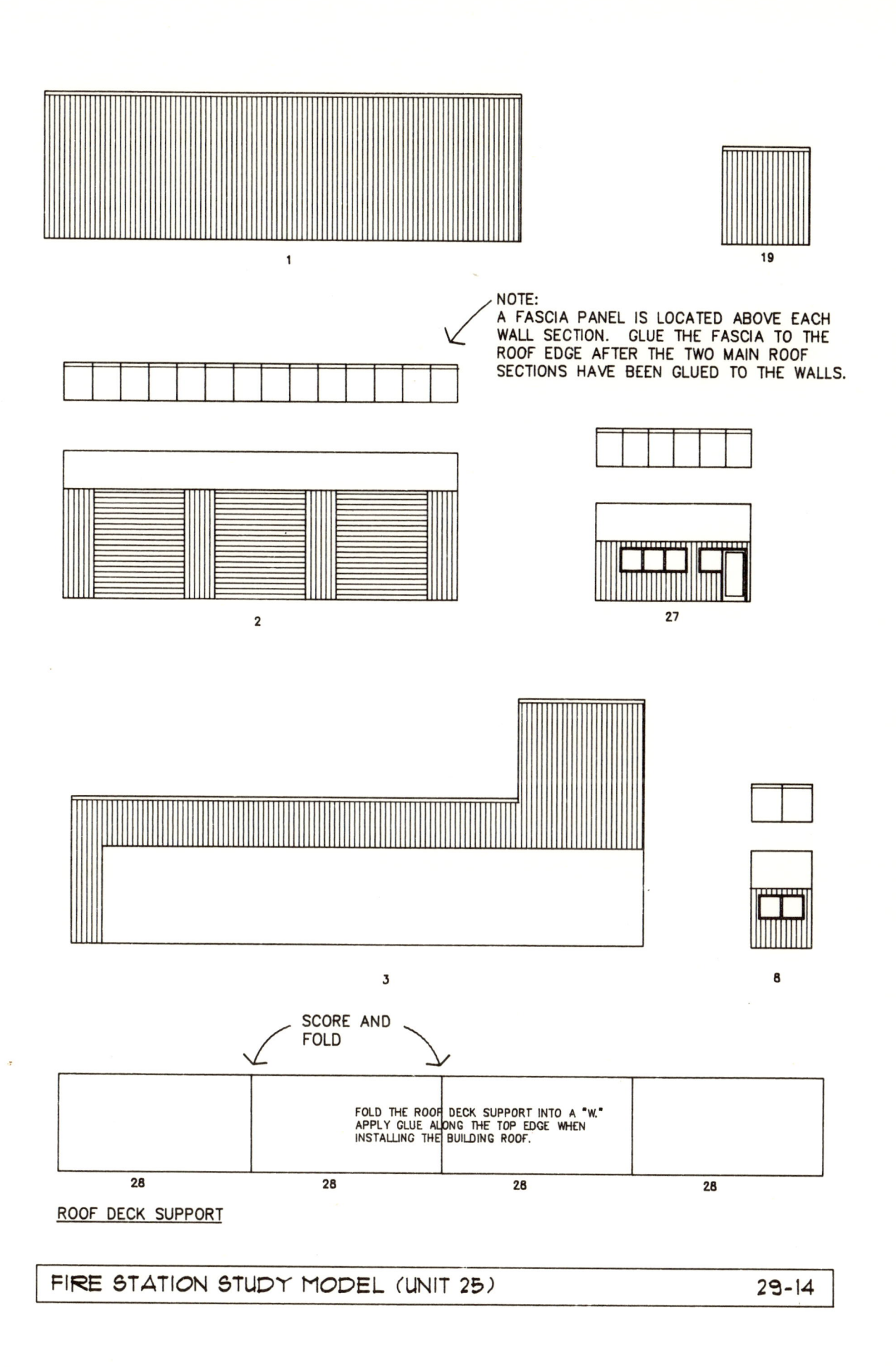

NOTE:
A FASCIA PANEL IS LOCATED ABOVE EACH WALL SECTION. GLUE THE FASCIA TO THE ROOF EDGE AFTER THE TWO MAIN ROOF SECTIONS HAVE BEEN GLUED TO THE WALLS.

SCORE AND FOLD

FOLD THE ROOF DECK SUPPORT INTO A "W." APPLY GLUE ALONG THE TOP EDGE WHEN INSTALLING THE BUILDING ROOF.

ROOF DECK SUPPORT

FIRE STATION STUDY MODEL (UNIT 25)

29-14

FIRE STATION STUDY MODEL (UNIT 25)

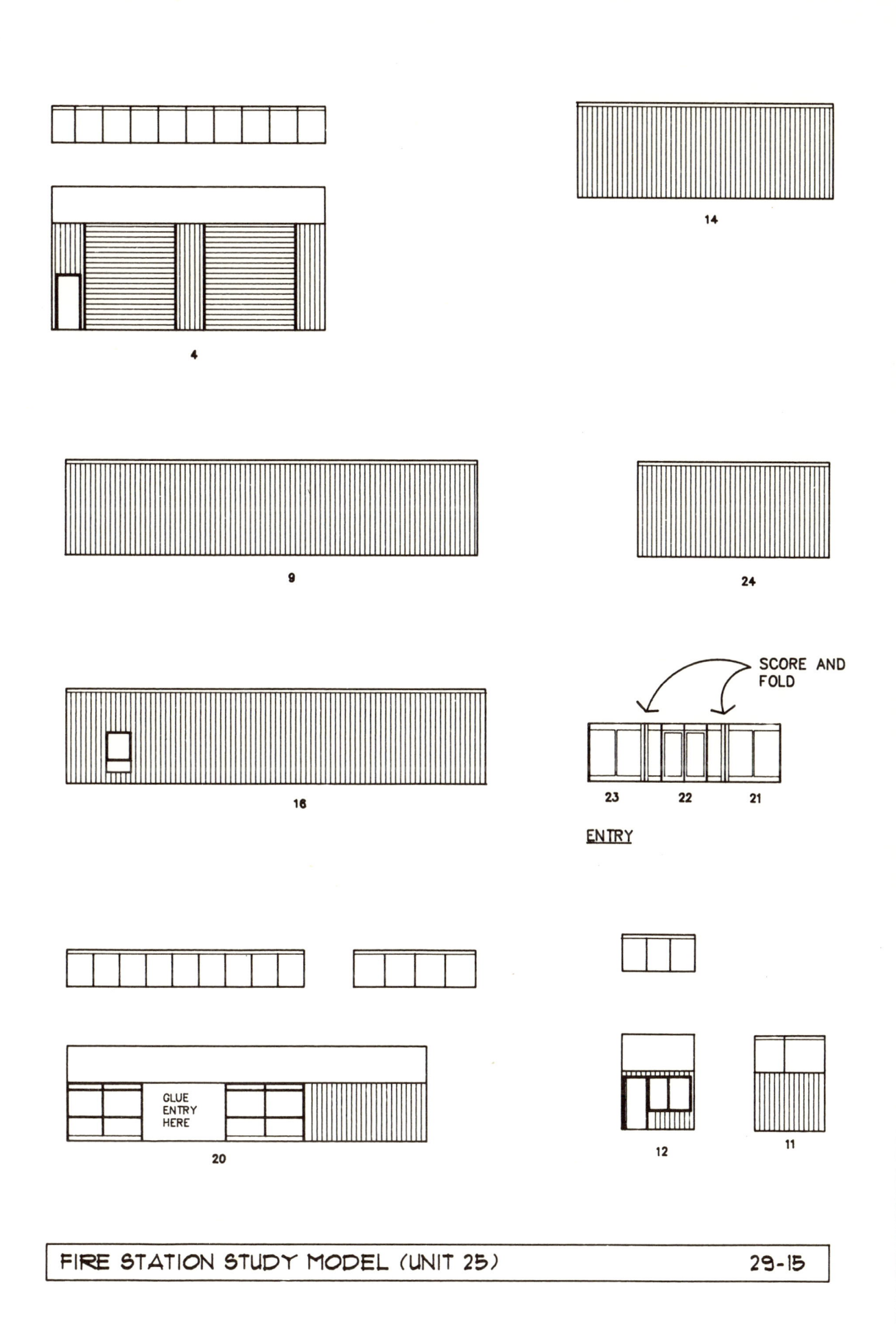

29-15

APPARATUS ROOM ROOF

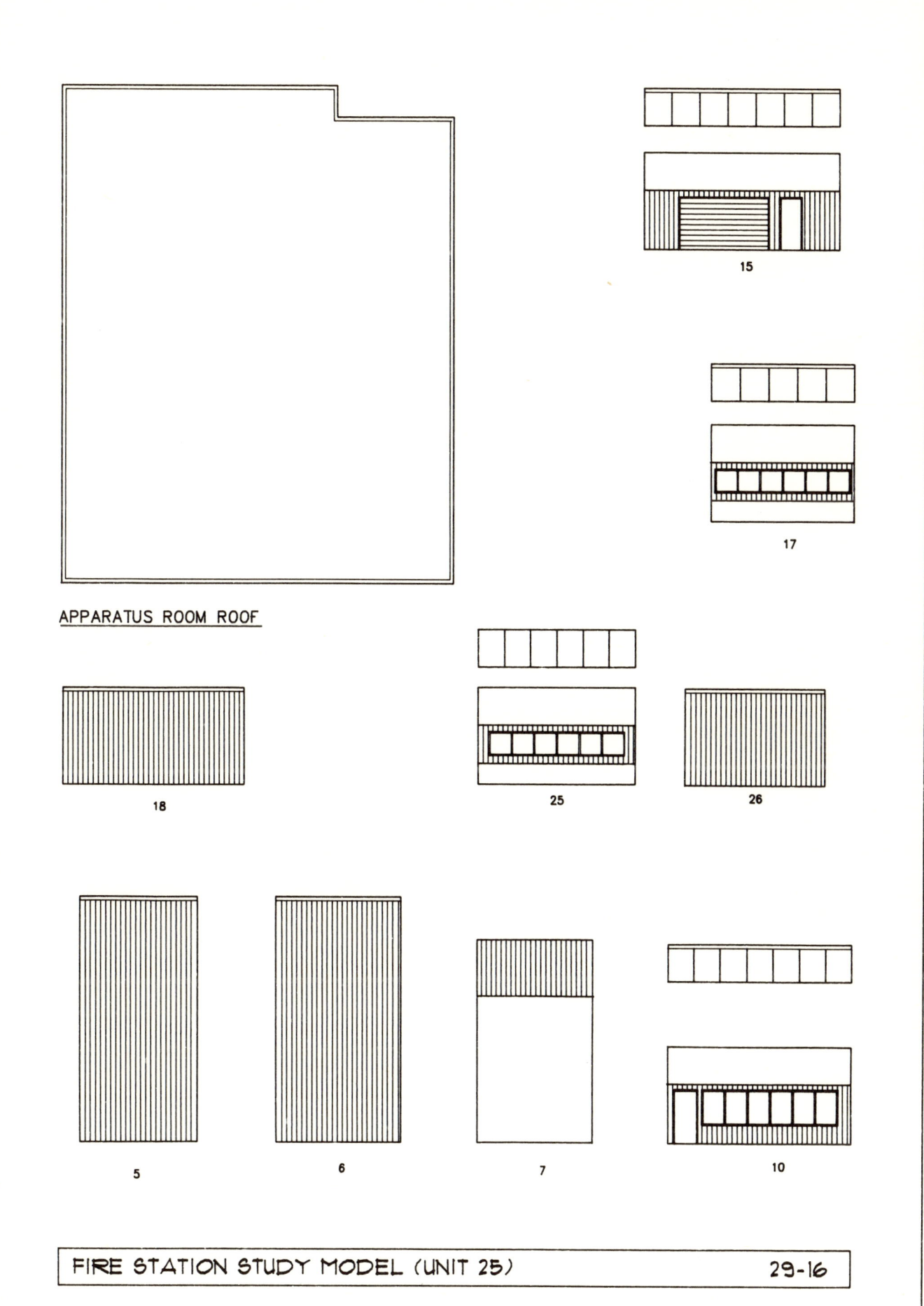

15

17

18 25 26

5 6 7 10

FIRE STATION STUDY MODEL (UNIT 25)   29-16

LOWER BUILDING
ROOF

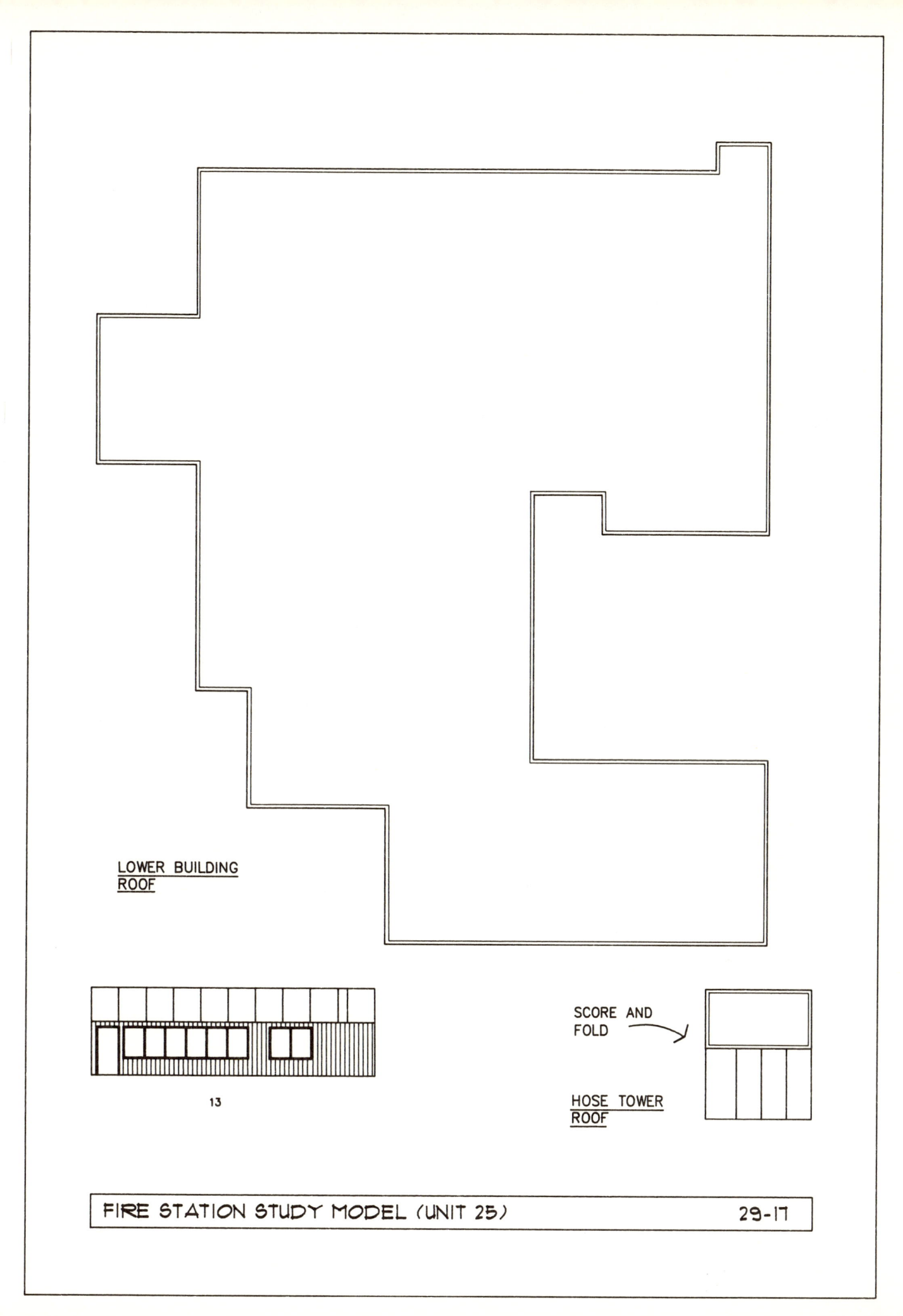

13

SCORE AND
FOLD

HOSE TOWER
ROOF

FIRE STATION STUDY MODEL (UNIT 25)   29-17

RAIL 5

RAIL 4

TAB C

RAIL 1

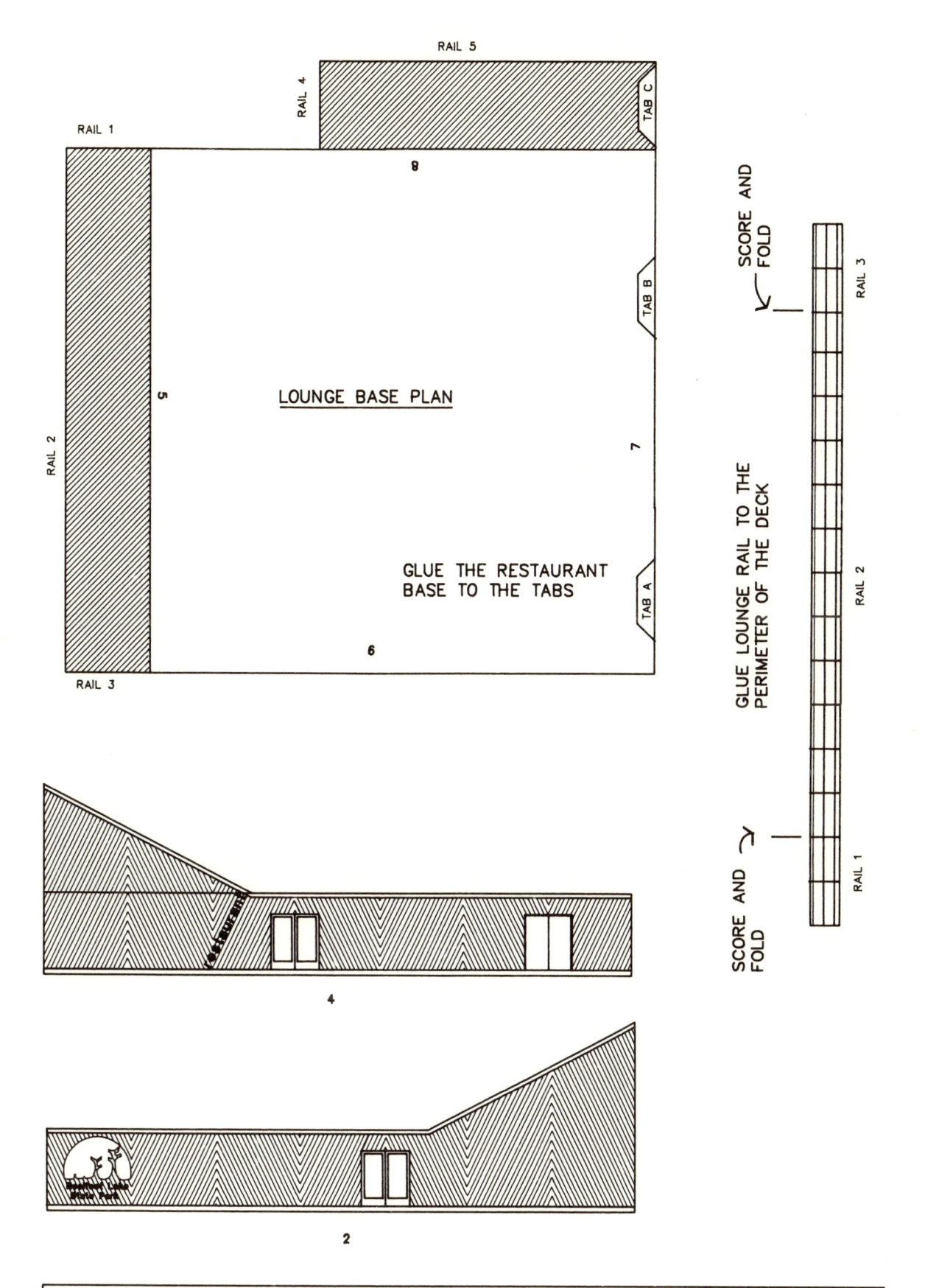

8

SCORE AND FOLD

RAIL 2

5

TAB B

LOUNGE BASE PLAN

RAIL 3

7

RAIL 2

GLUE LOUNGE RAIL TO THE PERIMETER OF THE DECK

GLUE THE RESTAURANT BASE TO THE TABS

TAB A

6

RAIL 3

RAIL 1

SCORE AND FOLD

4

2

MOTEL AND RESTAURANT STUDY MODEL (UNIT 26)   29-18

RAIL 12

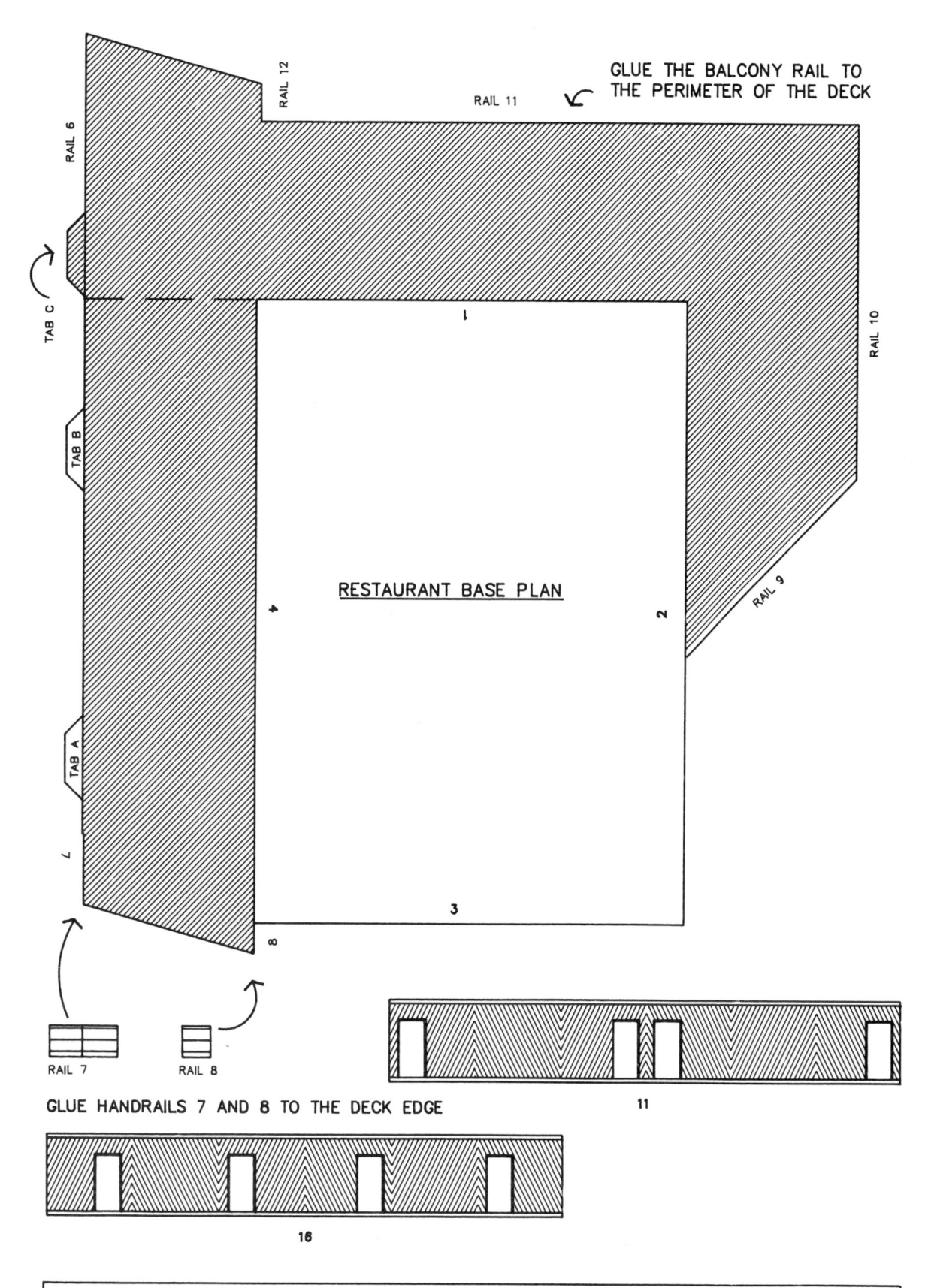

RAIL 11

GLUE THE BALCONY RAIL TO
THE PERIMETER OF THE DECK

RAIL 6

RAIL 10

TAB C

TAB B

RAIL 9

RESTAURANT BASE PLAN

TAB A

RAIL 7   RAIL 8

GLUE HANDRAILS 7 AND 8 TO THE DECK EDGE

11

16

MOTEL AND RESTAURANT STUDY MODEL (UNIT 26)   29-19

DECK 16

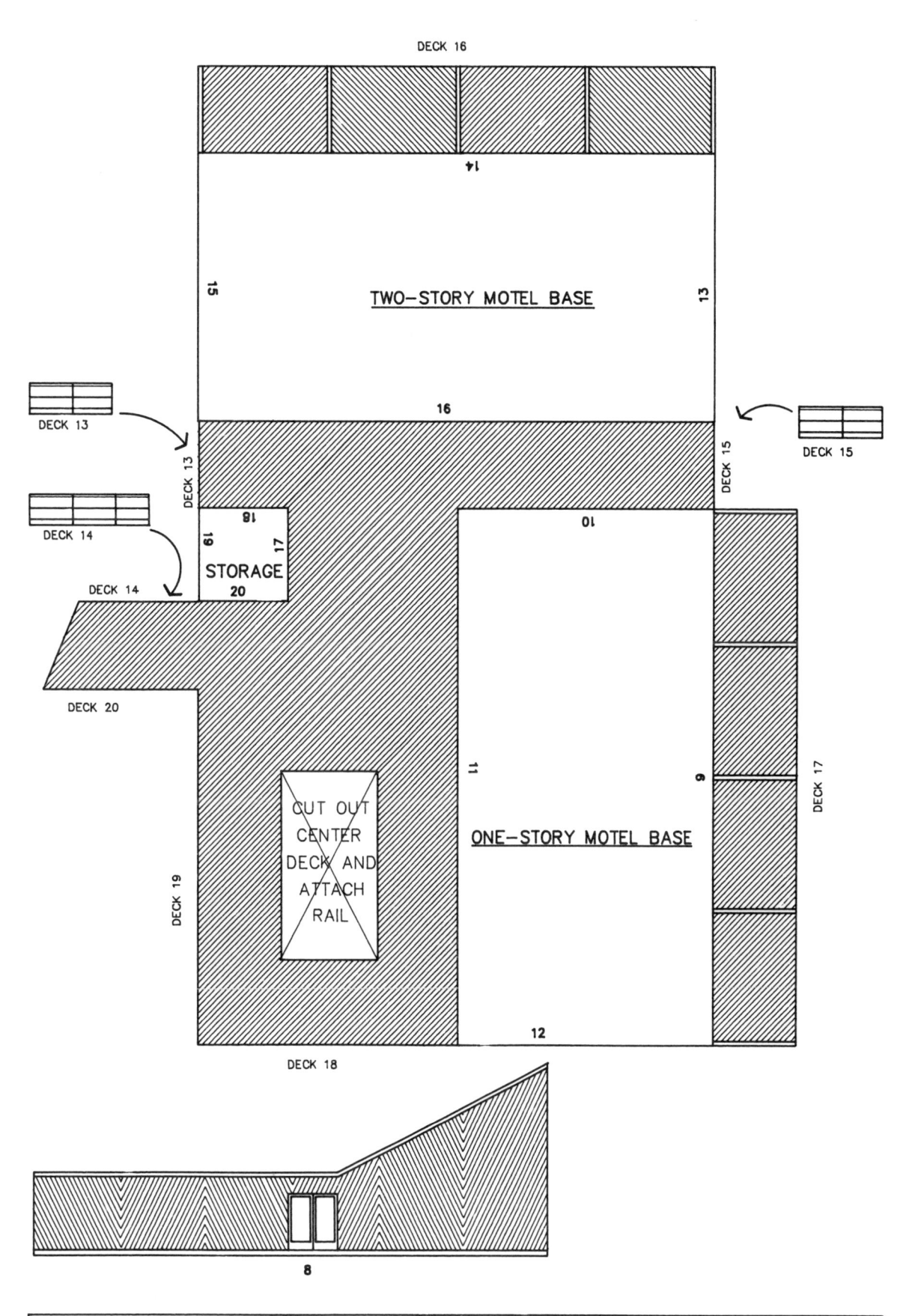

TWO-STORY MOTEL BASE

15 | 13

16

DECK 13 → DECK 13

DECK 15 ← DECK 15

DECK 14 → DECK 14

STORAGE

DECK 20

CUT OUT CENTER DECK AND ATTACH RAIL

DECK 19

ONE-STORY MOTEL BASE

DECK 17

DECK 18

8

MOTEL AND RESTAURANT STUDY MODEL (UNIT 26)   29-20

CUT TO END OF LINE AND FOLD ROOF UP

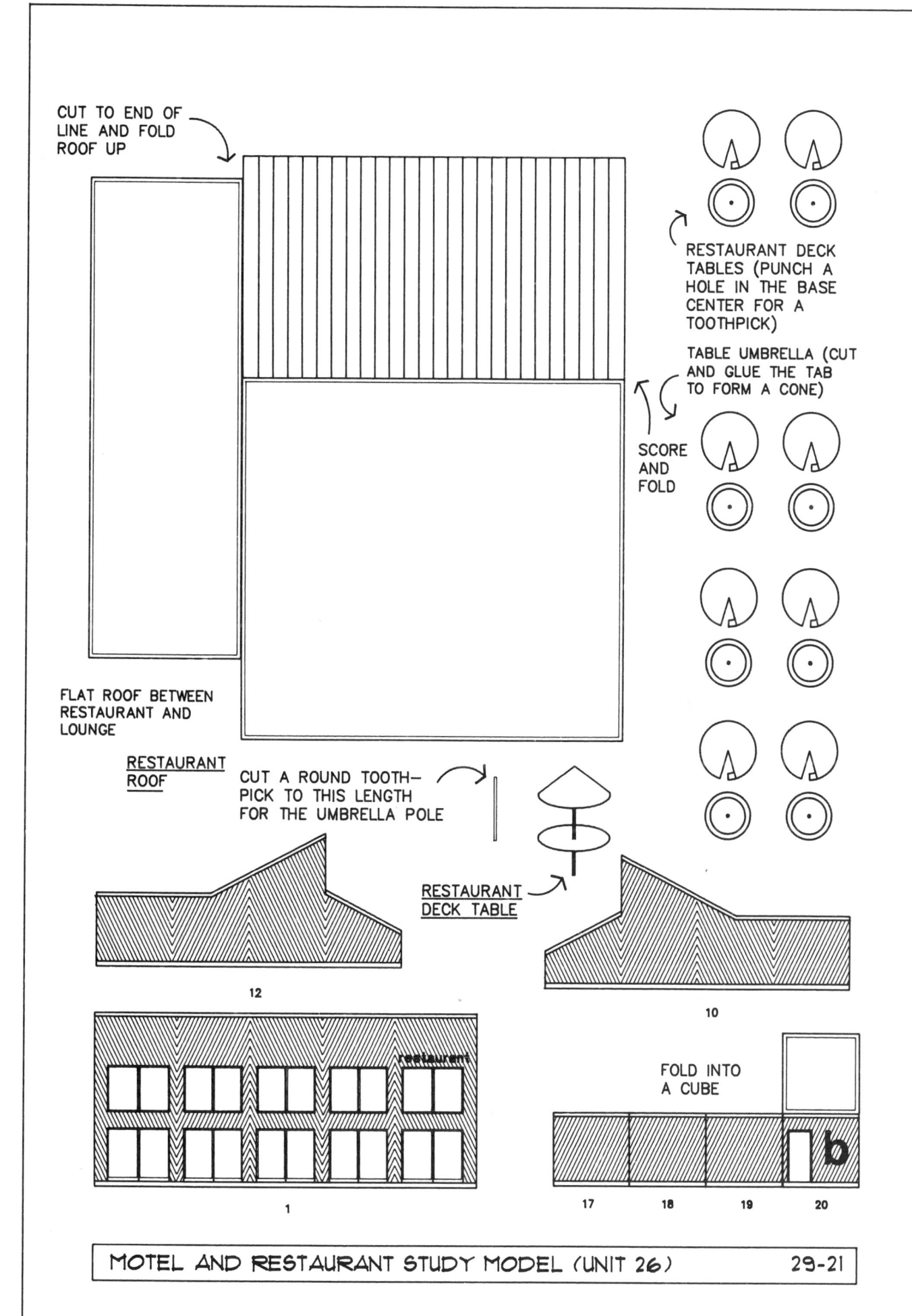

RESTAURANT DECK TABLES (PUNCH A HOLE IN THE BASE CENTER FOR A TOOTHPICK)

TABLE UMBRELLA (CUT AND GLUE THE TAB TO FORM A CONE)

SCORE AND FOLD

FLAT ROOF BETWEEN RESTAURANT AND LOUNGE

RESTAURANT ROOF

CUT A ROUND TOOTHPICK TO THIS LENGTH FOR THE UMBRELLA POLE

RESTAURANT DECK TABLE

12

10

1

FOLD INTO A CUBE

17 18 19 20

MOTEL AND RESTAURANT STUDY MODEL (UNIT 26)   29-21

SCORE AND FOLD — ONE-STORY MOTEL ROOF

SCORE AND FOLD — TWO-STORY MOTEL ROOF

SCORE AND FOLD | SCORE AND FOLD | SCORE AND FOLD

GLUE THE BALCONY RAIL AROUND THE MOTEL CENTER DECK PERIMETER

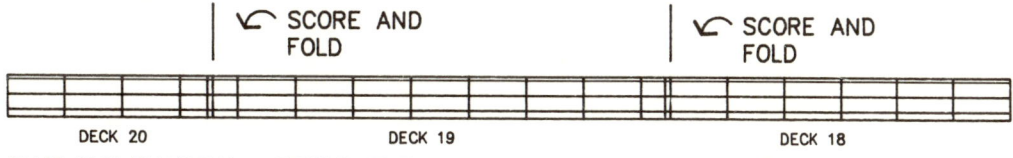

SCORE AND FOLD | SCORE AND FOLD

DECK 20   DECK 19   DECK 18

GLUE THE HANDRAIL AROUND THE PERIMETER OF THE MOTEL DECK

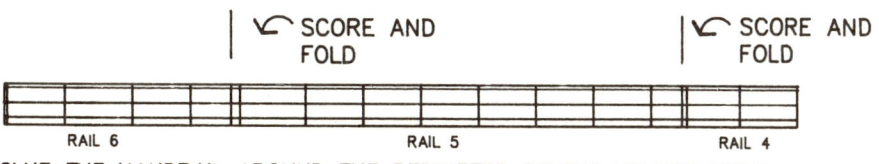

SCORE AND FOLD | SCORE AND FOLD

RAIL 6   RAIL 5   RAIL 4

GLUE THE HANDRAIL AROUND THE PERIMETER OF THE LOUNGE DECK

MOTEL AND RESTAURANT STUDY MODEL (UNIT 26)   29-22

LOUNGE ROOF

SCORE AND FOLD

SCORE AND FOLD

SCORE AND FOLD
CUT TO END OF LINE AND FOLD ROOF UP

GLUE WEDGE BETWEEN THE FLAT AND SLOPED ROOFS

GLUE HANDRAIL AROUND THE PERIMETER OF THE RESTAURANT DECK

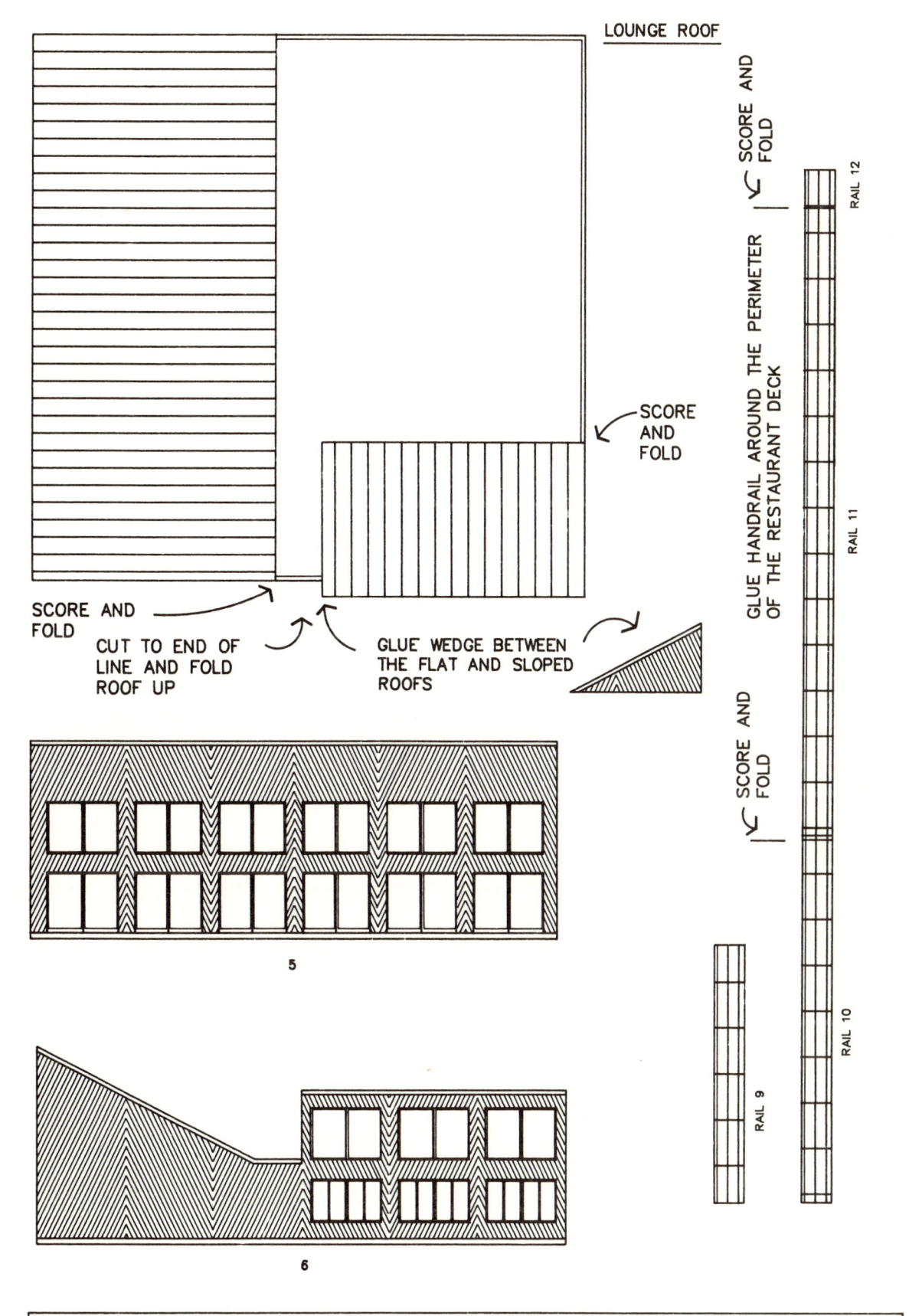

SCORE AND FOLD

RAIL 12

RAIL 11

RAIL 10

RAIL 9

5

6

MOTEL AND RESTAURANT STUDY MODEL (UNIT 26)   29-23

13

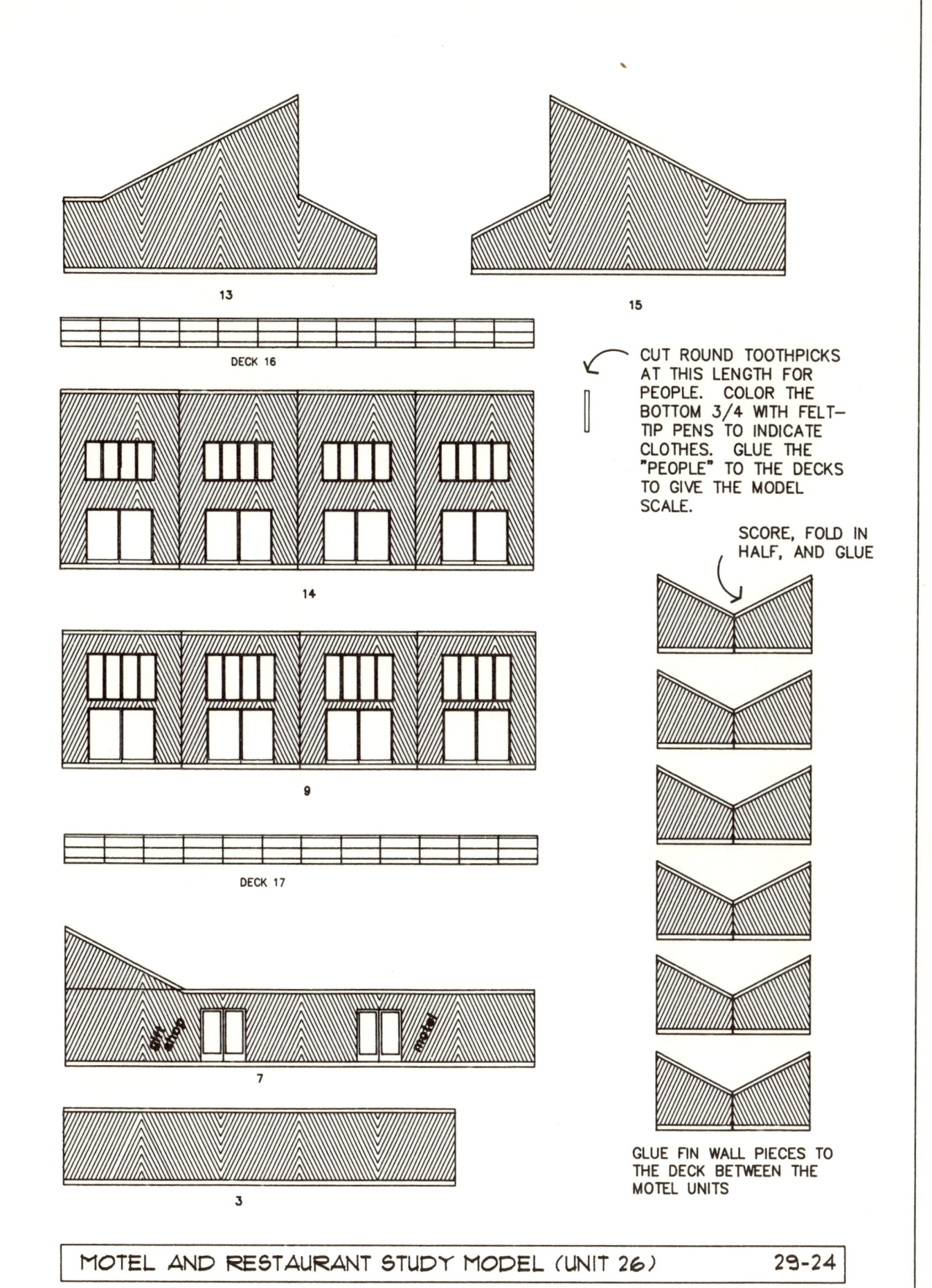

15

DECK 16

14

9

DECK 17

7

3

CUT ROUND TOOTHPICKS AT THIS LENGTH FOR PEOPLE. COLOR THE BOTTOM 3/4 WITH FELT-TIP PENS TO INDICATE CLOTHES. GLUE THE "PEOPLE" TO THE DECKS TO GIVE THE MODEL SCALE.

SCORE, FOLD IN HALF, AND GLUE

GLUE FIN WALL PIECES TO THE DECK BETWEEN THE MOTEL UNITS

MOTEL AND RESTAURANT STUDY MODEL (UNIT 26)   29-24

GLUE UPPER-LEVEL BASE HERE

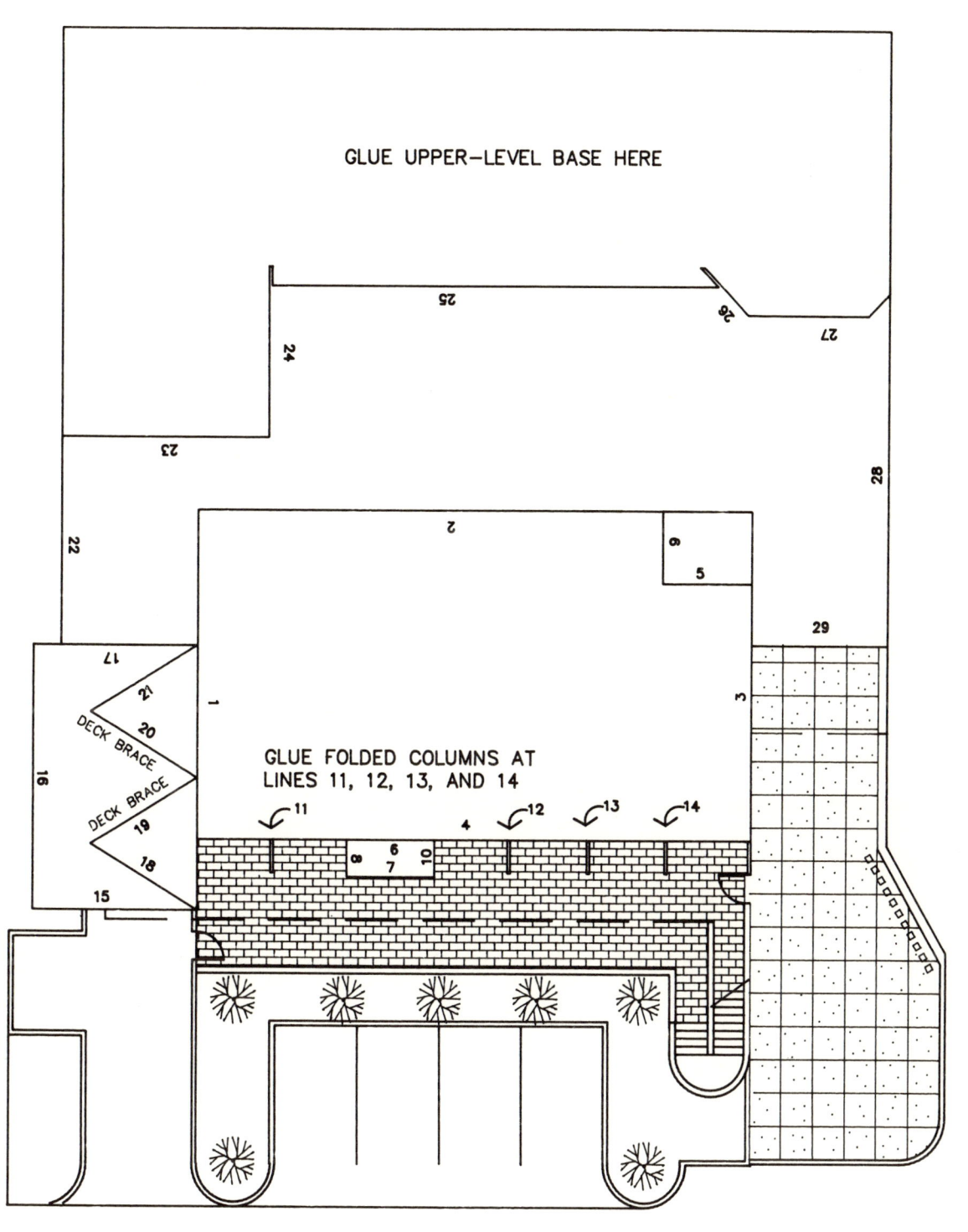

GLUE FOLDED COLUMNS AT
LINES 11, 12, 13, AND 14

BASE

STUDENT LIBRARY STUDY MODEL (UNIT 27)   29-25

STUDENT LIBRARY STUDY MODEL (UNIT 27)

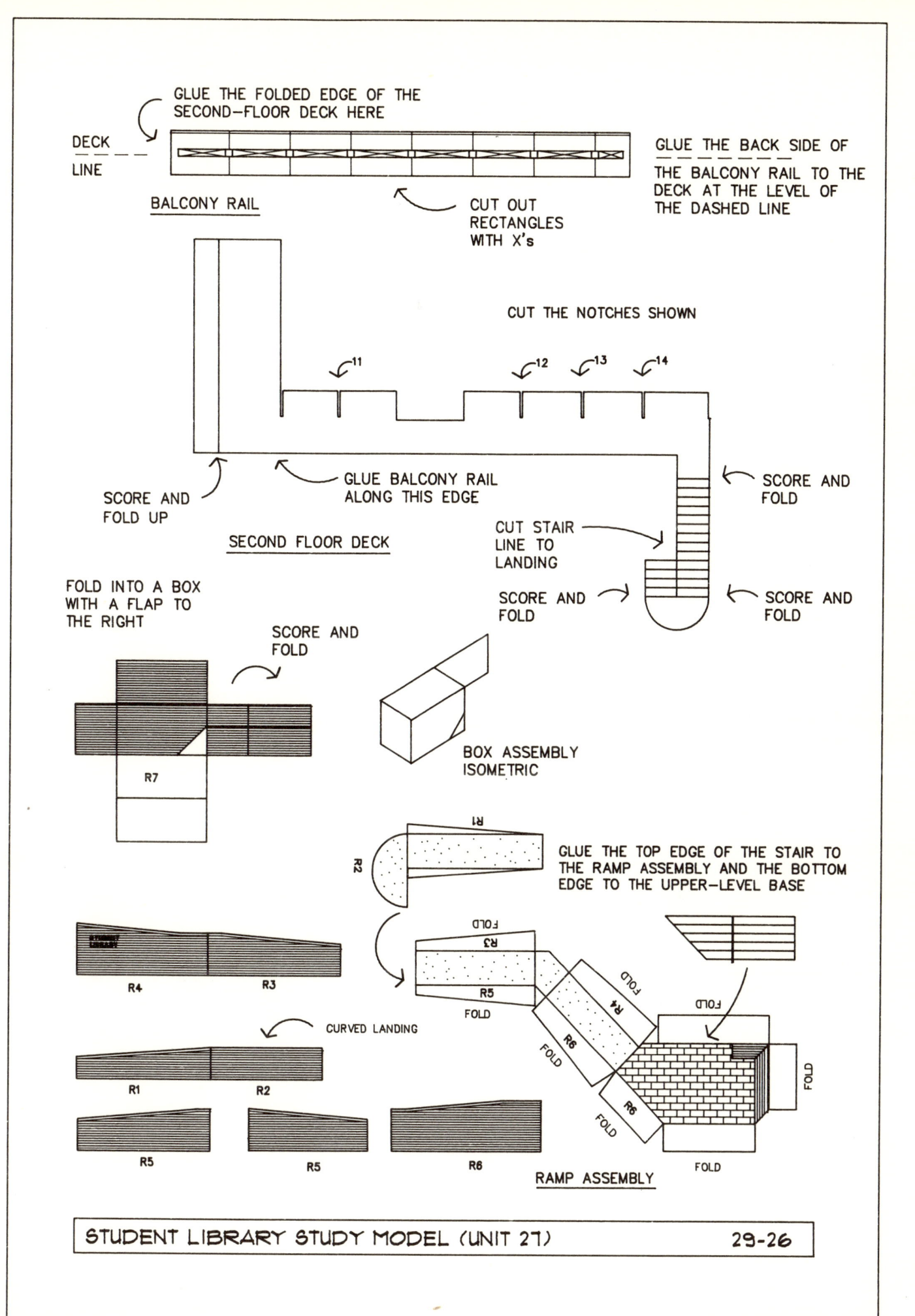

29-26

CUT TO LINE

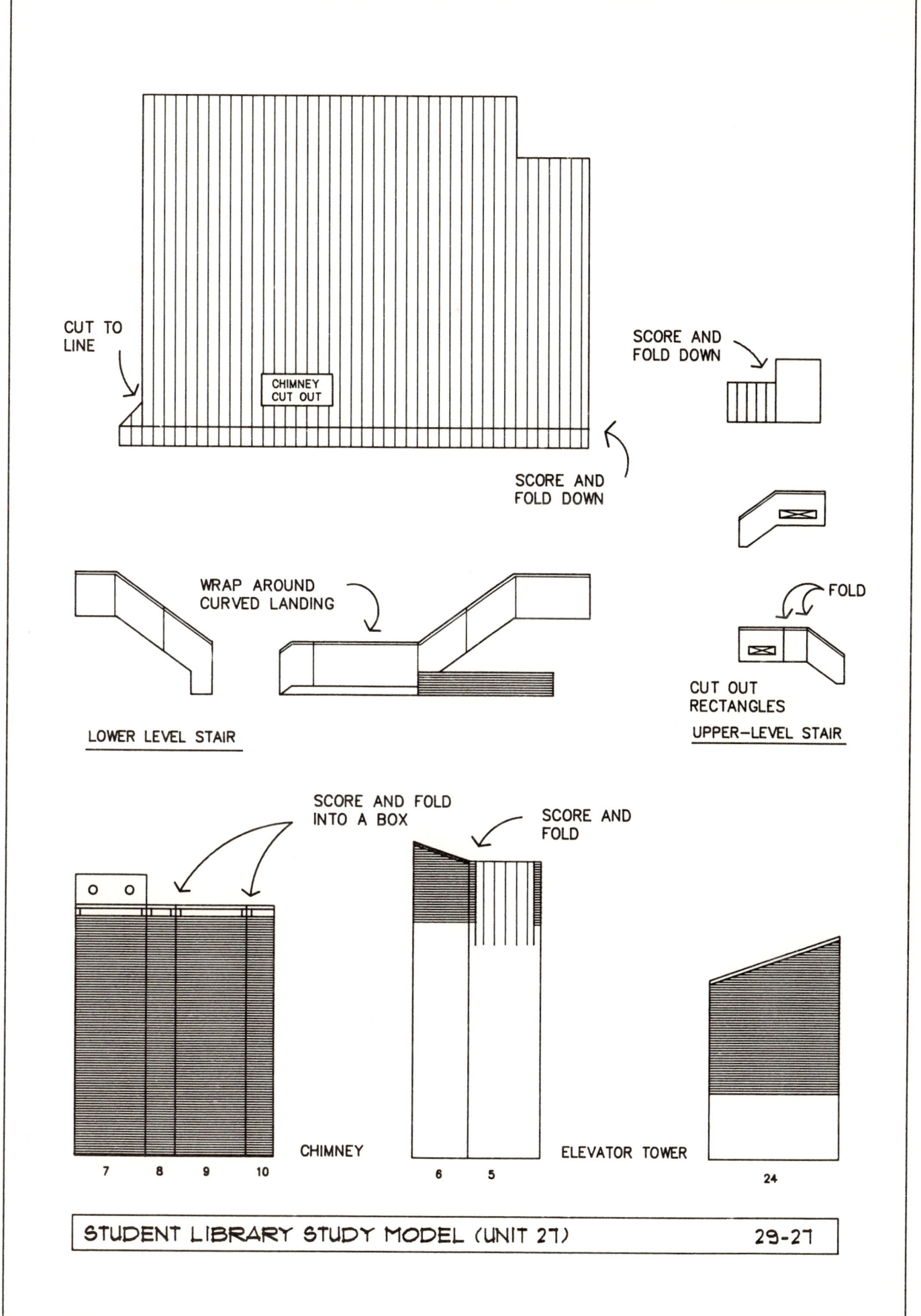

CHIMNEY CUT OUT

SCORE AND FOLD DOWN

SCORE AND FOLD DOWN

WRAP AROUND CURVED LANDING

FOLD

CUT OUT RECTANGLES

LOWER LEVEL STAIR

UPPER-LEVEL STAIR

SCORE AND FOLD INTO A BOX

SCORE AND FOLD

CHIMNEY

7   8   9   10

6   5

ELEVATOR TOWER

24

STUDENT LIBRARY STUDY MODEL (UNIT 27)

29-27

SCORE AND FOLD

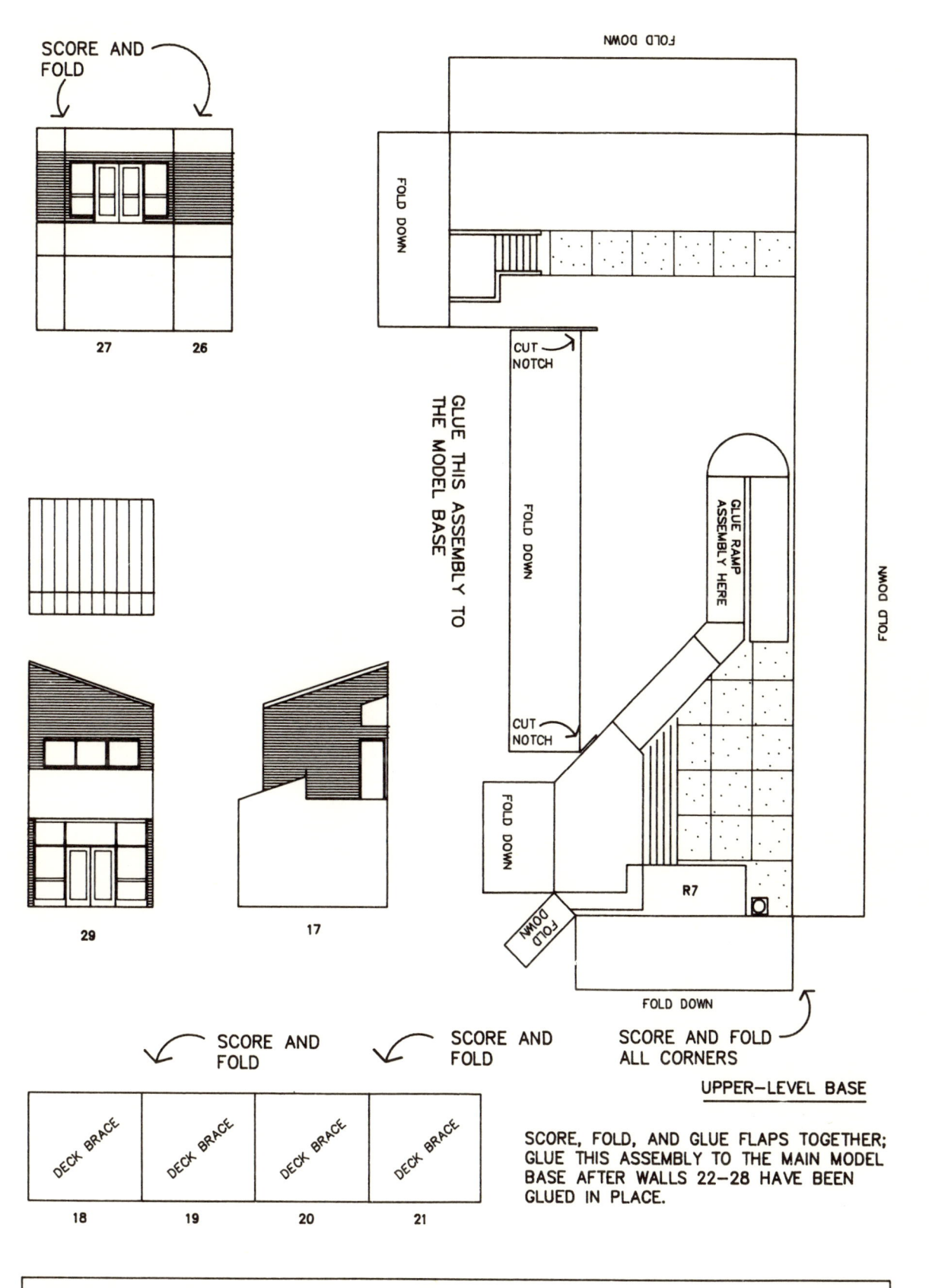

FOLD DOWN

FOLD DOWN

27 26

CUT NOTCH

GLUE THIS ASSEMBLY TO THE MODEL BASE

FOLD DOWN

GLUE RAMP ASSEMBLY HERE

FOLD DOWN

CUT NOTCH

FOLD DOWN

FOLD DOWN

R7

FOLD DOWN

29 17

FOLD DOWN

SCORE AND FOLD ALL CORNERS

UPPER-LEVEL BASE

SCORE AND FOLD

SCORE AND FOLD

DECK BRACE	DECK BRACE	DECK BRACE	DECK BRACE
18	19	20	21

SCORE, FOLD, AND GLUE FLAPS TOGETHER; GLUE THIS ASSEMBLY TO THE MAIN MODEL BASE AFTER WALLS 22–28 HAVE BEEN GLUED IN PLACE.

STUDENT LIBRARY STUDY MODEL (UNIT 27)   29-28

STUDENT LIBRARY STUDY MODEL (UNIT 27)   29-29

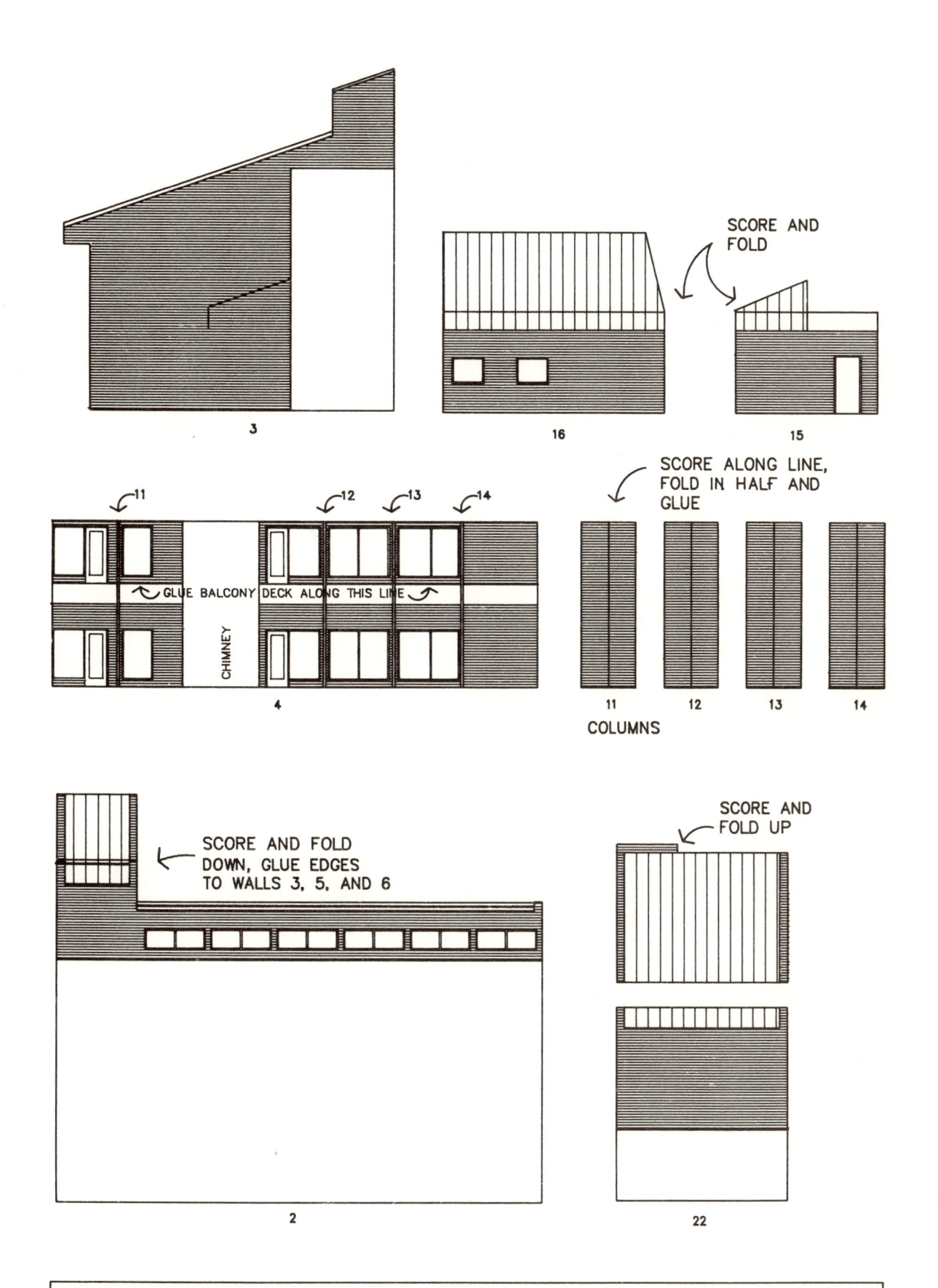

SCORE AND FOLD

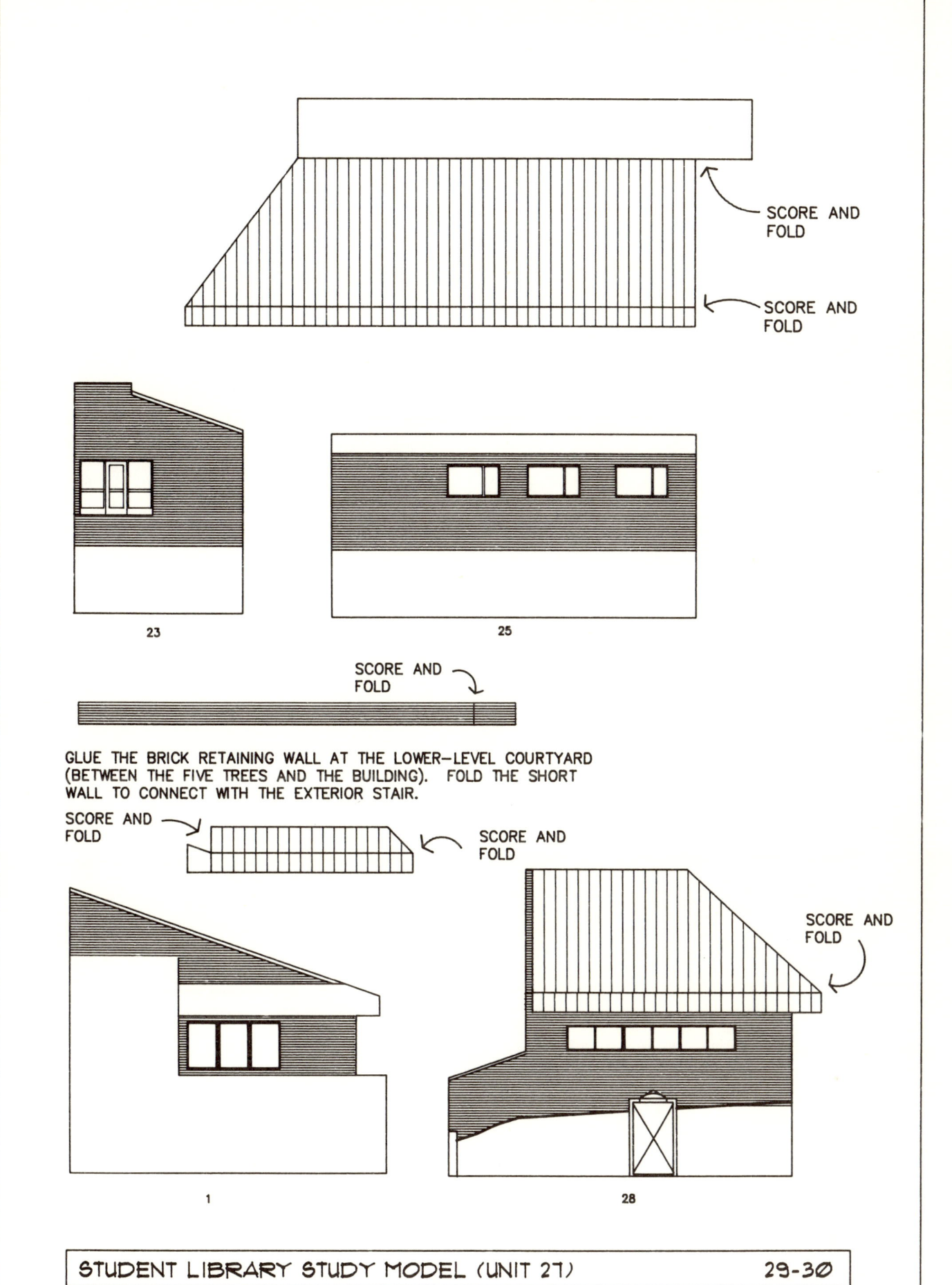

SCORE AND FOLD

23

25

SCORE AND FOLD

GLUE THE BRICK RETAINING WALL AT THE LOWER-LEVEL COURTYARD (BETWEEN THE FIVE TREES AND THE BUILDING). FOLD THE SHORT WALL TO CONNECT WITH THE EXTERIOR STAIR.

SCORE AND FOLD

SCORE AND FOLD

SCORE AND FOLD

1

28

STUDENT LIBRARY STUDY MODEL (UNIT 27)   29-30

GLOSSARY

AGGREGATE STONE OR GRAVEL USED IN IN CONCRETE AND ASPHALT.

AIR SPACE A VOID SPACE IN A WALL SEPARATING BUILDING COMPONENTS.

ANCHOR BOLT A BOLT USED TO SECURE WOOD OR STEEL STRUCTURAL MEMBERS TO CONCRETE.

ANGLE AN "L" SHAPED STEEL STRUCTURAL PIECE SHAPED TO FORM A 90° ANGLE.

APRON A PAVED STRIP ALONG A DRIVE ADJACENT TO A GARAGE DOOR OPENING.

ASHLAR MASONRY SQUARE-SHAPED STONE OR CAST CONCRETE LAID WITH A HORIZONTAL MORTAR JOINT.

ASPHALT A PETROLEUM-BASED MATERIAL INSOLUBLE IN WATER AND USED FOR WATERPROOFING, SHINGLES, ROAD SURFACES, AND ROOFING.

ASPHALTIC CONCRETE A BLACK BITUMINOUS-BASED PRODUCT MIXED WITH AGGREGATE USED FOR DRIVEWAYS.

ASPHALT SHINGLE ROOF SHINGLE MADE FROM ASPHALT-IMPREGNATED FELT OR FIBERGLASS AND COVERED WITH MINERAL GRANULES.

AWNING WINDOW A WINDOW UNIT THAT IS HINGED ALONG THE HEAD (TOP SIDE).

BACKFILL GRAVEL, COARSE DIRT, OR SAND PLACED IN A TRENCH AROUND A BUILDING FOOTING AND FOUNDATION WALL.

BAFFLE A SHIELD (TYPICALLY METAL) USED TO PREVENT INSULATION FROM PLUGGING EAVE VENTS.

BALLOON FRAME A TYPE OF WOOD FRAME CONSTRUCTION IN WHICH VERTICAL STUDS RUN UNINTERRUPTED FROM THE FOUNDATION TO THE ROOF. THIS TYPE OF FRAMING WAS POPULAR PRIOR TO THE 1940S AND IS FOUND IN OLDER HOUSES.

BAND JOIST A FLOOR JOIST SET ALONG THE EDGE OF THE FOUNDATION WALL PARALLEL TO OTHER JOISTS (ALSO CALLED A RIM JOIST).

BAR JOIST STRUCTURAL FRAMING JOIST MADE FROM BAR- AND ROD-SHAPED STEEL.

BASE A TRIM PIECE LOCATED AT THE INTERSECTION OF THE FLOOR AND WALL IN A ROOM.

BASE COURSE THE BEGINNING ROW OF BRICK OR BLOCK IN A MASONRY WALL.

BATT A RIGID FIBERGLASS SLAB THAT IS FORCE-FIT BETWEEN STUDS, RAFTERS, OR ROOF JOISTS.

BATTEN A VERTICAL STRIP OF WOOD USED TO COVER THE SEAM ON SIDING.

BATTER BOARD HORIZONTAL BOARDS USED TO SET THE LOCATION OF A BUILDING FOUNDATION. THE BOARDS ARE PLACED AT AN EXACT ELEVATION AND DISTANCE FROM THE FOUNDATION FOR MEASUREMENT.

BAY A STRUCTURAL AREA ON A BUILDING PLAN USUALLY DEFINED AS THE SPACE BETWEEN COLUMNS OR GRID LINES.

BEAM A HORIZONTAL STRUCTURAL MEMBER (WOOD, STEEL, OR CONCRETE) USED TO SUPPORT FLOOR, ROOF, OR WALL LOADS.

BEARING WALL A WALL THAT SUPPORTS A STRUCTURAL FLOOR OR ROOF LOAD.

BENCH MARK A KNOWN VERTICAL REFERENCE POINT USED TO SET BUILDING FOOTING, FLOOR, AND ROOF HEIGHTS.

BIFOLD DOOR A FOLDING DOOR FASTENED TO EACH SIDE OF THE FRAME OPENING.

BLOCKING SHORT WOOD MEMBERS USED TO TIE JOISTS AND STUDS TOGETHER

BOARD FOOT A UNIT OF MEASURE FOR WOOD, A BOARD FOOT IS 1" x 12" x 12".

BOND BEAM A "U"-SHAPED CONCRETE BLOCK FILLED WITH REINFORCED CONCRETE, USED TO STRENGTHEN MASONRY WALLS.

BRICK VENEER A SINGLE COURSE BRICK WALL (NONLOAD-BEARING) THAT IS BACKED BY A SECOND STUD OR MASONRY WALL.

BTU BRITISH THERMAL UNIT, A UNIT OF MEASURE FOR HEATING AND COOLING MECHANICAL EQUIPMENT, THE ENERGY NEEDED TO RAISE ONE POUND OF WATER ONE DEGREE FAHRENHEIT.

BUILDING PAPER ASPHALT-IMPREGNATED FELT USED BETWEEN SHEATHING AND EXTERIOR SIDING, MEASURED BY ITS WEIGHT PER SQUARE (100 SQ FT).

BUILT-UP ROOF A FLAT ROOF ASSEMBLY MADE OF THREE OR MORE LAYERS OF ASPHALT FELT BONDED TOGETHER WITH HOT ASPHALT, PITCH, OR COAL TAR.

BUTT A DOOR HINGE.

CAISSON A CONCRETE-FILLED SHAFT DRILLED INTO THE GROUND USED FOR STRUCTURAL COLUMN SUPPORT.

CALLOUT A NOTE DEFINING DETAIL THAT IS USED WITH A LEADER LINE ON A DRAWING.

CANT STRIP A WEDGE-SHAPED PIECE MADE OF WOOD OR INSULATION PLACED AT THE INTERSECTION OF A FLAT ROOF AND WALL.

CASEMENT WINDOW A WINDOW UNIT THAT IS HINGED AT THE JAMB (SIDE).

CASING A WOOD TRIM STRIP AROUND A WINDOW OR DOOR.

CATCH BASIN AN EXTERIOR DRAIN BUILT INTO A CONCRETE CURB AND CONNECTED TO A STORM SEWER.

CALK A FLEXIBLE ELASTOMERIC COMPOUND USED TO SEAL CONSTRUCTION JOINTS.

CAVITY WALL TWO WALLS (TYPICALLY MASONRY) SEPARATED WITH AN AIR SPACE.

CEMENT A FINE POWDER OF BURNED LIMESTONE USED IN MAKING CONCRETE.

CENTER TO CENTER A MEASUREMENT TERM MEANING THE DISTANCE FROM THE CENTER OF ONE OBJECT TO THE CENTER OF THE NEXT, AS IN JOIST AND STUD SPACING.

CHAIR A METAL SUPPORT MADE FROM BENT HEAVY-GAUGE WIRE TO HOLD STEEL REINFORCING DURING THE POURING OF CONCRETE.

CHANNEL A "C"-SHAPED STEEL MEMBER USED FOR STRUCTURAL BEAMS.

CHASE A HOLLOW WALL CAVITY BUILT TO HOUSE MECHANICAL PIPES AND DUCTS.

CHORD THE HORIZONTAL OR DIAGONAL MEMBER OF A TRUSS OR BAR JOIST.

CLAPBOARD A BEVELED HORIZONTAL SIDING THAT OVERLAPS THE BOARD BELOW IT.

CLERESTORY A HIGH WINDOW, OFTEN PLACED BETWEEN TWO ROOF LEVELS.

COLUMN A VERTICAL WOOD, STEEL, OR CONCRETE POST THAT SUPPORTS A STRUCTURAL LOAD.

CONCRETE A CONSTRUCTION MATERIAL MADE FROM CEMENT, SAND, AGGREGATE, AND WATER.

CONTROL JOINT A MASONRY WALL VERTICAL EXPANSION JOINT.

COPING A MASONRY CAP PLACED AT THE TOP OF A BRICK OR BLOCK PARAPET WALL.

CORNICE A ROOF OVERHANG AT THE TOP OF OF A WALL.

COUNTERFLASH A FLASHING PIECE USED UNDER ROOF FLASHING TO PROVIDE A WEATHERPROOF ASSEMBLY.

COURSE A CONTINUOUS HORIZONTAL ROW OF CONSTRUCTION MATERIALS SUCH AS SHINGLES, BLOCK, OR BRICK.

CRAWL SPACE A HOLLOW-CAVITY SPACE BETWEEN FLOOR JOISTS AND THE GROUND.

CRICKET A WEDGE-SHAPED ROOF BUILT TO DIVERT DRAINAGE AT THE INTERSECTION OF A SLOPED ROOF AND CHIMNEY.

CRIPPLE A SHORT STUD WALL, SUCH AS THE WALL UNDER A WINDOW.

CURE THE TIME IT TAKES MATERIALS SUCH AS CONCRETE OR SEALANT TO MEET THEIR DESIGN STRENGTH.

CURTAIN WALL A NONLOAD-BEARING EXTERIOR WALL BRACKETED TO A STRUCTURAL FRAME.

DECKING WOOD, METAL, OR CONCRETE USED TO FORM A FLOOR OR ROOF.

DORMER A BUILDING FORM THAT PROJECTS FROM A SLOPED ROOF.

DOUBLE HUNG A WINDOW UNIT THAT IS DIVIDED IN HALF HORIZONTALLY; THE UPPER AND LOWER HALVES SLIDE PAST EACH OTHER TO PROVIDE VENTILATION.

DRIP A GROOVE OR PROJECTING PIECE USED TO DIVERT RAINWATER.

DRY ROT DECAY IN WOOD CAUSED BY A FUNGUS THAT CAUSES THE MATERIAL TO DEGRADE.

DRYWALL SHEET GYPSUM BOARD ATTACHED TO STUDS IN A WALL ASSEMBLY.

EASEMENT A PORTION OF A SITE THAT CANNOT BE BUILT UPON DUE TO LEGAL RESTRICTIONS THAT TYPICALLY INVOLVE UTILITY ACCESS (SEWER, WATER, OR POWER).

EAVE THE LOWER PART OF A ROOF THAT PROJECTS FROM THE INTERSECTION WITH THE OUTSIDE WALL.

EGRESS A BUILDING EXIT.

ELEVATION (1) A VERTICAL HEIGHT ON A BUILDING MEASURED ABOVE A BENCH MARK, (2) THE ORTHOGRAPHIC VIEW THAT SHOWS VERTICAL HEIGHT AND HORIZONTAL WIDTH.

GLOSSARY

EPDM ETHYLENE PROPYLENE DIENE MONOMER, A SINGLE-PLY RUBBER ROOF MEMBRANE.
EXCAVATION A CAVITY DUG BELOW GRADE IN PREPARATION FOR CONSTRUCTION.
EXPANSION JOINT A JOINT IN A WALL OR FLOOR WHICH ALLOWS BUILDING MOVEMENT.

FABRICATION ASSEMBLY OF CONSTRUCTION COMPONENTS AWAY FROM THE JOB SITE.
FACADE THE EXTERIOR SURFACE OF A BUILDING.
FACE BRICK BURNED-CLAY MASONRY THAT IS HARD-BURNED AND MADE FROM CLAY THAT WILL WITHSTAND FREEZING WEATHER CONDITIONS.
FASCIA THE HORIZONTAL MEMBER ON THE LOWER EDGE OF A ROOF.
FELT ASPHALT-IMPREGNATED BUILDING PAPER USED AS AN UNDERLAYMENT FOR SIDING AND SHINGLES.
FILL GRAVEL, SAND, OR DIRT USED TO RAISE THE LEVEL OF A CONSTRUCTION SITE.
FINISHED LUMBER WOOD THAT HAS BEEN MILLED TO A FINAL DIMENSION.
FIREBRICK HARD-FIRED BRICK THAT WITHSTANDS HIGH TEMPERATURES, USED TO LINE FIREPLACES.
FIRE DOOR A FIRE-RATED DOOR THAT WILL SEPARATE BUILDING AREAS FROM FIRE FOR A RATED TIME.
FIRE WALL A WALL CONSTRUCTED FROM MATERIALS THAT WILL SEPARATE BUILDING AREAS FROM FIRE FOR A RATED TIME.
FLASHING METAL OR SINGLE-MEMBRANE SHEET USED TO PREVENT WATER LEAKING THROUGH THE INTERSECTION OF CONSTRUCTION MATERIALS.
FLAT ROOF A DEAD-LEVEL ROOF OR A ROOF SURFACE WITH A SLOPE OF LESS THAN 1/8" PER FOOT.
FLUE AN ENCLOSED CHIMNEY USED TO LEAD SMOKE OR GASSES TO THE OUTSIDE.
FOOTING A CONCRETE STRUCTURAL MEMBER AT THE BOTTOM OF A FOUNDATION WALL USED TO SPREAD THE BUILDING WEIGHT TO THE EARTH.
FOUNDATION A BELOW-GRADE WALL SYSTEM USED TO CONNECT AND SUPPORT THE BUILDING WEIGHT WITH THE FOOTING.
FROST LINE THE DEPTH AT WHICH FROST PENETRATES THE SOIL.
FURRING A SEPARATE WALL BUILT OUT FROM A MAIN WALL.

GABLE A ROOF SYSTEM IN WHICH TWO SLOPING PLANES INTERSECT AT A COMMON RIDGE.
GALVANIZED IRON IRON COATED WITH A ZINC SURFACE USED TO RESIST RUST.

GAMBREL A ROOF SYSTEM WITH TWO SLOPED PLANES THAT CONNECT AT A RIDGE.
GIRDER A HORIZONTAL STRUCTURAL BEAM USED TO SUPPORT SECONDARY STRUCTURAL MEMBERS.
GLUE-LAMINATED BEAM (GLU-LAM) A WOOD STRUCTURAL MEMBER FABRICATED FROM LAYERS OF LUMBER GLUED TOGETHER.
GRADE GROUND LEVEL AROUND A BUILDING.
GRADE BEAM A CONCRETE BEAM POURED BELOW GRADE AND SUPPORTED BY FOOTINGS OR CAISSONS SPACED AT INTERVALS.
GRAVEL STOP A METAL STRIP AT THE PERIMETER OF A FLAT ROOF USED TO RETAIN GRAVEL.
GROUT CEMENT MORTAR USED FOR LEVELING STRUCTURAL BEARING PLATES, ALSO USED TO FILL THE CRACKS IN FLOOR TILE.
GUSSET A PLATE USED TO CONNECT TRUSS CORD MEMBERS.
GYPSUM BOARD FLAT BOARD STOCK MADE FROM GYPSUM AND COVERED WITH PAPER, USED FOR INTERIOR WALL SYSTEMS.

HANGER A METAL BRACKET OR WIRE USED TO ATTACH STRUCTURAL MEMBERS.
HARDBOARD WOOD FIBERS COMPRESSED INTO A SHEET USED AS UNDERLAYMENT.
HEAD THE TOP PART OF A WINDOW OR DOOR.
HEADER A HORIZONTAL STRUCTURAL BEAM USED OVER DOOR AND WINDOW OPENINGS.
HEADER COURSE A HORIZONTAL MASONRY COURSE THAT EXPOSES THE SHORT END OF THE BRICK.
HEARTH A FIRE-RESISTANT FLOOR THAT EXTENDS 1'-6" IN FRONT OF A FIREPLACE.
HIP THE OUTSIDE EDGE FORMED BY TWO INTERSECTING ROOF PLANES.
HOSE BIBB A WATER FAUCET WITH A THREADED CONNECTOR FOR A GARDEN HOSE.
H.V.A.C. HEATING, VENTILATING, AND AIR CONDITIONING (MECHANICAL SYSTEM)

I BEAM A GENERIC TERM FOR A STRUCTURAL STEEL BEAM ROLLED IN AN AMERICAN STANDARD SHAPE.
INSULATION A CONSTRUCTION MATERIAL USED TO REDUCE CONDUCTION HEAT TRANSFER OR SOUND TRANSFER.
INVERT ELEVATION THE ELEVATION ABOVE SEA LEVEL OF THE FLOW LINE OF A STORM OR SANITARY SEWER PIPE.

JACK RAFTER A SHORT ROOF RAFTER CUT TO ALLOW FOR AN OPENING IN THE ROOF.
JAMB THE VERTICAL MEMBER OF A DOOR OR WINDOW FRAME.
JOIST A HORIZONTAL STRUCTURAL MEMBER TYPICALLY SPACED AT SHORT INTERVALS TO SUPPORT FLOOR, CEILING, OR ROOF LOADS.

GLOSSARY

KICK PLATE A sheet metal plate fastened to the bottom of a door to protect the surface.

KILN DRYING A process of reducing the moisture content in wood by placing it in a kiln or oven.

KIP A unit of measure used by structural engineers, one kip equals a thousand pounds.

KNEE WALL A wall with a short height.

LALLY COLUMN A structural steel pipe column used to support floor loads on a footing.

LAMINATE Thin sheets of material, such as plywood, that are glued into one solid sheet.

LATH A backer sheet for plaster or stucco (the sheet can be diamond-mesh steel, gypsum, or wood).

LAVATORY A bathroom sink.

LEDGER A horizontal support fastened to a wall, used to attach rafters, joists, or a roof soffit.

LINTEL A structural support (beam) that is located above an opening.

LOOKOUT A structural support for a roof eave.

LOUVER A mechanical grill used to move air into a space.

MASTIC Architectural-grade glue.

MESH Steel-wire fabric reinforcing used in a concrete slab.

METAL TIE A corrugated strap used to tie brick veneer to a backer wall.

MILLWORK Prefabricated wood products such as kitchen cabinets.

MINERAL WOOL Insulation made from glass or rock that is melted and spun into thin fibers.

MOISTURE BARRIER A sheet (typically plastic) used in a wall assembly that will restrict the flow of water vapor.

MOLDING A strip used to cover the intersection of two building products or surfaces.

MORTAR A cement-based product mixed with lime, sand, and water, used to bond masonry units.

MULLION A window frame used to separate two window units.

NAILER A wood piece attached to a construction surface that is used for attaching other materials.

NOMINAL DIMENSION The dimension of a building product rounded up to the next whole number.

NOSING The rounded front edge of a stair tread.

ON CENTER The distance from the center of one object to the center of the next object.

OUTRIGGER A support attached to a wall that is used to attach the roof overhang fascia.

OVERHANG The horizontal distance of a roof projection beyond the wall line.

OVERLAY DRAFTING A drafting technique that involves placing several layers of drawing sheets together.

PARAPET An exterior building wall that extends above the level of the roof.

PARGING A coat of plaster or cement that is troweled on a wall surface (also called stucco).

PARTITION An interior wall that separates spaces.

PARTY WALL An interior wall that divides building occupancies such as two apartment units.

PENNY The length of a nail, designated by a lower-case "d."

PIER A structural support that is engaged in a foundation wall.

PILASTER A column that is built into a wall assembly.

PILING A structural support that is driven below grade to support the weight of a building, typically a steel beam or treated wood post.

PITCH The angle of a roof, measured by the horizontal distance (run) and vertical height (rise).

PLASTER A wall treatment paste made from cement, line, sand, and water.

PLAT A legal description of a site showing the dimensions of the lot.

PLATE The horizontal members of a stud wall (the top plate, and the sill plate).

PLENUM A supply duct used to mix and transport air from the building mechanical system.

PLOT A building site.

POCHE A method of shading a presentation drawing of a building.

PORTLAND CEMENT A type of cement made from silica, lime, and aluminum.

POST A structural column.

POST-TENSION Structural concrete built on-site with stressed steel reinforcing.

PRECAST A concrete product that has been formed off-site and moved to the building location.

PREFABRICATED Building products that are manufactured off-site and moved to the project location.

GLOSSARY G-4

PRESTRESSED A CONCRETE STRUCTURAL MEMBER REINFORCED WITH STEEL THAT HAS BEEN PLACED IN TENSION.

PRIME COAT THE FIRST COAT OF PAINT, TYPICALLY APPLIED AT THE FACTORY IN PREFABRICATED PRODUCTS.

PROGRAM AN ARCHITECTURAL DESIGN STATEMENT THAT DEFINES THE SCOPE OF A PROJECT.

PURLIN A SECONDARY STRUCTURAL BEAM, TYPICALLY SUPPORTED BY A MAIN BEAM.

QUARRY TILE UNGLAZED CLAY TILE FLOOR MATERIAL.

RABBET A GROOVE CUT ON THE EDGE OF A BOARD.

RAFTER A STRUCTURAL MEMBER USED TO SUPPORT A SLOPED ROOF.

RAKED JOINT A RECESSED MASONRY MORTAR JOINT.

REBAR A STEEL BAR USED TO REINFORCE POURED CONCRETE, MEASURED IN 1/8" UNITS (A NUMBER "5" BAR IS 5/8" IN DIAMETER).

REGLET A NARROW MOLDING USED TO CONNECT FLASHING TO A WALL.

REINFORCED CONCRETE POURED CONCRETE WITH STEEL REINFORCING TO RESIST TENSION IN THE BEAM OR SLAB.

RENDERING AN ARTISTIC PRESENTATION OF A BUILDING, TYPICALLY SHOWN IN PERSPECTIVE WITH TREES AND PEOPLE.

R-FACTOR A UNIT MEASURING THE RESISTANCE TO CONDUCTION HEAT FLOW THROUGH A BUILDING MATERIAL.

RIDGE THE TOP EDGE OF TWO INTERSECTING ROOF PLANES.

RIDGE BOARD A HORIZONTAL BOARD AT THE TOP RIDGE OF INTERSECTING ROOF RAFTERS.

RIM JOIST A FLOOR JOIST AT THE PERIMETER OF THE STRUCTURE THAT RUNS PARALLEL TO THE OTHER JOISTS.

RISE THE VERTICAL DISTANCE USED WHEN MEASURING A RAMP OR ROOF PITCH.

RISER THE VERTICAL MEMBER IN A STAIR THAT CONNECTS TWO TREADS.

ROLL ROOFING ASPHALT-IMPREGNATED ROOFING THAT IS PLACED ON THE ROOF DECK BY ROLLING LAMINATES IN LAYERS.

ROOF DRAIN A DRAIN MOUNTED ON A FLAT ROOF DECK THAT IS CONNECTED TO AN INTERIOR DRAINAGE PIPE.

ROUGH-IN PRELIMINARY PREPARATION OF A FRAME WALL TO RECEIVE PLUMBING OR ELECTRICAL INSTALLATION.

ROUGH OPENING THE UNFINISHED OPENING SPACE BETWEEN FRAMING MEMBERS THAT ALLOWS THE INSTALLATION OF WINDOW OR DOOR FRAMES.

RUN THE HORIZONTAL DISTANCE USED WHEN MEASURING A RAMP OR ROOF PITCH.

SADDLE A WEDGE-SHAPED ROOF BUILT TO DIVERT DRAINAGE AT THE INTERSECTION OF A SLOPED ROOF AND CHIMNEY (ALSO CALLED A CRICKET).

SASH A WINDOW FRAME.

SCHEDULE A LIST CONTAINING COMPILED DATA ON SIMILAR PRODUCTS SUCH AS ROOM FINISHES.

SCRATCH COAT THE FIRST OF THREE LAYERS FOR STUCCO APPLICATION.

SCREED A STRAIGHT BOARD USED TO LEVEL POURED CONCRETE SLABS.

SCUTTLE AN OPENING IN A ROOF OR CEILING THAT ALLOWS ACCESS TO THE SPACE ABOVE.

SEASONING A MECHANICAL OR AIR-DRYING PROCESS THAT LOWERS THE MOISTURE CONTENT IN WOOD.

SECTION AN ORTHOGRAPHIC DRAWING THAT SHOWS A VERTICAL CUT THROUGH A BUILDING.

SEISMIC FORCES CAUSED BY AN EARTHQUAKE.

SETBACK A BUILDING ZONING REQUIREMENT THAT SETS THE MINIMUM DISTANCE THAT A BUILDING CAN BE PLACED BACK FROM THE PROPERTY LINE.

SHAKE A HAND-SPLIT CEDAR SHINGLE.

SHEATHING A SHEET BOARD MATERIAL ATTACHED TO STUDS OR RAFTERS, USED AN UNDERLAYMENT FOR SIDING OR SHINGLES.

SHIM A PIECE OF BUILDING MATERIAL WEDGED INTO A SPACE, USED TO ADJUST THE HEIGHT OF A PRODUCT.

SHIPLAP A HORIZONTAL SIDING MATERIAL WITH A RABBETED EDGE THAT ALLOWS THE CONNECTION OF PIECES.

SILL (1) A HORIZONTAL MEMBER AT THE BOTTOM OF A STUD WALL, (2) THE BOTTOM PIECE OF A WINDOW FRAME.

SKYLIGHT A ROOF WINDOW.

SLAB A POURED CONCRETE FLOOR DECK.

SLAB-ON-GRADE A CONCRETE SLAB THAT IS POURED ON GROUND LEVEL.

SLEEPERS WOOD SHIMS PLACED OVER A CONCRETE SLAB TO SPACE A FLOOR SYSTEM ABOVE THE SLAB.

SLUMP A TEST FOR CONCRETE THAT MEASURES THE WATER/CEMENT RATIO.

SOFFIT THE HORIZONTAL SURFACE OF A ROOF OVERHANG.

SOIL BORING A SOIL TEST MADE BY DRILLING A CORE SAMPLE INTO THE GROUND.

SOIL STACK A MAIN VERTICAL WASTE-WATER PIPE IN A PLUMBING SYSTEM.

SOLE PLATE A HORIZONTAL FRAMING MEMBER AT THE BOTTOM OF A STUD WALL.

SPACKLE A PASTE JOINT COMPOUND USED TO COVER A GYPSUM BOARD JOINT.

SPECIFICATION A WRITTEN DOCUMENT DEFINING QUALITY THAT ACCOMPANIES ARCHITECTURAL WORKING DRAWINGS.

SQUARE A UNIT OF MEASURE FOR ROOFING MATERIALS, 1 SQUARE = 100 SQUARE FEET.
STAND PIPE A VERTICAL PLUMBING LINE.
STILE A VERTICAL MEMBER OF A CABINET.
STIRRUP A "U"-SHAPED STEEL REINFORCING BAR PLACED IN A CONCRETE BEAM TO RESIST SHEAR.
STRINGER A DIAGONAL MEMBER OF A STAIR THAT SUPPORTS THE TREADS AND RISERS.
STUD THE VERTICAL MEMBER IN A FRAME WALL.
SUBFLOOR THE FLOORING SHEET MATERIAL THAT IS LAID ON THE FLOOR JOIST AND SERVES AS A BASE FOR THE FINISHED FLOOR
SUMP A RESERVOIR SERVING AS A RECEPTACLE FOR WASTE WATER.
SUSPENDED CEILING A CEILING THAT IS WIRE-HUNG BELOW THE UNDERSIDE OF A BUILDING STRUCTURE.

TAMP TO COMPACT OR COMPRESS SOIL OR CONCRETE.
THRESHOLD A RAISED PLATE FIXED TO THE FLOOR AT A DOOR OPENING.
TOENAILING A NAILING TECHNIQUE THAT ATTACHES WOOD MEMBERS BY DRIVING A NAIL AT AN ANGLE.
TONGUE AND GROOVE A JOINT IN WHICH THE EDGE OF ONE PIECE FITS INTO A GROOVE OF THE NEXT PIECE.
TRANSOM A WINDOW FRAME ABOVE A DOOR OPENING.
TREAD THE HORIZONTAL STEP MEMBER OF A STAIR
TRIMMER A JOIST OR RAFTER USED TO FRAME AN OPENING IN A FLOOR OR ROOF.
TRUSS A PREFABRICATED STRUCTURAL MEMBER FORMED OF TRIANGULAR CORD SHAPES, USED FOR LONG-SPAN ROOF CONDITIONS.

UNDERLAYMENT PLYWOOD OR PARTICLE BOARD FLOORING MATERIAL THAT ACTS AS A BASE FOR CARPET OR TILE.

VALLEY THE INTERNAL CORNER FORMED BETWEEN TWO INTERSECTING ROOF PLANES.
VAPOR BARRIER A PLASTIC SHEET MATERIAL LOCATED ON THE "WARM" SIDE OF A WALL ASSEMBLY THAT ACTS TO BLOCK THE FLOW OF WATER VAPOR
VENEER A THIN SHEET OF OUTER COVERING OR A NONLOAD-BEARING BRICK OUTER "SKIN" ON A WALL ASSEMBLY.
VENT STACK A VERTICAL PLUMBING PIPE THAT EQUALIZES THE VACUUM IN A WASTE LINE.
VESTIBULE A SMALL ENCLOSED ENTRANCE OR LOBBY SPACE.

WAINSCOT TILE OR PANELING APPLIED TO THE LOWER PORTION OF A WALL.
WALLBOARD SHEETS OF GYPSUM BOARD ATTACHED TO A STUD WALL.
WEATHER STRIP A FLEXIBLE MATERIAL PLACED ALONG THE MOVABLE EDGE OF A WINDOW OR DOOR TO REDUCE AIR INFILTRATION.
WEEP HOLE A SMALL TUBE PLACED AT THE LOWER PORTION OF A BRICK CAVITY WALL TO ALLOW DRAINAGE OF TRAPPED WATER.
WEEP WICK A ROPE PLACED AT THE LOWER PORTION OF A BRICK CAVITY WALL TO REMOVE TRAPPED WATER.
WELDED WIRE FABRIC STEEL WIRE REINFORCING IN A POURED CONCRETE SLAB.
WYTHE THE HOLLOW SPACE IN A CAVITY WALL OR THE SPACE ENCLOSED BETWEEN TWO SHEETS OF GLASS.

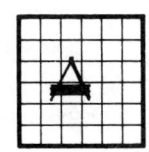

APPENDIX

GEOMETRIC CONSTRUCTION

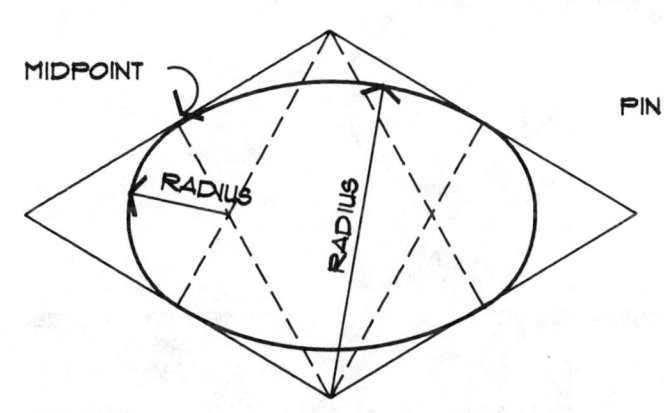

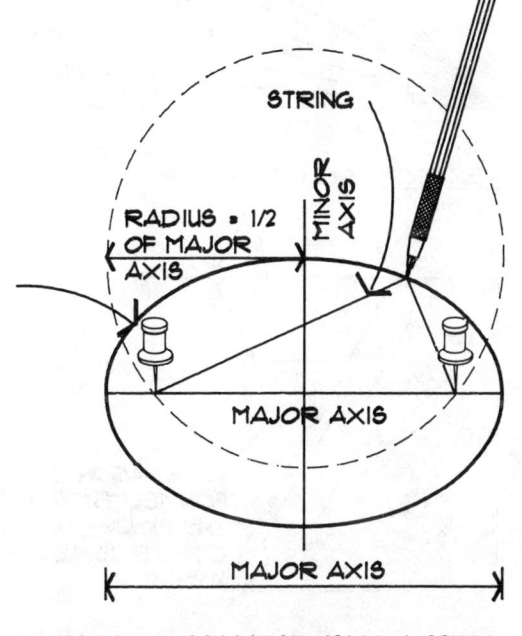

ELLIPSE

CONSTRUCT AN ELLIPSE BY DRAWING A PARALLELOGRAM THAT WILL OUTLINE THE FIGURE. CONNECT THE CORNERS TO THE MIDPOINT OF THE OPPOSITE SIDES. USE THE INTERSECTING LINES AS CENTER POINTS FOR A CIRCLE DRAWN WITH A BOW COMPASS.

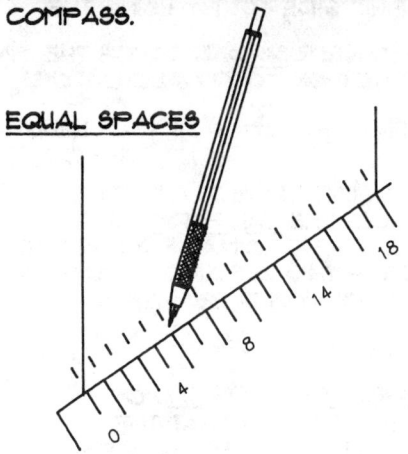

CONSTRUCT AN ELLIPSE USING A STRING AND TWO PUSH-PINS. BEGIN BY DRAWING A CIRCLE WITH A RADIUS OF ONE-HALF THE LENGTH OF THE MAJOR AXIS OF THE ELLIPSE. LOCATE THE CENTER OF THE CIRCLE AT THE INTERSECTION OF THE MINOR AXIS AND THE ELLIPSE. THE PINS ARE LOCATED AT THE INTERSECTION OF THE CIRCLE WITH THE MAJOR AXIS.

EQUAL SPACES

TO DIVIDE A SPACE INTO EQUAL PROPORTIONS, PLACE AN ARCHITECT'S SCALE BETWEEN THE TWO END LINES. SET THE "Ø" POINT OF THE SCALE ALONG ONE LINE AND ROTATE THE SCALE TO THE DESIRED NUMBER OF SPACES. (THE EXAMPLE DIVIDES THE DISTANCE INTO 19 EQUAL SPACES.) PLACE A TICK MARK AT EACH POINT WITH YOUR LEAD HOLDER

ROOF PITCH

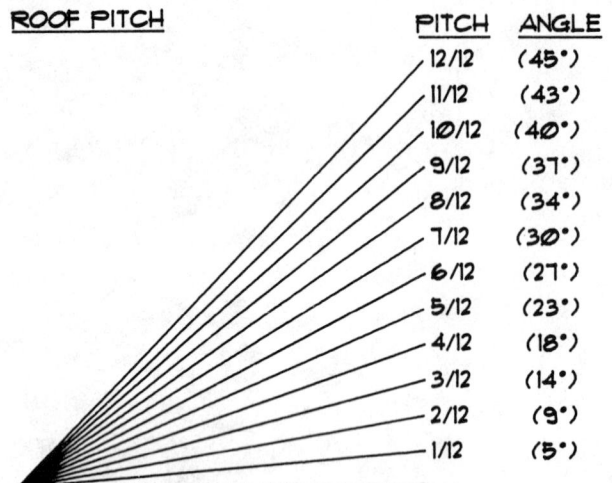

PITCH	ANGLE
12/12	(45°)
11/12	(43°)
10/12	(40°)
9/12	(37°)
8/12	(34°)
7/12	(30°)
6/12	(27°)
5/12	(23°)
4/12	(18°)
3/12	(14°)
2/12	(9°)
1/12	(5°)

(NOTE: ANGLES ARE ROUNDED OFF TO THE CLOSEST DEGREE.)

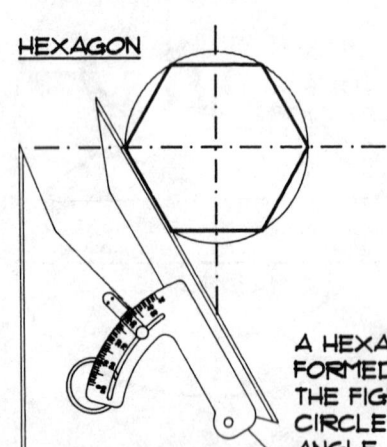

HEXAGON

A HEXAGON CAN BE FORMED BY INSCRIBING THE FIGURE IN A CIRCLE USING A 60° ANGLE.

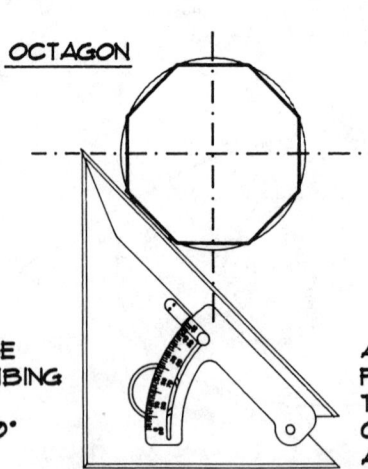

OCTAGON

AN OCTAGON CAN BE FORMED BY INSCRIBING THE FIGURE IN A CIRCLE USING A 45° ANGLE.

CONSTRUCT ANY POLYGON BY DIVIDING THE NUMBER OF SIDES OF THE FIGURE INTO 360°. SET YOUR ADJUSTABLE TRIANGLE TO THE ANGLE AND INSCRIBE IT IN A CIRCLE.

TRIGONOMETRIC FUNCTIONS

$$\text{SIN } \Theta = \frac{B}{C}$$
$$\text{COS } \Theta = \frac{A}{C}$$
$$\text{TAN } \Theta = \frac{B}{A}$$

HYPOTENUSE (C)
OPPOSITE (B)
ADJACENT (A)

EXAMPLE 1: IF YOU KNOW THAT ANGLE Θ IS 30° AND SIDE "B" IS 12', YOU CAN FIND SIDE "C" BY USING THE <u>SIN FORMULA</u>.

SIN 30° = .5 (ENTER 30 AND TOUCH THE SIN KEY ON YOUR CALCULATOR)

SIN $\Theta = \frac{B}{C}$ OR $.5 = \frac{12'}{C}$ = 24' (THE LENGTH OF SIDE "C")

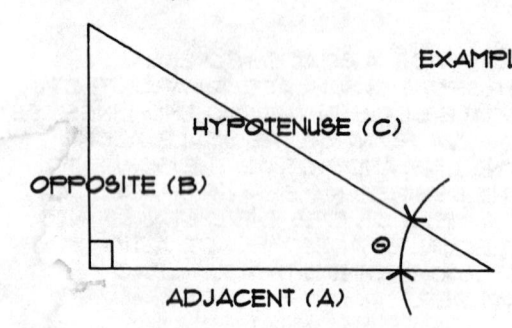

EXAMPLE 2: FIND ANGLE Θ IF SIDE "A" IS 12' AND SIDE "C" IS 6'-11 1/8". USE THE <u>TAN FORMULA</u> TO FIND THE ANGLE. (THE DECIMAL EQUIVALENT OF 11 1/8" = 0.9271 — THIS IS FOUND BY DIVIDING 11 1/8 BY 12 — 6'-11 1/8" WOULD BE 6.9271')

TAN $\Theta = \frac{B}{A}$ OR TAN $\Theta = \frac{6.9271}{12}$ = .577

USE THE <u>ARCTANGENT KEY</u> (TAN^{-1}) ON YOUR CALCULATOR TO FIND THAT THE ARCHTANGENT OF .577 IS A 30° ANGLE.

APPENDIX   A-2

AREA

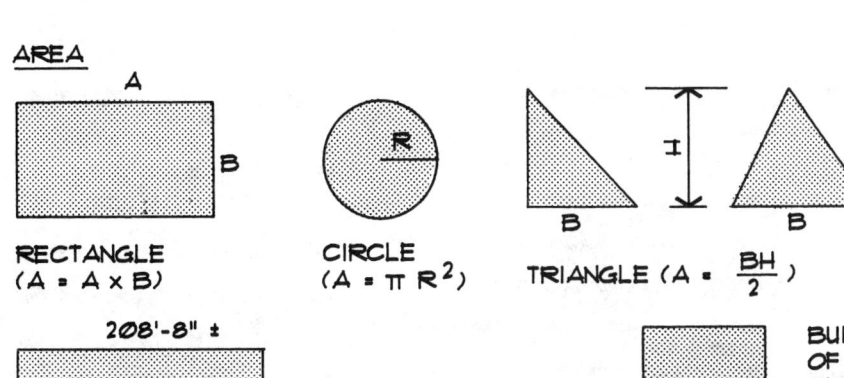

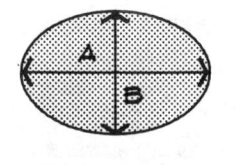

RECTANGLE (A = A × B)

CIRCLE (A = πR^2)

TRIANGLE (A = $\frac{BH}{2}$)

ELLIPSE (A = .7854 × A × B)

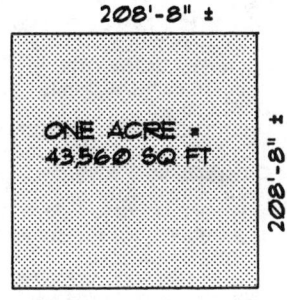

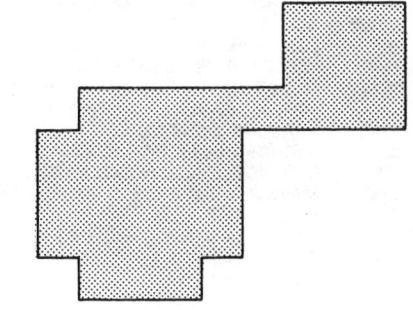

208'-8" ±
208'-8" ±
ONE ACRE = 43,560 SQ FT

ACRE

BUILDING AREA IS THE SUM OF THE AREAS ON THE FLOOR PLAN, MEASURED TO THE OUTSIDE OF THE EXTERIOR WALLS. ADD THE AREA OF ALL FLOORS (INCLUDING STAIR TOWERS AND ELEVATOR SHAFTS). TWO-STORY AREAS, SUCH AS COURTYARDS AND AUDITORIUMS, SHOULD BE MEASURED ONLY ONCE.

C.S.I. FORMAT

DIVISION 1 - GENERAL REQUIREMENTS

- 01010 SUMMARY OF WORK
- 01020 ALLOWANCES
- 01025 MEASUREMENT AND PAYMENT
- 01030 ALTERNATES
- 01040 COORDINATION
- 01050 FIELD ENGINEERING
- 01060 REGULATORY REQUIREMENTS
- 01070 ABBREVIATIONS
- 01080 IDENTIFICATION SYSTEMS
- 01090 REFERENCE STANDARDS
- 01100 SPECIAL PROJECT PROCEDURES
- 01200 PROJECT MEETINGS
- 01300 SUBMITTALS
- 01400 QUALITY CONTROL
- 01500 CONSTRUCTION FACILITIES AND TEMP. CONTROLS
- 01600 MATERIAL AND EQUIPMENT
- 01650 STARTING OF SYSTEMS
- 01700 CONTRACT CLOSEOUT
- 01800 MAINTENANCE

DIVISION 2 - SITEWORK

- 02010 SUBSURFACE INVESTIGATION
- 02050 DEMOLITION
- 02100 SITE PREPARATION
- 02140 DEWATERING
- 02150 SHORING AND UNDERPINNING
- 02160 EXCAVATION SUPPORT SYSTEMS
- 02170 COFFERDAMS
- 02200 EARTHWORK
- 02300 TUNNELING
- 02350 PILES AND CAISSONS
- 02450 RAILROAD WORK
- 02480 MARINE WORK
- 02500 PAVING AND SURFACING
- 02600 PIPED UTILITY MATERIALS
- 02660 WATER DISTRIBUTION
- 02680 FUEL DISTRIBUTION
- 02700 SEWERAGE AND DRAINAGE

DIVISION 2 - SITEWORK (CONT.)

- 02760 RESTORATION OF UNDERGROUND PIPELINES
- 02770 PONDS AND RESERVOIRS
- 02780 POWER AND COMMUNICATIONS
- 02800 SITE IMPROVEMENTS
- 02900 LANDSCAPING

DIVISION 3 - CONCRETE

- 03100 CONCRETE FORMWORK
- 03200 CONCRETE REINFORCEMENT
- 03250 CONCRETE ACCESSORIES
- 03300 CAST-IN-PLACE CONCRETE
- 03370 CONCRETE CURING
- 03400 PRECAST CONCRETE
- 03500 CEMENTITIOUS DECKS
- 03600 GROUT
- 03700 RESTORATION AND CLEANING
- 03800 MASS CONCRETE

DIVISION 4 - MASONRY

- 04100 MORTAR
- 04150 MASONRY ACCESSORIES
- 04200 UNIT MASONRY
- 04400 STONE
- 04500 RESTORATION AND CLEANING
- 04550 REFACTORIES
- 04600 CORROSION-RESISTANT MASONRY

DIVISION 5 - METALS

- 05010 METAL MATERIALS
- 05030 METAL FINISHES
- 05050 METAL FASTENING
- 05100 STRUCTURAL METAL FRAMING
- 05200 METAL JOISTS

DIVISION 5 - METALS (CONT.)

- 05300 METAL DECKING
- 05400 COLD-FORMED METAL
- 05500 METAL FABRICATIONS
- 05580 SHEET METAL FABRICATIONS
- 05700 ORNAMENTAL METAL
- 05800 EXPANSION CONTROL
- 05900 HYDRAULIC STRUCTURES

DIVISION 6 - WOOD AND PLASTIC

- 06050 FASTENERS AND ADHESIVES
- 06100 ROUGH CARPENTRY
- 06130 HEAVY TIMBER CONST.
- 06150 WOOD-METAL SYSTEMS
- 06170 PREFABRICATED STRUCTURAL WOOD
- 06200 FINISH CARPENTRY
- 06300 WOOD TREATMENT
- 06400 ARCHITECTURAL WOODWORK
- 06500 PREFABRICATED STRUCTURAL PLASTICS
- 06600 PLASTIC FABRICATIONS

DIVISION 7 - THERMAL AND MOISTURE PROTECTION

- 07100 WATERPROOFING
- 07150 DAMPPROOFING
- 07190 VAPOR AND AIR RETARDERS
- 07200 INSULATION
- 07250 FIREPROOFING
- 07300 SHINGLES AND ROOFING TILE
- 07400 PREFORMED ROOFING AND CLADDING/SIDING
- 07500 MEMBRANE ROOFING
- 07570 TRAFFIC TOPPING
- 07600 FLASHING AND SHEET METAL
- 07700 ROOF SPECIALTIES AND ACCESSORIES
- 07800 SKYLIGHTS
- 07900 JOINT SEALERS

APPENDIX

A-3

DIVISION 8 - DOORS AND WINDOWS

- 08100 METAL DOORS AND FRAMES
- 08200 WOOD AND PLASTIC DOORS
- 08250 DOOR OPENING ASSEMBLIES
- 08300 SPECIAL DOORS
- 08400 ENTRANCES AND STOREFRONTS
- 08500 METAL WINDOWS
- 08600 WOOD AND PLASTIC WINDOWS
- 08650 SPECIAL WINDOWS
- 08700 HARDWARE
- 08800 GLAZING
- 08900 GLAZED CURTAIN WALLS

DIVISION 9 - FINISHES

- 09100 METAL SUPPORT SYSTEMS
- 09200 LATH AND PLASTER
- 09230 AGGREGATE COATINGS
- 09250 GYPSUM BOARD
- 09300 TILE
- 09400 TERRAZZO
- 09500 ACOUSTICAL TREATMENT
- 09540 SPECIAL SURFACES
- 09550 WOOD FLOORING
- 09600 STONE FLOORING
- 09630 UNIT MASONRY FLOORING
- 09650 RESILIENT FLOORING
- 09680 CARPET
- 09700 SPECIAL FLOORING
- 09780 FLOOR TREATMENT
- 09800 SPECIAL COATINGS
- 09900 PAINTING
- 09950 WALL COVERINGS

DIVISION 10 - SPECIALTIES

- 10100 CHALKBOARDS AND TACKBOARDS
- 10150 COMPARTMENTS AND CUBICLES
- 10200 LOUVERS AND VENTS
- 10240 GRILLES AND SCREENS
- 10250 SERVICE WALL SYSTEMS
- 10260 WALL AND CORNER GUARDS
- 10270 ACCESS FLOORING
- 10280 SPECIALTY MODULES
- 10290 PEST CONTROL
- 10300 FIREPLACES AND STOVES
- 10340 PREFABRICATED EXTERIOR SPECIALTIES
- 10350 FLAGPOLES
- 10400 IDENTIFYING DEVICES
- 10450 PEDESTRIAN CONTROL DEVICES
- 10500 LOCKERS
- 10520 FIRE PROTECTION SPECIALTIES
- 10530 PROTECTIVE COVERS
- 10550 POSTAL SPECIALTIES
- 10600 PARTITIONS
- 10650 OPERABLE PARTITIONS
- 10670 STORAGE SHELVING
- 10700 EXTERIOR SUN CONTROL DEVICES
- 10750 TELEPHONE SPECIALTIES
- 10800 TOILET AND BATH ACCESSORIES
- 10880 SCALES
- 10900 WARDROBE AND CLOSET SPECIALTIES

DIVISION 11 - EQUIPMENT

- 11010 MAINTENANCE EQUIPMENT
- 11020 SECURITY AND VAULT EQUIPMENT
- 11030 TELLER AND SERVICE EQUIPMENT
- 11040 ECCLESIASTICAL EQUIPMENT
- 11050 LIBRARY EQUIPMENT
- 11060 THEATER AND STAGE EQUIPMENT
- 11070 INSTRUMENTAL EQUIPMENT
- 11080 REGISTRATION EQUIPMENT
- 11090 CHECKROOM EQUIPMENT
- 11100 MERCANTILE EQUIPMENT
- 11110 COMMERCIAL LAUNDRY AND DRY CLEANING EQUIPMENT
- 11120 VENDING EQUIPMENT
- 11130 AUDIO-VISUAL EQUIPMENT
- 11140 SERVICE STATION EQUIPMENT
- 11150 PARKING CONTROL EQUIPMENT
- 11160 LOADING DOCK EQUIPMENT
- 11170 SOLID WASTE HANDLING EQUIPMENT
- 11190 DETENTION EQUIPMENT
- 11200 WATER SUPPLY AND TREATMENT EQUIPMENT
- 11280 HYDRAULIC GATES AND VALVES
- 11300 FLUID WASTE TREATMENT AND DISPOSAL EQUIPMENT
- 11400 FOOD SERVICE EQUIPMENT
- 11450 RESIDENTIAL EQUIPMENT
- 11460 UNIT KITCHENS
- 11470 DARKROOM EQUIPMENT
- 11480 ATHLETIC, RECREATIONAL AND THERAPEUTIC EQUIPMENT
- 11500 INDUSTRIAL AND PROCESS EQUIPMENT
- 11600 LABORATORY EQUIPMENT
- 11650 PLANETARIUM EQUIPMENT
- 11660 OBSERVATORY EQUIPMENT
- 11700 MEDICAL EQUIPMENT
- 11780 MORTUARY EQUIPMENT
- 11850 NAVIGATION EQUIPMENT

DIVISION 12 - FURNISHINGS

- 12050 FABRICS
- 12100 ARTWORK
- 12300 MANUFACTURED CASEWORK
- 12500 WINDOW TREATMENT
- 12600 FURNITURE AND ACCESSORIES
- 12670 RUGS AND MATS
- 12700 MULTIPLE SEATING
- 12800 INTERIOR PLANTS AND PLANTERS

DIVISION 13 - SPECIAL CONSTRUCTION

- 13010 AIR SUPPORTED STRUCTURES
- 13020 INTEGRATED ASSEMBLIES
- 13030 SPECIAL PURPOSE ROOMS
- 13080 SOUND, VIBRATION, AND SEISMIC CONTROL
- 13090 RADIATION PROTECTION
- 13100 NUCLEAR REACTORS
- 13120 PRE-ENGINEERED STRUCTURES
- 13150 POOLS

DIVISION 13 - SPECIAL CONSTRUCTION (CONT.)

- 13160 ICE RINKS
- 13170 KENNELS AND ANIMAL SHELTERS
- 13180 SITE CONSTRUCTED INCINERATORS
- 13200 LIQUID AND GAS STORAGE TANKS
- 13220 FILTER UNDERDRAINS AND MEDIA
- 13230 DIGESTION TANK COVERS AND APPURTENANCES
- 13240 OXYGENATION SYSTEMS
- 13260 SLUDGE CONDITIONING SYSTEMS
- 13300 UTILITY CONTROL SYSTEMS
- 13400 INDUSTRIAL AND PROCESS CONTROL SYSTEMS
- 13500 RECORDING AND INSTRUMENTATION
- 13550 TRANSPORTATION CONTROL INSTRUMENTATION
- 13600 SOLAR ENERGY SYSTEMS
- 13700 WIND ENERGY SYSTEMS
- 13800 BUILDING AUTOMATION SYSTEMS
- 13900 FIRE SUPPRESSION AND SUPERVISORY SYSTEMS

DIVISION 14 - CONVEYING SYSTEMS

- 14100 DUMBWAITERS
- 14200 ELEVATORS
- 14300 MOVING STAIRS AND WALKS
- 14400 LIFTS
- 14500 MATERIAL HANDLING SYSTEMS
- 14600 HOISTS AND CRANES
- 14700 TURNTABLES
- 14800 SCAFFOLDING
- 14900 TRANSPORTATION SYSTEMS

DIVISION 15 - MECHANICAL

- 15050 BASIC MECHANICAL MATERIALS AND METHODS
- 15250 MECHANICAL INSULATION
- 15300 FIRE PROTECTION
- 15400 PLUMBING
- 15500 H.V.A.C.
- 15550 HEAT GENERATION
- 15650 REFRIGERATION
- 15750 HEAT TRANSFER
- 15850 AIR HANDLING
- 15880 AIR DISTRIBUTION
- 15950 CONTROLS
- 15990 TESTING, ADJUSTING, AND BALANCING

DIVISION 16 - ELECTRICAL

- 16050 BASIC ELECTRICAL MATERIALS AND METHODS
- 16200 POWER GENERATION
- 16300 HIGH VOLTAGE DISTRIBUTION
- 16400 SERVICE AND DISTRIBUTION
- 16500 LIGHTING
- 16600 SPECIAL SYSTEMS
- 16700 COMMUNICATIONS
- 16850 ELECTRIC RESISTANCE HEATING
- 16900 CONTROLS
- 16950 TESTING

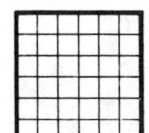

INDEX

A

ABBREVIATIONS, 5-14
   FOR DIMENSIONS, 6-4
ACRYLIC SEALANT, 12-46
ADJUSTABLE CURVE, 2-4
ADJUSTABLE TRIANGLE, 2-1
AIR DRYING, 12-3
AIR ENTRAINMENT TEST,
   FOR CONCRETE, 12-20
AIR FILM, 12-29
ALUMINUM, 12-41 TO 12-42
AMERICAN INSTITUTE OF ARCHITECTS
   (AIA), 10-4
AMERICAN STANDARD BEAM, 12-13
AMES LETTERING GUIDE, 4-8
ANALYSIS PROCESS, 24-3 TO 24-4.
   SEE ALSO SITE ANALYSIS
ANGLE, 12-13
ANNEALING, 12-39
ARCHITECT'S SCALE, 2-5, 2-9, 6-1 TO 6-2
<u>ARCHITECTURAL GRAPHIC STANDARDS</u>,
   5-10, 10-2, 10-4 TO 10-5
ARCHITECTURAL PRINTING.
   SEE PRINTING, ARCHITECTURAL
<u>ARCHITECTURAL RECORD</u> MAGAZINE, 24-7
ARCHITECTURAL SYMBOLS.
   SEE SYMBOLS, ARCHITECTURAL
<u>ARCHITECTURE</u> MAGAZINE, 24-7
AUTOCLAVING, 12-24
AXNOMETRIC VIEW, 1-6

B

BAR JOISTS, 7-14 TO 7-15, 12-14
BAYS, 11-3
BEAM COMPASS, 2-6
BENCH MARK, 6-11, 13-3
BENDING FIBER
   STEEL, 12-12
   WOOD, 12-2, 12-12
BIDDING PHASE, 1-4
BILLET, 12-12
BIRCH LAKE CABIN. SEE CABIN PROJECT
BLOCK COURSE, 6-13
BOARD, 12-4
BOARD FEET, 12-9 TO 12-10
BOLLARD DETAIL, 9-3, 9-5, 13-16
BOW COMPASS, 2-3
BRASS, 12-44
BRICK AND BLOCK. SEE MASONRY
BRONZE, 12-44
BUBBLE DIAGRAM, 24-4

BUILDING MATERIALS
   CONCRETE, 12-16 TO 12-22
   GLASS, 12-38 TO 12-41
   GYPSUM, 12-35 TO 12-38
   INSULATION, 12-27 TO 12-31
   MANUFACTURERS' DATA ON, 10-6 TO 10-7
   MASONRY, 12-22 TO 12-27
   NONFERROUS METALS, 12-41 TO 12-45
   REFERENCE SOURCES, 10-1 TO 10-10
   RESEARCH STEPS, 10-11 TO 10-14
   ROOFING, 12-31 TO 12-35
   SEALANTS, 12-45 TO 12-48
   FOR STAIRS, 18-3 TO 18-4
   STEEL, 12-11 TO 12-15
   WOOD PRODUCTS, 12-1 TO 12-11
BUILDING SECTIONS
   CABIN PROJECT, 21-6 TO 21-7
   CHECKLIST, 16-9
   COMMERCIAL PROJECTS, 16-5 TO 16-8
   DETAILS, 16-9 TO 16-12
   FIRE STATION, 7-8, 25-10 TO 25-11
   IMPORTANCE, 16-1
   LIBRARY PROJECT, 27-18 TO 27-21
   LOCATION RULES, 16-2
   MOTEL/RESTAURANT COMPLEX, 26-18 TO 26-21
   RESIDENTIAL PROJECTS, 16-2 TO 16-4
   SKYWAY HOUSE, 23-10 TO 23-13
   12/12 PITCH ROOF HOUSE, 16-2 TO 16-4,
      22-12 TO 22-13
BUILT-UP ROOFS, 12-32

C

C. S. I. (CONSTRUCTION SPECIFICATION
   INSTITUTE), 10-1 TO 10-2, A-3 TO A-4
CABIN PROJECT
   CAD DRAWINGS, 8-9 TO 8-13
   DESCRIPTION, 21-1
   EXTERIOR ELEVATIONS, 15-1 TO 15-4,
      21-6 TO 21-7, 28-1 TO 28-2
   FLOOR PLAN, 14-1 TO 14-5, 21-2 TO 21-3
   FRAMING AND DETAILS, 21-4 TO 21-5
   ISOMETRIC VIEW, 28-6
   PERSPECTIVE VIEW, 28-6 TO 28-11
   SITE PLAN, 13-8, 21-2 TO 21-3
   STUDY MODEL, 29-3 TO 29-4
CAD. SEE COMPUTER AIDED DRAFTING (CAD)
CALCULATORS, POCKET, 2-6
CEDAR SHAKE ROOFING, 12-33
CELLULOSE, 12-29
CEMENT, 12-16
CHANNEL (STRUCTURAL STEEL), 12-13
CHISEL POINT LETTERING, 4-4
CIRCLE TEMPLATE, 2-4

INDEX 1

CIRCLES, 3-12
CLAY TILE ROOFING, 12-33
CLERE STORY WINDOW DETAIL, 9-17, 20-15
CLIENT PHASE, 1-1
CLOSET DETAIL, 14-10
COKE, 12-11
COMMERCIAL PROJECTS. SEE ALSO FIRE
    STATION PROJECT; LIBRARY PROJECT;
    MOTEL/RESTAURANT PROJECT
  BUILDING SECTIONS, 16-5 TO 16-8
  DESIGN PHASE, 24-16 TO 24-22
  DETAIL ASSEMBLY, 20-8 TO 20-13
  DIMENSIONING, 6-9, 6-12
  DRAWINGS, ORGANIZATION OF, 7-5
  EXTERIOR ELEVATIONS, 15-5 TO 15-8
  FLOOR PLAN ASSEMBLY, 7-6
  FLOOR PLANS, 14-5 TO 14-8
  ROOF DETAILS, 9-23 TO 9-30
  SITE PLANS, 13-5 TO 13-7
  STAIRS, CODE REQUIREMENTS, 18-2
  STAIRS, DESIGN, 18-8 TO 18-9
  STUDY MODELS, 29-13 TO 29-30
  WALL DETAILS, 9-18 TO 9-22
  WALL SECTIONS, 17-7 TO 17-13
COMMUNITY CENTER PROJECT,
  24-16 TO 24-17
COMPASS
  BEAM, 2-6
  BOW, 2-3
  USE TIPS, 3-12
COMPRESSION TEST, FOR CONCRETE, 12-19
COMPUTER AIDED DRAFTING (CAD)
  ARRAY COMMAND, 8-1, 8-6, 8-12
  ARROWHEADS, 8-2
  BLOCK COMMAND, 8-2, 8-10
  BLOCK PLACEMENT, 8-7
  BREAK COMMAND, 8-3
  CABIN PROJECT, 8-9 TO 8-13
  CHANGE COMMAND, 8-12
  COPY COMMAND, 8-3
  CUSTOMIZATION FEATURES, 8-8
  "CUT-AND-PASTE," 8-3
  DIMENSIONING, 8-2
  ERASE COMMAND, 8-5
  GRID SETTING, 8-2, 8-8
  HATCH COMMAND, 8-3
  IMPORTANCE, 8-1
  LAYER TASK, 8-4
  LIBRARY, 8-2, 8-6
  LINE TYPES, 8-2, 8-11
  MIRROR COMMAND, 8-3
  MOVE COMMAND, 8-5, 8-13
  OFFSET TASK, 8-2
  PEN TABLE, 8-10, 8-11
  POLY LINE COMMAND, 8-12
  ROLE OF, 2-8
  ROTATE COMMAND, 8-5
  SCALE FACTOR, 8-9
  SCALE TASK, 8-3, 8-9, 8-12
  SNAP COMMAND, 8-5, 8-10
  SOFTWARE PACKAGES, 2-8, 8-6

COMPUTER AIDED DRAFTING (CAD) (CONT.)
  SYMBOLS, 8-6
  TRIM COMMAND, 8-3
  ZOOM COMMAND, 8-5
COMPUTERS, ROLE IN ARCHITECTURE, 2-8
CONCRETE, 12-16 TO 12-22
CONCRETE BENCH DETAIL, 13-15
CONCRETE BLOCK, 12-22 TO 12-24, 12-29
CONDUCTION HEAT TRANSFER, 12-27
CONIFEROUS TREES, 12-1
CONSTRUCTION PHASE, 1-1, 1-4 TO 1-5
CONSTRUCTION SPECIFICATION INSTITUTE
  (C. S. I.), 10-1 TO 10-2, A-3 TO A-4
CONTRACT, ARCHITECTURAL
  DRAWING SET DOCUMENT, 1-4
  PHASES OF, 1-1
CONVECTION HEAT TRANSFER, 12-27
COPPER, 12-43, 12-44
CORNERS, 3-11
COR-TEN STEEL, 12-12
COUNTER SPACE, 4-5
CROSSHATCHING, 1-8, 5-1
  MATERIALS, 5-1 TO 5-4
CURB DETAIL, 9-2, 13-15
CURVES, DRAWING TOOLS, 2-4

D

DECIDUOUS TREES, 12-1
DECK DETAIL, 14-10
DESIGN PROCESS
  ANALYSIS, 24-3 TO 24-4
  DESIGN STATEMENT, 1-2
  DEVELOPMENT PHASE, 1-3
  MASSING, 1-6, 24-7 TO 24-10
  ORGANIZATION AND PLANNING, 24-5 TO 24-7
  PROGRAMMING PHASE, 24-2 TO 24-3
  PURPOSE OF, 24-1
  STUDY MODELS, 24-11
DETAILS
  ASSEMBLY PROCESS, 20-1 TO 20-5
  BUILDING SECTIONS, 16-9 TO 16-12
  CHECKLIST, 20-14
  COMMERCIAL ROOFS, 9-23 TO 9-30, 24-22
  COMMERCIAL WALLS, 9-18 TO 9-22,
    20-8 TO 20-13, 24-22
  DOORS, 9-8, 9-9, 9-11
  ELEVATOR FRAME, 18-15
  EXAMPLES, 20-14 TO 20-16
  EXTERIOR ELEVATIONS, 15-9 TO 15-11
  FLOOR PLANS, 14-9 TO 14-13
  LINTEL AND DOOR CONDITIONS, 9-10 TO 9-12
  MOTEL/RESTAURANT COMPLEX,
    26-30 TO 26-33
  RESIDENTIAL WALLS, 9-15 TO 9-17, 20-6
  SCHEDULES, 7-2, 7-7, 9-7
  SITE PLANS, 9-2 TO 9-6, 13-13 TO 13-16
  SKYWAY HOUSE, 20-6 TO 20-7
  STAIRS, 9-13 TO 9-14, 13-13, 14-11, 18-12 TO 18-15
  WALL SECTIONS, 17-14 TO 17-16
DIMENSION LUMBER, 12-4

DIMENSIONING
   ABBREVIATIONS, 6-4
   BUILDING ELEVATION, 6-11
   FOR BUILDING SECTIONS, 16-4, 16-8
   WITH CAD, 8-2
   COMMERCIAL SITE PLAN, 6-12
   COMMERCIAL STRUCTURE PLANS, 6-9
   DETAIL CHART, 6-6
   FLOOR PLANS, 14-4, 14-7
   GROUND RULES, 6-2 TO 6-4
   LAYOUT TIPS, 6-5 TO 6-6
   MASONRY, 6-13 TO 6-14
   PROPERTY, 6-12
   RESIDENTIAL PLANS, 6-7 TO 6-8
   SCALES, 6-1 TO 6-2
   SITE PLAN, 13-12
   STUDENT LIBRARY PLAN, 6-10
   TERMINATION SYMBOLS, 6-2
   WALL SECTIONS, 17-6, 17-13
DOORS
   DETAILS, 9-8, 9-11
   SCHEDULES, 7-2, 7-7, 9-7, 19-3 TO 19-4, 26-33
DRAFTING BRUSH, 2-2, 3-12
DRAFTING INK, 2-7
DRAFTING LEAD, 2-5, 3-3
DRAFTING TAPE, 2-3
DRAWING SET. SEE WORKING DRAWINGS
DRAWINGS. SEE ALSO PRESENTATION DRAWINGS
   ABBREVIATIONS, 5-14
   ARCHITECTURAL SYMBOLS, 5-9
   DETAIL DEVELOPMENT, 9-1
   IMPORTANCE OF, 1-5
   LAYERS OF, 4-5 TO 4-6, 8-4
   LINE QUALITY IN, 3-1 TO 3-3
   LINE TYPES, 3-11
   LINE WEIGHTS, 3-3 TO 3-7
   MATERIAL HATCHING, 5-3 TO 5-4
   NOTE PLACEMENT, 4-7, 6-5
   ORTHOGRAPHIC, 1-5, 1-6
   PRECISION IN, 3-1
   SHORTCUTS, 3-8 TO 3-9
   SOURCES OF, 10-7
   STANDARD SIZES, 5-10 TO 5-13
   THREE-DIMENSIONAL, 1-5 TO 1-6
DRY ROT, 12-5
DRY WALL, 12-37

E

ELECTRIC ERASER, 2-5
ELEVATIONS, 1-6, 1-8, 3-3
   DIMENSIONS, 6-11
   EXTERIOR. SEE EXTERIOR ELEVATIONS
   INTERIOR, 7-3
   SHEET LAYOUT, 7-20
   SPOT, 6-11
   SYMBOLS FOR, 5-6, 5-7, 5-8
   TOPOGRAPHIC SURVEY, 13-3

ELEVATORS
   CHECKLIST, 18-12
   DETAILS, 18-15
   HYDRAULIC, 18-10 TO 18-11
   SECTION DETAIL, 16-11
   TRACTION, 18-10
ENGINEERED JOISTS, 12-9
ENGINEER'S SCALE, 2-5, 6-2
ENTRY DETAIL, 14-12
E P D M ROOF, 12-32
ERASERS
   ELECTRIC, 2-5
   VINYL, 2-4
ERASING SHIELD, 2-6, 2-9
ETHAFOAM, 12-47
EXTERIOR ELEVATIONS, 7-3
   CABIN PROJECT, 21-6 TO 21-7
   CHECKLIST, 15-8
   COMMERCIAL PROJECTS, 15-5 TO 15-8, 24-16, 24-19 TO 24-21
   DETAILS, 15-9 TO 15-11
   FIRE STATION, 7-7, 15-5 TO 15-8, 25-10 TO 25-13
   LIBRARY PROJECT, 27-14 TO 27-17
   MOTEL/RESTAURANT COMPLEX, 26-13 TO 26-17
   PRESENTATION DRAWINGS, 28-1 TO 28-2
   RESIDENTIAL PROJECTS, 15-1 TO 15-4, 24-12, 24-13, 24-15
   SKYWAY HOUSE, 23-10 TO 23-11
   12/12 PITCH HOUSE, 22-10 TO 22-11
EXTRUSION PROCESS, 12-42

F

FACE BRICK, 12-25
"FALLING WATER" HOUSE, 24-9
FASCIA PROBLEM, 11-5 TO 11-6
FELT-TIP PEN, 2-7
FIBERGLASS, 12-29
FIRE BARRIER, 12-36
FIRE STATION PROJECT
   BUILDING SECTIONS, 16-5 TO 16-8
   EXTERIOR ELEVATIONS, 7-7, 15-5 TO 15-8, 25-10 TO 25-13
   FLOOR PLANS, 7-6, 25-6 TO 25-9
   FRAMING REQUIREMENTS, 7-13 TO 7-15
   INTERIOR PLAN AND ELEVATIONS, 7-7
   ISOMETRIC VIEW, 7-5
   ROOM FINISH SCHEDULES, 19-2 TO 19-3
   SCHEDULES, 7-7
   SHEET LAYOUT, 7-18 TO 7-22
   SITE PLANS, 7-6, 13-5 TO 13-6, 25-2 TO 25-5
   STUDY MODEL, 29-13 TO 29-17
   WALL DETAILS, 20-12 TO 20-13
   WALL SECTIONS, 17-7 TO 17-13, 25-14 TO 25-21
FIREPLACES
   DETAIL, 14-11
   SECTION DETAIL, 16-11
FLAGPOLE DETAIL, 9-5, 13-14
FLAKE BOARD, 12-8
FLANGE, 12-12

FLOAT GLASS, 12-39
FLOOR FRAMING, PROBLEM-SOLVING
    EXAMPLE, 11-1 TO 11-3
FLOOR PLANS
    CABIN PROJECT, 14-1 TO 14-5, 21-2 TO 21-3
    CHECKLIST, 14-9
    COMMERCIAL PROJECTS, 7-6,
        14-5 TO 14-8, 24-17
    IN DESIGN PROCESS, 24-5 TO 24-7
    DETAILS, 14-9 TO 14-13
    FIRE STATION, 25-6 TO 25-9
    IMPORTANCE, 14-1
    LIBRARY PROJECT, 27-6 TO 27-13
    MATERIAL HATCHING, 5-1 TO 5-2
    MOTEL/RESTAURANT COMPLEX,
        14-5 TO 14-8, 26-6 TO 26-13
    REPRESENTATIONS IN, 1-8
    RESIDENTIAL PROJECTS, 14-1 TO 14-5,
        24-12 TO 24-14
    SHEET LAYOUT, 7-19
    SKYWAY HOUSE, 7-4, 23-6 TO 23-9
    12/12 PITCH ROOF HOUSE, 22-6 TO 22-9
FRAMING
    CABIN PROJECT, 21-4 TO 21-5
    COMMON TECHNIQUES, 7-9 TO 7-10
    FIRE STATION, 7-13 TO 7-15
    FLOOR, 11-1 TO 11-3
    LAYOUT TIPS, 7-13
    PLANS, 7-2
    RESIDENTIAL, 7-10 TO 7-13
    ROOF, 7-14 TO 7-15
    SKYWAY HOUSE PROJECT, 23-4 TO 23-5
    12/12 PITCH ROOF HOUSE, 22-2 TO 22-3
FRENCH CURVE, 2-4, 2-9

G

GALVANIZED IRON, 12-44
GEOMETRIC CONSTRUCTION, A-1 TO A-3
GLASS, 12-29, 12-38 TO 12-41
GLAZING COMPOUNDS, 12-39
GLUE, 2-6, 29-1
GLUE LAM BEAM, 12-8 TO 12-9
GRADING
    BAR JOISTS, 12-14
    GLUE LAM BEAMS, 12-9
    LUMBER, 12-4 TO 12-5
    PLYWOOD, 12-6
    WOOD, 12-2
GREEN ROCK, 12-37
GRIDS, IN CAD, 8-2, 8-8
GYPSUM, 12-35 TO 12-38
GYPSUM BOARD, 12-29
GYPSUM ENCLOSED STEEL COLUMN, 12-13

H

HANDICAP DETAILS, 9-6, 13-16, 14-12
HARD WOOD, 12-1
HATCHING. SEE CROSSHATCHING
HEADER, 11-3

HEAT-REDUCING GLASS, 12-40
HEAT TRANSFER, 12-27
HIGH-PERFORMANCE GLASS, 12-40

I

I BEAM, 12-13
INSULATED SHEATHING, 12-8
INSULATING GLASS, 12-29, 12-40
INSULATION, 12-27 TO 12-31
INTERIOR ELEVATIONS, 7-3
ISOMETRIC VIEW, 1-6, 7-5, 15-1, 28-3 TO 28-6

J

JOINT FILLERS, 12-47

K

KITCHENS
    CABINET DETAILS, 14-11
    EQUIPMENT SCHEDULE, 19-7 TO 19-8

L

LAMINATED BEAMS, 12-8 TO 12-9
LATEX SEALANT, 12-46
LATH, 12-37
LAYER TASK, IN CAD, 8-4
LEAD HOLDER, 2-1
    FOR PRINTING, 4-3
    USE TIPS, 3-2, 3-10
LEAD POINTER, 2-2
LEAD WEIGHTS, FOR PRINTING, 4-3
LIBRARY PROJECT
    BUILDING SECTIONS, 27-18 TO 27-21
    DIMENSIONING, 6-10
    ELEVATIONS, 27-14 TO 27-17
    ELEVATOR PLAN, 18-11
    FLOOR PLANS, 27-6 TO 27-13
    MISCELLANEOUS DETAILS, 27-34 TO 27-37
    SITE PLANS, 27-2 TO 27-5
    SKYLIGHT PLACEMENT, 10-13
    STAIRS AND REFLECTED CEILINGS,
        27-30 TO 27-33
    STONE BALCONY HANDRAIL DETAIL, 10-14
    STUDY MODEL, 29-25 TO 29-30
    WALL DETAILS, 20-8 TO 20-9
    WALL SECTIONS, 27-22 TO 27-29
LINE QUALITY, 3-1 TO 3-3
LINE TYPES, 3-11, 8-2, 8-11
LINE WEIGHTS
    FOR PLAN VIEW, 3-4 TO 3-6
    FOR SECTION VIEW, 3-6 TO 3-7
    TYPES, 3-3 TO 3-4
LOFT DETAIL, 14-13
LOW E GLASS, 12-40
LUMBER, GRADES OF, 12-4 TO 12-5

INDEX

M

MASONRY
    BRICK, 12-24 TO 12-26
    BRICK PAVERS AND CURB DETAIL,
        9-3, 13-15
    BRICK SCALES, 6-14
    CATEGORIES, 12-22
    CONCRETE BLOCK, 12-22 TO 12-24
    CONSTRUCTION PRECAUTIONS, 12-26
    DIMENSIONING, 6-13 TO 6-14
    MORTAR, 12-26
MASONRY CEMENT, 12-26
MASONRY ENCLOSED STEEL COLUMN, 12-13
MASSING, 1-6, 24-7 TO 24-10
MAT KNIFE, 2-7
MATERIAL HATCHING, 5-1 TO 5-4
MECHANICAL PENCIL, 2-2, 3-11
METAL ROOFING, 12-33 TO 12-34
MICRO-LAM BEAM, 12-9
MIRRORED GLASS, 12-40
MODULAR BLOCK, 12-24
MOISTURE CONTENT, OF WOOD, 12-3
MORTAR, 12-26
MOTEL/RESTAURANT PROJECT
    BUILDING SECTIONS, 26-18 TO 26-21
    DOOR SCHEDULE, 26-33
    ELEVATIONS, 26-13 TO 26-17
    FLOOR PLANS, 14-5 TO 14-8,
        26-6 TO 26-13
    KITCHEN EQUIPMENT SCHEDULE,
        19-7 TO 19-8
    MISCELLANEOUS DETAILS,
        26-30 TO 26-33
    PARKING PLAN, 13-7
    SITE PLANS, 26-2 TO 26-5
    STUDY MODEL, 29-18 TO 29-24
    WALL DETAILS, 20-10 TO 20-11
    WALL SECTIONS, 26-22 TO 26-29
MYLAR DRAFTING FILM, 4-8

N

NONFERROUS METALS, 12-41 TO 12-45
NOTES
    FOR BUILDING SECTIONS, 16-4, 16-8
    IN CAD, 8-4, 8-11
    FLOOR PLANS, 14-4, 14-7
    PLACEMENT OF, 4-7
    SITE PLANS, 13-12
    WALL SECTIONS, 17-4, 17-6, 17-9, 17-13

O

ORTHOGRAPHIC PROJECTION
    DEFINED, 1-5
    DRAWING, 1-6
OSB (ORIENTED STRAND BOARD), 12-8
OVERLAY DRAFTING, 3-8 TO 3-9

P

PARALLEL BAR, 2-7
PARKING FACILITIES
    LIGHT DETAIL, 13-16
    SITE PLANS, 13-6 TO 13-7
PARTICLE BOARD, 12-6
PASTE-UP DRAFTING, 3-8
PAVERS, 12-25
PENCILS
    MECHANICAL, 2-2, 3-11
    POINT OF, 3-10
PENS
    FELT-TIP, 2-7
    TECHNICAL, 2-2, 3-4, 3-11
PERSPECTIVE VIEW, 1-6, 28-6 TO 28-11
PIG IRON, 12-11
PIN BAR STRIP, 3-8
PLAN VIEW
    DESCRIBED, 3-4
    LINE WEIGHTS FOR, 3-4 TO 3-6
PLANS. SEE ALSO FLOOR PLANS; SITE PLANS
    DEFINED, 1-6
    IN WORKING DRAWINGS, 1-7 TO 1-9
PLASTER, 12-37
PLASTER OF PARIS, 12-35
PLASTIC DRAFTING FILM (MYLAR), 4-8
PLYWOOD, 12-6 TO 12-7
POCKET CALCULATOR, 2-6
POLISHED PLATE GLASS, 12-39
POLYSTYRENE, 12-29
POLYSULFIDE SEALANT, 12-46
POLYURETHANE, 12-29, 12-46
PORTLAND CEMENT ASSOCIATION, 12-16
POST AND BEAM CONSTRUCTION, 7-9
PRESENTATION DRAWINGS. SEE ALSO
    DRAWINGS; WORKING DRAWINGS
    ASSEMBLY TIPS, 28-12
    ELEVATIONS, 28-1 TO 28-2
    EXAMPLES, 28-13 TO 28-18
    ISOMETRIC VIEW, 28-3 TO 28-6
    PERSPECTIVE VIEW, 28-6 TO 28-11
    PURPOSE, 28-1
    SHADES AND SHADOWS, 28-6
PRIMERS, 12-47
PRINTING, ARCHITECTURAL
    CHISEL POINT LETTERING, 4-4
    IMPORTANCE OF, 4-1, 4-6
    LEAD WEIGHTS FOR, 4-3
    LETTER STYLES, 4-1
    SPACING, 4-5
    STYLING TIPS, 4-2 TO 4-5
    TIPS, 4-9
    TOOLS, 4-8
PROGRAMMING, 24-2 TO 24-3
PROGRESSIVE ARCHITECTURE MAGAZINE, 24-7
PROPERTY PIN, 13-2

INDEX

R

R FACTOR, 12-28
RADIATION HEAT TRANSFER, 12-27
REFERENCE SOURCES
   FOR BUILDING MATERIALS, 10-1 TO 10-10
   FOR DESIGN SOLUTIONS, 24-7
REFLECTIVE GLASS, 12-40
RENDERINGS. SEE PRESENTATION DRAWINGS
RESIDENTIAL PROJECTS. SEE ALSO CABIN PROJECT; SKYWAY HOUSE PROJECT; 12/12 PITCH ROOF HOUSE PROJECT
   BUILDING SECTIONS, 16-2 TO 16-4
   DESIGN PHASE, 24-2 TO 24-7, 24-12 TO 24-15
   DIMENSIONING, 6-7 TO 6-8
   DRAWINGS, ORGANIZATION OF, 7-2 TO 7-3
   EXTERIOR ELEVATIONS, 15-1 TO 15-4
   FLOOR PLANS, 14-1 TO 14-5
   FRAMING, 7-10 TO 7-13
   MASSING, 1-6, 24-7 TO 24-10
   SITE PLANS, 13-1 TO 13-4, 13-8 TO 13-11
   STAIRS, CODE REQUIREMENTS, 18-1 TO 18-2
   STAIRS, DESIGN, 18-5 TO 18-7
   STUDY MODELS, 24-11, 29-3 TO 29-12
   WALL DETAILS, 9-15 TO 9-17
   WALL SECTIONS, 17-1 TO 17-6
RESTAURANT COMPLEX PROJECT, 24-18 TO 24-22. SEE ALSO MOTEL/RESTAURANT PROJECT
RETAINING WALL DETAIL, 9-4
ROOF PITCH, 15-2
ROOFING FELT, 12-32
ROOFS
   ASPHALT-BASED, 12-31, 12-32
   CEDAR SHAKE, 12-33
   CLAY TILE, 12-33
   COMMERCIAL DETAILS, 9-23 TO 9-30
   COPPER, 12-43
   DESIGNS OF, 24-9, 24-10
   DETAILS, 20-14 TO 20-16
   FASCIA PROBLEM EXAMPLE, 11-5 TO 11-6
   FLAT, 12-31, 12-32
   FRAMING, 7-14 TO 7-15
   METAL, 12-33 TO 12-34
   OVERHANG PROBLEM EXAMPLE, 11-4 TO 11-5
   PITCHED, 12-31
   SHINGLES, 12-33
ROOM FINISH SCHEDULES, 3-8, 7-2, 7-7, 9-7, 19-1 TO 19-3
   FIRE STATION, 25-9

S

SAFETY GLASS, 12-39
SCALE
   BUILDING SECTIONS, 16-9
   IN CAD, 8-3, 8-9, 8-12
   COMMERCIAL PLANS, 7-7

SCALE (CONT.)
   EXTERIOR ELEVATIONS, 15-2
   SECTION CUTS, 1-9, 7-5
   STAIRS, 18-12
   WALL SECTIONS, 17-1 TO 17-6
   WALL TYPES, 19-5
   WINDOWS, 19-6
SCALES
   ARCHITECT'S, 2-5, 2-9, 6-1 TO 6-2
   BRICK, 6-14
   ENGINEER'S, 2-5, 6-2
SCHEDULES
   CHECKLIST, 19-8
   DOOR, 7-2, 7-7, 9-7, 19-3 TO 19-4, 26-33
   KITCHEN EQUIPMENT, 19-7 TO 19-8
   PURPOSE, 19-1
   ROOM FINISH, 3-8, 7-2, 7-7, 9-7, 19-1 TO 19-3, 25-9
   WALL TYPE, 19-5
   WINDOW TYPE, 19-5 TO 19-6
SCHEDULING, 11-9 TO 11-11
SCHEMATIC DESIGN PHASE, 1-2
SCHEMATIC DRAWINGS, 1-2
SEALANTS, 12-45 TO 12-48
SEASONING, OF WOOD, 12-3
SECTION VIEW
   DESCRIBED, 3-6
   LINE WEIGHT FOR, 3-6 TO 3-7
SECTIONS. SEE ALSO BUILDING SECTIONS; WALL SECTIONS
   DEFINED, 1-6
   LOCATION, 7-3
   SCALES, 1-9, 7-5
   SYMBOLS FOR, 5-6, 5-7, 5-8
SHEET GLASS, 12-39
SHEET LAYOUT
   DEFINED, 7-16
   FIRE STATION, 7-18 TO 7-22
   GUIDELINES, 7-17
   SIZES, 7-16
SHEET ROCK, 12-37
SHINGLES, 12-33
SILICONE SEALANT, 12-46
SITE ANALYSIS, 1-2
   CHECKLIST, 13-9 TO 13-10
   FOR DESIGN, 24-3 TO 24-4
SITE PLANS, 1-7
   CABIN PROJECT, 21-2 TO 21-3
   CHECKLIST, 13-13
   COMMERCIAL PROJECTS, 4-6, 13-5 TO 13-7, 24-16, 24-18
   DATA FOR, 13-1
   DESIGN CRITERIA, 13-8 TO 13-10
   DETAILS, 9-2 TO 9-6, 13-13 TO 13-16
   DIMENSIONS, 6-12
   FIRE STATION, 7-6, 13-5 TO 13-6, 25-2 TO 25-5
   LIBRARY PROJECT, 27-2 TO 27-5
   MOTEL/RESTAURANT COMPLEX, 26-2 TO 26-5
   PARKING FACILITIES, 13-6 TO 13-7
   RESIDENTIAL PROJECTS, 7-2, 13-1 TO 13-4, 13-8 TO 13-13

SITE PLANS (CONT.)
   SKYWAY HOUSE PROJECT, 7-2, 13-9 TO 13-10, 23-2 TO 23-3
   SURVEY DATA, 13-2
   SYMBOLS USED FOR, 5-9
   TOPOGRAPHIC, 13-3 TO 13-4
   12/12 PITCH ROOF HOUSE, 22-2 TO 22-3
SIZES
   BRICKS, 12-25
   CONCRETE BLOCK, 12-23, 12-24
   CONSTRUCTION LUMBER, 12-4
   SHEET LAYOUT, 7-16
   STANDARD, 5-10 TO 5-13
SKETCH PAPER, 2-3
SKYWAY HOUSE PROJECT
   DESCRIPTION, 23-1
   DETAILS FOR, 20-6 TO 20-7
   ELEVATIONS, 23-10 TO 23-11
   FLOOR PLAN, 23-6 TO 23-9
   FRAMING AND DETAILS, 23-4 TO 23-5
   SITE ANALYSIS, 13-9 TO 13-10
   SITE DRAWING ASSEMBLY, 13-11
   SITE PLAN, 7-2, 23-2 TO 23-3
   STUDY MODEL, 29-9 TO 29-12
   WALL SECTIONS, 17-1 TO 17-6, 23-12 TO 23-13
SLUMP TEST, FOR CONCRETE, 12-19
SOFT WOOD, 12-1
SOUND TRANSMISSION CLASS (STC), 12-36
SPACING, 4-5
SPALLING, 12-20
SPECIFICATIONS, ARCHITECTURAL, 10-8 TO 10-10
SPOT ELEVATIONS, 6-11
SPRAY-ON STEEL BEAM (FIREPROOFING) 12-13
STAIRS
   CHECKLIST, 18-12
   CODE REQUIREMENTS, 18-1 TO 18-2
   COMMERCIAL DESIGN, 18-8 TO 18-9
   DESIGN TERMS, 18-3
   DETAILS, 9-13 TO 9-14, 13-13, 14-11, 18-12 TO 18-15
   LAYOUT PROBLEM EXAMPLE, 11-7 TO 11-8
   LIBRARY PROJECT, 27-30 TO 27-33
   MATERIALS FOR, 18-3 TO 18-4
   RESIDENTIAL DESIGN, 18-5 TO 18-7
   SECTION DETAILS, 16-10, 16-12
   TYPES OF, 18-1
STC (SOUND TRANSMISSION CLASS), 12-36
STEEL, 12-11 TO 12-15
STRIKING THE JOINT, 12-26
STRUCTURAL FRAMING. SEE FRAMING
STUDY MODELS
   ASSEMBLY TIPS, 29-2
   CABIN PROJECT, 29-3 TO 29-4
   FIRE STATION, 29-13 TO 29-17
   LIBRARY PROJECT, 29-25 TO 29-30
   MOTEL/RESTAURANT COMPLEX, 29-18 TO 29-24

STUDY MODELS (CONT.)
   PURPOSE, 24-11
   SKYWAY HOUSE, 29-9 TO 29-12
   TOOLS FOR, 29-1 TO 29-2
   12/12 PITCH ROOF HOUSE, 29-5 TO 29-8
SUBSTRATES, 12-47
SUNROOM DETAIL, 9-17
SURVEYS
   PROPERTY, 13-2
   TOPOGRAPHIC, 13-3
SWEET'S CATALOG FILE, 10-2 TO 10-4
SYMBOLS, ARCHITECTURAL
   IN CAD LIBRARY, 8-6
   DIMENSION STRINGS, 6-2
   DRAWING TIPS, 5-9
   SITE DRAWINGS, 5-9
   STANDARD, 5-5 TO 5-8

T

TAPE, DRAFTING, 2-3
TAPE CIRCLES, 2-3
TAR PAPER, 12-32
TECHNICAL PEN, 2-2, 3-4, 3-11
TEE (STRUCTURAL STEEL), 12-13
TEMPERED GLASS, 12-39
TEMPLATES
   CIRCLE, 2-4
   TOILET, 2-3
   USE TIPS, 2-9
TERNE, 12-33
THREE-DIMENSIONAL DRAWINGS, 1-5 TO 1-6, 28-3 TO 28-11
TICK MARKS, 3-1
TIMBER, 12-4
TIME MANAGEMENT, 11-9 TO 11-11
TIN, 12-44
TJI JOIST, 12-9
TOILETS
   DETAILS, 14-12
   TEMPLATE, 2-3
TOOLS
   DRAFTING, 2-1 TO 2-8
   PRINTING AIDS, 4-8
   USE TIPS, 2-9, 3-10 TO 3-12
TOPOGRAPHIC CONTOURS, 1-7, 13-4
TOPOGRAPHIC SURVEY, 13-3
TRACING PAPER OVERLAY, 4-6
TRASH RECEPTACLE DETAIL, 13-15
TREE ROOTBALL DETAIL, 9-2, 13-14
TRIANGLE, 2-1
   AS PRINTING AID, 4-8
TRUS JOIST, 12-9
TUBE SHAPE COLUMN, 12-13
12/12 PITCH ROOF HOUSE PROJECT
   BUILDING SECTIONS, 16-2 TO 16-4, 22-12 TO 22-13
   DESCRIPTION, 22-1
   ELEVATIONS, 22-10 TO 22-11
   FIREPLACE REQUIREMENTS, 10-12
   FLOOR PLANS, 22-6 TO 22-9

12/12 PITCH ROOF HOUSE PROJECT (CONT.)
   FRAMING AND DETAILS, 22-4 TO 22-5
   SITE PLAN, 22-2 TO 22-3
   STUDY MODEL, 29-5 TO 29-8
   TIME MANAGEMENT, 11-9 TO 11-11

U

U FACTOR, 12-28

V

VAPOR BARRIERS, 12-28, 12-30
VENEER, 12-6
VERMICULITE, 12-29

W

WALL SECTIONS
   CHECKLIST, 17-14
   COMMERCIAL PROJECTS, 17-7 TO 17-13, 24-17
   DETAILS, 17-14 TO 17-16
   FIRE STATION, 17-7 TO 17-13, 25-14 TO 25-21
   LIBRARY PROJECT, 27-22 TO 27-29
   MOTEL/RESTAURANT COMPLEX, 26-22 TO 26-29
   RESIDENTIAL PROJECTS, 17-1 TO 17-6
   SKYWAY HOUSE, 17-1 TO 17-6, 23-12 TO 23-13
WALLS
   BRICK VENEER, 12-25 TO 12-26
   COMMERCIAL DETAILS, 9-18 TO 9-22
   DETAILS, 9-9
   FIRE AND SOUND SEPARATION CHART, 12-36
   FIRE STATION BLOW-UPS, 7-8
   HOUSE PROJECT MARKINGS, 7-4
   INTERSECTION CLEANUP (CAD), 8-7
   RESIDENTIAL DETAILS, 9-15 TO 9-17
   SHEET LAYOUT, 7-20, 7-21, 7-22
   TYPE SCHEDULE, 19-5
WEB, 12-12

WELDED GLASS, 12-40
WIDE FLANGE BEAM, 12-13
WINDOWS
   CLERE STORY, 9-17, 20-15
   TYPE SCHEDULE, 19-5 TO 19-6
WIRE GLASS, 12-39 TO 12-40
WOOD
   CATEGORIES OF, 12-1 TO 12-2
   DEFECTS, 12-6
   GRADING, 12-2
   INSULATION USE, 12-29
   MEASUREMENT UNITS, 12-9 TO 12-10
   MILLING, 12-2 TO 12-4
   PLANING, 12-4
   PRESERVATIVE METHODS, 12-5
   PRESSURE-TREATED, 12-5 TO 12-6
   PRODUCT TERMINOLOGY, 12-4
   PRODUCTS, 12-6 TO 12-10
   SEASONING, 12-3
   STRENGTH MEASURE, 12-2
WOOD BENCH DETAIL, 13-14
WORKING DRAWING PHASE, 1-3 TO 1-4
WORKING DRAWINGS. SEE ALSO DRAWINGS; PRESENTATION DRAWINGS
   COMMERCIAL PROJECTS, ORGANIZATIONAL PATTERN, 7-5
   AS CONTRACT, 1-4, 1-9, 7-1
   DEFINED, 1-7
   IMPORTANCE, 7-1
   ORGANIZATIONAL PATTERN, 7-2 TO 7-3
   PROBLEM SOLVING, 11-1 TO 11-8
   SHEET LAYOUT, 7-16 TO 7-22
   SITE, ASSEMBLY, 13-11 TO 13-13
   TIME MANAGEMENT, 11-9 TO 11-11
WRIGHT, FRANK LLOYD, 24-9

Z

ZINC, 12-44